APPROACHING DEMOCRACY

FOURTH EDITION

LARRY BERMAN
UNIVERSITY OF CALIFORNIA, DAVIS

BRUCE ALLEN MURPHY
LAFAYETTE COLLEGE

Prentice Hall

UPPER SADDLE RIVER, NEW JERSEY 07458

Library of Congress Cataloging-in-Publication Data

Berman, Larry.
    Approaching democracy/Larry Berman, Bruce Allen Murphy.—4th ed.
        p.cm.
Includes bibliographical references and index.
    ISBN 0-13-110251-6
    1. United States—Politics and government. 2. Democracy—United States.
I. Murphy, Bruce Allen. II. Title.

    JK274.B524 2003
    320.473—dc21   2002035548

VP, Editorial Director: Charlyce Jones Owen
Senior Acquisitions Editor: Heather Shelstad
Editorial Assistant: Jessica Drew
Director of Marketing: Beth Mejia
Marketing Manager: Claire Bitting
AVP, Director of Manufacturing and Production: Barbara Kittle
Executive Managing Editor: Ann Marie McCarthy
Developmental Editor: Barbara Heinssen
Production Liaison: Fran Russello
Project Manager: Jennifer Murtoff
Copy Editor: Megan Hill
Prepress and Manufacturing Manager: Nick Sklitsis
Prepress and Manufacturing Buyer: Ben Smith
Creative Design Director: Leslie Osher
Interior Design: Ximena Tamvakopoulos
Cover Design: Ximena Tamvakopoulos
Cover and Approaching Democracy Art: Jeremy Wolff/Graphistock
Director, Image Resource Center: Melinda Reo
Manager, Rights and Permissions: Zina Arabia
Interior Image Specialist: Beth Boyd-Brenzel
Cover Image Specialist: Karen Sanatar
Image Permission Coordinator: Fran Toepfer
Photo Researcher: Kathy Ringrose
Electronic Art Manager: Guy Ruggiero
Electronic Art Creation: Maria Piper
Cover Image: Jean-Marc Truchet/Getty Images, Inc

This book was set in 10/12 New Baskerville by Lithokraft II
and was printed and bound by Von Hoffman Press, Inc.
The cover was printed by Phoenix Color Corp.

©2003, 2001, 1999, 1996 by Pearson Education
Upper Saddle River, New Jersey 07458

Printed in the United States of America

10   9   8   7   6   5   4   3   2

ISBN 0-13-110251-6

Pearson Education LTD., London
Pearson Education Australia PTY, Limited, Sydney
Pearson Education Singapore, Pte. Ltd
Pearson Education North Asia Ltd, Hong Kong
Pearson Education Canada, Ltd., Toronto
Pearson Educación de Mexico, S.A. de C.V.
Pearson Education—Japan, Tokyo
Pearson Education Malaysia, Pte. Ltd
Pearson Education, Upper Saddle River, New Jersey

TO OUR OWN TEACHERS AND
THEIR EXTENDED LEGACY—
OUR STUDENTS

Brief Contents

PART I
FOUNDATIONS OF AMERICAN DEMOCRACY

1. Approaching Democracy 2
2. The Founding and the Constitution 26
   The Constitution of the United States of America
3. Federalism 78   Constructing a New Ideal Democracy 113

PART II
INSTITUTIONS OF AMERICAN DEMOCRACY

4. Congress 114
5. The Presidency 162
6. The Judiciary 200
7. The Bureaucracy 244

PART III
PROCESSES OF AMERICAN DEMOCRACY

8. Public Opinion 278
9. Political Parties 310
10. Participation, Voting, and Elections 346
11. Interest Groups 382
12. The Media 416

PART IV
LIBERTIES AND RIGHTS IN AMERICAN DEMOCRACY

13. Civil Liberties 446
14. Civil Rights and Political Equality 488

PART V
POLICY MAKING IN AMERICAN DEMOCRACY

15. Domestic and Economic Policy 526
16. Foreign Policy 562

Contents

Boxed Features   xv

Preface   xix

About the Authors   xxvii

PART I / FOUNDATIONS OF AMERICAN DEMOCRACY

1 APPROACHING DEMOCRACY   2

Approaching Democracy Case Study: Sí Se Puede: "It Can Be Done"   2

Introduction: Democracy as an Evolutionary Process   5

Forming a Picture of Democracy   9

Direct and Indirect Democracy   12

The Roots of Democracy   14

The Ideals of Democracy   15

Freedom and Equality   15 • Order and Stability   16 • Majority Rule and Protection of Minority Rights   17 • Participation   18

The Elements of Democracy   19

Summary   23

Key Terms   25

PoliSim Activity   25

Suggested Readings   25

2 THE FOUNDING AND THE CONSTITUTION   26

Approaching Democracy Case Study: The Constitution in Times of Crisis   26

Introduction: The Road to Democracy   28

The Seeds of American Democracy   29

Early Colonial Governments   29 • Social Contract Theorists   30

First Moves Toward a Union   32

Rebellion: Causes and Consequences   32

The Sugar and Stamp Acts   33 • The Townshend Revenue Acts   34 • The Boston Massacre   34 • Committees of Correspondence   35 • The Boston Tea Party   35

Revolution and the Stirrings of a New Government   36

The First Continental Congress   36 • "The Shot Heard 'Round the World"   37 • The Second Continental Congress   37 • *Common Sense*   38 • The Declaration of Independence   38

The First New Government: A Confederation of States   40

The Articles of Confederation (1781–1789)   41

The Need for a More Perfect Union   42

The Constitutional Convention   43

The Task   44 • The Participants   44 • The Major Players   45 •

Plans for a New Government   46 • Debate and Compromise: The Turning Point of the Convention   48 • The Issue of Slavery   50 • The Nature of the Presidency   51

The Miracle: Results of the Convention   53

A Republican Form of Government   53 • The Governmental Powers   54 • The Articles of the Constitution   57

Ratification: The Battle for the Constitution   61

The Federalist Papers   61 • Federalists versus Antifederalists   62 • Ratification by Way of Compromise: A Bill of Rights   64 • Politics the Old-Fashioned Way: A Look at the Battle for Ratification   65 • Adoption of the Bill of Rights   66

Updating the Constitution   67

Updating the Constitution through the Amendment Process   68 • Updating the Constitution by Judicial Interpretation   69 •

The Gettysburg Address and America's Approach to Democracy   71

Summary   73

Key Terms   75

PoliSim Activity   75

Suggested Readings   75

THE CONSTITUTION OF THE UNITED STATES

3 FEDERALISM   78

Approaching Democracy Case Study: Rebuilding New York City   78

Introduction: Federalism and Democracy   80

Federalism Defined   80

Federalism: Advantages and Disadvantages   81

Federalism in the Constitution   84

The Triad of Powers   84

The Division of Powers   86

The Development of Federalism   89

Debating the National Role: Hamilton versus Jefferson   89 • Asserting National Power: *McCulloch v. Maryland*   90 • Expanding National Power Further: *Gibbons v. Ogden*   90 • Asserting State Power: Nullification   91 • Developing a System of Separation: Dual Federalism   91 • Creating a Cooperative System: The New

Deal Era   93 • Seeking Uniformity: Federalism in the Post–New
Deal Era   94 • Federal Grants and Federal Mandates: Federalism
Since 1930   95

Presidents and Federalism   100
Roosevelt, Truman, and Eisenhower: The Era of Cooperative
Federalism, 1930–1963   100 • Lyndon Johnson: The Era of
Creative Federalism, 1963–1968   100 • Richard Nixon's New
Federalism, 1969–1974   102 • Creative Federalism Returns Under
Jimmy Carter, 1977–1980   102 • Ronald Reagan's "New New
Federalism," 1981–1988   103 • The Bush Years, 1989–1992
105 • Bill Clinton and New(t) Federalism, 1993–2001   105 •
George W. Bush, 2001–Present   106

The Rehnquist Court and the Future of Federalism   106
Federalism and Approaching Democracy in the Twenty-First
    Century   108
Summary   111
Key Terms   112
Suggested Readings   112

CONSTRUCTING A NEW IDEAL DEMOCRACY   113

PART II / INSTITUTIONS OF AMERICAN DEMOCRACY

4 CONGRESS   114

**Approaching Democracy Case Study: Negotiating
    the Legislative Labyrinth   114**
Introduction: Congress and Democracy   116
The Structure and Powers of Congress   117
What the Framers Had in Mind   117 • Limits on Congress's
Power   118
The Members of Congress   120
Who Are the Members?   120 • Congressional Districts   123 •
Majority–Minority Districts and the Approach to Democracy   124 •
Delegates versus Trustees   126 • Name Recognition and the
Incumbency Factor   127 • The "Two Congresses:" The Public's
View of Congress   129
How Congress Organizes Itself   130
Congressional Leadership   130 • Congressional Committees:
The Laboratories of Congress   133 • Why Does Congress Use
Committees?   135 • The Rise of Subcommittees   137
Congress in Session   138
The Rules and Norms of Congress   138 • How Members Make
Voting Decisions   144
How a Bill Becomes Law   146
The Congressional Agenda   147 • Congress Considers the Bill
147 • Obstacles to Passage of a Bill   149 • Overcoming the
Legislative Obstacles   151
Additional Functions of Congress   152
**The 106th and 107th Congress: Whither the "Republican
    Revolution"?   153**
Congress After the 2002 Election   155
Summary   158
Key Terms   159
PoliSim Activity   160
Suggested Readings   160

5 THE PRESIDENCY   162

**Approaching Democracy Case Study: The First Year
    of the Bush Presidency   162**
Introduction: The Presidency and Democracy   164

The Constitutional Design   166
Who Is Eligible to Be President?   167 • The Presidential
Powers   167
The Functional Roles of the President   175
Two Views of Executive Power   180
**Expanding Presidential Power: Moving Beyond
    the Constitution   182**
Congress Delegates Power to the President   182 • Conducting
Foreign Policy and Making War   184 • Going Public   187
The Institutionalized Presidency   190
The White House Office   190 • The Executive Office of the
President   191 • The Cabinet   193 • The Vice Presidency   194
Summary   197
Key Terms   198
PoliSim Activity   198
Suggested Readings   198

6 THE JUDICIARY   200

**Approaching Democracy Case Study: The Real Rehnquist
    Court Legacy?   200**
Introduction: The Courts and Democracy   202
The Origins and Development of Judicial Power   203
Creating the "Least Dangerous Branch"   203 • *Marbury v. Madison:*
The Source of Judicial Power   203 • Judicial Review: The Court's
Ultimate Power   204 • Other Powers of the Supreme
Court   205 • Independence of the Judiciary   205
The Organization of the American Court System   206
Types of Courts   208 • Types of Cases   209 • Organization of the
Federal Courts   209
Court Appointments: The Process and the Politics   211
The Supreme Court Appointment Process   211 • The Impact of
Presidential Appointments on the Supreme Court   216 • Staffing
the Lower Federal Courts   217
How the Supreme Court Operates   219
Selecting Cases   221 • The Solicitor General: "The Government's
Lawyer"   223 • The Process of Deciding Cases   223 • Marshaling
the Court: The Opinion-Drafting Process   228 • The
Announcement of Opinions   228 • The Chief Justice's Role   229
Analyzing Supreme Court Decisions   230

The Use of Precedent and Other Legal Factors   230 • The Mindset of Individual Justices   231 • Judicial Character   233 • Voting Blocs 233 • Limitations of Court Analysis   235

Implementing Supreme Court Decisions   235
The President and the Court   236 • Congress and the Court 236 • The Impact at State and Local Levels   237 • Public Opinion and the Supreme Court   237

The Court's Independence in Approaching Democracy   238

Summary   240

Key Terms   241

Suggested Readings   241

7 THE BUREAUCRACY 244

Approaching Democracy Case Study: Creating a New Department During a National Crisis: The Department of Homeland Security   244

Introduction: Bureaucracy and Democracy   246

Background on the Bureaucracy   247
Growth of the Federal Bureaucracy   249 • Evolution of the Bureaucracy: Creating the Civil Service   252

Meet the Bureaucracy   255
What the Bureaucracy Does   256 • The Structure of the Federal Bureaucracy   259 • Constraints on the Bureaucracy and Bureaucratic Culture   262

Bureaucratic Accountability   265
Presidential Control   265 • Congressional Control   267 • The National Security Bureaucracy   268

What the Public Thinks of the Bureaucracy   270
Are the Criticisms Justified?   270

Reforming the Bureaucracy   272

Summary   275

Key Terms   276

PoliSim Activity   276

Suggested Readings   276

PART III / PROCESSES OF AMERICAN DEMOCRACY

8 PUBLIC OPINION 278

Approaching Democracy Case Study: Landon Defeats Roosevelt—The Voice of the People?   278

Introduction: Public Opinion and Democracy   280

What Is Public Opinion?   281

Measuring Public Opinion   282

Political Socialization   285
The Role of Family   286 • Schooling   287 • Peers   288 • Television   288

Social Variables That Influence Opinion Formation   289
Class and Income   290 • Race and Ethnicity   290 • Religion 291 • Region   293 • Gender   294

American Political Culture   295
Core Values   295 • Political Ideology   297 • Culture and Lifestyle   299

The State of American Public Opinion   299
Political Awareness and Involvement   299 • How Are Political Opinions Formed?   301 • Stability and Change in Public Opinion 302 • How Changeable Is Public Opinion?   304

From Public Opinion to Public Policy   304

Summary   307

Key Terms   308

PoliSim Activity   308

Suggested Readings   309

9 POLITICAL PARTIES 310

Approaching Democracy Case Study: Jim Jeffords' Declaration of Independence   310

Introduction: Political Parties and Democracy   312

A Brief History of the American Party System   313
The First Party System (1790s–1820s)   313 • The Second Party System (1820s–1850s)   315 • The Third Party System (1850s–1890s)   315 • The Fourth Party System (1896–1932) 315 • The Fifth Party System (1932–1968)   316 • A Sixth Party System?: 1968 to Present   317

Functions of American Political Parties   319
Parties Organize the Election Process   319 • Parties Represent Group Interests   320 • Parties Simplify Political Choices   321 • Parties Organize Government and Policy Making   321

Party Organization   321
Parties at the Grass Roots   321 • The Party Machine   323 • National Party Organization   324 • Party Similarities and Differences   325

Nominating a President: Parties and Elections   325
Nominating Candidates   325

Reforming the Nominating Process   329

Why a Two-Party System?   335
Institutional Factors   335 • Cultural Factors   336 • Party Identification   336

Minor Parties   337
Why Minor Parties Appear   337 • Minor Party Performance   337 • Functions of Minor Parties   339

The Party in Government   339
The Importance of Party Ideology   340

Political Parties and the 2002 Election   341

Summary   343

Key Terms   344

PoliSim Activity   344

Suggested Readings   345

10 PARTICIPATION, VOTING, AND ELECTIONS   346

Approaching Democracy Case Study: The Motor-Voter Law, 1995–2002   346

Introduction: Political Participation and Democracy   348

Who Participates?   348

A Brief History of Voting in the United States   349

Voting   351
Voter Turnout   352 • Explaining Low Turnout   353 • Nonvoting 357 • Who Votes?   359 • A Voting Trend: Direct Democracy   359

Voting Choice   360
Party   360 • Candidate Appeal   361 • Policies and Issues   361 • Campaigns   363

Other Forms of Political Participation   363
Campaign and Election Activities   363 • Seeking Information 365 • Protest, Civil Disobedience, and Violence   365

Congressional Elections   366
Presidential Coattails   367

Presidential Elections   367
The Electoral College: The Framers' Intention   368 • The Electoral College and Strategies for Campaigning   371 • Electoral College Reform?   372 • Interpreting Presidential Elections   372

Money and Elections   373
Federal Matching Funds   375 • Campaign Finance Reform   376

Summary   379

Key Terms   380

PoliSim Activity   380

Suggested Readings   380

11 INTEREST GROUPS   382

Approaching Democracy Case Study: A Million Moms vs. the NRA and the Second Amendment Sisters   382

Introduction: Interest Groups and Democracy   384

Interest Groups: A Tradition in American Politics   385
What Is an Interest Group?   385 • A Long History of Association 386 • Recent Trends   387

Functions of Interest Groups   388
Interest Groups Allow for Collective Action   389 • Interest Groups Provide Information   390

Types of Interest Groups   392
Economic Interest Groups   393 • Public Interest Groups   395 •

Government Interest Groups   396 • Ideological Interest Groups 397 • Religious Interest Groups   397 • Civil Rights Interest Groups 398 • Single-Issue Interest Groups   399

Characteristics of Interest Groups   399
Interest Group Membership   399 • Other Characteristics of Interest Groups   401

Interest Group Strategies   402
Lobbying   402 • Grass-Roots Activity   404 • Using the Courts and Lobbying the Political Branches   406

Political Action Committees   407

Regulation of Interest Groups   408

Assessing the Impact of Interest Groups   409

Interest Groups of the Future   410

Interest Groups and the 2002 Election   411

Summary   412

Key Terms   414

PoliSim Activity   414

Suggested Readings   414

12 THE MEDIA   416

Approaching Democracy Case Study: The Media and the War on Terrorism   416

Introduction: The Media and Democracy   418

The Emergence of the Media   419
Newspapers   420 • Magazines   422 • Radio   423 • Television 423 • New Media Technologies   425

Functions of the Media   427
Surveillance   427 • Interpretation   430 • Socialization   431

Limits on Media Freedom   432
Regulating the Media   433 • Prior Restraint versus the Right to Know   434

Ideological Bias and Media Control   435
Media Diversity   436 • Media Ownership and Control   437 • Media-Government Symbiosis   438

The Media and Elections   438
Press Coverage   439 • Polling   439 • Talk Shows   439 • Television and Presidential Elections   440 • Political Advertising   441

Summary   444

Key Terms   445

Suggested Readings   445

PART IV / LIBERTIES AND RIGHTS IN AMERICAN DEMOCRACY

13 CIVIL LIBERTIES   446

Approaching Democracy Case Study: The Constitution and the War on Terrorism   446

Introduction: Civil Liberties and Democracy   448

Defining and Examining Civil Liberties and Civil Rights   449

The Dawn of Civil Liberties and Civil Rights in America   449

A History of the Application of Civil Liberties to the States   450

The Fourteenth Amendment   451 • The Clear and Present Danger Test   452 • The Beginnings of Incorporation   454 • Selective Incorporation of the Bill of Rights   455

Freedom of Religion   456
Establishment of Religion   457 • Free Exercise of Religion   461

Freedom of Speech   463
Political Speech   464 • Public Speech   464 • Symbolic Speech   465

Freedom of the Press   466
Prior Restraint   466 • Libel   467 • Obscenity   468

The Rights of Defendants   469
The Fourth Amendment   470 • The Fifth and Sixth Amendments   475

The Expanding Nature of Implied Rights   479
Privacy   479 • Abortion   482 • The Right to Die   484

Summary   485

Key Terms   486

PoliSim Activity   486

Suggested Readings   486

14   CIVIL RIGHTS AND POLITICAL EQUALITY   488

Approaching Democracy Case Study: Divided We Stand: Whither Affirmative Action?   488

Introduction: Civil Rights and Democracy   490
Defining Civil Rights   491

Establishing Constitutional Equality   492
The *Dred Scott* Case   492 • The Civil War and

Reconstruction   494

Creating Legal Segregation   495
Separate But Equal?   495 • The Disenfranchisement of African American Voters   495

Establishing Legal Equality   496
The White House and Desegregation   496 • Seeking Equality in the Schools   497 • State and Federal Responses   498

The Civil Rights Movement   499
The Civil Rights Acts   500 • The Supreme Court and Civil Rights   501 • De Jure versus De Facto Discrimination   501

Affirmative Action   505
Seeking Full Equality: Opportunity or Result?   505 • Affirmative Action in the Reagan-Bush Era   507 • The Future of Civil Rights   508

Women's Rights   509
Two Steps Forward, One Step Back   509 • The Struggle for Suffrage   510 • The Road to Equality   511 • Seeking Equality Through the Courts   511

Civil Rights and Other Minorities   516
Hispanic Americans   516 • Native Americans   517

Emerging Minority Groups Seek Prominence   518
Americans with Disabilities   518

Civil Rights and the War on Terrorism   521

Civil Rights and Approaching Democracy   523

Summary   523

Key Terms   524

PoliSim Activity   524

Suggested Readings   525

PART V / POLICY MAKING IN AMERICAN DEMOCRACY

15   DOMESTIC AND ECONOMIC POLICY   526

Approaching Democracy Case Study: Tax Cuts and Approaching Democracy: "The First Major Achievement of a New Era"   526

Introduction: Public and Economic Policy and the Democratic Process   528
Types of Policies   528

The Policy-Making Process   531
The Life Cycle of Policy Making   531 • Getting onto the Public Agenda   533 • Getting onto the Formal Agenda   534 • Implementing a Policy   535 • Evaluating a Policy   536 • Terminating a Policy   536 • Continuing a Policy   536

Regulatory Policy   537
Regulating the Environment   538

Social Welfare Policy   541
The Social Security Act   541 • The War on Poverty   542

Economic Policy   545

The Goals of Economic Policy   547

The Politics of the Federal Budget   547
The President Proposes, Congress Disposes   547 • How the Budget Is Prepared   548

Taxing   552
Sources of Tax Dollars   552 • Tax Reform   553

Spending   554

The Politics of International Economic Policy   554
The GATT Uruguay Round   556 • The NAFTA Treaty   556 • The Need for International Policy Coordination   556

Summary   558

Key Terms   560

PoliSim Activity   560

Suggested Readings   560

16   FOREIGN POLICY   562

Approaching Democracy Case Study: Operation Enduring Freedom: Building an International Coalition to Defeat Terrorism   562

Introduction: Foreign Policy and Democracy   564

An Overview of American Foreign Policy   565
Isolation and Regionalism   565 • World War I   566 • World War II   567 • Globalism and the Cold War   568 • The Post–Cold War Era   573

The Constitution and Foreign Policy   579
The President versus Congress   579

The Foreign Policy Bureaucracy   581
The Department of State   581 • The Department
of Defense   581 • The National Security Council   582 • The CIA
and Intelligence Gathering   583 • The Agencies Behind Economic
Policy Making   583

Democratic Checks on Foreign Policy   585
The Press   585 • The Public   586

Summary   588
Key Terms   589
PoliSim Activity   589
Suggested Readings   590

Appendix 1: Presidents and Congresses,
1789–2000   592

Appendix 2: Supreme Court Justices   594

Appendix 3: Declaration of Independence   596

Appendix 4: *The Federalist,* No. 10, James
Madison   598

Appendix 5: *The Federalist,* No. 51, James
Madison   601

Appendix 6: Introducing the Concept of Approaching
Democracy   603

Glossary   605

Notes   615

Photo Credits   629

Index   631

BOXED FEATURES

THE ROAD TO DEMOCRACY

The Back of the Bus	22
Balancing Congressional and Presidential Powers	58
And Then There Was One: Lowering the Confederate Flag	98
Crackup of the Congressional Committees	136
From the Imperial to the Imperiled to the Impervious Presidency	185
The "Borking" of the Federal Judiciary	220
Engineering a Disaster	262
Chicago, 1968, to Philadelphia and Los Angeles, 2000: The Vanishing Presidential Convention	332
Elections in Zimbabwe	364
Half a Century of Student Protest	390
The Internet Scoop That Started It All	428
Questioning the Death Penalty	458
Jackson, Mississippi: Freedom Rides the Span of 40 Years	502
Where Have You Gone, Joe Camel?	530

DEMOCRACY IN THE NEW MILLENNIUM

The Web and Dissent in the Twenty-First Century	24
The Constitution and the Computer	73
Paying the Bill for Fighting Terrorism	110
Surfing the "Digital Divide"	157
FirstGov.org: Three Clicks to Service	196
Justice in Wartime	239
"Bureaucracy on the Web" Has a Positive Connotation	274
Do "Likely" Voters Make It to the Voting Booth on Election Day?	307
Democrats Gain Ground in the Internet Race for Voters	342
Voting on the Internet in the Digital Age	377
Growing Better Grass-Roots through Cyber-Lobbying	412
The Impact of New Technology on Journalism	443
Preserving DNA Privacy?	484
Engineering a New Diversity	522
Making On-Line Calculations for a Secure Retirement	558
The U.S.–Afghanistan War and New Military Technology	587

APPROACHING DIVERSITY

The 2000 Census: "Never Have We Been so Diverse"   6
Abigail Adams: The First Feminist?   39
Of Gay Marriages, Civil Unions, and States' Rights   82
States and the Violence Against Women Act   108
Nancy Pelosi Makes History—Twice!   145
The Bush Executive Office   172
F.W.O.T.S.C.: Sandra Day O'Connor   214
Fairness of the Federal Merit Promotion Process   254
The Gender Gap in the 2000 Elections   295
Courting the Hispanic Vote   334
Gender Still Counts   355
Building a Latino Power Base   406
Young People Up to Speed on Terrorism News   432
Courting Justice: Gay Rights and the Supreme Court   480
Leveling the Playing Field   512
No Child Left Behind Act of 2001: Reauthorization of the Elementary
    and Secondary Education Act   531

APPROACHING DEMOCRACY AROUND THE GLOBE

The Freedom Gap   11
A Century of Freedom   63
Three Countries, One Continent: Federalism Crosses the Canadian Border   92
The Incoming Tide of Democracy in the Twenty-first Century   121
Mexico and Vicente Fox   180
Democracy and Judicial Independence   207
Polling in Riyadh   286
The Rise and Fall of Taiwan's Nationalist Party   322
Democracy Sweeps Africa   352
The Perils of International Democracy Assistance   398
The Proliferation of the Internet   429
Justice, China Style   470
Women of the House: Britain vs. Afghanistan   515
A Global Education Plan for All   555
An Alliance with a Future: Vaclav Havel's Vision   575

ADDITIONAL BOXES

Shays's Rebellion	40
Law Clerks: The Real "10th Justices"?	224
The INS Fiasco: Student Visa for September 11 Terrorists Renewed	250
Know Your Grasp of the Hatch Act	255
The National Science Foundation: A Model for Efficiency	261
Overhauling Bureaucracy: A "Transformation Plan" for the United States Postal Service	264
Our Ailing Bureaucracy	273
The Major American Parties	317
Caltech/MIT Voting Technology Report: What Is; What Could Be	354
Best Practices in Managing Voter Registration	357
Federal Elections	358
Voters Rate Themselves on the 2000 Election	368
How the Electoral College Works	370
Lobbying Gone Bad: Lessons from Enron	394
Tools of the Trade: How TV News Gathering Evolved	426
The Rehnquist Court: Jurists or Activists?	474
Orwell's Justice: The War on Drugs and Terrorism	476
Apologizing for the Past: Considering Slavery Reparations	493
Echoes from Ghost Ridge: *Cobell v. Norton*	519
Your Hamburger: 41,000 Regulations	543
Understanding the ABM Treaty	570
The Slow Odyssey of China	577

PREFACE

Welcome to the fourth edition of *Approaching Democracy!* From the moment eight years ago when the first edition went to press, the "professor" in each of us began mentally updating and modifying the original theme of the textbook. Now with the enormous challenges facing our country in the "war on terrorism," and institutional changes in the government that are underway, we face the task of using our theme of "approaching democracy" as a standard to test the democratic nature of this nation's quest to balance security and liberty. In making this effort, we have learned so much from the hundreds of students enrolled in our classes, as well as those who e-mailed or contacted us through our home page. We have also listened to our undergraduate readers throughout the country. From both of us we extend a heartfelt thank you!

Why *Approaching Democracy?*

The fourth edition of *Approaching Democracy* remains an exploration of the American experiment in self-governing. A great deal has happened in American politics since we published the first edition in 1996; we have tried to capture those changes not only factually, but thematically as well.

Our title and theme come from Vaclav Havel, a former dissident Czechoslovakian playwright once imprisoned by his country's communist government and later elected its president. Addressing a joint session of the U.S. Congress on February 21, 1990, Havel noted that with the collapse of the Soviet Union, millions of people from Eastern Europe were involved in a historically irreversible process, beginning their quest for freedom and democracy. And it was the United States of America that provided the model, the way to democracy and independence, for these newly freed peoples. But Havel put his own spin on the notion of American democracy as a model. "As long as people are people," Havel explained, "democracy, in the full sense of the word, will always be no more than an ideal. In this sense, you, too, are merely approaching democracy. But you have one great advantage: You have been approaching democracy uninterruptedly for more than two hundred years, and your journey toward the horizon has never been disrupted by a totalitarian system."[1]

The United States has been endeavoring to approach democracy for over two hundred years. In spite of its astonishing diversity and the consequent potential for hostility and violence, the United States has moved closer to the democratic ideal than any other country. But the process of approaching democracy is a continual one, and the debate about how to achieve democratic aspirations drives our politics. In other words, American democracy remains very much a work in progress.

We believe the political history of the world in which we live has validated this democratic experiment in self-government. In the early 1990s Samuel Huntington wrote about the "third wave" of the world's democratization that began in Portugal in 1974. He argued that the first wave of democratization extended from the American Revolution and ended with the fall of the empires at the close of World War I, and that the second wave resulted from the world's de-colonization movement at the end of World War II. While Huntington posited that each of these democratization movements would be followed by the rise of autocratic forms of

---

[1]Congressional Record–House, February 21, 1990, p. H392–95.

government, such as fascism or socialism, this time the end of the third wave of democratization has been different. Countries in Eastern Europe, South America, and elsewhere have either developed or retained their democratic regimes, or have moved more in that direction. The number of democracies worldwide increased from a few dozen in the 1950s to 121 of the 192 independent countries by mid-2002. As a result, writes Joshua Muravchik of the American Enterprise Institute, "Democracy has become an expectation, its claims hard to resist. . . .[D]emocracy has established itself as a universal norm."[2]

Clearly, we live in an age of democratic aspiration, and for many around the world who seek to achieve democracy, the United States represents a model of the democratic process. As Havel expressed, the triumph of democratic ideas in Eastern Europe was inspired by America's example of freedom and democracy. We are the laboratory for those who have broken from their totalitarian past and for those who dream of doing so. Notice how many Afghan men shaved their beards and how many women removed their burkas and smiled after the rout of the Taliban. The difference between living under a political system that promotes freedom and one that enslaves its citizens is easy to identify. What is less clear involves designing a system that will foster liberty and freedom, even when one disagrees with the government that is setting the rules.

But now we can see that our laboratory of democracy must continually operate. In many respects, the earliest edition of this book was written with an eye toward measuring whether the emerging democracies from the breakup of the Soviet Union would remain democratic. In this edition, what was once an external examination of the nature of democratic governments has become an internal examination of the nature of America's own democracy, as the government forms its policies for fighting its "war on terrorism." Since the terrible attacks of September 11, 2001, political discussion has raged over how to protect this country and still remain true to the ideals of the democracy as expressed by the Declaration of Independence, the Constitution, and the Bill of Rights. The world is watching us as we face this test. We have found that this book's theme of "approaching democracy" is the ideal scheme for evaluating whether, after so many tragic efforts over the last two centuries of sacrificing liberty in order to gain a measure of security, this nation will be able to find the proper, measured balance between these two goals in defending itself. Our challenge then, has been to use our "approaching democracy" theme in the fourth edition both to evaluate the impact on America's democracy in fighting terrorism, while also offering a vision of what America will look like in the future. Various chapters in this book examine the American approach to democracy—sorting out the ideals, studying the institutions, processes, and policies, and analyzing the dilemmas and paradoxes of freedom.

Organization

Part I presents the foundations of American government. Our theme is introduced in Chapter 1, where we identify the goals and elements that can be used to evaluate America's approach to democracy. We introduce a few widely accepted "elements of democracy" that serve as markers to identify progress toward the democratic ideals we identified earlier.

Part II explores the institutions of American democracy. It describes the various governmental arenas—the judiciary, the Congress, the executive branch, and the bureaucracy—where the struggle over democratic ideals is played out.

Part III focuses on the processes of American government and democracy. Through the avenues of public opinion, political parties, elections, interest groups, and the media, citizens can access and direct their government to achieve their desired goals.

---

[2]Joshua Muravchik, "Democracy's Quiet Victory," *New York Times*, August 19, 2001.

Part IV provides a detailed analysis of various issues of civil rights and liberties. They include the most fundamental rights of Americans, such as freedom of speech and religion, and are considered by many to be the foundation of our democracy.

Part V addresses the policy-making process and its consequences. How well national policy makers respond to the challenges of policy making—and how democratic the policies are—remain crucial questions as American government continues the process of approaching democracy.

Instructional Features

We hope readers will take advantage of the unique features of this book, which have been redesigned and refocused to better illustrate our theme of approaching democracy.

Case Studies open each chapter with a full-length discussion that integrates our theme and lays the groundwork for the material that follows. We have taken special care in selecting cases that provide anchors for the material covered in each chapter. Topics like the life and politics of Cesar Chavez, the Congress's passage of the U.S.A. Patriot Act, as well as campaign finance reform, the creation of a Department of Homeland Security, and President George W. Bush's leadership in building an international coalition aimed at defeating terrorist networks provide an opportunity for students to examine political events within the context of approaching democracy.

Democracy in the New Millennium concludes each chapter and examines how the constantly changing technological and political innovations, such as those on the Internet and with computers, have opened up—and sometimes even threatened—the process of American government to student and citizen involvement.

Each of these boxes offers websites that can be searched for more information. Topics such as the effect of the new copyright laws on the availability of information, the ways in which administrators are trying to "engineer diversity" to avoid the legal problems of affirmative action, internet voting, the federal government's new official web gateway http://www.firstgov.com/, the dangers to privacy presented by combining the human genome project and changes in the rules for access to the government's medical data base illustrate this theme.

The Road to Democracy examines the approach to democracy in a historical fashion, using a "That Was Then" and "This Is Now" theme. Here we study points in the development of the American political system in which a choice had to be made. The search for reparations for slavery by African Americans, the effect of the changes in Title IX of the Federal Education Act on women's sports and women's rights, and the changes in the use of the Confederate flag in the South are examples of these critical points in American political development.

Approaching Democracy Around the Globe examines the approach to democracy from a comparative perspective by studying changes in the governmental systems in other parts of the world. Features of the American political system like the Constitution and judicial independence are compared with those of other countries, while the role of women in Afghanistan and Great Britain, the lack of defendants' rights in China, and elections under the autocratic regime of President Robert Mugabe of Zimbabwe are compared to the United States.

Approaching Diversity boxes examine the difficulties that many groups have endured in their effort to be included in the American democratic experiment. Subjects explored include the efforts of political parties to reach out to the growing Latino community, the dramatic changes in the nation's public education system created by the Bush administration's 2001 "No Child Left Behind Act," the changing nature of gay rights as well as the effect of Vermont's Civil Union law on the nation's marriage laws, the changing composition of the federal workforce, and the gender gap in American politics.

Chapter Pedagogy

Each chapter contains a chapter outline, questions for reflection after each opening case study and throughout the chapter, a running glossary in the margin, key terms listed at the end of the chapter, a summary, and a list of suggested readings. A list of the Supreme Court Justices and a transcript of Vaclav Havel's address to Congress have been added to the materials in our appendix, which also include the founding documents and the list of Presidents and Congresses.

Although an introductory course in American government is not solely a course on current events, students are always interested in what is going on around them. Throughout the text, we use examples that are at the forefront of the news so that students have background information to draw from. Examples in the text put today's headlines into meaningful context, from the governments "war on terrorism" to the effects of campaign finance reform.

Technology Initiatives

With the development of new technologies, we have discovered more ways of helping students and instructors to further understand and analyze information. In this edition, we have made every effort to give both instructors and students a large array of multimedia tools to help with both the presentation and the learning of material.

- **New PoliSim version 2.0 (0-13-111573-1)**

    PoliSim is a dynamic series of multilevel simulations developed by Prentice Hall exclusively for American government that require students to make politically charged decisions based on the evaluation of data and information obtained from a variety of authentic sources. Students will use information such as real election results, demographics, maps, and voting score cards from actual Senators to complete simulations in a highly interactive, fully multimedia environment. Some of the simulations enable a Web browser so that students are encouraged to do additional research in order to make intelligent decisions. Simulations are current as of the midterm elections of 2002.

    PoliSim 2.0 features several improvements over version 1.0. Most notably, there are six new simulations for a total of 17, including a simulation on running for Congress and the Civil Rights Timeline (PoliSim simulations are incorporated into the table of contents for your convenience). A new user interface featuring a results reporter has been added to track progress and outcomes of each simulation for easy grading. For your added convenience, PoliSim is integrated into the end-of-chapter material of *Approaching Democracy*.

    PoliSim is included free with all new copies of the text and is CD-ROM based. A Web browser is required for the successful completion of some simulations. For complete hardware requirements, please refer to the end of the book.

- **New and Improved Evaluating Online Resources for Political Science with Research Navigator™**

    Prentice Hall's Research Navigator™, the newest addition to the reliable Internet guide for political science, keeps instructors and students abreast of the latest news and information, and helps students create top-quality research papers. From finding the right articles and journals, to citing sources, drafting and writing effective papers, and completing research assignments, Research Navigator™ simplifies and streamlines the entire process. Complete with extensive help on the research process and three exclusive databases full of relevant and reliable source material including EBSCO's ContentSelect™ Academic Journal Database, *The New York Times* Search-by-Subject Archive, and "Best of the Web" Link Library. A unique access code for Research Navigator™ is provided on the inside front cover of the booklet. Evaluating Online Resources for Political Science with Research Navi-gator™ is free when packaged with *Approaching Democracy* and available for stand-alone sale. Take a tour on the web at http://www.researchnavigator.com.

- **Improved Companion Website™ www.prenhall.com/berman**

    Students can now take full advantage of the World Wide Web to enrich the study of American government through the Approaching Democracy Website. Created by Larry Elowitz, the site features interactive practice tests, chapter objectives and overviews, additional graphs and charts, and over 150 primary source documents that are referenced in the text. Interactive Web exercises guide students to do research with a series of questions and links. Students can also tap into information regarding the midterm elections of 2002, writing in political science, career opportunities, and internship information. Students and instructors will benefit from material providing the latest news from highly regarded media outlets. Finally, a special feature allows instructors to create a customized syllabus for *Approaching Democracy* and post it conveniently online.

■ **Course Management and Distance Learning Solutions**

For instructors interested in managing their courses online, whether locally on campus or in a distance learning environment, Prentice Hall offers fully customizable online courses in both WebCT and Blackboard platforms. Ask your local Prentice Hall representative for details or visit our special demonstration site at http://www.prenhall. com/cms for more information.

■ **Course Compass Edition (0-13-110256-7)**

For instructors who would like to implement the use of course management software to organize their course and communicate with students, Prentice Hall is pleased to offer Approaching Democracy Course Compass Edition, featuring a host of organizational tools, such as gradebook management, an interactive syllabus, test preparation, and preloaded instructional content supporting the text. Instructors can save a great deal of time preparing for lectures and managing their course.

Supplements Available for the Instructor

■ **New Instructor's Resource CD-ROM (0-13-183074-0)**

The new Prentice Hall Instructor's Resource CD-ROM allows you maximum flexibility as you prepare your lectures and manage your class. For presentation use, this CD contains a database featuring most of the art from the text, more than 30 video and audio segments of classical and contemporary political science footage, and several simulations from PoliSim. An easy to use interface (organized logically by chapter) allows you to customize your lectures with your own original material and the assets we've provided. For your convenience, we've gotten you started with an entirely new pre-built PowerPoint presentation created especially for *Approaching Democracy*. To allow for optimum organization, we have also included the Instructor's Resource Manual in MS Word format to allow you to customize resources depending on how you organize your course.

■ **Instructor's Manual with Test Item File (0-13-110252-4)**

For each chapter, a summary, review of concepts, lecture suggestions and topic outlines, and additional resource materials—including a guide to media resources—are provided. An electronic version is also included on the Instructor's Resource CD-ROM. Thoroughly revised to ensure the highest level of quality and accuracy, the test item file offers over 1800 questions in multiple choice, true/false, and essay format with page references to the text.

■ **Prentice Hall Test Manager (0-13-110254-0)**

A computerized test bank contains the items from the Test Item File. The program allows full editing of questions and the addition of instructor-generated items. Suitable for Windows and Macintosh operating systems.

■ **American Government Transparencies, Series VI (0-13-011764-1)**

This set of over 100 full-color transparency acetates reproduces illustrations, charts, and maps from the text, as well as from additional sources. An instructor's guide is also available.

■ **Prentice Hall Custom Video: How a Bill Becomes a Law (0-13-032676-3)**

This 25-minute video chronicles an environmental law in Massachusetts from its start as one citizen's concern to its passage in Washington, D.C. Through narrative and graphics, students see the step-by-step process of how a bill becomes a law.

■ **PowerPoint Gallery**

For each chapter, the PowerPoint Gallery provides electronic files for each figure and table in the text, along with ready-to-customize PowerPoint slides. With the use of this tool you may create a dynamic PowerPoint presentation or print your own customized 4-color transparencies. The PowerPoint Gallery is included on the Instructor's Resource CD-ROM.

■ **Films for the Humanities and Social Sciences**

With a qualifying order of textbooks from Prentice Hall, you may select from a high-quality library of political science videos from Films for the Humanities and Social Sciences. Please contact your local Prentice Hall representative for a complete listing.

Supplements Available for the Student

■ **Study Guide (0-13-110257-5)**

Includes chapter outlines, study notes, a glossary, and practice tests designed to reinforce information in the text and help students develop a greater understanding of American government and politics.

■ **Supplementary Books and Readings for American Government**

Each of the following books features specialized topical coverage allowing you to tailor your American government course to suit the needs of your region or your particular teaching style. Featuring contemporary issues or timely readings, any of the following books are available for a discount when bundled with *Approaching Democracy*. Please visit our Online Catalog at http://www.prenhall.com/berman for additional details.

Government's Greatest Achievements: From Civil Rights to Homeland Security
Paul C. Light, Brookings Institution
ISBN: 0131101927 © 2004

American Politics: Core Arguments—Current Controversy, 2nd Edition
Peter Wooley, Fairleigh Dickenson University
Albert Papa, University of New Jersey
ISBN: 0130879193 © 2002

Contemporary Readings in American Government
Mark Rozell, The Catholic University of America
John White, The Catholic University of America
ISBN: 0130406457 © 2002

Issues in American Political Life: Money, Violence, and Biology, 4th Edition
Robert Thobaben, Wright State University
Donna Schlagheck, Wright State University
Charles Funderburk, Wright State University
ISBN: 0130336726 © 2002

Choices: An American Government Reader—Custom Publishing
Gregory Scott, University of Central Oklahoma
Katherine Tate, University of California—Irvine
Ronald Weber, University of Wisconsin—Milwaukee
ISBN: 013090399X © 2001

Civil Rights and Liberties: Provocative Questions and Evolving Answers
Harold Sullivan, The City University of New York
ISBN: 0-13-084514-0 © 2001

Sense and Non-Sense: American Culture and Politics
J. Harry Wray, DePaul University
ISBN: 0-13-083343-6 © 2001

21 Debated Issues in American Politics
Gregory Scott, University of Central Oklahoma
Loren Gatch, University of Central Oklahoma
ISBN: 0-13-021991-6 © 2000

Government and Politics in the Lone Star State: Theory and Practice, 4th Edition
L. Tucker Gibson, Trinity University
Clay Robison, The Houston Chronicle
ISBN: 0-13-034050-2 © 2002

Rethinking California: Politics and Policy in the Golden State
Matthew Cahn, California State University–Northridge
H. Eric Schockman, University of Southern California
David Shafie, Ohio University
ISBN: 0-13-467912-1 © 2001

The *Real Politics in America* series is another resource for contemporary instructional material. To bridge the gap between research and relevancy, we have launched a new series of supplemental books with the help of series editor Paul Herrnson of the University of Maryland. More descriptive than quantitative, more case study than data study, these books span all topics to bring students relevant details in current political science research. From exploring the growing phenomenon of direct democracy to who runs for the state legislature, these books show students that real political science is meaningful and exciting. Available for a discount when bundled with *Approaching Democracy*. Please see your Prentice Hall representative or access http://www.prenhall.com/berman for a complete listing of titles in the series.

ACKNOWLEDGMENTS

For the fourth edition of our text, we have accumulated a number of debts to the many talented and committed folks who constitute the Prentice Hall team. It is a pleasure to acknowledge our friends here. First, we owe much to the continual enthusiastic support of Heather Shelstad for this revision. Her vision for revising this edition of the book, as well as her understanding of our commitment to the theme of approaching democracy helped us bring this new edition of the text to completion. Heather's assistant Jessica Drew did a great job managing the traffic between two authors and their publisher.

We are especially indebted to Barbara Heinssen for her incredible herculean efforts in guiding the development of the new edition and saving us not only from ourselves but also from many errors. Our thanks also go to the book's talented production team for its skill in helping us to overcome the challenges of producing the most up-to-date book including the 2002 election results. We are especially grateful to Jennifer Murtoff, our project manager, for her professionalism and grace under pressure in supervising the entire effort, to Megan Hill for her skilled copyediting, to Verna Ansel for creating the fine page layout, to Ximena Tamvakopoulos for creating the spectacular new design for the book, and to Guy Ruggiero for his talented supervision of rendering art. We would also like to thank Chris Cardone for keeping us on our time schedule, and it was very good to be working again with the talented Rochelle Diogenes on this edition. Our deep appreciation also goes to our photo researcher, Kathy Ringrose, for her dedicated efforts to visually tell the story of "approaching democracy." Without the diligent efforts of all of these people, revising this book would not have been possible. We are also very grateful to James Corey, who added the annotations to the Constitution. We are, as always, thankful for the continuing support of Charlyce Jones Owen and marketing director Beth Mejia. When the most important questions were on the table, this leadership team supported the concept of *Approaching Democracy*. No authors can really ever ask for more.

We also wish to thank the many reviewers of the four editions of *Approaching Democracy* for their valuable suggestions.

Robert Jacobs, Central Washington University
Rebecca Britton, California State University, Chico
E. Terrence Jones, University of Missouri, St. Louis
William Bianco, Pennsylvania State University
Mark A. Cichock, University of Texas at Arlington
Stacy B. Gordon, University of Nevada, Reno
Henneth G. Hartman, Longview Community College
Rebekah Herrick, Oklahoma State University
Diana Owen, Georgetown University
Kelly D. Patterson, Brigham Young University
Dan Shea, Allegheny College
Robert L. Silvey, John Jay College/CUNY
Shirley Anne Warshaw, Gettysburg College

Larry Berman would like to thank his students at UC Davis for their many ideas for revising the book. He is also most appreciative of his former graduate students who are teaching American government using the book and always providing feedback. He especially thanks Professors Linda Valenty, Monte Freidig, Drew Froelinger, and Stephen Routh in this regard. Jason Newman performed his usual duty as a great research assistant, and now that he is gainfully employed in the academy, his loss to the next edition is compensated only by knowing how many students will benefit from Jason's presence in the classroom. Berman also thanks UC Davis undergraduate Erika Sy for her research on education policy and for her contribution to the boxed feature on the *No Child Left Behind Act*. Berman's administrative assistant at the UC Washington Center, Channa Threat, did more than he can possibly thank her for in the capacity of researching, writing, organizing, and helping him manage his day job. Channa is about as close one gets to the meaning of "indispensable." Also at the Center, Mary Byrne helped with the flow of UPS packages and copying of chapters when Channa was in class. Dianne Lessman and Michael Sesay used their technological know-how to print whatever map or table I requested. Rodger Rak, Manager of Information Services, and Karen Akerson, Associate Director, always knew when not to bother me because I was "updating" *Approaching Democracy*.

Bruce Allen Murphy wishes to recognize his undergraduate students in his Government 101 course at Lafayette College for their many suggestions and critiques for revising the textbook. Thanks also go to assistant Carmela Karns and secretary Ruth Panovec for helping to keep him on track. The incomparable Kirby Library research librarian, Mercedes Sharpless, deserves heartfelt gratitude for providing countless answers to desperate and seemingly impenetrable late-night questions. Once again, colleague John Kincaid was good enough to offer another comprehensive critique of the Federalism chapter. Sincere appreciation goes to Fred Morgan Kirby and his family for their generous support of the chair that he now holds. Finally, thanks go to his colleagues at Lafayette College, most especially Government and Law Department Head John McCartney, for helping to make his work environment so pleasurable and productive.

Since no two scholars can master all of the fields in the political science discipline, we express gratitude to all of our colleagues for the many academic contributions upon which we drew for the writing of this book. We would both like to express appreciation for the generations of students at the University of California and Lafayette College for the continuing flow of unique questions and ideas that spurred us in the writing of this and other editions of the book. We would also like to thank those colleagues in the discipline who have provided us with suggestions for improving the volume after teaching with the first three editions, thus improving this new revision.

Finally, but most importantly, we would both like to recognize our families without whom this existence of clippings, updating, and collaborative writing would not be possible. Bruce Allen Murphy thanks his wife, Carol Lynn Wright, and his children, Emily and Geoffrey, both of whom are now college students themselves and reading textbooks in their own chosen fields of study, for their never-ending love, patience, and encouragement throughout the revision process.

Larry Berman joins Murphy in the affections to family, adding only what he expressed in previous editions: Scott and Lindsay are constant reminders that our theme "approaching democracy" works, and Nicole is living proof that life only gets better.

Larry Berman
Bruce Allen Murphy

ABOUT THE AUTHORS

Larry Berman is Professor of Political Science at the University of California, Davis, and since 1999 has served as the founding Director of the University of California, Washington Center, http://www.ucdc.edu. Berman is the author or co-author of ten books and numerous articles. His research and publications have focused on the presidency, foreign policy, and the war in Vietnam. The most recent book, *No Peace, No Honor* has been featured on C-Span's *Book TV,* the History Channel's *Secrets of War,* reviewed prominently in *The New York Times, Washington Post, Boston Globe, Sacramento Bee,* and *Washington Times.* In addition, he has appeared on a number of broadcasts, including Bill Moyers' PBS series, *The Public Mind,* and David McCullough's *American Experience* series, *Vietnam: A Television History.*

Berman has been awarded fellowships from the Guggenheim Foundation, the American Council of Learned Societies, the National Science Foundation, as well as several research grants from presidential libraries. He has been a Fellow at the Woodrow Wilson International Center for Scholars in Washington, D.C., and a scholar in residence at the Rockefeller Foundation's Center in Bellagio, Italy.

Berman has received the 1996 Outstanding Mentor of Women in Political Science Award from the Women's Caucus for Political Science. He received the 1994 Bernath Lecture Prize, given annually by the Society for Historians of American Foreign Relations to a scholar whose work has most contributed to our understanding of foreign relations.

His class on the American presidency is cited in Lisa Birnbach's *New and Improved College Guide* as one of the most recommended classes for undergraduates at UC Davis. Berman has often conducted a series of live interactive television programs from Washington with his undergraduate classes at UC Davis on the American presidency and American government. The programs are available from PBS Adult Learning.

In addition to his work in political science, Berman is an authority on integrating and reengineering liberal arts education with technology. He regularly presents seminars and workshops on the subject to educators across the United States and has lectured in Australia, China, Germany, Israel, France, the Netherlands, and Vietnam on American politics, foreign policy, and multi-media technology in the classroom.

Bruce Allen Murphy is the Fred Morgan Kirby Professor of Civil Rights in the Department of Government and Law at Lafayette College. He is a nationally recognized judicial biographer and scholar on the American Supreme Court, civil rights and liberties, judicial behavior, and judicial biography.

Murphy is the author of many publications, including his newest judicial biography *Wild Bill: The Legend and Life of William O. Douglas, America's Most Controversial Supreme Court Justice,* which has been selected by the Book-of-the-Month and History book clubs. He also wrote *Fortas: The Rise and Ruin of a Supreme Court Justice,* which was nominated for both the Pulitzer Prize and the National Book Award. His bestselling *The Brandeis-Frankfurter Connection: The Secret Political Activities of Two Supreme Court Justices,* which received the American Bar Association's Certificate of Merit, was listed among *The New York Times'* Best Books for 1983 and was serialized by *The Washington Post.* In addition, he edited *Portraits of American Politics: A Reader.*

Murphy has received numerous teaching awards for his courses in American politics, civil rights and liberties, and Constitutional law. He has been a finalist in the Council for the Advancement and Support of Education's national Professor of the Year competition and was cited as a Best Professor in Lisa Birnbach's *New and Improved College Guide.* He is listed in both *Who's Who in America* and *Who's Who in the World.*

APPROACHING DEMOCRACY

1 APPROACHING DEMOCRACY

CHAPTER OUTLINE

Approaching Democracy Case Study:
  Sí Se Puede—"It Can Be Done"

Introduction: Democracy as an Evolutionary
  Process

Forming a Picture of Democracy

The Roots of Democracy

The Ideals of Democracy

The Elements of Democracy

APPROACHING DEMOCRACY CASE STUDY

Sí Se Puede—"It Can Be Done"

Cesar Chavez read the telegram sent to him by Dr. Martin Luther King, Jr., in March 1968, praising the fasting labor leader in Delano, California, for his tireless efforts in fighting for racial equality. "You and your valiant fellow workers have demonstrated your commitment to righting grievous wrongs forced upon exploited people. We are together with you in spirit and in determination that our dreams for a better tomorrow will be realized." Like King, Chavez had fought for economic equality since the civil rights movement started in the early

1950s. Chavez would continue to lead boycotts and stand at picket lines to fight for the rights of farm workers for the next quarter-century.

Working in the fields since the age of ten and leaving school in the eighth grade because his father became injured, Chavez joined the other 300,000 Mexican Americans who annually migrated from Washington state to southern California in search of a better life. Chavez met an organizer for the Community Services Organization, a Mexican American self-help group, while working in a fruit orchard outside of San Jose in 1952. Chavez became a full-time organizer for the group joining hundreds of other Mexican Americans to create voter registration drives and campaign against racial discrimination. Through tireless travel across the farms and fields of the West, Chavez politicized migrant Mexican Americans and their communities to stand up for their rights as American workers. In 1965, Chavez led his organization of 1,200 workers to join the AFL-CIO strike against the grape and wine producers of Delano, California. Despite ups and downs, Chavez would keep up the boycott for the next ten years.

In 1970, the United Farm Workers (UFW), under Chavez, finally organized the grape-growing industry field workers, enlisting over 60,000 dues-paying members at its highest point in 1972. In the process of fighting the grape growers, Chavez forged a powerful coalition of unions, church groups, nonprofit organizations, students, minorities, and consumers to extend protective labor legislation to farm workers. Jerry Brown, a sympathetic Democratic governor in California, helped pass the Agriculture Labor Relations Act in 1975 enabling UFW members to sign contracts with their employers for the first time.

Question for Reflection: Groups of underrepresented workers exist in America today—home health aides for the elderly, nannies and au pairs. What actions might they take to increase their rights?

Chavez continued to fight to enforce statutes and called for boycotts of table grapes and lettuce. He also expanded into other areas of farm-worker abuse, targeting the use of dangerous pesticides in farm-worker communities. Demonstrating his resolve through the Ghandian spirit of nonviolence, he conducted several hunger strikes while subsisting on UFW pay of $5,000 a year.

When he died of heart failure in 1993, over 44,000 people attended his funeral. He received the Presidential Medal of Freedom posthumously in 1994, the highest civilian honor bestowed in the United States. Considered the "Dr. Martin Luther King" of the Hispanic civil rights movement, and the most visible political icon in the Latino community, Chavez also attracted the attention of other Americans who wanted to improve American democracy.

Seven years following Chavez's death in 1993, a surge in Hispanic voters in Arizona, California, Texas, and Florida created a powerful force compelling the passage of new state holidays in the name of Chavez. California passed a state holiday in his name, reflecting the new political voice represented by Latino voters in that state and revealed the profound political impact of demographic changes in the makeup of the American electorate. "When children learn about the great life of Martin Luther King, they will also learn about the great life of Cesar Chavez," said California's Governor Gray Davis.[1] The University of California has renamed its administrative holiday in honor of Cesar Chavez. Cesar Chavez Day will be observed the last Friday of March and be phased into all university locations by the year 2005. The first Cesar Chavez holiday was observed Friday, March 29, 2002.

Today the sons and daughters of the Cesar Chavez generation have become a more politically active group even than their parents. In fact, during the 1990s, the combined population of African Americans, Native American Islanders, and Hispanic/Latinos in the United States grew at 13 times the rate of the white population. Hispanics are concentrated in high-immigration gateway cities such as Los Angeles, New York City, and Miami. There are large Hispanic populations in Texas (6.7 million), New York (2.9 million), and Florida (2.7 million). Illinois, Arizona and New Jersey have more than 1 million Hispanics each. But California has the largest Hispanic population, with almost 11 million—nearly one of every three Americans in California is of Hispanic/Latino origin (see Figure 1.1).[2]

As Hispanics gain more political power due to population increase, they have altered the American electorate, in a way that captures the essence of what we

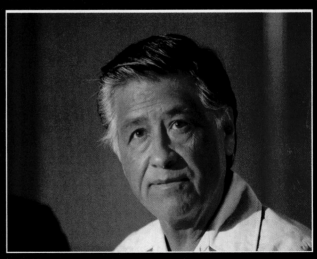

▲ The late Cesar Chavez championed the cause of largely Hispanic migrant workers. Several states have initiated drives for a holiday honoring him.

Figure 1.1
California's Population
The number of Hispanics in California grew dramatically in the last decade, while the number of non-Hispanic whites declined.
Source: U.S. Census Bureau.

Total population			
1990	29,760,021		
2000	33,871,648		

Non-Hispanic	Population		Percent change
White	15,816,790		-7.1%
Black	2,181,926		+4.3%
American Indian	178,984		-2.8%
Asian/Pacific Islander	3,752,596		+38.5%
Other	71,681		+27.8%
Multiracial	903,115		(NA)
Hispanic (any race)	10,966,550		+42.6%

mean by approaching democracy. While the nation's black and Hispanic populations are roughly equal, blacks hold almost twice as many Congressional seats. According to the 2000 U.S. Census the Hispanic/Latino population documented phenomenal growth (see Table 1.1). The political challenge facing Hispanics is that in 122 of the nation's 435 Congressional districts, Hispanics exceeded the national share of the Hispanic population, which is 12.5%. The Congressional Hispanic Caucus has created a political action committee for the sole purpose of recruiting Hispanic congressional candidates in order to gain a larger voice in the House of Representatives.

Question for Reflection: What can the current Congressional Hispanic Caucus learn from the activism of Cesar Chavez?

Table 1.1 ■ Resident Population of the U.S. by Age, Gender, Race/Ethnicity, and Region				
	1990		**2000**	
	Number	**Percent**	**Number**	**Percent**
Total Population	248,709,873	100.0	281,421,906	100.0
Under age 18	63,604,432	25.6	72,293,812	25.7
Ages 18 to 64	153,863,610	61.9	174,136,341	61.9
Ages 65 and over	31,241,831	12.6	34,991,753	12.4
Males	121,239,418	48.7	138,053,563	49.1
Females	127,470,455	51.3	143,368,343	50.9
White, non-Hispanic*	188,128,296	75.6	194,552,774	69.1
Black, non-Hispanic*	29,216,293	11.7	33,947,837	12.1
Hispanic	22,354,059	9.0	35,305,818	12.5
Asian, non-Hispanic*	6,968,359	2.8	10,476,678	3.7
American Indian, non-Hispanic*	1,793,773	0.7	2,068,883	0.7
Some other race, non-Hispanic*	249,093	0.1	467,770	0.2
Two or more races, non-Hispanic*	N/A	N/A	4,602,146	1.6

Note: N/A=Not Available.
*For 2000, excludes people who identified with two or more races.

Source: Reprinted by permission of Population Reference Bureau.

This case tells us much about America's approach to democracy. Cesar Chavez, the son of migrant workers, fought for the rights of farm workers, nearly all Hispanic, who constituted the backbone of California's agricultural economy. Most of us associate democracy with an expansion of the range of freedoms enjoyed by citizens. Although democracies do expand certain freedoms, they do not always protect basic human rights, political rights, and civil liberties. Citizens and migrant workers have sometimes been denied their rights to obtain an education, to choose where to live, or to decide which occupations to pursue, simply because of their race, ethnicity, religion, gender, or sexual orientation. American democracy has been remarkably open, over the long run, to expanding rights and liberties for all its citizens—even if those rights and liberties have been achieved only with struggle, sacrifice, and occasional failure. And the struggle never ends.

In this first chapter we begin by providing you with a template for evaluating the very idea of "approaching democracy," so that you can start formulating your own criteria and questions about the degree the United States currently meets the standards of a truly democratic society. We want you to keep in mind that social policy in the United States has traditionally been shaped by categories in census data. "From 1790 to roughly 1960, the social policies were essentially detrimental to racial minorities, that is they were first about slavery and sustaining the slave system, and then in the late nineteenth century, they became about trying to establish the principles of racial superiority and inferiority," observed Kenneth Prewitt, director of the U.S. Census Bureau from October 1998 to January 2001. "Then in 1960 those policies shifted 180 degrees . . . You get equal opportunity programs, quota programs, affirmative action programs, the Voting Rights Act—a whole series of public policies that are trying to right some wrongs that have been in place for the entire nation's history. The classification system was still important because you did this with the basic principle of statistical proportionality. If there is 12.5 percent of the population that is African American, but they make up only 2 percent of the population, then something is wrong."[3] The new challenge for minorities in their approach to democracy comes in the prevailing sense that with 63 race categories (or 126 if you include Hispanic origin), it will be almost impossible to design public policy upon a racial classification system.

INTRODUCTION: DEMOCRACY AS AN EVOLUTIONARY PROCESS

Democracy has evolved over time in America—and is still evolving. To illustrate, consider how many of your classmates have the power to vote and participate in politics. Virtually all of you do now. On the other hand, how many of your classmates are free white males over the age of twenty-one who also own land? This small handful of people in your class would have been the only ones entrusted with the vote at the time of the framing of the Constitution. When you realize the incredible openness of American politics now, you can appreciate the changes that have occurred in American politics. As a result, today the United States stands as a beacon throughout the world for those seeking freedom and democratic government.

One of the most eloquent statements on the evolutionary nature of American democracy was made by Vaclav Havel, a former dissident Czechoslovakian playwright once imprisoned by that country's Communist government and later, following the end of communism, elected Czechoslovakia's president. Addressing a joint session of the U.S. Congress on February 21, 1990, Havel noted that with the collapse of the

APPROACHING DIVERSITY

The 2000 Census: "Never Have We Been so Diverse"

"America is probably the most diverse society on earth; it is certainly the most diverse industrialized one," writer Peter Schuck asserts in his book *Diversity in America*. When the Census Bureau released the results of the decennial census, the authors of the Census narrative observed, *"never have we been so diverse; never have we been so many; never have we been so carefully measured."*

In 1790 the census divided the population into three racial groups: whites, slaves, other persons (American Indians). By 1820 "free colored persons" was added to the classification scheme. After the civil war, "mulatto," "quadroon," and "octoroon" were shades of color classifications further defining "free colored people." Mexican first appeared as a category in 1930 but was dropped when the government of Mexico complained that Mexican was not a race. Mexicans were counted as white until 1970, when Hispanic origin became a category. As the chapter opening Approaching Democracy box showed, in 2000, for the first time in American history Hispanics overtook African Americans as the nation's largest minority. The following table shows the evolution of identity from 1860 to 2000.

▲ Bush and Muslim leaders meet in the aftermath of 9–11 in an effort to foster tolerance towards the Muslim community. President Bush denounced domestic attacks on Middle Eastern people.

Source: Jonathan Rauch, "Diversity in a New America." *The Brookings Review* (Winter 2002, Vol. 20, No. 1) pp. 4–5. See also www.ameristat.org.

The Evolution of Identity

Here are the categories used in the decennial counts from 1860 to 2000, as presented by AmeriStat (www.ameristat.org).

1860	1870	1880	1890[1]	1900[2]	1910	1920	1930	1940	1950
White	White	White	White	White	White	White	White	White	White
Black	Black	Black	Black	Black	Black	Black	Black	Black	Negro
Mulatto	Mulatto	Mulatto	Mulatto	(Negro descent)	Mulatto	Mulatto			
	Chinese	Chinese	Chinese	Chinese	Chinese	Chinese	Chinese	Chinese	Chinese
	Indian	Indian	Indian	Indian	Indian	Indian	Indian	Indian	Amer. Indian
			Quadroon						
			Octoroon						
			Japanese	Japanese	Japanese	Japanese	Japanese	Japanese	Japanese
						Filipino	Filipino	Filipino	Filipino
						Hindu	Hindu	Hindu	
						Korean	Korean	Korean	
							Mexican		
						Other	Other	Other	Other	Other

Bold letters indicate first usage since 1860.

NOTE: Before the 1970 Census, enumerators wrote in the race of individuals using the designated categories. In subsequent censuses, respondents or enumerators filled in circles next to the categories with which the respondent identified. Also beginning with the 1970 Census, people choosing American Indian, other Asian, other race, or for the Hispanic question, other Hispanic categories, were asked to write in a specific tribe or group. Hispanic ethnicity was asked of a sample of Americans in 1970 and of all Americans beginning with the 1980 Census.

[1]In 1890, mulatto was defined as a person who was three-eighths to five-eighths black. A quadroon was one-quarter black and an octoroon one-eighth black.

[2]American Indians have been asked to specify their tribe since the 1900 Census.

Sources: AmeriStat, "200 Years of U.S. Census Taking: Population and Housing Questions 1790–1990," U.S. Census Bureau. Copyright ©2001 *The Washington Post.* Reprinted by permission.

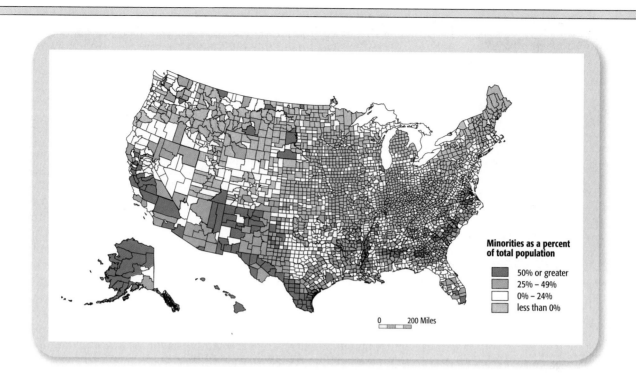

Minorities as a percent of total population

- 50% or greater
- 25% – 49%
- 0% – 24%
- less than 0%

0   200 Miles

1960	1970	1980	1990	2000
White	White	White	White	White
Negro	Negro or Black	Black or Negro	Black or Negro	Black, African American or Negro
Chinese	Chinese	Chinese	Chinese	Chinese
Amer. Indian	Indian (Amer.)	Indian	Indian (Amer.)	Amer. Indian or Alaska Native
	Japanese	Japanese	Japanese	Japanese
Filipino	Filipino	Filipino	Filipino	Filipino
		Asian Indian	Asian Indian	Asian Indian
	Korean	Korean	Korean	Korean
Aleut		Aleut	Aleut	
Eskimo		Eskimo	Eskimo	
Hawaiian	Hawaiian	Hawaiian	Hawaiian	Native Hawaiian
Part Hawaiian				
		Vietnamese	Vietnamese	Vietnamese
		Guamanian	Guamanian	Guamanian or Chamorro
		Samoan	Samoan	Samoan
	E		**Other Asian Pacific Islander**	**Other Asian**
				Other Pacific Islander
Other	T	Other	Other	Other race	Some other race
	H	Mexican	Mexican, Mexican Amer.,	Mexican, Mexican Amer.,	Mexican, Mexican Amer.
	N		**Chicano**	Chicano	Chicano
	I	**Puerto Rican**	Puerto Rican	Puerto Rican	Puerto Rican
	C	**Central/So. American**			
	I	**Cuban**	Cuban	Cuban	Cuban
	T	**Other Spanish**	Other Spanish/Hispanic	Other Spanish/Hispanic	Other Spanish/Hispanic/Latino
	Y	**(None of these)**	Not Spanish/Hispanic	Not Spanish/Hispanic	Not Spanish/Hispanic/Latino

▲ The Statue of Liberty has frequently been called the "Goddess of Democracy." This 2001 NYC Thanksgiving parade carried the Statue's likeness in a "Tribute to America."

Soviet Union, millions of people from Eastern Europe were involved in a "historically irreversible process," beginning their quest for freedom and democracy. And it was the United States of America that represented the model, "the way to democracy and independence," for these newly freed peoples. But Havel put his own spin on the notion of American democracy as a model:

> As long as people are people, democracy, in the full sense of the word, will always be no more than an ideal. In this sense, you too are merely approaching democracy. But you have one great advantage: you have been approaching democracy uninterruptedly for more than 200 years, and your journey toward the horizon has never been disrupted by a totalitarian system.[4]

This image of an America "approaching democracy" inspired the theme for this textbook and an excerpt of Havel's address is reprinted in the *Appendix*. Like Havel, we believe that the United States is still approaching democracy and that we constitute the world's great experiment in self-government as well as a beacon for freedom and opportunity. The pure joy on the faces of the men and women of Afghanistan when the rule of the Taliban ended was evident and the experiment in constructing a government with democratic forms began. Who would ever actually choose to live under the conditions of Taliban rule rather than under freedom and liberty? "No people on earth yearn to be oppressed or aspire to servitude or eagerly await the midnight knock of the secret police. If anyone doubts this, let them look to Afghanistan, where the Islamic street greeted the fall of tyranny with the song of celebration," President George W. Bush stated in his 2002 State of the Union address.

We live in an era of democratic aspiration. The number of democracies worldwide is on the rise (see Figures 1.2 and 1.3). The ideal of American democracy certainly influenced the hundreds of thousands of Chinese students who demonstrated in Tiananmen Square during the spring of 1989, with hopes of reforming their totalitarian government. These so-called dissidents identified their movement as "pro-democracy." They carried a statue similar to the Statue of Liberty through the square, calling it the "Goddess of Democracy," and proclaimed their inalienable rights to life, liberty, and the pursuit of happiness. Their demonstrations revealed something other than the desire to achieve democratic ideals; they also showed the difficulty of doing so under a repressive system. The student movement was crushed by the state, though for many in China or Zimbabwe, the dream of democracy endures. In Afghanistan, the joy of being free from tyranny is followed by the challenge of building systems that will maintain and nurture freedom and liberty. This is the challenge facing Afghanistan's new leaders as they "approach democracy" because, as a Freedom House study shows, there is an expanding "democracy gap" between Islamic countries and the rest of the world as illustrated in Figure 1.4 on page 10.[5]

QUOTE... UNQUOTE

"No one pretends that democracy is perfect or all-wise. Indeed, it has been said that democracy is the worst form of government except all those other forms that have been tried from time to time."

Winston Churchill

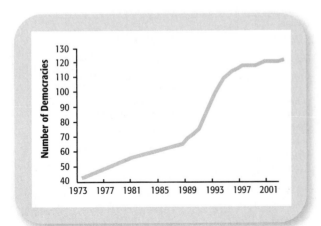
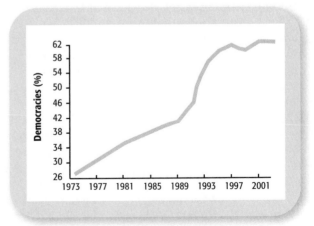

Figure 1.2 Tracking Democracy
Source: Reprinted by permission of The Freedom House.

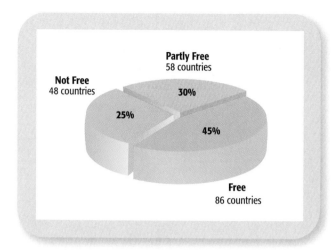

Figure 1.3a Status of Freedom in the World
Source: Reprinted by permission of The Freedom House.

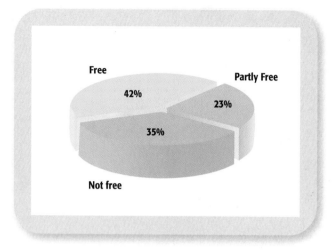

Figure 1.3b World Population by Free, Partly Free, Not Free

Forming a Picture of Democracy

One of the most astute observers of the American experiment in self-government was Alexis de Tocqueville. In 1835 he published a book of observations, *Democracy in America,* based on his journey throughout this new nation. "In America I sought more than America," he wrote. "I sought there the image of democracy itself, with its inclinations, its character, its prejudice, its passions, in order to learn what we have to fear or to hope from its progress." This eminent French writer wanted to do more than just describe one nation. "America was only the frame," Tocqueville later told the English philosopher John Stuart Mill. "My picture was Democracy."[6]

Our goal is a similar one. We wish to portray democracy as a system by showing how it works in the world's oldest democratic state. The United States has been making efforts to move toward democracy for more than two hundred years. In spite of its astonishing diversity and the consequent potential for hostility and violence, the United States has approached closer to the democratic ideal than nearly any other country, certainly closer than any other country of comparable heterogeneity and size. But the process of approaching democracy is a continual one. Indeed, even models of democracy, like Sweden, engage in a "democratic audit" aimed at taking stock of democratic gains. As Vaclav Havel made clear, the work of democracy is never finished. Understanding that evolutionary process in America begins with a discussion of the term *democracy* itself.

Webster's Dictionary defines **democracy** as "a government by the people, either directly or through elected representatives; rule by the ruled." The central idea is that democracies place key political powers in the hands of the people. At a minimum, citizens in a democracy choose their leaders freely from among competing groups and individuals. In highly developed democracies, the rights of the people extend well beyond this simple act of choosing leaders. Voters in advanced democracies are free to propose a wide array of public policy options and to join groups that promote those options. When Cesar Chavez joined the Community Services Organization in 1952, his crusade for improved worker conditions began. Eventually specific public policy legislation like the Agriculture Labor Relations Act of 1975 followed. Voters may even directly determine through **referenda** (proposed policy measures submitted for direct popular vote) which policy options will become the law of the land. This pattern contrasts sharply with that of an **authoritarian regime,** in which government stands apart from the people, oppressing citizens by depriving them of their basic freedom to speak, associate, write, and participate in political life without fear of punishment. Notice how many Afghan men shaved their beards and how many women removed their burkas after the rout of the

▼ A brave Chinese man faces down a column of tanks intent on reaching the democratic student protesters in Tiananmen Square. Eventually the man was pulled away by bystanders, saving his life, but allowing the tanks to roll toward the protesters.

democracy A system of government in which the people rule, either directly or through elected representatives.

referenda Proposals submitted by a state legislature to the public for a popular vote.

authoritarian regime An oppressive system of government in which citizens are deprived of their basic freedom to speak, write, associate, and participate in political life without fear of punishment.

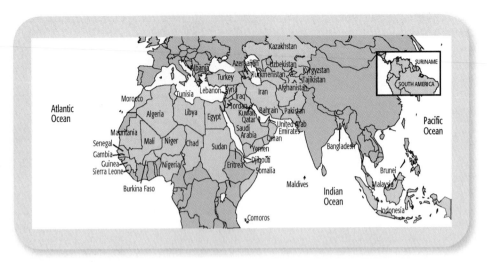

Figure 1.4   A Spectrum of Governments in the Islamic World
Countries with majority Muslim populations have greatly varying forms of government, ranging from democracy to monarchy and theocracy.

Democracy
Characterized by direct, free elections without restrictions on political parties; includes both parliamentary and republican systems.
Bangladesh; Senegal; Sierra Leone; Suriname; Turkey.

Emerging Democracy
Constitution provides for democratic, multiparty rule, but notable deficiencies remain.
Albania; Gambia; Indonesia; Lebanon; Niger.

Limited Democracy
Includes direct elections of at least one branch of legislature, but characterized by authoritarian rule with leaders elected by referendum or overwhelming majorities. Some had recent elections marred by opposition boycotts or serious irregularities.
Algeria; Azerbaijan; Burkina Faso; Chad; Djibouti; Egypt; Guinea; Kyrgyzstan; Kazakhstan; Maldives; Mali; Mauritania; Tajikistan; Tunisia; Turkmenistan; Uzbekistan; Yemen.

Authoritarian
Military or other authoritarian rule, with no elections or merely nominal ones.
Iraq; Libya; Syria.

Monarchy
Based on hereditary rule, with no elected legislative body; an asterisk denotes movement toward greater openness, with parliamentary elections planned within two years, or limited democratic experimentation under way.
Bahrain*; Brunei; Oman*; Qatar*; Saudi Arabia; United Arab Emirates.

Monarchy/Limited Democracy
Based on hereditary rule, but with an elected parliament with some power.
Jordan; Kuwait; Malaysia; Morocco.

Theocracy
Supreme leadership based on religious criteria, even if elections and some democracy coexist.
Iran.

Transitional
From military rule to civilian rule, as in Nigeria; or democratic practices suspended by seizure of power, as in Pakistan; or a transition government in place, but without full control of territory, as in Somalia.
Comoros; Eritrea; Nigeria; Pakistan; Somalia; Sudan.

No Functioning Central Government (in 2001)
Afghanistan.

Sources: C. A. World Factbook 2001: U.S. State Department. Reprinted by permission of *The New York Times.*

▼ With the Taliban rule over, Afghan women uncovered their faces with no fear of punishment.

Taliban. The difference between living under a political system that promotes freedom with one that enslaves its citizens is easy to identify. What is less clear involves designing a system that will foster liberty and freedom even when one disagrees with the government that is setting the rules.

Although political power in a democracy is in the hands of the people, not all democracies are alike. Let us look at two types: direct and indirect democracy.

APPROACHING DEMOCRACY AROUND THE GLOBE

The Freedom Gap

In an annual study of Freedom in the World 2001–2002, Freedom House concluded that there was a dramatic, expanding gap between Islamic countries and the rest of the world in their levels of freedom and democracy. "In the wake of the terrorist attacks against the United States on September 11, it is imperative that policymakers around the globe give serious attention to the democracy gap in the Islamic world," said Freedom House chairman, Bill Richardson. A non-Islamic country is more than three times likely to be democratic than an Islamic state. "This freedom and democracy divide exists not only between Islamic countries and the prosperous West. There is a growing chasm between the Islamic and the rest of the world. While most Western and non-western countries are moving towards greater levels of freedom, the Islamic world is lagging behind," observed Adrian Karatnycky, Freedom House president and coordinator of the survey.

In the organization's annual survey, 86 countries representing 2.54 billion people (or 41.40 percent of the world's population) receive a rating of Free. Their inhabitants enjoy a broad range of rights. The 2001–2002 study yielded mixed results. Seventeen countries registered significant gain in freedom, while another seventeen registered setbacks in political rights and civil liberties. One country, Peru, moved from Partly Free to Free, after open democratic elections resulted in a victory for Alejandro Toledo. Two countries, Gambia and Mauritania moved from Not Free to Partly Free. Both countries demonstrated marked improvements in their election procedures. Trinidad and Tobago migrated from Free to Partly Free amid a disputed national election. Liberia and Zimbabwe moved from Partly Free to Not Free amid widespread violence against political opponents and civil society.

Source: Freedom House, *The Washington Post*, 2001. Reprinted with permission. Freedom House is a clear voice for democracy and freedom around the world. Founded nearly sixty years ago by Eleanor Roosevelt, Wendell Willkie, and other Americans concerned with the mounting threats to peace and democracy, Freedom House has been a vigorous proponent of democratic values and a steadfast opponent of dictatorships of the far left and the far right.

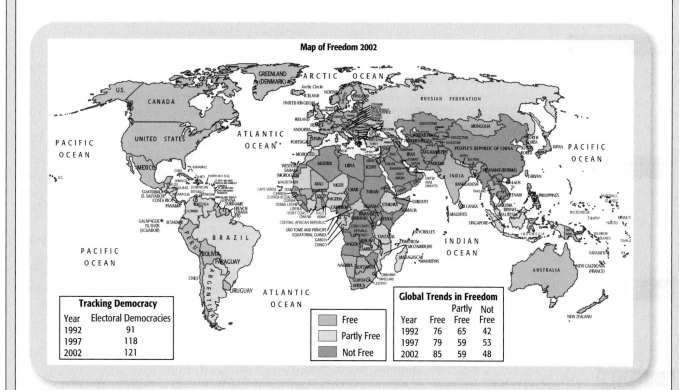

Map of Freedom 2002

Tracking Democracy	
Year	Electoral Democracies
1992	91
1997	118
2002	121

Legend:
- Free
- Partly Free
- Not Free

Global Trends in Freedom

Year	Free	Partly Free	Not Free
1992	76	65	42
1997	79	59	53
2002	85	59	48

Map of Freedom 2002
Source: Reprinted by permission of The Freedom House.

Direct and Indirect Democracy

Some democratic systems give their citizens direct political control; others allow them only indirect power. **Direct democracy** assumes that people can govern themselves. The people as a whole make policy decisions rather than acting through elected representatives. In an **indirect democracy,** voters designate a relatively small number of people to *represent* their interests; those representatives then meet in a legislative body and make decisions on behalf of the entire citizenry.

Direct Democracy   The political system of Athens and similar Greek city-states of ancient times can be thought of as an elite-based, direct democracy. Even though most people in Athens were not considered citizens, the small fraction of the population that was eligible to participate in political life met regularly, debated policy, and voted directly on the issues of the day. They needed no intermediaries and made all political decisions themselves. In contrast, the later Roman republic was an indirect, representative democracy, closer to the structures we have become used to in the United States.

The closest American approximation of direct democracy is the New England **town meeting,** a form of governance dating back to the early 1700s. In these meetings, town business has traditionally been transacted by the consent of a majority of eligible citizens, all of whom have an equal opportunity to express their views and cast their votes at an annual gathering. When it came into being, this method of direct participation represented a startling change from the undemocratic dictates of King George III of England and the authoritarian traditions of European politics in general. The town meeting system proved durable, even today representing the primary form of government in more than 80 percent of the townships in New England.

The town meeting instituted two of the indispensable features of effective democracy—equality and majority rule. **Equality** in this case means that all participants have equal access to the decision-making process, equal opportunity to influence the decisions made, and equal responsibility for those decisions. For this reason, the central premise of the Declaration of Independence is that "all men are created equal." Under **majority rule,** when more than half of the voters agree on an issue, the entire group accepts the decision, even those in the minority who voted against it. There is group consensus on a key procedural norm: majorities make the rules. Acceptance of this norm allows the government to operate. If minorities failed to abide by the law as determined by the majority, the result would be anarchy or even civil war. But democracy is about the struggle of the minority for their right to be equal and their perspective to be recognized. Recall the political challenge of increasing Hispanic representation mentioned earlier in the chapter. As the Hispanic population inches towards the majority, the need for increased representation in government increases.

Note that minorities accept majority rule for the same reason that majorities accept minority rights. Those in the minority hope to become the majority some day, and when they do, they will want that day's minority to obey the laws they pass. At a minimum, then, obedience to any majority-approved law represents a crude calculation of future self-interest. But for many in a democracy, this constant shifting between majority and minority positions broadens one's perspective. It produces an understanding of, even empathy for, the positions of people in the opposite political camp. The result is a degree of tolerance for different political points of view, an openness to others' opinions that lies at the heart of the democratic ideal.

Direct democracy (like the system prevailing in New England town meetings) works well for small, homogeneous groups of people. Once a population grows and diversifies, however, direct democracy can become cumbersome, even impossible to operate. One form of direct democracy—statewide balloting—is still used in states such as California. This procedure allows voters in the state to express their views

direct democracy A type of government in which people govern themselves, vote on policies and laws, and live by majority rule.

indirect democracy A type of government in which voters designate a relatively small number of people to represent their interests; those people, or representatives, then meet in a legislative body and make decisions on behalf of the entire citizenry.

town meeting A form of governance dating back to the 1700s in which town business is transacted by the consent of a majority of eligible citizens, all of whom have an equal opportunity to express their views and cast their votes at an annual meeting.

equality A state in which all participants have equal access to the decision-making process, equal opportunity to influence the decisions made, and equal responsibility for those decisions.

majority rule A decision-making process in which, when more than half of the voters agree on an issue, the entire group accepts the decision, even those in the minority who voted against it.

on policy matters (through referenda) or on changes in the state constitution or to state statutes (through initiatives).[7] However, individuals in a large community cannot realistically all gather in the same place at the same time to discuss policy matters, as citizens in smaller communities can at town meetings. Approximately 281 million people live in America; bringing all these Americans together to meet and make collective decisions would be impossible. With large numbers of people and a varied population, an indirect form of democracy makes more sense.

Indirect Democracy   As the size of the country grew, then, democracy became less pure and direct. The town meeting gave way to *representative town meetings,* a form of indirect democracy in which voters designate a few people to attend town meetings and vote on issues for the entire community. But even this system was ineffective. Myriad decisions needed to be made on a daily or weekly basis, and towns would come to a standstill if they had to call daily or weekly town meetings. The business of government was too complex and demanding even for this approach. To expedite matters, towns voted for "selectmen," who would conduct routine town business in the periods between full town meetings.

This new system of **representative democracy** became the means by which a larger and more diverse group of people could govern themselves. Under this system, voters select representatives to make the decisions of government for them. In theory, citizens still retain the ultimate decision-making power, since periodic elections allow them to eject representatives who don't carry out their wishes. Still, the day-to-day operations of government and the workaday flow of policy decisions no longer rest directly in the people's hands. Immediate power to run the government now resides with elected officials, delegates of the people. The resulting system is related to, but still something different from, the framework of direct citizen rule.

Given the choice between direct versus representative democracy, the framers of the Constitution chose the latter, fearing that direct rule by the people—pure democracy—would mean rule by the mob. As John Adams once wrote: "Remember, democracy never lasts long. It soon wastes, exhausts, and murders itself. There never was a democracy yet that did not commit suicide."[8] Seeking to keep their new democratic system from committing suicide, the framers decided to create a **republic,** a governing structure that places political decision makers at least one step away from the citizens they are governing. For instance, citizens grouped into several hundred districts elect the members of the U.S. House of Representatives. Each district is allowed to vote for one individual to represent its wishes and interests in an assembly at the nation's capital.

To further dilute the political influence of the American people, the framers placed other units of government even further from their direct control. The Senate would not be chosen directly by the people but by state legislators. The people would not vote directly for president, but for members of an electoral college who would then name the president. The Supreme Court would be even further removed from the people's will—chosen for life tenure by the indirectly elected president and confirmed by the indirectly elected Senate. Thus, the highest court in the land would be three times removed from the popular will.

Although the framers clearly opted for an indirect and representative form of democratic governance, over the years the system they devised has developed in ways that make it much closer to the Athenian ideal of direct democracy than it was originally. Still, we must marvel at how well the original structures, set up more than two hundred years ago, have held up. Everywhere in the country today, we see the system of representative democracy at work: in local, state, and national governments. Something in the original scheme seems to have met with the ideals and goals of the American democratic spirit: equality, freedom for all, a representative democracy based on majority rule and minority rights, a system of total participation.

representative democracy A system of government in which the voters select representatives to make decisions for them.

republic A system of government that allows indirect representation of the popular will.

(?) **Question for Reflection:** If a low level of U.S. voter turnout continues, how will the minority voting populace electing our government representatives impact democracy in America?

The Roots of Democracy

Precisely why American democracy has endured and advanced is one of the most interesting and complex questions of our time. To begin to answer this question, it helps to understand the origins of democracy and how it took root in America. Democracy did not begin in America; rather, it was the logical progression of a movement with a long history. Its seeds were first sown in the fertile soil of the ancient Greek city-state of Athens. The term *democracy* is derived from the Greek words *demos* and *kratia,* meaning literally "rule by the people." In Athenian democracy, roughly five centuries before Christ, the people were expected to participate actively in political life. To facilitate this participation, Athens organized government around the Assembly (*Ekklesia*). This body, composed of all native-born adult male property owners, met forty times a year to discuss the pressing issues of the day. From Plato and Aristotle we know that Athenian democracy involved such characteristics as citizen participation, rule of law, and free and open political discussion. It thus provided the world's first model of what a democratic political system might look like.[9]

Athenian democracy was far from perfect, however. It was based on two conditions, one of which is virtually impossible, the other undesirable, in modern democracies. First, this city-state was small, comprising no more than fifty thousand people, with perhaps six thousand of them eligible to participate in the political process. Thus, democracy in Athens emphasized face-to-face political discussion and decision-making. Most modern states contain millions of citizens, so, as we've seen, an Athenian town meeting style of government is simply out of the question. Second, Greek democracy was highly exclusive. Women, slaves, and immigrants—who together formed the majority of residents—were barred from participating in the *Ekklesia*. Modern democracies guarantee equal political rights to nearly every adult citizen, thus ensuring a boisterous political life and a much more complex set of institutions than was needed by a simple, small republic like Athens.

What is the American conception of democracy? Some of its ideals clearly derive from the Athenian model. One example can be found in Thomas Jefferson's famous phrase from the Declaration of Independence, that America is a government whose "just powers" are derived "from the consent of the governed." Also borrowed from Athens is the idea of freely conducted debates and, following those debates, elections, with majority rule forming the basis for determining actual public policy.

Despite the influence of the Athenian model of democracy, however, when our early leaders met to draft the United States Constitution, they clearly hoped to avoid some of its weaker elements. James Madison, for instance, spoke out strongly against the kind of pure democracy represented by Athens. He insisted that it was inherently unstable and prone to self-destruct:

> Such democracies have ever been spectacles of turbulence and contention; have ever been found incompatible with personal security or the rights of property; and have in general been as short in their lives as they have been violent in their deaths.[10]

It is true that Athenian democracy was short-lived. Its death has often been attributed to a series of citizen decisions that led to disastrous consequences, even though those decisions were made in a perfectly democratic manner. In America, the framers wished to avoid a system in which the immediate desires of average citizens had an instant impact on the policies of the state. The democratic model they chose was less inclusive, but turned out to be more durable than the Athenian ideal of direct decision making.

The Ideals of Democracy

America's commitment to democracy rests on its profound belief in an idealistic set of core values: freedom, equality, order, stability, majority rule, protection of minority rights, and participation. If the United States could uphold these values at all times, it might be regarded as the "perfect democratic system." It doesn't, however, even today, and it fell short of these ideals even more frequently in the past. Still, it was these worthy ideals, and the country's long and continuing efforts to move toward them, that led Vaclav Havel to see America as "approaching democracy."

Freedom and Equality

Two of the key values that American democracy claims to safeguard often lead in contradictory directions. Frequently, the more freedom citizens have, the less equality they are likely to achieve, and vice versa. Each of these admirable ideals, when applied to real-world circumstances, can produce contradictory results, depending on how one interprets their meaning. The dilemmas that arise when pursuing these two goals, both individually and together, are many.

To begin, take that quintessential American value, **freedom.** This value suggests that no individual should be within the power or under the control of another. We often take freedom to mean that we should have *freedom from* government interference in our lives. But to complicate matters, the notion of freedom means different things to different people. As the noted historian Isaiah Berlin has argued, freedom can be understood in two ways, either negative or positive.[11] Negative freedom implies freedom from government intervention. People have a right to certain liberties, such as freedom of speech, and government cannot violate or interfere with that right. For this reason, the First Amendment begins with the famous words "Congress shall make no law" and goes on to list several key citizen rights that government cannot restrict—notably, the rights to speak, write, assemble, and worship freely.

Contrast that approach with positive freedom, or *freedom to,* such as the freedom to exercise certain rights guaranteed to all U.S. citizens under the Constitution. Some examples might be the right to vote, the right to legal counsel, and the right to equal protection under the law.

Note how these two views of freedom lead to different roles for government. To ensure negative freedom (freedom *from* restrictions), government is expected to do nothing, to keep its hands off. It is, in a short phrase made popular by Supreme Court Justice William O. Douglas, the "right to be left alone." For instance, a person can say and write practically anything he or she wants about any political official, and government agencies in a democracy will do nothing—or at least, they are supposed to do nothing.

On the other hand, to secure rights involving freedom *to,* government is often expected, and even required, to take positive action to protect citizens and ensure that those rights can be exercised. In the 1960s, for instance, the federal government had to intervene with a heavy hand in the South to ensure that African Americans could exercise one of the basic freedoms of a democratic citizen: the right to vote. Thus, some elements of freedom require a weak or even nonexistent government, while others require a strong and interventionist one.

Similar contradictions arise in attempting to maximize the key democratic value of equality. This ideal suggests that all citizens, regardless of circumstance, should be treated the same way by government. What equal treatment means in practice, however, is not always easy to say. Does it mean equality of opportunity or equality of result? Underlying the goal of **equality of opportunity** is the idea that "people

freedom A value that suggests that no individual should be within the power or under the control of another.

equality of opportunity The idea that "people should have equal rights and opportunities to develop their talents," that all people should begin at the same starting point in a race.

▶ Reflecting America's diverse heritage, children pledge allegiance as part of a nationwide "Pledge Across America."

should have equal rights and opportunities to develop their talents." This idea implies that all people should have the chance to begin at the same starting point. But what if life's circumstances make that impossible, placing people from different situations at different starting points, some much farther behind than others? For example, the person born into a poor family in which no one has ever graduated from high school will be less prepared for college than the son or daughter of generations of college professors. Even more dramatic is the difference in life opportunities available to the children of poor black families, compared with the children of wealthy white families. Equalizing opportunities for all Americans would clearly take an enormous effort, which is why Cesar Chavez organized the farm workers into the United Farm Workers of America, AFL-CIO.

The difficulty of achieving equal opportunity for all has led some people to advocate another kind of equality. They promote **equality of result,** the idea that all forms of inequality, including economic disparities, should be eradicated. Policies aimed at maximizing this goal place less stress on helping people compete and more stress on redistributing benefits after the competition has taken place. Equality of result would produce a redistribution of goods, services, and income—taking from those who have more and giving to those who have less. These two forms of equality—equality of opportunity and equality of result—are often in conflict and represent different notions of what a democratic society would look like.[12]

Besides these internal contradictions, freedom and equality conflict with each other in a number of ways. For instance, if your view of freedom is freedom *from* government intervention, then equality of any kind will be an extremely difficult goal to achieve. If government stays out of all citizen affairs, some people will become extremely wealthy, others will fall through the cracks, and economic inequalities will multiply. On the other hand, if you wish to promote equality of *result,* then you will have to restrict some people's freedoms—the freedom to earn and retain an unlimited amount of money, for example.

Order and Stability

The values of freedom and equality, central to a democracy, often stand in tension with the power of the state to control its citizens. Every society, to be successful, must maintain **order** and provide social **stability,** so that citizens can go about their

[margin handwriting: More level playing field for people →]

equality of result The idea that all forms of inequality, including economic disparities, should be completely eradicated; this may mean giving some people an advantage at the start so that everyone will complete the race at the same point.

order A condition in which the structures of a given society and the relationships thereby defined among individuals and classes comprising it are maintained and preserved by the rule of law and police power of the state.

stability A condition that is resistant to sudden change or overthrow.

business in a secure and predictable manner. Governments make use of laws, regulations, courts, the police, and the military to prevent societal chaos. This need for order does, however, place limits on individual freedom, and it frequently violates certain notions of equality.

Think, for example, about one of the more obvious controls that government places upon us to prevent social disorder: the need for a state-approved driver's license before we are allowed to operate a motor vehicle. Americans who wish to drive a car cannot simply get into a car and start driving. They must first fill out a number of forms, write a check to a government agency, pass a written examination created by government officials, and then prove to other government officials through a driving test that they actually know how to drive a car. There are perfectly valid reasons for each of these steps, springing from the desire to make society orderly and safe, but government policies that derive from these goals do have the effect of limiting (very modestly, of course) the values of both freedom and equality.

The limit on personal freedom is obvious; we can't do what we want (drive a car) without satisfying certain government requirements. The limit on equality is perhaps less severe but is still there; not everyone is allowed to drive a car (those under a certain age, those who fail the various tests, those whose eyesight is weak, those who have violated certain laws, and so forth). This modest example suggests dozens of additional cases in which state powers aimed at ensuring order stand in conflict with some individual desires for freedom and equality. The constant tension between individual rights and state power creates a great deal of controversy in a democracy and gives rise to numerous policy disputes, many of which we examine in this text.

Majority Rule and Protection of Minority Rights

Just as democracies must balance freedom and equality with order and stability, so must they also strike a balance between the rule of the majority (*majoritarianism*) and the protection of minority rights. Whenever disagreement arises in a democracy, each party to the dispute seeks to persuade more than half of the populace in its favor. To accomplish this end, supporters of each position must agree among themselves on the desired goal; they must achieve some kind of internal *consensus*. In successful democracies, political scientist E. E. Schattschneider argued, consensus develops out of debate and persuasion, campaigning and voting, rather than being imposed by dictate. The minority becomes the majority, in other words, only through open procedures that encourage popular input and rational argument, not through some small group's authoritarian decision to impose its policy preferences on everyone else.[13]

Furthermore, policy questions in a democracy are rarely settled "once and for all." The minority remains the majority only as long as it can keep persuading all its members of the rightness of its positions. Those in the minority are constantly trying to influence the majority to change its mind. Free to express their views without fear of harm, proponents of the minority opinion will speak out persuasively, hoping to see their ideas become the majority perspective. Hence, majorities in a vibrant democracy can never feel secure for long. They must always defend themselves from the continuing arguments of the minority; they must always imagine that that same minority will replace them some day in the majority position.

To make matters more complicated still, note that few people ever find themselves in the majority on all issues. One may hold the majority viewpoint on prayer in public schools and on nuclear power but find oneself in the minority on the minimum wage issue. Democracy is never static; it is an elusive, dynamic, and constantly shifting process. For that reason, everyone in a democracy will at times be part of the majority; but just as surely, everyone at many other times will take an unpopular, minority position.

Knowing that majority status must inevitably be temporary, members of any majority must be careful. They must be reasonable in their demands and programs, seeking not to antagonize the minority excessively, since they would have to expect retribution when leaders of an oppressed minority become part of next week's or next year's majority. The knowledge that one might become the minority any day has a profound effect, leading the current majority in a democratic system to treat minorities fairly.

Question for Reflection: Reflecting upon the U.S. 2000 Census data, what groups are moving to the minority from a population standpoint? What impact might this have on their representation within our democracy?

The idea of **minority rights** springs from this perspective. We give rights to the minority because when we end up in the minority, as inevitably we must, we want to enjoy those rights ourselves rather than endure the repression that is the usual fate of minorities in non-democratic systems. Thomas Jefferson understood this idea well. When in the minority, his Democratic-Republican party, had been victimized by the Alien and Sedition Acts passed by the majority Federalist party in 1798, in part to restrain the Democratic-Republicans' views. When Jefferson himself entered the majority as president in 1801, he stressed the importance of majority restraint, referring in his first inaugural address to the "sacred principle that though the will of the majority is in all cases to prevail, that will to be rightful must be reasonable."[14]

When those in the minority band together into groups based on particular interests and seek to influence policy by allying with other groups, we have a system of **pluralism.** Continual competition among groups in a democracy ensures that power moves around in shifting alliances of interests. One year it might be the religious and education groups that unite on the question of government assistance to schools; the next year those groups might split on the issue of teachers' wages, with the labor unions and taxpayer interest groups weighing in with their own views.

In a system of democratic pluralism, maintaining a cohesive majority becomes more and more difficult. Coalitions constantly shift, and new majorities appear on every issue. In these circumstances the ephemeral majorities of the day are bound to respect minority rights and pay close attention to unpopular opinions. The large number of groups and the strong likelihood that everyone will frequently be in the minority diminishes the chance that one dominant oppressive group will form. The framers of our Constitution worried a good deal about "the tyranny of the majority," but in a modern, complex democracy this problem seems relatively minor. Indeed, the excessive power of minorities, including special-interest groups, seems more of a worry to many observers today—an issue we examine carefully in later chapters.

Participation

Since democracy is rule by the governed, *all* citizens must have an opportunity to influence the activities of government. That opportunity is best expressed by **universal suffrage,** a right to vote that extends to all adults. Democracy also requires that this vote be meaningful; that is, voters must have real choices at the polls, and their choices must be reflected in governmental policies. Beyond voting, democracies must provide citizens with ample opportunities to participate in and influence the direction of their government. Such participation may involve serving in the government, lobbying for governmental action, or simply reading and talking about government actions.

Participation is a central democratic ideal, and the United States has approached it over the years by continually expanding opportunities for Americans to participate in and influence their government. Only a minority of people—free, white, landowning males over the age of twenty-one—could exercise full citizenship rights in 1787. The expansion of citizenship rights toward inclusiveness

minority rights Rights given to those in the minority; based on the idea that tyranny of the majority is a danger to human rights.

pluralism A system that occurs when those in the minority band together into groups based on particular interests and seek to influence policy by allying with other groups.

universal suffrage The requirement that everyone must have the right to vote.

1. U-S citizen
2. 18
3. no felonies

has continued for two centuries. The amendment structure of the Constitution, in particular, facilitated this expansion. The Thirteenth and Fifteenth Amendments eliminated slavery and involuntary servitude and gave the freed African Americans the right to vote (though as you will learn, it was years before state laws were changed to ensure this goal); the Seventeenth Amendment gave the people the right to vote for their senators directly; the Nineteenth Amendment gave women the right to vote; the Twenty-third Amendment gave residents of the District of Columbia residential electoral college votes; the Twenty-fourth Amendment ended the practice of charging people a "poll tax" before they could vote; and the Twenty-sixth Amendment lowered the minimum voting age from twenty-one to eighteen. Today, the opportunity exists for nearly every adult American to participate in the political life of American society.

A Brookings Institution Study of the Federal Government's Top 50 Acts (see Table 1.2) identified the 3 of the top 5 greatest achievements as being those that brought us closer to the democratic ideal—expanding the right to vote, promoting equal access to public accommodations, and reducing workplace discrimination—an achievement the UFW was instrumental in promoting. The top achievement was rebuilding Europe after World War II; the other top 5 finisher was reducing disease. In later chapters you will learn about the ten statutes that both expanded and protected the right to vote, including the Twenty-fourth Amendment outlawing the poll tax, the Twenty-sixth lowering the voting age to 18, the Voting Rights Act of 1965 and the Civil Rights Act of 1964. You will also read about the three-statute endeavor originating in the Civil Rights Act of 1964, the Open Housing Act of 1968 and the 1990 Americans With Disabilities Act that together promoted access to public accommodations. With respect to the effort to eliminate workplace discrimination based on race, color, religion, gender, national origin, age or disability, you will read about the 1964 Civil Rights Act, the Age Discrimination Act of 1967, and the Americans with Disabilities Act of 1990. Collectively, these acts represent the glorious story of America's approach towards democracy; individually, each represents a struggle that was often built not just on ideas, but also the blood, sweat and tears of those Americans seeking a better life for all.

▲ Supporters of the Equal Rights Amendment chained themselves to the White House fence to demonstrate their support for the ERA.

The Elements of Democracy

Following the struggle for democracy in Poland, Adam Michnik, an early leader in the Solidarity movement, noted that "dictatorship has been defeated and freedom has been won, yet the victory of freedom has not yet meant the triumph of democracy. Democracy is something more than freedom. Democracy is freedom institutionalized."[15] Throughout this text we examine those characteristics of American democracy that have helped to "institutionalize freedom." Free elections, competitive political parties, a free press, interest groups, an independent judiciary, civilian control of the military, and a commitment among citizens to the rule of law and a set of democratic ideals—are indispensable for the preservation of democracy. The institutions and traditions of the American system have allowed it to develop toward democracy, a democracy that has not yet "committed suicide," as John Adams feared it would.

How closely have we approached the ideals of true democracy? Scholars are constantly trying to define and categorize democracy, using one or another set of objective indicators. While there is still healthy debate about the nature of these indicators, we have chosen to stress five widely accepted elements of democracy. These institutional elements will serve as markers to identify progress toward the democratic ideals discussed earlier. Only political systems that meet or at least approach those ideals can be considered democratic. Using the following elements, you can measure the strength and robustness of American democracy or any democracy.

Table 1.2 ■ Government's 50 Greatest Endeavors

1. Rebuild Europe After World War II	26. Protect Endangered Species
2. Expand the Right to Vote	27. Reduce Exposure to Hazardous Waste
3. Promote Equal Access to Public Accommodations	28. Enhance the Nation's Health Care Infrastructure
4. Reduce Disease	29. Maintain Stability in the Persian Gulf
5. Reduce Workplace Discrimination	30. Expand Home Ownership
6. Ensure Safe Food and Drinking Water	31. Increase International Economic Development
7. Strengthen the Nation's Highway System	32. Ensure an Adequate Energy Supply
8. Increase Older American's Access to Health Care	33. Strengthen the Nation's Airways System
9. Reduce the Federal Budget Deficit	34. Increase Low-Income Families' Access to Health Care
10. Promote Financial Security in Retirement	35. Improve Elementary and Secondary Education
11. Improve Water Quality	36. Reduce Crime
12. Support Veterans' Readjustment and Training	37. Advance Human Rights and Provide Humanitarian Relief
13. Promote Scientific and Technological Research	38. Make Government More Transparent to the Public
14. Contain Communism	39. Stabilize Agricultural Prices
15. Improve Air Quality	40. Provide Assistance for the Working Poor
16. Enhance Workplace Safety	41. Improve Government Performance
17. Strengthen the National Defense	42. Reform Welfare
18. Reduce Hunger and Improve Nutrition	43. Expand Job Training and Placement
19. Increase Access to Post-Secondary Education	44. Increase Market Competition
20. Enhance Consumer Protection	45. Increase the Supply of Low-Income Housing
21. Expand Foreign Markets for U.S. Goods	46. Develop and Renew Impoverished Communities
22. Increase the Stability of Financial Institutions and Markets	47. Improve Mass Transportation
23. Increase Arms Control and Disarmament	48. Reform Taxes
24. Protect the Wilderness	49. Control Immigration
25. Promote Space Exploration	50. Devolve Responsibility to the States

Source: http://www.brook.edu/dybdocroot/GS/CPS/50ge/50 greatest.htm. Reprinted by permission of The Brookings Institution.

A System for Popular Participation The United States provides numerous opportunities for citizen involvement in politics. In the course of two centuries, an increasing number of people gained the opportunity to participate in public life. The institutions that most clearly allow people to influence government are elections. All adult citizens now have the chance to participate in regularly scheduled **elections,** where at least two opposing groups have some likelihood of winning. By voting in elections, citizens can convey their desires to government and can expect government to act with those desires in mind. Over 100 million voted in the 2000 election, with the winner of the popular vote actually losing the electoral vote and the legitimacy of the process did not lead to a national rebellion. America's constitution worked!

The right to vote has been expanded over the years through constitutional amendments and court rulings, as you've seen, so that it now can be exercised by nearly everyone over the age of eighteen. Voting itself would not be sufficient to influence government, however, if voters could not make meaningful choices at the polling booth. The institution of free, competing **political parties** enables this element of choice to be exercised. Stable political parties exist and, once elected to office, seek to impose their will on policy makers. Parties allow like-minded members of the population to join together and magnify their individual voices into a focus for government action.

elections The institutions that give people the opportunity to participate in public life.

political parties Institutions that exist to allow like-minded members of the population to group together and magnify their individual voices to promote individual candidates and government action.

Important as they are, political parties are never the only outlet for citizen participation in a developed democracy. Citizens must be free to join a wide array of groups that promote particular interests. That situation has long been true in the United States, where a vigorous civil society allows public and private **interest groups** to thrive. These groups allow citizens to meet, organize, plan strategy, and lobby government for action. They even allow people to protest government policies, without fear that government will punish them.

A Commitment to Preserve Freedom and Equality for All

For democracy to flourish, the government must work to safeguard democratic ideals for all its citizens. That goal implies several kinds of action. First, it means that government stays out of the personal lives of its citizens, who have an inherent **right to privacy.** Furthermore, citizens must have access to a vigorous **free press** and other means of open exchange of information. Debate must be encouraged and fueled by freedom of speech and thought, not to mention freedom of information.

In a secure democracy, people must be free to think for themselves, inform themselves about governmental policies, and exchange information. A totalitarian government, using the state to maintain total authority over all citizens, suppresses open communication so as to maintain an iron grip over the minds of its populace.

An Independent Judiciary

Central to functioning democracies are the rule of law and the protection of civil liberties. Only an independent judiciary, free of political influence, can safeguard citizen rights, protecting both the majority and minorities at the same time. Like other federal courts, the U.S. Supreme Court possesses a unique power, **judicial review** that makes it the final interpreter of the Constitution. The day after the Supreme Court ruled that Florida would have to cease its recount of contested ballots, the Vice President of the United States and the winner of the popular vote, conceded the election to Governor George W. Bush. We will study this election later, but for now just think about what this peaceful transition says about the values that constitute our system of laws.

To protect individual freedoms, the federal judiciary has often used this power to strike down government actions. Independent state courts have also acted to preserve the rights of individuals. Courts have used their authority to make a powerful statement about equality and the rule of law: *All are equal under the law,* and no one, not even the president of the United States, is above it.

Civilian Control of the Military and the Police

In dictatorships, political parties come and go, but the group that controls the military and the police is the real power. The nation's nominal leader may be irrelevant. Saddam Hussein's dictatorship in Iraq is dependent upon the willingness of the military Republican National Guard to continue to back him. This kind of arbitrary military power does not happen in the United States or in any advanced democracy. Thanks in part to the example of George Washington, who resigned from the military following the end of the Revolution, the American military is controlled by the civilian government. Military leaders take no policy actions other than those they are directed to take by civilian political leaders; the commander in chief is the president. Furthermore, the military does not intervene in civilian political affairs. Since 1800, when the defeated John Adams turned over power to Thomas Jefferson, every losing political party has simply turned control over to its winning competitors. Never have civilian leaders, rejected by the voters, called on the military or police to keep them in office. Never have the military or police intervened to keep in office a candidate or party that has come up short at the polls. Both occurrences are common in countries where democratic institutions are weak.

As a result of this tradition of civilian control of the military, President Harry Truman was able to fire General Douglas MacArthur for insubordination during the

[handwritten margin note: Judicial branch — Supreme court has final say — determines the law or const. has been violated]

interest groups Formal organizations of people who share a common outlook or social circumstance and who band together in the hope of influencing government policy.

right to privacy The right to have the government stay out of the personal lives of its citizens.

free press Media characterized by the open reporting of information without censorship by the government.

judicial review The power of the Supreme Court established in *Marbury v. Madison* to overturn acts of the president, Congress, and the states if those acts violate the Constitution. This power makes the Supreme Court the final interpreter of the Constitution.

THE ROAD TO DEMOCRACY

The Back of the Bus

Today it is hard to believe that anyone would be required by law to sit in the back of a public bus. Imagine what it would be like for you to wait for public transportation, pay your fare, and be required to sit in a special section or forced to give up your seat to someone of the racial majority. Well, that is the way it was in Montgomery, Alabama, in 1955. The white majority in the city, abiding by the 1896 Supreme Court decision *Plessy v. Ferguson,* which held that state facilities could be "separate" for white and black citizens as long they were "equal" in quality, had constructed a complicated system for riding the bus. White citizens always rode in front; if there were no whites on the bus, those seats were left vacant. Black citizens sat or stood in the back of the bus. The middle of the bus was not assigned to either race. If there was no demand from the white customers, black customers could ride there. But if a black rider was seated in the middle and a white rider demanded the seat, the black rider was required by Alabama law to move to the back of the bus.

On December 1, 1955, Rosa Parks, a forty-two-year-old African American seamstress sat in the middle of the bus, but as the bus filled up, a white patron demanded her seat. Three other black riders vacated their seats, but Parks refused to move. The driver told Parks that she had to move to the back. When she did not move, he had her arrested.

Parks later explained: "I simply decided that I would not get up. I was tired, but I was usually tired at the end of the day, and I was not feeling well, but then there had been many days when I had not felt well. I had felt for a long time, that if I was ever told to get up so a white person could sit, that I would refuse to do so."

Parks had decided that Alabama's bus segregation law was unfair, but the courts offered her no justice. Although the United States Constitution guarantees citizens a trial by a jury of their peers before an impartial judge, such was not the case for blacks in the South in 1955. The state judges were all local white lawyers who, like the white majority, supported the "separate but equal" doctrine. They implemented the laws and regulations of the white state legislatures and the white city councils. Through unfair election laws, blacks were almost entirely excluded from voting. Thus, they had little say in who passed or administered the laws they had to live under. Since juries were chosen from the voting rolls, jurors were almost all white. No wonder that Parks was quickly convicted of violating the Alabama ordinance requiring the segregation of buses and sentenced to pay a $14 fine. As a result of this case, Parks lost her job and eventually had to leave the South.

But while Rosa Parks lost in the courts, civil rights activists were determined that she and others like her would not lose in the court of public opinion. These activists decided to use this incident to seek change and justice for African Americans. They asked the twenty-six-year-old son of a Baptist minister, Martin Luther King, Jr., with his

---

Korean War. Moreover, Americans did not have to worry that the same George Bush who commanded the American armed forces in the Persian Gulf War of 1991 would, following his electoral defeat in November 1992, use his powers as commander in chief to call off the election and surround the White House with an army. Or that Vice President Gore would do the same during the uncertain period following the November 2000 election. Indeed, these hypothetical examples, common enough in many nations, seem so outrageously unlikely in the American setting as to be laughable. Yet we must understand why they are so unlikely. They seem far-fetched precisely because Americans believe deeply in the norm of civilian control over the military and the police, a norm that is vital to the democratic process. After all, how democratic could a society be if the people's decisions could be arbitrarily set aside by the whims of a powerful few?

A Cultural Commitment to Democratic Ideals among All Levels of Society

Democracy doesn't just happen. People in general and leaders in particular must believe in it, understand how it works, and abide by its norms. All levels of society must agree on a set of common governmental ideals. In the United States, those ideals include reverence for the Constitution, the pursuit of freedom and equality, the value of minority rights, and the rule of law. This commitment to the rule of law is indispensable for maintaining stability. It produces a remarkable result, one found only in a democratic society. Americans unhappy with their government complain but almost never take up arms. That is why Timothy McViegh and the

compelling voice and hypnotizing command of the spoken word, to speak at a mass meeting of the newly formed protest group known as the Montgomery Improvement Association. Turnout was impressive.

Speaking from a few notes hastily scribbled on a piece of paper, King observed, "We are here in a general sense because first and foremost—we are American citizens—and we are determined to apply our citizenship—to the fullness of its means. But we are here in a specific sense—because of the bus situation in Montgomery." As he spoke about the injustices suffered by African Americans, the crowd was visibly moved. Finally, King boomed out: "And you know, my friends, there comes a time when people get tired of being trampled over by the iron feet of oppression."

THAT WAS THEN. . .

After boycotting for more than a year, the bus segregation policy was overturned by a panel of federal judges who found it unconstitutional. This ruling was affirmed without opinion by the U.S. Supreme Court in 1956. Rosa Parks' willingness to stand up for human justice won her the title of "Mother of the Civil Rights Movement."

THIS IS NOW. . .

Today, Rosa Parks is the recipient of the Congressional Gold Medal. She is known as a woman who changed a nation. She remained a committed activist, working to stop apartheid in South Africa during the 1980s and creating a career center for black youth in Detroit. Among her tributes are the NAACP's highest honor, the Spingarn Medal and the Presidential Medal of Freedom, the highest honor that the U.S. government can give a civilian.

Sources: Based on Taylor Branch, *Parting the Waters: America in the King Years, 1954–63* (New York: Simon & Schuster, 1988), pp. 124–42; David J. Garrow, *Bearing the Cross: Martin Luther King, Jr., and the Southern Christian Leadership Conference* (New York: Morrow, 1986), pp. 11–47.

▲ Mrs. Rosa Parks is fingerprinted in Montgomery, Alabama, in February 1956 for refusing to give up her seat to a white passenger and move to the back of the bus.

bombing of the Federal Building in Oklahoma City or Unibomber Ted Kaczynskil are considered aberrations of the values by which American have chosen to live. Americans tend to organize and wait for the next election and then vote the ruling party out of power.

SUMMARY

1. Throughout the world democracy has become increasingly prevalent. The United States is often viewed as a model of the democratic process. However, the formal institutions of a democracy do not by themselves guarantee the protection of individual liberties.

2. The term *democracy* means government by the people, either directly or through elected representatives. Citizens in a democracy choose their leaders freely from among competing groups and individuals. In highly developed democracies, voters are free to propose public policy options and join groups that promote those options. In contrast, in an authoritarian regime, government deprives citizens of the freedom to participate in political life.

3. In a direct democracy, the people as a whole make policy decisions. In an indirect democracy, voters designate a few people to represent their interests; those people meet in a legislative body and make decisions on behalf of the entire citizenry. Such a system of representative democracy makes it possible for a larger and more diverse group of people to govern themselves.

DEMOCRACY IN THE NEW MILLENNIUM

The Web and Dissent in the Twenty-First Century

Political dissenters in the twenty-first century are finding that the electronic revolution furthers free speech in ways unforeseen a generation ago. Following the September 11 suicide attacks and the U.S. response "Enduring Freedom," those peace activists who disagreed with the U.S. bombings found it difficult to utilize the usual channels of television and the radio to "protest" the war in Afghanistan.

But a small group of dissenters sitting at their computers in 2001–2002 successfully projected their views faster and more thoroughly to a wider audience using the Internet. In the process they also gained greater numbers and support from pockets of dissenters around the globe. According to one anonymous peace activist, the Internet removes the fear and confusion associated with holding views that one thinks nobody else believes: "Knowing that there were other people out there with my opinions made it a lot easier . . . It's just really nice to know that you're not alone."

Like mass-mailing, the Internet spreads a great deal of information all at once, though the Net reaches a much wider audience for a fraction of the cost. Examples of a how the Net was utilized to spread "anti-war" sentiment during the war on Afghanistan included the downloading of pamphlets and short articles sent abroad to be mass-reproduced and disseminated at public meetings, the sending of online

petitions simultaneously to countries around the world, and the discovery of peace organizations by average Americans who simply pressed "protest" into their search engines.

Brian Becker, a leader of the Internal Action Center, noted that the Internet reduced the necessity for the centralization of organizational efforts that guided peace movements in the past. "The character of political action organizing has completely shifted since the Gulf War . . . Instead of a physical location like our office, the Web site has become our mobilization headquarters." With the web accessible at literally hundreds of thousands of locations across the United States, political dissenters easily found like-minded individuals to plan protests for peace. E-mail addresses served as calling cards, giving dissenters more encouragement to voice their views in a context free from public and government reprisal. For further study see the following web sites:

U.S. Census Bureau: www.census.gov and http://factfinder.census.gov

Population Reference Bureau and Social Science Data Analysis Network: www.AmeriStat.org

Source: Amy Harmon, "The Dissenters: Demonstrators Find That the Web Is a Powerful Tool," November 21, 2001, *NYT,* B8.

4. Freedom and equality are core values of American democracy, but they often pull in contradictory directions. The more freedom citizens have, the less equality they are likely to achieve, and vice versa. Both of these ideals can be seen as requiring that government take no action. Conversely, they can be viewed as requiring governmental intervention to protect individual freedom or guarantee equal treatment. The desire for order and stability places limits on freedom and equality.

5. A democracy must strike a balance between the rule of the majority and the rights of the minority. In successful democracies a consensus is reached through debate, persuasion, campaigning, and voting. In a pluralist system those in the minority band together based on particular interests and seek to influence policy by allying with other groups.

6. In a democracy all citizens must have an opportunity to influence the activities of government. Influence is achieved through universal suffrage and other opportunities for political participation, such as serving in the government or lobbying for governmental action.

7. A republic places political decision makers at least one step away from the citizens it is governing. Thus, in the United States voters originally chose electors and state legislators, who in turn chose the president and U.S. senators, who then chose the justices of the Supreme Court. Over the years this system has been modified in ways that bring it closer to direct democracy.

8. Among the basic elements of American democracy is a system for popular participation consisting of regularly scheduled elections; free, competing political parties; and public and private interest groups. Another basic element is the commitment to preserve freedom and equality, which implies a right to privacy, a free press, and freedom of speech. Additional elements are an independent judiciary (including the power of judicial review), civilian control of the military and the police, and a cultural commitment to democratic ideals.

9. Democracy is a process whereby conflict is resolved and consensus achieved between a ruling majority and a minority that has a right to be heard but also accepts the legitimacy of majority rule. The United States has been approaching democracy for more than two hundred years and continues to do so today.

KEY TERMS

democracy	representative democracy	pluralism
referenda	republic	universal suffrage
authoritarian regime	freedom	elections
direct democracy	equality of opportunity	political parties
indirect democracy	equality of result	interest groups
town meeting	order	right to privacy
equality	stability	free press
majority rule	minority rights	judicial review

POLISIM ACTIVITY

The Freedom Map Simulation

Freedom and democracy are not absolutes; they can develop in stages. No country allows its citizens complete freedom and no country can completely eliminate it. The map in this simulation describes countries as free, partly free, or not free. You will finish the map by describing the countries in white as "free," "partly free," or "not free" based on the criteria of political rights—right to vote, free and fair elections, participation of minorities, etc.

SUGGESTED READINGS

CRONIN, THOMAS E. *Direct Democracy: The Politics of Initiative, Referendum, and Recall.* Cambridge, Mass.: Harvard University Press, 1989. An informative account of how ballot measures affect democratic politics. Cronin examines the strengths and weaknesses of these measures.

DAHL, ROBERT A. *Democracy and Its Critics.* New Haven, Conn.: Yale University Press, 1989. One of the most prominent political theorists of our era on the assumptions of democratic theory. The book provides a justification for democracy as a political ideal by tracing modern democracy's evolution from the early nineteenth century to the present.

INKELES, ALEX, ed. *On Measuring Democracy.* New Brunswick, N.J.: Transaction Publishers, 1991. Articles by social scientists on political democracy, revealing that it is not only conceptually but also empirically distinct from various social and economic patterns and outcomes.

MURCHLAND, BERNARD. *Voices of Democracy.* Chicago, IL.: University of Notre Dame Press, 2001. This book builds on conversations the author had with many leading political scientists of our time on the subject of democracy.

RAVITCH, DIANE, and ABIGAIL THERNSTROM, eds. *The Democracy Reader.* New York: HarperCollins, 1992. The enduring issues of democracy in a collection of documents, essays, poems, declarations, and speeches.

SCHUDSON, MICHAEL. *The Good Citizen: A History of American Civic Life.* New York: Free Press, 1998. A history of citizenship in the United States of America in which the new citizens of America must be "monitors of political danger rather than walking encyclopedias of governmental news."

TISMANEDNU, VLADIMIR. *Reinventing Politics: Eastern Europe from Stalin to Havel.* New York: Free Press, 1992. A well-balanced account of the factors leading to the revolutions of 1989 and the evolution of democratic institutions in Eastern Europe.

WOLIN, SHELDON S. *Tocqueville Between Two World: The Making of a Political and Theoretical Life.* Princeton, N.J.: Princeton University Press, 2001. The book connects Tocqueville's political and theoretical lives while also providing commentary on the course of Western political life over the past two hundred years.

2 The Founding and the Constitution

CHAPTER OUTLINE

- Approaching Democracy Case Study: The Constitution in Times of Crisis
- Introduction: The Road to Democracy
- The Seeds of American Democracy
- First Moves Toward a Union
- Rebellion: Causes and Consequences
- Revolution and the Stirrings of a New Government
- The First New Government: A Confederation of States
- The Need for a More Perfect Union
- The Constitutional Convention
- The Miracle: Results of the Convention
- Ratification: The Battle for the Constitution
- Updating the Constitution
- The Gettysburg Address and America's Approach to Democracy

APPROACHING DEMOCRACY CASE STUDY

The Constitution in Times of Crisis

"Tonight we are a country awakened to danger and called to defend freedom. Our grief has turned to anger, and anger to resolution. . . . I know there are struggles ahead and dangers to face. But this country will define our times, not be defined by them." So spoke President George W. Bush before a joint session of Congress on September 20, 2001. The horrific attack on the World Trade Center's Twin Towers in New York, the Pentagon in Washington D.C., and the plane which crashed in rural

Pennsylvania after a battle between the hijacking terrorists and the passengers, led the President to declare war on terrorism at home and abroad. It was a challenge unlike any faced by a previous president, with no historical markers to guide the president in creating the nation's policy.

But where does the Constitution stand in such times of crisis? "Generally, Chief Executives in wartime are not very sympathetic to the protection of civil liberties," Chief Justice William Rehnquist has written. Early in the Civil War, President Abraham Lincoln authorized the establishment of martial law or military rule, arresting approximately 2,000 southern sympathizers in border regions such as Maryland and Tennessee and suspending their writ of *habeas corpus,* by which the Court could command that the prisoners be brought before it for a hearing on the nature of the charges against them. During World War I, President Woodrow Wilson's Administration prosecuted opponents of the draft and the war from individuals in the national news like socialist leader, Eugene Debs, to a journalist for a small German language newspaper in Missouri, who wrote a series of articles critical of the U.S. draft. These prosecutions resulted in a series of court rulings that raised questions as to whether opponents of the war effort had any First Amendment rights, or whether they raised, in Justice Oliver Wendell Holmes' words, "a clear and present danger" of an evil that Congress had a right to prevent. Shortly after the Japanese attack on Pearl Harbor on December 7, 1941, President Franklin D. Roosevelt, acting on the advice of the military, subjected 120,000 Japanese-American citizens on the West Coast of the United States to a curfew, only to later remove them to internment camps in the Southwest in the belief that it would prevent acts of treason and espionage.

The chief executives in these times were operating under the Roman rule of *"Inter arma silent leges,"* or "In time of war, the laws are silent." But the Court, in applying the Constitution to these actions, did not always agree with these decisions. Chief Justice Roger Brooke Taney ordered the release of a farmer and former Maryland state legislator, John Merryman, who was suspected of a railroad bridge burning, declaring that President Lincoln did not have the power to suspend the writ of *habeas corpus.* Chief Justice Taney cited Article I, Section 9, Paragraph 2 of the Constitution, which states: "the privilege of the writ of *habeas corpus* shall not be suspended, unless when in cases of rebellion or invasion the public safety may require it." Lincoln, however, refused to comply, arguing before Congress that "To state the question more directly, are all the laws but one to go unexecuted, and the government itself go to pieces, lest that one be violated?"

The answer to Lincoln's question has come in two parts. Chief Executives and Congress have done what

they believed to be necessary during times of crisis, and it has become commonplace for the government to either confess or admit to their errors years later. After Lincoln was dead, the Supreme Court ruled that his abolition of *habeas corpus* was beyond the president's constitutional powers. Decades after Woodrow Wilson's First Amendment restrictions the Court changed the legal standard in such cases to one prohibiting speech only if it led to "imminent and lawless action," thus allowing the KKK to burn a cross at a rally in Ohio. And, after a set of hearings on the Japanese-American internment policy in 1988, Congress apologized for the policy and created a program offering reparations to victims of this policy.

The Bush Administration initially moved quickly to shore up the domestic effort against further terrorist acts. On October 26, 2001, Congress passed the U.S.A. Patriot Act granting power for secret search and seizures, "roving" wiretaps of suspects, the tracking of Internet and voice mail use, and defining as a terrorist, even retroactively, anyone who knew or should have known that an individual was engaged in or about to be engaged in terrorist acts. On November 13, 2001, President Bush by executive order proposed a system of military tribunals to try those suspected of terrorism. Only a two-thirds vote of a panel of military judges would be required for the imposition of the death penalty, with appeals after a conviction being barred; the President would retain "a final decision by me" on the results of these trials. Meanwhile, thousands of noncitizens were brought in for questioning by Immigration and Justice Department officials in an effort to develop leads in the anti-terrorism investigation. When questions were raised about the constitutionality and human rights issues in these policies, Attorney General Ashcroft told Congress: "To those ... who scare peace-loving

▲ A man across from the Washington National Cathedral after the attack on September 11, 2001, makes his position clear.

people with phantoms of lost liberty, my message is this: Your tactics only aid terrorists, for they erode our national unity and diminish our resolve. They give ammunition to America's enemies and pause to America's friends. They encourage people of good will to remain silent in the face of evil." While many raised objections to the First Amendment free speech problems with this statement, Ashcroft continued to argue that the administration's program was necessary to prevent further attacks on American soil.

Unlike previous administrations as you will learn in the case study in Chapter 14, the Bush administration got less than it was seeking from the start. Still, the policies enacted grant sweeping new powers to a government at war and will become the benchmark by which future presidents deal with crises under a Constitutional government.[1]

(?) Question for Reflection: How much do our constitutional rights in times of crisis depend on the nature of the attacks? That is, if there are no further attacks, can the administration claim that the restriction of rights was successful? Would a future attack result in even greater restrictions of rights? On the other hand, if the war is successfully concluded, would there be a demand for a re-establishment of the original level of constitutional rights?

INTRODUCTION: THE ROAD TO DEMOCRACY

Democracy took root early in America. Because of the tremendous distance from the British empire and the rough-and-tumble character of frontier existence, early colonial settlers were forced to devise some form of self-government. Drawing on a shared commitment to individual security and the rule of law, the frontier governments provided models on which the constitutional structure of American government was eventually built. To trace the development of American democracy from the early settlements to an independent United States, this chapter explores the ideas that inspired the American Revolution, including the impact of European political thinking on the founding and the struggle for independence from England.

To understand democracy in America, it also helps to understand where the idea of democracy got started. Although the colonists began their fight for independence in 1775, the idea of democracy that inspired them originated much earlier. As we discussed in Chapter 1, democracy in America resulted from the logical progression of an idea over time. Democracy first emerged in the Greek city-state of Athens. The Athenians devised a political system called *demokratia,* meaning "rule of the people." But it was the Roman **republic,** allowing indirect representation of the popular will, that attracted the founders. In fact, the framers of the U.S. Constitution looked to the Roman republic (rather than to Greece, because Athens appeared to be ruled by mobs) as a model of democracy. In *The Federalist,* no. 55, James Madison argued that, "had every Athenian citizen been a Socrates, every Athenian assembly would still have been a mob." Later, you will see how this fear of democracy led the founders to create a system of government that limited direct popular participation.

Characteristics of the British government also strongly influenced America's political arrangement. Britain's Magna Carta, formulated in 1215, limited the exercise of power by the monarch; the notion of limited government accompanied the early colonists to North America. Its impact is visible on the Mayflower Compact, the Declaration of Independence, and the Articles of Confederation.[2]

republic A system of government that allows indirect representation of the popular will.

The Seeds of American Democracy

Although the colonists drew extensively on the historic forms of democracy, America's political system was as much homegrown as it was imported.[2] The actions and experiences of the early settlers established a foundation for the emergence of a peculiarly American form of democracy, one that is still developing. In this section we examine some of the early attempts to establish a society under law in the early days of the American colonies. It is during this period that the first and most enduring seeds of democracy were sown, germinating in the fertile soil of a rugged frontier existence far from the British homeland.

Early Colonial Governments

Most of the New England colonies (including Plymouth, the Providence Plantations, the Connecticut River towns, and New Haven) based their first governments on the idea of a **compact,** a type of agreement that legally binds two or more parties to enforceable rules. Compacts developed directly from Puritan religious theory. Pilgrims, like those who would settle Plymouth Colony, felt that just as they had entered into a covenant with God to found a church and secure their own salvation, so, too, they could forge a covenant or compact among themselves to protect those "natural" liberties provided by God.[3]

Other colonies were created by charters granted to trading companies for the purpose of exploiting the resources of the New World. In 1629, the Massachusetts Bay Company, a private business venture, was chartered by King Charles I. The charter provided for the creation of a governing council that would include a governor, a deputy governor, and eighteen assistants, as well as a General Court composed of the "freemen" of the company, those with property and wealth. In the Cambridge Agreement of 1629, the stockholders in the venture transferred all governing authority from the trading company in England to the Massachusetts Bay Company in the colonies. Thus, Massachusetts Bay became de facto independent of the authority of any British corporation, and the new council became the exclusive government. The stockholders voted John Winthrop, a lawyer, to be their first governor.

Not all of the colonies were based on a compact or evolved from an English trading company. Maryland, New York, New Jersey, Pennsylvania, Delaware, the Carolinas, and Georgia developed from *royal grants*. In these cases, as a way of discharging the Crown's debts, the king issued a warrant granting land and full governing rights to a lord or baron. The recipient of the grant became sole proprietor of the grant of land, enjoying virtually absolute authority over its jurisdiction. Any settlement established there became known as a *proprietary colony*, and the original proprietor determined the nature of the local government of the colony. Thus, in 1632 Lord Baltimore was granted territory in Maryland, and in 1664 the Duke of York was granted the territory of New York.

Given that the proprietors of these territories enjoyed the power and authority of kings, the proprietary colonies made an unlikely but important contribution to emerging American democracy by importing parliamentary systems. The legislatures of the proprietary colonies borrowed their form from England's Parliament, with its bicameral houses of Lords and Commons, its committee system, and its procedures. A **bicameral legislature** is a representative lawmaking body consisting of two chambers or two houses. In the United States, the Senate and the House of Representatives are the two legislative chambers.

The bicameral colonial legislatures had an upper house, whose members were appointed by the Crown (or by the proprietor on recommendation of the royal governor), and a lower house, whose members were elected based on the traditional English suffrage requirement of a "forty-shilling freehold," meaning that to vote one had to own at least forty shillings' worth of land. Thus, only men who owned land or other property were viewed as sufficiently responsible to vote. Women were

compact A type of agreement that legally binds two or more parties to enforceable rules.

bicameral legislature A legislative system consisting of two houses or chambers.

not allowed to vote. Many of the colonies prohibited certain religious groups, such as Catholics and Jews, from voting, and the southern colonies barred "Negroes and mulattoes" from voting, as well as Native Americans and indentured servants.

The colonial legislatures claimed the right to control local legislation, taxes, and expenditures, as well as to fix the qualifications for and judge the eligibility of house members. They also desired freedom of debate, immunity from unrest, and the right to choose their own assembly speakers. To the colonists, these were their rights as English citizens living under British domain in America. However, the British Parliament claimed these rights for itself as the only representative body of a sovereign nation, viewing the colonies as subordinate entities with no inherent **sovereignty**, or independent authority. In Britain's eyes, the colonial legislatures were entitled only to the privileges the king or Parliament chose to give them. It was this fundamental clash between colonial legislatures and the power of the British Parliament and Crown that was to erupt into the war that would separate the fledgling colonies from the British Empire forever.

Every colony had a governor, the principal executive authority acting as the representative of the Crown. The Crown traditionally appointed colonial governors, although Rhode Island and Connecticut chose their own. The governors wielded an absolute veto, had the power of appointment, and commanded the colony's military forces. They also had the power to call the colonial assembly into session and dismiss it, to create courts, and to name and remove judges. The origins of the modern American presidency can, in part, be found here. The governors were assisted by a council whose members they nominated for life. Almost all judicial authority rested in this council.

But confrontations between the colonial assemblies and the governor occurred frequently. Because the colonial governor was the symbol of royal authority within the colonies and represented Britain's interests, such tension was inevitable, particularly since the colonists developed an extreme suspicion of executive power. In addition, the colonists saw advantages to spreading governmental responsibilities among separate compartments of government rather than concentrating power in the hands of one potentially despotic ruler. In this respect, the thinking of the French philosopher Charles de Montesquieu (1689–1755) was influential. Montesquieu viewed the separation of powers as the best way to counteract tendencies toward despotism. He felt that freedom could be best preserved in a system of checks and balances through which the powers of government are balanced against and checked by one another. Montesquieu's writings, particularly *The Spirit of Laws* (1748), eventually helped the framers of the Constitution formalize a three-part government divided into executive, legislative, and judicial functions.

Social Contract Theorists

Democracy developed and flourished in America because of the experience of the new settlers with self-government as well as the emergence of influential new theories of governing. Just as religious leaders of the day derived a notion of social compact from the natural order of life under God, a group of European philosophers known as **social contract theorists** reasoned that individuals existed in a state of nature before the creation of a society or an organized government. Social contracts provide the philosophical foundation for the obligations that individuals and states have toward each other. If a citizen violates the social contract, the state is legally empowered to enforce appropriate punishment in the name of the people. If the state breaks the social contract, the citizens have a right to revolt against its excessive authority and even to form another government in its stead. This theory provided a philosophical foundation for the Declaration of Independence.

Thomas Hobbes (1588–1679) was the first of the major social contract theorists. In the *Leviathan* (1651) Hobbes described the early state of nature as "nasty, brutish and short." People needed the authority of the state as protection from one another. Hobbes described people's relationships with each other as "war of all against all

sovereignty The independence and self-government of a political entity.

social contract theorists A group of European philosophers who reasoned that the most effective way to create the best government was to understand human nature in a state prior to government.

. . . a general inclination of all mankind, a perpetual and restless desire of power after power, that ceaseth only in death." In Hobbes's view, life without authority brings no security or liberty; he reasoned that human beings require a Leviathan, or authoritarian leader, to produce harmony and safety.

Hobbes also proposed a comprehensive theory of government. Since life in the state of nature was so threatening, individuals surrendered freedom in return for a government that provided protection and order in the form of a supreme authority, the *sovereign,* to whom all were subject. This embrace of absolute power in the form of a sovereign has led many to dismiss Hobbes as a legitimate founding thinker of modern democratic thought. Yet Hobbes clearly stated that even the authority of the sovereign must be carefully codified into a body of laws, and that those laws must be applied to all with absolute equality. It was this notion of equality under the law, even in the harsh frontier world of the colonial era, that was Hobbes's most significant contribution to social contract theory.

The most influential social contract theorist, though, was John Locke (1632–1704). Locke published extensively on a number of subjects, but his most significant political works are his *Two Treatises on Government,* published in 1690. Here, Locke rejected the notion of a Hobbesian Leviathan or even a divine right to rule. In the *Second Treatise,* Locke explained his theory of a social contract among citizens to create government and protect property, and for the right to revolt against an unjust government. Locke believed that governments exist to preserve the rights already present in society under nature: specifically, the protection of life, the enjoyment of personal liberty, and the possession and pursuit of private property. For Locke, these rights were inalienable, emanating from God's natural law. To deny any individual life, liberty, or property was to take away that which had been granted by God, either through birth, social status, or individual effort and ability.

Above all, and in support of the growing merchant class in England, Locke insisted that government was necessary to protect property, for property represented all that was noble in the human embodiment of God, the talents and energy that are the tools of divine will on earth. Because Locke recognized property as a result of individual ability and energy, he also accepted inequality in the distribution of that property. However, as with Hobbes, Locke believed that all individuals must be equally subject to the laws constituting the social contract between all citizens under government.

Along with the principle of an inalienable right to life, liberty, and property, Locke asserted the importance of limited government based on popular consent. By **limited government,** Locke meant that the powers of the government should be clearly defined and bounded, so that governmental authority could not intrude in the lives of private citizens. Unlike Hobbes, Locke did not see the necessity for an absolute sovereign but argued instead for a strong legislature. His model was, of course, the British Parliament, whereas Hobbes's sovereign bore more resemblance to the British Crown. But, like Hobbes, Locke insisted that whenever government oversteps its role, that is by not acting in the interests of the people, the people have a right to react. Because the government has thus broken its part of the social contract, the people may revolt against the leader to create a new government that acts more in line with their interests. Locke's limited government is strong enough to provide protection for all citizens and their property but not so strong that it infringes on individual liberty.

? Question for Reflection: Were Presidents Lincoln, Wilson, Roosevelt, and Bush breaking or preserving the social contract when they placed limits on American citizen's personal freedoms during times of crisis?

Locke's *Second Treatise on Civil Government* was such a clear statement of the themes just outlined that much of the Declaration of Independence draws from his rationale to justify severing ties with a tyrannical king. Locke's idea of limited government is also embedded in the Constitution. The separation of governing powers

Rousseau — right to vote

limited government A type of government in which the powers of the government are clearly defined and bounded, so that governmental authority cannot intrude in the lives of private citizens.

and the numerous guarantees of individual liberties found in the Bill of Rights are derived from the Lockean notion of limited government based on popular consent.

For the government of Britain, under which both Hobbes (for most of his life) and Locke lived, the theory of the social contract was just a theory. In the American colonies of the seventeenth century, however, each colonial territory was in part a miniature experiment in the practical application of that theory. Coming to a land that indeed often rendered life "nasty, brutish and short," with little real governmental authority reaching directly into their lives, the colonists did live in something like the "state of nature." And, just as both Hobbes and Locke theorized they must, the colonists entered into binding contracts, established laws and ruling bodies, and formed governments. The Mayflower Compact, the Fundamental Orders of Connecticut, and even the rather Hobbesian regimes established in the proprietary colonies all required the willing entry of individuals into a legally ordered arrangement of power—a society under the rule of law.

First Moves Toward a Union

By 1753, the Board of Trade in London requested that the colonies "enter into articles of union and confederation with each other for the mutual defense of His Majesty's subjects and interests in North America, as well in time of peace as war." The goal was to protect the economic interests of the empire.

French expansionism in the backwoods of America led to increasing conflict and to the French and Indian War (1754–1763), which spread to Europe two years later as the Seven Years' War. Following the outbreak of fighting on the frontier, northern colonies were advised by Britain to sign a treaty with the Iroquois, and a meeting was called in Albany for this purpose. On May 9, 1754, the *Pennsylvania Gazette* published a lead article and cartoon authored by Ben Franklin to illustrate the perils of disunity. At the meeting in Albany, Franklin proposed a plan of union calling for a self-governing confederation for the colonies. A **confederation** is a league of sovereign states that delegates powers on selected issues to a central government. The plan proposed a forty-eight-member Grand Legislative Council in which all colonies would be represented; its responsibilities would include raising an army and navy, making war, and regulating trade and taxation. The plan also called for a chief executive, to be called president-general of the United Colonies, appointed by the Crown.

The delegates unanimously endorsed Franklin's so-called Albany Plan, but individual colonial assemblies soon rejected it because it appeared to give too much power to the Crown. It was also rejected by the British Crown, which claimed it gave too much power to the colonists. Franklin later wrote, "If the foregoing plan, or something like it, had been adopted and carried into execution, the subsequent separation of the colonies from the mother country might not so soon have happened."[4] Some twenty years later Franklin's design would resurface in an early draft of the Articles of Confederation.

Rebellion: Causes and Consequences

With the end of the French and Indian War in 1763, France's claim to power and territory in North America came to an end, and Britain took control of the interior to the Mississippi River. But Britain was deeply in debt from financing the war. To alleviate this debt, it turned to the colonies with a program of direct taxation. Prior to 1763 the British were interested in the colonies primarily as new markets and sources of raw materials. Now undertaking a new policy of imperialism, Britain sought more efficient political and military control in the New World. To this end, several units of British soldiers were dispatched to protect the colonial frontier, at great annual expense to the Crown.

▲ Benjamin Franklin's 1754 "Join or Die" woodcut was originally designed to symbolize the need for the colonies to unite for their common defense against the French. The symbol became popular again during the revolutionary period, when the colonies confronted the British.

confederation A league of sovereign states that delegates powers on selected issues to a central government.

◄ On July 9, 1776, after the Declaration of Independence was read to assembled troops in Bowling Green, New York, the soldiers, joined by New York patriots, pulled down a gilt equestrian statue of King George III. The statue had been the laughing-stock of New York because its sculptor, Wilton of London, failed to put stirrups on the horse that the king is riding. The statue was then melted down and used to make bullets.

To generate revenues sufficient to defray the expense of British occupation and control, the "first lord of the Treasurey," George Grenville, was elected to raise taxes, first on the already burdened British and then on the American colonists, whose taxes had been relatively modest to this point. Such direct taxation of the colonists without their consent and without representation in Parliament had grave consequences. Resistance to British control and to what the colonists perceived as unjust taxation led to revolution and then to independence.

The Sugar and Stamp Acts

The British viewed taxation as part of the sovereign's inherent authority and sought to extend its influence and extract revenue from the colonists through a series of acts, most notably the Sugar Act of 1764 and the Stamp Act of 1765. The **Sugar Act** extended taxes on molasses and raw sugar to include foreign refined sugar and various other goods imported into the colonies. The preamble of the Sugar Act stated that the tax was to be used for "defraying the expenses of defending and securing the colonies." This was how the British saw it. The colonists, however, viewed the act as a revenue measure imposed on them by the sovereign, without their consent, that would cut into their profits.

On February 13, 1765, Lord Grenville proposed before Parliament another measure to raise money from the colonies—this time to pay the cost of stationing British troops in America. The **Stamp Act** was quickly passed by Parliament in March; it required that revenue stamps be placed on all printed matter and legal documents, including newspapers, almanacs, bonds, leases, college diplomas, bills of sale, liquor licenses, insurance policies, playing cards, and dice. The tax would be felt in every aspect of commercial life in the colonies, its influence extending well beyond that of the sugar tax by affecting more people directly. The act was scheduled to go into effect on November 1, 1765.

Most colonists opposed the Stamp Act, and public protest against it raged throughout the spring and summer of 1765. Since the American colonists had no representative in Parliament, they reasoned that Parliament had no right to tax them. To counter the colonists' demand of "no taxation without representation," Parliament offered the idea of "virtual representation," explaining that members of Parliament represent the interests of the whole empire, whether the whole of Ireland or American colonies. In addition, many new and old boroughs and cities in

Sugar Act A British act of 1764 that levied a three-penny-per-gallon tax on molasses and other goods imported into the colonies.

Stamp Act A British act of 1765 that required that revenue stamps be placed on all printed matter and legal documents, making it felt in every aspect of commercial life in the colonies.

England did not yet have representation in Parliament. Thus, there was no practical difference between Charleston, South Carolina, and Manchester, England: neither had a representative in Parliament, but each was nevertheless represented by virtue of Parliament's concern for all British subjects.

The colonists' experiences with their town meetings and colonial assemblies led them to reject the idea of virtual representation. "A mere cobweb, spread to catch the unwary, and entangle the weak," argued Maryland legislator Daniel Dulany. If Manchester was not represented in Parliament, "it ought to be," said Boston attorney James Otis. Ideas about compacts, natural rights, and social contracts informed colonial reaction. The colonists, by virtue of written constitutions and documents, expected to be granted the rights of freeborn Englishmen, arguing that a legislature should be "an actual representation of all classes of the people by persons of each class" to be a "true picture of the people." And although they accepted the supremacy of Parliament, they embraced the doctrine of limited government, saying Parliament had no claim to a power that would violate the natural rights and laws to which all free people hold claim.

The colonists had some support in Parliament. Edmund Burke argued, "The British Empire must be governed on a plan of freedom, for it will be governed by no other." In the House of Commons William Pitt argued, "Taxation is no part of the governing or legislating power"; the idea of virtual representation is one of "the most contemptible ideas that ever entered the head of man."[5]

But in March 1766, Parliament repealed the Stamp Act. At the same time, however, it passed the Declaratory Act, granting the king and Parliament complete legislative authority to make laws binding to the colonies "in all cases whatsoever."

The Townshend Revenue Acts

In 1767 Parliament sought to impose yet another series of taxes on glass, lead, tea, and paper imported into the colonies. The preamble of the **Townshend Revenue Acts** stated that these acts were intended for "the support of civil government, in such provinces as it shall be found necessary." Revenues would also be used to pay salaries for governors and other officers, thereby diluting the strength of colonial assemblies, which until then had controlled governors' salaries.

Few colonists protested Parliament's authority to regulate trade among the colonies of its empire, but most felt that only the colonial assemblies had the authority to directly tax the colonies. The Townshend Acts provoked numerous boycotts and mob action as well as the fourteen "Letters of a Farmer in Pennsylvania," an eloquent and moderate interpretation of the colonial position written by John Dickinson. "The cause of Liberty is a cause of too much dignity to be sullied by turbulence and tumult," Dickenson cautioned. Appearing in the *Pennsylvania Chronicle*, the letters challenged British authority. "For who are a free people? Not those over whom government is reasonably and equitably exercised, but those, who live under a government so constitutionally checked and controlled, that proper provision is made against its being otherwise exercised."

The Boston Massacre

Meanwhile customs commissioners had found it increasingly difficult to collect tax duties, and they asked Parliament to send troops. The redcoats arrived in Boston in October 1768, where their presence further incited anger. The cause of revolution was soon to have its first martyrs. On March 5, 1770, British soldiers fired a volley of shots into a crowd of hecklers. Five colonists were killed, including Crispus Attucks, son of a black father and Indian mother. The first colonists had now lost their lives protesting taxation without representation. **The Boston Massacre** aroused intense public protest. Within a month, all the Townshend duties were repealed except the tax on tea. The massacre also alerted the colonists to a dramatic truth—organized local resistance revealed the impotence of imperial power in the colonies.

Townshend Revenue Acts A series of taxes imposed by the British Parliament in 1767 on glass, lead, tea, and paper imported into the colonies.

Boston Massacre A 1770 incident in which British soldiers fired a volley of shots into a crowd of hecklers who had been throwing snowballs at the redcoats; five colonists were killed, including their leader, Crispus Attucks.

◄ Paul Revere's dramatic engraving of the Boston Massacre depicts the initial bloody conflict between British troops (redcoats) and Boston laborers. Months after the shooting, prints of the massacre could be found all over the colony. Revere added the words "Butcher's Hall" over the Customs House, which helped incite those who called the incident a massacre.

Committees of Correspondence

The fact that the colonists were able to publicize Parliament's encroachment on their rights helped fuel revolutionary fervor. In 1772 Samuel Adams emerged as a major agitator for colonial independence by forming the Boston Committee of Correspondence, which published a statement of rights and grievances warning colonists that Britain could disband colonial legislatures and take away individual rights. Similar committees quickly sprang up throughout Massachusetts and the other colonies. **Committees of Correspondence** thus became the first institutionalized mechanism for communication among the colonies, greatly advancing their cooperation. One loyalist (a person loyal to Britain) called the committees (no doubt a tribute to their effectiveness) "the foulest, subtlest, and most venomous serpent ever issued from the egg of sedition."

The Boston Tea Party

The British East India Company had fallen on hard times. Before the Townshend Acts, the company had been the chief supplier of tea to the colonists. In an effort to avoid paying the Townshend duty, colonists started smuggling in tea from the Netherlands, thus cutting deeply into the East India Company's profits. With 17 million pounds of tea in its warehouses, the company asked Parliament for help. Parliament allowed the company to sell tea to the colonies at a price below market value. The Tea Act, passed in May 1773, retained the hated and symbolic duty on tea.

The colonists were in an uproar, realizing that colonial tea merchants would be undercut. Even worse, no one knew which commodity might be next. Colonial women, among the principal consumers of tea, led a boycott against it. An organization of colonial women known as the Daughters of Liberty committed itself to agitation against British policies, proclaiming that "rather than Freedom, we'll part

Committees of Correspondence
Formed in Boston in 1772, the first institutionalized mechanism for communication within and between the colonies and foreign countries.

with our Tea." Parliament's actions also provoked a famous incident, the **Boston Tea Party.** At midnight on December 16, 1773, colonists disguised as Native Americans dumped 342 chests of tea into Boston Harbor.

To punish Massachusetts for the tea party and send a message to the other colonies, the king and his ministers legislated the Coercive Acts. The colonists dubbed this series of punitive measures, passed by Parliament in the spring of 1774, the **Intolerable Acts.** In addition to closing Boston Harbor until the tea was paid for and requiring the quartering of British soldiers in private homes, the acts created the position of military governor. General Thomas Gage, commander in chief of British forces in North America, was named to the post. Gage's consent was necessary for convening most town meetings, making him all but a dictator. In addition, he could use **writs of assistance** to search every part of a house for evidence of a crime, whether real or perceived.

Question for Reflection: How different was the English Parliament's legislation of the Coercive Acts from President Abraham Lincoln's establishment of martial law during the Civil War?

Rather than forcing the colonists to submit to the will of King George III, the Intolerable Acts helped to unify the colonies against the Crown. Massachusetts's plight inspired other colonies to defend its cause. A young member of Virginia's Committee of Correspondence, Thomas Jefferson, proposed setting aside June 1, the date of the closing of Boston Harbor, as a day of fasting and prayer in Virginia, hundreds of miles to the south. With this first instance of one colony's empathy for another's plight, a new nation was beginning to emerge. On learning of Jefferson's proposal, the Virginia royal governor immediately dissolved the assembly, whose members went down the road to the Raleigh Tavern and drew up a resolution calling for a congress with representation from all the colonies.[6]

Revolution and the Stirrings of a New Government

In the wake of the Boston Tea Party, the colonists' differences with the Crown moved far beyond the taxation issue. While the tax policies of Lord Grenville had served to ignite the first intense clash between Britain and America, the heavy-handed response of the Intolerable Acts revealed the real basis of the schism between Crown and colonies. The British wanted order and obedience; the colonists wanted greater liberty. "Although Liberty was not the only goal for Americans in the 1770s and 1780s," writes political scientist James MacGregor Burns, "they believed also in Independence, Order, Equality, the Pursuit of Happiness—none had the evocative power and sweep of Liberty, or Freedom—two terms for the same thing. To preserve liberty was the supreme end of government."[7] In Boston, this sentiment had taken the form of standing up to the hated British troops stationed there and dumping tea into the harbor. At the First Continental Congress, the signs of both revolution and American democracy were visible. In a speech before the Virginia Convention on March 23, 1775, Patrick Henry cried out, "Is life so dear, or peace so sweet, as to be purchased at the price of chains and slavery? Forbid it, Almighty God! I know not what course others may take; but as for me, give me liberty, or give me death!"

The First Continental Congress

On September 5, 1774, fifty-six elected delegates from provincial congresses or conventions of all the colonies except Georgia met in the **First Continental Congress** at Philadelphia's Carpenters Hall. They initially sought to reestablish more cordial relations with the British Crown, although still insisting on the restoration of their

Boston Tea Party A 1773 act of civil disobedience in which colonists dressed as Native Americans dumped 342 chests of tea into Boston Harbor to protest increased taxes.

Intolerable Acts A series of punitive measures passed by the British Parliament in the spring of 1774 as a response to the Boston Tea Party.

writs of assistance Blanket permission for British customs officials to search every part of a colonist's house for customs violations and any evidence of a crime, real or perceived.

First Continental Congress The meeting of fifty-six elected members (from provincial congresses or irregular conventions) that took place in Philadelphia's Carpenters Hall in 1774. It resulted in a resolution to oppose acts of the British Parliament and a plan of association for the colonies.

rights as English citizens. The delegates included Samuel Adams and John Adams of Massachusetts; John Jay of New York; John Dickinson of Pennsylvania; and Patrick Henry and George Washington of Virginia. Before leaving for Philadelphia, Washington wrote to a friend expressing the intensity of feelings common to those attending the Congress: "The crisis is arrived when we must assert our rights, or submit to every imposition, that can be heaped upon us, till custom and use shall make us as tame and abject [as] slaves, as the blacks we rule over with such arbitrary sway."[8]

The First Continental Congress issued the Declaration of American Rights, claiming in the name of the colonies exclusive legislative power over taxation and "all the rights, liberties, and communities of free and natural-born subjects within the realm of England." The Congress also rejected a plan of union introduced by George Galloway of Pennsylvania that closely resembled Franklin's Albany Plan of twenty years earlier. It did endorse the plan delivered from Suffolk County, Massachusetts, by a silversmith, Paul Revere. These Suffolk Resolves declared the Intolerable Acts null and void, supported arming Massachusetts to defend itself against Britain, and urged economic sanctions on Britain. The delegates agreed to meet again in May 1775 if Britain did not restore the rights it had taken away. Most delegates still hoped to avoid war with Britain; few were ready to publicly declare a war for American independence.[9]

"The Shot Heard 'Round the World"

Following the Boston Tea Party, Parliament had declared Massachusetts to be in open rebellion, giving British troops the right to shoot rebels on sight. General Gage was determined to put down this rebellion, so on the night of April 18, 1775, he marched west to Concord, near Boston, to destroy ammunition and gunpowder being stored by the local militia. Paul Revere and others rode furiously through the night to give warning. While Revere was captured, William Dawes was able to alert the colonists. Just after dawn, when the British reached Lexington, they were met by seventy minutemen—as the local militia were called because they were to be ready to take up arms at a minute's notice. Gage ordered the militia to disperse. A stray shot was fired, the British opened fire, and eight Americans were killed. The British continued their march on to Concord where they clashed with minutemen at Concord's North Bridge. At Lexington there had been no return fire, but at Concord, in Longfellow's words, was fired "the shot heard 'round the world," the first armed resistance by Americans. By day's end, 250 British troops and 90 Americans were dead or wounded. The colonies were now at war with the powerful British Empire, and the American War of Independence was under way.

The Second Continental Congress

Three weeks after the clashes at Lexington and Concord, the **Second Continental Congress** convened on May 10, 1775, with all thirteen colonies represented. The purpose of the Congress was to decide whether to sever the bonds with England and declare independence. The brief but dramatic skirmishes at Lexington and Concord were still fresh in the minds of the delegates. In the absence of any other legislative body, without any legal authority to speak of, and in the midst of growing hostility toward the British, the Congress had little choice but to assume the role of a revolutionary government. It took control of the militia gathered around Boston and named George Washington general and commander in chief of this ragtag army. Then, on June 17, the first major confrontation between the colonials and British forces occurred—the Battle of Bunker Hill. Still, the delegates hoped for a reconciliation, sending the "Olive Branch Petition" to King George III. But the king refused to receive it, and Parliament rejected it as well. The course toward American independence was now fixed.

Second Continental Congress A meeting convened on May 10, 1775, with all thirteen colonies represented. The purpose of the Congress was to decide whether or not to sever bonds with England and declare independence.

Common Sense

At the same time, Thomas Paine's pamphlet of January 1776, **Common Sense** (published anonymously to avoid charges of treason) helped crystallize the idea of revolution for the colonists. Paine, who would later serve with General Washington during the war, moved beyond merely stating the colonists' claims against Parliament to questioning the very institution of monarchy. He also concluded that the colonies needed to separate from England immediately. Paine wrote:

> A government of our own is our natural right; and when a man seriously reflects on the precariousness of human affairs, he will become convinced, that it is infinitely wiser and safer to form a constitution of our own in a cool deliberate manner, while we have it in our power, than to trust such an interesting event to time and chance. . . .
>
> Ye that tell us of harmony and reconciliation, can ye restore to us the time that is passed? Can ye give to prostitution its former innocence? Neither can ye reconcile Britain and America. The last cord now is broken.

In addition, *Common Sense* enumerated the advantages of republican government over monarchy and argued that an American republic would be a laboratory for a political experiment, in which citizens would enjoy full representation and equality of rights.

Common Sense profoundly influenced thinking in the colonies. As George Washington observed, "*Common Sense* is working a powerful change in the minds of men." More than 150,000 copies of the pamphlet were sold within three months of its first printing. Virtually every colonist had access to it, and the demand for independence escalated rapidly.

"O.K., the third of July is out. How about the fourth?"

© The New Yorker Collection 1996 Peter Steiner from cartoonbank.com. All rights reserved.

Common Sense Thomas Paine's pamphlet of January 1776, which helped crystallize the idea of revolution for the colonists.

Declaration of Independence A formal proclamation declaring independence, approved and signed on July 4, 1776.

The Declaration of Independence

On June 7, 1776, a resolution for independence was introduced by Richard Henry Lee, a Virginia delegate to the Continental Congress:

> Resolved, that these United Colonies are, and of right ought to be, free and independent States, and that they are absolved from all allegiance to the British Crown, and that all connection between them and the State of Great Britain is, and ought to be, totally dissolved.

No longer was the reestablishment of their "rights as Englishmen" sufficient for the colonial leaders attending the Congress; it was to be independence or nothing. Lee's resolution for independence was considered and finally passed when the Congress reconvened on July 2. Writing to his wife, Abigail, John Adams predicted that July 2 "will be the most memorable epoch in the history of America." In the meantime a committee had already been formed to draft a formal proclamation declaring independence. This committee included John Adams, Ben Franklin, and Thomas Jefferson. It was the thirty-three-year-old Virginian, Jefferson, who drafted the final document on which the Congress voted. On July 4, after three days of vigorous debate, the Declaration of Independence was approved and signed. According to legend, John Hancock, the first to sign, wrote his name so large because "I want John Bull to be able to read my signature without spectacle."

The **Declaration of Independence** renounced allegiance to the British Crown, justified the Revolution, and provided a philosophical basis for limited government based on popular consent. Clearly echoing social contract theorist John Locke, the Declaration proclaimed that the colonists were "created equal" and were endowed, by God, with certain natural rights—the inalienable rights to life, liberty, and the pursuit of happiness. The Declaration also proclaimed that government was instituted to secure these rights and derived its just powers from the consent of the governed. When governments become destructive of these ends, the people have the right to reconstitute it. The Declaration listed the colonists' many grievances against King George III and concluded that he had become "a Tyrant" who was "unfit to be the ruler of a free People." Thus, the colonies "are, and of right ought to be Free and Independent States."

By instituting government based on popular consent, in which power is exercised by representatives chosen by and responsive to the populace, the eighteenth-century revolutionaries sought "to become republican." Political power would come from the people, not a supreme authority such as a king. The ultimate success of a government would be dependent on the civic virtue of its citizenry. The key assumption was that "if the population consisted of sturdy, independent property owners imbued with civic virtue, then the republic could survive."[10] As James Madison later wrote, "No other form would be reconcilable with the genius of the people of America; with the fundamental principles of the revolution; or with the honorable determination, which animates every votary of freedom, to rest all our political experiments on the capacity of mankind for self-government."

However, the delegates' support of freedom and the social contract, and their opposition to tyranny, did not extend everywhere. Jefferson's initial draft complained that King George had "waged cruel war against human nature itself, violating its most sacred rights of life & liberty in the persons of a distant people, who never offended him, captivating and carrying them into slavery in another hemisphere, or to incur miserable death in their transportation thither, this piratical warfare, the opprobrium of *infidel* powers, is the warfare of the *Christian* king of Great Britain, determined to keep open a market where MEN should be bought & sold . . . " In short, Jefferson, a slave owner himself, was complaining about the practice of slavery in the colonies and seemingly trying to argue that these men should

APPROACHING DIVERSITY

Abigail Adams: The First Feminist?

In the early decades of America's history the voices of women were largely unheard. No women attended the Continental Congress, nor were any involved in the drafting of the Declaration of Independence. Women did, however, play an essential role in campaigns to boycott British goods in protest against the taxes imposed by Parliament. They were also active behind the scenes during the Revolution; women plowed fields, managed shops, and melted down pots to make shot. Yet they played virtually no part in political affairs; women could not vote, nor could they hold elective office. The only route open to them was to persuade their husbands to act on their behalf in Congress and the state assemblies.

The situation of women in the late eighteenth century is illustrated in a letter from Abigail Adams to her husband, John, who was attending the Continental Congress. "I desire you would remember the Ladies," she wrote, "and be more generous and favourable to them than your ancestors." Although she conceded the traditional dominance of men, women were "beings placed by providence under [male] protection," she issued a challenge, if only half seriously: "If perticuliar care and attention is not paid to the Ladies we are determined to foment a Rebellion, and will not hold ourselves bound by any laws in which we have no voice, or Representation."

John was amused by his wife's remarks on behalf of "another Tribe more numerous and powerfull than all the rest. . . . After stirring up Tories, Landjobbers, Trimmers, Bigots, Canadians, Indians, Negroes, Hanoverians, Hessians, Irish Catholicks, Scotch Renegadoes, at last [the members of the Congress] have stimulated the ladies to demand new Priviledges and threaten to rebell." But he was quick to point out that such a rebellion would lead nowhere: "Depend upon it, We know better than to repeal our Masculine systems" and submit to "the Despotism of the Peticoat."

In part, Abigail appears to have been teasing her husband; she did not directly challenge the prevailing notion of male superiority. But we may see in her correspondence a glimmer of what would ultimately emerge as modern feminism. Although it would be more than a century before the beginning of the "Rebelion" she warned of and it would be nearly two centuries before women would serve on the Supreme Court and as Secretary of State, in her gentle way she sounded a chord that has reverberated through the years.

Source: Diane Ravitch, *The Democracy Reader,* (New York: Harper-Collins 1972), pp. 103–04.

be equal as well. But the southern delegates did not agree, and by forcing the convention to strike this clause from the draft, in order to ensure that a unanimous call would be made against the King, left this controversial issue to be resolved by a Civil War more than three quarters of a century later.

By signing the Declaration, these revolutionaries were risking "our Lives, our Fortunes and our sacred Honor." The Declaration itself was an act of treason against the Crown, punishable by death. After he put his signature to the document, Ben Franklin is alleged to have remarked, "We must, indeed, all hang together, or most assuredly we shall hang separately."

The First New Government: A Confederation of States

Even before the War of Independence was won, Americans faced the challenge of devising a new government. To do this, they drew from their experiences with compacts, social contract theory, separation of governmental powers, and natural rights. Between 1776 and 1780, all states adopted new constitutions except Rhode Island and Connecticut, which simply struck from their original governing charters any mention of colonial obligation to the Crown. Seven of the state constitutions contained a separate bill of rights guaranteeing citizens certain natural rights and

Shays's Rebellion

Even before Jefferson penned the words of the Declaration of Independence, those ideals were inspiring Americans to fight for them. One of the fighters was a farmer and militia captain from western Massachusetts, Daniel Shays, who fought at Bunker Hill, near Boston, on June 17, 1775.

Shays fought in two revolutions in his lifetime. The first was the Revolutionary War, ending with the Treaty of Paris in 1783, which freed the colonists from English rule and recognized American independence. The second, in 1786–1787, was a protest against the new American government. Both times Shays fought for change, for "a new order of the ages," as inscribed on the seal of the United States.

This second revolution took root as economic conditions in the new nation deteriorated, particularly for farmers, who lacked markets and could not pay off their debts. They were often forced to pay exorbitantly high interest rates, and those who could not pay faced prison or indentured servitude. Between 1784 and 1786 in Hampshire County, Massachusetts, about a third of all males over sixteen were involved in debt cases, a figure typical for the entire country. During the same period, seventy-three men in Hampshire County were thrown into debtors' prisons.* Making matters worse, the farmers lacked government representation for their interests because the Massachusetts state legislature was dominated by merchants from the eastern part of the state (most farmers were from the western part).

The spirit that led the farmers to revolt against the British a decade earlier inspired them to organize and protest once again, in a populist uprising now remembered as Shays's Rebellion. Now the "tyrant" was not a distant monarch, but other Americans of a different socioeconomic class. The farmers succeeded in shutting down several local courts, setting some ablaze. (A court closed or burned could not foreclose.) They also demanded that the Massachusetts legislature print cheap paper money—as Rhode Island had done—that would be acceptable to creditors. The legislature refused and instead legislated new taxes.

Shays, like many farmers, was desperate. After unsuccessful protests and petitioning against taxation, the farmers rebelled. Shays led a force of 2,500 men against the state militia. Ironically, members of the militia included men who had fought with Shays at Bunker Hill. After a series of confrontations, the Shaysites were finally repelled by General Benjamin Lincoln, a hero of the Revolution. Massachusetts governor James Bowdoin described the farmers as engaging in "riot, anarchy, and confusion."

The populist rebellion horrified most of the new nation's political leaders, who were also of the wealthy, propertied class. To them, Shays's Rebellion symbolized lawlessness, as a mob of wild men took the law into their own hands. Had revolution failed to produce anything but democracy run amuck? Many believed that America was on the brink of anarchy.

Fear stemming from the rebellion pushed some antidemocratic sentiments to the center of political debate. On

protection from their government. The Virginia Bill of Rights, for example, provided for the right of revolution, freedom of the press, religious liberty, separation of powers, free elections, prohibition against taxation without consent, and fair legal procedures such as the right to trial by jury and moderate bail.

None of these state constitutions contained any provision for a central governmental authority that would help define the thirteen states as a nation. Thus, a few days after the Declaration of Independence was signed, a committee was called to draft a plan to bring the colonies together as a confederation. Fighting a war for independence necessitated a central direction, a plan for union.

The Articles of Confederation (1781–1789)

On July 12, 1777, after six drafts, the **Articles of Confederation** were presented to the Continental Congress. Following several months of debate, on November 15, 1777, the plan was adopted by the Congress and submitted to the individual states for ratification. The Articles formally took effect on March 1, 1781, after being ratified by all of the states.

The colonists were not about to jeopardize the power and freedom they had won, so the Articles sought to limit the powers of the government. The confederation they created was a loosely knit alliance of thirteen independent states agreeing to cooperate in certain instances. The central government was extremely weak. All

Articles of Confederation The first constitutional framework of the new United States of America. Approved in 1777 by the Second Continental Congress, it was later replaced by the current Constitution.

October 27, 1786, John Jay wrote to Thomas Jefferson that "a spirit of licentiousness has infected Massachusetts. . . . I feel for the cause of liberty, and for the honour of my countrymen who have so nobly asserted it, and who, at present, so abuse its blessings." George Washington was equally distressed and expressed his uneasiness to James Madison: "There are combustibles in every state which a spark might set fire to. . . . If government cannot check these disorders, what security has a man for life, liberty, or property?" Not all leaders agreed with the perspective of Jay and Washington. From Paris, Thomas Jefferson wrote to a friend back home, "The tree of liberty must be refreshed from time to time with the blood of patriots and tyrants."

Although most Americans wondered whether their new nation could survive the unrest, it is clear that Shays's Rebellion served an important purpose. It helped strengthen the position of those advocating stronger centralized government. To these people, the Shaysites were living proof that tyranny had many sources. Most citizens of the day linked liberty with security of property. By threatening the institutions created to protect property (the banks and courts), the Shaysites appeared to threaten liberty and replace it with anarchy.† The revolt was put down, but it would have a lasting impact on the construction of American democracy.

▲ Daniel Shays's rebels take control of a courthouse in western Massachusetts in 1786 to prevent farm foreclosures by creditors.

---

*Christopher Collier and James Lincoln Collier, *Decision in Philadelphia* (New York: Random House, 1986), p. 11.

†See Robert A. Feer, *Shays's Rebellion* (New York: Garland, 1988), pp. 504–29; and David Szatmary, *Shays's Rebellion* (Amherst: University of Massachusetts Press, 1980), pp. 120–34.

of the national power—executive, legislative, and judicial—was housed in a single house of Congress in which each state had one vote. Fearing a new king, the writers of the Articles did not create a separate executive branch.

Under the Articles, the states reigned supreme in a "league of friendship." They retained almost total sovereignty over their affairs. The powers of Congress were strictly limited. It was not given the power to tax, though it could coin its own money. And though it could declare war, it could not raise an army. Thus, after the Revolution was won, Congress was unable to act when the British refused to decamp from their forts on the Great Lakes in 1783; it was also powerless when the Spanish closed off the Mississippi River and the port of New Orleans to United States trade and when both Spain and Britain began arming Native Americans in the hope that they would attack frontier settlements. Their Congress had no power over interstate or international commerce and no power to make treaties with foreign governments. Instead, each state could make its own foreign policy. Congress could not even make laws; it was limited to passing resolutions or regulations. It took the agreement of nine states to pass any legislation, and a unanimous vote of all thirteen states was required to amend the Articles. Unable to raise funds, the Congress was forced to borrow vast sums of money from France and Holland to pay for the war with Britain. Unable to defend itself without the voluntary support of state militias and powerless to legislate, the new central government was simply too weak to govern effectively.

The problems of the confederation of states seemed to grow, ranging from financial and commercial difficulties to civil disorder. The political chaos that inevitably resulted made the new United States appear not so much a nation as an organization of thirteen little kingdoms, each directed by a state legislature. The irony here, of course, is that the Articles did exactly what they were devised to do. Independent state legislatures often acted against each other, even levying duties on trade that crossed state lines. James Madison summed up the problem: "Experience had proved a tendency in our governments to throw all power into the Legislative vortex. The Executives of the State are in general little more than Cyphers: the legislatures omnipotent. If no effectual check be devised for restraining the instability and encroachments of the latter, a revolution of some kind or other would be inevitable."

With the "omnipotent" state legislatures operating to the advantage of their individual interests, certain states flourished economically. Agricultural exports doubled and the national debt was so low that states were paying back principal as well as interest. The states were cooperating in their trade policies to keep out British goods and were working together to raise money for capital improvements. But when a crisis arose, the central government proved incapable of handling it. This was clearly demonstrated in the case of Shays's Rebellion. When skyrocketing interest rates and taxes forced many farmers into bankruptcy and ultimately revolt, the central government could not respond when asked by Massachusetts to do so. Instead, private citizens hired soldiers to put down the insurrection.

The Need for a More Perfect Union

After six years of confederation, it became clear that a stronger, more centralized government was needed. Shays's Rebellion led the colonists to fear anarchy and desire order. Even George Washington recognized that the Articles were founded on a too trusting view of human nature. The states seemed incapable of ensuring order, let alone promoting the common good.

Even as Shays's Rebellion was gaining momentum, delegates from five states, largely at the instigation of James Madison, met at Annapolis, Maryland, to find a way to solve the problems of economic competition among the states and promote interstate commerce. When the dozen men present found that they could do nothing, Madison and Alexander Hamilton, who emerged as leaders, clearly saw that the

◀ The American Revolution was fought on the twin principles of liberty and equality, but slavery became the practice of the land. Several leaders of the Revolution owned slaves. Shown here, a slave auction in Virginia, where human beings of all ages were sold to the highest bidder.

problems could not be solved by mere commercial agreements. So, they persuaded the delegates to issue invitations to all of the states to send delegates to a convention in Philadelphia in May 1787 to discuss more than just trade issues, but also to "perfect" the Articles of Confederation by considering all issues required "to render the constitution of the federal government adequate to the exigencies of the Union."

After five states agreed to send delegates, on February 21, 1787, the Confederation Congress endorsed the meeting "for the sole and express purpose of revising the Articles of Confederation." But most delegates knew that mere revision of the Articles would not be enough. The complex mix of economic, political, and other problems plaguing the confederation required not a loose arrangement of individual states struggling to sink or swim on their own but a centralized authority for the common protection and prosperity of all.

The Convention met in the East Room of the State House, the same room in which the Second Continental Congress had met in May 1775 and the Declaration of Independence had been signed in 1776. It opened on May 14, but nothing could be done for lack of a quorum, and delegates continued straggling in until well into the summer. Four months later they would accomplish what is frequently described as "the Miracle at Philadelphia." Table 2.1 summarizes the key events that produced this "miracle."

The Constitutional Convention

The unique nature of the American Constitution, and its success both in forging a nation that was becoming fragmented under the Articles of Confederation and in guiding that nation for centuries to come, can be explained in many ways. Part of the answer lies in the democratic political theory of the time, theory that was applied to the problems facing the government. However, theory does not govern a nation. People do. So the framing of the Constitution in 1787 is better understood by examining the circumstances under which various theories were advanced in debate and the people who were debating and making the compromises that made success possible.

FYI

Was there a spy at the Constitutional Convention? Scholars disagree whether total and absolute adherence to the secrecy rule was maintained. With so many of the delegates in financial distress, there is speculation that one of the delegates tried to sell information on the proceedings to a British agent. Whether this happened cannot be proven conclusively, but it is possible.

Table 2.1 ■ The Founding: Key Events	
1620	Mayflower Compact signed. Plymouth Colony founded.
1630	Massachusetts Bay Colony founded.
1760	King George III assumes the throne of England.
1764	Sugar Act passed by Parliament.
1765	Stamp Act passed by Parliament. Delegates to Stamp Act Congress draft declaration of rights and liberties.
1766	Stamp Act repealed. Declaratory Act issued.
1767	Townshend Acts passed.
1770	Boston Massacre. Townshend Acts limited to tea alone.
1772	First Committee of Correspondence formed by Samuel Adams.
1773	Boston Tea Party.
1774	Coercive Acts against Massachusetts passed. First Continental Congress convened.
1775	Skirmish at Lexington and Concord officially begins the War of Independence. Second Continental Congress convened.
1776	Common Sense published. Declaration of Independence signed.
1781	Articles of Confederation adopted.
1783	Peace of Paris. Great Britain formally recognizes the independence of the United States.
1786	Shays's Rebellion.

The Task

The problems of governing under the Articles of Confederation made it clear that a stronger central government was needed. But the mission of the Constitutional Convention was not quite so clear. Several states had already authorized their delegates "to render the constitution of government adequate to the exigencies of the Union." Some of the delegates came to the Convention with an understanding that the Articles needed to be scrapped altogether, and they were prepared to propose a new form of government from the outset.[11] Their success in doing so would be decided by whichever of the fifty-five men attending the Convention happened to be present during those debates. But it was not a success that was preordained, as William Grayson, representative from Virginia in the Confederation Congress, wrote: "What will be the result of their meeting I cannot with any certainty determine, but I hardly think much good can come of it: the people of America don't appear to me to be ripe for any great innovations."[12]

The Participants

While many have come to see the participants of the Constitutional Convention as legends, the delegates are better understood as skilled and ambitious politicians. What resulted came about not from a singular theoretical vision of a government but from a series of brilliant political compromises and fortuitous events.

The delegates came from a very narrow band of American society, the elite aristocracy. This fact should not be surprising, since less than 5 percent of the total population (150,000 of 3.9 million people) were the free, white males, over the age of twenty-one who owned land, and thus possessed the right to vote. Many rich men were present, and a variety of professions were represented. More than half were lawyers, another quarter were large plantation owners, eight were judges, and the rest were doctors, merchants, bankers, clergymen, and soldiers. All of the delegates owned property, and several owned slaves. Although it was a young group, with more than three-fourths under the age of fifty, what really distinguished this group was its experience in politics. There were several former members of the Continental Congress, forty-two members of the Confederation Congress, and seven former governors.

◄ Second Street in Philadelphia as the framers saw it. In the center of this view in the late 1700s is Christ Church, where the drafters of the Constitution went to pray for divine guidance in the successful conclusion of their Convention.

From their efforts at drafting earlier political documents, these experienced statesmen brought with them an understanding of the issues and the need for compromise. Six delegates had signed the Declaration of Independence; nine more, including George Mason of Virginia, Alexander Hamilton of New York, and John Rutledge of South Carolina, had drafted their state's constitution. Both Roger Sherman of Connecticut and John Dickinson of Delaware had played a major role in drafting the Articles of Confederation, while three other members—Elbridge Gerry of Massachusetts, and Gouverneur Morris and Robert Morris of Pennsylvania—had been among its signers.

Although elite and experienced, the delegates were far from representative of the general population. Only two delegates were farmers, even though 85 percent of the people of the United States lived on small farms. There were no members of the working class, no artisans, businessmen, or tradesmen among the delegates. African Americans, Native Americans, and women were nowhere to be found in the meeting either. More than 600,000, or just under 18 percent of the total population, was African American, about 520,000 of whom were slaves living in the South, while most of the rest were poor, working-class laborers in the northern cities.[13] Native Americans did not participate because they were not citizens; viewed as foreigners, they were specifically excluded from the Constitution, except in the "interstate commerce" power of Article I, Section 8, where they were lumped with the foreign nations as possible trading partners. Few Catholics or Jews were among the political elite from which the delegates were drawn.[14] For all practical purposes, women in American society had no political rights. Since they did not have the vote, participation in politics, much less the Convention was inconceivable. Thus, no woman attended a single state ratifying convention or voted for a state convention delegate. Despite this lack of diversity at the Convention, however, the framers crafted a constitution capable of including women and other groups over time.

The Major Players

The proponents of a strong national government (called *nationalists*) were led by James Madison, who would later be called "the Father of the Constitution." A short, thin, painfully shy, thirty-six-year-old bachelor from Virginia, Madison was one of

▲ James Madison (1751–1836), a political scientist and prolific note-taker at the Constitutional Convention, was very influential in the framing of the Constitution, which applied his theories of government.

Virginia Plan A plan presented to the Constitutional Convention; favored by the delegates from the bigger states.

legislative branch The branch of the government that makes laws.

executive branch The branch of the government that executes laws.

judiciary The branch of the government that interprets laws.

checks and balances Systems that ensure that for every power in government there is an equal and opposite power placed in a separate branch to restrain that force.

separation of powers State in which the powers of the government are divided among the three branches: executive, legislative, and judicial.

proportional representation A system of representation popular in Europe whereby the number of seats in the legislature is based on the proportion of the vote received in the election.

the best political theorists of his day. He spent months preparing for the Convention, studying and developing a new plan for a strong, central national government to counteract the problems of the Articles of Confederation.

Opposing Madison were the states' rights proponents (called *antinationalists*), led by New Jersey's William Paterson. The son of a shopkeeper and a lawyer by trade, Paterson believed that as a representative of the state of New Jersey, all his actions should take into consideration the needs of small states. He argued that the power and position of individual states had to be protected from the proposed central government. Joining Paterson was his old friend Luther Martin. The most prominent lawyer in his native Maryland, Martin's characteristic heavy drinking, leading to his nickname of "Lawyer Brandy Bottle," had a negative effect on his persuasiveness at the Convention. For Martin, states were sovereign entities deserving greater protection than people.

The wide gulf between the nationalists and the antinationalists made Roger Sherman of Connecticut a major player in the discussions. The third oldest delegate to the convention at age sixty-six, Sherman had spent nearly all of his life in public service. As the only man to have signed all of the new nation's formative documents, Sherman was a cautious, careful politician who bargained for the common ground that would secure a negotiated compromise.

Plans for a New Government

Governor Edmund Randolph of Virginia opened the formal debate on May 29, 1787, with a four-hour speech containing fifteen resolves, or resolutions, for a "strong consolidated union" rather than a federal one with continued state power. When the delegates agreed the next day to debate these resolves, the Convention was no longer a debate about improving the Articles of Confederation; it was about creating an entirely new form of government.

Once it was decided that the Articles of Confederation would be replaced, two central questions guided debate:

- How powerful would the new national government be?
- How powerful would the states be?

Of five plans submitted to the delegates for consideration, debate centered mainly on two of them: the Virginia Plan and the New Jersey Plan. The differences between these two proposals show clearly the divisions among the large-state and the small-state advocates.

The Virginia Plan   The **Virginia Plan** was presented by Governor Randolph and was so named because he and its author, James Madison, came from Virginia. This proposal was favored by the delegates from the bigger states. It was based on the following propositions designed to remedy the perceived defects in the Articles of Confederation:

1. It called for three branches of government: a **legislative branch** that makes laws, an **executive branch** that executes the laws, and a **judiciary** that interprets the laws. Since Madison feared the negative effects of power, his plan championed a system of **checks and balances.** For every power in government, there would be an equal and opposite power placed in a separate branch to restrain that force. This idea presumed another feature of the new government, the **separation of powers,** meaning that the powers of government are divided among the three branches, thus preventing the accumulation of too much power in any one branch.

2. Operating from a belief that the ultimate power to govern resides in the people, Randolph proposed a system of **proportional representation,** meaning that the size of each state's delegation in both houses of Congress would be based on the size of its population, rather than the one-state, one-vote rule in the Articles

of Confederation. The size of Virginia's population (691,737) would give it more than ten times as many members in Congress as Delaware (population 59,096).

3. Congress would have a bicameral legislature, consisting of two houses, both apportioned on the basis of population. A state would send members to the lower house, elected directly by the people. The lower house would elect the upper house from nominees provided by the state legislatures.

4. The executive, whose size was yet to be determined, would be elected for a maximum of one term by Congress.

5. The judiciary, which would consist of one or more supreme courts and other national courts, would be staffed by life-tenured judges.

6. There would also be a **council of revision,** a combined body of judges and members of the executive branch, having a limited veto over national legislation and an absolute veto over state legislation.

7. The legislature would have the power to override state laws.

It is not hard to see the impact of the Virginia Plan. It centered power in the national government, giving it authority over the states. And by placing much of the governing and appointment powers in a legislature chosen by proportional representation, states with the largest population would dominate that branch. Since the executive branch was put in place by Congress, the big states would dominate there as well, thus giving them control over the central government.

The New Jersey Plan   For the representatives of the small states, the Madisonian notion of proportional representation was unacceptable because it gave populous states the ability to force their will on smaller states. "New Jersey will never confederate on the plan," William Paterson said. "She would be swallowed up. . . . Myself or my state will never submit to tyranny or despotism." This reaction infuriated Pennsylvania's James Wilson, who asked, "Does it require 150 [voters of my state] to balance 50 [of yours]?"[15] The small-state delegates countered with a series of resolutions advanced by Paterson called the **New Jersey Plan.** This plan was designed to refine and strengthen the Articles of Confederation rather than to replace it, and in so doing, it protected the interests of the smaller, less populous states. The New Jersey Plan proposed the following:

1. The power of the national government would be centered in a **unicameral** (one-house) **legislature,** and, to minimize the impact of population, each state would have one vote.

2. A multiperson executive board would be elected by the legislature for one term only, and authorized to enforce national laws even in the face of opposition from the states. The executive could be removed by a majority of state governors.

3. A supreme court would be appointed by the executive board and be empowered to deal with impeachment of national officers, foreign policy questions, and tax and trade problems.

4. The power to tax imports would be taken away from the states and given to the national government.

5. The legislature would be empowered to tax state governments on the basis of population and collect the money by force if an unspecified number of states agreed.

6. All congressional acts would become "the supreme law of the respective states," with the executive board being authorized to use force to "compel an obedience to such acts" if necessary.

Although this plan increased the power of the central government, it clearly left a great deal more power in the hands of the states. In this way, the New Jersey Plan was much closer to what the delegates were originally sent to do at the Convention. And with each state having an equal voice in many government actions, the small

council of revision A combined body of judges and members of the executive branch having a limited veto over national legislation and an absolute veto over state legislation.

New Jersey Plan A plan presented to the Constitutional Convention of 1787 designed to create a unicameral legislature with equal representation for all states. Its goal was to protect the interests of the smaller, less populous states.

unicameral legislature A legislative system consisting of one chamber.

In 1790 the population of New Jersey was only 184,139, making it the fifth least populous state of the original thirteen. Two hundred years later, New Jersey's population was 7,730,188, making it the ninth most populous state of fifty. Do you think the representatives from that state would be proposing the small-state plan now?

states would continue to play a prominent role. In spite of the state-centered philosophy of this plan, its provision making congressional acts "supreme law" and compelling obedience to national acts (not found in the Virginia Plan) became an early version of what is known as the **supremacy clause** of the Constitution. This clause holds that in any conflict between federal laws and treaties and state laws, the will of the national government always prevails. Just as when the government moved against the Communist threat in the 1940s and 1950s, a good part of the effort was left to the national government. If a dispute were to arise between the national and state governments in dealing with terrorism, it would be the national government's policy that would prevail. Provisions like this one, along with granting the central government the power to tax, made it possible for compromise to be reached with the strong central government advocates of the Virginia Plan.

Whether the New Jersey Plan could have successfully governed America, or whether, as some think, it was a proposal designed specifically to thwart the notion of proportional representation at the convention, remains a matter of some debate.[16] Table 2.2 provides a quick overview of the differences between the Virginia and New Jersey Plans.

Swayed by an impassioned speech by James Madison, the delegates chose the Virginia Plan over the New Jersey Plan by a vote of 7 to 3. The representatives of the small states then turned their attention to achieving some influence for their states in the new government. Only by securing a compromise on the proportional representation aspects of the Virginia Plan, they reasoned, would their states have any voice in the government. Thus, it was over this issue that the Convention's success would turn.

Debate and Compromise: The Turning Point of the Convention

The Articles of Confederation failed because the prospect of a veto by each state over the actions of the central government had resulted in a powerless Confederation Congress. Thus, the composition of the new Congress and its means of selection were critical issues at the Convention. Would it be one house (unicameral), as before, or two houses (bicameral), as some delegates now preferred? Would the members be apportioned by the population of each state (proportional representation), as in the Virginia Plan; or would each state have the same number of representatives (one-state, one-vote), as in the New Jersey Plan? By the middle of June the Convention had split into two opposing groups: the "big states" composed of Massachusetts, Pennsylvania, Virginia, New York, the Carolinas, and Georgia (the southern states sided with the big states, believing that given their large size, proportional representation would eventually be in their interest), against the rest of the states, whose only hope for influence lay in the equal representation scheme.

supremacy clause A clause in Article IV of the Constitution holding that in any conflict between federal laws and treaties and state laws, the will of the national government always prevails.

Table 2.2 ■ Differences Between the Virginia and New Jersey Plans		
Issue	**Virginia Plan**	**New Jersey Plan**
Source of legislative power	Derived from the people and based on popular representation	Derived from the states and based on equal votes for each state
Legislative structure	Bicameral	Unicameral
Executive	Size undetermined, elected and removable by Congress	More than one person, removable by state majority
Judiciary	Life-tenured, able to veto state legislation in council of revision	No power over states
State laws	Legislature can override	Government can compel obedience to national laws
Ratification	By the people	By the states

Repeatedly in the early debates the small states failed to pass the New Jersey Plan, partly because Maryland's Luther Martin had alienated his colleagues by giving a virulent, two-day speech against proportional representation. Martin's effort backfired when the delegates quickly approved proportional representation for the legislature. However, when the delegates also voted to establish a bicameral legislative branch to provide some sort of balance of power, the issue now became how the upper house of Congress, known as the Senate, would be apportioned.

During this debate, Georgia delegate Abraham Baldwin later recalled, "The convention was more than once upon the point of dissolving without agreeing upon any system."[17] At this turning point in the debate, it was the selfless action of Baldwin and several other delegates that narrowly averted the complete failure of the Convention. The large-state delegates sought proportional representation in both the Senate and in the House of Representatives, as the lower house was called, giving them total control over the Congress, while the small-state delegates pressed for the old Articles of Confederation system of equality of votes in the legislature. Because of their numbers, the large states expected to win the issue by a narrow margin.

But well-timed absences and changes of heart by Baldwin and other delegates during key votes ended the big states' chances for dominance in the Senate and in the process saved the Convention from failure. When the vote was taken on the question of Senate representation, Maryland's Daniel of St. Thomas Jenifer, who otherwise had an exemplary record of attendance for the Convention, deliberately stayed away, keeping Maryland allied with the small states. Then, the three Georgia delegates conspired to switch their state's vote from the big-state position to the small-state position. Two of them suddenly left the Convention, and the third delegate, Abraham Baldwin, voted for the small-state position. Thus, proportional representation in the Senate failed.

With compromise now possible, a committee consisting of one member from each state was formed to prepare suggestions for resolving the question of representation in the Senate. When the selection process for the committee was finished, it turned out that every member favored the small states' position, so the result was preordained. What would emerge was a plan acceptable to the small states but capable of being passed by the large states as well.

This plan has become known as the **Great Compromise** (also called the **Connecticut Compromise**), based on a plan advanced by Roger Sherman of Connecticut. This compromise upheld the large-state position for the House of membership based on proportional representation and balanced that decision by upholding the small-state position of equal representation in the Senate, where each state, regardless of size, would have two votes. Since all legislation would have to pass through *both* houses, neither large nor small states could dominate. The compromise also stated that *money bills,* or measures that raise revenue, must begin in the House, to keep the power to tax with the people. This arrangement would prevent an alliance of small states in the Senate voting for programs that had to be paid for by the large states.

The composition and purpose of the two houses of Congress would be very different. Members of the House of Representatives would be chosen based on a state's population; there would be one representative for every 40,000 people, as determined by periodic census (at the request of George Washington this number was changed to 30,000 on the last day of the Convention). The House was constructed to be closest to the people and to reflect their desires. The Senate, with its equal representation and indirect method of selection by state legislatures, was intended as a more deliberative council of the political and economic elite. This body would serve as an advisory council to the president and would eventually be entrusted with reviewing presidential appointments and treaties.

Delegates voted in favor of the Connecticut Compromise by the narrowest of margins—5 to 4—with one state delegation tied. The compromise effectively ended the debate between the large and small states by giving each a balanced stake in the

Great Compromise (also called the **Connecticut Compromise**)   A plan presented at the Constitutional Convention that upheld the large-state position for the House, its membership based on proportional representation, balanced by the small-state posture of equal representation in the Senate, where each state would have two votes.

legislature of the new centralized national government. Acceptance of the compromise meant that the states would never again be seen as sovereign entities but would be part of one national government.

The Constitution was on its way to being realized, but there were still two vexing questions to resolve: one dealing with the issue of slavery and the other with the nature of the new executive.

The Issue of Slavery

Although the word *slavery* was never mentioned in the Constitution, it was very much on the minds of the framers. Since the 1600s, Africans had been brought over to the New World and sold as slaves. Without slave labor, southern plantations could not operate. While some delegates wanted to abolish slavery, citing the inalienable human rights of freedom and equality, they understood that such a call would lose much southern support and doom the convention to failure. So the institution of slavery was not debated directly. Instead, it was discussed indirectly through the question of how to distribute the sixty-five seats in the First Congress. Since membership in the Congress was based on population, how to count the slaves, who constituted almost 18 percent of the population, became a point of contention. If the slaves were not included in the count, southern states would have only 41 percent of the House seats; including all of the slaves would give them 50 percent of the seats.

After much debate, the Convention delegates arrived at the **three-fifths compromise,** which stated that the apportionment of taxes and representatives by state should be determined "by adding to the whole Number of free Persons . . . three-fifths of all other Persons" (Article I, Section 2). Since the phrase "all other persons" was a euphemism for slaves, this meant that it would take five slaves to equal three free people when counting the population for representation and taxation purposes. Although Convention delegates understood the political compromise being affected here, the stated rationale for this partial counting of slaves was that they produced less wealth.

three-fifths compromise A compromise which stated that the apportionment of representatives by state should be determined "by adding to the whole number of free persons . . . three-fifths of all other persons" (Article I, Section 2); meaning that it would take five slaves to equal three free people when counting the population for representation and taxation purposes.

◄ Few at the Constitutional Convention in Philadelphia in 1787 doubted that its leader, George Washington, would one day lead the nation as President.

This compromise represented a victory of political expediency over morality. Since slaves could not vote, their numbers were simply being used to add to the South's political power. Some have argued that even though the compromise kept the Constitutional Convention on track, it was immoral because it denigrated blacks by suggesting that they were only three-fifths as valuable and productive as whites. Others, though, have pointed out that while it did increase southern influence in the Congress and thus the presidential electoral count, this unique political compromise actually weakened the power of the southern states while also ensuring the Constitution's passage. As a result of the compromise, the slave states ended up with only 47 percent of the seats in Congress, thus keeping them in the minority and making it possible to outvote them on slavery issues.[18] As part of the compromise, Congress was barred from legislating on the international slave trade for twenty years, thus allowing slaves to be imported until at least 1808 (Article I, Section 9). Finally, a provision was added without much discussion that allowed the return of fugitive slaves to their masters (Article IV, Section 2).

In leaving it to later generations to address the practice of slavery and put an end to it, were the framers condoning slavery? Were they hypocrites for protecting slavery while discussing the high principles of freedom and equality? One response is that while they were hypocritical, their thinking reflected the vast majority of public opinion at the time; most people were indifferent to slavery. However, we must also realize, just as Thomas Jefferson discovered when he was forced to strike his criticism of slavery from the draft of the Declaration of Independence, that a successful outcome for the Constitutional Convention would not have been possible without compromise on the slavery issue. Had the southern states walked out, as they surely would have had slavery been banned, the nation would have been doomed to continue operating under the defective Articles of Confederation or perhaps to falter entirely.

The Nature of the Presidency

One of the most original contributions made by the framers of the American Constitution was their blueprint for the presidency, including the means for filling the job. (The presidency is described more fully in Chapter 5.)

The framers were ambivalent about the nature of the position they were creating, fearing that it would lead to a new monarchy in democratic clothing. This fear was reflected in the weak executive branches proposed in the Virginia and New Jersey Plans, which consisted of boards subservient to the legislature. To correct this approach, Charles Pinckney of South Carolina called for the creation of a "vigorous executive," because, in his words, "our government is despised because of the loss of public order." However, Edmund Randolph of Virginia, who favored instead a board of executives, expressed his fear that Pinckney's call for a single executive represented the "foetus of monarchy," or the beginnings of the reinstatement of a British Crown in America.[19]

It was James Wilson of Pennsylvania, fearing an all-powerful legislature similar to those in some of the states under the Articles of Confederation, who proposed a plan creating a national executive much like the powerful governor of New York—a one-person executive with substantial powers, such as a veto over legislation. This plan was not debated by the delegates but was instead submitted to the Committee on Detail, which was charged with organizing the resolutions passed by the Convention into a coherent document. Since Wilson and three other strong national government advocates sat on this five-person committee, the matter was settled in his favor. The powerful single executive that came out of that committee was adopted by the Convention three months later.

Although the delegates agreed on a one-person executive, they disagreed over the length of the term of office for the new president and how to select that powerful person. Some delegates proposed a three-year term with reelections possible, while others sought a single term of seven years. Originally, the Convention narrowly voted for a single seven-year term. This was eventually revised to a four-year term, with reelection possible. Nothing was said about the number of terms a president could serve.

The vital question of how to select the right person for the office of president led to yet another compromise in the form of the **electoral college system.** In an attempt to ensure the selection of statesmen like George Washington, whom everyone in the Convention expected to become the first president, the framers took the selection away from the voters. Instead, they designed a selection system of "electors" chosen by the states using means of their own choosing in numbers equal to the total number of senators and representatives from that state. The electors would vote for two people, at least one of whom could not be from their own state, with the highest overall vote-getter becoming the president and the runner-up, the vice president. The intention here was that the best-known and most-qualified person for president would appear somewhere on the ballots of the most electors from around the country. A tie vote would be sent to the House of Representatives for selection, with each state delegation having one vote.

Such a system struck a compromise between the large and small states. The president would not be chosen by direct popular vote or by the legislature because those methods would have favored the large states. Still, the large states would have some advantage, because the proportional representation feature of Congress would affect the number of electors from each state. On the other hand, if the matter was sent to the House because of the lack of a majority vote in the electoral college, as the delegates fully expected, the small states would get the one-state, one-vote system that favored them. (More will be said about the electoral college in Chapter 10.) This idea mandated that a presidential candidate would have to get a spread of support from large and small states around the country. In the 2000 Presidential election, for instance, if Al Gore had gotten the support of his home state of Tennessee he would not have to have depended on winning the Florida state electoral vote count to win the Presidency.

After nearly four months of debate, on September 17, 1787, the new Constitution was drafted. The eldest delegate, eighty-two-year-old Benjamin Franklin,

electoral college system Votes in the national presidential elections are actually indirect votes for a slate of presidential electors pledged to each party's candidate. Each state gets one elector for each of its representatives and senators. The winning slate of electors cast their votes in their state's capital after the public election. Election of the president and vice president in the United States is dependent upon receiving a majority (270) of the votes cast in the electoral college.

moved that the draft be approved, saying, "I consent to this constitution because I expect no better, and because I am not sure that it is not the best." To encourage even those who disagreed with the results to sign it, those who affixed their names became "witnesses" to the document. Even so, several of the delegates refused to sign, and only thirty-nine names were penned. Perhaps the best blessing on the whole enterprise was Franklin's, when the weeping old man told his fellow delegates that he had long puzzled over the half-sun design on the back of the Convention president's chair. Was the design of a rising or setting sun, he often wondered. "Now at length I have the happiness to know that it is a rising and not a setting sun," he told the delegates.[20] With that, George Washington penned in his journal: "The business being closed, the members adjourned to the City Tavern, dined together and took a cordial leave of each other."[21] But, they would soon discover, the battle had just begun.

QUOTE ... UNQUOTE

"It appears to me, then, little short of a miracle, that the Delegates from so many different States (which States you know are also different from each other), in their manners, circumstances, and prejudices, should unite in forming a system of national Government, so little liable to well founded objections."

George Washington

The Miracle: Results of the Convention

The purpose of the Constitution is laid out in the eloquent preamble:

> We the People of the United States, in Order to form a more perfect Union, establish Justice, insure domestic Tranquility, provide for the common defense, promote the general Welfare, and secure the Blessings of Liberty to ourselves and our Posterity, do ordain and establish this Constitution for the United States of America.

The goals of the framers' exercise in democracy were outlined in this one sentence. America was now one people rather than thirteen individual states. This nation had certain hopes—for justice, tranquility, and liberty. They were placing their sovereign power in a new constitution that would guide a new national government, a union more perfect than the one that existed under the Articles of Confederation.

The new constitution was unlike any seen before. It created a republican government, granting indirect power to the voting public, whose desires would be served by a representative government. Until that time, such a system seemed possible only for small countries like Greece or Switzerland.

A Republican Form of Government

At the end of the Convention, a woman asked Ben Franklin what kind of government the delegates had created—a republic or a monarchy? "A republic, Madam," responded Franklin, "if you can keep it."[22]

Believing that the people are more interested in their own welfare than the good of the whole, and realizing that the size of the new nation prevented implementing a pure democracy, the framers created a republican form of government with built-in checks and balances, in which the people hold an indirect voting power over their elected officials. Instead of governing themselves, the people elect representatives to protect their interests. These representatives could, however, vote against the desires of their constituents if it was for the good of the whole nation. Because the framers feared the instincts of the people, they devised a series of filters to minimize the effects of the popular vote. Only the House of Representatives would be elected directly by the people, with voting qualifications being determined by individual states. The people were given an indirect voice in the choice of the Senate, which would be chosen by the state legislatures, and their say in the choice of a president would be even more indirect because of the electoral college system. Finally, the people would have only the most indirect voice in the selection of the judiciary, which would be chosen by the already indirectly selected president and Senate. Since the framers did not fully trust the instincts of the representatives in the republican government either, they further limited this indirect power through the systems of separation of powers and checks and balances.

One of the main constitutional changes in the American system of government over the years has been a shift from the purely republican system of government created by the framers to a system that is much more democratic and inclusive of more people. Six times in our history, the Constitution has been amended to extend the voting base in federal elections, thus giving more people a direct voice in their government. These changes were: the Fifteenth Amendment which extended the vote to the newly freed slaves, the Seventeenth Amendment which provided for the direct popular election of the Senate, the Nineteenth Amendment which extended the right to vote to women, the Twenty-third Amendment which gave voters in the District of Columbia representation in the electoral college to vote for President, the Twenty-Fourth Amendment which abolished the poll tax by which people had to pay for the right to vote, and the Twenty-sixth Amendment which extended the vote to citizens over the age of eighteen. Finally, fewer representatives now act as independent "trustees," choosing instead to serve as "delegates" instructed by the voters through public opinion polls, mail counts, and the media (see Chapter 4). In these ways, the American republic has indeed approached democracy.

In moving closer to a system of pure democracy, is the republican system designed by the framers to protect liberty in danger? Not at all. The Constitution's mechanisms for limiting power provide an adequate check on the actions of the leaders and the demands of the people. A judiciary more powerful than the framers could ever have imagined, using the Constitution and its amendments to preserve liberty, also keeps the republic strong. In the end, just how far the country actually goes toward direct democracy depends on how much confidence the people have in the motives and wisdom of their leaders.

The Governmental Powers

You can better understand the results of the framers' efforts by taking two different approaches to studying the Constitution and the distribution of power: a horizontal view and a vertical view.

Horizontal Powers   Governmental powers are apportioned horizontally among the branches of the national government—the executive, legislative, and judicial branches—according to the system of *separation of powers* (see Figure 2.1). Each of the major branches of government was given a separate set of powers so that no one branch could become too powerful. The first three articles of the Constitution are concerned solely with the powers, responsibilities, and selection processes for each separate branch and include specific prohibitions against a person becoming a member of two branches at the same time.

But James Madison understood that separating the powers among three distinct branches would not be sufficient unless each branch was given the power to "check" the other, preventing encroachment into its own sphere. For this reason, a system of *checks and balances* was incorporated into the structure, giving each branch the power to approve, disapprove, or alter what the other branches do. "Ambition must be made to counteract ambition," Madison counseled in *The Federalist,* no. 51, on checks and balances (printed in its entirety in the Appendix). "If men were angels," he explained, "no government would be necessary. If angels were to govern men, neither external nor internal controls on government would be necessary. In framing a government which is to be administered by men over men, the great difficulty lies in this: You must first enable the government to control the governed; and in the next place oblige it to control itself."[23] With the checking powers outlined in Figure 2.1, no one branch can take control and run the government.

Although the president nominates ambassadors, cabinet officials, and justices, the Senate can reject those choices by refusing to give the majority vote required for its "advice and consent." Congress passes laws, but the president can then veto them. Congress can react by overriding a presidential veto with a two-thirds vote of

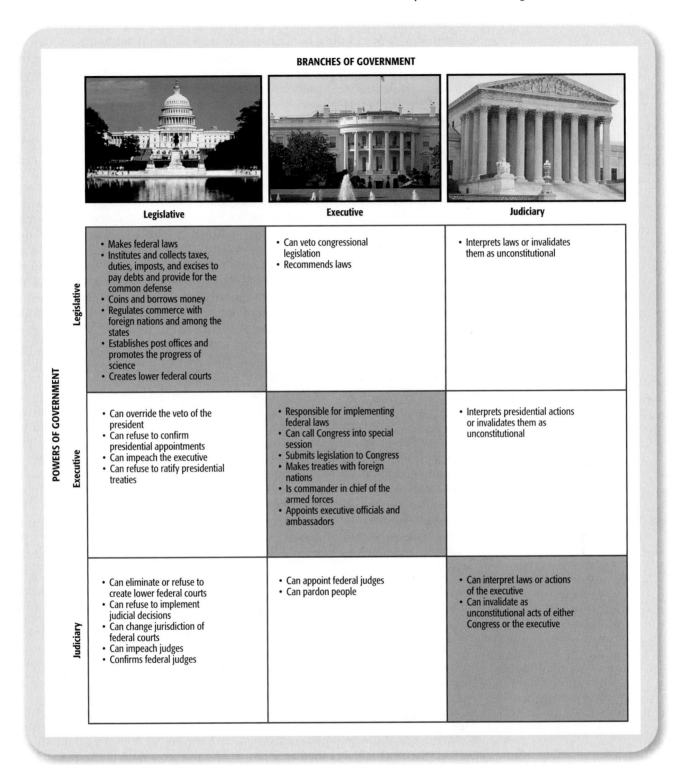

BRANCHES OF GOVERNMENT

		Legislative	Executive	Judiciary
POWERS OF GOVERNMENT	**Legislative**	• Makes federal laws • Institutes and collects taxes, duties, imposts, and excises to pay debts and provide for the common defense • Coins and borrows money • Regulates commerce with foreign nations and among the states • Establishes post offices and promotes the progress of science • Creates lower federal courts	• Can veto congressional legislation • Recommends laws	• Interprets laws or invalidates them as unconstitutional
	Executive	• Can override the veto of the president • Can refuse to confirm presidential appointments • Can impeach the executive • Can refuse to ratify presidential treaties	• Responsible for implementing federal laws • Can call Congress into special session • Submits legislation to Congress • Makes treaties with foreign nations • Is commander in chief of the armed forces • Appoints executive officials and ambassadors	• Interprets presidential actions or invalidates them as unconstitutional
	Judiciary	• Can eliminate or refuse to create lower federal courts • Can refuse to implement judicial decisions • Can change jurisdiction of federal courts • Can impeach judges • Confirms federal judges	• Can appoint federal judges • Can pardon people	• Can interpret laws or actions of the executive • Can invalidate as unconstitutional acts of either Congress or the executive

Figure 2.1   Constitutional Powers

The blue portions of this figure display the powers allotted to each of the branches and show the separation of powers. The remainder of the diagram indicates the powers that each of the branches holds as a check on the other branches. While each of the branches has primary responsibility in the executive, legislative, or judicial realms, each also shares powers with the other two branches.

both houses. Theoretically, the president can then refuse to execute the new law, but the president is kept in check by the fact that Congress has an impeachment power if "treason, bribery, or High Crimes or Misdemeanors" are committed. The judiciary has the power to interpret laws or use the power of *judicial review* to judge the constitutionality of, and thereby check the actions of, the other branches (a power which is not in the Constitution but was established by the Court itself in 1803). We saw this in the Supreme Court's ruling against Abraham Lincoln and his abolition of the writ of *habeas corpus* as well as its changing the legal standard for restricting First Amendment rights in reaction to Woodrow Wilson's actions during the First World War. Meanwhile, the judiciary itself is checked by the president's prerogative of nominating justices (with the advice and consent of the Senate) and Congress's power to create lower federal courts or change the Supreme Court's appellate jurisdiction.

At times the functions of government require the creation of independent agencies or actors to accomplish tasks that mix the functions of the three branches. Such is the case with the Securities and Exchange Commission, which regulates the activities of Wall Street, and the Federal Reserve Board, which regulates the monetary and banking system. One other such agency, which became the subject of great debate, was the special prosecutor system, developed during the Watergate crisis of 1974 to investigate the activities of President Richard Nixon. To get an independent investigation of allegedly illegal activities—such as the Whitewater land deal in Arkansas connected to Bill and Hillary Clinton and the campaign finance activities of President Clinton and Vice President Gore during the 1996 election—Attorney General Janet Reno first had to conduct two separate investigations. If she decided that the case should be pursued, then a panel of federal appeals court judges was convened to choose a special prosecutor, who would have wide investigatory powers. The proliferation of calls by Congress for the appointment of special prosecutors, the subsequently lengthy and expensive investigations, and the lack of concrete results (as shown by Special Prosecutor Kenneth Starr's multi-year effort to unravel the Whitewater/Monica Lewinsky controversy) illustrate the serious problems that can occur in horizontal powers. As a result, Congress decided in 1999 not to renew the law creating the position. Even in the absence of this law, Democrats continued to call for an independent investigation, including the subpoena of related documents, into allegations of the Bush Administration's connection to officials of the Enron Corporation before its collapse in 2002. At the same time Congress's General Accounting Office began efforts to sue the administration in an effort to uncover those documents.[24]

Because the framers deliberately allowed for elasticity in each branch's powers, the government that resulted was destined to become one in which powers overlap. As Justice Robert Jackson described it: "While the Constitution diffuses power the better to secure liberty, it also contemplates that practice will integrate the dispersed powers into a workable government."[25] The result over the years has not been a strict separation of powers but, as political scientist Richard Neustadt has said, a "government of separated institutions sharing powers." By this, he means that each institution frequently exercises the powers of the others: judges can make laws, Congress can interpret laws, and presidents can do both.[26]

? Question for Reflection: Knowing this, if you were on the Supreme Court how far would you let a President go in withholding information from Congress in forming policy that deals with the war on terrorism and how would that differ from your answer in other policy areas?

Vertical Powers Vertical powers refer to the relationship between the centralized national government and the individual state governments. This distribution of power is known as **federalism.** We cover the subject of federalism more extensively in the next chapter.

During the framing, the delegates tried to create the right balance of power between the national government and the state governments. Having seen that the confederation of states did not work, they wanted to give the national government sufficient authority to govern while leaving the state governments enough power to

federalism The relationship between the centralized national government and the individual state governments.

accomplish what they needed at the local level. The framers created a national government of **delegated powers,** meaning powers that are expressly granted or enumerated and limited in nature, while leaving the state governments with general **reserved powers,** or the remainder of the authority not specifically delegated to the national government. For example, to avoid the problem of various states under the Articles of Confederation conducting their own foreign policy, that power was delegated to the national government. However, if state governments wish to go to a foreign government seeking business investments, they may do so using the power to improve the economic welfare of their citizens, a power reserved for the states. Additionally, the federal government was not given the power to regulate relations among its citizens, as in marriage laws, or the power to create a criminal code. These **police powers,** or the power to regulate the health, morals, public safety, and welfare of citizens, were left to the states.

By viewing the Constitution from a vertical perspective, a number of other features become apparent. For instance, to remedy the lack of central control over the economy under the Articles of Confederation, Congress has the power over commerce *among* the states, while the states individually are left to govern commerce *within* their own boundaries. To handle a rebellion, such as Shays's Rebellion, the president was made commander in chief, and Congress was given power both to raise and support an army and to send it into battle. States, however, retained their own powers over a police force to keep order at home. The most important element of the vertical power is the so-called *supremacy clause* (Article VI), which states that in any controversy between the states and federal laws, Constitution, or treaties, the *federal dictates will always prevail.* With the acceptance of this provision came the guarantee that sovereign states would never again be the dominating power that they were under the Articles of Confederation.

The success of this reordering of governmental priorities between the national and state governments depends on one's point of view. Many of these powers have been interpreted to expand the national power to such a degree that individual states today have much less power than many of the framers ever intended. Some praise the uniformity and comprehensive nature of such a government, while others express concerns about the burgeoning size and remoteness of the national government and the need for policy innovation by the individual state governments. As you will learn in Chapter 4, this debate continues to this day with the issue of **devolution,** or returning governmental programs and powers to the states to reduce the size and authority of the national government. What is gained by the limitation of the size of the national government, however, may come at the expense of vastly different rights and protections from state to state, as in the early twentieth century and before.

The Articles of the Constitution

The Constitution is divided into seven articles, each with a unique purpose. The first three apportion power among the three branches of national government; two others (Articles IV and VI) apportion power between the national and state governments; the remaining two articles (Articles V and VII) lay out the procedures for amending and ratifying the Constitution. Gaps were deliberately left in each of these articles, and the language was given a certain elasticity to allow the Constitution to expand and evolve as the nation needed.

Article I   Article I sets forth the powers of the legislative branch. For the framers, this was the most important article (and therefore the first) because it sought to expand the powers of the old Confederation Congress while still preventing it from achieving the omnipotent power of the state legislatures under the Articles of Confederation. This intent is clear from the limiting nature of the first words of the article: "All legislative Powers herein granted shall be vested in a Congress of the United States." The article then contains a long list of specific and narrowly drawn powers. Those powers include the power to declare war, borrow and coin money,

delegated powers Powers that are expressly granted or enumerated in the Constitution and limited in nature.

reserved powers Powers not assigned by the Constitution to the national government but left to the states or to the people, according to the Tenth Amendment.

police powers Regulation by the states of the health, morals, public safety, and welfare of their citizens.

devolution Reducing the size and authority of the federal government by returning programs to the states.

THE ROAD TO DEMOCRACY

Balancing Congressional and Presidential Powers

Congress can request that members of the Executive Branch, such as the Director of Homeland Security, Tom Ridge, appear before them to testify, but what if their request is refused?

THAT WAS THEN. . .

President Bush is not the first chief executive to face the problems dealing with Congress's requests for information. Richard Nixon was compelled by the Supreme Court in the 1974 *U.S. v. Nixon* case to reveal the Oval Office tapes to Congress and the Judiciary. Nixon had claimed that the tapes of conversations with his advisors in the White House should remain secret because of the "executive privilege" power, which keeps those conversations private due to the need for confidentiality to get proper advice on such issues as national security and military secrets. The Court ruled that while "executive privilege" exists, Nixon was not trying to hide military or national security secrets in this instance, but trying to evade valid Congressional investigation or an on-going judicial case. So, it was left to federal judge John Sirica to determine in private whether these tapes should be revealed.

William Jefferson Clinton also faced the question of "executive privilege" when his administration tried to prevent both the secret service agents protecting him and his White House lawyer, Deputy White House Counsel Bruce Lindsey, from being compelled to testify about the President's relationship with Monica Lewinsky. The agents had already been compelled to testify in special prosecutor Kenneth Starr's Grand Jury hearing into the President's actions in the face of objections by both Clinton and former President George Bush that the chief executive's security could be compromised if secret service agents were forced to appear. In both cases, the Supreme Court let stand the lower federal court ruling that the agents and lawyers had to testify.

THIS IS NOW. . .

Despite George W. Bush's status as a war-time President and his high public approval rating, he has faced some of the same balance-of-powers disputes with Congress that his predecessor, Bill Clinton, faced. When the Senate Appropriations Committee requested that Tom Ridge appear before them to speak about the $38 billion, double the present government funding, that the Administration was requesting for new domestic security programs, Ridge refused. Ridge argued that his was a White House position similar to that of National Security Advisor Condoleeza

---

regulate interstate commerce, and raise and support an army. But the list is not as restrictive as it seems at first; the article also mandates that Congress can "make all Laws which shall be necessary and proper for carrying into Execution the foregoing Powers." As we will see in the next chapter, this **necessary and proper clause,** with its vague grant of power, has allowed a broad interpretation of Congress's powers under the Constitution. It is such built-in flexibility that makes the Constitution just as viable today as it was in 1787.

From the vertical perspective, Article I, Section 9, denies Congress the power to place a tax or duty on articles exported from any state. Moreover, under Section 10 states are denied the power to execute treaties, coin money, impair the obligation of contracts, and lay any imposts or duties on imports or exports without the consent of Congress.

Article II   Article II outlines the powers of the executive. At first glance, it seems to limit the president's power to simply granting pardons, making treaties, receiving foreign ambassadors, nominating certain officials, and being the "Commander in Chief" of the army and navy. But, as with the legislative branch, the executive was granted an elastic clause in the ambiguous first sentence of the article: "The executive Power shall be vested in a President of the United States of America." As you will see in Chapter 5 on the presidency, a broad interpretation of the words *executive power* provides a president with considerable power. For example, should the life of a Supreme Court justice or a member of Congress be threatened, it is within the "inherent powers" of the president to provide protection using a United States marshal. It is the executive power that allows presidents to decide to "make war" by

necessary and proper clause A clause in Article I, Section 8, Clause 18, of the Constitution stating that Congress can "make all Laws which shall be *necessary and proper* for carrying into Execution the foregoing Powers."

Rice and Economic Advisor Lawrence B. Lindsey, meaning that he was not a Cabinet Official confirmable by Congress. As an advisor to President Bush he was not answerable to nor should he have to testify before Congress.

But Senators from both sides of the aisle disagreed. "You are the single executive branch official with the responsibility to integrate the many complex functions of the . . . homeland defense programs," complained Senators Robert C. Byrd (D.-WV) and Ted Stevens (R-AL), "Your views and insights on the policies necessary to meet these objectives are critical to the [Appropriations] committee and the nation."

The Bush administration's refusal to keep Congress informed was evident in other areas. Members of Congress filed suit against Vice President Dick Cheney when he refused to give them information after the collapse of the Enron Corporation on the administration's contacts with Enron's company executives in drawing up the nation's energy plans. Then, the administration refused to inform Congress about the use of a Cold War era plan to create a shadow government of between seventy-five to one hundred officials to keep the government running in case of a catastrophic attack. The administration argued that this information was too sensitive to share with Congress. Members of Congress objected to this policy, with Republican Chuck Hagel (NE) arguing: "I don't think that is a wise way to do these things. The fact is we are a co-equal branch of government to the executive [branch]."

Lost in all of the discussion about President George W. Bush's problems with Congress was whether the notion of "executive privilege" was meant to cover topics such as plans to spend $38 billion in the domestic war on terrorism, an administration's connection to the collapsed Enron Corporation, and the "shadow government" contingency plans. Instead, these fights were all about politics, and it is not unusual for many of these issues to come before the Supreme Court of the United States to be resolved. As Brookings Institution scholar Thomas Mann argues: "The whole notion is, 'Hey, I'm in charge. I have my advisors, I'll make my decisions and we'll move on.'" But members of Congress, such as Bush supporter Rep. Ernest J. Istook, Jr. (R-OK) disagreed: "This is not minor. [Homeland Security] involves billions of taxpayer dollars. More importantly, it involves millions of lives." So, Ridge's offer to give briefings to two Republican-controlled committees but not formally testify was refused by the Senate.

In the end, the dispute was avoided when President Bush proposed making the Homeland Security Department a cabinet post. Tom Ridge, who would eventually be appointed the Cabinet Secretary, did testify on that issue.

Sources: Alison Mitchell, "Letter to Ridge is Latest Job in Fight Over Balance of Powers," *New York Times*, March 5, 2002, p. A8; Nick Anderson, "Ridge's Refusal to Testify Irks Lawmakers," *Los Angeles Times*, March 16, 2002; and Steve Lash, "Supreme Court Gives President a Double Defeat," *Houston Chronicle*, November 10, 1998.

sending troops to foreign countries, even in the absence of a formal declaration of war by Congress, or create policies like the U.S.A. Patriot Act and the military tribunal policy of 2001 which granted sweeping new powers to a government at war.

This article also gives the president the power to make judicial appointments. Article I also confers on that office the power to "return" (*veto*) bills passed by both houses of Congress. These powers enable the president to check the powers of the other two branches. Article II has additional elasticity built into it in Section 3, which states: "[The President] shall take Care that the Laws be faithfully executed." A president who disagrees with congressional legislation can "faithfully" execute the law by reinterpreting it or by devising a new law. For instance, if Congress appropriates too much money for a program, the president can "take Care" by *impounding*, that is, either delaying or refusing to spend, the full appropriation. Thomas Jefferson did this in 1803, when he withheld money for gunboats on the Mississippi. However, when Richard Nixon tried to expand this power, using it not to save money but to derail programs with which he disagreed, both Congress and the Supreme Court later overturned his action.

The presidential power to limit spending was expanded in 1996 when the Republican-controlled Congress, seeking to lower the deficit as part of its Contract with America, passed into law a line item veto, granting the president the power to strike certain kinds of specific spending or tax break provisions from a proposed piece of legislation, rather than having to reject the entire bill. Presidents had sought this power since the time of Ulysses S. Grant. Clinton used the line item veto 82 times over the next 18 months, arguing in many instances that by doing so he could balance the budget, though critics argued that these decisions were being made for political reasons.

The constitutionality of this dramatic shift of power between Congress and the president was tested in the Supreme Court in 1998. By a 6 to 3 vote, the justices, speaking through John Paul Stevens, struck down the line item veto, ruling that the law violated the Constitution's requirement that the president must unconditionally accept or reject an entire bill as passed by Congress. The Court viewed the change to allow a president to veto only specific provisions of spending bills as an unconstitutional shift in the separation of powers between the legislative and executive branches.

Article III Article III outlines the powers of the judicial branch. As we will see in more detail in Chapter 6, the framers provided the vaguest grant of powers to the judiciary because they could not agree on the role of this branch. This article establishes only a Supreme Court and grants Congress the power to "ordain and establish" inferior federal courts. Federal judges are to serve for life, as long as they maintain good behavior, and are removable only by impeachment. They have the power to decide "Cases, in Law and Equity" arising under the Constitution and also to interpret federal laws and federal treaties.

Articles IV–VII Article IV establishes guidelines for interstate relations. Under the Articles of Confederation, no such guidelines existed. A state could disregard the laws of other states; it could also treat its own citizens one way and citizens of other states another way. This article establishes uniformity by guaranteeing that "full Faith and Credit" must be granted by all states to the "public Acts, Records, and Judicial Proceedings of every other State." In addition, citizens of all states must receive the same "Privileges and Immunities" of citizens of "the several States." Because of this provision, divorces in one state must be recognized by all, and a decision to avoid repaying a state-financed college loan or even a parking fine by crossing state boundaries is ill advised. Those obligations are in force in all states of the union, as individuals who try to avoid paying child support or contest legal custody of children by moving out of state are discovering.

An interesting debate over the effect of interstate recognition of laws is arising from the passage by 35 states, including most recently Colorado, Nebraska and Nevada, of bans against same-sex marriages. These laws and Proposition 22 of California, which specifically denies the protection of laws governing marriages to same-sex couples who were married in other states, raise a constitutional issue in the face of the passage by Vermont of a civil union law, which provides benefits much like those of marriage to same-sex partners. Realizing that under Article IV of the Constitution, all other states would be bound to recognize such marriages and confer the same rights and benefits to same-sex couples; Congress in 1996 had also passed the Defense of Marriage Act, which withdraws federal recognition of same-sex marriages. Thus California, 35 other states, and Congress were signaling to the Supreme Court that they would ignore the "full faith and credit" provision in this area, leading some to think that this will become a future issue for decision by the Justices.

Article V outlines the procedure for amending the Constitution. The framers understood that changes in their original document might be necessary to correct imperfections in their work or to update it for use by future generations, as, for example, with the debate over the Equal Rights Amendment in the 1970s.

Article VI deals with federal-state relations and the financial obligations of the new government. This article not only contains the supremacy clause, affirming the predominance of the national government, but also ensures that all prior debts against the United States shall be valid. Moreover, it states that all national officers must swear an oath of office supporting the Constitution and cannot be subjected to a religious test.

Article VII explains the process for ratifying the Constitution.

Ratification: The Battle for the Constitution

Drafting the Constitution was just the first step toward creating a new government. The vote for or against the new document was now in the hands of the various state conventions. According to Article VII, nine of the thirteen states had to ratify the Constitution for it to take effect. Realistically, though, everyone understood that unless the most populous states ratified—Pennsylvania, Massachusetts, New York, and Virginia—the Constitution would never succeed.

Ratifying the Constitution involved hardball politics. This reality is often surprising for those who believe that creating the Constitution was a nonpartisan and academic process of debating the philosophical issues concerning a new government. A close look at this political crisis is instructive both for seeing how the nation was formed and understanding why the arguments over constitutional issues continue to rage today.

As in every good political fight, the side that was best organized at the beginning had the advantage. Those in favor of the Constitution, many of whom were nationalists at the Convention, took the lead by calling themselves the **Federalists.** Thus, they stole the semantic high ground by taking the name of supporters of the federal form of government under the Articles of Confederation. The true supporters of the federal form of government, the states' rights advocates, had to call themselves the **Antifederalists.** Among the members of this group were most but not all of the Convention's antinationalists.

The Federalist Papers

The debate over the Constitution raged in newspapers and hand-distributed pamphlets, the only source of communication in that period. Federalists Alexander Hamilton, James Madison, and John Jay wrote eighty-five essays in New York newspapers under the pen name of *Publius* (a Latin term meaning "public man") seeking to influence the debate in the New York state convention in favor of ratification. All these articles were intended to answer the arguments of the states' rights advocates that the new central government would be too powerful and too inclined to expand further, and thus likely destroy liberty. Hamilton, Madison, and Jay argued instead that without this new Constitution, the states would break apart and the

Federalists Those in favor of the Constitution, many of whom were nationalists at the Convention.

Antifederalists Strong states' rights advocates that organized in opposition to the ratification of the U.S. constitution prior to its adoption.

nation would fail. With it, they reasoned, the government would act in the national interest while also preserving liberty. Later collected under the title of *The Federalist Papers: A Commentary on the Constitution of the United States,* these pieces offer us what historian Henry Steele Commager calls a handbook on how the Constitution should operate. While these essays had little effect on the ratification debate, generations of judges, politicians, and scholars have considered them, together with Madison's notes of the Convention, to indicate "the intent of the framers" in creating the Constitution. (See, for example, *The Federalist,* nos. 10 and 51, in the Appendix.) For this reason, many scholars believe *The Federalist Papers* to be the most important work of political theory in U.S. history.

In opposition, the Antifederalists made their case in scores of articles such as those authored by Robert Yates, who wrote the *Letters of Brutus;* Luther Martin, who wrote *Genuine Information;* and Mercy Otis Warren, who wrote *Observations on the New Constitution . . . by a Columbian Patriot.* While these critics understood that the central government needed more power than it had under the Articles of Confederation, they feared that the structure established in the Convention would supersede the state governments, rendering them obsolete. By placing too much power in the hands of a government so far removed from the people, they argued, the new government would likely expand its power and rule by force rather than by the consent of the governed. They sought ways to establish a better balance between the power of the central government and the states by placing further checks on the newly established central government.

Federalists versus Antifederalists

The difference between the Federalists and the Antifederalists can be found on the most fundamental theoretical level. Since the Federalists, led by Hamilton and Madison, believed that *the people* had created the Constitution, and not *the states,* they argued that a strong central government was the best representation of the sovereignty of the people. The Federalists sought energy and leadership from a centralized government that would unite the entire nation, thus safeguarding the interests of the people. They also argued that the powers of the central government should be expandable to meet the needs of the people and to enable the government to respond to any emergencies that arise.

The Antifederalists argued that the Constitution was created by the states, meaning that the national government's power was carved out of the states' power. Accordingly, they insisted that the states should remain independent and distinct, rather than be led by a supreme national government. The Antifederalists sought to preserve the liberty and rights of the minorities by bolstering individual state governments that would be closer to the people.

In addition to the theoretical differences between Federalist and Antifederalist views, the two groups differed over who would have the authority for solving practical, real-world problems. The Federalists, supporters of a strong central government, realized that some problems spill over state boundaries and need to be resolved by a neutral, national arbiter. These problems include fishing rights in interstate waterways, the coinage of money, and interstate roadways. Federalists believed that a single solution to these problems would be more sensible and cost-effective than having each state devise and pay for its own program. They reasoned that the states would place their economies at a competitive disadvantage by attempting to resolve problems by themselves. While the Federalists were thinking of interstate commerce here, such problems as organized crime and pollution control would arise later to prove them correct about the need for a centralized source of authority.

Not surprisingly, the Antifederalists disagreed with the Federalists. To them, the government that was closer to the people, and thus more accountable to them, could best be trusted to tailor solutions to problems to fit each state. In addition,

APPROACHING DEMOCRACY AROUND THE GLOBE

A Century of Freedom

What twentieth-century development most altered the human condition? Was it the automobile, antibiotics, the airplane, the computer, radio, or television? In fact, the greatest change in the human condition comes from the explosion of freedom. In a century of concentration camps, dictators, gulags, and secret police, the spread of freedom and the changing nature of that freedom are cutting a swath of change throughout the world.

In 1900, huge empires carved up the world. The British Empire alone, characterized by colonial domination, embraced 400 million people, a quarter of the world's population. "Human subjugation was the rule, not the exception," says economist Robert Samuelson. But the situation now is very different. In 1999, Freedom House classified 88 of the world's 191 countries—2.4 billion people, or about 40 percent of the world's population—as free. These nations had a free press, civil rights and liberties, and free elections. Freedom, of course, varies from place to place. In Russia, for instance, the people were only "partially free" because, as for 1.6 billion other people, their system of elections and civil liberties protection was compromised.

Beyond the spread of freedom, the nature of freedom has also evolved. Now we talk not just about "freedom from," as in freedom from government oppression, but also about "freedom to" or the notion of "self-realization." People want the freedom to become whoever they want to be. As a result, the debate in many countries has changed to combining individual rights for women and minorities with the notion of "entitlements," such as health care, education, and welfare, which are seen as necessary for self-realization.

This evolution in freedom comes from two sources—war and economic progress. The tens of millions of people who died in the two World Wars ended up bringing about the end of the colonial empires. The same trend occurred when prosperity spread. Since 1990, the world's population has quadrupled, from 1.6 billion to 6 billion. At the same time, global production of goods and services—from food to steel to health care—had increased by nearly 15 times. As nations got richer, the traditional nature of freedom was no longer enough. People, with their needs for food and shelter and the ability to make a living satisfied, turned to self-esteem and spiritual issues such as justice and beauty. People could not consider themselves to be free without realizing these larger yearnings. Those desires are spread throughout the world by television. "Freedom is a great blessing," concludes Samuelson, "but it has never been easy—and never will be."

Source: Robert J. Samuelson, "Century of Freedom," *Washington Post,* December 22, 1999, p. A33. © 1999, *The Washington Post.* Reprinted with permission.

---

states were seen as the best protectors of personal liberty, as the fear existed that the new central government would be just as oppressive toward individual rights as King George III had been.

Out of these two opposing groups, two political parties would emerge. George Washington's Federalist party, supporting a strong nationalist government, was an outgrowth of the Federalist position. This party evolved, first, into the Whig party and then the Republican Party. The Antifederalists emerged in the Democratic-Republican Party of Thomas Jefferson, which supported states' rights and later became the Democratic Party.

(?) Question for Reflection: Would the current labels of Republican and Democrat still fit these descriptions?

It is clear from their arguments that the Federalists and Antifederalists were motivated by different fears. In one of the most famous of *The Federalist Papers,* no. 10, James Madison tried to explain how the new democratic government would overcome political differences that are "sown in the nature of man." The nation, he argued, is divided into **factions,** "a number of citizens, whether amounting to a majority or a minority of the whole, who are united and actuated by some common impulse or passion or . . . interest."[27] These groups of people, much like interest groups today, were united largely along the lines of property classifications—for example, farmers versus the manufacturing class—and would seek to have the

factions According to James Madison in *The Federalist,* no. 10: "A number of citizens, whether amounting to a majority or a minority of the whole, who are united and actuated by some common impulse or passion or . . . interests."

government protect their own interests to the exclusion of all others. Madison then sought to explain, in this article and later in *The Federalist,* no. 51, how the new government was designed to prevent an "interested and overbearing majority" of the citizens taking away the liberty of those in the minority. Since there was no way to eliminate the divisive *causes* of factions (there will always be rich versus poor and city dwellers versus farming interests), Madison explained how the new system of representative government was designed to control the harmful *effects* of factions. The key was to increase the size of the political unit, or "extend the sphere" from the smaller states, in which minorities could easily be outnumbered and oppressed, to the larger central government, where with a greater "number of electors" and thus "tak[ing] in a greater variety of parties and interests." As a result, they had a better chance for political protection.

In *The Federalist,* no. 51, Madison expanded his argument to show how the separation of powers would protect liberty by allowing each of the parts of the government to "be the means of keeping each other in their proper places." Because of the two-year term of the popularly elected House of Representatives, the six-year term of the Senate (elected by state legislatures), and the four-year term of the president (elected by the electoral college), each branch of government would represent different groups. The common people's voice in the House would turn over quickly and be restrained by the long-term elite, aristocratic view of the Senate and the national perspective of the president. Moreover, the powers of each branch would check the others. When combined with the system of federalism, in which national and state governments checked each other, it was hoped that no one majority faction could dominate American politics because every group would have effective representation somewhere. Those in a minority in one branch of the national government or in one state might find a representative in another branch of government or in another state.

At the other end of the spectrum, the Antifederalists argued that the central government was not to be trusted; they feared that the Constitution had traded English tyranny for tyranny by the central government at home. Worried that the central government would overrun the states and the rights of those in the minority, they asked what guarantees the Constitution contained to protect and preserve the rights of all Americans.

As far apart as these two groups were at the time of the drafting of the Constitution, some means had to be found to secure an agreement between them if the new document was to be ratified. The answer was the addition of a protective list of rights to the new constitution.

Ratification by Way of Compromise: A Bill of Rights

Though the Convention delegates had repeatedly refused to include in the new Constitution a long list of rights to be protected, the issue did not end with its signing. The Antifederalists in various states insisted during the ratification debate that a list of amendments be included, guaranteeing that the new central government could not restrict certain rights. The Federalists argued that a constitutional guarantee of rights was unnecessary since citizens were already adequately protected by the Constitution or by the constitutions of the individual states.

The debate over adding amendments to the Constitution presented an interesting philosophical dilemma. If the new government did not in fact already protect these rights, then many felt that it should not have been created in the first place. If it did in fact protect them, then why was it necessary to repeat those rights in a series of amendments? In the end, philosophy gave way to politics. Following the tradition of the Magna Carta, compacts, social contracts, and state bills of rights, it was agreed that the people would see their rights guaranteed in writing in the Constitution. In fact, the expectation of such amendments helped sell the Constitution.

◄ In this rare 1789 woodcut, members of Congress stood on the wall of the fort at Bowling Green in New York City to celebrate the ratification of the Constitution and cheer the float honoring Alexander Hamilton, one of the leaders at the Constitutional Convention.

Politics the Old-Fashioned Way: A Look at the Battle for Ratification

You might be surprised by the tactics used once the ratification debates moved from being a secret discussion among aristocratic political elites into the public arena. The debates were hardly genteel. Initially, ratification seemed inevitable. After all, the Federalists had the dual advantages of an existing document that defined the terms of the debate and an opposition movement that was disorganized. Within eight months after the Constitution had been signed, eight states had ratified the document. However, the battles in two of them—Pennsylvania and Massachusetts— indicated just how difficult it would be to get the critical ninth state, not to mention the two large-state holdouts—Virginia and New York.

The lengths that proponents of the Constitution were willing to go to achieve success were made clear in Pennsylvania. Ben Franklin forced the State Assembly, which was about to adjourn, to appoint a ratifying convention even before enough copies of the Constitution arrived for everyone to read. Seeking to derail this effort, the Antifederalists hid, thinking they might deny Franklin a voting quorum. The sergeant at arms was directed to take the necessary action to make a vote possible. A mob of angry Federalists volunteered to help him, roaming the streets of Philadelphia looking for any missing assemblymen they could find. They eventually found two assemblymen hiding in their rooms over a local tavern and, after dragging them through the streets of Philadelphia, threw them into the assembly hall while a mob of Constitution supporters blocked their escape. Not surprisingly, these two men cast their votes against a ratifying convention, but the measure passed by a vote of 44 to 2.

Protests against such strong-arm tactics were ignored. Mobs of Federalists used similar tactics to ensure that the final ratifying vote favored the Constitution by a 2 to 1 margin. The damage to the Federalists' prestige in Philadelphia was so great that James Wilson, a leading Federalist, was nearly beaten to death by a mob of angry Antifederalists weeks later.

In Massachusetts, clever political strategy rather than strong-arm tactics turned the tide. Three hundred and fifty delegates, many of them from the less populous western part of the state where the Antifederalists dominated, met in Boston on

January 8, 1788. The opponents of the Constitution held a slight numerical advantage. Governor John Hancock, a Federalist but also a cagey politician, was so unsure of how the vote would go that he decided to stay away, complaining of the gout. To convince Hancock to join them, the Federalists dangled the possibility that if Virginia failed to ratify the Constitution, it would leave George Washington outside the new nation; then Hancock would be the most likely prospect for the presidency of the country. With that, Hancock's gout miraculously abated, and he was carried to the convention as a hero, with his legs wrapped in flannel. There he proposed a series of amendments protecting such local concerns as taxation and merchants' rights. These amendments, an early version of what would later become the Bill of Rights, changed the terms of the debate. Now those who supported the Constitution could vote for it, and those who opposed it could vote for the document as amended. On February 6, 1788, Massachusetts ratified the Constitution by only nineteen votes (187 to 168). Hancock's amendment strategy was later used by other states to smooth the way to ratification.

By June 2, 1788, with only one state needed to ratify the Constitution and put it into effect, the eyes of the nation turned to Virginia, where some found the notion of "the people" running a democratic government preposterous. Patrick Henry, the leader of the Antifederalists, argued that even the first three words of the document were wrong: "Who authorized them to speak the language of *We the people,* instead of, *We the states?* States are the characteristics and the soul of a confederation."[28] But James Madison, thoroughly convinced of the need for a national government, saw no danger to the states, saying that the national government's "delegated powers" would keep it within limits. This sentiment could not persuade George Mason, who had refused to sign the Constitution: "Where is the barrier drawn between the government, and the rights of the citizens?"[29]

The key to success was Edmund Randolph, the politically ambitious thirty-four-year-old governor of Virginia, who had proposed the Virginia Plan in the Convention and then, unhappy with the outcome of the debates, refused to sign the final version of the Constitution. He switched to Madison's side in the ratification debate, arguing that he would "assent to the lopping [of his right arm] before I assent to the dissolution of the union." Randolph urged the acceptance of subsequent amendments to the document just as Hancock had done in Massachusetts. Randolph's argument proved decisive. On June 25, 1788, by a narrow margin of ten votes, the Constitution was ratified in Virginia. New Hampshire had moved more quickly, becoming the ninth state to ratify, but although tenth, Virginia's size made its action important in securing the success of the new government.

A week after Virginia's vote, New York State ratified the Constitution by a razor-thin 30 to 27 margin. North Carolina waited until after the Bill of Rights had been sent to the states for ratification before adding its assent in November 1789. And Rhode Island continued to take its time, waiting until May 29, 1790, to ratify the Constitution by a narrow 34 to 32 vote.

This highly political debate over the Constitution was proof that the new system would work because democracy had worked. The American people had freely and peacefully debated and chosen their new form of government. They had put aside their individual needs and local interests for the common good. As Benjamin Rush, a Philadelphia physician who signed the Declaration of Independence and lived to see the Constitution ratified, said, "'Tis done, we have become a nation."[30]

Adoption of the Bill of Rights

When the First Congress convened in 1789, Representative Roger Sherman of Connecticut, the only man to sign all three of this nation's founding documents then serving as a member of a select committee appointed by the House of Representatives to sift through more than two hundred amendments proposed in state debates to compose a possible Bill of Rights consisting of 11 amendments.[31] The Committee never mentioned this draft, instead choosing to send seventeen amendments to Congress for its consideration, with twelve being passed and sent to the states for ratification. Ten were ratified in 1791, becoming known as the **Bill of Rights.** As you can see from Table 2.3, the first eight amendments drafted by the First Congress guaranteed a variety of rights against government control and provided procedural safeguards in criminal trials and against arbitrary governmental action. The Ninth and Tenth Amendments were intended to describe the new constitutional structure, assuring that rights not listed in the Constitution, or powers not delegated to the national government, would be retained by the people or the states. The amendments placed limits on government power by prohibiting the *national* government from intruding on fundamental rights and liberties. However, the rights of the people against *state* intrusion would be left to the individual state constitutions and legislatures. As we will see in Chapter 13, though, over time America would further approach democracy as the Supreme Court applied all but a few of the provisions of the Bill of Rights to the states as well.

Updating the Constitution

The framers viewed the Constitution as a lasting document, one that would endure long after the debates and ratification. They did not believe, as Thomas Jefferson and George Washington did, that a new constitution should be written

---

Table 2.3 ■ The First Ten Amendments to the Constitution (The Bill of Rights)

Safeguards of Personal and Political Freedoms

1. Freedom of speech, press, and religion, and right to assemble peaceably and to petition government to redress grievances

2. Right to keep and bear arms

Outmoded Protection Against British Occupation

3. Protection against quartering troops in private homes

Safeguards in the Judicial Process and Against Arbitrary Government Action

4. Protection against "unreasonable" searches and seizures by the government

5. Guarantees of a grand jury for capital crimes, against double jeopardy, against being forced to testify against oneself, against being deprived of life or property without "due process of law," and against the taking of property without just compensation

6. Guarantees of rights in criminal trials including right to speedy and public trial, to be informed of the nature of the charges, to confront witnesses, to compel witnesses to appear in one's defense, and to the assistance of counsel

7. Guarantee of right of trial by a jury of one's peers

8. Guarantees against excessive bail and the imposition of cruel and unusual punishment

Description of Unenumerated Rights and Reserved Powers

9. Assurance that rights not listed for protection against the power of the central government in the Constitution are still retained by the people

10. Assurance that the powers not delegated to the central government are reserved by the states, or to the people

Bill of Rights The first ten amendments to the Constitution, added in 1791.

every generation, or twenty years or so. To create a lasting document, the framers drafted a constitution that included an amendment process to allow for adjustments to their handiwork. In addition, the Supreme Court would play a role, along with the pressures of social and political change, to alter a flexible and responsive constitution. This way, the Constitution could be kept timely and current. But the Constitution is not easy to alter, no matter how strong, compelling, or passionate the need.

Updating the Constitution through the Amendment Process

The framers deliberately made the amendment process difficult, thus placing the Constitution beyond the temporary passions of the people, but they did not require unanimity, which had already failed in the Articles of Confederation. Clearly, the amendment process was designed to be used only for the most serious issues.

The framers established a two-stage amendment process, resembling the one used to approve the Constitution. First, there must be a **proposal** for a change that the states must then **ratify.** The framers wanted to ensure that each new amendment would be considered carefully. Thus, they required a powerful consensus of political and social support for amendments, known as a **supermajority.** This means that each stage of the process has to be approved by more than the simple majority of 50 percent plus one. The proposal stage requires either a two-thirds vote of both houses of Congress or an application from two-thirds of the states for a constitutional convention. Ratification is accomplished by a vote of three-quarters of the state legislatures or a three-quarters vote of specially created state ratifying conventions. While the framers reserved this extraordinary voting requirement for other important tasks, such as overriding a presidential veto and ratifying a treaty, here alone the supermajority has to be mustered twice on the same issue. The amendment process is illustrated in Figure 2.2.

No formal time limit was placed on ratifying amendments, but a limit can be included in the body of the amendment, as it was in the ERA, and Congress can extend the limit if it wishes. Although the Supreme Court has been reluctant to rule on the constitutionality of such time limits, in 1921 it did rule that the seven-year limit placed in the Eighteenth Amendment was "reasonable."[32]

Although proposed several times, to date no amendment has been approved by constitutional convention. All have been proposed in Congress, and all except the Twenty-first Amendment repealing Prohibition have been ratified using state legislatures. Since there has been only one Constitutional Convention, a variety of interesting questions remain about the prospects for another such event. How would the delegates be selected? How would the votes be apportioned among the fifty states? Is there a need to ensure that all social groups are represented, and is there a way of doing so? And even if a convention is called to consider a specific proposal, is there a chance of a runaway convention resulting in reconsideration of the entire Constitution, as happened to the Articles of Confederation in 1787? The answers to these questions are unknown, and since the only example in this country was a runaway convention, few are willing to risk having another one. In 1911, thirty-one states called for a convention to consider the direct election of the Senate. A fearful Congress quickly proposed such an amendment in 1912, and after ratification by the states in 1913, it became the Seventeenth Amendment.

If you look at the ratified amendments you will see how remarkably few changes have been made in the Constitution, with all of them grouped around four purposes: to expand rights and equality; to correct flaws in, or revise, the original constitutional plan for government; to make public policy; and to overturn Supreme Court decisions. The amendments and their effects are outlined in Table 2.4 on page 70.

At times, the amendment proposal process can be used in an attempt to reverse Supreme Court decisions. For example, after the Supreme Court struck down state

proposal The first stage of the Constitutional amendment process, in which a change is proposed.

ratify An act of approval of proposed constitutional amendments by the states; the second step of the amendment process.

supermajority A majority vote required for constitutional amendments; consists of more than a simple majority of 50 percent plus one.

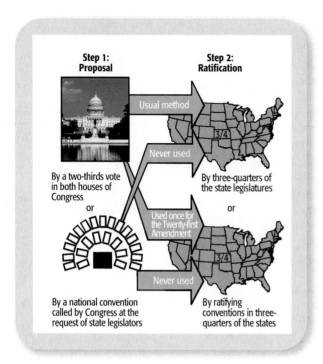

Figure 2.2   Procedures for Amending the Constitution
Although the framers provided four ways to amend the Constitution, only one method is usually used: proposal of an amendment by two-thirds of each house of Congress and ratification by three-quarters of the state legislatures. The sole exception was the Twenty-First Amendment repealing Prohibition. Ratification of this amendment took place in special state conventions.

and federal laws designed to outlaw burning the American flag, an amendment to accomplish the same thing was unsuccessfully proposed. In 1997, when the Supreme Court refused to allow states to impose term limits on candidates for congressional office, and Congress failed to pass a federal term limits law, the idea that this goal could be accomplished by constitutional amendment was considered.

The history of the disastrous Eighteenth Amendment and the Twenty-first Amendment repealing it best illustrates the problems that result when a special interest group takes over a process designed to express the wishes of the vast majority. The Prohibition era of the 1920s began when temperance (antiliquor) groups around the country pressured Congress in 1917 to pass, and the states to ratify two years later, an amendment banning the manufacture, sale, and transportation of liquor. Through a quirk of the process, most of the ratification support came from the less-populous western states, meaning that the amendment was ratified by thirty-six states having a total of 9 million fewer people than the other twelve states. The result was a conflict between a minority seeking virtue through abstinence and a majority who still wanted to drink. So drink they did. By 1929 thirty amendments repealing Prohibition had been proposed in Congress, with one finally being passed on February 20, 1933. In December of that year, the Twenty-first Amendment was ratified by state conventions—the only time in American history that that particular route was taken to pass an amendment.[33]

There have been other efforts by special interest groups and political parties to amend the Constitution so as to shape the morality of the nation or further their political agenda. For example, the amendment process has recently been used in an attempt to ban abortions, to reestablish prayer in public schools, to protect the rights of crime victims, to ban flag burning, and to deny citizenship to native-born children of illegal aliens. But the double supermajority feature of the amendment process usually prevents such uses by special interest and political groups, reserving amendments for the expression of the overwhelming desires of the vast majority.

Updating the Constitution by Judicial Interpretation

How has the Constitution managed to remain vibrant and current even though it has been amended only twenty-seven times? The answer to this question has to do

Table 2.4 ■ The Constitutional Amendments				
NO.	Proposed	Ratified	Subject	Purpose
11	1794	1795	To sue a state in federal court, individuals need state consent	Overruled a Supreme Court decision
12	1803	1804	Requires separate electoral college votes for president and vice president	Corrected a government plan flaw
13	1865	1865	Prohibits slavery	Expanded rights
14	1866	1868	Gives citizenship to freed slaves, guarantees them due process and equal protection of the laws, and protects their privileges and immunities	Expanded rights
15	1869	1870	Grants freed slaves the right to vote	Expanded voting rights
16	1909	1913	Grants Congress power to collect income tax	Overruled a Supreme Court decision
17	1912	1913	Provides for direct election of the Senate (formerly elected by state legislatures)	Expanded voting rights
18	1917	1919	Prohibited the manufacture, sale, and transportation of intoxicating liquor	Public policy
19	1919	1920	Grants women the right to vote	Expanded voting rights
20	1932	1933	Changes presidential inauguration date from March 4 to January 20, and opening date of Congress to January 3	Revised a government plan
21	1933	1933	Repeals the Eighteenth Amendment	Public policy
22	1947	1951	Limits the president to two terms in office	Revised a government plan
23	1960	1961	Grants citizens of Washington, D.C., status in electoral college to vote for president	Expanded voting rights
24	1962	1964	Prohibits charging a poll tax to vote	Expanded voting rights
25	1965	1967	Provides for succession of president or vice president in the event of death, removal from office, incapacity, or resignation	Revised a government plan
26	1971	1971	Grants the right to vote to eighteen- to twenty-year olds	Expanded voting rights
27	1789	1992	Prohibits a pay raise voted by Congress from going into effect until the following session	Public policy

judicial review The power of the Supreme Court established in *Marbury v. Madison* to overturn acts of the president, Congress, and the states if those acts violate the Constitution. This power makes the Supreme Court the final interpreter of the Constitution.

both with the brilliant ambiguity built into the Constitution and the power of the Supreme Court to interpret it.

But where did the Court get such power? As you will learn in Chapter 6, on the judiciary, in the 1803 case of *Marbury v. Madison*, the Court, under Chief Justice John Marshall, ruled that since the Supreme Court interprets laws and the Constitution is a law, then the Court has the power to be the final interpreter of the Constitution. This power, **judicial review,** enables the Court to overturn acts of the other two branches of government if those acts are ruled to be in violation of the Constitution as we saw in the case of Lincoln's suspension of the writ of *habeas corpus* and Wilson's prosecution of opponents of the military draft during World War I. In doing so, the Supreme Court interprets the Constitution, giving new meaning to the phrases and provisions written in 1787. Since overturning a constitutional ruling by the Supreme Court can only be done by the Court itself or through a constitutional amendment, these rulings, in effect, change the meaning of the Constitution. In exercising this power, the justices take on the role of modern constitutional framers, trying to define what the document should mean in the modern age. Throughout American history, scholars have debated the Court's role, with some believing that the justices should uphold the framers' original meaning of the Constitution and others maintaining that they should continue to update the document using a modern perspective.

The Gettysburg Address and America's Approach to Democracy

The most remarkable feature of the Constitution is how it has adapted to the times, changing along with an ever-changing nation. The world has changed dramatically from that of 1787, when it took four days for German immigrant Jacob Shallus to write the Constitution by hand on four pieces of stretched vellum with a quill pen and ink made from oak galls and dyes. Now we can create a version of the same document in just a few seconds using computer software. We have gone from a nation of a little more than the population of Los Angeles to one of over 280 million people, from a geographic base of thirteen seashore colonies to fifty states spread across more than three thousand miles. In 1787, wars took months to develop as ships crossed vast oceans; now, one press of a button can mean instant annihilation. Yet, as Supreme Court Justice Byron White has argued, the Constitution still survives because, "From the summer of 1787 to the present the government of the United States has become an endeavor far beyond the contemplation of the Framers. But the wisdom of the Framers was to anticipate that the nation would grow and new problems of governance would require different solutions."[34]

Over time, actions taken by the different branches of government have changed the nature of the government's structure without changing the Constitution. The framers originally gave Congress the power to declare war, but the speed of modern warfare has created the need for quicker responses. Now the president has the power to make war. The Korean and Vietnam wars, along with a host of other conflicts, were presidential wars. The framers also intended, despite the creation of a system of checks and balances, for Congress to be the predominant branch. But certain presidents have enlarged the powers of the executive. Thomas Jefferson directed the purchase of the Louisiana Territory; Abraham Lincoln imposed martial law and freed the slaves; Woodrow Wilson and Franklin D. Roosevelt extended the powers of their offices during world wars; and a host of other presidents exercised powers well beyond those delegated to them by Congress. For this reason President George W. Bush could commit troops to Afghanistan and the "war on terrorism" without congressional declarations of war. While it is doubtful that Madison and Franklin would recognize much of the government today, they would appreciate the fact that their handiwork allowed this evolution to take place.

As you have seen, the original Constitution was hardly a testament to full participatory democracy. It begins with the words, "We the People," but in the beginning the "we" who drafted the document were the fifty-five delegates to the Constitutional Convention in Philadelphia and the elite landowners they represented. The Constitution did not fully protect the rights of all citizens, and the framers did not seek to use their 4,400-word document to advance social or political equality. Slavery was not banned; in fact, it seemed to be condoned. The feminine pronoun never appeared in the document, and women had no more rights under the Constitution than they had under the Articles of Confederation. Most Americans could not vote and had essentially no voice in the operation of their government. Perhaps for this reason some of the framers anticipated that this document would have to be revised within a couple of decades as the nation expanded. In that sense, as Vaclav Havel said so eloquently, democracy in America only began in 1787, and the approach to democracy would have to continue.

President Abraham Lincoln continued that evolution in 1863 when he ventured to Gettysburg, Pennsylvania to dedicate the new Civil War cemetery there. In his short 271-word speech, Lincoln began by referring to the Declaration of Independence when "Fourscore and seven years ago our fathers brought forth on this continent a new nation, conceived in liberty and dedicated to the proposition that all men are created equal." But now, he argued, by the men who given their "last full measure of devotion" on the battlefield, that promise had become "that this nation, under God, shall have a new birth of freedom—and that government of the people, by the people, for the people, shall not perish from the earth." This concept represented a "Second Declaration of Independence." Suddenly, the governmental vision created by free, white men over the age of 21 who owned land had become a more inclusive democracy promising a vision of democracy for all people. As author Garry Wills argued, "If all men are created equal, they cannot be property. They cannot be ruled by owner-monarchs. They must be self-governing in the minimal sense of self-possession. Their equality cannot be denied if the nation is to live by its creed, and voice it, and test it, and die for it."[35] By applying this new concept of a "people's government" to the Constitution it was now possible for the American government to better approach democracy.

The Constitution is a highly elastic document that over the years and in response to the times would become more democratic. The paradox of the foundation of American democracy, then, is that a Constitution written in secret by representatives of less than 5 percent of the population established processes that have led to the most openly democratic nation in the world. The Bill of Rights included in the document protects the rights of most citizens. When a supermajority of the public demands change in the Constitution, change can occur through the amendment process. The Constitution can also evolve through judicial decisions and political action. In short, as new generations press for their rights and a greater voice in their government, the Constitution can change and expand, or if need be in times of crisis contract to protect itself, in order to fit the time and circumstances, thus allowing the nation to approach democracy in the long run. Even when these mechanisms do not work as they should, for example, when African Americans were not able to secure their promise of a right to vote and full equality, the legislative and judicial institutions created in the Constitution a way to seek redress.

This evolutionary process has continued in recent times with Ruth Bader Ginsburg's efforts in the 1970s to convince the Supreme Court to extend constitutional protection for women under the Fourteenth Amendment, Sandra Day O'Connor's appointment to the Supreme Court in 1981, Colin Powell's appointment as Secretary of State, Condoleeza Rice's appointment as George W. Bush's National Security Advisor, and Alberto Gonzales's appointment as Bush's White House counsel in 2001. Without the efforts of these people pushing for legal, political, and constitutional change—and in the process, changing the way public policy is viewed—we might never have heard of the changes sought by groups who had no voice in American government when the Framers labored on the founding documents. In this manner, the words of the Constitution might remain the same, but their meaning changes in response to the demands of each new generation.

The framers hoped that their Constitution would lead to a stable republic, an improvement over the Articles of Confederation. They did not seek to establish a system of pure democracy, relying instead on the notion of a representative government. That task would be left to the government itself, the people it represented, and the Supreme Court's interpretation of the Constitution. Yet the constitutional convention was truly "the Miracle" described by Catherine Drinker Bowen, not only because these men were able to reach some sort of compromise on the shape of a new government but also because the compromise they reached would create a system of government that continues to govern, even in times of crisis such as we now face, in ways that the framers could not fully anticipate.

Question for Reflection: How might legislators field-test potential acts to weigh the long-term constitutional ramifications of their implementation prior to approval?

DEMOCRACY IN THE NEW MILLENNIUM

The Constitution and the Computer

What do Leonardo DaVinci's statue of *David,* information on breast cancer, the Dave Matthews Band, and J.D. Salinger's *Catcher in the Rye* have in common for America's approach to democracy in the twenty-first century? The answer is that they all raise the question of how the computer revolution has led to constitutional issues that the quill-scratching Supreme Court Justices of the 18th century could never have imagined. This became clear in December, 2000, when well-intentioned legislators, seeking to ban child pornography on the Internet, passed the Child Internet Pornography Act (CIPA) requiring that schools and libraries using the Internet install pornography filters to block access to Websites which are considered to be harmful to minors. While the federal court overturned this law, the proposal itself still had negative effects. The problem here, in the words of American Library Association President, John W. Berry is that "with more than 27 million Websites, and the average Web page turning over every 44 days, the Internet is a very dynamic tool. Filters are technologically incapable of making the fine distinction between information that is *good* and that which is *bad.* They do not work today, and they will not work in the future." So, the filter that screens for pornographic sites will also prevent an art student from viewing photos of the nude statue of *David* or an inquisitive teen-ager from accessing informative sites on preventing breast cancer.

New problems arose when Congress, upon seeing the ease by which CD writers allowed people to copy and distribute copyrighted intellectual property such as popular music, computer games, software, and DVDs, passed the Digital Millennium Copyright Act (DMCA) of 1998. This act sought to protect intellectual property (IP) by prohibiting the violation of digital copyrights, and also any effort to bypass, or even describe how to bypass, the encryption measures that protect those copyrights. As a result, libraries are now finding that they cannot offer certain magazines, journals or e-books because the copyright laws prevent them from being distributed. A Russian computer programmer, Dmitri Sklyarov, was arrested for creating and distributing a program that allowed people to crack the protective encryption devices on Adobe e-books. So while the music of the Dave Matthews Band and other groups is now protected, Salinger's *Catcher in the Rye* may not be as available to readers because libraries will not be able to circulate electronic versions of these volumes for fear of violating the new copyright law.

These ultra-modern First Amendment issues relating to computers, and more, can be analyzed on sites such as www. prospect.org, www.ala.org, www.aclu.org, and www. educause. edu.

SUMMARY

1. The governments of some American colonies were based on the idea of a compact, an agreement legally binding two or more parties to enforceable rules. Other colonies evolved from royal grants of land and that gave governing rights to a lord or baron, who became the colony's proprietor.

2. Frequent conflicts between the governors and the colonial legislatures made the colonists highly suspicious of executive power. The colonists were also influenced by the ideas of Charles de Montesquieu, who saw the separation of executive, legislative, and judicial powers as the best way to counteract any tendency toward despotism, and by the ideas of social contract theorists such as Thomas Hobbes and John Locke—especially the latter, who asserted the importance of limited government based on popular consent.

3. Slowly American colonists recognized the need for cooperation. Benjamin Franklin proposed a plan that called for a self-governing confederation, a league of sovereign states that would delegate specific powers to a central government. However, in 1754, Franklin's plan was rejected by both the Crown and the colonial assemblies.

4. After 1763, Britain imposed a series of direct taxes on the American colonies. The Sugar Act retained a tax on molasses and extended duties to other goods imported into the colonies; the Stamp Act required that taxes be placed on all printed matter and legal

documents. The Townshend Revenue Acts imposed taxes on glass, lead, tea, and paper imported into the colonies.

5. The tax on tea especially irritated the colonists. The most famous protest against this tax was the Boston Tea Party of December 16, 1773, in which colonists dumped chests of tea into Boston Harbor. Parliament responded by passing the Coercive Acts, which closed Boston Harbor and required the quartering of British soldiers in private homes. In September 1774 representatives of twelve colonies met in Philadelphia to act in concert as they demanded restoration of their English rights.

6. Hostilities broke out in the spring of 1775 when British troops attempted to destroy ammunition stored by colonial militias. Three weeks after the battles at Lexington and Concord, the Second Continental Congress convened, becoming in effect a revolutionary government. The next year, the Continental Congress approved and signed the Declaration of Independence.

7. On November 15, 1777, the Continental Congress adopted the Articles of Confederation and Perpetual Union. Under the Articles the central government lacked the power to impose taxes, raise an army, or regulate commerce. Hence it was unable to protect either citizens or private property.

8. Although the stated goal of the Constitutional Convention was to revise the Articles of Confederation, some delegates believed that the Articles needed to be scrapped altogether and replaced by an entirely new document. Debate at the convention centered on two major proposals. The Virginia Plan called for a system of proportional representation in which the legislature would consist of two chambers, or "houses," and each state's representation in both houses would depend on its population. The New Jersey Plan proposed a unicameral (one-house) legislature in which each state would have one vote. The delegates voted to use the Virginia Plan as the basis for further discussion.

9. A key debate at the Convention dealt with representation in the two houses of Congress. States with large populations sought proportional representation in both houses, while those with smaller populations called for an equal number of votes for each state. In the Great (or Connecticut) Compromise the delegates decided that representation in the House of Representatives would be based on each state's population, while each state would have two votes in the Senate.

10. Another important debate was over slavery. The southern states wanted slaves to be counted as part of the population when determining representation in Congress; the northern states wanted slaves to be excluded from the count. The outcome of the debate was the three-fifths compromise: each state's representation would be determined by adding three-fifths of the number of slaves to the number of free citizens in that state.

11. The delegates were also divided over the nature of the presidency. Some favored a single national executive with the power to veto legislative acts, while others were concerned that a single executive would hold too much power and called instead for a board of executives. Eventually they agreed on a single executive.

12. The new Constitution created a republican form of government, in which the people hold an indirect voting power over elected officials. Originally, only members of the House of Representatives would be elected directly by the people; senators would be chosen by the state legislatures, and the president by an electoral college. Over the years the people have gained a more direct voice in the government through a series of constitutional changes such as popular election of senators and extension of the right to vote to all people over the age of eighteen.

13. The Constitution established a system of separation of powers in which different powers are granted to the three major branches of government. In addition, it set up checks and balances, giving each branch the power to approve, disapprove, or alter what the other branches do. It also distributed powers between the central government and the state governments. The powers of the central government are delegated—expressly granted and limited in nature—while all remaining powers are reserved to the states. The supremacy clause states that the dictates of the national government take precedence over those of any state government.

14. Supporters of the Constitution called themselves *Federalists;* opponents took the name *Antifederalists*. The Federalists claimed that the new government was designed to represent the sovereignty of the people, while the Antifederalists believed that the states

should remain independent of the central government. The Constitution was finally ratified after the Federalists agreed to the addition of the Bill of Rights.

15. The Constitution can be amended through a two-stage process. First, there must be a proposal for a change, which requires either a two-thirds vote of both houses of Congress or a request by two-thirds of the states for a constitutional convention. Then the amendment must be ratified by a vote of three-quarters of the state legislatures or a three-quarters vote of specially created state ratifying conventions. The primary source of constitutional change, however, is judicial interpretation in response to political and social changes.

KEY TERMS

republic
compact
bicameral legislature
sovereignty
social contract theorists
limited government
confederation
Sugar Act
Stamp Act
Townshend Revenue Acts
Boston Massacre
Committees of
   Correspondence
Boston Tea Party
Intolerable Acts
writs of assistance
First Continental Congress

Second Continental Congress
Common Sense
Declaration of Independence
Articles of Confederation
Virginia Plan
legislative branch
executive branch
judiciary
checks and balances
separation of powers
proportional representation
council of revision
New Jersey Plan
unicameral legislature
supremacy clause
Great (or Connecticut)
   Compromise

three-fifths compromise
electoral college system
federalism
delegated powers
reserved powers
police powers
devolution
necessary and proper clause
Federalists
Antifederalists
factions
Bill of Rights
proposal
ratify
supermajority
judicial review

POLISIM ACTIVITY

The Constitution
The democratic principles that guide this nation are embodied in the Constitution, or are they? In this simulation, it is 1789 and you have been asked to make final revisions on the Constitution. You will be challenged to apply some of the principles, both modern and traditional, to the original Constitution. Decide whether or not to include these principles and see how your choices might affect the Constitution and American history.

SUGGESTED READINGS

BAILYN, BERNARD. *The Ideological Origins of the American Revolution.* Cambridge, Mass.: Harvard University Press, 1967. An excellent study of the ideas that forged the Revolution.
BAILYN, BERNARD, ed. *The Debate on the Constitution.* 2 vols. New York: Library of America, 1993. The complete primary documentary record of all of the arguments that occurred among the general public and various legislatures in the states during the ratification process.
BEARD, CHARLES A. *An Economic Interpretation of the Constitution of the United States.* New York: Macmillan, 1913. Presentation of the famous argument that the framers acted out of economic self-interest in drafting the Constitution.
BOWEN, CATHERINE DRINKER. *The Miracle at Philadelphia: The Story of the Constitutional Convention, May to September 1787.* Boston: Little, Brown, 1966. A highly readable account of the Constitutional Convention.
BURNS, JAMES MACGREGOR. *The Vineyard of Liberty.* New York: Random House, 1982. A brilliant interpretation of the American attempt to preserve liberty during the founding.

COLLIER, CHRISTOPHER, and JAMES LINCOLN COLLIER. *Decision in Philadelphia: The Constitutional Convention of 1787*. New York: Random House, 1986. A popular account of the Constitutional Convention using all of the latest scholarship to bring it to life.

ELLIS, JOSEPH. *Founding Brothers: The Revolutionary Generation*. New York: Alfred A. Knopf, 2000. A study of the founders views on, and actions in, the democracy that they created during the remainder of their lives.

FARRAND, MAX, ed. *The Records of the Federal Convention of 1787*. 4 vols. New Haven, Conn.: Yale University Press, 1931–37. The definitive set of primary documents recording the events of the Constitutional Convention.

FLETCHER, GEORGE P. *Our Secret Constitution: How Lincoln Redefined American Democracy*. New York: Oxford University Press, 2001. A study of the meaning of the Gettysburg address for the expanding nature of American democracy.

FONER, ERIC. *The Story of American Freedom*. New York: W. W. Norton, and Company, 1998. A wonderful history of the evolution of American democracy through the study of key events in American political history.

HAMILTON, ALEXANDER, JAMES MADISON, and JOHN JAY. *The Federalist Papers*. New York: New American Library, 1961. The compelling arguments by three framers on behalf of the Constitution, and the starting point for our understanding of the meaning of that document.

HUTSON, JAMES H., ed. *Supplement to Max Farrand's "The Records of the Federal Convention of 1787."* New Haven, Conn.: Yale University Press, 1987. An update of the Farrand volume, containing many useful letters and documents from the framers in the Constitutional Convention period.

JENSEN, MERRILL. *The Articles of Confederation*. Madison: University of Wisconsin Press, 1940. The best treatment of the Articles and their shortcomings.

KAMMEN, MICHAEL. *A Machine That Would Go of Itself: The Constitution in American Culture*. New York: Knopf, 1986. A lively and highly informative cultural history of the Constitution.

KURIAN, GEORGE T. *A Historical Guide to the U.S. Government*. New York: Oxford University Press, 1998. A valuable collection of material on the founding of constitutional government.

LAZARE, DANIEL. *The Velvet Coup: The Constitution, the Supreme Court, and the Decline of American Democracy*. London: Verso, 2001. An analysis of the nature of the effect of the 2000 presidential election on the Constitution and American democracy.

LIPSET, SEYMOUR MARTIN. *The First New Nation*. New York: Basic Books, 1963. An interesting analysis of nation building by a political sociologist.

MAIER, PAULINE. *American Scripture: Making the Declaration of Independence*. New York: Vintage Books, 1997. A complete iconographic analysis of the Declaration of Independence, including its change from the original draft, and its meaning for America.

McCULLOUGH, DAVID. *John Adams*. New York: Simon and Schuster, 2001. A sweeping Pulitzer-prize winning biography of the Founder that some believe to be just as important, if not moreso, than Thomas Jefferson, including a fine account of the nation's founding period.

McDONALD, FORREST. *Novus Ordo Seclorum: The Intellectual Origins of the Constitution*. Lawrence: University of Kansas Press, 1985. The definitive analysis of the intellectual roots of the Constitution.

MEE, CHARLES L., Jr. *The Genius of the People*. New York: Harper & Row, 1987. A fascinating account of the Constitutional Convention supplemented by the riveting story of the ratification process.

RAKOVE, JACK. *Original Meanings: Politics and Ideas in the Making of the Constitution*. New York: Vintage Press, 1996. The Pulitzer Prize-winning analysis of the making of the Constitution and the "original intent" of the framers.

ROSSITER, CLINTON. *1787: The Grand Convention*. New York: Norton, 1966. The classic account of the Constitutional Convention by one of the great scholars of presidential power.

VILE, JOHN. *Encyclopedia of Constitutional Amendments, Proposed Amendments, and Amending Issues, 1789–1995*. Santa Barbara, Calif.: ABC-CLIO, 1996. A comprehensive review of the entire amendment field of study.

WEST, THOMAS G. *Vindicating the Framers: Race, Sex, Class, and Justice in the Origins of America*. New York: Rowman and Littlefield, 1997. A neoconservative critique of the founding period that offers an alternative interpretation of participation in the American founding.

WILLS, GARRY. *Inventing America: Jefferson's Declaration of Independence.* New York: Random House, 1978. An original and provocative account of the writing of the Declaration of Independence.

WILLS, GARRY. *Lincoln at Gettysburg: The Words That Remade America.* New York: Simon and Schuster, 1992. The Pulitzer prize winning account of the true meaning of the Gettysburg Address for the evolution of American Democracy.

WOOD, GORDON S. *The Creation of the American Republic, 1776–1787.* Chapel Hill: University of North Carolina Press, 1969. A fascinating study of the political thought in America during the time of the framing.

The Constitution
of the United States

THE PREAMBLE

We the People of the United States, in Order to form a more perfect Union, establish Justice, insure domestic Tranquility, provide for the common defence, promote the general Welfare, and secure the Blessings of Liberty to ourselves and our Posterity, do ordain and establish this Constitution for the United States of America.

"We, the people." Three simple words, yet of profound importance and contentious origin. Every government in the world at the time of the Constitutional Convention was some type of monarchy, wherein sovereign power flowed from the top. The Founders of our new country rejected monarchy as a form of government and proposed instead a republic, which would draw its sovereignty from the people.

The Articles of Confederation that governed the U.S. from 1776 until 1789 started with: "We the under signed Delegates of the States." Early drafts of the new constitution started with: "We, the states . . . " But again, the Founders were not interested in another union of states but rather the creation of a new national government. Therefore, "We, the states" was changed to "We, the people." The remainder of the preamble describes the generic functions of government. These would apply to almost any type of government. Some have proven more critical than others. For example, "promote the general welfare" has been cited as the authority for social welfare programs of the federal government.

ARTICLE I—THE LEGISLATIVE ARTICLE

Legislative Power

The very first article in the Constitution established the legislative branch of the new national government. Why did the framers start with the legislative power instead of the executive branch? Under the Articles of Confederation, the legislature was the only functional instrument of government. Therefore, the framers truly believed it was the most important component of the new government.

Section 1 All legislative Powers herein granted shall be vested in a Congress of the United States, which shall consist of a Senate and House of Representatives.

Section 1 established a bicameral (two-chamber) legislature, or an upper (Senate) and lower (House of Representatives) organization of the legislative branch.

House of Representatives: Composition; Qualifications; Apportionment; Impeachment Power

Section 2 Clause 1. The House of Representatives shall be composed of Members chosen every second Year by the People of the several States, and the Electors in each State shall have the Qualifications requisite for Electors of the most numerous Branch of the State Legislature.

This section sets the term of office for House members (2 years) and indicates that those voting for Congress will have the same qualifications as those voting for the state legislatures. Originally, states limited voters to white property owners. Some states even had religious disqualifications, such as Catholic or Jewish. Most property and religious qualifications for voting were removed by the 1840s, but race and gender restrictions remained.

Clause 2. No Person shall be a Representative who shall not have attained to the Age of twenty five Years, and been seven Years a Citizen of the United States, and who shall not, when elected, be an Inhabitant of that State in which he shall be chosen.

This section sets forth the basic qualifications of a representative: at least 25 years of age, a U.S. citizen for at least 7 years, and a resident of a state. Note that the Constitution does not require a person to be a resident of the district he or she represents. At the time the Constitution was written, life expectancy was about 43 years of age. So a person 25 years old was middle aged. Considering today's life expectancy of about 78 years, the equivalent age of 25 would be about 45. The average age of a current representative is 53. Because of the specificity of the Constitution as to the qualifications for office, the U.S. Supreme Court ruled that term limits could not be imposed.

Clause 2 does not specify how many terms a representative can serve in Congress. One provision of the Republican House *Contract with America,* "The Citizens Legislature Act," called for term limits for legislators. This provision was not enacted. Subsequently, some states passed legislation to limit the terms of their U.S. representatives. Because of the specificity of the qualifications for office, the Supreme Court ruled in *U.S. Term Limits, Inc. v. Thornton,* 514 U.S. 779 (1995), that term limits for U.S. legislators could not be imposed by any state but would require a constitutional amendment.

Clause 3. Representatives and direct Taxes[1] shall be apportioned among the several States which may be included within this Union, according to their respective Numbers, which shall be determined by adding to the whole Number of free Persons, including those bound to Service for a Term of Years, and excluding Indians not taxed, three fifths of all other Persons.[2] The actual Enumeration shall be made within three Years after the first Meeting of the Congress of the United States, and within every subsequent Term of ten Years, in such Manner as they shall by Law direct. The Number of Representatives shall not exceed one for every thirty Thousand, but each State shall have at Least one Representative; and until such enumeration shall be made, the State of New Hampshire shall be entitled to chuse three, Massachusetts eight, Rhode-Island and Providence Plantations one, Connecticut five, New-York six, New Jersey four, Pennsylvania eight, Delaware one, Maryland six, Virginia ten, North Carolina five, South Carolina five, and Georgia three.

This clause contains the Three-Fifths Compromise, wherein American Indians and Blacks were only counted as 3/5 of a person for congressional representation purposes. This clause also addresses the question of congressional reapportionment every 10 years, which requires a census. Since the 1911 Reapportionment Act, the size of the House of Representatives has been set at 435. This is the designated size that is reapportioned every 10 years. Based on changes of population, some states gain and some states lose representatives. This clause also provides that every state, regardless of population, will have at least one (1) representative. Currently, seven states have only one representative.

Clause 4. When vacancies happen in the Representation from any State, the Executive Authority thereof shall issue Writs of Election to fill such Vacancies.

This clause provides a procedure for replacing a U.S. representative in the case of death, resignation, or expulsion from the House. Essentially, the governor of the representative's state will assign a successor. Generally, if less than half a term is left, the governor will appoint a successor. If more than half a term is remaining, most states require a special election to fill the vacancy.

Clause 5. The House of Representatives shall chuse their Speaker and other Officers; and shall have the sole Power of Impeachment.

Only one officer of the House is specified—the Speaker. All other officers are decided by the House. This clause also gives the House authority for impeachments (accusations) against officials of the executive and judicial branches.

Senate Composition: Qualifications, Impeachment Trials

Section 3 Clause 1. The Senate of the United States shall be composed of two Senators from each State, *chosen by the Legislature thereof,*[3] for six Years; and each Senator shall have one Vote.

This clause treats each state equally—all have two senators. Originally, senators were chosen by state legislators, but since passage and ratification of the 17th Amendment, they are now elected by popular vote. This clause also establishes the term of a senator—6 years—three times that of a House member.

Clause 2. Immediately after they shall be assembled in Consequence of the first Election, they shall be divided as equally as may be into three Classes. The Seats of the Senators of the first Class shall be vacated at the Expiration of the second Year, of the second Class at the Expiration of the fourth Year, and of the third Class at the Expiration of the sixth Year, so that one third may be chosen every second Year; *and if Vacancies happen by Resignation, or otherwise, during the Recess of the Legislature of any State, the Executive thereof may make temporary Appointments until the next Meeting of the Legislature, which shall then fill such Vacancies.*[4]

To prevent a wholesale election of senators every six years, this clause provides that one-third of the Senate will be elected every two years. Senate vacancies are filled in the same way as the House—either appointment by the governor or by special election.

Clause 3. No Person shall be a Senator who shall not have attained to the Age of thirty Years, and been nine Years a Citizen of the United States, and who shall not, when elected, be an Inhabitant of that State for which he shall be chosen.

This clause sets forth the qualifications for U.S. senator: at least 30 years old, a U.S. citizen for at least nine years, and a citizen of a state. The equivalent age of 30 today would be 54 years old. The average age of a U.S. senator at present is 58.3 years.

Clause 4. The Vice President of the United States shall be President of the Senate, but shall have no Vote, unless they be equally divided.

The only constitutional duty of the vice president is specified in this clause—president of the Senate. This official only has a vote if there is a tie vote in the Senate; then the vice president's vote breaks the tie.

Clause 5. The Senate shall chuse their other Officers, and also a President pro tempore, in the Absence of the Vice President, or when he shall exercise the Office of President of the United States.

---

[1]Modified by the 16th Amendment
[2]Replaced by Section 2, 14th Amendment

[3]Repealed by the 17th Amendment
[4]Modified by the 17th Amendment

One official office in the U.S. Senate is specified— temporary president, who fills in during the vice president's absence (which is normally the case). All other Senate officers are designated and selected by the Senate.

Clause 6. The Senate shall have the sole Power to try all Impeachments. When sitting for that Purpose, they shall be on Oath or Affirmation. When the President of the United States is tried, the Chief Justice shall preside: And no Person shall be convicted without the Concurrence of two thirds of the Members present. Clause 7. Judgment in Cases of Impeachment shall not extend further than to removal from Office, and disqualification to hold and enjoy any Office of honor, Trust or Profit under the United States: but the Party convicted shall nevertheless be liable and subject to Indictment, Trial, Judgment and Punishment, according to Law.

The Senate acts as a trial court for impeached federal officials. If the accused is the president, the Chief Justice of the U.S. Supreme Court presides. Otherwise, the vice president normally presides. Conviction of the charges requires a 2/3 majority vote of those senators present at the time of the vote. Conviction results in the federal official's removal from office and disqualification to hold any other federal appointed office. Removal from office does not bar further prosecution under applicable criminal or civil laws, nor does it apparently bar one from elected office. A current representative, Alcee L. Hastings, was removed as a federal district judge. He subsequently ran for Congress and now represents Florida's 23rd Congressional District.

Congressional Elections: Times, Places, Manner

Section 4 Clause 1. The Times, Places and Manner of holding Elections for Senators and Representatives, shall be prescribed in each State by the Legislature thereof; but the Congress may at any time by Law make or alter such Regulations, except as to the Places of chusing Senators.
Clause 2. The Congress shall assemble at least once in every Year, *and such Meeting shall be on the first Monday in December, unless they shall by Law appoint a different Day.*[5]

The states determine the place and manner of electing representatives and senators, but Congress has the right to make or change these laws or regulations, except for the election sites. Congress is required to meet annually, and now, by law, annual meetings begin in January.

Powers and Duties of the Houses

Section 5 Clause 1. Each House shall be the Judge of the Elections, Returns and Qualifications of its own Members, and a Majority of each shall constitute a Quorum to do Business; but a smaller Number may adjourn from day to day, and may be authorized to compel the Attendance of absent Members, in such Manner, and under the Penalties as each House may provide.

This clause enables each legislative branch to essentially make its own rules. Normally, to take a vote, a quorum is necessary. But if no votes are scheduled, fewer than a quorum can convene a session.

Clause 2. Each House may determine the Rules of its Proceedings, punish its Members for disorderly Behaviour, and, with the Concurrence of two thirds, expel a Member.

Essentially, each branch promulgates its own rules and punishes its own members. The ultimate punishment is expulsion of the member, which requires a 2/3 vote. Expulsion does not prevent the member from running again.

Clause 3. Each House shall keep a Journal of its Proceedings, and from time to time publish the same, excepting such Parts as may in their Judgment require Secrecy; and the Yeas and Nays of the Members of either House on any question shall, at the Desire of one fifth of those Present, be entered on the Journal.

An official record called the Congressional Record, House Journal, etc., is kept for all sessions. It is a daily account of House and Senate floor debates, votes, and members' remarks. However, a record is not printed if a proceeding is closed to the public for security reasons. Many votes are by voice vote, and if at least 1/5 of the members request, a recorded vote of Yeas and Nays will be conducted and documented. This procedure permits analysis of congressional role-call votes.

Clause 4. Neither House, during the Session of Congress, shall, without the Consent of the other, adjourn for more than three days, nor to any other Place than that in which the two Houses shall be sitting.

This clause prevents one branch from adjourning for a long period of time or to some other location without the consent of the other branch.

Rights of Members

Section 6 Clause 1. The Senators and Representatives shall receive a Compensation for their Services, to be ascertained by Law, and paid out of the Treasury of the United States. They shall in all Cases, except Treason, Felony and Breach of the Peace, be privileged from Arrest during their Attendance at the Session of their respective Houses, and in going to and returning from the same; and for any Speech or Debate in either House, they shall not be questioned in any other Place.

This section ensures that senators and congressional representatives will be paid a salary from the U.S. Treasury. This salary is determined by no other than the legislature. According to the Library of Congress legislative Web site THOMAS: "The current salary for members of Congress is $145,100. A small number of leadership positions, like Speaker of the House, receive a somewhat higher salary." In addition, members of Congress receive many other benefits: free health care, fully funded retirement system, free gyms, 26 free round trips to their home state or district, etc. This section also provides

---

[5]Changed by the 20th Amendment

immunity from arrest or prosecution for congressional actions on the floor or in travel to and from the Congress. For example, few members of Congress have ever been charged with drunk driving.

Clause 2. No Senator or Representative shall, during the Time for which he was elected, be appointed to any civil Office under the Authority of the United States, which shall have been created, or the Emoluments whereof shall have been encreased during such time; and no Person holding any Office under the United States, shall be a Member of either House during his Continuance in Office.

This section prevents the U.S. from adopting a parliamentary democracy, since congressional members cannot hold executive offices and members of the executive branch cannot be members of Congress.

Legislative Powers: Bills and Resolutions

Section 7 Clause 1. All Bills for raising Revenue shall originate in the House of Representatives; but the Senate may propose or concur with Amendments as on other Bills.

This clause specifies one of the few powers specific to the U.S. House—revenue bills.

Clause 2. Every Bill which shall have passed the House of Representatives and the Senate, shall, before it becomes a Law, be presented to the President of the United States; If he approve he shall sign it, but if not he shall return it, with his Objections to that House in which it shall have originated, who shall enter the Objections at large on their Journal, and proceed to reconsider it. If after such Reconsideration two thirds of that House shall agree to pass the Bill, it shall be sent, together with the Objections, to the other House, by which it shall likewise be reconsidered, and if approved by two thirds of that House, it shall become a Law. But in all such Cases the Votes of both Houses shall be determined by yeas and Nays, and the Names of the Persons voting for and against the Bill shall be entered on the Journal of each House respectively. If any Bill shall not be returned by the President within ten Days (Sundays excepted) after it shall have been presented to him, the Same shall be a Law, in like Manner as if he had signed it, unless the Congress by their Adjournment prevent its Return, in which Case it shall not be a Law.

The heart of the checks and balances system is contained in this clause. Both the House and Senate must pass a bill and present it to the president. If the president fails to act on the bill within 10 days (not including Sundays), the bill will automatically become law. If the president signs the bill, it becomes law. If the president vetoes the bill and sends it back to Congress, this body may override the veto by a 2/3 vote in each branch. This vote must be a recorded vote.

Clause 3. Every Order, Resolution, or Vote to which the Concurrence of the Senate and House of Representatives may be necessary (except on a question of Adjournment) shall be presented to the President of the United States; and before the Same shall take Effect, shall be approved by him, or being disapproved by him, shall be repassed by two thirds of the Senate and House of Representatives, according to the Rules and Limitations prescribed in the Case of a Bill.

This clause covers every other type of legislative action other than a bill. Essentially, the same procedures apply in most cases. There are a few exceptions. For example, a joint resolution proposing a new congressional amendment is not subject to presidential veto.

Powers of Congress

Section 8 Clause 1. The Congress shall have Power To lay and collect Taxes, Duties, Imposts and Excises, to pay the Debts and provide for the common Defence and general Welfare of the United States; but all Duties, Imposts and Excises shall be uniform throughout the United States.
Clause 2. To borrow Money on the credit of the United States;
CLause 3. To regulate Commerce with foreign Nations, and among the several States, and with the Indian Tribes;
Clause 4. To establish an uniform Rule of Naturalization, and uniform Laws on the subject of Bankruptcies throughout the United States;
Clause 5. To coin Money, regulate the Value thereof, and of foreign Coin, and fix the Standard of Weights and Measures;
Clause 6. To provide for the Punishment of counterfeiting the Securities and current Coin of the United States;
Clause 7, To establish Post Offices and post Roads;
Clause 8. To promote the Progress of Science and useful Arts, by securing for limited Times to Authors and Inventors the exclusive Right to their respective Writings and Discoveries;
Clause 9. To constitute Tribunals inferior to the supreme Court;
Clause 10. To define and punish Piracies and Felonies committed on the high Seas, and Offences against the Law of Nations;
Clause 11. To declare War, grant Letters of Marque and Reprisal, and make Rules concerning Captures on Land and Water;
Clause 12. To raise and support Armies, but no Appropriation of Money to that Use shall be for a longer Term than two Years;
Clause 13. To provide and maintain a Navy;
Clause 14. To make Rules for the Government and Regulation of the land and naval Forces;
Clause 15. To provide for calling forth the Militia to execute the Laws of the Union, suppress Insurrections and repel Invasions;
Clause 16. To provide for organizing, arming, and disciplining, the Militia, and for governing such Part of them as may be employed in the Service of the United States, reserving to the States respectively, the Appointment of the Officers, and the Authority of training the Militia according to the discipline prescribed by Congress;

These clauses establish what are known as the "expressed" or "specified" powers of Congress. In theory, they serve as a limit or brake on congressional power.

Clause 17. To exercise exclusive Legislation in all Cases whatsoever, over such District (not exceeding ten Miles square) as may, by Cession of particular States, and the Acceptance of Congress, become the Seat of the Government of the United States, and to exercise like Authority over all Places purchased by the Consent of the Legislature of the State in which the Same shall be, for the Erection of Forts, Magazines, Arsenals, dock-Yards, and other needful Buildings,—And

This clause establishes the seat of the federal government, which was first started in New York.

It eventually was moved to Washington, D.C., when both Maryland and Virginia ceded land to the new national government, which then established the District of Columbia.

Clause 18. To make all Laws which shall be necessary and proper for carrying into Execution the foregoing Powers, and all other Powers vested by this Constitution in the Government of the United States, or in any Department or Officer thereof.

This clause, known as the "Elastic Clause," provides the basis for the doctrine of "implied" congressional powers, which was first introduced in the U.S. Supreme Court case of *McCulloch v. Maryland*, 1819. This doctrine tremendously expanded the power of Congress to pass legislation and make regulations.

Powers Denied to Congress

Section 9   Clause 1. The Migration or Importation of such Persons as any of the States now existing shall think proper to admit, shall not be prohibited by the Congress prior to the Year one thousand eight hundred and eight, but a Tax or duty may be imposed on such Importation, not exceeding ten dollars for each Person.

This clause was part of the Three-Fifths Compromise. Essentially, the new Congress was prohibited from stopping the importation of slaves until 1808, but it could impose a head tax not to exceed ten dollars for each slave.

Clause 2. The Privilege of the Writ of Habeas Corpus shall not be suspended, unless when in Cases of Rebellion or Invasion the public Safety may require it.

Congress cannot suspend the writ of habeas corpus except in cases of rebellion or invasion. The writ of habeas corpus permits a judge to inquire about the legality of detention or deprivation of liberty of any citizen.

Clause 3. No Bill of Attainder or ex post facto Law shall be passed.

This provision prohibits Congress from passing either bills of attainder (forfeiture of property in capital cases) or ex post facto laws (retroactive crimes after passage of legislation). Similar restrictions were enshrined in many state constitutions.

Clause 4. No Capitation, or other direct, Tax shall be laid, unless in Proportion to the Census or Enumeration herein before directed to be taken.[6]

This clause prevents Congress from passing an income tax. Only with passage of the 16th Amendment in 1913 did Congress gain this power.

Clause 5. No Tax or Duty shall be laid on Articles exported from any State.

This section establishes free trade within the U.S. The federal government cannot tax state exports.

Clause 6. No Preference shall be given by any Regulation of Commerce or Revenue to the Ports of one State over those of another; nor shall Vessels bound to, or from, one State, be obliged to enter, clear, or pay Duties in another.

This clause also applies to free trade within the U.S. The national government cannot show any preference to any state or maritime movements among the states.

Clause 7. No Money shall be drawn from the Treasury, but in Consequence of Appropriations made by Law; and a regular Statement and Account of the Receipts and Expenditures of all public Money shall be published from time to time.

This provision of the Constitution prevents any expenditure unless it has been specifically provided for in an appropriations bill. At the beginning of most fiscal years, Congress has not completed its work on the budget. Technically, the government cannot spend any money according to this provision and would have to shut down. So Congress normally passes a Continuing Resolution Authority providing temporary authority to continue to spend money until the final budget is approved and signed into law.

Clause 8. No Title of Nobility shall be granted by the United States: And no Person holding any Office of Profit or Trust under them, shall, without the Consent of Congress, accept of any present, Emolument, Office, or Title, of any kind whatever, from any King, Prince, or foreign State.

Feudalism would not be established in the new country. We would have no nobles. No federal official can accept a title of nobility (even honorary) without permission of Congress.

Powers Denied to the States

This section sets out the prohibitions on state actions.

Section 10   Clause 1. No State shall enter into any Treaty, Alliance, or Confederation; grant Letters of Marque and Reprisal; coin Money; emit Bills of Credit; make any Thing but gold and silver Coin a Tender in Payment of Debts; pass any Bill of Attainder, ex post facto Law, or Law impairing the Obligation of Contracts, or grant any Title of Nobility.

This particular clause is a laundry list of denied powers. Note that these restrictions cannot even be waived by Congress. States are not to engage in foreign relations or acts of war. A letter of marque and reprisal was used during these times to provide legal cover for privateers. The federal government's currency monopoly is established. The sanctity of contracts is specified, and similar state prohibitions are specified for bills of attainder, ex post facto, etc.

Clause 2. No State shall, without the Consent of the Congress, lay any Imposts or Duties on Imports or Exports, except what

---

[6]Modified by the 16th Amendment

may be absolutely necessary for executing its inspection Laws: and the net Produce of all Duties and Imposts, laid by any State on Imports or Exports, shall be for the Use of the Treasury of the United States; and all such Laws shall be subject to the Revision and Controul of the Congress.

This section establishes the monopoly control of the national government in matters of both national and international trade. The only concession to states is health and safety inspections.

Clause 3. No State shall, without the Consent of Congress, lay any Duty of Tonnage, keep Troops, or Ships of War in time of Peace, enter into any Agreement or Compact with another State, or with a foreign Power, or engage in War, unless actually invaded, or in such imminent Danger as will not admit of delay.

This final section of the Legislative article establishes the war monopoly power of the national government. The only exception to state action is actual invasion or threat of imminent danger.

ARTICLE II—THE EXECUTIVE ARTICLE

This article establishes an entirely new concept in government—an elected executive power.

Nature and Scope of Presidential Power

Section 1 Clause 1. The executive Power shall be vested in a President of the United States of America. He shall hold his Office during the Term of four Years, and, together with the Vice President, chosen for the same Term, be elected as follows

This clause establishes the executive power in the office of the president of the United States of America. It also establishes a second office—vice president. A four-year term was established, but not a limit on the number of terms. A limit was later established by the 22nd Amendment.

Clause 2. Each State shall appoint, in such Manner as the Legislature thereof may direct, a Number of Electors, equal to the whole Number of Senators and Representatives to which the State may be entitled in the Congress: but no Senator or Representative, or Person holding an Office of Trust or Profit under the United States, shall be appointed an Elector.

This paragraph essentially establishes the electoral college to choose the president and vice president.

Clause 3. The Electors shall meet in their respective States, and vote by Ballot for two Persons, of whom one at least shall not be an Inhabitant of the same State with themselves. And they shall make a List of all the Persons voted for, and of the Number of Votes for each; which List they shall sign and certify, and transmit sealed to the Seat of the Government of the United States, directed to the President of the Senate. The President of the Senate shall, in the Presence of the Senate and House of Representatives, open all the Certificates, and the Votes shall then be counted. The Person having the greatest Number of Votes shall be the President, if such Number be a Majority of the whole Number of Electors appointed; and if there be more than one who have such Majority and have an equal Number of Votes,

then the House of Representatives shall immediately chuse by Ballot one of them for President; and if no Person have a Majority, then from the five highest on the List the said House shall in like Manner chuse the President. But in chusing the President, the Votes shall be taken by States, the Representation from each State having one Vote; A quorum for this Purpose shall consist of a Member or Members from two thirds of the States, and a Majority of all the States shall be necessary to a Choice. In every Case, after the Choice of the President, the Person having the greatest Number of Votes of the Electors shall be the Vice President. But if there should remain two or more who have equal Votes, the Senate shall chuse from them by Ballot the Vice President.[7]

This paragraph has been superseded by the 12th Amendment. The original language did not require a separate vote for president and vice president. This resulted in a tied vote in the electoral college in 1800 when both Thomas Jefferson and Aaron Burr received 73 electoral votes. The 12th Amendment requires a separate vote for each. Only one of the two can be from the state of the elector. This means that it is highly unlikely that the presidential and vice presidential candidates would be from the same state. This question arose in the 2000 election when Dick Cheney, who lived and worked in Texas, had to reestablish his residence in Wyoming.

The original language provided for a House election in the case of no majority vote or a tie vote among the top five candidates. The amendment lowered the number of candidates to the top three. The Senate is to select the vice president if a candidate does not have an electoral majority or in the case of a tie vote. The Senate considers only the top two candidates. The amendment also clarifies that the qualifications of the vice president are the same as those for president.

Clause 4. The Congress may determine the Time of chusing the Electors, and the Day on which they shall give their Votes; which Day shall be the same throughout the United States.

Congress is given the power to establish a uniform day and time for the state selection of electors.

Clause 5. No Person except a natural born Citizen, or a Citizen of the United States, at the time of the Adoption of this Constitution, shall be eligible to the Office of President; neither shall any Person be eligible to that Office who shall not have attained to the Age of thirty five Years, and been fourteen Years a Resident within the United States.

The qualifications for the offices of president and vice president are specified here—at least 35 years old, 14 years' resident in the U.S., and a natural-born citizen or citizen of the U.S. The 14th Amendment clarified who is a citizen of the U.S., a person born or naturalized in the U.S. and subject to its jurisdiction. But the term "natural-born citizen" is unclear and has never been further defined by the judicial branch. Does it mean born in the U.S. or born of U.S.

---

[7]Changed by the 12th and 20th Amendments

citizens in the U.S. or somewhere else in the world? Unfortunately, there is no definitive answer.

Clause 6. In Case of the Removal of the President from Office, or of his Death, Resignation, or Inability to discharge the Powers and Duties of the said Office, the Same shall devolve on the Vice President, and the Congress may by Law provide for the Case of Removal, Death, Resignation or Inability, both of the President and Vice President, declaring what Officer shall then act as President, and such Officer shall act accordingly, until the Disability be removed, or a President shall be elected.[8]

This clause has been modified by the 25th Amendment. Upon the death, resignation, or impeachment conviction of the president, the vice president becomes president. The new president nominates a new vice president, who assumes the office if approved by a majority vote in both congressional branches. The president is also now able to notify the Congress of his inability to perform his office.

Clause 7. The President shall, at stated Times, receive for his Services, a Compensation, which shall neither be encreased nor diminished during the Period for which he shall have been elected, and he shall not receive within that Period any other Emolument from the United States, or any of them.

This section covers the compensation of the president, which cannot be increased or decreased during his office. The current salary is $400,000/year.

Clause 8. Before he enter on the Execution of his Office, he shall take the following Oath or Affirmation:—"I do solemnly swear (or affirm) that I will faithfully execute the Office of President of the United States, and will to the best of my Ability, preserve, protect and defend the Constitution of the United States."

This final clause in Section 1 is the oath of office administered to the new president.

Powers and Duties of the President

Section 2 Clause 1. The President shall be Commander in Chief of the Army and Navy of the United States, and of the Militia of the several States, when called into the actual Service of the United States; he may require the Opinion, in writing, of the principal Officer in each of the executive Departments, upon any Subject relating to the Duties of their respective Offices, and he shall have Power to grant Reprieves and Pardons for Offences against the United States, except in Cases of Impeachment.

This clause establishes the president as Commander-in-Chief of the U.S. armed forces. George Washington was the only U.S. president to actually lead U.S. armed forces, during the Whiskey Rebellion. The second provision provides the basis for cabinet meetings that are used to acquire the opinions of executive department heads. The last provision provides an absolute pardon or reprieve power from the president. The provision was controversial, but

---

[8]Modified by the 25th Amendment

legal, when former President Clinton pardoned fugitive Marc Rich.

Clause 2. He shall have Power, by and with the Advice and Consent of the Senate, to make Treaties, provided two thirds of the Senators present concur; and he shall nominate, and by and with the Advice and Consent of the Senate, shall appoint Ambassadors, other public Ministers and Consuls, Judges of the supreme Court, and all other Officers of the United States, whose Appointments are not herein otherwise provided for, and which shall be established by Law: but the Congress may by Law vest the Appointment of such inferior Officers, as they think proper, in the President alone, in the Courts of Law, or in the Heads of Departments.

This clause covers two important presidential powers: treaty making and appointments. The president (via the State Department) can negotiate treaties with other nations, but these do not become official until ratified by a 2/3 vote of the U.S. Senate. The president is empowered to appoint judges, ambassadors, and other U.S. officials (cabinet officers, military officers, agency heads, etc.) subject to Senate approval. The Congress can and does delegate this approval to the president in the case of inferior officers. For example, junior military officer promotions are not submitted to the Senate, but senior officer promotions are.

Clause 3. The President shall have Power to fill up all Vacancies that may happen during the Recess of the Senate, by granting Commissions which shall expire at the End of their next Session.

This provision allows recess appointments of the officials listed in Clause 2 above. These commissions automatically expire unless approved by the Senate by the end of the next session. Presidents have used this provision to fill jobs when the nomination process is stalled. Some of these appointments have been very controversial. The regular nomination was stalled because the Senate did not want to confirm the nominee.

Section 3 He shall from time to time give to the Congress Information of the State of the Union, and recommend to their Consideration such Measures as he shall judge necessary and expedient; he may, on extraordinary Occasions, convene both Houses, or either of them, and in Case of Disagreement between them, with Respect to the Time of Adjournment, he may adjourn them to such Time as he shall think proper; he shall receive Ambassadors and other public Ministers; he shall take Care that the Laws be faithfully executed, and shall Commission all the Officers of the United States.

This section provides for the annual State of the Union address to a joint session of Congress and the American people. The president is also authorized to call special meetings of either the House or Senate. If there is disagreement between the House and Senate regarding adjournment, the president is empowered to adjourn them. This would be extremely rare. The president formally receives other nations' ambassadors. The next to last provision to faithfully execute laws provides the basis for the whole administrative apparatus of the presidency. All officers of the U.S. receive a formal commission

from the president (most of these are signed with a signature machine).

Section 4 The President, Vice President and all civil Officers of the United States, shall be removed from Office on Impeachment for, and Conviction of, Treason, Bribery, or other high Crimes and Misdemeanors.

This section provides the constitutional authority for the impeachment and trial of the president, vice president, and all civil officers of the U.S. for treason, bribery, or other high crimes and misdemeanors (the exact meaning of this phrase is unclear and is often more political than judicial).

ARTICLE III—THE JUDICIAL ARTICLE

Judicial Power, Courts, Judges

Section 1 The judicial Power of the United States, shall be vested in one supreme Court, and in such inferior Courts as the Congress may from time to time ordain and establish. The Judges, both of the supreme and inferior Courts, shall hold their Offices during good Behaviour, and shall, at stated Times, receive for their Services, a Compensation, which shall not be diminished during their Continuance in Office.

This section establishes the judicial branch in very general terms. It specifically provides only for the Supreme Court. Congress is given the responsibility of creating the court system. It initially did so in the Judiciary Act of 1789, when it established 13 district courts (one for each state) and 3 appellate courts. All federal judges hold their offices for life and can only be removed for breaches of good behavior—a very nebulous term. Federal judges have been removed for drunkenness, accepting bribes, and other misdemeanors. To date, no justice of the U.S. Supreme Court has ever been removed.

The salary of federal judges is set by congressional act but can never be reduced. Although the American Bar Association and the Federal Bar Association consider federal judges' salaries inadequate, most Americans would probably disagree. Federal district judges earn $145,100/year, appellate judges $153,900, and Supreme Court justices $178,300. The Chief Justice is paid $186,300. These are lifetime salaries, even upon retirement.

Jurisdiction

Section 2 Clause 1. The judicial Power shall extend to all Cases, in Law and Equity, arising under this Constitution, the Laws of the United States, and Treaties made, or which shall be made, under their Authority;—to all Cases affecting Ambassadors, other public Ministers and Consuls;—to all Cases of admiralty and maritime Jurisdiction;—to Controversies to which the United States shall be a Party;—to Controversies between two or more States—between a State and Citizens of another State;[9]—between Citizens of different States;—between Citizens of the same State claiming Lands under Grants of different States, and between a State, or the Citizens thereof, and foreign States, Citizens, or Subjects.

---

[9]Modified by the 11th Amendment

Clause 2. In all Cases affecting Ambassadors, other public Ministers and Consuls, and those in which a State shall be Party, the supreme Court shall have original Jurisdiction. In all the other Cases before mentioned, the supreme Court shall have appellate Jurisdiction, both as to Law and Fact, with such Exceptions, and under such Regulations as Congress shall make.

Clause 3. The Trial of all Crimes, except in Cases of Impeachment, shall be by Jury; and such Trial shall be held in the State where the said Crimes shall have been committed; but when not committed within any State, the Trial shall be at such Place or Places as the Congress may by Law have directed.

This section establishes the original and appellate jurisdiction of the U.S. Supreme Court. With the Congress of Vienna's 1815 establishment of "diplomatic immunity," the U.S. Supreme Court no longer hears cases involving ambassadors. Since 1925, the Supreme Court no longer hears every case on appeal but can select which cases it will accept, which is now only about 150 cases per year. This section also establishes the right of trial by jury for federal crimes.

Treason

Section 3 Clause 1. Treason against the United States, shall consist only in levying War against them, or in adhering to their Enemies, giving them Aid and Comfort. No Person shall be convicted of Treason unless on the Testimony of two Witnesses to the same overt Act, or on Confession in open Court.

Clause 2. The Congress shall have Power to declare the Punishment of Treason, but no Attainder of Treason shall work Corruption of Blood, or Forfeiture except during the Life of the Person attainted.

Treason is the only crime defined in the U.S. Constitution. Congress established the penalty of death for treason convictions. Note that two witnesses are required to convict anyone of treason. Even in cases of treasonable conduct, seizure of estates is prohibited.

ARTICLE IV—INTERSTATE RELATIONS

Full Faith and Credit Clause

Section 1 Full Faith and Credit shall be given in each State to the public Acts, Records, and judicial Proceedings of every other State. And the Congress may by general Laws prescribe the Manner in which such Acts, Records and Proceedings shall be proved, and the Effect thereof.

This section provides that the official acts and records of one state will be recognized and given credence by other states, e.g., marriages and divorces.

Privileges and Immunities; Interstate Extradition

Section 2 Clause 1. The Citizens of each State shall be entitled to all Privileges and Immunities of Citizens in the several States.

This clause requires states to treat citizens of other states equally. For example, when driving in another state, a driver's license is recognized. One area not so clear is that of charging higher tuitions for out-of-state students at educational institutions.

Clause 2. A person charged in any State with Treason, Felony or other Crime, who shall flee from Justice, and be found in another State, shall on Demand of the executive Authority of the State from which he fled, be delivered up, to be removed to the State having Jurisdiction of the Crime.

Extradition is the name of this clause. A criminal fleeing to another state, if captured, can be returned to the state where the crime was committed. But this is not an absolute. A state's governor can refuse, for good reason, to extradite someone to another state.

Clause 3. No person held to Service or Labour in one State, under the Laws thereof, escaping into another, shall, in Consequence of any Law or Regulation therein, be discharged from such Service or Labour, but shall be delivered up on Claim of the Party to whom such Service or Labour may be due.[10]

This clause was included to cover runaway slaves. It has been made inoperable by the 13th Amendment, which abolished slavery.

Admission of States

Section 3   Clause 1. New States may be admitted by the Congress into this Union; but no new State shall be formed or erected within the Jurisdiction of any other State; nor any State be formed by the Junction of two or more States, or Parts of States, without the Consent of the Legislatures of the States concerned as well as of the Congress.

Clause 2. The Congress shall have Power to dispose of and make all needful Rules and Regulations respecting the Territory or other Property belonging to the United States; and nothing in this Constitution shall be so construed as to Prejudice any Claims of the United States, or of any particular State.

This section concerns the admission of new states to the Union. In theory, no state can be created from part of another state without permission of the state legislature. But West Virginia was formed from Virginia during the Civil War without the permission of Virginia, which was part of the Confederacy. With fifty states now part of the Union, this section has not been used for many decades. The only future use may be in the case of Puerto Rico or perhaps Washington, D.C.

Republican Form of Government

Section 4   The United States shall guarantee to every State in this Union a Republican Form of Government, and shall protect each of them against Invasion; and on Application of the Legislature, or of the Executive (when the Legislature cannot be convened) against domestic Violence.

This section commits the federal government to guarantee a republican form of government to each state and to protect the states against foreign invasion or domestic insurrection.

---

[10]Repealed by the 13th Amendment

ARTICLE V—THE AMENDING POWER

The Congress, whenever two thirds of both Houses shall deem it necessary, shall propose Amendments to this Constitution, or, on the Application of the Legislatures of two thirds of the several States, shall call a Convention for proposing Amendments, which, in either Case, shall be valid to all Intents and Purposes, as Part of this Constitution, when ratified by the Legislatures of three fourths of the several States, or by Conventions in three fourths thereof, as the one or the other Mode of Ratification may be proposed by the Congress; Provided that no Amendment which may be made prior to the Year One thousand eight hundred and eight shall in any Manner affect the first and fourth Clauses in the Ninth Section of the first Article; and that no State, without its Consent, shall be deprived of its equal Suffrage in the Senate.

Amendments to the U.S. Constitution can be originated by a 2/3 vote in both the U.S. House and Senate or by 2/3 of the state legislatures asking for a convention to propose amendments. Proposed amendments, by either route, must be approved by 3/4 of state legislatures or by 3/4 of conventions convened in the states for purposes of ratification. Only one amendment has been ratified by the convention method—Amendment 21 to repeal the 18th Amendment establishing Prohibition.

Thousands of amendments have been proposed; few have been passed by 2/3 vote in each branch of Congress. The Equal Rights Amendment was one such case, but it was not ratified by 3/4 of state legislatures. There have only been 27 successful amendments to the U.S. Constitution.

ARTICLE VI—THE SUPREMACY ACT

Clause 1. All Debts contracted and Engagements entered into, before the Adoption of this Constitution, shall be as valid against the United States under this Constitution, as under the Confederation.

This clause made the new national government responsible for all debts incurred during the Revolutionary War. This was very important to banking and commercial interests.

Clause 2. This Constitution, and the Laws of the United States which shall be made in Pursuance thereof; and all Treaties made, or which shall be made, under the Authority of the United States, shall be the supreme Law of the Land; and the Judges in every State shall be bound thereby, any Thing in the Constitution or Laws of any State to the Contrary notwithstanding.

This is the National Supremacy Clause, which provides the basis for the supremacy of the national government.

Clause 3. The Senators and Representatives before mentioned, and the Members of the several State Legislatures, and all executive and judicial Officers, both of the United States and of the several States, shall be bound by Oath or Affirmation, to support this Constitution; but no religious Test shall ever be required as a Qualification to any Office or public Trust under the United States.

This clause requires essentially all federal and state officials to swear or affirm their allegiance to and support of the U.S. Constitution. Note that a religious test was prohibited for federal office. However, some states used religious tests for voting and office qualification until the 1830s.

ARTICLE VII—RATIFICATION

The Ratification of the Conventions of nine States, shall be sufficient for the Establishment of this Constitution between the States so ratifying the Same.

Done in Convention by the Unanimous Consent of the States present the Seventeenth Day of September in the Year of our Lord one thousand seven hundred and Eighty seven and of the Independence of the United States of America the Twelfth. *In Witness whereof We have hereunto subscribed our Names.*

AMENDMENTS

Realizing the unanimous ratification of the new Constitution by the 13 states might never have occurred, the framers wisely specified that only 9 states would be needed for ratification. Even this proved to be a test of wills between Federalists and Anti-Federalists, leading to publication of the great political work *The Federalist Papers.*

THE BILL OF RIGHTS

[The first ten amendments were ratified on December 15, 1791, and form what is known as the "Bill of Rights."]

The Bill of Rights applied initially only to the federal government and not to state or local governments. Beginning in 1925 in the case of *Gitlow v. New York*, the U.S. Supreme Court began to selectively incorporate the Bill of Rights, making its provisions applicable to state and local governments. There are only three exceptions, which will be discussed at the appropriate amendment.

AMENDMENT 1—RELIGION, SPEECH, ASSEMBLY, AND POLITICS

Congress shall make no law respecting an establishment of religion, or prohibiting the free exercise thereof; or abridging the freedom of speech, or of the press; or the right of the people peaceably to assemble, and to petition the Government for a redress of grievances.

This is the godfather of all amendments in that it protects five fundamental freedoms: religion, speech, press, assembly, and petition. Note that the press is the only business that is specifically protected by the U.S. Constitution. Freedom of religion and speech are two of the most contentious issues and generate a multitude of Supreme Court cases.

AMENDMENT 2—MILITIA AND THE RIGHT TO BEAR ARMS

A well-regulated Militia, being necessary to the security of a free State, the right of the people to keep and bear Arms, shall not be infringed.

This amendment is the favorite of the National Rifle Association. This amendment also has not been incorporated for state/local governments; that is, state and local governments are free to regulate arms within their respective jurisdictions. There is also controversy as to the meaning of this amendment. Some believe that it specifically refers to citizen militias, which were common at the time of the Constitution but now have been replaced by permanent armed forces. Therefore, is the amendment still applicable? Do private citizens need weapons for the security of a free state?

AMENDMENT 3—QUARTERING OF SOLDIERS

No Soldier shall, in time of peace be quartered in any house, without the consent of the Owner, nor in time of war, but in manner to be prescribed by law.

It was the practice of the British government to insist that colonists provide room or board to British troops. This amendment was designed to prohibit this practice. Today, military and naval bases provide the necessary quarters.

AMENDMENT 4—SEARCHES AND SEIZURES

The right of the people to be secure in their persons, houses, papers, and effects, against unreasonable searches and seizures, shall not be violated, and no Warrants shall issue, but upon probable cause, supported by Oath or affirmation, and particularly describing the place to be searched, and the persons or things to be seized.

This extremely important amendment is designed to prevent the abuse of state police powers. Essentially, unreasonable searches or seizures of homes, persons, or property cannot be undertaken without probable cause or a warrant that specifically describes the place to be searched, the person involved, and the suspicious things to be seized.

AMENDMENT 5—GRAND JURIES, SELF-INCRIMINATION, DOUBLE JEOPARDY, DUE PROCESS, AND EMINENT DOMAIN

No person shall be held to answer for a capital, or otherwise infamous crime, unless on a presentment or indictment of a Grand jury, except in cases arising in the land or naval forces, or in the Militia, when in actual service in time of War or public danger; nor shall any person be subject for the same offence to be twice put in jeopardy of life or limb; nor shall be compelled in any criminal case to be a witness against himself, nor be deprived of life, liberty, or property, without due process of law; nor shall private property be taken for public use, without just compensation.

Only a grand jury can indict a person for a federal crime. This provision does not apply to state/local governments. This amendment also covers double jeopardy, or being tried twice for the same crime in the same jurisdiction. Note that since the federal government and state governments are different jurisdictions, one could be tried in each jurisdiction for essentially the same crime. For example, it is a federal crime to kill a congressperson. It is also a state crime to murder anyone. Further, this amendment also covers the prohibition of self-incrimination. Pleading the 5th Amendment used to be common in Mafia cases but recently was used by Enron witnesses. The deprivation of life, liberty, or property by any level of government is prohibited unless due process of law is applied. Finally, private property may not be taken under the doctrine of "eminent domain" unless the government provides just compensation.

AMENDMENT 6—CRIMINAL COURT PROCEDURES

In all criminal prosecutions, the accused shall enjoy the right to a speedy and public trial, by an impartial jury of the State and district wherein the crime shall have been committed, which district shall have been previously ascertained by law, and to be informed of the nature and cause of the accusation; to be confronted with the witnesses against him; to have compulsory process for obtaining witnesses in his favor, and to have the Assistance of Counsel for his defence.

This amendment requires public trials by jury for criminal prosecutions. Anyone accused of a crime is guaranteed the rights to be informed of the charges; to confront witnesses; to subpoena witnesses for their defense; and to have a lawyer for their defense. Currently, the government must provide a lawyer for a defendant unable to afford one.

AMENDMENT 7—TRIAL BY JURY IN COMMON LAW CASES

In Suits at common law, where the value in controversy shall exceed twenty dollars, the right of trial by jury shall be preserved, and no fact tried by a jury shall be otherwise re-examined in any Court of the United States, than according to the rules of the common law.

This amendment is practically without meaning in modern times. Statutory law has largely superseded common law. Federal civil law suits with a guaranteed jury are now restricted to cases that exceed $50,000. The Bill of Rights, which includes the right to trial by jury, applied originally only to the national government. Beginning in 1925, the Supreme Court began a selective process of incorporating provisions in the Bill of Rights and making them applicable to state/ local governments as well. There are just a few provisions that have not been thus incorporated. Trial by jury is one. Some state/local governments have trials by judges, not by juries.

AMENDMENT 8—BAIL, CRUEL AND UNUSUAL PUNISHMENT

Excessive bail shall not be required, nor excessive fines imposed, nor cruel and unusual punishments inflicted.

Capital punishment is covered by this amendment, which also prohibits excessive bail. But this is relative. Million-dollar bails are not uncommon in some cases. One federal judge offered voluntary castration for sex offenders in lieu of jail time. Higher courts held this to be a cruel or unusual punishment. But it is the death penalty that generates the most heated controversy. Court cases challenging the constitutionality of capital punishment cite this amendment's language prohibiting cruel and unusual punishment. For a period of 4 years, the Supreme Court banned capital punishment. When states modified their statutes to provide a two part judicial process of guilt determination and punishment, the Supreme Court allowed the reinstitution of capital punishment by the states.

AMENDMENT 9—RIGHTS RETAINED BY THE PEOPLE

The enumeration in the Constitution, of certain rights, shall not be construed to deny or disparage others retained by the people.

This amendment implies that there may be other rights of the people not specified by the previous amendments. Indeed, the Warren Court established the right to privacy even though it is not specifically mentioned in any previous amendment. Some would claim that persons have a right to adequate medical care and education.

AMENDMENT 10—RESERVED POWERS OF THE STATES

The powers not delegated to the United States by the Constitution, nor prohibited by it to the States, are reserved to the States respectively, or to the people.

The 10th Amendment was seen as the reservoir of reserved powers for state governments. If the national government had been limited only to expressed powers in Article 1, Section 8, of the Constitution, this would have been the case. But the doctrine of implied national government powers, which was established by the U.S. Supreme Court in *McCulloch v. Maryland* in 1819, made the intent of this amendment almost meaningless. Any reserved powers that were retained by the states were virtually removed by the U.S. Supreme Court's decision in the *Garcia v. San Antonio Metropolitan Transit Authority* case in 1985, which basically told state/local governments not to look to the courts to protect their residual rights but rather to their political representatives. In subsequent cases, the Supreme Court has retreated somewhat from this position when the court found the federal government encroaching in state jurisdictional areas.

AMENDMENT 11—SUITS AGAINST THE STATES

[Ratified February 7, 1795]

The Judicial power of the United States shall not be construed to extend to any suit in law or equity, commenced or prosecuted against one of the United States by Citizens of another State, or by Citizens or Subjects of any Foreign State.

Article 3 of the U.S. Constitution originally allowed federal jurisdiction in cases of one state citizen against another state citizen or state. This amendment removes federal jurisdiction in this area. In essence, states may not be sued in federal court by citizens of another state or country.

AMENDMENT 12—ELECTION OF THE PRESIDENT

[Ratified June 15, 1804]

The Electors shall meet in their respective states, and vote by ballot for President and Vice-President, one of whom, at least, shall not be an inhabitant of the same state with themselves; they shall name in their ballots the person voted for as President, and in distinct ballots the person voted for as Vice-President, and they shall make distinct lists of all persons voted for as President, and of all persons voted for as Vice-President, and of the number of votes for each, which lists they shall sign and certify, and transmit sealed to the seat of the government of the United States, directed to the President of the Senate;—The President of the Senate shall, in the presence of the Senate and House of Representatives, open all the certificates and the votes shall then be counted;—The person having the greatest number of votes for President, shall be the President, if such number be a majority of the whole number of Electors appointed; and if no person have such majority, then from the persons having the highest numbers not exceeding three on the list of those voted for as President, the House of Representatives shall choose immediately, by ballot, the President. But in choosing the President, the votes shall be taken by states, the representation from each state having one vote; a quorum for this purpose shall consist of a member or members from two-thirds of the states, and a majority of all the states shall be necessary to a choice. And if the House of Representatives shall not choose a President whenever the right of choice shall devolve upon them, *before the fourth day of March next following*, then the Vice-President shall act as President, as in the case of the death or other constitutional disability of the President.[11] The person having the greatest number of votes as Vice-President, shall be the Vice-President, if such a number be a majority of the whole numbers of Electors appointed, and if no person have a majority, then from the two highest numbers on the list, the Senate shall choose the Vice-President; a quorum for the purpose shall consist of two-thirds of the whole number of Senators, and a majority of the whole number shall be necessary to a choice. But no person constitutionally ineligible to the office of President shall be eligible to that of Vice-President of the United States.

This was a necessary amendment to correct a flaw in the Constitution covering operations of the electoral college. In the election of 1800, Thomas Jefferson and Aaron Burr, both of the same Democratic-Republican Party, received the same number of electoral votes, 73, for president. Article II of the original Constitution specified that each elector would cast two ballots. It did not specify for whom. This amendment clarifies that the electoral vote must be specific for president and vice president. The original Constitution provided that if no candidate received a majority of electoral votes, the House would decide from the candidates with the top five vote totals. This amendment reduces the candidate field to the top three vote totals. If the House delays in this selection past the fourth day of March, the elected vice president will act as president until the House selects the president. The original Constitution provided that the candidate with the second highest number of electoral votes would become vice president.

This amendment, which requires a separate vote tally for vice president, provides for selection by the U.S. Senate if no vice presidential candidate receives an electoral vote majority.

AMENDMENT 13—PROHIBITION OF SLAVERY

[Ratified December 6, 1865]

Section 1   Neither slavery nor involuntary servitude, except as a punishment for crime whereof the party shall have been duly convicted, shall exist within the United States, or any place subject to their jurisdiction.

Section 2   Congress shall have power to enforce this article by appropriate legislation.

This is the first of the three Civil War amendments. Slavery is prohibited under all circumstances. Involuntary servitude is also prohibited unless it is a punishment for a convicted crime.

AMENDMENT 14—CITIZENSHIP, DUE PROCESS, AND EQUAL PROTECTION OF THE LAWS

[Ratified July 9, 1868]

Section 1   All persons born or naturalized in the United States, and subject to the jurisdiction thereof, are citizens of the United States and of the State wherein they reside. No State shall make or enforce any law which shall abridge the privileges or immunities of citizens of the United States; nor shall any State deprive any person of life, liberty, or property, without due process of law; nor deny to any person within its jurisdiction the equal protection of the laws.

This section defines the meaning of U.S. citizenship and protection of these citizenship rights. It also establishes the Equal Protection Clause that each state must guarantee to its citizens. It extended the provisions of the 5th Amendment of due process and protection of life, liberty, and property and made these applicable to the states.

Section 2   Representatives shall be apportioned among the several States according to their respective numbers, counting the whole number of persons in each State, excluding Indians not taxed. But when the right to vote at any election for the choice of electors for President and Vice President of the United States, Representatives in Congress, the Executive and Judicial officers of a State, or the members of the Legislature thereof, is denied to any of the male inhabitants of such State, being twenty-one[12] years of age, and citizens of the United States, or in any way abridged, except for participation in rebellion, or other crime, the basis of representation therein shall be reduced in the proportion which the number of such male citizens shall bear to the whole number of male citizens twenty-one years of age in such State.

---

[11]Changed by the 20th Amendment

[12]Changed by the 26th Amendment

This section changes the Three-Fifths Clause of the original Constitution. Now all male citizens, 21 or older, will be used to calculate representation in the House of Representatives. If a state denies the right to vote to any male 21 or older, the number of denied citizens will be deducted from the overall state total to determine representation.

Section 3 No person shall be a Senator or Representative in Congress, or elector of President and Vice President, or hold any office, civil or military, under the United States, or under any State, who, having previously taken an oath, as a member of Congress, or as an officer of the United States, or as a member of any State legislature, or as an executive or judicial officer of any State, to support the Constitution of the United States, shall have engaged in insurrection or rebellion against the same, or given aid or comfort to the enemies thereof. But Congress may by a vote of two-thirds of each House, remove such disability.

This section disqualifies from federal office or elector for president or vice president anyone who rebelled or participated in an insurrection against the Constitution. This was specifically directed against citizens of southern states. Congress by a 2/3 vote could override this provision.

Section 4 The validity of the public debt of the United States, authorized by law, including debts incurred for payment of pensions and bounties for services in suppressing insurrection or rebellion, shall not be questioned. But neither the United States nor any State shall assume or pay any debt or obligation incurred in aid of insurrection or rebellion against the United States, or any claim for the loss or emancipation of any slave; but all such debts, obligations and claims shall be held illegal and void.

Section 5 The Congress shall have power to enforce, by appropriate legislation, the provisions of this article.

Sections 4 and 5 cover the Civil War debts.

AMENDMENT 15—THE RIGHT TO VOTE

[Ratified February 3, 1870]

Section 1 The right of citizens of the United States to vote shall not be denied or abridged by the United States or by any State on account of race, color, or previous condition of servitude.

Section 2 The Congress shall have power to enforce this article by appropriate legislation.

This final Civil War amendment states that voting rights could not be denied by any states on account of race, color, or previous servitude. Unfortunately, it did not mention gender. Accordingly, only male citizens 21 or over were guaranteed the right to vote by this amendment.

AMENDMENT 16—INCOME TAXES

[Ratified February 3, 1913]

The Congress shall have power to lay and collect taxes on incomes, from whatever source derived, without apportionment among the several States, and without regard to any census or enumeration.

Article I, Section 9, of the original Constitution prohibited Congress from enacting a direct tax (head tax) unless in proportion to a census. Congress in 1894 passed an income tax law, levying a 2 percent tax on incomes over $4,000. In 1895, the U.S. Supreme Court in a split decision (5–4) found that the income tax was a direct tax not apportioned among the states and was thus unconstitutional. Thus, Congress proposed an amendment allowing it to enact an income tax. Once this amendment was ratified, the flow of tax money to Washington increased tremendously.

AMENDMENT 17—DIRECT ELECTION OF SENATORS

[Ratified April 8, 1913]

The Senate of the United States shall be composed of two Senators from each State, elected by the people thereof, for six years; and each Senator shall have one vote. The electors in each State shall have the qualifications requisite for electors of the most numerous branch of the State legislatures.

When vacancies happen in the representation of any State in the Senate, the executive authority of such State shall issue writs of election to fill such vacancies: Provided, That the legislature of any State may empower the executive thereof to make temporary appointments until the people fill the vacancies by election as the legislature may direct.

This amendment shall not be so construed as to affect the election or term of any Senator chosen before it becomes valid as part of the Constitution.

Prior to this amendment, U.S. senators were selected by state legislatures. Now U.S. senators would be selected by popular vote in each state. Further, the governor of each state may fill vacancies, subject to state laws.

AMENDMENT 18—PROHIBITION

[Ratified January 16, 1919. Repealed December 5, 1933 by Amendment 21]

Section 1 After one year from the ratification of this article the manufacture, sale, or transportation of intoxicating liquors within, the importation thereof into, or the exportation thereof from the United States and all territory subject to the jurisdiction thereof for beverage purposes is hereby prohibited.

Section 2 The Congress and the several States shall have concurrent power to enforce this article by appropriate legislation.

Section 3 This article shall be inoperative unless it shall have been ratified as an amendment to the Constitution by the legislatures of the several States, as provided in the Constitution, within seven years from the date of the submission hereof to the States by the Congress.[13]

This amendment was largely the work of the Women's Christian Temperance Union and essentially banned the manufacture, sale, or transportation of alcoholic beverages. Unintended consequences

---

[13]Repealed by the 21st Amendment

of this attempt to legislate morality were the brewing of "bathtub gin" and moonshine liquor, the involvement of the mob in importing liquor from Canada, and the "Untouchables" of Eliot Ness. Fortunately, this ill-fated social experiment was corrected by the 21st Amendment. This is also the first amendment where Congress fixed a period for ratification— 7 years.

AMENDMENT 19—FOR WOMEN'S SUFFRAGE

[Ratified August 18, 1920]

The right of the citizens of the United States to vote shall not be denied or abridged by the United States or by any State on account of sex.

Congress shall have power to enforce this article.

At long last, women achieved voting parity with men.

AMENDMENT 20—THE LAME DUCK AMENDMENT

[Ratified January 23, 1933]

Section 1 The terms of the President and Vice President shall end at noon on the 20th day of January, and the terms of the Senators and Representatives at noon on the 3d day of January, of the years in which such terms would have ended if this article had not been ratified; and the terms of their successors shall then begin.

Section 2 The Congress shall assemble at least once in every year, and such meeting shall begin at noon on the 3d day of January, unless they shall by law appoint a different day.

Section 3 If, at the time fixed for the beginning of the term of the President, the President elect shall have died, the Vice President elect shall become President. If a President shall not have been chosen before the time fixed for the beginning of his term, or if the President elect shall have failed to qualify, then the Vice President elect shall act as President until a President shall have qualified; and the Congress may by law provide for the case wherein neither a President elect nor a Vice President elect shall have qualified, declaring who shall then act as President, or the manner in which one who is to act shall be selected, and such person shall act accordingly until a President or Vice President shall have qualified.

Section 4 The Congress may by law provide for the case of the death of any of the persons from whom the House of Representatives may choose a President whenever the right of choice shall have devolved upon them, and for the case of the death of any of the persons from whom the Senate may choose a Vice President whenever the right of choice shall have devolved upon them.

Section 5 Sections 1 and 2 shall take effect on the 15th day of October following the ratification of this article.

Section 6 This article shall be inoperative unless it shall have been ratified as an amendment to the Constitution by the legislatures of three-fourths of the several States within seven years from the date of its submission.

Called the Lame Duck amendment, this amendment fixes the dates for the end of presidential and legislative terms. A new president is elected in November, but the current president remains in office until January 20 of the following year. Thus,

the term "lame duck." Legislative terms begin earlier, on January 3.

AMENDMENT 21—REPEAL OF PROHIBITION

[Ratified December 5, 1933]

Section 1 The eighteenth article of amendment to the Constitution of the United States is hereby repealed.

Section 2 The transportation or importation into any State, Territory, or possession of the United States for delivery or use therein of intoxicating liquors, in violation of the laws thereof, is hereby prohibited.

Section 3 This article shall be inoperative unless it shall have been ratified as an amendment to the Constitution by conventions in the several States, as provided in the Constitution, within seven years from the date of the submission hereof to the States by the Congress.

This unusual amendment nullified the 18th Amendment. The amendment called for the end of Prohibition unless prohibited by state laws.

AMENDMENT 22—NUMBER OF PRESIDENTIAL TERMS

[Ratified February 27, 1951]

Section 1 No person shall be elected to the office of the President more than twice, and no person who has held the office of President, or acted as President, for more than two years of a term to which some other person was elected President shall be elected to the office of the President more than once. But this article shall not apply to any person holding the office of President when this article was proposed by the Congress, and shall not prevent any person who may be holding the office of President, or acting as President, during the term within which this article becomes operative from holding the office of President or acting as President during the remainder of such term.

Section 2 This article shall be inoperative unless it shall have been ratified as an amendment to the Constitution by the legislatures of three-fourths of the several states within seven years from the date of its submission to the states by the Congress.

This amendment could be called the Franklin D. Roosevelt amendment. It was FDR who broke the previously unwritten rule of serving no more than two terms as president. Democrat Roosevelt won an unprecedented four terms as president. When the Republicans took control of the Congress in 1948, they pushed through the 22nd Amendment, limiting the U.S. president to a lifetime of two full four-year terms of office.

AMENDMENT 23—PRESIDENTIAL ELECTORS FOR THE DISTRICT OF COLUMBIA

[Ratified March 29, 1961]

Section 1 The District constituting the seat of government of the United States shall appoint in such manner as the Congress may direct:

A number of electors of President and Vice President equal to the whole number of Senators and Representatives in Congress to which the District would be entitled if it were a state, but in no event more than the least populous state; they shall be in addition to those appointed by the states, but they shall be considered, for the purposes of the election of President and Vice President, to be electors appointed by a state; and they shall meet in the District and perform such duties as provided by the twelfth article of amendment.

Section 2 The Congress shall have power to enforce this article by appropriate legislation.

This amendment gave electoral votes to the citizens of Washington, D.C., which is not a state and thus not included in the original scheme of state electoral votes. Currently, Washington, D.C., has 3 electoral votes, bringing the total of presidential electoral votes to 538. Puerto Ricans are citizens of the U.S. but have no electoral votes.

Amendment 24—The Anti-Poll Tax Amendment

[Ratified January 23, 1964]

Section 1 The right of citizens of the United States to vote in any primary or other election for President or Vice President, for electors for President or Vice President, or for Senator or Representative in Congress, shall not be denied or abridged by the United States or any state by reason of failure to pay any poll tax or other tax.

Section 2 The Congress shall have power to enforce this article by appropriate legislation.

The poll tax was a procedure used mostly in southern states to discourage poor white and black voters from registering to vote. Essentially, one would have to pay a tax to register to vote. The tax was around $34/year. But for a poor white or black voter, this might not be disposable income. As part of the assault against disenfranchisement of voters, the poll tax was abolished. Literacy tests, another device to disqualify voters, were abolished by the Voting Rights Act of 1965.

Amendment 25—Presidential Disability, Vice Presidential Vacancies

[Ratified February 10, 1967]

Section 1 In case of the removal of the President from office or of his death or resignation, the Vice President shall become President.

Section 2 Whenever there is a vacancy in the office of the Vice President, the President shall nominate a Vice President who shall take the office upon confirmation by a majority vote of both Houses of Congress.

Section 3 Whenever the President transmits to the President pro tempore of the Senate and the Speaker of the House of Representatives his written declaration that he is unable to discharge the powers and duties of his office, and until he transmits to them a written declaration to the contrary, such powers and duties shall be discharged by the Vice President as Acting President.

Section 4 Whenever the Vice President and a majority of either the principal officers of the executive departments, or of such other body as Congress may by law provide, transmit to the President pro tempore of the Senate and the Speaker of the House of Representatives their written declaration that the President is unable to discharge the powers and duties of his office, the Vice President shall immediately assume the powers and duties of the office as Acting President.

Thereafter, when the President transmits to the President pro tempore of the Senate and the Speaker of the House of Representatives his written declaration that no inability exists, he shall resume the powers and duties of his office unless the Vice President and a majority of either the principal officers of the executive department, or of such other body as Congress may by law provide, transmit within four days to the President pro tempore of the Senate and the Speaker of the House of Representatives their written declaration that the President is unable to discharge the powers and duties of his office. Thereupon Congress shall decide the issue, assembling within forty-eight hours for that purpose if not in session. If the Congress, within twenty-one days after receipt of the latter written declaration, or, if Congress is not in session, within twenty-one days after Congress is required to assemble, determines by two-thirds vote of both Houses that the President is unable to discharge the powers and duties of his office, the Vice President shall continue to discharge the same as Acting President; otherwise, the President shall resume the powers and duties of his office.

President Woodrow Wilson's final year in office was marked by serious illness. It is rumored that his wife acted as president. There was no constitutional provision to cover an incapacitating illness of a president. This amendment provides a procedure for this eventuality. The president can inform congressional leaders of his incapacitation, and the vice president then takes over. When the president recovers, he can inform congressional leaders and resume office.

The amendment also recognizes that the president may not be able or wish to indicate this debilitation. In this case, the vice president and a majority of cabinet members can inform congressional leaders, and the vice president takes over. When the president informs congressional leadership that he is back in form, he resumes the presidency unless the vice president and a majority of the cabinet members disagree. Then Congress must decide who is to be president. The likelihood that this procedure will ever be used is relatively small.

The most immediate importance of this amendment concerns the office of vice president. The original Constitution did not address the issue of a vacancy in this office. The 25th Amendment established the procedure just in time! This amendment was ratified in 1967. In 1973, the sitting vice president, Spiro Agnew, resigned his office. Under the provisions of this amendment, President Nixon nominated Gerald Ford as vice president. As a former member of the House, Ford was quickly approved by the Congress. But a year later, President Nixon also resigned. Now Vice President Ford became President Ford, and he in turn appointed Nelson Rockefeller as the new vice president. For the first time in our history, we had both a president and vice president, neither of whom was elected by the electoral college.

AMENDMENT 26—EIGHTEEN-YEAR-OLD VOTE

[Ratified July 1, 1971]

Section 1 The right of citizens of the United States, who are 18 years of age or older, to vote, shall not be denied or abridged by the United States or by any state on account of age.

Section 2 The Congress shall have power to enforce this article by appropriate legislation.

During the Vietnam War, 18 year olds were being drafted and sent out to possibly die in the service of their country. Yet they did not even have the right to vote. This incongruity led to the 26th Amendment, which lowered the legal voting age from 21 to 18.

AMENDMENT 27—CONGRESSIONAL SALARIES

[Ratified May 7, 1992]

No law varying the compensation for the services of the Senators and Representatives shall take effect until an election of Representatives shall have intervened.

This is a "sleeper" amendment that was part of 12 amendments originally submitted by the first Congress to the states for ratification. The states only ratified 10 of the 12, which collectively became known as the Bill of Rights. But since Congress did not set a time limit for ratification, the other two amendments remained on the table. Much to the shock of the body politic, in 1992, 3/4 of the states ratified original amendment 12 of 12. This reflected the disgust of seeing Congress continuing to increase its salary and benefits. The amendment delays any increase of compensation for at least one election cycle.

3 FEDERALISM

CHAPTER OUTLINE

Approaching Democracy Case Study:
  Rebuilding New York City

Introduction: Federalism and Democracy

Federalism Defined

Federalism in the Constitution

The Division of Powers

The Development of Federalism

Presidents and Federalism

The Rehnquist Court and the Future
  of Federalism

Federalism and Approaching Democracy
  in the Twenty-First Century

APPROACHING DEMOCRACY CASE STUDY

Rebuilding New York City

"Our skyline will rise again. The people are going to be whole again." So spoke former New York City mayor Rudy Giuliani after viewing the horrific sight following the September 11, 2001, attack on the World Trade Center. Rebuilding New York City was a certainty, but who would make the decisions and provide the money? The answers came in the coordinated financial efforts of New York City, New York State, and the United States Government, led by the political partnership of Mayor Rudolph Giuliani, Governor George Pataki, President George W. Bush, and the United States Congress.

For Mayor Giuliani, the moments after the attack began with arriving at the WTC only to learn that the city's state-of-the-art government command center bunker at 7 World Trade Center was being evacuated. As he ventured from building to building trying to set up the city's government, the Mayor quickly realized that with the Pentagon blazing from another plane attack, and the White House being evacuated, except for federal military air cover, for the moment he was on his own in trying to deal with the crisis in his city. Then the South Tower, with its massive radio antenna, collapsed, temporarily trapping the Mayor and his team in a building on Barclay Street. Against the advice of his subordinates, the Mayor insisted on venturing out of the building to search for yet another place from which to run their government. As he did so, the Mayor conducted a series of walking press conferences seeking to reassure his city and a shocked nation. A few new command centers, countless improvised decisions, and dozens of informal press conferences and speeches later—only 16 hours had passed and the Mayor was already preparing to rebuild his beloved city. Guiliani became, in the words of *Time* magazine, "America's homeland-security boss," a "gutsy decision maker," "crisis manager" and "consoler in chief." In time, every speech the Mayor gave, always with New York Governor George Pataki standing silently behind him, he promised that his city would rise from the ashes. "Tomorrow New York is going to be here. And we're going to rebuild, and we're going to be stronger than we were before . . ."

The immediate rescue and recovery efforts by the people of New York City were awe-inspiring, but the question of how to pay for it all needed an answer. Hundreds of millions of dollars in goods, services, and donations overwhelmed the city. The three levels of government most involved—New York City, New York State, and the United States Government—would determine how to pay the monetary price for the attacks, which would reach in the scores of billions of dollars. Within days, the United States Congress pledged $40 billion in rebuilding funds as, what Majority Leader Tom Daschle called, "a down payment" on the effort. Everyone understood that it might cost $100 million to repair the Pentagon, but no one could predict the cost of restoring New York City to its original luster. By the end of October 2001, Governor Pataki was estimating the damage to New York State's economy as being $9 billion dollars, more than double what the state collects each year in business taxes. Knowing that the city and the state did not have the money to make up for this shortfall in a downturned economy, the Governor proposed a "Rebuild NY—Renew America" plan that called for an overall rebuilding plan of $54 billion dollars, which included $2 billion in tax-free bonds, $3 billion in aid to the victims' families, $3 billion in transportation project financing, and $12 billion in federal aid to compensate the city and state for lost tax revenue.

In time, federal money did flow to the city and the state. By mid-January 2002, Governor Pataki had $700 million in federal aid to hand out to crippled businesses and $400 million in federal mass transit money available for the building of a new PATH terminal near what was once the site of the World Trade Center towers, now Ground Zero. Small businesses crippled by the attack received another $371 million in federal aid, and another $285 million in federal grants, loans, and tax incentives flowed into New York City to help retain jobs and attract corporations to return to the city's financial district. By the end of that month, the Governor was asking the New York state legislature for the authority to oversee the more than $10.4 billion in expected federal aid. Since the money had not yet arrived, state legislators were reluctant, in the words of Assembly speaker Sheldon Silver, to "sign off on a blank check, what the purposes are for this money, how we are using it." The legislature was concerned that, after granting the governor blanket authority to distribute $5 billion in federal aid in September 2001, only $375 million in federal disaster relief had been passed through to the city of New York by January 2002. They argued that Congress had already put tight restrictions on the spending purposes of the $10.4 billion in city relief aid so there was no reason to give the Governor such latitude in spending. Much of this promised money consisted of block grants, including stipulations as to how it should be spent. So many guidelines were placed on the use of this money by Congress that Kevin Quinn, from Governor Pataki's budget office said, "The vast majority of these funds are simply passed on to New York City to meet their rebuilding and recovery needs." So, with the American people and their

▲ President George Bush and New York Governor George Pataki console New York City Mayor Rudy Giuliani as they survey the wreckage at Ground Zero.

elected representatives in Congress providing the money to rebuild New York, it will be left to negotiations among federal, state and local leaders, in the persons of President George W. Bush, New York Governor George Pataki, and the newly elected New York City Mayor Michael Bloomberg, as to just how that feat will be accomplished.[1]

Question for Reflection: What role should leaders at different levels of government play in times of crisis? Who should determine how federal money should be spent—Congress, the state through which the money is sent, or the cities and localities where the money is needed? Has the government done enough to help the attack sites recover, and if not, what more can be done?

INTRODUCTION: FEDERALISM AND DEMOCRACY

This case study illustrates the workings of the classic partnership among Congress, seeking a broad vision of national interests, the states, trying in this case to preserve **states' rights,** and localities, trying to resolve any differences between those visions while applying the larger policies to their region. At the heart of these negotiations over policy is the concept of federalism.

Few subjects in American government are as likely to serve as a cure for insomnia as federalism, yet few subjects are more important. If you doubt this, glance at the daily paper and see how many articles deal with the relations among the national, state, and local governments. A typical front page of a local newspaper might cover the new national crime bill that provides funding for state and local police; a state road that will not be funded because of changes in a bill dealing with the national highway system; or a flood hitting a local town and leading to a request for national assistance. All of these are examples of federalism in action.

This chapter begins with a definition of federalism. It then looks at federalism as outlined in the Constitution and how it has developed over the years. Finally, it examines the dynamic and changing nature of the federal structure. As you will see, as a result of a series of Supreme Court decisions and public policies, the government system we have now is far different from that envisioned by the framers. Federalism is one of America's unique contributions to democratic theory and republican government. Only by understanding how the system works can you come to understand how it has helped the United States approach democracy.

Federalism Defined

Federalism is a political system in which two or more distinct levels of government share and exercise power over the same body of citizens. The American system consists of an overarching national government sharing power with governmental subdivisions such as state and local governments.

To understand the nature of the federal system in America, it is important to know the framers' intentions in constructing it. The framers rejected the *unitary* system of government, one in which all of the power is vested in a central authority that could compel the state governments to respond. This was the relationship between the English monarchy and the American colonies. The framers also rejected the *confederation* system of government, in which the power to govern is decentralized among sovereign states, and the national government has such limited powers that it must respond to state dictates. This was the system of government under the Articles of Confederation. Instead, the framers sought to create a structure that combined the best features of both systems—a central government, strong

states' rights Those rights that have neither been granted to the national government nor forbidden to the states by the U.S. Constitution.

federalism A political system in which two or more distinct levels of government share and exercise power over the same body of citizens.

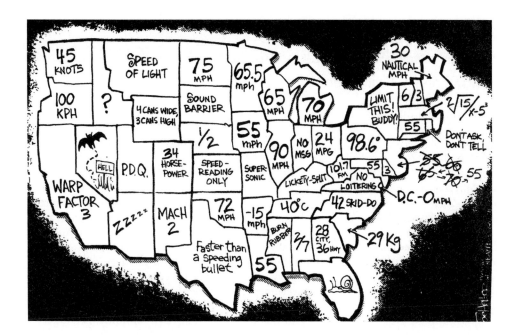

When Congress allows states to set their own speed limits.

Hiller's View, The Boston Globe.

enough to deal with the larger national problems, and a decentralized government at the state level, able to address the needs of the people at the state and local levels.

Building flexibility into the federal structure was also the intent of the framers. They wanted to delegate enough powers to the central government to allow it to govern the entire nation, thus correcting the weaknesses inherent in the Articles of Confederation. But they also saw functional reasons for maintaining powerful states within that system. As James Madison explained in *The Federalist*, no. 10: "The federal Constitution forms a happy combination in this respect; the great and aggregate interests being referred to the national, the local and particular, to the state legislatures."[2] In other words, the federal system was designed to consist of a national government limited to areas of common concern, while the power to make particular policy would remain with the states. Over the years, the gaps deliberately left in the Constitution regarding allocation of powers between the two levels of government have been filled by the experience of dealing with political problems. As a result, a new relationship was forged, leaving the national government as the controlling partner in the structure.

Federalism: Advantages and Disadvantages

National policy is the same for everyone, but state and local policy varies widely by region. Variations are found in tax policy, public programs, and services such as police and education. As we see in the box on civil unions and states' rights, the decision by the state of Vermont to allow gay "civil unions," with five other states considering following this policy, while 35 other states, including California, Colorado, and Oregon, and the federal government are adopting "defense of marriage" laws that seek to remove legal and constitutional protections from homosexuals, illustrates the need at times for an overarching national governmental policy to resolve a conflict. On the other hand, there are times when giving the states a chance to experiment with policy, as has been the case with affirmative action programs and welfare, produces programs adopted at the national level.

Advantages   There are many advantages to federalism. Rather than one uniform policy for everyone, diversity among policies and programs is ensured by the large number of different governments. Diverse policies are needed to accommodate a diverse populace across a vast country.

▲ Alabama governor George Wallace blocks the doorway of the all-white University of Alabama in 1963 to prevent two African American students from enrolling. The photo was all for publicity. With Deputy U.S. Attorney Nicholas Katzenbach looking on, Wallace then quietly stood aside, allowing the two students to enter. At the end of his life, Wallace, who had benefited from African American votes in later election successes, apologized.

APPROACHING DIVERSITY

Of Gay Marriages, Civil Unions, and States' Rights

Peter Harrigan and Stan Baker were thrilled to have the celebration of their union recognized not only by the guest attending their wedding ceremony on a Lake Champlain cruise ship dubbed "The Spirit of Ethan Allen," but by their state as well. As one of three same-sex couples who successfully persuaded the state of Vermont to pass a law in April, 2000 permitting same-sex couples to enjoy the "benefits and responsibilities" of marriage, they sparked a nationwide debate over gay rights by formalizing their "civil union." The Vermont law was passed in response to a December, 1999 state supreme court ruling ordering the legislature to provide gay couples the same rights that heterosexual couples enjoyed in marriage, everything from insurance coverage to golf memberships.

Vermont state officials were uncertain as to the effect this decision would have on the national gay rights debate. The Vermont decision had reversed the momentum of state decisions in Hawaii and California against gay rights. In Hawaii, the state supreme court upheld a 1998 amendment to the state constitution barring gay marriages. In California, the voters did the same by approving an initiative called Proposition 22 in the 2000 election, which barred the state from recognizing all same-sex marriages, even those legalized by other states. While supporters of the California measures claimed the initiative supported "family values," their vote effectively banned same-sex marriages and denied same-sex couples a series of benefits of marriage available to heterosexual married couples.

After the Vermont civil union law's passage, changes both within and outside the state of Vermont were significant. Over an 18 month period, from July 1, 2000 to January 4, 2002, 3,471 civil union licenses were issued in the state of Vermont; over two-thirds of the licenses were issued to female couples. In early 2002, the Vermont Supreme Court rejected a legal challenge to the law that it forced town clerks to issue such licenses in violation of their religious beliefs. The greatest question for the American federal system of government, however, is just what impact a law promising traditional marriage benefits to same sex marital-like relationships in one state will have on other governmental structures from the local and state, to the national level. While five states considered adopting either a civil union or a gay marriage bill, thirty-five other states and the U.S. Congress have passed so-called "defense of marriage" laws that define marriage as being solely an institution for heterosexual couples. Thirty-two states have banned outright same-sex marriages, with no state giving same-sex couples the right to marry. Congress, in its Defense of Marriage Act, denies federal recognition of same-sex marriages and permits states to ignore same-sex unions licensed by other states. A group calling itself the Alliance for Marriage announced that it would campaign for a United States Constitutional amendment banning same-sex marriages.

So, will the civil union law in Vermont have any effect on the rights of those couples in other states? Under the "full faith and credit clause" of the Constitution, which requires

Policy diversity also minimizes policy conflict. If groups are unsuccessful in passing their programs at the national level, they can try again at the state or local level, thus minimizing pressure on the national government for action. But should action fail at the state level, then the focus of attention can shift back to the national government. The greater the number of centers of power for implementing policy, the greater the opportunity for government to respond to the needs and desires of the people. One example of this pattern can be seen in the area of health care reform. When successive efforts to pass a national health insurance program covering everyone failed in the 1960s and 1970s, Vermont, Massachusetts, and Oregon passed their own programs. However, these state programs and others failed because of lack of financial resources and various political problems, thus shifting pressure for action back to the national government. As a result, President Bill Clinton pushed for national health care reform in 1994.[3] After Clinton's comprehensive proposal failed to pass, several states attempted again to establish their own health care programs. A more recent example comes from the field of education reform. In December of 2001 President Bush signed into law his "No Child Left Behind Act," an education reform act that was modeled on the President's home state of Texas's education plan which tests students to measure public school performance. Under this plan, states would receive over $26 billion in federal funds for education assistance especially for low income children, but in return they would have to institute additional student testing to measure the performance of the schools. While some

one state to observe the decrees and judgments of other states, gay rights advocates argue that once a state allows same-sex unions, then the benefits of marriage should be extended by other states. But others argue that the term "civil union" is a separate category that need not be observed by other states.

Indeed, the civil union is different from marriage. Under the Vermont law, only marriages are "sanctified" by clergy or justices of the peace, whereas civil unions are to be "certified." To end a marriage requires a divorce; same-sex couples can end their relationship by "dissolution." But the benefits of civil union for couples are very clear. Same-sex partners will be able to make decisions about their partner's health care and have their health care coverage cover both people. The new relationship would likely have an effect on custody fights and adoption requests. Couples in civil unions get breaks in inheritance and property taxes but would have to pay the increased "marriage penalty" that heterosexual couples pay for income taxes.

In Massachusetts seven gay couples, including one who had entered into a Vermont civil union, began the process of trying, through the state judicial system, to force the state to become the first to allow full same-sex marriage by suing in state court seeking the right to marry. "This is definitely the most important development of its kind in the area of gay rights," said Harvard Law school constitutional expert Laurence Tribe. "If people try to make a Vermont civil union portable to other states, it will wind up before the courts." Just what the United States Supreme Court will say when legal challenges under the Vermont or any future similar statutes reaches them is not clear. What is

▲ After the Vermont Supreme Court ordered lawmakers to provide gay couples with the same rights as married people, demonstrators marched in Montpelier to oppose the civil union bill then under consideration in the state capitol. The bill was eventually passed.

clear, though, is that any such decision will change the face of federalism in the United States.

Sources: Carlos Frias, "Ga. Court rejects same-sex bond," *The Atlanta Constitution,* January 26, 2002; Pamela Ferdinand, "With Vermont in the Lead: Controversy Progresses: Battle Over Same-Sex Unions Moves to Other States," *Washington Post,* September 4, 2001; Pamela Ferdinand, "Vermont Legislature Clears Bill Allowing Civil Unions," *Washington Post,* April 26, 2000, p. A3; and Fred Bayles, "Vermont Gay Union Bill Leaves Questions Unanswered," *USA Today,* April 17, 2000, p. 7.

praised the law's reliance on the education testing plan developed in Texas, others feared that this would become the means by which the federal government would take more control over the traditionally state-led education policy.[4]

Federalism also results in a healthy dispersal of power. The framers, concerned about a national government with too much power, reserved certain powers for the states. This dispersal of political power creates more opportunity for political participation. Individuals or political parties that cannot take power nationally have the opportunity in the federal structure to establish bases of power at state and local levels. Thus, the Republican party, which had no foothold in the national government in the early 1960s, was able to build a base of power at the state level and retake the White House in 1968 and the Congress in 1994.

America's system of federalism also enhances the prospects for governmental experimentation and innovation. Justice Louis D. Brandeis described this possibility when he wrote: "It is one of the happy incidents of the federal system that a single courageous state may, if its citizens choose, serve as a laboratory and try novel social and economic experiments without risk to the rest of the country."[5] Thus, the national government can observe which of the experimental programs undertaken by various states are working and perhaps adopt the best of those ideas for the rest of the nation. The Social Security Act, for example, was passed in 1935 to provide economic security for those over age sixty-five and unemployment insurance for the millions thrown out of work by the Depression. It was based on an unemployment program being used at the time in Wisconsin. Such was the case when the Bush Administration based its "No Child Left Behind Act" education reform plan on that of the state of Texas.

Disadvantages   But federalism has its disadvantages. The dispersal of power and opportunities for participation within the federal structure allows groups in certain regions to protect their interests, sometimes with the undemocratic result of obstructing and even ignoring national mandates. For example, into the 1960s, the southern states tried to perpetuate policies of segregation by citing states' rights. Ultimately legal discrimination in civil rights, housing, voting, and schools came to an end by federal law.

There are also inequities in a federal system. Poor regions cannot afford to provide the same services as wealthier ones. Thus, governmental programs at the local level can vary dramatically. Schools in the rich suburb of Scarsdale, New York, are very different from those in the poorer sections of south-central Los Angeles.

It takes a proper balance of national and state powers to realize the benefits of federalism and minimize its drawbacks. What, then, constitutes this proper balance? That question has been debated since the framers' day.

Federalism in the Constitution

Let us now look at the vertical powers the framers outlined in the Constitution and their effect on the relationship between the national and state governments. Three constitutional provisions are particularly important—the interstate commerce clause, the general welfare clause, and the Tenth Amendment—because they continually shift the balance of power between the national and state governments. We refer to these three provisions as the **triad of powers.**

The Triad of Powers

Each power in the triad has a specific function. Two of them—the interstate commerce clause and the general welfare clause—have been used to expand the powers of the national government. The third—the Tenth Amendment—has been used to protect state powers.

The Interstate Commerce Clause   In Article I, Section 8, the framers gave Congress the power "to regulate Commerce with foreign Nations, and among the several States." This clause sought to rectify the inability of the national government under the Articles of Confederation to control the movement of goods across the state lines. But it really did much more. Using the interstate commerce clause, the framers designed a national government with the power to provide some uniformity of policy among the states. A broad interpretation of this clause—and the change from self-contained states to commercial enterprises linked across state lines—would ultimately provide the means for expanding national power even within state borders. Using this power, the national government could keep the states from penalizing each other while encouraging them to work together.

To demonstrate how the national government can use the commerce clause to achieve uniform policy, let's say that restauranteur Joe Bigot is determined to discriminate against minorities in his world-famous, fast-food hamburger business. "Joe's Best Burgers" franchises are sold everywhere. One franchise is located on a train club car that travels between New York and Connecticut, another on an interstate highway between Texas and Oklahoma. Clearly, the national government would be able to bar discrimination in these restaurants because the restaurants serve interstate travelers, and thus affect interstate commerce.

Thoroughly dismayed, Joe is so determined to do business his way that he sells his franchise, moves to his hometown high in the Rocky Mountains, and opens a

triad of powers Three constitutional provisions—the interstate commerce clause, the general welfare clause, and the Tenth Amendment—that help to continually shift the balance of power between the national and state governments.

restaurant in an area that hasn't seen an interstate customer since the wagon trains brought the gold rush settlers to California in the 1800s. Can the federal government bar discrimination here, too? The answer is yes, because the meat Joe serves, his kitchen machinery, and his eating implements were all imported from out of state. Since those purchases affect interstate commerce, federal regulations apply. This example is based on two Supreme Court cases upholding Congress's use of its interstate commerce power as the basis for the 1964 Civil Rights Act, which expanded the rights of African Americans and barred discrimination in public accommodations.[6]

As you can see from this example, a broad interpretation of the interstate commerce clause can give the national government tremendous power to reach policy areas previously reserved to the states. Using the interstate commerce clause, the national government can, if it so desires (and it invariably does), regulate the wages and work hours on your campus; the admissions and scholarship rules, including the apportionment of scholarships between men and women on college sports teams; campus housing regulations; and campus codes of conduct. Off campus, the food you eat in a restaurant, the operations of the local government, and the operations of the businesses you patronize can all be regulated by the national government's use of its interstate commerce power.

The General Welfare Clause   Also in Article I, Section 8, of the Constitution, the framers granted Congress the power to "lay and collect Taxes, Duties, Imposts and Excises, to pay the Debts and provide for the common Defense and general Welfare of the United States." The combination of this spending power with the necessary and proper clause (also known as the elastic clause) in Article I, Section 8, enabled the national government to indirectly influence state policy through the power of the pocketbook. This power has expanded the national government's reach into formerly state-controlled areas via "carrot-and-stick" programs. The "carrot" is the money that the federal government provides for states that abide by national programs; the "stick" is the threatened loss of money if they do not. This sort of approach to spending was evident in 1974, when Congress passed a law that national highway funds could be received by a state only if it abided by the fifty-five-mile-an-hour speed limit (a law that was repealed in 1987), and again when the increased education funding money was made available to the states in 2001 in return for adoption of the student achievement testing program. Should the national government ever try to ban cell phone use on the highways, they would likely have to do so through the states using the threat of withdrawing highway funds as the "stick." The most visible evidence of the carrot-and-stick approach to policy making is the manner in which the legal drinking age was changed around the country. Before 1984, the drinking age varied from state to state, sometimes even from county to county. In 1984, however, Mothers Against Drunk Driving (MADD) demanded that the drinking age be raised nationally to twenty-one. MADD pointed out that 9,500 Americans under the age of twenty-five were dying annually in alcohol-related driving accidents. Only by imposing a uniform national drinking age of twenty-one, they argued, could drinking and driving be discouraged among young people. But liquor sales meant big business in various states, a formidable obstacle to a policy change. Congress used the carrot-and-stick approach to prevail. If states did not raise their drinking age to twenty-one, they would lose 5 percent of their 1986 federal highway funds and 10 percent of the 1987 total. Not surprisingly, near uniformity on the new legal drinking age was achieved almost immediately.[7]

▲ After Congress allowed states to raise the speed limit on interstate highways to sixty-five miles per hour, state workers changed signs on Interstate 80 in Vacaville, California.

? Question for Reflection: What are some of the potential pitfalls of this "carrot and stick" approach? How might the General Welfare clause be used to forward a particular social agenda? Is there a balance to this power?

The Tenth Amendment   What was it that kept the national government from dominating the federal structure from the beginning? The answer can be found in the Tenth Amendment, which states: "The powers not delegated to the United States by the Constitution, nor prohibited by it to the States, are reserved to the States respectively, or to the people." With this amendment, the framers intended to preserve the individuality of the states and restrict the national government to its delegated powers.

This amendment has been at the center of the shifting balance of power between the national government and the state governments. Between 1877 and 1937, the Tenth Amendment was used by state-centered federalism advocates on the Supreme Court as a barrier to national intrusion of power into state activities. Because manufacturing and mining took place entirely within state boundaries, the national government was assumed to have no power to reach them.[8] After the change in the direction of the Court brought on in the aftermath of Roosevelt's "court-packing plan," however, the new Roosevelt appointees on the Supreme Court declared that the Tenth Amendment "states but a truism," and thus cannot restrict Congress's desire to control commerce and economic activities within state boundaries.[9]

The Tenth Amendment has gained new prominence in recent years as a basis for the *devolution* of power from the national government to the states. Both the Congress since 1995 and a five-person conservative majority under William Rehnquist on the Supreme Court since 1992 are inclined to use this amendment as a means of shifting power to the states, in line with their commitment to reduce the role of Washington in administering and funding local programs.[10]

The Division of Powers

The framers were careful to express in the Constitution a series of powers that preserve the independence of each of the two levels of government. You will recall from Chapter 2 that the **supremacy clause** upholds national laws and treaties as the "supreme Law of the Land." This clause establishes the predominance of national laws whenever national and state legislation overlap. There are also powers granted to, and limits placed on, the states. Those provisions are outlined in Table 3.1. Carefully detailed are the powers delegated to the national government, the powers reserved to the states, and the powers that apply to the two governments concurrently (see Figure 3.1 on page 88).

First are the **delegated powers,** those delegated specifically to the national government. Generally, these are the powers that the framers saw were lacking in the old Articles of Confederation. The framers reasoned that a nation must speak with one voice when negotiating with foreign countries; it also needs a uniform monetary system for its economy to function. Thus, only the national government can declare war, raise and support an army, make treaties with other nations, and coin money.

Another category of powers comprises the **implied powers,** those not specifically enumerated in the Constitution but that can be inferred from the delegated powers. Many can be justified through the elastic clause. For example, the national government's power to tax and spend can be extended by the necessary and proper clause to cover construction of a national system of roads. In addition, there are **inherent powers,** which do not appear in the Constitution but are *assumed* because of the nature of government. Thus, only the national government has the power to conduct foreign relations, make war even in the absence of a formal declaration, and protect its officials against bodily harm or threats.

Those powers not assigned to the national government are left with the states. These **reserved powers** are guaranteed in the Tenth Amendment and protect the role of the states in the federal system. Among the reserved powers are the so-called **police powers,** or the ability to regulate the health, morals, public safety, and welfare of state citizens. Such regulations include speed limits on highways, but they also involve education, marriage, criminal law, zoning regulations, and contracts.

supremacy clause A clause in Article VI of the Constitution holding that in any conflict between federal laws and treaties and state laws, the will of the national government always prevails.

delegated powers Powers delegated specifically to the national government by the Constitution.

implied powers Powers not specifically stated in the Constitution but can be inferred from the delegated powers.

inherent powers Powers that do not appear in the Constitution but are assumed because of the nature of government. Also refers to a theory that the Constitution grants authority to the executive, through the injunction in Article II, Section 3, that the president "take Care that the Laws be faithfully executed."

reserved powers Powers not assigned by the Constitution to the national government but left to the states or the people, according to the Tenth Amendment.

police powers The powers to regulate the health, morals, public safety, and welfare, which are reserved to the states.

Table 3.1 ■ Constitutional Guarantees of and Limits on State Power

Guarantees	Limits
1. State Integrity and Sovereignty	
No division of states or consolidation of parts of two or more states without state legislative consent (Art. IV, Sec. 3)	States cannot enter into treaties, alliances, or confederations (Art. I, Sec. 10)
Guarantee of republican form of state government (Art. IV, Sec. 4)	No interstate or foreign compacts without consent of Congress (Art. I, Sec. 10)
Protection against invasion and against domestic violence (Art. IV, Sec. 4)	No separate coinage (Art. 1, Sec. 10)
Powers not delegated to national government reserved for states (10th Amend.)	National constitution, laws, and treaties are supreme (Art. VI)
State equality in Senate cannot be denied (Art. V)	All state officials bound by national Constitution (Art. VI)
	No denial of privileges and immunity of citizens (14th Amend.)
	No abridgment of right to vote on basis of race (15th Amend.)
	No abridgment of right to vote on basis of sex (19th Amend.)
2. Military Affairs and Defense	
Power to maintain militia and appoint militia officials (Art. I, Sec. 8, 2d Amend.)	No maintenance of standing military in peacetime without congressional consent (Art. I, Sec. 10)
	No engagement in war without congressional consent, except in emergency (Art. I, Sec. 10)
3. Commerce and Taxation	
Equal apportionment of direct federal taxes (Art. I, Secs. 2, 9)	No levying of duties on vessels of sister states (Art. I, Sec. 9)
No export duties imposed on any state (Art. I, Sec. 9)	No legal tender other than gold or silver (Art. I, Sec. 10)
No preferential treatment for ports of one state (Art. I, Sec. 9)	No impairment of the obligations of contract (Art. I, Sec. 10)
Reciprocal full faith and credit among states for public acts, records, and judicial proceedings (Art. IV, Sec. 1)	No levying of import or export duties without congressional consent, except the levying of reasonable inspection fees (Art. I, Sec. 10)
Reciprocal privileges and immunities for citizens of different states (Art. IV, Sec. 2)	No tonnage duties without congressional consent (Art. I, Sec. 10)
Intoxicating liquor may not be imported into states where its sale or use is prohibited (21st Amend.)	
4. Administration of Justice	
Federal criminal trials to be held in state where crime was committed (Art. III, Sec. 2)	No bills of attainder (Art. I, Sec. 10)
Extradition for crimes (Art. IV, Sec. 2)	No ex post facto laws (Art. I, Sec. 10)
Federal criminal juries to be chosen from state and district where crime was committed (6th Amend.)	Supreme Court has original jurisdiction over all cases in which state is a party (Art. III, Sec. 2)
Federal judicial power extends to controversies between two or more states, between a state and citizens of another state, and between a state or its citizens and a foreign nation or its citizens (Art. III, Sec. 2)	No denial of life, liberty, or property without due process of law (14th Amend.)
	No denial of equal protection of state laws to persons within its limits (14th Amend.)

Source: From Table 2.2, pp. 42–43 from *American Federalism: A View from the States,* 3rd Ed. by Daniel J. Elazar. Copyright © 1984 by Harper & Row, Publishers, Inc. Reprinted by permission of Pearson Education, Inc.

Over time, it has been necessary to shift some of these powers to the national government. For example, some state criminal law powers have been supplemented by congressional acts and Supreme Court decisions to provide more uniformity among the states and prevent criminals from escaping punishment simply by crossing state boundaries. The "Lindbergh" law, for example, gave the national government power to investigate and prosecute kidnapping cases that involve the crossing of state lines.

There are also powers that are *shared* by both levels of government; they are known as **concurrent powers.** Both levels can regulate commerce, levy taxes, run a

concurrent powers Powers that are shared by both national and state levels of government.

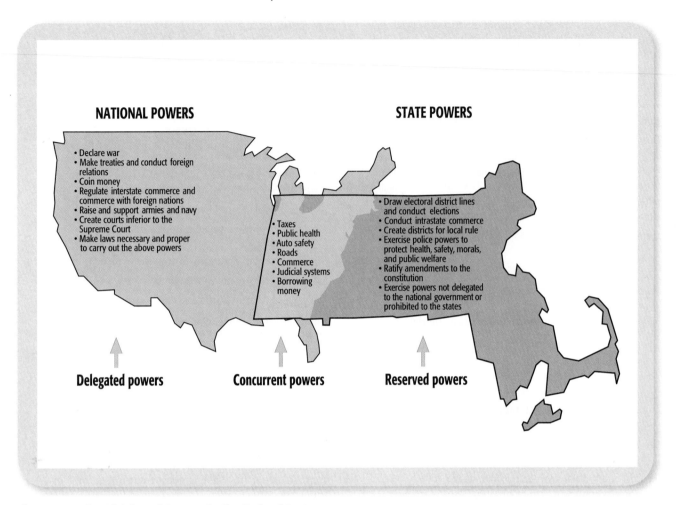

NATIONAL POWERS

- Declare war
- Make treaties and conduct foreign relations
- Coin money
- Regulate interstate commerce and commerce with foreign nations
- Raise and support armies and navy
- Create courts inferior to the Supreme Court
- Make laws necessary and proper to carry out the above powers

STATE POWERS

- Taxes
- Public health
- Auto safety
- Roads
- Commerce
- Judicial systems
- Borrowing money

- Draw electoral district lines and conduct elections
- Conduct intrastate commerce
- Create districts for local rule
- Exercise police powers to protect health, safety, morals, and public welfare
- Ratify amendments to the constitution
- Exercise powers not delegated to the national government or prohibited to the states

Delegated powers   **Concurrent powers**   **Reserved powers**

Figure 3.1   The Division of Powers in the Federal System

road system, establish their own elections, and maintain their own judicial structure. Sometimes these overlapping powers give citizens an additional forum in which to seek support or to secure their rights. For instance, as the box on pages 82–83 illustrates, when the national government tried to discourage the move toward same-sex marriages, civil unions, and gay adoptions through the Defense of Marriage Act of 1997, couples sought recourse in different state judicial systems.

Despite the existence of concurrent powers, the national government can, if it chooses, use the authority in the supremacy clause to force upon states policies which are in the best interests of the entire nation or *preempt* state action in areas where both governments have legislative authority.[11] Over the years, the federal government, looking to impose uniform policies over the entire country, has devised laws that have superseded state action in areas such as pollution control, transportation, nutrition labeling, taxation, and civil rights. In 2002, President Bush and Congress decided, over the objections of Nevada's state government and United States Senators to approve the burial of 77,000 tons of high level radioactive waste, currently stored around the country, under the Yucca Mountain, near Las Vegas. And, reminiscent of the era when the national government took over anticommunist policies from the states, in reaction to the attacks on September 11, 2001, the national government has used its pre-emption power over foreign affairs to prevent state and local governments from revealing the names of alleged terrorism suspects and witnesses who are being held in jail without legal representation.[12] The Bush Administration did receive a setback in its attempt to impose its will on the states, however, when a federal court judge denied Attorney General John

Ashcroft the power to use federal drug laws in an attempt to prevent the state of Oregon from implementing its "assisted-suicide" program under its "death with dignity" law, by threatening to prosecute doctors for prescribing massive doses of proscribed drugs.[13]

In addition to granting powers, the framers *denied* certain powers to both levels of government. Fearful of creating an all-powerful central government that would override the rights of the states and the people, the framers withheld from the national government powers that might have that result. For example, Article I, Section 9, denies the national government the right to place an export tax on products from the states and the power to impose a direct tax on the people unless it was levied proportionally to each state's population (a provision that was overridden by the Sixteenth Amendment, allowing for the creation of a national income tax). The Bill of Rights, beginning with the words "Congress shall make no law . . ." can also be seen as a long list of powers denied to the national government in areas such as freedom of speech, freedom of religion, freedom of the press, and defendants' rights.

The powers denied to the states were designed to keep their functions separate from those of the newly established national government. Limits on state powers, some of which can be overridden by Congress, are outlined in Article I, Section 10, of the Constitution. Among the prohibited powers are those delegated exclusively to the national government: the power to declare war, make treaties, and coin money. In addition, states are denied the power to impair the obligations of contracts, thus preventing them from wiping out any debts, including those that existed prior to the formation of the Constitution. As the "Civil Unions" box shows, it remains to be seen how the Supreme Court will rule under the "obligation of contracts" and the "full faith and credit" provision of Article IV, Section I, on the question of whether "same-sex" couples from one state can require other states to provide them with the benefits of marriage.

Finally, the framers denied to both the national and state governments certain powers deemed offensive based on their British experience. These include the power to grant titles of nobility, pass bills of attainder (which legislate the guilt of an individual without the benefit of a trial), and pass ex post facto laws (which declare an action to be a crime *after* it has been committed).

The Development of Federalism

Despite this enumeration of powers in the Constitution, the framers omitted many problem areas in mapping out the relationship between the national and state governments. That relationship had to be developed over time by policy makers at both levels and by the judicial system. Many of those decisions were made in response to crises faced by the nation.

Debating the National Role: Hamilton versus Jefferson

How much leeway would Congress have to legislate beyond its enumerated constitutional powers, thereby increasing the national government's power over the states? The debate began in the Washington administration over the creation of a national bank. At issue here was Article I, Section 8, Clause 18, of the Constitution (the elastic clause), which grants Congress the power "to make all Laws which shall be necessary and proper for carrying into Execution" its enumerated powers. Thus, Secretary of the Treasury Alexander Hamilton argued in 1791 that the national government could build on its power to coin money, operate a uniform currency system, and regulate commerce by chartering a national bank. Secretary of State Thomas Jefferson, however, opposed this idea, arguing that since no explicit power to charter banks was written into the Constitution, that power was reserved to the states.

This debate over the constitutionality of creating a bank represented two very different visions of federalism. Hamilton's argument favoring a national bank suggested the prospect of a whole new series of implied powers for the national government. Jefferson's argument was that such a broad interpretation of the clause would give Congress unlimited power to, in his words, "do whatever evil they please," with the result that the national government would "swallow up all the delegated powers" and overwhelm the states. In the end, President Washington was more persuaded by the expansive national powers position of Hamilton, and the bank was chartered in 1791. But was the bank constitutional?

Asserting National Power: *McCulloch v. Maryland*

After a second national bank was chartered in 1816, the state of Maryland challenged the bank's operation by imposing a state tax on it. When the bank refused to comply, the Supreme Court was asked in 1819 to rule, in **McCulloch v. Maryland,** on both the constitutionality of Congress's chartering the national bank and the constitutionality of a state's tax on that bank.[14]

Chief Justice John Marshall, an advocate of strong, centralized national power, wrote a resounding unanimous opinion supporting the power of Congress to charter the bank. Marshall turned to the necessary and proper clause of the Constitution and found there the implied power for the national government to do what was convenient to carry out the powers delegated to it in Article I, Section 8. According to Marshall, the powers of the national government would now be broadened considerably: "Let the end be legitimate, let it be within the scope of the Constitution, and all means which are appropriate, which are plainly adapted to that end, which are not prohibited, but consistent with the letter and spirit of the Constitution, are constitutional."

This was indeed the broadest possible definition of national power. Now Congress could justify any legislation simply by tying it to one of the delegated national powers in the Constitution. This ruling created the potential for the national government to expand its powers into many areas that had previously been thought to be reserved to the states.

Having established the constitutionality of the national bank, the Court also declared Maryland's tax on the bank unconstitutional, reasoning that states have no power to impede congressional laws. In this case, Marshall argued, "the power to tax involves the power to destroy" the bank, and thus limit congressional power. The Court's reading of the supremacy clause made the national government "supreme within its sphere of action," meaning that it was the dominant power in areas where its power overlaps with that of the states. It seemed that Jefferson was right in fearing that the national government was well on the way to "swallowing up" the states.

Expanding National Power Further: *Gibbons v. Ogden*

The Constitution states quite clearly that Congress has the power "to regulate Commerce . . . among the several States." But does the power to control commerce "among the several States" extend to control of commerce entirely within a state? And, if so, how extensive would that power be? In the 1824 case of **Gibbons v. Ogden,** John Marshall once again interpreted the Constitution broadly, ruling in favor of expanding national power.[15]

This case involved a license to operate steamboats in the waters between New York and New Jersey. One man, Aaron Ogden, had purchased a state-issued license to do so in New York waters, while his former partner, Thomas Gibbons, had gone to the national government for a federal coasting license. It was left to the Supreme Court to decide whether the central government's power over *interstate*

McCulloch v. Maryland The 1819 decision by Chief Justice John Marshall that expanded the interpretation of the "necessary and proper" clause to give Congress broad powers to pass legislation and reaffirmed the national government's power over the states under the supremacy clause.

Gibbons v. Ogden The 1824 decision by Chief Justice John Marshall that gave Congress the power, under the "interstate and commerce" clause, to regulate anything that "affects" interstate commerce.

commerce (commerce among states) predominated over an individual state's power to regulate *intrastate* commerce (commerce within a state boundary). Marshall used this opportunity to give the interstate commerce clause the broadest possible definition, holding that the national government had the power to regulate any "commercial intercourse" having an effect in two or more states. This meant that the national government could now reach activities that affect interstate commerce even within state boundaries. All that was left to the states, then, was the power to regulate commerce that was wholly within one state. But with the growth of industries such as mining and food production, it would soon be hard to find such enterprises. This ruling made states' rights advocates unhappy. Slaveholders in the South, for example, feared national incursion into their peculiar form of labor "commerce."

Asserting State Power: Nullification

Inevitably, there was an organized response to Marshall's strong central power position in the *McCulloch* and *Gibbons* cases. In the 1820s and early 1830s, southerners such as John Calhoun of South Carolina objected to the national government raising tariffs on raw materials and manufactured goods, thereby protecting northern industries but forcing southerners to pay higher prices. Lacking the numbers in Congress to reverse this direction, Calhoun adopted the theory of **nullification** (initially proposed by Jefferson and Madison in 1798 in opposition to the Alien and Sedition Acts), which held that states faced with unacceptable national legislation could declare such laws null and void and refuse to observe them. South Carolina, for example, declared the national tariffs null and void in 1832 and threatened to *secede* (leave the Union) over the issue. A crisis was averted when President Andrew Jackson lowered the tariff while also threatening to use military force to prevent secession.

However, nullification reared its head again over attempts by the national government to restrict slavery. This time the South did secede, and the Civil War was the result. This war was a turning point in American federalism, because the North's victory ensured that the Union and its federal structure would survive. No longer could states declare national laws unconstitutional or threaten to secede.

Developing a System of Separation: Dual Federalism

After the Civil War, the prevailing view of federalism was one of **dual federalism,** in which each level of power remains supreme in its own jurisdiction, thus keeping the states separate and distinct from the national government. Dual federalism prevailed during this period as a result of two factors. Supreme Court rulings between 1877 and 1937 fueled a state-centered view of federalism. In addition, industrial expansion created an economic environment opposed to government interference and regulation, thereby limiting the national government's power over industry and giving states the upper hand in the federal structure. For instance, in 1895 the Court ruled that the national government had no power to regulate the monopoly of the sugar-refining industry, which, while national in scope, had factories located in the state of Pennsylvania. The Court ruled in *United States v. E. C. Knight* that the national government had the power to regulate the shipment of sugar, which constituted interstate commerce, but it did not have the power to regulate the manufacture of sugar, because that was local in nature and thus wholly within the supreme power of the states.[16]

In another ruling in 1918, the Court placed additional restrictions on national power. With the 1916 Keating Owen Act, Congress sought to limit child labor. But in overturning this act in *Hammer v. Dagenhart,* Justice William R. Day indicated just how state-centered the Court had become. He wrote: "The grant of authority over a purely federal matter was not intended to destroy the local power always existing and carefully reserved to the States in the Tenth Amendment to the Constitution."[17]

nullification A nineteenth-century theory which holds that states faced with unacceptable national legislation can declare such laws null and void and refuse to observe them.

dual federalism A system in which each level of power remains supreme in its own jurisdiction, thus keeping the states separate and distinct from the national government.

after civil war

APPROACHING DEMOCRACY AROUND THE GLOBE

Three Countries, One Continent: Federalism Crosses the Canadian Border

When newly elected President Vincente Fox of Mexico looked in 2000 to reform his country's highly centralized government under the long ruling Institutional Revolutionary Party (PRI) to make it more like the federal structure outlined in the Mexican Constitution, he asked Canadian Prime Minister Jean Chretien to show them how. By 2001 one-third of Mexico's states were governed by Fox's National Action Party and the leftist Democratic Revolutionary Party. This change in state governorships enabled Fox to institute federalist policies reflective of those employed in Canada's provinces.

The late twentieth century in Canada saw the turbulent rise of the independence movement of Quebec, a sort of "revolution tranquille," the increasing efforts of the western provinces, most notably Alberta and British Columbia, to separate themselves from the central government as political and economic players. The central province of Ontario also sought to separate itself from the central government.

To accommodate the increasing diversity among the provinces and a tendency toward separation, the central government changed its intergovernmental fiscal arrangements. A "Social Union" was created using an "equalization formula," under which the Canadian central government has poured money into the provinces to implement each one's own version of the welfare state, while also allowing some of the provinces to raise their own taxes to fund programs tailored to their particular needs. The provinces are allowed to tax anything they want (with the exception of international and interprovincial trade) and so tax along with the central Canadian government both income and sales. Since some provinces are wealthier than others, this leads to a variation of resources available to finance programs across the country. Thus it is left to the Canadian central government to fund federal-provincial transfers such as the Canada Health and Social Transfer (CHST) and the equalization transfer to make the government funding more equitable. Another set of federal payments goes directly to individuals, such as old age pensions, a child benefit program, and a major public sector pension based on a payroll tax. While there are no differences in these program expenditures across the country, because some regions have more people in different categories (such as senior citizens), some provinces receive more federal money than others. Another important financial equalization effort comes in the form of a federal unemployment insurance program, which has been renamed the EI, or "Employment Insurance," program. Funded by payroll taxes, this program supports those who are out of work, meaning that some provinces with higher levels of unemployment will benefit more than others.

The taxation program also helps to keep the nation together. Since each province can set its own tax rate and base, as well as collect the tax itself if it wishes, each has the funding to support its own programs. As a result, personal income tax rates vary widely, with Newfoundland, for instance, having a 17 percent higher tax rate than Alberta. While tax rates are also higher in Quebec, citizens in that region pay a 16.5 percent lower federal tax than in other provinces because of a national government agreement in 1960 acknowledging that existing provincial programs duplicate some federal ones and make them unnecessary. The independence movement in Quebec led the Canadian national government to grant that province even more concessions. Quebec is constitutionally required to provide some services in its own language. The province has its own payroll tax-based pension plan that is used to promote the region's economic development and business ownership by native speakers. Also, Quebec is alone among the provinces in its power to screen and approve immigrants, which has created some problems with the main immigrant-receiving provinces of Ontario and British Columbia. Like the United States, Canada is able to use the power of the central government to create both diversity and equality by supporting and managing its provinces in a way that acknowledges the diversity of the regions and creates a means for maintaining the unity of an overarching governmental structure. Still, the future of federalism in Canada is uncertain.

Some say that the idea of Canada's equalization formula by which the federal government redistributes money and services to even out the financial resources of the provinces might be the perfect model for Mexico. Others, however, argue that the Canadian system would never work in Mexico because the governmental administrative responsibilities delegated to the provinces is not matched by the level of federal money offered to support them. A new report on Canadian federalism by Yves Seguin, a former Quebec Cabinet Minister, argues that the Canadian federal government is collecting too much in sales taxes and giving too little money to the provinces to provide services such as health care. As a result, Seguin recommended the replacement of the Canadian system of transferring money from the federal to the provincial governments for health care and social services in favor of allowing provinces to keep sales tax money collected in their own provinces. As the United States' North American neighbors continue to develop their approaches to federalism, it remains to be seen whether the common problems of economics and anti-terrorism programs will lead to the creation of what some are calling a "North American Community," with common policies on the borders of all three countries.

Source: Don MacPherson, "Fixing Federalism: Seguin Report Comes Up with Canadian Solutions to Fiscal Problems," *Montreal Gazette,* March 8, 2002; April Lindgren, "PM to Sell Federalism in Mexico," *Montreal Gazette,* November 14, 2001; and Richard M. Bird and Francois Vaillancourt, "The Role of Intergovernmental Fiscal Arrangements in Maintaining an Effective State in Canada," revised version of a paper prepared for the Conference on the Role of Intergovernmental Fiscal Relations in Shaping Effective States Within Fragmented Societies, Fribourg, Switzerland, February 10–12, 2000, presented at Lafayette College, Easton, Pa., April 25, 2000.

◀ A group of young doffer and spinner boys comprised the labor force in a textile mill in Fall River, Massachusetts, in January 1912. In the early 1900s over 1.5 million children worked for as little as twenty-five cents for a twelve-hour day, and many exhausted young workers fell asleep on the job and were mutilated by their machines.

In this classic statement of dual federalism, the states' reserved powers now represented a limitation upon the national government.

Creating a Cooperative System: The New Deal Era

The Great Depression of the 1930s and President Franklin D. Roosevelt's New Deal eventually put an end to dual federalism. In 1932 the country was in the throes of the worst economic depression in its history. To relieve the suffering, Roosevelt promised Americans a "New Deal," which meant taking immediate steps to get the economy moving and create jobs. At Roosevelt's behest, Congress passed programs involving tremendous new powers for the national government, such as creating large national administrative agencies to supervise manufacturing and farming. These programs produced an increase in spending by the national government, a large number of regulations, and even larger numbers of bureaucrats to administer the regulations.

Initially, the Supreme Court used the rulings of the dual federalism era to restrict Roosevelt's programs, arguing that the problems they addressed were local in nature and not in the province of the national government.[18] But the nation's needs were so great that the Supreme Court's position could not endure. A highly critical President Roosevelt proposed a "court-packing plan," whereby he sought to add one new justice for each one over the age of seventy up to a total of fifteen justices. While the plan was before Congress, the Supreme Court, in what became known as "the switch in time that saved nine," suddenly began ruling in favor of the New Deal programs, with Chief Justice Charles Evans Hughes and Justice Owen Roberts changing their mind about federalism to allow the national government to prevail over the states.

In a 1937 case, *National Labor Relations Board (NLRB) v. Jones and Laughlin Steel,* the Court upheld the national government's right to impose collective bargaining by unions and ban certain unfair labor practices. The Court was now willing to support the use of national power and allow the national government to control manufacturing, production, and agricultural activities through the interstate commerce powers. As a result, the court-packing plan was abandoned.[19]

② Question for Reflection: If Roosevelt had carried out his "court packing plan" and almost doubled the size of the Supreme Court, what impact would this have had on dual federalism and the country in other areas of law?

But what of the Tenth Amendment, which reserves to the states powers not delegated to the national government? A Supreme Court that was in the process of being completely remade by eight new Roosevelt appointees seemingly put an end to dual federalism in 1941. In *United States v. Darby Lumber Co.*, which upheld the national government's power to regulate the wages and hours of the lumber industry under the interstate commerce power, the Court ruled that the Tenth Amendment "states but a truism that all is retained which has not been surrendered."[20] In short, this amendment was no longer seen as a limitation on the national government or a bar to the exercise of its power, even wholly within state boundaries.

A new era in the federal relationship had been ushered in by the New Deal, one of cooperation between the national and state governments rather than of the separation of governments and functions. This system is known as **cooperative federalism.** Solutions for various state and local problems were directed and sometimes funded by the national government and were then administered by the state governments according to national guidelines as was the case in the rebuilding of New York City after the attacks of September 11.[21]

The national government was supreme in the federalism partnership despite the fleeting return of dual federalism in response to a Court challenge in 1976 that was overturned nine years later. In 1976 the Supreme Court signaled a possible return to dual federalism in the case of *National League of Cities v. Usery*, which dealt with extending national wages and hours legislation to state and municipal workers. Writing for a slim majority, Justice William Rehnquist banned national regulation of "core" state functions. Nine years later, however, the Court overturned *Usery* in the case of *Garcia v. San Antonio Metropolitan Transit Authority*, which also dealt with wages and hours legislation. The Court shifted its position back to favoring national predominance, arguing that states must rely on Congress rather than the Court to decide which of their programs should be regulated by the national government. This ruling was reaffirmed by the Court in *South Carolina v. Baker*.[22] But, as you will see at the end of the chapter, the Supreme Court is once again reassessing and redefining the nature of the relationship between the two levels of government.

What were the results of this partnership between the national and state governments? States came to look to the national government for help and funding to deal with problems viewed as beyond their means. Similarly, citizens began to look to Washington for solutions to their problems rather than to their state and local governments. The result was an increase in the power of the national government and a drive to achieve uniformity of programs throughout the country, often at the expense of state power and innovation.

Seeking Uniformity: Federalism in the Post–New Deal Era

A major judicial movement in the 1950s and 1960s created a new role for the national government in the federal system, that of protector of personal rights guaranteed by the Constitution. Prior to the 1930s, defendants' rights had been a power reserved to the states. This arrangement resulted in variations in policy, particularly with regard to minorities, who were often denied personal liberties and legal protection in certain states. The Supreme Court ruled to extend most of the protections of the Bill of Rights to the states (the Bill of Rights originally applied to the national government only) to ensure uniformity from one state to another and help end inequality. The Court did this by ruling that certain guarantees in the Bill of Rights are part of the due process right guaranteed by the Fourteenth

cooperative federalism A cooperative system in which solutions for various state and local problems are directed and sometimes funded by both the national and state governments. The administration of programs is characterized by shared power and shared responsibility.

everyone work together

Amendment against state government intrusion. This process was called the **incorporation** of the Bill of Rights.

Uniformity of the judicial process was thus established around the country. For instance, in the 1932 *Scottsboro* case, in which a group of young African Americans had been convicted of rape and sentenced to death without a fair trial, the Supreme Court ruled that the Sixth Amendment's right to counsel should be extended to all future state capital trials like this one to ensure fairness.[23] States could still operate their judicial systems, but to guarantee personal rights, they had to adhere to national standards regarding constitutional protections. In Chapter 13 we discuss the full extent of this incorporation process in detail.

The national government also sought to impose national standards regarding equality. Social equality was promoted through a series of Court decisions, such as *Brown v. Board of Education of Topeka* in 1954, which called for the end of segregation in public schools,[24] and later cases that promoted integration. Political equality was sought through a series of cases, such as *Reynolds v. Sims* in 1964. This case established the "one-person, one-vote" standard in which the number of voters in each district was made roughly the same, thus giving people an equal say in the operation of their government.[25] Personal equality was guaranteed by a series of First Amendment cases granting citizens the same rights of speech, press, assembly, religion, and thought no matter where they live. Economic equality was the goal of a series of welfare, educational, and social programs adopted by Congress as part of the "War on Poverty" program initiated by the Johnson administration in the 1960s.

These judicial decisions and political actions establishing uniformity of rights have helped America approach democracy because a final recourse for seeking constitutional rights was guaranteed to residents in all states. Once the partnership between the national government and the state governments was established, the question of how the two levels of government would interact remained. For example, in 1997 some states were reluctant to take one kind of welfare aid from the national government because a minor provision had set aside $250 million requiring that children be taught about sexual abstinence.[26]

Federal Grants and Federal Mandates: Federalism Since 1930

Federal spending and power began to grow during the 1930s in response to the Depression. When the Supreme Court ruled during the New Deal that the national power to spend was not limited to the enumerated grants of power in the Constitution, further growth was inevitable.[27] Since then, national power has continued to grow, particularly in the last three decades. At issue in this federal system is how much money will be spent by the national government and under what conditions it may be used by the states (with the answers usually being "lots" and "according to specific guidelines"). We now look at the different types of federal grants and then at how various administrations have worked with the grant-in-aid system.

Federal Grants   There are a variety of national spending programs. The most frequently used is the **grant-in-aid,** money paid to states and localities to induce them to implement policies in accordance with federally mandated guidelines. Money is made available through an *intergovernmental transfer,* but only if it is spent by the states in certain policy areas. If the states do not wish to abide by the **conditions of aid** or national requirements, they can refuse federal funds. These conditions come in a variety of forms. Some require that a grant be spent in a certain fashion, while others try to accomplish additional policy goals. For instance, in October 2000, President Bill Clinton signed into law a bill requiring all states to pass by September 2003, a uniform .08 blood alcohol standard for driving "under the influence" that applied to first time offenders, or lose an increasing amount of their federal highway funding assistance. Usually, with the deep pockets of the national

incorporation The process whereby the protections of the Bill of Rights have been found by the Supreme Court to apply to the states.

grant-in-aid Money paid to states and localities to induce them to implement policies in accordance with federally mandated guidelines.

conditions of aid National requirement that must be observed.

government and states being forever short of funds, refusal of aid rarely happens. However, in this case while 32 states had complied by passing this legislation by April 2002, 16 other states, led by Wisconsin, which is retaining its sliding standard starting at .10, began losing funding because they had not passed the uniform national standard into state law.

The number of such grants is vast and has been rising steadily for the last decade. National grants to states and localities rose from 594 to nearly 660 in the years from 1993 to 1999. Simultaneously, the size of grant outlays rose by 1998 to $251 billion, an increase of 29 percent from the $194 billion in 1993.[28] Medicaid growth was the principal cause of increase (from $75.8 billion to $88.4 billion), but another large outlay went for the disaster assistance programs of the Federal Emergency Management Agency (see Figure 3.2).[29] These grant outlays, though, were due for considerable change with the election of the Bush Administration in 2000 and the terrorist attacks a year later. President Bush's fiscal year 2002 budget called for nearly a 7% reduction in grant-in-aid spending with eventual plans to reduce that spending by another 11.2% by fiscal year 2011. Some of the largest cuts, revealing the administration's new policy choices, were proposed in the environmental protection agency, highways aid, and state criminal alien assistance programs. Coincidentally with these domestic cuts, just two months after the September 11 attacks, President Bush signed Congress's anti-terrorism package providing another $20 billion in emergency funding and security programs, with $10.4 billion alone promised in federal aid to New York City and State for their recovery efforts.[30]

Grants-in-aid come in a wide variety of types. **Categorical grants** are the most common and are given for specific purposes, usually with strict rules attached. Categorical grants usually require the state or local government or a nonprofit organization to come up with matching funds, of 10 percent, for example, since the grant is supposed to cover only part of the costs. In this way, the grants induce increased spending by states for desired programs and encourage cooperation. Approximately 89 percent of the national aid to the states and localities comes in the form of categorical grants. This is such a fast-growing form of national assistance that we now have the largest number of categorical grants in history, with the "catalog of federal domestic assistance" listing in 2002 some 1,044 different forms of federal

categorical grant The most common type of federal grant, given for specific purposes, usually with strict rules attached.

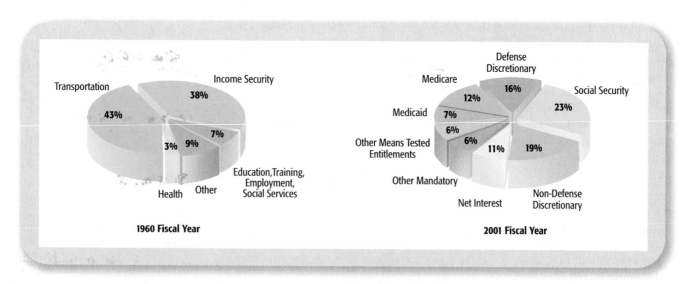

Figure 3.2   The Changing Functions of National Grants to States and Localities
Over the last forty years, there has been a dramatic shift in the purposes for national grants. In short, national funding for transportation and welfare programs has been replaced by a system of health care programs and funding for job training.
Sources: U.S. Advisory Commission on Intergovernmental Relations, Characteristics of Federal Grant-in-Aid Programs to State and Local Governments, 1995 (Washington, D.C.; ACIR, January 1996), p. 16 and Lawrence Mishel, "Changes in Federal Aid to State and Local Governments," as proposed in the Bush Administration FY 2002 Budget, Economic Policy Institute, found at http://www.epinet.org/briefingpapers/.

assistance programs to the states and localities.[31] Categorical grants come in three types: **formula grants, project grants,** and combined **formula/project grants.**

Formula grants are allocations of federal money to states and localities based on a prescribed legislative distribution formula for continuing activities which are not confined to a specific project. Depending on their policy aim, such formula grants can take into account a wide variety of factors, such as total population, median family income, miles of coastline, total enrollment in education, and miles of highways and railways. Governmental units meeting the strict rules for distribution automatically qualify for the grant.[32]

The project grant is not based on a formula but is distributed for specific purposes after a fairly competitive application and approval process for a fixed period of time. These are sometimes called *discretionary grants* because they are distributed at the discretion of a designated legislator or administrator. Given the desire of legislators to maintain more control over the operation of these programs, the vast majority of categorical grants, 83.5 percent in 2002, are project grants, representing an increase of over 11% since 1995.[33]

In recent years a combined formula/project grant has been developed in which competitive grants are awarded, but they are also restricted by the use of a formula. For example, limits may be placed by Congress on the amount of grant money that can be awarded to a state or region of a state.

As grants proliferated and became more complex, a new type of grant was created in 1966 to simplify the process. President Lyndon Johnson created **block grants,** which consolidate several smaller grants into one large grant that provides money for broad functional program areas, and the funds may be used at the recipient governmental level's discretion. Compared with the vast number of categorical grants, in 2002 only 33 block grants were available, up from fifteen in 1993, and covering such diverse areas as low income home energy assistance, local law enforcement assistance, community development assistance, Hispanic serving institutions assisting communities, Native American housing, and preventative health and health services. One new program, created in 2000, made $25 million in funds available to states and localities under a new block grant to enforce the newly adopted national underage drinking law which made the 21-year-old drinking age mandatory around the nation.[34]

By examining the direction of the spending using all of these types of federal grants in specific issue areas one can see clearly the shifting spending priorities of Congress in the years to come. For example, a recent Congressional Budget Office study of "Federal Spending on the Elderly and Children," those people below the age of 18 and over the age of 64, concluded that the federal government was spending in fiscal year 2000 just over one-third of its budget (up from just 22% in 1971), or about $615 billion on the elderly and just under 10% or $175 billion on children. If present spending rates hold, though, by 2010 about half of the federal budget will be spent on these two groups, with four-fifths of that amount being devoted to the elderly. The importance of this spending priority, due to the aging Baby Boomer population, was demonstrated by the number of governmental spending programs for the elderly, which numbered only 46 in 1971, rose to 360 in 1990, nearly doubled to 615 in 2000, and was expected to rise to a staggering 1,050 (equal to the number of all current domestic programs now) by 2010.[35]

One major change in the welfare area was expected to be the **"devolution revolution,"** a term signifying the shift in policy-making responsibility to the states. In this way, former Speaker of the House Newt Gingrich argued, "power" could be restored to the individuals first, then to state and local governments as the next best option. Some research by noted federalism expert John Kincaid has now indicated that because of political opposition little such devolution is now evident. Rather, there has been a process of *de facto* devolution, instead of one accomplished by law. The federal government's defunding of urban programs as policies is no longer directed toward places but instead is directed more toward persons, and the rights of

formula grant A grant based on a prescribed legislative formula to determine how money will be distributed to eligible governmental units (states or big cities).

project grant A grant not based on a formula but distributed for specific purposes after a fairly competitive application and approval process.

formula/project grant A grant in which competitive grants are awarded, but also restricted by use of a formula.

block grant A federal grant that provides money to states for general program funding with few or even no strings attached.

"devolution revolution" A trend initiated in the Reagan administration and accelerated by Newt Gingrich as Speaker to send programs and power back to the states with less involvement by the national government in the hopes of first restoring power to individuals and later to state and local governments.

Tennesse Volunteers

individuals, such as social welfare, rather than the interests of state and local governments, such as transportation and urban aid programs. In the words of Senator Carl Levin (D-MI), "There's no political capital in intergovernmental relations. Helping out mayors or county officials gets me very few votes."[36]

The extent to which grants-in-aid provide a means for this country to approach democracy is highly debatable. Faced with the prospect that certain regions of the country are not spending in a manner that reflects the needs of their citizens, the national government can take tax money from one region of the country and redistribute it to another region. Dictating the spending of governmental resources in this way has helped to remove some inequalities, but it has political costs for the states. Because all national money carries with it certain strings, the national government is able to dominate the federal-state partnership once more by dictating the way state governments must act to receive the money they need. More than that, states very quickly grew to depend on national money, thus further impelling them to allow the national government to dictate their policy direction. Some argue that

---

THE ROAD TO DEMOCRACY

And Then There Was One: Lowering the Confederate Flag

THAT WAS THEN . . .

Few decisions are more central to the symbolism of a state, and more central to the diverse decision making of a state, than the nature of its symbols. In the beginning of the 1990s four southern states still officially displayed some version of the confederate flag with its rebel cross (a blue cross with 13 white stars)—Alabama, South Carolina, Georgia and Mississippi. Then all four states came under attack because what was seen as the symbol of slavery still flew on the dome of their Statehouses and throughout their borders. The call to remove the flag was unsettling to those citizens who saw it as a symbol of their "courage, pride, and honor," not to mention the region's history.

The first state to resolve the dispute was Alabama, where, in 1963, former segregationist Governor George Wallace had raised the confederate battle flag along with the state and federal flags above the Alabama capitol building in protest of the Kennedy administration's desegregation policies. Thirty years later, a federal judge ruled that only the Alabama state flag, which does not have the rebel cross, and the United States flag, could fly above the state Capitol building. So in 1993 the Confederate battle flag was removed.

The controversy then shifted to South Carolina where the confederate battle flag flew over its Capitol Dome. The Confederate flag was first flown above the state capitol in South Carolina in 1962 as an observance of the Civil War dead. Like Alabama, though, the Confederate flag remained flying through the 1960s as a gesture of defiance toward the national government's civil rights policies. As the twentieth century drew to a close, various civil rights groups including the NAACP, urged the removal of the Confederate flag to demonstrate the more inclusive politics of the "New South." Nearly every business group and religious organization in the state of South Carolina added their voice to the call for the removal of the Confederate flag on the basis of the state's changing racial climate and to improve business prospects for the state.

THIS IS NOW . . .

Seeking to lower the flag, the mayor of Charleston, Joseph P. Riley, led a 120-mile protest march from the seacoast to Columbia. Scores of sporting and cultural events, as well as conventions, began boycotting the state. The issue became even more heated in mid-January of 2000 on the birthday of Martin Luther King, Jr., when 46,000 people marched on the South Carolina state house in Columbia to demand that the flag be removed, creating the largest civil rights demonstration since the 1960s. Over and over the crowd sang, "The flag is coming down today," to the tune of "We Shall Overcome." "Not everyone in South Carolina is still living in the eighteenth century. We are going to send a clear message to those who have the authority to deal with the placement of the Confederate battle flag. Let it be clearly understood that we live in the sovereign state of South Carolina, and not in the Confederate States of America," said James Gallman, president of the South Carolina NAACP. The issue even took centerstage in the 2000 Republican Presidential nomination race with both George W. Bush and John McCain refusing to take a stance on the question because it was a matter of states' rights. Only after he had lost the Republican primary race did McCain apologize for not commenting on the flag issue, saying that he "chose to compromise my principles" in his search for political victory.

grants are a recession from democracy because they decrease democratic account-ability for government spending, decrease governmental efficiency, increase govern-mental spending, and change state and local spending priorities. For this reason, some students of fiscal federalism argue for minimizing intergovernmental transfers.

Federal Mandates—Funded and Unfunded Congress can exercise considerable control over the states by attaching to federal money certain **federal mandates.** States may be required to create programs that accord with federal policy goals. For example, a program to increase employment might have a provision setting aside 10 percent of the grants for minority hirings, or a national health grant may place restrictions on teenage smoking. Since these mandates are uniformly imposed by the national gov-ernment, they lead to some very unusual policy choices in different regions. In 1994, to receive federal funding for its water supply, the city of Chicago continued to observe a federal mandate requiring it to test its water for two pesticides present only in the Hawaiian water supply, where they are used on the pineapple crops.

federal mandate A direct order from Congress to the states to fulfill.

Eventually the pressure had an impact. The South Car-olina government forged a compromise whereby the Confederate battle flag would be removed from the state-house dome and placed adjacent to a thirty-foot monument honoring the Confederate dead that stands in front of the statehouse. The compromise was not completely accept-able either to the NAACP or to the South Carolinians who supported removal of the Confederate flag because huge spotlights on the flag made it clear that the flag was still a valued symbol, yet by no longer flying it in a position of sov-ereignty and placing it on the ground, it did not carry the weight of the government's backing.

The question of how Georgia and Mississippi states' rights would be resolved with respect to their flags re-mained. Each state went in the opposite direction. Fearing an economic boycott of Georgia similar to that of South Carolina, lawmakers and Governor Roy Barnes secretly designed a new flag that significantly reduced the size of the confederate symbol. When the new Georgia flag was quickly accepted, all eyes turned to Mississippi. There, the state Supreme Court ruled that because of a legislative bu-reaucratic oversight dating back to 1906, the state now had no official state flag, and after a 17-member commission was appointed to design a new flag, legislators decided instead to hold a voter referendum to determine which flag would fly over the Capitol. After a new flag was pro-posed which eliminated the rebel cross, Mississippi voters overwhelming chose to retain their 107-year-old flag promi-nently displaying the confederate cross in the upper left corner.

With Mississippi now the only state in 21st century still displaying the Confederate flag over its Capitol, the move-ment for change there took a new political turn, over and above the symbolism and states' rights issues involved, when it became clear that Governor Roy Barnes of Georgia was unexpectedly defeated in the 2002 election largely be-cause of his support for changing his state's flag.

▲ Supporters lobby for the retention of Mississippi's old Confed-erate flag in a voter referendum considering the adoption of a new flag.

Sources: Paul Duggan, "Mississippi Keeps Its State Flag; Confeder-ate Symbol Wins in Landslide," *Washington Post,* April 18, 2001, David Firestone, "South Carolina Senate Votes to Remove Con-federate Flag," *New York Times,* April 13, 2000, p. 1; "Flag Compro-mise Resisted in South Carolina House," *New York Times,* April 14, 2000, p. A18; and "46,000 March on South Carolina Capitol to Bring Down Confederate Flag," *New York Times,* January 18, 2000, p. A14.

States frequently complain that federal mandates are underfunded or unfunded, meaning that the requirements are imposed on them without providing the funds to make compliance possible. Thus the national government controls policy but shifts the financial burden to the states.[37] By 1995, state and local governments were spending approximately 25 percent of their budgets to meet federal mandates.[38] State officials object to these unfunded mandates because it means they have to raise the tax revenue to support them. This leads to voter backlash against local officials rather than the members of Congress who vote the policy into effect but do not pay for it. In response to state and local officials' complaints that the national government's use of unfunded mandates was overburdening their budgets, the Republican Congress in 1995 passed the Unfunded Mandates Reform Act of 1995 as part of its Contract with America. This bill said that Congress had to assess the fiscal effect of a federal mandate on state and local governments, and if it was valued at over $100 million annually, then any member of Congress could challenge it with a point of order that could lead to a separate vote on the mandate and consideration of its possible funding by Congress.[39] In addition, the Advisory Commission on Intergovernmental Relations (ACIR) was asked by Congress to review the impact of particularly controversial unfunded mandates. Of the first fourteen reviewed, half were suggested for elimination and the rest faced proposed modifications. More than two hundred other mandates were then proposed for review.[40]

Question for Reflection: What criteria would you propose for the evaluation of unfunded mandates attached to federal funding to determine whether or not the national government should be imposing policy without accounting for the financial burden to the state that the policy generates?

Because of the continual demand by the states for national funding, the willingness of the national government to provide it, and the growing presence of complicated restrictions on the spending of that money, the grant-in-aid system has spiraled out of control. An examination of the history of this system will illustrate how presidents in the last sixty years initially used federal grants to change the relationship between the national and state governments and then sought to bring that system under control.

Presidents and Federalism

Roosevelt, Truman, and Eisenhower: The Era of Cooperative Federalism, 1930–1963

As you have learned, the system of cooperative federalism began during the Great Depression in the 1930s. Congress authorized a large number of new grants-in-aid beyond the fifteen that already existed for state support. By 1939, total federal outlays were fifteen times greater than they had been in 1933.

As public demands for greater government action increased following the New Deal, the national grant-in-aid became the major tool for responding. The Truman administration created seventy-one separately authorized grant programs involving areas such as education, health, and transportation. The increase in grants-in-aid even continued through the conservative Eisenhower administration. By 1960, 132 grants were consuming $6.8 billion—a 250 percent increase in federal outlays. As the number and size of national grants grew, so did the conditions attached to these grants.[41]

Lyndon Johnson: The Era of Creative Federalism, 1963–1968

In the 1960s President Lyndon B. Johnson launched his Great Society program, which involved using federal programs to create a smoother functioning social welfare system. Johnson used what is called **creative federalism,** an initiative that expanded the concept of the partnership between the national government and the states. The national government would now work with cities, countries, school districts, and even nonprofit organizations to provide social services.

Under creative federalism the central government was thrust into a number of areas that had been neglected by the states. Johnson directed his administration to attack poverty, promote equal opportunity in education, solve the "urban crisis" through direct aid to the big cities (bypassing the states), and guarantee equal rights for minority groups. His Great Society initiative led to a rapid increase in new programs, most significantly Medicare and Medicaid, which provided national health care assistance for the aged and the impoverished; the Elementary and Secondary Education Act (ESEA), which provided national funding for public education; and Model Cities, which was aimed at rejuvenating the inner cities. Broad national guidelines were attached to these programs, but it was left to the states and localities to implement the programs. For instance, the Medicaid program included national guidelines such as the level of income that would qualify a person for assistance, but the states determined who would be eligible, how broad health coverage would be, and how health care providers would be reimbursed.

In the 1960s, the focus of the grants-in-aid program shifted from needs that were perceived by the states and pressed on the national government to needs perceived by the national government and pressed on the states. In addition, national spending increased dramatically. Between 1960 and 1967, the number of grants increased from 132 to 379. Public as well as private resources were mobilized and pooled in an effort to meet a variety of goals, including improving farming, combating drug abuse, securing disaster relief after a flood or a storm, and improving education. As a result of these programs, the national government became bloated and overloaded. Bureaucracies to administer the spending programs were enlarged at both the national and state levels. States engaged in the "grantsmanship game," tailoring their applications to fit national requirements rather than their own policy needs. Moreover, the American people became accustomed to looking to the national government for solutions to their problems.

This effort to use federalism creatively helped the nation to approach democracy by empowering groups that had been voiceless for years. Grants were given for programs aimed at improving the quality of life for the handicapped, migrant workers, and neglected children. Other programs promoted bilingual education and desegregation. States that had previously ignored the needs of certain groups in their region found that they could attract additional national funds by being attentive to those groups' needs. In short, it was now in the states' financial interest to promote democracy.

As you will learn in Chapter 15, while the goals of creative federalism were laudable, the very nature of the American federal structure served to thwart these goals. The size of the programs, the sharp disagreements among groups about their goals, and the lack of proper governmental oversight doomed them to failure. For instance, the Model Cities program was originally designed for twelve major cities, but it could not be passed until members of Congress from around the country got a piece of the pie for their own region, thus expanding the program to an unmanageable 150 cities.[42]

By the end of the 1960s there was widespread disenchantment with the Great Society and the national government's efforts to make sweeping social changes.[43] However, many of the programs from that era still exist, such as the Head Start program, which provides preschool instruction for poor children; the Legal Services program, which provides legal assistance for the indigent; and food stamps, which provide national funding to feed the poor. But with poverty still an enduring problem in America, the question of whether the benefits of the Great Society exceeded its administrative costs continues to be debated.[44]

creative federalism An initiative that expanded the concept of the partnership between the national government and the states under President Lyndon Johnson in the 1960s.

Richard Nixon's New Federalism, 1969–1974

President Nixon's **New Federalism** program, so labeled because it was designed to return fiscal power to the states and localities, was, in essence, a reaction to the excesses of Johnson's creative federalism. The cornerstone of this policy was **general revenue sharing (GRS),** in which money would be given to the states with no restrictions on how it could be spent. Also important was **special revenue sharing,** in which groups of categorical grants-in-aid in related policy areas such as crime control or health care would be consolidated into a single block grant.

After the passage of revenue sharing in 1972, $30 billion was distributed among the states and local governments, but the program was not a complete success. One-third of the funds were given to the states according to a complicated formula taking into account poverty levels and city size; the remaining two-thirds were paid directly to local governments, such as the cities of New York, Dallas, and San Francisco. The list of allowed expenditures was so general that rather than using the revenue-sharing money to replace old grant-in-aid programs, many states and localities began using it to cover their basic operating expenses, such as the salaries of public officials. As a result, many program areas that were once funded by categorical grants-in-aid now went unfunded.

Paradoxically, while it was intended to return power to the states, the GRS in fact further extended the influence of the national government. Even though GRS money had few funding restrictions, since the money went into the general treasury of each jurisdiction, states were now subject to national regulations in such areas as civil rights, affirmative action, and fair wages.

In the area of special revenue sharing, Nixon tried to create several block grants in community development, employment and training, and social services to replace the increasing number of more specific categorical grants. Contrary to his conservative image, Nixon spent freely in the domestic area, with the amount rising from 10.3 percent of the gross national product (GNP) at the beginning of his term of office and ending with 13.7 percent six years later. Seeking to induce state and local officials to support his New Federalism initiatives, Nixon added extra block grant money on top of what would have been available from the bundled categorical grants. Nixon was engaged in an ambitious process of grouping all of the operating and capital categorical grants into a handful of block grants in such areas as welfare and health care, and transferring the responsibility for income transfers (welfare, health care, school lunches, and food stamps) to the national government, when Watergate ended his effort.[45]

The movement toward increased dominance of the national government in the federal structure could not be reversed. Although Presidents Richard Nixon and Gerald Ford attempted through consolidation to slow the growth of national grants, by 1976 the total number of federal aid programs actually increased by 250 percent. Because there was a layer of unrestricted revenue-sharing money in addition to an increasing number of categorical grant programs, national spending expanded. Unhappy with its lack of control over both the amount and nature of this spending, Congress abolished revenue sharing to the states in 1981, then did the same for revenue sharing to the localities in 1986.

With more time in the White House, the state-oriented Republican party might have been able to carry out its plan to reform and reduce the categorical grants program. But the Democrats returned to the White House in 1976.

Creative Federalism Returns Under Jimmy Carter, 1977–1980

President Carter tried to combine the best aspects of Johnson's creative federalism and Nixon's New Federalism to more precisely target federal aid to the most hard-pressed communities. He also sought to use public funds to encourage private investment for certain problems. With these two goals, Carter hoped to mount a

New Federalism A program under President Richard Nixon that decentralized power as a response to New Deal centralization.

general revenue sharing (GRS) A system of the New Federalism program in which money was given to the states with no restrictions on how it could be spent.

special revenue sharing A system of the New Federalism program in which groups of categorical grants-in-aid in related policy areas such as crime control or health care are consolidated into a single block grant.

full-fledged attack on governmental red tape. As a result of these efforts, federal aid to the states and localities leveled out and, in the last years of Carter's term, even began to decrease. But while Carter had begun to reverse the trend toward increased national involvement in the American federal system, once more the failure to win reelection cut short a reform effort.

Ronald Reagan's "New New Federalism," 1981–1988

When Ronald Reagan ran for president in 1980, he promised to restore the power and authority of the state governments. In his first Inaugural Address, Reagan vowed "to curb the size and influence of the federal establishment and to demand recognition of the distinction between the powers granted to the federal government and those reserved to the States or to the people."[46] Reagan's logic was simple: Why should the national government tax the people and then ship the money back to the states? Why not simply let the states do the taxing and administer the programs?

Reagan's crusade against big government was approached from several different angles. In a speech to Congress several weeks later, Reagan presented his economic recovery strategy in an Omnibus Budget Reconciliation Act, which consisted of tax cuts, vast budget cuts, and cuts in federal regulations—all of which were designed to give "local government entities and states more flexibility and control."[47] The president faced stiff opposition from those who would be affected by the cuts. State governors began to balk when the cuts proved to be deeper than anticipated. Interest groups speaking for the recipients of grant money also pressed for continued funding. Nevertheless, Congress consolidated seventy-seven categorical programs into nine block grants. Although funding for the national programs was cut by less than half of what the administration had requested, Reagan's first year in office marked a significant break with the past. Figure 3.3 illustrates the rise and fall in national funding of state and local budgets from 1958 to 1998.

To further his reforms, in January 1982 Reagan proposed a complete reordering of the national spending priorities. First, there would be a "swap and turnback program" in which the national government would take over Medicaid, while the states, in turn, would take over sixty programs such as Aid to Families with Dependent Children (AFDC) and food stamps. Relying on its budget estimates, the White

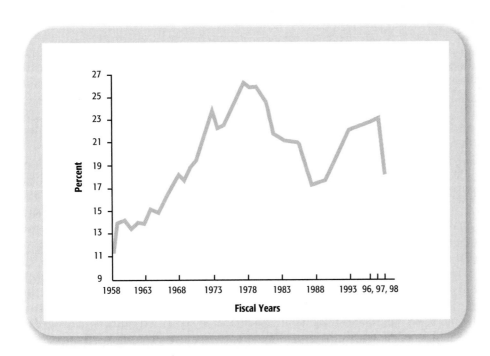

Figure 3.3
National Aid to States, 1958–98

Sources: "Giving Power to Fifty Little Washingtons," *Newsweek,* February 6, 1995, pp. 18–19; *The Book of the States, 1994–1995,* vol. 30 (Lexington, Ky.: Council of State Governments, 1996), pp. 580–581; *The Book of the States, 1988–1989,* vol. 24, p. 439; *The Book of the States, 1996–1997,* vol. 31, p. 494; *The Book of the States, 1998–1999,* vol. 32, pp. 287–289; *The Book of the States, 1997–1999,* vol. 32, pp. 287–89; and *The Book of the States, 2000–2001,* vol. 33, pp. 312–321.

House promised that the swap would not result in increased expenditures for the states, and since the health costs taken over by the national government were destined to rise sharply, the result would likely represent future savings for the states.

Stiff resistance quickly developed over these new reforms. While states wanted greater control over spending for programs, they also wanted the security of guaranteed national funding. And while the national government wanted to reduce its level of spending, a transfer of program responsibilities to the states would mean a loss of control over tax revenues. In short, this attempt to move away from national dominance in the federal partnership threatened to send a hesitant government into uncharted waters.

As a result, Reagan's new brand of New Federalism achieved mixed results. While the "swap and turnback program" was never introduced in Congress, there was an $8 billion absolute reduction in national spending from the budget cuts, and 140 national grant programs were cut or consolidated. However, after 1982 the number of federal grants began rising again, from 400 in 1982 to 492 in 1988. Reagan also won adoption of nine new block grants in areas such as the prevention and treatment of substance abuse and maternal and child care. Over time, just as in the Nixon years, these block grants lost dollar value as inflation increased faster than their rise in funding.

Reagan's New New Federalism created challenges and dilemmas for states now faced with doing more with less.[48] While it is true that overall national grant funding dropped from 25 percent of state budgets in the late 1970s to less than 17 percent in the late 1980s, in fact only once during the Reagan years was there a real dollar reduction in federal aid. In every other year federal aid in real-dollar terms actually increased.[49] The appearance of a lack of federal aid to the states was due to other factors. First, there was a statistical increase in the revenue-growth of states and localities in the period from 1978 to 1988, thus lowering the percentage of federal aid as it related to state and local governments revenue, budgets and outlays. States such as New Jersey, California, Massachusetts, New York, and Pennsylvania found that despite their increased state revenue, the increased programmatic responsibilities delegated to them due to the "turnback" program and the increased costs due to the downturned economy led to rapidly escalating state budget deficits. In response, governors argued that large tax increases had to be adopted or important programs, such as funding for college education, had to be cut significantly. Despite these problems, the potential for greater state innovation as a result of funding cuts did offer some hope for the future of policy reform.

The Bush Years, 1989–1992

President George Bush sought to continue the Reagan downsizing of government. He called for personal volunteerism to address social ills and encouraged state and local governments to pick up the costs of certain national programs, such as wastewater treatment plants and mass transit. In addition, Bush tried to lower welfare spending and find other ways to pay for environmental protection and education programs. Despite these funding cuts, however, sharp increases in the cost of Medicaid, now the responsibility of the national government after the Reagan reform, led to national grant increases from $101.2 billion to $166.9 billion, or an average increase of 9.2 percent per year.[50] Because of these escalating costs and the huge budget deficits, the Bush administration was unable to carry out its plans to refocus domestic initiatives.[51] In 1992 Bush tried to consolidate $20 billion in categorical grant programs into a single block grant and turn it back to the states, but the proposal was not enacted.

The experience of the Bush administration, like that of the Reagan administration, revealed the difficulty of reversing heavy national financial involvement in the federal partnership. Rising budget deficits, the public's demands for increased services and lower taxes, and the inability of financially strapped states to meet policy expectations made successful implementation of reforms difficult. With the budget deficit out of control and Medicaid expenses continuing to add to the deficit, choices had to be made about which grant programs to fund. These choices were not easy, as various interest groups remained ready to do battle over any cuts or reforms.

Bill Clinton and New(t) Federalism, 1993–2001

Bill Clinton took office facing an escalating national budget deficit and the dilemma that the vast majority of Americans wished to retain the national programs they had come to expect over the years but had become less willing to pay for. Medicaid expenses alone amounted to 40 percent of the one-quarter trillion dollars that the federal government now paid to states and localities. Clinton knew from his experience as governor of Arkansas of the states' ability to devise new programs if given the funds.

Clinton was elected on a campaign promise to be a **"New Democrat"**—a conservative Democrat who supports states' rights and a less activist national government that provides people with tools to help themselves, such as job training, rather than with an array of expensive social services. But Clinton's first two years in office left him looking more like an "Old Democrat" from the liberal wing of the party, which maintains that the national government should provide people with a safety net, even if it means that government will grow. National grant funding rose steadily in his term of office until it reached 23 percent of state budgets by the late 1990s.

The election of a Republican House under Speaker Newt Gingrich and a Republican Senate under Majority Leader Bob Dole forced the president to think about ways to reorganize government in the direction of the states. Clinton's initial step, his 1994 health care package, although aimed at reducing escalating health costs, failed largely because of the perception that it would foster big government. In 1996 Clinton signed into law a welfare bill that gave much more control over welfare to the states and forced recipients back to work after a two-year period of assistance, with an overall limit of five years of support in one's lifetime. As a result, the nature and amount of welfare assistance varied from state to state, with millions of people being dropped from the rolls.[52]

But then Clinton went the other way on May 1, 1998, by reversing a 1987 executive order by Ronald Reagan that was designed to prevent federal meddling in state and local affairs. He quietly laid the groundwork for increased federal power by signing Executive Order 13803, which allowed federal agencies to consult more with state and local officials and also created nine justifications for federal intervention in policy matters. Local officials as well as conservative members of Congress immediately charged that this order seriously eroded federalism, leading the president to suspend the order pending further review.

The last eighteen months of the Clinton administration brought changes in the legal aspects of federalism, though not as great as some expected. On August 5, 1999, President Clinton issued an executive order requiring all departments in the executive branch to take into account the "fundamental federalism principles" in creating policies, including federal regulations that "can inhibit the creation of effective solutions" to societal problems. This action undermined the legal doctrine of "preemption" by which Congress can, under the supremacy clause, signal that it will be the only legislative body to govern in a policy area. By this means a uniform policy can be achieved. So Clinton's executive order was designed to allow states and local governments to develop their own policies to govern certain commercial enterprises. Critics of the executive order, argued that this move away from a uniform policy could create such diversity of regulations that it would become a national problem.

However, Congress's attempt to allow for such diversity of policies did not succeed. The House passed a Federalism Act, and a Senate Committee passed the Federalism Accountability Act of 1999, which would require the Congress to consult with state and local officials prior to the consideration of any federal regulations

"New Democrat" A conservative Democrat who supports states' rights and a less activist national government.

that could interfere with traditional state and local rights and spell out both how the new law might preempt state and local law and why it would be a good idea. The attempt to allow for diversity in governmental regulation, however, united three normal sets of foes—the Chamber of Commerce (small businesses), labor unions, and environmental protection advocates—in derailing the measure in the House because of the maze of governmental regulations that would result in their area.

George W. Bush, 2001–Present

That such measures protecting the states will be reconsidered is likely now because of the 2002 congressional elections.[53] There was little doubt that George W. Bush would have continued the pro-states' rights programs of his father and Ronald Reagan. All of the plans were derailed temporarily in mid-2001 when Senator Jim Jeffords of Vermont left the Republican Party to become an Independent, thus enabling the Democratic Party to control the Senate. Then, the terrorist attack on September 11, 2001 turned the president's agenda away from the domestic affairs and toward foreign and military issues. Viewed from a distance, the one major domestic initiative of the Bush administration during this period, the "No Child Left Behind Act" reforming public education by making federal money available to public schools in return for states implementing more extensive achievement testing and holding schools accountable for performance, had the appearance of a grand federal program. Even here, though, individual states were given wide latitude to spend the federal money targeted for low-income students in a manner best suited for their region. In other domestic areas, the Bush administration began calling for cutbacks in spending. While the lack of a Republican Senate and the anti-terrorism fight made it difficult for President Bush to move the country quickly in such a states' rights and reduced domestic spending direction, much of the change in the first area was being effected by the decisions of the Rehnquist Court. The latter area will be a focus of discussion by the Republican-led 108th Congress.

The Rehnquist Court and the Future of Federalism

What does the future hold for our federal system? In addition to presidential and congressional policies that have sought to devolve power to the states, Supreme Court and lower court rulings have recently begun to redefine federalism in the direction of more state power. In 1992, the Supreme Court had ruled, in *New York v. United States,* that a 1985 congressional statute regulating the disposal of low-level radioactive waste should be struck down because of its "take title" provision. If states and localities did not provide for the disposal of all such waste created in their region by a specific date, they were required to take possession and responsibility for it. Justice Sandra Day O'Connor and the majority found this statute to be a violation of the Tenth Amendment: "Whatever the outer limits of [state] sovereignty may be, one thing is clear. The Federal Government may not compel the States to enact or administer a federal regulatory program. The Constitution . . . [does not] authorize Congress simply to direct the States to provide for the disposal of radioactive waste generated within their borders."[54]

In its 1994–95 term, ruling in the case of *United States v. Lopez,* a narrow five-person majority of the Supreme Court overturned a section of the 1990 federal Gun-Free School Zones law making it a crime to possess firearms within one thousand feet of a school zone. Congress argued that its power to regulate such behavior came from the interstate commerce clause, because violent crime around a school could affect the national economy through higher insurance costs and self-imposed limits on travel. Although this justification would have worked in the past, during oral argument, Justice David Souter warned: "Presumably there is nothing left if

Congress can do this, no recognizable limit." In overturning the law, the Court appeared ready to establish new limits on congressional authority by requiring Congress, for the first time in fifty years, to justify the link between a law and the commerce clause. Speaking for what has become a hard five-person conservative majority on the Court in favor of state power, Chief Justice William Rehnquist said that this regulation "neither regulates a commercial activity nor contains a requirement that the possession be connected in any way to interstate commerce."[55] This decision represented a real shift in decision-making, because for more than fifty years the Court had not even pushed for a clear connection between a law and the commerce power in approving federal extensions of authority. In 1996 Congress resurrected the Gun-Free School Zones Act in its Omnibus Appropriations Act but this time with one key difference—now it was a federal crime either to knowingly carry a gun within a 1,000 feet of a school or fire a weapon in that area.

That this decision represented a watershed in the direction of more state power was made clear in a series of later rulings.[56] Shortly after the decision to overturn the 1990 federal Gun-Free School Zones law, the same five-person conservative majority limited Congress's power to make states subject to federal lawsuits because of the Eleventh Amendment. In this case, the state of Florida was freed from suit by a Seminole Indian tribe challenging negotiations over its desire to create gambling interests on its tribal lands because of the states' sovereign right of immunity from lawsuits by citizens.[57] Finally, in 1997 the Supreme Court invalidated those portions of the federal Brady handgun control law that required local sheriffs to perform background checks on handgun purchasers until a national investigation database could be established. In this case, while Justice Antonin Scalia could not find anything in the Constitution requiring such a decision, he still did so based on the "historical understanding and practice, in the structure of the Constitution, and in the jurisprudence of this Court." Using The Federalist Papers and a study of early American history, Justice Scalia argued that the national government "at most" had been able to impose some duties on state court judges, but had never been able to do more than "recommend" that other actions be performed by state government officials. That this reading of history is controversial, however, was made clear by Justice David Souter in dissent, who defended Congress's power to adopt the Brady bill by quoting from Alexander Hamilton in *The Federalist,* no. 27, that: "The legislatures, courts, and magistrates, of the [states] . . . will be incorporated into the operations of the national government as far as its just and constitutional authority extends, and will be rendered auxiliary to the enforcement of its laws."[58]

Only the Court's refusal in its 1999 term to allow states to sell personal information such as names and addresses from their motor vehicle records to various commercial databases represented a restriction on state authority in this period. There, it was the privacy interests of the public in computer databases that, for the Court, appeared to take precedence over the interests of the states in making millions of dollars by selling the information to commercial retail outlets. Then, as seen in the Approaching Diversity box, the Court returned in 2000 to leaving it to states to prosecute "gender-induced" attacks by striking down the federal law on the issue. And, that same year, the Court narrowed the decision in the Brady bill case a bit by ruling that the federal government, under the Drivers Privacy Protection Act, could prevent states from selling personal information about people with motor vehicle licenses and who owned cars as a means of raising money.[59]

At the heart of these Supreme Court cases are questions about who decides—the national government or the states. For now, there appears to be a five-person majority willing to extend state powers, but a change of one of those votes through presidential appointment might well send the Court in a different direction. So these questions about the American federal system will continue to be explored as President George Bush appoints new justices to the Court.[60] With President Bush on the record as saying that his favorite Supreme Court justices are avowedly pro-states' rights advocates Antonin Scalia and Clarence Thomas, there seems to be little

APPROACHING DIVERSITY

States and the Violence Against Women Act

Sometimes the road to democracy takes a U-turn back to the old ways of earlier generations. Few realized that in 1994 when Christy Brzonkala, a college student at Virginia Polytechnic Institute, claimed she was raped in her dorm room by two Virginia Tech football players, Antonio J. Morrison and James L. Crawford, it would lead to a major Supreme Court ruling that turned back the clock on the federalism issue to an earlier era of greater state power within the federal structure, continuing a decade long trend under conservative Supreme Court Chief Justice William Rehnquist.

Ms. Brzonkala brought suit in federal court against her two attackers after they were allowed to return to Virginia Tech despite being found guilty by the school's disciplinary system; their continued presence on campus caused her to decide to drop out of school. Ms. Brzonkala brought suit under a provision of the 1994 Violence Against Women Act (VAWA) that allows women to sue their attackers in federal court in cases "motivated by gender," rather than in state court, which was their only previous outlet, for monetary damages under the civil law. Although this type of crime was ordinarily remedied by state criminal laws, Congress used a nearly sixty-year tradition of Supreme Court decisions in the interstate commerce field to expand federal power in this area, arguing that such attacks represented a significant effect on business transactions among various states. Beyond that, Congress argued that this sort of "gender-motivated violence" represented harm to the equal protection of women, which was safeguarded by the Fourteenth Amendment. While Congress was passing the law, however, Chief Justice William Rehnquist argued that the general power to control crime should be left at the states' level.

When the alleged attackers argued that the congressional Violence Against Women Act was a violation of the Constitution by its changing the nature of the federal process, the legal battle began. Thirty-six states joined the federal government in arguing in favor of the law, citing the billion-dollar costs associated with violence against women. To them, the costs were compounded by the suffering of the victims, which could only be lessened by increased emergency, medical, welfare, and insurance payments—all of which would be borne at the state level. Solicitor General Seth Waxman cited various studies showing that there was a "pervasive bias" in the state criminal justice systems against women who had been attacked and were unsuccessfully seeking to use the equal protection of the laws provision of the Constitution to preserve their rights. On the other side, the attorneys for the football players argued that if Congress were allowed to pass such a law it would lead to an increase in the federal government's meddling in traditionally local and state activities, such as criminal law and individual relations, thus upsetting the nation's basic constitutional framework.

While for decades after the court-packing plan of 1937 the Supreme Court had routinely agreed with Congress's use of the interstate commerce clause and other constitutional provisions to expand national powers, in nine major rulings since 1992 the Rehnquist Court ignored such claims and restored power to the states. These decisions were all handed down by a narrow 5-4 majority. The provision of the VAWA allowing suits for crimes "motivated by gender"

doubt that given a chance he will attempt to place on the Court jurists with similar points of view.

Federalism and Approaching Democracy in the Twenty-First Century

The debate over federalism and the proper balance of power between national and state governments is ongoing. "We need a certain administrative discretion," argues political scientist Don Kettl: "You can't run everything from Washington." Political historian Todd Gitlin responds that "the argument for local difference was always disingenuous. . . . They are afraid of the onslaught of secular humanism, or pointy-headed bureaucrats."[61] That has been the nature of the debate for more than two centuries. There's usually agreement that there are problems to be dealt with: commerce, crime, the economy, health care, the environment and now the fight against the terrorism threat. The disagreement, however, comes over

to be taken to federal court was struck down by another 5-4 vote. The Court declared that "the Constitution requires a distinction between what is truly national and what is truly local." To accept Congress's claims of support under the interstate commerce and equal protection clauses for this law, argued Rehnquist, "would allow Congress to regulate any crime as long as the nationwide, aggregated impact of that crime has substantial effects on employment, production, transit or consumption." For Rehnquist, a general power by the states in the criminal area is something "which the founders denied the national government and reposed in the states." In a footnote, however, Rehnquist hinted that another provision of VAWA that made it a crime to cross state lines to engage in domestic violence or stalk women would be constitutional because of its multistate character. In dissent, Justice David Souter noted that even the states wanted this law and urged his colleagues to let the political system work out the problem instead of creating the irony in this ruling that "the states will be forced to enjoy the new federalism whether they want it or not." For Souter, "it is clear that some Congressional conclusions about obviously substantial, cumulative effects on commerce are being assigned lesser values." This decision became, then, only the second time since 1935 that a crime was ruled to have so little connection to commerce that it must be left to the states rather than Congress to regulate.

Under these rulings, the diverse nature of state actions rather than a national approach to issues that predominated prior to the rulings of the Warren Court in the 1960s will likely continue. This was made clear in 2000 when Congress reauthorized the VAWA and even expanded the law to cover date rape, but, following the Supreme Court's ruling, refused to reinstate the provision of the law permitting victims to sue their attackers in federal court.

▲ The suit of former Virginia Polytechnic Institute student, Christy Brzonkala, against two football players alleging that she was raped resulted in a landmark Supreme Court decision dealing with federalism.

Sources: This box is based on Linda Greenhouse, "Women Lose Right to Sue Attackers in Federal Court," *New York Times,* May 16, 2000, p. 1; Joan Biskupic, "States' Role at Issue in Rape Suit," *Washington Post,* January 10, 2000, p. A17; Marcia Coyle, "New Federalism Litmus," *National Law Journal,* January 24, 2000, p. 1; and Stuart Taylor, Jr., "The Tipping Point," *National Journal,* June 10, 2000, pp. 1810–19. and Herman Schwartz, "Supreme Court: Assault on Federalism Swipes at Women," *Los Angeles Times,* May 21, 2000).

which level of government, or whether any government at all, should address such matters. Generally more and more people argue that the government that is closest to the people is the best government to handle these issues. But with the terrorist threat, the question may well be how much financial support and political guidance will be needed and will be offered by the federal government.

Where one stands in the federalism debate reveals a lot about one's political ideology. In this century, Franklin D. Roosevelt's New Deal put the liberal Democrats firmly in the position of the nation-centered party, upholding that only the national government can provide a basic standard of living and uniform democratic rights for all citizens. Lyndon Johnson's Great Society is a classic example of this position. He used the powers of the national government to create a welfare state aimed at helping the underprivileged, solving civil rights problems, improving education, and so forth. Conservative Republicans, on the other hand, advocate a state-centered approach, arguing that solutions are best left either to the state governments or to the private sector. These conservatives were understandably overjoyed with Ronald Reagan's election in 1980; his platform opposing big government and advocating the return of power to the states was more to their taste. Reagan sought to dismantle the welfare state and to cut national spending. Now the Bush administration's call for tax cuts and its need to spend money on the war in Afghanistan and the anti-terrorism fight is likely to lead to further calls for cuts in spending to states and localities. As a result, Democrats and liberals continue to express worries about the potential consequences of a shrunken national role. To some, then, a stronger national government means more democracy, while to others it means less.

America's experience with federalism has involved a continual shifting of power from the states to the federal government, and now, with the Rehnquist Court's decisions in the last decade and the current Bush administration, power is shifting back to the states. The nature of the federal structure continues to change. Although the national government predominates, in recent years due to the budget deficit there has been less money in its coffers, meaning less leverage over the states and a new role for the states as they try to figure out ways to make more efficient use of whatever federal monies come their way. Through it all, in exercising its political role, each level of government plays an important part in ensuring that our federal structure, the result of a careful compromise forged by the framers in Philadelphia, continues to function and thrive in dealing with America's new policy needs.

DEMOCRACY IN THE NEW MILLENNIUM

Paying the Bill for Fighting Terrorism

Two of the biggest questions over the next few years may well be who pays the bills for the antiterrorism efforts at the state and local level, and how effective are those governments at spending the money? With state budget surpluses a thing of the past as nearly every state faces revenue shortfalls, with more than three-quarters of the states having gone through a series of hiring freezes and budget cuts, and with more than half of the states having spent their rainy day funds, they must now attempt to design state level programs to deal with the terrorism threat. The hope of many state officials is that with Tom Ridge, the former Governor of the State of Pennsylvania as the new Secretary of the Department of Homeland Security, and former Texas Governor George W. Bush as President, federal financial help might be forthcoming.

But the problem that states currently face is a lack of guidance from Washington. The state of Oklahoma recently tested its new homeland defense plan; its agencies responded to a suspected smallpox outbreak in the state. Before the crisis ended, state and federal officials disputed whether the federal government's use of "yellow" as the code for this type of threat (a significant threat of a terrorist strike) as opposed to "orange" (a higher risk of attack) was appropriate.

The pervasiveness of the threat of attacks on our nation has motivated Congress to make federal money available for some state and local programs. The federal government has made $3.5 million in antiterrorism aid available to the states, but few states know how to apply for the money and many do not yet know how to use it. The Department of Justice must first sanction the states's "domestic preparedness strategy" before requests for money are approved. Then, the state must demonstrate that it has already spent at least one-third of any money previously received for antiterrorism programs. Finally, the state must show its organizational plan for the relevant governmental departments involved in antiterrorism efforts. For the state of Massachusetts, this meant organizing the response strategies of the state's 48,000 state and local fire, police, public works, and emergency services personnel. Prerequirements of this type translate into delays; four years after Congress authorized money for emergency response, the Office of Justice Programs still had not awarded over half of the $243 million earmarked for state and local fire, police, and emergency response agencies.

The models for dealing with the terrorist threat are as varied as the states. North Carolina has established a new homeland security office but left the duties to existing law enforcement agencies. Georgia has established a $1 million intelligence-gathering and analysis operation. "There is little question that federal support will determine whether local homeland initiatives succeed," argues *USA Today*. As the various levels of government labor to strengthen security and improve response times in battling terrorism, the question of how effectively the state and local governments are able to spend federal money to meet the threats at their level remains.

For more on this question, see www.nemaweb.org/Trends in Terrorism Preparedness/index.htm and www.nasulgc.org/.

Sources: Kevin Johnson, "U.S. is all over the map on Homeland Defense," *USA Today,* April 23, 2002; and Ralph Ranalli, "State Slow to Apply for Federal Terror Aid," *Boston Globe,* April 23, 2002. And Francis X. Clines, "Painful Choices for States Facing Wider Budget Gaps," *New York Times,* February 8, 2002, p. A 17.

SUMMARY

1. The term *federalism* refers to a political system in which two or more distinct levels of government exercise power over the same body of citizens. Federalism differs from a *confederation*, in which the power to govern is decentralized among sovereign states.

2. Among the advantages of federalism are the ability to accommodate a diverse population, a tendency to minimize policy conflict, dispersal of power, and enhanced prospects for governmental innovation. Such a system also has disadvantages: groups that wish to protect their interests may obstruct national mandates, and the system may produce inequities among different regions.

3. The most important powers shared by federal and state government are the ability to regulate commerce and the right to collect taxes to provide for the general welfare. Also important are the powers reserved to the states by the Tenth Amendment to the Constitution. These three constitutional protections help create a balance of power between the two levels of government.

4. The Constitution delegates certain powers exclusively to the national government; these include the power to declare war, raise and support an army, negotiate with foreign countries, and coin money. The powers reserved to the states include regulation of the health, morals, public safety, and welfare of state citizens. Concurrent powers are shared by the two levels of government; in addition to the power to regulate commerce and impose taxes, they include the power to regulate elections and maintain a judicial structure.

5. A few powers are denied both to the national government and to the states. These include the power to grant titles of nobility and to pass bills of attainder and ex post facto laws.

6. Efforts in the early 1800s to expand the power of the national government were hotly debated, leading to a Supreme Court decision upholding the dominance of the national government in areas where its powers overlapped with those of the states. One response was the theory of nullification, which held that states could refuse to observe national legislation that they considered unacceptable.

7. After the Civil War the concept of dual federalism prevailed; each level of power was viewed as separate and supreme within its own jurisdiction. During the Great Depression the national government regained its dominance despite numerous Supreme Court rulings setting limits on its activities. Eventually a new approach, known as cooperative federalism, emerged. Since the 1930s Supreme Court decisions have sought to ensure uniformity in policies involving the rights of individuals and to impose national standards to reduce inequality.

8. A grant-in-aid gives money to states and localities to induce them to implement policies favored by the national government. Categorical grants are given for specific purposes and are usually accompanied by strict rules. Federal mandates are national requirements that must be observed by the states.

9. In the 1960s creative federalism was used to address problems in areas that had been neglected by the states, resulting in rapid growth in the size and cost of the federal bureaucracy.

10. President Nixon's New Federalism included the policy of general revenue sharing, by which money was given to the states with no restrictions on how it could be spent; and special revenue sharing, by which categorical grants in related policy areas were consolidated into a single block grant. President Carter attempted to combine this approach with creative federalism, while President Reagan attempted to do away with revenue sharing and restore power to the state governments, a policy that was continued by President Bush.

11. At present, federalism is caught in a dilemma resulting from conflicting desires—to reduce spending by the national government, on the one hand, and to maintain national assistance to the states, on the other.

KEY TERMS

states' rights	*McCulloch v. Maryland*	project grant
federalism	*Gibbons v. Ogden*	formula/project grant
triad of powers	nullification	block grants
supremacy clause	dual federalism	devolution revolution
delegated powers	cooperative federalism	federal mandates
implied powers	incorporation	creative federalism
inherent powers	grant-in-aid	New Federalism
reserved powers	conditions of aid	general revenue sharing (GRS)
police powers	categorical grant	special revenue sharing
concurrent powers	formula grant	"New Democrat"

SUGGESTED READINGS

BANFIELD, EDWARD. "Federalism and the Dilemma of Popular Government." *In Here the People Rule: Selected Essays.* 2d ed. ed. Edward Banfield, pp. 57–88. Washington, D.C.: American Enterprise Institute, 1991. An intriguing explanation of how the nation-centered view of federalism originated and developed.

BEER, SAMUEL H. *To Make a Nation: The Rediscovery of American Federalism.* Cambridge, Mass.: Harvard University Press, 1993. A highly readable account tracing the philosophical origins of federalism from the British experience, through the constitutional founding, to the use of federalism today.

BERGER, RAOUL. *Federalism: The Founder's Design.* Norman: University of Oklahoma Press, 1987. An interesting depiction of the philosophical basis for the state-centered federalism position, arguing that since the states preceded the national government they still have sovereign power.

DYE, THOMAS R. *American Federalism: Competition Among Governments.* Lexington, Mass.: Lexington Books, 1990. An intriguing picture of American federalism as a system of competition among the national and state governments.

ELAZAR, DANIEL J. *American Federalism: A View from the States.* 3d ed. New York: Harper & Row, 1984. A very helpful and comprehensive examination of American federalism from the perspective of state governments.

GOLDWIN, ROBERT, ed. *A Nation of States.* Chicago: Rand McNally, 1961. A series of classic essays by experts on federalism.

GRODZINS, MORTON. *The American System.* Chicago: Rand McNally, 1966. The classic account of the "marble-cake" image of cooperative federalism.

KINCAID, JOHN. "De Facto Devolution and Urban Defunding: The Priority of Persons Over Places," *Journal of Urban Affairs,* Volume 21, Number 2, (1999) pp. 135–167. A highly informative and well-researched analysis of what really became of the promised "devolution revolution."

OSBORNE, DAVID. *Laboratories of Democracy.* Boston: Harvard Business School, 1988. A highly readable series of case studies on state governors and governments operating to solve public policy problems.

PRESSMAN, JEFFREY, and AARON WILDAVSKY. *Implementation.* Berkeley: University of California Press, 1973. An excellent account of how the democratic processes in federalism thwarted the implementation of one of Johnson's economic development projects in Oakland, California.

REAGAN, MICHAEL D., and JOHN G. SANZONE. *The New Federalism.* 2d ed. New York: Oxford University Press, 1981. A comprehensive and classic analysis of fiscal federalism outlining both the grant-in-aid and revenue-sharing systems.

RIKER, WILLIAM H. *The Development of American Federalism.* Boston: Kluwer Academic, 1987. Essays on the continuity of American federalism, written over a thirty-year period by Riker and his colleagues.

STEWART, WILLIAM H. *Concepts of Federalism.* Lanham, Md.: University Press of America, 1984. A comprehensive dictionary on the meanings of, and metaphors for, federalism.

WALKER, DAVID B. *Toward a Functioning Federalism.* Cambridge, Mass.: Winthrop, 1981. An in-depth examination of the intergovernmental-relations system, offering a series of suggestions for reform.

Constructing
a New Ideal Democracy

The new nation of Islandia has asked the student readers of *Approaching Democracy* for help. Islandia is an
island in the Pacific of one million people whose
demographic, geographic, and political views are fair-
ly diverse. Fully 70% of the people on the island live on the eastern
side, with only 20 miles separating it from the nearby island Expatria,
a new nation of people who left Islandia to live very different lives.

There are other differences on the island. The northern part of
the island is mainly urban, with people living in fairly large villages
intent on making fishing nets and the clothing. The southern part of
the island is largely agricultural, with people growing vegetables
and coconuts. The inhabitants of the northwest and southeast
sections of the island base their religion on worshipping the sun,
while those in the northeast and southwest sections of the island
base their religion on worshipping the moon. A significant portion
of the population of the eastern part of the island makes clothing,
while the western part of the island has developed a significant boat
and weapon-making operation.

The biggest issue on the island is food. This means protecting
the fishing rights for the people, who rely on this for their primary
food source. The best fishing areas are along the fishing banks off of
the western side of the island. While there is good fishing off of the
eastern banks, neighboring Expatria creates major problems when it
sends armed fishing boats to try to take over the fishing banks between the two islands.

An astonishing revolution by descendants of the founder of Islandia has broken up the dictatorial government and replaced it
with leaders from the new democratic movement. You and your
team of students have been asked to draft a new constitution and
design a government for Islandia that would best "approach
democracy" based on a model of the American Constitution and
its federal structure. Design the government and constitution for
Islandia.

To accomplish this result you need to do the following. First,
read *The Federalist*, No. 10 in the appendix of the book and figure out
how many states should be created and where those states should
be. Then, after re-reading the American Constitution, especially
Articles I and IV, along with the 9th and 10th Amendments, you
need to figure out how much power the states and the overall island
government should possess. Finally, you need to read *The Federalist*,
No. 51 and determine how many branches of government there
should be for the entire island government, which powers each will
possess, and whether or not to separate them in the same way as in
the American government.

Once all of this is done, what will happen to your new government when it becomes apparent that the western part of the island
wants to ban the use of nets to fish in order to preserve their food
supply, but the eastern part of the island does not? Likewise, what
will happen when the eastern part of the island finds that it needs
the help of the weapon-making ability of the western part of the island to protect its fishing banks from the raiders from Expatria, but
that assistance is likely to be denied because their food source is adequately protected already?

4   CONGRESS

CHAPTER OUTLINE

Approaching Democracy Case Study:
   Negotiating the Legislative Labyrinth

Introduction: Congress and Democracy

The Structure and Powers of Congress

The Members of Congress

How Congress Organizes Itself

Congress in Session

How a Bill Becomes a Law

Additional Functions of Congress

The 106th and 107th Congress:
   Whither the "Republican Revolution"?

Congress After the 2002 Election

APPROACHING DEMOCRACY CASE STUDY

Negotiating the Legislative Labyrinth

S omething was wrong with the Campaign Finance Law passed in 1974 to regulate money
flow into the election process. While the law
regulated how much "hard money" contributors could
donate directly to a candidate's election campaign, unlimited "soft money" could be donated to the candidate's party. Abuse of this loophole allowed President
Bill Clinton to raise tens of millions of dollars in soft
money from large contributors by allowing them to
spend a night in the Lincoln bedroom. In 2000, the
Democratic and Republican parties raised more than

$500 million dollars in soft money. "Issue advocacy ads" thus funded were beyond government control and appeared frequently. Senators John McCain (R.-AZ) and Russell Feingold (D.-WI) criticized the use of soft money as being corruptive of the election process, but conservative Senators including Mitch McConnell (R.-KY) and Trent Lott (R.-MS) defended it as being protected by the First Amendment. After McCain and Feingold introduced reform legislation that got nowhere in 1995, in 1997 they tried again, proposing a routine amendment to the Campaign Finance Law limiting or banning the use of the soft money and issue ads.

The McCain-Feingold bill introduced to the Senate on January 21, 1997, was not considered that year because McCain and Feingold failed to get 60 votes for cloture to end a three-day filibuster led by conservative Republicans. They tried reintroducing the bill again the following February. Again the bill failed.

Meanwhile, in the House of Representatives, Christopher Shays (R.-CT) and Marty Meehan (D.-MA) tried to get their own campaign finance bill, through the House. With the Republicans in control of the House and Majority Whip Tom Delay (R.-TX) vocally opposing the bill, the Democrats could not move the bill out of committee. On October 24, 1997, House Democrats threatened to pass a rarely used discharge petition that would bring the measure out of committee and onto the floor of Congress for consideration. Republicans sidetracked this maneuver, promising to bring the measure to the floor by March 1998. But they broke this agreement.

In mid-summer 1998 the House bill finally made it to the floor, despite opposition from 53 interest groups and attempts by conservative members of Congress to kill the measure by forcing votes on nearly four dozen amendments, many of them so-called "poison pill" amendments designed to make even the bill's original supporters unwilling to vote for it. In August 1998, the measure passed the House. But a companion bill still had to be passed in the Senate before the measure could be sent to President Clinton for signature. When the House-approved Shays-Meehan Bill made it to the Senate, it was replaced by the McCain-Feingold Bill. This attempt at Senate approval was stalled by another filibuster led by Mitch McConnell, and Campaign Finance Reform died once again. By now it was clear, unless McCain, Feingold, Meehan and Shays could muster 60 votes in the Senate, campaign finance reform was never going to pass in Congress.

The polarized legislative climate in Congress had to change to assure passage. The antagonistic relationship of the two political parties, the undue influence of political interest groups, the impact of the media, and a presidency weakened by scandal were all factors affecting the bill's passage. The Republicans believed that they could raise more soft money and were thus unwilling to limit it. The Democrats, however, were trying to regulate the process in a way that would preserve their election chances. Still, neither party wanted to be perceived as corrupt, so appearing to be in favor of reform was desired. Thus, some in the House voted for the Shays-Meehan Bill believing that it would never get through the Senate.

Special interest groups fought hard against reform, believing a soft money ban would impair their ability to influence the votes of legislators and regulation of issue ads would impair their ability to get their messages to the public. The National Right to Life Committee made it clear that a vote for campaign reform would be considered a vote against them.

The national media whipped up a circus-like frenzy over this fight, making it impossible for some members of Congress to change their views. Much was written about Republican Christopher Shays, who was portrayed as the reformist "David" slinging his rocks, against the "Goliath" of big money interests and his own political party.

Then there was the Monica Lewinsky scandal, which would turn into an impeachment struggle, making Bill Clinton a weak leader on legislative issues. When Clinton recommended that Congress pass the McCain-Feingold Bill, or the Shays-Meehan Bill, no one listened.

In 2001 the issue re-emerged. House Democrats decided to utilize the discharge petition, getting the Shays-Meehan Bill onto the floor and passed. The way success was achieved in the House angered Republicans, inspiring them to fight the bill even harder in the Senate. Yet another filibuster in the Senate ended reformists' hopes of keeping the bill alive that term.

The political climate changed in 2001 for various reasons. First, several of the bill's most vocal opponents were not returning to their Congressional seats after the

▲ Representatives Christopher Shays (R.-CT) and Marty Meehan (D.-MA) and Senator John McCain (R.-AZ) (l. to r.), along with Senator Russell Feingold (D.-WI), led the successful fight to enact campaign finance reform in 2002.

2000 election. Second, Senator John McCain had made clear in his presidential run that campaign finance reform was his top priority and he was prepared to force his colleagues to vote the measure up or down early in the Bush presidency. Third, Senator Jim Jeffords' decision to leave the Republican party and become an Independent moved control of the Senate body to the Democrats, making it possible for Majority Leader Tom Daschle to push reform. Finally, in early 2002, the Enron Corporation, an energy company, collapsed, causing political outrage after company officials were revealed to have sought help from political officials, some in the new administration, who had received significant amounts of "soft money" during the 2000 election. Recognizing the shifting political dynamic, President Bush gave signals that he would not veto a reform bill.

But even with the changed climate, passing the Bipartisan Campaign Reform Bill into law was not easy. With Senate passage considered possible, the bill's House opponents staged a mighty fight against the Shays-Meehan Bill. Despite repeated efforts by the Republicans and interest group lobbyists to have just one of dozens of amendments passed to alter the bill from the Senate measure, thus forcing a conference committee and allowing one more chance to kill it, the House measure passed in mid-February 2002 by a 240–189 vote.

The bill, which was passed five weeks later by a 60–40 vote in the Senate, banned the raising of soft money by the national political parties after the November 2002 election, and changed the amount of money individuals could contribute to candidates and state and local political parties. It also prohibited unions, corporations, and nonprofit groups from paying for issue advocacy ads that run within 30 days of an election primary or 60 days of a general election.

But not even a successful journey through the legislative labyrinth could guarantee the future of Campaign Reform. Even in defeat Senator Mitch McConnell vowed, "Today is not the end. There is litigation ahead. I am consoled by the obvious fact that the courts do not defer to Congress on matters of the Constitution."[1]

Question for Reflection: In considering the long journey to pass campaign finance reform, should Congress be designed to efficiently promote the passage of laws or make it difficult to pass laws, thus promoting democratic consideration of the issues involved?

INTRODUCTION: CONGRESS AND DEMOCRACY

The legislative journey of the 2002 Bipartisan Campaign Finance Reform law illustrates the complex route bills must follow to become law. Each newly introduced bill faces a daunting set of obstacles. This became clear to the Bush administration in May 2001 when Republican Senator Jim Jeffords of Vermont abandoned his party and tilted the perfectly balanced Senate to the Democrats. This allowed them to take control of the body's leadership positions and dictate the legislative agenda, derailing President George Bush's plans for the moment. After the terrorist attacks in September 2001, a bipartisan Congress allowed the Republican President to pass the U.S.A. Patriot Act with record speed and helped him to pass the sweeping Education Reform Act that he had promised in his election campaign. By the end of the first session of the 107th Congress, in 2001, of the 120 votes on which President Bush made his position clear, he won 104 of them, making his the most successful record with Congress for bill passage since President Lyndon B. Johnson in 1965. Still, one is left wondering what the Republicans could have accomplished if Jeffords had remained in their party.

In changing the pace and direction of its work, Congress was working exactly as the framers intended, with the House providing an immediate response to public will and the Senate behaving as the "saucer that cooled" the House's tea by offering its evaluation more deliberatively.

There are many stages in the legislative process. Countless actors play a role in the drama of lawmaking, and enemies of every proposal lurk in a dozen or more places. It often seems amazing that any bill ever passes. Occasionally, however, a "breakthrough moment" arrives, such as that when the U.S.A. Patriot Act was rushed into law in a matter of weeks, when Congress finds the political will to work like a well-oiled machine. This chapter looks at how Congress has helped, and at times thwarted, America's approach to democracy as it transforms public demands into governmental action.

The Structure and Powers of Congress

The United States Congress is among the world's most powerful legislatures. If the dominant congressional faction is large and determined enough, it can override presidential vetoes and make national policy entirely on its own. Presidents cannot force Congress to do their bidding. Neither can they simply ignore it. And they cannot get rid of Congress by dissolving it and calling for new elections. In nondemocratic nations, executives can do all these things, and their legislatures are little more than puppets under authoritarian leadership.

The U.S. Congress is a major power within the American constitutional system, but it is also a democratic body. Its members are elected by the American people. These two facts—that Congress is powerful *and* democratic—may seem obvious, but they are worth stressing for their significant political implications. If Congress is powerful, then it makes sense for citizens to focus on this body if they wish to influence national policy outcomes.

Congress is pluralistic and decentralized.[2] Each of its 535 members has real power in the sense that each has *one* vote. That means, in essence, 535 power points. The result is that the decision-making process is much more complex than it would be if power were concentrated in the hands of a few people. Those wishing to influence Congress must persuade a large number of people who have different outlooks, who are found at different points in a complex structure, and whose impact on policy outcomes can vary dramatically.

What the Framers Had in Mind

Believing that Congress would become the predominant branch of national government, the framers took steps to prevent it from becoming the tyrannical force that the state legislatures had been under the Articles of Confederation. We have already seen in Chapter 2 the way the Constitution limits Congress's power (through the Bill of Rights, for example) and the way other institutions (the president and the Supreme Court) can check its actions.

But the framers went further. Through the Connecticut Compromise, which based state seating in the House on population but equalized the seating in the Senate at two per state, the Constitutional Convention devised a way to make Congress check itself by striking a balance between the interests of the large states and the small states. They divided Congress into **bicameral** (two-chambered) **legislature,** and gave each chamber the power to inhibit the other's actions. Each house was to have a very different structure and purpose.

James Madison referred to the House of Representatives as "the great repository of the democratic principle of government," that is, the one most sensitive to public opinion. The House would be made up of popularly elected representatives serving two-year terms. The entire body would have to face the electorate every other year, so it would by nature reflect shifts in public opinion. This requirement was supposed to ensure that representatives would reflect the popular will. This requirement also places members of Congress in an eternal "election mode" making their

bicameral legislature A legislative system consisting of two houses or chambers.

need for campaign finances a constant necessity. And being based on population, this House would also favor the larger states.

The Senate, in contrast, was designed as a brake on the public's momentary passions, or as Madison put it, a "necessary fence" against the "fickleness and passion" of the people. The equal number of senators per state would give more power to the small states, making it an adequate counterbalance to the overrepresentation of the large states in the House of Representatives. Since senators were originally selected not by the voting public but by the state legislatures, the Senate was designed to be a more aristocratic group. It was intended to be an advisory council to the president—a judicious group of wise elder statesmen, one step removed from the passions and demands of the people. This distinction between the two chambers was based on the British tradition, in which the House of Commons represents the masses and the House of Lords the aristocracy.

Until 1913 most members of the Senate were chosen by their state legislatures (some western states had direct elections), ensuring that they were, in fact, somewhat removed from the mass electorate. This design for the Senate changed when, in our more democratic age, senators, like House members, are now directly elected by their state's residents. It is not clear whether the use of popular election for the Senate has made it more democratic or just created a body that is more hostile to centralization and federalism.

Even though their six-year term would seem to make senators more removed from popular desires, the fact that their reelection campaigns are often more competitive than those of the House increases their chances of being turned out of office, increasing an incumbent's desire to have ample campaign financing at their disposal. It also ensures that they will reflect shifts in public thinking more closely than when they were selected by state legislatures. However, since their terms are staggered, so that only one-third of the Senate is subject to election every two years, Senate membership is more stable than that of the House. After any given election, two-thirds of the Senate—those whose terms did not expire that year—automatically remain in place.[3]

In allocating legislative powers, the framers went to great lengths to specify the powers of Congress in the Constitution in order to avoid the chaos that had prevailed in the state legislatures under the Articles of Confederation. In Article I, Section 8, they gave Congress authority in three broad areas: economic affairs, domestic affairs, and foreign affairs (see Table 4.1). The power to impeach and remove a high official from office is divided between the two chambers, with the House drafting and voting on articles of impeachment that are then tried in the Senate. Additional differences between the two houses of Congress are outlined in Table 4.2 on page 120.

Although the framers wished to limit the powers of Congress, they realized that it was impossible to foresee all the issues and emergencies that were likely to arise in the future. Therefore, they included in Article I, Section 8, the so-called **necessary and proper clause,** also called the *elastic clause,* which grants Congress the power to "make all Laws which shall be necessary and proper" to carry out all the other powers specified in Article I, Section 8. This sweeping language has been interpreted by the Supreme Court to allow Congress to develop its role broadly with regard to regulating commerce, borrowing money, and collecting taxes.[4]

Limits on Congress's Power

Although extensive, Congress's powers are limited in many ways. As with every agency of the U.S. government, Congress is checked at the most essential level by what the public will tolerate. In addition to regularly scheduled elections, which force members of Congress to be responsive to the will of the people, voters can ignore hated laws or even force Congress to rescind them. Congress is also limited by important elements of the Constitution. It cannot infringe on a number of state

necessary and proper clause
Clause of the Constitution that grants Congress the power to "make all Laws which shall be necessary and proper" to carry out all other powers specified in Article I, Section 8; also called the elastic clause.

Table 4.1 ■ The Key Powers of Congress
To lay and collect taxes, duties, imposts, and excises
To borrow money
To regulate commerce with foreign nations and among the states
To establish rules for naturalization and bankruptcy
To coin money, set its value, and punish counterfeiting
To fix the standard of weights and measures
To establish a post office and post roads
To issue patents and copyrights to inventors and authors
To create courts inferior to the Supreme Court
To define and punish piracies, felonies on the high seas, and crimes against the law of nations
To declare war
To raise and support an army and navy and make rules for their governance
To provide for a militia
To exercise exclusive legislative powers over the District of Columbia and over places purchased to be federal facilities
To "make all Laws which shall be necessary and proper for carrying into Execution the foregoing Powers, and all other powers vested by this Constitution in the Government of the United States"

powers, beginning with an essential one: Congress cannot abolish or change the boundaries of any state without that state's consent.

In theory, the enumerated powers of Article I, Section 8, are not just grants of power to Congress but also limits. The framers argued that Congress (and the federal government) had delegated powers that could be used only when specifically granted such authority. In all other cases, the authority would remain in the states or in the people—a restriction made clear in the Ninth and Tenth Amendments.[5] Furthermore, in the exercise of its powers, Congress is subject to the Supreme Court, which is seen as the final interpreter of the Constitution. Thus, under its judicial review power, the Supreme Court can legitimately void legislation that in its view is contrary to the Constitution. This has been done by the Court nearly three dozen times since 1995. For example, this is the basis upon which the Supreme Court overturned the Communications Decency Act of 1995, the line item veto legislation in 1998, and Section 3501 of the 1968 Omnibus Crime Control Act in 2000.[6] In the case of the Communications Decency Act, the Court ruled that the law was too vague to enforce constitutionally under the First Amendment freedom of speech guarantee. The Court ruled that the line item veto was an unconstitutional violation of the separation of powers by giving the president too much of Congress's lawmaking power.[7] In June 2000 the Court continued this trend by overturning the anti-*Miranda* ruling law, Section 3501 of the Omnibus Crime Control Act, which instructed judges to examine whether a defendant's confession to police was made "voluntarily" rather than after police warnings of the rights to silence and counsel.[8]

Beyond these checks, perhaps the most important day-to-day limit on Congress's power is the president. No matter what the party lineup, Congress and the president are continually playing complex games of power politics that involve competition and cooperation. Both institutions must work together if government is to operate, yet each can check the other quite dramatically. The president has an array of powers that can stymie the will of Congress, including his role as commander in chief of the military, his appointment powers, his control of the national bureaucracy, and his veto powers.

Table 4.2 ■ Differences Between the House and Senate	
House	**Senate**
435 members	100 members
Two-year term	Six-year term
Smaller constituencies	Larger constituencies
Fewer personal staff	More personal staff
Equal populations represented	States represented
Less flexible rules	More flexible rules
Limited debate	Virtually unlimited debate
More policy specialists	Policy generalists
Less media coverage	More media coverage
Less prestige	More prestige
Less reliance on staff	More reliance on staff
More powerful committee leaders	More equal distribution of power
Very important committees	Less important committees
More partisan	Less partisan
Nongermane amendments (riders) not allowed	Nongermane amendments (riders) allowed

The Members of Congress

Who Are the Members?

When the First Congress met in 1789, there were only sixty-five representatives and twenty-six senators—all of them from the most elite families in America. They were rich, white, and male. Superficially, members of Congress today differ little from that first group. They are still disproportionately rich, white, and male, and they come overwhelmingly from the fields of law, banking, and big business. A third of the Senate and one-seventh of the House are millionaires. Over the last two decades, at least thirty times more millionaires serve on Capitol Hill than are found in American society in general. On the other hand, the number of lawyers in Congress has recently been dropping. Thirty years ago more than half the members of Congress had a law degree, but that number has now been cut in half.[9] Some ask, "How can such a group claim to be a representative body?" Others respond, "Does it matter whether the country's representatives are rich or poor, white or black, male or female, as long as they support policies its citizens want and oppose those they don't?"[10]

Some of the wealthiest members of Congress, such as Ted Kennedy and Jay Rockefeller, claim to represent the interests of the poor. And many male members of Congress work diligently to promote the welfare of women. Still, it seems reasonable to conclude that a healthy democracy would include leaders from all social groups. How does Congress shape up in this regard?

? Question for Reflection: With campaign finance reform now a reality, what, if any impact will it have on the number of millionaires found within the Houses of Congress?

Because of Supreme Court decisions and the redistricting that has taken place at the state level, Congress approached democracy in the twentieth century by increasing the ethnic diversity of its membership. When we compare the present

APPROACHING DEMOCRACY AROUND THE GLOBE

The Incoming Tide of Democracy in the Twenty-first Century

From the Middle East to South America and from West Africa to East Asia, democracy is becoming more prevalent as citizens vote to throw out long-standing dictatorial regimes and replace them with democratic ones. The reasons for this change are many. In some areas, developing nations have begun to restructure their governments in order to better compete in today's high-tech global economy. In other areas, though, democratic regimes were launched after various economic crises weakened the authoritarian regimes that held power.

Perhaps the most dramatic change occurred on the island of Taiwan when the reformist opposition leader, Chen Shui-bian, ousted the longtime Nationalist Party. But this event has been repeated throughout the world. In Indonesia, a moderate Muslim cleric, Abdurraham Wahid, defeated the ruling party in October 1999 to create the first freely elected government in that country since the 1950s. While the transition to power in Indonesia was bloody, Wahid is now pushing political and economic reforms to diminish the power of the military and business elite that ruled during President Suharto's thirty-two-year dictatorship. The Suharto regime ended as a result of the Asian financial crisis, which brought the nation to its knees and led to pro-democracy protests and riots in 1998. When the International Monetary Fund required Indonesia to reform its economy in order to receive the necessary bailout loans, Suharto's protégé, B. J. Habibie, drastically cut the number of legislative seats that were controlled by the military. As a result, the groundbreaking election occurred in which Habibie lost to Wahid and the democratic reformers took over the entire government. The ripple effect of these economy-driven reforms continued as East Timor was able to achieve its democratic-led independence from Indonesia after a series of bloody riots. On top of that, Wahid continued the reform by dismissing long-standing defense minister General Wiranto, replacing him with the first civilian leader in that post in forty years, and then purging the army of the Suharto followers. These changes in Taiwan and Indonesia (the world's fourth most populous nation) could become beacons for democratic change throughout the developing world.

Change seems also to be coming in the Middle East. Iran's religious regime is under attack from a developing democratic movement. Change began in 1997 with the election of President Mohammad Khatami, and continued in February 2000 with the dramatic victory in parliament of candidates allied with Khatami. As a result, the young people in Iran have been pushing for democratic reforms. While Iran's supreme leader, Ayatollah Ali Khameni, is still in charge, if the younger generation continues to push for Western-style democratic reforms, many wonder whether the ruling religious clans can continue to maintain power. While this is good for the democratic movement, the direction of the reforms in Iran has many of its Middle Eastern neighbors, where true democracy is rare, worried as to whether it will threaten their ruling elites as well. "It gives Arab states the idea of making change from within, making the system elastic enough to absorb all movements under the slogan of democracy," said Lahib Kamhawi, a prominent scholar of Jordan. "The democratic takeoff in Iran has begun," adds Fahmi Howeidi, an Islamic writer in Egypt, "and no objective observer can doubt its credibility."

Meanwhile, in Africa, Nigeria has added to the movement with an election in February 1999 that ended the brutal and corrupt military regime of General Sani Abacha, who had died unexpectedly in June 1998, was replaced by the first civilian leader in more than fifteen years with the election of Olusegun Obasanjo. The election took place only because many of Abacha's own generals were so disturbed by the corruption of his rule, which had made the nation an international pariah. If this election holds in Nigeria, which is one of the region's most populous nations, it may serve as a beacon for the spread of democratic reforms throughout the African continent. It will also affect the international oil industry, since Nigeria is the world's sixth largest exporter of oil. Also, in tiny Senegal, a West African nation, President Abdou Diouf surprised his people by accepting the results of a runoff election that ended the forty-year rule of his Socialist party in the parliament.

Finally, in South America, democratic reform is taking place in Venezuela with the election of populist Hugo Chavez in December 1998. His leftist coalition defeated the two traditional parties in the assembly when he campaigned as an outsider seeking to make the government more democratic and responsive to the poor. The newly elected delegates then wrote the country's new governing charter, fired hundreds of judges who were accused of corruption, and appointed a new supreme court, attorney general, and national elections board. While Chavez was accused of developing his own dictatorial regime, the assembly was accused of overstepping its powers, the reformers argued that they were simply attempting to break up the long-standing ruling oligarchy. This move toward democracy is highly significant in Venezuela, which has the largest oil reserves outside the Middle East.

The tide of democracy is definitely coming in around the world, usually beginning at the very top positions and then spreading to the legislative branch. Whether this tide will continue, though, is yet to be seen. The question will be whether these new democratically elected regimes will be able to improve the lives of the peoples of their nations by accomplishing economic reforms as well.

Source: Thomas Wagner, "Democracy Is Making Strides Around the World," *Allentown Morning Call,* April 9, 2000, p. 10; and Hamza Hendawi, "Iran's Reform Process Worries Arab Neighbors," *Allentown Morning Call,* April 9, 2000, p. A10.

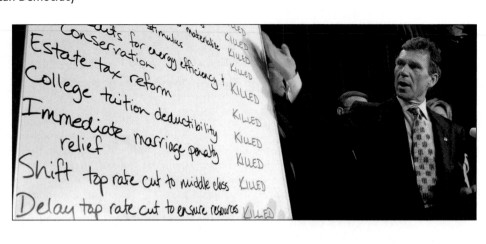

► Some argue that Senator Tom Daschle's (D.-SD) trademark "calm demeanor" and negotiating style with the Republicans cost his party control of the Senate and lost him his seat as Senate Majority Leader.

LITTLE-KNOWN FACT

There have been only twenty-six female senators in U.S. history. In addition, only seven states have ever had two female senators: Maine, Alabama, California, Louisiana, Nebraska, South Dakota, and Washington.

makeup of Congress with its composition a few decades ago, we see that the institution is becoming far more diverse. In 1952 the House included only two African Americans and ten women; the Senate had no African Americans and only one woman. In 2003 thirteen women are in the Senate, a record number, including Hillary Rodham Clinton, representing New York, the first First Lady in history to serve in Congress; two Asian Americans, Daniel K. Inouye and Daniel K. Akaka; and the first Native American senator, Ben Nighthorse Campbell. The 2003 membership of the House included thirty-seven African Americans, nineteen Hispanics, fifty-nine women, and four Asian Americans, as well as naturalized citizens from Cuba, Kenya, and Korea. Thus, in the past five decades African Americans have increased their numbers on Capitol Hill by 2,000 percent. The nineteen Hispanic Americans elected in 2002 represents the same number of Hispanics as in the previous Congress.[11]

Although the 108th Congress is just as diverse as its predecessors, it still falls short of reflecting the population as a whole. The increasingly diverse demographics of Congress do have an impact on the legislative agenda. The large African

▲ In 1916 Jeannette Rankin of Montana became the first woman to be elected to Congress.

▲ Several members of Congress celebrate their victory after the House of Representatives rejected a gun control bill that would have weakened government controls over sales at gun shows.

American Caucus has had an impact both on President Bush's policies towards affirmative action and limiting racial profiling in the War on Terrorism. At the same time, the increasing numbers of women in Congress have attacked such questions as the role of females in the military, gun control, and the shifting of medical research funds on cancer and heart problems to include women as well. Table 4.3 suggests what Congress would look like if its members represented a true cross section of the nation.

Congressional Districts

The racial and ethnic makeup of Congress is strongly influenced by the nature of the districts from which its members are elected. The way the boundaries of these districts are drawn can determine a candidate's chances of election, making determining the size and the geographic shape of any legislative district a political act.

Article I, Section 2, of the Constitution arbitrarily set the size of the first U.S. House of Representatives at 65 members and apportioned those seats roughly by population. Later, after the 1790 census, the size of the House was set at 105 seats, with each state given one seat for each 33,000 inhabitants. As the nation's population grew, so did the number of representatives. By the early twentieth century, the House had expanded to 435 members, each with a constituency of approximately 200,000 people. At that point members agreed that the House had reached an optimum size. The Reapportionment Act of 1929 formalized this sentiment; it set the total House membership at 435, a number that has remained stable to this day. But because the nation's population has almost tripled since then, each congressional district now contains about 635,000 citizens.

Population growth and shifts within each of these 435 districts vary dramatically over time. To keep the numerical size of districts relatively equal, it becomes necessary to redraw district lines from time to time, and even to adjust the number of representatives allotted each state. This process is known as **reapportionment.** Each reapportionment of House seats reflects the nation's population shifts since the last census.[12] Reapportionment occurs every ten years, always producing "winners" and "losers." Because of population growth in the South and Southwest, states such as California, Arizona, Texas, and Florida picked up seats after the 2000 census; population loss in the industrial North and Northeast led to a reduction in the number of representatives from states such as New York, Pennsylvania, Connecticut, and Ohio.

Table 4.3 ■ To What Extent Does the House Mirror Society?				
Social Group	**Number in the House if it were Representative of American Society at large**	**Number in the 106th Congress**	**Number in the 107th Congress**	**Number in the 108th Congress**
Men	184	379	376	376
Women	226	56	59	59
African Americans	52	35	34	37
Hispanics	30	19	18	19
People in Poverty	65	0	0	0
Lawyers	2	239	234	228
Americans under Age 45	300	136	140	154

Source: Calculated from Congressional Quarterly and Statistical Abstract of the United States.

reapportionment A process of redrawing voting district lines from time to time, and adjusting the number of representative allotted each state.

The responsibility for redrawing a state's congressional districts falls to the legislatures of the fifty states, pending the approval of the Justice Department to ensure that election districts are drawn fairly. This means that the party composition of state legislatures and the state governorships after the 2000 census was central to the future makeup of Congress.

Within these 435 districts, one finds every imaginable variation. Each has its own character; none is an exact replica of the larger society. Because of their particular social composition, some districts view Democrats more favorably, while others lean toward Republicans. The social composition of a district cannot be understood only in terms of the financial and socioeconomic status of that district. Some rich districts might be liberal and some poor districts might be conservative because of the influence of other social factors, such as religion, education, and cultural background.

An enormous political struggle ensues when a new census changes the number of seats a state will receive. State governments, either through their legislatures, judicial panels, or specifically designed commissions, must then redraw the boundaries of their congressional districts. This process is not simply a matter of counting voters and redrawing boundaries to make the districts equal. There are, after all, many ways to carve out numerically equal congressional districts. Some of those ways will help Democrats get elected, while others will help Republicans. Boundary lines can be drawn to make a large ethnic group the majority within a single district or to dilute that group's influence by dispersing its members into two, three, or more districts, where they can be outvoted by the majority in each era. **Redistricting,** as the process is called, therefore becomes very political. State legislators naturally seek to establish district boundaries that will favor candidates from their own party.

The term **gerrymander** is used to describe the often bizarre district boundaries set up to favor the party in power. This word was coined in the early nineteenth century after Republican governor Elbridge Gerry of Massachusetts signed a redistricting bill that created a weirdly shaped district to encompass most of the voters who supported his party. One critic looked at the new district and said, "Why, that looks like a salamander!" Another said, "That's not a salamander, that's a gerrymander" (see Figure 4.1). The term is now used to describe any attempt to create a *safe seat* for one party, that is, a district in which the number of registered voters of one party is large enough to guarantee a victory for that party's candidate.

Majority–Minority Districts and the Approach to Democracy

Sometimes the redistricting process has been used to further social as well as political goals, such as increasing diversity in Congress—an interesting example of America's meandering approach to democracy. After the 1990 census, states with histories of racial discrimination were required by law to draw new district boundaries that would give minority candidates a better chance of election. The mandated redistricting was meant to ensure representation for nonwhites living in white-dominated areas. Such African American and Hispanic majority districts were called **majority-minority districts.** As a result of the redistricting, nineteen new black and Hispanic members were added to Congress in 1992. Proponents point to these gains as evidence that the new districts made Congress more representative of the general population, but critics claim that they constitute "racial gerrymandering."[13]

North Carolina's Twelfth Congressional District was one of those created to strengthen the voting power of African Americans. However, it was so narrow in some places that it spanned only one lane of Interstate Highway 85. This District was disallowed by the Supreme Court in 1993 in the case *Shaw v. Reno*. Although the Court sidestepped the general question of racial gerrymandering, it did prohibit racially based redistricting in the case of "those rare districts [like North Carolina's

redistricting The redrawing of boundary lines of voting districts in accordance with census data or sometimes by order of the courts.

gerrymander Any attempt during state redistricting of congressional voting boundaries to create a safe seat for one party.

majority-minority district A congressional district that has been drawn to include so many members of a minority group that the chance for a minority candidate to be elected is greatly improved.

Figure 4.1
The Gerrymander

An 1812 cartoon lampooning the original "Gerry-Mander" of a Massachusetts district. This district was redrawn to guarantee a Republican victory, and gerrymander soon became a standard political term.

Twelfth] that are especially bizarre." It added acidly that the district "bears an uncomfortable resemblance to political apartheid"[14] (see Figure 4.2).

In 1992 Cynthia McKinney, an African American, was elected to the House of Representatives from Georgia's Eleventh District. In a 5 to 4 decision in 1995, the Supreme Court struck down the "race-based" redistricting plan in Cynthia McKinney's 260-mile-long district.[15] Saying that this Justice Department–directed plan to create three black majority districts in the state out of the previous eleven such

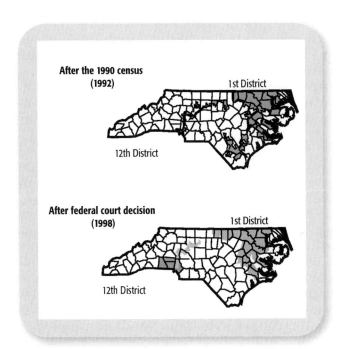

Figure 4.2
Gerrymandering in the 1990s: North Carolina's First and Twelfth Districts

Source: Reprinted from Roger H. Davidson and Walter J. Oleszek, *Congress and Its Members,* 7th ed. (Washington, D.C.: Congressional Quarterly Press, 1999), p. 55.

districts violated the equal protection rights of white voters because it was based predominantly on race, the Court put similar plans throughout the nation (mainly in the South) in jeopardy by ruling that they must all be "narrowly tailored to achieve a compelling [state] interest." In other words, although race can be a factor in redistricting, it cannot be the overriding consideration.

A year later, the Supreme Court upheld another redistricting scheme coming out of Georgia. The Court approved the plan by the district court to create a single black majority district for the 1996 elections, saying that a single such district is enough, because any attempt to create more of them would have to be based on race and would thus violate both the Voting Rights Act and the "one person, one vote" standard in *Reynolds v. Sims* for interpreting Article I, Section 2, of the Constitution. Speaking for the Court, Justice Anthony Kennedy reaffirmed that race "must not be a predominant factor in drawing the district lines."[16]

Since these rulings, the electoral results in these areas have been interesting. Across the South in the 1996 election, McKinney and other redistricted minority candidates won reelection with huge majorities of black votes plus an average of 30 percent of white votes. Some argue that these results offer evidence that the traditional bias against voting for minority candidates in predominantly white districts is lessening, while others interpret the results as affirming the value of incumbency experience.[17] This issue continued after the 2000 elections. In a recent case the Supreme Court unanimously offered the states "very significant breathing room" in redistricting, using the 2000 election results.[18] In Mississippi, the Bush administration stepped in, using the Voting Rights Act to block a state court ordered redistricting plan that would have created a congressional district with 37.5% African American voting age population in favor of one mandated by the Federal court with only 30.4% African American voters. The result was that while the Federal court plan was used for the 2002 election, the U.S. Supreme Court accepted an appeal to review this decision.[19] With so many federal, state, and local racially gerrymandered districts in existence and all of the Supreme Court decisions being decided by a narrow 5-4 majority with Sandra Day O'Connor in the swing seat, it was inevitable that the Court would decide to revisit this question.

Delegates versus Trustees

If Congress is to function as a representative institution, individual members must represent their constituents. In theory, legislators may view themselves as either delegates or trustees. **Delegates** feel bound to follow the wishes of a majority of their constituents; they make frequent efforts to learn the opinions of voters in their state or district. But how does a legislator represent minority groups in the district or raise issues of national importance that are not a high priority for constituents? For example, should a representative with only a few African American constituents vote for an affirmative action program that is opposed by an overwhelming majority of voters in the district?

In these situations many legislators see themselves not as delegates but as **trustees,** authorized to use their own judgment in considering legislation. The trustee role was best expressed by the English philosopher Edmund Burke (1729–97), who as a member of Parliament explained to his constituents that representatives should never sacrifice their own judgment to voter opinion. After hearing that Burke did not intend to follow their wishes, his constituency promptly ejected him from Parliament.

In Congress, the role of trustee, which often leads to policy innovations, is more likely to be favored by representatives from safe districts, where a wide margin of victory in the past makes future reelection likely by discouraging potential opponents and their contributors. Legislators from marginal districts tend to be delegates, keeping their eyes firmly fixed on the electorate. They apparently wish to avoid Burke's fate.

delegates Congress members who feel bound to follow the wishes of a majority of their constituents; they make frequent efforts to learn the opinions of voters in their state or district.

trustees Congress members who feel authorized to use their best judgment in considering legislation.

In practice, members of Congress combine the roles of delegate and trustee. They follow their constituency when voters have clear, strong preferences, but they vote their own best judgment either when the electorate's desire is weak, mixed, or unclear, or when the member has very strong views on an issue. This approach to voting is called the *politico* role. Members of Congress frequently have to balance votes on issues of national importance against votes on issues that are important to their constituents.[20]

— both

A particularly poignant example of this dilemma arose during the early civil rights era. Lawrence Brooks Hays, an Arkansas moderate member of Congress from 1943 to 1959, was caught between his integrationist beliefs and his district's segregationist views. After he chose to act as a trustee—voting in favor of a civil rights bill—his constituents replaced him in the next election with someone closer to their own views. This case illustrates a problem all elected officials ultimately face. Do they do what is popular or what they believe is right? Sometimes when legislators do what they believe is right, it costs them so dearly that they lose their seat, a situation John F. Kennedy labeled "profiles in courage."[21]

Name Recognition and the Incumbency Factor

Incumbents are individuals who currently hold public office. Since the 1950s, an average of over 92 percent of House incumbents and 80 percent of Senate incumbents seeking reelection won those elections.[22] Despite the anti-incumbent sentiment of the 1994 election, over 90 percent of the House and 80 percent of the Senate incumbents who sought reelection still won in that election and each of the four that followed.

The advantage of incumbency is a relatively recent phenomenon. Before the Civil War, almost half of each new House session and one-quarter to one-third of each entering Senate class were composed of new members (a fact that can also be explained by the high number of members who voluntarily chose not to run for reelection). Despite high incumbency reelection rates, many members voluntarily leave office, either due to unhappiness with their jobs or a desire to turn the seat over to someone new. When combined with the change wrought by the so-called Republican Revolution in 1994, a majority of the members of the House and the Senate have been newly elected since 1990.

Incumbents enjoy a number of significant advantages in any election contest.[23] They nearly always enjoy greater name recognition than their challengers. They can hold press conferences for widespread publicity, participate in media events such as town meetings, and maintain offices back home that keep their names in the spotlight. Challengers must struggle for, and often fail to achieve, the kind of publicity and recognition that come automatically to an incumbent. Incumbents also often benefit from favorable redistricting during reapportionment.

Incumbents can increase their visibility through use of the **franking privilege**—free mailing of newsletters and political brochures to their constituents. These mailings solicit views and advice from constituents and serve to remind them of the incumbent's name and accomplishments. The use of franked mail has grown over the years. In 1994 House members seeking reelection sent out 363 million pieces of mail, nearly two items for every person of voting age. Because of excesses by members such as Dan Rostenkowski, former Democratic member from Illinois who served time in jail for violations of his mail privilege, reforms were instituted, such as caps on mailing and counting the franking privilege as part of the member's overall office expense allowance.

Another advantage for incumbents is their staff, which helps them do favors for constituents. These services, known as **casework,** may involve arranging for the repair of potholes, expediting payment of Social Security benefits, or providing a tour of the Capitol. Casework is at the heart of the power of incumbents. Realizing that every voter remembers these little favors, members of Congress often have several

incumbents Individuals who currently hold public office.

franking privilege The free mailing of newsletters and political brochures to constituents by members of Congress.

casework Favors done as a service for constituents by those they have elected to Congress.

— special privilege

▲ Making a clean sweep of it? Republican candidates for Congress used this symbol in 1994 to symbolize their desire to pass term limits as part of their Contract with America. Once they were elected, however, their fervor cooled considerably. Term limits are yet to be passed by either house of Congress.

term limits A legislated limit on the amount of time a political figure can serve in office.

full-time staff members who deal with cases involving individual constituents.[24] This kind of experience allows incumbents campaigning for reelection to "point with pride" to favors done for their districts. Although the direct impact of casework on voting may be minimal, it does help name recognition and avoids any negative backlash from constituents if requests are ignored. More than that, casework is a strategy to gain positive feedback from constituents, which enables members to take stands on legislative issues that might be unpopular with their constituents.[25]

Incumbents also have the advantage of legislative experience. They sit on committees with jurisdiction over issues of particular importance to their constituents. Former rock star turned representative, Sonny Bono of the Palm Springs district in California, was made a member of the Judiciary Committee's Subcommittee on Courts and Intellectual Property because copyright issues are a significant issue for the record and motion picture industry in his district. When Bono died in a skiing accident in early 1998, his wife Mary took advantage of reflected name recognition to win a special election for his seat and was then asked to take his seat on the Judiciary Committee.

Perhaps the greatest advantage held by incumbents is financial. Parties, interest groups, and individuals tend to back known candidates because they have the best chance of winning, while relatively unknown challengers have great difficulty raising money. In 2000, House incumbents spent about $400,000 more than their challengers, while Senate incumbents spent over $2 million more than their challengers.[26]

House races frequently cost about $666,000; Senate races average $5.6 million, with the Senate race in New Jersey between Democrat Jon Corzine and Republican Robert D. Franks costing $70 million, with the vast majority of it being spent by Corzine, the eventual winner. Incumbents can raise that kind of money with little difficulty, but most challengers cannot.[27] However, challengers usually do not have to raise as much money as incumbents just to be competitive in the election. All they really have to do is pass a threshold of about $400,000 for a House seat in order to make a credible run for the office.

? Question for Reflection: How might the next version of Campaign Finance Reform deal with the inequitable campaign spending of incumbents versus relatively unknown challengers?

Seeking to change this pattern, many voters now favor some form of **term limits,** usually a maximum of twelve years in each house. With polls in 1994 showing that 80 percent of the public want term limits, twenty-three states passed legislation limiting the length of time their senators and representatives can serve in Congress. Underlying these measures is the growing public perception that incumbent legislators, feeling confident of reelection, become either complacent or corrupt.

In 1995 the Supreme Court overturned the power of the state of Arkansas—and thus *all* states—to impose term limits on congressional candidates (in this case a limit of no more than three terms for the House and two terms for the Senate). As a result similar laws in 22 other states were voided. Justice John Paul Stevens explained that states could not add a new requirement for office to the three requirements for office—age, citizenship, and residency—specified in the Constitution. If term limits on congressional candidates was going to have to happen it would have to be done by constitutional amendment.[28] Two years later, the Court *disallowed* (by refusing to hear on appeal) the attempt by Arkansas and eight other states to signify on the ballot through a so-called scarlet letter provision those candidates for Congress who did not adhere to voluntary term limits.[29]

Despite the Supreme Court rulings, the term limits movement continues to have an effect. In 1995 the 104th Congress approved term limits for its leaders—four consecutive terms for the Speaker and three consecutive terms for committee chairs. In addition, twenty states had passed term limits for their state legislatures. These laws began having such an impact that in California one entire house of its legislature has turned over since 1990.[30]

Although over nine out of ten incumbents in the 2002 election were reelected, the actual turnover rate in Congress, including seats vacated because of deaths, retirements, and decisions to run for other offices, was well more than 15 percent— almost the same as it has been for more than the last two decades.

The movement seemed to be stalling when only Nebraska voted state legislative term limits into effect in 2000. Then, a year later, term limits were ruled unconstitutional in Oregon. When the Idaho legislature voted in early 2002 to become the first state to repeal its term limits law (a decision later ratified by voters in the 2002 election), only 17 states still had term limits on their legislatures. However, the term limits movements in the states refused to slip from view. This was made clear when voters in a California special election, by a 58–42% margin, defeated Proposition 45, which would have weakened the legislative term limits in effect in the state by allowing every member of the legislature the chance to run for an additional four years in office.[31]

The "Two Congresses:" The Public's View of Congress

The American public has generally had a "Love my congressman, hate the Congress" view of the institution. For scholars in the field, this is known as the **Two Congresses** phenomenon. Congress as an institution is, and generally always has been, held in low regard by the public. Surveys conducted from the 1960s to the late 1990s revealed a steady decline in the proportion of respondents rating Congress positively. As you can see in Figure 4.3, by 2002 a National Opinion Research Center poll revealed that the number of Americans saying that they had "a great deal" of confidence in Congress had risen to 22 percent, up from the less than 10 percent figure that it received five years earlier.[32] But if Americans are negative about Congress as an institution, most still feel a strong sense of loyalty to their individual senators and representatives. In a 1998 poll, respondents approved of the performance of their individual member of Congress more than 20 points higher than they did of Congress as an institution.[33]

There are many reasons for such a wide discrepancy between the public's love of their own member of Congress and disdain for the institution as a whole. Individual members are able to serve constituents and act quickly, while the overall Congress tends to move much more slowly and focus on complicated national issues. Individual members are popular because they are able to direct government spending and projects to their home districts, while Congress as a whole is generally criticized for its overall spending practices. The national media are also much more critical of Congress as a whole, focusing on scandals and conflicts, while the local press tends to deal with the individual members in a much friendlier fashion. Finally, an individual member is able to speak clearly on policy with one voice, while the overall

Two Congresses A term denoting the differing views the public has toward Congress as a whole and their representative individually, noting that the opinions are more positive for the individual representative than for the body as a whole.

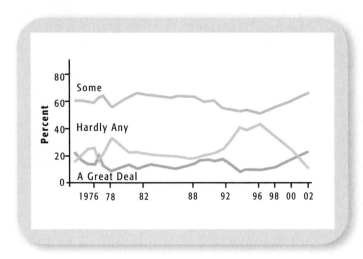

Figure 4.3
Confidence in Congress
Source: Harris Poll #6, 1/30/02, accessed at www.//harrisinteractive. com/harris poll/; see also National Opinion Research Center. Reported in *National Journal*, January 17, 1998, p. 111.

Congress speaks with many voices, and sometimes there are no voices at all.[34] Because of this paradox of the "Two Congresses," it is not uncommon even for incumbent members from both parties who are seeking reelection to criticize their colleagues for going in the wrong direction or at the wrong speed.

How Congress Organizes Itself

Since the Constitution says very little about how each house of Congress should be organized, those structures have evolved over the decades. The result has been a tension between the centralizing influence of the congressional leadership and the decentralizing influence of the committees and the subcommittees.

Congressional Leadership

Leadership in the House   The Constitution designates only one presiding officer of the House, the **Speaker of the House.** One of the most powerful officeholders in the U.S. government, the Speaker is usually seen as the voice of the House of Representatives, and sometimes even of the overall Congress. Though the Constitution does not specify that this person must be a member of Congress, traditionally, he or she is the leader of the party with a majority of the seats. Currently, the Speaker is J. Dennis Hastert of Illinois.

The Speaker's formal duties are to preside over the House when it is in session; to appoint all of the members to the Policy Committee, a representative body of the party conference that handles committee assignments and plans the legislative agenda;[35] to appoint the party's legislative leaders and senior staff members; and to control the assignment of bills to committees. When the majority party in the House is different from the president's party, the Speaker is often considered the minority party's national spokesperson.[36]

Speaker of the House The only presiding officer of the House mentioned in the Constitution. The leader of the majority party in Congress and third in line for the presidency.

▶ Years of partisan bickering were ended temporarily on September 11, 2001, as the so-called "Gang of Five" (l. to r.) House Speaker J. Dennis Hastert (R.-IL), Senate Majority Leader Tom Daschle (D.-SD), President George W. Bush, House Minority Leader Richard Gephardt (D.-MO), and Senate Minority Leader Trent Lott (R.-MS), exhibited solidarity seeing the president off on his trip to China.

The power of the Speaker has varied over time. Around the turn of the twentieth century, Speakers Thomas Reed and Joseph Cannon were so powerful that they could personally appoint all committee chairs and determine committee membership, thus enabling them to block legislation and punish those who opposed them. Cannon's powers, though, were diluted by a House revolution in 1910. It was Speaker Sam Rayburn of Texas who exemplified, from 1940 until his death in 1961 (with the exception of four years when the Republicans controlled the House), the use of all the formal and informal powers of the office. Rayburn's powers, however, were limited by the competing interests of entrenched conservative committee chairs.

A series of reforms in the 1970s made the speakership of Thomas ("Tip") O'Neill (1977–87) even more powerful on paper. The Speaker was now able to dictate the selection of the committee chairs, committee members from the Speaker's party, and party members of the powerful Rules Committee. In addition, the office was given more power to refer bills to committees and dictate the order of the floor proceedings. O'Neill became far more powerful than any Speaker since Cannon, but there were limits on his powers. O'Neill often could not dissuade southern Democrats in Congress, the so-called "boll weevils," from backing President Ronald Reagan's conservative policies. On one occasion, in 1981, when Reagan's administration substitued a one-thousand-page bill that contained dozens of drastic funding cuts at the last moment before a vote, all O'Neill could do was use the "bully pulpit" of his position to object in a speech. Noticing that the "cut and paste" bill had the name of a woman and her phone number in the margin, a likely source for one of the cuts, O'Neill objected, "Why are we enacting this woman into law?" But no one listened, and the bill passed anyway.[37]

Though the powers of the office had not changed, the prestige and effectiveness of the office declined when O'Neill's successor, James Wright of Texas, tried to use his powers for partisan goals, only to be forced to resign by a House revolt, led by Newt Gingrich. Ironically, Gingrich thought he would restore the Speaker's position to greater luster in 1995, but eventually he, too, contributed to the weakening of the office. He voluntarily stepped down from the speakership after party members charged him with ethics violations and responsibility for the poor Republican showing in the November 1998 elections. When Bob Livingston of Louisiana was forced to resign almost immediately after being chosen to replace Gingrich, he was replaced with J. Dennis Hastert of Illinois.

Next in line after the Speaker is the **House majority leader,** in 2003 Tom Delay of Texas. The majority leader is elected by the **party caucus,** a conference of party members in Congress, and serves as the party's chief strategist and floor spokesperson. The majority leader also schedules bills and attempts to persuade members of the majority party to vote according to the party's official position on pending legislation.

The minority party is headed by the **minority leader,** in 2003 Democrat Nancy Pelosi of California. Should the minority party become the majority in Congress, the minority leader is likely to be a candidate for Speaker of the House.[38] When the Republicans gained a majority in the House in 1994 and minority leader Robert Michel retired, Newt Gingrich was able to make the dramatic move from his former position as party whip.

Both the majority and minority party leaders work with the support of **whips,** who are charged with counting prospective votes on various issues and making certain that members have the information they need for floor action. *Whip* is a foxhunting term applied to the legislative process. During a fox hunt the whipper-in keeps the sniffing dogs from straying by whipping them back into the pack. The majority whip in 2003 is Roy Blunt of Missouri; the minority whip is Steny Hoyer of Maryland, who won the office in his second race for the position. They are aided by a complex system of more than ninety deputy whips, assistant regional whips, and at-large whips.

House majority leader The person elected by the majority party caucus who serves as the party's chief strategist and floor spokesperson.

party caucus A conference of party members in Congress.

minority leader The leader of the minority party in Congress.

whips Congress members charged with counting prospective votes on various issues and making certain that members have the information they need for floor action.

▲ Senate Majority Leader Lyndon Baines Johnson (D.-TX) makes a point forcefully with Senator Theodore F. Green (D.-RI). In what colleagues called the "Johnson Treatment," he would lean into colleagues and use his full 6 foot 5 inches to dominate their space.

president of the Senate The vice president of the United States.

president pro tempore The majority party member with the longest continuous service in the Senate, who serves as the chief presiding officer in absence of the vice president.

Senate majority leader A senator selected by the majority party whose functions are similar to those of the Speaker of the House.

Leadership in the Senate   Other than making the vice president the **president of the Senate,** the Constitution does not specify a leadership structure for the Senate. The vice president presides over the Senate only on rare occasions—most commonly when a tie vote seems likely on a key piece of legislation. If a tie does ensue, the vice president can cast the deciding vote. Except for the occasional ceremonial event, the vice president rarely enters the Senate. To guide that body's day-to-day activities, the Constitution allows the election of a **president pro tempore.** This position is essentially honorary and goes by tradition to the majority party member with the longest continuous service. In 2003, Ted Stevens of Alaska first appointed senator in 1968, holds the office. It is the president pro tempore who, in theory, presides over the Senate, although the position provides little political clout. The day-to-day task of the Senate presiding officer is usually farmed out to a wide range of senators, often junior ones who use the job to gain experience and "pay their dues."

The structure of party leadership in the Senate differs only slightly from the structure of the House. The majority party selects a **Senate majority leader**—currently Trent Lott of Mississippi—whose functions are similar to those of the Speaker of the House.[39] Lott returns to the position he had lost in 2001 as a result of Vermont Republican Jim Jeffords's switch to an Independent, thus changing the majority in the Senate to the Democrats. The majority leader is responsible for scheduling legislation, directing committee assignments, and persuading members to vote along party lines. There is also a minority leader in the Senate—currently Tom Daschle of South Dakota—who works with the majority leader to establish the legislative agenda. As in the House, the majority and minority leaders are aided by whips, who help organize and count votes. In 2003, the majority whip is Mitch McConnell of Kentucky; the minority whip is Harry Reid of Nevada.

The Senate majority leader is usually an influential politician. If the president is from the same party, the majority leader can be a valuable ally and spokesperson on Capitol Hill, as Republican majority leader Trent Lott will be for George Bush during the 108th Congress (2003–05). But a majority leader who is a member of the opposing party can be among the president's toughest critics, as Robert Dole was for Bill Clinton from 1995 to 1997.

One of the most persuasive Senate majority leaders in recent history was Lyndon Baines Johnson of Texas, a Democrat who served as Senate leader from 1955 until he became vice president in 1961. In what became known as the "Johnson treatment," he would corner fellow senators in search of a vote and badger them with his charismatic charm and large size until he got an agreement.[40] Johnson always said that the Senate was like an ocean, with whales and minnows; if he could persuade the "whales" (powerful senators) to follow him, the "minnows" (weaker members) would follow along in a school. Nothing stood in Johnson's way. Once, when Senator Hubert Humphrey of Minnesota was caught in a holding pattern flying over Washington and was needed for a key vote, Johnson ordered the air traffic controllers to clear the plane for immediate landing. On another occasion, when Senator Allen Frear of Delaware opposed a bill, Johnson stood up on the floor of the Senate and yelled, "Change your goddamn vote!" Frear immediately complied.[41]

Several other leaders are important in the Senate. The leaders of each party's campaign committee help to determine what kind of support will be provided for reelection campaigns. In 2003, Senator George Allen of Virginia chairs the Republican Campaign Committee, and Jon Corzine of New Jersey is expected to chair the Democratic Campaign Committee. When the members of each party meet in their conference committee, the chair helps to determine their legislative agenda. Senator Rick Santorum of Pennsylvania chairs the Republican Conference; Tom Daschle has retained control of this position in the Democratic party.

Congressional leaders since the 1960s, particularly in the Senate, are persuaders rather than dictators. They must be skilled at the give-and-take of bargaining and consensus building. Former Majority Leader Robert Byrd spoke of this difference from Johnson's world, describing the Senate not as an ocean of whales and minnows to be led but instead as a forest. "There are 99 animals. They're all lions. There's a waterhole. They all have to come to the waterhole. I don't have power but . . . I'm in a position to do things for others."[42]

Congressional Committees: The Laboratories of Congress

The success of a Speaker or a Senate majority leader depends now on how well he or she works with the leaders and members of the "laboratories of Congress"—its committees and subcommittees. Some of Congress's most important work is done in committee and subcommittee. As Woodrow Wilson put it, "Congress on the floor is Congress on public exhibition; Congress in committee is Congress at work."[43]

There are four types of congressional committees: standing, select or special, conference, and joint. Seats on all committees are allocated to each party in proportion to its representation in the entire House or Senate. Thus, the majority party in each house generally controls a corresponding majority in each committee. The assignment of members to committees is controlled by the party leadership. Table 4.4 lists the key committees in Congress.

The most important committees in both houses of Congress are the **standing committees.** These permanent committees—sixteen in the Senate, nineteen in the House—determine whether proposed legislation should be sent to the entire chamber for consideration. Virtually all bills are considered by at least one standing committee and often by more than one. When Congress considered Bill Clinton's proposals for health care reform in 1994, the matter came before five standing

standing committees Permanent congressional committees that determine whether proposed legislation should be sent to the entire chamber for consideration.

– where bills are decided

Table 4.4 ■ Standing Committees in the House and Senate, 2002	
House Committees	**Senate Committees**
Agriculture	Agriculture, Nutrition, and Forestry
Appropriations	Appropriations
Armed Services	Armed Services
Budget	Banking, Housing, and Urban Affairs
Education and the Workforce	Budget
Energy and Commerce	Commerce, Science, and Transportation
Financial Services	Energy and Natural Resources
Government Reform	Environment and Public Works
House Administration	Finance
International Relations	Foreign Relations
Judiciary	Governmental Affairs
Resources	Health, Education, Labor, and Pensions
Rules	Judiciary
Science	Rules and Administration
Small Business	Small Business and Entrepreneurship
Standards of Official Conduct	Veterans' Affairs
Transportation and Infrastructure	
Veterans' Affairs	
Ways and Means	

▲ Senator Strom Thurmond (R.-SC), now retired, listened to the arguments of Senator Patrick Leahy (D.-VT) (far left) and his colleagues during an impromptu debate after they were evacuated from their offices because of an anthrax scare in 2001.

committees: Ways and Means, Energy and Commerce, and Education and Labor in the House; Finance and Labor and Human Resources in the Senate. (The committees have been reorganized with the names changed since then.)

Select or **special committees** are established on a temporary basis to conduct investigations or study specific problems or crises. These committees possess no authority to propose bills and must be reauthorized by each new Congress. The creation and disbanding of these special committees mirror political forces in the nation at large. When a given issue is "hot" (for example, concern about drug use or security), pressures on Congress grow. Setting up special committees to investigate may be one of Congress's responses. When the problem appears to be solved or interest in the issue dies away, the committee set up to deal with the problem also meets its end. On the other hand, if the original problem and the concerned constituency continue to grow, a new standing committee may be created, thus providing power and institutional permanence for those concerned with the issue.

Conference committees are formed to reconcile differences between the versions of a bill passed by the House and the Senate. A conference committee can be very small, usually composed of the chairs of the relevant committees and subcommittees from each chamber. [44] On some major bills, however, as many as 250 representatives and senators may be involved. Conference committees rarely stay in existence for more than a few days.[45]

Since both houses jealously guard their independence and prerogatives, Congress establishes only a few **joint committees.** These groups, such as the Joint Economic Committee, consist of members from both chambers who study broad areas that are of interest to Congress as a whole. More commonly, joint committees oversee congressional functioning and administration, such as the printing and distribution of federal government publications.

select committees (or special committees) Temporary congressional committees that conduct investigations or study specific problems or crises.

conference committees Committees that reconcile differences between the versions of a bill passed by the House and the Senate.

joint committees Groups of members from both chambers who study broad areas that are of interest to Congress as a whole.

Why Does Congress Use Committees?

Committees enable Congress to do its work effectively by allowing it to consider several substantive matters simultaneously. Because each committee is concerned with a specific subject area, its members and staff develop knowledge and expertise. Committees also provide a place for ideas to be transformed into policies based on research and expert testimony. By providing multiple points of access for citizens and interest groups, committees serve as mini-legislative bodies representing the larger House or Senate.

Because committees play a major role in the operation of Congress, members actively seek seats on particular committees. In doing so, they have three goals in mind: to get reelected, to make good public policy, and to gain influence within the chamber.[46] The ideal committee helps them do all three. A seat, for instance, on the House Ways and Means Committee or the Senate Finance Committee, which pass on tax legislation, or on the House or Senate Appropriations Committees, which dictate spending priorities, ensures internal influence and authority.[47] The House Rules Committee and the Judiciary Committees of both houses were once seen as powerful and thus desirable. Now, though, the House Rules Committee is merely a tool of the Speaker, and the Judiciary Committees of the House and Senate handle such controversial legislation that serving on them often creates only trouble for members.

The changing role of committee chairs also demonstrates the approach to democracy in Congress. In the 1950s and 1960s, when conservative southern Democrats controlled the chairs because they had the most seniority, they were able to block liberal civil rights legislation by bottling it up in committee. That power was diminished after the 1974 "post-Watergate class" of legislators enacted a series of reforms lessening the discretionary power of the chairs to block legislation and determine the number and membership of subcommittees. However, the chairs still had enough power to keep the Speaker from working his will if they so desired.

After the 1994 election, Newt Gingrich moved quickly to take back much of the Speaker's power by slashing the number of committees and delegating much of the power of the chairs to the Speaker. This move allowed him to direct the fight for his proposed Contract with America. After his personal problems weakened his leadership in 1996, power was returned to the chairs, and once again they began to dictate the direction and pace of legislation.[48]

Despite this appearance of a return to the all-powerful chairs of earlier decades, the enactment by the Republicans in 1995 of term limits for chairs and other congressional leaders of no more than three consecutive terms reduced their power to control legislation and has led to a periodic changeover in congressional leadership. As a result, some leaders, such as Republican Tom Delay of Texas faced the loss of his Majority Whip seat, but instead became Majority Leader when Dick Armey (R.-TX) retired, and the Republicans maintained control of the House after the 2002 election.

Other committees help members serve their districts directly. A representative from rural Illinois or California, both large agricultural states, might seek a seat on the Agriculture Committee. Membership on such a committee would increase the legislator's chances of influencing policies affecting constituents and thus be helpful at election time. As a former member who was on the Public Works Committee (now Public Land and Resources) explains, "I could always go back to the district and say, 'Look at that road I got for you. See that beach erosion project over there? And those buildings? I got all those. I'm on Public Works.'"[49]

The committee system also provides opportunities for career advancement and name recognition. A strong performance at these televised hearings can impress constituents, increase name recognition, and convey a positive image. But such visibility can also backfire. Consider the House Judiciary Committee, which received tremendous national visibility in 1998 during the hearings on President Bill Clinton's impeachment. California Republican James Rogan, a member of that

THE ROAD TO DEMOCRACY

Crackup of the Congressional Committees

Why does there appear to have been such chaos in Congress in recent years, and why have so few bills actually passed both houses? Political reporters observing the institution think they have the answer. Says Richard E. Cohen, "From the scant handful of major bills passed by the House and Senate [in 1999], one unmistakable fact emerges: The congressional committees have lost their long-standing preeminence as the center of legislative ideas and debates."

THAT WAS THEN . . .

In 1999 alone, both the House and the Senate considered major gun control bills that were neither written nor reviewed by the Judiciary Committee of either chamber. When then-Majority Leader Trent Lott, a Republican from Mississippi, was pressed by Senate Democrats to act on a patients' rights bill, he selected for the floor debate a bill that had been written by key Democrats rather than a committee dominated by Republicans. The Republicans' version of the bill was prepared by a Senate Republican task force, rather than a standing committee. And in the area of tax cuts, both houses considered measures that had been reviewed by the tax-writing committees but were written instead by a minority of the members in consultation with their senior aides. Complained moderate Republican Michael N. Castle, of Delaware, "There was virtually no discussion of the bill with members."

What's going on? "Congress in session is Congress on public exhibition, whilst Congress in its committee rooms is Congress at work. Whatever is to be done must be done by, or through, the committee," wrote Woodrow Wilson in 1885. But this is no longer true. Now the kind of ad hoc legislating using task forces and individual members belies the textbook model for congressional lawmaking. No longer are committees the places where compromises on legislation are forged. No longer are members of those committees recognized for their seniority and expertise. No longer are chairs of committees recognized for their growing and continual power.

Instead, over the last three decades committee power has eroded to the point that committees have largely collapsed. The committees began to lose power during the Democratic control era, but the death warrant came in 1995 with the reforms instituted under Speaker Newt Gingrich. Once he began reforming committees with term limits for chairpersons, and with his top-down management style of creating task forces to draft bills that reflected the wishes of the congressional leadership rather than the committees, the committee structure began to collapse.

THIS IS NOW . . .

When J. Dennis Hastert took over as Speaker in 1999, he promised to restore the committee structure, but it has not worked out that way. He tried to follow a return to "regular order" whereby the committees would be set free to consider legislation in their own way. Indeed, one member has said, "There is a stronger sense that our members are charting their own course." But time and again, Hastert has found that a return to legislating-as-usual has not worked out well.

In the Senate, where Majority Leader Tom Daschle was more comfortable in his post and with the committee structure, he tried to use the normal legislative method more often. However, Senate committees found, like their House counterparts, that because of their own lack of deliberation on issues, or their own ineffectiveness, they were being ignored by the Senate leadership. Committees "will become increasingly irrelevant from the standpoint of legislation," argued political conservative activist Gordon S. Jones.

As a result of this trend away from committee involvement, legislation came to the floor of the House or the Senate that had neither been properly reviewed nor had gathered the necessary support from a majority of the members because of the compromises forged therein. Speaking of this practice, Martin Frost of Texas, then chairman of the House Democratic Caucus said, "It's an everyday occurrence now for committees to lose control." "[The Republican leaders] have danced on the edge several times and are flirting with disaster. You can't always cram for the final exam and get A's. Plus, their incompetence emboldens our side to go after them."

Indeed, one result of the creation of these insufficiently backed and prepared bills was the increasing number of measures being filibustered in the Senate. Because of this constant hamstringing of measures, it has been difficult for either party to present a coherent party platform to the voting public.

Thus the 108th Congress may be the time for both parties to begin to explore which model of legislative order should govern the operation of the Congress.

Source: Richard E. Cohen, "Crackup of the Committees," *National Journal,* July 31, 1999, pp. 2210–2217.

committee and the one who led the House fight against Clinton, lost his 2000 reelection bid, in one of the most expensive congressional campaigns ever after more than $10 million was spent.

The Rise of Subcommittees

Much of the legislative work of Congress is done in **subcommittees,** the smaller working groups that consider and draft legislation. In early 2003 the nineteen standing committees of the House included eighty-eight subcommittees, while the sixteen Senate standing committees had sixty-eight.[50] Subcommittees provide a further division of congressional labor. By narrowing the topic that members focus on, these groups allow for greater specialization. They also provide more opportunities for public access to the legislative process. Subcommittees hold hearings to obtain a broad range of testimony from local administrators, group leaders, and individuals. Such hearings would be impossible for the whole House and difficult for a large committee, but they are ideally suited to the smaller arena of the subcommittee.

Before 1970 congressional committees operated largely behind closed doors. The power of legislative decision making was concentrated in a few powerful chairs, traditionally appointed based on seniority, who were not representative of rank-and-file members. In the 1970s a revolution of sorts occurred. The younger rank-and-file members of Congress demanded and won more control over the policy agenda. In a crucial change, House Democrats made it technically possible to replace committee chairs by a secret ballot of the entire caucus. They proceeded to strengthen that newly gained power by voting to replace three long-standing conservative chairs who were deemed to be seriously out of touch with the national party's much more liberal perspectives. Most Democratic chairs responded quickly to that lesson. They became remarkably open to rank-and-file concerns; only a handful got into trouble again while Democrats controlled the House. But Speaker Gingrich also learned this lesson, and upon taking power in 1994 he bypassed seniority to put his ideological allies in as chairs of key committees, such as Robert L. Livingston (R.-LA) for Appropriations, and Henry J. Hyde (R.-IL) for Judiciary, thus bypassing more senior members, such as twenty-two-year veteran Carlos J. Moorhead (R.-CA).

Another crucial change adopted in the 1970s reform era brought a radical decentralization of power to the House. Usually referred to as the "Subcommittee Bill of Rights," it created additional subcommittees and seats on existing subcommittees.[51] Each House committee with more than twenty members had to create at least four standing subcommittees, and the committee chair could not easily tamper with subcommittee powers. Each subcommittee had its own chair, based largely on seniority, not political favoritism. Subcommittees had the right to hire permanent staff, and they could not be disbanded at the whim of the committee chair. All bills had to be referred to a subcommittee within two weeks of reaching the chair, thus preventing the chair from killing bills by ignoring them. With this reform, subcommittee chairs became powerful, owing their position to no one person, heading groups that could not be easily dissolved, and commanding staff resources to support their work.

One additional fact ensured further decentralization of power in the House. No one was allowed to head more than one subcommittee. Thus, instead of the handful of powerful barons that ran Congress in the 1950s, scattered knights now held power in the 1980s as heads of the more than one hundred House and eighty Senate subcommittees. A more recent reform in 1997 reduced the number of subcommittees by nearly one hundred panels and limited the number of panels on which an individual member could serve.

The proliferation of subcommittees has had effects beyond decentralizing congressional power. For one thing, interest groups can now influence bills by supporting and persuading only the legislators on a particular committee or subcommittee. For example, campaign contributions from the tobacco industry were targeted to give the industry a favorable hearing. In 1998, Thomas J. Bliley, Jr., (R.-VA) who as the new chair of the House Commerce Committee was in a position to affect legislation on smoking, got the most campaign support, $159,416 over a six-year period.

FYI

According to the German leader Otto von Bismarck, there are two things one should never watch being made—sausage and legislation.

subcommittees The subgroups of congressional committees charged with initially dealing with legislation before the entire committee considers it.

On the other hand, Henry A. Waxman (D.-CA), a vocal critic of the industry, received nothing.[52]

At the same time, these changes made the legislative process more unwieldy, giving many individual members a veto over legislation. For example, thirty committees and seventy-seven subcommittees played a role in shaping the 1992 defense budget. Moreover, as the number of subcommittees has grown, so has the amount of time a legislator must devote to committee business. Many find it impossible to even read the bills, and so must rely on staff members and lobbyists to provide them with information about pending legislation.[53] As a result of these drawbacks, the decentralization of power represented by subcommittee government, once heralded as an important reform, came under strong attack by the Republican Congress of 1995.

Question for Reflection: Has the committee system approached or receded from democracy after the changes reducing the power of the senior chairpersons of the 1950s and 1960s to control the flow of legislation as opposed to the current decentralized system based on more power of individual committee members?

Congress in Session

Together with the power and influence of congressional leaders and committee and subcommittee chairs, the procedures of the House and Senate shape the outcomes of the legislative process.[54]

The Rules and Norms of Congress

The formal rules of Congress can be found in the Constitution, in the standing rules of each house, and in Thomas Jefferson's *Manual of Parliamentary Practice and Precedent*. Congressional rules, for example, dictate the timing, extent, and nature of floor debate. Imagine what might happen without rules. If, for example, each of the 435 members of the House tried to rise on the floor and speak for just one minute on just one bill, debate would last at least seven hours, not taking into account the time needed for amendments, procedural matters, and votes.

The House Rules Committee As noted earlier, the House Rules Committee plays a key role, directing the flow of bills through the legislative process. Except for revenue, budget, and appropriations bills, which are *privileged legislation* and go directly to the House floor from committee, bills that have been approved in committee are referred to the Rules Committee. The **rules** issued by the House Rules Committee determine which bills will be discussed, how long the debate will last, and which amendments will be allowed.[55] Rules can be either *open,* allowing members to freely suggest related amendments from the floor; *closed,* permitting no amendments except those offered by the sponsoring committee members; or *restrictive,* now the most commonly used procedure, which limits amendments to certain parts of a bill and dictates which members can offer them. By refusing to attach a rule to a bill, the Rules Committee can delay a bill's consideration or even kill it.

During the 1950s the Rules Committee was dominated by conservative members who succeeded in blocking civil rights, education, and welfare legislation, even though it was favored by a majority of House members.[56] Today, however, as a result of the democratizing reforms described above, the Rules Committee has become what one member of Congress has called "the handmaiden of the Speaker," directing the flow and nature of the legislative process according to the majority party's wishes.[57] If the Speaker favors a bill, the rule is passed; if not, the rule is denied. If a long debate would prove embarrassing to the majority party, only a short debate under a closed rule will likely be allowed. Thus, contrary to earlier days when whole sessions of Congress would pass without a vote on a key issue, Speaker Newt

rules The decisions made by the House Rules Committee and voted on by the full House to determine the flow of legislation—when a bill will be discussed, for how long, and whether amendments can be offered.

Gingrich used his total control over the Rules Committee to direct the House to vote on each of the points of the Contract with America in the first one hundred days of the 104th Congress.

Because the Senate is smaller and more decentralized than the House, its rules for bringing a matter to the floor are much more relaxed. There is no Rules Committee; instead, the majority leader has the formal power to do the scheduling, but informal agreements are usually reached with the minority leader. Scheduling is accomplished by **unanimous consent agreements,** a waiver of the rules for consideration of a measure by a vote of all of the members. With no central traffic cop to control the flow of legislation, some bills are considered on the floor of the Senate for weeks, even overlapping with the consideration of other measures, often at the expense of the substance of the measure.

Amendments to a Bill   A key procedural rule in the House requires that all discussion on the floor and all amendments to legislation must be *germane,* that is, relevant to the bill being considered. The Senate, in contrast, places no limits on the addition of amendments to a bill.

The ability to attach unrelated **riders** to a bill can sometimes help a senator secure the passage of a pet project by attaching it to a popular proposal. Another important consequence of riders is that committees cannot serve the gatekeeper function on legislative wording as in the House; Senate committees are less important in this function than their counterparts in the House. However, the use of riders has led to problems. When budget bills were considered, members sometimes added so many riders, each containing spending provisions desired by those individual members, that the result was known as a "Christmas tree bill," laden with financial "ornaments." The president was required to either sign or veto a bill in its entirety, a requirement that led to spending bills containing expensive pet projects inserted by legislators. When Congress passed the **line item veto** in 1996, it allowed specific provisions of select taxing and spending bills to be vetoed independently of the rest of the bill. When the Supreme Court ruled the line item veto unconstitutional in 1998, the power of riders returned.

Filibusters and Cloture   There are few restrictions on debate in the Senate. It is possible to derail a bill by means of a **filibuster.** This technique allows a senator to speak against a bill—or just talk about anything at all—to "hold the floor" and prevent the Senate from moving forward with its business, as was seen by the multiple filibusters used to derail the campaign finance reform legislation. He or she may yield to other like-minded senators, and the marathon debate can continue for hours or even days.

The record for the longest individual filibuster belongs to Senator Strom Thurmond of South Carolina, who spoke against the Civil Rights Act of 1957 for an uninterrupted twenty-four hours and eighteen minutes.

Over time the Senate has made filibusters less onerous, first by interrupting them when the Senate's workday ended, and then by allowing them to be interrupted by a vote to consider other work. In recent years, senators have begun using a scheduling rule called a **hold** on legislation to stall a bill. This century-old practice was once a courtesy used just to keep a piece of legislation from being debated until a member could return to the chamber for the discussion. In recent years, however, senators have used holds to secretly indicate not that they wanted a chance to discuss the legislation, but that any debate on a bill was pointless because they intended to filibuster it, either because of their objection to it or because concessions had not yet been offered in its wording by the bill's supporters.[58] Senator Jesse Helms (R–NC) used this tactic as chair of the Senate Foreign Relations Committee to block forty-three ambassadorial appointments because he disagreed with the State Department's policies. By the end of 1999, Senator Herb Kohl (D.-WI)

QUOTE... UNQUOTE

"Vote without debating is perilous, but to debate and never vote is imbecile."

Sen. Henry Cabot Lodge, R.–MA

unanimous consent agreement The process by which the normal rules of Congress are waived unless a single member disagrees.

rider An amendment to a bill in the Senate that is totally unrelated to the subject of that bill but is attached to a popular measure in the hopes that it too will pass.

line item veto The power given to the president to veto a specific provision of a bill involving taxing and spending. Previously the president had to veto an entire bill. Declared unconstitutional by the Supreme Court in 1998.

filibuster A technique that allows a senator to speak against a bill, or talk about nothing at all, just to "hold the floor" and prevent the Senate from moving forward with a vote. He or she may yield to other like minded senators, so that the marathon debate can continue for hours or even days.

hold A request by a senator not to bring a measure up for consideration by the full Senate.

▶ Senate Majority Leader Trent Lott (R.-MS) (left) shakes hands with his predecessor Tom Daschle (D.-SD) knowing that he has been given a rare second chance at the Senate's top leadership position.

announced that he would place a hold on all legislation, including spending bills, unless dairy legislation that he opposed was allowed to die. At one point, several members threatened a hold on the adjournment vote unless legislation they wanted was supported.[59]

Through the use of a hold, several bills can be blocked indefinitely, with the rule now in effect that sixty votes, rather than a simple majority, are needed for passage. After witnessing the use of this tactic to block a $145 billion highway bill in late 1997, Majority Leader Trent Lott explained, "This is the Senate. And if any senator or group of senators want to be obstructionist, the only way you can break that is time."[60]

Between 1940 and 1965, only nineteen filibusters were employed for major legislation, but between 1992 and 1994 the Republicans conducted twenty-eight filibusters to derail the Democrats, who outnumbered them in the Senate. In fact, there were more filibusters in this period than in the previous sixty years (see Figure 4.4).

After Majority Leader Trent Lott took control of the Senate in 1996 and contended with Democrats who were doing to him what Republicans had done to them four years earlier by filibustering everything, he complained: "We are completely balled up and it's not my fault. I want us to sober up here now and get on with the business of the Senate."[61] But when the control of the Senate changed over to the Democrats in May 2001, Trent Lott and the other Republicans were back using the same tactics to slow down the agenda of Tom Daschle and the Senate Democrats. As evidenced in Figure 4.4, while the number of filibusters dropped from 35 in 1999 to 22 in 2000, they remained at 22 the following year.

How does the Senate get any work done under these conditions? In 1917 it adopted a procedure known as **cloture,** through which senators can vote to limit debate and stop a filibuster. Originally cloture required approval of two-thirds of

cloture A procedure through which a vote of sixty senators can limit debate and stop a filibuster.

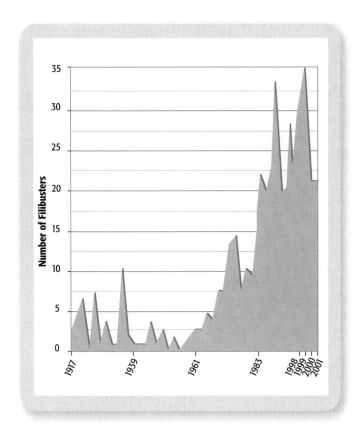

Figure 4.4
Senate Filibusters, 1917–2001

Source: Courtesy of Senate Historical Office, 6/14/02.

the senators present and voting (sixty-seven members if all were present), but when such a vote proved too difficult to achieve, the required majority was reduced to three-fifths of the members, or sixty votes.

Although the majority required for a cloture vote can be difficult to muster, the number of successful cloture votes has increased in recent years. Even if cloture has been voted, however, a postcloture filibuster can still continue for thirty more hours.[62] The value senators place on this technique was evident in the 104th Congress when, despite the continual bogging down of the body in concurrent filibusters, the members refused to reform the technique further. As a result, there have been cloture votes in the double digits, many of them unsuccessful as was the case with the Campaign Finance Reform bill, throughout the rest of the 1990s, on the majority leader's motion to bring legislation to the floor.

? Question for Reflection: Few congressional rules raise such interesting questions about Congress's ability to approach democracy as the Senate's filibuster and cloture devices. Does the ability to talk a bill to death, or to silence those seeking to do so, promote or hinder the democratic process?

Liberals who objected to the use of filibusters to stall civil rights legislation took advantage of that same tactic to combat and sometimes defeat key measures of the Contract with America. Some argue that cloture and filibusters empower minorities, while others claim they are stalling tactics that obstruct the will of the majority.

To place the filibuster in perspective, remember that although it is abused on occasion, senators use it only on major issues where a large minority is intensely opposed to what the majority is trying to do. Unhappy minorities should not necessarily win all they want, but neither should any political system systematically neglect the demands of a large minority. Filibusters force the majority to hear the minority and perhaps respond to some of its demands. All in all, the benefits of the filibuster in giving voice to minorities probably outweigh the frustrations it creates for the majority.

Informal Rules and Norms   In addition to its formal rules, Congress, like most large organizations, has informal, unwritten rules that facilitate its day-to-day operations. High among these is the rule of **seniority.** A members rank in both the House and Senate depends on how long he or she has served in that chamber. In the past the only way to become chair of a committee was by accumulating more years of continuous service on that committee than any other majority party member. Even membership on committees was tied to seniority.

A companion to this norm once was the norm of *apprenticeship,* whereby younger members were expected to sit quietly and learn their legislative craft from their elders. "To get along, go along" was the wisdom that Speaker Sam Rayburn once preached to junior members in persuading them to follow his lead.

Another traditional norm of Congress, designed to keep friction to a minimum, has been that debates on the floor and in committees are conducted with the utmost civility. One member never speaks directly to another; instead, members address the presiding officer, who may deflect damaging comments by ruling them out of order. In addition, whenever debates occur between members, titles, not names, are used, as in "I would like to commend the Representative from State X." Political scientist Donald Matthews has labeled such adherence to unwritten but generally accepted and informally enforced norms as "the folkways of the Senate."[63] Even the most bitter of political rivals still refer to each other as "the distinguished senator from . . . " or "my good friend and esteemed colleague" before proceeding to attack everything they hold dear.

As you might expect, there are occasional breakdowns in this norm. In recent years, as the two parties have become partisan and their ideologies have drifted further and further apart, the notion of civility has broken down on numerous occasions. Stories abound of members of Congress trading insults with, or shouting at, each other in hearings or in debates on the floor. In 1996 a highly agitated Representative Sam Gibbons (D.-FL) called his Republican colleagues "a bunch of fascists" and "dictators" before stalking out of a hearing room and yanking on the necktie of a California colleague. In 1997, one debate on the House floor ended with House Majority Whip Tom DeLay (R.-TX) forcibly shoving Representative David R. Obey (D.-WI) before the two men were separated.[64] This lack of civility, however, has been the reason for many of the more moderate members leaving their positions early.[65]

The result of these changes, Congressional scholar Burdett Loomis has written, has meant a change for the Senate, as we saw in the Bipartisan Campaign Finance Reform case study. Thus Loomis said with respect to the prospects of legislative passage: "However much we may want to romanticize the world's greatest deliberative body,' the cold fact remains that the 1980s and 1990s have witnessed a consistent growth in partisan behavior and position-taking in the U.S. Senate." Fewer and fewer members of Congress, it is charged, seem to put the national interests ahead of those of their own party, making it harder for the two parties to find a point of compromise.[66]

Thus, a new norm, political party loyalty, might be replacing seniority, apprenticeship and civility, at least in the House.[67] When over one-half of the freshmen members in the 104th Congress made their maiden floor speech in the opening session in January 1995, it was clear that the apprenticeship norm was dying, and it has been long since dead in the Senate.

The Senate is currently more traditional than the House in its regard for seniority. In 1953, some dilution of seniority rights began when Senate Minority Leader Lyndon Johnson instituted what became known as the "Johnson rule," which provided that no Democratic senator would receive more than one major committee assignment until everyone had one. Republicans adopted a similar rule in 1965. Thirty years later, however, when Republicans once again controlled the Senate, Majority Leader Bob Dole decided instead to let seniority determine every committee chair, even though several Republican colleagues were uncomfortable with

seniority An informal, unwritten rule of Congress that more senior members (those who have served longer than others) are appointed to committees and as chairs of committees. This "rule" is being diluted in the House as other systems are developed for committee appointments.

some of the results—most notably, archconservative Jesse Helms of North Carolina chairing the Foreign Relations Committee, and ninety-two-year-old Strom Thurmond of South Carolina chairing the Armed Services Committee.

Two other norms used to push legislation through Congress are *specialization* and *reciprocity*. Legislators are expected to develop a certain expertise on one or more issues as a way to help the body in its lawmaking role. Members who lack expertise in a particular policy area defer to policy specialists with more knowledge, with the understanding that the favor will be reciprocated.

When reciprocity is applied to votes on key measures the result is called **logrolling,** which helps legislators cooperate effectively. The term comes from a competition in which two lumberjacks maintain their balance on a floating log by working together to spin it with their feet. In congressional logrolling, legislators seek the assistance of colleagues by offering to support legislation the colleagues both favor. For example, a Democratic senator from California might support a flood control project in Mississippi that has no relevance to West Coast voters, provided that the Republican senator from Mississippi promises to support a measure delaying the closing of an army base in California.[68] On the other hand, two sets of representatives with linked interests might make such a deal. The House leadership's "Freedom to Farm" Act in the 104th Congress, which continued farm subsidies for sugar, peanuts, and milk, passed without trouble because it was paired with a food stamp program that brought it the votes of the liberal Northeast representatives.[69] In an era of government spending cuts, however, the notion of reciprocity has faded somewhat.

A traditional form of the logrolling norm is called **pork-barrel legislation,** special interest spending for members' districts or states. It is named for the practice of distributing salt pork as a treat to sailors on the high seas. In this case, members of Congress see their job as "bringing home the bacon" in the form of support for jobs and programs in their districts: dams and highways, military bases, new federal buildings, high-tech company support, or even research grants for local colleges and universities. The distribution of district or state pork-barrel spending tends to follow power. Thus it is not surprising that Mississippi, the home state of Majority Leader Trent Lott, got the most pork in 1997, receiving nearly $850 billion, or an average of $310 per capita. The state of Wyoming, with no powerful legislators, received only an average of 83 cents per capita. But these benefits are not limited by party. Leetown, West Virginia, hometown of Senate Appropriations Committee ranking Democrat Robert Byrd, was awarded $6 million for the National Center for Cool and Cold Water Aquaculture, winning it a 1998 annual "oinker" award from the Citizens Against Government Waste.[70]

It is not uncommon for revenue bills to contain their own version of pork: tax loopholes and breaks for companies in specific districts. Given the program-cutting mood of Congress in recent years, a new form of "negative pork" has been developed to distribute the cuts in different areas. Sometimes the cuts have been so contentious, such as military base closings, that special bipartisan commissions had to be created by Congress to recommend them.

Although many people criticize these spendthrift ways, attracting federal spending is traditionally the way that members of Congress represent their districts. In many districts, federal buildings and roads are named for local members of Congress, thus solidifying their reelection support. The deadlock over the 1997 Omnibus Highway Spending Bill was eventually broken by an agreement with House Transportation Committee Chair Bud Shuster (R-PA) to secretly dole out more than $9 billion in spending for highways and bridges in states and districts around the country. It was labeled by one legislator "a pork barrel bill—I fear—to end all pork barrel bills for the decade."[71] As "Tip" O'Neill explained, "All politics is local." These are the expensive practices that the line item veto was designed to eliminate. But given the Supreme Court's 1998 decision, this option is no longer available, unless it is passed by constitutional amendment.

logrolling A temporary political alliance between two policy actors who agree to support each other's policy goals.

pork-barrel legislation Policies and programs designed to create special benefits for a member's district, such as bridges, highways, dams, and military installations, all of which translate into jobs and money for the local economy and improve reelection chances for the incumbent.

How Members Make Voting Decisions

Political scientists have long sought to understand why members of Congress vote as they do. Their research suggests seven major sources of influence.

Personal Views The personal views and political ideology of members of Congress are the central variables in determining their voting decisions. When members care deeply about a policy matter, they usually vote their own preferences, sometimes risking their political careers in the process. Party leaders recognize the importance of personal convictions. "I have never asked a member to vote against his conscience," said former Speaker of the House John McCormack. "If he mentions his conscience—that's all. I don't press him any further."[72]

Sometimes such votes show the best aspects of congressional representation. In early 1995, Republican Senator Mark Hatfield was so unwilling to provide his party with the winning vote to pass the Balanced Budget Amendment, saying he opposed "tinkering with the Constitution," that he offered to resign instead. Majority Leader Robert Dole declined his offer. These personal views, however, can be influenced by other factors on an issue—most notably the desires of a member's constituents.

Constituents In votes with high visibility, constituents have a significant influence on their representative's voting decisions.[73] No representative wants to lose touch with the district or appear to care more about national politics than about the people back home. This was why Oklahoma Representative Mike Synar—a four-term liberal Democrat who supported gun control and the Family Leave Act while opposing a measure requiring parents to be notified if a teenaged daughter has an abortion—was defeated in a 1994 primary in his conservative district. A former supporter explained that Synar had "lost touch." To avoid these situations, members regularly conduct surveys and return to their districts to learn how constituents feel about issues on the congressional agenda.

On votes of lesser importance, or everyday activities in which the general public is not paying much attention, the members tend to follow other cues. However, they remain aware that their votes might be cited by opponents or a rival interest group in the next election.

Party Affiliation A member's vote can often be explained by political party affiliation. The number of times that members of Congress vote based on party position has steadily increased, from below 60 percent in 1970 to over 80 percent in the 1990s.[74] Sometimes, though, members do not vote according to party.[75] In the 104th Congress, six Democrats, including Alabama Senator Richard Shelby and Colorado Senator Ben Nighthorse Campbell, found themselves voting so many times with the opposition party that they switched to the Republican party.

If the national party leadership or the president is committed to a particular vote, the chances of a vote along party lines are even greater. If the party's position runs counter to the member's personal views, however, it is less likely to influence the way he or she votes.[76]

The President Sometimes the president seeks to influence a member's vote by calling him or her to the White House for a consultation. The president may offer something in return (support for another piece of legislation or a spending project in the member's district) or threaten some kind of punishment for noncompliance. If the line item veto had been accepted by the Supreme Court, the president's influence over members' votes might have been strengthened. Without it, the president cannot negotiate votes from members who oppose him by threatening to eliminate some pork-barrel legislation of interest to them. Sometimes the purpose of the consultation with the president is simply to make the member look important to the voters back home, but even that serves as a political favor, inducing the member to look more kindly on presidential requests for legislative support.[77]

APPROACHING DIVERSITY

Nancy Pelosi Makes History—Twice!

When House Representative Nancy Pelosi (D.-CA), a mother of five and grandmother of five more was handed a large black leather whip by outgoing Democratic minority whip David Bonior and charged with counting votes to make sure that Democrats followed the leadership, she knew she had made history. In November of 2001 she became the highest-ranking woman in a leadership position in either House of Congress in American history. Then the number two person in the House Democratic leadership, she worked with Minority Leader Dick Gephardt, hoping to retake control of Congress.

The journey to this lofty position was not an easy one. All Pelosi, a homemaker in the mid-1980s, had been thinking of doing was running for Mayor of San Francisco. Toward that end she helped the Democratic party raise money by chairing the state party and serving as the finance chair for the Senate Democrats in 1986. When Sala Burton, the widow of California Democratic Representative Philip Burton, who had won her husband's seat upon his death, announced that she herself was critically ill, she handpicked Pelosi to take her seat. "Hardly any women in Congress determine who [their] successor is," observed Pelosi, "Lots of men do."

Once in Congress Pelosi served with distinction on the powerful Appropriations and Intelligence Committees, but when a vacancy opened for the number three seat in the Democratic caucus, Pelosi passed on the prospect, telling a colleague, "I'm running for whip." When Democratic Whip David Bonior of Michigan left the House to run for governor, she had her opportunity. Running against

Maryland Rep. Steny H. Hoyer, Pelosi argued that her organizing and fund-raising skills, enabling her to help the party raise some $4 million in the 2000 election, made her the best candidate for the job. Other Democrats, though, also saw that by choosing a woman for the position they were providing evidence of the party's commitment to diversity.

It was a hard-fought campaign, with Pelosi demonstrating her whip skills by organizing a get-out-the-vote system for her own colleagues complete with 7:30 a.m. wake up calls to make sure that they showed up to vote in the election. Eventually, she won the race 118 to 95. Hoyer argued that her 32 member delegation from California also gave her an edge. Perhaps the best indication of her unique skills for this leadership position, is the fact that one of her admirers is ultra-conservative Tom Delay (R.-TX), the majority party leader, who got to know her during a tour investigating the AIDS crisis. If she needs any help learning how to use her new whip to keep her fellow party members in line, Delay has said that he will pull out his black leather whip, given to him when he was the whip, to teach her: "I'll show her how to pop one."

But Pelosi had served as whip for only one year when she made history again. After Richard Gephardt chose not to run for re-election as Minority Leader in the wake of his party's losses in the 2002 election, Pelosi was elected to the position, a first for a woman, thus putting her in line to become Speaker if the Democrats should retake control of the House.

Source: Juliet Eilperin, "Pelosi Finds Her Place in the House," *Washington Post,* November 13, 2001, p. A25.

Presidential lobbying of undecided or politically exposed members can be a key factor in the outcome of a vote. First-term Democratic representative Marjorie Margolies-Mezvinsky of Pennsylvania learned this lesson in the summer of 1993, when her party's congressional leadership pressed her to support a deficit-reduction bill that would raise taxes and offend her predominantly Republican constituents. On the day of the vote, Margolies-Mezvinsky decided to oppose the bill. However, when the vote was tied at 217 to 217 (which meant that the bill would fail), President Clinton implored her to back the bill for the good of the country and the party. After casting the deciding vote in favor of the bill, she lost the 1994 election to the very same Republican she had beaten two years earlier.[78]

Interest Groups Important interest groups and political action committees that have provided funds for past elections try to influence a member's vote by lobbying intensely on key issues. In addition, lobbying organizations seek access to members of Congress through personal visits and calls. Sometimes they apply pressure by generating grass-roots campaigns among the general public, jamming members' phone lines and fax machines, and filling their mailbags. In the end, interest groups and their financial political action committees (PACs) are much less relevant on votes than on access to the members to influence their thinking on an issue.

▲ Rep. Nancy Pelosi (D.-CA) received a whip from Rep. David E. Bonior (D.-MI) when she became the first woman elected House Minority Whip, and one year later she again made history by becoming the first woman to be elected House Minority Leader.

In considering tax legislation, for instance, so many prominent and well-dressed financial lobbyists prowl the Capitol seeking to influence the outcome that the halls are nicknamed "Gucci Gulch," for the fancy leather shoes they wore in the hallway button-holing members to lobby them.[79] But there were some extraordinary cases in which interest groups have been highly influential in the final votes. In 1987 both liberal and conservative groups prevailed on followers to pressure the Senate concerning controversial Judge Robert Bork's nomination for the Supreme Court. So many calls came in during this debate that some members' telephone switchboards literally broke down.

Congressional Staff   One of the functions of congressional staff members is to sort through the various sources of pressure and information. In so doing, they themselves become a source of pressure on members to vote in a particular way. Staff members organize hearings, conduct research, draft bill markups and amendments, prepare reports, assist committee chairs, interact with the press, and perform other liaison activities with lobbyists and constituents. In addition, as important players in the political game, they have their own preferences on many issues. With their expertise and political commitments, they can often convince members of Congress to vote for the bills they favor. However, since members of Congress normally hire people whose political views reinforce their own, most often staff people simply help members of Congress be more efficient at what they want to do anyway: please their constituents, promote their party, and vote their convictions.[80]

Congressional staffs proliferated in the 1960s as the federal government grew in size and complexity. Members of both houses of Congress became increasingly dependent on staff for information about proposed legislation. Moreover, in an effort to stay closer to voters, members established district-based offices staffed by aides.[81]

Colleagues and the "Cue Structure"   What does a legislator do when all these influences—personal convictions, voters, party leadership, the president, interest groups, and staff—are sending contradictory messages about how to vote on a particular bill? And what does a member do when there is not enough time to gather the necessary information about an issue before voting on it? To help them make quick decisions about how to vote, members develop a personal intelligence system that scholars label a *cue structure*. The cues can come from a number of sources: members of Congress who are experts, knowledgeable members of the executive branch, lobbyists, or media reports.[82] Sometimes the cues come from special groups within Congress, such as the Black or Women's Caucuses, the Democratic Study Group, or the Republicans' Conservative Opportunity Society. Members also get cues from their particular "buddy system:" other members whom they respect, who come from the same kinds of districts, and who have similar goals. In voting, members generally look first for disagreement among their various cues and then try to prioritize the cues to reach an acceptable vote. This "consensus model" suggested by political scientist John Kingdon does seem to hold when members vote on issues of average importance, but on highly controversial issues that may affect their reelection prospects, members are far more likely to follow their own opinions.[83]

How a Bill Becomes a Law

Spread over several square blocks of Washington, D.C., are six buildings housing congressional offices. An underground subway carries members of Congress from their offices to the Capitol, a magnificent structure that includes the Senate and House chambers where the 535 elected senators and representatives work when Congress is in session.

As you know from the case study at the beginning of the chapter, transforming a bill into a law is a long and complicated process. In order to succeed, a bill must win

218 votes in the House, 51 votes in the Senate, and one presidential signature. The process may take years because of disagreements among the two houses or the need to muster 60 votes to break a filibuster in the Senate. In the most controversial cases, members know that if the president is adamantly opposed to a bill and will not negotiate, then a two-thirds vote of both Houses will be needed to override the anticipated veto. Conflicting policy goals, special interests, ideology, partisanship, and political ambitions often delay or obstruct the passage of legislation. Most bills never even reach the House or Senate floors for debate.[84] Yet some bills manage to make their way through the administrative and political maze. Let's see how that can happen.

The Congressional Agenda

When a member of Congress drafts and submits a piece of legislation dealing with a particular issue, that issue is said to be on the **congressional agenda.** While much of the agenda consists of mandated business—such as reauthorizations of earlier actions or appropriations for government spending—a new issue must gain widespread public attention to be viewed as important enough to require legislative action.[85] Often issues rise to prominence in response to a perceived national crisis, such as terrorist attacks and the costs of providing homeland security. Other issues, such as health care or a balanced budget, build momentum slowly for years before reaching the level of national consciousness that ensures congressional action. Ideas for bills can come to the attention of Congress from a number of sources, including the president, cabinet, research institutes, scholars, journalists, voters, and sometimes from **lobbyists** (people paid to further the aims of some interest group among members of Congress).[86] Any citizen can draft legislation and ask a representative or senator to submit it. Only members of Congress can introduce a bill.

Congress Considers the Bill

Once a bill has been introduced in Congress, it follows a series of steps on its way to becoming law (see Figure 4.5). In the House, every piece of legislation is *introduced* by a representative, who hands it to the clerk of the House or places it in a box called the "hopper." In the Senate, a senator must be recognized by the presiding officer to announce the introduction of a bill. In either case, the bill is first *read* (printed in the *Congressional Record*) and then referred to the appropriate committee (or committees if it is especially complex) by the Speaker of the House or the Senate majority leader.

After a bill has been assigned to a committee, the chair of that committee assigns it to a subcommittee. The subcommittee process usually begins with **hearings,** formal proceedings in which a range of people testify on the bill's pros and cons. Witnesses are usually experts on the subject matter of the bill; sometimes they are people who have been or will be affected by the issue, including various administration officials and highly visible citizens. Subcommittee chairs can influence the final content of a bill and its chances of passage by arranging for a preponderance of either friendly or hostile witnesses or by planning for the type of testimony that will attract media attention.

After hearings, the subcommitte holds a **markup session** to revise the bill. The subcommittee then sends the bill back to the full committee, where additional discussion, markup, and voting occur. Approval at this level enables the bill to be sent to the full House, but most bills must first move through the House Rules Committee, which schedules the timing, length, and conditions of debate, such as whether amendments would be allowed, under which bills are debated on the House floor.

Once a bill reaches the House floor, its fate is still far from certain. Debate procedures are complex, and many votes are taken (usually on proposed amendments) on measures containing almost indecipherable language before the bill secures final acceptance. To expedite matters, the House or the Senate can act as a

congressional agenda A list of bills to be considered by Congress.

lobbyists People paid to pressure members of Congress to further the aims of some interest group.

hearings Formal proceedings in which a range of people testify on a bill's pros and cons.

markup session A session held by a subcommittee to revise a bill.

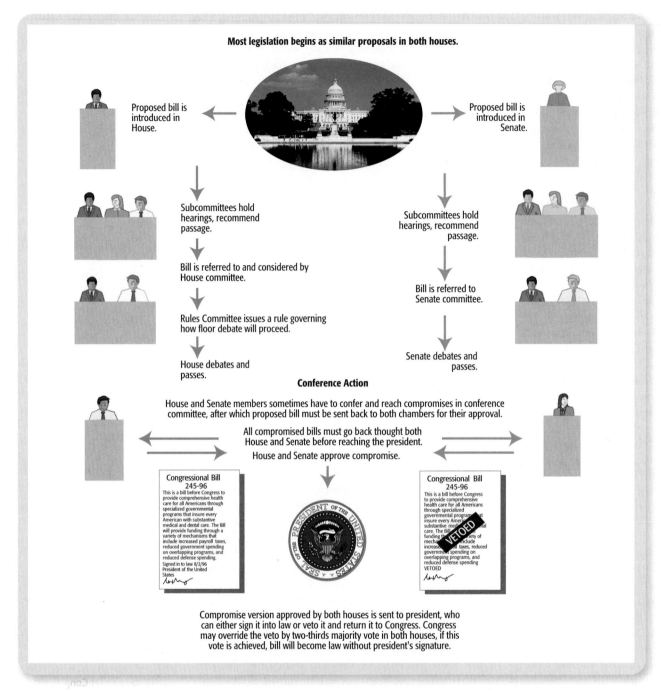

Figure 4.5   How a Bill Becomes a Law

committee of the whole in which all members can function as a committee rather than as a formal legislative body. Committee rules are looser and less formal than those that apply to the full House. For instance, only 100 House members need be present when the House is operating as the Committee of the Whole, whereas normally it takes 218 representatives on the floor to conduct business. Opponents have numerous opportunities at this stage to defeat or significantly change the wording, and thus the impact, of the bill.

Being much smaller than the House, the Senate is an intimate body that operates with much less formality. After committee deliberation, bills are simply brought to the floor through informal agreements among Senate leaders. Individual senators can even bring bills directly to the floor, bypassing committees altogether. They do this by offering their bill as an amendment to whatever bill is then pending, even if the two are unrelated.

The House of Representatives uses an *electronic voting system* that posts each member's name on the wall of the chamber. Members insert a plastic card into a box attached to the chairs to vote "yea," "nay," or "present." The results of the vote then appear alongside each legislator's name. The electronic voting system has increased participation at roll calls, and watchdog groups have been known to keep a close eye on legislators who are frequently absent on important roll calls. In addition, legislators find the electronic system handy; it enables them to check how their colleagues are voting. But even if successful in the House and Senate, proposed legislation still faces hurdles. To become law, the bills passed in both houses of Congress must be worded identically. As mentioned earlier, a conference committee composed of both House and Senate members reconciles the differences in language and creates a single version of the bill.[87]

When the differences between versions of a bill have been ironed out, the final version is returned to both houses for approval. If it is then approved by both chambers, it becomes an **enrolled act,** or **resolution,** and is sent to the White House for the president's signature or veto. Measures that require spending are offered in one of thirteen **appropriations bills,** based on authorized amounts that are passed by Congress. Thus, the Congress has two opportunities to debate a measure: first the measure itself, then the funding of it.

The President Considers the Bill   Once Congress has voted and sent a bill on to the president, four scenarios are possible. The president can sign the bill, and it becomes law. Or the president can **veto** it; that is, return the bill to Congress with a statement of reasons for refusing to sign it. At that point, Congress can **override** the president's action with a two-thirds vote in both the House and Senate. Congress can rarely muster this level of opposition to a sitting president, so vetoes are overridden less than 10 percent of the time.[88] Of President Clinton's 25 vetoes in his first five years of office, only one was overridden. While President Bush has repeatedly used the threat of a veto to try to enforce his spending priorities on the Democrats, such as when he threatened to block their efforts to add $40 million in counter-terrorism spending in late 2001 and threatened in April of 2002 to use his veto power to force Congress to stay within its spending limits, by the end of 2002 he had not issued a single veto. Still, such threats have an effect on members who realize that it might now take a two-thirds vote to pass legislation.

Two other outcomes are also possible. Once a bill reaches the president's desk, the president can simply do nothing, in which case the bill automatically becomes law after ten legislative days (not counting Sundays, and providing that Congress is still in session) in spite of remaining unsigned. The president can also refuse to sign a bill that Congress passes in the last ten days of its session. If Congress has adjourned, the unsigned bill automatically dies. This is called a **pocket veto.**

From time to time, even if the president reluctantly signs a bill, a signing statement might also be released that seems to undercut some aspects of the measure. This action is taken in anticipation of a Supreme Court challenge to the measure, knowing that the Court may use this statement in deciding whether to uphold the measure.

Obstacles to Passage of a Bill

This textbook approach to passing a bill rarely works smoothly because there are so many obstacles lying in the path of success. The backers of any bill must win support at each stage of the lawmaking process. They must find majorities in each committee, they must find enthusiastic backers during each formal discussion, and so forth. Opponents of the bill have a much easier job. They can kill it at any step along the way. Sometimes they do not even need a majority; one unfriendly legislator in the right place may be sufficient.

enrolled act (or resolution) The final version of a bill, approved by both chambers of Congress.

appropriations bill A separate bill that must be passed by Congress to fund measures that require spending.

veto Presidential power to forbid or prevent an action of Congress.

override The two thirds vote of both houses of Congress required to pass a law over the veto of the president.

pocket veto Presidential refusal to sign or veto a bill that Congress passes in the last ten days of its session; by not being signed, it automatically dies if Congress adjourns.

Imagine how you, as a member of Congress, could stop a bill you disliked. Here are some of the ways you could take action.

1. Lobby members of your party conference or caucus to stop, or at least slow down, consideration of the bill.
2. Convince the Speaker to stop, or slow down, consideration of the bill.
3. Lobby committee and subcommittee members to oppose the bill in committee hearings, deliberations, markups, and votes.
4. Lobby the Rules Committee to oppose giving the bill a rule, which dictates the timing and terms of a bill's debate.
5. Lobby colleagues on the House floor not to vote for the rule, thus preventing the bill from ever reaching floor discussion.
6. Call press conferences and give interviews trying to build a grass-roots or interest group coalition against the bill.
7. Propose a series of amendments that weaken the bill or make it less attractive to potential supporters. Then vote for unattractive amendments at every opportunity.
8. If the bill does gain passage in the House, use the same tactics to stop it in the Senate, mustering opposition in committees and on the Senate floor. Be sure to have Senators also gain media attention against the bill, whipping up negative reaction to its possible passage.
9. Find senators who hate the bill and persuade them to filibuster, or place a hold on the bill yourself.
10. If both House and Senate pass the bill, work against it in the conference committee, if one is needed.
11. If Congress passes the bill, seek allies in the White House who might persuade the president to veto it.
12. Once the bill becomes law, use similar steps to prevent Congress from funding the measure.
13. If the bill becomes law and is funded, work to rescind the law or to keep funding too low for it to be effective. Or, lobby the executive branch to delay the implementation of the bill.
14. If all else fails, have faith that some group opposed to the bill will mount a constitutional challenge to the law, going all the way to the Supreme Court if necessary.

This array of blocking options favors those who oppose change. What you think of this system depends on how you like the status quo. A majority of congressional liberals in the 1960s often felt frustrated by the difficulty in working their agenda through a conservative minority of Republicans and southern Democrats. Today, however, some of those same liberals find some value in these legislative obstacles.

The best example of the operation of all of these obstacles is what happened to the Republican Congress's effort after the 1994 elections to pass the Contract with America. Speaker Gingrich had vowed that the first one hundred days of the 104th Congress would be devoted to passing ten major items: a Balanced Budget Amendment, a line item veto, dealing with crime and closing loopholes in the death penalty, reforming welfare, dealing with "deadbeat parents" who failed to support children, creating school voucher programs, creating a middle-class tax cut, restricting the United Nations' ability to command U.S. troops, reforming Social Security, cutting capital gains taxes, reforming the legal system and product liability/malpractice suits, and establishing congressional term limits.

House Republicans were unified in passing nearly all of these promises, but the Senate considered these measures at a much more leisurely pace and greatly increased the time that it took to pass many of the measures. In addition, all of the measures had to be greatly watered down to have any chance of Bill Clinton signing them. The Balanced Budget Amendment failed twice by a single vote. And the term limits proposal was defeated by a combination of amendments and vigorous lobbying.

Another example of legislative obstacles, as outlined in the case study, was the effort to block the reform of campaign finance by limiting soft money contributions and creating electoral spending limits. This measure was killed in 1998 and again in 1999 by Majority Leader Trent Lott's substituting a less attractive amended bill and enforcing a cloture vote to shut off an anticipated filibuster. Campaign finance reform garnered only fifty-one votes in 1998, nine votes short of the sixty votes needed for cloture.[89] It lost again by a narrower margin in 1999, despite the fact that a majority in the Senate appeared to be willing to pass campaign finance reform. But in 2002, a combination of both the Jeffords party switch and the Enron scandal changed the climate, thus allowing the obstacles to passage to be overcome.

Overcoming the Legislative Obstacles

In recent years, the Republican Congress has sought ways to overcome the traditional obstacles to passing legislation.[90] With all of the various blocking points that threaten to doom single pieces of legislation, party leaders in Congress have begun to package the biggest and most important legislation into so-called **omnibus legislation,** which some refer to as "megabills" or "packages." The idea here is to hide controversial pieces of legislation inside packages of related bills that have a very high likelihood of successful votes. The president then will have to sign the entire bill. Members of Congress are provided with cover in supporting the controversial legislation, interest groups and their financial PACs are less likely to punish supporters for their votes, and the media sometimes lose track of the controversial issues.

This trend toward fewer but longer and more complex bills is demonstrated by the fact that over the last half century the sheer size of the laws has increased from 2.5 pages to 16.2 pages.[91] The Welfare Reform Bill of 1996, with all of its different provisions to limit the amount of time people could receive welfare and encourage them to work, was just such a piece of omnibus legislation. In order to pass this comprehensive measure, Republicans had to drop the cutbacks in such "safety net" items as school lunches, and turn to the more moderate Senate version of the bill before President Clinton would sign it. This strategy is not foolproof, however, as was indicated by the doomed health care reform effort in 1994, when the complex provisions of the bill offered multiple targets for medical interest groups to attack.

With many controversial appropriations measures to be passed each year under the budgeting procedure, leaders have had to resort to the passage of **continuing resolutions** that provide stop-gap funding to keep the government running. These resolutions must be passed by both houses of Congress and do not require a presidential signature, thus making them apparently veto-proof. Such resolutions were once common for temporary funding of one to three months for a handful of agencies. But learning from the late 1980s, when the procedure was used for all thirteen major appropriations measures, the Republican Congress used this technique to overcome delays in approving the budget. The attempt backfired in late 1995 and early 1996 when disagreements between Congress and the president forced the government to shut down twice because even continuing resolutions could not be agreed upon and passed. Because of the political damage to Republicans in Congress, in 1997 an automatic continuing resolution was created to keep the government going in the event that the two parties disagreed on future funding. The same technique was used that year for emergency legislation that provided disaster relief for the states and funded the peacekeepers in Bosnia.[92]

From time to time, when faced with highly controversial legislative subjects, congressional leaders bypass the normal procedures for drafting bills, preferring instead to handle problems by creating ad hoc **task forces.** Such task forces, groups of legislators charged with drafting legislation and coordinating strategy to forge a

omnibus legislation A large bill which combines a number of smaller pieces of legislation.

continuing resolution A bill passed by Congress and signed by the president which enables the federal government to keep operating under the previous year's appropriations.

task force An informal procedure used by Congress to get groups of legislators together to draft legislation and negotiate strategy for passing a bill.

consensus on an issue, increase the communication among members and thus speed the passage of controversial legislation. While this technique had been used occasionally in the past, Newt Gingrich used it most successfully to push portions of the Contract with America along. In recent years Speaker Hastert has abandoned the use of task forces in the House, while then-Majority Leader, Trent Lott created in 2000 the bipartisan Senate National Security Working Group to examine possible legislation dealing with topics such as missile defenses and weapons control.

Even with all of these strategies, members of Congress often resort to presenting their cases directly to the media either to push or to block legislation. In the old days, legislators would use an *inside strategy* of lining up votes. But now they often resort to an *outside strategy* of giving speeches, press conferences, and interviews to try to mobilize public opinion and interest group assistance on their behalf.

Additional Functions of Congress

Aside from enacting legislation, two of the most important functions of Congress are **oversight** and budget control. Congressional oversight involves monitoring the effectiveness of laws passed by Congress. The Legislative Reorganization Act of 1946 specifically directs the committees of Congress to exercise "continuous watchfulness" over the agencies of the executive branch that carry out the laws, and to supervise them to see that the laws are implemented as Congress intended. This oversight can be either *legislative* (in the form of pilot programs, special studies, or cost/benefit analysis) or *investigative* (in the form of hearings to examine possible legal or ethical infractions).[93] Examples of oversight investigations include the 1974 hearings on Watergate, which toppled Richard Nixon, and the 1987 hearings on the Iran-Contra affair, which threatened Ronald Reagan.[94] More recently, the 2002 investigation by ten Congressional Committees into the causes of the collapse of the Enron corporation led to calls for changes in the government's regulations of businesses and energy corporations.

One of the ways that Congress maintains control over administrative implementation of its mandates without having to exercise control on a day-to-day basis is the **legislative veto.** The legislative veto allows the president or an executive agency to act subject to the later approval or disapproval of either one or both houses of Congress, or sometimes even the committees in one or both houses. In 1983 the Supreme Court ruled that many such legislative vetoes, in this case one dealing with the Immigration and Naturalization Service, are unconstitutional because they represent a violation of the separation of powers of the government branches and the presentation clause of the Constitution, which requires that all legislation must be presented to the president for signature.[95] In response, however, Congress eliminated some legislative vetoes and modified others, but continued to pass new bills with this feature in them.

Congress's budget-control powers are contained in the Constitution. All tax legislation (the raising of money) must originate in the House, but tax bills, along with appropriations bills (the spending of money), need approval from both House and Senate. This "power of the purse" is central to Congress's role. Through its influence on money matters, Congress can shape nearly every policy undertaken by the national government.

In 1974 Congress passed the Congressional Budget and Impoundment Control Act. This legislation created the **Congressional Budget Office (CBO),** permanent budget committees in the House and Senate, and a new budget timetable. The act was intended to expand congressional control over the national budget at a time when the president usually dominated the process. The House and Senate Budget Committees review the president's annual budget in light of the projections made by the CBO. The CBO establishes budget totals and spending outlays, loan obligations; and deficit-reduction strategies.[96]

oversight Congressional function that involves monitoring the effectiveness of laws by examining the workings of the executive branch.

legislative veto A legislative action that allows the president or executive agencies to implement a law subject to the later approval or disapproval of one or both houses of Congress.

Congressional Budget Office (CBO) A governmental office created by Congress in 1974 to analyze budgetary figures and make recommendations to Congress and the president.

The most extreme form of oversight by Congress is **impeachment,** by which the House can vote charges against the president, other executive officials, or members of the judiciary for committing "High Crimes and Misdemeanors." Only three times in our history have presidents faced impeachment—Andrew Johnson in 1868, Richard Nixon in 1974, and Bill Clinton in 1998. Should articles of impeachment be voted by the House, a trial is held in the Senate, chaired by the chief justice of the United States. (In Nixon's case, he resigned after articles were voted by the House Judiciary Committee.) When Special Prosecutor Kenneth Starr finished his investigation of President Bill Clinton and intern Monica Lewinsky, that information was turned over to Judiciary Committee Chair Henry J. Hyde (R.-IL). The decision by the committee and the full House was to initiate an impeachment investigation. While articles of impeachment were voted in the House, the president was not convicted in the Senate.

In the end, the entire process works more or less as the framers intended. With the Constitution silent on all but a few rules of Congress, this complex legislative system slowly evolved to ensure that no idea can break through the maze of political roadblocks without securing wide general support of both the short- and long-term interests from many segments of society. Observes congressional scholar Ross Baker, "If James Madison were to come back and sit in the gallery of the House and Senate, he'd be pretty pleased with the way things are working."[97]

The 106th and 107th Congress: Whither the "Republican Revolution"?

The last two terms of Congress have been among the most remarkable in the nation's history, but not for the reasons that anyone expected. When Newt Gingrich took over as Speaker of the House in 1995 for the 104th Congress, he had an overwhelming twenty-five seat majority in the House, bolstered by the Republican control of the Senate under Majority Leader Trent Lott of Mississippi. Everyone expected that the so-called "Republican Revolution" would be solidified for a generation to come even with a Democrat in the White House because of the party's ability to dictate the legislative agenda. Instead, the body degenerated into much partisan and bitter wrangling, as illustrated by the 1998 impeachment attempt of Bill Clinton. The result was that by 2000 Gingrich was gone, the margin in the House was only five seats for the Republicans, Democrats in the Senate under Minority Leader Tom Daschle had successfully employed a variety of tactics to slow down the Republicans' legislative agenda, and the partisan rancor in both Houses had increased to the point that moderate legislators were leaving the body. Other members could not work with each other, and many wondered whether the Republicans would retain control of either body after the 2000 election.

As a result of this partisanship and balance in Congress, little was accomplished in the 106th Congress. Speaker J. Dennis Hastert, while proving to be personally popular among the members despite the fact that he was not a dynamic leader, was not able to fashion the Republicans into the disciplined legislative machine that existed during the Gingrich Speakership. Meanwhile, the Senate wrangled over issues such as Campaign Finance Reform, a series of investigations of the White House, and the rate at which Bill Clinton's judicial and executive appointments were being confirmed.

All in all, the Congress in 1999 passed only thirty-nine bills into law, thirty-four of them on unanimous voice vote (of which nine were simply to rename federal buildings and three to reappoint the regents to the Smithsonian). "This Congress has a rendezvous with obscurity," said one congressional expert. "I've been here 25 years, and I've never seen this place so ineffective," argued Democrat Patrick J. Leahy (VT). Even the members on the other side of the aisle were unhappy. Representative Michael N. Castle, a Republican from Delaware, argued: "It's pretty frustrating for those of us who actually want to get things done. . . . It's a real shame, and it's a

impeachment The process by which government actors can be removed from office for committing "High Crimes and Misdemeanors," treason, or bribery. The House of Representatives first votes on the charges, and then the trial takes place in the Senate.

collective shame." And it did no better the following year as rather than pass major laws, each party in Congress seemed determined to use its votes to highlight issues that created an agenda for the upcoming 2000 election.

Gingrich's Republican Revolution stalled in the final days of the 2000 election and was derailed, at least for the moment, in May, 2001. After more than $500 million was spent on Congressional elections nationwide, the balance in the Senate came down to a count of absentee ballots in the Washington Senate race between incumbent Slade Gorton, a Republican and relatively unknown dot.com executive, Maria Cantwell, a Democrat. No one could have predicted that this race would have mattered so much, but in the final days of the election campaign four other senior Republican Senators—Spencer Abraham of Michigan, John Ashcroft of Missouri (who lost to the deceased Missouri governor, Mel Carnahan), Rod Grams of Minnesota, and William Roth of Delaware—all ran into trouble in their campaigns. After all of these Senators, who were avowed conservatives and vocal opponents of the campaign finance bill lost, it came down to the Washington State race to determine whether the Senate would be perfectly balanced in a 50–50 margin, meaning that Vice President Dick Cheney would have to cast the tie-breaking vote. Cantwell's narrow win made this a reality and gave the Democrats hope for the future.

The Republican majority in both Houses during the 107th Congress had narrowed to the smallest margins since the late 1950s. In the House, the Republicans eventually took 222 seats, four greater than a majority of the House and the Democrats took 211 seats, with two Independents (one who consistently voted with the Democrats and the other one with the Republicans). In the Senate, Republican control was shaky. Both senior Republican Senators Strom Thurmond (SC) and Jesse Helms (NC) were ill and would be replaced by Democratic state governors if forced to resign.

With both Houses poised for deadlock and perhaps even stalemate, everything changed in May 2001 when, as outlined in Chapter 9, moderate Republican Jim Jeffords of Vermont, angered by his lack of influence with the Bush administration, changed his party affiliation to Independent, thus awarding control of the Senate to the Democrats. As Majority Leader Tom Daschle of the Democratic party sought to advance his own party's agenda, and a return to divided government was clear. Using the tactics of his predecessor, Trent Lott of Mississippi, he sought to derail the Bush administration's legislative agenda. Things got interesting when Republican John McCain, who had promised an extended filibuster unless the first order of business was an up or down vote on his and Democrat Russell Feingold's campaign finance reform bill, promised that there would "be blood on the floor of the

▶ Senator Joseph Biden (D.-DE) delivers an impromptu foreign policy lecture to a group of high school students on the Capitol steps.

Senate" if his demand was not met. McCain's private meeting with Daschle in Arizona gave rise to speculation that the Democrats might have more ammunition than previously thought in dictating the direction of the Senate even despite their narrow margin of party control.

For a time after Jeffords' switch, moderate members from each party appeared ready to reach across the aisle in search of compromise to accomplish their legislative goals. Daschle and Trent Lott even reached a unique power-sharing arrangement in the Senate in an effort to frame legislation in a nonpartisan manner. But not as much agreement between the parties could be reached as was hoped.

Then came September 11. Suddenly Congress was united and spoke with one voice. While House leaders, Speaker J. Dennis Hastert and Minority Leader Richard Gephardt, had not been speaking for several months at the end of the 106th session of Congress, now they and the two Senate leaders, Daschle and Lott, combined with President Bush in what the press called the "Gang of Five" to lead the nation. When members of Congress were forced to flee their buildings in response to the anthrax scare, it only further united the membership. Bonded together, members of Congress shepherded to passage the U.S.A. Patriot Act and the sweeping Education Reform Act. The result was a short period of bipartisanship, unique in the modern era. Said Congressional scholar Thomas Mann of the Brookings Institution of the 107th Congress: "This is a session of Congress without historical precedent. Agendas changed as radically as I have ever seen them change."[98]

Congress After the 2002 Election

The 2002 election determined whether or not the "Republican Revolution" was truly over, if a bipartisan era would continue, or if the old bitter partisan legislative wars would resume. Even after the 2000 redistricting, which many expected to be used by state parties to ensure their members' ability to win election, Congressional election expert Charles Cook argued that only 44 of the 435 House seats up for election would be competitive in the 2002 election. This meant that the Democrats needed to retain all of the seats that they anticipate winning and win a large majority of the contested seats in order to gain the six seats needed for control of the House, which became seven seats when conservative Democrat Ralph M. Hall of eastern Texas announced that he would vote for the Republican Speaker if his vote became the decisive one. The Republicans challenge to retake the Senate appeared to be a difficult one. Of the 34 Senate seats being contested in 2002, the Republicans needed to defend 20 of them, while the Democrats needed to defend only 14.

The 2002 Congressional election finally broke the deadlocked result from the two previous years by enabling the Republicans to take control of both the House and the Senate, making this the first time in over 50 years that this party controlled both Houses of Congress and the Presidency. To accomplish this feat, President George W. Bush went on the campaign trail, traveling to 25 battleground states in the last month of the campaign. Bush, bolstered by a nearly 70% approval rate, made this election a referendum on his presidency, arguing that the Democrats had obstructed the passage of his plan to create a Department of Homeland Security and failed to confirm many of his judicial appointments. For their part, the Democrats, led by Senate Majority Leader Tom Daschle (D.-SD) and House Minority Leader Richard Gephardt (D.-MO), did not articulate any alternative to Bush's foreign policy, hoping that voters would make their decisions on such issues as the downturn in the economy, a plan for providing prescription drugs for senior citizens, and education reform.

The distinction between the political parties blurred as candidates from both sides appeared to be moderates, leaving people with no reason to make a change. As a result, the Republicans widened their control of the House, taking at least 228 seats, with 204 going to the Democrats, one Independent seat, and two seats still to be determined but leaning Republican. Even this, though, may not prove to be the final result of the election. Richard Gephardt chose not to run again for House Minority Leader; some said it was because of his failed campaign strategy failure, while he argued that it was to run for President. When liberal Nancy Pelosi (D.-CA) became the first woman to be elected Minority Leader to succeed Gephardt, setting up a policy-making battle with the new conservative Majority Leader, Republican Tom Delay (R.-TX), many predicted more defections by conservative southern Democrats to the Republican party, thus increasing their governing majority. Nevertheless, Congressional expert Charles Cook points out that the election of 2002 was amazingly close, as a shift of about 94,000 votes out of nearly 76 million votes cast nationwide would have led to a Democratic party-controlled House and Senate. The fact that President Bush was able to tilt the balance so decisively for his party led liberal commentator Paul Begala to say, "The President stitched himself some coattails on election day."

The race over the control of the Senate met with several unexpected events during the campaign. Senator Robert Torricelli (D.-NJ) abandoned his re-election bid because of ethics violations and was replaced on the ballot by 78-year-old Frank Lautenberg, a former New Jersey Senator. Senator Paul Wellstone of Minnesota, the Senate's most liberal member, died in an airplane crash shortly before the election, leading Democrats to replace him on the ballot with 74-year-old Walter Mondale, a former Senator, Vice President for President Jimmy Carter, and Presidential candidate in 1984. In Georgia, the race for the Senate took a particularly ugly turn when Saxby Chambliss (R.-GA) ran an ad against Senator Max Cleland (D.-GA), a veteran who had lost three limbs during the Vietnam War, depicting Osama Bin Laden and claiming that Cleland was obstructing passage of President Bush's Department of Homeland Security. The implication was that Cleland was soft on terrorism, when in fact he and other Democrats sought to labor union protection for 40,000 civil service employees who would work in the new Department before supporting the bill. Of these three seats, the Republicans won two: Minnesota and Georgia.

When the Democrats failed to hold onto their seat in Missouri and to take open seats in New Hampshire and North Carolina, they lost their narrow control of the Senate. The Republicans took 51 seats, while the Democrats took 47, with one Independent, Jim Jeffords (I.-VT), and one seat, in Louisiana, to be determined by a run-off election. As a result, Senator Trent Lott (R.-MS) retakes control of the Majority Leader's position and the committee chairs return to many of the same Republicans who lost their positions after Jim Jeffords (R.-VT) switched affiliation in 2001. With Democrats having to defend four more Senate seats than the Republicans in the 2004 election, it appears to be an uphill climb for that party to retake control of the Senate in the future. Still, with their narrow majority many expected that it would be difficult for the Republicans to govern the Senate in the 108th Congress given the need for 60 votes to break a Democratic-led filibuster and the several moderate voters in its party, such as Lincoln Chafee (R.-RI), Olympia Snowe (R.-ME), and Arlen Specter (R.-PA), and maverick John McCain (R.-AZ). However, Republicans began planning to make parts of their legislative agenda "filibuster proof," such as a new prescription drug plan. This can be done by including such measures, so long as they involve revenue or spending changes for programs such as Social Security or Medicare, in a budgetary "reconciliation bill," the final omnibus budgetary bill that resolves the differences among the annual spending bills passed by each of the committees. Once that is done, according to the "Byrd Rule," named for West Virginia Senator Robert Byrd (D.-WV), so long as the desired measure is "merely incidental" to the overall policy goals of the bill, which cannot itself be filibustered, it will be included. Thus, such new policy measures might be passed over the minority party's objections without any prospect of a filibuster.

Major changes will occur in the Senate Committee structure as a result of the 2002 Congressional election, allowing the Republican party to take over all of the chairmanships and a majority of the seats on each committee. Judicial confirmations

DEMOCRACY IN THE NEW MILLENNIUM

Surfing the "Digital Divide"

In the Congressional world where all legislators think they are equal, when it comes to the Internet some are more equal than others. The Congress Online Project evaluated all 605 House and Senate Websites and concluded that just 10% were above average. This so-called "digital divide" in which very few sites are much better than all the rest means that some members of Congress are more successful in getting their message out than others. House Republican Conference Chairman J.C. Watts (R.-OK), who retired from the House in 2002, developed a Website for his party that received 1.7 million visits by allowing the visitors to create their own version of the Web page, and Sen. Jeff Bingaman (D) of New Mexico has a site featuring a fancy map of his home state linking the visitor to all of the relevant information from his office. On the other hand, Rep. James A. Traficant, Jr. (D.-OH) who was convicted in federal court and sent to prison for bribery and racketeering, and expelled from Congress, had a site featuring a cartoon-like image of him waving a sign that read, "Bangin' Away in D.C." Many of the sites seemed to be filled with excessive self-promotion, hard-to-download information, and outdated content.

Party affiliation did not dictate who had the edge in technological savvy, as an examination of the top two dozen House sites revealed that 79% of them were done by Republicans while the remainder were done by Democrats. However, when the top sites from the Senate were examined, 73% of them were done by the Democrats while the remainder was done by the Republicans.

Still, constituents' choice of contact method for their legislators has changed from the letter and the occasional phone call. Members such as Rep. Mike Honda, (D.-CA) now realize that they are getting more communications via the Internet than phone, fax, and mail combined. So, the next time you want to contact your Congressman, search for his or her website and start typing!

You can begin your Congressional surfing with these sites: http://www.gop.org, http://www.democrats.org. Or to contact individual members of Congress try http://www.house.gov/[last name of your member of Congress]/. For your Senator try this: http://[last name of your Senator].senate.gov. If you do not find them, perhaps you are in the "digital divide."

Source: Juliet Eilperin, "Most Web Sites on the Hill Unimpressive, Survey Finds," *Washington Post,* January 28, 2002, p. A19.

---

for the Bush Administration will become much easier as a result of the takeover of the Senate Judiciary Committee by pro-governmental power advocate Republican Orrin Hatch (R.-UT) instead of individual rights–oriented Democrat Patrick Leahy of Vermont. Republican Pete Domenici (R.-NM) will be the center of two changes. In taking over the Senate Energy and Natural Resources Committee, which oversees the nation's energy policy, such as the controversial proposal to drill for oil and natural gas in the Arctic National Wildlife Refuge, Domenici, who supports drilling on behalf of domestic energy production, replaces pro-environmentalist Jeff Bingaman, a Democrat from New Mexico. But in making this move, Domenici announced that he would not seek the chairmanship of the Senate Budget Committee, which oversees budget balancing and tax cut legislation, thus allowing Don Nickles (R.-OK) to take over, which will facilitate the Bush Administration's push for greater tax cuts and domestic spending cuts. Another major change, though, will come in the Environment and Public Works Committee, which deals with air pollution and environmental protection rules. The Committee was chaired before the election by Senator Jim Jeffords (I.-VT), who is very pro-environmental protection. But now the chairman will be Senator James M. Inhofe (R.-OK), who is opposed by environmental groups and will be supported by a White House likely looking to get even with Jeffords for switching parties from the Republicans to become an Independent, thus denying them a majority in the Senate in 2001.

Just where the 108th Congress goes next is unclear. Will the bitter partisanship and stalemated chambers return, or will President Bush be able to create a bipartisan agenda? The passage of the Bipartisan Campaign Finance Bill in 2002 showed that even the thorniest of legislative measures could be worked through the "legislative labyrinth." However, with difficult issues such as a possible war in Iraq, creating a Department of Homeland Security, balancing the budget, keeping the nation secure in the "war on terrorism" while also protecting liberty, and social security reform still on the horizon, it remains to be seen whether this relatively harmonious and productive period can be extended. Only then will we see whether Congress can help the nation approach democracy in this time of crisis.

The complexity of the legislative process we have just explored was intended not to prevent the passage of legislation, but to encourage compromise. The bicameral system, committees, complicated rules of Congress, conference committees, and the president's signature on legislation were all designed to allow differing views to be heard before legislation could be passed. Although members of Congress are often sincere, honest, hardworking, and dedicated to doing a difficult job under trying circumstances, the institution in which they serve continually faces criticism.

Does Congress help America approach democracy? Certainly it is the branch most responsive to the public will. However, much of the criticism of Congress has resulted from the institution being too responsive to specific segments of the public. This "don't upset anyone" attitude makes it much more difficult to find the compromises that might not please everyone but would make it possible to effectively legislate. Lawmakers tend to spend more time blaming government for various problems—a view they know will resonate with the voters—than finding ways to solve problems. Perhaps the actions of the more united Republican Congress will help to change that perception, but it positions Congress in an unaccustomed role as the leading generator of public policy.

In recent years, Congress has faced criticism in fights such as the Campaign Finance reform debate, as being hopelessly inefficient, fragmented, and paralyzed by gridlock. When Congress takes strong actions, as it did in the U.S.A. Patriot Act, it is accused of overreaching its powers. Clearly the truth lies somewhere between these extremes. The strength of Congress, indeed its very constitutional purpose in American democracy, is its closeness to the people and its representational base. "To express the public views" remains the principal responsibility of the national legislature and its most pressing challenge, as Congress and America approach democracy during the twenty-first century.

SUMMARY

1. The Constitution established a bicameral Congress consisting of a House of Representatives whose members serve two-year terms and a Senate whose members serve six-year terms. Congress was given numerous major powers, including the power to collect taxes, declare war, and regulate commerce. The necessary and proper clause enables it to interpret these powers broadly.

2. A disproportionate number of Congress's members are rich white males drawn from the fields of law, banking, and big business. The ethnic diversity of Congress increased in the twentieth century, but it still falls short of that of the population as a whole.

3. Today, each congressional district contains about 570,000 citizens. The number of representatives from each state is adjusted after each census (reapportionment). In states that gain or lose seats, district boundaries must be redrawn (redistricting). The term gerrymander is used to describe the often bizarre district boundaries that are drawn to favor the party in power.

4. Members of Congress sometimes find themselves torn between the role of delegate, in which they feel bound to follow the wishes of constituents, and the role of trustee, in which they use their best judgment regardless of the wishes of constituents. In practice, they tend to combine these roles.

5. Incumbents have several advantages over their challengers in an election, including greater name recognition, the franking privilege, the services of staff members, legislative experience, and greater financial backing. These advantages have led critics to call for legislation limiting the length of time members may serve in Congress.

6. The presiding officer of the House is the leader of the majority party and is known as the Speaker of the House. Next in line is the House majority leader, who serves as the party's chief strategist. The minority party is headed by the minority leader, and both party leaders are assisted by whips. In the Senate, the majority party elects a president pro tempore, but this is essentially an honorary position. As in the House, there are majority and minority party leaders and whips.

7. There are four types of congressional committees: standing (permanent), select or special (temporary), conference, and joint. Much of the legislative work of Congress is done in subcommittees. The power of the subcommittees since the 1970s has made the legislative process rather unwieldy, prompting calls for reform.

8. In the House, the Rules Committee determines what issues will be discussed, when, and under what conditions. In the Senate, scheduling is done by the majority leader in consultation with the minority leader. In the Senate there are no limits on floor debate. As a result, it is possible to derail a bill by means of a filibuster, in which a senator talks continuously to postpone or prevent a vote. Filibusters can be halted only by cloture, in which sixty or more senators vote to end the discussion.

9. The voting decisions of members of Congress are influenced by personal views, constituents, party affiliation, the president, interest groups, and congressional staff. Members also get cues about how to vote from their "buddy system" of other members whom they respect.

10. A member of Congress places an issue on the congressional agenda by drafting a bill and submitting it to the House or Senate. The bill is then referred to the appropriate committee, whose chair assigns it to a subcommittee. After holding hearings on the proposed legislation, the subcommittee holds a markup session in which the language of the bill is revised. It then returns the bill to the full committee. If the committee approves the bill, it is then sent to the full House or Senate. If the two chambers pass different versions of a bill, it is sent to a conference committee, which reconciles the differences and creates a single bill. If the final version is approved by both chambers, it goes to the president to be signed or vetoed.

KEY TERMS

bicameral legislature	president of the Senate	pork-barrel legislation
necessary and proper clause	president pro tempore	congressional agenda
reapportionment	Senate majority leader	lobbyists
redistricting	standing committees	hearings
gerrymander	select (or special) committees	markup session
majority-minority district	conference committees	enrolled act (or resolution)
delegates	joint committees	appropriations bill
trustees	subcommittees	veto
incumbents	rules	override
franking privilege	unanimous consent	pocket veto
casework	agreement	omnibus legislation
term limits	rider	continuing resolution
Two Congresses	line item veto	task force
Speaker of the House	filibuster	oversight
House majority leader	hold	legislative veto
party caucus	cloture	Congressional Budget Office
minority leader	seniority	(CBO)
whip	logrolling	impeachment

POLISIM ACTIVITY

Running for Congress
You are a Republican or Democratic party leader and the hottest campaign manager in American politics. You can have your pick of candidates you will work for in the upcoming congressional elections, but your help is most needed in Missouri. You will have to guide your candidate through the general election. Research the district and help your candidate raise money and create a strong media-based campaign. Good luck!

SUGGESTED READINGS

BAKER, ROSS K. *House and Senate.* 2d ed. New York: Norton, 1995. An excellent study of the political and stylistic differences between two very different legislative bodies.

BARRY, JOHN N. *The Ambition and the Power: The Fall of Jim Wright—A True Story of Washington.* New York: Viking Press, 1989. An engagingly written account of the tenure of Democratic Speaker James Wright and his downfall in 1989, revealing how Congress really operates.

BINDER, SARAH A., and STEVEN S. SMITH. *Politics or Principles? Filibustering in the United States Senate.* Washington, D.C.: Brookings Institution, 1997. A revealing study of the growing use of the filibuster and other delaying tactics to derail legislation in the Senate.

BRADLEY, BILL. *Time Present, Time Past: A Memoir.* New York: Knopf, 1996. A former Rhodes Scholar, professional basketball player, and presidential candidate looks back on his years in the Senate, but with an eye toward the lessons for himself and America.

CARO, ROBERT A. *Master of the Senate.* New York: Alfred A. Knopf, 2002. The third volume, covering the Majority Leader years, of the masterful four-volume series on Lyndon B. Johnson.

CWIKLIK, ROBERT. *House Rules: A Freshman Congressman's Initiation to the Backslapping, Backpedaling, and Backstabbing Ways of Washington.* New York: Villard Books, 1991. A window into the world of a member of Congress, tracking Nebraska Democrat Peter Hoagland's first year in office (1989).

DAVIDSON, ROGER H. *The Postreform Congress.* New York: St. Martin's Press, 1992. Readings examining how Congress changed as a result of reforms in the 1970s.

DAVIDSON, ROGER H., and WALTER J. OLESZEK. *Congress and Its Members.* 8th ed. Washington, D.C.: Congressional Quarterly Press, 2002. A comprehensive text on the operations of Congress.

DEERING, CHRISTOPHER, and STEVEN S. SMITH. *Committees in Congress.* 3d ed. Washington, D.C.: Congressional Quarterly Press, 1997. A complete text on the operations of committees in Congress, showing how they are the "laboratories" of the legislative process.

DODD, LAWRENCE C., and BRUCE I. OPPENHEIMER. *Congress Reconsidered.* 5th ed. Washington, D.C.: Congressional Quarterly Press, 1993. A revealing series of articles on facets of Congress's operations.

DREW, ELIZABETH. *Showdown: The Struggle Between the Gingrich Congress and the Clinton White House.* New York: Simon & Schuster, 1996. A behind-the-scenes look at the titanic political battle in 1995 and 1996 between Bill Clinton and the Republican revolutionaries in Congress under Newt Gingrich and Bob Dole.

FENNO, RICHARD. *Congressmen in Committees.* Boston: Little, Brown, 1973. An analysis based on comprehensive interviews with members of Congress and their staffs, describing how committees are staffed and organized, and how they operate.

———. *Home Style: House Members in Their Districts.* Boston: Little, Brown, 1973. A study showing how members of the House deal with their constituents.

GINGRICH, NEWT. *Lessons Learned the Hard Way.* New York: HarperCollins, 1998. An interesting memoir of the Speaker's experiences, with an eye toward creating a powerful Republican party.

KILLIAN, LINDA. *The Freshmen: What Happened to the Republican Revolution?* Boulder, Colo.: Westview Press, 1998. A highly readable account of the tribulations of the conservative members of Congress elected in 1994 to fulfill Newt Gingrich's legislative vision.

LOOMIS, BURDETT, ed. *Esteemed Colleagues: Civility and Deliberation in the U.S. Senate.* Washington, D.C.: Brookings Institution Press, 2000. A very interesting collection of essays investigating the changing nature of the modern Senate away from civility and more toward partisanship.

MARTIN, JANET M. *Lessons from the Hill: The Legislative Journey of an Education Program.* New York: St. Martin's Press, 1994. An account of how key education legislation was passed and reconsidered by later Congresses, written by a political science professor after working in two congressional offices.

RUDMAN, WARREN. *Combat: My Twelve Years in the U.S. Senate.* New York: Random House, 1996. An independent-minded Republican former senator from New Hampshire focuses on his role in the balanced budget controversy, ethics investigations, the Iran-Contra investigation, and the David Souter nomination to show what life was like during the Reagan and Bush years.

SCHROEDER, PAT. *24 Years of Housework . . . And the Place Is Still a Mess.* New York: Andrews McMeel, 1998. An entertaining memoir by the 12-term congresswoman depicting how Congress really works.

SIMPSON, ALAN. *Right in the Old Kazoo: A Lifetime of Scrapping with the Press.* New York: William Morrow, 1997. A highly readable memoir by one of the most outspoken members of the Senate.

WALDMAN, STEVEN. *The Bill: How Legislation Really Becomes Law: A Case Study of the National Service Bill.* New York: Penguin, 1996. Account of how Americorps was debated and passed in Congress, illustrating how tortuous this process can be.

5

THE PRESIDENCY

CHAPTER OUTLINE

Approaching Democracy Case Study: The
First Year of the Bush Presidency
Introduction: The Presidency and Democracy
The Constitutional Design
The Functional Roles of the President
Two Views of Executive Power
Expanding Presidential Power: Moving
Beyond the Constitution
The Institutionalized Presidency

APPROACHING DEMOCRACY CASE STUDY

The First Year of the Bush Presidency

George W. Bush entered office as the forty-third President on January 20, 2001, amidst intense scrutiny, having failed to win the popular vote and the Supreme Court halting a recount of disputed ballots in Florida, where his younger brother, Jeb, served as governor. The new President had no electoral mandate to govern and many believed the election outcome was tainted; others questioned whether or not the Texas governor was up to the new job of being President of the United States.

Table 5.1 ■ First Year of a Changed Presidency	
Jan. 20	George W. Bush is sworn in as the 43rd president.
March 31	Faces first foreign policy crisis as American spy plane makes an emergency landing in China after colliding with a Chinese fighter jet.
June 7	Signs $1.35 trillion tax cut into law, fulfilling a major campaign promise.
Aug. 9	Announces he will allow federal money for limited research on existing stem cells.
Sept. 11	Addresses the nation after the terrorist attacks on the World Trade Center and the Pentagon.
Sept. 14	Visits rescue workers at the World Trade Center site.
Sept. 20	In an address to a joint meeting of Congress, warns the Taliban to turn over Osama bin Laden or face military attack.
Oct. 7	Announces the beginning of American military action against Afghanistan.
Oct. 11	Gives his first formal East Room news conference, saying he would welcome a role for the United Nations in rebuilding Afghanistan.
Nov. 10	Tells the United Nations General Assembly that all its member countries must join the fight against terrorism.
Nov. 13	Signs order allowing the use of military tribunals for terrorism suspects.
Dec. 13	Notifies Russia that the United States will withdraw from the Antiballistic Missile Treaty.

Source: *The New York Times.* January 1, 2002. Reprinted by permission of *The New York Times.*

One year later, President George W. Bush's legitimacy was unchallenged; his performance as a war leader had won great praise; his job approval rating hovered above eighty percent. The story of Bush's first year in office points (see Table 5.1) to the remarkable powers possessed by the leader of the executive branch, particularly in times of war and national emergency when presidents have claimed broad inherent powers in the interest of protecting security at home and abroad.

After his swearing in, the new President faced the daunting task of establishing public credibility amidst a downturn in the American economy and unforeseen international incidents. Bush's first six months in office were rife with bipartisan wrangling because the new president set out to govern as if he had actually won an electoral mandate. Presidential initiatives in the areas of privatization of health care, the opening of borders with Mexico, and education reform were met with resistance by a politically divided Congress that was fairly reflective of opinions of the American public. International incidents common to all presidential administrations plagued the Bush White House almost immediately. In February of 2001, a U.S. submarine off Hawaii sunk a Japanese ship. In March, Bush pulled the United States out of the 1997 Kyoto Agreement to decrease global warming. In April, the Chinese captured a high-tech American surveillance plane and held the crew for eleven days. In one of the biggest blows to the new administration's domestic agenda, Vermont Senator Jim Jeffords defected from the Republican party in June, stunning the White House by ending six years of Republican control in the Senate and elevating Tom Daschle (D.-SD) to Senate Majority Leader. The signing of an historic ten-year $1.35 trillion tax cut on June 16 saved the first six months of the Bush presidency from political mediocrity.[1]

September 11 completely altered the presidential power equation. In the President's own words, "I had the responsibility to show resolve. I had to show the American people the resolve of a commander in chief that was going to do whatever it took to win. No yielding. No equivocation . . . It was also vitally important for the rest of the world to watch . . . I understand the job of the president. And the job of the president is to lead a nation in a long and difficult struggle, and this is going to be a very long and difficult struggle."[2]

▲ Just four days following 9-11, the former President George H.W. Bush reaches for his son President Bush during a prayer service at Washington National Cathedral.

In his address to a Joint Session of Congress and the American people on September 20, 2001, President Bush observed that, "Americans are asking, why do they hate us? They hate what we see right here in this chamber—a democratically elected government. Their leaders are self-appointed. They hate our freedoms—our freedom of religion, our freedom of speech, our freedom to vote and assemble and disagree with each other." To paraphrase and expand, they hate our continuing experiment with democracy; our approach to democracy. Yet, within our own country, the president's actions ignited serious debate about separation of powers, checks and balances, civil liberties and the role of the media.

Introduction:
The Presidency and Democracy

Consistent with the actions of his predecessors, the president claimed the right and the authority to deal with the national emergency. For Abraham Lincoln, the very survival of the Union justified extraordinary claims to executive power. For Franklin Delano Roosevelt the banking and financial crisis of the Great Depression in the 1930s along with the Japanese attack on Pearl Harbor many years later, justified extraordinary actions that at other times might be unconstitutional but were justified by the crisis at hand. The President moved to reorganize the Immigration and Naturalization Service without congressional approval. The President signed a directive legalizing the use of military tribunals to try al-Qaeda soldiers taken into custody in Afghanistan and imprisoned at the American naval base in Guantanomo, Cuba. In cooperation with Attorney General John Ashcroft, the President narrowed the legal rights and civil liberties of aliens living in the United States, making it easier to profile and round-up those suspected of terrorist connections. Roving wire taps and limits on congressional access to intelligence information also were instituted in the war against terrorism. In the view of Press Secretary Ari Fleischer, "The way our nation is set up, and the way the Constitution is written, wartime powers rest fundamentally in the hands of the executive branch. . . . It's not uncommon in time of war for a nation's eyes to focus on the executive branch and its ability to conduct the war with strength and speed."[3]

The great paradox of the presidency is that nowhere in America is there an office that unites so much power as well as purpose to help Americans approach their democratic potential, yet also poses the most serious threats to the ideals of democracy. The framers of our government designed the presidency so that its potential for energy would be encouraged and its potential for tyranny would be minimized. Accomplishing both of those ends entailed the creation of a complicated separation and distribution of powers. But, in the intervening two centuries, that distribution has been altered; presidents have gained power by formal grants of congressionally delegated power, court-sanctioned expansions of power, and popularly based assumptions of power. The President now speaks for America's interests and security.

Like the Constitution's designers, Americans believe, like Lord Acton, a British historian and political figure that, "power tends to corrupt and absolute power corrupts absolutely." That belief has not changed much since the eighteenth century; what has changed, however, is the role government plays in American life. Americans have delegated increasing amounts of power to the national government and to the presidency; their expectations of both the government and the chief executive have risen proportionately. The office of president lies at the center of countless demands, many of them contradictory, some impossible to achieve under any conditions. The mere energy required to hold the position and carry out its duties puts it far beyond the average person's capacity (see Figure 5.1 for Bush's activities

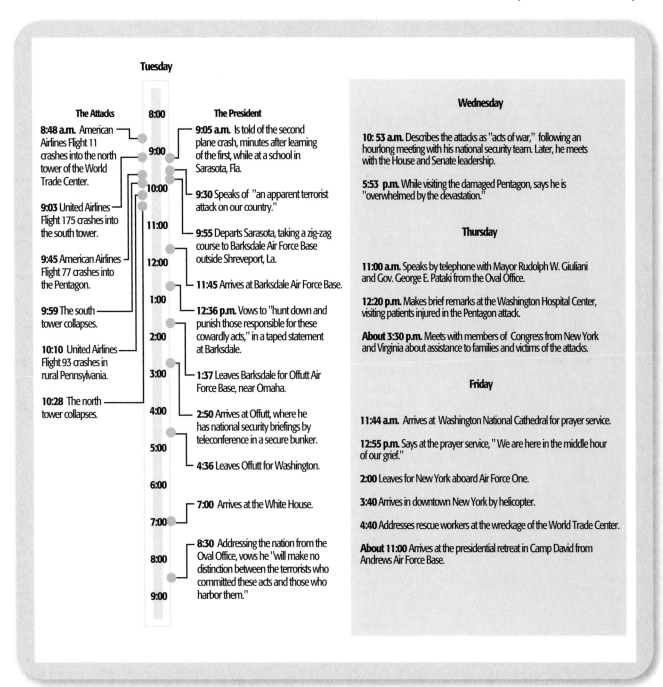

Figure 5.1   A President During a Time of Crisis
Some of the main movements and statements of President Bush.
Source: Reprinted by permission of *The New York Times.*

from 9/11/01 to 9/14/01). The office has broken several presidents; many have been diminished by it and thus have diminished the office. Even those who have risen to its challenge, whose records from the distance of history we admire, faced scathing criticism and fought determined foes throughout their tenure in the White House. Still, some have thrived in the office, and a number of presidents have achieved greatness. It is impossible to predict who will or will not succeed at the job, but one thing is certain: the presidency is at the core of the American democratic system. To understand how the American presidency can foster an approach to democracy, we must carefully examine this unique and powerful office.

Question for Reflection: How does the power of the presidency in the United States differ from the presidential powers in countries like France, Russia or Mexico?

The Constitutional Design

The creation of the presidency may be the framer's most original contribution. In a world of kings and emperors, many of whom left office feet first or on the wrong end of a bloody revolution, the president in America was to be unlike any other world leader. In creating this unique position, the framers sought to avoid a monarchy like the one in England they had rebelled against, but they also wanted a strong, independent executive for the nation as a whole. They were appalled at the results of legislative omnipotence in the states, as had been the case under the Articles of Confederation.

In creating a source of power independent of the Congress but capable of balancing its powers, the framers based the presidency on seven key principles:

1. They set up a *single presidency.* To ensure its strength and energy, executive power was to center on one individual, not some group like a council or a cabinet.
2. The selection of president would be made neither by the Congress nor by the people. A president chosen by Congress could become its puppet; one chosen by the people could become a demagogue and tyrant. Creating an independent body of individual electors selected by the state legislatures (the *Electoral College*) would make the president independent of the two branches.

Question for Reflection: How did the 2000 presidential election test this selection process?

3. The president was given a *fixed term of office.* The genius of this idea lies in its assurance of both stability and constraint. Executives serve four years, with the possibility of reelection. They cannot be forced from office by arbitrary "no-confidence" votes in Congress (votes that force the early resignation of entire governments in parliamentary systems). On the other hand, presidents will not be reelected unless they have broad popular support. And if they commit "Treason, Bribery, or other High Crimes and Misdemeanors," they may be impeached and removed from office. It was this impending sequence that forced President Nixon's resignation.
4. The president would be eligible for *more than one term of office,* making the executive a source of potential power to balance or check congressional power. (This is no longer the case. The Twenty-second Amendment restricts the president to two terms.) If presidents remained popular and their policies successful; they could win reelection. Thus, Congress would always have to take the president into account.
5. The president could be removed from office only by a cumbersome *process of impeachment* involving both houses of Congress; thus, a president would have to be continually reckoned with. On the other hand, the impeachment by the house of ex-President Clinton demonstrates that impeachment does indeed represent an ultimate check.
6. The president was given a *veto power,* enabling the executive to say no to Congress. This single provision makes the president a central player in the legislative process because a president's wishes must be taken into account as Congress goes about its work.
7. The president was not required to appoint an advisory council. Thus, presidents were allowed to act on their own, at least within their own constitutional realm of the executive arena.

FYI

John Kennedy was this country's youngest elected president (43 years and 236 days old at his inauguration). Teddy Roosevelt was the youngest president, having succeeded from vice president to president on the death of William McKinley when he was 42 years and 322 days old.

The effect of this set of principles was to establish a strong but constrained executive, a single, symbolic head of the nation, possessed of serious means for exercising power but operating under law and restricted in power by the countervailing institutions of Congress and the Supreme Court.[4]

Who Is Eligible to Be President?

The Constitution specifies only three requirements for becoming president: a president must be at least thirty-five years old, must have lived in the United States for at least fourteen years, and must be a natural-born citizen.

The framers set up the minimum-age requirement of thirty-five (which at that time represented "middle age") to guarantee that a president would be reasonably mature and experienced in politics. The fourteen-year-residence condition was set up to guard against the possibility of a president with divided loyalties between England and the United States—an obvious concern in the years following the American Revolution. For the same reason, the framers stipulated that presidents be natural-born citizens (born in the United States or to American citizens abroad).

▲ There are no gender specifications for the job of president, but thus far all American presidents have been men. Victoria Woodhull, shown here, was the first woman presidential candidate. A stockbroker and newspaper editor from New York, Woodhull ran for president in 1872 as a member of the Equal Rights party.

Some Presidential Statistics

Tallest
Abraham Lincoln stood 6 feet 4 inches.

Shortest
James Madison stood 5 feet 4 inches, a full foot shorter than Lincoln.

Heaviest
William Howard Taft weighed between 300 and 350 pounds. He was so large that a specially built bathtub had to be installed in the White House to accommodate him.

Oldest
Ronald Reagan was the oldest man to become president, at 69. And, at 91 he has lived longer than any other president.

Youngest
Theodore Roosevelt was 42 when he succeeded to the presidency after the assassination of William McKinley.

Most Children
John Tyler had 15 children by two wives.

Least Children
None of these presidents had children:

George Washington

James Madison

Andrew Jackson

James Polk

James Buchanan

Warren Harding

The Presidential Powers

What powers does the president possess to accomplish the office's broad range of responsibilities? The Constitution has remarkably little to say on this point. Only one-third of Article II is devoted to formal presidential powers. This brevity reflects the framers' uncertainty on the subject. Trusting that George Washington would almost certainly be the first president, the framers assumed that he would establish precedents for the office.

What the framers did write into the Constitution can be categorized in two ways. First, in clear simple language they gave the president some very specific powers.

▶ Surrounded by a bipartisan coalition of supporters, President Bush signs a $26 billion education bill at Hamilton High School in Hamilton, Ohio.

veto Presidential power to overrule an action of Congress.

pocket veto Presidential refusal to sign or veto a bill that Congress passes in the last ten days of its session; by not being signed, it automatically dies if Congress adjourns.

Second, and more important, they also gave the executive some broad, even sweeping, powers written in vague language subject to individual interpretation.

The Veto Power   Perhaps the president's most potent legal constitutional weapon is the **veto,** a Latin word meaning "I forbid." The power to forbid or prevent an action of Congress gives the president a central role in the legislative process. When Congress passes a bill or joint resolution, the legislation goes to the White House for presidential action. The president then has four options. First, the president can sign the bill, at which point it becomes law. Second, the president can do nothing, allowing the bill to become law without a signature in ten days. Third, if Congress adjourns before those ten days pass, by refusing to sign legislation the president can kill the bill by what is known as a **pocket veto.** Finally, the president can veto the bill, returning it to the house of origin with a message stating reasons for the veto. Congress then has the option to override the veto by a two-thirds vote in each house.

The framers saw the veto as a bulwark of executive independence, a basic building block in their efforts to separate and check power. Alexander Hamilton made this position clear in *The Federalist,* no. 73: "The primary inducement to conferring [the veto] power upon the executive is to enable him to defend himself; the second one is to increase the chances . . . against the passing of bad laws, through haste, inadvertence, or design." The veto was thus conceived as a "negative" by which an executive could defend against legislative excesses.[5]

Presidents can sometimes affect the wording or passage of a law by announcing ahead of time that they intend to veto a pending bill. The strategy is akin to the story of a farmer who used "friendly persuasion" to get his mule to move, but first had to whack it on the head "to get its attention." In 1985 President Ronald Reagan dared Congress to raise taxes. Borrowing from Clint Eastwood, he said such actions would "make my day" and be met by a quick veto. Using a similar tactic, President Bill Clinton warned Congress during a nationally televised State of the Union Address: "If you send me legislation that does not guarantee every American private health insurance that can never be taken away, you will force me to take this pen [and] veto the legislation." President George W. Bush threatened Congress that he would veto any health care legislation containing a patient's bill of rights, unless the Senate made dramatic changes to legislation passed by the House. Table 5.2 shows the number of presidential vetoes from 1789 through 2002. Table 5.3 on page 171 shows how President Clinton specifically used the veto from 1995–2000.

The Appointment Power   This is another specific and important power granted the president. The appointment power affects the president's ability to staff the executive branch with trusted allies. Article II, Section 2, of the Constitution gives the president, "by and with the Advice and Consent of the Senate," the power to appoint ambassadors, public ministers, and consuls; judges of the Supreme Courts; and "other Officers of the United States, whose Appointments are not herein otherwise provided for, and which shall be established by Law."

The power of appointment allows a president to recruit people who will help promote his policies. Although appointment is an important administrative power of the president, more than two thousand presidential appointments require Senate confirmation, which is sometimes difficult to obtain.

President George W. Bush was able to use a "backdoor" procedure know as recess appointment to secure two nominees after they failed to win Senate confirmation. The constitution authorizes the President to fill vacant positions when the Senate is in recess. Appointees can serve without Senate confirmation until the end of the congressional season at the end of the year. However, a majority of Senators can remove appointees at any time. Both Otto J. Reich, appointed as Assistant Secretary of State for Western Hemisphere Affairs and Eugene Scalia, Labor Department Solicitor were recess appointments by the President. Reich, a Cuban exile and the State Department's top advisor on Latin America, opposes trade with Cuba, a position that places him in opposition with many farmers, members of Congress, business executives and even Republicans who favor trade with Cuba. Reich and others insist that Cuba itself must "approach democracy" by releasing political prisoners and holding free elections before any trade with the United States will occur. Representative Jo Ann Emerson, Republican from Missouri, observed that the recess appointment of Reich stood in stark contrast to prevailing views in the House: "There's no doubt that a majority of our colleagues in the Senate and the House support more trade with Cuba and lifting the travel ban, which is the heart of it all."[6]

Perhaps the single most important appointment presidents can make is a nomination to fill a vacancy on the Supreme Court. On average, a president names only two justices during any four-year term of office; it is a rare president who ends up naming a majority of Court members. Nevertheless, since the Court is usually split ideologically, even one or two appointments can affect the outcome of important constitutional cases well beyond the president's term of office. Some presidents, such as Jimmy Carter, never had the opportunity to appoint a justice to the Supreme Court, while his successor, Ronald Reagan, appointed four. President Clinton appointed both Ruth Bader Ginsburg (1993) as well as Stephen G. Breyer (1994) to the Court. President Bush is awaiting the chance to make his first nomination to the Court.

The Treaty Power   The Constitution also gives presidents the power to negotiate treaties with other nations. **Treaties** are formal international agreements between sovereign states. But the framers foresaw a system of consultation between the

treaties Formal international agreements between sovereign states.

Table 5.2 ■ Presidential Vetoes, 1789–2002

	Regular Vetoes	Pocket Vetoes	Total Vetoes	Vetoes Overridden
Washington	2	—	2	—
Madison	5	2	7	—
Monroe	1	—	1	—
Jackson	5	7	12	—
Tyler	6	3	9	1
Polk	2	1	3	—
Pierce	9	—	9	5
Buchanan	4	3	7	—
Lincoln	2	4	6	—
A. Johnson	21	8	29	15
Grant	45	49	94	4
Hayes	12	1	13	1
Arthur	4	8	12	1
Cleveland	304	109	413	2
Harrison	19	25	44	1
Cleveland	43	127	170	5
McKinley	6	36	42	—
T. Roosevelt	42	40	82	1
Taft	30	9	39	1
Wilson	33	11	44	6
Harding	5	1	6	—
Coolidge	20	30	50	4
Hoover	21	16	37	3
F. Roosevelt	372	263	635	9
Truman	180	70	250	12
Eisenhower	73	108	181	2
Kennedy	12	9	21	—
L. Johnson	16	14	30	—
Nixon	26	17	43	7
Ford	48	18	66	12
Carter	13	18	31	2
Reagan	39	39	78	9
Bush	29	17	46	1
Clinton	36	0	36	2
G. W. Bush	0	0	0	0

Sources: *Statistical Abstract of the United States, 1986,* p. 235; Senate Library, *Presidential Vetoes* (Washington, D.C.: Government Printing Office, 1960), p. 199. From *The Paradoxes of the American Presidency* by Thomas E. Cronin and Michael A. Genovese. Copyright © 1998 by Oxford University Press, Inc. Used by permission of Oxford University Press, Inc.; updated by authors.

branches such that the executive's negotiation would involve the Senate's "advice and consent." When President George Washington went to Congress to solicit advice on an Indian treaty, however, he was made to stay several hours and answer questions that he believed had little bearing on the treaty. Irked by this experience, Washington resolved not to repeat it. Henceforth, while required to secure

Table 5.3 ■ Clinton's Use of the Veto			
Bill	**Description**	**Vetoed**	**Congressional Response**
1995			
HR 1158	FY95 supplemental spending/rescissions	June 7	
S 21	Lift Bosnia arms embargo	Aug. 11	
HR 1854	FY96 legislative branch spending	Oct. 3	
HR 2586	Temporary increase in public debt limit	Nov. 13	
H J Res 115	FY96 continuing appropriations	Nov. 13	
HR 2491	$245 billion tax cut over seven years	Dec. 6	
HR 1977	FY96 Interior spending	Dec. 18	House sustained, 239–177
HR 2099	FY96 VA-HUD spending	Dec. 18	
HR 2076	FY96 Commerce-Justice-State spending	Dec. 19	House sustained, 240–159
HR 1058	Limitation on lawsuits by disgruntled shareholders	Dec. 19	House overrode, 319–100 Senate overrode, 68–30
HR 1530	FY96 defense authorization	Dec. 28	House sustained, 240–156
1996			
HR 4	Welfare system overhaul	Jan. 10	
HR1833	Ban on "partial birth" abortion	April 10	House overrode, 285–137 Senate sustained, 57–41
HR1561	State Department authorization	April 12	House sustained, 234–188
HR 956	Limit on awards in product liability lawsuits	May 2	House sustained, 258–163
HR 743	Ease regulation of labor-management teams	July 30	
HR 2909	Land acquisition in wildlife refuge	Oct. 2	
1997			
HR 1469	FY97 supplemental spending	June 9	
HR 1122	Ban on "partial-birth" abortion	Oct. 10	House overrode, 296–132 Senate sustained, 64–36
HR 2631	Restore spending struck by line-item veto from FY98 military construction law	Nov. 13	House overrode, 347–69 Senate overrode, 78–20
1998			
S 1502	District of Columbia school vouchers	May 20	
HR 2709	Punish nations giving missile aid to Iran	June 23	
HR 2646	Expand education savings account benefits	July 21	
HR 4101	FY99 agriculture spending	Oct. 7	
HR 1757	State Department authorization	Oct. 21	
1999			
HR 2488	$792 billion tax cut over 10 years	Sept. 23	
HR 2587	FY00 District of Columbia spending	Sept. 28	
HR 2606	FY00 foreign operations spending	Oct. 18	
HR 2670	FY00 Commerce-Justice-State spending	Oct. 25	
HR 3064	FY00 D.C./Labor-HHS-Education spending	Nov. 3	
2000			
S 1287	Rules for Nevada nuclear waste storage site	April 25	Senate sustained, 64–35
HR 4810	Alleviate tax code's "marriage penalty"	Aug. 5	House sustained, 270–158
HR 8	Repeal of taxes on estates, gifts and trusts	Aug. 31	House sustained, 274–157
HR 4733	FY01 energy and water spending	Oct. 11	
HR 4516	FY01 Treasury-Postal Service and legislative branch spending	Oct. 30	
HR 4392	FY01 intelligence authorization	Nov. 4	
HR 2415	Consumer bankruptcy overhaul	Dec. 19	(Congress had adjourned)

Sources: U.S. Congress, Secretary of the Senate, *Presidential Vetoes, 1789–1988* (Washington: GPO, 1992), 595 pp. S. Pub. 102–12; U.S. Congress, Secretary of the Senate, *Presidential Vetoes 1989–1991* (Washington: GPO, 1992), 12 pp. S. Pub. 102–13; Gary L. Galemore, CRS Report 98–156. *The Presidential Veto and Congressional Procedure;* Gary L. Galemore, CRS Report 98–148. *Presidential Vetoes, 1789–Present: A Summary Overview;* Gary L. Galemore, *President Clinton's Vetoes;* http://www.house.gov/rules/98-157.pdf. Reprinted by permission of Congressional Quarterly Press, through the Copyright Clearance Center.

APPROACHING DIVERSITY

The Bush Executive Office

President Bush appointed women and minorities in numbers that more closely resemble the Clinton cabinet than his father's administration. Significantly, President Bush appointed women to more influential positions than any prior president including "the most powerful woman ever to work on a White House staff," National Security Advisor Condoleeza Rice and Margaret La Montagne, director of the Domestic Policy Council. Placing women in highly visible positions, particularly in the case of National Security Advisor, confirms the advancement of women in political positions traditionally considered exclusively male. The de-genderization of political positions in the United States should lead to a continued increase in the number of women working in the Executive branch.

President Bush's minority appointments are substantially greater than all those of his immediate predecessors and the expanded role of Hispanic's within the Bush administration demonstrates the President's recognition of the increasing Latino population in the U.S., as well as his Texas roots.

The Executive Office of the President
The "A" Team: Reagan 1981, Bush 1989, Clinton 1993, and Bush 2001

	Reagan 1981 N=61	Bush 1989 N=50	Clinton 1993 N=72	Bush II 2001 N=65
Average Age	45	43	45	45
% Women	5	14	29	28
% Minorities	3	8	8	11
% Home State	26	10*	10	29
Most Common Job Experience	Exec. Branch	Exec. Branch	Capitol Hill	Pres. Campaign

Source: Kathryn Dunn Tenpas and Stephen Hess, "Bush's 'A Team': Just Like Clinton's, but more so." *Washington Post,* January 27, 2002, B5. Jeffrey E. Cohen, *The Politics of the U.S. Cabinet* (Pittsburgh: University of Pittsburgh Press), 1998. Bradley H. Patterson, Jr., *The Ring of Power* (New York: Basic Books), 1998.

---

the consent of the Senate in ratifying treaties, he did not encourage senators to contribute their sometimes dubious "advice"—and later presidents have followed that model.

Treaty approval is by no means a foregone conclusion, partly because it requires a two-thirds majority of senators present and voting. In addition, the Senate may attach amendments to treaties. Treaty rejections do occur. The most dramatic example took place in 1919, when the Senate failed to ratify Woodrow Wilson's Treaty of Versailles ending World War I. The defeat of this treaty, which included membership in Wilson's cherished League of Nations, was seen as a direct slap in the president's face by a hostile Congress. It not only undermined Wilson's authority at home but helped doom the League—the predecessor of today's United Nations—to ineffectiveness abroad.

Most treaties are approved without modification, and the Senate has defeated only 1 percent of the treaties submitted to it. However, that record of success is misleading, since presidents have withdrawn 150 treaties that seemed headed for defeat. Still, the possibility of treaty rejection gives the Senate a potential power, just as the possibility of a veto does for the president.

Treaties have declined as a potential congressional check on presidential power because presidents have increasingly turned to a less formal means for conducting foreign affairs. **Executive agreements,** diplomatic contracts negotiated with other countries, allow presidents or their agents to make important foreign policy moves without Senate approval. These agreements appeal to harried presidents in their role as world leader. Unlike treaties, which are covered by the media, generate controversy, and take time to ratify executive agreements are usually negotiated in secret, making them a particularly powerful foreign policy tool. By executive agreement William McKinley ended the Spanish-American War and Theodore Roosevelt restricted Japanese immigration to the United States.

? Question for Reflection: What, if any, impact do you think the war on terrorism will have on the likely increase of secret agreements in the conduct of U.S. foreign policy?

Presidents may conclude an executive agreement on any subject within their constitutional authority as long as the agreement is not inconsistent with legislation enacted by Congress in the exercise of its constitutional authority. Scholars agree that although not explicitly outlined in the Constitution, the president's right to conduct foreign policy through executive agreement rests on several sound constitutional bases. These include the president's authority as chief executive to represent the nation in foreign affairs, the president's authority to receive ambassadors and other public ministers, the president's authority as commander in chief, and the president's authority to "take Care that the Laws be faithfully executed." Presidents are increasingly finding that executive agreements, unlike treaties, give them the flexibility they need to make foreign policy.[7]

In 1997 President Clinton sought "fast-track" authority to negotiate new trade agreements to open markets for U.S. exporters. Congress cannot amend these executive-negotiated trade agreements; Congress can only vote for or against the agreement. Former Republican President Gerald R. Ford strongly endorsed fast-track for a Democratic president because it "is essential for continued U.S. leadership on all issues . . . The United States must lead the world toward a more open, prosperous global economy. But without fast-track, the United States is relegated to the sidelines."[8]

In his 2002 State of the Union address, President Bush pushed for Senate passage of Trade Promotion Authority (TPA), a fast-track authority that would allow the President to negotiate good trade deals that will open markets, increase opportunities for American farmers, workers, consumers, and business. Supporters of fast-track trade promotion see it as the key test of America's international leadership. Opponents argue that it undermines hard fought legislative protections.[9] Table 5.4 shows trade agreements approved under Fast track.

Executive Privilege   President Dwight Eisenhower once said that, "any man who testifies as to the advice he gave me won't be working for me that night." He invoked executive privilege 40 times in his 8 years in office.[10]

To what extent may a president withhold information from Congress or the courts? **Executive privilege** is the implied or inherent power (depending on which president is making the claim) to withhold information on the ground that to release such information would affect either national security or the president's ability to discharge his official duties. The important question is not necessarily whether privilege should exist, but rather who should determine its extent—the president, the legislative branch, or the courts.

The Constitution does not mention executive privilege; the first discussion of privilege occurred in 1792. A special House investigation committee requested that President Washington turn over materials pertaining to an Indian massacre of troops under the leadership of General Arthur St. Clair. Washington called a special cabinet meeting to establish standards for the executive branch's responses. The House Committee had requested that Secretary of War Henry Knox turn over all

---

**Table 5.4 ■
Trade Agreements Approved under Fast Track**

Fast track has been invoked just five times during the two decades it was in effect for a small minority of the trade agreements reached during that period.

■ Tokyo Round GATT Agreements—1979

■ U.S.–Israel FTA—1985

■ U.S.–Canada FTA—1988

■ North American Free Trade Agreements—1993

■ Uruguay Round WTO Agreements—1994

Source: http://www.brook.edu/comm/policybriefs/pb91.htm.

---

executive agreement A government-to-government agreement with essentially the same legal force as a treaty. However, it may be concluded entirely without the knowledge and/or approval of the Senate.

executive privilege The implied or inherent power of the president to withhold information on the ground that to release such information would affect either national security or the president's ability to discharge his official duties.

original letters and correspondence pertaining to St. Clair's mission. In the first case of a president's refusing to supply Congress with a document, Washington denied the request, giving both constitutional and pragmatic reasons.

Several of George Washington's successors followed his precedent of withholding information. President Jackson refused to turn over documents that would have disclosed his reasons for removing government deposits from the Bank of the United States. The best-known case of executive privilege involved President Richard Nixon's claim that tapes of confidential conversations between himself and his aides were within the province of the White House. In a unanimous decision, the Supreme Court acknowledged a constitutional basis for executive privilege, but not in Nixon's case. The Court did not view the power to protect presidential communications as absolute. The privilege of confidentiality had to derive from the supremacy of the executive branch within its assigned areas of constitutional duties.

Neither the doctrine of separation of powers, nor the need for confidentiality of high-level communications, can sustain an absolute, unqualified presidential privilege of immunity from judicial process under all circumstances. The President's need for complete candor and objectivity from advisers calls for great deference from the courts. However, when the privilege depends solely on the broad undifferentiated claim of public interest in the confidentiality of such conversations, a confrontation with other values arises. During the Clinton Presidency this involved controversies between the President and his attorney as well as the Secret Service during the Monica Lewinsky investigation and impeachment.

President Bush invoked executive privilege for the first time when he rejected a congressional subpoena for prosecutor's records on a thirty year old Boston mob case as well as for documents on the Clinton campaign finance probe. In both cases Bush cited threats to "national interest" that might be threatened with disclosure. Representative Dan Burton (R.-IN) challenged Bush: "the Legislative branch has oversight responsibility to make sure that there is no corruption in the executive branch."[11]

The collapse of Enron brought another claim of privilege. The Bush administration refused to release details of energy policy meetings between corporate executives and a task force chaired by Vice President Cheney that was setting energy policy guidelines. The Government Accounting Office (GAO), the legislative arm of Congress, filed suit to obtain that information, the first time in history such an action is being taken. "The collapse of Enron in no way, shape or form affects the basic principles we're trying to protect here." Vice President Cheney told CNN. "This is about the ability of future presidents and vice presidents to do their job."[12]

In late September 2002, lawyers for the GAO and the Vice President sparred before a federal judge over which branch of government's claim to information was paramount—the legislature's right to investigate how public money is spent, as well as the names of industry officials who helped develop energy policy, or the executive's right to maintain confidential records as a matter of privilege.

While democracy requires openness, arguably there are legitimate needs for government secrecy that pertain to national security. Each of us can debate the extent of privilege over access to information and where or where not the national interest is truly at stake. The level of secrecy already demonstrated by the Bush presidency raises several important issues in thinking about our theme of approaching democracy. The government has refused to release the names or nationalities of the Taliban and al-Qaeda fighters imprisoned in Guantanamo Bay or even to reveal the names and locations of immigrants detained as suspected terrorists or having links with terrorist organizations. The Bush administration is also refusing to give Congress information on the counting of the 2000 census; the President signed an Executive Order restricting access to the papers of former presidents and now in the Enron case, according to Bush, "we're not going to let the ability for us to discuss matters between ourselves become eroded. It's not only important for us, for this administration. It's an important principle for future administrations."[13]

Other Constitutionally Designated Powers   The Constitution gives the president additional specific powers, such as the right to grant pardons (President Ford pardoned Richard Nixon for any crimes he may have committed as president and President Clinton issued, and later admitted regretting some controversial pardons during his last day in office) and the right to convene Congress in extraordinary circumstances. Perhaps the most important specific power granted to the president by the Constitution is the power of commander in chief of the armed forces. As this case study showed, presidents who use this power effectively can dramatically enhance their national and international stature.[14]

Beyond specific grants of power, the Constitution gives the president a vague mandate to run the executive branch of government. Different presidents have interpreted that mandate in very different ways. We shall soon see that that vagueness in the Constitution has allowed presidents a good deal of leeway in expanding the powers of the chief executive during the two centuries since the framers wrote the Constitution. But first, we'll look at the various roles that define the job of chief executive.

The Functional Roles of the President

Presidential behavior depends only partly on laws that require action or prohibit it. Beyond formal legalities, all presidents are constrained and directed by informal or functional role expectations. When leaders are expected to take an action, they do it—whether or not permission for the action is contained somewhere in a legal document. As leader of a vocal, democratic people, the president stands at the center of a mass of such expectations.

The President as Chief of State   The president acts as a ceremonial chief of state, symbolizing the national government to people in this country and other nations. At world gatherings the chief of state is put on the same high protocol rank as kings. Presidents greet foreign ambassadors, pin medals on heroes, hold barbecues on the White House lawn, and give state dinners. Virtually all these opportunities help dramatize and personalize a presidency. From meeting astronauts to making an entrance to the tune "Hail to the Chief," presidents bask in the glory and often hide behind the pomp and circumstance of their office.

The President as Commander in Chief   Presidents have more than ceremonial duties, however. They hold awesome powers, particularly in their military leadership role. As commander in chief, the president is charged with providing national security and defense. When necessary, the president must defend American interests by committing troops to combat. The war against international terrorism provides a case in point. This role is reinforced by the president's oath of office to "preserve, protect, and defend the Constitution of the United States." A president who fails to respond forcefully to a threat is seen as weak or indecisive, as was the case with President Carter's response, or lack thereof, to the seizure of the United States embassy in Tehran, which resulted in an extended hostage crisis. On the other hand, President Bush did a magnificent job, taking quick and decisive action following the events of September 11, 2001.

The President as Crisis Leader   The president also comes to the forefront of the nation's attention during periods of crisis such as natural disasters, civil unrest, and military or terrorist attacks against the United States. George W. Bush's September 14th visit to the site of the World Trade Center attack unified our nation and gave comfort to a people in mourning. After natural disasters or events such as the terrorist attacks of September 11th, the attention of the nation turns to the president. He is the only leader capable of bringing about timely action in such circumstances.

FYI

The president travels in Air Force 1, a $200 million Boeing 747 built in 1990. The plane is equipped with 85 telephones, 19 television sets, and can travel 7,000 miles without refueling. It carries 70 passengers with a crew of 23. In June 1998, the president's plane disappeared from radar screens for a few seconds, causing panic in traffic control booths.

► Among the President's many roles is the one Professor Berman dreams about—throwing out the first pitch of a World Series game at Yankee Stadium.

In times of crisis, Congress generally acquiesces to the president. Moreover, during such episodes, presidential actions are generally accompanied by a noticeable jump in popularity. For example, on the heels of the Persian Gulf War, former President George Bush's popularity rating soared well above 85 percent, the highest rating of any president until his son's rating in January 2002. This relationship between crisis and presidential support has become known as the "rally effect" because the country is seen as rallying around the president in response to a crisis.

The President as Chief Diplomat   Presidents must be international diplomats as well as warriors. Maintaining smooth relations with allies and a tough stance with potential or real enemies is expected of all presidents. President's are often asked to serve as brokers between warring parties, which President Bush was reluctant to do between Israel's Ariel Sharon and the PLO's Yasser Arafat in April 2002.

Indeed, so important is foreign policy that many presidents direct foreign relations from the Oval Office more than through the State Department. This power shift reflects the significance of the president's role as world leader. President John Kennedy once said, "The big difference [between domestic and foreign policy] is that between a bill being defeated and the country [being] wiped out."

The President as Chief Legislator   Despite numerous constraints, however, presidents do play a major role in domestic matters. Congress and the American public expect the president to send legislative initiatives to Congress and to work with Congressional leaders in forging legislation that will improve the quality of life in America. Indeed, most legislation addressed by Congress originates in the executive branch, but when President Dwight Eisenhower chose not to submit a program in 1953 (his first year in office), he was chided by a member of Congress: "Don't expect us to start from scratch . . . That's not the way we do things here. You draft the bills and we work them over."[15] In January 2002, President Bush signed bipartisan legislation providing the broadest rewriting of federal education policy in decades, the No Child Left Behind Act.

Besides such proactive involvement in the legislative process (proposing policies and lobbying for them), the president also has negative legislative power. As you've seen, presidents can thwart congressional attempts at legislation through the veto or threats of a veto.

The President as Chief Executive   As the nation's chief executive, the president signs *executive orders* and presidential decrees setting the administrative direction and tone for the executive branch. The Bush presidency has made extensive use of Executive Orders to achieve its policy goals (see Table 5.5). As chief administrator or chief bureaucrat, the president oversees an army of officials, thousands of executive branch workers trying to carry out presidential policies effectively and quickly. And in this executive capacity, presidents do not act in a vacuum. They are closely monitored by interest groups throughout the country, all eager to see that the executive branch promotes policies and interpret laws to their liking.

▲ From the Oval Office, President Bush speaks with New York City Mayor Rudolph W. Giuliani and Governor George E. Pataki and pledges to visit New York on September 14, 2001.

The President as Moral Leader   Increasingly, the question of presidential character has been identified as essential. It has generally been assumed that the president must also set a high moral tone for the American people, even if it is folklore. George ("I cannot tell a lie") Washington and Abraham ("Honest Abe") Lincoln are the models a president is expected to emulate. Even though few citizens see politics as a fair and moral game, and even though no one can become president except through politics, Americans still seemed to hold the president to higher public standards than most politicians—or most citizens for that matter. Presidents were expected to be truthful, to deal openly with problems, to keep their word—and even to set high standards in their personal lives.

One of the most interesting components of President Clinton's approval ratings was that a majority of Americans recognized that he had serious character flaws. These were not considered an impediment to his being an effective president.

The President as Party Leader   As long as presidents remain in office, they are the chief architects of their political party's fortune. The Constitution makes no reference to party leadership—indeed, it makes no reference to parties at all—but today's presidents must never forget that their party put them in the Oval Office. A president's every action will either help or hurt that party, and its members will keep a close eye on the president to make sure that their party's ideas and fortunes are promoted.

Still, in campaigning and speaking for the party, the president must be careful. By playing that role too zealously, the president will come to be perceived as narrowly partisan and lose the image as leader of the entire nation. Presidents who act more like partisans than national leaders are asking for public disapproval. As details came to light of President Clinton's fund-raising efforts on behalf of the Democratic party that took place in the White House, questions of credibility quickly arose, not to mention violations of law.

The President as Manager of Prosperity   The public expects the president to act as an economic superhero who will stave off both depression and inflation while keeping the economy at full employment. When presidents act in this capacity, they adopt the role that was described by political scientist Clinton Rossiter as "Manager of Prosperity."[16] The chief executive is, in a sense, the nation's chief economist. The political lessons of the Great Depression are clear. No president can preside over hard times without being blamed. Herbert Hoover was soundly defeated after failing, in the public's eyes, to deal competently with the economic setbacks of that time. George Bush was sent into retirement because, in the words of political strategist James Carville, "It's the economy, stupid."[17] Democratic presidents have also suffered at the polls from the public's perception that they couldn't keep soaring inflation rates in check. Largely for that reason, Harry Truman lost his Democratic

Table 5.5 ■ Executive Orders Issued by President Bush, Jan. 29, 2001 to Oct. 7, 2002

Date	Executive Order	Date	Executive Order
2002		Nov. 16	National Emergency Construction Authority Executive Order
Oct. 7	Creating a Board of Inquiry to Report on Certain Labor Disputes Affecting the Maritime Industry of the United States	Nov. 13	Military Order
		Nov. 9	Citizen Preparedness in War on Terrorism Executive Order
Sep. 18	Environmental Stewardship and Transportation Infra-structure Project Reviews	Oct. 22	Dept. of Health and Human Services
Aug. 29	Further Amending Executive Order 10173, as Amended, Prescribing Regulations Relating to the Safeguarding of Vessels, Harbors, Ports, and Waterfront Facilities of the United States	Oct. 16	Critical Infrastructure Protection
		Oct. 12	Educational Excellence for Hispanic Americans Commission
		Oct. 8	Establishing Office of Homeland Security
Aug. 13	Proper Consideration of Small Entities in Agency Rulemaking	Oct. 3	Excellence in Special Education
		Oct. 1	Continuance of Federal Advisory Committees
Jul. 9	Establishment of the Corporate Fraud Task Force	Oct. 1	President Signs PCAST Executive Order
Jul. 3	Expedited Naturalization	Sep. 24	Terrorist Financing
Jul. 3	Taliban	Sep. 14	Ready Reserves of Armed Forces to Active Duty
Jun. 20	Executive Order	Aug. 17	Export Control Regulations
Jun. 20	President's Council on Physical Fitness and Sports	Jul. 31	Energy Efficient Standby Power Devices
Jun. 20	Activities to Promote Personal Fitness	Jul. 2	Executive Order
Jun. 6	Amendment to Executive Order 13180, Air Traffic Performance-Based Organization	Jun. 20	21st Century Workforce Initiative
		Jun. 19	Community-Based Alternatives for Individuals with Disabilities
Apr. 29	President's New Freedom Commission on Mental Health	Jun. 6	Amendment to Executive Order 13125
Apr. 12	Amendments to the Manual for Courts-Martial, U.S.	Jun. 1	Executive Order
Mar. 21	Homeland Security Council	May 28	President's Task Force to Improve Health Care Delivery for Our Nation's Veterans
Mar. 19	Order of Succession in the Environmental Protection Agency and Amending Certain Orders on Succession	May 23	Additional Measures with Respect to Prohibiting the Im-portation of Rough Diamonds from Sierra Leone
Feb. 12	Advisors for Historically Black Colleges and Universities	May 18	Actions Concerning Regulations That Significantly Affect Energy Supply, Distribution, or Use
Feb. 7	Amendment to Executive Order 13227, President's Commission on Excellence in Special Education	May 18	Actions to Expedite Energy-Related Projects
		May 2	President's Commission to Strengthen Social Security
Jan. 30	Establishing the USA Freedom Corps	Apr. 30	Establishment of the President's Task Force on Puerto Rico's Status
Jan. 17	Amendment to Executive Order 13223		
Jan. 7	Exclusions from the Federal Labor-Management Relations Program	Apr. 6	Amendment to Executive Order 13202
		Apr. 5	Further Amendment to Executive Order 10000
2001		Apr. 4	Termination of Emergency Authority For Certain Export Controls
Dec. 28	Succession in the Department of Veterans Affairs		
Dec. 28	Succession at the Department of State	Mar. 9	Establishing an Emergency Board
Dec. 28	Succession at the Department of Labor	Feb. 21	Preservation of Open Competition and Government Neu-trality Towards Government Contractors' Labor Relations on Federal and Federally Funded Construction Projects
Dec. 28	Succession at the Department of Housing and Urban Development		
Dec. 28	Succession at the Dept. of Health and Human Services	Feb. 21	Notification of Employee Rights Concerning Payment of Union Dues or Fees
Dec. 28	Succession at the Department of Interior		
Dec. 28	Succession at the Department of Commerce	Feb. 21	Revocation of Executive Order on Nondisplacement of Qualified Workers under Certain Contracts
Dec. 28	Succession at Department of Agriculture		
Dec. 28	Adjustments of Certain Rates of Pay	Feb. 21	Labor-Management Partnerships
Dec. 28	Succession in Department of Treasury	Feb. 12	Information Technology Advisory Committee
Dec. 28	Succession in Federal Agencies	Jan. 29	Agency Responsibilities with Respect to Faith-Based and Community Initiatives
Dec. 21	Council of Europe in Respect of the Group of States Against Corruption		
		Jan. 29	Establishment of White House Office of Faith-Based and Community Initiatives
Dec. 20	Establishing An Emergency Board		
Dec. 14	Afghanistan Combat Zone Executive Order		
Dec. 6	Federal Government Closure on Dec. 24		
Nov. 28	Creation of the President's Council on Bioethics		
Nov. 27	Waiver of Dual Compensation Provisions of the Central Intelligence Agency Retirement Act of 1964		

Source: http://www.whitehouse.gov/news/orders/.

majority in Congress during the 1946 election, and Jimmy Carter's fate might have been different if he could have averted the double-digit inflation of his last years in office. It remains to be seen whether the recession of 2002 will undo the President's high approval.

The President as Juggler of Roles   The president must play all of these roles—and others besides. Yet doing so, for all practical purposes, is an impossibility because the roles often conflict. How can one be both a partisan politician and a national unifier? For that matter, can one be a politician at all and still act as an inspirational leader to the nation? Can one be both a legislator and an administrator of laws? And how is it possible to reconcile the president's role in world affairs as both soldier and diplomat? How can a president seem fair and effective in the eyes of a multitude of constituencies? Finally, just finding the time and energy to carry out these expected tasks is surely beyond the capacity of any mortal. Political scientists Thomas Cronin and Michael Genovese have divided the job description into "three subpresidencies" (see Table 5.6).

The job of president is daunting, all the more so because the powers granted the person we expect to accomplish these multiple roles fall far short of any imaginable capacity to carry them out. In fact, even though we expect Herculean accomplishments of presidents, we hedge them with restrictions so that they look less like Captain Marvel and more like Gulliver, tied down by a thousand tiny ropes. We set up a perfect system for failure: a presidency with exaggerated expectations and a political-legal system of restraints. How, then, can anyone fill all the expected roles of the presidency? Let us examine two reactions to this system: presidents who accept the restraints and live within them, and presidents who chafe at the restraints and invent ways to surpass or abolish them.

Table 5.6 ■ The Presidential Job Description

Types of Activity	The Three "Subpresidencies"		
	Foreign Policy and National Security	Macroeconomics	Domestic Policy and Programs
Crisis management	Wartime leadership; missile crisis, 1962; Gulf War, 1991	Coping with recessions, 1982, 1992	Confronting coal strikes of 1978; LA riots, 1992; LA earthquake, 1992
Symbolic and morale-building leadership	Presidential state visit to Middle East or to China	Boosting confidence in the dollar	Visiting disaster victims and building morale among government workers
Priority setting and program design	Balancing pro-Israel policies with need for Arab oil	Choosing means of dealing with inflation, unemployment	Designing a new welfare program, health insurance
Recruitment leadership (advisers, administrators, judges, ambassadors, etc.)	Selection of secretary of defense, UN ambassador	Selection of secretary of treasury, Federal Reserve Board governors	Nomination of federal judges
Legislative and political coalition building	Selling Panama or SALT treaties to Senate for approval	Lobbying for energy-legislation package	Winning public support for transportation deregulation
Program implementation and evaluation	Encouraging negotiations between Israel and Egypt	Implementing tax cuts or fuel rationing	Improving quality health care, welfare retraining programs
Oversight of government routines and establishment of an early-warning system for future problem areas	Overseeing U.S. bases abroad; ensuring that foreign-aid programs work effectively	Overseeing the IRS or the Small Business Administration	Overseeing National Science Foundation or Environmental Protection Agency

Source: From *The Paradoxes of the American Presidency* by Thomas E. Cronin and Michael A. Genovese. Copyright © 1998 by Oxford University Press, Inc. Used by permission of Oxford University Press, Inc.

APPROACHING DEMOCRACY AROUND THE GLOBE

Mexico and Vicente Fox

While he still favors his trademark blue jeans and cowboy boots, Vicente Fox, Mexico's first National Action Party (PAN) president in more than 70 years, now wears a suit and tie with his boots. His campaign catch phrases of "a democratized market economy, a deepened political democracy and capable government serving the little guy" are still evident but they have lost some of their luster and he sits atop a bickering and often paralyzed administration. The people of Mexico have grown impatient for Fox's promised improvements to their daily lives, resulting in a steady slip in his support. As political commentator Gabriel Guerra Castellanos states, "Mexico is essentially a conservative country that likes its president in a suit, well dressed and well behaved. But what the people really want is a more focused and organized president."

Unemployment in Mexico rose in early 2002 due to the slowdown in consumption north of the border and there have been a rash of kidnappings and robberies that had security officials acknowledging the rising crime rate. Despite these problems however, Fox has an approval rating of between 50–60 percent for the simple fact that the economy had not collapsed in contrast to the economies of other Latin American countries. Rather than talking about improved relations with the United States (a key issue of Fox's first year in office), Fox began talking about the domestic economy and domestic issues, promoting his new Federal Office of Investigation, an organization similar to the FBI and one Fox hopes will combat the rising crime rate. Fox has taken a more proactive approach in his relationship with the National Congress, which is exercising new power in Mexico's evolving democracy. In addition, Mexico's new president has opened a new chapter in the government's relationship with society and the media in an effort to bolster his image. He is looking to improve the rocky relationship he has had with Mexican journalists who in the past have accused him of being shallow and talking too much.

▲ U.S. and Mexican Presidents share an affinity for Western wear. Here, President Vicente Fox and his wife are horseback riding. President Fox wears his trademark boots to most state dinners.

In his own words President Fox states, "I have to recognize the public and the media demand a very serious presidency that doesn't joke around, and I have learned—I am correcting that aspect." In his second year as President in a new era in Mexican politics, Vicente Fox is staying close to home, looking to strengthen the economy and to combat the rising crime rate—all in a suit and cowboy boots.

Sources: Washington Post, January 9, 2002, A15; See also *New York Times,* July 4, 2000, http://specials.ft.com/1n/specials/spc886.htm, and Kevin Sullivan, "Mexico's Fox Finds Campaign Promises Hard to Keep," *Washington Post,* January 23, 2002, A22. Also, Unger, Roberto Mangabeira. "In Mexico, a New Era and . . . a New Deal?" http://www.robertounger.com/fox.htm.

(?) Question for Reflection: How realistic are the expectations for the president to fulfill all these roles? How would you amend the position to assure that democracy is best served?

Two Views of Executive Power

How strong should a president be? How much power does the office really possess? The Constitution is silent on this matter. Article II begins with the ambiguous sentence, "The executive Power shall be vested in a President of the United States of America." What did the framers mean by this elusive phrase, "the executive Power"? Did it refer to a mere designation of office, or did it imply a broad and sweeping mandate to rule? Scholars and politicians alike have long debated the question, but have come to no agreement. History has left it up to each president to determine the scope of executive powers, given a president's personality, philosophy, and the political circumstances of the time.

This executive power "wild card" has allowed many a president to go beyond what is narrowly prescribed in the Constitution when conditions call for extraordinary action—or when the president thinks such action is necessary. Activist presidents find ways to justify sweeping policy innovations even if no specific language in the Constitution allows for those policies.

Franklin Roosevelt exemplified this approach in his Inaugural Address on March 4, 1933. With the country on the brink of economic collapse because of the Great Depression, Roosevelt declared in one of history's most memorable speeches, "Let me first assert my firm belief that the only thing we have to fear is fear itself—nameless, unreasoning, unjustified terror which paralyzes needed efforts to convert retreat into advance." Roosevelt then turned to the issue of means: "I shall ask the Congress for the one remaining instrument to meet the crisis—broad executive power to wage a war against the emergency, as great as the power that would be given to me if we were in fact invaded by a foreign foe."[18] Roosevelt then took a number of dramatic actions that included closing the banks by executive order, forbidding payments of gold, and restricting exports.

Not all presidents have made as sweeping claims to executive power as Franklin Roosevelt. Considering their different approaches to the use of power, we can categorize presidents in office as either stewards or constructionists. The **stewardship** approach to presidential power was articulated by Theodore Roosevelt and based on the presidencies of two of his predecessors, Abraham Lincoln and Andrew Jackson. Theodore Roosevelt believed that the president had a moral duty to serve popular interests. The president, in his eyes, was "a steward of the people bound actively and affirmatively to do all he could for the people." Roosevelt did not believe that the president needed specific authorization to take action:

> I did . . . many things not previously done by the President. . . . I did not usurp power, but I did greatly broaden the use of executive power. . . . I acted for the common well being of all our people. . . . in whatever manner was necessary, unless prevented by direct constitutional or legislative prohibition.[19]

Teddy Roosevelt held an activist, expansionist view of presidential powers. In a classic example of the stewardship model, he engineered the independence of Panama and the subsequent building of the Panama Canal. As he put it, "I took the [Panama] Canal Zone and let Congress debate, and while the debate goes on the canal does too."[20] Over the years, activist or steward presidents have used their powers broadly. Thomas Jefferson presided over the Louisiana Purchase in 1803, which almost doubled the size of the country. Lincoln assumed enormous emergency powers during the Civil War, justifying them on the grounds of needing to take quick, decisive action during an extraordinary national crisis. During World War I, Woodrow Wilson commandeered plants and mines, requisitioned supplies, fixed prices, seized and operated the nation's transportation and communication networks, and managed the production and distribution of foodstuffs.

In contrast to this stewardship view of executive power is the **constructionist** view espoused by William Howard Taft. Taft believed that the president could exercise no power unless it could be traced to or implied from an express grant in either the Constitution or an act of Congress. He scoffed at the idea of some "undefined residuum of power" that a president can exercise "because it seems to him to be in the public interest." The president, he believed, was limited by a strict reading of the Constitution. Unless that document gave the executive a specific power, that power was beyond the scope of legitimate presidential activity. Taft cringed in horror at Theodore Roosevelt's view that the president could "do anything that the needs of the nation demanded."[21]

Because of this restricted view of presidential power, Taft was a passive executive, reluctant to impose his will or the power of his office on the legislative process.[22] He

LITTLE-KNOWN FACT
William Howard Taft was the only person to serve as both president of the United States and chief justice of the Supreme Court. At 321 pounds, he was also the country's largest president. Taft had an oversized bathtub specially constructed for the White House.

stewardship An approach to presidential power that was articulated by Theodore Roosevelt and based on the presidencies of Lincoln and Jackson, who believed that the president had a moral duty to serve popular interests and did not need specific constitutional or legal authorization to take action.

constructionist A view of presidential power espoused by William Howard Taft, who believed that the president could exercise no power unless it could be traced to or implied from an express grant in either the Constitution or an act of Congress.

did not exert strong party leadership in Congress, nor did he embark on the ambitious and "extra-Constitutional" exercises of power typical of Teddy Roosevelt. Other presidents besides Taft have pursued this constructionist line, at least in certain situations. For example, Herbert Hoover was reluctant to exercise presidential powers to manipulate the economy during the Great Depression, appearing very much the constructionist—at least in economic policy. Indeed, it was this very reluctance that caused many voters to see him as indifferent to their economic plight.

On the whole, Americans have sided with an activist interpretation of the presidency. They expect dynamic leadership from the office. Almost none of the presidents regarded as "great" by either historians or the public has adopted a passive, constructionist approach to the job (see Table 5.7). The men who did much to create our idealized view of the presidency—Washington, Jefferson, Lincoln, the two Roosevelts—did not reach lofty status by minding their own business. They crossed and stretched constitutional boundaries in the name of the national interest. Their achievements stand as models, if not monuments. Current presidents invoke their names and strive to fill their shoes, while voters measure current occupants of the White House against these past giants. Few hope that the next president will behave like William Howard Taft, and it is unlikely that anyone will seek that office promising "to govern in the spirit of Franklin Pierce." President George W. Bush is known to admire and even fashion his presidency after the active Republican steward Teddy Roosevelt.[23]

At the beginning of the twenty-first century, with the United States as the world's only superpower, presidents can hardly be anything but activist stewards of the nation. While we may not all agree with Woodrow Wilson that, "the President has the right, in law and conscience, to be as big a man as he can be," the president can no longer be a passive actor in the political system. Many now believe that the health of American democracy, not only in the United States but worldwide, rests in the hands of an activist executive who represents democracy's interests.

Expanding Presidential Power: Moving Beyond the Constitution

Congress Delegates Power to the President

Presidents in our time have all gained the potential to exercise power far beyond that available to executives in the past. One major reason has been legislative acquiescence. Congress has willingly legislated broad delegations of power to the executive. Between 1933 and 1939, with the approval of Congress, President Franklin Roosevelt set up one agency after another to help remedy the economic problems of the Depression. These agencies—including the Civilian Conservation Corps (1933), the Public Works Administration (1933), the Resettlement Administration (1935, later absorbed into the Farm Security Administration), and the National Labor Relations Board (1935)—were given control over many important public policy decisions. Although they were originally set up to deal with the "emergency" of the Depression, many of these agencies and the policies associated with them continue to exist.

In non-emergency situations, it is quite common for Congress to pass laws that give only general guidelines and then leave it to the executive to "fill in the details." For example, Congress may pass a bill requiring all companies to provide their employees with a "safe working environment." It is then the responsibility of an executive agency (in this case, the Occupational Safety and Health Administration, or OSHA) to set the specific standards for workplace safety. Since presidential appointees usually run these executive agencies, the president can exercise quite a bit of influence over the administration, regulation, and interpretation of laws. In many cases, by having direct control over the details, the agencies of the executive branch can actually shape the laws to fit the president's program.

Table 5.7 ■ How Historians Rank the Presidents Now

	Overall Ranking	Public Persuasion	Moral Authority	Crisis Leadership	Inter-national Relations	Vision/ Setting an Agenda	Economic Management	Administrative Skills
Abraham Lincoln	1	3	2	1	4	1	3	1
Franklin Delano Roosevelt	2	1	4	2	1	2	1	3
George Washington	3	6	1	3	2	3	2	2
Theodore Roosevelt	4	2	3	5	3	4	4	4
Harry S. Truman	5	12	7	4	5	7	7	5
Woodrow Wilson	6	9	6	6	6	5	6	6
Thomas Jefferson	7	8	8	12	16	6	13	8
John F. Kennedy	8	5	15	8	13	9	9	13
Dwight D. Eisenhower	9	10	5	10	9	18	8	7
Lyndon Baines Johnson	10	13	28	17	36	11	12	9
Ronald Reagan	11	4	11	15	14	8	21	32
James K. Polk	12	16	20	9	15	10	10	10
Andrew Jackson	13	7	14	7	19	12	24	23
James Monroe	14	17	17	18	7	14	20	14
William McKinley	15	14	16	14	17	17	14	15
John Adams	16	24	9	13	10	19	11	19
Grover Cleveland	17	15	18	16	18	16	19	12
James Madison	18	18	13	19	24	15	15	18
John Quincy Adams	19	33	12	21	11	13	16	22
George Bush	20	19	19	11	12	28	23	16
Bill Clinton	21	11	41	20	21	22	5	21
Jimmy Carter	22	30	10	28	20	20	33	26
Gerald Ford	23	31	21	22	23	31	25	24
William Howard Taft	24	25	22	25	22	26	18	20
Richard Nixon	25	28	40	23	8	21	17	17
Rutherford B. Hayes	26	23	26	26	26	23	22	27
Calvin Coolidge	27	20	23	31	30	33	26	28
Zachary Taylor	28	26	27	24	27	25	29	31
James Garfield	29	21	25	32	38	24	30	34
Martin Van Buren	30	32	29	34	28	27	34	25
Benjamin Harrison	31	35	30	33	29	30	28	30
Chester Arthur	32	34	33	29	34	29	27	29
Ulysses S. Grant	33	22	31	30	33	36	37	39
Herbert Hoover	34	37	24	39	25	37	41	11
Millard Fillmore	35	36	32	27	32	32	32	35
John Tyler	36	38	35	35	31	34	31	33
William Henry Harrison	37	29	34	36	41	35	39	36
Warren G. Harding	38	27	39	38	35	38	36	41
Franklin Pierce	39	39	36	40	39	40	38	38
Andrew Johnson	40	41	37	37	37	39	35	40
James Buchanan	41	40	38	41	40	41	40	37

Source: C-Span, reported in *The Washingtonian*, April 2000, p. 55.

The constitutionality of this congressional delegation of power has been challenged several times. With only a few exceptions, however, the Supreme Court has upheld the decision of Congress to give up some control over the administration of its laws. In the past, Congress has tried to reassert some of its administrative and legislative control through different measures. One was the *legislative veto,* a statutory provision that allowed Congress to delay administrative actions for two or three months. During this time Congress could vote to approve or disapprove the administrative action altogether. Use of the legislative veto expanded rapidly during the Nixon-Ford-Carter years, but then died a swift death at the hands of the Supreme Court. In the case of *INS v. Chadha* (1983), the legislative veto was ruled unconstitutional on the grounds that it circumvented the president's own veto power.[24]

Conducting Foreign Policy and Making War

Although the president's power has grown in domestic affairs, it is the role as head of the nation in an increasingly complex and dangerous world that has produced the greatest enlargement of executive branch powers. At a time when key diplomatic and military decisions must often be made in hours, even minutes, presidents as single individuals with great authority have enormous advantages over a many-headed, continuously talking institution like Congress. At times national survival itself may require nothing less than rapid and unfettered presidential action. Congress, along with the rest of the nation, recognizes that reality. Even more clearly than in the domestic arena, it has delegated broad and sweeping powers that allow presidents to act in foreign affairs with few congressional restraints. In the days immediately following September 11th, the Senate voted 96-0 and the House 422-0 to give President Bush $40 billion to help rebuild lower Manhattan and the Pentagon as well as to launch his global war on terrorism. The Senate voted 98-0 to give the President virtually unlimited powers to prosecute the war against terrorism.

It is not Congress alone that defers to the president in foreign affairs. The executive's preeminence in this field has even been recognized and legitimized by the Supreme Court. Its position was enunciated in the 1936 case of *United States v. Curtiss-Wright.* Associate Justice George Sutherland's opinion provides the rationale for an active presidential role by distinguishing between foreign and domestic affairs and the powers apportioned to each. While domestic power comes only from an express grant in the Constitution, he argued, in foreign affairs the president is sovereign. Sutherland concluded that the grant of foreign policy power to the president did not depend on any constitutional provision but rather on the sovereignty of the national government. In sweeping language Sutherland stated: "In this vast external realm, with its important, complicated, delicate and manifold problems, the President alone has the power to speak or listen as a representative of the nation."[25]

Presidential War Powers   In theory, then, both Court and Congress see the president as the dominant force in foreign policy. This perspective is bolstered by the president's constitutionally delegated role as commander in chief of the American armed forces. Presidents have used this military role in a variety of ways to achieve their policy ends and expand the power of their office.

Some presidents have left the actual conduct of war to professional military personnel, while using their commander in chief role to set broad national and international policy. That policy often seemed far removed from urgent military matters. Abraham Lincoln, for instance, issued the Emancipation Proclamation "by virtue of the power in me vested as Commander-in-Chief of the Army and Navy" and "warranted by the Constitution upon military necessity." In short, Lincoln used his command over the military to abolish slavery. It was a worthy goal, but represents a broad interpretation of the commander in chief powers.

In times of crisis, some presidents have gone even further than Lincoln. As noted in the opening case, following Japan's bombing of Pearl Harbor, Franklin Roosevelt ordered more than 100,000 Japanese Americans living on the West Coast evacuated

▲ President Bush greets the peacekeeping troops at Camp Bodsteel, a U.S. military base in Kosovo.

THE ROAD TO DEMOCRACY

From the Imperial to the Imperiled to the Impervious Presidency

Thomas Jefferson, in 1797, referred to the presidency as "a splendid misery." In the last four decades, eight men have served as president. Despite winning the Cold War, landing on the moon, establishing several beachheads of peace around the globe, and other achievements, Gerald Ford, Jimmy Carter, and former President George Bush were voted out of office, John Kennedy was assassinated, Ronald Reagan shot, Richard Nixon resigned in disgrace, Lyndon B. Johnson chose not to seek reelection fearing defeat, and Bill Clinton was impeached.

THAT WAS THEN . . .

With the Vietnam War raging and the Watergate scandal unfolding, historian Arthur M. Schlesinger, Jr., described and deplored "the expansion and abuse of presidential power" in his 1973 book, *The Imperial Presidency*. In several respects, however, that vivid, cautionary phrase imperial presidency has become anachronistic, as formal and informal measures have sought to curb what Schlesinger referred to as the "runaway presidency."

The passage by Congress of the War Powers Act in 1973, the Budget and Impoundment Control Act in 1974, and the Independent Counsel Act in 1978 all served notice to the executive branch that other government entities were monitoring the involvement of the military in hostile situations, the spending of appropriated money, and the conduct of the presidents and their appointed subordinates.

Moreover, Supreme Court decisions (notably *United States v. Nixon* in 1974 and *Clinton v. Jones* in 1997) made it clear to presidents that their standing in potentially criminal matters was the same as any other citizen's. In the Nixon case, claims of executive privilege did not prevent surrender of his Oval Office tapes about Watergate. With Clinton, the argument of presidential immunity for an allegation of sexual harassment before taking office failed to delay court proceedings that involved Paula Corbin Jones and, ultimately, Monica Lewinsky.

At the same time that the high court and Congress were imposing checks of different kinds on the presidency and on individual presidents, the news media was dramatically changing its approach to and attitude toward White House coverage. In the post–Watergate climate of unblinking scrutiny, any suggestions of scandal or personal peccadilloes received sustained attention. As journalists became more probing and, at times, adversarial, previously taboo subjects such as health or sex partners became fair yet controversial game. Aiding and abetting this tell-all atmosphere is the loose-lipped coterie of White House officials and assistants who would leak anonymous, insider information to willing reporters or leave government service and write revealing, behind-the-doors memoirs about their former bosses still in office.

THIS IS NOW . . .

Considered collectively, the governmental, journalistic, and cultural changes of the past twenty-five years result in more of an investigated or imperiled presidency rather than an imperial one. At a time when the United States is the world's only superpower, whoever occupies the Oval Office faces new constraints that, to a degree, weaken the institution. The presidency is still a combination of chief executive, head of state, commander in chief, principal diplomat, legislative agenda setter, crisis manager, and party leader, but these roles have become more difficult since Vietnam and Watergate.

The checks and balances that operate between the executive and legislative branches date back more than 200 years to the ratification of the Constitution, deliberately limiting the powers of each branch of government. Theodore Roosevelt once remarked, "Oh, if I could only be president and Congress too for just 10 minutes." That lament could serve as the hopeful wish of any president.

Source: Excerpted and adapted from Robert Schmuhl, "The Presidency: Full of Peril or Possibility?" *The Boston Globe*, 1/2/2000. Reprinted by permission of the author.

to interior places of internment, citing national security. He thus used his military powers to establish de facto concentration camps. Roosevelt also issued an ultimatum in a speech to Congress on September 7, 1942. Should legislators not repeal provisions within the Emergency Price Control Act, he stated that he would "accept the responsibility and act." Roosevelt's claim here is impressive: that acting in his capacity as commander in chief, he could make domestic policy unrestrained by the wishes of Congress. Even more impressive, perhaps, is the fact that the American people strongly supported him on this matter.

The commander in chief role is also used by presidents to make war, and congressional delegation of power to the president has allowed for expansion of this role. Lyndon Johnson, for example, committed ground troops to Vietnam on the basis of a loosely worded congressional resolution of August 7, 1964. The Southeast Asia Resolution, remembered now as the Tonkin Gulf Resolution, stated that, "the Congress approves and supports the determination of the President, as Commander in Chief, to take all necessary measures to repel any armed attack against the forces of the United States and to prevent further aggression." President Johnson later described the resolution as being like grandma's nightshirt—it covered everything![26]

Using his powers as commander in chief, Richard Nixon later ordered the Vietnam War expanded into Laos and Cambodia, neutral countries at the time. Hundreds of enemy sortie reports were falsified to justify the president's actions. Congress and the public were kept in the dark. The House Judiciary Committee considered an article of impeachment against Nixon that cited his deliberate misleading of Congress "concerning the existence, scope, and nature" of the American operation in Cambodia. This article was dropped, however, suggesting just how reluctant Congress is to curb a president's powers, even those of an extremely unpopular one, as long as the president appears to be acting in the commander in chief capacity.[27]

Still, military power does not make the president a dictator, and commanders in chief have at one time or another been restrained by both Congress and the Supreme Court. In *Youngstown Sheet and Tube Company v. Sawyer* (1952), the Supreme Court struck down President Truman's seizure of the domestic steel industry. He had claimed that his powers as commander in chief in wartime (the Korean War) allowed him to seize and run the steel mills to ensure the ongoing efficacy of the war effort. The Court ruled that only a pressing national emergency, which in its opinion did not exist at the time, could justify such a sweeping action in the domestic sphere without approval of Congress.[28]

Congress, too, has challenged the president in military affairs. After all, the Constitution assigns Congress the power to declare war, order reprisals, raise and support armies, and provide for the common defense. Doesn't that give it the legal authority to commit American forces to combat and oversee their actions? Many legislators believed so and worked to assert Congress's constitutional prerogatives after the unpopular Vietnam War. The result was passage of the War Powers Resolution in 1973, over President Nixon's veto.[29]

The resolution requires that the president "in every possible instance" report to Congress within forty-eight hours after committing U.S. troops to hostile action if no state of war has been declared. If Congress disagrees with the action, the troops must be removed within ninety days. Actually the troops must be withdrawn within sixty days unless the president requests thirty additional days to ensure their safety. Since *INS v. Chadha* (discussed earlier), Congress can no longer stop the military commitment by *concurrent resolution* (a resolution passed by both houses in the same form).

The effectiveness of the resolution has been "to legalize a scope for independent presidential power that would have astonished the framers." The first test occurred in May 1975, when President Gerald Ford ordered the marines and navy to rescue the U.S. merchant ship *Mayaguez*, without any prior consultation with members of Congress. The ship, carrying both civilian and military cargo, was seized by Cambodian ships for being in Cambodia's territorial waters. In his report to Congress, submitted *after* the troops had been withdrawn, President Ford cited both his inherent executive power and his authority as commander in chief.[30]

These examples illustrate that a congressional declaration of war is no longer needed for a president to send American troops into combat. While the Constitution grants Congress the power "to declare War," history, practice, precedent, and popular expectation have given the president authority to "make war." Presidents have often ordered troop actions, leaving Congress with few options but to support them. Appropriations cutoffs expose legislators to charges of having stranded soldiers in the field. Perhaps these facts explain why presidents have committed troops abroad in dozens of combat situations, while Congress has actually declared war only five times.

As the war on terrorism escalates, the President's war-making powers are once again expanding. After much debate over the need for him to seek Congressional approval for a war on Iraq, President Bush introduced a bill to Congress that would give him the power to use military force if necessary to rid Iraq of its chemical and biological weapons and to dismantle its nuclear weapons program. The House approved Joint Resolution 114 with a vote 296 to 133 (3 not voting) and the Senate in a 77 to 23 vote the following day. The resolution was signed into effect on October 16, 2002. House Joint Resolution 114 requires the president to notify Congress before or within 48 hours of an attack, explaining its necessity and how military action will not hurt the war on terror, but it still allows him to act unilaterally. President Bush then received unanimous backing from the UN Security Council, which approved a resolution he formulated in his September 12th speech entitled "A Decade of Deception and Defiance." In it he outlined 16 Iraqi violations of UN regulations over the last decade and asked the Security Council to mandate new weapons inspections whose failed compliance could trigger military action.[32]

Going Public

We have seen that the growing importance of America's role in the world has helped increase the president's power; an American president is a world leader. Given the singular nature of the office, a president can use modern means of communication to curry public support for his policies. As individuals in an age of personality, they are in a position to manipulate the media to enhance their reputation, which most members of Congress are unable to do.

During the early years of the Republic, presidents promoted themselves through the prevailing means of communication: public speeches, pamphlets, and articles. Although nearly all of the early presidents had some experience in mass persuasion, it was by no means considered vital to the office.

◀ Former President Clinton is joined by James Roosevelt and Anna Eleanor Roosevelt for the unveiling of a statue of the thirty-second President in his wheelchair.

Throughout the nineteenth century most presidents, with the conspicuous exception of Andrew Johnson, communicated to Congress in formal, written addresses. Public speeches were suspect, to be avoided as demagoguery. Indeed, one of the impeachment charges against Johnson read that he "did . . . make and deliver with a loud voice certain intemperate, inflammatory, and scandalous harangues . . . particularly indecent and unbecoming in the chief Magistrate of the United States." These charges seem laughable today, when effective speechmaking has become a requirement of the presidency.

It was not until the twentieth-century presidency of Theodore Roosevelt, in fact, that presidents assumed the role of preachers in what Roosevelt called "the bully pulpit." Great American oratory—what there was of it—had always come from Congress, out of the mouths of speakers like Stephen Douglas, Daniel Webster, and Henry Clay. Roosevelt changed all that, at least for the duration of his term. He spoke loudly and often, but only when compared with presidents of his day, not presidents of ours.

Woodrow Wilson was the first twentieth-century president to use mass persuasion for a particular policy goal. Facing serious opposition in Congress after World War I, Wilson toured the country in search of support for the League of Nations. He was unsuccessful, but the presidency thereafter became a national theater with the chief executive the most visible actor on the stage. That supreme thespian, Franklin D. Roosevelt, would soon be expertly using the presidency as a forum for mass persuasion.

A master of public communication, Roosevelt used that expertise to increase the power of the national government and in particular the presidency. He did this in part by personalizing the office. When listening to his "fireside chats" on radio, people felt that they knew and understood the president as a person, not just as a chief executive. What Roosevelt began, other presidents continued. While varying widely in their skill as communicators, no president since Roosevelt has attempted to govern without also attempting to create and maintain mass support.

Presidents see popular opinion as a source of power. Yet the need for public support is also a constraint. Presidents must now be seen to be governing for people to believe that they are governing. Presidents must therefore be attentive to their approval ratings and dedicate increasing amounts of time to the public side of their office (see Tables 5.8 and 5.9). As a result, the office has become increasingly more ceremonial and less deliberative than the framers ever intended.

Nonetheless, presidents have long recognized the advantages of what political scientist Samuel Kernell calls **going public,** promoting themselves and their policies to the American people. The strategy includes televised press conferences, prime-time addresses, White House ceremonies, and satellite broadcasts. Rather than bargain directly with Congress, presidents appeal to the American public, hoping to generate popular pressure for their policy aims. In one nationally televised speech, for example, President Ronald Reagan once appealed to the public to "contact your senators and congressmen. Tell them of your support for this bipartisan [tax] proposal."[33] During the 2003 midterm elections, President George W. Bush used his extraordinary approval ratings, as well as the perks of his office (Air Force One), to campaign for Republican candidates throughout crucial battleground states. The strategy worked, bringing Republican control to the Senate and increasing the Republican majority in the House. Going public secured great political advantage for the President.

Going public may appear to be an easier strategy than bargaining or negotiation, but it is a far riskier one. Members of Congress may feel themselves ill disposed toward a president who bypasses them and goes directly to the people. Going public thus carries risks for the often tenuous lines of communication between the White House and Capitol Hill. Generally, negotiators must be prepared to compromise, and bargaining proceeds best behind closed doors. By fixing a firm presidential position on an issue through public posturing, however, the strategy of going public may serve to harden a president's bargaining position and make later compromise with other politicians difficult.

▲ Ronald Reagan was an expert at communicating with the American people, and no president better understood how to make the best of a photo opportunity. The former movie actor was ideally suited for television.

going public Actions taken by presidents to promote themselves and their policies to the American people.

Table 5.8 ■ First Year Average Job Approval Ratings, Truman to Bush

President	Dates	Average	Ratings
Truman	Apr 20, 1945–Jan 19, 1946	77.3	3
Kennedy	Jan 20, 1961–Jan 19, 1962	76.4	15
Johnson	Oct 20, 1963–Jan 19, 1964	76.3	3
Eisenhower	Jan 20, 1953–Jan 19, 1954	68.8	14
George W. Bush	Jan 20, 2001–Jan 19, 2002	67.1	33
Bush	Jan 20, 1989–Jan 19, 1990	65.9	13
Carter	Jan 20, 1977–Jan 19, 1978	61.8	26
Nixon	Jan 20, 1969–Jan 19, 1970	61.4	20
Reagan	Jan 20, 1981–Jan 19, 1982	57.1	20
Ford	Jul 20, 1974–Jan 19, 1975	51.1	9
Clinton	Jan 20, 1993–Jan 19, 1994	49.3	29

Source: Gallup Poll Analyses–http://www.gallup.com/poll/releases/, 1/17/02 p. 3 of 5.

Table 5.9 ■ What Are Bush's Approval Ratings?

Approval among	July 2002	Oct. 9, 2001
Republicans	95%	99%
Independents	66%	92%
Democrats	51%	88%

Source: ABC *Washington Post* poll, July 24–28. http://www.abcnews.com.

President Bush's skyrocketing popularity and support emanates from a revision in voters' attitudes since September 11. Support for the President's handling of the war on terrorism was almost 90 percent and this positively impacted views of Bush on domestic efforts because people felt more secure at home. According to a March 21, 2002, Gallup poll, in the six months since September 11, 2001, George Bush's approval rating fell slightly, to 80%. Bush's 10-percentage-point drop six months after his high point (90%) compares favorably to the average archives back to Dwight Eisenhower. The average decline in job approval at the six-month mark following the date of each president's high score is 16 points. In the cases of John F. Kennedy, Lyndon Johnson, and Richard Nixon, the decline was less than 10 points. Table 5.10 shows each president's high score and where his job approval rating stood six months after he received it:

Table 5.10 ■ Presidential Job Approval Ratings, High Score and Decline Over Six Months

President	High Score	Date	Score	Six Months Later Date	Difference
Eisenhower	79%	Dec 14–19 '56	63%	June 27–Jul 2 '57	16
Kennedy	83	Apr 28–May 3 '61	79	Nov 17–22 '61	4
Johnson	79	Feb 29–Mar 4 '64	70	Nov 20–25 '64	9
Nixon	67	Nov 12–17 '69	59	May 21–26 '70	8
Ford	71	Aug 16–19 '74	39	Feb 28–Mar 2 '75	32
Carter	75	Mar 18–21 '77	59	Sep 30–Oct 3 '77	16
Reagan I	68	May 8–11 '81	49	Nov 13–16 '81	19
Reagan II	68	May 16–19 '86	47	Dec 4–5 '86	21
Bush	89	Feb 28–Mar 3 '91	70	Sep 5–8 '91	19
Clinton	73	Dec 19–20 '98	57	Jun 25–27 '99	16
G. W. Bush	90	Sep 21–22 '01	80	Mar 8–9 '02	10

Source: http://www.gallup.com/poll/releases/pr021018.asp.

The Institutionalized Presidency

One individual, the president, is expected to manage a national government of some 2 million employees. To describe this position is to define the problem. Presidents must effectively manage not only the national government but also their staff. The bureaucratic aspects of this job are daunting.[34]

Before 1939 presidents relied on a few clerks for general staff assistance. One of President Washington's first decisions was to hire his nephew Lawrence Lewis as a clerical assistant. Lewis, the president's sole employee, was paid out of Washington's own pocket. That tradition continued for seventy years until Congress appropriated funds for the president's household staff in 1833.

Andrew Jackson was the first president to receive an allowance for a departmental clerk, who was authorized only to sign land patents. For day-to-day functions such as writing letters or speeches, however, the president was still left to his own resources. Not until 1857 did Congress fund the first official household staff budget, including a private secretary ($2,000 a year), an executive mansion steward ($1,200), messengers ($900), and a contingency fund ($750).

Little had changed by 1937, when the administrative aspects of an expanded modern government and the proliferation of New Deal agencies overwhelmed Franklin Roosevelt, who had a secretary, a press secretary, and a handful of aides. Believing that expanded government requires management tools equal to the task, Roosevelt commissioned the Committee on Administrative Management, usually referred to as the Brownlow Commission. This group recommended that the president have a permanent staff for managing the executive branch. Its report began with a clarion call, "The President needs help," and recommended that the president receive both personal and institutional assistance.

The Brownlow Report displayed keen insight and sensitivity with regard to the potential dangers of installing unelected and anonymous staff in a White House office. It recognized that the effectiveness of presidential assistants could be directly proportional to their ability to discharge their functions with restraint. Therefore, they were to remain in the background, make no decisions, issue no orders, make no public statements, and never impose themselves between cabinet officers and the president. These assistants were to have no independent power base and should "not attempt to exercise power on their own account." In the famous words of the Brownlow Report, they were to have a "passion for anonymity."

As presidential aides have multiplied, the Brownlow Report's admirable goals have become difficult to maintain. Staff members have grown in power, along with the presidency, and in an open democracy few people with power can maintain anonymity for long. Many of them have come to hold important powers, despite being unmentioned in the Constitution. The number of people working directly for the president has become so large that we need complex organizational charts merely to keep track of them.

FYI

When a president delivers the State of the Union Address, all but one cabinet member attends. The lone nonparticipant stays behind to represent the country should the Capitol be attacked.

The White House Office

Closest to the president are those who work in the White House, where the president both lives and works. Thus, White House staff are never far from their employer. The White House is located at 1600 Pennsylvania Avenue NW, Washington, D.C. The first family sleeps upstairs; the president works downstairs in the West Wing Oval Office. Presidential staff also work downstairs in both the East and West Wings. The president's chief lieutenants operate nearby in the West Wing. Also located in the West Wing are the Situation Room, the Oval Office, the National Security Council staff, the vice president's office, assistants to the president, and the Cabinet Room. The East Wing houses the First Lady's office, congressional relations staff, and various social correspondence units.

All presidential assistants in the White House tread a thin line between the power they derive from being close to the president and their actual role as assistants and underlings. An office in the White House can transform the most sensible person into someone who cannot resist barking into a phone, "This is the White House calling," Jack Valenti, a special assistant to President Johnson from 1963 to 1966, explains the temptations:

> You sit next to the Sun King and you bask in his rays, and you have those three magic words, "the President wants." All of a sudden you have power unimagined by you before you got in that job. And if you don't watch out, you begin to believe that it is your splendid intellect, your charm and your insights into the human condition that give you all this power. . . . The arrogance sinks deeper into their veins than they think possible. What it does after a while is breed a kind of insularity that keeps you from being subject to the same fits of insecurity that most human beings have. Because you very seldom are ever turned down. You are seen in Washington. There are stories in *Newsweek* and *Time* about how important you are. I'm telling you this is like mainlining heroin. And while you are exercising it, it is so blinding and dazzling that you forget, literally forget, that it is borrowed and transitory power.[35]

The size of the staff has increased with the growth of government. As presidents are expected to solve more and more problems, the number of specialists on the White House staff has come to look like "a veritable index of American society," in political scientist Thomas Cronin's words.[36] These men and women come from every imaginable background. Because their loyalty is solely to the president and not to an administrative agency, they seem more trustworthy to the president than cabinet members or high-level officials from the civil service. The president therefore puts them to work running the everyday operations of the presidency. White House staff members often end up usurping the policy-making power normally held by cabinet secretaries, their staffs, and the staffs of various independent executive agencies.

The Chief of Staff   The White House **chief of staff** is now the president's de facto top aide. Often earning a reputation as assistant president, this individual is responsible for the operation of the White House and acts as gatekeeper to the president. The chief of staff also plays a key role in policy making. During the Eisenhower years, Chief of Staff Sherman Adams was so influential that the following joke became popular: "Wouldn't it be awful if Ike died, then we'd have Nixon as president?" Response: "But it would be even worse if Sherman Adams died. Then Eisenhower would be president." In like manner, H. R. Haldeman, Nixon's chief of staff, was once described as "an extension of the President."[37] President Bush's chief of staff, Andrew Card, has a very firm idea about the way things should work in the White House. He did not want the president referred to as POTUS, the long-used acronym for President of the United States. Staffers were told not to use it. Card also established dress codes for staffers in the West Wing. It's not quite as casual as during the prior eight years.

The Executive Office of the President

This title is somewhat misleading, since there is no single Executive Office Building. Instead, the **Executive Office of the President (EOP)** consists of staff units that serve the president but are not located in the White House. Some of these units include the National Security Council, the Council of Economic Advisers, and the Office of Management and Budget, among others. The Bush administration made two significant additions to the EOP: the Office of Strategic Initiatives led by Karl Rove, the President's leading political advisor and the Office of Faith-Based and Community Initiatives, now directed by Jim Towey, demonstrates Bush's commitment to "compassionate conservatism."

chief of staff The president's top aide.

Executive Office of the President (EOP) Created in 1939, this office includes all of the staff units that serve to support the president in his administrative duties.

▶ On September 11, 2001, in Sarasota, Florida, Chief of Staff Andrew Card whispers news of the attacks to President Bush.

The National Security Council   The National Security Council (NSC) was established in 1947, and its formal membership consists of the president, vice president, and secretaries of defense and state. The special assistant to the president for national security affairs is the council's principal supervisory officer. The NSC's job is to advise the president on all aspects of domestic, foreign, and military policy that relate to national security.

The Council of Economic Advisers   The Council of Economic Advisers (CEA) was created by the Employment Act of 1946. The legislation was intended to give the president professional, institutionalized, economic staff resources. Today, the CEA is responsible for forecasting national economic trends, making economic analyses for the president, and helping to prepare the president's annual economic report to Congress. The CEA chair is appointed by the president with the advice and consent of Congress. The recently created National Economic Council is responsible for coordinating high-priority economic policy matters for the president.

Although the CEA is a valuable resource, the president actually gets most economic advice from a group referred to as the "troika"—a functional division of labor among the secretary of the treasury (revenue estimates), the CEA (the private economy), and the Office of Management and Budget (federal expenditures). When the chair of the Federal Reserve Board is included in the group, it is referred to as the "quadriad."

Office of Management and Budget   Observers of American politics have long recognized the central role that the Office of Management and Budget (OMB)

◄ The morning after the September 11 attacks, President Bush meets with his National Security Council and begins the strategic planning for striking back.

plays.[38] While the OMB's primary responsibility is to prepare and implement the budget, the office is also responsible for evaluating the performance of federal programs. As such, it reviews management processes within the executive branch, prepares executive orders and proclamations, plans the development of federal statistical services, and advises the president on the activities of all federal departments. The OMB also helps promote the president's legislative agenda with Congress. As the most highly developed coordinating and review unit in the Executive Office, the OMB is also the most powerful. It acts as the central institutional mechanism for imprinting (some would say inflicting) presidential will over the government.

The OMB began as the Bureau of the Budget (BOB) in 1921. It acted at first only as a superaccountant, keeping track of the executive branch's books. Over the years, BOB's powers continued to grow until, in 1970, a major executive office reorganization transformed BOB into OMB, with greatly expanded powers. Given its array of responsibilities and powers, OMB's influence now extends into every nook and cranny of the executive branch.

The Cabinet

Cabinet officers act as a link between the president and the rest of the American political system. Cabinet departments have been created by Congress, which has given them specific legal responsibilities and political mandates. Department heads are confirmed by the Senate and are frequently called to testify before congressional committees (see Table 5.11 on page 195).

As an institution, the cabinet itself is unusual. It is not mentioned in either the Constitution or in statutory law, yet it has become a permanent part of the presidency. The framers considered but eventually rejected adding a council of any kind to the executive. Thus, the cabinet as such does not legally exist. Nevertheless, the idea of a cabinet surfaced early. Newspapers began using the term in the 1790s to describe the relationship between President Washington and his executive officers.

In its most formal meaning the **cabinet** refers to the secretaries of the major departments of the bureaucracy and any other officials the president designates (such as the OMB director). An informal distinction is often made between the inner and outer cabinet. Members of the *inner cabinet* are the most visible and enjoy more direct access to the president. Typically, this inner cabinet is composed of the secretaries of state, defense, treasury, and justice. These being the most powerful positions, presidents tend to staff them with close political allies.

Cabinet officers are responsible for running their departments as well as advising the president on matters of policy. Although many of its members have been quite distinguished, the cabinet has rarely served as a collective source of advice. John

cabinet Group of presidential advisers including secretaries of the major departments of the bureaucracy and any other officials the president designates.

Kennedy, for instance, scoffed at calling full cabinet meetings; he saw no reason to consult the postmaster general about matters of war and peace. Lincoln viewed his cabinet with something approaching disdain. On the occasion of signing the Emancipation Proclamation, he looked around his cabinet table and said, "I have gathered you together to hear what I have written down. I do not wish your advice about the main matter. That I have determined for myself."[39]

A president who took cabinet meetings most seriously was Dwight D. Eisenhower. Not only did his cabinet meet regularly with a set agenda, but Eisenhower also created the position of Cabinet Secretariat to serve as a liaison with the president. He also expanded the size of the official cabinet to include such important aides as U.S. ambassador to the United Nations, budget director, White House chief of staff, and a national security affairs assistant. Still, most presidents have followed a different pattern. Cabinet members end up as glorified bureaucrats, running their department and consulting with the president individually about their specialized activities.

President Bush's most recent cabinet innovation was the creation of the "war cabinet" that is composed of the top national security officials in the White House, CIA, State Department, and Pentagon. The creation of the cabinet level office of Homeland Security (OHS) headed by former Pennsylvania Governor Tom Ridge is also an important innovation. Ridge also leads the Homeland Security Council.[40]

The Vice Presidency

? Question for Reflection: How would the role of vice president change if the Constitution was amended to include specific responsibilities for the office?

The second highest elected official in the United States, the **vice president,** has few significant constitutional responsibilities. Indeed, the only powers actually assigned to the vice president by the Constitution are to preside over the Senate (except in cases of impeachment) and cast a vote when the Senate is deadlocked. Even that job is one that most vice presidents shun. Few have wished to spend all day listening to senators talk. The vice president's most important job is the one Americans hope he never takes—succeeding to the presidency in case of death, resignation, or removal. (Table 5.12 outlines the line of succession to the presidency.) As Woodrow Wilson once wrote, "There is very little to be said about the vice-president. . . . His importance consists in the fact that he may cease to be vice-president."

The actual work of the vice president ends up being whatever the president decides it will be. In recent years presidents have done more to bestow authority than to remove it. The growth in their own responsibilities has led them to turn to the vice president for help. For that reason the office of vice president, like that of the president, is becoming institutionalized. Between 1960 and 1980, vice presidential staff grew from twenty to more than seventy and largely parallels the president's, with domestic and foreign policy specialists, speech writers, congressional liaisons, and press secretaries.

Recent occupants of the office have been deeply involved in substantive matters of policy. Nelson Rockefeller chaired President Ford's Domestic Council. Walter Mondale served as a senior presidential adviser on matters of Carter administration policy. President Reagan appointed George Bush to lead the administration's crisis management team. Dan Quayle played an important role as chair of the Bush administration's Council on Competitiveness. Al Gore, Jr., was placed in charge of President Clinton's ambitious program to "reinvent government" by downsizing the bureaucracy, streamlining procedures, updating systems, and eliminating some subsidies and programs.

Dick Cheney's experience in Washington, his formidable role during the 2000 presidential transition, and the support and counsel he offered President Bush in

▲ Vice President Cheney has become the most influential power broker and presidential confidant in history. Cheney has had a distinguished career as a businessman and public servant, serving four Presidents.

vice president The second highest elected official in the United States.

Table 5.11 ■ President Bush's Cabinet
The Cabinet
Secretary of Agriculture Ann Veneman
Secretary of Commerce Don Evans
Secretary of Defense Donald Rumsfeld
Secretary of Education Rod Paige
Secretary of Energy Spencer Abraham
Secretary of Health & Human Service Tommy Thompson
Secretary of Housing & Urban Development Mel Martinez
Secretary of Interior Gale Norton
Attorney General John Ashcroft
Secretary of Labor Elaine Chao
Secretary of State Colin Powell
Secretary of Transportation Norman Mineta
Secretary of Treasury Paul O'Neill
Secretary of Veterans Affairs Anthony Principi
Cabinet Rank Members
The Vice President, Richard B. Cheney
President's Chief of Staff, Andrew H. Card, Jr.
Environmental Protection Agency, Christie Todd Whitman
Office of Homeland Security, Tom Ridge
Office of Management and Budget, Mitchell E. Daniels, Jr.
Office of National Drug Control Policy, John Walters
United States Trade Representative, Robert B. Zoellick

Source: http://www.whitehouse.gov/government.
This information current as of August, 2002.

Table 5.12 ■ Presidential Line of Succession

1. Vice president
2. Speaker of the House of Representatives
3. Senate president pro tempore
4. Secretary of State
5. Secretary of the Treasury
6. Secretary of Defense
7. Attorney General
8. Secretary of the Interior
9. Secretary of Agriculture
10. Secretary of Commerce
11. Secretary of Labor
12. Secretary of Health and Human Services
13. Secretary of Housing and Urban Development
14. Secretary of Transportation
15. Secretary of Energy
16. Secretary of Education
17. Secretary of Veterans Affairs

the period immediately after September 11, have elevated the vice presidency to new heights—even when this often stealth-like VP spends his evenings at an "undisclosed location." Table 5.13 shows a typical day for the vice president. It was Cheney who recommended and formulated the plan to set up the Office of Homeland Security. His two top aides Mary Matalin and Lewis Libby are also "Assistants to the President." More than any other vice president in history, Cheney has become the supreme last voice the President wants to hear before making a decision, "What does Dick think?" is what counts. In August 2002, Cheney said that his health was so good that he looked forward to serving as vice president during a second Bush administration from 2005–2009.[41]

In our study of the presidency we have seen the dynamics of a democratic society at work. The Executive Office of the President was created and expanded to help a twentieth-century president deal with managing a modern government. Yet despite this increase in the potential for power, presidents are seriously constrained by the context in which they are embedded. While great, their powers are far from absolute. Except in rare cases of clear emergencies, presidents do not act alone. They must seek and obtain the approval of Congress, the courts, and the people. And those people have high expectations. No other office of government represents the elements of democracy to Americans more than the presidency.

Table 5.13 ■ A Pre-9–11 Day at the Office

Tuesday, May 8, 2001, was a typical busy day for Vice President Dick Cheney.

Tuesday, May 8	
5:30	Wake up
7:10	Intelligence briefing at residence, Naval Observatory
	Intelligence and national security briefings with President Bush and Condoleezza Rice at White House
	Budget meeting with the president, Oval Office
10:20	Meet with I. Lewis Libby, chief of staff
10:45	Live interview on CNN
12:15	On Capitol Hill: meet with Rep. Jerry Lewis (Calif.), Rep. Norman Dicks (Wash.)—they want Pentagon to build more B-2 bombers
12:30	Meet with Senators Harry Reid and John Ensign (Nev.) about energy issues.
	Policy lunch with Senate Republicans
2:10	Meet with House Republican moderates on energy, environment
	Back to White House; review the final report on energy policy
	Meet with officials from Freedom House, a group of human rights organizations
6:15	Leave White House for residence
7:00	Dinner with Lynne Cheney and friends

Source: Reprinted by permission of *The New York Times.*

DEMOCRACY IN THE NEW MILLENNIUM

FirstGov.org: Three Clicks to Service

Presiding over the official e-launch in the Eisenhower Executive Office Building, Vice President Cheney said that the new and improved site was an attempt to "remedy one of the government's oldest problems: the slow, confusing and often ineffective ways in which it responds to the public." In a letter to the American people on March 14, 2002, President George Bush extended a "welcome to the government of the twenty-first century." Introducing the "Front Door" to his administration's e-government initiative, the Website was intended to make "your government more accessible to all Americans."

FirstGov is a one-stop, easy-to-use web portal to all government online services. This means that you can click onto the web site and quickly find and conduct business without needing to know which department or agency provides it. FirstGov helps you cut through governmental red tape to find online services that matter to you. The site has been enhanced from one that provided information about the government to one that provides solutions for people.

The idea of three clicks involves the categories citizens, business and government. Boundaries between agencies have been eliminated at the site. The Bush Presidency has also completely revamped the White House Web page at www.whitehouse.gov and, as you may have noticed, much material used in this textbook comes from data on that page.

Sources: From Ellen Nakashima, "Transition on the Web: The Cyber House Rules," *Washington Post,* January 19, 2001, p. A35; Ellen Nakashima, "FirstGov Web Site Again Is Clicking," *Washington Post,* March 1, 2002.

Some disenchantment with presidential performance in office seems almost inevitable, no matter who is president. Tensions between the promise and the limitations of this unique office are likely to continue to present the biggest challenges for this institution's approach to democracy.

SUMMARY

1. The framers designed the presidency to be independent of the legislature. This separation was achieved by creating a single executive who would be selected neither by Congress nor directly by the people. The president would serve a fixed term of office but be eligible to serve more than one term. The framers also made it very difficult to remove the president from office.

2. The veto power gives the president a central role in the legislative process. The president also has the power to appoint officials of the executive branch and nominate justices of the Supreme Court. Treaties with other nations are negotiated by the president but must be approved by a two-thirds majority of the Senate. To avoid seeking Senate approval, modern presidents have made increasing use of executive agreements and executive privilege.

3. The president performs a variety of roles, both formal and informal. Among these are chief of state, commander in chief, crisis leader, chief diplomat, chief legislator, chief executive, moral leader, and party leader. The president is also viewed as the manager of the nation's prosperity.

4. Activist presidents go beyond the powers prescribed in the Constitution when they feel that extraordinary action is required; this view of the presidency is referred to as stewardship. Constructionist presidents, in contrast, exercise no powers other than those that are expressly granted by the Constitution or an act of Congress. The theory of inherent powers holds that the Constitution grants broad authority to the executive during times of national emergency.

5. Congressional grants of power to the president have greatly increased the power of the presidency. The greatest enlargement of executive branch powers has occurred in the areas of foreign and military policy. Bowing to the president's constitutionally delegated role as commander in chief of the armed forces, Congress has largely acquiesced to the president in matters related to war. In 1973, however, it passed the War Powers Resolution, which requires that the president report to Congress within forty-eight hours after committing U.S. troops to hostile action.

6. Advances in communications technology have increased the president's influence by enabling the president to reach ever-larger numbers of people more quickly. Modern presidents promote their policies to the people through televised press conferences, prime-time speeches, and the like.

7. In recent decades the president's staff has grown steadily, and staff members have come to hold important powers. The White House chief of staff is responsible for White House operations but also plays a key role in policy making. The special assistant for national security affairs may also have considerable influence. The Office of Management and Budget plays a central role in executive policy because it is responsible for evaluating the performance of federal programs as well as budget formation.

8. The cabinet consists of the secretaries of the major departments of the federal bureaucracy and any other officials designated by the president. The inner cabinet consists of the secretaries of state, defense, treasury, and justice. Cabinet officials are responsible for running their departments as well as advising the president on matters of policy.

9. In the event of the death, resignation, or removal of the president, the vice president succeeds to the presidency. In recent administrations vice presidents have become increasingly more involved in substantive matters of policy.

10. One view of the presidency holds that the president's real power derives from the ability to persuade and bargain. Another view places more emphasis on the formal powers of the presidency but does not downplay the importance of leadership skills. As a result, modern presidents often go public, that is, attempt to persuade the people to put pressure on their legislators in support of the president's policies.

KEY TERMS

veto	stewardship	Executive Office of the
pocket veto	constructionist	President (EOP)
treaties	going public	cabinet
executive agreement	chief of staff	vice president
executive privilege		

POLISIM ACTIVITY

Who's Got the Power?

Although Presidents share with Congress the responsibility for making foreign policy, in practice a president has the primary responsibility to shape foreign policy. Presidents can bargain, negotiate, persuade, apply economic pressures, threaten, or even use armed force. In addition, the agencies that carry out foreign policy report directly or indirectly to the president. However, Congress can block the president's foreign policy and undermine the chief executive's decisions. In this simulation, as the president of the United States, you are expected to provide strong leadership in foreign policy matters. This will entail choosing policies and responding to international events. You will make decisions regarding three policies and respond to one international crisis. Your success or failure depends on which issues you choose to address and how well you can gain the support of the U.S. Senate.

Presidential Greatness? How Do We Judge Them?

Most Americans judge contemporary presidents against the standard of the Mount Rushmore presidents. We want presidents who can summon us to live up to our shared ideals of liberty and freedom and who will pay close attention to our immediate needs. In sum, we use varying and sometimes unfair standards when we judge presidents. The opinions of historians differ from what the general public believes. They rate presidents as outstanding, great, or near great on the basis of whether they brought about desirable changes and acted wisely guiding the nation through turbulent times. But why should historians have all the fun? In this simulation, we ask you to rate the last nine Presidents—from Dwight D. Eisenhower to William J. Clinton. Do some research first, to refresh your memory, then see how your opinions rate against some of the most respected presidential historians of our time.

SUGGESTED READINGS

BARBER, JAMES DAVID. *The Presidential Character: Predicting Performance in the White House.* Englewood Cliffs, N.J.: Prentice Hall, 1985. rev. ed. 1992. A provocative proposal that from the pattern a person followed in political life, we can predict how that person will perform as president.

BRUNI, FRANK. *Ambling into History: The Unlikely Odyssey of George W. Bush.* New York: Harper-Collins, 2002. New York Times reporter Frank Bruni's look at President George W. Bush from the campaign trail though the 9/11 tragedy.

COHEN, JEFFREY E. *Presidential Responsiveness and Public Policy-Making: The Public and the Policies That Presidents Choose.* Ann Arbor: University of Michigan Press, 1997. An examination of the way in which presidents have dealt with public opinion in policy making.

GREENSTEIN, FRED. *The Presidential Difference: Leadership Style from FDR to Clinton.* Princeton, New Jersey: Princeton University Press, 2000. A fascinating account of the qualities that have served well, in the oval office and those that haven't, from Franklin D. Roosevelt to the Presidency of George W. Bush.

KERNELL, SAMUEL. *Going Public: New Strategies of Presidential Leadership.* Washington, D.C.: CQ Press, 1993. rev. ed., 1997. Examination of presidential power in the context of political relations in Washington—particularly the strategy of bypassing bargaining on Capitol Hill and appealing directly to the American public.

KLEIN, JOE. *The Natural: The Misunderstood Presidency of Bill Clinton.* New York: Doubleday, 2002. An honest look at the strengths and weaknesses of the Clinton presidency and its affects on the military, economy, the American people, and the country.

NEUSTADT, RICHARD E. *Presidential Power and the Modern Presidents.* New York: Free Press, 1990. A classic study of presidential bargaining and influence that has set the agenda for a generation of presidency scholars.

SKOWRONEK, STEPHEN. *The Politics Presidents Make: Leadership from John Adams to George Bush.* Cambridge, Mass.: Harvard University Press, 1993. An important and innovative book that chronicles fifteen presidents and how they continually transformed the political landscape.

6

THE JUDICIARY

CHAPTER OUTLINE

Approaching Democracy Case Study:
The Real Rehnquist Court Legacy?

Introduction: The Courts and Democracy

The Origins and Development of Judicial
Power

The Organization of the American Court
System

Court Appointments: The Process
and the Politics

How the Supreme Court Operates

Analyzing Supreme Court Decisions

Implementing Supreme Court Decisions

The Court's Independence in Approaching
Democracy

APPROACHING DEMOCRACY CASE STUDY

The Real Rehnquist Court Legacy?

"**A**lthough we may never know with complete certainty the identity of the winner of this year's Presidential election, the identity of the loser is perfectly clear. It is the Nation's confidence in the judge as an impartial guardian of the rule of law." So spoke Supreme Court Justice John Paul Stevens in dissent in the case of *Bush v. Gore* on December 12, 2000. While Justice Stevens was objecting to the decision by five of his colleagues to rule in favor of George

W. Bush as the winner of the 2000 presidential election, he was also raising the question of whether, in the words of Conservative commentator, William Kristol, this decision would further "the politicizing of the Courts".

There is evidence this decision has had an impact on the relations among the Justices themselves. Justice Stephen Breyer argued in dissent that "[t]he Court was wrong to take the case" because in this case the Court "risk[s] a self-inflicted wound—a wound that may harm not just the Court, but the Nation." Later, in a Court reception for six judges from Russia, when one Russian judge said, "In our country, we wouldn't let judges pick the president," Breyer responded that the *Bush v. Gore* decision was "the most outrageous, indefensible thing," that the Court had ever done, adding, "We all agree to disagree, but this is different."

The *Bush v. Gore* decision, which ruled that due to the Equal Protection Clause of the Fourteenth Amendment it was not possible to fairly recount the Florida ballots to determine which candidate should receive that state's electoral college votes, effectively ended the recount and gave the presidency to Bush. This ruling resulted in widely divergent reactions. Fully half the nation's law school professors signed an advertisement in the *New York Times* criticizing the Supreme Court Justices for acting as "political proponents for candidate Bush, not as judges." Still, conservative Court of Appeals Judge Richard Posner argued in a book on the case that while the decision was badly reasoned and written, the Court majority had issued a "kind of rough justice" that avoided a political crisis which he believed would have resulted from the "banana republic" like decisions of the Florida Supreme Court. Despite all the academic controversy however, a Gallup poll showed that public confidence in the Supreme Court had rebounded to 62% public approval in July 2001, the same approval rating the Court received three months before their 2000 presidential election decision.

But the 2000 election was just one of a number of decisions that had analysts questioning the real legacy of the Rehnquist Court. Much like the 1930s activist Supreme Court thwarting President Franklin D. Roosevelt's New Deal policies with a series of decisions overturning Congressional depression-relief laws, the Rehnquist Court has become, often by a one-vote decision margin, one of the most activist conservative Courts in U.S. history. While in the nation's first 200 years the Supreme Court overturned only 127 federal laws, in the seven years between 1995 and 2002 the Rehnquist court has overturned 31 federal laws.

So the key question concerning the Rehnquist Court legacy may well not be the nature of its specific decisions, with some critics complaining that it is "a court in search of a theme," but whether it has wounded the institution's prestige. The question of whether the Court has created a "self-inflicted wound" is not new. *Miranda v. Arizona,* which ruled that suspects must be informed of their rights before police custodial interrogation, was considered in 1966 to be a "self-inflicted wound" by the Warren Court, and the *Roe v. Wade* pro-abortion decision was seen by some as wounding the Burger Court. Others see the *Dred Scott* decision upholding slavery in 1857, the *Plessy v. Ferguson* decision upholding racial segregation if it is "separate but equal" in 1896, and the *Korematsu v. United States* upholding the Japanese internment policy in 1943, as being further examples of "self-inflicted wounds" that damaged the Court's prestige. Perhaps the most illuminating precedent occurred in 1877, when the disputed presidential election was awarded to Rutherford B. Hayes, because the swing seat on the investigating Commission was held by Justice Joseph P. Bradley, who voted for his own political party.

In time, we will learn the true impact of *Bush v. Gore* and the Rehnquist Court's activism on the judical body's prestige. But we do so realizing the validity of the words of Justice Anthony Kennedy, another of the "swing justices" on the Court: "Ultimately, the power and the prestige and the respect of the Court depends on trust. My colleagues and I want to be the most trusted people in America." Whether they are or not, will greatly affect America's continued approach to Democracy.[1]

 Questions for Reflection:

1. Do you believe the Supreme Court should have heard and decided the *Bush v. Gore* case, or would American democracy have been better served if the decision were left to other branches of government, e.g. Congress or possibly the Governor of Florida?

▲ **Supporters of the Presidential candidates, George Bush and Al Gore, hold their own "oral argument" outside the United States Supreme Court Building while the disputed Florida voting case is being argued inside.**

2. Knowing the possibility of a "self-inflicted wound" to the Court's prestige, is it worth it to decide a case that might prevent further damage to the nation (as argued by the *Bush v. Gore* majority justices), or lead a reluctant nation in a direction that it might not otherwise go (e.g. *Brown v. Board of Education,* 1954)?

INTRODUCTION:
THE COURTS AND DEMOCRACY

Disputes brought to the Supreme Court by people like George W. Bush and Al Gore illustrate why we should be attentive to the workings of the American court system. All Bush and Gore wanted was justice as each of them saw it, which meant to win the presidency. So did Steven Engel, Estelle Griswold, Jane Roe, Dolores Mapp, Ernesto Miranda, Linda Brown, James E. Swann, and Michael Hardwick. Some of these names may be unfamiliar to you now, (Roe, Miranda, and Brown were all mentioned in the opening case study) but lawyers and scholars of the court immediately recognize their connection with some of the most important Supreme Court cases in the history of this country. (We cover these cases in greater detail in Chapters 13 and 14.)

The judicial decisions made in the cases of these individuals resulted in fundamental changes in our society. Steven Engel's 1962 case resulted in the banning of state-employed teacher-led prayer in public schools. Before Estelle Griswold's case in 1965, the only contraceptive devices available for sale in some states were found on the black market. Before Jane Roe's case in 1973, to have an elective abortion procedure performed women would often have to leave their state, or even the country, or violate the law. Dolores Mapp's and Ernesto Miranda's cases in the 1960s placed limits on police who search a residence or question an individual about crimes. Linda Brown's case in 1954 outlawed segregation in public schools, while James Swann's case in 1971 legitimated busing as a means for achieving school integration.

Whether or not you approve of these changes, they all resulted from decisions made by the Supreme Court. It falls to the Court to interpret definitively the Constitution. In the process, the Court can create new rights or expand, and even dramatically alter, existing ones.

One of the ironies in American democracy is that the Supreme Court, which interprets the Constitution, is the most undemocratic of the three branches of government. Operating in total secrecy, nine unelected, life-tenured jurists sit at the top of a complex legal structure designed to limit rather than encourage appeals, and they have almost total power to say what the law is. But as you will see, despite its undemocratic mode of operating, in the last sixty years the Court has actually helped to expand and protect the rights of Americans. As a result, the Court has helped America approach democracy.

Nearly all issues that make their way to the Supreme Court are raised initially in the lower federal courts or the state judicial systems. The prospect that state courts and federal courts can disagree with each other makes it necessary for a single Supreme Court to resolve those differences.

In this chapter we examine the developing powers of the Supreme Court, the organization of the American court system, the appointment of justices, and the means by which cases are appealed to and then decided by the Supreme Court. We also look at how judges arrive at decisions and, perhaps most important, how those decisions affect both public policy and democracy.

QUOTE ... UNQUOTE

"We are very quiet ... but it is the quiet of a storm center, as we all know."

Justice Oliver Wendell Holmes

The Origins and Development of Judicial Power

Of the three branches of government created by the framers in the Constitution, the judiciary is the least defined, both in its organization and in the nature of its powers. Instead, it was left to the Court to define the nature of its power through its own rulings.

Creating the "Least Dangerous Branch"

The framers outlined the nature of the federal judicial branch in Article III of the Constitution: "The judicial Power of the United States shall be vested in one supreme Court, and in such inferior Courts as Congress may from time to time ordain and establish." As you can see, the framers were vague about the structure of the courts and about how powerful they wanted the courts to be. And in establishing only a Supreme Court, they left it to Congress to design a lower federal court system.

The jurisdiction, or sphere of authority, of the federal courts was also left relatively undefined. Article III establishes that the Supreme Court and the lower federal courts shall decide all legal disputes of a federal nature or those arising under the Constitution, U.S. law, and treaties. In some cases, such as those involving disputes between or among states of the union or involving foreign ambassadors, the Supreme Court will have **original jurisdiction;** that is, it will be the first court to hear the cases. For all other disputes, such as those involving the United States as a party, admiralty or maritime claims, disputes between citizens of two or more different states, and between a citizen and a state, the Court will hear cases on **appellate jurisdiction,** or after the matter has been argued in and decided by a lower federal or state court.

Although the full extent of the Supreme Court's powers was not specified, the framers designed the judiciary to be the least influential and weakest of the three branches of government. Some framers believed that in a representative government, the courts should not have much power because they do not have an explicitly political or representative role. Alexander Hamilton made this argument in *The Federalist*, no. 78: "The judiciary . . . will always be the least dangerous to the political rights of the Constitution. . . . The judiciary . . . has no influence over either the sword or the purse . . . [and it] may be truly said to have neither FORCE nor WILL, but merely judgment."[2]

The framers left it to Congress to be more specific about the organization and jurisdiction of the judiciary. In the Judiciary Act of 1789, Congress established a three-tiered system of federal courts, consisting of district or trial courts, appellate courts, and one Supreme Court. The act also defined more fully the jurisdiction of the Supreme Court, granting it, among other things, the power to review state court rulings that reject federal claims.

Still, the Supreme Court remained weak, and often it had no cases to decide. Chief Justice John Jay (1789–95) was so distressed by the "intolerable" lack of prestige and power of his job that he quit to take a better one—as governor of New York. But the relative weakness of the Court changed in 1803 with the decision in *Marbury v. Madison*.[3]

Marbury v. Madison: The Source of Judicial Power

When the Federalist party lost the election of 1800, outgoing president John Adams, with the help of a lame duck Congress which passed two judiciary acts and confirmed judicial appointments in the Senate, tried to pack the federal courts with appointments from his own party by issuing a number of commissions the night before leaving office. When one of those commissions, the appointment of William

original jurisdiction The authority of a court to be the first to hear a case.

appellate jurisdiction The authority of a court to hear a case on appeal after it has been argued in and decided by a lower federal or state court.

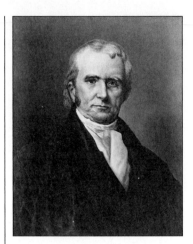

▲ Chief Justice John Marshall (1755–1835) served from 1801 to 1835. His ability to forge unanimous majorities for a series of Supreme Court decisions transformed America from a confederation of states into a nation.

Marbury as justice of the peace for the District of Columbia, was denied by the incoming Jefferson administration, Marbury sued for his post. The case became the landmark *Marbury v. Madison* decision.

The issue in this case was whether the Supreme Court has the power to order federal officials to carry out their official duties, in this case to deliver a judicial commission. This power had been given to the Court by the Judiciary Act of 1789. Chief Justice John Marshall (1801–35), himself an Adams midnight appointee, wrote the Court's opinion. After conceding that the commissions were valid, he then proceeded to move beyond the issue to review the constitutionality of the Judiciary Act of 1789. Since no power to review the constitutionality of any law can be found in the Constitution, Marshall brilliantly used this case to establish just such a power. He argued that since courts interpret law, and the Constitution is a form of law, then the Supreme Court can interpret the Constitution. ·

Thus, Marshall invoked the power of **judicial review,** the power of the Supreme Court to overturn acts of the president, Congress, and the states if those acts violate the Constitution. In assuming the absolute and final power to say what the Constitution means, Marshall helped define the powers of the Court and placed it on an equal footing with the other branches. Marshall then used his newfound judicial review power to deny Marbury his commission. As a result, there was no judicial order for the Jeffersonians to reject, so Marshall's establishment of judicial review stood unchallenged.

Few decisions in the early years of the nation had such a tremendous impact on America's approach to democracy. The Supreme Court now had the power in the system of checks and balances to negate potentially oppressive majority actions taken by the other political branches. Thus, minorities would have a place to go for relief. With the power of judicial review, the Supreme Court was also able to bring various state government actions, both political and judicial, into harmony with the national Constitution, thus altering the federal structure.

Judicial Review: The Court's Ultimate Power

Judicial review has been referred to as the Court's ultimate power because it is awesome and absolute. Professor Edward S. Corwin has called this power "American democracy's way of hedging its bet," meaning that wayward actions by the political branches can always be corrected by the Court.[4] Moreover, judicial review has allowed the Supreme Court to update the Constitution by continually reinterpreting its words to fit new situations.

Over the years, judicial review has become a feature of American government accepted by the political branches, the lower judiciary, and the general public. Since 1803, the Supreme Court has declared around 1,200 provisions of state laws and state constitutions unconstitutional, while exercising the same power with respect to 110 federal executive branch actions and the provisions of nearly 160 federal laws (of more than 95,000 passed).[5] This power can also be used to expand states' rights, as it was at the end of the 1998–99 term when the court voted 5-4 in three separate cases and expanded state immunity from federal claims brought by private parties. Since 1995 the Court has overturned thirty-one federal laws—a record pace—and many of them by a narrow five-to-four majority, a controversial legacy of the Rehnquist Court.

Is judicial review a democratic power? While advocates of judicial review hold that someone has to have the final say over the meaning of the Constitution, others argue that this power is undemocratic because life-tenured, appointed justices can, by a five-vote majority, overrule the collective will of the elected branches. With few mechanism to countermand judicial review directly—the passage of new or modified legislation by Congress, constitutional amendment, or Court reversal—that power is significant. However, although it may appear that judicial review provides the Court with unlimited power, the political branches and the general public do possess considerable power to rein in the Court.

Marbury v. Madison The 1803 case in which Chief Justice John Marshall established the power of judicial review.

judicial review The power of the Supreme Court established in *Marbury v. Madison* to overturn acts of the president, Congress, and the states if those acts violate the Constitution. This power makes the Supreme Court the final interpreter of the Constitution.

Other Powers of the Supreme Court

The Court has two other important powers in addition to the power of judicial review. Using its power of **statutory construction,** the Court can interpret or reinterpret a federal or state law. Since the wording of a law is not always clear, the justices must determine the law's true meaning and apply it to the facts in a specific case. Midway through the 2001 term, in a case involving a woman who claimed that her carpal tunnel syndrome prevented her from gripping the tools on a Toyota assembly line and thus entitled her to benefits under the 1990 federal Americans with Disabilities Act, a unanimous Supreme Court interpreted the word "disabled" to mean that the worker had to prove that he/she was impaired in one or more "major life functions" and not just a particular job. By reading the law narrowly, the Court was using its interpretation of Congress's real intentions from its reading of the preamble of the law to narrow by several times the number of people who would be able to claim benefits under this law.[6]

The power used most frequently by the Supreme Court, though, is the power to do nothing by *refusing to review a case,* thus leaving a lower-court judgment, even one from the states, in force. This the Court did in early 2002 when it refused to hear an appeal by Terry Nichols. Nichols, who had already been convicted and received life in prison in federal court for bombing the Alfred P. Murrah Federal Building in Oklahoma City which killed 168 people, argued that by being tried and facing the death penalty in Oklahoma State criminal court for the bombing, he was being subjected to double-jeopardy in violation of the Fifth Amendment. In its refusal to hear the case, the Court left the lower Oklahoma Court of Criminal Appeals decision against Nichols' claim in force. By refusing to hear Terry Nichols' case, the Court implied that either: 1.) It agreed with the lower-court ruling, 2.) That the issue presented was not significant enough to review, or that 3.) The Court was not yet ready to hear that issue. In using this power to do nothing, the Court can develop its constitutional doctrine incrementally and as it sees fit.

Independence of the Judiciary

The extent of a court's power depends on its independence, that is, to make decisions free of outside influences. The framers were aware of the importance of the court's independence and placed several provisions in the Constitution to keep the Supreme Court free of pressures from the people, Congress, and the president:

1. Justices are appointed not elected; thus, they are not beholden to voters.
2. The power to appoint justices is shared by the president and the Senate; thus, the Court is not beholden to any one person or political party.
3. The justices are guaranteed their position for life, as long as they exhibit "good Behaviour." Even in cases of bad behavior, justices can be impeached only for "High Crimes and Misdemeanors," thus ensuring that the Court cannot be manipulated by the political branches.[7]
4. The Constitution specifies that justices' salaries "shall not be diminished during their Continuance in Office," meaning that Congress cannot lower the Court's salary to punish it for its rulings.

But how much independence does the Court really possess? A great deal, although the Court is not completely shielded from outside influences. Presidents can change the direction of the Court with new appointments. Congress can attack the judiciary's independence through some or all of the following: abolishing all lower federal courts, refusing to raise salaries, using its power to remove certain classes of cases from the appellate docket (thus leaving lower-court rulings in force), changing the number of justices on the Supreme Court, passing a law to reverse a Court decision, trying to impeach a sitting justice, and attacking the Court in speeches.

"Hi, I'm your court-appointed lawyer—whoa! Don't tell me you've been executed already."

statutory construction The power of the Supreme Court to interpret or reinterpret a federal or state law.

QUOTE ... UNQUOTE

"The Supreme Court is like putting nine scorpions in a bottle."

Yale Law Professor Alexander Bickel

Only in a few rare instances has Congress attempted to use any of these methods to threaten the Court's independence. In 1804, impeachment proceedings were brought against rabid Federalist Justice Samuel Chase for his intemperate political remarks against President Thomas Jefferson, but the Senate trial resulted in acquittal, further solidifying the independence of the judiciary. Another effort came in 1957, when a Congress displeased with judicial limits placed on its investigative powers considered the Jenner-Butler Bill, which would have weakened the Court by removing several classes of cases from its appellate docket. Only the efforts of powerful Senate Majority Leader Lyndon Johnson prevented passage of the bill.

At times, mere threats to judicial independence can have an impact on Court decisions. Franklin Roosevelt's court-packing plan failed, but it still resulted in a change of direction among the justices in favor of his New Deal programs. And although the Jenner-Butler Bill failed, Justices Felix Frankfurter (1939–62) and John Marshall Harlan (1955–71) changed their positions and began to uphold Congress's power to investigate.

In 1997, the independence of the judiciary came under serious attack by congressional Republicans led by Congressman Tom DeLay (R.-TX) and Senator Jefferson Beauregard Sessions (R.-AL), the latter a failed judicial nominee. Unhappy with what he called "the liberal activism" of President Clinton's federal judicial appointments, DeLay told the press that federal judges need to be intimidated. "If they don't behave, we're going to go after them in a big way."[8] And go after them, the Republicans did. Judicial nominees found their confirmations delayed or voted down. Some judges were threatened with impeachment; bills were introduced to end life tenure and split the liberal Ninth Circuit Court of Appeals into two circuits, thus giving conservative judges a chance to exercise more power. Other bills were introduced to remove classes of cases from the federal judicial docket, and no salary raises were passed by Congress for the judiciary.[9]

While Congress did routinely delay President Clinton's court appointments, at the end of his eight year term of office he had succeeded in getting 374 federal judges confirmed, comparable to the 382 for Ronald Reagan in his eight years and greater than George Herbert Walker Bush's 193 in his four year term. With George W. Bush in the White House, Senate Majority Leader Trent Lott and Judiciary Committee Chairman Orrin Hatch intended to move quickly on judicial appointments, only to be thwarted by Vermont Senator Jim Jeffords' change in May, 2001 from Republican to Independent status. Jefford's move changed the Senate majority to the Democrats and put Democrat Patrick Leahy of Vermont in charge of the Judiciary Committee. While Senate consideration of President Bush's nominees, especially those with a conservative ideology, slowed considerably during his first year in office, by the end of 2002 a record 94 of the President's 130 nominees to the federal court had been confirmed.

In the end, the Court's greatest protection from political threats to its independence has always come from the people themselves. As long as justices are careful not to get too far ahead of public opinion in their decisions, the public is generally supportive of this branch of government. An independent judiciary that secures the rights and liberties of citizens is a cherished part of the American political landscape, in which the rule of law is paramount. It is also one of the measures of true democracy, as you learned in Chapter 1. Thus, it remains to be seen how long the public will allow this Senate version of political payback to be accepted in the judicial confirmation process.

The Organization of the American Court System

The American judicial system consists of two separate and parallel court systems: an extensive system of state and local courts in which the vast majority of cases are decided, and a system of national or federal courts. Figure 6.1 on page 208 illustrates

APPROACHING DEMOCRACY AROUND THE GLOBE

Democracy and Judicial Independence

In the United States, the concept of judicial independence means that judges are free to make decisions in support of civil liberties and press freedom based on the law and do not feel compelled to comply with the wishes of powerful political leaders. But the degree of judicial independence varies in other nations.

As the accompanying map shows, there is a strong correlation between judicial independence, civil liberties and press freedom support, and democratic government. In democratic countries, judges are usually chosen on the basis of merit rather than politics and cannot be removed from office because of the nature of their decisions. In contrast, in authoritarian regimes judges are more likely to follow the dictates of political leaders and to be disciplined if they do not.

The link between stable, democratic government and full judicial independence can be seen in nations like Australia, Great Britain, Japan, and Scandinavia. The governments of many other nations, such as India, Argentina, Italy, and France, while democratic, are less stable, and their judicial systems have less independence.

The least independent judicial systems are found in countries with authoritarian governments, like China, North Korea, and many African nations. The limited court systems of these countries make few decisions, and the decisions they do make can be overruled by military and party leaders. Judges who make unpopular decisions risk being removed, jailed, or even killed.

And when governments reform, as they have recently in Mexico, Peru, and Afghanistan, one of the first places that change is evident is the increasing independence of the judicial branch.

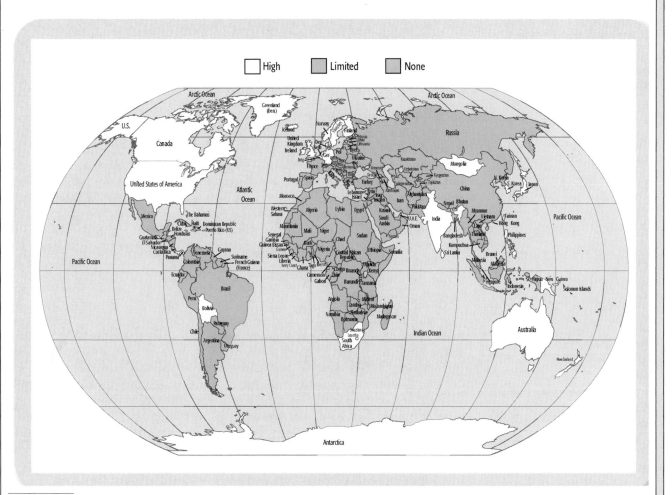

Source: From "Freedom in the World, 2001–2002," Freedom House, at www.freedomhouse.org/research/survey2002.htm. Copyright © 2002 Freedom House. Reprinted by permission.

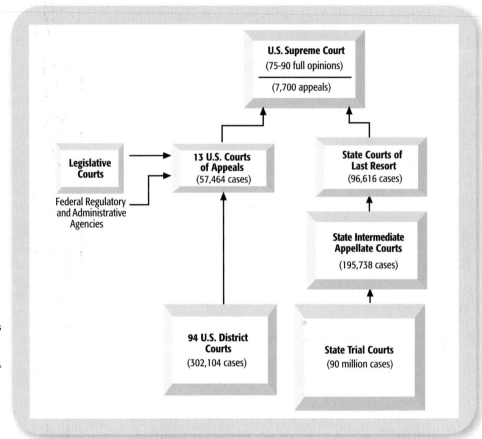

Figure 6.1

Structure of the American Court System

Sources: Federal Judicial Workload Statistics (Washington, D.C.: Administrative Office of the U.S. Courts, 2001); Administrative Office of the U.S. Courts Website, http://www.uscourts/gov; National Center for State Courts, Williamsburg, VA, http://www.ncsonline.org; http://www.ncsc.dni.us/2000AnnlRept.htm/; and 2001 Year End Report on the Federal Judiciary, http://www.supremecourtus.gov/publicinfo/.

how the American court system is structured. These two judicial systems operate independently of each other most of the time. State courts deal with state laws and constitutions, and federal courts deal with federal laws and the U.S. Constitution. But when the state courts handle issues touching on the U.S. Constitution or federal laws, it is possible for a litigant to shift over to the federal system. The extensive lower-court system (all courts beneath the Supreme Court) functions as a gatekeeper, restricting the flow of appeals to the Supreme Court. Appeals come to the Supreme Court from both the highest courts in the fifty states and from the federal appellate courts.

Types of Courts

Federal and state courts are divided into trial and appellate courts. A **trial court** (also known as a *petit court*) is often the point of original entry in the legal system, with a single judge and at times a jury deciding matters both of fact and law in a case. Deciding issues of fact in a case involves determining what actually happened; deciding issues of law involves applying relevant statutes and constitutional provisions to the evidence and conduct of a trial. For instance, in a murder case, deciding a matter of fact would involve the jury's determining a defendant's guilt or innocence based on the evidence admitted into trial. Deciding a matter of law would involve the judge's determining whether certain pieces of evidence, such as a particular witness's testimony, should be admitted into the proceedings.

An **appellate court** reviews the proceedings of the trial court, often with a multijudge panel and without a jury. The appellate court considers only matters of law. Thus, in a murder case the appellate court would not be concerned with the jury's verdict of guilty or innocent; instead, it could reconsider the legality of the trial, such as whether the judge was correct in admitting some of the evidence into trial.

trial court The point of original entry in the legal system, with a single judge and at times a jury deciding matters of both fact and law in a case.

appellate court The court that reviews an appeal of the proceedings of the trial court, often with a multi-judge panel and without a jury; it considers only matters of law.

An appellate court ruling could lead to a new trial if certain evidence is deemed inadmissible.

Types of Cases

Trial and appeals courts hear both criminal and civil cases. In **criminal cases,** decisions are made regarding whether to punish individuals accused of violating the state or federal criminal (or penal) code. Murder, rape, robbery, and assault are covered by the criminal law, as are some nonviolent offenses such as embezzlement and tax fraud. The vast majority of criminal cases are dealt with at the state level, though in recent years Congress, outraged at the nature of some illegal actions, has created many more federal crimes, such as the 1994 Freedom of Access to Clinic Entrances Act that made it a federal crime to prevent access to abortion clinics, the 1996 Church Arson Prevention Act that made burning a church a federal crime, and the 2001 U.S.A. Patriot Act that created a new category of federal crimes of terrorism against mass transit. By 1998, Chief Justice Rehnquist was complaining that "The trend to federalize crimes that traditionally have been handled in state courts . . . threatens to change entirely the nature of our federal system. . . . Federal courts were not created to adjudicate local crimes, no matter how sensational or heinous the crimes may be."[10]

More than 90 percent of criminal cases never come to trial but instead result in private conferences called **plea bargains,** in which the state agrees to press for either a reduced set of charges or a reduced sentence in return for a guilty plea. Plea bargains eliminate the need for a time-consuming trial, thus helping to keep the court system from becoming overloaded.[11]

In **civil cases,** courts resolve private disputes among individuals over finances, property, or personal well-being. Malpractice suits, libel suits, breach of contract suits, and personal injury suits are examples of civil cases. Judicial remedies in such cases can involve a judicial decree, requiring that some action be taken or money be awarded. If a monetary award is involved, it can require both *compensatory damages,* which reimburse a litigant for the harm done by another's actions, and *punitive damages,* which go beyond compensation to punish intentional or reckless behavior that causes harm, seeking to discourage such action in the future. In 2000, a Miami, Florida jury ordered cigarette makers to pay $144.8 billion in punitive and compensatory damages to a large group of Florida smokers who suffered from tobacco-related illnesses.[12]

Large groups of people affected by an action can unite in a **class action suit,** a single civil case in which the results are applicable to all participants. Often class action suits, such as the one mentioned above in Florida are used to compensate victims of large corporations. Sometimes, though, these cases have important policy implications as well. In 2002, a group of seven Bucks County, Pennsylvania, relatives of victims of the September 11th World Trade Center attack filed a class action lawsuit against Osama Bin Laden and his terrorist network, in seeking to dry up their monetary funds worldwide. When the American government froze $80 million, together with the $150 million already frozen, it seemed more possible to fight back against terrorism in this way.[13] As with criminal cases, a great many class action suits and civil cases generally never come to trial because they are settled out of court.

? Question for Reflection: If the majority of criminal and civil cases are settled out of court, how might the organization of the American court system be revised to accommodate this reality and improve the speed with which justice is rendered?

Organization of the Federal Courts

As you've seen, the federal judiciary is organized in three tiers—the U.S. district courts at the bottom, the courts of appeals in the middle, and the Supreme Court at the top. These are all **constitutional courts,** so called because they are mentioned in

criminal cases Cases in which decisions are made regarding whether or not to punish individuals accused of violating the state or federal criminal code.

plea bargains Agreements in which the state presses for either a reduced set of charges or a reduced sentence in return for a guilty plea.

civil cases Noncriminal cases in which courts resolve disputes among individuals and parties to the case over finances, property, or personal well-being.

class action suit A single civil case in which the plaintiff represents the whole class of individuals similarly situated, and the court's ruling applies to this entire class.

constitutional courts Courts mentioned in Article III of the Constitution whose judges are life-tenured.

Article III of the Constitution, the judicial article. All federal constitutional courts are staffed by life-tenured judges or justices.

The **U.S. district courts** are the trial courts serving as the original point of entry for almost all federal cases. There are ninety-four district courts, with at least one in every state, staffed in 2002 by 664 judges. These courts serve as the workhorses of the federal judicial system. More than 302,000 civil and criminal cases are filed here every year. District courts hear cases arising under federal law, national treaties, and the U.S. Constitution, and they review the actions of various federal agencies and departments. In roughly half of the cases, juries are used. Since appealing cases to the next level is expensive and time consuming, for roughly 85 percent of the cases decided at the district court level, the judgment is final.

The next rung on the federal judicial ladder is the **U.S. court of appeals,** consisting in 2002 of 167 judges in thirteen courts. Twelve of these appeals courts are geographically based, eleven of them in multistate geographic regions called *circuits* (see Figure 6.2), so named because Supreme Court justices once literally "rode the circuit" to hear cases. The U.S. Court of Appeals for the Ninth Circuit, for example, covers more than 50 million people in California, Arizona, Nevada, Oregon, Washington, Idaho, Montana, Alaska, and Hawaii. The twelfth circuit court is the U.S. Court of Appeals for the District of Columbia, which hears appeals from federal regulatory commissions and agencies. Because of the important nature of the cases arising from federal agencies and departments, the Court of Appeals in the District of Columbia is viewed by many as the second most important federal court after the Supreme Court. The U.S. Court of Appeals for the Federal Circuit is the thirteenth appeals court; it specializes in appeals involving patents and contract claims against the national government.

Decisions from various circuits vary widely, depending on the political orientation of the judges of those courts. The ninth circuit, containing a majority of liberal Carter and Clinton Democrats, once had twenty-five of twenty-six appeals reversed by the conservative Rehnquist Court, whereas now, the fourth circuit in the Virginia

1. Supreme Court

2. **U.S. district courts** The trial courts serving as the original points of entry for almost all federal cases.

3. **U.S. court of appeals** The middle appeals level of judicial review beyond the district courts; in 2002, consisted of 167 judges in 13 courts, 12 of which are geographically based.

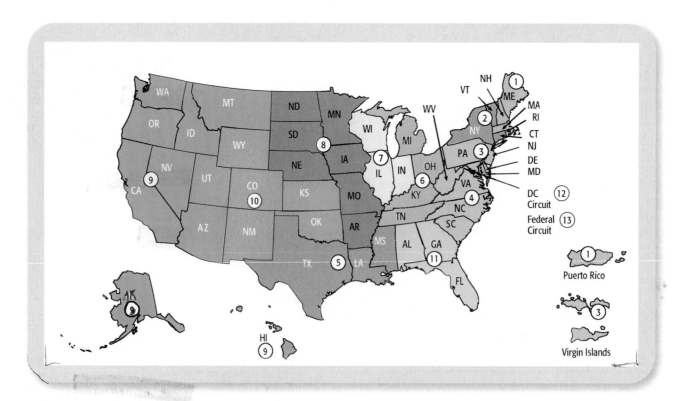

Figure 6.2   The Thirteen Federal Judicial Circuits
Source: Administrative Office of the United States Courts, September 1991.

and Carolina regions and dominated by highly ideological Reagan-Bush conservatives is finding more and more of its controversial decisions accepted for an expected positive review.[14]

Appeals courts usually hear cases in three-judge panels, although sometimes cases are decided in **en banc** proceedings, in which all of the appeals judges in a particular circuit serve as a tribunal. The court of appeals receives more than 57,000 appeals in a year. For the remaining cases, the district court's judgment is left in force.[15] Because so few cases proceed to the Supreme Court, the court of appeals has been described by one prominent judicial scholar as a "mini Supreme Court in the vast majority of cases."[16] This is important because recently the high volume of appeals has led judges to resort to one-word opinions resolving cases, just to clear their dockets—thus creating a two-level justice system for tens of thousands of cases.[17]

In addition to these constitutional appeals courts, the federal judiciary includes **legislative courts** of appeal. Legislative courts are called Article I courts because they are established by Congress based on Article I, Section 8, of the Constitution. These courts are designed to provide technical expertise on specific subjects. Unlike judges on constitutional courts, who are appointed for life, legislative court judges serve for a fixed term. Legislative courts include the U.S. Court of Military Appeals, the U.S. Tax Court, the U.S. Court of Veterans Appeals, and various territorial courts. Any decision by legislative courts can usually be appealed to the constitutional court system. It is under the executive power, though, as outlined at the end of this chapter that President Bush created the new system of Military Tribunals to try selected dangerous terrorism suspects, but here the cases cannot be appealed to the federal civilian court system.

Court Appointments: The Process and the Politics

The process for appointing judges to the federal courts is stated clearly in Article II, Section 2, of the Constitution. There the president is charged with making the appointments, and the Senate is charged with confirming those appointments by majority vote (its "advice and consent" role). While the framers wanted only the most "meritorious" candidates to be selected, politics plays an important part in the process and helps determine which judges end up on the federal bench.

The Supreme Court Appointment Process

At any given time, of the hundreds of people who are qualified for the Supreme Court, only about two dozen people are actively mentioned to fill a vacancy. How does an individual rise to the top and secure an appointment? The process for appointing Supreme Court justices varies depending on the president and the candidate involved, but in general it begins with the collection and sifting of names. When a vacancy occurs, suggestions for the new appointment come into the White House and the Justice Department from politicians, senators, governors, friends of the candidates, the candidate themselves, and even sitting and retired federal judges. This list is then winnowed down to a few top names. A member of the attorney general's staff or the White House staff is then charged with gathering information on these top names. This information-gathering process involves a background check by the Federal Bureau of Investigation (FBI) to determine suitability of character and to uncover any potentially damaging information that might lead to problems with confirmation. A short list of candidates is then forwarded to the president for consideration.

A seat on the Supreme Court is the juiciest plum in the presidential patronage garden. It can go to a highly visible candidate or to someone close to a president. But an equally important consideration is partisanship. Presidents tend to be partisan in their choices, seeking both to reward members of their own party and to see

▲ Ruth Bader Ginsburg signs the Supreme Court's oath card on October 1, 1993, with Chief Justice William Rehnquist and President Bill Clinton looking on. Ginsburg has proven to be not as liberal on the Court as she had been in practicing law.

en banc Proceedings in which all of the appeals judges in a particular circuit serve as a tribunal.

legislative courts Courts designed to provide technical expertise on specific subjects based on Article I of the Constitution.

their own political ideology mirrored on the Court. In addition, representativeness comes into play as do other players, such as the American Bar Association and the Senate.

The Role of Party   Well over 90 percent of the appointees to the Supreme Court have been from the president's own political party. In general, Democrats tend to appoint judges who are willing to extend constitutional and legal protections to the individual and favor government regulation of business. Republicans, on the other hand, tend to appoint judges who are less attentive to individual rights and more willing to defer to the government unless the issue is business, where they favor less government control. Republican George Herbert Walker Bush, appointed David Souter and Clarence Thomas to the Supreme Court, two jurists with philosophies inclined to uphold lower-court and regulatory agency decisions. Democrat Bill Clinton turned instead to Ruth Bader Ginsburg, a leader of the women's rights movement, and Stephen G. Breyer, a strong advocate of individual rights.

But even in trying to fill the Court with people of a similar mind-set, presidents are sometimes unpleasantly surprised. What a person *was* can be a poor predictor of what he or she *will become* on the Supreme Court. Although some scholars estimate that over 70 percent of the time presidents get exactly the sort of appointee they are expecting, but miscalculations do happen.[18] Conservative president Dwight Eisenhower appointed Earl Warren (1953–69) and William Brennan (1956–90) to the Court on the assumption that they were conservatives. Warren's prior work as California governor and Brennan's as a New Jersey State Supreme Court justice turned out to reveal little about how they might decide cases. They became two of the Court's great liberals. When asked at the end of his career what he thought in retrospect about the Warren appointment, Eisenhower replied: "It's one of the two biggest mistakes I made in my administration." (The other, Ike indicated elsewhere, was Brennan's appointment.)[19] Essentially, the immense responsibilities of the office, the weight of the history of a Court seat, and interaction with new colleagues on the bench can all combine to create a very different kind of jurist than expected.

Recently, presidents have tried to sharpen their ability to predict the ideology of their Supreme Court appointments and improve their chances for Senate confirmation by selecting candidates who are judges on the courts of appeals, where their prior judicial records might offer some clues regarding future decisions. This changes the kind of Court that is assembled. For instance, while the 1941–42 Roosevelt Court consisted of a Harvard law professor, two U.S. senators, a chair of the Securities and Exchange Commission, three former attorneys general, a solicitor general, and a U.S. attorney, the 2002 Court consists of a Justice Department official, a state Court of Appeals judge (prior to that the majority leader of the state senate), and seven U.S. court of appeals judges. The result is a Court that operates in a more bureaucratically judicial fashion as the Justices take fewer cases, decide them in an incremental fashion, and write the opinions very narrowly.

Seeking to accomplish the aim of a more ideologically-suitable set of judicial appointments, President Bush has put White House counsel Alberto Gonzales, a Hispanic attorney who many rate highly as a possible appointee to the Supreme Court should a vacancy occur, in charge of vetting possible nominees as to their conservative judicial philosophy. To accomplish this goal, Gonzales has assembled an ad hoc group of 15 to 20 staffers and Justice Department appointees to review the credentials of, and interview, possible nominees in order to prepare lists of appointment prospects for Attorney General Ashcroft and President Bush.

Seeking a More Representative Court   Over the years the representative nature of the Court has become an issue, and a number of categories have emerged to guide presidents in selecting nominees. These include geography, religion, race, and gender. Presidents have used these factors to create a sort of "balanced" Court that keeps various constituencies satisfied.

▲ The efforts of White House Counsel Alberto Gonzales to lead the staffing of the federal judiciary will be greatly benefited by the Republicans' takeover of the Senate after the 2002 election, and some think may lead to his appointment as the first Hispanic member of the Supreme Court.

FYI

The oldest justice ever to serve on the Court was Oliver Wendell Holmes, at age ninety, while the youngest was Joseph Story in the early 1800s, at age thirty-two. The longest-serving jurist on the Court was William O. Douglas (thirty-six years, seven months), while the shortest tenure was served by James F. Byrnes (fifteen months).

An effort has always been made to have all geographical regions of the country represented on the Court. "Wiley, you have geography," Franklin Roosevelt told Iowan Wiley Rutledge (1943–49) when explaining his impending appointment to a Court whose only "non-Easterner," William O. Douglas (1939–75), had been raised in Yakima, Washington, although he actually lived on the East Coast since his law school years.[20] Religion also plays a role. For more than one hundred years there was a so-called Catholic seat on the Court. The appointment of Louis Brandeis (1916–39) created a Jewish seat that remained until 1969 (and some believe was resumed in 1993). An African American seat was established by Thurgood Marshall's appointment (1967–91). Clarence Thomas (1991–present), also an African American, was appointed to fill that seat when Marshall retired. Sandra Day O'Connor's appointment (1981-present) seems to have established a female seat. There is now a growing movement within the Hispanic community for the establishment of a new seat for that ethnic group.

Judicial scholars continue to debate whether considering such representational factors is the proper way to staff the Court.[21] Many believe that merit should be the primary consideration. Some argue that given the small number of Court seats and the large number of interest groups, satisfying everyone is virtually impossible. It is believed that the recent appointments of Ruth Bader Ginsburg, the second woman on the Court, and Stephen Breyer, the Court's other Jewish member, were based on merit, and that merit may be beginning once again to outweigh representational factors. Most appealing about Ginsburg were her accomplishments as a leading lawyer in the women's movement. In Breyer's case, his background as an effective appeals court judge played a greater role than his religion. Still, political considerations are unavoidable in a democracy. Recent administrations have tried to appease their constituencies by mentioning during the initial winnowing-down process that candidates from various categories are "under consideration." But they then select appointees based on other factors.

The Role of the American Bar Association   It used to be the case that a short list of candidate names was submitted by the president to the American Bar Association (ABA), a national association for the legal profession, for an informal review by its Standing Committee on the Federal Judiciary, before making an appointment. This review is performed by attorneys who canvas judges and lawyers throughout the country regarding the nominees' qualifications. Based on these inquiries, ratings for nominees for the Supreme Court fall into the categories of "highly qualified," "not opposed," or "not qualified." Candidates for the lower courts are rated on a scale of "well qualified," "qualified," or "not qualified."[22] Although the intent is to seek out information on the nominee's professional qualifications, personal and ideological considerations inevitably arise as well.

In general, since there is no requirement to consult the ABA, if the president has settled on a nominee, a negative rating by this group will have little effect.[23] Conservatives became unhappy with the ABA after it issued a mixed review for Robert Bork in 1987 and four years later gave its worst rating ever for Clarence Thomas, with George Herbert Walker Bush, still appointing him to the Court, calling Thomas the "most-qualified lawyer in America." Because of the Republican Senate's unhappiness with the results of the ABA's judicial surveys, the Senate Judiciary Committee, under Republican Orrin Hatch (R.-UT), stopped using their reports. When the political orientation of the presidency and the Senate Judiciary Committee shifted in 2001, with the election of Republican President George W. Bush and the political party switch of Jim Jeffords which changed the Senate to Democratic control, the President announced that, despite the half-century tradition, he would no longer use the ABA review process. Instead, the reports were sent to the Senate Judiciary Committee for use by the Democrats.

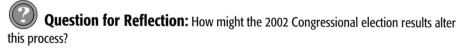 **Question for Reflection:** How might the 2002 Congressional election results alter this process?

▲ Judge Robert Bork testifies before the Senate Judiciary Committee in a nationally televised confirmation hearing in 1987, saying that serving on the Court would be an "intellectual feast." Bork was eventually denied his seat on the Court.

APPROACHING DIVERSITY

F.W.O.T.S.C.: Sandra Day O'Connor

In the 1980 presidential election, Ronald Reagan promised to appoint a woman to the Supreme Court. And, when he made good on that promise, what a difference it has made. By 2001, she was universally being recognized as "The most powerful woman in America." Ever since she arrived on the Court, Sandra Day O'Connor has called herself the F.W.O.T.S.C., or the First Woman on the Supreme Court. She used to tell a joke about herself and what women were like on the Supreme Court: "If you've seen one, you've seen 'em all."

Since that time she has been the woman in the middle, most often holding the key swing vote for the narrowly balanced Court—including in the *Bush v. Gore* decision. It was her vote in 1993 that made the crucial difference on the issue of whether the abortion decision, *Roe v. Wade,* would be overturned. The same has been true on the issue of sexual harassment in the schools. In that case there was a memorable scene as members of the Court presented their views. O'Connor and Justice Anthony Kennedy both summarized their majority and dissenting views and seemed to have much in common. Both were westerners in their 60s, both Stanford University graduates, both appointees of Ronald Reagan, and each the parent of three grown children. But their difference in gender made for very different opinions in this case. Justice O'Connor spoke for the majority in ruling that public school districts should be held accountable for the sexual harassment by one student on another because severe harassment can affect the learning environment in the classroom. Kennedy argued that the federal government had no reason to intrude into the local schools on this matter, but he could only get three votes for his dissent. The fact that the two jurists were long-time allies on the question of states' rights made their differences here even more remarkable.

Once Ruth Bader Ginsburg joined the Court she amplified the differences of having two women on the Court. Both had graduated from top law schools—Columbia for Ginsburg and Stanford for O'Connor—only to find the top jobs in the legal profession closed to them. O'Connor only got offers as a legal secretary, and Felix Frankfurter said of Ginsburg's application for his clerkship that she could not have it because she "did not wear pants."

Years later, the two women could end this bias from the Court. During the announcement of the end of the gender bias of the Virginia Military Institute, Ginsburg looked across at Sandra Day O'Connor as the Court ruled the all-male school unconstitutional. Later she would note that in citing O'Connor's 1982 ruling against the exclusion of males from the Mississippi University for Women, an all-female nursing school, that decision was 5-4, while the VMI ruling was 7-1. "What occurred in the intervening years in the Court, as elsewhere in society?" asked Ginsburg. Then citing Shakespeare, the justice added, "Haply a woman's voice may do some good."

▲ Sandra Day O'Connor, the first woman to be appointed to the U.S. Supreme Court and a moderate conservative, frequently casts the deciding vote in cases now being reviewed by the Court, resulting in 5–4 conservative decisions.

Some Court observers now think that the presence of two women on the Court makes change even easier for both of them. "Having two makes a huge difference," says law professor Peter J. Rubin. "It just makes it a lot easier. It's only human nature. You're in an insulated environment. You're not out there on the ground. When two colleagues who have had different experiences say that here is a problem to be taken very seriously, it's bound to have an impact." But, as Justice O'Connor made clear after the *Bush v. Gore* decision, the job is not an easy one. "It was a difficult case. It's too bad that it came up," she told NBC correspondent Jane Pauley, "[W]e don't enjoy being thrust into the middle of political controversy. We don't always have a choice in what comes here."

One can only imagine what a difference it will make on the Court if the next president chooses to appoint an Hispanic to the Court, or appoint Justice O'Connor, who expresses "no present plans to retire" to replace a retiring William Rehnquist as Chief Justice.

Source: Adapted from Linda Greenhouse, "From the High Court, a Voice Quite Distinctly a Woman's," *New York Times,* May 26, 1999, p. 1. ————"O'Connor: *Bush v. Gore* Difficult Decision to Make," *Houston Chronicle,* January 27, 2002; and Jeffrey Rosen, "A Majority of One," *New York Times,* June 3, 2001.

The Role of the Senate   As we saw earlier, the Constitution charges the Senate with confirming Supreme Court appointments by majority vote. The Senate confirmation process begins with a Senate Judiciary Committee hearing designed to elicit views about a candidate. The committee then makes a recommendation for or against a candidate prior to a vote of the full Senate. Over the years, Senate confirmation has proven to be a significant hurdle, resulting in the rejection of nearly one in five presidential nominations.

In general, the president initially has the upper hand in the appointment process, but the Senate can oppose a nominee for a variety of reasons. Some rejections are due to unhappiness with the candidate's competence or political views. The Senate rejected G. Harrold Carswell in 1971, citing a lack of competence—but not before Nebraska senator Roman Hruska defended Carswell by saying: "Even if he is mediocre there are a lot of mediocre judges and people and lawyers. They are entitled to a little representation, aren't they?"[24]

Other rejections have to do with partisan politics. A Democratic Senate may oppose the conservative candidate favored by a Republican president. In 1987, Republican president Ronald Reagan's appointee Robert Bork was confronted by a Senate Judiciary Committee controlled by the opposing Democratic party. After a massive media campaign by a coalition of liberal interest groups, vigorous questioning from the Judiciary Committee, and with the tide of public opinion turning against him, the intellectually qualified Bork was defeated because of his ultraconservative views, well documented in a trail of paper that spanned his entire career.[25] Some rejections may result from Senate opposition to the president or may be intended to send a message of opposition to the current direction of the Court.

Timing seems to be important in the success of a nomination. If a nomination comes early in a president's term or during a period of presidential popularity, the Senate is more likely to allow a nomination to succeed. Should it come late in the term or be made by a weak president, however, there is greater potential for a difficult confirmation. For instance, Bork's troubled nomination came in the next-to-last year of Reagan's presidency, while neither of Bill Clinton's nominations, made in his first two years in office, met with significant opposition.

Sometimes a nominee is challenged because of information uncovered in the Judiciary Committee investigation. When Clarence Thomas was nominated by George Herbert Walker Bush, in 1991, charges were launched by law professor Anita Hill that she had been sexually harassed by Thomas while working for him in the Equal Employment Opportunity Commission (EEOC). The televised hearings were dramatic, with Senator Arlen Specter accusing Professor Hill of "flat-out perjury," and women's rights groups demanding that the nomination be defeated. In the end, Thomas was confirmed by a razor-thin 52 to 48 margin.[26]

In the twentieth century, the Senate sought greater influence in the confirmation process. After approving all Supreme Court candidates for nearly forty years, the Senate began to use its "advice and consent" role to such an extent that since 1968 it has turned down four nominees (Abe Fortas, G. Harrold Carswell, Clement Haynsworth, and Robert Bork), forced the withdrawal of another (Douglas Ginsburg), and significantly attacked two other candidates (William Rehnquist for chief justice, and Clarence Thomas).[27] The recent increase in importance of the Senate in this process has come about because of a heightened interest by the general public in Supreme Court confirmations since the Bork battle in 1987. Moreover, the televising of confirmation hearings and floor debates has made senators more conscious of the politics of the appointment process. Finally, the increased lobbying activity of interest groups, which now mount election-style media campaigns, has whipped up considerable public pressure on voting senators.

To counter this newfound willingness by the Senate to question seriously and even reject nominees, presidents have devised new appointment strategies. First, they have searched for "safe" candidates, ones lacking a large body of writing or decisions that are easy targets for attack. Seeking to avoid the problems faced by the highly visible and widely published legal scholar Bork, two years later President George Herbert Walker Bush, appointed a little-known Court of Appeals judge from Weare, New Hampshire, David Souter. Because there was no paper trail to provide any inkling of Souter's leanings, he became known as the "stealth candidate."

Presidents have also appointed friends and protégés of prominent senators, in hopes that the senator will lead the confirmation fight in the Senate. Clarence Thomas's nomination was greatly helped by his mentor, Republican Senator John Danforth of Missouri, while Stephen Breyer's nomination was helped along by the advocacy of a fellow Massachusetts resident, Senator Ted Kennedy. President Clinton consulted with powerful members of the Senate, including opposing party members, prior to any appointment, seeking to eliminate any names that might cause difficulty. Thus, Secretary of the Interior Bruce Babbitt was dropped from the appointment list in 1994, when conservative Republican Senator Orrin Hatch of Utah objected to his liberal philosophy.[28]

This search for "safe" candidates could have an impact on the nature of the Court. Highly qualified but also highly controversial legal scholars are now being passed over for appointment by presidents fearful of Senate rejection. In the past, controversial candidates such as Felix Frankfurter and William O. Douglas had a tremendous impact on the Court's direction. Some judicial scholars wonder whether this avoidance of talented but risky candidates will result in a Court that is unwilling to expand its decision-making role or make controversial decisions. Such a trend is impossible to predict, of course, because of the politics of appointment and the development of jurists once on the Court.

? Question for Reflection: How has the process of selecting Supreme Court Justices in the twentieth century affected the types of candidates considered? How does this approach conform with Article II, Section 2 of the Constitution and the framers' desire that the most "meritorious" candidates be selected?

The Impact of Presidential Appointments on the Supreme Court

Although every appointment to the Court is important, not every appointment changes the direction of the Court. Commonly a Supreme Court is named after its chief justice, such as the Rehnquist Court, but because philosophical directional changes occur within those years, it would be better to categorize a Court according to the president who redirected it through judicial appointments.

In recent history, three presidents—Kennedy, Nixon, and Reagan—have dramatically changed the direction of the Court. In 1962, Democratic president John F. Kennedy shifted an ideologically balanced moderate-conservative Court to a more liberal one by replacing the moderate-conservative Justice Frankfurter with the more liberal Arthur Goldberg (1962–65). In doing so, Kennedy assured a solid 5 to 4 vote in favor of civil rights and liberties cases. After Richard Nixon was elected on a "law and order" platform in 1968, his four conservative appointments to the Supreme Court—William Rehnquist, Lewis Powell, Harry Blackmun, and Warren Burger—moved the Court in a more conservative direction, away from individual rights. After his election to the presidency in 1980, Ronald Reagan's four appointments—Sandra Day O'Connor, Antonin Scalia, Anthony Kennedy, and William Rehnquist as chief justice—created a Court able to reverse earlier rulings in such areas as defendants' rights. Thus, the rights of Americans can expand and contract as a result of their president's choices.

Although presidents expect their legacy of Supreme Court appointments to live long after them (with the exception of William Howard Taft, who appointed sixty-six-year-old Edward White as chief justice, hoping that he would die shortly and leave the opening for Taft himself—which, in fact, did happen), fate sometimes dictates otherwise. The much-celebrated New Deal Court changed direction in late

1949 when liberals Frank Murphy (1940–49) and Wiley Rutledge (1943–49) died suddenly, to be replaced by moderate conservatives Tom Clark (1949–67) and Sherman Minton (1949–56). The current Rehnquist Court has been reshaped by two retirements—conservative Democrat Byron White and Republican Harry Blackmun, who was expected to be a conservative but evolved into a liberal.

Thus far, Bill Clinton's appointments of moderate liberals Ruth Bader Ginsburg and Stephen Breyer have failed to move a conservative court toward the moderate center. This conservative trend, often by 5 to 4 votes, occurs because Justices Anthony Kennedy and Sandra Day O'Connor have shifted to the conservative side, to vote frequently with Justices Rehnquist, Scalia, and Thomas. Clinton's hope of redirecting the Court toward a more moderate, and perhaps more liberal, direction went unfulfilled. With three Justices on the evenly balanced Supreme Court over 70 years old and rumors floating that Chief Justice Rehnquist, and perhaps others, might step down, the Republicans' takeover of the Senate after the 2002 election will give President Bush an opportunity to change the direction of the Court through his future appointments, relatively unimpeded by the partisan confirmation process.

Staffing the Lower Federal Courts

The real impact of the presidential appointment power comes not so much at the Supreme Court level as at the lower federal court level. With hundreds of appointments of life-tenured judges here, and more than 99.9 percent of all federal cases never reaching the Supreme Court, these appointments determine the direction of American law for many years to come. The legacy of a president's lower-court appointments will last for about two decades after the end of that president's term of office.[29]

The formal selection process for the lower federal courts is roughly the same as for the Supreme Court. Guided by officials in the Justice Department and White House, the president nominates candidates who have first been screened by the FBI. The candidates' names are then sent to the Senate Judiciary Committee, which consults the ABA report in beginning the confirmation proceedings. But there is one important difference in the selection process for lower-court judges. For federal district court appointments, presidents observe the practice of **senatorial courtesy** by submitting the names of nominees to senators from the same political party who are also from the nominee's home state. Failure to do so might lead to a senator declaring that a candidate is "personally obnoxious," dooming the appointment. Other senators, wishing to preserve the practice of senatorial courtesy for their own use in the future, will follow the first senator's lead and vote against the nomination. In these ways, senatorial courtesy has forced presidents to share their nomination power with the Senate.[30] In fact, in many cases the names of prospective candidates are forwarded to the White House by the senators from the president's party and the candidate's state (and sometimes even from powerful senators in the other party) prior to the nomination decision. These candidates often become the nominee.

A president's ability to use the appointment power to shape the lower federal court is determined by length of service in the White House, the number of vacancies that arise during that time, and whether the Senate confirms the nominees. There is also the possibility that Congress can expand the lower-court system, creating new seats to be filled. One-term President Jimmy Carter made 258 appointments, while two-term president Ronald Reagan made 382. When Republican George Herbert Walker Bush's 193 appointments are combined with the holdovers from previous Republican administrations, we see that approximately 65 percent of the lower federal judiciary was appointed by the Republican party. By the end of Bill Clinton's first term of office, he had filled over one-fifth of the federal judiciary. By the end of Clinton's administration he had appointed 374 judges, or roughly 45 percent of the federal court judges. However, even at that time, there were still well

senatorial courtesy A procedure in which a president submits the names of judicial nominees to senators from the same political party who are also from the nominee's home state for their approval prior to formal nomination.

over 40 percent of the appointees from the Reagan/Bush administrations left on the federal bench.

Recent presidents have clearly sought to leave their mark on the composition of the federal bench. President Jimmy Carter sought to make the court system more representative of the general population. After years of largely white male appointments, in 1976 Carter created merit selection panels for choosing nominees to the appeals courts. Charged with searching for more diverse candidates as opposed to those that were just politically well connected, these panels identified qualified female, African American, and Hispanic prospects. As a result, more than one-third of Carter's appointments were from these underrepresented groups.[31]

The Reagan administration abandoned the merit selection process, seeking instead to correct a perceived liberal bias on the federal courts. The President's Committee on Federal Judicial Selection was created to give the administration centralized ideological control over the selection process. In addition to the usual background checks, extensive written surveys and lengthy personal interviews were conducted to determine the nature and degree of the conservatism of the candidates. The result was, in the words of one judicial selection expert, "the most consistent ideological or policy-orientation screening of judicial candidates since the first term of Franklin Roosevelt."[32] And the change in the gender and ethnic composition of nominees was dramatic. Far fewer women, African Americans, and Hispanics were nominated (see Figure 6.3). Although the George Herbert Walker Bush administration ended the overt screening of candidates for conservatism, ideology remained as much a consideration as under the Reagan administration. Nonetheless, the Bush administration appointed more women to the federal bench than even Carter had (19.5 percent to 15.5 percent). Over 25 percent of Bush's appointments to the federal bench were women and minorities.

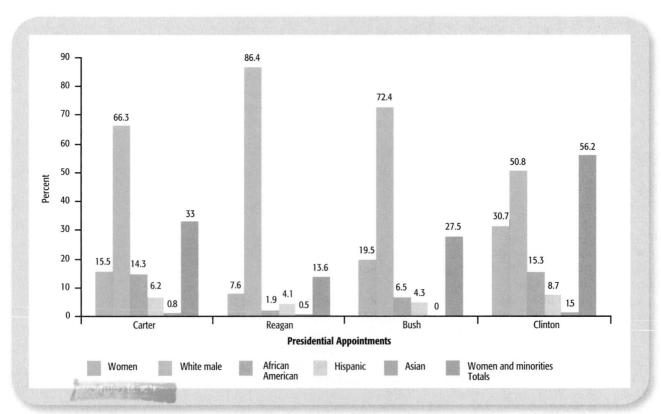

Figure 6.3   Presidential Appointments of Minorities on the Lower Federal Courts

Source: Sheldon Goldman, et al., "Clinton's Judges: Summing Up the Legacy," *Judicature,* vol. 84, #5, Mar./Apr. 2001, pp. 228–54. Sheldon Goldman and Matthew D. Saronson, "Clinton's Nontraditional Judges: Creating a More Representative Bench," *Judicature 78,* no. 2 (September/October 1994), pp. 68–73; Sheldon Goldman and Elliot Slotnick, "Clinton's First-Term Judiciary: Many Bridges to Cross," *Judicature 80,* no. 6 (May/June 1997), p. 254; Sheldon Goldman and Elliot Slotnick, "Picking Judges Under Fire," *Judicature 86,* no. 6 (May/June 1999), pp. 265–278.

In his eight years of office, Clinton sought to make the courts even more representative and in the process made history because of the highly representative nature of his federal judicial appointments. Compared with the last four presidential administrations, Clinton appointed the greatest percentage of African American and female judges, resulting in historic highs in each category. Well over one of every two of his appointments were women and minorities, resulting in a federal judiciary in which 32 percent of the judges in 2002 now come from these groups (representing a 68 percent increase during Clinton's presidency).[33] Although these percentages do not mirror the proportion of these groups in the total population, the percentage of women on the federal bench is now much closer to the percentage of women in the legal profession, and the percentage of African Americans on the bench is more than two times the proportion of African Americans in that profession.[34]

As outlined in the Road to American Democracy box, since the Robert Bork failed Supreme Court nomination in 1987 presidents have found it increasingly difficult to reshape the federal judiciary due to Senate opposition. The Democratic-controlled Senate Judiciary Committee refused to confirm fifty-two of George Herbert Walker Bush's nominees, affording incoming president Bill Clinton the opportunity to fill 13 percent of the judiciary seats. After the 1996 Congressional elections, the Republican-dominated Judiciary Committee, led by Utah's Orrin Hatch, held up Bill Clinton's appointments even to the point of not allowing hearings on many names. The result was a backlog of nearly one hundred vacancies on the lower federal judiciary, or 12 percent. Senate Republicans urged the new, President George W. Bush, to send forward nominations as quickly as possible to staff the judiciary with conservatives. When the Democratic Party took control of the Senate in early 2001, Democratic Senator Patrick Leahy led the Judiciary Committee to slow down consideration of the President's nominations to the point that by early 2002 there were roughly 100 vacancies on the federal bench. This apparent "court-blocking" strategy, as it has been labeled by political scientists Sheldon Goldman and Elliot Slotnick, has put great pressure on the independence of the judiciary, much in the fashion of Roosevelt's court-packing plan of 1937. It also raises questions of whether there will be a political "payback" if the Republicans retain control of the Senate and the Democrats should retake control of the White House in 2004.[35]

 Question for Reflection: How is this politically motivated approach to appointing judges affecting our democracy? What could be done to alter the "court blocking" strategy employed by the opposition party to presidential nominations?

How the Supreme Court Operates   *Important*

How many times have you heard someone involved in a legal dispute proclaim defiantly, "I'm going to appeal this case all the way to the Supreme Court!"? Because of the importance of his lawsuit for the nation, George W. Bush had the opportunity to do this, but the chances of someone else following in his footsteps are less than those of being struck by lightning. In other words, a successful appeal to the Supreme Court is extremely rare. The reason, as you have already learned, has to do partly with the number of cases that are decided conclusively on their way to and through the intermediate appeals level. But it also has to do with the methods the Supreme Court uses to select the cases it will hear.

Each year the Supreme Court receives well over 7,000 appeals. Of these, just over 1 percent, or roughly seventy-five to ninety cases, are placed on the Court's **docket,** or agenda, having been accepted for full review with oral argument. Nearly all of these cases are decided by a full written opinion. But a few will be decided *per curiam,* in a brief, unsigned, generally unanimous opinion by the Court. The lower-court judgment is left in effect for cases not accepted by the Court for review.

docket The Supreme Court's agenda of cases to consider.

THE ROAD TO DEMOCRACY:

The "Borking" of the Federal Judiciary

"Forgive and remember!" According to former New York Senator Daniel Patrick Moynihan, this is the slogan that now governs Washington. Nothing proves the slogan better than the effect the rejection of conservative former Court of Appeals Judge Robert Bork for the pivotal 1987 Supreme Court vacancy created by the retirement of swing justice Lewis Powell had on the confirmation process. Consideration and rejection of nominees based on ideology rather than on the merit of the candidate were the lessons learned from that battle and were still being applied in March of 2002, when District Court judge Charles W. Pickering became a candidate for the Fifth Circuit Court of Appeals.

THAT WAS THEN . . .

The 1987 Bork nomination was the turning point in the confirmation process of federal court judges when the Democratically-controlled Judiciary Committee, chaired by Senator Joseph Biden (D.-DE), used everything at its disposal to defeat the nomination. In confirmation hearings run on prime time television, a coalition of liberal interest groups, called People for an American Way, under the chairmanship of Ralph Neas, and the Alliance for Justice, under Nan Aron, charged that Bork would move the constitution in a conservative direction, using ads in newspapers and on television that created more of a circus-like election atmosphere than an inquiring Senate confirmation hearing environment. At one point, journalists even attempted to secure the list of Bork's video rentals seeking to make statements about his views and morals.

The rejection of Bork's nomination in a close vote did not end this confirmation practice as Democrats then attacked Clarence Thomas's nomination to the Supreme Court in 1991, accusing him of once sexually harassing Professor Anita Hill. After Thomas complained that he was being subjected to a "high-tech lynching," he was confirmed by a narrow four vote margin.

With the Republicans, under Utah's Orrin Hatch, in control of the Senate Judiciary Committee, Bill Clinton found it difficult to get his nominees for the federal courts confirmed, or even considered, by the committee. As a result scores of vacancies in the judicial system went unfilled. One of the main examples of this practice came when Missouri Supreme Court Justice Ronnie White was rejected by a 54 to 45 margin for the federal District Court because of the opposition of both of his then home state Senators, Christopher "Kit" Bond and John Ashcroft. Ashcroft objected to White's "indications of potential activism" and a "very serious bias against the death penalty."

THIS IS NOW . . .

As George W. Bush's administration began in 2000 with a Republican-controlled Senate, quick confirmation of judicial nominations was anticipated. However, Vermont

► The only known photograph of the Supreme Court hearing oral arguments was taken secretly in June 1932 by Dr. Erich Solomon, who smuggled a camera into the courtroom. From left to right are Justices Owen Roberts, Pierce Butler, Louis D. Brandeis, Willis Van Devanter, Chief Justice Charles Evans Hughes, George Sutherland, Harlan Fiske Stone, and Benjamin Cardozo. The empty seat was that of Justice James C. McReynolds.

Nearly all of the Court's cases come from its *appellate jurisdiction,* cases that have already been reviewed and decided by one or more federal or state courts. About 90 percent of the appellate cases come from the lower federal courts, with most coming up the one step from the court of appeals. The 10 percent of cases coming from state courts must raise a *federal question* and have exhausted all possible state appeals in order to jump to the Supreme Court. This usually means that state cases come

Senator Jim Jeffords' party allegiance switch from Republican to Independent in 2001 put the Democrats in charge of the Senate and the Judiciary Committee, trapping President Bush's judicial nominations in the same sluggish confirmation process that both Bill Clinton and his father, George Herbert Walker Bush, had seen. After approving 42 nominees to federal courts, albeit very slowly in the minds of Republicans, Judiciary Committee head Senator Patrick Leahy and the Democrats decided to make a stand on Federal District Court Charles W. Pickering's nomination for the Fifth Circuit Court of Appeals. Charges were made in a month long battle leading up to a fight in the Judiciary Committee about Pickering's lack of judicial competence, resulting in a series of reversals of his decisions by the Fifth Circuit Court of Appeals that he now sought to join, and that he was not sensitive to the claims of African Americans in his Court, often inserting his personal views into his opinions. Research by Neas' and Aron's liberal interest group organizations uncovered a 1959 law review article by Pickering that promoted means by which a Mississippi law against interracial marriage could be strengthened. Republicans, complaining that opponents were trying to tar Pickering as a racist, pointed out that he had prosecuted the KKK in the late 1960s and had many African-American supporters from his home state of Mississippi. Fearing the future vote, President Bush complained, "We are seeing a disturbing pattern where too often judicial confirmations are turned into ideological battles that delay justice and hurt our democracy." It was the same claim that Democrats had been making about the Republicans in the Senate during Bill Clinton's presidency. In the Pickering nomination though, there never was a Senate vote because a straight line party vote, in March 2002, resulted in Pickering's nomination not even getting out of committee. When Republicans complained about this treatment, Democrats in the "forgive and remember" philosophy, cited the case of their nominee Michael Schattman, who never got a hearing for his judicial nomination over a three year period and finally withdrew his name.

But a Presidential counselor, Karl Rove, made clear to the Family Research Council, a key Christian political action committee, that for the administration the fight was just beginning: "... This is not about a good man, Charles Pickering. This is about the future. This is about the U.S. Supreme Court. And this is about sending George W. Bush a message that, 'You send us somebody that is a strong conservative, you're not going to get him.'" But Rove added, defiantly, "Guess what? ... They sent the wrong message to the wrong guy." Indeed, with the Republican takeover of the Senate as a result of the 2002 elections, experts predicted that Charles Pickering and other conservative appointees who had languished in the Judiciary Committee would soon be sent to the floor for a vote. With the President calling for reform of the confirmation process, there was also speculation as to whether Chief Justice William Rehnquist would step down, leading to a conservative replacement.

Source: Edward Walsh, "Confirmation Fight: Replay and Review," *Washington Post,* March 14, 2002; ———, "Judicial Game Cycles On," *Los Angeles Times,* January 21, 2002; and Jay Bookman, "GOP 'Borkers' Righteously Slam 'Borking,'" *Atlanta Constitution,* March 21, 2002.

from the state court of last resort, though they need not do so. The second source of Court cases is its *original jurisdiction,* which as you learned earlier, involves cases seeking to resolve disputes among states and cases affecting foreign ambassadors. The Court hears few original jurisdiction cases today.

Selecting Cases

The rules for appealing a case to the Court have been established by congressional legislation. Appellate cases come to the Court through a formal writ called a **writ of certiorari,** a Latin term meaning "to be made more certain." Established in 1925, this discretionary writ enables the Court to accept cases for review only if there are "special and important reasons therefore." Essentially, the Court will consider accepting a case for review if it raises issues that affect society or the operation of government. You will recall that the *Bush v. Gore* case was accepted for review to determine the winner of the 2000 Presidential election, even though some thought that it was a "political question" best left to the determination of political bodies such as Congress. Following legislation passed by Congress in 1988, the Court now has virtually total discretion over the cases it will hear.

All of the justices (except John Paul Stevens, whose own clerks assist him) rely on a group of law clerks in a "cert pool" to do the initial screening of the appeals. The clerks divide up all of the petitions, summarize a portion of them in memo form,

writ of certiorari A Latin term meaning "to be made more certain;" this is a writ that enables the Court to accept cases for review only if there are "special and important reasons therefore."

and then submit their recommendations for acceptance or rejection to the justices.[36] This procedure now appears to some to make the law clerks into an intermediate court of review, as the justices form their own judgments about which cases are worthy of review on the basis of these initial evaluations.

The justices meet twice weekly to decide which appeals to accept. To speed up the decision process, appeals deemed worthy of consideration are placed on a "discuss list" by the chief justice at the request of any member of the Court. The remainder of the appeals are put on a "dead list," and unless at least one justice asks for further consideration, those appeals are denied by the Court without further discussion. The Court then votes on the cases on the discuss list. In what is known as the **rule of four,** a vote by at least four justices to hear the case will grant the petition for a writ of certiorari and put the case on the Court's docket.

Since the Court never explains why it accepts or rejects particular cases, political scientists have tried to discover what cues guide the Court's choices. One researcher found that during the period 1947–57 the Court tended to accept civil liberties cases, cases in which the national government was asking for a review of a lower federal court decision, and cases in which there was a difference of opinion among two or more lower federal courts.[37] Recently, though, Chief Justice Rehnquist (1972–present) reports, and political science research confirms, that if there is a set of conflicting rulings on an issue in the courts below, a misapplication of an earlier Supreme Court ruling by a lower court, or a request from certain interest groups that a case be heard, the justices will be inclined to give serious consideration to the appeal petition.[38] New research, however, indicates that the value system and inexperience of the law clerks may well be affecting the Court's appellate choices. For instance, far fewer important economic cases are being accepted for review (and far fewer cases overall as well) since the law clerks' cert pool has increased in importance.[39]

Using its agenda-setting power to decide what cases to hear, the Court frequently waits for the ideal case or cases raising precisely the constitutional or legal issue it wants to rule on. For example, the Court ruled in the 1964 case *Escobedo v. Illinois*[40] that criminal suspects have the right to have an attorney present during police questioning if they ask for one. The Court then considered sixty-six cases over the next two years before finding the one with just the right facts. *Miranda v. Arizona*[41] stated that police would have to inform suspects of the right to an attorney before custodial interrogation.[42]

Recent Trends in Case Selection Since the late 1980s, the Supreme Court has been accepting and deciding fewer and fewer cases. Although the number of appeals to the Court has increased by 85 percent in the last twenty-five years, the percentage of cases actually accepted by the justices has dropped dramatically. In the late 1970s and early 1980s, several hundred cases were decided yearly by either full opinions or unsigned orders. Of the 7,700 appeals coming to the Court in 2001–2002, only 75 cases were decided by full opinion, 4 less than in the year before and the fewest number of full decisions in any term since the early 1950s.[43] Reflecting the narrow balance of the Court, over one fourth of these decisions were made by 5–4 votes. Even with this small number of cases, though, the Court can still impose its will by the nature of its selection process and the region of the country from which it takes the cases. In the 1996–97 term, twenty-six of the eighty cases, or nearly 40 percent, came from the Ninth Circuit Court of Appeals, one of the most liberal judging panels in the country, and the conservative Rehnquist Court reversed an amazing twenty-five of those decisions.[44]

There are several explanations for the Court's shrinking docket. First, recent congressional legislation on federal jurisdiction eliminated nearly all categories of constitutional cases that the Court was once required to review. Second, the staffing of the vast majority of the lower federal courts with conservatives by the Reagan and Bush administrations has meant that a fairly conservative Supreme Court has had fewer lower-court opinions with which it disagrees. Third, political scientist

rule of four A means of determining which cases will be heard by the Supreme Court; at least four justices must vote to hear a case and grant the petition for a writ of certiorari for the case to be put on the Court's docket.

David O'Brien discovered that an old practice called "Join 3," whereby a justice would vote to review if three of his colleagues were willing to do so, thus increasing the number of appeal acceptances, has recently been abandoned.[45] Fourth, it is also possible that after the bruising confirmation fights over Robert Bork and Clarence Thomas, and the controversial *Bush v. Gore* decision, the justices may be consciously trying to lower the profile of the Court for a while by accepting fewer cases. But the most likely explanation is that the law clerks reviewing the petitions in the cert pool are far less interested in taking cases than reviewing justices were in the past. "You stick your neck out as a clerk when you recommend to grant a case," explains Justice John Paul Stevens. "The risk-averse thing to do is to recommend not to take a case. I think it accounts for the lessening of the docket."[46] Whether this is a long-term change or just a cyclical trend remains to be seen.

The Solicitor General: "The Government's Lawyer"

One of the most important outside players influencing the Supreme Court's work, including its selection of cases, is the **solicitor general.** The third-ranking official in the Justice Department (after the attorney general and deputy attorney general), the solicitor general is appointed by the president and charged with representing the U.S. government before the Supreme Court. The solicitor general decides which federal cases to appeal from the lower courts, prepares those appeals, files briefs for accepted cases, and appears before the Court for oral argument. In cases that do not involve the national government as a party, the solicitor general may file **amicus curiae briefs,** or "friend of the court" briefs. Amicus briefs enable groups or individuals, including the national government, who are not parties to the litigation but have an interest in it, to attempt to influence the outcome of a case. All in all, the solicitor general is involved in about two-thirds of the cases before the Supreme Court.

The solicitor general has become so powerful and influential that the position is sometimes informally referred to as "the tenth justice." The willingness of the solicitor general to become involved in a case alerts the justices to the need to hear that appeal. In this way, the solicitor general serves as eyes and ears for the Court and can play a role in setting the Court's agenda.

The solicitor general is often pulled in two directions. As a presidential appointee, he or she must be sensitive to the policy preferences and interests of the White House. At the same time, the solicitor general is an officer of the Court, representing the interests of both the judiciary and the entire national government. At times politics prevails. During the Ronald Reagan and George Herbert Walker Bush years the solicitor general's office took hard-line conservative positions on controversial issues, such as abortion, favored by the administration. Clinton's acting solicitor general in the 1996–97 term, Walter Dellinger (his name was never sent to the Senate for confirmation because of the opposition of Senator Jesse Helms), tried as an officer of the Court to represent the position of the national government and judiciary. However, the White House occasionally forced him to modify his liberal stance on certain issues for political reasons.[47] Dellinger's replacement, Seth Waxman, faced fewer challenges in presenting the Clinton administration's legal agenda due to his more moderate point of view.[48] Now, though, President Bush's solicitor general, Theodore Olson, the attorney who successfully argued the President's case in the *Bush v. Gore* litigation, will be arguing war on terrorism cases with the Justices being fully aware that his wife Barbara was killed in the crash of the plane hijacked and crashed into the Pentagon.

The Process of Deciding Cases

Once a case is accepted for review, it passes through a number of stages as it is being considered. Each of these stages is designed, first, to inform the jurists, and then to give them a chance to organize a final decision.

solicitor general The third-ranking official in the Justice Department, appointed by the president and charged with representing the U.S. government before the Supreme Court.

amicus curiae briefs Legal briefs that enable groups or individuals, including the national government, who are not parties to the litigation but have an interest in it, to attempt to influence the outcome of the case; literally, "friend of the court" briefs.

Law Clerks: The Real "Tenth Justices"?

Justice Louis D. Brandeis once said that the Supreme Court was respected because "the justices are almost the only people in Washington who do their own work." But that no longer appears to be true. A book by Harry Blackmun's law clerk Edward Lazarus and an investigation by Supreme Court reporter Tony Mauro have revealed that a much greater role is played by these assistants in the appeals selection and opinion writing processes than previously suspected.

Law clerks are chosen for this $45,823 a year job in their second year of law school, and they generally come from the elite law schools. The overwhelming majority are white males. Before working at the Supreme Court, they serve a year's clerkship with federal court of appeals judges. Certain appeals judges, such as Michael Luttig of the fourth circuit, Laurence Silberman of the D.C. circuit, and Alex Kozinski of the ninth Circuit, have proven to be the major "feeder judges" for Supreme Court law clerks. Clerks are expected to adhere to a "code of conduct" preventing them from revealing privileged information about their work, and were at one time instructed not to speak with any journalist for more than 90 seconds.

Once on the Court, these assistants become participants in the "cert pool," which largely shapes the decision-making docket for eight of the nine justices (John Paul Stevens being the exception). "When I tell clients who have cases with hundreds of millions of dollars on the line that a bunch of 25-year-olds is going to decide their fate, it drives them crazy," says Carter Phillips, who knows this to be true since he served as a former law clerk for Chief Justice Warren Burger.

This intervention by the law clerks may well be one explanation for why so few cases, and a much smaller percentage of economic cases, are being accepted by the Court, as the law clerks lack both the knowledge of history and the confidence to accept more cases.

Decision making is still done by the justices, but the writing of first drafts of opinions, a most influential part of the process, is left largely to law clerks. It is not unusual for some opinions to come through the writing process without being significantly changed by the justice whose name appears on the opinion. Justice John Paul Stevens, once a law clerk to Wiley Rutledge in the 1940s, acknowledges this change: "I had a lot less responsibility than some of the clerks now. They are much more involved in the entire process now."

Judicial opinions now are a lot longer, much more fragmented, and much less clear in their legal explanation than previously. Court of Appeals Judge Richard Posner likens the increased dependence on law clerks to "brain surgeons delegating the entire performance of delicate operations to nurses, orderlies, and first-year medical students." Indeed, in a world in which every word of an opinion will be interpreted by lower courts, lawyers, legal scholars, and the general public for instruction on how to apply the law, this delegation of responsibilities has serious consequences.

Recent research indicates that groups of law clerks have in the past been able to influence the direction of the Supreme Court. Ed Lazarus writes of an ideological battle waged by conservative law clerks during the 1988–89 term to influence the Court to favor right-wing positions. This group devised an e-mail system to communicate with each other, found ways to influence some of the justices, and were so opposed to death row appeals that they had a champagne party when serial killer Ted Bundy was put to death. Lazarus quotes one conservative law clerk as saying: "Every time I draw blood, I'll think of what they did to Robert H. Bork."

When their year with the Supreme Court is done, many of these clerks go on to major jobs in law firms, some with signing bonuses of over $50,000. Others become teachers at the best law schools in America, where they then train and recommend future law clerks. Making this job search even more troubling is the fact that many of the law firms recruiting those clerks do so knowing that those same young men and women may well be writing the opinions in cases that their firm has just argued before the Court.

Many legal scholars have been calling for a reform of this initial screening system to take back some of the

---

briefs Written arguments to the court outlining not only the facts and legal and constitutional issues in a court case, but also answering all of the anticipated arguments of the opposing side.

The Filing of the Briefs When a case is accepted for the argument, the attorneys for all sides are asked to submit **briefs.** These are hundreds of pages of written arguments outlining not only all the facts and legal and constitutional issues in the case but also answering the anticipated arguments of the opposing side.

These written arguments were once strictly legal in nature, but now it is common for attorneys to present extensive sociological, psychological, scientific, and historical arguments to bolster their legal documentation. In the case of *Brown v. Board of Education,*[49] which in 1954 raised the issue of desegregating public schools, the Court was presented with evidence from social psychologist Kenneth Clark that African-American youngsters were psychologically harmed by segregated school systems.[50] As you will see in Chapter 14, it was primarily this evidence that contributed to the Court's decision to ignore legal precedents and rule that segregated schools are inherently unconstitutional.

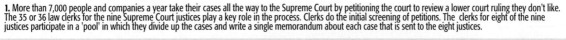

1. More than 7,000 people and companies a year take their cases all the way to the Supreme Court by petitioning the court to review a lower court ruling they don't like. The 35 or 36 law clerks for the nine Supreme Court justices play a key role in the process. Clerks do the initial screening of petitions. The clerks for eight of the nine justices participate in a 'pool' in which they divide up the cases and write a single memorandum about each case that is sent to the eight justices.

Justice John Paul Stevens does not participate in the pool. He says his own clerks dispose of most cases without sending him a memo. For the rest, his clerks write memos or he reviews the petitions himself.

Clerks for Chief Justice Rehnquist | Clerks for Justice Breyer | Clerks for Justice O'Connor | Clerks for Justice Ginsburg | Clerks for Justice Kennedy | Clerks for Justice Scalia | Clerks for Justice Souter | Clerks for Justice Thomas | Clerks for Justice Stevens

2. The pool memos summarize the facts and the issues and often recommend whether the case should be accepted by the court for review. In most cases, the justices who receive the pool memos dispose of the cases without further study.

3. Based on the clerks' memoranda and occasional independent research, all nine justices meet privately to decide whether to accept or deny a petition for review. If four of the nine justices say a case warrants review, it is docketed for oral arguments. Fewer than 100 cases are accepted each term.

4. Before a case is argued, some justices have clerks write a bench memo that summarizes the case and may also suggest questions the justice could ask during oral arguments.

5. After a case is argued, the justices meet in private to take an initial vote and assign the writing of the majority and dissenting opinions. Clerks usually write the first drafts.

6. Drafts are circulated to other justices for editing and revision. Clerks are often the conduits for communicating and negotiating between justices about the final wording.

7. When the opinions are finished, they are handed down under the names of the justices. Clerks are never mentioned.

Source: Copyright 1998, *USA Today.* Reprinted with permission.

responsibility and give it to the justices. "The fact that any power at all is vested in someone who is one or two years out of law school is incredible," says a former law clerk who was also Vice President Al Gore's assistant, Ronald Klain. However, the Supreme Court, as always, is very resistant to change.

Sources: Tony Mauro, "Justices Give Pivotal Role to Novice Lawyers," and "Corps of Clerks Lacking in Diversity, "*USA Today,* March 13, 1998, pp. 1A, 12–13A; see also Ed Lazarus, *Closed Chambers* (New York: Times Books, 1998).

Oral Argument   Once briefs are submitted, oral arguments follow. One of the most exciting and impressive events in Washington, D.C., is the public oral argument before the Supreme Court. Typically, the arguments are heard during the first three days of the first two weeks of each month from October through April. Lawyers from all sides, on occasion the solicitor general, and in the most important cases other interested parties, including those who have submitted amicus curiae briefs, are allowed to come before the justices and present their case. Each side is usually given only thirty minutes to speak, with time limits kept so carefully by the chief justice that during one Court session, a lawyer was interrupted in the middle of the word *if.*

Although lawyers come prepared with statements, they must stop to answer questions from the justices. Justices have very different questioning styles. Ruth Bader Ginsburg asks carefully sculpted questions designed to keep counsel from avoiding

▲ Members of the U.S. Supreme Court gathered in the East Conference Room of the Court Building. From left to right they are Chief Justice William H. Rehnquist and Justices John Paul Stevens, Sandra Day O'Connor, Antonin Scalia, Anthony M. Kennedy, David H. Souter, Clarence Thomas, Ruth Bader Ginsburg, and Stephen G. Breyer.

issues, while Stephen Breyer usually waits until the end of counsel's time before asking one or two lengthy questions designed to crystallize the central issue in the case. By contrast, Clarence Thomas asked no questions during his first eighteen months on the bench.

The most combative person on the bench in this role, however, is Antonin Scalia. Much as he did as a law professor, Scalia asks many rapid-fire questions and tries to lead the argument in his direction in an effort to educate his fellow justices. At one point in a case, Scalia appeared ready to argue the case himself for an attorney who would not answer his question to his satisfaction, only to have Chief Justice William Rehnquist interject: "I think he's capable of answering himself." "Well, he's not capable," Scalia responded. One attorney who has faced this barrage says of Scalia: "I've seen some lawyers really thrown off. At the end, they look dizzy." In responding to these questions, lawyers have to be careful to pitch their arguments to the more centrist, swing justices in the voting—Anthony Kennedy, Sandra Day O'Connor, and David Souter.[51]

The appellate and oral argument process is such a specialized skill that it can cost as much as $500,000 to take a case to the Supreme Court. For a solo practitioner to take a case to the Court *pro bono*, or for free, can result in having to close down a practice for six months to prepare for the argument. More and more, an elite group of less than two dozen Washington, D.C., litigators who specialize in Supreme Court argumentation, some of them former U.S. solicitors general and Supreme Court law clerks, are being hired by corporations, states, and even other law firms to take their cases this final step.[52] Sometimes the willingness of these attorneys to take a case or not makes them another gatekeeper in deciding which appeals will be made to the Court.

What role does oral argument play in the decision-making process? For some justices, oral presentations highlight problems with the issue being raised by the written briefs and suggest possible avenues for decision. For others, written briefs weigh more heavily. For this reason it is often difficult to predict how the Court will rule based on the nature of its questioning during oral argument.

The Decision-Making Stage: The Conference After the justices read the briefs and listen to oral arguments, the decision-making process begins with the *judicial conference.* These conferences take place on Wednesday afternoon for cases argued on Monday, and all day Friday for cases argued on Tuesday and Wednesday. At these meetings, the justices discuss both the cases under consideration and which appeals to grant in the future.

The meetings take place in total secrecy in an oak-paneled conference room, with only the justices present. Proceeding from the chief justice down to the most junior justice, the justices indicate both their views and how they will vote. Opinions expressed at this time constitute a preliminary vote.[53]

In recent years, the conference stage has changed dramatically. Harlan Fiske Stone (chief justice, 1941–46) conducted exhausting judicial conferences that went on for hours and often extended from Friday into Saturday. During these long meetings clerks recall hearing Felix Frankfurter and William O. Douglas screaming at each other so loudly that their voices carried down the hall. Recently, though, the conference stage has become briefer and less heated. "Not very much conferencing goes on," explains Justice Antonin Scalia. "In fact, to call our discussion of a case a conference is really something of a misnomer. It's much more a statement of the views of each of the nine justices, after which the totals are added and the case is assigned [for the drafting of the opinion]."[54] "Bam, bam, bam" is how one justice describes the current speed of voting in conference.[55]

Assignment of Opinions Once the discussion and voting are over, if the chief justice is in the majority he assigns one of the members voting in the majority to draft an **opinion,** the written version of the decision. Sometimes the chief justice will write the opinion in the hope of expressing an even stronger view from the Court. If the chief justice is not in the majority, the senior justice in the majority makes the assignment or writes the opinion.

Assignments are based on a number of factors. The expertise of certain members of the Court, their speed in drafting opinions, their ability to forge a consensus, and their current workload may be considered. At times, personal and symbolic considerations govern the choice. Earl Warren liked to give the most interesting opinions to his colleagues; his successor, Warren Burger, was known to assign the least interesting opinions to the justices with whom he was unhappy. To the great annoyance of colleagues such as William O. Douglas, Burger occasionally tried to assign opinions even though he was not in the majority.[56] Though he was a vocal critic of the *Miranda* police interrogation protections case, in 2000 Chief Justice Rehnquist assigned the *Dickerson* opinion upholding that decision to himself, likely because of its historic importance and his desire to limit the scope of its holding.

The assignment of opinions is important because such choices determine the tone of Court opinions and their reception by the public. A classic example of this tone-setting power was Chief Justice Harlan Fiske Stone's reassignment of the *Smith v. Allwright*[57] opinion. That 1944 case barred all-white Democratic party primaries in Texas. After initially assigning the case to Felix Frankfurter, a political independent from New England, Stone realized the potential for the opinion to arouse resentment in the Democratic party and in the South, where a white primary was considered a cherished right. So he reassigned the opinion to Stanley Reed (1938–57), an avowed conservative Democrat from the border state of Kentucky. The opinion was still controversial, but it was more acceptable because of Reed's role.[58]

Sometimes the voting lineup—and thus the decision in a case—hinges on who is assigned the opinion. In 1992, five justices—Thomas, Scalia, Rehnquist, White, and Kennedy—seemed ready to overturn the *Roe v. Wade*[59] abortion decision in the case of *Planned Parenthood of Southeastern Pennsylvania v. Casey.*[60] When conservative Chief Justice Rehnquist assigned the opinion to himself because of the importance of the case, and drafted a very harsh opinion toward the Roe precedent, Kennedy decided to vote in a more moderate direction, joining in an opinion with David Souter and

FYI

According to a survey in 1998, of the 394 law clerks hired by the members of the Court, just 1.8 percent were African American, 1 percent were Hispanic, 4.5 percent were Asian, and 24.3 percent were women. In the 2002–2003 group of clerks, 35 in total number, there are two African Americans, four Asian Americans, and thirteen women, the largest number of minorities ever.

opinion A written version of the decision of a court.

Sandra Day O'Connor upholding the precedent.[61] (In his book *Closed Chambers,* former law clerk Ed Lazarus charges that this switched vote became so sensitive that Kennedy told the law clerk working on this case to hide his work even from other clerks to avoid pressure as a result of this defection.)[62]

Marshaling the Court: The Opinion-Drafting Process

After the judicial conference, the justice assigned to write the opinion takes weeks, and sometimes months, to develop a draft to circulate among the other justices. Special care is taken because conference votes are tentative, and justices will lobby to change their colleagues' positions. As justice William Brennan used to say to his law clerks while wiggling all of the fingers of his hand in the air: "Five votes. Five votes can do anything around here."[63] And each side attempts to muster those five votes.

At any point, right up to the public announcement of the opinion, a justice can change a vote. That occasionally happens, but the language of opinions nearly always changes, sometimes even dramatically in controversial cases, as a result of lobbying efforts. Each opinion goes through multiple drafts, with justices negotiating with each other over changes on which the final votes may depend. Such negotiations take time. For this reason, opinions for major cases argued in the fall of a judicial term might not be issued until the spring of the following year. Often, these negotiations come in the form of written comments on various opinion drafts, personal memos, and even personal lobbying. Justices have different styles in such lobbying efforts. Frankfurter used the "carrot" approach, often praising a justice for his brilliance (while saving less gracious comments for his personal diary). On the other hand, Justice James McReynolds (1914–41), sarcastically referred to as the Court's "Mr. Congeniality," used the "stick" approach, once writing on a colleague's draft, "This statement makes me sick."[64]

Years ago such lobbying took place through personal interaction, but in recent years what little lobbying has taken place is usually done by argumentative memos. Despite such efforts, however, evidence suggests that votes change in less than 10 percent of the cases.[65]

Sometimes the frustration of these unsuccessful negotiations is reflected in the final opinion. In one abortion case, Justice Antonin Scalia, by all accounts a charming man in person, once described Justice Sandra Day O'Connor's opinion as "perverse," "irrational," and "not to be taken seriously."[66] When Scalia could not convince the Court to abandon its prevailing test in establishment of religion cases—the so-called *Lemon* test, taken from the case *Lemon v. Kurtzman*—he wrote: "Like some ghoul in a late-night horror movie that repeatedly sits up in its grave and shuffles abroad, after being repeatedly killed and buried, *Lemon* stalks our Establishment Clause jurisprudence once again, frightening little children and school attorneys."[67]

Only after there is an agreement by all justices on the wording of the final opinion is it ready to be announced.

The Announcement of Opinions

The vote on any case is final only when the decision or opinion is announced in open court. The Court's opinion not only states the facts of a case and announces the decision, but since this will be the only public comment on the case, it contains supporting logic, precedents, and rationale to persuade the public of the merits of the judgment. In addition, the language used in an opinion is designed to be used later by lower courts, federal and state politicians, and the legal community to interpret similar cases in the future.

The Court makes it decision based on a majority (five votes of nine), called a **majority opinion,** which represents the agreed-upon compromise judgement of all the justices in the majority. This opinion is almost always signed only by its authors.

majority opinion A decision of the Supreme Court that represents the agreed-upon compromise judgment of all the juices in the majority.

In cases where less than a majority agrees on the wording, a **plurality opinion** will be issued. This plurality opinion announces the opinion of the Court, but it does not have the same binding legal force as a majority opinion.

If a justice agrees with the majority decision of the Court but differs on the reasoning, a **concurring opinion** can be written. From this literary platform a single justice, or a small group of them, can show where the majority might have ruled. A careful reading of the concurring opinions thus can reveal the true sentiments of the Court majority. In the landmark 1971 freedom of the press case *New York Times Co. v. United States*,[68] the Court allowed two newspapers to publish the Pentagon Papers, a classified study of the decision-making process of America's involvement in Vietnam. However, the six concurring opinions revealed that if the government had sought to punish the *Times* editors after publication, and if there had been a statute which outlawed such a publication, rather than by preventing publication through prior censorship, a majority of the Court would have approved.

When a justice disagrees with the holding of the Court, frequently he or she will write a **dissenting opinion,** speaking for that justice alone or a few of the members of the Court. In the *Dickerson* case, Justice Scalia used his dissent to attack Chief Justice Rehnquist's majority opinion by using language from confession cases that Rehnquist himself had decided nearly three decades before. From the stewardship of Chief Justice Marshall until the early 1920s, justices avoided dissents, fearing a diminution of the public authority of the Court. The increase in the practice came in the 1940s when dissents occurred in 70 percent of the cases, as opposed to 22 percent of the cases in the previous decade. Now either as a result of less personal conferencing by the justices, weaker leadership by the chief justice, a greater role in the drafting process by the law clerks, or a greater desire by the individual jurists to be heard, many more dissents are being issued. Since the mid-1970s, the practice of joint dissents became so common that assignments were made by senior judges for the writing of them, much like in majority opinion assignments. A recent study discovered that frequent dissenter William Brennan made such assignments in 477 cases based on the workload of his colleagues rather than based on their ideological orientation.[69]

One must pay attention to these statements because the dissents of today can become the majority opinions of tomorrow with the change of a few members on the Court. The decision rule proposed in dissents by Oliver Wendell Holmes and Louis D. Brandeis in the First Amendment free speech cases of the early twentieth century, and Justices Hugo Black and William O. Douglas in the 1950s, later became the law of the land. Similarly, much of the current Court's restriction of defendants' rights was first expressed in solo dissents by William Rehnquist in the early 1970s.

The Chief Justice's Role

The chief justice is first among equals on the Supreme Court, with substantial powers to influence the Court's direction by assigning opinions, leading the judicial conference, and acting as the social and intellectual leader of the Court. In addition, as chief justice of the United States, he or she also heads, represents, and lobbies for the entire federal judiciary.

There has been much variation in the leadership styles of chief justices. Some have been more effective as leaders of the Supreme Court than others. The austere Charles Evans Hughes (1930–41) moved the Court along with military precision. His replacement, the gregarious Harlan Fiske Stone (1941–46), lost control of the Court during judicial conferences. Fred Vinson (1946–53) was mismatched with the high-powered, egocentric Roosevelt appointees, leading to considerable rancor on the Court in those years. On the other hand, the relative harmony that followed came during the tenure of the politically skilled former governor of California, Earl Warren (1953–69), known to his admiring colleagues as "the Super Chief." This period was in contrast to the sharply split Court under Warren Burger (1969–86), who

plurality opinion Less than a majority vote on an opinion of the Court; does not have the binding legal force of a majority opinion.

concurring opinion A written opinion of a justice who agrees with the majority decision of the Court but differs on the reasoning.

dissenting opinion A written opinion of a justice who disagrees with the holding of the Court.

was reputed to be an uninspiring leader.[70] Currently, the highly popular and respected William Rehnquist has proven to be capable of forging and maintaining the Court's narrow conservative coalition.

Analyzing Supreme Court Decisions

To analyze and understand any Supreme Court decision, it helps to be aware of the following considerations: the Court's use of precedent and other legal factors, the mind-set of the individual justices, the personalities of the justices, and the voting blocs on the Court at a particular time.

The Use of Precedent and Other Legal Factors

Judges throughout the entire legal system often decide cases on the basis of the doctrine of **stare decisis,** which means "to let the decision stand" or to adhere if at all possible to previously decided cases, or **precedents,** on the same issue. Federal and state courts, for example, are supposed to follow Supreme Court precedents in making their own decisions. The Supreme Court often rules based on its own precedents. By following the rulings of their predecessors, all courts, including the Supreme Court, seem to be nonpolitical, impartial arbiters, making incremental changes based on past decisions.

But following precedent is not as restrictive as it sounds. Since in practice precedents need interpretation, judges can argue about the meaning of an earlier case or whether the facts of the current case differ substantially from those of past cases, thus requiring a different ruling. In one case, the *Bowers v. Hardwick* case, dealing with the privacy rights of gays in the bedroom, both Justices Blackmun and White cited the same case of *Stanley v. Georgia,*[71] a privacy and pornography case, as a major precedent upholding their opposing positions on the constitutionality of the Georgia anti-sodomy law. On some occasions, justices will give the appearance of upholding precedent, when in fact they are deliberately ignoring it or consciously reinterpreting it to reach a different result.

Only in the most extreme cases is the Court willing to overturn an earlier decision, thus declaring it invalid. Precedents are usually overturned if they prove to be unworkable from a public policy standpoint, outmoded, or just plain unwise. Sometimes, though, the Court will overturn a precedent simply because of a change in personnel, thus changing the Court's direction, or because of a change in public opinion. For example, in 1991 the Court overruled two earlier Eighth Amendment capital punishment decisions barring the use of statements by victims in the penalty phase of a capital trial. The arrival of new conservative members made these rulings possible but led frustrated liberal Thurgood Marshall to argue before retiring from the Court, "Power, not reason, is the new currency of this Court's decision making."[72] In actuality, however, the Court rarely overrules its own precedents. Of the tens of thousands of decisions issued by the Court, it has overruled its own precedents in less than 300 cases.[73]

A favorite technique for circumventing precedent without reversing a previous decision is to *distinguish* cases, that is, to claim that the earlier case and a more recent case are very different (even though they are in fact similar), thus requiring different decisions. The Court has been able to dilute the original ruling in the 1966 *Miranda* case using such a technique. That case established rules governing police conduct during the interrogation of witnesses. Though it was not overruled in the *Dickerson* case, the Court created so many exceptions to it when ruling in similar cases that the original ruling is now much less protective of defendants' rights.

stare decisis A doctrine meaning "let the decision stand," or that judges deciding a case should adhere if at all possible to previously decided cases that are similar to the one under consideration.

precedents Previously decided court cases on an issue similar to the one being considered.

Justices also look at a variety of factors beyond precedent to decide an issue, including the meaning of a law, the meaning of part of the Constitution, the lessons of history, and the possible impact on public policy. Justices may look carefully at the wording of a statute or a portion of the Constitution, using *strict construction*, interpreting the law as closely as possible to the literal meaning of the words in the text. When the wording is vague, justices will then search for historical context—or for the so-called intent of the framers who wrote the law and the Constitution—to determine the true meaning of both. Proponents of the *original intent* theory with respect to the Constitution, such as Judge Robert Bork, argue that it is the Court's duty to adhere solely to the original meaning of the framers. The effect is to limit the power of Supreme Court justices. Others, however, argue that society has changed since the drafting of the Constitution, and that the Court's decisions should thus reflect the needs of a continually changing society. Sometimes justices examine the general history of an issue and the public policy impact of their decision. In the *Bush v. Gore* case, the Court majority argued that many factors led them to rule that the initial certification of the presidential vote by the Florida Secretary of State should stand, thus effectively ending the election in Bush's favor. As outlined in the case study, though, many believed that this decision was influenced more by politics than by law.

The Mindset of Individual Justices

Personal factors also need to be considered when analyzing judicial decisions. It is helpful to look at a judge's mindset—his or her political ideology, jurisprudential posture, or a combination of the two.

Political Ideology   Although some observers of the Court would prefer that justices decide cases on the basis of neutral principles, the individuals sitting on the Court are human beings influenced by their own biases.[74] A comprehensive study by two political scientists found a strong correlation between justices' votes on the Court and their ideological views as expressed in newspaper articles written during the appointment process.[75]

Like members of political parties, justices tend to be grouped ideologically as conservative, liberal, or moderate. Conservatives tend to support the government's position instead of the individual's in civil rights and liberties, while liberals tend to defend or even expand the rights of the individual instead of the government. On economic questions, conservatives tend to oppose government regulation while allowing for *laissez faire* business existence, while liberals tend to vote for a more intrusive government regulatory role. Moderates often flip back and forth between these two positions, depending on the issues. On the current Court, Justices O'Connor and Kennedy, both moderate conservatives, often switch back and forth in their votes on various issues, thus determining the direction of the Court's decision.

Labeling jurists this way is helpful but in no way definitive. There are many varieties of liberals and conservatives and many legal issues that do not fit clearly into those groupings. Political ideology, then, is only a starting point for understanding a jurist's mind-set. We must also consider the willingness of the justices to use their power.

Jurisprudential Posture   Justices have a certain jurisprudential posture, meaning how willing they are to use their power on the Court. Some practice self-restraint, others are activists. Those justices who believe in **judicial restraint** see themselves as appointed rather than elected officials, who should defer to the elected legislature and uphold a law or political action if at all possible. "If the legislature wants to go to hell, I'm here to tell them they can do it," said Oliver Wendell Holmes. The

> ❝ **QUOTE ... UNQUOTE**
>
> "Justice Douglas, you must remember one thing. At the constitutional level where we work, ninety percent of any decision is emotional. The rational part of us supplies the reasons for supporting our predilections." ❞
>
> Chief Justice Charles Evans Hughes

judicial restraint An approach in which justices see themselves as appointed rather than elected officials, who should defer to the legislature and uphold a law or political action if at all possible.

classic expression of judicial self-restraint is that of Felix Frankfurter in dissent in a case forcing the children of Jehovah's Witnesses to salute the flag in contravention to their religious beliefs:

> One who belongs to the most vilified and persecuted minority in history [Frankfurter was Jewish] is not likely to be insensible to the freedoms guaranteed by our Constitution. . . . As a member of this Court I am not justified in writing my private notions of policy into the Constitution, no matter how deeply I may cherish them or how mischievous I may deem their disregard.[76]

In deferring to the legislature, the Court can arrive at some unexpected rulings. In 1968, the Supreme Court upheld an amendment to the Selective Service Law banning the knowing destruction or mutilation of a draft card, despite the freedom of speech claim of the defendant, David Paul O'Brien, who had burned his card in a Vietnam War protest. In ruling that the draft card was an administrative document necessary to the operation of the draft, the Court ignored the clear evidence that some in Congress were passing this regulation with the clearly unconstitutional purpose of discouraging antiwar protests.[77]

Judges who practice **judicial activism** believe that they have a duty to reach out and decide issues even to the point, some critics charge, of writing their own personal values into law. Judicial activists are more willing to strike down legislation, reject a presidential action, or create rights not specifically written in the Constitution. For example, William O. Douglas's ruling in the case of *Griswold v. Connecticut*[78] fashioned a right of privacy even though such a right is not explicitly in the Constitution. Douglas's classic description of the activist posture came in a dissent to a case in which the Court would not rule to protect the environment in the Sierra Nevada Mountains of California against the bulldozers of Walt Disney Corporation, which was seeking to build a ski resort:

> Inanimate objects are sometimes parties in litigation. . . . So it should be as respects valleys, alpine meadows, rivers, lakes, estuaries, beaches, ridges, groves of trees, swampland, or even air that feels the destructive pressures of modern technology and modern life.[79]

For Justice Douglas, nature should have the right to sue, too. The activist posture often leads to the charge by conservatives that the Court is acting as a "superlegislature," overruling duly elected bodies.[80]

Activists come in many varieties and are given a number of labels. *Result-oriented* justices begin with the result they intend to reach in mind and simply announce that judgment, paying little attention to justifying their decision in the opinion. Another kind of activist, the *absolutist*, believes that the rights in the Constitution are paramount, and no contrary interest of the state can be used to justify overruling them. Hugo Black (1937–71), a New Deal justice, once stated, in reference to the First Amendment's ban on any law abridging freedom of speech, "No law means NO law!"[81]

The Four-Cell Method for Classifying Justices

It is often revealing to assess justices according to a four-cell categorization that takes into consideration both political ideology (whether a judge is liberal or conservative) and jurisprudential posture (whether a judge is self-restrained or an activist). This scheme, illustrated in Figure 6.4, helps us better understand that self-restrained liberals and self-restrained conservatives on the Court have much in common because neither will be inclined to break new ground. For instance, New Deal appointee Felix Frankfurter was frequently criticized by liberal colleagues because his self-restrained opinions upholding the letter of the law made him look too conservative. However, the activists on either side of the political spectrum can differ dramatically, as liberal activists are willing to reach beyond the law and write new individual rights into the Constitution, conservative activists sometimes seek to substitute their vision of the constitution for that of the legislators. Thus, the conservative activists on the

Figure 6.4   The Four-Cell Method for Classifying Justices

It is useful to assess justices by looking at their politics (whether they are liberal or conservative) and at their judicial philosophy (whether they are activist or self-restrained). We learn, as a result, that both types of self-restrained justices share an inclination to avoid innovation, while activists in the two camps can differ dramatically with regard to the goals of their activism.

judicial activism An approach in which justices create new policy and decide issues, to the point, some critics charge, of writing their own personal values into law.

Rehnquist Court have been able to overturn 31 Congressional laws over the last seven years, oftentimes claiming to be adhering to the "original intention" of the framers of the Constitution.

But concentrating solely on the political and judicial views of a justice is not enough to understand decisions. Instead, in dealing with a life-tenured Court an additional angle needs to be considered: judicial character.

Judicial Character

The personalities of individual justices and how the justices interact with each other play a large role in the direction of the Court. Justice William Brennan explains: "In an institution this small, personalities play an important role. . . . How those people get along, how they relate, what ideas they have, how flexible or intractable they are, are all of enormous significance."[82] A justice can shade an opinion to secure the agreement of a colleague, or perhaps remain silent rather than write a dissent, in the interest of interpersonal harmony. On the other hand, a justice can, for personal or professional reasons, simply chart a separate course, possibly creating friction on the Court.

Like any group, members of the Court can be divided into leaders, team players, and loners. The leader does not necessarily have to be the chief justice. One political scientist argued that on every Court there are "task leaders," who see that the work gets done, and "social leaders," who keep life on the Court harmonious.[83] Sometimes these two types of leaders can be rolled into one, as in the case of Justice Brennan, who during his tenure became known as a "playmaker," or the justice who unites a ruling majority on the Court. That role continued even during the highly conservative Rehnquist Court years, where the liberal Brennan's elfin, affectionate style enabled him to continue amassing five-person majorities. Then there are the team players, those justices usually willing to go along with the majority. On the present Court, one team player is Justice Clarence Thomas, who nearly always follows the conservative position of Justices Rehnquist and Scalia. In contrast are the loner justices, who are willing to take a stand even if it means issuing frequent sole dissents and angering colleagues. Justice William O. Douglas and, in his early years, Justice Rehnquist adopted this role with such frequency that each was called "the Lone Ranger." Now liberal Justice Stevens appears willing to adopt this role, frequently issuing solo dissents on civil rights and liberties questions. While the conservatives now lack the kind of vote-unifying playmaker that the liberals had in Brennan, the increasing willingness of Justices Kennedy and O'Connor to vote with them many times functions in the determinative playmaker role on such issues as affirmative action, federalism issues, and freedom of religion.

Voting Blocs

To analyze Court decisions, it helps to group the whole Court into blocs of like-minded jurists. Such blocs can be defined by ideology as conservative, liberal, and moderate (see Table 6.1). Although justices sometimes shift within these blocs, more frequently change results from vacancies filled in a way that alters the balance of the Court. For the *Dickerson* case, we see three conservatives (Rehnquist, Scalia, Thomas) and three liberals (Stevens, Ginsburg, Breyer) with three justices (Souter, Kennedy, O'Connor) holding the moderate swing votes. When all of the moderates voted to uphold *Miranda* as a valid precedent, taking one conservative, Chief Justice Rehnquist, with them, the result was the 7 to 2 majority. These blocs are not absolute determinants of votes, however, since the views of a justice, and thus the justice's position within a bloc, frequently vary according to the issue under consideration.

Bloc analysis can be helpful in predicting which justices may become the swing votes that determine the outcome in a case. Law firms appearing before the Court

Table 6.1 ■ Judicial Voting Blocs

	LIBERAL	MODERATE	CONSERVATIVE
Eisenhower Court (1961)	Warren	Whittaker	Frankfurter
	Brennan	Harlan	Stewart
	Black		Clark
	Douglas		
Kennedy Court (1963)	Warren	Harlan	Stewart
	Brennan		Clark
	Black		White
	Douglas		
	Goldberg		
Johnson Court (1969)	Warren	Harlan	Black*
	Brennan		Stewart
	Douglas		White
	Fortas		
	Marshall		
Nixon Court (1974)	Brennan	Powell	Burger
	Douglas	Blackmun	Rehnquist
	Marshall		Stewart
			White
Ford Court (1976)	Brennan	Powell	Burger
	Marshall	Blackmun	Rehnquist
		Stevens	Stewart
			White
Reagan Court (1989)	Brennan	Kennedy	Rehnquist
	Blackmun†	O'Connor	Scalia
	Marshall	Stevens	White
Bush (41) Court (1993)	Blackmun	Kennedy	Rehnquist
	Stevens	Souter	Scalia
		O'Connor	White
			Thomas
Bush (43) Court (2002)	Stevens		Rehnquist
	Ginsburg		Scalia
	Breyer		Thomas
	Souter‡		Kennedy‡
			O'Connor‡

*The liberal Hugo Black became conservative after a stroke.

†It is interesting to note that when appointed in 1970, Blackmun was very conservative. By 1973, he had become a moderate, and later in his career he became a liberal.

‡These moderate, swing justices have tended over the last several years to vote more frequently with these groups, thus accounting for the frequent 5–4 conservative votes.

make this kind of analysis so they can pitch their oral argument to one or two justices they deem critical to their case.

Replacing one of the members of a leading bloc of the Court with a member suited to the other bloc will sharply tip the balance of the Court. So while new Supreme Court appointments are always important, some of them take on greater importance because they have the potential to change the entire direction of the Court. That was why the prospect of replacing Warren Burger with Antonin Scalia in 1986—a conservative for a conservative—did not have nearly the impact and was not as controversial as the attempted replacement of the moderate Powell with the highly conservative activist Robert Bork a year later. It is highly likely that President Bush will have the opportunity to make a court appointment that will change the direction of the evenly balanced institution.

Limitations of Court Analysis

Although the preceding tools for analyzing Supreme Court decisions help us understand how the Court may have arrived at a decision, they have limitations as predictors of Court rulings. Because of the nature of the Court's independent role, the constantly evolving philosophies of the individuals on it, the hidden role of law clerks, and the shifting nature of the personnel on it, the Court does not always head in the direction that seems obvious or that the experts predict. Harry Blackmun was expected to become a conservative on the Court much like his friend Warren Burger, but instead he evolved into one of its most liberal members. John Paul Stevens was appointed by Republican President Gerald R. Ford, but while his views did not change appreciably, with the retirement of liberals William Brennan and Thurgood Marshall, he became known as the most liberal member of an increasingly conservative Court. Republican President George Herbert Walker Bush's additions of conservatives David Souter and Clarence Thomas were expected to make the Court extremely conservative, but initially in the 1991–92 Court term Souter teamed up with two Reagan appointees, Anthony Kennedy and Sandra Day O'Connor, to create a controlling centrist bloc that frequently thwarted the conservatives. Thomas, as expected, sided with the conservatives.

While President Clinton's two moderate-liberal appointments—Ruth Bader Ginsburg and Stephen Breyer—were expected to move the Court left, instead two of the moderate-conservative swing justices—Sandra Day O'Connor and Anthony Kennedy—began in the 1996–97 term to ally with the three solid conservatives on the Court—Rehnquist, Scalia, and Thomas. By the 1998–99 term, they had formed a consistent but narrow 5 to 4 majority on key questions such as favoring states' rights, diluting defendants' rights, and opposing affirmative action. It is this same narrow majority, most often with Sandra Day O'Connor casting the determining vote, that decides cases now. When George W. Bush gets an appointment to the Court, the question of whether this appointment would affect the ideological direction of the Court will depend once again on which member is being replaced. Only if the vacancy is created by the loss of one of the members of the five-person conservative group, to be replaced by a Democratic party president, might there be a resulting shift in policy direction. On the other hand, the loss of a liberal member to be replaced by a Republican president would solidify the conservative majority.

Implementing Supreme Court Decisions

When the Supreme Court issues its judgments, in theory they become the law of the land, and one might expect compliance to be automatic. But that does not always happen. Some decisions are so controversial that they are ignored in many places.

As a school board member in Deming, New Mexico, put it in defying the Court's ban on prayer in public schools: "Until those justices come down here and tell us to change, we'll do things our own way."[84]

Possessing neither "sword" nor "purse," the Supreme Court must maintain the support of political actors such as the president, the Congress, the state and local governments, and public opinion to implement its decisions. This means that the Court, although an unelected body, cannot operate in a political vacuum when making its decisions.

The President and the Court

Compliance with a decision is influenced by whether the president is willing to lend the weight of his office to mobilize favorable public opinion. When state and local officials in Little Rock, Arkansas, resisted the *Brown v. Board of Education* school desegregation decision in 1957, President Eisenhower sent federal troops to help implement it.[85] It was Catholic president John F. Kennedy's support for the Court's 1962 decision outlawing school prayer that helped to build public support on behalf of that decision.[86]

While most often presidents have nothing to say about Court decisions, their occasional opposition can have an impact. The classic expression came in 1832 with a Supreme Court ruling in favor of the legal rights of the Cherokee Indians. The old frontier fighter President Andrew Jackson was reputed to have said: "Well, John Marshall has made his decision, now let him enforce it!"[87] Since the state of Georgia also opposed the rights of the Cherokee Indians, it would be left to the federal judiciary and Congress to safeguard their rights.

In the long run, however, presidents who do not support the direction of Court rulings can have a greater impact on the Court through appointments than through direct confrontation.

Congress and the Court

Frequently, Congress will say nothing about Court rulings, the majority of which interpret or define their laws. But if Congress disagrees with the Court's statutory ruling, it has four routes to convey its discontent:

1. It can pass a new law or a revised version of an old law restating its original intentions.
2. It can pass resolutions expressing disagreement with the Court.
3. It can threaten to use one of its constitutional powers to attack the Court directly.
4. It can propose a constitutional amendment.

Generally, Congress will choose to overturn statutory interpretations by passing another version of the law that has been struck down. For instance, in response to six anti-civil rights decisions by the Court in 1991, Congress passed new versions of the same laws guaranteeing those civil rights to citizens.

Less frequently, Congress attempts to reverse constitutional decisions by passing new laws limiting their effect. Section 3501 of the Omnibus Crime Control Law in 1968, which was reviewed in the *Dickerson* case, was just such an example of Congress trying to overrule the Court by substituting the old "voluntariness" rule for the *Miranda* warnings in determining the admissibility of confessions. In 1993 Congress sought to use legislation to overturn a 1990 case that ruled that the state of Oregon could deny unemployment compensation to two Native Americans who, in smoking peyote in a religious ritual, violated state antidrug laws.[88] When this ruling was then applied in more than sixty other cases to restrict free exercise of religion, Congress passed, and President Clinton signed into law, the Religious Freedom Restoration Act (RFRA), which required the states to show a "compelling state interest," or a very high level of proof, before it could interfere with freedom of religion.[89]

Those and similar efforts to overturn a constitutional decision by the Court through legislative means risk review by the Court in the future. Indeed, in the 1996 term, the Supreme Court did overturn RFRA, arguing that "the power to interpret the Constitution in a case or controversy remains in the Judiciary. . . . Our national experience teaches that the Constitution is preserved best when each part of the government respects both the Constitution and the proper actions and determinations of the other branches."[90] Citing the Court's judicial review ruling in *Marbury,* Justice Anthony Kennedy added, "If Congress could define its own powers by altering the Fourteenth Amendment's meaning, no longer would the Constitution be 'superior paramount law, unchangeable by ordinary means.' . . . [Instead] shifting legislative majorities could change the Constitution and effectively circumvent the difficult and detailed amendment process contained in Article V."[91] Of course, this is exactly what critics of the Supreme Court charge is being done by their decisions on the basis of shifting five-person majorities. Indeed, as indicated in the *Dickerson* case, where the Court overturned the congressionally passed Section 3501, an activist conservative majority has overturned thirty-one federal laws since 1995. With the Court choosing to strike down a law, however, Congress as always retains the option of proposing a constitutional amendment. While a lack of congressional support can weaken or undermine Supreme Court rulings, congressional displeasure with Court rulings is most often apparent during confirmation hearings for judicial vacancies.

The Impact at State and Local Levels

The implementation of Supreme Court decisions, especially those that are controversial and complex, requires the cooperation of a large number of state and local officials. Often compliance is not immediate; it takes time for decisions to filter through the system and be made a workable part of everyday life.

Lower federal and state court judges play a role. They are empowered to apply Supreme Court rulings to new cases in their jurisdiction. Because Supreme Court decisions are sometimes couched in vague language, they are open to significant interpretation. Thus, lower courts have tremendous power to establish how a Supreme Court ruling will be applied.

Governors, state legislatures, local governments, and even school boards also play a role in the implementation of Supreme Court decisions. Even local law enforcement has considerable impact. Decisions limiting the power of the police to search for evidence will be implemented only if the police and prosecutors choose to observe them and state judges decide to enforce them. Although the vast majority of decisions are implemented without question, a handful of highly controversial ones are not, illustrating the problems the Court faces when issuing decisions. More than four decades after the *Brown* desegregation ruling, many American school systems still remain segregated. And three decades after the decision striking down prayer in public schools, students in many public schools still participate in some form of devotional service. Although *Roe v. Wade* legalized abortion, state legislatures around the country have placed a wide variety of restrictions on that right.

Public Opinion and the Supreme Court

Finally, supportive public opinion plays an important part in implementation. Although the Supreme Court is an unelected body and does not need to consult public opinion polls when making its rulings, the views of the American people do play a role in its decision making. Should the Court fail to capture the conscience of the public with the persuasiveness of its reasoning, the decision might never be fully implemented. The sharp public division over the abortion decision in *Roe v. Wade*, for example, has affected its level of acceptance.

Research has revealed the Court's general willingness to adhere to majority public sentiment in nearly 60 percent of its decisions.[92] In addition, when it makes bold innovative decisions, public opinion is taken into account in that these decisions are often counterbalanced by a series of later, more conservative judgments to encourage acceptance. The Court is aware that if it gets too far out in front of public opinion, it risks losing support (see Figure 6.5). Thus, the Court will change the law, and thereby public policy, incrementally to encourage implementation. After granting defendants the right to state-appointed attorneys in serious felony trials in the *Gideon* decision,[93] the Court was very slow to extend that right to other types of trials.

Should the Court lead or follow public opinion? The complete answer is that ideally it should do both. In general it is best to be attentive to the views of those implementing the decisions and to the general public, but at times the Court must lead when others in the political arena are unwilling to take the initiative. In this respect, the Court's independence is indispensable if it is to help America approach democracy.

The Court's Independence in Approaching Democracy

The Supreme Court, said political scientist (and later president) Woodrow Wilson, is "the balance wheel of our whole constitutional system."[94] Like the balancing middle wheel that keeps a machine running smoothly, the Supreme Court takes into consideration the demands of the president, Congress, the bureaucracy, the fifty states and its protectorates, and the American public, and attempts to arrive at decisions that bring them all into harmony.

The paradox is that this vital balancing role is being filled by one of the least democratic institutions in the world. In other countries, leaders who are unelected, hold office for life, and rule in complete secrecy are either kings or dictators; in America they are Supreme Court justices. In theory, the justices can make any decisions they like, but as you have seen, in reality the judiciary is restrained by the possibility that its decisions will meet resistance or not be implemented at all.

Figure 6.5
Confidence in Political Institutions

While generally a higher percentage of the public has consistently said it has a "great deal of confidence" in the Supreme Court than in the presidency and Congress, since the terrorist attacks on September 11, 2001, for the first time the President has been outpolling the Supreme Court in the public's level of confidence.

Source: Compiled from Harris Poll #6, January 30, 2002, Harris Poll Library, www.//harrisinteractive.com/harris_poll/ and data by John R. Hibbing and James T. Smith "What the American Public Wants Congress to Be," in *Congress Reconsidered,* 7th ed., by Lawrence Dodd and Bruce I. Oppenheimer, eds., Congressional Quarterly Press 2001, as it appeared in *National Journal,* June 10, 2000, p. 1818.

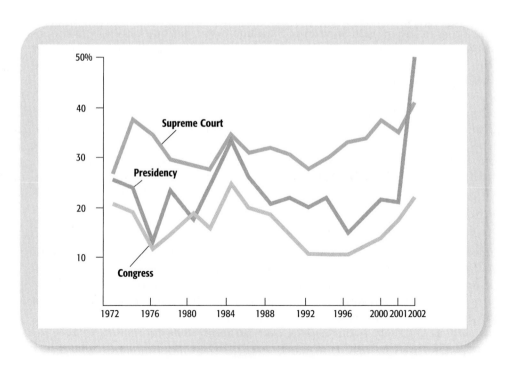

DEMOCRACY IN THE NEW MILLENNIUM

Justice in Wartime

"The mass murder of Americans by terrorists, or the planning thereof, is not just another item on the criminal docket. This is a war against terrorism. Where military justice is called for, military justice will be dispensed." So spoke Vice President Dick Cheney in presenting the case for establishing a new kind of court system, military tribunals, established by President George W. Bush on November 13, 2001 by executive order, for dealing with "real foreign terrorists who violated the laws of war and engaged in unlawful belligerency against the U.S." By using a military system of justice, with military judges and a lower level of individual rights for these suspects, it was hoped that justice could be made more swift and sure, while also retaining a level of security for the prosecutors, the judge, the jury and the general public.

This is not the first time that America had used military tribunals rather than civilian courts to prosecute its enemies and protect its shores. During the Revolutionary War, British secret agent John Andre was convicted by a military commission of collaborating with traitor Benedict Arnold. During the Civil War, at least 4,271 military commission trials were held by the Union army against those who created civil disorder that aided the Confederacy; the most important of these being the trial of the alleged assassins of Abraham Lincoln, resulting in the hanging of Mary Surratt. But the most famous precedent came during World War II, when a military commission investigated and sentenced to death eight German marines who landed via submarine on the American shores of Long Island and Florida, seeking to sabotage military factories and bridges. This procedure was tested when the Germans' lawyer got a writ of *habeas corpus,* in spite of an executive order that denied them access to the civilian courts, in seeking an appeal to get them a civil trial. While the Supreme Court upheld the use of military trials in this case, in the case of *Ex Parte Quirin* (1942), it did so with such speed that the opinions in the case were not written and published until after the convicted men had been executed.

Employing these precedents and operating on the concept that terrorists are not lawful prisoners of war and as such have no right to the traditional American judicial protections, the Bush administration created a system of military tribunals to try the top Taliban and terrorism leaders. Unlike in the civilian federal court where one has the right to a "speedy trial," one's own attorney, a jury of 12 people who must vote unanimously for a conviction, protection by the federal rules of evidence, and the right to appeal through the federal courts to the Supreme Court if necessary, the new tribunals offer fewer legal protections. In the military tribunals the accused can be held indefinitely and can either accept a provided military attorney or pay for one of their own choosing. The accused also has a jury of between 3 to 7 military officers (with 7 required for a death penalty case), and can be convicted by a 2/3 vote unless a death penalty case is involved. Appeals can only be made to a military review panel, which could include civilians temporarily appointed as military officers.

How this program will operate remains to be seen. Whether the President has the right to create such a judicial system given Congress's law-making power and constitutional power over the federal court system is an important question being raised. Secretary of Defense Donald Rumsfeld argues that, "We have made every reasonable effort to establish a process that is just, one that protects both the rights of the defendant to a fair trial but also protects the rights of the American people to lives as they were meant to live, in freedom and without fear of terrorists." On the other hand, Laura W. Murphy, the executive director of the American Civil Liberties Union professes to be "deeply disturbed" by this program and argues that Congress should step in before the "Bill of Rights in America is distorted beyond recognition."*

For more on the Bush administration's plan to use military tribunals to deal with the "war on terrorism," consult www.aclu.org, www.cato.org and www.usinfo.state.gov.

---

*Elisabeth Bumiller, and Steven Lee Myers, "Senior Administration Officials Defend Military Tribunals for Terrorist Suspects," *New York Times,* November 15, 2001, p. B6; William Safire, "Military Tribunals Modified," *New York Times,* March 21, 2002, p. A37; John Mintz, "Tribunal Rules Aim to Shield Witnesses," *Washington Post,* March 22, 2002, p. A1; and John Mintz, "U.S. Adds Legal Rights in Tribunals," *Washington Post,* March 21, 2002, p. 1.

What, then, is the role of an independent Supreme Court in the American system of democracy? Attempts to answer this question have led to a long-standing debate about whether the Court should actively make policy or whether it should practice judicial restraint. Should the Court adhere to the letter of the law and leave policy making to the elected Congress and president? Should it be an architect of public policies that advance human rights? Or should the Court simply reflect the desires of the populace?

Over the years, the willingness of the Supreme Court and the lower federal courts to use the full extent of their power has varied based on the nature of the legal issues, the number of cases heard, the political situation, and who the justices are. What will be the impact of the *Bush v. Gore* case on the willingness and ability of the Supreme Court to hear and decide cases in other areas of law? Recalling the negative reaction to the *Brown v. Board of Education* desegregation decision in 1954 and the *Roe v. Wade* abortion decision in 1973, it remains to be seen whether the Court will be compelled by the wartime posture of the terrorism crisis to back off of issues that they would otherwise like to resolve now. Whatever happens, we can be assured that the actions of the judiciary in America's democracy will continue to have powerful implications for both government and individual rights.

SUMMARY

1. The federal courts decide all legal disputes arising under the Constitution, U.S. law, and treaties. In cases involving disputes between states or involving foreign ambassadors, the Supreme Court has original jurisdiction. For all other federal cases, it has appellate jurisdiction.

2. In the 1803 case of *Marbury v. Madison*, Chief Justice Marshall argued that the Supreme Court has the power to interpret the Constitution. This power, known as judicial review, enables the Court to overturn actions of the executive and legislative branches and to reinterpret the Constitution to fit new situations. The power of statutory construction enables the Court to interpret a federal or state law.

3. The power to appoint justices to the Supreme Court is shared by the president and Congress. The justices are appointed for life and can be impeached only for "High Crimes and Misdemeanors." The president can influence the Court by appointing justices who support a particular philosophy. Congress can change the number of justices or pass a law to reverse a Court decision.

4. Most cases enter the judicial system through a trial court consisting of a single judge and, at times, a jury. The proceedings of the trial court are reviewed by an appellate court consisting of a multijudge panel but no jury. Criminal cases involve violations of state or federal criminal law; civil cases involve private disputes. Most criminal cases are resolved by plea bargains, in which the state agrees to reduce the charges or sentence in return for a guilty plea.

5. The federal judiciary is organized in three tiers. At the bottom are the ninety-four district courts, at least one of which is located in each state. At the next level are the courts of appeals, which hear cases from thirteen circuits, or regions, usually in three-judge panels. District and circuit courts are constitutional courts, but the federal judiciary also includes legislative courts, courts established by Congress.

6. Candidates for the Supreme Court are suggested by senators, governors, the candidates themselves, their friends, and federal judges, and they are screened by the FBI and the American Bar Association. Most nominees to the Court are members of the president's party and share the president's political philosophy.

7. The confirmation process begins with a hearing by the Senate Judiciary Committee, which makes a recommendation prior to a vote by the full Senate. These procedures can constitute major hurdles, resulting in the rejection of nearly one in five presidential nominations.

8. For nominations to district courts, the tradition of senatorial courtesy gives senators what amounts to a veto power. Often, however, candidates are suggested by senators who are members of the president's party. Recent presidents have attempted to make the federal judiciary more representative of the population as a whole.

9. The solicitor general decides which federal cases to appeal from the lower courts, prepares the appeals, and represents the United States before the Supreme Court. Appellate cases come to the Supreme Court through writs of certiorari. If at least four justices

vote to hear a case, it is placed on the docket. In recent years the Court has decided fewer cases, even though the number of appeals reaching it has increased dramatically.

10. When the Court accepts a case, attorneys for all sides submit briefs, or written legal arguments. They then present oral arguments before the Court. The justices hold a conference to discuss and vote on the case, and one of the justices voting with the majority is assigned to draft the opinion, or written version of the decision. The opinion must be approved by at least five justices. A justice who agrees with the majority decision but differs on the reasoning may write a concurring opinion. When a justice disagrees with the Court's ruling, he or she may write a dissenting opinion.

11. Interpretation of a law or a portion of the Constitution as closely as possible to the literal meaning of the words is known as strict construction. When the wording is vague, some justices attempt to determine the original intent of the framers. In some cases, justices consider the effect a ruling would have on public policy. Some justices believe in judicial restraint, deferring to the other branches of government whenever possible. Others are judicial activists, believing that judges have a duty to further certain causes.

12. Decisions of the Supreme Court become the law of the land. However, compliance with a decision is influenced by the extent to which the president supports it. It may also be circumvented by Congress, which can pass a new law or propose a constitutional amendment restating its original intentions.

KEY TERMS

original jurisdiction	constitutional courts	briefs
appellate jurisdiction	U.S. district courts	opinion
Marbury v. Madison	U.S. courts of appeals	majority opinion
judicial review	en banc	plurality opinion
statutory construction	legislative courts	concurring opinion
trial court	senatorial courtesy	dissenting opinion
appellate court	docket	stare decisis
criminal cases	writ of certiorari	precedents
plea bargains	rule of four	judicial restraint
civil cases	solicitor general	judicial activism
class action suit	amicus curiae briefs	

SUGGESTED READINGS

ABRAHAM, HENRY J. *The Judicial Process.* 7th ed. New York: Oxford University Press, 1998. An outstanding text on every facet of the judicial process. Includes a comparative perspective and is chock-full of interesting details and quotations.

————.*Justices, Presidents and Senators: A History of the U.S. Supreme Court Appointments from Washington to Clinton.* Lanham, MD: Rowman and Littlefield, 1999. A complete history of presidential appointments to the Supreme Court and the decision-making that resulted.

BAUM, LAWRENCE. *Supreme Court.* 7th ed. Washington, D.C.: Congressional Quarterly Press, 2001. A highly informative and readable text on the workings of the United States Supreme Court.

BRONNER, ETHAN. *Battle for Justice: How the Bork Nomination Shook America.* New York: Norton, 1989. An inside account of the Robert Bork nomination by a Boston Globe reporter, including the means used by liberal interest groups to defeat the nomination.

DEAN, JOHN W. *The Rehnquist Choice: The Untold Story of the Nixon Appointment that Redefined the Supreme Court.* New York: Free Press, 2001. The behind-the-scenes story of the judicial appointment process that brought William Rehnquist to the Supreme Court by the former counselor to Richard Nixon who helped to bring down his presidency.

EPSTEIN, LEE, et al. *The Supreme Court Compendium: Data, Decisions and Developments*. 3rd ed. Washington, D.C.: Congressional Quarterly Press, 2002. A comprehensive almanac full of useful data on the Supreme Court's history, environment, decisions, and members, including material from the U.S. Supreme Court Judicial Database.

EPSTEIN, LEE, and JACK KNIGHT. *The Choices Justices Make*. Washington, D.C.: CQ Press, 1998. An analysis of the strategically political manner in which justices decide cases.

GOLDMAN, SHELDON. *Picking Federal Judges: Lower Court Selection from Roosevelt Through Reagan*. New Haven, Conn.: Yale University Press, 1997. Findings from thirty years of study by the nation's expert on the lower federal court judicial selection process into how nine presidents have undertaken this process.

GREENYA, JOHN. *Silent Justice: The Clarence Thomas Story*. Fort Lee, N.J.: Barricade Books, 2001. A revealing biography of the enigmatic Justice including a detailed account of the bitter confirmation fight in 1991 that brought him to the Supreme Court.

HOWARD, J. WOODFORD, JR. *Courts of Appeals in the Federal Judicial System*. Princeton, N.J.: Princeton University Press, 1981. An excellent study on the workings of the U.S. Courts of Appeals.

JACOB, HERBERT. *Law and Politics in the United States*. 2d ed. New York: HarperCollins, 1994. An introductory textbook on the operations of the American legal system, showing the connections to the larger political system.

LAZARUS, EDWARD. *Closed Chambers*. New York: Times Books, 1998. Not only a revealing look inside the Court in the 1998–89 term by a former Blackmun law clerk, but a potentially damaging account of the increased role of law clerks in the Court's work.

LEWIS, ANTHONY. *Gideon's Trumpet*. New York: Vintage Press, 1964. A study of the *Gideon v. Wainwright* case that is still the best short, single volume on the progress of a case through the Supreme Court.

MENAND, LOUIS. *The Metaphysical Club: A Story of Ideas in America*. New York: Farrar, Giroux, and Straus, 2001. A fascinating history of an informal discussion club that met in Cambridge, Massachusetts in 1872, including such members as Oliver Wendell Holmes and John Dewey which traces how the ideas spawned by the Civil War eventually evolved into the free speech ideas in the 1919 war cases, such as *Abrams v. U.S.*

MURDOCH, JOYCE and DEB PRICE. *Courting Justice: Gay Men and Lesbians v. the Supreme Court*. New York: Basic Books, 2001. A highly readable history of the Supreme Court's effort to avoid and then mishandle the issue of gay rights in cases throughout the decades.

O'BRIEN, DAVID. *Storm Center: The Supreme Court in American Politics*. 6th ed. New York: Norton, 2002. A highly revealing text on the internal politics of the Supreme Court using sources from justices' papers in historical archives.

PERRY, H. W., JR. *Deciding to Decide: Agenda Setting in the United States Supreme Court*. Cambridge, Mass.: Harvard University Press, 1991. A wonderful analysis of the process by which the Supreme Court accepts cases, based on detailed interviews with sixty-four former law clerks and several Supreme Court justices.

PHELPS, TIMOTHY, and HELEN WINTERNITZ. *Capitol Games: Clarence Thomas, Anita Hill, and the Story of a Supreme Court Nomination*. New York: Hyperion Books, 1992. A fascinating account of the Clarence Thomas confirmation battle by one of the reporters who broke the Anita Hill story that reveals how the press can affect the process.

POLENBERG, RICHARD. *The World of Benjamin Cardozo*. Cambridge, Mass.: Harvard University Press, 1997. A revealing biographical study of one of the nation's most private Supreme Court justices, whose judicial legacy far exceeds the brief time that he served on the bench.

PRITCHETT, C. HERMAN. *Constitutional Civil Liberties*, and its companion, *Constitutional Law of the Federal System*. Englewood Cliffs, N.J.: Prentice Hall, 1984. Still a classic account of how the Supreme Court's doctrine has developed.

REHNQUIST, WILLIAM H. *The Supreme Court: How It Was, How It Is?* New York: William Morrow, 1987. A highly readable explanation of how the Supreme Court operates by an author in the best possible position to speak authoritatively on this question.

SAVAGE, DAVID. *Turning Right: The Making of the Rehnquist Supreme Court.* New York: Wiley, 1992. An inside account by the court reporter for the *Los Angeles Times* of the people who make up the Rehnquist Court and the ways their personal views and interactions shape public policy.

SUNSTEIN, CASS R. *One Case at a Time.* Cambridge, Mass.: Harvard University Press, 1999. A persuasive argument that the current Supreme Court decides cases in a "minimalist," or incremental, fashion.

VILE, JOHN R. ed. *Great American Lawyers: An Encyclopedia.* Santa Barbara, CA, 2001. A fascinating biographical encyclopedia of the lawyers who have helped to shape this nation.

WOODWARD, BOB, and SCOTT ARMSTRONG. *The Brethren: Inside the Supreme Court.* New York: Avon Books, 1979. A highly controversial study of the inside workings of the Supreme Court from 1969 through 1975. Uses anonymous law clerk interviews and Court papers.

7 THE BUREAUCRACY

CHAPTER OUTLINE

Approaching Democracy Case Study:
Creating a New Department During
a National Crisis: The Department
of Homeland Security

Introduction: Bureaucracy and Democracy

Background on the Bureaucracy

Meet the Bureaucracy

Bureaucratic Accountability

What the Public Thinks of the Bureaucracy

Reforming the Bureaucracy

APPROACHING DEMOCRACY CASE STUDY

Creating a New Department During a National Crisis: The Department of Homeland Security

Following the September 11, 2001, attack on the World Trade Center and the Pentagon by al-Qaeda operatives, President Bush used an executive order to create an Office of Homeland Security. Selected to protect the domestic front from terrorism, Tom Ridge, a former prosecutor, congressman, and two-term Republican governor of Pennsylvania (and a close friend and political supporter of President Bush and his father), was selected to run the new office and assigned the title Assistant to the President for Homeland Security.

Ridge was given a high profile office in the west wing, an initial staff of 80 and a broad agenda for overseeing eleven major subject areas. Ridge's cabinet responsibilities include coordinating the activities of over 40 federal agencies and departments. The new cabinet office was mandated to protect 20,000 miles of U.S. borders and to coordinate 46 separate federal agencies to fight terrorism. The challenge is to streamline the organizational coherence of the new cabinet post without creating another management or supervisory bureaucratic unit (see Figure 7.1).

Ridge identified four broad areas his office would target: a quick response plan to enable local officials to acquire necessary resources during a terrorist attack, a coherent anti-biological security program, a program to secure the national air space, and a reconfigured early-warning system to stem future terrorist attacks. When assuming office, Ridge emphasized that close oversight and department coordination were integral to making his new job work: "My job is to step back from all of these different agencies, take a look at all their moving parts. Then I can see where there can be some refining, some strengthening and some improvements."[1]

The creation and development of the Office of Homeland Security within the context of the September 11 attacks reveals the complex challenge our democracy faces in attempting to manage and lead a bureaucratic entity within the web of our existing federal bureaucracy. In the weeks following September 11, Ridge helped to coordinate a remarkable infrastructure involving the FBI, FEMA, Department of Energy, Environmental Protection Agency, Coast Guard, Army National Guard, Departments of Justice, Transportation, and other agencies of the federal government. After several weeks in office Ridge was able to take stock of where he was and where he wanted to be: "I think one of the challenges that the Office of Homeland Security has is to make sure that it becomes a permanent part of how the federal government does business. For a long time whether it was perceived or real, there was a notion that when you took a look at Washington D.C., different departments and different agencies, in many respects, kind of siloed their communication, their information and the like. But since September 11, there has been extraordinary collaboration and cooperation. And one of the responsibilities I believe we have in the Homeland Security Office is to make sure that not just the principals are cooperating—and I see that every day at every level, I might add—the FBI and the Attorney General and the CIA and the Department of Defense and Customs, working with INS. I mean, it's happening naturally. But I think our long-term best interests will be served if we create structures and relationships that just become a permanent part of how we do business and

how the government provides service and security for the long-term."[2]

On June 6, 2002, we learned just how permanent a structure was envisioned for homeland security when President Bush announced a proposal for the creation of a new cabinet department for domestic defense. In the President's words, "we have concluded that our government must be reorganized to deal more effectively with the threats of the twenty-first century. So tonight I ask the Congress to join me in creating a single permanent mission—securing the homeland and protecting the American people. . . . Tonight I propose a permanent cabinet-level Department of Homeland Security to unite essential agencies that must work more closely together . . . What I am proposing tonight is the most extensive reorganization of the federal government since the 1940's."[3]

The next day President Bush predicted a difficult fight ahead for the plan because it involved so many bureaucratic turf battles. "This is going to be a tough battle, because we're going to be stepping on some people's toes . . . when you take power away from one person in Washington, it tends to make them nervous. So we're just going to have to keep the pressure on the people in the United States Congress to do the same."[4]

The legislative bottleneck disappeared in the aftermath of the Republican electoral victory in November 2002. By a vote of 299 to 121, the House of Representatives passed legislation on November 13 establishing a new Department of Homeland Security. By a vote of 90–9, the Senate quickly followed suit on November 19. President Bush soon thereafter signed the bill into law, thereby creating the Homeland Security Department (see Figure 7.2).

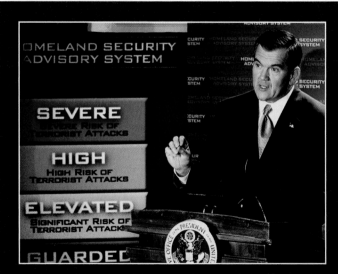

▲ Homeland Security Advisor Tom Ridge stands beside the color-coded Homeland Security Advisory System, which is a means to disseminate information regarding the risk of terrorist acts to federal, state, and local authorities, and to the American people.

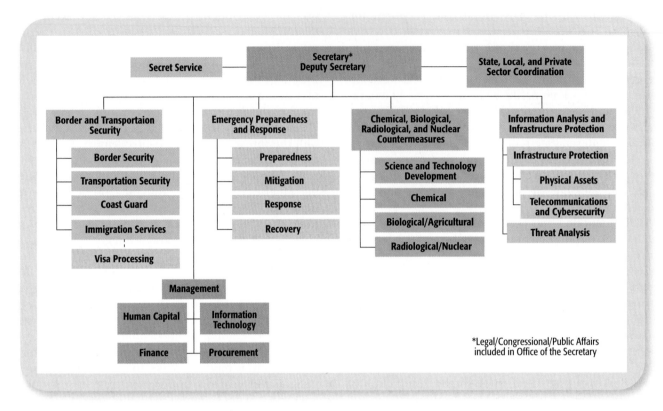

Figure 7.1   Organization of the Department of Homeland Security
Source: http://www.naco.org/pubs/cnews/02-06-17/Articles/02bush.html.

Question for Reflection: Early in the twentieth century the United States developed agencies to combat threats to our way of life both at home and abroad. The FBI and CIA were established to fight crime and coordinate intelligence data. Based on the evolution of these two agencies, what predictions might be made for the future of the Department of Homeland Security?

INTRODUCTION: BUREAUCRACY AND DEMOCRACY

In this chapter we look at some of the contradictions that arise between bureaucratic necessity and democratic ideals. We want you to be thinking about how it is that a necessary, but inherently secretive bureaucratic organization such as the Department of Homeland Security can gain legitimacy and function without public disclosure of activities. After all, democracy requires plurality; traditional bureaucracy requires unity. Democratic society is organized around the principle of equality, while bureaucratic organization is hierarchical. A fundamental element in any democracy is openness, but bureaucratic operations often demand secrecy, especially when national security is involved. A democratic political system ensures equal access to participation in politics, but bureaucratic participation depends on institutional authority. Finally, democracy assumes the election and subsequent public accountability of all officials, but bureaucrats are appointed and the agencies they lead are created without congressional action and thus are not subject to public accountability.

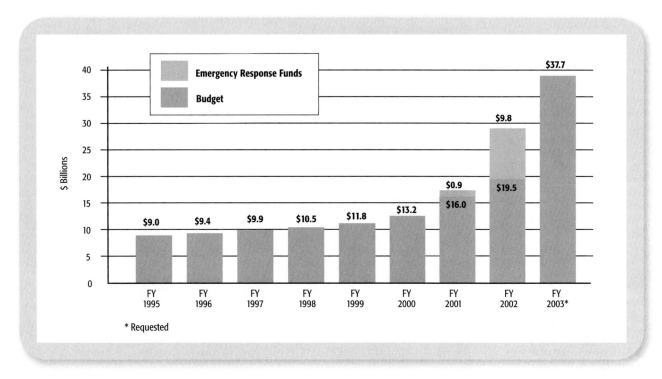

Figure 7.2   Funding for Homeland Security
Source: Office of Management and Budget.

Though the bureaucracy is an institution that is often scorned for its enormous size and lack of responsiveness or accountability, this "fourth branch" of government is charged with an important function that makes it indispensable in America's approach to democracy: carrying forth the work of the federal government. The Department of Homeland Security has the responsibility of developing and coordinating a national strategy to secure the United States from terrorist threats or attacks. The President's most important job is to protect and defend the American people. The Coast Guard has assumed expanded duties to safeguard our shores and ports. The National Guard has increased its surveillance. New licensing requirements have been instituted to ensure safer transportation of hazardous materials. New federal anti-terrorism laws have been passed, giving law enforcement officers tools to track terrorists. Tighter controls are being instituted on immigration. Many of these actions challenge core values such as freedom and liberty. All Americans want Tom Ridge to succeed in his mission and most of us would be willing to compromise some of our democratic principles if it meant achieving the greater good—the survival of our nation and the eradication of terrorist networks. Thinking about these issues will help you to conceptualize the challenge of approaching democracy.

FYI

Former Alabama governor and presidential candidate George Wallace, never a fan of the bureaucracy, once commented, "Send me to Washington and I will push those pointy-headed bureaucrats off their bicycles and throw their briefcases in the Potomac River."

Background on the Bureaucracy

It is difficult to imagine a world without bureaucracy. Americans usually measure the performance of bureaucratic agencies not by their routine successes but by the impact of their failures. "Bureaucracy is the cod-liver oil of social institutions. It smells bad and leaves a nasty aftertaste, but sometimes it is just what you need."[5] Part of the suspicion Americans feel about their bureaucracy comes from the realization that most government agencies function, most of the time, with little or no restraint from the American people. Indeed, the bureaucracy has been called the "fourth branch of government"—as powerful as Congress, the president, and the

▶ On November 19, 2001, President Bush signed into law the Aviation and Transportation Security Act (ATSA), which among other things created a new Transportation Security Administration (TSA) within the Department of Transportation. This act established a series of challenging but critically important milestones toward achieving a secure air travel system. The improvements include that by November 19, 2002, screening of individuals and property in the United States will be conducted by TSA employees and companies under contract with TSA. This requires enhanced qualifications, training, and testing of individuals who perform screening functions. It also requires that federal law enforcement officers be present at screening locations.

bureaucracy A large and complex organizational system in which tasks, roles, and responsibilities are structured to achieve a goal.

bureaucrats People who work in a bureaucracy, not only the obscure, faceless clerks normally disparaged by critics of government, but also "street-level bureaucrats" such as police officers, social workers, and schoolteachers.

specialization A principle that in bureaucracy, specific tasks should be delegated to individuals whose training and experience give them the expertise to execute them. Also refers to a norm used to push legislation through Congress in which members who lack expertise in a particular policy area defer to policy specialists with more knowledge.

hierarchy A clear chain of communication and command running from an executive director at the top down through all levels of workers.

formal rules In a bureaucracy, clearly defined procedures governing the execution of all tasks within the jurisdiction of a given agency.

Supreme Court, but operating without the regular elections and/or oversight committees that keep these institutions responsive to public opinion.

A **bureaucracy** is a large and complex organizational system in which tasks, roles, and responsibilities are structured to achieve a goal. The term is rooted in the eighteenth-century French word for a woolen cloth (*burel*) used to cover a writing desk, or *bureau*. **Bureaucrats,** the people who work in a bureaucracy, include not only the obscure, faceless clerks normally disparaged by critics of government but also "street-level" bureaucrats, such as police officers, social workers, and schoolteachers.[6]

German sociologist Max Weber (1865–1920) is considered the father of modern bureaucracy. He modeled his "ideal type" of bureaucratic organization on the Prussian government of the early twentieth century. He believed that the purpose of a bureaucracy was to improve efficiency, and that efficiency could be promoted in three ways—through specialization, hierarchy, and a system of formal rules.[7]

The principle of **specialization** means that specific tasks should be delegated to individuals whose training and experience give them the expertise to execute them. As the responsibilities of government increase, so too does the need for more specialization, or more experts in various areas.

Bureaucratic organization also requires **hierarchy,** a clear chain of communication and command running from an executive director at the top down through all levels of workers, such as the mailroom clerks in the middle and janitors at the bottom. The hierarchy facilitates decision-making and establishes clear lines of authority within a large, complex organization. As new bureaucratic organizations that involve the coordination and collaboration of multiple agencies, such as the Department of Homeland Security, are created, new approaches to hierarchy are needed.

? Question for Reflection: What type of hierarchy would be effective for the Department of Homeland Security?

In addition to specialization and hierarchical authority, bureaucratic organizations use **formal rules,** clearly defined procedures governing the execution of all tasks within the jurisdiction of a given agency. Sometimes called *standard operating procedures (SOP)*, these rules simplify and routinize complex procedures, curtail favoritism, and improve the decision-making process by allowing bureaucrats to respond to a broad array of situations with a minimum of delay and confusion. Such formal rules also apply to the professional lives of bureaucrats. There are clearly defined steps for job advancement, specific descriptions of job duties, and specific qualifications for salary increases.

Problems Inherent in the Bureaucratic Form   Specialization, hierarchy, and formal rules are all designed to improve the performance of bureaucracy. Usually this structure works. Likewise, although we sometimes hear horror stories about mail going undelivered, the U.S. Postal Service remains one of the most efficient public bureaucracies in the world. And for all of our moaning and groaning about taxes and the Internal Revenue Service, most of us receive our tax returns from the IRS promptly—through the U.S. mail. In fact, when some people died and others were infected with anthrax in the fall of 2001, the Postal Service continued to process 30 billion pieces of mail daily. Postal employees took extra precautions, but they came to work and did their jobs, always knowing that another contaminated letter could arrive at any time at any postal facility within the United States.

Indeed, the very nature of specialization within a bureaucracy can sometimes impede rather than improve performance, rendering an agency relatively efficient in some tasks but inflexible in others. Weber warned that bureaucratic organization might turn workers into "specialists without spirit," motivated only by narrowly defined tasks and unable to adapt to changing circumstances. You can probably think of an applicable case from your own daily dealings with bureaucracy at college, local government, or even during a summer vacation at your favorite national park administered by the National Park Service.

Question for Reflection: What if the management of the border patrol was placed under the Department of Homeland Security rather than the Justice department? What ramifications would this have on the existing bureaucracy and the balance of powers?

Growth of the Federal Bureaucracy

The bureaucracy commands the most attention when something goes wrong—when sacks of undelivered mail are discovered in some musty Chicago basement, or when a string of successes is marred by a tragic disaster. Despite their problems, bureaucracies are necessary and have come to characterize modern industrialized societies. Large-scale bureaucratic organizations allow for high levels of productivity and the coordination of government programs, such as road building, air traffic control, environmental management, the postal system, and telecommunications. Nevertheless, bureaucracies pose serious problems in terms of accountability and power. For example, how can organizations such as the Federal Bureau of Investigation (FBI) and the Central Intelligence Agency (CIA) have sufficient enforcement power to thwart terrorism without compromising the rights of innocent civilians who are rounded up and jailed because they fit a profile? How can the Internal Revenue Service (IRS), responsible for processing several million tax returns annually, be sufficiently restrained not to prey on innocent citizens by terrifying them into paying taxes they don't owe or by ruining them financially if they cannot pay what they do owe?

America's early bureaucracy hardly resembled today's Leviathan. George Washington's budget for the entire bureaucracy in 1790 was just under $1.5 million per year, and the money funded just three departments—State, War, and Treasury. The largest of these, the Department of the Treasury, employed 70 workers in 1790, minuscule by modern standards. The federal government's rapid growth began in the late nineteenth century. At that time, industrial expansion was increasing the size

The INS Fiasco: Student Visas for September 11 Terrorists Renewed

In one of the most shocking and embarrassing incidents of the Bush presidency, the Immigration and Naturalization Service in March of 2002 sent letters to a Florida flight school renewing the student visas held by dead al-Qaeda operatives who bombed the World Trade Center on September 11, 2001.

How could it happen? That is the question every American asked when the story broke. Angry politicians from both major parties called for a total overhaul of the beleaguered INS—under intense fire for years of poor performance. Cecilia Munoz, a leader of the National Council of La Raza, noted that "It's a given that the agency needs to be reformed, the question is how." Representative F. James Sensenbrenner Jr., head of the powerful House Judiciary Committee, argued that the INS could never be fixed. Most Republican leaders wanted to divide the enormous responsibilities of the agency into two separate entities: one agency under the Justice Department to patrol the borders to enforce immigration law, the other under the INS to administer benefits to immigrants. Only in this way could a nation built by immigrants handle its own mandate to accept new people from around the globe.

Conflicting responsibilities, an out-dated infrastructure, and a large workload plague the INS. The United States has some of the longest borders of any nation in the world. Immigrants who legally enter the United States must be tracked according to a cumbersome and lengthy administration process. The system is so broken that there are over 500,000 pending cases. INS officials attempted in the 1990s to reform the administration but made little headway.

The Bush administration opposed the idea of separating the INS due to the costs involved and the increase in size of bureaucratic units and staff. The administration faced a political bind, however. If the September 11 attacks meant that American borders need increased policing, then why not separate the functions of the INS to increase national security? The credibility of presidential appointments was also at stake. President Bush wanted James W. Ziglar, INS czar, to have a chance to reform the organization. But as Ziglar's predecessors learned, reforming government bureaucracies once they are created is no easy task. As the functions of the INS in the future become more police-orientated in the interests of protecting the nation from resistance abroad, it will become even more practically difficult—and politically impossible—to reform the agency. In mid-April 2002, Congress took the first steps towards overhauling the INS by preparing a bill that would abolish the INS and split its functions into two bureaus, one for enforcement, the other for services.* The Department of Homeland Security will absorb the operation of the INS and will bring the major border security and transportation operations under one roof.

Sources: Eric Schmitt, "Agency Finds Itself Under Siege, With Many Responsibilities and Many Critics," *The New York Times,* March 15, 2002, p. A11; Doris Meissner, "Two Jobs for One INS," http://www.washingtonpost.com, March 28, 2002, p. A29.

*See Eric Schmitt, "Congress Set to Break Up Beleaguered Agency," *New York Times,* April 10, 2002, p. A13; Cheryl Thompson, "Congress Eyes Plan to Dismantle INS," *Washington Post,* April 10, 2002, p. A21.

and complexity of the economy and destabilizing American social life. As corporations became more powerful, the popular call for increased regulation of business and a larger role for government in protecting the welfare of its citizens intensified. Among those calling for change were the Progressives, and in the early twentieth century they became successful advocates for increased popular participation in government and administrative reform at the local level. The Progressives thought government ought to assume broad regulatory powers over corporations, thus initiating the modern trend toward viewing government involvement in a positive light. The belief in limited government that had prevailed through the nineteenth century began to yield to the idea of "an active government that would be without limitation, with power to pursue social and economic justice."[8]

This new faith in the power of government peaked during the thirty-year period in which government mobilized the nation's resources to fight the Great Depression, wage World War II, and combat domestic poverty and racial discrimination. The public's commitment to activist government paved the way for the astonishing growth of the federal bureaucracy in the twentieth century. The greatest growth was evident in the 1930s and 1940s, during the emergence of what has become known as the "welfare state."

The Welfare State   Beginning in 1933, Franklin D. Roosevelt's New Deal involved the government in everyday economic affairs and dramatically increased the size of the government's work force and the scope and power of federal responsibilities.

FYI

How large is the bureaucracy? President Carter tried to find out, but after three months of searching, a White House official told him, "We were unable to obtain any single document containing a complete and current listing of government units which are part of the federal government." The United States Government Organization Manual, which runs to more than eight hundred pages, scarcely begins to convey the size and complexity of the U.S. government.

The New Deal was devised in response to the Great Depression, which brought massive unemployment—at times as much as a quarter of America's labor force was out of work—and a growing awareness of the need to provide more security for American citizens, both on the job and after retirement.

The New Deal consisted of a series of legislative acts, executive orders, and proclamations creating large-scale federal programs that sought to provide retirement insurance, health care, economic security, and poverty relief for Americans. New Deal programs were aimed at creating jobs and jump-starting a stagnant economy. They also laid the legislative foundation for liberal Democratic policies. The Civilian Conservation Corps (CCC) granted millions of dollars to the states to pay young people to work at forestry, irrigation, and land projects; by 1935 more than 500,000 youths were at work under the auspices of the CCC. The Tennessee Valley Authority (TVA) provided funds to build dams and reservoirs, creating thousands of jobs and bringing electricity to new areas. The Wagner Act established the National Labor Relations Board (NLRB) and gave workers the right to unionize and bargain collectively. The Social Security Act established a federally funded financial safety net for the elderly, infirm, and unemployed.

Roosevelt, building upon the work done earlier in the century by his cousin President Theodore Roosevelt, also used the power of the government to increase regulation of finance and commerce. Responding to a wave of bank failures and lost deposits, Roosevelt's administration established the Federal Deposit Insurance Corporation (FDIC) to insure most bank deposits. Roosevelt's administration also created the Securities and Exchange Commission (SEC), the Federal National Mortgage Association (FNMA, or "Fannie Mae"), and the Federal Communications Commission (FCC), to regulate the stock exchanges, the interstate mortgage market, and the public airwaves, respectively.

The New Deal programs became the core of the modern **welfare state.** Although designed as temporary emergency programs to relieve the suffering of the Depression, most New Deal agencies became a permanent part of a dramatically enlarged federal bureaucracy. In addition to expanding the bureaucracy, the New Deal era led to a growing dependence upon that bureaucracy to administer and regulate many of the essential functions of modern American life.

Similarly, during World War II the federal government hired hundreds of thousands of temporary employees to plan and coordinate the vast assembly of personnel and machinery used to defeat the Axis Powers. After World War II, many of these "temporary" employees remained at work in government and were absorbed by agencies that redefined their civilian missions more broadly. But neither the growth of the bureaucracy nor the dependence upon it by increasing numbers of Americans stopped with the end of the Great Depression and World War II. Since then the size of the federal bureaucracy has been relatively stable, although hardly stagnant.

The slight growth in the 1960s was the result of President Johnson's Great Society, an ambitious assault on racial injustice and poverty, which created scores of new government agencies. At the request of the president, Congress enacted programs to provide medical care, job opportunities, and business loans to the poor and to improve the quality and availability of education at all levels. In addition, Congress enacted programs to conserve water, air, and natural resources.

During the 1970s, growing citizen awareness of the problems of consumer safety and environmental degradation led to creation of the Consumer Product Safety Commission (CPSC) and the Environmental Protection Agency (EPA), and, thus, more bureaucratic growth. In the wake of the OPEC oil embargo, the old Office of Emergency Preparedness was systematically expanded. First it became the Federal Energy Office (FEO), then the Federal Energy Administration (FEA), and finally the cabinet-level Department of Energy (DOE). Mounting concern over safety in the workplace, coupled with evidence that corporations were not willing to adopt appropriate safety measures without government prodding, led to the creation of the Occupational Safety and Health Administration (OSHA).

welfare state A social system whereby the government assumes primary responsibility for the welfare of its citizens.

Expansion of the responsibilities of government during the 1960s and 1970s brought major increases in the federal budget, largely because of increases in *transfer payments*—that is, money paid to individuals in the form of Social Security benefits, welfare payments, and the like—thereby "transferring" money from one segment of society to another.

One of the key campaign promises made by virtually all presidential candidates since the 1970s is to reduce the size and scope of the federal government. Throughout their campaigns, candidates attack big government, but once in office they find it very difficult to reduce the number of federal workers. One of the most dramatic attempts at downsizing was made by former president Ronald Reagan, but even this conservative icon found it difficult to reduce the scope of bureaucratic power. Reagan's failure to curtail the bureaucracy says more about bureaucracy than it does about the former president. Reagan encountered something presidents throughout American history have had to accept: the bureaucracy is a constantly evolving, growing, largely independent realm of government. Perhaps the final irony of the bureaucracy's vengeance on the Reagan legacy came in 1997 with the opening of the largest new federal building in Washington, D.C. Taking up the size of several football fields and housing thousands of federal workers, the new federal building is named the Ronald Reagan Building and International Trade Center. Only the Pentagon building is larger.[9]

Evolution of the Bureaucracy: Creating the Civil Service

Since the early days of the republic, the federal bureaucracy has grown enormously. There has also been a corresponding change in its character. Prior to the presidential election of Andrew Jackson in 1828, a small, elite group of wealthy, well-educated white males dominated the bureaucracy. Jackson, a populist, was determined to make the federal workforce more representative by opening up jobs to the masses.

"H.U.D. called the F.A.A. The F.A.A. called the S.E.C. The S.E.C. called G.S.A. G.S.A. called O.M.B. O.M.B. called Y-O-U."

He instituted a new system based on the declaration of his friend, Senator William Marcy: "To the victor go the spoils."[10] The emergence of this **spoils system** meant that Jackson and his subordinates would award top-level government jobs and contracts on the basis of party loyalty rather than social or economic status or relevant experience.

Jackson's opponents in the Whig party recognized the advantages of using government jobs for patronage purposes, and when Jackson's Democrats were voted out of office, the bureaucracy was restaffed by those loyal to the Whigs. Later on, as the government grew, supporters of the spoils system found that if a thousand patronage jobs were beneficial, ten thousand or twenty thousand would be even more welcome.

The spoils system survived until the assassination of President James Garfield by Charles Guiteau in 1881, who was bitter about his inability to find a job in Garfield's administration. In response, Congress passed the Pendleton Act of 1883, which created a **civil service,** a system of hiring and promoting employees based on professional merit, not party loyalty. Such a system was designed to protect government employees from political threats to their job security. The act also created a three-person Civil Service Commission to oversee the implementation of the merit principle throughout the federal work force. The Civil Service Commission evaluated job applicants on the basis of their performance on civil service examinations. Employees achieved permanent status after a probationary period, and they were promoted only with strong performance evaluations from supervisors. The Civil Service Commission functioned until 1978, when, under the Civil Service Reform Act, it was replaced by two agencies. One, the Office of Personnel Management, administers civil service recruitment and promotion procedures; the other, the independent Merit Systems Protection Board, conducts studies of the merit system and holds grievance and disciplinary hearing for federal employees.

Today, merit-based hiring and advancement have eliminated much of the corruption and cronyism of the old patronage system. The civil service system encourages the hiring of people with high levels of skill and expertise and provides procedures for evaluating the qualifications and job performance of federal workers. There is, however, a downside to the civil service. For one thing, it insulates federal employees from many of the pressures of a competitive, private sector job market. For example, the process for disciplining a federal employee is long and complicated, making it difficult to dismiss or demote a civil servant. The employee must receive written notice at least thirty days in advance, detailing the reasons for, and specific examples of, the conduct prompting the action. The employee may then appeal the action to the Merit Systems Protection Board (MSPB), which must grant a hearing, at which point the employee has the right to legal counsel. If the MSPB rejects the appeal, the employee may take the case to the U.S. Court of Appeals. The process has become so burdensome that, rather than attempt to fire unproductive employees; supervisors have learned to live with them. Debate on the Homeland Security legislation centered on President Bush's push for greater freedom from civil service rules versus union opposition to political management control over federal employees.

Civil service guidelines not only insulate the federal work force, they also tend to instill in some agencies a sense that they are "untouchable," whatever the periodic changes in the political climate of the country. One common remark associated with career civil servants when they are asked about a change in presidential administration is that while presidents are temporary employees, careerists in the bureaucracy stay for life. Research has shown that most civil servants tend to conform to the policy directives of administrations as they come and go, but determined resistance to presidential initiatives can hamper a president's agenda considerably.

The Hatch Act To make the bureaucracy more responsive to the policy directives of changing presidential administrations and to move it in the direction of greater political neutrality, Congress passed the **Hatch Act** in 1939, named for its author,

In this political cartoon by Thomas Nast, President Andrew Jackson is riding the hog of political patronage, implying that those who win office can help those who support them with jobs, money, and power.

spoils system A system in which government jobs and contracts are awarded on the basis of party loyalty rather than social or economic status or relevant experience.

civil service A system of hiring and promoting employees based on professional merit, not party loyalty.

Hatch Act Approved by Congress in 1939, and named for its author, Senator Carl Hatch of New Mexico, a list of political dos and don'ts for federal employees; designed to prevent federal civil servants from using their power or position to engage in political activities to influence elections, thereby creating a nonpartisan, nonpolitical, professionalized bureaucracy.

APPROACHING DIVERSITY

Fairness of the Federal Merit Promotion Process

In 2002 a private report revealed that federal employees are dissatisfied with the system of promotion and believe that pay raises and job promotions do not follow the merit system written into the legal code. The report was produced by the Merit Systems Protection Board, a nonpartisan agency that conducts studies of federal workers for both the White House and Congress. The report's findings stemmed from questionnaires filled out by 1,144 supervisors, 189 union officials, and 1,636 employees.

According to the study, the federal government allocates $238 million dollars annually to make the "promotion process" work, though public and private critics contend that the funding fails to fix the promotion problem. The study revealed that 48 percent of federal employees surveyed contend that they were bypassed for promotion that they felt they deserved (28 percent alleged that this had occurred within the past two years). Over 75% of respondents also stated that the supervisors handpicked the applicant before the job opening was even announced. Approximately 52% of employees believed that they were never given an adequate chance to prove their capabilities. Over half of the employees wanted someone from their own organization to receive a job promotion before an outsider was considered.

For their part, supervisors took a different opinion of the promotion problem. Supervisors stated that they relied solely upon merit and job capability to promote federal employees both within and outside of their organizations. Ninety-eight percent stated that technical qualifications were the single most important criteria for job selection. They admitted, however, that over half of the time they select a person for a new job *before* announcing the opening of the position. In response, over sixty percent of employees reported that acting loyal to the supervisor equated with job performance in receiving a promotion.

Union officials who were also polled noted that government promotion of individuals stemmed primarily from contacts within the administration and the permanent federal bureaucracy. Over 62% of union operatives believed that people within the organization should be promoted over outsiders (only 30% of supervisors thought so). Approximately two-thirds of union officials believed that seniority should play the primary role in promotion. (40% of supervisors agreed).

The most important conclusion of the study entails the lack of communication between supervisors and employees within the federal government. According to the MSPB report, "The perception of fairness may not be completely attainable... We simply may not be able to completely eliminate or even reduce employee concerns about the fairness of the merit promotion process unless we can develop better ways to help supervisors identify who among a group of best qualified applicants is in fact the best candidate for the job."

Source: Stephen Barr, "Survey Tries to Show the Score in the Game of Federal Promotions," *The Washington Post*, February 17, 2002.

Senator Carl Hatch of New Mexico. It is a list of political do's and don'ts for federal employees. The act was designed to prevent federal civil servants from using their power or position to influence elections, thereby creating a nonpartisan, nonpolitical, professionalized bureaucracy. Under the Hatch Act, bureaucrats may express opinions about issues and candidates and contribute money to political organizations, but they cannot distribute campaign information, nor can they campaign actively for or against a candidate. A federal employee may register and vote in an election but cannot run as a candidate for public office.

Although the authors of the Hatch Act believed it necessary to restrict the political liberties of government employees to preserve the neutrality of the growing maze of federal agencies and programs, these restrictions illustrate one area where bureaucracy clashes with democratic ideals. Nearly 3 million American civilians who work for the federal government have their rights to full participation in the nation's political process sharply curtailed. In the box "Know Your Grasp of the Hatch Act," test your knowledge of what federal employees are allowed to do. Although many civil servants and constitutional scholars have denounced the Hatch Act as unconstitutional, the Supreme Court has disagreed with them.

Critics of the law have found some sympathy in Congress. In 1993 it amended the act to allow federal employees to participate more actively in partisan politics, with several restrictions. They cannot be candidates for public office in partisan elections, use official authority to influence or interfere with elections, or solicit

Know Your Grasp of the Hatch Act

Test your Hatch Act IQ. Knowing the right answers could keep you from losing your job, being fined or suspended, or maybe even going to jail. Federal employees may do the following (true or false):

1. Sign a nominating petition for a partisan candidate.
2. Assist in voter registration drives.
3. Hold office in a political club or party.
4. Contribute money to a political organization and attend political fund-raisers.
5. Wear a political button at work.
6. Distribute political party literature at a polling place on election day.
7. Solicit contributions to a partisan political fund-raiser.
8. Park a car with a political bumper sticker in a federally owned or subsidized parking lot.
9. Participate in partisan political activity if employed by the Office of Personnel Management, the Commerce Department, the Bureau of Indian Affairs, or the Health Care Finance Administration.
10. Participate in partisan political activity if employed in a low-level job by the Central Intelligence Agency, the National Security Council, the FBI, or the Contract Appeals Boards.
11. Wear a political button on a government-issued uniform if off duty or on vacation or other approved leave.

Answers

1. True
2. True
3. True
4. True
5. False
6. True
7. False
8. True
9. True
10. False
11. False

funds from or discourage the political activity of any person undergoing an audit, investigation, or enforcement action. However, federal workers can register and vote as they choose, assist in voter registration, participate in campaigns when off duty, and seek and hold positions in political parties or other political organizations.

All these changes in the Hatch Act are intended to allow federal workers to exercise more of the rights and privileges of political participation open to other American citizens. But as federal employees are granted more freedom to participate in politics, there is the potential for the reappearance of the kinds of partisanship that prompted the passage of the Pendleton and Hatch Acts in the first place. Language in the Homeland Security bill would allow creation of a federal personnel management system that is "flexible," "contemporary," and "grounded in the principles of merit and fitness." Critics see this as threatening the civil service protections we have discussed throughout this section.

Question for Reflection: How would you amend the Hatch Act to enable federal workers greater involvement in their democratic system of government?

Meet the Bureaucracy

What does the federal workforce look like? Among the *civilians* employed by the federal government, there are more than 15,000 official categories of employees, ranging from electricians to paperhangers, from foreign service officers to postal service workers. There are nearly 100,000 regulators; 150,000 engineers; hundreds of thousands of analysts, clerks, and secretarial staff; 15,000 foresters; 2,300 veterinarians; 3,000 photographers; and 500 chaplains. Surprisingly, nearly 90 percent of federal employees work outside Washington, D.C. California alone has almost as many federal employees as does the nation's capital.[11]

All told, nearly 176 million civilian employees now work for the federal government. This force is spread among 1,800 departments, agencies, commissions, and government corporations in 400,000 government-owned buildings throughout the United States and abroad. We want to expose one myth with fact: today's federal worker is better educated and better compensated than at anytime in history. Government is not a bastion of clerks with pointy pencils. In a study conducted by the Congressional Budget Office, from 1985–2000, employment in clerical jobs dropped from 377,400 to 135,000. This steep drop relegated clerical workers to constituting only 9% of the civil service. During this same period, the number of professional, administrative, or technical members of the civil service increased from 79% to 87% in white-collar jobs, with 56% in professional or administrative jobs. In 1985, 30% had a BA degree; by 2000 that number had increased to 40%. All of this has resulted in dramatically higher pay grades for civil servants.[12] The CBO study, *Changes in Federal Civilian Employment: An Update* is available at the CBO Website, www.cbo.gov.

What the Bureaucracy Does

Americans today share a tradition as old as their government: animosity toward "those faceless bureaucrats" in Washington, their state capitol, or their local city hall. Yet those bureaucrats perform many essential functions that we take for granted. Bureaucrats direct the flow of air traffic, patrol U.S. borders to control the flow of people and drugs, and deliver the mail. Civil servants are typical working Americans whose jobs, although hardly glamorous, are important to the smooth functioning of society. Whenever a letter is delivered on time, an application for governmental financial aid is processed, or a highway is repaired, the bureaucracy has done its job.

Because bureaucrats have been facing pressure from private competitors, they have found it in their interest to be more attentive to public opinion and more open to useful suggestions from within the organization. This development has occurred in spite of the fact that their institutional authority is based on professional expertise. Most bureaucratic specialists feel—often rightly—that they know more than other bureaucrats and more than the general public about an issue.

Although bureaucrats are appointed rather than elected, the evidence shows that they are surprisingly similar to the public in terms not only of demographic characteristics but even in terms of their general values . . . Those allegedly "faceless bureaucrats," then, look very much like the United States they serve.[13]

The bureaucracy performs three key governmental tasks: implementation, administration, and regulation.

Implementation   One of the primary tasks of the bureaucracy is to implement the policies established by Congress and the executive. Think back to the opening case study and the task of homeland defense. **Implementation** means providing the organization and expertise required to put into action any policy that has become law. When Congress passed legislation establishing the Head Start program of early childhood care and education in the 1960s, a new agency was established to "flesh out" the guidelines of the program, hire and train employees, and disburse the federal monies appropriated to the program. Tom Ridge, as head of the Office of Homeland Security, has the task of fleshing out numerous proposals that will protect our borders and skies, from all forms of terrorist threats made to our national security.

Implementation can involve a considerable amount of bureaucratic autonomy. In implementing legislation, administrators are able to exercise **administrative discretion,** which refers to the latitude that an agency, or even a single bureaucrat, has in interpreting and applying a law. When passing legislation, Congress often does

implementation The act of providing the organization and expertise required to put into action any policy that has become law. Also refers to the actual execution of a policy.

administrative discretion The latitude that an agency, or even a single bureaucrat, has in interpreting and applying a law.

little more than declare policy goals, assign their implementation to an agency, and make money available to the agency. Lack of statutory specificity may be necessary to get a bill over the hurdles of the legislative process, but it makes for poorly defined policy directives. After a bill is passed, bureaucratic managers must step in and, exercising administrative discretion, draft detailed guidelines for all the various procedures required to turn policies into workable programs.

Even when Congress and the bureaucracy are well intentioned, there are many points at which implementation can go awry. Frequently, interest groups at state and local levels resist new policies or raise questions—for example, about clean air and water laws—that make the implementation of such policies difficult if not impossible. In 1994–95, citizens in Maine, Pennsylvania, and Texas protested the implementation of strict auto emissions tests ordered by the Environmental Protection Agency. As a result, legislatures in all three states suspended the programs, preferring the wrath of the EPA to the wrath of their constituents.

Administration Another bureaucratic task is **administration,** which involves performing the routine tasks associated with a specific policy goal. Bureaucrats exercise a lot less administrative discretion at this stage. If we look at the post September 11 activities of the federal government we can see that virtually every government agency contributed to the relief effort. Just think about the administrative task that was the responsibility of the federal government in New York alone—the Federal Emergency Management Agency, FEMA sent eight 62 member Urban Search and Rescue teams to New York, working closely with the Army Corps of Engineers, the Government Services Administration and the Environmental Protection Agency.[14] The federal government was asked to determine whether the water was safe to drink, whether other structures were safe from collapse, and whether or not that section of New York City should be declared a Superfund site, thereby providing additional clean-up money. Health and Human Services provided grants for child care, elderly assistance, mental health care and other services for those left homeless or bereft following the collapse of the Trade Towers. The Departments of Justice and Treasury were called in to administer improved airport security. U.S. Customs administered additional scrutiny at our borders. The Internal Revenue Service extended the filing of income taxes to all involved in the search and rescue efforts. The Department of Housing and Urban development processed FHA loans to the thousands in need of assistance. The so-called "simple" administrative tasks of bureaucracy became the vital link for survival to those immediately affected by the terrorist attack in New York. Now start to expand this list to include the Pentagon and you can get a sense of the responsibilities given to our fourth branch of government.

Question for Reflection: Our democracy depends upon the coexistence of federal and state governments, each with their own bureaucratic systems. In the wake of the attacks of September 11, how might the administration of relief efforts and protection affect this coexistence?

Regulation Another important bureaucratic task is **regulation.** Regulation involves the making of rules, their enforcement, and the adjudication of disputes about them. In many areas of American life, the bureaucracy establishes and enforces guidelines regulating behavior and enforcing punishments for violation of those guidelines.[15]

Administrative regulation is pervasive in America. Americans wake up in the morning and eat breakfast food whose quality is regulated by the U.S. Agriculture Department. The FDA is responsible for a labeling rule that seeks to regulate, for example, the booming diet supplement industry. After a hard day, Americans may decide to flip on the television to watch programming whose content must fall within guidelines established by the Federal Communications Commission. Finally, at the end of the day, Americans crawl into bed and snuggle under blankets certified

administration Performance of routine tasks associated with a specific policy goal.

regulation The making of rules by an administrative body that clarify and interpret legislation, its enforcement, and the adjudication of disputes about it.

as fire resistant by the Consumer Product Safety Commission. When Americans get into their cars, they buckle their seat belts because it is the law, and it is the law because the Federal Highway Administration withholds federal funds from states that do not require seat-belt use. Americans also drive to work in autos that do minimal harm to the air because of the catalytic converters mandated by the Environmental Protection Agency. At work, Americans conform to the anti-discrimination guidelines established by the Equal Employment Opportunity Commission. When shopping for dinner, they may choose to purchase organic products, which are regulated by the Department of Agriculture. Some watchdog groups are wary of the adverse effects that will come from a decrease in such areas as air traffic control and food safety inspection. "Right now, people eat meat at their own risk,: said Arthur Hill, an Agriculture Department inspector who estimates that an additional 9000 inspectors are necessary to meet federal law guidelines.[16]

Whether implementing, administering, or regulating, bureaucrats exercise a great deal of autonomy and have power over our lives. Given the complex demands upon the bureaucracy, such power is inevitable. But, some ask, whose interests do the bureaucrats serve? Are they responsive to the needs of the public? In fact, many bureaucrats do heed the voices of ordinary citizens and seek to stay in the good graces of the two government institutions most responsive to public opinion: Congress and the presidency. Yet federal morale is clearly down and federal employee's are reporting less satisfaction wit their own work and the work of their agencies. Figure 7.3 shows the results of a recent Brookings Institution survey that shows declining levels of morale, with one exception—the Department of Defense.

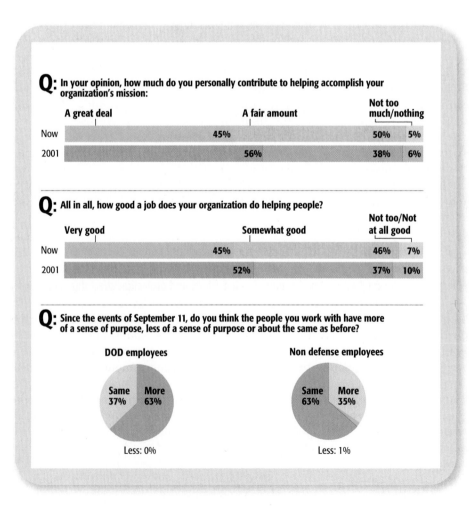

Figure 7.3
Federal Morale Down

Source: Surveys conducted for the Brookings Institution's Center for Public Service. As reported in *The Washington Post*, April 12, 2001, p. A29. Reprinted by permission of the Brookings Institution.

The Structure of the Federal Bureaucracy

The institutions that constitute the federal bureaucracy are part of the executive branch. There are four such government institutions: cabinet departments, independent agencies, independent regulatory commissions, and government corporations.

Cabinet Departments **Cabinet departments** are major administrative units responsible for conducting a broad range of government operations. Originally, the heads of these departments—usually called *secretaries*—were the president's closest advisers, though today the president's personal White House staff is more likely to command the president's attention. Each department is subdivided into smaller units called divisions, sections, agencies, and offices. The current cabinet departments are State, Treasury, Defense, Interior, Justice, Agriculture, Commerce, Labor, Health and Human Services, Housing and Urban Development, Transportation, Energy, Education, Veterans Affairs, and Homeland Defense. Although each of the departments has jurisdiction over a specific policy area, sometimes their responsibilities overlap, as when State and Defense address the diplomatic and strategic aspects of U.S. foreign policy.

For fiscal year 2003, the Bush administration has used an OMB ranking of Department performance.[17] The $2.13 trillion budget plan that President Bush sent to Congress on February 4, 2002, for the first time formally assessed the performance of government agencies and programs and linked their financing to the grades they receive. An internal review conducted by the Office of Management and Budget assigned uniformly poor marks to all the major cabinet departments in five categories of management, including personnel and finances. The five categories are personnel, using competition to hold down costs, financial management, using technology to increase efficiency, and matching the effectiveness of programs to the financing they receive. The Department of Energy's fossil energy research and development programs were judged ineffective and duplicative and had their budget slashed to $58 million from $101 million, a 43 percent reduction. The Agriculture Department's system of 5,600 county field offices was rated ineffective and had its budget increase limited to about 2 percent, or $59 million, probably not enough to keep pace with inflation. But the National Weather Service's hurricane and tornado warning program was deemed highly successful, and the administration will seek a budget increase for it of $32 million, or 4.2 percent.

The effort grew out of a campaign promise by Mr. Bush to make government more accountable for its performance and follows similar efforts in Congress to find ways to measure bang for the taxpayer's buck. It dovetails with the ideological push by many Republicans, including Mitchell E. Daniels Jr., the White House budget director, to weed out what they consider to be wasteful, duplicative, and inefficient programs in their drive to reduce the size of government.

As shown in Figure 7.4, there were three categories of performance. A green light indicated that a department met all standards for success in that area. The review yielded only one green light: the National Science Foundation's financial management was judged to be up to par. A yellow light signified that the department had met some but not all of the criteria. The Departments of Agriculture, Commerce, Labor and Transportation all got at least one yellow light, as did agencies like NASA and the Small Business Administration.[18]

Independent Agencies **Independent agencies** are usually smaller than cabinet departments and have a narrower set of responsibilities. Generally, they exist to perform a service. Congress may establish an independent agency so that it can keep particularly tight control over that agency's functions. For example, an independent agency may be established in response to demands from interest groups that wish to see a government function performed with care and attention rather than

▲ Secretary of Labor Elaine L. Chao is responsible for carrying out the department's mission of inspiring and protecting the hardworking people of America.

cabinet departments Major administrative units whose heads are presidential advisers appointed by the president and confirmed by the Senate. They are responsible for conducting a broad range of government operations.

independent agencies Government agencies that are usually smaller and have a narrower set of responsibilities than cabinet departments.

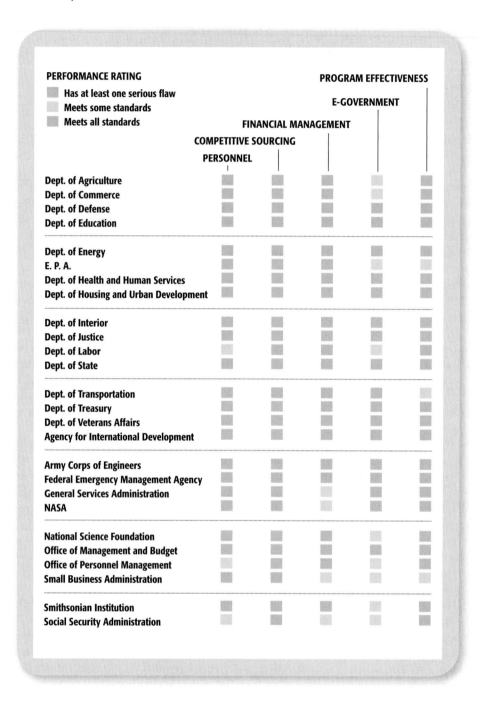

Figure 7.4
Rating Government's Performance

Source: Office of Management and Budget.

by some indifferent department. Among the major independent agencies are the Central Intelligence Agency (CIA), the Environmental Protection Agency (EPA), the National Aeronautics and Space Administration (NASA), the Small Business Administration (SBA), the Peace Corps, and the General Services Administration (GSA), which manages federal property.

Independent Regulatory Commissions   Independent regulatory commissions are agencies established to regulate a sector of the nation's economy in the public interest. For example, an independent regulatory commission might guard against unfair business practices or unsafe products. They are generally run by a board whose members have set terms, although some of the newer regulatory bodies are headed by a single individual, making the label "commission" something of a misnomer. These bodies establish rules, enforce the rules, and adjudicate disputes

independent regulatory commissions Agencies established to regulate a sector of the nation's economy in the public interest.

The National Science Foundation: A Model for Efficiency

The Office of Management and the Budget rated the different departments within the federal bureaucracy in early 2002. The results indicated that the National Science Foundation has become a model of efficiency among the 26 separate federal agencies currently in place. The success story of the agency reveals the necessity and importance of bureaucratic reform within government.

The positive rating came in the form of a green dot signaling compliance with Bush administration criteria. In five categories of review, the NSF received a green dot for its management of finances. Other agencies were not so lucky—most received either red (major problems) or yellow (some problems fixed) from the OMB.

The NSF rated highly due primarily to its sophisticated use of modern technology. Web and the Internet have been the key. The NSF has amazingly downsized its immense load of paperwork by enabling scientists to apply for grants for research by using the web. Cyberspace meetings between scientists working with the NSF around the globe are now routine. The NSF receives roughly 30,000 research proposals each year, a number that is climbing and can only be handled with increased technology.

Further strong points included keeping overhead low (only 4.5% of the 5.1 billion dollar NSF budget for 2003 goes to pay for the salaries of employees). Unlike most agencies, the NSF has not increased the number of employees for several years. It has consistently relied on a core group of workers—1,200 employees, 300 temporary contractors, and 100 scientists who rotate through the agency.

The inspector general of the agency gave it a "clean" bill of health in part because the NSF complied totally with two essential bureaucratic reform acts: the 1982 Federal Financial Managers Integrity Act, and the 1996 Federal Financial Management Improvement Act. This was no easy task. Of the 26 agencies reviewed by the Bush administration, only 18 earned "clean" opinions (five opinions received a qualified rating and two possessed disclaimers).

According to Thomas N. Cooley, the chief financial officer for the NSF (he started as a part-time employee in 1979), his department's ability to earn high marks stems from the hard work of NSF employees over several administrations: "You don't build systems overnight . . . "

Source: Stephen Barr, "It's Not Easy Getting Green: NSF Alone at Top of Bush Scorecard," *Washington Post*, February 10, 2002.

---

about them. In so doing they perform all of the traditional functions of government—legislative, executive, and judicial. These agencies develop a great deal of expertise in a particular policy area, although sometimes they become too closely identified with the businesses they are charged with regulating. Congress and the courts rely on their expertise and are usually loath to overrule them. Among the more important independent regulatory commissions are the Federal Communications Commission (FCC), which regulates radio and television; the Federal Reserve Board (FED), whose members function as a central bank for the United States; the Federal Trade Commission (FTC), which regulates advertising and labeling; the National Labor Relations Board (NLRB), which enforces the laws governing labor-management disputes; and the National Transportation Safety Board (NTSB). The NTSB is charged by Congress, with investigating every civil aviation accident in the United States and significant accidents in the other modes of transportation—railroad, highway, marine, and pipeline—and issuing safety recommendations aimed at preventing future accidents. The NTSB is responsible for maintaining the government's database on civil aviation accidents and also conducts special studies of transportation safety issues of national significance.

Government Corporations   A **government corporation** is a semi-independent government agency that administers a business enterprise and takes the form of a business corporation. Congress creates such agencies on the assumption that they will serve the public interest and gives them more independence and latitude for innovation than it gives other government agencies. A government corporation can raise its own capital and devise its own personnel system; it can determine, within the limits of the charter Congress gives it, the kind of services it provides; and when the occasion seems favorable, it may develop new services. The Tennessee Valley Authority (TVA), a government corporation originally set up to control flooding

government corporation A semi-independent government agency that administers a business enterprise and takes the form of a business corporation.

THE ROAD TO DEMOCRACY

Engineering a Disaster

THAT WAS THEN . . .

The successful launch of the first space shuttle in April 1981 marked the beginning of a new era for the National Aeronautics and Space Administration (NASA), a long-established but somewhat neglected public bureaucracy. The shuttle was designed to cut the cost of delivering various hardware payloads such as satellites into space and to encourage public support for future research projects in space. The shuttle's first twenty-four missions went off almost flawlessly. Their success revived NASA's image and led to increased federal funding. However, mission number twenty-five was to be different. Early on the morning of January 28, 1986, with temperatures well below freezing, NASA launched the space shuttle Challenger from the Kennedy Space Center in Florida.

Seventy-three seconds after lift-off, Challenger exploded before millions of television viewers and stunned NASA officials. All seven astronauts on board died. One was Christa McAuliffe, a grade-school teacher whose training for the mission had been followed by schoolchildren all over the United States. It was the worst disaster in the history of the space program.

President Ronald Reagan appointed a commission, headed by a former secretary of state, William Rogers, to investigate the disaster. The Rogers Commission concluded that most of the blame lay with NASA's bureaucratic culture. NASA's "can-do" atmosphere and its strict adherence to the principles of engineering had produced a string of historic accomplishments in aerospace exploration—the Apollo flights, the moon landings, and the first shuttle missions—but that same culture sometimes led the agency to push too far too fast.

The Rogers Commission discovered that on the bitterly cold night before the fateful launch, officials from NASA and Morton Thiokol Industries (MTI), the designer of the shuttle's solid rocket booster system, debated the wisdom of launching Challenger. MTI engineers in Utah tried desperately to convince NASA officials in Florida and at the Johnson Space Center in Houston, Texas, to scrub the Challenger mission because the rocket booster system was not designed to withstand subfreezing temperatures. The O-ring seals that joined the sections of the fuel tanks had never been used below 53 degrees Fahrenheit. In laboratory experiments performed at freezing temperatures, the seals had disintegrated.

Given the warnings from MTI officials, how could NASA have allowed the disaster to happen? The decision to ignore MTI's advice and launch Challenger arose from a combination of problems within NASA that are all too common in large public bureaucracies. NASA officials were overconfident in light of the previous successes of the shuttle program. They worried about the public image problems that might arise from a scrubbed mission and insinuations of technical failure. They wanted to guard

---

and provide electricity to the area within the Tennessee River watershed, now manages the artificial lakes it created for recreational purposes, runs economic development programs, and experiments with alternative energy development.

In addition to possessing much of the flexibility of a private company, a government corporation also has the authority of government. It can take land, levy fees, and make rules that govern the public. Though these agencies have more leeway in establishing the nature and cost of the services they provide, they generally remain subject to more regulation than private corporations do. Besides the TVA, other major government corporations include the Postal Service, the Corporation for Public Broadcasting, the Federal Deposit Insurance Corporation, United Parcel Service, the Export-Import Bank, and Amtrak.

Constraints on the Bureaucracy and Bureaucratic Culture

The bureaucracy faces three major constraints that shape its behavior: bureaucratic agencies do not control revenue; decisions about how to deliver goods and services must be made according to rules established elsewhere; and other institutions mandate goals. Because of these constraints, bureaucrats and bureaucracies behave differently from employees and companies in the private sector. Certain *norms,* or unwritten rules of behavior, have developed, creating a unique bureaucratic culture.

against possible budget cutbacks if Congress concluded that technical flaws threatened the shuttle program. And they were concerned about costs. A postponed shuttle mission would be enormously expensive; the solid rocket fuel alone, which would have been lost in the event of a scrubbed launch, was valued at half a million dollars. Finally, decision makers were not sufficiently knowledgeable to assess the potential risk of the launch, and they chose to ignore the evidence of the engineers and other experts outside of NASA.

THIS IS NOW . . .

Seventeen years after the tragic Challenger mission, NASA is experiencing a revival in its image with the successful completion of more than 83 shuttle missions. However, the death of Chista McAuliffe, the grade school teacher aboard the Challenger shelved NASA's Teachers in Space program and with it, as costs associated with space travel increase, plans for civilian space travel. But that doesn't mean the opportunity for civilian space travel has disappeared. Today, if you are a private citizen with $20 million, the Russian Space Agency is offering rides aboard its shuttles to the International Space Station. Recently, those rides have gone to the American investment manager Dennis Tito, South African Internet millionaire Mark Shuttleworth, and plans are in the completion stage for the American N'Sync band member Lance Bass. If you still want to have the zero-g experience without the $20-million price tag, NASA does have special programs that offer rides on its KC-135 plane, which

▲ The space shuttle Challenger exploding seventy-three seconds after lift-off on January 28, 1986.

is used to train astronauts and the Arlington, VA–based Space Adventures sells rides aboard the Russian Space Agency's equivalent plane, the IL-76, for $5,000.

Sources: http://www.space.com/missionlaunches/sts109_update_020128.html 8/20/02; http://cbc.ca/news/indepth/background/spacetourist.html 8/20/02; and http://www.nytimes.com/aponline/arts/AP-Russia-Space-Lance-Bass.html 8/20/02. James Q. Wilson, *Bureaucracy: What Government Agencies Do and Why They Do It* (New York: Basic Books, 1989), pp. 104–5.

First, Congress does not allow agencies to keep money left over when the fiscal year ends. Furthermore, an agency that ends the year with a surplus demonstrates to Congress that it can get by on less than the current year's budget. As a consequence, bureaucrats have no incentive to conserve funds. In fact, there is every incentive to spend with abandon as the fiscal year draws to a close on September 30, in hopes of showing Congress that there is no surplus and that, in fact, more money is needed for the next year. In addition, since bureaucrats are not supposed to profit from their dealings with government, they focus on other non-monetary incentives such as prestige. The bigger the budget and the larger the agency, the more prestige a bureaucrat acquires, providing managers with another reason to put political pressure on Congress to allow their agencies to grow.

FYI

Senator Dale Bumpers of Arkansas described the bureaucracy as "a 700 pound marshmallow. You can kick it, scream at it, and cuss it, but it is very reluctant to move."

(?) **Question for Reflection:** What, if any, impact might the Bush administration's use of the Office of Budget Management performance rankings have on these spending practices?

Second, to ensure fairness, efficiency, and comprehensive coverage of a program, decisions about hiring, purchasing, contracting, and budgeting must be made according to rules established by Congress and the president. Since the end of World War II, Congress has passed an array of such rules: for example, the Administrative Procedure Act of 1946, a comprehensive set of regulations governing the way an agency makes rules, publicizes its operations, and settles disputes; the Freedom of Information Act of 1966, assuring that most agency records are available to interested citizens on demand; the National Environmental Policy Act of 1969, requiring federal agencies to prepare environmental impact statements for all actions that significantly affect the environment; the Privacy Act of 1974, a law that limits the circumstances in which information about individuals can be released to other agencies and to the public; and the Government in the Sunshine Act of 1976, mandating open meetings of most regulatory decision-making bodies.

Such a system breeds rule-following managers, not managers who take initiative. It is no wonder that surrounded by such a thicket of regulations and laws bureaucratic managers worry more about violating procedure than about marching boldly ahead to promote the public good. After all, managers can always explain poor outcomes by claiming that they were just following the rules.

Finally, bureaucratic agencies do not control their own goals, which are set by Congress and the president. Congress has told the United States Postal Service that it must charge one rate to deliver a first-class letter no matter where the letter goes. Furthermore, the Postal Service must deliver newspapers, magazines, and junk mail below cost, and it must keep small post offices open even though they may not be economical to operate. Cost-conscious, practical business decisions that might be made in the private sector, are now being considered at the Postal Service.[19]

Despite the constraints imposed by the unique character of public service, some administrative institutions flourish. A determined leader can install a sense of mission even in employees of an organization whose offices are scattered across the

Overhauling Bureaucracy: A "Transformation Plan" for the United States Postal Service

In a move that may write a new chapter in bureaucratic reform, the United States Postal Service may become more privatized under a plan proposed by the Bush administration in early 2002. Unreformed since 1972 and mandated with a weighty responsibility to deliver the nation's mail, the Post Office is beset with problems inherent to a cumbersome and under funded federal agency. It is in debt to the tune of $11 billion. It employs more civilians than any other organization except Wal-Mart, requiring the payment of $32 billion in insurance and pension costs. Anthrax attacks have now required a two- to three-billion-dollar technological upgrade to scan the mail and protect the American people. The Postal Service is an independent regulatory agency that does not typically receive taxpayer money for operations.

Politicians from both political parties agree that major changes need to be made. Corporations are happy about the idea of making the Post Office more like them. According to Gene Del Polito, president of the Association for Postal Commerce, privatizing the post office promises to improve its ability to function: "The idea that the Postal Service really needs to be transformed into a more businesslike structure is something we applaud. Now it's going to be up to Congress to figure out how to get it done."

Cost-cutting will be crucial: The Post Office needs to cut over five billion dollars in operating expenses, a vital move given that costs are annually outstripping revenues. That's the problem—unless the Post Office switches to more privatized, free market solutions to budgetary problems, the American people will lose out. Either way, the American people will pay more for services and postage. On June 30, 2002, the cost of postage for a first class stamp rose from 34 cents to 37 cents in a move that was intended to generate an additional $4.2 billion a year.

The plan proposed by the Bush administration emphasizes making the Post Office function more like a business and less like a government agency. Republican mistrust of the size and cost of the federal government gave the Bush administration added clout in attempting to push through Post Office reforms during a time when the American people welcomed any executive moves to safeguard the nation.

The privatization plan includes stipulations to increase the flexibility of the Post Office to negotiate contracts with supply companies. Currently, the Post Office must adhere to government guidelines to purchase goods at high prices from select companies. The Bush administration also wanted to decrease the power of binding arbitration to settle disputes with unions representing Postal Service workers.

Although a system of bureaucracy remains central to the smooth functioning of government in a complex federal system, it remains a difficult process to mold to meet the needs of the American people.

Sources: Stephen Barr and Ellen Nakashima, "Postal Service Plans Massive Overhaul of Its Operations—Skyrocketing Costs Forcing First Changes in 30 Years," http://www.washingtonpost.com, Friday, April 5, 2002, p. A21; Bill Miller, "Postal Service Customers Accept June 30 Rate Rise," *Washington Post*, January 7, 2002, p. A15.

nation. The Social Security Administration is such a mission-driven agency. Its personnel officers recruit potential employees who show an orientation to customer satisfaction, and managers constantly invoke an ethic of service when they talk to employees. Bureaucrats who work for the Social Security Administration take pride in their jobs and do them well.

Bureaucratic Accountability

The story of late twentieth-century American politics is in large part the story of attempts by the White House and Congress to control the powerful federal bureaucracy and make it more accountable to the people. Perhaps the most disturbing example of this challenge occurred in 1997 when the nation's attention focused on the congressional hearings concerning the Internal Revenue Service. We learned of horrifying instances of taxpayer harassment and intimidation and a culture of abusive tax collection methods and abuse by individual agents within the organization. Witnesses before the congressional investigating committee told of IRS agents who sought out lower-income individuals for audits, destroyed credit ratings, and sought to punish people through the audit process. We heard stories of IRS agents snooping through computer files to read the tax forms of the famous, their neighbors, their former spouses, and even prospective dates. President Clinton quickly jumped aboard a congressional plan to create a citizen oversight board that would monitor IRS activities. On July 22, 1998, Clinton signed into law a major overhaul of the IRS. Yet, in February 2000, Clinton was calling for more tax revenue and asking IRS agents to be more aggressive in identifying tax cheaters.

Still, American bureaucracy has made major strides toward democratic accountability. Today, few bureaucracies operate outside the law, as the FBI did under J. Edgar Hoover in the 1950s and 1960s. Today's administrators, influenced by modern business management techniques, spend as much time listening to their employees and to their customer, the public, as they do giving orders. Although few administrative rules are made according to a democratic voting process, the policymaking process has broadened to include a variety of perspectives in recent years. Rule-making agencies take care to notify not only businesses subject to regulation about upcoming hearings, but also to invite consumer and civil rights groups to testify.[20]

On secrecy, the picture is less clear. While the Administrative Procedure Act, the Freedom of Information Act, and the Government in the Sunshine Act have opened up routine administrative decisions to public scrutiny, the national security establishment continues to operate behind closed doors. The attack on America has only created more layers of official secrets in the name of national and homeland security. As we saw in Chapter 5, the Bush administration has done virtually everything it can to claim the privilege of confidentiality and maintain official secrets.[21]

Presidential Control

One of the most common complaints a president makes is that aligning the objectives of the federal bureaucracy with the priorities of the administration is terribly difficult. President Harry Truman once complained, "I thought I was the president, but when it comes to these bureaucrats, I can't do a damn thing." Truman may have been exaggerating, but presidential control of the bureaucracy is not as easy as most incoming chief executives either thought or hoped.[22]

As the federal bureaucracy has grown, so, too, has the amount of energy expended by presidents to rein in the agencies that oppose their objectives. After a grueling election, the president enters office with a policy agenda that was presumably supported by at least a plurality of the American people. To pursue that policy agenda, the president must try to convince not only Congress but, the various agencies of the federal government to cooperate with the White House. There are four main strategies a president can use: the appointment power, reorganization, the budget, and the power of persuasion.

The Appointment Power   The president must be clear about the goals of the policy agenda. And to advance that agenda, the president can use a powerful weapon, the **appointment power.** As we learned in Chapter 5 on the Presidency, the president can nominate some three thousand agency officials, of whom about seven hundred are in policy-making positions, such as cabinet and sub-cabinet officials and bureau chiefs. The rest are lower-level appointees who can provide the president with valuable information and a source of political patronage hearkening back to the old spoils system. A president who can secure loyalty from these appointed bureaucrats has overcome a major obstacle in pursuing the White House policy agenda.

But when using the appointment power to control the bureaucracy, the president must know what is going on within it. One of the presidents who did just that was Franklin Roosevelt. He filled federal agencies with people who were more loyal to him than to each other. Although his appointees battled each other over policy questions, they ultimately referred their disagreements to the president, who resolved them and in doing so exercised effective control over bureaucratic policy making. Roosevelt's administration funneled information and decision-making authority to the top, and because Roosevelt had the intellectual capacity to understand the arguments of the specialists, he was able to settle their disputes with dispatch. This form of management is impossible today, given the size of government. Current trends lean more towards collaboration and cooperation and shared communication amongst the different department and agencies, evidenced by Director Ridge's early success in coordinating an elaborate infrastructure involving over forty federal agencies and departments.

Reorganization   Having the power to move some programs around within specific agencies, presidents can also influence the bureaucracy through reorganization. For example, a president opposed to pesticide regulation might shift that program from the EPA, which favors regulation, to the Department of Agriculture, where pro-agriculture forces would tend to limit such regulation.

A president may also choose to elevate an agency to cabinet level, thereby expanding its scope and power as President Bush did with the Department of Homeland Security. This office involves a number of different agencies within the federal government. As this new office evolves, it may lead to some agency reorganization. In 1979, President Carter elevated one of the offices of the Department of Health, Education and Welfare to cabinet level, creating the Department of Education. He hoped that this reorganization would improve the prestige and status of the office and underscore the importance of education as a national priority. Conversely, as we noted previously, a president can remove an agency's cabinet status and thus potentially reduce its power and prestige. Upon succeeding Carter, Reagan sought several ways to reduce the power of the Department of Education, including an unsuccessful attempt to demote the agency from the cabinet level. The Reagan administration saw the department as wasteful and inefficient and as an inappropriate extension of federal government into state and local realms. But the department dug in its heels and outlasted Reagan.[23]

The Budget   One formidable tool for presidential control of the bureaucracy is the **Office of Management and Budget (OMB).** Established in 1921, transferred to the newly created Executive Office in 1939, and renamed OMB as part of the major executive office reorganization in 1970, the OMB's main responsibilities are to prepare and administer the president's annual budget. It is through the budget process that a president and the OMB can shape policy, since the process determines which departments and agencies grow, get cut, or remain the same as the year before. During the budget-preparation cycle, officers from OMB—all specially

appointment power The president's power to name some three thousand agency officials, of whom about seven hundred are in policy-making positions such as cabinet and subcabinet officials and bureau chiefs.

Office of Management and Budget (OMB) The unit in the Executive Office of the President whose main responsibilities are to prepare and administer the president's annual budget. It is through the budget process that a president and the OMB can shape policy, since the process determines which departments and agencies grow, get cut, or remain the same as the year before.

trained to assess government projects and spending requests—are in constant touch with government agencies to make sure that the agencies are adhering to the president's policies. Because the budget has a profound effect on an agency's ability to function and survive, it is rare for an administrator to defy the OMB.[24]

President Bush assigned OMB Director Mitchell Daniels the responsibility of weeding out programs that he considered wasteful, duplicative, and inefficient. Since defeating international terrorism and defending Americans is now the nation's number 1 priority, programs of lesser priority must prove their value. With $48 billion in increased spending for the military, other programs were slashed dramatically by OMB, the "Dr. No" of the administration.

The Power of Persuasion   Lastly, presidents can use the power to persuade in an attempt to control the bureaucracy. Some presidents, such as John F. Kennedy, sought to inspire the bureaucracy with a vision of public service as a noble activity. Even though he was frequently thwarted by and frustrated with bureaucratic procedures, Kennedy saw the bureaucracy as capable of innovation. He was able to reorganize the space program and convince its employees that despite the string of failures in attempting to launch unmanned rockets, NASA would put a man on the moon before the decade was out, which it did. But persuasion only gets a president so far and most turn to their limited command powers for getting the bureaucracy to move—or they shift responsibility into the Executive Office of the President— creating yet another bureaucratic layer, but one that is loyal to the interests of the President and not divided between the President and "the natives."[25]

Congressional Control

Congress is responsible for much of the oversight that keeps bureaucratic power in check (also see Chapter 4). To perform this task, Congress has several mechanisms at its disposal. Most important is the *power of the purse*. Congress appropriates all funding for each federal agency. If there are problems, Congress can, and occasionally does, curb funds or even eliminate entire projects.

One classic example of the assertion of control over a runaway program is Congress's treatment of the Department of Energy's (DOE) super-conducting super-collider project. Projected in 1982 to cost taxpayers $4.4 billion, the total budget for the huge particle accelerator, designed to allow scientists to learn more about atomic structure, ballooned to more than $11 billion by 1993. When the DOE carried out its own investigation of the Texas-based project, officials discovered a history of free-spending waste, including an expense of $56,000 for potted plants to adorn the project's offices. Finally, in late 1993, and after the expenditure of $2 billion, Congress canceled the entire program.

Congress also has the power of *administrative oversight*, the practice of holding hearings and conducting investigations into bureaucratic activity. As a consequence of these hearings, Congress can rewrite the guidelines for an agency to expand or narrow the scope of its responsibilities. Finally, through its "advice and consent" role, the Senate can shape the direction of federal agencies by confirming or rejecting presidential nominees for top positions in the bureaucracy.

Although Congress has many tools to fulfill its oversight functions, it often chooses not to use them. Why would Congress not want to keep the bureaucracy under close control? One answer can be found by examining the mutually beneficial political relationship between federal agencies and members of Congress.

Legislators have the ability to keep federal agencies alive and funded. Those agencies provide goods and services—such as contracts, exemptions, and assistance—that members of Congress use to please their constituents. Legislators from agricultural states, for example, work hard to keep crop subsidies in the federal budget, thus ensuring a future for the Department of Agriculture and its employees. In turn, the department can give special consideration to the crops grown in a member's district, thus helping to ensure a member's reelection.

These relationships have been characterized as **iron triangles.** An iron triangle is a strong interdependent relationship among three crucial actors in policy making: legislators, particularly those on the relevant subcommittees with jurisdiction over the policy in question; lobbyists for specific interests affected by the policy; and bureaucrats at the agencies with jurisdiction over the implementation and administration of relevant policies. Iron triangles are resistant to democratic accountability. The interlocking interests of its parts are so strong that few presidents and few members of Congress who are not a part of the triangles ever try to bring them under control.

Similar to but broader than iron triangles are **issue networks,** which are composed of political actors in a particular policy area. These networks usually include bureaucrats, congressional staffers, interest groups, think tank researchers or academic experts, and media participants, all of whom interact regularly on an issue. Issue networks dominate the policy-making process, and different issue networks exist for different policy areas.

The National Security Bureaucracy

The national security bureaucracy has been resistant to efforts to bring it under the control of Congress and the president. The agencies that form this bloc include the Central Intelligence Agency (CIA), the Federal Bureau of Investigation (FBI), the Defense Intelligence Agency (DIA), and the National Security Agency (NSA). In this agency "alphabet soup" we should also include the Bureau of Alcohol, Tobacco and Firearms (ATF), the Drug Enforcement Administration (DEA), the Immigration and Naturalization Service (INS) and, most recently, the Office of Homeland Defense (OHD).

The sheer size of the national security bureaucracy is daunting and makes control and accountability difficult. A comprehensive examination of the entire national security bureaucracy is nearly impossible. Much of the statistical data about expenditures and various activities are unavailable; they are kept secret and "off-budget," purportedly to protect national security. Yet it is difficult to imagine a nation as large as the United States, in a world as unstable as that of the last half-century, maintaining the security of its borders and its internal stability without such a bureaucracy. Nevertheless, its growth and complexity have created some embarrassing moments for the federal government and resulted in some genuine concern about the security of the civil liberties of American citizens.

Two agencies whose transgressions have garnered particular public attention are the FBI and the CIA. The FBI was created in 1924 under the directorship of J. Edgar Hoover. The bureau soon developed a reputation as the nation's toughest crime-fighting agency. Much of this prestige was directly orchestrated by Hoover, who publicized the arrests or prominent criminals such as John Dillinger in 1930 and cooperated extensively in a series of Hollywood motion pictures celebrating the bureau's tough, efficient, crime-busting image.

By the 1950s Hoover had gained so much power—largely as a result of using the bureau to assemble files on most of the prominent political figures of the day—that he could turn the FBI's scrutiny virtually wherever he pleased. Hoover deployed agents and government resources to investigate a seemingly endless labyrinth of communist "cells," many of which were established by FBI agents themselves to lure potential "subversives." As vigorous a racist as he was an anticommunist, Hoover also used the FBI to infiltrate or attack every African-American organization during the 1960s, and he mounted a personal attack on the reputation of civil rights leader Dr. Martin Luther King, Jr.

During the 1980s the FBI dramatically expanded its undercover operations. The subjects included Washington legislators caught taking bribes by undercover FBI agents as well as labor leaders and students. In the wake of the April 1995 bombing

iron triangles The informal three-way relationships that develop among key legislative committees, the bureaucracy whose budgets are supervised by those committees, and interest groups with a vested interest in the policies created by those committees and agencies.

issue networks Networks of political actors in a particular policy area, usually including bureaucrats, congressional staffers, interest groups, think tank researchers or academic experts, and media participants, all of whom interact regularly on an issue.

of a federal building in Oklahoma City, a public debate ensued about whether the agency's investigative powers should be expanded even further to aid efforts to combat terrorism.

Most recently the FBI has been embarrassed by the revelation that Robert P. Hanssen, a counterintelligence agent, was spying at the FBI for over two decades. Security at the FBI appears to have been very lax and file clerks often had access to top-secret information. A special Justice Department panel, chaired by former FBI Director William Webster, concluded that, "the FBI's approach to security policy has been as fragmented as the operations of its security programs." In accepting the report, Attorney General John Ashcroft said that, "much remedial work remains to be done . . . the lessons learned for the Hanssen case present a historic opportunity to make substantial, durable improvements to the FBI's internal security."[26]

Created as part of the National Security Act of 1947 to coordinate international intelligence data, the CIA gradually assumed a shadowy life of its own as America's chief covert operations apparatus. With nearly 20,000 employees and a budget of $3 billion, the CIA has vast responsibilities. Since 1981, when Ronald Reagan signed an executive order empowering it to do so, the CIA has used its large array of intelligence-gathering and counterespionage resources to scrutinize American citizens within the borders of the United States. With many of its expenditures "off-budget" and its agents buried in false identities around the world, the CIA is among the most difficult of federal agencies to effectively track. The CIA and its Director George Tenet (the only holdover from the Clinton Administration) have a remarkably close relationship with President Bush. Tenet meets regularly with the President and has unusual access to the White House. Still, in the wake of the September 11 attacks, many Americans asked aloud whether or not the CIA has been asleep at the wheel in not detecting any signals for planned terrorist attacks against the United States. The Bush administration's 2003 budget proposed an increase in almost 2 billion to pay for the CIA's increased role in the war on terrorism.[27]

◄ George John Tenet was sworn in as Director of Central Intelligence on July 11, 1997, following a unanimous vote by both the Senate Select Committee on Intelligence and the full Senate. In this position he heads the Intelligence Community (all foreign intelligence agencies of the United States) and directs the Central Intelligence Agency. In March of 2001 President Bush visited the agency headquarters and thanked CIA employees for their efforts. The President's father, former President George Bush was Director of Central Intelligence and head of the Central Intelligence Agency from January 30,1976, to January 20, 1977.

Question for Reflection: How can a democracy in a pluralist society effectively manage its national security operations without jeopardizing their secret intelligence?

What the Public Thinks of the Bureaucracy

Americans tend to be suspicious of the administrative state, and politicians often exploit the public's distrust of government.[28] A few years ago members of Congress made headlines with stories about Defense Department purchases of $435 hammers and $91 screws. The stories, though exaggerated, confirmed long-held suspicions about government waste. But following the bombing of the Federal Building in Oklahoma City, many critics of government began to see their antigovernment statements as delegitimizing the very idea of government.

Many Americans feel that government is expensive and wasteful. Each year the federal government spends a good deal of money unwisely. Highly publicized examples of government waste include the Department of Agriculture sending subsidy checks to wealthy recipients in Beverly Hills, Chicago, and Manhattan. Retired federal employees have been found to live at a level of luxury far beyond that of the ordinary taxpayer because the government guarantees them cost-of-living adjustments pegged to exaggerated calculations of the rate of inflation. And while the Commerce Department helps tobacco growers market their products, the surgeon general works toward the goal of reducing the number of smokers in society. As a consequence of such stories, Americans have an exaggerated notion of the extent of government waste (see Table 7.1).

One of the most common complaints is that government is not responsive to citizens. In implementing policies agencies should be attentive to the needs and circumstances of individual taxpayers. But too often, red tape prevents such flexibility. **Red tape** refers to the excessive number of rules and regulations that government employees must follow. While many employees chafe under the burden of these regulations, others welcome them. Rigid adherence to the rules relieves bureaucrats of the burden of thinking about individual cases and shelters employees from being criticized by their supervisors for making wrong decisions. One consequence of the proliferation of red tape in government is that citizens with unusual circumstances encounter delays while their cases are bumped up to higher levels for official rulings. Businesses complain that the bureaucracy hobbles them with unnecessary regulations and paperwork. Every time a company wants to expand its operations or use a new method for manufacturing its products, it must apply for permission from a host of government agencies and fill out a great many forms.[29]

Are the Criticisms Justified?

Bureaucracy is a modern-day inevitability. And despite the criticisms, many Americans have come to rely on the goods and services that the bureaucracy provides. Although many of the criticisms are valid, there are two sides to every story about an institution as large as the federal government. Although bureaucratic waste is real, it is less prevalent than the public believes. And it is important to keep in mind that government expenditures exist for reasons that many Americans would support. For example, most citizens want to ensure that no official awards a contract on the basis of personal friendship or bribery, so agencies are required to use costly bidding procedures on federal contracts. Most citizens would support programs that train people who lack skills to find jobs in the public sector. Such policies add to the cost of government, but ultimately, many citizens agree with the rationale for the expenditures. While some agencies never accomplish the tasks given to them by

red tape The excessive number of rules and regulations that government employees must follow.

Table 7.1 ■ Government Management Report Card

	Agency grade	Managing for results	Financial management	Human resources management	Information management	Physical assets management	
National Weather Service	A	A	A	A	A	A	Results-focused management coordinated throughout agency and across functions to achieve mission success.
Postal Service	A	A	A	C	B	A	Management is focused on results and coordinated throughout the agency, but it is hampered by serious problems with human resources and communications.
Administration for Children and Families	B	B	B	B	B	N/A	Agency with strong service ethos rising to the challenge of managing for results in a devolved, welfare-reform environment.
NASA	B	B	C	B	B	B	Strong "can do" culture aimed at technical excellence is marred by weakness in mission definition and measurement of outcomes.
Bureau of Consular Affairs	C	C	C	C	B	N/A	Agency benefited from inspired leadership and increased funding but lacks systematic practices needed to sustain momentum.
Forest Service	C	C	D	B	C	C	Conflicting missions and decentralized systems have created systematic weaknesses that management is committed to addressing.
Bureau of Indian Affairs	D	D	C	C	D	D	Long-standing management deficiencies acknowledged, but improvements difficult and slow in high-pressure/low-resource environment.

The group surveyed 100 managers in each of the agencies it rated. Here's how they graded their agencies in "managing for results":

Administration for Children and Families	B
Bureau of Consular Affairs	B
NASA	B
National Weather Service	B
Postal Service	B
Bureau of Indian Affairs	C
Forest Service	C

Source: Washington Post, April 12, 2001, p. A29. Copyright © 2001 *The Washington Post.* Reprinted by permission.

Congress, the Social Security Administration has sustained a remarkable record for competence. It assigns a number to, and maintains a lifetime earnings record for, each taxpayer in the country, then mails a benefit check for everyone who becomes eligible for Social Security.

Although businesses are dismayed by government rules and regulations, those guidelines almost always serve an important purpose. Automobile manufacturers complain about the $100 million added to production costs by the government's requirement that cars have rear-window brake lights, but that requirement prevents $900 million in property damage and a great deal of human suffering. Furthermore, though chemical manufacturers may not like to fill out government forms specifying where they dump hazardous materials, most citizens would no doubt be reassured by the fact that manufacturers have to comply with that particular annoyance.[30]

Reforming the Bureaucracy

There is no shortage of ideas on how to reform the federal bureaucracy. Some advocates of reform have called for a partial return to the patronage system used up until the passage of the Pendleton Act in 1883. These political observers argue, just as Andrew Jackson did more nearly two centuries ago in 1828, that patronage appointments will improve efficiency and democratic accountability by translating popular support for the objectives of an incoming president into actual policy. But, as the reformers who abolished patronage in the 1880s pointed out, patronage leads to widespread corruption, disorganization, and underqualified personnel in the bureaucracy.

Other reforms seek to address charges of an inert, unproductive work force in federal agencies. One effort to improve innovation and productivity was the Civil Service Reform Act in 1978, which created the *Senior Executive Services (SES),* a group of upper-management bureaucrats with access to private-sector incentives such as bonuses but also subject to measurable job-performance evaluations. Those who failed to achieve high ratings could be fired. The idea was that the senior bureaucrats would respond positively to productivity incentives and become more responsive to presidential policy leadership. The effects of the program have been unclear. While innovation has occurred, some career officers find exposure to political pressure uncomfortable. Few members of the SES have been fired, but many have left their jobs with a bad taste in their mouths.

Another reform aimed at making the bureaucracy more effective and accountable is the *Whistle-Blower Act,* passed by Congress in 1989. This act encourages civil servants to report instances of bureaucratic mismanagement, financial impropriety, corruption, and inefficiency. It also protects civil servants from retaliation—from being fired, demoted, or relocated, for example. The act has been effective in helping to identify and root out problems in the bureaucracy. In February 1998 the FBI agreed to pay a settlement of $1.16 million to a whistle-blower whose report brought about an overhaul of its crime laboratory. Frederick Whitehurst exposed the FBI lab for flawed scientific work and inaccurate, pro-prosecution testimony in many cases, including the Oklahoma City and the 1993 World Trade Center bombings. Whitehurst was suspended following his charges of FBI incompetence.

Still, the 1989 Whistleblower Protection Act has often been narrowly interpreted by the U.S. Court of Appeal's for the Federal Circuit to "exclude employees who first take their allegations to supervisors or co-workers." At a 2002 Paul Revere Forum, in honor of the Revolutionary War hero who rode through Massachusetts to warn that the British were coming, the National Whistleblower Center called for tougher legislation that would protect the messenger.[31]

Some have proposed drastically reducing or even eliminating the bureaucracy altogether through privatization. **Privatization** involves turning over public responsibilities for regulation and for providing goods and services to privately owned and operated enterprises. Some economists argue that private enterprises could do a superior and less costly job of implementing, administering, and regulating government programs. Advocates of privatization point to the success of United Parcel Service and Federal Express, and compare these two private companies with the

"I had to switch your lie detector test this afternoon from 3 to 1 because you're scheduled to leak some information at 2!"

Cartoon by Wayne Stayskal (1983), from *Chicago Tribune.*

privatization The turning over of public responsibilities to privately owned and operated enterprises for regulation and for providing goods and services.

stickers to liscence plates

Our Ailing Bureaucracy

From the overburdened Immigration and Naturalization Service to the cumbersome and expansive Department of the Interior, fundamental flaws became so serious that major government action was undertaken during the Bush administration in 2002. According to Paul C. Light, director of the government studies program at the Brookings Institution, "every week brings new examples of federal agencies not just performing poorly, but performing stupidly."

Many agencies are teetering on the brink of operational breakdown and public disenchantment with poor performance. The Department of the Interior, mandated with the responsibility of protecting Native American natural resources, has thoroughly mismanaged leasing, royalty rights, and trust fund accounts, depriving billions of dollars from Indian tribes since the mid-nineteenth century. The Bureau of Indian Affairs within the Department also came under fire: it received a "C" or "D" grade in all categories of efficiency utilized by a Bush administration study. Embattled in 1999 and 2000, the Internal Revenue Service decided to focus on small business owners rather than the wealthy to see who is cheating on their taxes. In one of the most hurtful and glaring examples of bureaucratic dysfunction, the Immigration and Naturalization Service and the Federal Aviation Administration mistakenly mailed visa and flight-school applications to the dead bombers of 9–11.

Lois A. Clark, executive director of a nonprofit watchdog organization called the *Government Accountability Project* that protects "whistle-blowers" (employees who reveal government problems), noted that "before September 11, there was a bit of a blasé attitude of, 'O.K., the government screwed up again . . . ' Now people see the consequences on their lives, and see the necessity of government functioning well." Most federal employees interviewed by the Brookings Institution contend that they lacked sufficient resources to perform adequately in the workplace. Except for the Defense Department, the problem of bureaucratic inefficiency is worsening, according to the study.

▲ Gale Norton, a lifelong conservationist, public servant, and advocate for bringing common-sense solutions to environmental policy, was sworn in as the 48th Secretary of the U.S. Department of the Interior in January 2001. The first woman to head the 153-year-old department, Norton has made what she calls the Four C's the cornerstone of her tenure: Consultation, Communication, and Cooperation, all in the service of Conservation. At the heart of the Four C's is the belief that for conservation to be successful, the government must involve the people who live and work on the land.

Source: Eric Schmitt, "Is This Any Way to Run a Nation?" *The Nation*, April 26, 2002.

more costly and less efficient U.S. Postal Service. They view this comparison as evidence that shifting services from governmental to private hands will greatly improve both quality and cost effectiveness. But defenders of the Postal Service argue that such comparisons are unfair, since private companies, unlike the Postal Service, are not limited by costly congressional policy mandates.

The very people who have grown comfortable with the status quo—relevant legislators and the bureaucrats themselves—are responsible for developing, implementing, and administering the programs that would improve bureaucratic performance, democratize the bureaucracy, and enhance accountability. For this reason more than any other, attempts to reform the bureaucracy dramatically have

Table 7.2 ■ National Performance Review Accomplishments, 1993–2000
Savings total $137 billion.
Federal agencies have published more than 4,000 customer service standards for more than 570 organizations and programs.
Agencies have eliminated more than 640,000 pages of regulations. President Clinton will shortly sign an Executive Order requiring the rest to be rewritten in plain English.
Government was reduced by 351,000 positions. Reductions occurred in 13 or 14 departments. (Justice increased crime fighting.)
Nearly 1,200 Hammer Awards have been presented to teams of federal workers and their partners in industry and state and local governments for using reinvention principles to create a government that works better and costs less.
About 850 reinvention labs are reengineering government processes and using technology to unleash innovations that excite customers and employees alike with more flexible internal systems and improved services to the public.
The Congress has passed and President Clinton has signed 85 laws so far enacting NPR recommendations.

Source: Reinvention Accomplishments http://www.npr.gov/accompli/index.html.

encountered bristling opposition and met with only partial success. For a list of former Vice President Al Gore's successes, see Table 7.2.

In conclusion, bureaucratic organizations are inherently undemocratic. Democracy requires plurality; traditional bureaucracy requires unity. Though the bureaucracy is an institution that is often scorned for its enormous size and lack of responsiveness or accountability, this "fourth branch" of government is charged

DEMOCRACY IN THE NEW MILLENNIUM

"Bureaucracy on the Web" Has a Positive Connotation

More Americans conducted business with a government Website during 2001 than paid a credit card bill or traded stocks online. Nearly 55% of adults with Internet access visited a government web site and 21% of those visitors conducted a government transaction online. "There's a huge range of things people are doing online now—car registration, voter registration, paying fines, enrolling in schools, filing taxes . . ." said Charles Colby, president of the company conducting the survey. The study suggests that the Internet may offer citizens an alternative mode for interacting with government bureaucracy. "It's inconvenient to interact with the government in traditional ways, and you can provide via the Internet services, especially information services, that weren't available before. For the government, it's faster, cheaper and more efficient," said Roland Rust, the Director of the Center for e-Service at the University of Maryland. Rust provided the example of Virginia's Department of Motor Vehicles, which posted its first online business transaction—registration renewal—on the Web in May 1999. Nearly 4000 people used the service that month and the rate has now increased to 21,000 persons a month.

FirstGov, the official site for U.S. Government information, services, transactions and forms:

http://www.firstgov.org

The White House's main Web page:

http://www.whitehouse.gov

Fed Stats, official statistical information available to the public from the Federal Government:

http://www.fedstats.gov

Source: Ellen McCarthy, "Government Sites Draw Web Traffic," *Washington Post,* January 9, 2002, p. E5.

with an important function that makes it indispensable in America's approach to democracy: just as the creation of the Department of Homeland Security is intended to protect the very survival of our democratic society.

Developing federal plans for preventing and responding to terrorist attacks and then coordinating those blueprints with state and local governments is an enormous undertaking. Bringing together 170,000 employees from 22 agencies is likely to produce resistance from the prevailing bureaucratic cultures and lead to new institutional rivalries. "The continuing threat of terrorism, the threat of mass murder on our own soil, will be met with a unified, effective response," said President Bush at the bill signing in the East Room of the White House. "Dozens of agencies charged with homeland security will now be located within one cabinet department with the mandate and legal authority to protect our people."[32] It will take much more than a presidential stroke of a pen to achieve these goals, and the true test lies in personal leadership and response of a bureaucratic entity charged with ensuring the safety of our democratic policy.

SUMMARY

1. A bureaucracy is a large and complex organizational system in which tasks, roles, and responsibilities are structured to achieve a goal. Bureaucracies are characterized by specialization, hierarchy, and a system of formal rules. Bureaucratic failures often result from too-rigid adherence to one or more of these characteristics.

2. The federal bureaucracy began growing rapidly in the late nineteenth century, spurred by industrial expansion. The size of the bureaucracy has increased dramatically during the twentieth century, largely as a result of efforts to create a welfare state. Recent growth has resulted from legislation to address racial injustice, environmental degradation, and other problems in American society.

3. Before 1828 the federal bureaucracy was dominated by a small elite of wealthy, well-educated white males. Under the "spoils system" instituted by President Andrew Jackson, government jobs were awarded on the basis of party loyalty. In 1883 Congress passed the Pendleton Act, which created a civil service—a system that hires and promotes employees on the basis of professional merit and protects them from political threats to their job security.

4. The Hatch Act of 1939 established standards for federal employees. The political liberties of government employees were restricted to preserve the neutrality of federal agencies. Recent amendments allow federal employees to participate more actively in partisan politics, although they cannot run for office.

5. One of the primary tasks of the bureaucracy is to implement the policies established by Congress and the president. Administrators have considerable discretion in implementing legislation. As a result, the actual impact of a policy may be quite different from what was intended.

6. The administration of a policy involves the performance of routine tasks associated with a specific policy goal. Another task of bureaucratic agencies—regulation—consists of making rules, enforcing them, and adjudicating any disputes that arise as a result.

7. Cabinet departments are major administrative units responsible for conducting a broad range of government operations. Each department has jurisdiction over a specific policy area and is headed by a secretary who is also a member of the president's cabinet.

8. Independent agencies are smaller than cabinet departments and have a narrower set of responsibilities; they generally exist to perform a service such as space exploration or intelligence gathering. Independent regulatory commissions are established to regulate a sector of the nation's economy in the public interest and are generally run by a board whose members have set terms.

9. A government corporation is a semi-independent government agency that administers a business enterprise. It takes the form of a business corporation but possesses the authority of government.

10. Agencies of the federal bureaucracy are subject to three major constraints. They lack control over their revenues, over decisions about how to deliver goods and services, and over the goals they must attempt to achieve.

11. Presidents attempt to control the bureaucracy through the appointment power, which enables them to appoint agency officials who will support their policies. Reorganization is another tool available to presidents seeking to control the bureaucracy. The Office of Management and Budget, which administers the federal budget, can be used to control government agencies. Presidents can also seek to influence the bureaucracy through persuasion.

12. Congressional oversight of the bureaucracy occurs largely through the power of the purse, which gives Congress the power to appropriate all funding for federal agencies. Congress also has the power of administrative oversight, and the Senate can confirm or reject presidential nominees for top positions in the bureaucracy.

13. The term *iron triangle* is used to refer to a strong interdependent relationship among legislators, lobbyists, and bureaucrats concerned with a particular area of public policy. Iron triangles are resistant to democratic accountability.

14. The American public has a negative view of the bureaucracy, believing that government is expensive and wasteful and that the bureaucracy is incapable of achieving its goals. It is widely believed that the bureaucracy hobbles businesses with unnecessary regulations, that government is not responsive to citizens, that federal bureaucrats take advantage of the taxpayer, and that the growth of the bureaucracy is out of control.

15. Efforts to reform the bureaucracy led to the creation of the Senior Executive Service, which was intended to increase innovation and productivity in the federal work force. Another proposed reform is privatization, or turning over certain governmental responsibilities to private enterprises. Current reform efforts focus on reorganizing "reinventing government:" shrinking agencies, reducing budgets, and making the bureaucracy more efficient.

KEY TERMS

bureaucracy	implementation	appointment power
bureaucrats	administrative discretion	Office of Management and
specialization	administration	Budget
hierarchy	regulation	iron triangles
formal rules	cabinet departments	issue networks
welfare state	independent agencies	red tape
spoils system	independent regulatory	privatization
civil service	commissions	
Hatch Act	government corporation	

POLISIM ACTIVITY

Bureaucracy

Congratulations on your appointment as Deputy Director of the Census Bureau! With the change in administration you will help to rebuild a democracy that was shaken up during the transition from the previous administration. One of your responsibilities is to shield the Director from the routine problems that arise in any bureaucratic organization. As bureaucratic problems arrive on your desk you must make the decisions that will establish you as a seasoned administrator.

SUGGESTED READINGS

BOZEMAN, BARRY. *Bureaucracy and Red Tape.* Upper Saddle River, N.J.: Prentice Hall, 2000. A very useful guide to understanding the complexity of government regulations as well as solutions for making government more efficient.

DOWNS, ANTHONY. *Inside Bureaucracy.* Prospect Heights, Ill.: Waveland Press, 1994. Interesting theories and insights into bureaucratic decision making.

GOODSELL, CHARLES T. *The Case for Bureaucracy: A Public Administration Polemic.* 3d ed. Chatham, N.J.: Chatham House, 1993. Myths about the bureaucracy and evidence that it usually does a better job than we give it credit for.

NEIMAN, MAX. *Defending Government: Why Big Government Works.* Upper Saddle River, N.J.: Prentice Hall, 2000. This book addresses the benefits of well-designed, democratically inspired public policies. It provides a very thoughtful analysis of the public sector, economic performance, and personal liberty.

WILSON, JAMES Q. *Bureaucracy: What Government Agencies Do and Why They Do It.* New York: Basic Books, 1989. A lively, "bottom-up" view of bureaucracy and an explanation of why some agencies work well, while others fail.

8

PUBLIC OPINION

CHAPTER OUTLINE

Approaching Democracy Case Study: Landon Defeats Roosevelt—The Voice of the People?

Introduction: Public Opinion and Democracy

What Is Public Opinion?

Measuring Public Opinion

Political Socialization

Social Variables that Influence Opinion Formation

American Political Culture

The State of American Public Opinion

From Public Opinion to Public Policy

APPROACHING DEMOCRACY CASE STUDY

Landon Defeats Roosevelt—The Voice of the People?

Beginning about 1916, the magazine *Literary Digest* made what was then the most sophisticated use of polling for political data. The magazine mailed surveys to a large number of Americans asking for opinions on a host of important issues. Using their responses, the magazine claimed a high degree of accuracy in predicting election outcomes. Indeed, in 1932 the *Literary Digest* poll came within 1 percent of the actual vote in predicting Roosevelt's victory over Herbert Hoover. So impressive was this predictive ability that Democratic National Chair James Farley proclaimed just prior to the election: "I consider [the poll results] conclusive evidence as to the desire of the people of this country for a charge in the national government. The *Literary Digest* poll is an achievement of no little magnitude."[1] This was high praise for a magazine whose editorial policy and readership were decidedly sympathetic to the Republican party.

But a major mistake by the *Literary Digest* in 1936 changed everything and signaled the beginning of a new era in how polling is done. Today we take it for granted that the New Deal was generally popular, that Roosevelt's policies were widely supported, and that Roosevelt himself was beloved by millions. Nothing is clearer than hindsight. But at the time, before the advent of sophisticated polling techniques, it was unclear to most political observers what the outcome of the 1936 election would be. Indeed, the most respected polling outfit of the day, *Literary Digest,* predicted Roosevelt's sound thrashing in his reelection bid by his Republican opponent, Kansas governor Alfred Landon.

Now if Alf Landon doesn't immediately strike you as a household name, you are correct. Landon suffered perhaps the worst election defeat in American history and promptly faded into obscurity, while Roosevelt went on to win two more presidential elections in the next eight years. With such convincing evidence of public support for the president and the New Deal, how could anyone have assumed, in the fall of 1936, that Americans would back a little-known mid-western governor and a return to the Republican policies widely viewed as responsible for bringing on the Depression?

Prior to the election that year, the *Literary Digest* poll predicted a landslide win for Landon and claimed Roosevelt would gain only 41 percent of the vote to Landon's 55 percent, with 4 percent going to a third-party candidate, William Lemke. A disgusted James Farley, who had praised the *Digest* only four years earlier, now entirely discounted the poll results, predicting instead a Roosevelt sweep of all but eight electoral votes. His prediction was exactly right, and the rest is history. Landon carried only two states, while FDR garnered 61 percent of the popular vote. How could *Literary Digest* have been so wrong?

The answer is simple. The *Digest* worked with a biased sample. As with its earlier polls, in 1936 the magazine sent out millions of informal surveys to people whose names had been culled from automobile registration lists and telephone books. Altogether 10 million ballots were sent out, and nearly 2.4 million were returned— large numbers, but a response rate of under 25 percent. But in 1936, these respondents were no longer representative of the total American public as they had been in 1932. They were wealthier, for one thing. In a period of grinding economic depression, they could still afford the luxury of an automobile and a telephone. They were also better educated than the average American in 1936.

These two factors ensured a built-in bias against Roosevelt, since wealth and education have long been correlated with support for Republicans. Many people in this group were motivated to return their ballots because they wanted to get rid of Roosevelt. Despite their large numbers, they were hardly typical of the American public as a whole.

In addition to these problems, participants in the poll were self-selected. They were picked not at random but simply on the basis of whether they chose to return the questionnaire. Since the individuals most motivated to respond to a political survey are almost never representative of the wider population, the results from such a self-selected survey are not reliable.

The editors of the *Literary Digest* openly confessed their chagrin in the post-election issue and vowed to rethink their methodology in subsequent polling efforts. Being contrite, however, did them little good. Their magazine was already a luxury during the Depression. Under the further weight of this highly publicized embarrassment, the *Digest* went broke within a year. This incident marked an end to the era of unscientific polling and pushed survey researchers to fine-tune their methods. It opened the door to today's much more sophisticated—and reliable—survey models.

Question for Reflection: If the individuals motivated to respond to a political survey are almost never representative of the wider population, how might pollsters attract a broader percentage of the general populace to participate in their surveys?

▲ **President Franklin D. Roosevelt during inauguration ceremonies, January 20, 1937. The president is pictured on the porch of the Hermitage, a replica of the home where Andrew Jackson lived.**

INTRODUCTION: PUBLIC OPINION AND DEMOCRACY

This case study was selected in order to make a point about measuring public opinion. Public opinion is the keystone of democracy. No government can claim to be the legitimate voice of a people unless public opinion plays an integral role in the choice of political leaders and the development of public policy. Thus, the gathering of information about public opinion becomes a vital task for a democracy. Using sophisticated polling techniques, survey analysts are able to provide a relatively accurate snapshot of what Americans think and feel about specific issues, events, and candidates.

While not all Americans are politically active and informed, all have the opportunity to be, and millions do take advantage of that opportunity. Leaders are continually made aware of what citizens are thinking; they are particularly well informed about voter desires through a constant barrage of scientific public opinion polls and a never-ending series of popular elections. Knowledgeable about what citizens want, leaders are likely to heed the public's wishes, a result that is central to any idea of democracy.

Americans are sufficiently informed and participatory to keep leaders in touch with their desires, sufficiently open and tolerant to live together peacefully within a diverse and complex culture. To gauge the strength of democracy, leaders need to know what citizens desire, how well they communicate those desires through political activity, and how well political leaders respond to those desires. For any democratic system, not just in America, to be democratic, its leaders must at the very least hear "the voice of the people." For example, a *Jerusalem Post* opinion poll on April 1, 2002, revealed that seventy-two percent of Israeli's support the Sharon government's decision to wage wide-scale war in the territories. With this type of public approval, Sharon was in a better position to ignore President Bush's call for an immediate ceasefire and withdrawal. But Bush was feeling pressure of another sort. A *Washington Post*–ABC News poll (see Figure 8.1) of April 23, 2002, showed an American public wary of seeing the United States assume a broker's role between warring sides.[2]

This leader–follower connection is central to democratic theory in democratic societies such as Israel and the United States. Citizens in a democracy express their preferences through informed political activity, and leaders listen with a keen interest to those expressed preferences. If the masses are inactive or if the leaders consistently ignore their desires, democracy falters. To begin to understand the impact of public opinion, we examine how it is measured, where opinions on political issues come from, and the nature of public opinion in America.[3]

© 1995 Creators Syndicate Inc.
Richmond Times-Dispatch 11/95.
Bob Gorrell.

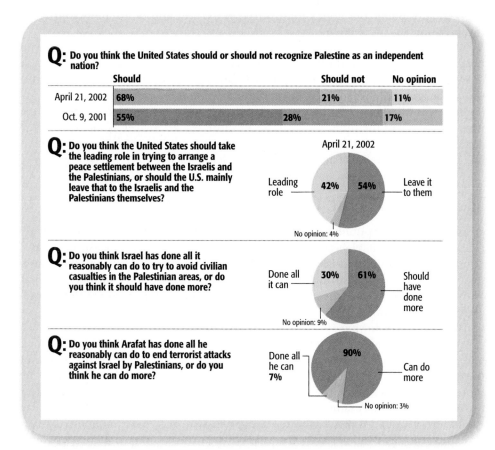

Q: Do you think the United States should or should not recognize Palestine as an independent nation?

	Should	Should not	No opinion
April 21, 2002	68%	21%	11%
Oct. 9, 2001	55%	28%	17%

Q: Do you think the United States should take the leading role in trying to arrange a peace settlement between the Israelis and the Palestinians, or should the U.S. mainly leave that to the Israelis and the Palestinians themselves?

April 21, 2002

Leading role 42% 54% Leave it to them

No opinion: 4%

Q: Do you think Israel has done all it reasonably can do to try to avoid civilian casualties in the Palestinian areas, or do you think it should have done more?

Done all it can 30% 61% Should have done more

No opinion: 9%

Q: Do you think Arafat has done all he reasonably can do to end terrorist attacks against Israel by Palestinians, or do you think he can do more?

Done all he can 7% 90% Can do more

No opinion: 3%

Figure 8.1
America's Views on Mideast Strife

Source: The Washington Post, April 23, 2002. Copyright © 2002 *The Washington Post.* Reprinted by permission.

What Is Public Opinion?

Public opinion is the collective expression of attitudes about the prominent issues and actors of the day. The concept of a "public" holding "opinions" on various issues is almost as old as politics itself. Plato, for instance, saw public opinion as a danger if it meant the free expression of individual desires by the mass of citizens. According to Plato, popular opinions were good only when they reflected the will of the state and its rulers. A very different view was expressed centuries later by John Stuart Mill, who in his essay *On Liberty* (1859) argued in favor of a populace free to express its diverse political views. Only by giving all individuals the maximum liberty to state their opinions, said Mill, could a society ever arrive at the "truth." Where Plato wanted to shape and control opinions, Mill advocated free rein to their expression.

James Madison took something of a middle stance between Plato and Mill. In *The Federalist,* no. 10, Madison acknowledged the inevitable diversity of opinion that would develop in a free society but feared that competing opinions could lead to hostile factions that would divide rather than unify or improve society:

> A zeal for different opinions . . . [has] divided mankind into parties, inflamed them with mutual animosity, and rendered them . . . disposed to vex and oppress each other.[4]

Like most of the framers, Madison was concerned that an overzealous majority might inflict its irrational, prejudiced, or uninformed wishes on a political minority. Hence, the framers made sure to install constitutional safeguards (such as the Electoral College, the Senate, and the Supreme Court) against the too easy implementation of public passions. On the other hand, they also allowed many outlets for the

public opinion The collective expression of attitudes about the prominent issues and actors of the day.

expression of public opinion: voting, a free press, the right of assembly, and other forms of political participation.

How deeply public opinion should be taken into account, then, has long been the subject of intense political debate, but today there are clear parameters for this debate. No longer can a legitimate public figure argue, as Plato did, that the public should be ignored or manipulated in political decision-making. The only real argument now is whether the public's will should prevail "all of the time," "most of the time," or "some of the time." The public, in short, is a key player in the democratic game of politics. For that reason, discovering and publicizing the public's opinion has become a key political activity in modern democracies.

Measuring Public Opinion

While the notion of public opinion has been with us for centuries, we have only recently developed reliable ways to measure it. The first attempts at measuring public opinion began in the mid-1800s, with a variety of **straw polls.** A straw poll is a nonscientific method of measuring public opinion. It springs from the farmer's method of throwing straw up into the air to gauge the strength and direction of the prevailing breeze. In a straw poll, one wishes to measure which way and how strong the political breezes are blowing.

As we saw in the case study, straw polls have inherent flaws that make them inappropriate as scientific indicators of public opinion. Their main problem is that they fail to obtain a **representative sample** of the public. A valid sample must be representative, meaning it must include all the significant characteristics of the total population. A sample of Americans that included no women, for instance, would obviously be invalid. A non-representative sample like the infamous *Literary Digest* poll of 1936, which underrepresented poor and average-income people, is worthless.

After the 1936 fiasco, professional pollsters began a determined effort to make their work more scientific. George Gallup and Elmo Roper, among others, helped meet the growing demand for information about public attitudes. Applying modern statistical techniques, they found it possible through interviews with small but representative samples of voters to predict the behavior of the overall voting population.

To obtain a representative sample, some requirements must be met. First, the number of people in the sample should be at least several hundred. Second, the people to be polled must be chosen through a technique known as random sampling. In addition, pollsters must guard against sampling bias.[5]

Sample Size   Most pollsters produce results of high reliability. Their findings are accurate at least 95 percent of the time, within a margin of error of about 3 percent. **Margin of error** reflects the validity of the results obtained by a poll given the sample size. For example, a poll with a 3 percent margin of error suggests that, on average, the results of the poll would differ by plus or minus 3 percent if the entire population were polled, rather than just a sampling of that population.

Another component of a good poll is sample size. Generally, the larger the sample the better, because larger samples reduce the margin of error. Most reputable national polls have sample sizes of 1,500 to 2,000 respondents, a size that reduces the margin of error to plus or minus 3 percent. Using statistical methods, pollsters have determined that information from a sample of that size can be projected onto the entire population. The method does work, but there is a heavy burden on pollsters: "What's critical is that we all act with care gathering our data honestly and well: examining them fully and thoughtfully; chasing bias and conventional wisdom out the door; reaching for new, independent approaches and fresh understandings; keeping sight of the limitations as well as the possibilities of our work; and,

straw poll A nonscientific method of measuring public opinion.

representative sample A sample that includes all the significant characteristics of the total population.

margin of error The measure of possible error in a survey, which means that the number for the entire population of voters will fall within a range of plus or minus several points of the number obtained from the small but representative sample of respondents.

Gary Markstein, Copley News
Service © *The Milwaukee Journal
Sentinel.*

ultimately, producing the best, most thoughtful analysis of public opinion we can.
The times demand no less, observed Gary Langer, director of polling for ABC
news."[6]

Random Sampling   The second requirement for a good poll, random sampling,
is harder to achieve. In a **random sample,** every member of the population must
have an equal chance of appearing in the sample. Advancements in technology
have reduced the problems associated with randomness. Pollsters are increasingly
utilizing *random digit dialing* (RDD), which, through the use of computers, automatically selects phone numbers at random. The use of this technique allows for the selection of phone numbers that are both listed and unlisted, ensuring that all
individuals have the same chance of being selected for inclusion in a poll.

Pollsters make every effort to guard against **sampling bias.** They try to ensure
that no particular set of people in the population at large—rich or poor, black or
white, northerner or south westerner—is any more or less likely to appear in the
final sample than any other set of people. Recall that the major flaw in the *Literary
Digest* poll of 1936—the disproportionately high percentage of respondents who
were relatively wealthy and well educated—led to biased results.

Little room is left to interviewer discretion. Most polling organizations divide the
population of the United States into categories based on the location and size of
the city in which they live. Certain areas or blocks are then randomly selected and
interviewers are sent into the neighborhood. Using another technique, pollsters
carry out a survey using computer-generated lists of telephone numbers. Because
people are selected completely at random, these lists will reflect an approximation
of the entire nation. The result is that polls today come relatively close to meeting
the crucial requirement that every American have an equal chance of appearing in
any given pollster's sample.

Problems still occur, however. The reliance on telephones, while convenient and
inexpensive, does introduce a modest degree of sampling bias. For example, 1990
census figures indicated that 20 percent of Native American households lack telephone service of any kind, as do 15 percent of African American and Hispanic
households; by contrast, only about 5 percent of white households have no telephone. Altogether, nearly 5 million of America's 92 million housing units lack telephones. Since a strong statistical correlation exists between poverty and lack of
telephone facilities, it would appear that most "phoneless" housing units are in
areas of urban poverty. Polls based on telephone ownership are therefore likely to
under represent the urban ethnic poor.

general opinion

random sample A strategy required
for a valid poll whereby every member of the population has an equal
chance of appearing in the sample.

sampling bias A bias in a survey
whereby a particular set of people in
the population at large is more or
less likely to appear in the final sample than other sets of people.

Reliability   Another major concern of polling is reliability. Pollsters want to obtain results that are meaningful and consistent. Attention to *question wording* is essential for reliable results. Respondents can often be led into answers by the way a question is worded. For example, in 1992 Independent presidential candidate Ross Perot commissioned his own poll, which asked: "Should laws be passed to eliminate all possibilities of special interests giving huge sums of money to candidates?" Here was a case of a candidate framing a poll question to get the answer he wanted—99 percent of the respondents answered "yes." But if the question had been rephrased to ask, "Do groups have the right to contribute money to candidates they support?" it is likely the response would have been different from the loaded question asked by Perot.[7]

The type of answers solicited by pollsters can also affect the results. Generally, questions are either *open-ended,* where respondents are free to offer any answer to a question ("What do you think is the biggest problem facing the country today?") or *close-ended,* where the pollster provides a set of possible answers ("Would you consider welfare, crime, or environment to be the biggest problem facing the country?").

Pollsters confront a number of additional problems as they set out to conduct their polls. Interviewers must be carefully trained to avoid interviewer bias. They must be courteous, businesslike, and neutral so as to elicit responses from the public that are open and honest. Interviewers must also be persistent. Some people are rarely home; others may hesitate to answer questions. Interviewers must make every effort to contact potential respondents and draw them out; they must learn how to extract truthful answers from shy, hostile, or simply bewildered members of the voting public.

The Importance of Polls   Public opinion polls has emerged as an integral part of American politics. Accurate polls are one of the most important sources of information used by political leaders in the decision-making process. Polls today that are conducted by reputable national polling organizations do provide a reasonably accurate picture of the beliefs and desires of the American public. Without polls, an understanding of what the public thinks and wants would be difficult to achieve. In one of the most interesting post–September 11 polls on American attitudes, a Hart-Teeter telephone survey (see Figure 8.2) of 961 randomly selected adults from November 12 to November 19, 2001, found that many American's believed, e-government "has a critical role to play" in the war on terrorism. Large majorities believe that e-government will help federal and local agencies better coordinate a response to an emergency. The poll also revealed that Americans have mixed feelings about national identification cards.[8]

Virtually every news organization has association with a polling company and an in-house polling team. Many public officials, the president included, have professional pollsters on their staff—always prepared to check the pulse of the people. Lobby groups are constantly releasing the results of polls they have commissioned to "prove" that the public supports their particular policy preferences.

Polls are used by the media during campaigns to track the support of candidates over time. These types of polls are called **tracking polls.** The media also utilize **exit polls,** which target voters as they leave the voting booth in an effort to gauge the likely winner of an election before the results are announced. The use of exit polls is often criticized for lowering voter turnout, particularly in western states, because the media use exit polls to project winners well before voting booths have closed across the nation. In the 2000 primaries, exit polls were available on the Internet hours before voting ended. On election night 2000, the television networks, basing their announcement on exit polling in Florida, erroneously projected Al Gore as winning the election. Voter News Service, a consortium of news organizations that provide exit polls, erred in its statistical projections, not unlike *Literary Digest's* prediction of the 1936 presidential election results.

tracking polls Polls used by the media to track the support levels for candidates over time.

exit polls Polls that question voters as they leave the voting booth to predict the outcome of an election.

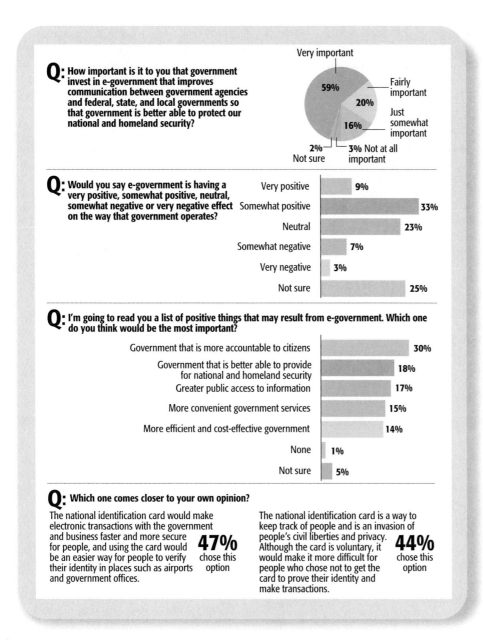

Figure 8.2
E-Government and the War on Terrorism

Source: The Washington Post, February 27, 2002. Copyright © 2002 *The Washington Post.* Reprinted by permission.

? Question for Reflection: Have you ever been contacted by pollsters for your opinion on political issues on either a national, state, or local level? Did you comply with their request for your feedback? If not, why, and would you reconsider your decision based on the impact polls have on our democratic system?

Political Socialization

Where do our ideas about politics come from? **Political socialization** refers to the process by which we learn about the world of politics and develop our political beliefs. Learning about politics begins early in childhood. Political thinkers have long observed that parent-child and sibling relationships shape the social and political outlook of future citizens. Other institutions—schools, peer groups, mass media—also serve as agents of socialization.

political socialization The process by which we learn about the world of politics and develop our political beliefs.

APPROACHING DEMOCRACY AROUND THE GLOBE

Polling in Riyadh

When Crown Prince Abdullah of Saudi Arabia raised the prospect that he possessed a peace plan for the Middle East, many foreign policy experts suggested that the Prince was primarily making a public relations gesture in order to repair U.S.–Saudi relations that had soured in the post–September 11th revelations that a majority of the terrorists were from Saudi Arabia. It seems, however, that the Prince was motivated by domestic public opinion polls revealing that the Arab-Israeli conflict could not only undermine the kingdom's relationship with the United States, but perhaps the stability of the kingdom itself.

Polling conducted inside Saudi Arabia in March 2002 revealed that the Saudi people were angry and frustrated at the U.S. role in the Arab-Israeli conflict. The problem for the Prince was that he wanted to assist the U.S. in the war on terrorism and to rein in radical Islamists. A survey of Saudi elites—media professionals, academics, and chamber of commerce members—revealed "43% said that their frustration with the United States would be completely removed, and 23% said they would be significantly reduced, if America brokered a just and lasting peace in the Arab-Israeli conflict." In a general opinion survey of the entire population conducted during the summer 2001, the Palestinian issue was identified as the single most important issue to them personally. "When asked if their attitudes towards the United States were mostly based on its policies or its values, 86% answered politics. Only 6% said values."

Thus, it appears that the Saudi peace effort is as much an effort to solve a real problem, as it is a public relations gesture. So long as there is no peace between Israel and its Arab neighbors, the Saudi's leaders have much to fear from the most radical elements in its own society and these threaten the long term stability of the kingdom—at least that is what their opinion polls show.

Source: Shibley Telhami, "Polling and Politics in Riyadh," *New York Times,* March 3, 2002. p. 4, Week in Review.

The Role of Family

Family influence is especially powerful in the development of political knowledge, understanding, and participation. Whether we grow up poor or rich, for instance, shapes our view of the world and bears heavily on the likelihood of our developing an interest in politics. Other family traits—education level, race, even geographic location—deeply affect our perspectives on the political world.

Around the age of ten, children begin to form their worldview, based significantly on family views toward politics. The role of family in political socialization is mostly informal. Parents rarely sit their children down and inform them that they are Democrats, supply-siders, or isolationists. In this sense, the family unit has a unique advantage for influence. Children absorb the casually dropped remarks of their parents and, over time, unthinkingly adopt those views as their own.

The influence of family also derives from the strong emotional bonds forged by the family connection. Children want to adopt the views of their beloved mentors. Close-knit families produce offspring whose views differ little from those of the parents. The power structure of the family provides an additional key to the early political socialization of children. Strong parental authority figures have an enormous impact on a child's values and attitudes. Many scholars believe, for instance, that harsh, punitive parents produce children who are more authoritarian, intolerant, and ultraconservative than the average American.

Because many variables affect political attitudes, it is difficult to trace the precise effects of family on the political opinions of adult Americans. In one area, however, parental impact seems clear and pronounced. Children tend to adopt the party loyalty of their parents. That's significant, because *partisan identification* helps people make sense of the political world and predicts their behavior within it. Interestingly, when each parent identifies with a different political party, children generally embrace the partisan affiliation of their mother. We are not certain why this is, but

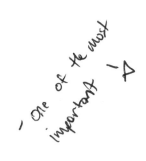
– One of the most important ↓

one possible explanation, which would certainly reinforce the importance of family socialization, is that children feel closer to their mother, from whom they received much early nurturing and affection.

Children, however, must adjust their values so they can adapt to a changing world. The concept of a *generation gap* describes the potential decline in family influence over children's values. It postulates that when children reach adulthood, they break away and may condemn their parents' political beliefs. The rebellious 1960s gave new credence to this theory. However, follow-up studies during the 1970s suggest that as the children of the 1960s grew older, many adopted some of their parents' political beliefs. What accounts for this transition? Among other things, we know that as people age, they settle down and grow slightly more conservative. The day-to-day responsibilities of a job, a family, and a home move individuals in the direction of preserving the status quo of society and politics. One cannot, after all, remain a rebellious youth forever.[9]

Still, no generation simply mimics the views of its parents. Analysts have observed a strong **generational effect** in the socialization patterns of the American public. The generation of adults who grew up during the 1960s does appear to have its own outlook, different from that of the previous generation. Its views are characterized by weaker ties to political institutions, weaker partisan identification, and a higher incidence of political independence or nonpartisanship. This pattern results from a host of factors, including the social dislocations of the 1960s, the Vietnam War, and the Watergate scandal—all of which made Americans more critical of their political system.

Schooling

Outside the family, the most powerful institutional influence on political socialization is education. In school children first learn the formal rules of social interaction and come face to face with institutional authority: teachers, staff, and principals. More specifically, they learn to develop positive attitudes toward citizenship through history and civics courses. Early primary education leads children to recognize the name and image of the president. Most children are taught to look at the president as a benevolent symbol of government and politics. This early socialization carries over strongly into adult life. Even after Richard Nixon's resignation from office in the midst of the Watergate scandal, most American adults still placed enormous faith in the office of the presidency and believed in the notion of a strong political leader in the White House.

Since schools are central to the socialization process, they have become the center of political controversy, as different sides of the political spectrum struggle for control of what schools teach. The issue of prayer in the public schools, for example, has sharply divided the American public and led to heated debate. This clash fits into a larger debate between educational conservatives and liberals on the role of schools in modern American society. Both sides wish to use schools to socialize students to the perspectives they hold dear. Conservative critics charge that schools are failing to provide students with the traditions and norms of American culture. Liberal critics fault the schools for perpetuating class, race, and gender divisions and for failing to teach about "diversity" and "multiculturalism." As these arguments suggest, Americans live in a complex and increasingly divided society. Debate about the way schools should socialize young Americans is therefore likely to continue for some time.

University training also represents a key element in the process of socialization. Most people believe that the experience of attending a university somehow "makes people more liberal." In fact, recent years have witnessed an increase in the number of self-identified conservatives among university students. Historically, university students were every bit as likely to be Republicans as Democrats; however, those who obtain both a university education and high socioeconomic status tend to be moderate or conservative, not liberal.

— the more education the more socialized you are

generational effect Socialization patterns in which a generation of adults who grew up during a certain decade or period appears to have its own outlook, different from that of the previous age.

Peers

A child's peers make up another important source of political socialization. We all absorb the ideas and outlook of our contemporaries, especially close friends. However, studies have found that although on matters of taste, dress, and style, teenage peer groups exert a significant impact, they do little more than reinforce parental and community values, at least when it comes to politics. Peer groups do appear to affect political attitudes on the rare public issues of special relevance to young people. The decision to resist the draft or to enlist in the 1960s, for example, would have been influenced by one's peer group. And "Generation X," young people of the 1990s, through a political action committee representing their political and economic needs (XPAC), identify Social Security reform as the core issue for this group.

In recent decades, many observers have described the emergence of a "youth culture." Urie Bronfenbrenner, for instance, has argued that children's peers and television are much more influential in American culture than they were in the past, due in large part to the breakdown of the family and the decrease in its traditional influence.[10] The youth culture, he fears, stresses immature, violent, and commercialized perspectives on life, shielded as it is from the more responsible perspectives of an adult world and deeply influenced by images on the television screen. A whole generation has now come of age heavily influenced by youth culture norms.

A landmark study by Robert Putnam suggests these consequences: Americans today are less prone to engage in civic activities, less trusting of others, and more cynical about the institutions of American society than they were in previous generations. The values propagated in the peer groups of young adults may have a role in this trend.[11]

A Pew Research Center study, in March 2002, found that the post–September 11 era had led to a dramatic and unparalled increase in national unity, patriotism, and nationhood. The evidence also shows that younger Americans in particular see government since September 11 as being more relevant today. Tables 8.1 and 8.2 show this trend.[12]

Television

Perhaps more than anything else in American culture, television has emerged to dominate the social and political landscape. The language, habits, values, and norms of American society seem to derive as much from exposure to the imagery of television as from any other socializing force.

Despite a considerable literature devoted to the effects of television on political attitudes and behavior, no consensus exists regarding just how and to what degree television affects Americans. Television has come under severe scrutiny because of its ubiquity, its demonstrated power to absorb viewer time for several hours a day, and its unique blend of immediacy, proximity, and audiovisual appeal. Perhaps the major criticism of television focuses on its power to divert our attention from the serious to the trivial.

Since the vast majority of television shows are devoted to amusement rather than information, and most people watch television for entertainment, its effect in shaping political attitudes must be indirect. One study concludes that, "politically relevant issues are now raised in virtually all types of programming."[13] The values conveyed by television—commercialism, tolerance for sex and violence, encouragement of an extreme form of rugged individualism—become, in other words, an unthinking part of the general culture. Viewers absorb these values and subconsciously draw on them when thinking about politics.

Despite all the criticism of television, however, many studies reveal a surprise. Although children watch an average of twenty-seven hours of television per week—close to the amount they spend in class—a significant amount of viewing actually

Table 8.1 ■ Post-9/11 Nationhood Reinvigorated			
	1999	**2000**	**2002**
Importance of the State of the Union address . . .	%	%	%
More Important	27	16	54
Less Important	16	22	4
Same	51	53	36
Don't know	6	9	6
	100	100	100

Number rating country's future optimistically	**Rated "Very High"**
2002*	52%
2001*	39%
1997	26%
1989	31%
1974*	29%
1959*	52%

*Source: Gallup trend. Reprinted by permission of The Pew Research Center for the People and the Press.

Table 8.2 ■ Post-9/11 News Interest			
	Total	**18-30**	**Over 30**
Interested in Political news	%	%	%
More	46	56	43
All kinds of news	26	41	21
War on terrorism	18	12	20
Both/DK	2	3	2
No Difference	50	35	54
Less	4	8	2
Don't know	1	1	1
	100	100	100

Source: Reprinted by permission of The Pew Research Center for the People and the Press.

increases exposure to and knowledge of politics and government. So while Americans are undoubtedly bombarded with huge daily doses of advertising, sports, and entertainment, television watching does at least expose young viewers to a considerable amount of political information as well.

Social Variables that Influence Opinion Formation

In learning about politics, we are all subject to the same general influences that shape the mind-set of our society. We learn from our families a common set of norms and values; we live together through major political and economic events;

we all go to school; and we are all bound together by the unifying force of television. Still, even within the same culture, people differ from each other in a number of ways. Different social circumstances—class and income, race and ethnicity, religion, region, and gender—produce very different life experiences that are bound to be reflected in differing political opinions.

Class and Income

Our relative standing in society shapes many of our social and political values. Class, or social status, rests high on every social scientist's list of the forces that mold behavior. Unfortunately, class is a complex and difficult variable to measure; no two analysts and no two citizens agree on its precise definition. Hence, we often resort to examining income, a key element in the concept of class and one that is far easier to define and study. As with class, people in different income groups often see the political world in very different ways. The impact of class and income, however, is mitigated through education. That is, those with higher education are more likely to be wealthy and of a higher class than those who are poorly educated. The impact of this relationship is particularly strong on voting behavior. The better educated, hence the wealthier, are much more likely to vote than the less educated, who are predominantly poor. We saw evidence of this connection in the *Literary Digest* presidential election poll of 1936, which represented opinions of the wealthier and better educated segments of the U.S. population.

As a general rule, the less money one makes, the more inclined one is to favor liberal economic policies that provide benefits to the less well off in society. These policies include a Social Security system, progressive taxation, minimum wage laws, generous unemployment benefits, and welfare payments to the disadvantaged. The more money one makes, the more one is likely to oppose such policies. Both positions reflect a degree of economic self-interest. Lower-income groups benefit from liberal economic policies, while the money to pay for these policies comes from higher-income groups. Nevertheless, these tendencies are only that—tendencies. Many individuals in each income category take positions opposite to what we would expect. Some millionaires are liberals, and some individuals at the lower end of the economic spectrum are conservatives.

Income level strongly influences voting patterns in the United States. Roughly stated, poor people vote for Democrats (the more liberal party on economic policy); rich people vote for Republicans (the more conservative party on economic policy); and middle-income people split their votes, depending on circumstance. To illustrate, if voting in 1996 had been restricted to people living in households with an annual income level of more than $50,000, Republican Robert Dole would have been handily elected, instead of running a poor second to incumbent Democrat Bill Clinton. In 1996, when Bill Clinton won a resounding reelection victory, the wealthiest voters in the country actually gave a majority of their votes to the loser, Republican Robert Dole. Income level, then, clearly affects one's perspective on the political process.

Race and Ethnicity

Income is but one of many social influences that produce different perspectives on politics. In addition, racial and ethnic background strongly affects the attitudes a person is likely to develop. Imagine how different your life experiences would have been, and how different the political attitudes you would have developed, had you been born into this world with a different skin color or a different ethnic heritage.

In most cultures, minorities are discriminated against. Hence, they can grow up feeling distrustful of and alienated from their society and its public authorities. These attitudes are expressed in politics in a number of ways. In the United States, for instance, blacks are clearly more alienated from the political process than whites are. As a result, they vote less frequently in elections and participate at a lower level in other areas of the political process. African Americans vote in large numbers for the party most associated with economic benefits for minorities and the less well off—that is, the Democrats. Race, America's most enduring social cleavage, produces the clearest of all social delineations between the two major political parties. The vast majority of black voters consider themselves Democrats, whereas white voters are more closely divided in party identification. Blacks consistently identify former President Bill Clinton as their greatest president.

Hispanics, too, tend to take a liberal position on economic issues and vote heavily for the Democratic party. However, the different groups within the Hispanic population are not as unified on issues as African Americans tend to be. Cuban Americans, for example, are wealthier than average and are among the more conservative of American voting blocs.

As a general rule, ethnic groups become conservative as they rise in social status. Asian Americans, whose income levels have risen significantly in recent decades, are now among the most conservative groups in the nation. The same is true for so-called "white ethnic" voters, people whose ancestors immigrated from Ireland, Italy, or Poland. This group was heavily Democratic for decades, but as members rose into the middle class, they developed more conservative outlooks. (We explore the political consequences of race and ethnicity in Chapter 10, when we examine voting patterns.)

Religion

Religious differences produce serious political differences in the United States, as in all countries. During the Republican 2000 primaries; candidate George W. Bush spoke at Bob Jones University, leading to an outcry from Catholics and others because of its ban on interracial dating, its ban on gay students, and Bob Jones University leader's statements calling the Catholic church a "satanic cult" and the Pope the "antichrist." Three general principles help explain the effect of religion on political attitudes. First, the less religious you are, the more liberal or "left" you are likely to be. In the United States, people with few religious connections are likely to take liberal stands on most social and economic questions and to vote Democratic. This pattern is not numerically significant, however, because most Americans profess religious belief of one kind or another.

More important for its political ramifications is the second principle: Members of any country's dominant religion tend to be more conservative. This stand makes sense, since these people have more investment in the status quo. By comparison, minority religious groups, especially the more oppressed ones, tend to favor liberal perspectives. This pattern can be seen clearly in the United States. Protestantism has long been the majority religion. Catholicism and Judaism were generally the religions of smaller minority groups who were discriminated against when they first immigrated to this country. As we would expect, over the years Protestants have been the most conservative religious group, while Catholics and Jews have been more liberal, and thus more likely to support Democrats. The way that the Catholic Church has handled the issue of sexual abuse of children by priests now threatens to undercut influence of the church on the political views of members (see Figure 8.3).

These are, of course, broad generalizations; many individuals within each category deviate significantly from the pattern. Furthermore, changing social circumstances are changing this pattern. Many Catholics have entered America's mainstream and have become conservatives. But Catholics who still belong to minority ethnic groups are still more liberal and more likely to support Democrats than are Protestants—or other Catholics for that matter. Jews remain the most liberal of all religious groups, but even they have moved modestly in a conservative direction as their economic situation has improved.

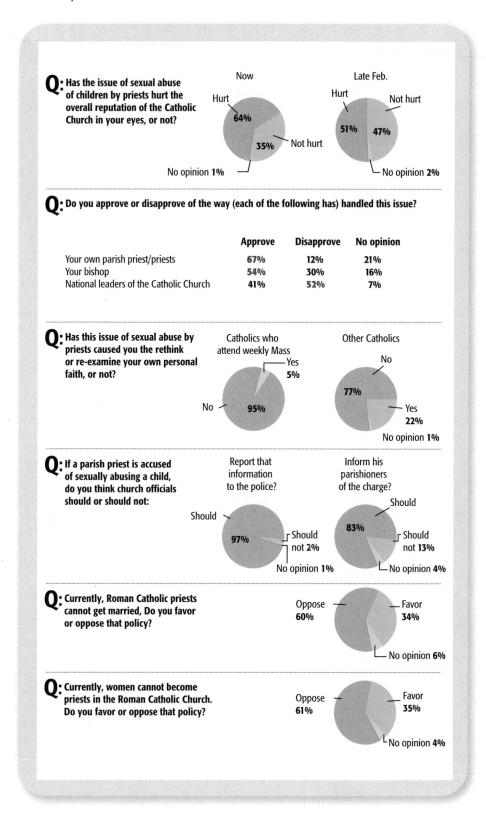

Figure 8.3
American Catholics Speak Out

Source: The Washington Post, April 4, 2002. Copyright © 2002 *The Washington Post.* Reprinted by permission.

A final principle helps further explain the effect of religion on political outlook. Generally, the more religious one is, the more conservative one is likely to be. Thus, ardent churchgoers and committed believers take a conservative outlook on life; in politics they gravitate toward the right side of the political spectrum. This tendency helps explain a key trend of this age: White evangelical Protestants, along with right-to-life supporters, have moved in significant numbers toward the Republican party and are moving the GOP more to the right.

A March 2002 poll, conducted by pollster John Zogby on "What Ethnic Americans Really Think: The Zogby Culture Polls," analyzed six distinct and diverse ethnic communities: African Americans, Asians/Pacific Americans, Hispanic Americans, Jewish Americans, Italian Americans, and Arab Americans. Zogby reported the following results:

Jewish Americans are most liberal.

African Americans are most proud of heritage, most discriminated.

Asians, Hispanics, Arabs are most supportive of global trade.

Italians, Hispanics are less likely pro-choice supporters.

All groups oppose racial preferences in hiring/college.

None of these American ethnic groups support using racial preference in hiring or college admissions, including African Americans and Hispanic Americans.

Jewish Americans (18%) are least likely to attend religious services at least once a week, compared to 43.8% of Italian Americans, 52.9% of Hispanic Americans, and 46.8% of African Americans.

African Americans (71.8%), Jewish Americans (58.9%), and Asians Americans (57.4%) have experienced discrimination because of ethnic heritage in greater numbers than Italian Americans (26.9%) or Arab Americans (39.1%).

A majority of Hispanic Americans (60.8%) would ban abortions except in cases where the mother's life is in danger, compared to 46.8% of Italian Americans, 44.2% of African Americans, and 20.7% of Jewish Americans.

Majorities of all ethnic groups favor treating 11–13 year olds who use a gun in a crime as adults including African Americans (52.5%), Hispanic Americans (55.8%), and Arab Americans (61.2%)

Asian Americans (71.7%) and Jewish Americans (70.7%) are more likely to have access to the Internet, compared to 54.4% of African Americans, 46.4% of Hispanic Americans, 64.9% of Italian Americans, and 64.3% of Arab Americans.

Asian Americans (68%) and Hispanic Americans (65.5%) significantly trail the other ethnic groups in voter registration. More African Americans (90.1%), Italian Americans (88.6%), and Arab Americans (88.7%), are registered voters.[14]

▲ Bob Jones University has been a traditional stop for Republicans during the South Carolina primary. In 2000, however, George W. Bush's visit prompted outcries from John McCain and others because of the university's position on interracial dating and the founder's statements about Catholics.

Region

The political outlook people develop is often influenced by the place in which they grew up and the area in which they now live. In the United States certain sections of the country have conservative traditions; other areas are more liberal. People from conservative areas are likely to be conservative, and those from liberal areas, liberal.

The South has always been America's most conservative region. Strongest among the many reasons for this pattern was that disheartened southern whites after the Civil War rejected all "northern" values, including industrial age liberalism. A firm stress on tradition, on order and hierarchy, and of course on religious fundamentalism have all helped keep the South a bastion of social—and now political—conservatism, especially for white residents of that area. By a quirk, however, the South remained Democratic for decades, a reaction against the Republicanism of Abraham Lincoln and the victorious North. In recent decades, however, the South has moved increasingly into the Republican camp, a trend especially strong during presidential elections and among white Protestant fundamentalists.

From a more general perspective, rural areas everywhere tend toward social and political conservatism. The reasons for this tendency are complex. It may have something to do with the traditionalism associated with longtime, stable communities, along with a sense, developed from years of working on the land, that permanence and stability are the most desirable patterns of life. For whatever reason,

1980	Reagan	Carter	Anderson
Men	55%	36	7
Women	47%	45	7

1984	Reagan	Mondale
Men	62%	37
Women	56%	44

1988	Bush	Dukakis
Men	57%	41
Women	50%	49

1992	Bush	Clinton	Perot
Men	38%	41	21
Women	37%	45	17

1996	Dole	Clinton	Perot
Men	44%	43	10
Women	38%	54	7

2000	Bush	Gore
Men	52%	42
Women	42%	54

Figure 8.4   The Gender Gap

The difference between a candidate's votes from men and his votes from women in presidential elections. Percentages may not add up to 100 because of other candidates.

Sources: From *The New York Times,* March 26, 2000. Copyright © 2000 by The New York Times Co. Reprinted by permission. Updated by authors.

gender gap A difference in the political opinions of men and women.

conservatives and Republicans are more numerous than average in smaller communities, in rural areas, and increasingly in the South (except among minorities). In contrast, one is much more likely to find liberal voters and Democrats in the urban areas of America, especially outside the South. In suburban areas, the two parties are closely matched and compete intensely for the moderate, middle-class vote.

Gender

Few forces shape one's world outlook as powerfully as gender. It should surprise no one that men and women differ in the way they see the world. That difference carries over into politics. Of all the trends in American public opinion, few are more striking than the consistent differences that pollsters find in the political opinions of men and women. In a pattern that has come to be known as the **gender gap,** women have consistently been more supportive of so-called "compassion issues" like school integration and social welfare programs than have men (see Figure 8.4). Compared with men, women "are more supportive of arms control and peaceful foreign relations; they are more likely to oppose weapons buildups or the use of force. They much more frequently favor gun control and oppose capital punishment."[15] Men, in contrast, are more likely than women to support military, police, and other sources of government force. In most cases, men take the tougher, more conservative stands. For instance, men are more likely than women to oppose environmental and consumer protection, busing and other forms of desegregation, and most programs to aid the sick, the unemployed, the poor, and ethnic minorities.[16]

The ultimate difference between men and women shows up at election time. Where candidates or parties show clear differences on issues of force and compassion, women vote, on average, from 4 to 8 percentage points further "left"— that is, for the more liberal position, candidate, or party (usually the Democrats). Thus, in the 1980 election between President Jimmy Carter and challenger Ronald Reagan, men voted strongly for Reagan, whereas women split their vote almost evenly. Indeed, the perception that Reagan was wildly popular is based largely on his enthusiastic backing by one key group in American society—white men. Women were frequently divided in their feelings about Reagan, and black men were clearly hostile. This gender gap continues to show itself in presidential elections. About 45 percent of women supported Bill Clinton in 1992, compared with 40 percent of male voters. This trend continued in the 1996 election. In the 2000 election, a majority of women (54%) voted for Gore; a majority of men (53%) for Bush.

In 1992, Clinton received overwhelming support from women voters often referred to as "soccer moms." Soccer moms—predominantly white suburban women between the ages of 35 and 45—replaced "angry white men" as the swing vote in 1996. They are wooed by candidates of both parties because they vote, but not along party lines. They are busy but not disinterested. Exit polls in 1996 showed soccer moms favored Clinton over Dole by 49 percent to 41 percent, with 8 percent for Perot. "Soccer dads" preferred Dole by 56 percent, Clinton by 34 percent, and Perot by 9 percent.

On some issues, however, men and women hold similar views. One finds almost no difference at all in their views on abortion. Interestingly, where male and female opinions do begin to converge, the direction of change follows the prevailing opinion preferences of women rather than men. This has been the case on issues ranging from environmental protection to defense spending. For various reasons, men have become more supportive of what had historically been a "female" position. These findings may point to women's increasing political clout.[17]

APPROACHING DIVERSITY

The Gender Gap in the 2000 Elections

Gender gaps, the differences found in the political opinions of male and female voters, were evident in most of the 2000 races, including the presidential contest as well as Senate, House and gubernatorial elections.

The Gender Gap in the Presidential Race

According to the nationwide election day voter polls conducted by Voter News Service (VNS), a 10 percentage point gender gap was evident in support for the Republican candidate, with 53% of men and 43% of women voting for George W. Bush. Similarly, a 12 percentage point gender gap was evident in support for the Democratic candidate, with 54% of women and 42% of men voting for Al Gore. Men and women were clearly divided in their preferences for president, with a majority of women (54%) voting for Al Gore and a majority of men (53%) voting for George W. Bush.

(The votes of women and men in the decisive state of Florida mirror those of women and men nationally. In Florida, 54% of men and 45% of women voted for George W. Bush; 53% of women and 42% of men voted for Al Gore.)

There was a gender gap among white women and white men of the same magnitude as for women and men overall. White women were evenly divided between the two presidential candidates (48% for Gore and 49% for Bush) while white men overwhelmingly preferred Bush to Gore (36% for Gore and 60% for Bush).

Working women overwhelmingly preferred Gore to Bush (58% for Gore and 39% for Bush).

The gender gap in the 2000 presidential race was of the same magnitude as the 11 percentage point gender gap in the 1996 presidential race and much larger than the 4 percentage point gender gap evident in the 1992 presidential race.

Source: http://www.gendergap.com/.

American Political Culture

Scholars have pored over a huge amount of data on public opinion and built up a picture of the American public's perspectives, or its **political culture.** They have discovered that American political culture is shaped by three key variables: core values, political ideology, and culture and lifestyle.

Core Values

At the deepest level, American values are remarkably homogeneous. Surveys reveal a broad consensus on the core issues and ideals of government: individual liberty, political equality, and the rule of law. These values ensure the stability of the political system. Support for them is rock solid, in sharp contrast to the vacillating winds of change evident on everyday political issues. The genius of the Constitution rests in its embodiment of these core ideals. The framers, recognizing that the Constitution must elicit strong support, wrote these central values into the document. Those three basic principles have been held in high esteem by generations of Americans who have sought to approach the democratic ideal.

Perhaps the leading American value is liberty. Central to the function of American government is the protection of basic individual rights that ensure freedom. Americans can, in theory, speak and act as they wish. These rights are legally guaranteed by the Bill of Rights clauses protecting freedom of speech, assembly, and religion. Liberty is also central to the American economic system. Americans overwhelmingly support the concept of a free enterprise, capitalistic economy.

political culture A political perspective based on core values, political ideology, culture, and lifestyle.

▶ In the post–9/11 climate, tolerance and respect for diversity often proved to be elusive. This group had its sign torn down and chose to gather at a New York State thruway exit ramp in order to send their message.

? **Question for Reflection:** How might our democracy change if Americans supported economic equality as strongly as they now support the concepts of free enterprise and a capitalistic economy?

The American belief in equality represents another key American value. Americans place enormous stress on the ideas of *political equality* and formal political rights, seeking to guarantee equal access to the political system, universal voting rights, and equality under the law. Americans do not particularly support *economic equality*, especially if defined as a guarantee of equal economic outcomes. They do, however, support equality of another kind, namely, *equality of opportunity*. Americans have even been willing to use government to achieve this goal—to level the playing field, so to speak. Yet in recent years, there has been a backlash against affirmative action, which, as we have seen, has produced a highly volatile issue in California and elsewhere in the United States. Americans want government to guarantee equal economic opportunities and to ensure that economic activity is free from coercion, but they definitely do not want government to guarantee that economic outcomes will be the same for all.

Public support for the Constitution and the democratic institutions it created represents another core American value, although support for this ideal may be weakening. Part of this decrease in confidence derives from a paradox of this era: Americans expect government to provide increasing services in an age of decreasing resources. Americans want lower taxes and blame government for their high tax bills, while still complaining about poor government service. The one government agency insulated from the public's increasing political negativism is the least democratic of all American institutions—the U.S. Supreme Court. Continued respect for that institution illustrates the value we place on the concept of rule of law.

Americans and Intolerance Is tolerance a core American value? Many Americans believe it is, yet the evidence regarding how open Americans are to a wide range of political viewpoints is mixed. Since before the Revolution, American political thinkers and European counterparts like Tocqueville feared the "tyranny of the majority." They worried that the "inflamed passions" of the majority might sweep away the opinions—and also the fragile liberty—of the minority, thus threatening the very core of American democracy. Think about how mobs in the aftermath of September 11, pursued, attacked, and harassed Arab Americans in this country. In a few cases, innocent people were killed by angry mobs seeking vengeance against someone who looked like Osama Bin-Laden.

How valid were the fears of the framers? Public opinion data on intolerance gives some credence to anxieties about the tyranny of the majority. Statistically, Americans remain among the least tolerant of all people in industrialized democratic societies; that is, many Americans are still reluctant to allow the same liberties and opportunities that they enjoy—and that are protected by government institutions—to be enjoyed by those with whom they disagree or whom they simply do not like. Racism, homophobia, gender discrimination, and fear of foreigners are still powerful forces in American culture. And many Americans still feel reluctant or even afraid to speak out against prevailing majority opinion. How dangerous is this pattern of conformity and intolerance?[18]

Political scientists studying the consequences of cultural conformity argue that intolerance in America constrains "the freedom available to ordinary citizens." Studies have found, for instance, that blacks are much more likely to feel "unfree" than are whites. Compared with Americans as a whole, African Americans feel less comfortable expressing unpopular opinions and more worried about the power of government, including the police.[19]

Similar studies also reveal a "spiral of silence" and a "spiral of intolerance" in America. Individuals sensing the prevailing opinions of those around them echo those opinions to avoid social ostracism.[20] Their silence has a reinforcing effect. An initial reluctance to express opinions counter to the majority continues in an ever-tightening spiral, with the result that many Americans are pressured into conforming to the dominant opinion, whether they agree with it or not. Public opinion thus becomes a form of social control.

Intolerance does constitute a serious problem, but it need not remain an inevitable feature of American society. Studies show that as socioeconomic status and level of education increase, so does tolerance for conflicting points of view and alternative lifestyles. Perhaps a "spiral of tolerance" will develop in which family, peers, community, and institutions reinforce rather than suppress tolerance. Over the years, programs such as school busing to break down segregation and affirmative action to ameliorate its negative impact have attempted to allow for the kind of socioeconomic and educational improvement that might, in time, reverse the spiral of intolerance. Teaching about "diversity" and "multiculturalism" (different perspectives and different ways of life) represents another attempt to combat intolerance, although this approach is meeting increased resistance in many communities.

Political Ideology

A second set of deep-seated public attitudes makes up our ideology. Technically, we may describe **political ideology** as a coherent way of viewing politics and government. Ideological perspectives include beliefs about the military, the role of government, the proper relation between government and the economy, the value of social welfare programs, and the relative importance for society of liberty versus order. Our political ideology provides an overarching frame that is used to organize our political beliefs and attitudes.

Ideologies of every kind abound. Each one offers a coherent and unified body of ideas that explain the political process and the goals sought by participants within that process. The most common ideologies among politically aware Americans are liberalism and conservatism. Although these two outlooks capture only a part of the diversity of political attitudes of the American public, they do serve to categorize most people in the mainstream; they also offer a useful introduction to political differences at the national level.

political ideology A coherent way of viewing politics and government; ideological perspectives include beliefs about the military, the role of government, the proper relation between government and the economy, the value of social welfare programs, and the relative importance for society of liberty and order.

These terms are often associated with political party affiliations—Democrats with liberalism, and Republicans with conservatism—but they go well beyond party allegiance. They express a political philosophy, a view of human nature and the proper role of government in society. On the whole, liberals support government intervention to minimize economic inequality. They support progressive taxes and minimum wage laws, for example, but oppose government actions that restrict cultural and social freedoms, such as censorship, prayer in school, and restrictions on abortion. Conservatives take precisely the opposite positions.

Political observers have long debated whether Americans are becoming more conservative. Many saw the success of Ronald Reagan in 1980 and 1984 as a clear signal that the nation had turned to the right. Scholars have questioned this claim, however, by pointing out that while Reagan enjoyed high personal popularity (he left office with 67 percent approval rating), the policies and ideas he advocated throughout his presidency had only limited success and modest public backing. His attempts to cut government, balance the budget, and implement school prayer all failed. On the day Reagan left office, polls showed that while the president remained enormously popular, more and more Americans favored a decrease in military spending and diverting that money to social programs, an outlook directly opposed to the one held by Reagan.

Still, Reagan's legacy of tax cuts and reforms, a strong military, and a reinvigoration of support for the presidency stands in contrast to his failures. Some saw renewed support for Reagan's conservative ideals in the wave symbolized by the Contract with America in 1994, but by the time of the 1996 election, that tide had ebbed. Today, President George W. Bush champions "compassionate conservatism" which blends Reagan's defense budgets with a commitment to education and welfare reform.

Analysis of twenty years of polling data shows that conservatives do (modestly) outnumber liberals in American society, but that the percentages in each category have scarcely changed from 1972 to 2000. Furthermore, "middle-of-the-roaders" always constitute the largest set of respondents in any poll.[21] Finally, the very terms *liberal* and *conservative* don't mean a great deal to many Americans, so their voting decisions may not reflect an ideological preference. Indeed, some scholars argue that the real trend of this age is alienation and a general withdrawal from politics.[22]

The terms *liberal* and *conservative,* then, may have little more than symbolic meaning to most Americans. At the political leadership level, these terms work well to define people, but average citizens adopt a variety of political stands from all points on the political spectrum. How does one categorize, for instance, an individual who favors conservative positions such as deregulation of business and cuts in the capital gains tax, but who also supports the liberal stand of a woman's right to choose an abortion? Many Americans defy easy classification. How can we accurately describe public opinion, then, if ideology proves a weak guide? Moreover, most Americans do not view themselves as either liberals or conservatives, but as moderates. The implication of this self-perception for governing is significant. Given that most voters see themselves in the center of the political spectrum, it should not surprise us to see that President Clinton, lagging in the polls, positioned himself as a "New Democrat" for the 1996 election—right in the shifting center of American politics.

In 2000, George W. Bush portrayed himself as a "compassionate conservative." Here is what he said: "we will carry a message of hope and renewal to every community in this country. We will tell every American, 'The dream is for you.' Tell forgotten children in failed schools, 'The dream is for you.' Tell families, from the barrios of LA to the Rio Grande Valley: 'El sueño americano es para ti.' Tell men and women is our decaying cities, 'The dream is for you.' Tell confused young people, starved of ideals, 'The dream is for you.' As Americans, this is our creed and our calling. We stumble and splinter when we forget that goal. We unite and prosper when we remember it. No great calling is ever easy, and no work of man is ever perfect. But we can, in our imperfect way, rise now and again to the example of St. Francis, where there is hatred, sowing love; where there is darkness, shedding light; where there is despair, bringing hope."

Culture and Lifestyle

Culture theory argues that individual preferences "emerge from social interaction in defending or opposing different ways of life." A "way of life" designates a social orientation, a framework of attitudes within which individuals develop preferences on the basis of how they relate to others and to the institutions of power. Recall the earlier discussion of intolerance that indicated that blacks tend to trust government less than whites do and to feel less free to express different opinions. That orientation cannot be explained by reference to liberal or conservative ideological positions. But in light of the disproportionately high number of African Americans who are arrested and imprisoned, the tendency to distrust and even fear government authority seems hardly surprising. This orientation is neither liberal nor conservative; rather, it reflects an outlook on life that might be characterized as suspicion of the law enforcement system and alienation from government in general. This explanation of political attitudes is cultural rather than ideological.

The State of American Public Opinion

We now have some idea of what lies at the heart of the average American's perspective on political life. But how interested are citizens in politics? How much do they know about politics, and how likely are they to participate? And how do Americans form their opinions on political issues? By turning to polling data, we can provide answers to these and other questions about the current state of American public opinion.

Political Awareness and Involvement

Knowledgeable insiders have often been appalled at the average citizen's poor grasp of public affairs. The respected journalist Walter Lippmann once wrote that the average American "does not know for certain what is going on, or who is doing it, or where he is being carried. . . . He lives in a world which he cannot see, does not understand and is unable to direct."[23] And scholar Joseph Schumpeter's view of citizens was even more caustic: "The typical citizen drops down to a lower level of mental performance as soon as he enters the political field. He argues and analyzes in a way he would readily recognize as infantile within the sphere of his real interests. He becomes a primitive again."[24] Lippmann and Schumpeter join a host of social scientists who have portrayed American voters as apathetic and poorly informed, their opinions unstable or even irrational.

Polling research from the 1940s and 1950s revealed that Americans did not know very much about important issues and that they tended to confuse the issue positions of various candidates during campaigns. At the height of the Cold War, for instance, many Americans believed that the Soviet Union—the foremost ideological enemy of the United States—was in fact part of the North Atlantic Treaty Organization (NATO), the military alliance to which the United States and its allies belonged. In poll after poll, more than half of Americans cannot make a single correct statement about either major political party, despite both parties having been at the core of American history for more than a century. In tests on knowledge of the Constitution and Bill of Rights, only a few respondents can correctly identify the preamble of the Constitution and the contents of the Bill of Rights. Typically, most Americans cannot even identify their own representatives and senators.

culture theory A theory that individual preferences "emerge from social interaction in defending or opposing different ways of life."

These data show that the American public falls short of the ideal advocated by democratic theorists—a well-informed citizenry. But it should not surprise us that citizens know little about politics because their interest in politics is minimal. No more than a third of the electorate ever claims to be seriously active in electoral politics. Even smaller percentages take part in the political activities that influence those in power: writing an elected official, joining a political group, attending a political rally. And as we'll see in Chapter 10, few vote.

Question for Reflection: Do you think the framers took the public's limited interest in politics into account as they fashioned the government? How might our nation change if the ideal advocated by democratic theorists of a well-informed citizenry was suddenly realized?

In addition, members of the general public seem to show little interest in the issues most hotly debated by politicians.[25] Over time, such issues as abortion rights, crime and violence, AIDS, racism, the environment, and arms control have dominated the political agenda of elected officials, party leaders, and interest group activists. During the same period, none of these issues was ever ranked by more than five percent of the general public as "the most important problem" facing the nation. Even when issues do catch the public's attention, citizens do not always perceive them with the same gravity and commitment as do political activists. For example, America's concern with drugs, while not insignificant, skyrocketed briefly after former President George Bush's declaration of a "war on drugs," only to drop to relatively low levels within a matter of months. The public's interest in economic issues such as the deficit, unemployment, and the general health of the economy is similarly unstable, mirroring the ebbs and flows of the business cycle. Until September 11th, surveys found that today's college freshmen were less interested in politics and participated less than any group of freshmen in the last three decades. One of the great paradoxes of democracy was that the information age had produced a relatively indifferent and apathetic group of young people.

Some scholars counter this image of the ignorant, apathetic citizen by asserting that the American people are generally well informed and that their opinions are as sensible as those of their leaders. These scholars see the public as more rational than many observers are willing to concede, arguing that, while Americans may not know all the names of the people and places of politics or the intricate details of every issue of the day, they do recognize and rationally distinguish between the alternatives presented to them, especially when they step into the voting booth. In *The Rational Public,* political scientists Ben Page and Robert Shapiro find that "public opinion as a collective phenomena is stable, meaningful, rational and able to distinguish between good and bad."[26] Indeed, surveys show that when presented with a list of names, rather than having to rely on their own recall of such names, most Americans can accurately identify their regional and national leaders.

Nonetheless, scholars continue to debate whether average citizens are politically informed and involved enough to make democracy work. We cannot supply a definitive answer here. Certainly few Americans live up to the ideal image of the citizen who is fully informed, ever alert, and deeply involved in the political process. Still, most citizens may be informed enough to make simple decisions on the small number of options presented to them on election day. Besides, the American system has a number of built-in safeguards in case citizens, for lack of information or other reasons, do not make the best decision. If people elect some candidate or some party they come to dislike, they can "turn the rascals out" at the next election. And no matter who is elected, no position within the U.S. government carries overwhelming power, and all positions are checked by a number of other positions and institutions. Given this system of multiple checks and frequent elections, the American public may well be sufficiently informed to keep the system working and reasonably democratic.

How Are Political Opinions Formed?

If people know little about politics and have little interest in it, how is it that they develop seemingly strong opinions on a variety of political issues? How do they know whom to vote for on election day? The answer is surprising. Average citizens develop broad orientations toward their world, including ways of thinking about politics, based on their entire set of life experiences. They then use these broad intellectual frameworks as shortcuts for processing new information.

These intellectual frameworks for evaluating the world, often called **schemas,** act as efficient filters or cues. When people encounter new issues or ideas, they frequently do not have the time or energy to study them in detail. It is simpler just to fit them into a preexisting perspective. Studies show, for instance, that Americans know nothing about the actual level of spending for foreign aid, nor do they have any idea which countries receive most U.S. foreign aid; nevertheless, they are still convinced that the United States spends too much abroad. That's because they have already developed a general orientation (opposition to government spending and fear or distrust of non-Americans, perhaps) that allows them to take a stand on foreign aid while knowing almost nothing about the subject.

As this example suggests, facts are often irrelevant in the development of opinions. Changing a deeply ingrained set of beliefs is psychologically painful. That's why people often avoid facts and resort to preexisting schemas. These schemas allow individuals to sift and categorize new information, so that it can be made "safe"—that is, congruent with an existing framework of attitudes. People ignore or explain away evidence that would undermine their carefully constructed world views.

Party Identification as a Schema   Despite the decline in the number of Americans who identify themselves with one of the major parties, party identification remains the strongest predictor of an individual's political behavior. Partisan identification provides a cue that individuals use to evaluate candidates and acts as a filter through which individuals view the political world. These party ties represent one of the most enduring of all political attitudes held by Americans. However, even this apparently stable indicator of opinion can change over the course of time or under the impact of dramatic events.

A broad-based change in partisanship is known as **realignment.** In a period of realignment, large groups of people shift allegiance from one party to another.[27] A realignment occurred in the 1932 election, when many people took their support—and their votes—from the Republican to the Democratic party. The resulting New Deal coalition was a strong electoral force that kept Democrats the majority party for decades. However, recent evidence suggests that grand realignments of this kind are rare. A more useful approach to understanding shifts in partisan identification suggests that it is a gradual process that is continually taking place through generational replacement. Specifically, this theory suggests that as a new generation reaches maturity and becomes involved in the political process, it will have been socialized around a set of values and issues different from those of the parent and grandparent generations. As each new generation becomes a larger segment of the electorate, it replaces older generations and produces shifts in the identification of certain groups within the party around the new issues and values.

Partisan identification and general political orientation can also change across generations. Several studies revealed a sharp decline of support for and trust in the institutions and actors of government following the Vietnam War and the Watergate scandal. It was at this time that pollsters began to track a decline in partisan identification, the rise of political *independents*—people declaring no allegiance to either party—and a growing suspicion of government in general.

Even with periodic realignments and generational change, political partisanship remains the most stable indicator of political preference. It is not, of course, the

> **QUOTE . . . UNQUOTE**
>
> "The working of the popular will . . . has always called for explanation . . . what Sir Robert Peel called 'that great compound of folly, weakness, prejudice, wrong feeling, right feeling, obstinacy, and newspaper paragraphs which is called 'public opinion.' Others have concluded that since out of drift and incoherence, settled aims do appear, there must be a mysterious contrivance at work somewhere above and over the inhabitants of a nation. They invoke a collective soul, a national mind, a spirit of the age which imposes order upon random opinion."
>
> Walter Lippmann, *Public Opinion*

schemas Intellectual frameworks for evaluating the world.

realignment A broad-based change in partisanship in which large groups of people shift allegiance from one party to another.

only schema to affect people's political thinking. Others include ideology, ethnic consciousness, and regional identification. And people occasionally change their minds or ignore "the party line" when it comes to specific issues, events, and actors. Nevertheless, to understand how any citizen feels about a host of political matters, begin by learning that individual's partisan allegiance.

Still, when a February 2002 Washington Post-ABC News Poll asked American's which party they trusted more to do a better job coping with the nation's main problems, Republicans emerged with a narrow 44 percent to 40 percent advantage. But when President Bush is pitted against Democrats in the same question, Bush got 62 percent support and Democrats got 31 percent. "The President's advantage extends across all the major demographic groups, even those that generally favor the Democrats, such as women and people with lower incomes"[28] (see Table 8.3).

Stability and Change in Public Opinion

Though many of our opinions remain stable over long periods of time, others do change. Many scholars believe that people are flighty and changeable; others point to the deep-seated, long-lasting nature of our opinions. To understand this difference in perspective, it helps to look at three factors: intensity, latency, and salience.

Table 8.3 ■ Whom Do You Trust with the Nation's Problems?				
Americans by . . .	**REPS. vs. DEMS.**		**BUSH vs. DEMS.**	
. . . sex				
Men	47%	33%	65%	27%
Women	41	46	59	34
. . . annual household income				
<$30,000	40	44	52	36
$30–$50,000	39	47	63	33
$50–$75,000	56	33	71	23
$75,000+	50	31	64	29
. . . age				
18–30	50	37	67	29
31–44	45	37	61	32
45–60	41	40	61	30
61+	40	48	58	32
. . . region				
East	43	42	60	36
Midwest	45	37	64	28
South	42	44	66	25
West	47	35	51	42
. . . union affiliation				
Union households	36	46	58	37
Non-union HH	47	38	62	30

This poll is based on telephone interviews with 1,507 randomly selected adults nationwide, conducted Jan. 24–27. Each of the two choices above was presented to a separate half of the total sample. The margin of error for each half sample is plus or minus 4 percentage points and somewhat larger for subgroups. Sampling error is only one of many potential sources of error in this or any other public opinion poll. Interviewing was conducted by TNS Intersearch of Horsham, Pa. Categories do not add to 100 percent because "both" and "neither" responses are not shown.

Source: Copyright © 2002 The Washington Post. Reprinted by permission.

◀ The World Economic Forum is an independent international organization committed to improving the state of the world. The Forum provides a collaborative framework for the world's leaders to address global issues, engaging particularly its corporate members in global citizenship. In February 2002 the International A.N.S.W.E.R. (Act Now to Stop war and End Racism) coalition called a teach-in and street demonstrations in New York City coinciding with the meeting of the Forum at the Waldorf-Astoria Hotel. These demonsrators displayed their concerns dressed as Lady Liberty.

Intensity   Opinions are not all equal. People feel some things more intensely than others, and that affects the strength and durability of their opinions. **Intensity** is a measure of the depth of feeling associated with a given opinion. It affects the way people organize their beliefs and express their opinions on a wide variety of issues. For some, the issue of a woman's right to choose an abortion elicits an intense reaction; others express their most intense political sentiments for or against gun control. Try visiting a local senior center and suggest cutting Social Security benefits! On the other hand, try getting just about anyone to speak out on soybean subsidies. Some issues elicit more intense reaction than others.

Issues that provoke intense feelings are often called *hot-button issues,* since they strike a nerve, a "hot button" that can elicit strong reactions and affect voting choices. In the 2000 election, abortion was just such an issue. The more intensely an opinion is felt, the more likely it is to endure and to influence policy decisions. Thus, we can assume that attitudes about race (a subject most Americans have intense opinions about) will not change much over the next decade or two. Attitudes about U.S. foreign policy toward Belize, on the other hand, could prove extremely volatile. Few Americans hold intense feelings about Belize, so short-term events (a communist takeover) or the sudden pronouncements of respected American leaders ("Let's help Belize, our democratic neighbor to the south") could dramatically affect how Americans feel about that nation.

Latency   Public opinion is not always explicit. **Latency** describes feelings that are hidden or unspoken, suggesting the *potential* for an opinion or behavior, but only when the right circumstances occur. Ross Perot's bid for the presidency in 1996 unleashed an avalanche of latent feeling. The American public's long-standing but often dormant distrust of government and politicians—and its admiration for successful entrepreneurs—leapt to the fore following a series of scandals, a sagging

how strong; intense or ~~you~~

intensity In public opinion, a measure of the depth of feeling associated with a given opinion.

latency In public opinion, feelings that are unspoken, suggesting the potential for an opinion or behavior, but only when the right circumstances occur.

economy, and a burgeoning federal budget deficit. Those latent opinions gave Perot the highest third-party vote since Theodore Roosevelt in 1912, even though Perot withdrew and then reentered the race.

Salience Opinions can be intense, latent, or even nonexistent, depending on whether a given issue touches one directly. **Salience** is the extent to which people see an issue as having a clear impact on their own lives. Salient issues stir up interest and participation. Proposition 209, which banned affirmative action programs in California, is an example. Similarly, the issue of base closings is more salient to residents of states such as California, where the local, regional, and state economies rely on the proximity of military bases or lucrative contracts for the production of military hardware. Politicians decrying base closures might get a strong following in California but be ignored in Chicago, where the issue lacks salience. To understand public opinion and how that opinion will affect citizen actions, one must know how salient a given issue is to a given population.

How Changeable Is Public Opinion?

Some research findings have suggested that individual political opinions are not firmly held. When respondents are asked the same questions again and again over relatively brief time periods, their responses tend to vary and even to contradict earlier responses. Is this evidence that we tend to offer random, meaningless answers when asked our opinions? Table 8.4 suggests otherwise; candidates get the voters they earn!

Many scholars see this pattern as proving the "irrationality" of the American voter. However, much of the apparent irrationality may actually stem from faulty polling methods. When the same question is asked differently, or when questions are worded vaguely, respondents are more likely to change their answers. This is not so much evidence of irrationality as an indication that people are trying to make the best sense of what they are asked, even when the questions are difficult to understand. On the other hand, when researchers phrase questions so that they contain the information necessary to formulate firm opinions, results show that individuals actually do have stable, "rational" opinions. While Americans may not be particularly intimate with political specifics, they nonetheless harbor enduring and meaningful political beliefs. It is up to the pollster to find the best way to elicit these opinions.

Yet we do know that people's opinions sometimes change. Changing circumstances trigger corresponding changes in public opinion. As incomes rise, so does support for shorter work weeks, higher minimum wages, and increasing expenditure for workplace safety and environmental protection.[29] As more women join the work force, there are more calls for women's rights. And awareness of rising crime produces a demand for tougher laws and more police officers in the street. Sudden events can also cause a change in opinions. In time of national crisis Americans are likely to feel more patriotic, to "rally around the flag" and the president; they are also likely to lower their levels of criticism of the government and national leadership.

Although it appears that Americans respond in an almost knee-jerk fashion to appeals from popular figures or to images presented in the media, the malleability of public opinion should not be overestimated. On many issues Americans maintain a deep-seated set of attitudes that they don't want to change, making them a "tough sell" when leaders solicit approval for actions that are not supported by the public.

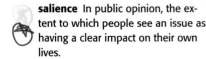

salience In public opinion, the extent to which people see an issue as having a clear impact on their own lives.

From Public Opinion to Public Policy

Public opinion is a crucial element in the political process. It can dramatically affect both the policies of government and government's legitimacy in the mind of the

Table 8.4 ■ Sharp Increase in Positive Voting				
	1988	**1992**	**1996**	**2000**
Voted ... *	%	%	%	%
Pro-Candidate	64	54	48	64
Anti-Candidate	28	20	33	23
Don't Know	4	3	3	2
Other Candidate/DK	4	23	16	11
	100	100	100	100

*For major party candidate.

Source: Reprinted by permission of The Pew Research Center for the People and the Press.

people. After all, the ultimate test of a democracy comes down to this: Do government actions, over the long run, reflect what citizens want?

At first glance, we are struck by a significant gap between what Americans say they want and what their leaders are doing. The United States would be quite a different place if public opinion set public policy. Over the years polls have shown consistent support for proposals that American political leaders do little to implement. For instance, the following policies would all have been in force today if American public opinion were translated into the law of the land. Seven in ten Americans support new campaign finance legislation (see Figure 8.5), but Congress has been slow to move on this and other prevailing opinions:

- Individuals would have the "right to die."
- Members of Congress would be limited to twelve years in office, and term limits would be placed on most other political offices as well.
- Stricter limits would be imposed on campaign spending.
- The death penalty would consistently be imposed for murder.
- Prayer would be permitted in public schools.
- Financial aid to other nations would be severely curtailed.
- Most affirmative action programs would be banned.
- Trigger locks would be installed on most handguns.

Why hasn't American public policy reflected these majority preferences? Translating the public will into public policy within a complex framework of divided powers takes time—often a good deal of time. Further slowing down the entire process is the persistent view of the framers of the Constitution that the "common will" of the people does not always stand for the "common good" of society.

How well has the U.S. government reflected its people's will over the last few decades? Has the United States approached democracy, in the sense that government is doing what Americans want it to be doing? There are no easy answers to these questions. Clearly, American government policy does not always reflect popular desires. But a perfect reflection of popular desires is surely beyond the capability of any government. Some aspects of the public will are simply unrealistic ("more services, lower taxes!"). Others are opposed by most political actors because they contradict the spirit of the Constitution. For example, a constitutional amendment allowing school prayer in public schools has been widely popular but until recently was opposed by most decision makers.

On any number of issues we find government policies reasonably close to the general direction of public opinion. The United States has been an activist world power in accordance with, not in opposition to, the will of the American people. Laws and policies designed to ensure gender equality have gradually been implemented as public attitudes shifted to favor them. Tough crime laws have increased

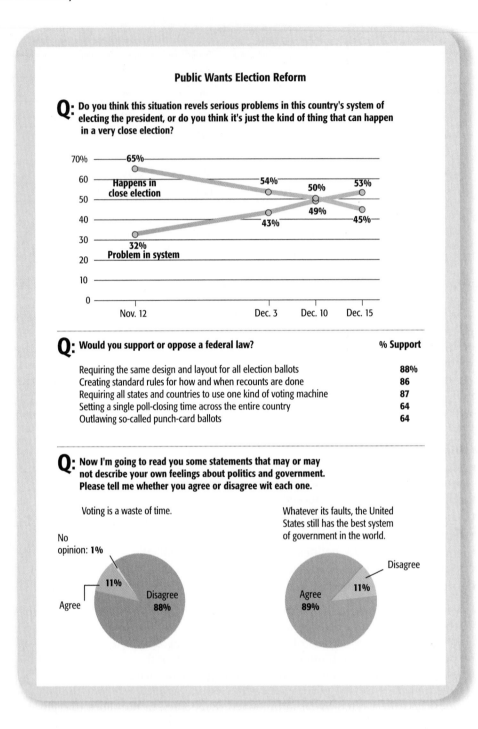

Figure 8.5
Public Wants Election Reform

Source: The Washington Post, December 18, 2000. Copyright © 2002 *The Washington Post.* Reprinted by permission.

in response to growing demands on government officials to "do something" about alarming crime rates. But as with school prayer, public desires are thwarted on occasion.

Keep in mind, too, that it takes time for an emerging public opinion to become government policy. On the whole, however, if a significant majority of the American people indicate over time that they believe government should act in a particular manner, the chances are good to excellent that government will accede to those wishes. For that reason, Americans remain loyal to their democratic political system.

DEMOCRACY IN THE NEW MILLENNIUM

Do "Likely" Voters Make It to the Voting Booth on Election Day?

Do "likely" voters really vote? Politicians need polls to identify segments of the population that will most likely cast their vote in an upcoming election. But the accuracy of polls conducted to identify these voters came into question during the 1998 congressional elections. Critics of then President Clinton complained that the Gallup Organization's daily tracking poll exaggerated the number of Democratic voters favoring the President, thereby skewing the poll results. Taking this objection seriously, Pew evaluated the well-known survey companies utilized by politicians since the 1950s, including Gallup and their own Pew Research Center, to discern if a more accurate method of polling likely voters should be developed.

Pew chose to focus on a very close political contest, the 1999 Philadelphia mayoral election. The race was one of the tightest in the city's history—Democrat John Street edged out Republican challenger Sam Katz by less than 9,500 votes. Pew conducted polls on two occasions and developed a data set for 2,415 registered voters to discover how they voted. One poll was taken two weeks prior to the election, the other one-week before the voters cast their ballots. Although the Pew researchers asked the respondents to provide answers to a litany of questions, they focused on the names and addresses given by the voters. This data was used to connect pre-election survey results with the exact voting record of the respondents gleaned from Philadelphia voting records. Pew researchers were then able to track 70% of the registered voters who were polled through Philadelphia voting returns to identify who of their respondents actually voted on election day.

The results of the survey delighted the Pew researchers. They were able to accurately predict the voting actions of 73% of the Philadelphia voters. Although 27% were not identified correctly, the accuracy of the poll remained high. Pew discovered that the older procedures guiding the Gallup surveys since the 1950s continue to function accurately despite changes in voter make-up and the increasing complexity of American politics since World War II. Pew then compared its latest study to conclusions formed following a similar survey conducted by Gallup in the 1984 presidential race. In that election, Gallup accurately predicted the voting behavior of 69% of registered voters. Pew researchers could only conclude in 2000 that the voter index continues to function as an accurate model for concerned politicians who want to know the preferences of people most likely to vote for them. For perhaps the very best source on public opinion, visit the Web site for the Pew Research Center for the People and the Press at http://people-press.org/.

Source: "Screening Likely Voters: A Survey Experiment," May 18, 2001, The Pew Research Center, http://www.people-press.org/reports.

SUMMARY

1. Public opinion is the collective expression of attitudes about the prominent issues and actors of the day. Discovering and publicizing the public's opinion has become a key political activity in modern democracies.

2. Political polling began in the mid-1800s with informal straw polls. These failed to obtain a representative sample of the population, which must be chosen through random sampling. In a random sample, every member of the population must have an equal chance of appearing in the sample. Efforts must be made to avoid sampling bias, in which particular subsets of the population are over- or underrepresented in the sample.

3. Political socialization refers to the process by which we learn about the world of politics and develop our political beliefs. It begins early in childhood, starting with the family. Children tend to adopt their parents' party loyalties and, to some extent, their political ideology. Political socialization continues in school, where children learn about citizenship, and in college, where students may modify their political ideology. Other important sources of political socialization are peers and the mass media.

4. Numerous social variables influence the formation of opinions. They include social class as represented by income and educational level, race and ethnicity, religious differences, region and place of residence, and gender.

5. The leading core values of Americans are liberty and equality. Although Americans generally are not troubled by economic inequality, they do support equality of opportunity. Another important value is rule by law. Americans are much less tolerant than citizens of

other industrialized democratic societies; intolerance is expressed in the form of racism, homophobia, gender discrimination, and fear of foreigners.

6. The most common ideologies among politically aware Americans are liberalism and conservatism. In general, liberals support government intervention to minimize economic inequality but oppose government actions that restrict cultural and social freedoms; conservatives take the opposite positions.

7. Culture theory argues that culture and lifestyle create a framework of attitudes within which individuals develop preferences. Lifestyle orientations explain more about political behavior than do ideological preferences.

8. Political opinions appear to be based on schemas—broad orientations toward the world based on previous life experiences. Schemas serve as cues for judging new issues or ideas. Among the strongest schemas is political partisanship. Even with periodic realignments and generational change, political partisanship remains the most stable indicator of political preference.

9. Intensity is a measure of the depth of feeling associated with a given opinion; issues that provoke intense feeling are often called "hot-button" issues. In contrast, latent feelings are unspoken, suggesting the potential for an opinion under the right circumstances. Whether an opinion is intense, latent, or nonexistent depends on the salience of the issue, that is, the extent to which people see it as having a clear impact on their lives.

10. The media's portrayal of events and actors can significantly influence public opinion. The media set the political agenda and influence opinions about who is to blame for various political events.

KEY TERMS

public opinion	exit polls	culture theory
straw poll	political socialization	schemas
representative sample	generational effect	realignment
margin of error	gender gap	intensity
random sample	political culture	latency
sampling bias	political ideology	salience
tracking polls		

POLISIM ACTIVITY

Public Opinion Simulation

The Opinion Outreach and Public Survey has been declining in recent years due to a lack of leadership and expertise. As the new Director of Research, your job is to correct the problems in questions, methods, and interpretation. Each survey question tries to make a generalization about a population (all the people being described) by interviewing a sample (all of the people actually surveyed). You will have a toolbox that contains all of the resources you need to fix the survey so that the report is reliable and valid. Your ability to produce a quality report will determine the fate of your organization.

Political Culture and Ideology

Political culture consists of widely shared beliefs, values and norms concerning the relationship of citizens to government and to one another. However, just because they are widely shared does not mean they are universally shared. To what degree do you share beliefs with the general population? with your generation? with your classmates? In this simulation you will complete a questionnaire to see how your political beliefs compare with those of people around you.

SUGGESTED READINGS

ASHER, HERBERT. *Polling and the Public.* Washington, D.C.: Congressional Quarterly Press, 1988. An explanation of the meaning and methods of public opinion research, using contemporary examples.

ERIKSON, ROBERT S., NORMAN R. LUTTBEG, and KENT L. TEDIN. *American Public Opinion: Its Origins, Content, and Impact.* 4th ed. New York: Macmillan, 1991. A comprehensive overview of the major aspects of American public opinion, including opinion formation, opinion distribution within society, and the influence of public opinion on public policy.

GINSBERG, BENJAMIN. *The Captive Public: How Mass Opinion Promotes State Power.* New York: Basic Books, 1986. An examination of the thesis that as it becomes a more prominent force in American politics, public opinion actually enhances the power of American government over its citizens.

GROSSMAN, LAWRENCE K. *The Electronic Republic: Reshaping Democracy in the Information Age.* New York: Viking, 1995. An examination of the changes in our democratic political system that have shrunk the distance between the governed and those who govern.

PAGE, BENJAMIN I., and ROBERT Y. SHAPIRO. *The Rational Public: Fifty Years of Trends in America's Policy Preferences.* Chicago: University of Chicago Press, 1992. A challenge to the assumption that American public opinion is "irrational" based on data revealing relatively steady public preferences over time, changing only under logical circumstances.

STIMSON, JAMES A. *Public Opinion in America.* Boulder, Col.: Westview Press, 1991. A major study of public opinion research and its link with major issues in American politics.

9

POLITICAL PARTIES

CHAPTER OUTLINE

Approaching Democracy Case Study: Jim Jeffords' Declaration of Independence

Introduction: Political Parties and Democracy

A Brief History of the American Party System

Functions of American Political Parties

Party Organization

Nominating a President: Parties and Elections

Why a Two-Party System?

Minor Parties

The Party in Government

Political Parties and the 2002 Election

APPROACHING DEMOCRACY CASE STUDY

Jim Jeffords' Declaration of Independence

"The horizon was clear; there were no clouds. No one saw it, and then it poured." So spoke a Bush White House aide after seeing their ability to govern with Republican control of both Houses of Congress evaporate when Senator Jim Jeffords of Vermont announced to Senate Majority Leader Trent Lott (R.-MS) in late May 2001 that he was leaving the Republican party to become an Independent. This action split the even balance of the United States Senate, shifting a one-seat advantage to the Democrats. As a result, the position of Majority Leader shifted to Democrat Tom Daschle of South Dakota, all 16 Senate Committee Chairs shifted to the Democratic party, the ratio of staff members for Committees shifted in favor of the Democrats, and hundreds of Republican staff members lost their jobs. The decision of one member of their political party required the Bush administration to adjust all of their legislative plans to account for the opposing party's control of the Senate. Just how could this happen, and why?

The answer stems from the month long efforts of Tom Daschle and the new majority whip, Harry Reid of Nevada; they persuaded Jeffords to switch his party affiliation. Jim Jeffords has always been something of a maverick. When he first came to Washington as a member of Congress in 1975, he lived in a camper in order to pay off his $40,000 campaign debt. He was also the only Republican who voted against Ronald Reagan's tax cut. His nature did not change after his 1988 election to the Senate. He was one of two Republicans to vote against the confirmation of Clarence Thomas for the Supreme Court and one of only five members of his party to vote against convicting Bill Clinton in the impeachment trial in 1999. Jeffords was a moderate, who over a fifteen year span opposed his party more than he supported it in legislative votes. By 2000 he was one of ten Republicans to receive the endorsement of the environmentally-protective Sierra Club.

After the Republicans won control of the Senate in 2000, Jeffords position within the party became even more tenuous. He was denied a seat on the Environment and Public Works Committee, where he would have a voice on the reauthorization of the Clean Air Act and work on the acid rain problem in Vermont. In April of 2000, Jeffords voted against President Bush's tax cut package, forcing the party to propose and pass a much more modest $1.35 trillion package. When some speculated that he might be punished for this decision, Jeffords himself raised the prospect of leaving the party by saying that he doubted any retribution would come because "it's a short walk across the aisle." When the administration focused in early 2001 on a comprehensive education bill, a particular passion of Jeffords, even though he had been the chairman of the Health, Education, Labor and Pensions Committee since 1997, conservative Judd Gregg from New Hampshire, the second ranking member of that committee, took control of the bill. Meetings were held among the committee's Republicans, but Jeffords was not invited. After Jeffords had arranged a deal with the White House in March 2001 for full funding from the federal budget of his special education program to support disabled students, the Individuals with Disabilities Education Act (IDEA), the arrangement fell apart on April 4. By now his requests for federal judgeship appointments were not receiving any attention. His friends on the "Mod Squad"—moderate Republican Senators Olympia Snowe (ME), Arlen Specter (PA), Susan Collins (ME),

and Lincoln Chafee (RI)—noticed that he was speaking to them less and less in their meetings.

Little did the Republicans in the Senate know that Jeffords had been negotiating with Democratic leaders Daschle and Reid for more than a month on the prospect of jumping parties. When Jeffords complained to Democratic Senator Chris Dodd of Connecticut, Dodd said, "Look, Jim, there's room for you over here." While Jeffords knew that he did not want to become a Democrat, he began to think that he could become an Independent who caucused with the Demcrats, thus changing the Senate to one controlled by the other party. Jeffords knew he was not held in favor by the White House when he was not invited to the April 23, 2001 Rose Garden ceremony honoring one of his constituents, Middlebury, Vermont high school social studies teacher Michele Forman as national teacher of the year. About that same time, rumors began flying that Senate Republican leaders were about to eliminate the Northeast Interstate Dairy Compact, a price support program benefiting the Vermont dairy farmers, and Gregg announced that he would be "spearheading" the reauthorization of the Elementary and Secondary Education Act. Congressional scholar Norman J. Ornstein warned, "Push Jeffords far enough and he can use the nuclear weapon he has in his arsenal." "I think he probably looked in the mirror and saw five more years of total misery, in addition to being completely ignored. And that's what really drove him," said one of his aides.

After a series of meetings with Senator Reid, it became clear that Jeffords would be allowed to chair the Environment and Public Works Committee in Democratically controlled Senate. In the end, meetings with Trent Lott, President Bush, and Vice President

▲ Senator Jim Jeffords (I.-VT) changed the entire direction of the early Bush Administration when he bolted from the Republican Party to become an Independent in May 2001, thus giving control of the Senate to the Democrats.

Cheney were arranged and calls and letters from campaign supporters in Vermont were attempted to try and persuade Jeffords not to leave the party. But it was too late. "Our party was the party of Lincoln," he told the press in Vermont, but for moderates like him in a conservative Senate "it has become a struggle for our leaders to deal with me and for me to deal with them." Senator Jim Jeffords declared his independence and the Republicans lost control of the Senate.[1]

 Questions for Reflection:

1. Do elected representatives have an obligation to follow their own political instincts, or the expressed wishes of those who voted for them, in making their decisions?

2. Is America's approach to democracy benefited or imperiled because the direction can be changed by solitary individuals?

Introduction:
Political Parties and Democracy

As Jim Jefford's decision to become an Independent shows, the balance of powers among the political parties lies at the heart of democracy, representing the crucial link between what citizens want and what government does.[2] That is why parties must continually change, adapt, and adjust to the popular forces of their time. They must stay in touch with the voters—from whom they derive their support and power—so that they can gain control of government and the policy-making process. Competitive and democratic political parties allow the peaceful entry into politics of a wide range of groups that might otherwise have to turn to illegitimate measures to gain their ends.

Political parties are a relatively new phenomenon, nonexistent until less than 200 years ago. Charlemagne needed no party nomination before heading the Holy Roman Empire. Parties did not vie for power under Henry VIII. The framers did not even mention political parties in the United States Constitution. The reason why parties played little role in history is simple: The general public played little role in the political process. For most of human history politics was a game for elites. It consisted of struggles for power among a small inner circle of leaders, people who were trying to become rulers or seeking to curry favor with those in power. The need for broad-based political parties arose with attempts to implement political equality in the eighteenth century, which led to an expansion in the number of people participating in the governing process. Parties became helpful in organizing the legislative factions and in making their attempts to seek power and influence effective. Today, political parties are massive, complex institutions, incorporating large numbers of citizens into the political process. By their very nature, parties are forces of democratization.

Political parties, then, are nongovernmental institutions that organize and give direction to mass political desires. They bring people together—people who think alike or who have common interests—and help them work toward common goals. The clearest goal of any political group is power—power to control government and thus implement their policy preferences. In an age of mass participation, power goes to those elites who can connect with the masses. Today, it frequently seems that the Democratic and Republican parties are having trouble making that connection.

In this chapter we look at party history, as well as at the functions, development, role, and future of American political parties. First, let's look at the history of American parties to see how the development of democracy is inextricably tied to the activity of political parties.

political parties Organizations that allow like-minded members of the population to group together and magnify their individual voices into a focus promoting individual candidates and government action.

A Brief History of the American Party System

Many of the framers, beginning with George Washington, feared the development of a political party system. James Madison, the strongest influence on the Constitution's final shape, shared this hostility to parties, seeing them as a direct threat to the common good of society because their promotion of specialized interests would subvert the general welfare.

Despite the framers' fears, political parties in the United States developed quickly. By 1800, they were already playing a major role in elections and governance. A party system began to emerge in the United States during the divisive and continuing debate between President Washington's secretary of the treasury, Alexander Hamilton, and his secretary of state, Thomas Jefferson. Hamilton, a supporter of a strong federal government, argued for a manufacturing sector that would allow the United States to become a wealthy and self-sufficient trading partner in the world economy. A strong federal government would have a national bank with sufficient power to borrow and spend money, develop international agreements, and protect the domestic economy. Conversely, Jefferson wished to see a United States that remained largely rural. He envisioned a nation that retained its republican roots built upon the base of a large working, agrarian class. These two visions for the country divided other leaders and the general public into *factions*—"the spirit of party" the framers had feared.

In the first few years of the republic, many of the framers denounced party divisions. Hamilton, for instance, declared that a faction dominated by Madison and Jefferson was "decidedly hostile to me and my administration, . . . and dangerous to the union, peace and happiness of the country."[3] George Washington warned "in the most solemn manner against the harmful effects of the spirit of party." This spirit, he asserted, demands "uniform vigilance to prevent its bursting into a flame." Washington's cautionary remarks about political parties may seem extreme by today's standards, but he was surely correct when he said that the "spirit of party" was "a fire not to be quenched."[4] While the party system in the United States has undergone many changes, the presence of political partisanship has been continuous from his day to ours.

Scholars have identified five different historical eras in which party influence, allegiance, and control have changed. These eras always begin with a party **realignment,** in which significant historical events or national crises cause a shift in fundamental party identification and loyalty. Realignments are the result of a change in public attitudes about the political system and the ability of each party to deliver favorable candidates and policies. They usher in new eras, which tend to be stable and lengthy in duration.[5]

The First Party System (1790s–1820s)

The Federalists, followers of John Adams and Alexander Hamilton, and the Republicans, led by Jefferson (also called the Jeffersonian Republicans and later the Democratic-Republicans), represented two competing groups. As such, they constituted America's first parties. Today's Democratic party, the direct descendant of Jefferson's party, is the oldest political party in the world. This party originally sided with rural and small-town forces in the struggle between promoters of agriculture and promoters of manufacturing. Its followers resisted the trend toward nationalization of power. They promoted Jefferson's belief that a nation of small property owners represents the best society, one likely to be virtuous and egalitarian.

The elections of 1789 and 1792 took place smoothly, since parties had yet to be formally established. On the first Wednesday of February in 1789, the newly established electoral college chose George Washington as the nation's first president. Washington was easily reelected in 1792. With his departure from the political scene after his second term, however, political tensions emerged as distinct factions.

realignment A shift in fundamental party identification and loyalty caused by significant historical events or national crises.

Federalist John Adams and Democratic-Republican Thomas Jefferson opposed each other in the closely contested elections of 1796 and 1800. Adams barely won the initial contest, while Jefferson triumphed in the rematch in 1800. The 1800 election was so pivotal that it became known as the **Revolution of 1800.** It was the first time anywhere in the world that the ruling elite in a nation changed without a death or a revolution and the loser left office voluntarily. But this election also illustrated how the party system affected the electoral system, as all of the Jeffersonian Party electors in the electoral college followed their instructions and voted for both Jefferson and his running mate, Aaron Burr, causing a tie and throwing the decision into the House of Representatives. With fears being heard of further intrigue and deals that might overturn the will of the electorate, the process was changed by the Twelfth Amendment, which mandated separate votes for the presidency and the vice presidency.

With Jeffersonians clearly dominating after Jefferson's reelection in 1804, Federalist support rapidly declined, and following the War of 1812, the party fell apart. In fact, during the presidency of James Monroe (1817–25), distinctions between the two parties disappeared. This so-called "Era of Good Feelings" was characterized by a lack of divisive issues and the rapid recovery of the American economy.

Question for Reflection: What do you think would be the impact on the current U.S. government and economy if the distinctions between the two parties suddenly disappeared? Would the result warrant the label, "Era of Good Feelings?"

The election of 1824 was the first in which popular votes were counted and the last to be settled by the House of Representatives. Four regional candidates could produce no electoral college winner (see Table 9.1). To become president, it is not sufficient to win more electoral college votes than anyone else—as Andrew Jackson clearly did in this election. According to the Constitution, a candidate must win a *majority* (more than 50 percent) of those electoral college votes; otherwise, the U.S. House of Representatives is delegated to choose from among the top three contenders. The winner and eventual president must receive a majority of state delegations, that is, twenty-six out of fifty states in our time, and thirteen out of twenty-four states in Jackson's day. Since Jackson won only 37.9 percent of the electoral college vote (more than anyone else, but short of a majority), the election was thrown into the House of Representatives for resolution.

Unpopular in Congress, where he was viewed as a political outsider and demagogue, Jackson found his popularity with the public did not help him. Henry Clay—his weakest rival in the election but a power in the House, where he served as Speaker—threw his support behind the second-place candidate, John Quincy Adams. Clay's influence gave Adams his barely needed thirteen states, making him president by the slimmest of margins. In return, Adams named Clay secretary of state. This "deal" came to be widely resented in the nation at large, a fact Jackson exploited as he continued to campaign for president over the next four years. Adams soon proved an unpopular leader. A National Republican who favored major increases in the power of the federal government to encourage domestic

Revolution of 1800 The first election in the world in which one party (the Federalist party of John Adams) willingly gave up power because of a lost election to another party (the Republican party of Thomas Jefferson) without bloodshed.

Table 9.1 ■ Results of the Presidential Election of 1824				
Candidate	**Popular Votes**		**Electoral College Votes**	
	Number	Percent	Number	Percent
Jackson	155,872	42.2	99	37.9
Adams	105,321	31.9	84	32.2
Crawford	44,282	12.9	41	15.7
Clay	46,587	13.0	37	14.2

economic development, he met tremendous opposition in Congress and thereby contributed to the rebirth of the two-party system.[6]

The Second Party System (1820s–1850s)

Outraged and galvanized by having the election of 1824 "stolen" from them, followers of Jackson organized to take power in the next election. Their grass-roots activism, under the energetic leadership of Jackson himself, reenergized the old Jeffersonian Party and sent it forth in a modern format, that of the populist Jacksonian Democrats. Formalized by Jackson's presidential victory in 1828, the Jacksonian Democrats sought to revive Jefferson's egalitarian principles. The party drew support from urban workers, westerners, and southern non-slaveholders.

Symbolic of this new democratic spirit, Jackson was chosen as a presidential candidate for his second term at a national party convention in which delegates, chosen by local party members throughout the country, selected a candidate by a two-thirds vote, adopted a statement of party principles, and generated party spirit. This nomination differed from the old system of nomination by a small group of national legislative leaders, known as the **"King Caucus."**

When Jackson sought to dismantle the national bank, business interests joined with slaveholding southerners to form the Whig party. Much like the Hamiltonian Federalists, Whigs supported an active federal government. Their ranks included Senators Henry Clay and Daniel Webster and Illinois lawyer Abraham Lincoln. This was an era of real two-party competition, with each party capturing a significant portion of political offices. The Whigs were particularly successful in winning congressional elections. Ultimately, the Civil War and the issues of slavery and the nature of the Union would lead to the disintegration of this second party system.

The Third Party System (1850s–1890s)

Slavery splintered not only the party system, but American society as well. The Supreme Court's Dred Scott decision established that a slave who resides in a free state or territory is still a slave. Denying African Americans the rights of citizenship added fuel to the fire, as did acrimonious congressional debates over the spread of slavery and actual clashes between proslavery and antislavery forces in the new western territories. Northerners, progressive whites, and many of those settling in the West, along with activists from former minor parties like the Liberty and Free Soil parties, came together in 1854 to form the Republican party, dedicated to abolishing slavery.

Lincoln, elected president in 1860 as part of this new political alignment, came to the Republican party from the Whigs. He and other Republican leaders developed policy platforms that stressed issues of moral conscience more than had previous political parties. The Whigs dropped from sight, while the Democratic party, weakened by its connection to the losing Confederate cause, kept its base in the South and Midwest, primarily among agricultural, rural voters. The Republican party dominated national politics until the 1890s by winning six consecutive presidential elections (1860–84). Grover Cleveland, in the very close elections of 1884 and 1892, was the lone Democrat to capture presidential office in this period.

Democratic politics at this time were conducted in what has often been derided as a "smoke-filled room" where party bosses from around the country met to select the candidate. Critics charged that nominations were being made by middle-aged, cigar-chewing white men, wheeling and dealing around some backroom table.

The Fourth Party System (1896–1932)

The era of the late nineteenth and twentieth centuries is frequently characterized as one of party government. During this time, the Democratic and Republican parties became highly developed, well organized, and successful in attracting a loyal body of voters. The huge influx of immigrants helped change the shape of

---

LITTLE-KNOWN FACT

One of the oldest and most familiar symbols of America's two-party system was not created by the parties themselves but by a witty and provocative commentator on American politics. The familiar Democratic donkey and Republican elephant, which can be seen adorning many of the trappings of major elections, were the brainchild of nineteenth-century political cartoonist Thomas H. Nast. His donkey and elephant captured what he saw as the essence of American party competition: the braying, obstinate rhetoric of the Democrats and the corpulent, smug Republican tycoons.

"King Caucus" The process of selecting candidates for president in the early nineteenth century in which the members of each party's delegation in Congress did the nominating.

▲ William Jennings Bryan, the "boy orator of the Platte," delivered his classic "Cross of Gold" speech in 1896 about the harm the monetary system did to farmers. His loss to William McKinley in 1896 ushered in a new period of Republican control of the White House.

domestic politics, leading to the growth of urban party "machines" and creating long-term alliances between various ethnic groups and political parties.

The election of 1896 did not dramatically change the domination enjoyed by Republicans in capturing the presidency or controlling the House of Representatives. It did, however, result in a long-term realignment of voters identifying with each party. Republicans consolidated their control of the North and West, while Democrats continued to control the South. In 1893, a depression occurred under Democrat Grover Cleveland. Already the stronger party, Republicans in 1896 held off the combined challenge of the Populists and Democrats, both of whom nominated "the Silver-Tongued Orator," William Jennings Bryan, as president. The victory of Republican William McKinley ended the Populist party and solidified a fundamental shift in Democratic and Republican constituencies.

Some Populist issues were taken up by the Progressives, reformers from both parties who argued that the process of nominating candidates should be shifted from the leaders in the "smoke-filled room" to the voters. While some states did adopt a **primary system,** with elections being held to nominate candidates, not enough of them did so to dictate the outcome of the process. Only one Democrat, Woodrow Wilson, who served from 1913 to 1921, held the office of president between 1896 and 1932. Economic expansion, industrialization, immigration, and the emerging status of the United States as a world power brought great prosperity in the early decades of the twentieth century. However, Republican domination ended abruptly in 1932, as the Great Depression brought the next realignment in party identification and power.[7]

The Fifth Party System (1932–1968)

By the summer of 1932, the Great Depression had left millions without work or economic relief. The incumbent president, Republican Herbert Hoover, did his best to assure a frightened American citizenry that prosperity was forthcoming; people just had to trust his leadership. Hoover clung relentlessly to faith in the gold standard and the need for a balanced budget; there would be no government handouts. Meanwhile, New York governor Franklin Delano Roosevelt accepted the Democratic party's nomination for president claiming, "I pledge you, I pledge myself, to a new deal for the American people."

On November 8, 1932, Governor Roosevelt defeated President Hoover. "A frightened people," wrote James David Barber, "given the choice between two touters of confidence, pushed aside the one they knew let them down and went for the one they prayed might not."[8] Roosevelt amassed a 472 to 59 electoral college majority and a popular vote margin of 22,809,638 to 15,758,901.

To gain this massive victory, Roosevelt brought together an alliance of Americans that came to be known as the **New Deal coalition.** The key components of this successful amalgam consisted of the urban working class, most members of the newer ethnic groups (especially Irish, Poles, and Italians), African Americans, the bulk of American Catholics and Jews, the poor, southerners, and liberal intellectuals. This broad-based coalition allowed Roosevelt to forge scores of new government programs that increased government assistance and brought him immense popular support. It also brought about a new set of beliefs and attitudes toward government.

Riding a wave of enthusiasm for the New Deal, Democrats went on to dominate national politics between 1932 and 1968. The nation chose only one Republican president during this period: World War II hero Dwight Eisenhower. Each of Roosevelt's Democratic successors kept the New Deal coalition alive. Lyndon B. Johnson (1963–69), in particular, gave renewed impetus to New Deal philosophy by expanding government economic assistance programs with his "Great Society."[9] In the pivotal 1968 election, however, conservative Richard Nixon was able to beat Vice President Hubert H. Humphrey, whose election was hampered by the bitter split among the Democratic party, and the Republicans took control of the White House.

primary system The system of nominating candidates in which voters in each state make the choice by casting ballots.

New Deal coalition Brought together by Franklin Roosevelt in 1932, a broad electorate made up of the urban working class, most members of the newer ethnic groups, the bulk of American Catholics and Jews, the poor, the South, and liberal intellectuals.

The Major American Parties

In the last 200 years, there have been only five political parties that have achieved and held a position in American politics for any amount of time. Of these five, only the Democrats and the Republicans hold such a position today.

1. *The Federalists.* This was the first American political party. Named after its leaders' outspoken defense of the federal Constitution during the ratification process, it had the support of merchants, landowners, and those of wealth and status in the Northeast and the Atlantic states. But it was limited by this narrow base and fell away before the successes of the next party, the Jeffersonians.

2. *The Jeffersonians.* This was a party of the small farmers, workers, and less wealthy citizens who were opposed to the nationalism of the Federalists and preferred the authority of the states. Its founder was Thomas Jefferson, and like him it espoused many of the ideals of the French Revolution, such as the idea of direct popular self-government. (At times this party was also called the Anti-Federalists, the Republicans, and the Democratic-Republicans.)

3. *The Democrats.* This was the first really broad-based, popular party in the United States. It represented less privileged voters, welcomed new immigrants, and stood up to nativist opposition to immigration; it also opposed national banking and high tariffs. The Democrats grew from the Jacksonian wing of the Jeffersonian party.

4. *The Whigs.* This party had a short life, during which it was the representative of many interests, among them nativism, property, and business and commerce. It had its roots in the old Federalist party and was formed in opposition to the strong presidency of Andrew Jackson.

5. *The Republicans.* This party grew out of northern opposition to slavery and came to power as the Civil War approached. It was the party of the Union, Lincoln, and the freeing of the slaves. From the Whigs it also took on a concern for business and propertied interests.

The figure below shows where each of these parties falls on a historical continuum from 1788 to 1900.

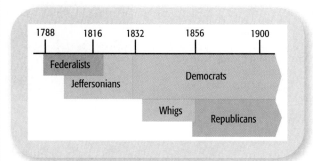

The Five Major American Political Parties
Five political parties have achieved a successful and competitive role in American politics. The Democrats and the Republicans have succeeded over the last 150 years where others have failed.

Source: Congressional Quarterly, Guide to Elections, 2d ed. (Washington, D.C.: Congressional Quarterly, 1985), p. 224.

A Sixth Party System?: 1968 to Present

Since 1968, the Republican Party has won six of the last nine presidential elections, with the two Democratic winners being conservative members of the party from the South. Yet until recently scholars have been reluctant to describe the post–1968 period as another realignment. Although Republican presidents Richard Nixon, Gerald Ford, Ronald Reagan, and George Herbert Walker Bush, won the presidency, all were unsuccessful in dismantling the New Deal and Great Society programs, which had proven broadly popular. Democrats retained majority control of the U.S. House of Representatives during a forty-year period from January 1955 to January 1995. In past realignments, the emerging dominant party swept to broad election victories in both Congress and the presidency as a result of its position on a highly controversial issue, and then took control in the majority of American states as well. But Republicans remained the minority party in state and local elections throughout the 1960s and 1970s era.

There are many signs, however, that partisan strengths are shifting. After taking control of both houses of Congress in 1994 for the first time in 40 years, Republicans succeeded in retaining control of both bodies in 1996 and 1998. However, party results in state races in the 1998 and 2000 elections, were mixed. Middle-of-the-road, pragmatic Republic conservatives won the governorships of twenty-three of the thirty-four contested races in 2000. As a result, going into the 2002 election

▶ Who gets the "sound bite" this time? While Senator Trent Lott (R.-Miss.) announces the Republican party's "hunt for bills" in the Democratic party-led Congress, Senator Bill Frist (R.-Tenn.) tries unsuccessfully to wrest a boom microphone out of the mouth of one of the bloodhounds brought in to lead the "search."

the Republicans held the governorships of 27 states and the Democrats held 21, with two independents.[10] In the 2002 election, the Democratic party picked up three governorships nationwide, including Pennsylvania, Michigan, and Illinois. However, Sonny Perdue became the first Republican governor in Georgia since Reconstruction, and Jeb Bush withstood a significant challenge to win re-election in Florida, setting up Republicans there for the 2004 election.

Since 1977, the story of the balance between the two parties has been the uninterrupted loss of voter support for the Democratic party. When Ronald Reagan took control of the White House in 1981, the percentage of people identifying with the Democratic party dropped below 40% for the first time. With the steady rise in Republican support during Reagan's presidency, the lead held by the Democratic party fell from 27% to only 9% in 1985. Between 1985 and 2001 the Democratic party lead in those identifying with its party dropped from 9% to a mere 5%. By January 2002, one poll revealed that the Republicans had taken a 3 point lead in party identification, a trend later confirmed by several other polls.[11] Evidence of this shifting balance between the parties is evident in the roughly 6,000 state legislative seats being contested. Prior to the 2000 election, the Democrats controlled both houses of the states legislatures in 19 states and the Republicans in 17. After the 2000 election, the state legislatures were even more evenly matched with the Republicans and the Democrats each controlling both houses of the legislature in 17 states. Another 14 states were split with each party controlling one House, with the state of Nebraska having a nonpartisan, single-chamber legislature.

As a result of these gains in state legislatures and its control of the state governorships, the Republicans managed the re-districting for 98 seats in the United States Congress, with the expectation that it would make it easier for the Republican party to defend its six-seat margin in Congress.[12] And the strategy worked, as the Republicans in the 2002 Congressional election defied the historic trend of sitting Presidents losing seats to such an extent that the Republicans gained five seats in Congress (with 2 seats still to be decided).

The reasons for this trend towards Republicanism over the last three decades are varied. The number of young conservatives entering the electorate has steadily increased, a potential boon to Republicans. The number of Democratic voters has been slowly declining for several years, due in part to the aging of its constituency and the declining power of labor unions, while the number of Independents has steadily risen. Indeed, polls taken through 1998 show the number of Independents rising steadily, with Republicans and Democrats losing traditional supporters. In 2001, however, while the number of Democratic and Independent voters declined, the Republican voter numbers increased slightly (see Table 9.2).[13] Realignment may well be taking place, and it may be that the United States has entered an era in which the Republicans are becoming the dominant political party. Or it could be that the weakness of the voters' identification with the major parties, coupled with the increase in the number of Independents and third party identifiers, will lead to a system of relatively balanced political party strength, making any prediction of election outcomes based solely on party identification uncertain.

Question for Reflection: What role has voters' frustration with "politics as usual" within the Republican and Democratic parties played in the reshaping of the party system in the last decade?

Functions of American Political Parties

The governing institutions of the United States were designed to fragment and decentralize power, and they have succeeded very well at that task. The only political institutions that work to pull people together—that exert a coherent, unified perspective on public affairs and attempt to govern in a reasonably cohesive manner—are the two major political parties.[14] The functions they perform within American society are varied and crucial for the health of our democracy.

Parties Organize the Election Process

A party's most basic role is to nominate candidates and win elections.[15] True, citizens need not belong to a political party to run for office, but to win high elective office, a candidate must, with few exceptions, belong to one of the two major American political parties. Every president since 1853 has been either a Democrat or a Republican. After Jim Jeffords' switch in 2001, 99 senators still belonged to one of those two parties, as did 433 of 435 representatives (the exceptions being Independents Virgil Goode of Virginia and Bernard Sanders of Vermont) and 49 of 50 governors (the exception being Minnesota's Jesse "the Body" Ventura, who ran on the Reform Party ticket and later changed to the Independence Party before deciding in June 2002 not to run for re-election). The stability of this pattern is impressive. For more than a century, the rule for any ambitious politician has been simple: To build a serious career in public life, first join either the Democratic or the Republican party. When dissatisfied, however, an elected politician can always switch parties, as Senator Richard Shelby of Alabama did in 1994 when he switched to the Republican Party after finding in the early Clinton years that he did not have the influence that he expected with the White House. But this change, which gave the Republicans a six vote margin in the Senate, did not have the profound impact on policy making ability that Jim Jeffords' switch in 2001 brought, changing the party balance of the entire Senate body (see Figure 9.1).

Table 9.2 ■ Trends in Party Identification										
	1988	**1989**	**1990**	**1991**	**1992**	**1993**	**1994**	**1996**	**1998**	**2001**
Republicans	27%	33%	32%	31%	28%	27%	29%	28%	28%	31%
Democrats	30	33	33	32	34	34	33	39	38	36%
Independents	38	34	30	33	34	34	35	33	34	22%

Source: http:harrisinteractive.com (July 2, 2002) Times Mirror Center for the People and the Press, *The New Political Landscape*, October 1994, p. 43; American National Election Studies, Center for Political Studies, University of Michigan; and Gallup Poll Election Survey, 1998.

Figure 9.1
Taking Control

When George W. Bush became the first new President since Franklin D. Roosevelt in 1934 to add seats in Congress, he restored control of both Houses of Congress that was lost when Sen. Jim Jeffords deserted the Republican party in 2001.

Source: The Washington Post, May 25, 2001.

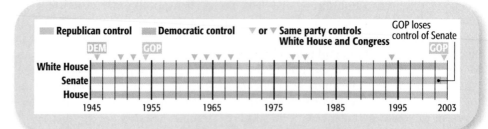

Since winning office is crucial to party fortunes, party members spend much time and energy on the election process. Parties select candidates, provide money to local, state, and national races, and arrange administrative support at all levels of electoral competition. They begin this work with the vital function of **recruitment.** Parties are continually looking for effective, popular candidates to help them win votes and offices. The search for good candidates never ends. In 2000, when highly regarded politicians chose not to run for reelection, both parties found it difficult to persuade rising political starts to run for Congress, even for open or highly winnable seats, because of the need to raise large campaign war chests and the stresses placed by such service on their families. For a time, however, it has seemed that in some states the term limits placed on state legislators improved this prospect somewhat as state politicians were forced to run for federal office in order to stay in public life.

In trying to find successful campaigners, parties perform another key function: *representation.* To win free, democratic elections, parties follow a crucial axiom: Find out what voters want and promise to give it to them. No matter who is elected, the winners attempt to remain committed to the popular programs on which they campaigned. Following this logic, parties must *act responsibly* and legislate the policies they promised. Parties elected under pledges to carry out a specific set of policies will be judged by voters at the next election. Did they do what they promised? If not, voters can (and often do) reject them in favor of their rivals. Knowing punishment of this sort can occur, parties are under serious pressure when writing their platforms. Backing away from or even flip-flopping on a public commitment can often produce a devastating backlash.

In the long run, this open competition for power serves the desires of the voting public. By recruiting good candidates, representing voter wishes, and being held responsible for their actions in office, the two parties help Americans approach the democratic ideal of government.[16]

Parties Represent Group Interests

In their struggle for power, parties speak for and unite different groups and their varied interests. Parties find that it pays to discover what groups want, then work with those groups to fulfill their desires. Thus, Republicans often work closely with business groups to articulate pro-business positions; Democrats do the same with labor union leaders. But parties must do more than speak for one narrow interest if they wish to gain the majorities needed to win public office; they must appeal to a wide range of social groups. In so doing, they learn to meld individual group interests into a larger whole with a coherent philosophy of governing.[17]

The need to combine a complex set of interests forces parties to become broad political coalitions. Republicans, for instance, must find a rationale for uniting the interests of multinational corporations and small businesses, rural evangelical Protestants and pro-life Catholics. Democrats, too, must unite a diverse set of factions that include small-town white southerners, urban black workers, and ethnic white suburbanites. In the process of building a coalition from social subgroups, both parties perform another democratic function—integrating various groups into public life and the democratic process. Parties thus help mute the conflicts that

recruitment The process through which parties look for effective, popular candidates to help them win votes and offices.

might arise if each interest group had its own separate party and fought the others at every election.

Parties Simplify Political Choices

By bringing together a wide range of groups and creating a coherent platform for voters at election time, parties simplify political choices for voters. Most voters do not study every issue in depth, nor do they know where each candidate stands on every issue. How, then, can they make rational decisions at the ballot box? Parties help by melding a series of complex issues into a broad, general perspective and explaining that perspective in simple, direct ways. By election day, most voters have been educated. They know that their choices are not merely between two individual personalities, but between two differing philosophies of governance. Consider what the alternative would be: a ballot listing only a long series of names unconnected to any party and without any hint of the candidate's position.

Parties Organize Government and Policy Making

Once elections are over, parties help organize the country's political institutions for governing. Public officials work together as organized members of the winning party. They try to carry out their party's aims and election pledges. The Republican takeover of Congress after the 1994 elections, for example, resulted in a set of policies very different from those that existed before that election, when Democrats were in the majority. In 2003 the Republican takeover of the Senate, reversing the effect of Jim Jeffords' switch from the Republican party, will help to promote the legislative agenda of President Bush. Policy decisions in the United States result from party leaders attempting to govern in the spirit of their party's philosophy. This work is in both parties' interest. After all, the party that solves political problems wins mass support at the next election.

Party Organization

Despite recent trends toward strengthening national party organizations, political parties are still relatively decentralized institutions. The flow of power moves upward—from local to state organizations, and from there to the national committees and conventions.

Parties at the Grass Roots

Parties at the grass roots consist of city, county, and state organizations. Party operations begin at the local level. The **local party organization** provides the initial point of entry for people seeking involvement in politics as volunteers, organizers, or candidates. Each local party is highly dependent on the level of interest demonstrated by its community. In some places awareness and interest are high. Party faithful eagerly fill slots as precinct chairs and election organizers, volunteer for administrative posts, and even run for slots to participate in state conventions. Where interest is low, party structures remain skeletal, with many posts going unfilled or a few party faithful keeping the organization going.

While linked to the national apparatus, local and state political parties have a great deal of independent power, often more than the national party. Local parties enjoy significantly higher personal interaction with members, are able to base their platforms on significant local issues, and can perform their duties without seeking huge monetary donations. It is also easier for citizens to become involved at the local level in such activities as donating money or working for a campaign.

Political activists are vital in a democracy; they have an important influence on the party platform and on political decision makers. Party activists are different from the population at large in that they tend to be wealthier and have higher levels of

local party organization The initial point of entry for those seeking involvement in politics as volunteers, organizers, or candidates.

APPROACHING DEMOCRACY AROUND THE GLOBE

Rise and Fall of Taiwan's Nationalist Party

The loss of 42 legislative seats and their majority completed the demise of Taiwan's Nationalist party in December 2001. In ending more than fifty years of rule by that party, it raised questions about the future of Taiwan relative to mainland China.

The Nationalist Party once controlled China and presided over the emergence of democracy in that nation. But it was those democratic forces that eventually overturned the party. The corruption of the Nationalist Party under Generalissimo Chiang Kai-shek in the mid twentieth century enabled Mao Zedong to lead the Communists in 1949 to defeat the Nationalists after a civil war and drive them to the offshore island of Taiwan. Since that time the United States has offered its protection of the island against an invasion by Communist China, thus allowing the Nationalist Party to rule with an eye toward its own aggrandizement. The party had no real ideological direction, and enforced its rule by killing or torturing its opposition. In addition, it imposed its ideas and language on Taiwan by forcing children to speak Mandarin Chinese and refusing to allow the teaching of local history.

The Nationalist Party was able to maintain power by redistributing land, promoting education, and helping the people to get rich by forming businesses. But this economic and educational revolution laid the seeds for the political revolution that would upend the Nationalists in the end.

By the 1980s, the Nationalists began responding to popular demands in permitting opposition party activities. On occasion, critics of the Nationalists were still tortured and even killed, and the Nationalists controlled the news media. In addition, the ruling party owned businesses, which gave it a huge economic advantage in national elections. Still, the opposition leaders began to win at the local level and built their power bases there.

After the death of Nationalist Party leader Chiang Ching-kuo in 1988, power passed uneasily to Lee Teng-hui, a Taiwanese, who became the country's new president. He changed the Nationalist Party by democratizing it, thus creating a more pluralistic environment in which the opposition party could flourish. Lee's theme of distancing Taiwan from mainland China was picked up by the opposing Democratic Progressive Party, which called for complete independence from mainland China. For its part, China began warning that the election of this party would mean war as it sought to return what it called this wayward province to the motherland.

In the March elections, Chen Shui-bian, a 49-year-old lawyer and mayor of Taipei, and the leader of the Democratic Progressive Party, won the three-way race for the presidency with 39 percent of the vote. For the Nationalist Party, though, the loss was much worse than the end of its

▲ Members of the Democratic Progressive party of Taiwan celebrate the end of fifty years of rule by the Nationalist party.

five-decade rule. The party had split with James Soong, who mounted an independent candidacy of such success that he took second place with a strong 37 percent of the vote, while Lien Chan, the Nationalist candidate, took a distant third place with a mere 23 percent of the vote.

While Chen tried to reach out to mainland China to prevent inflaming the separation between the two nations, tensions in Taiwan itself quickly rose. Thousands of disaffected supporters of the Nationalists battled police for hours as President Lee Teng-hui barricaded himself inside his party headquarters. Facing calls to resign immediately, Lee agreed to step down as party chairman in September, a year earlier than planned.

Analysts fear that both the election of the Democratic Progressive Party and the total unraveling of the ruling Nationalist Party at a time of great tension between Taiwan and mainland China may spell trouble for the island nation. But this prospect apparently did not worry voters as the losses in the legislature for the Nationalist Party were greater than expected. "It shows that it takes time to heal the wounds," said Shaw Yu-Ming, the chairman of the Nationalist Party's newspaper, *The Central Daily News.* However, the Nationalists may not be finished yet as it still has a chance of allying with the third largest party in the legislature in an effort to retake the majority.

Sources: Mark Landler "Nationalists Are Routed in Taiwan Legislative Election," *New York Times,* December 2, 2001, p. A8; Nicholas D. Kristof, "Party Undone by Liberty It Nutured," *New York Times,* March 19, 2000, p. 18; Erik Eckholm, "Taiwan Nationalists Ousted After Half-Century Reign," *New York Times,* March 19, 2000, p. 1; and Mark Landler, "Violent Protests in Taiwan Follow Election Defeat," *New York Times,* March 20, 2000, p. 1.

education. As a result of reforms in the methods the Democratic party uses to select delegates to the nominating conventions, the party has also encouraged increased activism on the part of women, minorities, and youth. And the Republican party has also opened its doors to these newer activists.[18] So while party activists have characteristics different from those of the population at large, party reform has resulted in a more demographically representative group.

The fifty **state party organizations** all have very different systems. Through their two key roles as organizers of elections and providers of the electoral college votes needed to win the presidency, state party organizations play a critical part in American national politics. They also play a significant role in state politics. The leaders in each state party's central committee supervise the various functions vital to state parties, such as raising funds, identifying potential candidates, providing election services, offering advice on reapportionment, and developing campaign strategies. State parties also act in conjunction with state governments to conduct the primary elections or caucuses that are used by most states to register preferences for presidential candidates.

Party structure varies dramatically from state to state. Some party organizations, like that of Pennsylvania, have permanent headquarters, a regular calendar of events, frequent meetings with local officials, and a central committee staffed with professional administrators, strategists, and fund raisers. Parties in other states are less impressive. California is known to have weak political parties. From these differences follows a common political rule: Where parties are weak, interest groups are strong.

The Party Machine

Local parties for many years constituted the main avenue for political party activity. From the final decades of the nineteenth century to the early or middle part of this century, an organizational style called **machine politics** flourished in New York City, Chicago, Philadelphia, Kansas City, and elsewhere.

At the heart of the system lay an ingenious scheme of reciprocal influence. Party leaders (bosses) traded jobs, money, and favors for votes and campaign support. Party workers would help bosses win office, receiving patronage jobs in return. Once in office, the party bosses had jobs to distribute. As for voters, those who supported the winning party could be assured of good local service, the occasional handout, the odd favor. The bosses, able to reach into the public till for party funds and personal enrichment, could use some of the purloined cash to keep voters and party workers happy.[19]

The system worked for a time to ensure strong, organized parties. It was based largely on an urban landscape of impoverished workers, often recent immigrants, who were more concerned with immediate benefits and simple economic survival than with the idealistic goals of effective and honest government. Urban dwellers who were poor, hungry, and uneducated found that support of the party boss and the machine could ensure them a job or at least an economic safety net in tough times. The party machine acted as a combination employment agency, social work provider, and welfare state. Naturally, the machine and the party bosses did not undertake these tasks merely for humanitarian reasons. They sought power, wealth, and privilege—primarily through the public coffers. Eventually their venality and corrupt behavior produced a backlash that swept them into oblivion.

The boss and the machine fell to several modernizing forces of the twentieth century. To begin with, the increasing wealth and education of Americans produced a citizenry supportive of a government that served people's interests and was less inclined to accept corrupt machine behavior. Candidates who ran against party bosses started getting elected in ever-larger numbers. Furthermore, in an increasingly wealthy society, people needed fewer of the favors that the bosses typically had at their disposal.

state party organizations Party organizations at the state level; they organize elections and provide the electoral college votes needed to win the presidency; they also supervise the various functions vital to state parties, such as fund raising, identifying potential candidates, providing election services, offering advice on reapportionment matters, and developing campaign strategies.

machine politics An organizational style of local politics in which party bosses traded jobs, money, and favors for votes and campaign support.

Four additional developments doomed the old machine system. First, the invention of the civil service robbed the party machine of those tangible and valued rewards for potential followers—government jobs. Second, the creation of the modern welfare state provided a safety net for the poorest citizens, meaning that bosses were no longer needed to serve that purpose. Third, the proliferation of primary elections removed decision making about candidates and nominations from the hands of party bosses and gave it to a mass electorate. With little power to control the struggle for high office and few rewards to dole out to anyone, the influence of party bosses crumbled, and nearly all of the traditional machines ground to a halt. Finally, the secret ballot helped speed the decline of party bosses' ability to intimidate voters.

Still, good organizations know how to adapt to changing circumstances. As the 2000 presidential nomination campaign revealed, party machines have not been dismantled but streamlined. Amid all the attention focused on the reform candidates—McCain and Bradley—it was the veritable army of precinct workers—some carrying on a partisan family tradition handed down over generations—"pounding the pavement," that got the vote out for the front-runners, Al Gore and George W. Bush. The downsized machines, operating on "walking around money" from the party organization, still continue to crank out voter loyalty, often quite successfully. The Bipartisan Campaign Finance Reform Act of 2002 may have an impact on how the party machinery raises money from individuals.

National Party Organization

The strength of the **national party organization** is most apparent during presidential elections. Even with the increasing democratization of the nominating process and the proliferation of interest groups and political action committees, the national party organization remains a crucial source of coordination and consensus building for both Republicans and Democrats.

Ostensibly, the national organization is the highest authority for each political party, but in fact, it has always been weak. For decades, the national organization's primary task was to organize the **national party convention** once every four years. The convention symbolizes the party's existence as a national institution. At this festive affair, party delegates from around the country come together to select presidential and vice presidential candidates for the coming election and to write the party's platform. At no other time is the national party much in evidence to the American public.[20]

A **party platform** is a statement of principles and policies, the goals that a party pledges to carry out if voters give it control of government. The platform announces positions on prominent issues of the day, such as gun control, abortion, taxation, and social spending. The platform is also important as a way of setting the tone for each party and distinguishing one party from another. As you can see in Table 9.3 on page 326, Democrats and Republicans differ from each other ideologically. These differences show up clearly in platform statements.

Although many people assume that party platforms mean little to the actual performance of the party in government, this is not the case. For example, when the platform of a president's party is analyzed, platform positions tend to mirror subsequent government expenditures quite closely. At times, though, candidates such as George W. Bush find that they have to differentiate their campaign rhetoric from the party platform in the search for votes. For the Republicans, it is often the strong anti-abortion stance of the platform that forces them to take this approach.

The day-to-day operations of the national party fall to the *national chair*. Each chair, selected by the presidential nominee of the party, is the actual administrator. The chair is responsible for personnel, fund raising, scheduling, and the daily activities of the party. Modern fund-raising techniques, such as computer-derived mailing lists and direct mail, have made both state and national party units more effective in recent years. Each party's ability to target specific voters—based on

▲ Republican National Committee Chairman Mark Racicot of Montana helped to craft the campaign strategy that led the Republican party to an historic victory in the 2002 Congressional election.

national party organization Party organization at the national level whose primary tasks include fund raising, distribution of information, and recruitment.

national party convention The national meeting of the party every four years to choose the ticket for the presidential election and write the platform for the party.

party platform The statement of principles and policies, the goals that a party pledges to carry out if voters give it control of the government.

geography, demographics, previous financial support, and precinct location—becomes more sophisticated with each election. Given the administrative responsibilities of the national chair's job, holders of this office tend to be relatively unknown rather than popular national political figures. The Democrats' appointment of former Clinton fundraiser Terry McAuliffe, as well as former Montana Attorney General Mark Rocicot's appointment by the Republicans, is evidence of this point.

Party Similarities and Differences

Although a great deal of the organizational structure is similar for both parties, each bases its structure on different goals. The Republican party stresses the creation and maintenance of effective administrative structures, especially at the national level, which can supply assistance and raise funds for candidates. As a result, Republicans tend to be more bureaucratically oriented than Democrats, but also benefit from less ideological discord. Conversely, Democrats stress representation by promoting voter mobilization, activism, and debate. Because it encourages pluralistic participation, the Democratic party ensures acrimonious argument regarding policy and the selection of candidates.

The Republican party seems more effective at fund raising. In a typical election year, Republicans raise and distribute to candidates about 250 percent more money than Democrats do.[21] This disparity caused problems for President Bill Clinton and Vice President Al Gore in 1997, when they were accused of raising money for the Democratic National Committee by phone calls from the White House in violation of a nineteenth-century law. Although no such violation was ever proved, there was little doubt that the fund-raising tactics of the White House, including the use of overnight stays in the Lincoln Bedroom to attract contributions from prominent party donors, caused harsh criticism of the process. In 2002, President Bush scheduled so many fund raisers for the spring and summer to fund the upcoming Congressional elections that by June he had raised over $100 million. Providing a sense of the magnitude of this fund-raising effort, it took President Bill Clinton ten years, from 1992 on, to raise $113 million for the Democratic party. As a result of the Bipartisan Campaign Finance Reform Act, this kind of "soft money" fund-raising will end after the 2002 election.[22] The issue ads which this money often funds will not be legal 30 days before the election primaries or 60 days before the general election.

▲ Democratic National Committee Chairman Terry McAuliffe put on a bold face after the Democrats suffered a devastating loss in the 2002 Congressional election but still faced the challenge of reorganizing and rejuvenating his party.

Nominating a President: Parties and Elections

Before a party can run the government and make public policy, it must win control of the top political offices. In the United States, that means the presidency in particular. Let us examine the process by which a Democrat or a Republican becomes a candidate for president of the United States.

Nominating Candidates

Before candidates can be elected to public office, they must first be nominated. **Nomination** can be thought of as the candidate's "sponsorship" by a political party. Party endorsement carries legal weight. Only one candidate per position can appear on any ballot with the word Democrat or Republican after his or her name. Since all other names on a ballot have next to no chance of getting elected, how the parties organize the nomination process matters a great deal. In the past, a small group of party leaders controlled nominations. That process has now been democratized, with major political consequences.

In the current American system, to gain a party's nomination for president, a candidate must win a majority of delegates at the party's national convention in the summer before the November presidential election. By tradition, the party currently

nomination A candidate's "sponsorship" by a political party.

Table 9.3 ■ The Parties' Platforms: How They Compared in the 2000 Election

Democrats	Republicans	Democrats	Republicans
Taxes		**Welfare**	
"Tax cuts would let families live their values by helping them save for college, invest in their job skills and lifelong learning, pay for health insurance, afford child care, eliminate the marriage penalty for working families, care for elderly and disabled loved ones, invest in clean cars and clean homes, and build additional security for their retirement."	"Replace the five current tax brackets with four lower ones, ensuring all taxpayers significant tax relief while targeting it especially toward low-income workers. Help families by doubling the child tax credit to $1,000, making it available to more families and eliminating the marriage penalty."	"One way we value and reward hard work is to modernize, strengthen and sustain the nation's unemployment compensation system. . . . The system serves far fewer working families than in the past, and many especially vulnerable workers—such as low-wage workers, seasonal employees, contingent workers and women—are especially likely to fall outside the system's protective safety net."	"Reward work with tax reform that takes 6 million families off the tax rolls, cuts the rate for those who remain on the rolls and doubles the child tax credit to $1,000. . . . Allow families receiving federal rental payments to apply one year's worth of their existing assistance money toward the purchase of their own first home."
Abortion		**Health Care**	
The party "stands behind the right of every woman to choose, consistent with *Roe v. Wade,* and regardless of ability to pay. We believe it is a fundamental constitutional liberty that individual Americans—not government—can best take responsibility for making the most difficult and intensely personal decisions regarding reproduction."	"The unborn child has a fundamental individual right to life which cannot be infringed. We support a human life amendment to the Constitution and we endorse legislation to make clear that the Fourteenth Amendment's protections apply to unborn children."	"We should guarantee access to affordable health care for every child in America. We should expand coverage to working families, including more Medicaid assistance to help with the transition from welfare to work. . . . Americans aged 55 to 65—the fastest-growing group of uninsured—should be allowed to buy into the Medicare program."	"It's time to modernize [Medicare] to match current medical science, improve the program's financial stability and cut back the bureaucratic jungle that is smothering it. . . . We will promote a health care system that supports, not supplants, the private sector; that promotes personal responsibility in health care decision-making; and that ensures the least intrusive role for the government."
Education		**Social Security**	
"By the end of the next presidential term, we should have fully qualified, well-trained teachers in every classroom in every school in every part of this country. . . . We should ensure that no high school student graduates unless they have mastered the basics of reading and math. . . . Parents across the nation ought to be able to choose the best public school for their children."	"Raise academic standards through increased local control and accountability to parents, shrinking a multitude of federal programs into five flexible grants in exchange for real, measured progress in student achievement. . . . Empower needy families to escape persistently failing schools by allowing federal dollars to follow their children to the school of their choice."	Use "the savings from our unprecedented prosperity to strengthen the Social Security Trust Fund in preparation for the baby-boom generation. . . . Al Gore has proposed the creation of Retirement Savings Plus—voluntary, tax-free, personally controlled, privately managed savings accounts with a government match."	"Anyone currently receiving Social Security, or close to being eligible for it, will not be impacted by any changes. . . . Real reform does not require, and will not include, tax increases. . . . Personal savings accounts must be the cornerstone of restructuring. . . . Any new options for Social Security should be voluntary."

Source: Washington Post, August 16, 2000, p. A20. Copyright © 2000 *The Washington Post.* Reprinted by permission.

holding the White House holds the later convention, usually in August. The challenging party holds its convention a month or so earlier, usually in July—perhaps on the theory that its candidate needs a running start to win the presidency.

Delegates in the past were often *uncommitted,* or under the control of party leaders who frequently withheld any commitments until a politically opportune moment at the convention itself. Even on the convention's opening day, the race might remain wide open. Today, however, nearly all delegates are *committed* long before the convention convenes. In fact, it is usually clear who the nominee will be long

◀ The Bushes and the Cheneys celebrated their win at the Republican National Convention little realizing that, thanks to Sen. Jim Jeffords of Vermont, it would be two years before they would take complete control of both Houses of Congress.

before the convention, which acts primarily as a formal ratifier of the obvious. Convention activities are now aimed less at choosing a candidate than at unifying the party faithful and gearing up for the fall election struggle.

Caucuses   Caucuses are meetings of party adherents who gather in precinct halls or private homes to discuss and deliberate, and finally throw their support to a candidate for president. They then select delegates who will represent their choices at higher-level state party meetings; eventually their votes are reflected at the national convention. Candidates or their representatives often attend caucuses to discuss issues and make appeals.

Caucus meetings may be all-day affairs that require a heavy investment of time. For that reason they are generally attended by only the most active and devoted party members. Any member of the party is by law allowed to attend, but this system makes it difficult for average citizens to play a role. It limits power to the more intensely political members of the voting public—usually people who are better off economically and well educated. For that reason, as American society approaches democracy, it has tended to prefer primary elections, which are more inclusive and democratic in nature than caucuses.

Primaries   Primary elections date from the beginning of the twentieth century. They were in large part a response to pressure from that era's reformers, the Progressives, who were tired of seeing their candidates pushed aside by political bosses and party machines. The Progressives argued that it was undemocratic to allow elites within the party to choose the party's candidate. Under pressure, the party leaders buckled, and the primary system slowly developed. A **primary election** is essentially a preelection, allowing all members of a party, not just its leadership, to select the party's candidates for the general election in the fall.

The acceptance of the primary system is widespread. Today political parties in about three-quarters of the states employ primaries to select candidates for national elections. Voters in presidential primaries vote for a specific candidate, and these votes are converted into delegates for that candidate. The delegates then attend the party's national convention, where they vote for the candidate they represent.

States that use primaries have employed various systems for parceling out delegates. Republicans allow greater variation than Democrats. In some places they use a **winner-take-all system** for the entire state; the winner of the primary gets all

caucus Meeting of party adherents who gather to discuss, to deliberate, and finally to give their support to a candidate for president. They then select delegates who will represent their choices at higher-level party meetings; eventually, their votes get reflected at the national convention itself. Also means a conference of party members in Congress.

primary election A preelection that allows all members of a party, not just its leadership, to select the party's candidate for the general election in the fall.

winner-take-all system A system in which the winner of the primary or electoral college vote gets all of the state's convention or electoral college delegates.

proportional representation A system of representation popular in Europe whereby the number of seats in the legislature is based on the proportion of the vote received in the election.

closed primary A system of conducting primary elections in which only citizens registered as members of a particular political party may participate in that party's primary.

open primary A system of conducting primary elections in which citizens vote in whichever party's primary they choose.

frontloading The process by which most party primaries and caucuses are held early in the nomination schedule so that the majority of the delegate support is locked up early.

the state's convention delegates. In other states they distribute delegates by congressional district, using a winner-take-all system for each district; thus, a state could split its delegates among several candidates. Finally, in some states Republicans use various systems of **proportional representation** to distribute delegates. Candidates who win, say, 20 percent of the statewide vote in the party primary will win about that same proportion of the state's delegates to the national convention.

In contrast to Republicans, Democrats employ a mandatory system of proportional representation to distribute delegates. Any candidate who wins at least 15 percent of the vote in any statewide primary must be allocated delegates to the national convention, and those delegates must reflect the exact percentage of primary votes received.

These generalizations about the delegate selection process only suggest the complexity of rules governing the winning of delegates. The arcane nature of the rules makes them comprehensible only to political insiders and specialists in the party organizations.[23]

There are different kinds of primaries. The closed primary is used by most states. In **closed primaries** only citizens registered as members of a political party may participate in that party's primary. A registered Republican, for instance, cannot cast a ballot in the Democratic primary. Conversely, **open primaries** allow all registered voters to vote in whichever party's primary they choose. Cross-party voting is thus possible. One reason why few states use open primaries is that this system may allow voters from one party to help decide who their rival party's nominee might be. An organized effort could produce crossover votes that select the opposition party's weakest candidate. This appeared to be the case in the 2000 campaign, when Democratic voters crossed over to vote for McCain in an effort to defeat George W. Bush before the general election. Two states, Washington and Alaska, have *blanket primaries,* which allow voters to choose either party on an office-by-office basis.

For nearly half a century the New Hampshire primary was the first big test of a candidate's legitimacy. Indeed, in ten straight presidential elections (from 1952 through 1988), nobody became president without first winning the party's presidential primary in New Hampshire. Why should this small and atypical American state assume a dominant role in the presidential selection process? Much of New Hampshire's influence stems from a simple fact: It always holds the first primary of each presidential election year. This race shows how a candidate fares in the "retail politics" of actually meeting the voters. While the Iowa caucus also held importance, since it tested candidates in the farm belt and preceded New Hampshire's primary, McCain's decision to skip this contest in 2000 may have diminished its importance for the future.

Being first has a powerful effect on voter and media perceptions, and thus on the fund-raising ability of the candidates. For instance, Bill Clinton was able to overcome questions about his personal life and his draft status to place second to Massachusetts Senator Paul Tsongas in the 1992 New Hampshire primary, and thus save his candidacy. Then, in the 1996 nominating process, Republican favorite Bob Dole barely defeated conservative candidate Pat Buchanan in the Iowa caucuses and lost to him in New Hampshire. As a result, Dole briefly considered dropping out of the race entirely. In 2000, George W. Bush's 19-point loss to McCain in New Hampshire nearly derailed him.

The traditional importance of Iowa and New Hampshire is diminishing, however. Many states, including some of the large ones, came to resent their power in selecting the nominee. To give themselves more political clout, many states changed the dates of their primaries. More than 75 percent of both parties' convention delegates are now chosen in a time frame from one to six weeks after New Hampshire's primary, a process known as **frontloading.** Thus, ambitious candidates must campaign in a number of states, in addition to New Hampshire, to have any chance of gaining their party's nomination. They cannot count on putting all their effort into winning New Hampshire and having a month or more, as they once did, to bask in that limelight and build national support. It is now harder for a dark horse to come out of nowhere, do well in New Hampshire, and go on to win a major party's nomination, as George McGovern did in 1972.

In 2000, the primary landscape changed dramatically. California decided to move its presidential primary from mid-June to March 7, when New York, Maryland, Colorado, Ohio, and five New England states were also holding their contests. March 7 is just one week before "Super Tuesday," the date when Florida, Texas, and the southern states hold their primaries. Predictions that as a result of these moves the nomination process would move closer to one big presidential primary, seemed to be borne out in 2002 when the Democratic party announced that any state would be able to hold primaries at any time after February 2, 2004. As a result, states such as Missouri and Wisconsin planned to move their primaries from March and April respectively, to February, and Iowa and New Hampshire, which have always led this process, were expected to move their delegate selection process ahead to late January 2004. This movement will favor candidates with the most early name recognition and prior fund raising. It will not allow candidates who misstep in an early primary to recover in the later contests. As one party official predicted, "The nomination likely will be won in 2003. Somebody's going to have to surge before Christmas of 2003." Indeed, throughout 2002, nearly a dozen Democratic party candidates kept "visiting" New Hampshire.[24] After the 2002 Congressional election, their challenge will be to persuade voters that the Democratic party now has a clear plan for governing the nation (see Figure 9.2).

After the long caucus and primary season (February to June), prospective nominees have several weeks before the parties meet for their national party conventions. If the race is still close, candidates use that time to keep pushing their nomination prospects. They seek to keep their committed delegates in line and to convince uncommitted delegates to declare for them. Negotiation, conciliation, and planning characterize this period.

Question for Reflection: What impact will the twenty-first century changes to the primary system have on party selection of a presidential candidate and our approach to democracy?

Reforming the Nominating Process

Since 1968 the presidential selection process has been radically altered. The Democrats' disastrously divisive convention in Chicago in 1968 fueled the impetus for change in the party's nomination process for presidential candidates.

The nomination race itself had foretold the problems. Senator Eugene McCarthy's anti-Vietnam War stance and narrow second-place finish in the New Hampshire

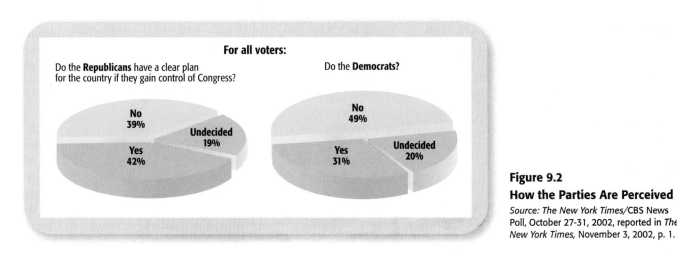

Figure 9.2
How the Parties Are Perceived

*Source: The New York Times/*CBS News Poll, October 27-31, 2002, reported in *The New York Times,* November 3, 2002, p. 1.

▶ Can you locate the presidential candidate? Bill Bradley, standing at far right, looks unhappy campaigning among commuters on a ferry boat near Seattle as he tries, unsuccessfully, to save his race for the Democratic nomination from certain defeat to Al Gore.

primary had convinced President Lyndon B. Johnson to end his reelection campaign. Then Senator Robert F. Kennedy entered the race, and though he was far behind, his victory in the winner-take-all primary in California seemed to indicate that he would be nominated. However, his assassination by Sirhan Sirhan right after the primary narrowed the race to McCarthy and Vice President Hubert Humphrey, who had entered no primaries at all but was amassing significant support from the caucuses and party leaders behind the scenes.

It was at the Democratic National Convention during several hot days in Chicago that holders of opposing perspectives clashed dramatically in front of the TV cameras. Inside the convention hall, party leaders, led by Chicago machine boss Mayor Richard Daley, tried to direct the party's nomination to their candidate, Hubert Humphrey. But outside, Vietnam War protesters, led by Tom Hayden, Jerry Rubin, and a group later known as the "Chicago Seven," clashed violently with police as they shouted, "The whole world's watching! The whole world's watching!" The party leaders were unable to contain the rising force of the next generation of political activists, who demanded more opportunity to participate in the nomination process. As the news broadcasts switched back and forth between the two scenes, clashes broke out inside the convention hall itself, and national broadcaster John Chancellor of NBC was escorted out when he tried to report on events Democratic party leaders did not want exposed.[25] As a result of this disaster, Humphrey got the nomination, but was too far behind in the election to win in November, as many party faithful sat out the early part of the campaign.

The Chicago convention was a watershed in American politics. Its most important accomplishment was to create widespread agreement that future party nominees had to depend on a deeper base of support than just the party hierarchy. Candidates at all levels in American politics since then have increasingly had to pass muster with the party rank-and-file in primaries before gaining the right to wear the party label in a general election.

Before the Chicago convention adjourned, activists succeeded in passing a resolution requiring that by 1972 all state parties "give all Democrats a full, meaningful, and timely opportunity to participate" in the selection of delegates. To create guidelines for compliance, the Democratic National Committee created the Commission on Party Structure and Delegate Selection, usually called the **McGovern-Fraser Commission** (after its chair, Senator George McGovern of South Dakota, and its vice chair, Representative Donald Fraser of Minnesota). This commission had far-reaching effects on the character of American politics. Its recommendations,

McGovern-Fraser Commission
Democratic party commission that after the 1968 national convention opened up meetings and votes to a large variety of party activists, made primaries rather than caucuses the common means of choosing convention delegates, weakened the power of party leaders, and set up rules to ensure that a wide range of party members could participate fully in all party operations.

largely adopted by the Democratic party, opened up meetings and votes to a large variety of party activists, made primaries rather than caucuses the common means of choosing convention delegates, weakened the power of party leaders, and set up rules to ensure that a wide range of party members—especially women, young people, and minority group representatives—could participate fully in all party operations.

Although Republicans did not adopt these same reforms in all the details, they did follow Democrats on the essential points. Most of their delegates to the national convention, as well as their nominees for most lower-level offices, are now also chosen through party primaries. No longer can a handful of leaders in either party dictate who the party will nominate for any office or what the party will stand for in an upcoming election.[26]

The Results of Reform   It is often said that every reform creates a series of unintended consequences, some of which may prove even less popular than the system the reform was designed to improve. States were so frustrated by the confusion and expense of implementing the many rule changes that they simply adopted a primary system. As a result, it became possible for a candidate such as George McGovern, who did not represent the mainstream of the Democratic party, to win the nomination in 1972 by bypassing the party and going directly to the voters. Many observers are dissatisfied with the post–1968 party reforms; they level particularly harsh criticism against the current dominance of primaries in the party nomination process.

As a result of this criticism, in 1984 the Democratic party revised its rules to bring elected and party officials back into the nominating process. They did this by creating a certain number of "independent" delegate spots (now over 650 of the more than 2,000 delegates) and allowing party and elected officials to attend the convention as unpledged **superdelegates.** The idea was that the presence of these superdelegates would get more media attention and provide a display of party unity. Because these delegates were not bound by primary elections, a candidate would still need the support of national party leaders to get the nomination. This process did not work as expected in 2000, Vice President Gore received the commitments of the vast majority of these delegates before a state vote was ever cast. This gave him a tremendous early advantage over Bill Bradley.

The winds of reform that swept through the presidential nomination system touched party processes at every level in both parties. In the past candidates gained party nominations by working within the party hierarchy, rising through party ranks, and demonstrating party loyalty to the inner circle of leaders. Anyone who now wishes to run for office in a partisan election anywhere in the United States must first win a party primary or caucus, one likely to be contested by other ambitious party figures. The implications of this change are enormous. Politicians stopped working within the party to please a small group of leaders and now work outside party structures to please a large mass of relatively uninformed voters.

As a result of this shift in focus from party elites to party masses, money became increasingly important in American politics. This development was another unexpected and unintended consequence of the democratization of candidate selection. Yet it stands to reason that it costs more to sway a large number of people than a small number. In the past those who desired party nominations needed to influence only a few people who had a say in the decision—at most a few hundred, more typically a few dozen, and in some cases a handful of party leaders. Today decision makers (that is, registered party voters) number in the millions.

The change is so great that nomination races are now decided well before the national conventions, which have become so reduced in importance that the national networks are debating whether to cover them on television. To reach today's decision makers, a prospective candidate needs to hire a team of campaign specialists, conduct polls, create and mail out an impressive array of literature, and, most important, buy time on television.

superdelegates Delegates to the Democratic National Convention who are not bound to vote for any particular candidate; usually prominent members of the party or elected officials.

THE ROAD TO DEMOCRACY

Chicago, 1968, to Philadelphia and Los Angeles, 2000: The Vanishing Presidential Convention

The presidential nomination process was changed forever as a result of the events at the 1968 Democratic National Convention in Chicago. The result of the 2000 election may change the process once again. National party conventions were once the centerpiece of American politics.

THAT WAS THEN . . .

In 1940 citizens captured the Republican convention with chants of "We Want Willkie" granting Wendell Willkie the opportunity to lose to Franklin D. Roosevelt. The same happened to Adlai Stevenson in 1952, who after not even running in the primaries for President, was chosen by the Democrats to run against Dwight Eisenhower. By 1968, though, the Democratic party was deeply divided: on the one side the peace advocates opposing the Vietnam war and protestors opposing the lack of civil rights for African Americans, on the other side southern conservatives and their states' rights agenda. Fueled by the opportunity to carry out their battle on national television, the recipe for political party disaster was evident in Chicago.

The field for the nomination appeared to be wide open after a turbulent nomination season. President Lyndon Johnson, stung by the intense criticism of his Vietnam and civil rights policies, and by his narrow margin of victory over antiwar Senator Eugene McCarthy in the New Hampshire primary, had announced on March 31 that he would not run for reelection. While Senator Robert Kennedy of New York seemed on his way to making a serious challenge for the nomination after winning the "winner-take-all" primary in California, his assassination reopened the nomination. So the race was left to the Establishment candidate, liberal Vice President Hubert Horatio Humphrey of Minnesota and antiwar Senator Eugene McCarthy.

▲ As police and anti–Vietnam demonstrators, led by Tom Hayden, Abbie Hoffman, and the "Chicago Seven," clashed violently outside the 1968 Democratic party convention, onlookers began chanting, "The whole world's watching! The whole world's watching!"

While African Americans, antiwar delegates, women, and young people prepared to vote and lobby in Chicago for McCarthy and the antiwar movement, Mayor Richard Daley prepared his own plan. Though Humphrey had entered no primaries (some said because he missed filing deadlines; others believed that he did so deliberately as not to endure defeats), he had won enough votes in the party elite-dominated caucus states, where the delegates are chosen only by meetings, many of which were secret, that he had the advantage going into the convention. Then

In addition, the electronic media have taken on a new and important role in American politics. To impress the large mass of the electorate that votes in primaries, candidates must invade their consciousness by appearing on the dominant media of the age. The centrality of television in modern political campaigns raises campaign costs and also changes politicians' behavior. Success on television does not always go to those who can craft clever sound bites and look attractive, but people with these skills are surely at an advantage in the struggle for power over those who lack them.

And increasingly, interest groups have become powerful and influential. Candidates need workers, support services, and money. They have found those resources in the variety of strong interest groups that have sprung up to promote specialized causes. Symbolic of this development is the growing influence of **political action committees (PACs),** which promote specific interest groups' agendas. Those who won elections in the past owed much to the traditional party hierarchy; now they owe much to their numerous interest group backers. Interest group and PAC lobbying has grown to such an extent that in the 2000 election the Democratic party

political action committees (PACs)
Committees formed as the fund-raising and distribution arm of a specific interest group.

Daley and the leaders excluded some state delegations and many activists for McCarthy. In addition, members of the press such as Tom Brokaw and Dan Rather were prevented from reporting on events while the process was rigged for Humphrey. Meanwhile, in Grant Park, some two miles from the convention hall, where Daley was keeping them bottled up with city policemen, antiwar protesters opposed the events in the convention while getting beaten by police and thrown into paddy wagons to be taken off to jail. "The whole world's watching! The whole world's watching!" they chanted, in news report scenes that were interspliced with scenes from inside the convention hall where events were being rigged for the democratic establishment candidate.

The American public was so horrified by what it saw that the Democrats were terribly split in their support. Humphrey got the nomination, but his candidacy for the presidency in the weeks following never got off the ground, and he narrowly lost a presidential election to Richard Nixon that could have been easily won by the Democrats. Some in fact believe that if the election season had gone just two weeks longer, the Democrats would have won. The controversy continued as the leaders of the antiwar convention protest—including Tom Hayden, Jerry Rubin, and Abbie Hoffman—the so-called "Chicago Seven," were defended by William Kunstler in a turbulent political trial.

Having seen the damage done by closing the convention and by its presidential selection process, the Democratic party created the McGovern-Fraser Commission, named for South Dakota Senator George McGovern and Minnesota Congressman Don Fraser, to reform the nomination process by opening it up. Women, minorities, and young people would now be included in a much more open process. The rules that were adopted were so complicated, though, that many states simply created a state primary system, which was much easier to operate. As a result, more than 70 percent of the delegate votes would now be chosen directly by the people. And, not coincidentally, the first

choice of those voters for the Democrats in 1972 would be for the man who knew the rules best—George McGovern—whose grass-roots campaign was led by a young director named Gary Hart, who refined the process of mobilizing circles of voters for a candidate. One day Hart himself would try to do the same for himself, but fail when scandal overtook him.

THIS IS NOW . . .

By 2000, largely because for years this reformed nomination process resulted in the clear selection of candidates beforehand, there was so little viewer interest in the Convention that network executives decided to greatly reduce the media's coverage of the convention. Each network covered the meeting for only a few hours a night, focusing on key speeches, the selection of a vice-presidential candidate, and the presidential candidates' acceptance speeches. The reason is clear. "These conventions are no longer what they used to be." Says veteran news anchor Bob Schieffer, "There was a time when all of these delegates came together, and you really saw something being decided at the convention. [Now] they're almost like a boat show. Both parties come along, they roll out the new model, we come out, look them over, listen to them, write stories about them, and that's about it."

The question is, with additional television networks like CNN, MSNBC, and FOXNEWS, whether there will be any extended television coverage of the meetings in the future, or, with the advent of electronic communication technology, whether there will be any meetings at all and instead the meetings will be held like the Reform Party's effort in the 2000 election, by satellite uplink, or perhaps on computers.

Sources: James Endrst, "Conventions Suffer Low Viewer Turnout" *The Hartford Courant*, July 27, 2000, and Robert Dallek, "The Real Race to the White House Begins," *Australian Financial Review*, July 21, 2000.

was able to raise $520 million, with about half of that coming from "soft money" donations, and the Republican Party raised $716 million, with a third of that as "soft money." With no limits placed on soft money fund-raising until after the November 2002 election by the new Bipartisan Campaign Finance Reform Act of 2002, the huge fund-raising efforts from these sources continued. Planning for the upcoming Congressional elections, three different Republican fund-raising committees raised $204 million, which was $86 million more than that raised by the parallel Democratic party fund-raising committees. When combined with the $100 million campaign war chest raised by President Bush, the Republicans were poised for their successful 2002 Congressional and state government electoral campaign.[27]

Finally, with the destruction of the old party leadership that once provided continuity and cohesion for the party, politicians who win high office now do so on their own and see themselves as independent of the discipline of party structures. The result is a decline in party cohesiveness. In particular, the Democratic party in recent years has appeared to many observers like an uneasy coalition of squabbling individualists rather than a unified group of like-minded team players. Politicians'

APPROACHING DIVERSITY

Courting the Hispanic Vote

The Republican Party has launched an all-out crusade to court the Hispanic vote for the 2004 presidential campaign. They are fueled by a single calculation—if Hispanics and other minority groups vote in the same proportions as they did in 2000, and nothing else changes, President Bush will lose by 3 million votes.

In the 2000 election Bush—despite his connection to his Hispanic sister-in-law (Governor Jeb Bush's wife), his serviceable Spanish, his relationship with the Hispanic voters in Texas as that state's governor, and his emphasis on public education in both English and Spanish for Hispanics—only received 35% of the Hispanic vote, while Al Gore received 62% of the Hispanic vote. "I know I have an image to battle," said the President, "It is definitely important . . . to reach out to voter groups that don't necessarily believe the Republican Party's message is meant for them." Part of the reason for this gap is that issues which traditionally are being advanced by the Democratic party—raising the minimum wage, education and increasing government services—also appeal to the Hispanic community. Since census and survey data show that the Hispanics are now 12% of the United States population, which is up from 9% in 1990, and with vast further increases in population predicted, Republicans fear that if changes are not made in their relationship to this community, they will soon have trouble in normally Republican states such as Colorado, Florida, Missouri, and Nevada, as well as in "swing states" that can go either way, such as Michigan and New Jersey, all states with growing Hispanic populations.

Realizing all of this, the Republican Party has launched a multi-faceted campaign to win over the Hispanic voter. First, the President is thinking seriously of granting legal residency status to the more than 3 million illegal immigrants in the country. He has also announced that he is thinking of appointing the first Hispanic to the Supreme Court when a vacancy occurs. Realizing that the Democratic party has registration tables outside of courthouses where new citizens are being sworn in, the Republican party has done the same thing. The White House is also looking into ways to improve business prospects for small businessmen in the Hispanic community, by teaching them English and business skills. In June 2001, the White House also decided to stop military exercises on the Puerto Rican island of Vieques. The President has ordered that one in ten administration jobs be filled by Hispanics and his Saturday radio addresses are re-recorded in Spanish for this community.

"For us to be successful . . . we've got to expand," says Jack Oliver, the deputy director of the Republican National Committee, "We have to make the Republican Party a place that is welcoming, and that's a long-term challenge." Changing the image will not be an easy. Republican Jeremy Gonzalez Ibrahim of Pennsylvania says "A lot of Latinos think the Republican Party is just for rich people," Still, as David Kramer, chairman of the Nebraska Republican Party says, "We're taking baby steps, but this is the beginning. What's at stake for the Republican Party is political survivability. What's at stake from the Hispanic perspective is significant political influence at the local, state, and national levels."

Source: Judy Keen and Richard Benedetto, "Republican Party on a Crusade to win over Hispanic, Americans," *USA Today,* August 7, 2001.

ability to get their own campaign money has enabled them to go their own way. In the 2000 election Democrat Jon Corzine contributed nine of every ten dollars to his campaign for the New Jersey Senate seat against Robert D. Franks, and won in a race in which over $70 million was spent. In the 27th District in California, surrounding Pasadena, Democrat Adam Schiff, a former political science professor at Glendale Community College and a U.S. Attorney, defeated Republican James Rogan, one of the leaders against Bill Clinton in his 1998 impeachment fight, in a race which cost $10 million, the most ever spent in a Congressional campaign.

Even what at first appeared to be a new development in party politics after the Republican takeover of Congress in 1994 now stands as another example of the fragmentation of American party politics characteristic of the post–Vietnam era. During the famous "first 100 days" of the 104th Congress in 1995, Speaker Newt Gingrich was able to fashion considerable party cohesiveness among the freshmen members. However, as his policies became more moderate on taxes, budget reform, and other social issues in order to compromise with President Clinton, the cohesiveness lessened considerably. This erosion of support continued as Gingrich became embroiled in an ethics scandal over his incorrect testimony to an investigating committee about the tax status of funds to support a college course he was teaching. As a result, Gingrich was sanctioned by the House and forced to pay a $300,000 fine (which he borrowed from Bob Dole), and after he was blamed for his party's unexpected loss of seats in the 1998 Congressional election he left the Speakership. Though he won re-election to his seat, he resigned from the body. The eventual successor to the Speakership, J. Dennis Hastert (IL) has found it challenging to keep the ultra-conservative members of his party in control in seeking to pass legislation. Before Jim Jeffords' party switch in 2001, then-Majority Leader Trent Lott (R.-MS), was also having trouble keeping the increasingly conservative and restive members of his Republican party under control. With the split in the Republican party between the independent reformers who followed John McCain in the 2000 election, the moderates who identified with Jim Jeffords, and the conservative establishment following the Bush administration, together with the split in the Democratic party between the old-style liberals like Ted Kennedy and the "new Democrat" progressive reformers like Tom Daschle (SD) and John Edwards (NC), this trend toward party fragmentation seems likely to continue.

Why a Two-Party System?

Throughout American history, two political parties have been the rule rather than the exception. Yet most democratic nations are characterized by a **multiparty system** in which five, ten, and sometimes even more parties regularly compete in elections, win seats, and have some chance of gaining power. Why is it that only two parties flourish in the United States?[28]

Institutional Factors

The most frequent explanation for the emergence and survival of the two-party system is the way the United States elects public officials. Known as the *single-member district electoral system,* it is widely believed to inhibit the development of third parties. In other democratic nations, districts are often, but not always, large enough to contain many representatives, and each party elects about as many representatives as its proportion of the vote in that large district. In a ten-member district, for instance, a party obtaining 10 percent of the vote gets one elected legislator. If that party averages 10 percent of the vote across the country, it will end up with 10 percent of the members of the national legislature. Then if it maneuvers sensibly, it may be asked to form part of a governing coalition. The upshot of such a multi-member district, or proportional representation system, is that small parties can gain seats and power, so there is an incentive for minor parties to form and contest elections.

In the United States, the incentives all favor the two large parties. The entire country is divided into **single-member districts,** and each district seat is awarded to the candidate with the most votes. Small parties, say one that wins 10 percent in every district across the nation, do not get a single seat in the legislature. With that performance, they would lose in each district to one of the two big parties. Hence, after every election, small parties end up with no seats and no power, and they gradually fade away as supporters grow discouraged. Potential supporters for a third party simply join one of the two big parties and promote their policy aims within a successful political grouping where those aims have some chance of being implemented.[29]

This system not only prevents the creation of third parties but also inhibits breakaway factions of the two major parties from setting up shop on their own. Disgruntled party subgroups have no incentive to leave and form their own parties, because doing so will lead to political impotence.

Another institutional element favoring two-party competition is the **electoral college.** By its very design, the electoral college puts smaller parties at a disadvantage. The system produces, in effect, fifty-one winner-take-all state (including the District

multiparty system A political system in which five to ten or more parties regularly compete in elections, win seats, and have some chance of gaining power. This is promoted by systems with proportional representation and is characteristic of most democratic nations.

single-member districts Districts in which a seat goes to the candidate with the most votes. In this system, small parties, say one that wins 10 percent in every district across the nation, do not get a single seat in the legislature.

electoral college The group of 538 electors who meet separately in each of their states and the District of Columbia on the first Monday following the second Wednesday in the December after a national presidential election. Their majority decision officially elects the president and vice president of the United States.

of Columbia) contests. Each state is allotted a certain number of electoral college votes, depending on its representation in Congress. Votes for president are then counted by state, and in all but two small states (Maine and Nebraska), whichever candidate comes in first in that state gains *all* of that state's electoral votes, no matter how close the contest, even if the winning candidate falls short of a majority of the ballots cast. There is no consolation prize for finishing second, much less third or fourth, in American politics. A candidate comes in first or gets nothing. For that reason, many voters are reluctant to "throw their vote away" on a candidate outside the mainstream. They tend, in the end, to align with one of the two major parties.

Occasionally, a significant portion of the electorate will cast off such inhibitions and risk supporting a third-party candidate, as in the case of Ross Perot. But consider the result of Perot's 1992 campaign. Although he captured some 20 million votes—about 19 percent of the total—he did not receive a single vote in the electoral college. The same was true in 1996, when Perot's overall support was cut by more than half to 9 percent of the voting electorate, and his nearly 8 million votes again gained him no electoral college votes at all. What matters, then, is where those votes are located. And remember that citizen votes do not make a president; only electoral college votes do. It is hardly surprising, then, that Perot-style candidacies have been the exception rather than the rule. Nevertheless, the votes received in the 2000 election by third-party candidates Patrick Buchanan for the Reform Party and Ralph Nader for the Green Party had such an impact on the presidential election that Nader's votes, most likely siphoned from the Al Gore's potential supporters might well have resulted in the presidential win by George Bush.

Cultural Factors

Some scholars believe that the American two-party system is built into prevailing cultural norms and values. They point to the United States' supposed traditions of moderation, deliberation, and compromise. Whereas the French or Italian political cultures—out of which have sprung vigorous multiparty democracies—are often described as volatile and fragmented, American culture is supposedly centrist, devoid of the ideological extremes, class divisions, and group hatreds that produce political fragmentation elsewhere. This theory suggests that with most citizens clustering at the center of the spectrum, the United States has no room for a variety of parties. These conditions produce a natural setting for a two party system, with each vying for the largest constituency of moderate voters.

This cultural explanation was accepted for decades, but in recent years scholars have begun to question it.[30] Particularly since the 1960s, American political culture appears to have become fragmented. Bitter struggles over civil rights, Vietnam, women's rights, and abortion have shattered the country's veneer of consensus and may help explain what many see as a weakening in the pattern of stable two-party dominance. In recent years, some of the most volatile issues tearing at the fabric of the two-party system and its stability have been essentially cultural—race, gender, sexuality, and family values.

Party Identification

Another attempt to explain the two-party system centers on electorate psychology. Explanations of this type stress the deep-seated, enduring nature of party attachments. Many voters develop lasting loyalty to a political party, often because that party served their needs on some crucial issue. Thus, Republicans gained the loyalty of millions in the 1860s by standing for national unity and the abolition of slavery. Democrats gained lifelong supporters in the 1930s with their attempts to mitigate the worst aspects of the Depression. Furthermore, voters have long memories. They stay faithful to their party for years, even for life, often passing these loyalties on to their children.

QUOTE ... UNQUOTE

"The political debate has settled into two familiar ruts. The Republicans are infatuated with the 'magic' of the market and reflexively criticize government as the enemy of freedom, and the Democrats distrust the market, preach government as the answer to our problems, and prefer the bureaucrat they know to the consumer they can't control."

Former Senator Bill Bradley

QUOTE ... UNQUOTE

"I have no personal agenda. My goal is to get them to do it, to educate voters and hope both parties repent and be reborn. But getting reborn takes a little time. They've got to deliver."

Ross Perot

This psychological orientation, the long-term propensity to think positively of and vote regularly for a political party, is what political scientists call **party identification.** It does not explain the origins of the U.S. two-party system, but it does help explain its persistence. The intense psychological ties that keep party voters faithful ensure both parties of long-term support. These old attachments hamper any new party trying to break through the status quo to gain followers.[31]

Minor Parties

Despite the power of the two major American parties, **minor** or **third parties** have made appearances in every decade of American history. Why do they appear, how have they performed, and what do they accomplish?[32]

Why Minor Parties Appear

With most Americans clustering in the middle range of the ideological spectrum, the two major parties take relatively moderate positions on most controversial policies. Any clear ideological stand far to the right or left of the average voter would alienate a large portion of the potential electorate. Since the major parties aim at winning votes and gaining office, they cast their nets as widely as possible for broad inclusiveness. Both major parties end up focusing on the same central segment of the electorate, but do not necessarily give equal emphasis to the same issues. Frequently, the emergence of a third party that is talking about issues the major parties seek to avoid will signal that a realignment of the voters, or at the very least a restructuring of the major parties, is about to occur.

In like fashion, the major parties cannot aim their appeals too obviously at just one subgroup of the population, be it farmers, union members, or gun owners. Since by definition any one social group represents a minority of Americans, any party that becomes identified as that group's champion risks alienating other segments of the population.

This lack of ideological purity and the absence of narrow group promotion directly affect the character and formation of the minor American parties. Third parties are formed when an issue arises of such intensity to some Americans that they just can't be satisfied by the relatively moderate stands taken by both Democrats and Republicans. They are also formed when some group feels totally ignored and left out of the mainstream political process. But third parties that result from the organization of these interests almost always remain minor, or sometimes have their platforms co-opted by one or both of the major parties.

Minor Party Performance

Third parties do, on occasion, make waves, usually when an issue or set of issues become joined to a popular or charismatic leader. Under these conditions, minor party efforts have done remarkably well. Theodore Roosevelt, a former president, turned in the best performance of any minor party candidate. In 1912 he ran on the Progressive ticket and garnered 27 percent of the popular vote, along with 88 electoral votes out of 531. Most remarkable about his achievement was placing second in the balloting ahead of an incumbent president, William Howard Taft.

Another significant minor party candidacy occurred in 1968, when Alabama's segregationist governor, George Wallace, a Southern Democrat, ran as an American Independent. Wallace captured 14 percent of the popular vote and 46 electoral votes. In 1980 a former Republican and member of the House of Representatives, John Anderson, ran as an independent candidate, receiving 7 percent of the popular vote but no electoral votes.

Texas billionaire H. Ross Perot stunned many observers when he ran in 1992 without any party affiliation, and after dropping out and later reentering the race,

party identification A psychological orientation, or long-term propensity, to think positively of and vote regularly for a particular political party.

minor parties (or third parties) Parties in the American system other than the current Democrats or Republicans.

▶ Consumer advocate Ralph Nader's campaign for the Presidency in 2000 as the candidate for the Green Party is credited by many as having tipped the election to the Republican party.

still won 19 percent of the popular vote. His organization, United We Stand America, however, was little more than a label attached to a group of amateur enthusiasts; at that time it was nothing like an organized party. In 1995 Perot's organization held a three-day national convention that once again raised the possibility of a third party, and by 1996 it had become the Reform Party. In a nominating convention held on August 18 that was beamed from Valley Forge, Pennsylvania, over cable TV, its members selected Perot as its presidential candidate over former Colorado Governor Richard Lamm. Today Reform Party members are frequently identified as a new "radicalized center" in American politics that Democratic and Republican Party leaders cannot afford to ignore.

Despite these modest successes, third-party candidates have rarely been a significant force in American national elections. As we have seen, they face the major psychological hurdle of party identification. Since most voters already feel an emotional link to one of the two major parties, voters are rarely eager to wrench themselves away from their traditional voting habits to support a new, little-known group with no governing track record.

Beyond psychology, candidates outside the two-party mainstream face serious procedural obstacles. To be listed on local and state ballots, minor party candidates must obtain a certain number of signatures that demonstrate a minimal level of support. With few activists and little public recognition, minor parties frequently can't even get on the ballot. At the national level, they have enormous difficulty meeting eligibility requirements for federal election campaign funds. They also face a key difficulty in simply making people aware of who they are and what they stand for. To capture national attention, candidates with little more than local or regional notoriety must court a national press often intent on following only the major candidates.

In the 2000 election a vivid example of these procedural obstacles was provided when the Reform and Green parties were denied permission to appear in the presidential debates unless they had 15 percent support in the public opinion polls. By also ruling that both third parties had failed to qualify for additional federal campaign support, the Federal Election Commission made it even more difficult for them to win.

Overall, the barriers to the creation of a successful third party are enormous.[33] Although the Reform Party is now a minor political party, its predecessor, United We Stand America, was more successful as a grass-roots public interest group whose goal was to make both political parties more responsive to the American people.

Functions of Minor Parties

Although minor parties rarely attain power in the United States, they do perform important functions in a democracy. In a way, they act as wake-up calls to the two major parties. If enough dissatisfaction exists to fuel a third-party movement, both Democrats and Republicans quickly pay close attention. Almost always one, and often both, parties adopt enough of the third party's proposals to defuse the grievances the third party represents—and incidentally deflate the chances of that third party ever gaining power.

A prime illustration of this process can be seen in the "radical" platform that Socialist Eugene Debs endorsed in his 1904 campaign for the presidency. It included such "subversive" promises as support for women's right to vote, an eight-hour day for factory workers, and an end to child labor. All of these ideas, and many others from the Socialist agenda of that era, have long since become mainstream concepts, accepted by both major parties and most of the American electorate. The same was true of George Wallace's "Law 'n' Order" campaign in 1968 for the American Independent party, which held very conservative views about the control of crime and the dismantling of civil rights programs. Richard Nixon adopted many of these views, becoming increasingly conservative in his campaign rhetoric and promising to appoint more strict constructionist federal judges to accomplish these goals, so that he began losing significant voter support to Democrat Hubert H. Humphrey. Finally, Ross Perot's constant call through the Reform party for budget deficit reduction led to the adoption of this proposal by both major parties.

By being the first to champion original ideas that may later become widely endorsed, minor parties perform a vital service for the democratic process. But even if their ideas never get adopted, they at least encourage open discussion of new proposals, force mainstream groups to rethink and justify the status quo, and give life to key democratic norms, such as free speech and the right of all citizens to organize to promote their interests.

▲ A supporter of Ross Perot, the candidate for president from the Reform party in 1996, protested when he was excluded from the second debate between President Clinton and Republican nominee Robert Dole. Perot had been allowed to participate in the 1992 debates, but his successor, Patrick Buchanan, was not allowed into the 2000 debates.

The Party in Government

Although not a word can be found in the Constitution about political parties, and the framers hoped that parties would play no role in the emerging republic, today government institutions at all levels are organized through the party system. Party leaders run administrations at the state and national levels; many act as city or town mayors or hold other executive offices in a variety of political settings. Members of Congress and legislators in each state hold party caucuses practically every day. These meetings help them decide the direction of party policy and the best tactics to gain their ends. In Congress and in most state legislatures, the leadership of the chamber, the committee chairs, and committee membership rolls all result from partisan votes, and party members usually sit together on opposite sides of the main aisle. Party is simply the first and dominant force in all of the upper-level institutions of American political life.

Among other things, party significantly influences the behavior of individual politicians. It proves to be, for instance, the single most powerful variable for predicting how American legislators will vote. The number of times that members of Congress vote based on party affiliation has steadily increased from below 60 percent in 1970 to over 80 percent in the 1990s. This was clearly seen during the Clinton impeachment battle of 1998 when the two parties voted as a unified group over

QUOTE ... UNQUOTE

"Television has changed the nominating conventions from deliberative, volatile bodies to orchestrated showcases."

George Comstock, "Television in America"

90% of the time. By 2000, the Republican members of Congress were voting based on party affiliation more than 85% of the time, while the Democrats were doing the same over 80% of the time.[34] Simply put, party ideology matters. Democrats don't vote the same way as Republicans do.

? Question for Reflection: The framers did not envision political parties in their original approach to democracy. How have parties affected the way democracy is shaped?

The Importance of Party Ideology

It often surprises outsiders to learn just how much party matters in governance. Yet why should we be surprised? We already know that Democrats and Republicans hold different ideologies and represent different segments of society. Given the reasonably clear party differences, we should logically expect the parties to create different public policies when they control government. That has indeed been the case. What government does changes sharply when power clearly shifts from one party to the other. Democrats create liberal policies; Republicans create conservative ones.

An excellent way to illustrate party difference is to compare the voting records of Republicans and Democrats. For this purpose, we can make use of a device called an *interest group rating scheme*. Many interest groups routinely rank members of Congress on a scale from 0 to 100, as a way of publicizing each member's level of support for the group's aims. (The closer to 100, the higher the level of support.) The best known of these groups, and indeed the one that started this practice back in the 1940s, is the liberal Americans for Democratic Action. The ADA, as it is known, each year gives each member of Congress a rating that represents the percentage of times that member voted as the ADA desired on the thirty or forty most important bills taken up by Congress that year. The resulting number provides a rough idea of how "liberal" a member of Congress is. Ratings of 60 or higher indicate a clear liberal. Ratings of 40 or lower suggest a conservative. Middle numbers delineate moderates.

No scheme of this sort can be perfectly precise. A difference of 5 or 10 points between two legislators may reflect little more than a vote or two missed because of illness. Still, major differences over time clearly indicate different voting patterns and different philosophies. Year after year, Democrats score between 60 and 80 on the ADA scale, while Republicans rank in the 10 to 20 range. There can be little

▶ Former House Minority Leader Richard Gephardt (D.-MO), here being observed by Democratic National Committee Chairman Terry McAuliffe, tried without success to rally his party, leading to his decision not to run for reelection to the Congressional leadership.

question about the basic pattern. Although some moderates can be found in both parties, the bulk of Republicans are conservative, while the bulk of Democrats are liberal. No Democrat, for example, signed onto the Republicans' Contract with America.

If this is the case, it really matters which party gains control of government. Committee chairs in Congress have a major impact on policy outcomes. They shepherd bills they like through the legislature and find ways to kill those they don't. The policies that emerge from party members acting in government greatly affect how the public views these organizations (see Figure 9.3).

Political Parties and the 2002 Election

David Broder, a leading American journalist, wrote a grim analysis several years ago of America's party system entitled *The Party's Over.*[35] He claimed that American political parties were disintegrating, that they had lost their traditional stabilizing power over the electoral and governmental processes and were being replaced by a proliferation of special interest groups and the imagery of television.

Is the party really over? Many argue that declining rates of party identification, voter apathy, and the lack of formal constraints to ensure party allegiance all indicate that American political parties are headed toward extinction. Optimists, however, see hope for the future of parties and even a role for them in the revival of a more participatory and stronger democracy. They argue that parties have responded reasonably well to the many sources of change over the past three decades. After

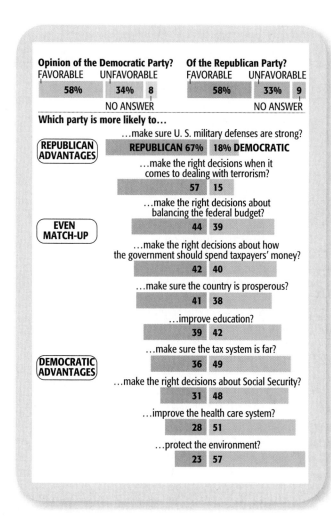

Figure 9.3
**Public Images
of the Two Parties**

Based on interviews conducted with 1,034 adults nationwide January 21 through 24. Those who gave other answers are not shown.

Source: The New York Times, January 27, 2002.

all, despite social upheavals, new forms of technology and communications, changing attitudes toward politics, institutional reforms in government, generational shifts in support for politics, and major crises in government, parties have stayed afloat and even maintained their hold over a large percentage of the American electorate. Could dying institutions have such staying power?

Political parties are crucial democratic structures that link the popular will to governmental outcomes. For the 2002 Congressional election one poll revealed that the American people, when asked what issue was "the number one problem," were most concerned about the economy (27%), terrorism (13%), and education (6%) a distant third.[36] These are all policies on which the two political parties disagree. While Democrats were bolstered by the history that the party in control of the White House nearly always loses seats in the off-year Congressional election, Republicans proved by their victory that the issues most important to the voters worked in their favor. Republicans demonstrated that the terrorism issue was still uppermost in the voters' minds in the 2002 election, as President Bush's policies maintained positive voter support. Democrats, on the other hand, were unable to link the Republicans to the on-going sluggish economy. Meanwhile, the Bush administration's support of education reform had an impact on the electoral picture as the voters were now split over which party they prefer on this issue, an issue the Democrats once dominated. In the end, though, it was the possible war with Iraq, homeland security, and the continuation of the tax cut that determined the outcome of the 2002 Congressional elections. Led by the heavy campaigning of President Bush, the Republicans gained control of both the House and the Senate, setting them up for the 2004 presidential race.

DEMOCRACY IN THE NEW MILLENNIUM

Democrats Gain Ground in the Internet Race for Voters

"Reach out and touch someone," a phone company used to use as the tag line to one of their advertising campaigns, and through the use of its new interactive website the Democratic party will seek to do exactly that. The new Website can automatically send tailored messages to voters. For years the Democrats have seen the Republican Party take the lead in reaching voters through direct mail campaigns, the use of comprehensive voter lists, computer email, and Web technology. Now, through the use of its new Website, Democratic party Chairman Terry McAuliffe promises that they are "ready to be a 21st century party."

The new Website asks visitors to answer a series of questions on their political views on such issues as women's rights, economic interests, and voting rights, and develops a profile of each user's political preferences. This profile can then be used to plot out an automatic series of messages that will be sent to the user targeted especially for them. Says McAuliffe, they can "hit a button and send out messages in 50 different languages, with fifty different messages: [such as] 'We need you to register voters,' . . . The goal always is to get new activists into the party and turn these activists into donors." This is quite an improvement from the old party communication system that sent out the same message to everyone, one message at a time.

One of the things that the new Website will allow the DNC to do is to court Hispanic voters. After polling potential Hispanic voters, the DNC can determine which issues are most important to their community and tailor direct messages that take account of the regional and/or ethnic preferences of these voters. Thus issues that are important to Puerto Ricans will not be directed toward Mexican-Americans and vice-versa.

The DNC learned this lesson in the crucial Florida vote during the 2000 Presidential campaign. The Republican Party was able to send out tens of thousands of "get out the vote" messages around the state through their advanced email system. Then, after the election was stalemated, it was this system that allowed the Republicans to mobilize their followers to ensure that the members of the party lobbied politicians and the courts to get the final vote count to weigh in their favor.

With the Democrats' new electronic system, the 2004 election will be a high-tech battle of evenly matched tools. For more see www.dnc.org and compare to www.rnc.org.

Thomas B. Edsall, "Democratic party Touts New Interactive Web Site," *Washington Post,* January 23, 2002, p. A23.

The point is clear, then, that beyond the outcome of the 2002 election, each party still has to do its best to fashion a position in the voters' minds that they hope will secure electoral support in the future.[37] But as Jim Jeffords' switch in 2001 showed, in an evenly balanced political situation, sometime the election is not over even after the votes have been counted. As the United States approaches democracy, power has shifted from the few to the many. But sometimes even the few matter greatly. Still, recent changes in the way parties operate are merely part of that ongoing process of democratization that is central to the current pattern of American political development.

SUMMARY

1. Political parties have played a role in American democracy since 1790. The first party system pitted Federalists (led by Hamilton) against Democratic-Republicans (led by Jefferson) and was so unstable that it disappeared between 1816 and 1824. The second party system began with the formation of the Jacksonian Democrats, actually an outgrowth of the Jeffersonian party. Seeking to make the electoral process more democratic, the Jacksonian Democrats replaced the system of nomination by party leaders with a national party convention. Opposition coalesced around a new party, the Whigs.

2. The third party system arose during the 1850s out of conflict over the issue of slavery. The new Republican party was devoted to abolishing slavery, while one branch of the Democratic party supported the Confederate cause. By this time, the Whigs had dropped from sight. The fourth party system began with a realignment in party constituencies in the 1890s and lasted until 1932. During this period the Democratic and Republican parties became highly developed and well organized.

3. The fifth party system began in 1932 with the realignment in party identification known as the New Deal coalition. This broad-based coalition supported the Democratic party and enabled it to dominate national politics until 1968. Although Republicans have won five out of seven presidential elections since then, it is unclear whether another realignment is taking place.

4. Political parties organize the election process by recruiting candidates for public office, representing the desires of voters, and attempting to ensure that their candidates carry out specific policies once in office. They also speak for and unite different groups and their varied interests through the formation of political coalitions. Other important functions of parties are to simplify political choices and organize government and policy making.

5. The local party provides the point of entry for those seeking involvement in politics. At the next level is the state party organization, which acts in conjunction with the state government to conduct primary elections. The national party organization is most active during presidential elections.

6. From the end of the nineteenth century to the middle of the twentieth, local parties often engaged in machine politics, in which party bosses traded jobs, money, and favors for votes and campaign support. Machine politics declined as a result of the creation of the civil service and the modern welfare state as well as the proliferation of primary elections.

7. At the national party conventions delegates from the state parties meet to select presidential and vice presidential candidates and write the party's platform—a statement of principles and policies that it will carry out if its candidates are elected.

8. Some state party organizations select candidates for presidential elections at a caucus, or meeting of party adherents. Other state parties hold primary elections that allow all of the party's members to vote for a candidate. In a closed primary, only citizens who are registered as members of a political party may participate in that party's primary. Open primaries allow registered voters to vote in whichever primary they choose, thus permitting cross-party voting.

9. Since 1968, the presidential selection process has been radically altered as a result of demands for "democratization." Reforms adopted by the Democratic party included selecting candidates by means of primaries rather than caucuses and increasing the diversity of

delegates to national conventions. Some of these reforms were also adopted by the Republican Party.

10. The greater power of rank-and-file party members has reduced the power of party bosses, increased the cost of conducting a campaign, reinforced the dominance of the electronic media in American politics, increased the power of interest groups and political action committees, and brought about a decline in party cohesiveness. The result is a trend toward candidate-centered, rather than party-centered, politics.

11. The single-member district system inhibits the development of third parties and thus produces and maintains a two-party system. In nations with systems of proportional representation, in which more than one member of the legislature can come from the same district, small parties can gain legislative seats and a multiparty system results. The electoral college favors a two-party system because the candidate who wins the most popular votes in a state receives all of that state's electoral votes.

12. Other explanations of the U.S. two-party system include cultural factors. Some believe that the two-party system is built into prevailing cultural norms and values; the tendency toward party identification leads voters to deep-seated, enduring affinity for the major parties.

13. Although minor or third parties usually have no hope of gaining real power, such parties occasionally arise when an issue is not adequately addressed by the major parties. When a minor party has a popular or charismatic leader, it can affect the outcome of elections and force the major parties to adopt or at least consider some of its proposals.

14. Although political parties are not mentioned in the Constitution, government institutions at all levels are organized through the party system. Party membership influences the behavior of individual politicians and leads to the creation of different public policies depending on which party is in control of the government.

KEY TERMS

political parties
realignment
Revolution of 1800
"King Caucus"
primary system
New Deal coalition
recruitment
local party organization
state party organizations
machine politics

national party organization
national party convention
party platform
nomination
caucus
primary election
winner-take-all system
proportional representation
closed primary
open primary

frontloading
McGovern-Fraser Commission
superdelegates
political action committees
  (PACs)
multiparty system
single-member districts
electoral college
party identification
minor (or third) parties

POLISIM ACTIVITY

The Great American Divide

Following the 1932 election, the New Deal Democrats—a coalition of union members, immigrant workers, and people hurt by the Great Depression—established a voting base which dominated the Congress until Newt Gingrich led Republican Revolution in 1994. Now, as memories of the New Deal fade and the agenda of American politics shifts, the alignments of the 1930s and 1940s hold less and less relevance. The Democrat Party will need to create a new voting base if it hopes to return to power. In this simulation, you will study the factors that led to the 1932 election and then try to decide where the Democrats had their support in the 2000 election.

The Political Horizon

Every four years, during the presidential election season, the parties write their platforms, which delineate their principles and policy position and proposals. While these platforms are not binding on individual candidates, they are a good indicator of what that party considers important. This simulation contains two parts. In the first part you can explore which party holds views closest to your own. In the second part you can test your knowledge of the issue positions espoused by the parties.

SUGGESTED READINGS

DICLERICO, ROBERT E. *Political Parties, Campaigns, and Elections.* Upper Saddle River, N.J.: Prentice Hall, 2000. A fine up-to-date textbook dealing with the state of political parties in the election process.

DREW, ELIZABETH. *Showdown: The Struggle Between the Gingrich Congress and the Clinton White House.* New York: Simon & Schuster, 1996. A wonderful recounting and analysis of how party politics has shaped the national political agenda in this study of the policy battles between the Democratic President Clinton and the Republican Congress elected in 1994.

GREEN, JOHN, and DANIEL SHEA. *The State of the Parties: The Changing Role of Contemporary American Parties.* 3d ed. Lanham, Md.: Rowman & Littlefield, 1999. An interesting study of the future of American political parties in a changing democratic system.

JEFFORDS, JAMES M. *My Declaration of Independence.* New York: Simon and Schuster, 2001. A very readable account of why and how Senator Jeffords decided to leave the Republican Party.

JOHNSON, HAYNES, and DAVID BRODER. *The System: The American Way of Politics at the Breaking Point.* Boston: Little, Brown, 1996. Two of America's finest political journalists examine how well the American political system is operating in a review of the political party dispute over the Clinton administration's efforts to create a system of universal health care.

KAYDEN, XANDRA, and EDDIE MAHE, JR. *The Party Goes On: The Persistence of the Two Party System in the United States.* New York: Basic Books, 1985. The first full-scale assessment of the strength of political parties and their impact on national political life.

KEY, V. O. *Southern Politics.* New York: Knopf, 1949. A classic account of one-party politics in the South.

POLSBY, NELSON. *Consequences of Party Reform.* New York: Oxford University Press, 1983. An excellent account of changes in party rules and the impact of those changes on party roles in government.

RANNEY, AUSTIN. *Curing the Mischief of Faction: Party Reform in America.* Berkeley: University of California Press, 1975. A detailed account of the effect of party reforms on politics, with a special focus on the 1972 changes. Should be read with the following:

SHAFER, BYRON E. *Quiet Revolution: The Struggle for the Democratic party and the Shaping of Post-Reform Politics.* Washington, D.C.: Brookings Institution, 1983. The story of party reform from 1968 to 1972 that produced a new era in national politics. The changes altered the very character of presidential politics, from campaign organization to grass-roots participation.

SUNDQUIST, JAMES L. *Dynamics of the Party System: Alignment and Realignment of Political Parties in the United States.* Washington, D.C.: Brookings Institution, 1973. An analysis of the party system and the meaning of realignments in American history.

THOMAS, EVAN, et al. *Back from the Dead: How Clinton Survived the Republican Revolution.* New York: Atlantic Monthly Press, 1997. The story of how the once-liberal Democratic President Bill Clinton repositioned himself in the American political landscape to forge an electoral victory in 1996.

WATTENBERG, MARTIN. *The Decline of American Political Parties, 1952–1996.* Cambridge, Mass.: Harvard University Press, 1989. A scholarly analysis of the declines in party identification, the rise in ticket splitting, and the challenges facing American political parties today.

10 PARTICIPATION, VOTING, AND ELECTIONS

CHAPTER OUTLINE

Approaching Democracy Case Study:
  The Motor-Voter Law, 1995–2002

Introduction: Political Participation
  and Democracy

Who Participates?

A Brief History of Voting in the United States

Voting

Voting Choice

Other Forms of Political Participation

Congressional Elections

Presidential Elections

Money and Elections

APPROACHING DEMOCRACY CASE STUDY

The Motor-Voter Law, 1995–2002

Democracy is a system in which the people govern themselves—or at the very least, play a major role in the governing process. In modern representative democratic systems, the core of popular participation is the vote. If all citizens can easily register to vote and exercise that right, then those candidates who are elected will represent the choice of the populace. Conversely, if most citizens do not have a chance to vote, then leaders will ignore them, leading to mass discontent and long-term disaffection from the political system.

The National Voter Registration Act (NVRA, P.L. 103–31), known as the Motor-Voter Law, was signed by President Bill Clinton in 1993 and went into effect on January 1, 1995. In September of 1995, Attorney General Janet Reno anounced that more than 11 million citizens, the largest single increase in history, registered to vote or updated their voting addresses by the time of the 1996 presidential election. States reported 142,856 registered voters nationwide, amounting to 73% of the voting age population. According to the Federal Election Commission, this was the highest percentage of voter registration since reliable records were first available in 1960.[1]

The Motor-Voter Law was designed to encourage voter registration by simplifying the registration process and, thus, it was hoped, increase voter turnout for elections. The law required states to provide registration services through driver's license agencies and public assistance and disability offices, and by mail-in registration. No citizen can vote without being registered, but in the past the registration process in most states was cumbersome, time consuming, and unpublicized. As a result, many citizens lost their right to vote by failing to get their names on the voting list. In all but a few states, Americans must register several weeks before an election if they wish to vote in it. On election day, when they suddenly decide that they want to vote, it is too late.

The Motor-Voter Law was a priority of the Clinton Administration after a similar bill was vetoed by President George Bush in 1992. Within weeks after Clinton took office, the Motor-Voter bill was reintroduced in the House, where it passed easily. In the Senate, however, it was threatened by a Republican filibuster. With only fifty-seven members in the senate, the Democrats lacked the necessary sixty votes to stop a filibuster.

Opponents of the law claimed that it would impose excessive expenses on financially strapped state governments and that it would increase opportunities for voter fraud. Underlying the oppositions was the belief that the law would benefit Democrats more than Republicans by making it easier for more inner-city and lower-income people to register. To win over enough Republican support to pass the bill, the Democrats needed to make some concessions, including new language that tried to ensure that recipients of public benefits were not pressured by welfare agency employees into registering to vote or registering for a particular party.

Opposition continued after the law was passed, with some states challenging its constitutionality. Republican Governor Pete Wilson of California refused to implement the act, claiming that it would cost more than $35 million and arguing states should not have to pay for unfounded mandates issued by federal government. Wilson also claimed that the law would increase voter fraud by encouraging ineligible voters, such as undocumented immigrants, to vote. The justice department responded by filing lawsuits against California and two other states

to force compliance. The U.S. Supreme Court later ruled that the Motor-Voter Law was not an infringement on the states' rights to govern, not an unfunded mandate, and not a tool for increasing voter fraud.

Unfortunately, the Motor-Voter Law has not produced an increase in voter turnout, only in registrations to vote. In fact, turnout in the 1996 presidential election was less than 50%—the lowest since 1924. Four years later, in November 2000, more than 105 million people cast a vote for president—9.5 million more votes than in 1996—but this was a mere increase from 49.0% to 51.0% in overall turnout. Perhaps when there is little expenditure of energy in the act of registration, people are less likely to engage in the act of voting. The research of political scientists Raymond Wolfinger and Jonathan Hoffman led them to conclude that "critics of the NVRA were correct in predicting class and racial disparities in the use of motor voter . . . our findings are consistent with the proposition that costless registration is associated with an increase in nonvoting registrants."[2]

The Motor-Voter Law represented an important step in America's approach to democracy, but it was only one step on the road to fully realizing the democratic process. With a majority of Americans registered to vote, the next step in the fulfillment of the democratic process is getting those who are registered to actually vote. The U.S. Census Bureau reported that in the 2000 presidential election, 7.4% of registered voters who did not vote (3 million people) identified trouble with their registration as the main reason they did not vote.[3]

Question for Reflection: A total of 78.7 million votes were cast on November 5, 2002, a turnout of 39.3 percent. Did you vote in the 2002 midterm elections? If you do not vote, why?

▲ Millions of voters have been added to the rolls since 1992, but the great challenge for democracy is to get these voters to actually go to the voting booth.

INTRODUCTION: POLITICAL PARTICIPATION AND DEMOCRACY

In this chapter we would like you to begin thinking about an issue that goes to the very heart of the democratic ideal. Democracy simply cannot work without mass political involvement, or **participation.** Citizens who have a say in the national decision-making process show greater levels of satisfaction with the political system as a whole. The very act of participation makes them feel a part of the system; in addition, citizens are gratified when they see that policy decisions, over the long run, reflect their desires. Although mass participation can produce political tension, as participants argue their various interests, in the long run it leads to democratic outcomes and acceptance of the system. A 2001 bipartisan National Commission on Federal Election Reform, co-chaired by former Presidents Gerald R. Ford and Jimmy Carter, concluded that, "for Americans, democracy is a precious birthright. But each generation must nourish and improve the processes of democracy for its successors."[4]

Who Participates?

Since the ancient Greek theorists first debated various types of government, political thinkers have held that a citizen's informed participation represents the highest form of political expression within democracy. Indeed, the Greek word *idiot* originally described someone who did not participate in politics—a definition showing how much importance the ancient Greeks placed on democratic involvement. In Athens, citizens not only discussed politics but served in government as well. They held no elections as such; instead, everyone eligible regularly drew lots to serve in the legislature and fill other posts.

In a nation as large as the United States, the Athenian kind of *direct* democracy is logistically impossible. Instead, the United States has evolved a *representative* form of government in which all eligible citizens may participate in electing officeholders to represent their opinions in government. And Americans have the opportunity to go to the polls frequently. The United States has more elections than any nation in the world, with more than 500,000 offices filled in any four-year election cycle!

The standards of self-governance assume most citizens participate in some form of political activity and that they base their participation upon a reasoned analysis of ideas, options, and choices. This link between widespread and informed participation, voting, elections, and public policy constitutes the fundamental component of democracy. Voting is but one form of political behavior essential to a democracy. Indeed, the right to choose *not* to vote is also essential to the workings of a successful democracy.

The ancient Greeks assumed that being a participant in a democratic society was a full-time job for males who had full citizenship and owned property. Citizens would spend a good deal of time familiarizing themselves with the issues of the day, then make policy decisions based on informed reason and factual knowledge. This ideal is clearly difficult to achieve in a modern, large-scale mass democracy where citizens spend much of their time earning a living. Also, individuals' interests vary, and it is unrealistic to expect that in their spare time all citizens will participate in political activity. On the other hand, not all Americans are apathetic and uninvolved. A large number do come close to the ideal of full-time political involvement, and many others meet some of the criteria for democratic citizenship.

A classic study of political participation levels of the American electorate by Sidney Verba and Norman Nie found that citizens fall along a continuum of political engagement, ranging from those who are totally uninvolved in politics to those who

▲ For days before national elections in India, this billboard reminded voters of the scorn the ancients felt toward nonvoters.

participation Mass political involvement through voting, campaign work, political protests, civil disobedience, among many other actions.

engage in it as a full-time occupation. They found that political participation is a many-sided activity in which citizens may choose to invest minimal or large blocks of time and effort. At the upper levels of effort, about a tenth of the population is deeply involved in the political process. Nearly half of American citizens are engaged in political activities of which the ancient Greeks would have approved: that is, those who work for candidates or issues at election time, and those who work in groups that support social issues. Almost 46 percent of the population engages in some kind of serious, politically oriented activity. In addition, another quarter of the population votes or contacts public officials for one purpose or another, leaving only about a fifth of American citizens completely inactive in the political process. We can debate whether this record could be improved upon, but it does not appear to be as lamentable a performance as many social commentators would make it.[5]

The disturbing element in the variation in participation rates concerns the different types of people likely to be found in each category. Generally speaking, in the continuum from low to high levels of political activism, one finds fewer low-income people and minority group members at the higher levels. Activists, for instance, are largely well-educated, middle- and upper-income voters. Inactives are disproportionately poorly educated and low-income. This is not to say that all active citizens are rich and educated, or that all inactive ones are poor and uneducated. The issue here is one of tendency.

These findings, replicated in study after study, lead many observers to wonder how well American society is approaching the democratic ideal of equal political participation by all.

A Brief History of Voting in the United States

Historically, American politics has been notable for the steady erosion of barriers to democratic participation. Voting in particular, and other avenues of participation more generally, were closed for many years to minorities, women, and young people. Today, many barriers to participation have been broken.

Politics in the United States began as an activity reserved for white, property-holding, tax-paying, middle- and upper-class males. Perhaps a quarter of the American adult population met those criteria. Thus, poor whites and women were disenfranchised. Slaves remained "property," retaining none of the citizenship rights that whites enjoyed; in fact, slaves were not even considered whole human beings. A compromise forged during the Constitutional Convention resulted in each slave being counted as three-fifths of a person for purpose of taxation and of representation in the U.S. House of Representatives.

Property requirements for voting were gradually relaxed over the decades, disappearing by the middle of the nineteenth century, when virtually all white males were enfranchised. The Fifteenth Amendment, passed in 1870 as part of the Civil War Amendments, guaranteed that, "The right of citizens of the United States to vote shall not be denied or abridged by the United States or by any State on account of race, color, or previous condition of servitude." The amendment's aim was to extend voting privileges to former slaves—and to African American males in general. Though it seemed to pave the way for broader political participation, the spirit underlying the Fifteenth Amendment was perverted to the narrow perspective of southern state and local interests intent on keeping African Americans from voting, by the end of the nineteenth century.

Racism led government officials in the South to devise a number of techniques that kept African Americans from the polls. First and foremost was the simple tactic of intimidation. Local African Americans were victims of threats, beatings, home burnings, or in many cases were lynched by anonymous mobs. Naturally, when people are living under the constant fear of violence, an unsubtle "suggestion" that they not exercise their right to vote will be enough to deter all but the bravest of them.

Southern officials also devised formal ways to keep the African American vote down. First, they required payment of a **poll tax,** a fee that had to be paid before one could vote. In several states, an unpaid fee continued to accrue from one election to the next until it became a sum beyond the means of poor African Americans. Southern election officials also made selective use of the **literacy test,** a requirement that voting applicants demonstrate some ability to read and write. African American college graduates might be asked to read and explain complex passages of the Constitution, while white citizens were given simple grade-school paragraphs to read. A third device was the **good-character test,** requiring those wishing to vote to get two or more registered voters to vouch for their integrity. Since African Americans found it difficult to register, they also found it difficult to find registered friends to vouch for them, and registered whites were unwilling to come to their aid. Southern states used a variety of other devices as well to limit African American political power.

These prohibitions were extremely successful. Since most African Americans lived in the South until well into the 1950s, southern interference with African American political rights effectively disenfranchised the vast majority of African Americans for decades. For the first half of the twentieth century, African Americans rarely participated in politics, few held public office, and less than 10 percent voted regularly.

Change came as the civil rights movement gained momentum in the 1950s and 1960s. The Voting Rights Act of 1965, providing protection to African Americans wishing to vote, and the Twenty-fourth Amendment (1964), outlawing the poll tax in federal elections, helped seal a new national commitment to equal opportunity in the political arena. The U.S. Supreme Court erased many barriers to African American participation, striking down state poll tax laws in 1966.

The movement for women's political equality has a lengthy history, beginning with the first women's rights convention at Seneca Falls, New York, in 1848. After decades of pressuring for suffrage and other legal rights, women finally won the right to vote with passage of the Nineteenth Amendment in 1920, although we should note that this was a rather slow approach to democracy because minority males won the vote in 1870—22 years after Seneca Falls; it would take another 50 years for women to finally gain the right to vote! The Nineteenth Amendment, guaranteed that, "The right of citizens of the United States to vote shall not be denied or abridged by the United States or by any State on account of sex."

poll tax A fee that had to be paid before one could vote; now unconstitutional.

literacy test A requirement that voting applicants demonstrate some ability to read and write, primarily used to prevent blacks from voting in the South.

good-character test A requirement that voting applicants wishing to vote get two or more registered voters to vouch for their integrity.

▶ Democracy's advance in Africa is evidenced by Malians lining up to vote for president in May 2002.

Further expansion of political participation came with ratification of the Twenty-third Amendment in 1961, which gave residents of the District of Columbia the right to vote in presidential elections, and the Twenty-sixth Amendment in 1971, which gave the right to vote to all citizens of the United States eighteen years of age or older. Extending suffrage rights is a key step toward approaching the democratic ideal of equal political participation by all and the primary reason why former presidents Ford and Carter co-chaired the 2001 National Commission on Federal Election Reform.

Question for Reflection: The 2001 National Commission on Federal Election Reform concluded, ". . . for Americans, democracy is a precious birthright. But each generation must nourish and improve the processes of democracy for its successors." Beyond the 1993 National Voter Registration Act, how might this generation contribute towards that goal?

Voting

As we have seen, participation in politics may take many forms, but the most central act in a democracy is the citizen's decision to vote. All other political acts cost more in terms of time, effort, and money, and none produces such a level of equality as the vote. Writing prior to the 2000 presidential election, Berman and Murphy noted in the previous edition of *Approaching Democracy* that "each citizen is truly equal to all others in the privacy of the ballot box; there each person has one vote, and all votes are counted the same. And votes in an election constitute the core political decision: who rules. Voting, then, is key to an understanding of the political process in a democracy, and we must therefore examine in some detail this vital political activity."[6] Yet, we know that all votes did not count and others were not counted in the 2000 presidential election.

Over 105 million ballots were cast and Vice President Al Gore received 539,897 more votes than George W. Bush, who won the electoral vote 271–266, but only after the Supreme Court, in a 5–4 decision, overruled the Florida Supreme Court order that would have allowed manual counting of ballots. An examination of over 175,000 Florida ballots that were not counted revealed that the ballots of those in Florida's black neighborhoods were most likely to go uncounted. "Overall, 136 out of every 1,000 ballots in heavily black precincts were set aside—a rate of spoiled ballots that was three times higher than in predominantly white precincts."[7] The disenfranchisement of black voters poses a challenge for a system like ours that rightfully prides itself in the great progress made in enfranchising voters in America.

A joint study conducted by Caltech/MIT in July 2001 found that between 4–6 million presidential votes were lost in 2000. Another 1.5 million votes were not

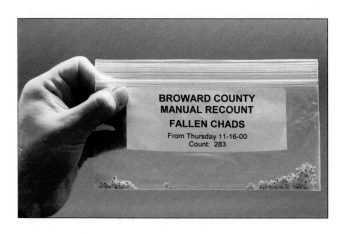

◄ Chads are the small pieces of paper that voters punch out with styluses to indicate their votes. In the Broward county recount, the small specks of paper were gathered up and examined by recounters who would try to decide voter intent.

APPROACHING DEMOCRACY AROUND THE GLOBE

Democracy Sweeps Africa

Over the past four decades, African nations, suffering from military dictatorships and rampant corruption, have searched for stability. In the 1980s, the military dictator and president of Zaire, Mobutu Sese Seko, proudly proclaimed, "Democracy is not for Africa." During the 1980s only four African countries held multiparty elections in a continent whose leaders held power through the barrel of a gun.

In the last ten years, however, 42 of the 48 nations in sub-Saharan Africa have participated in elections with multiple party participation—a hallmark of democratic government. The past decade marks a major turning point in African political consciousness, a change equally as momentous as the successful resistance of Africans against colonial European rule in the early 1960s. To some observers, the political changes currently taking place in Africa resemble the dismantling of communism by Eastern European nations following in 1991. Familiar problems have arisen with broader freedoms. Africans are freer than they were prior to 1990, but poorer too.

The recent election in Mali, one of the poorest nations in the world, is a case in point. In May of 2002, Mali citizens turned out to participate in an important election to determine the fate of the nation's presidency. After ten years in power, the ruling party lost the election and then held a press conference to announce its relinquishment of power. In the past, many African political parties ousted from power have used interpersonal and state-sponsored violence to reclaim political power. As elections in other nations reveal, however, times are changing in Africa.

Since 2000, the African nations of Senegal, Mauritius, Ghana, and Mali have thrown off the yoke of despotism. So have Mozambique, Senegal, and South Africa. Although Africans readily admit that the level of democracy they now enjoy pales in comparison to Western democracies, they also point out that their newfound freedom is a major improvement over the "freedom" to vote for one political party. The following figure shows the degrees to which Africans prefer democracy.

Elements of Democracy		Support for Democracy	
Expected effects		*More favorable than other forms*	
Provide basic necessities	89%	Botswana	84%
		Tanzania	83%
Education for everyone	89%	Nigeria	81%
		Uganda	80%
Provide jobs	87%	Ghana	77%
Majority rule	78%	Zambia	75%
Free to criticize government	75%	Zimbabwe	71%
		Malawi	65%
Regular elections	74%	Mali	60%
Two or more parties	72%	South Africa	60%
		Namibia	58%
Small gap, rich and poor	70%	Lesotho	40%

Democracy in Africa

Source: Afrobarometer, a research coalition of university and social agencies in Africa.

In May of 2002, African voters in Sierra Leone, suffering from years of some of the most serious internal political strife and violence in any civil war on the globe, peacefully

counted because of difficulties using voter equipment. The U.S. Census Bureau reported that 2.8 percent of registered voters who did not vote (1 million people) did so because of long lines, inconvenient hours, or the location of their polling place.[8]

Voter Turnout

Many observers of politics define the health of a representative democracy by the degree to which its citizens participate in elections. **Voter turnout** expresses the percentage of eligible voters who actually show up and vote on election day. Thus, a turnout rate of 80 percent for a given election means that 80 percent of all citizens legally entitled to vote actually did vote in that election.

Scholars have traced voter turnout in the United States over the years. Since 1860, voter turnout in presidential elections has shown a long, fairly steady decline. In 1860, those who voted in the presidential election constituted over 82 percent of the eligible adult population; in 2002, less than 40 percent voted. These numbers do not tell the whole story, but they paint a dismal picture of the trend in American

voter turnout The percentage of eligible voters who actually show up and vote on election day.

elected a new president. That same month voters in Lesotho also elected a new government without bloodshed. More change appears imminent since the leaders of Mozambique, Namibia, and Angola have declared their intention not to run for reelection.

But not all African nations can lay claim to democratic reforms in the election system. The nations of Zimbabwe, Kenya, and the Congo Republic remain mired in despotism. Nigeria underwent an election in 2002 during which the dictator of the nation used violence and military force to intimidate voters from reaching the polls. Those who did vote experienced fraud in the election returns. The result of the election was predictable to outside monitors and the Nigerian people: the ruling party remained in power.

Citizens of Mali, however, appeared hopeful that participating in a new democratic election would initiate a long-term process of healing for their war-torn nation. Poor shepherds and farmers in Mali continue to protest over the lack of food and the rampant political corruption from village governments to the halls of the nation's leadership. Although outside observers note the democratic turn in Mali's election, they also pointed out that rampant corruption infused the first round of election voting. The Mali Constitutional Court was forced under pressure to throw out approximately half a million votes due to charges of graft and double voting. According to Sulamo Djiguiba, a Mali elder, democracy appears destined to remain: "Justice prevails a little more . . . During the military regime, solders would just come and arrest us and make us work for the army or on their farms. Now that doesn't exist. We are free. We can go where we like."

The West has attempted to respond to Africa's yearning for democracy. But help has taken a glacial pace to arrive, given the long and bitter history of slave raids and the taking of raw materials from Africa by Britain, France, and Belgium. In June of 2002, African leaders met in Canada with the representatives of the most industrialized nations in the world. Neglected since the fall of communism made them minor players on the world scene in the 1990s, African nations yearn for increased U.S. and foreign funding to help them achieve the dream of democracy. To satisfy the political needs of the West for guarantees of democracy for future generations of African people, the leaders of South Africa, Nigeria, Senegal, and Algeria have created what they call the New Partnership for Africa's Development. Time will tell whether or not Africa will receive the help it needs to continue on the path toward approaching democracy.

Source: Rachel L. Swarns and Norimitsu Onishi, "Africa Creeps Along Path to Democracy," *New York Times,* June 2, 2002, p. 1.

▲ This woman waited a lifetime to exercise the right to vote in Mali's 2002 election, which ousted the governing party.

voting. The trend is particularly troubling to many political scholars (see Figure 10.1). True, a slight rise in turnout in 1992 was viewed as an encouraging sign, but it was still far below the figures for most of the late nineteenth and early twentieth centuries. The 1996 turnout, the first presidential election following implementation of the Motor-Voter Law, resulted in a 49.4 percent turnout. This was the lowest voter turnout in a presidential election since 1924![9]

Turnout is even lower when Americans elect members of Congress in nonpresidential, midterm elections. For these races, voter turnout averages between 35 and 40 percent of the eligible adult population. In the 2002 election, turnout rose slightly from 37.6 percent (in the previous midterm elections of 1998) to 39.3 percent of all voting-age citizens.

Explaining Low Turnout

How can we explain these low turnout rates in the world's oldest democracy? Nations such as Italy, the Netherlands, Belgium, Sweden, Australia, Germany, and

Caltech/MIT Voting Technology Report

What Is; What Could Be

The Problem

- The election process lost 4 to 6 million presidential votes in 2000.
- An estimated 1.5 million presidential votes were not recorded in 2000 because of difficulties using voting equipment.
- Up to 3.5 million Senate and governor votes were lost because of technology over the last election cycle for these offices.
- According to the US Census Bureau, in the 2000 election, 7.4 percent of registered voters who did not vote (approximately 3 million) reported that trouble with their registration was the main reason they did not vote.
- According to the US Census Bureau, in the 2000 election 2.8 percent of registered voters who did not vote (approximately 1 million) reported that long lines, inconvenient hours, or polling place locations were the main reason they did not vote.

Equipment

- There are five types of voting equipment: hand-counted paper, mechanical lever machines, punch card ballots, optically scanned paper, and electronic voting machines.
- Hand-counted and optically scanned paper have had the lowest rates of unmarked, uncounted, and spoiled ballots in presidential, Senate and governor elections over the last 12 years.

- Punch cards have the highest rate of unmarked, uncounted, and spoiled ballots over the last four presidential elections.
- Lever machines have the highest rate of unmarked, uncounted, and spoiled ballots in Senate and governor elections over the last 12 years.
- Electronic machines have the second highest rate of unmarked, uncounted and spoiled ballots in presidential, Senate, and governor elections over the last 12 years.

Voter Registration

- Voter registration is a large system to manage: There are about 150 million voter registrations in the United States.
- Counties maintain voter registration in almost all states.
- There are a large number of duplicate registrations. Michigan found 1 million duplicate registrations throughout the state when that state created a unified statewide registration system.

Absentee Voting

- Two decades ago, five percent of all ballots were cast absentee or early.
- In 2000, fourteen percent of all ballots were cast absentee or early.

Source: Copyright © 2001 Caltech/MIT Voting Technology Project. http://www.vote.caltech.edu/Reports/. Reprinted with permission.

**Figure 10.1
Voter Turnout
in Presidential
Elections (1960–2000)**

Source: http://www.
bettercampaigns.org/
documents/turnout.htm.

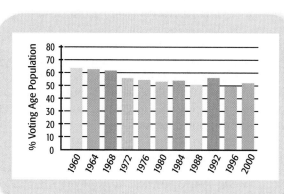

APPROACHING DIVERSITY

Gender Still Counts

Political races for president, senate, gubernatorial, and house offices reflected the iron-clad gender divide during the 2000 election—women tended to vote ten percentage points or higher than men for the Democratic Party, and men voted ten percentage points higher than women for the Republican Party regardless of the gender of the candidate. Although the gap is often invisible to the general public, it was strong enough to sway elections in all major contests. What does this mean for candidates, campaign managers, and special interest groups involved in the complex process of campaigning and election in a modern democracy?

The gender gap has been widening for the past decade to the delight and dread of office-seekers. In the 1990s, the gender gap in presidential support was evident at four percentage points. But in 1996 this jumped to eleven percent. In 2000 the figure was ten percentage points, with 43% of women and 53% of men voting for Texas Governor and Republican Presidential candidate George Bush. In contrast, 42% of men and 54% of women voted for Democratic Vice President and Presidential candidate Al Gore. Race, class, and ethnic background amazingly fail to alter the ratio of disparity between male and female voters in this pattern of party voting.

For citizens voting for female U.S. Senators, the results were very similar. Six women vied for the senatorial office. One, Hillary Clinton, campaigned for an open seat, while two other Senators ran against incumbents. The gender gap in voting determined four of the six elections. For instance, Hillary Rodham Clinton received sixty percent of the female vote, while her Republican opponent, Rick Lazio received 39%. In another instance where the gender divide proved true and determined an election outcome, Kay Bailey Hutchison (R.-TX) garnered more male (68%) than female (63%) votes.

Candidates for the House also showed a gender gap—nine percent points overall between men and women. For all House seats, 53% of women voted for Democratic candidates compared to 44% of men. Concerning majority voters, 53% of women voted for Democratic candidates and 53% of men voted for Republican candidates. Gubernatorial races were no different. Three women were elected governor. Two of the candidates, Jeanne Shaheen (D.-NH) and Ruth Minner (D.-DE) enjoyed more support from women than from men, enough to win the election. But Judy Martz (R.-MT) received more support from men (44%) than from women (33%), indicating that women and men *consistently* vote for a different political party in our two-party system.

Source: "Gender Gap in the 2000 Elections," *Center for American Women and Politics*, http://www.rci.rutgers.edu/~cawp/facts/elections/gg2000.html.

Norway boast an average turnout of over 80 percent in national elections (see Table 10.1). Some experts argue, however, that these figures are deceptive. Turnout data are not comparable from one nation to the next. Many nations make voting compulsory, and they fine people who do not vote. Naturally, their turnout will be higher than in nations where voting is voluntary. Furthermore, many foreign nations report turnout as a percentage of all registered voters, whereas turnout rates in the United States are usually given as a percentage of all adult citizens who are eligible to vote. These different bases skew U.S. voting rates so that they appear lower, since only about 70 percent of Americans are actually registered.[10]

To explain nonvoting, start with a simple axiom: Nothing in this life is free. Even the simplest political action has costs. Consider what it takes to exercise the right to vote in America. First, a citizen must register to vote. Unlike other democracies, registration in the United States is the individual's responsibility, requiring a conscious decision, and then the expenditure of time and energy, although less of both since implementation of the Motor-Voter Law.

Registering can be cumbersome. It usually means taking time to contact some government agency during business hours. Although re-registration is not required for every subsequent election, voters must reregister when they move to a new address. Thus, when they move out of a district, citizens lose the right to vote unless they make another conscious decision to get back on the voting list in their new community. One explanation for low voter turnout may be that the average American moves often—about every five years—and registering to vote is not the first

Table 10.1 ■ International Voter Turnout, 1991–2000

International voter turnout per year

Country	1991	1992	1993	1994	1995	1996	1997	1998	1999	2000	Average	System
Argentina	89%		78%		80%		78%				81%	PR
Australia			83%			82%					83%	PR***
Austria	80%			76%	79%						78%	PR
Belgium	85%				83%						84%	PR
Bolivia			50%				62%				56%	Mixed**
Brazil				77%							77%	PR
Canada			64%				56%				60%	District#
Chile			82%								82%	PR
Colombia	26%			29%				40%			32%	PR
Denmark				82%				83%			83%	PR
Dominican Republic				31%		62%					47%	PR
Ecuador				66%		68%		48%			61%	PR
Finland	71%				71%						71%	PR
France			61%				60%				61%	District$
Germany				72%							72%	PR*
Greece			86%			84%					85%	PR
Guatemala				14%	33%						24%	PR
Iceland	89%				88%						89%	PR
Ireland		74%					67%				71%	PR***
Italy		92%		91%	87%						90%	Mixed**
Luxembourg				60%							60%	PR
Mexico	50%			66%			54%			60%	58%	Mixed**
Netherlands				75%							75%	PR
Norway			74%				77%				76%	PR
Peru					58%						58%	PR
Portugal	78%				79%						79%	PR
Spain			77%			81%					79%	PR
Sweden	83%			84%							84%	PR
Switzerland	40%				36%						38%	PR
Thailand		58%			64%	65%					62%	District&
Turkey	80%				79%						80%	PR
United Kingdom		75%					69%				72%	District#
United States		55%		39%		49%		36%		47%	45%	District#
Venezuela			50%								50%	Mixed**

Data is based on Voting Age Population (VAP).

Blank spaces indicate missing data or no elections held that year.

* 50% by single-seat, plurality election $ Single-seat districts, with majority provision

** 75% by single-seat, plurality election & Multi-seat districts, elected by plurality

*** Choice Voting ~ Indicates compulsory voting

\# Single-seat districts, elected by plurality

Source: International Institute for Democracy and Electoral Assistance, as found on The Center for Voting and Democracy Website, www.fairvote.org/turnout/intturnout.htm. Reprinted by permission of The Center for Voting and Democracy.

thing on the mind of someone moving into a new home and adapting to a new community.

Registration laws in most states seem designed to depress election turnout rates. In all but a few states, citizens must register several weeks before the actual day of the election. Since many people don't pay much heed to an election until the campaign is in high gear two or three weeks before voting day, many of them lose the right to vote because by the time it occurs to them to register, it is too late.

As you would expect, states that do allow same-day registration and voting (such as Maine, Minnesota, and Wisconsin) have much higher turnout rates. But well over 90 percent of Americans live in states where registering to vote must be done well in advance of the election. Motor-voter laws, of course, ease the registration process.

Even registered voters, however, don't always get to the polls. Most detrimental to election turnout in the United States is the traditional day of voting—Tuesday. Most states keep their polls open from 8:00 a.m. to at least 7:00 p.m., but busy citizens with jobs, families, and errands to run often have difficulty finding the time to vote on a weekday.

In recent years most states have taken steps to minimize the costs of registering and voting. Registration can now be done closer to election day than in the past, and polls stay open longer than in the past. In some states, such as California, employers are required to give employees paid time off to vote. Frequently civic groups target universities and colleges, grocery stores, shopping malls, and other crowded areas to register people. Other creative suggestions have been put forth by a variety of citizen groups: keeping polls open for twenty-four or forty-eight hours, same-day registration in all states, making election day a national holiday, holding elections on weekends, and internet voting.

All in all, registering and voting still involve some costs, but the costs have been declining. To understand nonvoting, then, institutional factors are not sufficient. We must also look at subjective, psychological explanations.

Nonvoting

People have numerous reasons for failing to vote, and one is the possibility that they are satisfied with the way things are going and see no particular need to become involved politically. Today's nonvoters may decide to vote when a public controversy sears their conscience and forces them to act, as former Supreme Court justice Felix Frankfurter once argued. Thus, nonvoters may start showing up on election day if they become unhappy enough. This option of nonvoters to vote also keeps politicians relatively honest. They know that truly unpopular actions could bring

FYI

President Bush urged Americans to vote on Election Day, Nov. 5, 2002.

Dear friend,

America's the greatest country in the world and will remain so if Americans take seriously their right and responsibility to vote.

If you care about our culture, and the values we pass on to our children, about our country, then vote Tuesday and ask your friends and family to vote too.

One person can make a difference. Your vote matters. America's future will be decided by those who vote.

Sincerely,
George W. Bush

Best Practices in Managing Voter Registration

The Michigan Qualified Voter File (QVF)

The QVF provides electronic linkage for elections officials throughout the State of Michigan to an automated and integrated statewide voter registration database (http://www.sos.state.mi.us/election/qvf/index.html).

California "On-line" Voter Registration

California's "on-line" voter registration process allows for easy distribution of voter registration forms via the Internet (http://sosdev3.ss.ca.gov/votereg/OnlineVoterReg). The

system does not allow for truly "on-line" voter registration, as a paper-based signature is still required.

Orange County, Florida

County workers with laptop computers containing country-wide voter registration information assisted with voter authentication in the polling places, reducing registration problems at the polling places significantly.

Source: Caltech/MIT Voting Technology Project, http://web.mit.edu/newsoffice/nr/2001/bestpractice.pdf.

Federal Elections

Q: Why are federal elections held on the Tuesday after the first Monday in November?

A: The Tuesday after the first Monday in November was initially established in 1845 (3 U.S.C. 1) for the appointment of presidential electors in every fourth year. 2 U.S.C. 7 established this date for electing representatives in every even numbered year in 1875. Finally, 2 U.S.C. 1 established this date as the time for electing U.S. senators in 1914.

Why early November? For much of our history, America was a predominantly agrarian society. Lawmakers, therefore, took into account that November was perhaps the most convenient month for farmers and rural workers to be able to travel to the polls. The fall harvest was over (remember that spring was planting time and summer was taken up with working the fields and tending the crops), but in the majority of the nation the weather was still mild enough to permit travel over unimproved roads.

Why Tuesday? Since most residents of rural America had to travel a significant distance to the county seat in order to vote, Monday was not considered reasonable since many people would need to begin travel on Sunday. This would, of course, have conflicted with church services and Sunday worship.

Why the first Tuesday after the first Monday? Lawmakers wanted to prevent election day from falling on the first of November for two reasons. First, November 1 is All Saints Day, a Holy Day of Obligation for Roman Catholics. Second, most merchants were in the habit of doing their books from the preceding month on the first. Apparently, Congress was worried that the economic success or failure of the previous month might prove an undue influence on the vote!

Source: http://www.fec.gov/pages/faqs.htm, March 29, 2000.

out a horde of formerly silent citizens eager to vote them out at the next election. Thus, from this perspective, nonvoting does not threaten the survival of democratic processes in America. It simply maintains the status quo.

Another school takes issue with this perspective. It claims that nonvoting and nonparticipation in general undermine the health of democratic politics. Citizens who remain outside the political process may come to feel little connection with the laws of the land and the government that administers those laws. They feel alienated—that their vote doesn't make a difference, that the process of voting is too difficult, and that the parties do not offer true alternatives. Turnout has decreased in the United States as a consequence of these increased feelings of detachment from the political process.

In "The Mystery of Nonvoters and Whether They Matter," Michael Kagay of the *New York Times* concluded that the preferences of nonvoters did not differ significantly from voters and that while a 100% turnout would please democratic theorists, it would not alter election outcomes—only the margin of victory. In a statistical analysis of three presidential elections—1988, 1992, and 1996—counting nonvoter votes would have only increased the victor's margin.[11]

A poll conducted by the League of Women Voters in 1996 found that nonvoters were no more alienated than voters. This survey concluded that people do not vote because they do not grasp the significance or importance of elections to them, because the process of voting seems difficult and cumbersome, or because the costs of becoming informed are just too steep. This survey showed that nonvoting was not a product of alienation, but rather that nonvoters just do not see voting as being particularly important. When asked what they would do when given a choice between a once-a-year sale at their favorite store and voting, 30 percent of nonvoters choose the sale, compared with 6 percent of voters. When asked to choose between watching a new episode of their favorite television show and voting, 27 percent of nonvoters chose watching TV; only 3 percent of voters would stay at home. Voters and nonvoters were equally distrustful of government, but nonvoters just did not see their participation as mattering in the outcome.[12]

Who Votes?

The answer to the question "Who votes?" is crucial for understanding the political process, since it is natural for political leaders to pay more attention to voters (who determine politicians' fates) than to nonvoters (who play only a potential role in making or breaking governments). Many variables affect who votes. Education, according to every study, stands out as the leading influence. The more years of schooling one has, the more likely it is that one will consistently vote. Schooling increases one's ability to understand the intricacies of politics. In turn, the ability to understand public affairs helps one see the benefit of taking political action, like voting, to enhance one's interests.

Social status is another crucial variable that determines the likelihood of voting. Simply stated, the higher one's socioeconomic level, the more likely one is to participate in politics, especially to vote. Better-off people see themselves as having more of a stake in political outcomes. They also have the resources (money, connections, education) that allow them to understand the link between politics and their interests and then take effective political action to promote those interests.

Education and income frequently go together, of course, since it is becoming more difficult in modern society to gain economic success without an education. People who have both education and income possess two very strong motivators of political activity.

Social connections in general make political participation more likely. The more ties citizens have to their community, the more reason they see for getting involved in politics. They work to keep their property taxes low, help support a new school for their children, or promote their next-door neighbor's city council campaign. Older people are more likely to vote than younger people, and longtime community residents are more likely to vote than newcomers. Similarly, married people are more likely to vote than those who are single.

These variables describe tendencies, of course, not iron laws. Not all young people are uninvolved in politics, but as a group the pattern is clear: eighteen- to twenty-year-olds vote less than any other age group, followed by twenty-one- to twenty-five-year-olds, then twenty-six- to thirty-year-olds, and so on. People in their sixties, seventies, and even eighties, though they vote slightly less than middle-aged people do, are still far more likely to vote than people in their early twenties. This tendency helps explain the powerful influence of the senior-citizen lobby and its chief representative, the American Association of Retired Persons (AARP).

The continuing modest level of voting rates in the United States presents something of a puzzle to social observers. For four or five decades, Americans have been getting richer, older, and more educated. These demographic trends would suggest a pattern of increasing political participation and voting that has not materialized.

A Voting Trend: Direct Democracy

Those dissatisfied with American voting levels continue to explore creative ways to encourage voters to get to the polls. In recent years there has been increasing support for the use of initiatives and referenda. **Initiatives** are policy proposals placed on the ballot for voter consideration at the instigation of a group of citizens. Often they are ideas that have not met with success in a state's legislature or even contradict existing laws. Issues such as term limits have raised voter ire in recent years, leading to popular initiatives in the states. The initiative was designed to allow the public to take matters into its own hands. To qualify for the ballot, the initiative process requires that proponents obtain a number of signatures—usually representing 10 percent of all registered voters—that must be verified by the secretary of state. Once verified, the initiative is placed on the ballot and put to a popular vote.[13]

A **referendum** is a proposal submitted by the legislature to the public for a popular vote, often focusing on whether a state should spend money in a certain way. For example, in California the legislature often places bond issues before the voters,

> ## QUOTE ... UNQUOTE
> "Nobody will ever deprive the American people of the right to vote, except the American people themselves—and the only way they can do that is by not voting."
>
> Franklin D. Roosevelt

initiative A proposal submitted by the public and voted upon during elections.

referendum A proposal submitted by a state legislature to the public for a popular vote, often focusing on whether a state should spend money in a certain way.

asking them to approve the sale of state bonds to finance various programs, such as education and prisons. At other times, the legislature will place a referendum on the ballot to determine the public's sentiment on an issue.[14]

These two methods of consulting citizens on issues, like the primary system that you read about in Chapter 9, grew out of attempts to broaden political participation and decrease the influence of special interests. Many people see these options as ways to approach direct democracy. But initiatives and referenda have met with mixed success, and in recent years there has been criticism of both methods. "Where direct democracy becomes a more dominant force than representative government the result is whipsaw, without any long-term coherence," observed Brian Weberg, of the National Conference of State Legislatures. Some critics find that issues end up on the ballot even though they are too complex for simple yes or no decisions. Both initiatives and referenda have become costly, requiring expensive television campaigns, and are therefore subject to the influence of big business and special interest groups. Lastly, by involving people directly, these methods bypass the considered deliberations of representative political institutions.

Although the idea of direct democracy is appealing, studies have shown that even when given the opportunity to vote by initiative or referenda, voter turnout does not dramatically increase. Is direct democracy, then, an answer to the problems of voter turnout? Many predict that the United States will start using initiatives and referenda at the national level with the advent of sophisticated telecommunications and computer technology. Scholars and journalists now argue whether we should develop voting techniques that allow citizens to hear a discussion or debate over an issue and then vote electronically. Electronic democracy expands the conception of democracy and may provide a new approach to democracy.

Voting Choice

Although not everyone votes in every election, millions of Americans do vote with some regularity. When voters show up at the polls to make political choices, what determines their actual vote? Political scientists have long been studying the electoral process and the reasons why citizens vote as they do. We now have a good idea of the key influences on American voters: party, candidate appeal, policies and issues, and campaigns.

Party

More than five decades of study of the American electorate have shown that there is one overwhelming influence on voting decisions: party. Other things being equal, voters show up on election day and vote for candidates from the party to which they feel most connected. This idea of connection has been termed **party identification,** a concept we explored in Chapter 9. Party identification is a psychological phenomenon, a deep-seated feeling that a particular party best represents one's interests or best symbolizes one's lifestyle. Once party attachments develop, especially if they develop early, they tend to remain in place for a lifetime, since it is psychologically painful to change party allegiance.

Not all voters have strong party ties. Some are Independents, and others are weak party identifiers. For these voters, other considerations enter the voting decision. Frequently they may cast **split-ticket ballots,** meaning that they vote for candidates from more than one party. Those with strong party connections, however—still 25 to 30 percent of the electorate—can be counted on to go to the polls and vote for only one party, known as a **straight-party ticket.** Only in exceptional circumstances (a friend is running on the other party's label, a key issue of the day turns voters temporarily away from their party) do party loyalists break their long-standing commitment to their own party in an election.

But party is far from being the only determinant of voter choice. For one thing, some elections (usually local) are *nonpartisan,* so voters have to choose among

party identification A psychological orientation, a long-term propensity to think positively of and vote regularly for a particular party.

split-ticket ballots Ballots on which people vote for candidates from more than one party.

straight-party ticket Ballots on which people vote for candidates of only one party.

candidates whose party affiliation is unknown. Other elections involve primary contests. In a party primary, all candidates on the ballot belong to the same party and vie to represent that party in the general election. Hence, party primary voters must often choose from among a number of candidates without party to guide their decisions. Finally, many elections—for example, state constitutional amendments and referenda questions—involve issues. Party positions on these policy matters are not indicated on the ballot, and often parties take no clear position during the campaign. Hence, party cues are missing in these elections as well. For a full understanding of how voters make electoral decisions, we must go beyond the useful but still limited variable of party preference.[15]

Candidate Appeal

Personality has always played a major role in the individualist culture of the United States. Our political system has been deeply touched by key personalities of the day: George Washington, Thomas Jefferson, Andrew Jackson, Abraham Lincoln, Theodore Roosevelt, Woodrow Wilson, Franklin Roosevelt, and Ronald Reagan, to name just a few. Colorful, authoritative, or charismatic individuals at the local, state, or national level have often won office by drawing voters away from long-standing party loyalties and by picking up the bulk of the Independent vote as well. Republican Dwight Eisenhower, for instance, traded on his status as war hero to gain the votes of many Democratic loyalists in the 1950s. Ronald Reagan's movie star charisma and boyish charm, combined with a clear message of change, helped draw many traditionally Democratic voters into the Republican camp in 1980 and 1984.

Strong or popular personalities have a major advantage in any political campaign. Through force of personality they can grab a voter's attention, and even support, at the ballot box. After all, most voters know little about the specifics of political life, except their own party preferences, the top issues of the day, and the names of just a few of the top political leaders of the time. Thus, in a typical election, whatever the office being contested, neither candidate is likely to make much of an impact on average voters, who simply vote their usual party allegiances. Gaining name recognition means that candidates have a stronger chance of picking up support.

What are the attributes that help a candidate become attractive to the voting public? Likeability is surely important to Americans. A next-door-neighbor friendliness and a casual informality go a long way toward pleasing the American voter. It also helps to exude self-confidence, and especially to show a calm assurance when speaking in public. It does not hurt, of course, to be attractive. Studies show that while people vigorously deny it, they are clearly influenced to think better of individuals whose looks are above average. This finding may explain why celebrities, who are well known at least in part because of their good looks, often have an advantage if they choose to run for office.

Another important attribute is the candidate's message. No matter how attractive the candidate, or how folksy or self-assured, if he or she does not take policy positions that are popular with the electorate, the battle for office will be uphill. No election for public office is a simple popularity contest. Candidates cannot get through a campaign without stating where they stand on the issues or explaining what they will do once elected.

Policies and Issues

Ultimately, elections are about what government is going to do. Despite cynicism on the part of many observers about voters choosing candidates on the basis of their teeth or hairstyle, the electorate does make decisions quite regularly on the basis of issues. Issue voting is a central part of the political process, although that is not always clear because issue voting is a complex matter.

QUOTE ... UNQUOTE

"No country can approach the United States in the frequency and variety of elections, and thus in the amount of electoral participation to which its citizens have a right. No other country elects its lower house as often as every two years, or its president as frequently as every four years.... No other has as wide a variety of nonrepresentative offices (judges, sheriffs, attorneys general, city treasurers, and so on) subject to election.... The average American is entitled to do far more electing—probably by a factor of three or four—than the citizen of any other democracy. Thus, although the turnout rate in the United States is below that of most other democracies, American citizens do not necessarily do less voting than other citizens; most probably, they do more."

Ivor Crewe

Let's say a voter feels strongly about ten issues. He or she then looks for a candidate who takes the "right" stand on those issues. It may turn out, however, that one of the two leading candidates for the contested office takes the voter's favored position on just five of those issues, while the other candidate takes the preferred stand on the other five. This situation leaves the issue-oriented voter without much direction on how to vote. He or she may then consider other factors (like party or personality) to make a voting choice.

What if both candidates take convoluted or ambiguous stands on all ten issues, leaving no clear idea of what they would do on these matters once in office? Or what if both candidates take the same position on all ten issues? Or what if both candidates do a poor job of campaigning, or the media do a poor job of reporting, so that the voter fails to understand where the candidates stand on these ten issues? Or what if candidate A supports the two issues the voter cares most about, but candidate B supports the eight others? Do two favorable stands on the intensely held policy convictions outweigh eight favorable stands on the less intensely held ones? For issue voting to occur, then, a number of factors must exist at the same time and in the same election:

1. The voter must care intensely enough about one or more issues to become informed about which positions each candidate takes on these issues.
2. Issue differences on these specific policy matters must exist between the leading candidates for the office.
3. These issue differences must be communicated clearly to all voters.
4. The voter's preferred positions on issues must not be split between the candidates but rather should fall mostly toward one candidate and away from the other.
5. Other factors, such as party and personality, should not detract from the voter's focus on issues.

Since in many elections all these elements do not come together, observers often conclude that issues are irrelevant to average voters. In fact, issues are relevant to voters, but the structure of the voting situation may make issue voting difficult.

Those who criticize the American electorate for failing to take issues into account when voting may be missing another key point. Party voting, the key determinant of voting, is closely related to policy preferences and issue voting. Parties take positions on dozens, even hundreds, of current policy questions, so a party vote is a vote to support those positions. Party-line voters may not agree with everything their party stands for, but studies show that by and large party identifiers agree much more often with their own party on the key issues of the day than with the other party. Thus, a party vote is in many ways an issues vote.

A particularly powerful form of issue voting occurs when voters look back over the last term or two to judge how well an incumbent or the party in power has performed in office. This is known as **retrospective voting.** Generally, retrospective voting takes the form of a judgment by the voters of the incumbents' handling of the economy. The elections of 1992 and 1996 provide strong support for the retrospective voting model. In 1992, following the Persian Gulf War, former President Bush had the highest approval rating of any president in history. Unfortunately for Bush, the economy was perceived as sluggish in late 1991 and into the election year of 1992; Bush, the incumbent, was held responsible. The economy became the dominant issue of the 1992 campaign. In 1996 President Clinton was the beneficiary of a sound economy and easily defeated Bob Dole. Conversely, Gerald Ford's defeat in 1976 and Jimmy Carter's in 1980 represented negative voter evaluations.

If things are going well in the voters' eyes, if policy problems have been solved, if one's personal economic situation is good, if foreign or domestic crises have been skillfully addressed, then voters will reward the incumbents by returning them or their party successors to office.

retrospective voting A particularly powerful form of issue voting in which voters look back over the last term or two to judge how well an incumbent or the "in party" has performed in office.

Campaigns

A final influence on voting choice is the campaign itself. At least one-third, and sometimes as much as one-half, of the electorate makes up its mind during political campaigns. With fewer Americans holding deeply rooted attachments to parties, campaigns can take on special significance. Many voters can be swayed during the months leading up to election day. Issues and personalities of the day can move uncommitted voters in one direction or another with relative speed.

Campaigns also take on special significance for their ability to arouse voters' interest and get them to the polls. The candidate or party that inspires its supporters to vote on election day is the most likely to win, and citizens are most likely to turn out to vote after a well-organized and stimulating campaign. For these reasons, the last two decades have seen the rise of *campaign specialists*—public relations people, media consultants, and fund-raising experts. With the decline of the old party machine, a new world of political entrepreneurs has arisen to provide advice and direction to any candidate with the money and desire to hire them.

We should not conclude, however, that money and a strong public relations campaign alone can make a winning candidate. Remember that party and issues play key roles in voter decisions. There is not enough money in existence to catapult into office a minor party candidate taking unpopular positions on key issues. That assumes, of course, that such a candidate's opponent is reasonably competent and does not self-destruct through scandal or incompetence. Finding a way to package a message cleverly and present a candidate attractively are surely important, but the content of that message and the substance of a candidate's personality are even more important. If those do not impress voters, the chances of winning, despite all the slick packaging imaginable, are slim.

Other Forms of Political Participation

Voting in elections is the most common form of participation, but not the only form. There are many other avenues for participation in the United States, including campaign work, seeking information, protesting, civil disobedience, and even violence. In Chapter 11, we discuss participation through interest groups, but now we examine the other ways in which individuals become involved in the political process.

Campaign and Election Activities

Unlike the pattern in most countries, Americans do not expect to join political parties and become dues-paying members who regularly attend monthly meetings. Still, some Americans do volunteer to work for their party in election campaigns, although the work is hard, the hours long, and the material benefits negligible. Even with the increasing use of sophisticated electronic media, the backbone of most campaigns is still people. Successful campaigns require volunteers to answer telephones, handle mail, canvass the electoral district, distribute candidate or party literature, and discuss the candidates and issues with people in the neighborhood. Interested citizens find still other ways to be actively involved during campaigns. Some participate by displaying signs or bumper stickers or handing out literature of a favored party or candidate, hoping to induce others to echo such support at the polls. Others work as party volunteers in voter registration drives.

Why do people volunteer? They likely believe in what they are doing, feel an obligation to participate actively in the political process, or simply enjoy the game of politics. When all is said and done, the number of people who become involved in campaign activities is small. In recent years the number of people who wear a campaign button or put a bumper sticker on their car always falls below 10 percent of the adult population, as does the number who claim to have attended a political

THE ROAD TO DEMOCRACY

Elections in Zimbabwe

THAT WAS THEN . . .

While self-muzzled protesters held placards proclaiming violations of freedom of expression under the autocratic regime of President Robert Mugabe, the Zimbabwean legislature moved forward with legislation limiting the freedom of the press for the nation's largest independent newspaper. This came on the heels of weeks of economic decline, violence and government repression surrounding the presidential election of March 2002.

The election incidents in Zimbabwe, a nation that has elected only one president since its independence from Great Britain in 1978, underscore the complex relationship between the government and the press in modern nations struggling to balance censorship and individual freedom.

President Robert Mugabe at age 77 has been in office for 22 years, but faced the closest election of his political career in 2002. International criticism of his often dictatorial regime put watchdog groups on alert, including the U.N. Opposition parties, primarily the Movement for Democratic Change (MDC), gained greater support from the Zimbabwean people. His ruling party, which had given him wide latitude and much independence, now showed cracks, forcing the ruler to curb freedom of the press. The backlash continued when Mugabe ordered journalists to carry government-issued licenses, enabling his regime to keep track of journalists and their stories. If the government has a list of where reporters lived, it could intimidate the press into thinking that armed men would show up in the night to take them away.

In response to the crackdown, Mugabe's own party, the Zimbabwe African National Union-Patriotic Front (ZANU-PF), criticized its leader. Eddison Zvogbo, a ranking member of the party, stated "ask yourselves whether it is rational for a government in a democratic and free society to require registration licenses and ministerial certificates for people to speak." The European Union and the United States also threatened to freeze Mugabe's foreign assets should he ban international observers from monitoring the contested election. But outsiders had to be careful since Mugabe's supporters have been known to kill members of the MDC or others who get in the way of his regime.

On election weekend in early March, it was not surprising that Mugabe increased his manipulation of the media, the press, and the public to pull-off a victory. Along with the bill limiting the freedom of the press, Mugabe simply altered the voting structure to omit large swaths of voters.

Thousands of Zimbabwean voters were either left on the rolls or physically prevented from voting. Secretary of State Colin Powell soundly condemned the unfair elections, as did the international community.

In one of the most important elections since the jettison of apartheid and the election of Nelson Mandela in South African in 1991, Mugabe's tactics have sent a positive message to Africa's other struggling democracies—it is o.k. to use force to curtail political dissent to win victory. How this will shape future elections on the continent remains to be seen. Although the international community has rallied against the African ruler, it can do little other than freeze Mugabe's assets in foreign countries and curtail the modest amount of aid reaching his nation from foreign sources.

THIS IS NOW. . . .

As 2002 draws to an end, conditions in Zimbabwe continued to worsen. The Bush administration has called the rule of President Mugabe both illegitimate and irrational. Political dissidents, especially journalists and news organizations, continue to face harsh crackdowns for writing stories critical of the government after the passage of the new press law days before the March 9 elections. As part of his land redistribution plan, Mugabe's government began enforcing its law evicting thousands of white farmers from their property, in what he has suggested is the final piece required to complete the independence war. However, in a heavy drought year with nearly half of its 11 million citizens on the brink of starvation, international relief organizations are calling Zimbabwe's arrest of white farmers and seizure of their property, madness. Several Western nations have imposed travel and financial sanctions and the Commonwealth coalition of 54 African nations suspended Zimbabwe from its ranks in March, but both remain unable to change to course of action of the Zimbabwean government.

Sources: "Mugabe Steals the Election," www.theaustralian.com, March 15, 2002; Jon Jeter, "Zimbabwe Puts Curbs on Media," *Washington Post,* February 1, 2002, A20; "Zimbabwean Presidential Vote Begins," *The Associated Press,* http://printerfriendly.abcnews.com; Jon Jeter, "A Bitter Campaign Ends," *Washington Post,* March 10, 2002, A22; James Dao, "Bush Team is Campaigning to Muster Opposition in Africa to Mugabe's Rule," *New York Times,* August 21, 2002, A8; Jon Jeter, "Repression Lasts Long After Zimbabwe Vote," *Washington Post,* July 3, 2002, A16.

---

meeting in the last year. We should not let these small percentages mislead us, however. After all, 5 percent of the voting age population is close to 10 million people. Thus, millions of Americans regularly work at election time to influence other voters and elect policy makers.[16]

◀ The use of Websites by candidates has become one of the hottest ways of getting information out to potential voters. All candidates in the Democratic and Republican primaries had their own Websites in 2000.

Seeking Information

Political knowledge is important. The *World Wide Web* provides that information, and as the photo shows, candidates use the Web. No one can exercise an effective citizenship role without being well informed. For that reason, the simple act of gaining knowledge about public affairs constitutes a form of political activity. Certainly, a person who attends a meeting of public officials or the local government is participating in politics. In addition, every time a person reads a newspaper or news magazine, watches a news broadcast or political program, or enrolls in a political science class, he or she is actively seeking information that will assist in formulating political preferences and opinions. By just learning about politics, a citizen contributes to the overall knowledge base of the American political system. And each time a person discusses political events and issues of the day with friends and family or writes a letter to the editor to express an opinion on those events and issues, that person is participating in the continuous process of politics. Acknowledging the importance of information to the workings of a democracy, Thomas Jefferson once remarked that given the choice between a government without newspapers or newspapers without government, he would without hesitation choose the latter.

The most recent innovation in the continuing development of outlets for political information is the myriad television stations and programs that focus on political affairs, such as C-SPAN, Court-TV, and cable television channels that air state legislature sessions and city council meetings. Another innovation is the development of the World Wide Web and Internet, which enable interested individuals to obtain complete texts of presidential speeches, position papers, and analyses of these positions by political experts in seconds.

Question for Reflection: Technological advances have brought an unprecedented level of access to information to American voters. What are some of the best ways to analyze this material to determine its accuracy and bias?

Protest, Civil Disobedience, and Violence

When governments produce public policy, groups, institutions, and individuals in society invariably respond. This response may be simple support, such as accepting and participating in government-sponsored programs, voting in elections, paying taxes, or complying with new laws. But sometimes the actions of the government

▲ Protest and civil disobedience are characteristics of a free society. Here, demonstrators march to the Capitol urging debt forgiveness for poor countries.

▲ Sometimes protests can turn violent as they did in 1999's protests against the World Trade Organization and World Bank. Many sections of Seattle were declared security zones and placed in a state of emergency that barred protesters.

protest An expression of dissatisfaction that may take the form of demonstrations, letters to newspapers or public officials, or simply opting out of the system by failing to vote or participate in any other way.

civil disobedience Breaking the law in a nonviolent fashion and being willing to suffer the consequences, even to the point of going to jail, to demonstrate publicly that the law is unjust.

political violence Violent action motivated primarily by political aims and intended to have a political impact.

midterm elections Elections in which Americans elect members of Congress but not presidents; 2002, 2006, and 2010 are midterm election years.

may provoke strong expressions of dissatisfaction. Occasionally, these expressions take the form of organized protests and acts of civil disobedience, either against existing policies or conditions or as a response to actual or threatened change in the status quo.

Protest may take the form of demonstrations, letters to newspapers and public officials, or opting out of the system by failing to vote or participate in any other way. **Civil disobedience** is a more specific form of protest in which disaffected citizens openly but nonviolently defy existing laws that they deem to be unjust. Civil disobedience was commonly used in the 1960s by citizens seeking to protest continued U.S. involvement in the Vietnam War. Some draftees burned their Selective Service cards, and students organized boycotts of classes and "die-ins." Even disillusioned veterans marched on the Pentagon and the 1968 Republican and Democratic National Conventions to call attention to their opposition to the war.

Struggles for civil rights in the 1950s and 1960s were often carried out through active violation of existing segregation laws, on the basis that these laws were unjust, exclusionary, and racist. Civil disobedience was the principal means through which Martin Luther King, Jr., sought to bring equal justice to the political system. This civil disobedience included incidents in which African Americans asked for service at "whites-only" lunch counters and sat quietly on the lunch counter stools, knowing that these actions would provoke a reaction. By violating what they believed to be, and what were ultimately abolished as, morally unjust laws, they drew attention and support to their cause.

Seldom discussed in the context of political participation is the phenomenon of **political violence,** violent action motivated primarily by political aims and intended to have a political impact. When radical opponents of abortion bomb abortion clinics or shoot clinic workers, they claim that their actions are aimed at stopping the "murder of unborn citizens." It is often difficult to tell the true motives behind supposedly political acts of violence. The rise of white supremacist and neo-Nazi movement is certainly, in part, a response to social conditions. We know that violent intolerance follows in the wake of sustained economic downturns, when competition for jobs and scarce governmental resources is most troubling.

When the residents of south-central Los Angeles rioted in the summer of 1992 after four policemen were acquitted of assault charges stemming from the videotaped beating of black motorist, Rodney King, not all of them were looters and vandals. Some were seeking an outlet for genuine frustration over the apparent failure of the system to mete out appropriate justice, not only in the King case but in the treatment of minorities and the poor in general. It seems that most political violence is triggered by a combination of economic problems and political events but the vast majority of Americans strongly condemn criminal actions involving injury and property damage.

Congressional Elections

Under our Constitution, elections for the House and Senate are held every two years. Each of the 435 House members is up for reelection every two years, while just one-third of the senators (who serve six-year terms) are. Most candidates for Congress are not nationally known; they may not even be widely known within their own state or district. Although the U.S. Senate has included a former astronaut and a former movie actor, most national legislators come from somewhat less conspicuous, if equally wealthy, backgrounds. For that and other reasons, many constituents may have little information about who their elected representatives are, what they stand for, or even what sort of work they actually do.

Congressional elections do not generally receive the national media attention or voter turnout of the national contest for the presidency. In an off-year, or **midterm elections,** when there is no presidential contest to galvanize press and voter attention, the usual voter turnout hovers around one-third of registered voters, far below even the relatively modest turnout in recent presidential election years. Because of this, and because congressional elections are not federally subsidized like presidential elections, the race for House and Senate seats takes on a form decidedly different from a presidential campaign, although the 2002 midterm election proved to be an exception to this rule because President Bush nationalized the election and the issues. In doing so, the President maximized his strong approval ratings as a war leader and helped Republican candidates in many local and state elections.

Presidential Coattails

Over the years, an interesting pattern has emerged in congressional elections. Typically in presidential elections, the party of the winning presidential candidate also gains power in the legislature; conversely, in off-year elections, members of the incumbent president's party often find their reelection prospects diminished. This phenomenon varies somewhat over time, depending on the fortunes of the president, the state of the economy, and the possible flare-up of controversy or scandal. President George Bush's Republicans gained seats in the midterm elections of 2002, and in 1994, another midterm election ushered in the Contract with America and brought the Republicans to power in Congress for the first time since 1952.

When representatives or senators of a successful presidential candidate's party unseat incumbents, they are said to "ride the president's coattails" into office. Sometimes this **coattails effect** can be quite dramatic. For example, in 1980, when Ronald Reagan defeated Democratic President Jimmy Carter, he brought enough Republican senators into office on his coattails to wrest control of the Senate from the Democrats for the first time since 1955. But usually the coattails effect is not so dramatic. Despite Republican George H.W. Bush's presidential victory in 1988, Democrats retained control of both House and Senate. The same result occurred in the 1968 and 1972 presidential victories of Republican Richard Nixon. Thus, the coattails effect is not an absolute guarantee in American politics, and many scholars believe its importance is waning as voters become more unpredictable, less tied to party, and more willing to vote a split ticket.

During off-year elections, with voter turnout low and the public able to look back on two years of presidential performance with a skeptical eye, the sitting president's party typically loses seats in the House and Senate. The 1994 midterm election offered a dramatic example of that pattern, as the Democratic party saw itself ejected from its longtime control of Congress by an electorate motivated, at least in part, by unhappiness over a widespread perception of incompetence on Democratic President Clinton's part. The 1998 election was atypical in that Republicans lost five seats in the House and broke even in the Senate. This was the first time since 1934 that the president's party gained seats in a midterm election and the first time since before the Civil War that a president gained seats in the sixth year in office. In the 2002 midterm elections, Republicans increased their majority in the House from 12 to 24 and gained a two-vote majority in the Senate by winning 4 seats. President Bush's popularity was the critical factor; of twenty-three House members for whom Bush campaigned, 21 were victorious. Twelve of the 16 Senate candidates similarly won elections.

Presidential Elections

Following the national party conventions, which take place in summer every four years, the nation's attention turns to the presidential election. The pack of presidential contenders has usually been narrowed to two, although occasionally a serious third candidate competes.

The rules of the game at this stage are quite different from those of the nomination phase (see Chapter 9 for more on the nomination process). The timetable is compressed from two years to two months, and the fight is usually Democrat against Republican. Candidates who previously spent all their efforts wooing the party

coattails effect "Riding the president's coattails into office" occurs in an election when voters also elect representatives or senators of a successful presidential candidate's party.

Voters Rate Themselves on the 2000 Election

Despite intense controversy surrounding the contested Florida election, the campaign of 2000 was rated very high by voters according to a wide set of criteria. According to a poll taken one week following the election by the Pew Research Center, 1,113 voters polled from different parties were more satisfied overall with this election than any of the others since 1984.

In perhaps the most important category—making an informed choice—83% of voters reported that they could easily make distinctions between the different candidates. They also praised the election for less negative campaigning, more substantive discussions of important issues, and engaging presidential debates that were much improved from four years ago.

Not surprisingly, Republicans were happier than Democrats about the choice of candidates and the outcome of the election. Over eighty percent of Republicans were satisfied (compared to 60% of Democrats), an increase of nearly fifty percentage points since the victory of President Clinton in 1996. Also not surprising was the higher rating given to the debates by younger voters, 74% of whom reported being influenced compared to 57% of senior citizens. But women more so than men felt their voting choices were impacted by the debates. Although the debates were basically a tie, a large minority of voters (20%) reported that the debates swayed their decisions in a significant way. On the issue of presidential discussion of subjects vital to national interest, nearly five in ten voters reported that the election met their expectations. This figure was up from 36% in 1996.

But a negative view of the press was still evident. Only 29% gave the press a high grade, while forty percent gave the press a failing grade. Part of the miserable rating stems from the manipulation of the outcome of the election by news reporters who prematurely released inaccurate information about who was winning. Nearly seventy percent of voters believed that it was wrong for the press to declare George Bush the winner. Others think that the media's mistake in initially giving Florida to Gore may have influenced the rest of the nation, particularly the West, to vote in a particular fashion.

In what is perhaps the strongest mandate from the poll for future elections in the twenty-first century, nine out of ten voters want the networks to delay declaring the winner until all the votes are counted, a reasonable procedure in a democratic nation where voting is often whimsical and taken for granted. Eight in ten voters felt that news corporations jumped the gun because they wanted to be the first to claim to have released the winning results.

Source: The Pew Research Center, "Campaign 2000 Highly Rated," http//www.people-press.org/reports/display.php3?ReportID=23.

---

faithful to gain the nomination must now broaden their sights to the less committed party voters and Independents who will determine the election outcome. The fall campaign involves juggling a number of balls in the air successfully. Candidates must use federal funds strategically, define a clear campaign theme, anticipate any last-minute "October surprises" by opponents, avoid self-inflicted gaffes, attack opponents without seeming to mudsling, monitor the pulse of the nation, and manage a successful media campaign.

The Electoral College: The Framers' Intention

Until the 2000 presidential election, many voters were unaware that it is not they but the **electoral college** that actually chooses the president. That's how George W. Bush was elected president and why the outcome of the popular vote in Florida was so important.[17]

How did this little-understood institution come into being? The design for the electoral college was written into the Constitution from the beginning. The framers wanted to ensure that exactly the right type of person was chosen for the job, and they sought to clone the best aspects of the first presidential role model—George Washington. Rather than getting ambitious demagogues who cater only to the whims of the electorate or act as the mouthpiece of Congress, the framers wanted to ensure the selection of a statesman, someone wise enough to unify the people behind a program that was in their best interest. After considerable discussion, the framers chose not to have Congress select the president, fearing that the president would then become dependent on that body. They also decided not to let the

electoral college The group of 538 electors who meet separately in each of their states and the District of Columbia on the first Monday following the second Wednesday in the December after a national presidential election. Their majority decision officially elects the president and vice president in the United States.

people choose the executive, hoping thus to insulate that office from what they considered the popular passions and transitory fancies of the electorate.

Instead, they designed a system unlike any in the world, the electoral college, which provided an indirect election method. Legislators from each state would choose individuals known as *electors,* the number to be based on the state's representation in Congress. (A state with two senators and five representatives, for instance, would be allotted seven electors to the electoral college.) The framers expected that electors would be individuals with experience and foresight who would meet, discuss in a calm, rational manner the attributes of those candidates who were best suited for the presidency, and then vote for the best person to fill that post. Thus, presidents would be chosen by an elite group of state leaders in a sedate atmosphere unencumbered by political debts and considerations.

In practice, the electoral college has never worked as the framers had planned because the framers had not anticipated the emergence of political parties. Originally, the electors had nearly absolute independence. They had two votes to cast and could vote for any two candidates, as long as one of their two votes went for someone from outside their state. Today, this requirement ensures that the president and vice president cannot both be residents of the same state.

This odd system worked well only in the first two presidential elections, when victories by George Washington were foregone conclusions. After his departure, the beginnings of the first party system had, by 1796, ensured that electors were not, in fact, disinterested elder statesmen. They were instead factional loyalists committed to one of the two leading competitors of the day, John Adams or Thomas Jefferson. Thus, in a straight-line vote after the 1796 election, the electoral college chose Adams for president by a scant three votes over Jefferson. This made Adams president but Jefferson, his chief rival, vice president. A modern-day equivalent of this situation would be if Bob Dole, who came in second to Bill Clinton in the electoral voting of 1996, served under Clinton as vice president.

Things worsened in the election of 1800. By then, strong political parties with devoted loyal followers had arrived to stay, ensuring that members of the electoral college would vote the party line. Jefferson and Adams opposed each other again, but this time both chose running mates to avoid the anomaly of another Adams-Jefferson presidency. Jefferson's vice presidential selection was Aaron Burr, and their ticket combined to win more electoral votes than either Adams or Charles Cotesworth Pinckney, Adam's running mate. However, all of Jefferson's supporters in the electoral college had been instructed by party leaders to cast their ballots for Jefferson and Burr, and when they did, the two men ended up in a tie vote for the presidency. This result threw the choice of president into the House of Representatives. It took a good deal of intrigue in the House before Jefferson finally emerged the winner and was named president.

The absurdity of these two elections brought cries for reform. The Twelfth Amendment was quickly proposed and ratified, directing the electoral college to cast separate ballots for president and vice president. Under this system the party that wins a majority of electors can first elect the party's nominee for president, then go on to choose the party's nominee for vice president. No longer can a president from one party and a vice president from another be elected, nor can there be tie votes between two candidates from the same party. In a way this early reform preserved the electoral college system, since in nearly all subsequent American elections it has worked to give Americans the president who received the most votes. To this day, the electoral college remains a central part of the American political system.

How the Electoral College Works Today   When Americans go to the polls in a presidential election, most believe they are casting their ballots for president. In fact, they are voting for a slate of electors, individuals selected by state party leaders who are expected to cast ballots for their respective state's popular vote winner. Still, electoral college votes produce the occasional **faithless elector,** who casts his or her

faithless elector Member of the electoral college who casts his or her vote for someone other than the state's popular vote winner.

How the Electoral College Works

- Each State is allocated a number of Electors equal to the number of its U.S. Senators (always 2) plus the number of its U.S. Representatives (which may change each decade according to the size of each State's population as determined in the Census).

- The political parties (or independent candidates) in each State submit to the State's chief election official a list of individuals pledged to their candidate for president and equal in number to the State's electoral vote. Usually, the major political parties select these individuals either in their State party conventions or through appointment by their State party leaders while third parties and independent candidates merely designate theirs.

- Members of Congress and employees of the federal government are prohibited from serving as an Elector in order to maintain the balance between the legislative and executive branches of the federal government.

- After their caucuses and primaries, the major parties nominate their candidates for president and vice president in their national conventions traditionally held in the summer preceding the election. (Third parties and independent candidates follow different procedures according to the individual State laws). The names of the duly nominated candidates are then officially submitted to each State's chief election official so that they might appear on the general election ballot.

- On the Tuesday following the first Monday of November in years divisible by four, the people in each State cast their ballots for the party slate of Electors representing their choice for president and vice president (although as a matter of practice, general election ballots normally say "Electors for" each set of candidates rather than list the individual Electors on each slate).

- Whichever party slate wins the most popular votes in the State becomes that State's Electors-so that, in effect, whichever presidential ticket gets the most popular votes in a State wins all the Electors of that State. [The two exceptions to this are Maine and Nebraska where two Electors are chosen by statewide popular vote and the remainder by the popular vote within each Congressional district].

- On the Monday following the second Wednesday of December (as established in federal law) each State's Electors meet in their respective State capitals and cast their electoral votes-one for president and one for vice president.

- In order to prevent Electors from voting only for "favorite sons" of their home State, at least one of their votes must be for a person from outside their State (though this is seldom a problem since the parties have consistently nominated presidential and vice presidential candidates from different States).

- The electoral votes are then sealed and transmitted from each State to the President of the Senate who, on the following January 6, opens and reads them before both houses of the Congress.

- The candidate for president with the most electoral votes, provided that it is an absolute majority (one over half of the total), is declared president. Similarly, the vice presidential candidate with the absolute majority of electoral votes is declared vice president.

- In the event no one obtains an absolute majority of electoral votes for president, the U.S. House of Representatives (as the chamber closest to the people) selects the president from among the top three contenders with each State casting only one vote and an absolute majority of the States being required to elect. Similarly, if no one obtains an absolute majority for vice president, then the U.S. Senate makes the selection from among the top two contenders for that office.

- At noon on January 20, the duly elected president and vice president are sworn into office.

Source: http://www.fec.gov/pages/ecworks.htm.

electoral vote for someone other than the state's popular vote winner. In 1988, for example, one of the electoral delegates from West Virginia cast a vote for Republican Robert Dole rather than for the party's nominee, George Bush (41).

The electors selected in the presidential election meet in their respective state capitals on the first Monday after the second Wednesday in December. The term *electoral college* is deceptive, since the 538 electors never actually assemble en masse to cast their votes for president. Title 3, Chapter 1, of the U.S. Code provides that on the sixth day of January after every meeting of the electors—usually referred to as Certification Day—the electoral vote (which had been sent by registered mail to Washington) will be announced by the vice president before both houses of Congress. Not until that moment are the election results considered official—although the whole world has known these results unofficially for several weeks.

To become president, the winning candidate needs to receive a majority, or 270 of the 538 electoral votes. The 538 votes are made up of one vote for each of the 435 members of the U.S. House of Representatives, plus one vote for each of the 100 senators, plus three votes for the District of Columbia. If no candidate receives the required majority in the electoral college, a **contingency election** is held in the House. Under the guidelines for a contingency election, the House chooses among the top three candidates, with each state casting a single vote.[18]

The Electoral College and Strategies for Campaigning

Presidential campaigns are shaped by the rules governing the operations of the electoral college. Since the name of the game is winning 270 electoral votes to become president, parties need to campaign in such a way as to improve their chances of winning those votes. That leads to a simple strategy: Go where the votes are. Thus, the "big" electoral states are at the heart of a presidential contest (see Figure 10.2).

Going Where the Votes Are The strategy of "going where the votes are" is crucial because of a voting system that gives the large states extraordinary influence in presidential elections. In all but two small states (Nebraska and Maine), electors are chosen on a "winner-take-all" basis. Whichever candidate wins the highest number of popular votes wins all of a state's electors. The consequences can be dramatic. A 54 to 46 percent victory, for example, in a large state like Ohio would give a candidate all of Ohio's important twenty-one electoral votes and hence a 21 to 0 lead over an opponent. If electors were allocated by proportional representation with this same popular vote outcome, a candidate would hold a minuscule one vote (11 to 10) electoral college lead over a rival.

Most states long ago decided to adopt this winner-take-all system to bolster their political importance, so it has become ingrained in American political habits and seems unlikely to change. The result is to exaggerate the power of the large states, where all rational candidates will end up spending most of their campaign time, effort, and money. Naturally, candidates will take a state and its interests more seriously if that state can give candidates a large number of electoral votes. If its vote

contingency election A runoff presidential election held in the House if no candidate receives the required majority in the electoral college.

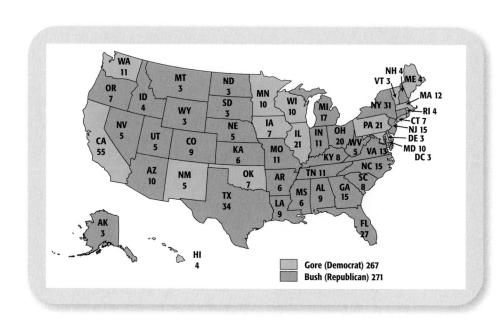

Figure 10.2
2000 Electoral Vote Distribution

The 2000 presidential election brought the electoral college to the forefront. Vice President Al Gore may have won the popular vote, but the electoral vote was another matter. This figure shows the distribution of 538 electoral votes.

Source: www.fec.gov/pubrec/map1.htm.

totals were to be split, they would represent very little advantage to the winner. The box on page 380 shows how the electoral college works.

Electoral College Reform?

The most favored alternative to the electoral college is a direct vote for election of the president. Four American presidents—Lyndon Johnson, Richard Nixon, Gerald Ford, and Jimmy Carter—endorsed a constitutional amendment that would replace the electoral college with direct election. The direct vote plan has its critics. What would happen, for instance, if four or five candidates ran for president, and someone with, say, 31 percent of the vote came in first? Would Americans accept someone for whom less than a third of the electorate had voted? To remedy that problem, most direct election proposals would require 40 percent of the vote to win. If no candidate won 40 percent, a run-off election between the top two candidates would be held.

Critics then argue that such rules would encourage many candidates to enter the race, some representing single-issue parties, hoping to come in first or second, even with a relatively small percentage of the votes. The winner of a run-off election might have gained a very low level of national support on the first ballot and still emerge as president. The adverse consequences for political legitimacy, and perhaps even political stability, would be quite significant in a nation that is unaccustomed to the idea of a runner-up winning the presidency.

? Question for Reflection: Would abolishing the electoral college bring us closer to or farther from the democratic ideal?

Interpreting Presidential Elections

The day after the election, virtually every politically interested citizen, including the president-elect, asks the same question: What message did voters send to their new (or reelected) leaders? The answer to that question is usually unclear.

Election outcomes are notoriously difficult to interpret. For one thing, never in United States history has a president been elected with a majority of those eligible to vote. As we know, only 50 to 55 percent of the electorate turn out to vote for president. Nearly every one of them would have to vote for the same candidate for that person to obtain a majority of all adult Americans as supporters. Naturally, this has never happened in a free society and never will. Indeed, more citizens choose "none of the above" by staying at home on election day than vote for the winning presidential candidate.

Given low voter turnout, we cannot say for certain after any given election that the winner was even the preferred candidate of the majority of the nation's citizens. That is all the more true in most other elections to political office in the United States, since turnout rates are even lower in races for offices other than the presidency. Many local elections occur with 20 to 30 percent turnout, meaning that many local officeholders are elected with the support of just a tiny fraction of their fellow citizens.

In an attempt to make more sense of presidential contests, political scientists use party realignment theory to classify elections as maintaining, deviating, or realigning (or critical) elections. **Maintaining elections** were the most common type throughout much of the last fifty years (1936, 1940, 1944, 1948, 1960, 1964, and 1976). In this pattern the majority party of the day wins both Congress and the White House, maintaining its long-standing control of government. In **deviating elections** the minority party captures the White House because of short-term intervening forces, and the country experiences a deviation from the expectation that power will remain in the hands of the dominant party. Deviating elections took

QUOTE ... UNQUOTE

Money invades politics "like ants in the kitchen—without closing all the holes, there is always a way in."

Bill Bradley

maintaining election Election in which the majority party of the day wins both Congress and the White House, maintaining its control of government.

deviating election Election in which the minority party captures the White House because of short-term intervening forces, and thus there is a deviation from the expectation that power will remain in the hands of the dominant party.

place in 1956, 1968, 1972, 1980, 1984, and 1988. **Realigning elections** are characterized by massive shifts in partisan identification, as in 1932 when the New Deal coalition was forged. Recent trends have been toward regional realignment in the South with Republican gains in 1992 and 1996.

The size of Ronald Reagan's 1984 electoral victory led many to speculate that it, too, represented a realignment that changed the electoral landscape. This interpretation was weakened, however, with the Democratic congressional victories of 1986, 1988, and 1992 and with Bill Clinton's triumph in the presidential races of 1992 and 1996. The realignment thesis was revived with the dramatic takeover of the House and Senate by the Republicans following the 1994 midterm elections, but the voters in 1998 did not continue a revolt against politics as usual. Analysts will need a few more years to assess the true nature of the voting changes occurring within the American electorate, but most do agree on one thing: Regional realignment has undoubtedly occurred in the South, particularly among white males. That group, formerly a bastion of support for the Democratic party, can now be safely categorized as solidly Republican.

As we learned in Chapter 9, some political scientists characterize the current era by the term **dealignment**—the moving away from partisanship. This term helps describe an increase in the number of self-styled Independents as well as the weakening of party ties among the many voters who still claim allegiance to one of the two major parties. This growing disaffection from the parties helps explain some recent elections, when strong party wins at the presidential level failed to produce comparable victories for the party in Congress. Instead, voters showed their growing independence of party by ticket splitting.

Money and Elections

It is often said that money is the mother's milk of politics. The 2000 presidential and congressional elections were the most costly in history. According to Federal Election Commission records, overall fund raising by the major parties in 2000 exceeded $880 million, a 73 percent increase since the presidential election cycle of 1992. Congressional campaign spending increased by more than 70 percent in the last decade, jumping from $450.9 million in 1985–86 to $765.3 million in 1999–2000. The average cost of winning a seat in the House of Representatives was $684,000 in 1996; the average cost of winning a Senate seat was $3.8 million.[19]

For the most part, a simple rule holds: Spend more money than your opponent, and you are likely to win the election. Candidates therefore spend a good deal of time and effort raising campaign dollars. Still, exceptions to the rule do occur. In the 1998 California gubernatorial primary, millionaire Al Checci spent $40 million of his personal fortune, but it did not buy him his party's nomination. Steve Forbes spent millions of his own funds in 2000, but failed to capture the Republican nomination.

Presidential elections are conducted under the guidelines of the Federal Election Campaign Act of 1971 (see Table 10.2). Before this campaign finance law was enacted, candidates could raise as much money as possible, with no limits on the size of individual contributions. Most of the money came from the large contributions of very wealthy individuals, corporations, and organized labor. For example, in the 1952 presidential contest, at least two-thirds of all the money raised and spent at the national level came from contributions of $500 or more (equivalent to $2,000 in 1996 dollars). This was the era of the political "fat cats," the wealthy capitalists who, along with rapidly growing labor unions, contributed most of the money and exerted most of the influence during campaigns.

The aftermath of the Watergate scandal led to the most significant election reform in history. The Federal Election Campaign Act of 1971 created the Federal

realigning election Election characterized by massive shifts in partisan identification, as in 1932 when the New Deal coalition was forged.

dealignment The moving away from partisanship.

Table 10.2 ■ Changes in the Way Political Campaigns Are Financed	
1907	With the urging of President Theodore Roosevelt, Congress passes the Tillman Act, banning campaign contributions from corporations.
1947	Congress overrides a veto by President Harry S. Truman to pass the Taft-Hartley Labor Act, co-sponsored by Senator Robert A. Taft, Republican of Ohio. The act includes a ban on political contributions by labor unions.
1947	In response to Watergate and its disclosures of illegal fundraising by President Richard M. Nixon, Congress amends the 1971 Federal Election Campaign Act, limiting contributions by individuals, parties and PAC's and creating the Federal Election Commission.
1976	Supreme Court strikes down as unconstitutional limits on campaign spending that were part of the 1974 amendments.
1978	An administrative ruling by the F.E.C. creates the loophole that the parties exploit to raise unlimited contributions from corporations, labor unions, and the wealthy. Such donations are called soft money.
1988	Soft money is raised aggressively by George H.W. Bush and Michael J. Dukakis in the presidential campaign.
1996	About $260 million in soft money is raised by national party committees, with some used for candidate-specific issue ads. The Clinton-Gore campaign is criticized for its fund-raising practices, including allowing big donors to stay in the Lincoln Bedroom in the White House.
1999	For the fourth year in a row, Senate Republicans led by Senator Mitch McConnell, Republican of Kentucky, block final votes on bills to overhaul the campaign finance laws.
2000	Senator John McCain, Republican of Arizona, makes campaign finance overhaul the cornerstone of his presidential bid. The parties raise almost $500 million in soft money.
2002	The Senate and President Bush passes Campaign Finance legislation that bans donations to national parties by corporations and unions and would place strict limits on individual donations.

Source: The New York Times, March 4, 2002. p. A16; additional sources: Professor Anthony Corrado, Colby College; Congressional Research Service; Federal Election Commission; Common Cause.

Election Commission (FEC), limited individual contributions, and instituted a new system of public financing through an income tax checkoff. The 1974 amendments were immediately challenged, leading to an important judicial ruling.

On January 30, 1976, in *Buckley v. Valeo*, the Supreme Court struck down the limits an individual can spend on his or her own campaign for political office. The Court ruled that the First Amendment gives each citizen the right to spend his or her money, no matter how much, in any lawful way, as a matter of freedom of speech. In a later ruling the Court also struck down legal limits on the amount of money an interest group can spend on behalf of a candidate, as long as the group spends its money independently of the candidate's campaign organization. Despite these rulings, however, the fundamentals of the act remained intact.[20]

The Court did back reformers on some crucial issues. It upheld contribution limits, disclosure rules, and public financing. Thus, individuals can give only modest amounts of money to campaigns, limiting the political power of the wealthy—in theory. Furthermore, the names of all who give money to any campaign are placed on public record through the disclosure provisions, meaning that under-the-table "buying" of political candidates seems unlikely to occur, given the certainty of publicity. These reforms, along with the public financing of presidential campaigns, led some to assume that American elections are approaching closer to the democratic ideal than in the days when a few wealthy groups and individuals surreptitiously paid for most of the candidates' expenses. However, the system is in crisis because of the ways that the law can be circumvented.[21]

◀ Large segments of the American populace favor campaign finance reform. One of the most well-known protesters is Doris Haddock, known as "Granny D," who walked from California to Washington, D.C., to protest soft money.

Federal Matching Funds

During the long road to the nomination before the convention, presidential candidates can opt for **federal matching funds.** That is, once they raise a certain amount of money in the required way, they apply for, and are given, a matching sum of money from the federal government. The rules that govern qualifying for these funds are relatively simple. A candidate must raise $100,000 in individual contributions of $250 or less, with at least $5,000 collected in twenty states. Once this is accomplished, the federal government will match all individual contributions of $250 or less, dollar for dollar. Individual contributions over the $250 limit are not matched. This stipulation has led candidates to concentrate on raising $250 from as many contributors as possible. The result is an increase in small contributors ("kittens"), compared with the large contributors ("fat cats") who had previously dominated campaign financing.

In return for federal funds, candidates must accept a total preconvention spending limit plus a percentage limit on fund raising, as well as spending limits in each state. A state's spending limit is calculated at sixteen cents for each resident of voting age, plus an adjustment for inflation. Thus, candidates who accepted matching funds have to develop careful strategies for where and when to spend.

Not all candidates accept matching funds. In 1996 Steve Forbes refused to accept the limitations on spending and therefore did not request federal funds. In 2000, Bush and Forbes chose not to accept federal matched funds. But this did not mean that either candidate was free of all financial restrictions. Although legally permitted to spend as much as they wanted of their own money in each state and had no overall spending limit, they were prohibited by federal law from accepting donations higher than $1,000 from individuals and $5,000 from political action committees (PACs).

Matching funds are cut off if a candidate does not receive 10 percent of the vote in two consecutive primaries. To re-qualify for funds, a candidate must receive 20 percent of the vote in another primary. The FEC requires twenty-five days' advance notification that a candidate is not participating in a particular primary. Candidates who run unopposed in the primaries, as Ronald Reagan did in 1984, are allowed to spend the legal limit anyway.

During the general election, candidates from each major political party are eligible for public funds for presidential elections. The money source is a three-dollar income tax check-off to the Treasury's Presidential Campaign Fund.

federal matching funds System under which presidential candidates who raise a certain amount of money in the required way are able to apply for and are given a matching sum of money from the federal government.

Campaign Finance Reform

The 1996 and 2000 election cycles highlighted the need for reform, based in part on efforts by both political parties to take advantage of loopholes in election laws. In 1996 the Democrats raised $123.9 million and the Republicans $38.2 million in soft money contributions. Another distinguishing component of the 1996 election was the role of foreign contributions, particularly those brought in by John Huang, a former Commerce Department official who raised millions of dollars from overseas donors.

Soft money is contributions that are used by state and local party organizations for "party-building" activities. These include party mailings, voter registration work, get-out-the-vote efforts, recruitment of supporters at the grassroots level, and so forth. This money is considered "soft" because it does not go directly into a specific candidate's campaign and are unrestricted donations. Therefore, it does not count toward the legal limits imposed on every presidential candidate who accepts federal matching funds. This provision allows candidates to get around legal spending limits, since the money, while intended to strengthen state and local parties, ends up (more than coincidentally) helping the party's national ticket as well. The soft-money loophole has allowed corporations, unions, and wealthy individuals to contribute as much as they want to political parties (see Figure 10.3).

Issue advocacy, the process of campaigning to persuade the public to take a position on an issue, has become like soft money, a mechanism for channeling huge amounts of money into the system. Moreover, these funds do not have to be disclosed publicly and are unregulated by the FEC.

Another loophole in the campaign finance law involves **independent expenditures,** funds that are dispersed independently by a group or person in the name of a cause, presumably not by a candidate. Thus, a group or even an individual can spend unlimited sums of money on advertising and TV time to promote policies favored by a particular candidate. Although these actions help that candidate's chance of success in the political campaign, they are entirely legal as long as the group and the candidate maintain separate organizations. The Supreme Court has ruled that in such cases, there can be no restrictions on individual or interest group spending.

soft money Contributions used by state and local party organizations for "party-building" activities.

issue advocacy The process of campaigning to persuade the public to take a position on an issue.

independent expenditures Loophole in the campaign finance law involving no limits to fund that are disbursed independently by a group or person in the name of a cause presumably not by a candidate.

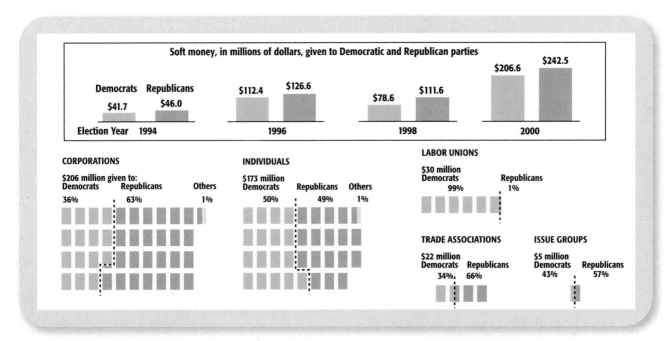

Figure 10.3 The Power of "Soft Money"
Source: Washington Post, February 13, 2002, p. A25.

The rise of political action committees should be understood in this context. PAC spending for candidates is unrestricted as long as it forms no part of the candidates' own campaign operations. Yet PACs naturally find it in their interest to have a president beholden to them, so they will surely spend large sums of money (unrestricted, after all) to back their favored candidates.

In March 2002, President Bush signed into law new campaign finance legislation that would ban donations to national parties by corporations and unions and would place strict limits on individual donations. The League of Women Voters President Carolyn Jefferson-Jenkins declared, "Passage of this legislation silences big money's political power and restores the public's faith and trust in American democracy."[22]

Yet, shortly after signing the bill, suits were filed in federal court challenging the constitutionality of the legislation on grounds that it tries "to regulate core political speech" and "would radically alter, in a fundamental and unconstitutional fashion, the ways that citizens, corporations, labor unions, trade associations, officeholders, candidates, advocacy groups, tax-exempt organizations, and national, state and local political party committees are permitted to participate in our nation's democratic processes."[23]

DEMOCRACY IN THE NEW MILLENNIUM

Voting on the Internet in the Digital Age

Incorporating the use of technology to advance the aspirations of the democratic process took a giant leap forward during the Arizona 2000 Democratic primary election. The Republican Party held most of statewide offices in Arizona, including both houses of the state legislature. Democrats found it difficult to secure state election funding and therefore hired *Election.com* to hold an Internet election. Instructions explaining the procedures to vote on the Internet and Personal Identification Numbers were sent to 821,000 registered Democrats in the state, as well as an application to receive a ballot. The day of the election, voters could cast their ballot from 124 official Democratic Party voting locations, as well as a paper ballot if they chose to do so.

Before the election could take place, however, a lawsuit was filed asking for an injunction against the Internet election by Voting Integrity Project of Virginia (VIP). They objected to the "Digital Divide" that has developed along racial and ethnic lines over the past decade. Many people don't have computers in their homes or in their neighborhoods. In response to the lawsuit, Arizona Democrats submitted their Internet voting plan for clearance by the Justice Department, which it received in February of 2000. A federal judge soon ruled that holding elections on the Internet did not violate the 1965 Voting Rights Act.

When the election took place, almost half of Arizona Democrats chose to vote on the Internet. Forty-one percent of votes cast on the net were from remote locations, while the remaining five percent from on-site Internet connection places. More than four out of five voters who cast a ballot on the Internet did so from their own homes, eight percent from their job site, and eight percent at work, one percent from a public library, and six percent from a combination of alternatives.

Limitations to the technology unfortunately prevented many Arizona Democrats from casting their ballots. Some computers failed to properly load the voting program, while in many cases the ballot did not appear due to problems associated with the dissemination of voting instructions, and some people complained that they did not receive a PIN number in the mail. But overall, the use of the Internet during the primary effectively increased voter-turnout, making the Internet a promising tool for approaching the goals of participatory democracy. Increasing numbers of local and state governments are now moving closer than ever towards using the Internet to hold elections.

Arizona could learn much from Britain, which has gone farther than any other country in using high-tech communications for voting. In over 6000 city council elections voters cast ballots over the Internet, on kiosks, over the phone, and by marking an *X* on the ballots. In an effort to increase participation by young people, several cites allowed citizens to vote by sending a text message from their cell phone. Voters even received a message right back saying, "Thanx 4 Ur Vote." What we see in the UK and Arizona is very probably the future of voting in the twenty-first century. Visit http://www.electiononline.org for your first stop on election reform information.

Source: Frederic I. Solop, "Digital Democracy Comes of Age in Arizona: Participation and Politics in the First Binding Internet Election," Paper read at American Political Science Association National Conference, Washington, D.C., August 31–September 3, 2000; TR Reid, "England cotes, but Not necessarily at the polls: cell phones, internet and touch-screen kiosks used by many in local election," *Washington Post,* May 3, 2002, p. A23.

In June 2002, the FEC approved the McCain-Feingold restrictions on soft money. Nevertheless, nonfederal (soft money) activity by the national political parties has been greater in the 2002 campaign than in the 2000 presidential cycle (see Figure 10.4 for soft money contributions from 1994 to 2000). According to the Federal Election Commision, Republicans raised $221.7 million and Democrats $199.6 million between January and October 16, 2002. National political party fundraising of hard money—contributions within the limits and prohibitions of the Federal Election Campaign Act was $416.5 million—43% over that of the 1997–98 midterm campaign.

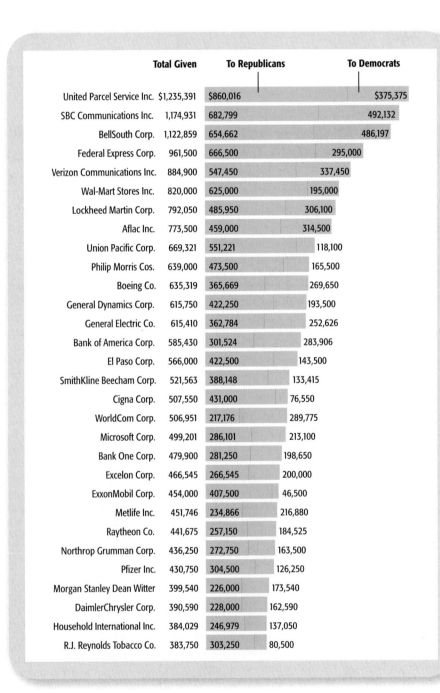

	Total Given	To Republicans	To Democrats
United Parcel Service Inc.	$1,235,391	$860,016	$375,375
SBC Communications Inc.	1,174,931	682,799	492,132
BellSouth Corp.	1,122,859	654,662	486,197
Federal Express Corp.	961,500	666,500	295,000
Verizon Communications Inc.	884,900	547,450	337,450
Wal-Mart Stores Inc.	820,000	625,000	195,000
Lockheed Martin Corp.	792,050	485,950	306,100
Aflac Inc.	773,500	459,000	314,500
Union Pacific Corp.	669,321	551,221	118,100
Philip Morris Cos.	639,000	473,500	165,500
Boeing Co.	635,319	365,669	269,650
General Dynamics Corp.	615,750	422,250	193,500
General Electric Co.	615,410	362,784	252,626
Bank of America Corp.	585,430	301,524	283,906
El Paso Corp.	566,000	422,500	143,500
SmithKline Beecham Corp.	521,563	388,148	133,415
Cigna Corp.	507,550	431,000	76,550
WorldCom Corp.	506,951	217,176	289,775
Microsoft Corp.	499,201	286,101	213,100
Bank One Corp.	479,900	281,250	198,650
Excelon Corp.	466,545	266,545	200,000
ExxonMobil Corp.	454,000	407,500	46,500
Metlife Inc.	451,746	234,866	216,880
Raytheon Co.	441,675	257,150	184,525
Northrop Grumman Corp.	436,250	272,750	163,500
Pfizer Inc.	430,750	304,500	126,250
Morgan Stanley Dean Witter	399,540	226,000	173,540
DaimlerChrysler Corp.	390,590	228,000	162,590
Household International Inc.	384,029	246,979	137,050
R.J. Reynolds Tobacco Co.	383,750	303,250	80,500

**Figure 10.4
Corporate PACs Give
$66 Million to Candidates**

Source: Washington Post, August 7, 2002, p. A19.

On November 6, 2002, the very day that the McCain-Feingold campaign finance law took effect, nineteen states filed a motion in the District Court of Columbia in support of the McCain-Feingold law that is facing challenges in federal court in the suit known as *Sen. Mitch McConnel v. Federal Election Commission*. The suit involves more than eighty plaintiffs and is scheduled for a December 4, 2002, oral argument. While a court ruling is expected several months later, both sides agree that the decision will be appealed to the United States Supreme Court. At stake is both the role of soft money in politics as well as the role of a political party in our democratic process.

We conclude with a truism about American democracy. Active citizen participation can move the United States closer to the ideal of a democratic political system. Through voting and other forms of political participation—campaigning, gathering information, joining groups, and protesting—Americans can involve themselves in the democratic process. Closed to the vast majority in the framers' day, American government has become accessible, open to the input of millions, representing every conceivable point of view. Dozens of outlets for effective political participation are available to any citizen who cares to make even a marginal effort to get involved.

SUMMARY

1. About one-tenth of American citizens are deeply involved in the political process, but nearly half engage in political activities such as campaigning for candidates or working in groups to support social issues. Another 20 percent vote but do not participate in other ways.

2. Today all citizens who are eighteen years of age or older are eligible to vote. Over the years many barriers to voting have been removed, including property requirements, poll taxes, literacy and good-character tests, and prohibitions based on gender and age.

3. Voter turnout rates for presidential elections have been declining since the mid-nineteenth century and are now below 50 percent.

4. Education is the leading influence on whether people vote, followed by social status; people with more education and income are more likely to vote. Social connections in general increase rates of political participation; thus, older people, married people, and people with ties to their community are more likely to vote.

5. In recent years there has been increasing support at the state level for the use of initiatives and referenda as ways to return to direct democracy. Initiatives are proposals by the public that are placed on the ballot for a popular vote; referenda are submitted by the legislature to the public for a popular vote.

6. The most important factor in voters' choices is identification with a political party. Voters who do not identify strongly with a party may cast split-ticket ballots, but those with strong party loyalty usually vote a straight-party ticket.

7. Other influences on voters' choices are the candidates' attractiveness, personality, and positions on key issues. Issue voting is likely to take the form of retrospective voting, in which voters judge how well the incumbent performed during the previous term. The skill with which the campaign is conducted also influences voter choice.

8. In presidential election years, the party of the winning presidential candidate often also gains power in the legislature; this effect is known as "riding on the president's coattails." In off-year elections, the president's party tends to experience some losses.

9. In a presidential election voters cast their ballots for a slate of electors who are expected to cast their ballots for the candidate who wins the most popular votes in their state.

10. To become president, the winning candidate must receive a majority of the 538 electoral votes (1 for each member of Congress, plus 3 for the District of Columbia). If no candidate receives a majority, a contingency election is held in the House of Representatives, in which each state casts a single vote.

11. Under the winner-take-all system, all of a state's electoral votes go to the candidate who wins the most popular votes in that state. Presidential campaigns therefore focus on the states with the largest numbers of electoral college votes.

12. Presidential elections are conducted under the guidelines of the Federal Election Campaign Acts of 1971 and 1974, which place limits on the amounts of money that may be contributed to candidates by individuals and interest groups. The system today is in crisis because of loopholes involving soft money, independent expenditures, and issue advocacy.

13. In March 2002 President Bush signed into law new campaign finance legislation that sought to ban soft money in politics.

KEY TERMS

participation	straight-party ticket	contingency election
poll tax	retrospective voting	maintaining election
literacy test	protest	deviating election
good-character test	civil disobedience	realigning election
voter turnout	political violence	dealignment
initiative	midterm elections	federal matching funds
referendum	coattails effect	soft money
party identification	electoral college	issue advocacy
split-ticket ballots	faithless elector	independent expenditures

POLISIM ACTIVITY

Election 2004

No presidential election in recent history illustrated not only the importance of every vote but the importance of a candidate's campaign tactics in accumulating votes and more importantly how those votes translate into electoral college votes than the 2000 election. Although the electoral college's continued existence has been hotly debated, it still forms the backbone strategy of anyone who is seriously considering a run at the presidency. Also playing a huge role in determining the outcome of the 2000 presidential campaign was the continued importance of raising money (lots of it) and the influence of third party candidates on the race. In this simulation, you will become the presidential campaign manager of either the Republicans or Democrats for the 2004 race. But watch out—you need to raise enough money and skillfully position your candidate on the issues to fendoff potential third party candidates to win the White House.

SUGGESTED READINGS

BERNS, WALTER, ed. *After the People Vote: A Guide to the Electoral College*. Lanham, Md.: University Press of America, 1992. An exceptionally useful guide to the operations of the electoral college.

CAMPBELL, ANGUS, PHILIP E. CONVERSE, WARREN E. MILLER, and DONALD STOKES. *The American Voter*. New York: Wiley, 1960. The classic study of voting, which even today should be the starting point for approaching the study of elections and politics.

NIE, NORMAN H., SIDNEY VERBA, and JOHN R. PETROCIK. *The Changing American Voter*. Cambridge, Mass.: Harvard University Press, 1976. An important study offering a fresh look at the classic 1960 study of the American voter.

PIVEN, FRANCIS FOX, and RICHARD CLOWARD. *Why Americans Don't Vote.* New York: Pantheon, 1988. A starting point for understanding the problems associated with the decline in voting in America.

POLSBY, NELSON, and AARON WILDAVSKY. *Presidential Elections.* New York: Scribner's Sons, 2000, 10th edition. An important book that provides a history and analysis of elections and American politics.

TEIXEIRA, RAY A. *The Disappearing American Voter.* Washington, D.C.: Brooking Institution, 1992. The reasons Americans don't vote and the effects of nonvoting on political life.

WOLFINGER, RAYMOND E., and STEVEN J. ROSENSTONE. *Who Votes.* New Haven, Conn.: Yale University Press, 1980. An important empirical analysis of voting, the results of which are then unified into a theory of voting behavior.

11

INTEREST GROUPS

CHAPTER OUTLINE

Approaching Democracy Case Study:
A Million Moms vs. the N.R.A.
and the Second Amendment Sisters

Introduction: Interest Groups
and Democracy

Interest Groups: A Tradition in American
Politics

Functions of Interest Groups

Types of Interest Groups

Characteristics of Interest Groups

Interest Group Strategies

Political Action Committees

Regulation of Interest Groups

Assessing the Impact of Interest Groups

Interest Groups of the Future

Interest Groups and the 2002 Election

APPROACHING DEMOCRACY CASE STUDY

A Million Moms vs. the NRA and the Second Amendment Sisters

Sometimes lobbying groups win a battle, but who wins the political war is uncertain. Such was the case when the Justice Department filed a brief with the Supreme Court on May 7, 2002, arguing that the federal court should abandon six decades of precedent and in two cases under consideration for appeal, interpret the Second Amendment to guarantee the rights of individuals, not just militias, to carry guns, in an effort to nullify two federal gun laws. The Democratic party, except for New York Senator Charles

Schumer, remained silent and it became clear that the "Million Mom March" organization's goal of influencing the retention and expansion of federal gun laws was still a long way off.

On Mother's Day, 2000, over 200,000 women from across the United States traveled to Washington D.C. marching along the National Mall passed the "wall of death," a sorrowful list of over 4,000 Americans, many small children, who died of gunshot wounds. The women shared stories of loved ones lost to gun-related violence, vowing to make the future safer for their children. American politicians received a wake-up call from their constituents that revealed anger over loose state and national gun control laws. In the wake of shootings by children and young adults at places like Columbine High School in Colorado, women used the march as a pulpit from which to voice concerns that gun-related violence was unraveling the fabric of American culture. Led by the popular actress, then-talk-show host, and mother Rosie O'Donnell, the rally made clear what it considered a connection between gun violence and the National Rifle Association. "We have had enough . . . of the NRA and their tactics. Enough of the stranglehold the NRA has in Congress and the Senate. . . . We are the voice of the majority of Americans, and it is time we are heard," said O'Donnell. Most of the gun control legislation advocated by the Million Mom group has existed in various states for years. *National* standards are what this group wishes to be developed and implemented. Their collective voice for gun restraint represented a new interest group whose influence on national politics was growing. American women, in general, make up an important and increasingly powerful voting bloc, whose influence could swing upcoming elections. Polls estimate that 65 percent of women favor some form of gun control.

But gun control advocates were not the only concerned mothers there on Mother's Day, 2000. On the opposite side of the Washington Monument, the Second Amendment Sisters passionately voiced their concerns for the future of their children and families. Some of these women had survived a violent assault and recommended increased training in firearms to prevent the continued abuse of women by men. Others stressed the traditional rights of American people to hunt and shoot for sport and also protect themselves from unwanted encroachments on their constitutional rights. Arguing that more unnecessary laws will not make society safer from criminals with guns, many of these mothers lamented the loss of their Second Amendment freedoms. The Second Amendment Sisters' solutions are tougher jail sentences, gun-safety training for youth, and the expanded right for citizens to carry firearms, with minimal background checks at gun shows and by gun dealers. Although the Second Amendment Sisters drew a crowd of only 3,000, they represent an interest group that is much stronger than many politicians realize.

The existence of the Million Mom group and the Second Amendment Sisters along with the NRA reveals the powerful influence of interest groups upon the American political framework. The Million Mom March rekindled the debate over firearms, demonstrating the degree to which the right to bear arms is a cherished symbol of American freedom. Although gun control advocates, as witnessed at the Million Mom March, embody a numerical majority of the electorate, they do not vote in large numbers on the issue. Rather, those who want to preserve their rights to firearms—NRA and Second Amendment Sisters members—turn out at the polls in droves when gun control issues dominate an election.

Hundreds of new Million Mom March chapters were organized throughout America, and the interest group grew, claiming more than 230 chapters across the nation. Said Mary Leigh Blek, president of the Million Mom March, "Ten kids die from gun violence every single day in this country. Gun violence is a major public health problem costing taxpayers hundreds of millions of dollars every year." The Million Mom March also targeted key congressional districts across the country for get out to vote efforts. In each of these states, Million Mom March organizers hoped to elect candidates who would support common sense gun control legislation that included not only licensing and registration, but also built-in locks on all guns and a ban on all military-style assault rifles.

But by early 2002 the Million Mom March organization had merged with another gun control lobbying group, the 500,000 member Brady Campaign to Prevent Gun Violence, named for James Brady, the Reagan press secretary who was injured in the assassination attempt against the President. Mother's Day 2002 came and went with no further protest. Little gun restriction legislation

▲ Hillary Rodham Clinton joined thousands of people in the Million Mom March in Washington, D.C., in a protest against gun violence and related issues.

had appeared in the national or state legislatures. The Democratic party seemed to have momentarily abandoned the issue in the hopes of gaining seats in the rural areas to take control of Congress. One notable exception was the Minnesota Million Mom chapter, which has held monthly vigils and was credited with blocking a state bill that would have allowed the carrying of concealed guns.

Nationally, the Supreme Court gave the Million Mom group renewed hope with two decisions. In mid-June, 2002, the Court refused to hear the two cases in which the Justice Department had been urging adoption of the "individual rights" interpretation of the Second Amendment. Just two weeks later, the Court by a narrow 5-4 decision in *Harris v. United States* permitted judges to increase the prison sentences of defendants who use guns while committing crimes, even if the defendant had not been convicted by a jury of any charge directly involving the use of the weapon.

Experts agree that only if the Million Moms and the Brady Group can show that gun control issues have real weight at the polls in 2002 they will be able to inject more power in their lobbying efforts. While the purpose of lobbying is to give voice to the people's call for governmental policy change, sometimes it is the governmental institutions themselves that help give voice to the lobbyists. Either way, the fight between the gun control groups and the NRA and the Second Amendment Sisters is sure to continue.[1]

? Question for Reflection: The Framers' plans did not explicitly include a note for lobbying groups in their outline for government. What impact has the public's increased participation in the crafting of laws had on approaching democracy?

INTRODUCTION: INTEREST GROUPS AND DEMOCRACY

Interest groups are formal organizations of people who share a common outlook or social circumstance and who band together in the hope of influencing government policy.[2] Americans often see corporate interest groups as sinister, selfish, high-pressure outfits that use illegitimate means to promote narrow ends at the expense of the public interest. But the truth is that we *all* belong to interest groups, whether we recognize it or not. Many of us are members of churches or synagogues, or perhaps we work in a unionized job. Students in colleges and universities might be surprised to learn that part of their student fees are sometimes used to support lobbying efforts. Even those of you who do not belong to any such organizations will recall signing petitions in the malls or on the streets supporting such causes as environmentalism.

Millions of people can band together and persuade political candidates, and thus governing officials, to make their agenda the new governmental agenda. The success or failure of the efforts of various groups can have an impact on the future direction of American politics.

Interest groups as a whole really don't run anything; they struggle against each other for influence with those who do run things. Each group wins some of the time and loses some of the time, but the statement that "some interest groups get some of what they want some of the time," while much more accurate than the overgeneralization that "special interests run this country," doesn't stir the emotional juices in the same way.

American suspicion toward interest groups is especially curious, given the evidence that they are a natural and inevitable presence in free societies. Interest groups are here to stay, and they play a key role in American politics. In fact, interest groups are crucial to democratic society. They provide an easy means for average

interest groups Formal organizations of people who share a common outlook or social circumstance and who band together in the hope of influencing government policy.

citizens to participate in the political process, thereby allowing all Americans to approach the democratic ideal. We need to look closely at interest groups to see how they broaden the possibilities for political participation. We also need to learn why these agents for democratic influence are often accused of distorting and even undermining the democratic system.

Interest Groups: A Tradition in American Politics

Foreign and domestic observers have long noted the propensity of Americans to form and join groups. "Americans of all ages, all stations in life, and all types of disposition," wrote Alexis de Tocqueville in 1831, "are forever forming associations."[3] This tendency has been attributed to causes ranging from calls for religious conformity to the need for community cohesion imposed by the rugged conditions of the country's early history. For whatever reasons, the desire to come together in social groups for common ends has been deeply embedded in American culture.

This value is enshrined politically in the First Amendment's freedom of association clause: "Congress shall make no law . . . abridging . . . the right of the people peaceably to assemble, and to petition the government for a redress of grievances." These simple words provide the legal framework for all citizen-based political activity in the United States. They ensure the existence of a vast array of interest groups, since government can literally do nothing ("Congress shall make no law") to interfere with people joining together ("peaceably to assemble") to try to influence government policies ("petition government for a redress of grievances"). Deeply ingrained in American culture, then, as well as in an entire body of legal precedents, is the norm that citizens may form any kind of group they please to try to influence government, as long as that activity is undertaken "peaceably."

To help Americans in their efforts to influence government, the Constitution also gives them, in the same sentence in the First Amendment, the rights of assembly and petition, the right to say what they want (freedom of speech), and to publish what they want (freedom of the press). And Americans have not been shy about using these rights. From the earliest days of the republic, they have formed groups of every type and description to defend common interests and obtain favorable government policies. The result has been a complex array of competing and cooperating interests that practically defines modern democracy. If you find a political regime today that does not allow competing interest groups, you will have found a political system that is *not* democratic.

What Is an Interest Group?

If interest groups are central to the democratic process, what precisely are they? Interest groups can take a wide variety of forms. One example is a labor union such as the United Auto Workers (UAW), which formed in 1935 to secure improvements in wages and working conditions for automobile factory workers. Another example is the National Rifle Association, a large affiliation of firearms owners who have organized a powerful lobby for the Second Amendment right to "keep and bear Arms." Groups can vary from large organizations with diffused goals, such as the American Association of Retired Persons (AARP), with its 35 million members and its broad aim of promoting the interests of the elderly, to small outfits with very specific goals, such as the American Women's Society of Certified Public Accountants.

Some political scientists have found it useful to distinguish between actual and potential interest groups. **Actual groups** have already been formed; they have a headquarters, an organizational structure, paid employees, membership lists, and the like. **Potential groups** are interests that could come into being under the right circumstances but as yet have no substantive form—and may never have one. Still,

actual groups Interest groups that have already been formed; they have headquarters, an organizational structure, paid employees, membership lists, and the like.

potential groups Interest groups that could come into being under the right circumstances; as yet, they have no substantive form and may never have one, but they cannot be discounted by political participants.

they cannot be discounted by political participants. Whenever substantial numbers of people share a common outlook or socioeconomic condition, they might well decide to join together to promote their mutual interests. Politicians who ignore potential groups for long may, in fact, be encouraging their formation.

Strongly held policy preferences are essential for interest group formation. Interest groups provide individuals who hold strong policy preferences with a way to disseminate information to legislators, make their preferences known, and work within the system to influence legislation.

Often it takes little more than one or a few dynamic leaders, called **policy entrepreneurs,** to create the conditions whereby a potential group becomes an actual interest group. Ralph Nader, who ran for President on the Green Party ticket in the 2000 election, stands as a classic example of a policy entrepreneur. Largely due to his untiring efforts, a number of consumer-oriented interest groups, such as Public Citizen Litigation Group and the Health Research Group, as well as various other Public Interest Research Groups (PIRGs), came into being in the 1970s, with a major impact on legislation at both the national and the state levels.

A classic example of a potential interest group becoming an actual group can be seen in the establishment of Mothers Against Drunk Drivers (MADD). For decades children had been killed or maimed by intoxicated motorists, creating the potential for bringing the parents of those children together to push for stricter laws to prevent and punish drunk driving. Yet no such group appeared until one woman, Candy Lightner, who lost a child to a drunk driver, decided to form such a group and devote her life to this work.

In a free society actual groups may form and even become powerful on very short notice. United We Stand America, an interest group formed to support Ross Perot's 1992 presidential candidacy, went from nonexistence to the status of major player in national politics in the space of a few short months and then became a full-fledged political party. Thus, politicians and observers of politics must always be aware of potential groups "out there" in the public.

Of course, not every potential group will become a major power in politics. As we will see, some groups are more likely to form and to gain political clout than others. In making policy, politicians consider numerous factors without constantly worrying whether an action they decide to take today could cause the formation of a group that will punish them tomorrow. Still, that possibility can never be wholly ignored and must play at least a modest role in the policy-making process.

A Long History of Association

From the very beginning of the republic, national leaders have wrestled with the idea of interest groups. In *The Federalist,* no. 10, James Madison wrote, "Liberty is to faction what air is to fire."[4] To put it in modern terms, he saw that the development and proliferation of interest groups were inevitable in a free society. But Madison also saw a basic flaw in democratic politics when it came to interests. He worried that one set of interests (a "faction"), whether a majority or a minority of the population, might gain control of the levers of power and rule society for its own aims, to the detriment of the collective good.

Concerned as he was about the negative potential of factions, Madison worked to control their effects, while warning against any effort to eliminate factions altogether—an action he knew would undermine Americans' precious liberties. He reasoned that the power of factions could be moderated by *diffusing* their influence. This diffusion would occur in two ways. First, the very act of joining the individual states into a large and diverse country undercut the power of any one faction. What group could successfully unite the industrial interests of the Northeast and the plantation interests of the South, small independent farmers, indentured servants, urban workers, artisans and merchants, hired hands, and all of the other groups in America at that time? The very size and complexity of the new nation would guard against the likelihood of any one faction controlling government.

policy entrepreneurs Leaders who invest in and create the conditions for a potential group to become an actual interest group.

Madison's second hedge against the triumph of any given faction was to make government complex. By *dividing* political power among several institutions representing different interests chosen at different times by different elements of the population, he strove to ensure that no one faction could ever gain control of all the key levers of power. As we know, Madison and the other framers were hugely successful at their task. Indeed, one of the major criticisms of the American political system is that the framers were too successful. America's national government is so hedged with restrictions on its powers and so open to the input of every imaginable faction or interest group that it can rarely develop a coherent set of national policies.[5]

Madison, then, strove to mitigate the worst effects of faction rather than eliminate the causes of faction altogether. As he saw it, the causes of faction are "sown in the nature of man." Given the human tendency toward disagreement and disharmony, factional differences will always exist. Thus, government can never eliminate the causes of faction; government can only eliminate or suppress faction itself. But governmental suppression of faction would destroy liberty, thus making the cure worse than the disease. Rather than try to suppress faction, Madison and the framers chose to allow a diversity of factions within a complex system of political and social pluralism, ensuring that all interests could be heard, while making it difficult for any one interest to gain tyrannical control of power.

From a modern perspective, Madison's view of faction was both wise and prescient. Tens of thousands of interest groups have formed and thrived since the early days of the republic, allowing widespread input into the policy process from millions of average citizens, yet no one group has ever gained full control of all the levers of political and social power. Setting group against group in relatively peaceful competition within a complex system of divided powers seems to have been a successful vision of the way to deal with the fissures and stresses that are inevitable in a free society.

Political parties formed in the very early years of the republic, and groups of every type and description began to flourish soon thereafter. Revivalist religious groups, social reform groups, peace groups, women's rights groups, abolitionist groups, temperance groups—these and hundreds of others that sprang up in the first half of the nineteenth century bore witness to Madison's expectation that the air of liberty would do nothing but nourish a swarm of factional organizations. It is hardly surprising that American political history is in many ways a history of diverse and competing interest groups.

The organizational ease with which groups are formed in the United States is generally attributed to its democratic culture. Americans, who often see themselves as equals, usually find it easy to work together in groups toward common ends. Tocqueville wrote that "in no other country of the world has the principle of association been more successfully used, or more unsparingly applied to a multitude of different objects, than in America."[6] While all modern democracies exhibit interest group activity, few have achieved the level of vibrant nongovernmental group life apparent in the American system.

Recent Trends

Even though interest groups have been central to American political history, the number of groups trying to pressure government has grown dramatically in the last three decades. The reasons for this development are complex. For one, government policies since the 1960s have resulted in greater regulation of society. Responding to demands that Washington "do something" about the problems of civil rights, the environment, education, conditions in the workplace, health, women's rights, and so forth, the national government has developed policies that affect all sectors of society. Government regulations now touch all Americans. Naturally, people whose livelihoods and values are affected by government actions find it

FYI

In 1831 Tocqueville noted the tendency of Americans to form groups for any purpose whatever. "There are," he wrote, "not only commercial and industrial associations . . . but others of a thousand different types—religious, moral, serious, futile, very general and very limited, immensely large and very minute."

▲ From Seattle to Washington, D.C., protests against the World Bank continued in April 2000. While remaining much more peaceful than the Seattle protests (shown here), Washington saw occasional clashes.

expedient to work together to influence those actions. Thus, as government's power to affect society grows, so, too, does the number of groups that aim to influence and pressure government.

Another explanation for the growth of interest groups stems from the success that liberal interest groups experienced starting in the 1950s. In the past, conservative groups rarely relied upon group activity to advance their aims because conservatives were already active in civic affairs, being on the average wealthier, better educated, and more likely to participate in politics than average citizens. Thus, they were already well represented in government and believed that it adequately responded to their needs. Conversely, those groups most underrepresented in political institutions were most likely to use interest groups to pursue policy goals. These groups tended to promote the liberal aims of civil rights groups, environmentalists, the poor, and women.

By the 1970s, liberal groups had gained many victories through the pressure they exerted on Congress, the executive branch, and the courts. Moreover, the federal government actually sponsored citizen-group involvement by reimbursing participants with seed money or outright grants. Federal domestic legislation included provisions for citizen participation that spurred group organizations such as environmental action councils, legal defense coalitions, health care organizations, and senior citizen groups.[7] Manufacturing and business leaders, along with ideological conservatives of every type, responded by forming their own interest groups. These conservative groups developed their own dynamism in reaction to the social-policy gains made previously by liberals. While Planned Parenthood, the American Civil Liberties Union, and other groups considered liberal fought battles to gain abortion and privacy rights, political conservatives countered in the late 1970s and 1980s with groups such as Operation Rescue and the Moral Majority. Thus, the success of liberal interest groups led to the rise of conservative counterpart groups.

A major impetus toward increasing group involvement in politics came in the early 1970s with campaign finance reform. Two acts (one in 1971 and its amendments in 1974) changed the nature of money in American politics. As you saw in Chapter 9, these laws limited the role of individual "fat cats" and expanded the power of **political action committees (PACs)**, groups whose main aim is to financially promote the political goals of particular interest groups. Rather than seeking large donations from a small number of very wealthy individuals, these groups raised small amounts of money from large numbers of contributors and combined them for maximum effectiveness.

Finally, increasing income and education levels have led to increased levels of political activity in the United States over the past sixty years. The United States now has a large middle class and upper middle class of educated, affluent voters who are vitally aware of the political process and how it affects them. Many of these people have become deeply involved in politics—especially in groups that promote their interests and concerns. No theory seeking to explain the rise in the number and power of American interest groups can fail to take into account this important social development. Figure 11.1 shows how membership in the NRA has risen over the years.

Functions of Interest Groups

political action committees (PACs) Committees formed as the fund-raising and financial distribution arm of specific interest groups.

Interest groups provide people with the opportunity to band together to influence public policy and are therefore central to the operations of democracy. They also provide policy makers with information; indeed, members of Congress have come to depend on the expertise and information provided by interest groups as part of their deliberative process.

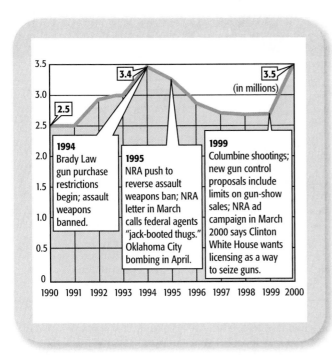

Figure 11.1
How NRA Membership Has Risen

Source: USA Today, May 18, 2000, p. 4A. Copyright © 2000 *USA Today.* Reprinted with permission.

Interest Groups Allow for Collective Action

People form and join interest groups because **collective action** (the action of many) is stronger, more credible, and more likely to influence policy outcomes than the isolated actions of individuals.[8] Imagine, for example, the modest influence you would have if you alone wrote a letter to your congressional representative to protest a new law. You would probably receive a form letter from a staff member expressing concern about the issue, to be followed later by another letter asking for a campaign donation. Your individual letter will not change policy. But what if you joined a group whose goal was to persuade several thousand others to write and complain about this law? Collective action of that sort would surely be taken more seriously than the actions of one or a few individuals. As the Approaching Democracy in the New Millennium box (see page 412) on the new "netizens" organizations and their protests on behalf of liberty on the Internet shows, this form of collective action lobbying resulted in the elimination of portions of the Communications Decency Act of 1996.

Collective action was effective in the protests of the early 1970s, when students temporarily shut down many colleges across the nation as part of their protest against the Vietnam War, or the 1960s, when civil disobedience by African Americans led to changes in our civil rights policies. And it is used now when groups of people demonstrate at environmental sites or collect money to buy threatened land areas in order to save them from development. In time, if enough people join such interest groups, they could have important consequences for election outcomes.

Group action is also more effective in politics, where the power of numbers carries special weight. Thus, interest groups serve a number of important functions in the American political system. They allow citizens to promote their specialized concerns. Through interest group activity, people can join with like-minded others rather than have to blend in under the common umbrella of a large political institution like a political party. In representing specific points of view in society, interest groups can project precise citizen demands into politics, bringing both government and the political parties closer to the people, thereby democratizing the national

collective action The political action of individuals who unite to influence policy.

THE ROAD TO DEMOCRACY

Half a Century of Student Protest

ew people realize that America's Approach to Democracy over the last 50 years has been fueled, and at times actually led, by college student protests. Americans have a proud history of student protests over the last half century. In the 1940s and 1950s labor unions mobilized student-run groups like the American Student Congress to help fight labor issues such as inadequate pay and racial discrimination. At the same time the American Communist party recruited student chapters on campuses. In time, professional activists in the NAACP began to recruit students to help in the fight for civil rights.

THAT WAS THEN . . .

On February 1, 1960 student protests reached a crossroads as four African-American students in North Carolina engaged in a sit-in, protesting the lack of civil rights for African-Americans, by refusing to leave a segregated lunch counter at F.W. Woolworth's in Greensboro, North Carolina. By May of that year the Student Nonviolent Coordinating Committee (SNCC) was formed to lobby for civil rights, naming as its president Marion Barry of Fisk University, later the mayor of Washington, D.C. This group helped to register minority voters in the South, often with bloody riots resulting. In June 1962, Tom Hayden of the University of Michigan, later a California State Senator, held a retreat in Port Huron, Michigan and drafted the manifesto for the Students for a Democratic Society (SDS). This group later protested against the Vietnam War and participated in the riots at the 1968 Democratic Convention in Chicago.

In March 1965 members and leaders of SNCC were beaten as they marched for civil rights from Montgomery to Selma, Alabama. The photos of the students being attacked, as they used Ghandi's nonviolent resistance technique, became the basis for the passage of the 1965 Voting Rights Act. When progress in civil rights was not as evident as some would like, new leaders for SNCC advocated a more violent protest approach, and another group, the Black Panthers, formed to achieve change "by any means possible." In time, an even more radical group of student dropouts formed a group called the Weather Underground to "make revolution."

By 1968 the focus of student protest changed from civil rights to ending America's involvement in the war in Vietnam. College-age students, who were too young to vote yet were old enough to fight in Vietnam, began to vigorously protest against the war. Student protests continued across the nation until on May 2, 1970, four students were killed and nine were injured by National Guardsmen at Kent State University in Ohio, many of whom were the same age as the student protestors. Eventually America's participation in the war ended, but before that time 18 to 21 year old Americans were given the right to vote by the adoption of the twenty-sixth Amendment

By 1985, student groups across the nation were back at work protesting the connection between the investment portfolios of their colleges and universities and the segregation-promoting apartheid government in South Africa. Students at Cornell and Penn State Universities built cardboard and tin buildings on their campuses to protest the shantytowns in which the blacks were forced to live in that country. While 1,000 students were arrested at Cornell, eventually, colleges and universities, as well as American companies, were forced to divest themselves of

agenda. It was through interest group activity that the perspectives of the abolitionist movement, which sought to end slavery, came to be absorbed into the political outlook of the pre-Civil War Republican party, just as the perspective of the civil rights movement of the twentieth century was largely absorbed by the post–New Deal Democrats.

Question for Reflection: Given this history and success of the student protest movement, one is left to wonder how will America's approach to democracy be affected in the twenty-first century by student actions?

Interest Groups Provide Information

Interest groups possess the expertise to provide relevant information about policy goals to party leaders, public officials, and bureaucrats who would otherwise not have these facts at their disposal. Through this function, interest groups provide an important avenue for broader participation in the actual policy-making process.

Interest groups provide government officials with a constant, reliable source of information about popular sentiment. Sometimes this information is technical in

holdings in South Africa and eventually, thanks to Nelson Mandella, Bishop Desmond Tutu, and their followers, apartheid was ended.

THIS IS NOW . . .

The 1990s represented a return to the links between students protestors and labor unions as students who would eventually work for large corporations joined the AFL–CIO's Union Summer to learn protest tactics. In the summer of 1998 Union Summer launched United Students Against Sweatshops to protest the cheap labor shops in foreign countries that were used to produce the logo-bearing clothing so popular on campuses throughout the United States. As a result of the growth of over 100 chapters of this group and their work against such companies as Nike, many colleges and universities changed their policies for dealing with these businesses.

The end of the millennium saw students in December 1999 join protestors in Seattle who sought to disrupt the meeting of the World Trade Organization in Seattle. When as many as 50,000 people marched in protest of the monetary gap between the industrialized countries and the Third World and the lack of attention given to poverty by the World Trade Organization, a riot ensued. Six hundred protestors were arrested, compromising the peaceful intentions of the majority. In the end, the meeting produced no new agreements and was called a failure by analysts.

After a twenty-day student sit-in protest in 2001, Harvard's administration agreed to create a commission to study the issue of raising the hourly wage for the school's janitors. What will the next student protest be?

▲ Students at Harvard University engage in a sit-in protest in 2001 on behalf of raising the hourly wage for the school's janitors.

Source: Based on Stephanie Gutmann, "Half a Century of Student Protest," "Education Life" section, *New York Times*, November 11, 2001, p. 29.

nature, educating public officials about the details of a topic; this information is always slanted, however, in the direction of an outcome that the group seeks. At other times the information is political in nature, educating public officials about the consequences among the voting electorate of making a decision one way or another. Since both of these types of information are important for policy makers, interest groups serve as a vital indicator of the system's responsiveness to citizen demands. The more public officials hear the varied voices of the people, the more likely they are to take those voices into account in formulating government policies.

While interest groups are an important element in American democratic life, many observers fear that their effects are not all positive. Because interest groups focus only on their own cause, they are said to downplay or ignore the public good. Furthermore, by creating a proliferation of competing demands and divisive rhetoric, the vast array of interest groups may drown out moderate voices of compromise and cooperation. The information supplied by interest groups can be biased, leaving officials and the public with just one perspective on an issue. Furthermore, interest groups are not all equal. The powerful groups tend to be those already in control of the major resources in society, especially money and property. Large corporations tend to dominate the sphere of interest group activity, and their activities often overwhelm groups trying to promote consumer safety, workers' welfare, and environmental protection.[9]

Interest groups thus represent a peculiar irony of democracy. While stimulating citizen action and political involvement, they can also create confrontation instead of cooperation, diatribe in place of reasoned debate. Although they allow a role for average citizens to promote their democratic goals, interest groups can also skew the political process to favor those who are already powerful and well off. The "factions" that so concerned Madison are now powerful, well-financed organizations. Can a modern democratic system preserve liberty—allowing groups free rein to promote their goals—without sacrificing the very essence of the democratic ideal—widespread access to power for all citizens? That is one of the central questions that American society continually confronts as it struggles to approach democracy.

Types of Interest Groups

Nearly 20,000 organized groups of every imaginable kind regularly seek to influence the policies of the American government. These groups take a wide variety of forms, but for simplicity we can divide them into a few major types: economic, public interest, government, ideological, religious, civil rights, single-issue, state, and local interest groups. Table 11.1 shows the different types of groups that participated in world trade protests in Washington, D.C., in April 2000.

Table 11.1 ■ World Trade Protest Groups

	Religious Groups	Environmental Groups	Organized Labor	Student Groups	Ad Hoc Coalitions
Some of the Main Groups	A movement known as Jubilee 2000, backed primarily by Catholics and Protestant churches.	Friends of the Earth, the Sierra Club, and the Rainforest Action Network.	The AFL-CIO, the United Steelworkers of America, and the Teamsters Union.	United Students Against Sweatshops and the U.S. Student Association.	Global Exchange, 50 Years Is Enough, and the Ruckus Society.
Among Their Main Complaints	That many of the poorest nations are overburdened with international debt and deserve debt forgiveness.	That the spread of free market capitalism is damaging forests, silting rivers, contributing to greenhouse gas emissions, and destroying the natural resources of poor nations.	That global trade will have a negative effect on workers' jobs in wealthy countries. Labor groups have pushed for stricter trade and labor standards worldwide.	That U.S. companies that make consumer products sometimes tolerate poor working conditions in overseas factories.	That globalization worsens social injustice, poverty, and animal rights, and speeds the erosion of indigenous cultures.
Why They Are Protesting the World Bank and the IMF	The World Bank and the IMF are among the leading lenders to the poorest countries. Many religious groups criticize these lenders for a slow and half-hearted response to the push for debt relief.	Some accuse the World Bank of funding energy and road projects that hasten environmental degradation. These groups contend that the IMF encourages governments to curtail spending on environmental protection in return for aid.	Some say the lenders encourage poor nations to develop big export-oriented industries, costing U.S. jobs. Labor's main goal, however, is to rewrite trade rules enforced by the World Trade Organization.	Some student groups accuse the World Bank and the IMF of protecting the interests of corporations over the rights of workers abroad and of forcing Third World corporations to open their doors to investment by multinational companies.	The World Bank and the IMF are seen as the main villains of globalization, capitalist enforcers trying to make the world safe for big corporations.

Source: From *New York Times,* April 15, 2000, p. 8. Copyright © by The New York Times Co. Reprinted by permission of *The New York Times.*

Economic Interest Groups

On a day-in, day-out basis, most observers would rate the power of economic interests as dominant in politics. The old saying, "Most people vote their pocketbooks" applies to group activity as well. Most people take political action to protect or enhance their economic well-being. Thus, groups whose main aim is to help their members make money or keep money will always play a central role in the political process of any democracy. Economic interest groups include business, organized labor, and similar groups.

Business   Corporations have long dominated interest group activity in American politics, as is clear from the lobbying efforts by the Enron Corporation. That pattern is hardly surprising in an environment of entrepreneurial capitalism. Calvin Coolidge made the point concisely: "The business of America is business." The United States' political process almost seems designed to illustrate Coolidge's observation. Over half the lobbies operating in Washington today represent corporate and industrial interests.[10] Sometimes those groups represent single businesses, but other times groups of businesses unite in trade associations, which lobby on a much broader range of issues. For individual business members of these associations, the group not only gives them additional clout from other allied companies but also multiple points of access to the political system at both federal and state levels.

▲ Members of the Black Farmers and Agriculturist Association protest USDA racism and discrimination in Little Rock, Arkansas.

Heading the list of business-oriented trade associations is the U.S. Chamber of Commerce, which represents 225,000 businesses across the nation, including manufacturers, retailers, construction firms, and financial, insurance, and real estate companies. With an annual budget of more than $65 million and a full-time staff of 1,400, the Chamber of Commerce carries considerable political clout. Other major business interest groups in this category include the National Association of Manufacturers (NAM) and the Business Roundtable. These were the groups that led the fight against Clinton's health care reforms in the mid-1990s. However, individual health maintenance organizations (HMOs) also played a role.

In addition to belonging to umbrella trade associations, many large and medium-sized companies, numbering some five hundred in Washington alone, such as IBM, Ford, General Motors, Exxon, and Xerox, maintain their own lobbyists to ensure that their voices are heard. Before the failed efforts of the Enron Corporation, one of the best examples of how individual business lobbying works was how various tobacco businesses spent tens of millions of dollars in seeking to influence tobacco-control legislation at both the federal and state levels. Corporate executives from the U.S. tobacco industry testified that smoking does not cause cancer. Later internal documents proved that their own research indicated that smoking causes cancer as well as other serious physical maladies such as emphysema and heart disease. And, like the problems faced by the Enron executives, the tobacco companies and their executives faced law suits and legislative control efforts across the country.

Organized Labor   Despite its power, business is not the only voice of organized economic interest. From the late nineteenth century until the middle of the twentieth, labor played a major role in American politics. Indeed, the influential economist John Kenneth Galbraith once called labor unions an important "countervailing power" that could stand up to and dilute the power of business.[11] But their power has declined in recent years. Unionized workers, who once represented nearly 36 percent of the work force, now account for less than 15 percent of it. Still, the AFL-CIO, labor's umbrella organization, continues to represent millions of workers and puts intense pressure on politicians for better wages, improved working conditions, job protection, social programs, and health insurance. Other major labor groups include the United Auto Workers, the United Mine Workers, and the Teamsters (a union representing workers in the transportation industry).

Although it often appears that business and labor are always at odds, they occasionally join forces. For instance, when the Chrysler Corporation was seeking

Lobbying Gone Bad: Lessons From Enron

Money cannot buy everything in politics, as the corporate officers at Enron Corporation learned. Sometimes, after all the money spent on lobbying, businesses and interest groups not only do not get what they want, but they find politicians backing away from them to avoid the public perception of being bought.

In late January 2002 ten House and Senate committees were investigating just how Enron, the seventh-largest company in the nation which traded in gas, electricity and other commodities to public utilities, virtually disappeared taking with it the jobs and retirement funds of thousands of its workers, while enriching its company executives and leading to the suicide of one of those executives.

Enron began in 1985 as a pipeline gas company based in Houston that promised to deliver natural gas to public utilities at a guaranteed price on a particular day. By 1992 the company was exempted from oversight by the Commodity Futures Trading Commission, then headed by Wendy Gramm, the wife of Senator Philip Gramm (R.-TX). She later became a member of the Enron board. When lobbying by senior Enron officials led to the electrical power markets being de-regulated, Enron Chairman Kenneth L. Lay expanded the company's trading to other commodities, such as electricity. At the same time, Arthur Andersen, one of the largest accounting companies in the world, developed Enron's financial statements which encouraged investment in the company, while some of its company officials took positions in Enron itself to manage its bookkeeping. By August of 2000 the company share price had risen to $90, up from a mere $20 a share in January of 1998 and company expansion continued.

By the 2000 election cycle Enron company members and its executives poured $1.7 million into various political campaigns. Over the years, over $500,000 was given to George W. Bush's various campaigns for office. At the same time, Enron grew into a hybrid company that worked much like a commodity exchange, buying energy from a supplying company and earning a profit on the deal, before selling that same energy to a utility and earning additional profit on this second transaction. This system assured that only Enron knew both the buying and selling prices of their energy.

Confidence in the company began to fall however, and the stock value dropped steadily in the final months of 2000 and the first seven months of 2001. Efforts were made to hide the company's expanding losses from public view, while one senior vice president of the company, Sherron Watkins, warned Chairman Kenneth Lay in an anonymous memo that Enron "might implode in a wave of accounting scandals." On September 26, 2001, Chairman Kenneth Lay sent an email to his employees claiming that the company's stock was "an incredible bargain" and predicted that the third quarter earnings would be very strong. Despite this claim, by October of 2001, the Enron house of cards began to collapse. Enron had spawned a number of large company partnerships to hide the enormous company debt. Senior Enron officials drew huge salaries and exercised their stock options as the stock prices fell, while company workers were prohibited from divesting themselves of the company stock that comprised their entire retirement portfolio. Arthur Andersen fired the head Enron auditor after charges that he had ordered key company documents to be shredded to frustrate a company audit.

In an attempt to contain these problems, Kenneth Lay tried to cash in on his campaign contributions calling on the Bush administration officials that he knew, among them Treasury Secretary Paul H. O'Neill and Commerce Secretary Donald L. Evans. Both men declined to help the company. However, the Bush administration did try to help the company divest itself of a power plant in India that was going bad for $2.3 billion. Vice President Cheney even

---

government loans in 1981, one of the most ardent backers of the loan program was the United Auto Workers, which hoped to preserve the tens of thousands of jobs its workers held in Chrysler plants.

Other Economic Interest Groups　It is probably no exaggeration to say that some kind of interest group exists to protect and promote the interests of every group of people who make their living in the United States. Beyond workers and businesspeople, groups exist to advance the interests of lawyers (the American Bar Association), doctors (the American Medical Association), teachers (the National Education Association), and so forth.

Farmers were once among the most powerful groups in the United States and are still solidly represented by such organizations as the American Farm Bureau Federation, the National Corn Growers Association, and the National Farmers Union. The power of agricultural interests has inevitably diminished as the number of farmers has steadily declined, mirroring a pattern in all industrial nations.

mentioned the company to India's Congress party leader Sonia Gandhi, during her visit to the United States.

With the company collapsing, the support that it had tried to build eroded. On October 16, 2001, Enron announced a $638 million loss for the third quarter. Its stock, then at 34, plummeted 25 points that month, and was reduced to 34 cents by January 23, 2002. As a result, billions of dollars in employee mutual funds were lost. Meanwhile, Arthur Andersen tried to distance itself from the disaster by saying that it would take "all appropriate steps" to defend its integrity. Attorney General John Ashcroft, who had received Enron money for his failed 2000 Senate campaign, recused himself from the Justice Department's investigation of the company. The White House denied any substantive connection with the company, despite the campaign contributions coming to them, and President Bush claimed that his own mother-in-law had lost money on the company.

By January 2002 all of their lobbying had done nothing for the company officials. Chairman Kenneth Lay resigned from his position on January 23, and CEO Jeffrey Skilling did the same earlier. Thousands of hard-working Enron employees lost their jobs and their entire retirement portfolios. Banks such as J.P. Morgan Chase, who had underwritten the company, lost nearly a billion dollars. Arthur Anderson suffered a severe client drain and laid off thousands of employees worldwide. Prominent politicians in both political parties announced that they would be returning the contributions they had received from the company, or contribute it to charity. With dozens of lawsuits being filed against the company around the nation, one judge contemplated freezing the assets of company executives to pay for possible judgments against them. In addition to the investigations of the collapse by Congress and the Department of Justice, the Securities and Exchange Commission launched an investigation. Officials at Arthur Andersen were found guilty of violating federal law in destroying documents and hiding the losses. And for all of the lobbying and government investigations, no one could figure out either how this could have happened, or how it might be

▲ Looking for work? The collapse of the huge energy corporation Enron in 2002 threw thousands of highly qualified people out of work, stripped them of their pensions consisting entirely of company stock, and caused chaos in the political world.

prevented in the future. With politicians beginning to return contributions from another failed company—WorldCom, a communications firm—one longtime lobbyist said of the Enron scandal's effect on his profession, "It's turning Washington upside down."

Source: "Enron: A Primer," *Washington Post,* January 24, 2002, p. A11; Gail Russell Chaddock, "Lobbyists Find a Tougher Sell After Enron," *Christian Science Monitor,* March 6, 2002.

People who make more than half their income through farming now represent less than 2 percent of the U.S. work force. Still, given the importance of this segment of the population, which provides food for Americans and many others around the world, it is safe to say that farm groups will continue to wield major political power for some time to come. This was shown in mid-2002 by members of the Black Farmers and Agriculturist Association protesting in the hopes of receiving the $50,000 payments promised them in order to remedy the allegations of racism by the USDA in awarding its agricultural grants.

Public Interest Groups

Economic self-interest, though a powerful force, represents just one of the reasons that people come together in groups to secure collective action from government. One of the most interesting developments in American government since the 1960s is the dramatic increase in **public interest groups.** These groups represent the

public interest groups Groups that focus not on the immediate economic livelihood of their members, but on achieving a broad set of goals that represent their members' vision of the collective good. Examples include the National Taxpayers Union, the League of Women Voters, and Common Cause.

interests of average citizens as consumers, as holders of individual rights, as proponents of various causes, and as the disadvantaged. Public interest groups focus not on the immediate economic livelihood of their members but on achieving a broad set of goals that represent their members' vision of the collective good. Their members and leaders seek substantive policy as their goal ("clean air"), not specific increments of economic well-being ("twenty cents more an hour for minimum wage workers").

Some of the best-known public interest groups include Citizens for Tax Justice, the Nature Conservancy, the Natural Resources Defense Council, the National Taxpayers Union, the National Organization for Women, the League of Women Voters, and Common Cause. Seeing their goal as the achievement of policy favorable to all citizens, public interest groups recruit widely and welcome the support of the general public.

Ralph Nader is one of the best-known public interest group advocates in the nation. A Harvard-trained lawyer, Nader became famous in the 1960s when he challenged General Motors and its Corvair automobile, which he considered unsafe. In 1965 he published *Unsafe at Any Speed* and later created the group Public Citizen, which is devoted to making the legal system more responsive to the public. In addition, in many states, Nader's Public Interest Research Groups (PIRGs) are popular with students. They provide oversight on auto safety, consumer issues, health issues, and the environment. Today there are more than two hundred such groups, and they claim among their victories nonsmoking rules on airlines, nutrition labels, and laws requiring smoke detectors in apartment buildings.

Perhaps the best-known public interest group is Common Cause, which promotes campaign reform, the abolition of political action committees (PACs), the elimination of unneeded bureaucratic institutions, and in other ways aims to achieve "good government." Common Cause has more than 250,000 members and an $11 million annual budget. Its central target has been the abuse of money in the political process.[12] Common Cause has been especially outraged by the cozy relationship between interest group contributions and political influence. It points, for instance, to the fact that the National Rifle Association can contribute money to members of the Senate Judiciary Committee, which has the job of reviewing firearms legislation, and that the American Medical Association and American Dental Association can contribute millions to members of Congress who serve on committees that consider regulations that affect business practices in these professions. Emphasizing that PAC expenditures on congressional races are at an all-time high, Common Cause recently sought to organize People versus PACs, a campaign designed to clean up the financing of congressional elections. Common Cause's long-time efforts to reduce or eliminate the influence of money in politics eventually led to the passage of the Bipartisan Campaign Finance Reform Act of 2002.

▲ Green Party presidential candidate Ralph Nader has spent his career as a public interest group advocate.

? **Question for Reflection:** Interest groups give a stronger voice to citizens' concerns. How might the isolation of interest groups be overcome to form a new, more unified multi-issue approach to democracy?

Government Interest Groups

A recent addition to the interest group mix has been government itself. Today, the National Conference of Mayors, the National League of Cities, the National Governors' Association, and other organizations composed of government officials compete alongside traditional interest groups for funding, policies, and attention.

Although questions have been raised about whether government interest groups should be competing for scarce resources, these groups are well funded, very influential, and easily able to gain access to the halls of Congress. Their right to act as interest groups was affirmed in an important 1985 Supreme Court case, *Garcia v. San*

Antonio Metropolitan Transit Authority. The opinion's author, Justice Harry Blackmun, refused to grant authority to the states to set their own compensation rates for municipal employees. States, he said, like private employers, would have to abide by the regulations governing wages established in the federal Fair Labor Standards Act. Blackmun argued that states were inherently well represented in Congress—through automatic representation in the Senate and secondary representation in the House—and were responsible for petitioning Congress to make laws in accordance with their wishes.[13] Immediately following the *Garcia* decision, a number of government interest groups successfully lobbied Congress to grant exemptions from the Fair Labor Standards Act to public employees. Government agencies and officials are under no constitutional restraints when it comes to forming their own interest groups to place pressure on other agencies and officials of our government, thereby strengthening the concept of federalism.

Ideological Interest Groups

Some people get into politics to promote deep-seated ideological beliefs. They are not satisfied with limited changes and solutions. They want nothing less than to transform society and the political process along the lines of some broad philosophical perspective. Such people form ideological interest groups. The best known is Americans for Democratic Action (ADA). Founded in 1947 by Hubert Humphrey, John Kenneth Galbraith, and Eleanor Roosevelt to oppose the more centrist policies of President Harry Truman, ADA has been pushing ever since for an entire set of policy proposals that would create a coherently liberal society. To counter ADA efforts, a group known as the American Conservative Union (ACU) sprang up a few years later to promote a conservative agenda. Other ideologically oriented groups include the American Civil Liberties Union (ACLU) on civil liberties issues, People for the American Way (liberal) on legal issues, and the Concord Coalition (conservative) on tax and budget issues.

In keeping with our American culture's tendency toward pragmatism, ideological interest groups have always been few in number and consist primarily of a small number of dedicated activists. Still, because these activists are energetic, well educated, well connected, and adept at raising money, ideological interest groups frequently wield a good deal more clout than one would expect from numbers alone. A prominent example of this clout came in 1987 when a group of liberal interest groups, such as the People for the American Way and the National Association for the Advancement of Colored People united to defeat Robert Bork's nomination to the Supreme Court.

Religious Interest Groups

A variant of the ideological interest group is the group that wishes to transform society along the lines of its religious beliefs. As you would expect in a society where most people take religion seriously, groups seeking to bring religious values into the political arena have at one time or another had powerful effects on American politics. Perhaps the most famous example of religion's impact was the Prohibition movement, which in the nineteenth and early twentieth century sought to ban the sale and consumption of alcohol. The movement was driven by church and religious groups throughout the nation. Among the more powerful religious groups today are the Christian Coalition, the Catholic Alliance, the National Council of Churches (mainstream Protestantism), B'nai B'rith's Anti-Defamation League (Judaism), and the Council of Catholic Bishops.

Sometimes these groups oppose each other, but when they unite on questions of freedom of religion, as they did in seeking to overturn a Supreme Court decision to create the Religious Freedom Restoration Act (RFRA) and to secure government vouchers for students to attend religious schools, they can be particularly effective with governing officials (see Chapter 13).

APPROACHING DEMOCRACY AROUND THE GLOBE

The Perils of International Democracy Assistance

While the operations of interest groups seem easy in America's democracy, trying to invest in the duplication of that system in other countries is fraught with peril. Sometimes you don't get what you pay for.

Those who tried to start a democratic regime in the Central Asian region of Kazakhstan in the early 1990s found this to be dangerous work. Opponents of the nation's president, Nursultan Nazarbayev, were brutally assaulted and intimidated by the secret police. Representatives of the International Republican Institute (IRI), which is identified with the Republican party in the United States, in nearby Caspia, were murdered. Under pressure from the West, Nazarbayev allowed a bit more freedom of the press and political pluralism, but still acted to preserve his political power.

In 1995, the Franklin Printing Company invested three million dollars of American taxpayer money in what the State Department declared to be "an emerging democracy" in Kazakhstan, an oil-rich country in Central Asia. The goal, through this "democracy assistance" was to improve the freedom of the press in this region in the hope that informed groups of people would organize in the country to promote democratic reforms. This kind of international assistance has been expanding for years, with the U.S. Agency for International Development (USAID) spending $649 million in democracy programs in 2000, up nearly half a billion dollars from 1991. Nations such as Yugoslavia, Slovakia, and Peru benefited from such democracy-building efforts.

But the campaign has not been as successful in Central Asia. After five years of spending, the dictatorial president of the Kazakh government became embroiled in a corruption scandal with allegations of multimillion-dollar deposits by international oil companies in Swiss bank accounts. The printing company, which is named for Benjamin Franklin, is owned by a firm linked to the Kazakh president's daughter. Whatever money is spent to increase political freedom, it seems, is insufficient to counteract the influence of entrenched leaders such as khans, commissars, and presidents-for-life.

Despite the lack of success of international democracy-building aid in this region, supporters of the policy plead for time to allow it to work. "We are building political parties, NGOs [nongovernmental organizations] and political activities," argues Eric Kessler, the representative in Central Asia for the National Democratic Institute (NDI), which is affiliated with the United States Democratic party. "We shouldn't turn our backs on the political activists of these countries just because the regimes will not let them be effective for many years."

Just how did the money happen to be spent in this region of the world? The Kazakh president, and his main political opponent, hired high-priced Washington lawyers, public-relations firms and political lobbyists to lobby for government money to be spent in that region for democracy-assistance. Millions of dollars were spent in this country using the lessons of democracy lobbying for money that theoretically would help create the conditions in Kazakhstan for developing democracy. Illustrating the questionable nature of the Kazakhstan leadership's effort towards democracy, some of this lobbying money was funneled through Liechtenstein-based foundations and offshore Caribbean banks.

Will this effort to nurture democracy in this Central Asian region be successful? Thomas Carothers, a Brookings Institution scholar, argues that democracy assistance is most effective "when a country is clearly moving forward to democracy," or at the moment of greatest political ferment, such as in Yugoslavia in recent years. In Central Asia, though, interest in democratic reform is low. In the end, says Natalia Chumakova, a Kazakh human rights observer, "it is not for USAID to create democracy here. Democracy must grow in our hearts. As long as it is not there, no amount of outside help will create it."

Source: Michael Dobbs, "Investment in Freedom is Flush with Peril; from Kazakhstan, A Cautionary Tale," *Washington Post,* January 25, 2001.

Civil Rights Interest Groups

Similar to ideological interest groups are groups that seek to promote the legal rights of minorities and others who have suffered discrimination. All of these groups seek to transform society to ensure legal equality and social justice for their members. They focus on creating an egalitarian society in which their members are given equal opportunities for advancement and are accepted into mainstream society without denigration. One of the best known of these groups is the National Association for the Advancement of Colored People (NAACP), which for decades was the driving force behind the black civil rights movement. Other well-known groups of this sort include the National Organization for Women (NOW), the

American Indian Movement (AIM), the Mexican-American Legal Defense and Educational Fund (MALDEF), and various organizations that protect and seek to advance the rights of gay Americans.[14]

Single-Issue Interest Groups

As the name implies, single-issue interest groups are organizations that represent citizens who are primarily concerned with one particular policy or social problem. For many participants in such interest groups, the one issue that drives them to political activity looms so large in their value scheme that all other issues seem insignificant by comparison. Hence, group members are both intense and uncompromising in promoting their aims.

Groups of this type that are currently powerful in American politics include the National Rifle Association (NRA), the National Coalition to Ban Handguns, the National Right to Life Committee, and the National Abortion Rights Action League (NARAL). Sometimes the single issue that leads to the creation of an interest group can expand to encompass a series of related issues, all with a single goal. Such is the case with the Sierra Club and the Environmental Defense Fund (EDF), both of which fight for the preservation of the environment. The multimillion-member Sierra Club began in the early 1970s in response to the threat of Walt Disney Corporation to create a ski resort known as the Mineral King Resort on the edge of the Sequoia National Forest in California. Not only was this group successful in this fight, but it has saved countless other pristine natural areas from destructive development since then.

Given their uncompromising beliefs, single-issue activists present a prickly problem for politicians, whose usual job consists of balancing competing demands and reaching judicious compromise solutions. Single-issue groups do not look kindly upon compromise. Their supporters often take a bipolar view of the world: if you're not with them, you're against them—an enemy to be crushed and defeated. Inevitably, single-issue groups raise political temperatures and exacerbate conflict whenever they get seriously involved in politics. Many politicians shudder at the prospect of having to deal with them.

Characteristics of Interest Groups

Although each interest group is unique, most share characteristics that distinguish them from other organizations in society. For instance, interest groups, unlike political parties, rarely try to get their leaders elected to major political positions, but they do target elected officials who are unsympathetic to their interests and support those who are sympathetic. Interest groups want to influence government, not *be* government, and they seek a government of policy makers who support their goals.

In addition, interest groups do not usually have as their main aim business, trade, or the making of money. They may promote business interests, and they may incidentally make money in one way or another (through the sale of books, maps, insurance policies, or other items for members), but profit is not their main focus. Interest groups are quintessentially government-influencing institutions. Their goal of pressuring government decision makers sets them apart from the other major structures of American society: government itself, political parties, business enterprises, and run-of-the-mill social groups that do not undertake political activities (such as the Lions Club or the Masons).

Interest Group Membership

Interest groups need members to survive and prosper, and in a democratic society, the more members a group has, the more political clout it will wield. Scholars have

FYI

Did you know there is a "Christian Left"? One such group, called Bread for the World, was founded in 1973 by Arthur Simon, a Lutheran pastor and brother of former U.S. Senator Paul Simon. BFW has approximately 40,000 members, mainly Catholic, Methodist, and Lutheran churches, and focuses on traditionally liberal issues, such as resolving hunger problems.

long sought to learn why some interest groups are more successful than others in attracting members. Closely related to that question is another: Why do some groups form and prosper while others never get started, or if they do, falter and disappear?

Maintaining Interest Group Membership An interest group forms when some citizens, be they few or many, perceive that the political arena is failing to provide the policy outcomes they prefer, or when some citizens have been adversely affected by technological change or by government policies. Many other factors influence the development of a particular interest group: the presence of strong, dynamic leaders, the financial and educational resources of the group, the geographic concentration of the group (it's easier to unite workers in one large factory than people who clean individual homes across a large city). Many factors help determine the likelihood that a group will become cognizant of itself and band together in a formal organization to promote a common interest.

Perhaps the central question about why people form and join interest groups follows from our earlier discussion about the likelihood of a potential group becoming an actual group. Just because people with a common interest exist, it does not automatically follow that they will form a group and become active in promoting its aims. No one is obliged to become an interest group member. As with all life choices, people must decide that the expenditure of time, money, and effort on interest group activity is worthwhile. And no one is obliged to remain a group member, as the ACLU learned when nearly half of its members resigned over the group's decision to support the free speech rights of the American Nazi party to march in Skokie, Illinois, a region populated by survivors of the Holocaust. Some groups that are united by common economic interests and goals, such as businesses, unions, and trade associations, do not have such problems organizing and maintaining memberships since they speak for people who are already in their group.

For other groups that people do not automatically support even if they do objectively represent their interests, group leaders must devote a major portion of their time to **group maintenance;** that is, they must constantly canvass for new members and provide benefits—both psychological and material—for current members. Although the advancement of favorable policies was the initial impetus for forming the interest group, policy efforts soon become just one part of the equation when the group considers how best to use its resources. The Sierra Club, for example, devotes a good deal of time, money, and energy to pleasing current members and recruiting new ones; the club organizes singles vacations to scenic areas and family package cruises, and offers discounts of many types for purchases of environmentally conscious products and subscriptions to its magazine. The same is true of the American Association of Retired Persons (AARP), which represents senior Americans on a wide variety of legislative issues. Only by offering benefits such as discount cards, insurance policy opportunities, and trips has that group been able to build its organization into a powerful legislative force. Finally, some groups speak for those whose interests are being represented whether individuals are members or not. The American Association of University Professors (AAUP), for instance, monitors a wide range of educational issues to the benefit of all academics, even though some professors are not formal dues-paying members.

? **Question for Reflection:** Check your postal and electronic mailboxes. How many pieces of mail are from interest groups? Why did you receive a mailing from this particular group? How actively are you involved in any interest group's activities?

group maintenance Activities by an interest group designed to affect policy. Includes enrolling new members and providing benefits for them.

The Free Rider The need to keep current and potential group members happy stems from an issue known as the *free rider*. Mancur Olson, Jr., a leading social theorist, has identified and described this issue.[15] To achieve a collective good, groups call upon their members for resources, time, expertise, and participation. But if everyone benefits anyway, why should people feel the need to put in any time or money? Members who do not invest but still share in the collective benefits of group action are known as **free riders.** Some union members, for instance, may reason that there's no point in going to interminable union meetings, since they will end up getting the same pay hikes and improved working conditions as members who spend all those hours attending meetings. The problem, of course, is that if everyone in the union thinks that way, management will realize that the union is ineffectual and will reduce, not increase, employee benefits. As a result of too many free riders, all members of a group may suffer, undermining the group's very reason for being.

If the benefits achieved by the group extend to nonmembers, an additional free-rider problem exists. The Sierra Club, for instance, has over half a million members, and its work to preserve the national parks benefits all Americans. So why should you join the club if you're guaranteed the benefits of its work anyway? In another example, all citizens will benefit if the National Taxpayers Union succeeds in persuading Congress to lower tax rates. Why, then, put in the time and money to join the National Taxpayers Union?

However, the free-rider may be exaggerated. It rests heavily on the argument that most people join groups for material gain. In fact, people undertake voluntary group activity for any number of reasons, and most do not engage in economic calculations before deciding whether their involvement in a group is "worth it." Many Americans are induced by feelings of moral obligation to contribute to a cause or get involved in a group. And when people commit themselves intensely to political action, it is likely that the rewards they gain are psychological rather than material. Thus, dedicated activists may be motivated by a variety of psychological incentives, including the desire to make social contacts, the wish to advance political career chances, the opportunity to participate in a fascinating game (politics), and the urge to help improve the quality of government. Most groups, then, can gain both supporters and active members without necessarily offering them a material reward for their participation.[16]

Other Characteristics of Interest Groups

Interest groups differ from each other in many ways. These differences help to explain why some groups will be more effective than others, be more or less inclined to use a grass-roots strategy, or be likely to operate at the state rather than the national level. One key difference centers on resources. Naturally, groups with money, connections, social prestige, and access to political elites will be greatly advantaged in the struggle to influence government. On the other hand, zeal and numbers can go a long way toward overcoming financial deficiencies. Any group that can get a large number of people writing letters, calling political leaders, and marching in the street can have a serious impact on the policy-making process.

Whether a group is concentrated or diffuse matters. A neighborhood association trying to block construction of a nearby prison will have a greater chance of success than a broad potential group of people who have recently lost jobs due to American free trade policies. The level of government at which a group needs to exert pressure is also crucial. It is easier to get results at the local level than at the national level. The leadership skill of group officers is also important. Naturally, the more forceful and persuasive the group leader, the more successfully that person can advance the group's cause and keep it in the public eye. Whether a skilled, dynamic leader will emerge for any given group is, of course, subject to circumstance. One wonders, for instance, whether the American civil rights movement could have been as successful as it was without Martin Luther King, Jr. These days, interest group organizations and medical research endeavors often use movie stars as the visible figures in their advertising campaigns, and Congressional testifying efforts in an attempt to get attention. Thus, the Parkinson's Disease research fund benefited

free riders Members who do not invest money or time in an interest group but still share in the collective benefits of group action.

▶ Gun-rights advocates march in support of their rights to maintain their guns and their constitutional protections.

from its attachment to the actor, Michael J. Fox, and the same was true for the paraplegic research groups, who were associated with actor, Christopher Reeves.

Interest Group Strategies

It is not always apparent how an interest group can best achieve its goals. A group must constantly make decisions about strategy: Where should it focus its energies? What issues should it push? With whom should it align itself? Should the group target a House subcommittee, the Senate majority leader, the president, a deputy undersecretary, or key governors and mayors? Issues cut across political arenas at the local, state, and national levels, so the best place to apply pressure is frequently unclear. Groups must also consider whether to push at the grass roots to create a populist groundswell for their ideas or to go directly to powerful public officials.

Lobbying

Lobbying represents the most common and effective way to influence public policy. **Lobbying** is the formal, organized attempt to influence legislation, usually through direct contact with legislators or their staff. The political use of the term *lobby* in the United States was first recorded in the annals of the Tenth Congress; in 1829 the term *lobby-agents* was used to describe favor seekers. President Ulysses S. Grant (1869–77) frequently walked from the White House to the Willard Hotel on Pennsylvania Avenue, and when he was relaxing with legislators in the Willard's comfortable lobby, individuals seeking jobs or favors would visit him in the lobby—hence the term *lobbyists*.[17]

Lobbyists have never ranked high in the eyes of the public. However, the distasteful caricature of a fat-cat special interest lobbyist who buys a vote by bribing a legislator is a gross distortion of what most lobbyists do. Outright bribery is rare; so, too, are other illegal attempts to gain the favor of political officials. The reason is simple. The rewards for corrupt behavior rarely outweigh the risks. After all, money leaves a trail that investigators can follow. Besides, people talk (especially people in politics), so keeping a political secret is no easy task. Astute reporters, of whom there are hundreds hoping to expose some juicy scandal, can ultimately uncover most bribery episodes. Furthermore, bribery is illegal, so not only are reporters out to uncover corruption, but so are state and federal legal officers.

lobbying The formal, organized attempt to influence legislation, usually through direct contact with legislators or their staff.

Who Are the Lobbyists?   Lobbyists are key players in the game of politics. Some are prominent Washington figures and major power brokers. Many are former government officials who have discovered that their expertise, access, influence, and good name are valuable assets, particularly to major industries. More than one public official has learned that it pays much better to be a lobbyist influencing policy from the outside than to be a public servant making policy on the inside. Former members of Congress are especially valued by interest groups, given their knowledge of government operations and their many contacts with the politically powerful. They command salaries well above what they were making in Congress, although ex-members are barred from lobbying Congress for a year after leaving that institution.

In 1961 there were 365 lobbyists registered in Washington. Today there are more than 23,000. "Everybody in America has a lobby," declared former House Speaker Thomas (Tip) O'Neill. The leading lobby registrants are businesses and corporations, trade associations, state and local governments, citizen groups, and labor unions. Even foreign governments are actively involved in lobbying as seen in the case of Kazakhstan, a republic in Central Asia. Japanese companies and the Japanese government spend more than $100 million to hire hundreds of lobbyists in Washington.[18]

Lobbying Tactics   How do lobbyists work with politicians to achieve their aims? The relationship between lobbyists and politicians is one of the least understood in politics. Most lobbyists neither bribe nor threaten politicians. Both tactics are self-defeating. What they do instead is inform, persuade, and pressure. And since most people dislike pressure, the smart lobbyist does as little of that as possible, and only as a last resort.

Persuasion starts (and often ends) with information, a lobbyist's most valuable resource. Legislators, whose staffs are small and usually stretched thin, often cannot get the vital information they need to make decisions about the possible impact of pending legislation. A good lobbyist gains access by providing this information. Naturally, the information will be skewed to favor the lobbyist's point of view. Still, it must never be an outright lie, or the interest group loses all credibility for future lobbying efforts. And even if lobbyists do not provide legislators with a well-rounded perspective on the issue, the information they do provide can be helpful. At a minimum it lets politicians know how key groups feel about the way pending legislation will affect their interests. And sensible politicians listen to a variety of groups and take a range of information into account before putting the final package of a given bill together.

◄ A group of disabled activists from twenty-six states gathers at the Lincoln Memorial prior to rolling across the Memorial Bridge to Arlington National Cemetery to lobby in favor of health care reform.

A lobby exists to get results, and most Washington-based lobbies seek to influence policy in similar ways. To begin, the interests represented by the lobby will make campaign contributions to members of Congress. They hope thereby to elect representatives who see the world as they do and who will vote for the issues they support. Failing that, they hope that campaign contributions will at least buy them access: time to present their case to the members whose campaigns they supported. That explains why many large interests donate money to both parties. By hedging their bets, they hope to gain an audience with whatever group ends up controlling Congress.

Access is crucial; lobbyists can't influence people if they can't grab their attention. Lobbyists are salespeople. If they can make their case one-on-one, they will be effective. Good lobbyists get to know the members of Congress and their key staff people so that they can talk to influential politicians when the need arises. In some cases lobbyists and legislators work together so closely that lobbyists actually draft the legislation and submit it to Congress through their legislative contacts.

Beyond pushing their legislative aims in Congress, lobbyists spend a good deal of time presenting their case formally and publicly. They put out reports, pamphlets, and press releases, all aimed at presenting arguments and evidence to support their group's policy goals. They also give speeches, appear on television and radio and at other public forums, and provide interviews—all in the hope that their message will be noticed and viewed favorably by those who have power or by those who can influence power holders. Among their many activities, lobbyists often testify before congressional committees about the policies they hope to persuade Congress to adopt. They often write amicus curiae briefs to the Supreme Court. Interest groups have also successfully used the lower courts to sue government and private industry and have had an impact on public policy in this way, especially in the environmental arena.

Grass-Roots Activity

Rallying the public behind their cause is a central element in most lobbyists' work, a strategy known as **grass-roots activity**.[19] As we see in Table 11.2, 80 percent of lobbyists engage in this activity. The reason is simple: just as nations with no army play little role in world affairs, lobby groups with no popular support play little role in a democracy. Those who make our laws gain office in a mass democratic election, so they pay particularly close attention to matters that the mass of the people in their electoral districts seem to care about. A lobbyist is just one person, but a lobbyist with the backing of hundreds or thousands of voters in a legislative district is a power to be reckoned with. Thus, the most effective lobbyists are those who can clearly show an ability to rally grass-roots support for their proposals.

Grass-roots pressure "greases the wheels" of the policy-making process. Lobbyists create this pressure by rousing constituents back home in a variety of ways: through political advertisements in newspapers, radio, and television, through speeches in local and national forums, and through rallies or letter-writing campaigns. These activities are meant to let politicians know that a large number of voters agree with the lobbyist, so that the politicians will come to believe that supporting the lobby group's goal is the only sensible and expedient action. Certain groups are especially adept at grass-roots activism. Surely the best example is the National Rifle Association and its battle to limit the inclusion of assault weapons in the Brady Bill. As will be made clear in the "Approaching Democracy in the New Millenium" box at the end of the chapter, the high-tech cyber methods used by various interest groups to reach out to, and mobilize, their followers on issues of importance to them, rank as among the most effective grass-roots campaigns in recent years.

Women's groups have recently gained prominence in the political arena. From the National Organization for Women (NOW) to the conservative antifeminist group Concerned Women for America, women have been making their policy positions on issues known, and in so doing they have influenced legislation. In addition,

grass-roots activity The rallying of group members, as well as the public, behind a lobby's cause.

Table 11.2 ■ What Lobbyists Do	
Activity	**Percent Who Use Technique**
Testify at hearings	99%
Have formal contact with public officials	98
Have informal contact with public officials	95
Present research information	92
Send letters to group members to update them on group activities	92
Enter into coalitions with other organizations	90
Attempt to shape the implementation of policy	89
Talk with the media	86
Consult with public officials to devise legislative strategy	85
Help to draft legislation	85
Sponsor letter-writing campaigns	84
Help shape the government's agenda by calling attention to problems	84
Mount grass-roots lobbying efforts	80
Have influential group members contact legislative offices	80
Help to draft agency regulations, rules, and guidelines	78
Serve on advisory commissions and boards	76
Alert legislators to the effects legislation will have on their districts	75
File suits or otherwise engage in litigation	72
Make financial contributions to campaigns	58
Assist officials by doing favors for them	56
Attempt to influence appointments to public office	53
Publicize candidates' voting records	44
Engage in direct-mail fund raising for the interest group	44
Use media advertisements to publicize the group's position on an issue	31
Contribute work, personnel, or services to electoral campaigns	24
Publicly endorse candidates for office	22
Engage in protests or demonstrations	20

Source: "Activities of Professional Lobbyists," from *Organized Interests and American Democracy* by Kay Lehman Schlozman and John T. Tierney. Reprinted by permission of Pearson Education, Inc.

two women's group PACs have been increasingly important in funding female candidacies: EMILY's List (*E*arly *M*oney *I*s *L*ike *Y*east; it makes the dough rise) for Democrats, and WISH (*W*omen *I*n the *S*enate and *H*ouse) for Republicans.

Interest groups use various strategies to appeal directly to group members or potential members for support and action. A group using a letter-writing campaign appeals to group members to "write your representative" and "express your support" for the group's position on a given issue. Congressional offices are periodically inundated by the cards, letters, telegrams, e-mail, and faxes from concerned group members and sympathizers—testimony to the effectiveness of this tactic.

The group may also use *direct-mail* to target citizens with mailings describing the group's cause, presenting its arguments, and requesting support or money. An important political function of the direct-mail campaign is that it provides valuable information to the recipients of mailings, although most mailings are decidedly skewed toward the group's avowed position. The group often provides voting cues by giving voters a checklist to take with them into the voting booth. Another grass-roots technique is to stage free concerts, speaking engagements, or even

APPROACHING DIVERSITY

Building a Latino Power Base

Comedian Woody Allen once said that "ninety percent of life is just showing up." For Republican Representative Constance A. Morella (MD), her future career in Congress depended on that very lesson as she faced re-election in her suburban Washington, D.C. district in the November 2002 election. Her race for re-election may serve as a model for future races as her chances for success depended on a virtual smorgasbord of political science topics: redistricting after the decennial census, labor union interest group activity, voter registration, voter turnout, political party appeal to minority groups, and luck.

With a six-seat margin in the House of Representatives, the Republican party needed to defend every seat they held. However, Democrats in control of the General Assembly in Maryland made it difficult for Republican Morella when they added Latino and African American precincts in Takoma Park, Silver Spring and Prince George's County to her district. As soon as that happened, two labor unions—the International Brotherhood of Electrical Workers and the Service Employees International Union—launched a drive to register as many Hispanic and African American voters as possible for their endorsed candidate, Democrat Mark K. Shriver. "The increase of African-American and Latino voters in this district, who are much more leery about splitting tickets and voting for Republican candidates than any other group, will be the decisive difference in this race." This led Morella and her staff to understand that because of the concerted effort of interest groups trying to mount opposition support from growing minority groups her re-election would be made more difficult.

But Morella is not alone. Fully 163 of the 435 seats in Congress have districts containing more than 10 percent Hispanic voters. As a result, registration drives were launched in states across the nation, from Nevada and California to Georgia. While the Republican National Committee has launched its own drive to register minorities favoring their views, teaching political lessons in Spanish to political leaders in key states, the fear is that the party's views do not appeal to these groups. The AFL-CIO had such success registering and encouraging voter participation by Hispanics in Southern California that polls that surveys of potential voters have been thrown off.

All of the work by the labor unions and minority interest groups to increase minority voter participation in Connie Morella's district succeeded as she became one of the handful of incumbents, especially Republicans, to lose her seat in Congress. Forty-three-year-old Christopher Van Hollen, Jr., a Democrat, spent so much money responding to significant White House support that more than $8 million was spent on the race, making it one of the most expensive in the nation. Meanwhile, the Hispanic vote was so significant that in California, two Hispanic sisters, Linda and Loretta Sanchez, both won seats in Congress, the first sisters to do so.

Source: Jo Becker, "Unions Target Minorities in Voter Drives: Democrats Woo Latinos in Morella's 8th District," *Washington Post,* June 15, 2002.

---

demonstrations. These events are often effective at raising both funds and citizens' consciousness of the group's cause, and they have the added advantage of attracting attention through news coverage.

Using the Courts and Lobbying the Political Branches

Although grass-roots strategies can often ignite large-scale popular support, interest groups must still reach the institutions of government—Congress and the executive branch—to meet their objectives. Even large-scale grass-roots movements sometimes fail to impress policy makers in Congress. Members of Congress may simply disagree with the group's goals; the constituents who voted them into office may not support these goals; the policy makers may be influenced by other powerful groups with opposing aims; or members of Congress may be listening to other, more powerful interest groups. Many grass-roots campaigns have failed to persuade Congress to produce the desired legislation. Consider, for example, these few recent failed campaigns: to limit congressional terms of office, to declare abortion illegal, and to reform the health care system.

Because of the difficulty of lobbying Congress, a growing amount of attention by interest groups is directed at the executive branch. Groups may try to get an appointment with the president or a member of the cabinet, or at least mount a letter-writing campaign in that direction. Far more likely, though, these groups will direct their efforts toward lower-level bureaucrats.

Despite the inevitability of setbacks, interest group leaders rarely give up easily. Groups unsuccessful in obtaining their goals from one institution often turn to another. The civil rights movement of the 1950s and 1960s is perhaps the best example of group persistence. Unable to persuade either Congress or southern state legislatures to eliminate discriminatory laws and practices, civil rights groups turned to the courts and to the executive branch, where they achieved great success. It was the Supreme Court, after all, not Congress, that finally declared school segregation unconstitutional, and it was a series of presidents who were willing to use federal troops to enforce that decision. These judicial and executive actions, initiated by interest group pressures, finally forced states to dismantle their segregated school systems and eliminate other previously legal forms of racial discrimination.

Today, conservative interest groups such as Operation Rescue, which seeks to restrict abortion, use the courts nearly as frequently as did liberal groups of the past, a strategy that makes sense given the growing conservative inclination of the courts. Operation Rescue has combined traditional grass-roots strategies with more aggressive tactics, such as blockades of abortion clinics and the intimidation of clinic workers and patients. But a third, and quite effective, strategy of this group has been the continued appeal to state and federal courts in an attempt to eliminate all laws permitting abortion. Coupled with the publicity garnered from their aggressive tactics, Operation Rescue has become a political force that even the supposedly nonpolitical courts can no longer ignore. The federal judiciary, then, has once again become a key target for interest group activity.[20]

Political Action Committees

Of all the trends related to interest groups, the most dramatic new development has been the proliferation of political action committees (PACs). The first PAC was created as early as 1948, when the AFL-CIO founded its Committee on Political Education (COPE) to channel union funds to prolabor candidates. In 1963 business created its first PAC, the Business-Industry Political Action Committee (BIPAC). But because campaign contributions were relatively unlimited until the 1970s, and recipients of large contributions were not required to report either the names of donors or the amount of money donated, most large industries and corporations simply funneled the money from corporate coffers directly to the campaigns of their chosen candidates or causes.

Things changed dramatically by the mid-1970s with passage of the Federal Election Campaign Act (FECA) of 1971, which placed a $1,000 limit on donations that individuals could make to any single campaign. The act did, however, allow labor unions, corporations, and other entities to create PACs that could donate up to $5,000 to any single campaign. The newly formed Federal Election Commission (FEC) provided regulation and oversight. By 1976, the FEC had granted authority for universities, museums, trade associations, cooperatives, and eventually for private citizens to form PACs. It was at this time that a virtual explosion in PAC formation and activity occurred. More than four thousand PACs have since been registered with the FEC.

PACs have taken the traditional lobbying role of interest groups and added a new way to gain access and influence: donating tremendous amounts of money in relatively small increments to congressional election campaigns. In the 1996 elections, the top fifty PACs donated nearly $64 million in unregulatable **soft money** to the Clinton and Dole campaigns, both national political parties, and all federal congressional election campaigns. All of these groups carefully hedged their bets by donating to candidates from *both* parties, thus giving them access no matter who wins the election.

Because PACs can legally donate more money than individuals, campaign fund raising has shifted away from seeking individual contributions to seeking money

soft money Campaign contributions directed to advancing the interests of a political party or an issue in general, rather than a specific candidate.

from PACs. As a result, the power of interest groups has increased, while the power of political parties has weakened. Politicians seeking elective office now turn to PACs for support rather than to party organizations. A Michigan Democrat running for the U.S. Senate, for instance, will be equally concerned with gaining the backing of state party officials as with soliciting support from the political action committees of the various unions that are powerful in that state, beginning with the United Auto Workers. As PACs decide which candidates will receive support, they usurp one of the traditional roles reserved for parties: the recruitment and selection of candidates for office.

This growth of PAC influence in the candidate selection process has created problems for American politics.[21] Most PACs focus on a narrow range of issues or even on a single issue. Candidates seeking scarce political resources for their increasingly expensive campaigns often court the favors of influential PAC groups with narrow agendas, while giving short shrift to the moderating perspective, broad-based public agenda, and amorphous ideology of political parties. The result, as we saw in Chapter 9, is the candidate-centered campaign, the subsequent weakening of traditional party power, and a growing number of elected officials with narrow viewpoints and confrontational operating styles.

As seen in Chapter 4, it was the concern by political observers and insiders alike about the growth of PAC influence that led to the campaign finance reform effort. And it was the power of the PACs that kept the legislation from being passed year after year. Now with the passage of the 2002 Bipartisan Campaign Finance Reform Act, it remains to be seen whether PACs will be seriously limited. Madison's admonition that removing the causes of faction reduces liberty still rings strong. PACs have a basic right to participate in the system, and they fight with all the considerable power they can muster against attempts to restrict their activities.

QUOTE ... UNQUOTE

"Excuse me, but this campaign to kill [special interests] . . . is snobbish, elitist, antidemocratic, and un-American. . . . Destroy the PACs and you constrict the voice of small business, and restrict the political access of the millions who support them—enhancing the clout of Big Media, Big Business, Big Labor, and their ilk who can afford to maintain permanent lobbying representation in Washington."

Patrick J. Buchanan

Regulation of Interest Groups

Since interest group activity is protected by the First Amendment, politicians have been cautious about proposals to regulate interest groups and their lobbyists. But the poor image many citizens have of special interests has produced periodic attempts at regulation. Some of these efforts have borne fruit and produced the occasional law aimed at reducing the scope of interest group influence. For the most part, however, these laws have been few and weak, leaving interest groups relatively unfettered.

The 1946 Federal Regulation of Lobbying Act stipulated that lobbyists seeking to influence congressional legislation must list all contributions, expenditures, and the names of anyone who received or contributed $500 or more. When the act was challenged on First Amendment grounds, the Supreme Court upheld the legislation but interpreted the registration requirement to apply only to groups whose "primary purpose" was to influence legislation.[22] Many large outfits such as the National Association of Manufacturers use this argument to avoid registering altogether. They claimed no need to register as lobbyists, since influencing legislation was not their principal reason for existing as a group. For that reason and others, the 1946 act turned out to be virtually useless. It also lacked enforcement powers and did not apply to lobbying the executive branch, to grass-roots organizing, or to indirect lobbying.

The 1971 and 1974 Federal Campaign Finance laws were much more effective in their efforts to regulate donations, but they also ensured an increase in the power and proliferation of PACs, which represent many citizens, thereby reducing the power of individual fat-cat financiers. Another congressional action that has had some effect on lobbying behavior was the 1978 Ethics in Government Act, which codified rules governing conflict of interests. A key section of this law was meant to prevent the kind of "revolving-door" activity in which government officials leave their posts and immediately use their insider knowledge and contacts to lobby the very people for whom they had just been working. The law prohibited former government employees from lobbying their former agency for a period of one year after leaving office and prohibited them from lobbying any department on an issue for which they clearly had direct responsibility for two years.

Efforts to regulate the operations and impact of lobbying have continued with varying degrees of success. Realizing that the 1971 Federal Election Campaign Act only covered lobbyists who seek to influence members of Congress, in December 1995 Congress passed the Lobbying Disclosure Act, which regulated those who sought to lobby members of the congressional staffs and policy-making members of the executive branch, including the president and his staff, even if they worked only part time at lobbying. Lobbyists are now required to register within forty-five days of either being hired or making their first contact with such officials and file reports twice a year about their activities. These reports must list the special interests for which they are lobbying and the offices that have been contacted (but not the names of the people contacted), and specify whether any action is being undertaken for a foreign government; the only groups exempted were grass-roots lobbying and tax-exempt religious organizations.[23]

Assessing the Impact of Interest Groups

The growth of interest groups presents new challenges and problems for the U.S. political system. As more interest groups participate in the political arena, do they open or close opportunities for individual influence? As groups continue to increase in number, will they become the only legitimate channel for political expression?[24]

Scholars have devoted much effort to understanding the role groups play in American politics. Nearly a century ago political scientist Arthur Bentley argued that groups lie at the very heart of the political process.[25] Indeed, in his eyes *all* political phenomena could be understood in terms of group activity. He saw politics as a perpetual struggle for power. Groups compete endlessly for public goods and services, and only the fittest prosper and survive. Government is simply the agency that sorts out which groups are winning or losing at any given time. From this perspective, interest group activity is synonymous with politics itself.

Another leading scholar, political scientist David Truman, argued in 1951 that groups play a stabilizing role in American politics.[26] Echoing both Madison and Bentley, Truman wrote that politics is best understood as a complex network of groups, each striving for access to government. In response to critics who felt that powerful economic interests have an advantage, Truman countered with two responses. First, most Americans have overlapping group memberships and are likely to belong to at least one group that benefits from government policies. Second, he pointed to the idea of potential groups. Certain issues could arise and galvanize unorganized citizens into cohesive groups as exemplified by the Million Mom March and the Second Amendment Sisters. Formerly disadvantaged people would thus be represented in the halls of power, and these new groups would provide a vital balancing mechanism to counter the influence of groups already representing the wealthier elements of society.

In yet another critique of the pluralist vision of group activity, political scientist Theodore Lowi maintained that contemporary group politics has fundamentally altered how the United States functions.[27] Lowi described a new political system, which he called *interest group liberalism,* in which interest groups have proliferated, expanding their control of legislative politics. Real policy making stems neither from voter preference nor from Congress. Instead, it flows from a set of tight connections among the bureaucracy, selected members of Congress (especially subcommittee chairs), and special-interest groups representing the upper stratum of

American society. Lowi and others have used the term **iron triangles** to characterize the typical cozy relationship among congressional elites, lobbyists, and bureaucrats.

The rapid proliferation of interest groups, all competing for influence over policy, could place excessive and conflicting demands on public officials. In the face of massive political pressure, government might grind to a halt or continue to implement the status quo, as all efforts at change or reform are stymied by the many competing claims of powerful interest groups. This produces **gridlock,** a condition in which major government initiatives are impossible because existing groups can veto any effort at change and will do so, for fear of losing their own already established connections and privileges.

Such pessimism is not universally accepted by interest group specialists. More optimistic scholars raise several points of objection. First, they claim that gridlock may derive less from the proliferation of interest groups than from American society's lack of consensus about which direction government policy should take. That lack of consensus has been a standard condition in American history, as one would expect in a diverse and complex culture. But when Americans do reach consensus on political aims, government can take dramatic action with amazing speed, despite all the talk about interest groups causing gridlock. That situation occurred in 1933 with the rapid approval of a vast range of New Deal programs, in 1941–42 with the United States' entry into World War II, in 1965 with passage of the Great Society programs, and in 1995 with the acceptance of many Republican Contract with America proposals. Group pressures did little to prevent those dramatic changes in national public policy. Perhaps interest groups do not create gridlock but merely take advantage of its existence in a complex and diverse society.

The *iron triangle* idea has also been criticized. As early as 1978 political scientist Hugh Heclo pointed to the rise of a range of issue experts who forced legislators, bureaucrats, and lobbyists to pay attention to other information and actors, thus undermining their cozy triangular relationship.[28] As a result, **policy networks** have formed. These networks are characterized by discussion of a wide range of options in the effort to resolve issues, conveying a more inclusive and less conspiratorial image of the policy process than do *iron triangles*.[29]

Other scholars have noted the vast array of new groups that have entered the political arena in recent years. This influx of groups has created conditions of uncertainty and unpredictability, helping to break up established connections among the principal actors of the old triangles. As the number of groups and interests operating in American society has dramatically expanded, political life has become more complex, making any generalization about how policies get made more difficult to substantiate.

Finally, we must remember that many of the new groups represent public interest activists, political participants who stand up for those segments of society not usually represented in the ongoing group struggles for power. Public interest lobbyists may be middle class, but their aims, at least in theory, would benefit all citizens, particularly those at the lower ends of the socioeconomic spectrum. Thus, the argument that the less well off are disadvantaged by interest group activity, while retaining a strong kernel of truth, is less accurate today than it might have been two or three decades ago.

Interest Groups of the Future

Because of a decision by the Supreme Court in 1996, the nature of interest group advertising in elections has changed dramatically. The dispute arose from Colorado's Democratic Senator Timothy Wirth's reelection campaign in 1986, when that state's Republican Federal Campaign Committee exceeded the spending limits on independent campaign contributions by political parties as outlined in the Federal Election Campaign Act of 1971. The Republicans, who had not yet picked their

iron triangles The informal three-way relationships that develop among key legislative committees, the bureaucracy, and interest groups with a vested interest in the policies created by those committees or agencies.

gridlock A condition in which major government initiatives are impossible because a closely balanced partisan division in the government structure accompanied by an unwillingness to work together toward compromise produces a stalemate.

policy networks Networks characterized by a wide-ranging discussion of options as issues are resolved, conveying a more inclusive and less conspiratorial image of the policy process than *iron triangles* do.

candidate when they ran $15,000 worth of radio ads against Wirth, claimed that they had a First Amendment freedom of speech right to spend what they wished on the election. Speaking for a seven-person majority, Justice Stephen Breyer agreed, arguing "We do not see how a Constitution that grants to individuals, candidates, and ordinary political committees the right to make unlimited independent expenditures could deny the same right to political parties."[30] Only if the party and the candidates were working together in the campaign spending would the federal limits apply. As a result, interest groups that helped the Republicans win back Congress in 1994 proliferated in the elections in the years ahead.

The creation of this loophole in the campaign expenditure law has spurred political parties and interest groups to continue to collect "soft money," the unregulated donations for "the good of the political parties" that could be used for a candidate's campaign, and begin running national **issue advertisements,** that talked about the issues rather than candidates directly. By thus making clear the organization's position about a particular issue rather than a specific candidacy, it could avoid federal regulation.[31] Various national interest groups continued to fund those ads, almost completely bypassing the candidates themselves. In June 2001 the Supreme Court, by a narrow 5-4 decision, ruled in a campaign finance reform case coming from Colorado that limits on coordinated campaign spending by political parties and candidates for federal office were constitutional because if they did not exist it would not be possible to establish limits on the spending for individual candidates' campaigns. It was this decision that gave supporters of campaign finance reform hope.[32] As the case study in Chapter 4 details, while the Bipartisan Campaign Finance Reform Act of 2002 now bans raising of unregulated "soft money" after the November 2002 election and limits the use of issue advertisements 30 days before an election primary and 60 days before the general election, it has yet to be seen how the inevitable First Amendment litigation challenges to this law will be ruled upon by the federal courts.

Interest Groups and the 2002 Election

Interest groups provide a vital link between citizens and public officials. They convey substantive information and public sentiment to policy makers, and they provide knowledge about government programs to citizens and assist them in gaining access to these programs. Interest groups even provide the inspiration necessary to stimulate citizen involvement in politics. It remains true that the most powerful, most influential, and most resourceful interests have advantages. Politics is rarely played on a level field. Business and corporate interests far outweigh public interest groups in most power struggles. And small but powerful interests often gain their ends from government, seemingly at the expense of the public good.

In the last federal election before the ban on "soft money" regulation in the Bipartisan Campaign Finance Reform Act of 2002 takes effect, Senate and House candidates raised $879 million for their races.[33] Already, though, new loopholes were being created by Federal Election Commission rulings, one of which would permit the national party to transfer "soft money" for "party building activity" to the unregulated state political parties. Also, members of Congress could raise "soft money" for state parties. Lacking individual state regulation of this fund-raising activity, more and more of the "soft money" and "issue ads" may come now from state rather than national party organizations.[34]

Despite their big money efforts to influence the direction of government, interest group activity is not the villain. Franklin Roosevelt once said that the only cure for the problems of democracy is more democracy. Along these lines, the only cure for the undue influence of some interests is for those currently unhappy with policy outcomes to take advantage of their own right to become a powerful interest group. Over time countervailing forces often do arise to give the system some degree of

issue advertisements
Advertisements in a political campaign funded by an interest group advocating a position on an issue but technically not supporting a specific candidate.

DEMOCRACY IN THE NEW MILLENNIUM

Growing Better Grass-Roots through Cyber-Lobbying

When Utah Representative James V. Hansen decided in mid-2002 to insert Title XIV into the Senate version of the Defense Appropriation Act, the Southern Utah Wilderness Alliance (SUWA) sprung into action with their cyber-lobbying grass-roots campaign effort. Title XIV sought to allow the Department of Defense to close public access in designated wilderness areas, deny the federal government the power to protect wildlife through water rights, and bar hundreds of thousands of acres of wilderness from being identified as Wilderness Study Areas. SUWA asked its followers on its Website to "PLEASE MAKE TWO PHONE CALLS TO YOUR U.S. SENATORS ... TELL YOUR SENATORS TO VOTE AGAINST ANYTHING RESEMBLING TITLE XIV."

The Utah group, which first developed this tactic to successfully lobby President Bill Clinton to establish the 1.7 million acre of federal land in Utah known as the Grand Staircase-Escalante National Monument. Other small grass-roots organizations say the Web is changing the dynamics of citizen involvement in government. Whereas low-budget organizations once took weeks to generate a few hundred letters or phone calls to Washington, they now can mobilize thousands of members almost instantly in a bid to compete against well-financed lobbies.

Established lobbying organizations, as well as small start-up groups, are using the Web to press their agendas on the Hill. The Christian Coalition's Website (www.cc.org) has a series of screens where religious conservatives can skim through issues before Congress, edit letters on those issues, and send the letters by e-mail to their representatives. The National Rifle Association's Website (www.nra.org) advises gun owners on setting up local grass-roots networks and phone banks, and contains legislative alerts on federal, state, and local issues across the country. On the other side,

the Million Mom March Organization's site (www.million mommarch.org) reports on victories against the gun lobby and news of actions by other anti-gun organizations. A site maintained by the National Federation of Independent Business (www.nfibonline.com) asks company owners to contribute accounts of how federal regulations have cost their firms money, fueling a campaign to scale back government requirements.

"The only thing public interest groups have that corporate interest don't is people, and now we have a way to mobilize them," said Tom Price, national grass-roots coordinator for the Utah alliance. "(Corporations) can buy ads; they can hire lobbyists, but now suddenly tiny little environmental groups in the middle of nowhere can bring thousands of people into play with very little capital. . . . The Web is an extraordinary tool for the democratization of American politics." What remains to be seen, however, is whether the World Wide Web will change the balance of power among competing interests, or if it will be just the latest high-tech tool used by all sides. Either way, predicts Jack Bonner, president of a grass-roots organizing firm, Bonner and Associates, "There will be a more informed electorate. I think the Web is very healthy for democracy."

To see the new cyber-lobbying techniques on these issues in action, visit sites such as http://www.suwa.org, and http://www.cc.org. For the latest positions on the hottest issues by your favorite lobbying organization, plug in their URL and see what is happening on their main Website. Or, if there are issues of great importance to you, why not develop your own Website and lobby others.

Source: David Hosansky, *Congressional Quarterly*. Reproduced with permission of Congressional Quarterly, Inc. via Copyright Clearance Center.

balance, if not perfect justice. The growth of public interest groups has helped give the voiceless and the powerless some modest victories, in the form of government policies that work to their advantage rather than to the benefit of those with money and status. Such groups help America approach democracy.

SUMMARY

1. Interest groups are formal organizations of people who share a common outlook or social circumstance and who band together in the hope of influencing government policy. Actual groups have a headquarters, an organizational structure, paid employees, and so forth; potential groups are interest groups that could come into being under the right circumstances. Those circumstances are often created by dynamic leaders known as policy entrepreneurs.

2. While all modern democracies exhibit interest group activity, few have achieved the level of nongovernmental group life found in the United States. The number of groups trying to pressure government has grown dramatically in recent years, partly owing to the growth and increased activity of the government and partly owing to higher average levels of education.

3. People form interest groups because collective action is stronger, more credible, and more likely to influence policy outcomes than the isolated actions of separate individuals. However, because interest groups focus on their own cause, they are said to skew or ignore the public good.

4. Economic interest groups include those representing big business, organized labor, farmers, and other economic interests. Public interest groups represent the interests of average citizens; they focus on achieving a broad set of goals that represent their members' vision of the collective good. Government interest groups compete alongside traditional interest groups for funding, policy goals, and attention. Other interest groups include ideological groups, religious groups, civil rights groups, and single-issue groups.

5. Interest groups are most likely to form when some citizens have been adversely affected by technological change or by government policies. Other factors, such as dynamic leaders and geographic concentration, also influence the development of an interest group.

6. Group leaders must devote much of their time to group maintenance—canvassing for new members and providing benefits for current members. In doing so they face the so-called free-rider issue, the tendency of individuals to share in the collective benefits of group action even if they do not themselves contribute to the group.

7. Lobbying is the formal, organized attempt to influence legislation, usually through direct contact with legislators or their staff. Lobbyists provide legislators with needed information and attempt to persuade, and sometimes pressure, them to support the interest group's goals. They also publicize the group's cause to the general public through published materials, speeches, television appearances, and the like.

8. A key aim of lobbying is to rally group members, as well as the public, to the cause—that is, to gain grass-roots support for the group's proposals. An often-used tactic is the direct-mail campaign, in which targeted citizens receive mailings describing the group's cause and requesting their support.

9. Leaders of interest groups learn that when they are unable to get a hearing for their cause in one branch of government, success sometimes can be achieved by looking for help elsewhere. Thus, in times when Congress and the president are unsympathetic, requests for help can be directed toward the Supreme Court, and vice versa.

10. An important trend is the proliferation of political action committees, groups whose main aim is to promote the political goals of particular interest groups. PACs donate large amounts of money to political campaigns, thereby undermining the role of political parties in recruiting and selecting candidates for office.

11. There are few legal restrictions on interest groups. Lobbyists must list their contributions and expenditures, but only if their "primary purpose" is to influence legislation. The Ethics in Government Act bars former government employees from lobbying their former agency for a year after leaving office and for two years on specific policy issues.

12. Interest group activity during congressional elections has evolved to the point that issue advertising sometimes proceeds without any reference to the candidates in the race. Such ads alert voters to the importance of the issues, but sometimes blur the real candidate identities in the race.

13. Some political scientists believe that policy making stems from the connections among the bureaucracy, selected members of Congress, and interest groups—so-called iron triangles. The rapid proliferation of interest groups has led to what some political scientists call "gridlock," or a harmful excess of competing demands. Policy networks, which are more broad-based than iron triangles, now characterize the process. There can be no doubt that the number of groups and interests now operating in American society has dramatically expanded, adding to the complexity of political life.

KEY TERMS

interest groups	collective action	soft money
actual groups	public interest groups	iron triangles
potential groups	group maintenance	gridlock
policy entrepreneurs	free riders	policy networks
political action committees (PACs)	lobbying	issue advertising
	grass-roots activity	

POLISIM ACTIVITY

Interest Groups

This activity allows you to try your hand at the "art" of lobbying. You will take on the role of being the newest lobbyist in Washington and you need to earn a reputation for success. As a representative of an influential interest group, you will be given a specific amount of time and money. Your job is to get your own legislation passed. How well you allocate your resources will determine whether or not you are successful!

SUGGESTED READINGS

BERRY, JEFFREY M. *The Interest Group Society.* 3d ed. New York: Longman, 1997. A very interesting examination of the development of interest group politics in American society.

CIGLER, ALLAN J., and BURDETT A. LOOMIS, eds. *Interest Group Politics.* 4th ed. Washington, D.C.: Congressional Quarterly Press, 1995. An excellent collection of readings on American interest groups.

DYE, THOMAS R. *Who's Running America? The Clinton Years.* 6th ed. Englewood Cliffs, N.J.: Prentice Hall, 1995. A description of the dominant political institutions of our time and the individuals who control them.

HEINZ, JOHN P., EDWARD Q. LAUMANN, ROBERT L. NELSON, and ROBERT H. SALISBURY. *The Hollow Core: Private Interests in National Policy Making.* Cambridge, Mass.: Harvard University Press, 1993. A scholarly examination of connections among interest groups, members of Congress, and bureaucrats that sheds doubt on the theory of iron triangles.

LOWI, THEODORE J. *The End of Liberalism: The Second Republic of the United States.* 2d ed. New York: Norton, 1979. A provocative perspective on American government, arguing that the tight connections between interest groups and government officials have created a new kind of American political system.

OLSON, MANCUR, Jr. *The Logic of Collective Action.* Cambridge, Mass.: Harvard University Press, 1965. An influential work that argues that rational citizens have few incentives to join groups, and consequently the interests of nonjoiners are poorly represented in politics.

RAUCH, JONATHAN. *Demosclerosis: The Silent Killer of American Government.* New York: Random House/Times Books, 1994. A popularization of the Lowi–Olson thesis that interest groups dominate American politics and create a government of institutionalized gridlock.

TRUMAN, DAVID B. *The Governmental Process.* New York: Knopf, 1951. A classic book, presenting the pluralist vision of how interest groups operate in American politics.

WALKER, JACK L., Jr. *Mobilizing Interest Groups in America: Patrons, Professions, and Social Movements.* Ann Arbor: University of Michigan Press, 1991. An excellent and wide-ranging discussion of interest groups in modern American political life.

WOLPE, BRUCE C., and BERTRAM J. LEVINE. *Lobbying Congress: How the System Works.* 2d ed. Washington, D.C.: Congressional Quarterly Press, 1996. An in-depth examination of how interest groups successfully influence the direction of Congress.

WRIGHT, JOHN R. *Interest Groups and Congress.* Boston: Allyn & Bacon, 1996. A well-written study of how political action committees and interest group lobbies influence the policy making of Congress.

12 THE MEDIA

CHAPTER OUTLINE

Approaching Democracy Case Study:
    The Media and the War on Terrorism
Introduction: The Media and Democracy
The Emergence of the Media
Functions of the Media
Limits on Media Freedom
Ideological Bias and Media Control
The Media and Elections

APPROACHING DEMOCRACY CASE STUDY

The Media and the War on Terrorism

Dateline Afghanistan—2002. In the wake of September 11 and the invasion of Afghanistan, the federal government, citing the need to maintain national security at home and abroad, moved to limit the amount and kinds of information reaching news reporters and the American public. In early October, President Bush, fearing the possible use of coded messages by al-Qaeda, requested American media sources to "exercise judgment" in broadcasting images of Osama Bin Laden; the network executives complied and ordered closer editing of war images in the future. While many Americans agreed with this decision and approved of the ensuing dearth of direct news on the escalating conflict, others, including reporters and photographers, worried that the war would continue the precedent first established in the 1991 Persian Gulf crisis. As one Pentagon official in early 2002 quipped of hidden airfields in central Asia, "We can put aircraft there where CNN can't film them taking off."[1]

During the Persian Gulf crisis in 1991, news blackouts and the official praise of "smart-bombs" revealed that the executive branch had learned a painful lesson: media coverage shapes, and can even determine, the successful execution of military actions abroad. This lesson was reinforced by television images of dead soldiers dragged through the streets of Mogadishu, Somalia, in 1996, prompting the pullout of American troops by President Clinton the following week, fearful of another Vietnam.

The issue of the role of the media in relation to foreign policy, military engagements, and the war on terrorism has come under intense debate within the American public. When air strikes on Afghanistan began on October 7, 2001, the international news media was shocked that reporters received less access from the Pentagon to the war than during the Persian Gulf conflict. To stifle war coverage, the Pentagon on October 11, four days after the bombing began, purchased the exclusive rights to Space Imaging, a corporation that produces satellite images of Earth. This was done to prevent the news media from receiving the most sophisticated satellite reports of bomb damage in Afghanistan. In Iraq and Kuwait in 1991, many reporters accompanied Army units in the field, including the Marine advance into Kuwait. Interviews with military officials, including General H. Norman Schwarzkopf, enabled the American public to hear first-hand the progress of the war from its military leaders.

During the Afghanistan invasion, American reporters were not allowed on the aircraft carriers of the strike force, nor were they able to accompany special forces units on their missions. General Tommy Franks, head of U.S. Central Command, kept silent. Although after the initial attack, the Pentagon eventually allowed reporters onto the carriers and other naval vessels, and General Franks began to make the circuit of TV news talk shows, it adamantly forbade any coverage, including delayed broadcasts, of special forces operations, the mainline American troop deployment in Afghanistan. In a similar move as coalition supporters, the British government disallowed media coverage of operations taking place in Diego Garcia, an air base in the Indian Ocean, which the British allowed the American government to use to bomb Afghanistan cities and troop positions. As a result, many of the initial images of the war reaching American television were nothing more than old army training films to give an impression of what the troops were doing in the "field."

Coverage of civilian casualties represented another flashpoint of controversy involving the public's right to know vs. the perceived need of the federal government to cloak its actions in the name of national security. Independent foreign news sources confirmed that two to four thousand Afghanistan civilians were accidentally killed during the heavy bombing of al-Qaeda and Taliban military positions in October and November of 2001. Although the White House side-stepped official reports of civilian deaths, President Bush ordered the bombing of the Al-Jazeera independent-based television station in Kabul, the capital of Afghanistan. Before the bombing, Al-Jazeera broadcasts reached most of the Arab world, frequently showing some of the only available images of Afghanistan.

When the heavy bombing of Afghanistan ceased in January of 2002, the American news media discovered that it had literally "missed the story" of the American military invasion of Afghanistan despite increased coverage of "hard news" (see Table 12.1). In response to the public's perception that the media gave the Bush administration only positive coverage of the war, news sources unleashed a backlash of critical reporting concerning the treatment of al-Qaeda prisoners, civilian casualties, and the accuracy of Pentagon briefings. Despite the criticism, the Pentagon continued to prevent American journalists from visiting "sensitive" areas, even threatening the use of deadly force should reporters violate the orders. According to Doug Struck, a *Washington Post* reporter denied access to a prison run by the American military in Afghanistan: "It shows the extremes the military is going to [to] keep this war secret, to keep reporters from finding out what's going on."[2]

▲ Nic Robertson of CNN and Steve Harrigan of Fox News report live from two separate locations in Afghanistan. Individual journalists as well as the networks face much greater pressure today than during the Persian Gulf conflict to scoop their rivals from the field.

Table 12.1 ■ How the War on Terrorism Changed the News Agenda		
Topics on the Evening News		
	Percentage of Newscast	
All Networks	**June**	**Oct**
Hard News	45.5%	80.2%
Celebrity News	4.7	0.0
Crime/ Law/ Courts	11.7	3.5
Business/ Economy	14.1	4.5
Science and Technology	4.2	10.9
Lifestyle Features	19.7	1.0
Total	100.0	100.0

Source: Project for Excellence in Journalism, "How the War on Terrorism Changed the News Agenda," Network Television, June–October 2001." http://www.journalism.org/publ_research/befandaft2.html. Reprinted with permission from Project for Excellence in Journalism.

Question for Reflection: How has the media's capability to report on events within moments of their occurrence by using the latest technology, affected the government's ability to manage access to information during times of military conflict?

INTRODUCTION: THE MEDIA AND DEMOCRACY

Perhaps no other chapter in this text raises issues that deal so directly with democracy. A nation based on democratic principles like the United States is going to great and unprecedented lengths to limit public access to field information about the war's progress. As George Orwell observed, censorship in "free" societies is necessarily more complex and calculated than in dictatorships; the latter merely issues an official ban backed by armed force to halt coverage, while the former must find more thorough means to assure that "unpopular ideas can be silenced."[3]

The tension between freedom of the press and government restrictions on that freedom is one of several key issues related to the role of the mass media in a democratic society. Indeed, one of the central components of a society's approach to democracy is whether the government allows freedom of the press—a press that is free to criticize the government without fear of being shut down and its editors thrown into prison. In April 2002, the government of Thailand shut down a cable television station which was giving airtime to a critic of Prime Minister Thaksin Shinawarta. By May 2002, Eritrea, a small country in the Horn of Africa, had imprisoned more journalists than any other African country. Freedom of the press became so unruly that the government closed all eight private newspapers in the country. Journalists working for the papers were picked up at home or work and imprisoned. "We were pushing the government ahead toward democracy and urging it to ratify the Constitution, which is still kept on a comfortable shelf."[4]

At a minimum, democracy requires that citizens receive objective information so they can make informed decisions about candidates, policies, and government actions. Yet the media responsible for transmitting that information are often characterized by bias, distortion, and sensationalism. The job of the media entails simplifying complex and detailed realities into symbols and images. Thus, the information reaching the citizen often consists primarily of sound bites and pictures that greatly simplify the definition of political reality for millions of Americans. Indeed, it is no exaggeration to say that for most people, politics has little reality apart from its media version.

In the United States, information about politics is routinely transmitted to the public through the electronic and print media as well as through faxes and electronic mail and online information sources. Americans can read local, regional, national, and international newspapers; and twenty-four-hour news stations and coverage of local, state, and national public officials on television provide a first-hand look at the political process. But in a democratic polity the media must do more than bring political information to a broad audience. They must report events accurately and truthfully, free from control or censorship by government agencies. Freedom of the press and other media is essential in a free society. Perhaps this explains the general outrage over disclosure that the Pentagon's Office of Strategic Influence planned to disseminate false information and stories to foreign journalists as part of America's war on terrorism.

No other nation in the world, even among the industrialized democracies, enjoys the degree of media freedom found in the United States. Yet, there are a variety of limits on the independence of the media. They range from government-imposed restrictions, both foreign and domestic, to more subtle forms of censorship resulting from the symbiosis between reporters and "official sources" within the government. Thus, while media freedom in the United States represents a closer approach to democracy than has been achieved in any other nation, it is far from absolute, evidenced by the limited access allowed the press during the early stages of the war on terrorism.

President John Kennedy once said, "The flow of ideas, the capacity to make informed choices, the ability to criticize, all of the assumptions on which political democracy rests, depend largely on communications."[5] Democracy requires an *informed* citizenry, and the communication of political information is an essential prerequisite for political participation. A free press stands as one of the defining features of any democratic political system. Figure 12.1 indicates which countries have a free or partly free press.

On the other hand, elites both inside and outside government recognize that they have a major stake in how the media report political information. The **spin** of the news—the interpretation placed on it by those presenting it—is often more important than the news itself. (The term *spin* derives from such sports as soccer, pool, and basketball in which, by giving the ball the correct spin, the players can make it go where they want.) Many experts believe that the effect of spin is to "erode the central requirement of a democracy that those who are governed give not only their consent, but their informed consent."[6]

The Emergence of the Media

A medium is a means of transferring or conveying something. By **mass media,** we mean the various means—newspapers, magazines, radio, television, the Internet—through which information is transferred from its sources to large numbers of people. Perhaps more than any other nation, the United States has become a mass media society. Today more than 40 percent of all adult Americans report that they read daily newspapers; slightly more than one in five regularly watch television's Cable News Network; and well over half make regular use of other cable television systems. In fact, during the 2000 presidential election, for the first time, voters cited cable news outlets as their primary source of information about the campaign than either network or local television news. More and more people also used the Internet to get their information.

FYI

Reporters covering the war in Vietnam used to refer to the official five o'clock press briefings as the "five o'clock follies," because much of the information given out by American officials was far removed from the actual battlefield experiences of the reporters.

spin The interpretation placed on the news by those presenting it.

mass media The various media—newspapers, magazines, radio, television, the Internet—through which information is transferred from its sources to large numbers of people.

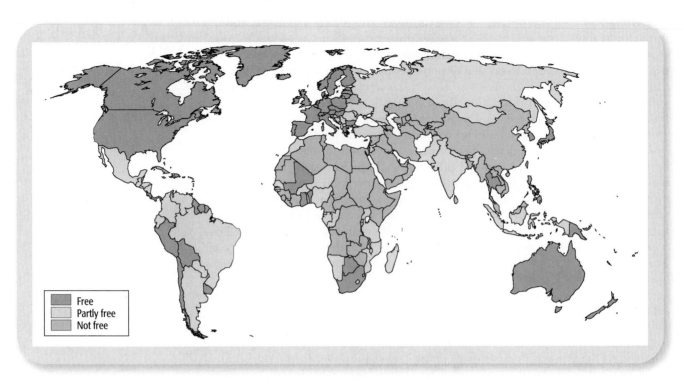

Figure 12.1   Map of Press Freedom
Source: World Press Freedom Committee (http://freedomhouse.org/pfs2002/pfs2002map.pdf). Reprinted by permission of The Freedom House.

Where a citizen gets his or her news—a newspaper, the Internet, television—influences their views on candidates and the election process. For most of the past two hundred years, the mass communication of political information has been dominated by newspapers and television; radio and magazines have been less influential, yet they have also played a role in the development of Americans' political attitudes. With the media occupying such a central place in political affairs today, it is important to understand how the media evolved over the course of American history.

Newspapers

The importance of the press in American politics dates from the revolutionary period, when newspapers served as effective tools for mobilizing public opinion. They were also the primary vehicle for the debate over ratification of the Constitution. *The Federalist Papers* of Alexander Hamilton, James Madison, and John Jay were originally published as articles in the *New York Independent Journal.*

Early political leaders saw the press as the key to educating the public about the new political system. Thomas Jefferson believed that the success of a participatory democracy depends on preventing citizens from making unwise decisions: "Give them full information of their affairs through the channel of the public papers, and . . . contrive that those papers should penetrate the whole mass of the people." In an address to Congress, President George Washington stressed the "importance of facilitating the circulation of political intelligence and information" through the press.[7]

In the period following revolution and independence, political leaders sought allies among newspaper publishers. As secretary of the treasury, Hamilton encouraged a staunch Federalist, John Fenno, to establish a newspaper that would espouse the administration's partisan positions. In return, Fenno was guaranteed financial assistance and printing jobs. Fenno moved from Boston to New York and then Philadelphia, publishing the *Gazette of the United States* from the national capital.

Not to be outdone, Jefferson and other Democratic Republicans urged Philip Freneau to publish a Democratic Republican newspaper, the *National Gazette.* Although neither paper was a financial success, a relationship was forged between editors and their benefactors. As late as 1860, the superintendent of the census classified 80 percent of the nation's periodicals, including all 373 daily newspapers, as "political in their character."[8]

The mass media revolution can be said to have begun with the September 3, 1833, issue of the *New York Sun,* which was sold on the streets for one cent, thereby earning the name "penny press." The paper was targeted at the masses and offered news of local events, along with human-interest stories and entertainment. Mass circulation was achieved through the low price (most newspapers at the time cost six cents) and availability; it could be purchased on virtually every street corner in New York.

In the period from 1850 to 1900, the number of daily papers multiplied from 254 to 2,226. Total circulation increased nearly sevenfold, from 758,000 to over 15 million. As you will see shortly, the development of newspapers as mass communicators influenced the way in which news was presented and even the definition of what constituted news.

Today there are about 1,700 daily newspapers in the United States, with a total circulation of over 63 million. The vast majority of daily papers are in the business of information and entertainment rather than politics. About 60 percent of a typical newspaper's space is taken up by advertising; human-interest stories, sports, reviews, recipes, and other features account for most of the remainder. The portion devoted to news and editorial coverage amounts to about 4 percent of the total.

Question for Reflection: Why do you think such a small percentage of a typical newspaper's space is devoted to news and editorial coverage?

Muckraking and Yellow Journalism   During the nineteenth century the style of journalism changed significantly, both in the way stories were reported and in the events that were considered newsworthy. The mass journalism that developed during that period included much less political and foreign affairs reporting and more local news and sensationalism. In particular, newspapers began to feature coverage of dramatic court cases and criminal activity, along with a strong dose of sex or violence or both. The new journalism also spawned two trends whose effects are still felt today: muckraking and yellow journalism.

The term **muckraking** is derived from the Man with the Muckrake, a character in John Bunyan's *Pilgrim's Progress* who could look only downward and rake the filth on the floor. The word is used to describe a style of reporting that was the precursor of what is now called investigative journalism. Muckraking journalists like Lincoln Steffens and Ida Tarbell and photographer Lewis Hine came to prominence during the early 1900s, a period characterized by reform movements and populist politics known as the Progressive era. They attempted to expose the power and corruption of the rich while championing the cause of workers and the poor. Their stories of political fat cats, machine politics, evil slumlords, and heartless millionaire industrialists enraged the political and social elite. Although these exposés inevitably suffered from subjectivity, not to mention bias, the muckrakers set a trend that continues today.

The darker side of the new journalism drew less on social conscience and more on the profit motive. **Yellow journalism**—named after the controversial "Yellow Kid" comic strip—is usually associated with the big-city daily newspapers of Joseph Pulitzer and William Randolph Hearst. In the late nineteenth century, Pulitzer and Hearst transformed the staid, rather dull publications of their predecessors into brash, colorful, well-illustrated, often lurid and sensationalized organs of half-truth, innuendo, and sometimes, outright lies. The writing style became more casual and colloquial and the stories more dramatic, with the emphasis on sex and violence.

muckraking A word used to describe a style of investigative reporting that uncovered many scandals and abuses.

yellow journalism Brash, colorful, well-illustrated, often lurid and sensationalized organs of half-truth, innuendo, and sometimes outright lies, usually associated with the big-city daily newspapers of Joseph Pulitzer and William Randolph Hearst.

Facts became less important than impact. If a story was not true, yellow journalists often left the onus on those most damaged by its publication, having little to fear from the ineffective libel and slander laws of the time.

The legacy of yellow journalism can be seen in many of today's daily papers and in the sensationalism of news Websites like the Drudge Report. More and more, newspapers are printing stories that were formerly reserved to tabloids such as *The National Enquirer*. Today, print media impacts the average citizen more than even TV and the Internet (see Table 12.2).

Magazines

Although they are less prominent than newspapers as a source of political information, magazines enjoy wide circulation, attentive readership, and an important place in the political education of Americans. Of all the major mass media, magazines as a whole offer the widest variety of subject matter and ideological opinion because each targets certain groups of readers on the basis of socioeconomic status, education, political views, or consumer habits. The proliferation of specialized magazines covering everything from aerobics to zoology is evidence of this strategy.

Of the major news magazines, the most widely read is *Time*. Originally, *Time* was the flagship of the publishing empire founded by Henry Luce. The son of a Presbyterian minister, Luce brought to the magazine his strident faith in the "American Century" and the exalted place of Western culture. According to journalist David Halberstam, Luce "was one of the first true national propagandists; he spoke to the whole nation on national issues, one man with one magazine speaking with one voice, and reaching an entire country."[9] Luce's domineering editorial stance revealed that the potential for ideological extremes was much greater for magazines than for the other mass media. For decades Luce's control of *Time* made him one of the most important and influential political forces in America.

Luce's impact on mass-readership magazines extended beyond politics. In addition to *Time*, his growing company published *Look, Life, Fortune,* and *Sports Illustrated*. But *Time* created an explosive popular appetite for news coverage. Luce's formula for the "modern" news magazine featured dramatic photographs, information, analysis, and opinion on the dominant issues of the day. *Time's* success soon produced a host of competitors, including *Newsweek* and *U.S. News & World Report*. These and similar publications continue to serve as "sources of record" for elected

---

Table 12.2 ■ Whom Each Medium Impacted

Where a citizen gets his or her news from is likely to influence the views they form about candidates and the election process. In a study conducted by the Project for Excellence in Journalism, television, not newspapers or the Internet, tended to cover campaign themes more than any other medium. This table shows the impact of each medium in the 2000 election.

Whom Each Medium Impacted	Print	TV	Internet
Citizens	32%	20%	23%
Politicians	59	70	68
Interest Groups	6	4	6
No Impact	3	6	3
Total	100%	100%	100%

Source: http://www.journalism.org/publ_research/campaign7.html. Reprinted with permission from Project for Excellence in Journalism.

officials, corporate executives, and informed citizens who pay close attention to political affairs. Besides the news magazines, there are numerous magazines of political opinion. The most widely read are the conservative *National Review,* the liberal *New Republic,* and the Progressive *Nation.* The ideological differences among these publications testify both to the targeting of readership and to the breadth of political opinion among magazine readers.

Radio

Radio enjoyed a brief but important heyday as a significant source of political information for the American public. Developed in the early twentieth century, radio technology underwent a revolution during World War I. From the 1930s until after World War II, radio was the dominant popular medium. Today's three major television networks—NBC, ABC, and CBS—began as radio networks.

Unlike print media, radio broadcasts could report events as they were happening. This quality of immediacy produced some of the most dramatic live reporting in history, including the horrifying account of the explosion of the German zeppelin *Hindenburg* in 1937. The degree to which radio had become a trusted medium was revealed in October 1938, when Orson Welles and his Mercury Theatre of the Air broadcast "War of the Worlds," a fictionalized invasion of the earth by Martians. So convincing were the dramatization's simulated "live" news reports that many Americans believed that the invasion was real.

Radio journalism picked up where print journalism left off. Many of radio's early news reporters had begun as newspaper or magazine reporters. The most successful of them combined the journalistic skills of print reporters with the effective speaking voice required by a medium that "spoke" the news. One of radio's premier news reporters, Edward R. Murrow, established standards of integrity and reportorial skill that continue to this day. He combined the investigative traditions of the early muckrakers with concise writing and a compelling speaking voice. Murrow's career would outlast the peak of radio's popularity; he enjoyed equal fame as a television journalist.

Probably the most successful use of radio by a politician was the famous series of "fireside chats" by President Franklin Roosevelt. An impressive public speaker, Roosevelt used these brief broadcasts to bolster American confidence—and his own popularity—as he pushed for major legislative reforms to combat the Great Depression. The immediacy of radio was also exploited by demagogues like the arch conservative Father Charles Coughlin of Michigan. While Coughlin never ran for public office, his broadcast "sermons" included strident attacks on communists and Jews, even implying support for the Nazi regime at a time when the United States was seriously contemplating entering the war against Germany.

Radio's popularity began to ebb after World War II. Its chief competition came not from newspapers and magazines but from a new, even more immediate and compelling medium—television. By 1948 three networks were broadcasting regular programming on television. But radio has not been entirely eclipsed. In recent years radio talk show hosts like Rush Limbaugh, Larry King, or Don Imus have become an important source of news and opinion, as well as entertainment, for the listening public. Many commuters tune in to such programs while traveling to and from work.

Television

Unlike newspapers, magazines, and radio, television developed primarily as a commercial medium, designed not so much to provide information or opinion but to entertain and stimulate mass consumerism. Thus, most Americans tend to think of television as a low-cost leisure activity rather than as a source of political information.

▲ President Franklin D. Roosevelt is shown here during a radio broadcast in 1938. Millions of Americans came to trust their president because of his extremely personal radio broadcasts, known as "fireside chats."

Television is more pervasive and effective than any other form of mass communication in the United States. Advances in broadcast technology have made possible virtually instantaneous transmission of information and greatly expanded the range of programs for viewers to choose from. As a result, according to political scientist Richard Neustadt, television is "at once the primary news source for most Americans, the vehicle for national political competition, a crucial means to sell consumer goods, and an almost universal source of entertainment."[10] Figure 12.2 shows how television can play a central role in political events.

Yet network television news viewing has declined in recent years. In fact, people appear to be less inclined to believe TV news and less inclined to watch it. Over the years there has been a steady decline in news viewership. In 1981 collective nightly newscasts commanded 84 percent of the viewing audience, in 2002 these same newscasts attract only 43 percent of potential viewers.[11] As more and more people access the Internet and view such cable news shows as Bill O'Reilly's *The O'Reilly Factor*, "maybe we are moving to a time when the major commercial broadcast networks, CBS and NBC as well as ABC, get out of the news business," PBS NewsHour host Jim Lehrer declared, "They go about the business of entertaining and leave the informing to others. With the coming of the two C-SPAN channels and the cable news channels—and the growing number of news Web sites . . . the issue may be only one of transition."[12]

Although most Americans see television as an entertainment medium, no public official or political candidate can afford to ignore its power as a means of communicating with the public. In fact, television plays a central role in elections, especially presidential campaigns. The Project for Excellence in Journalism reported

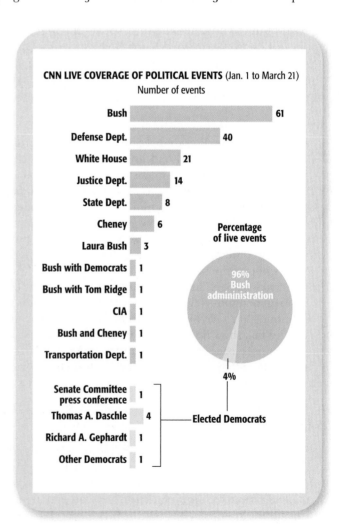

Figure 12.2
Tallying Air Time

Source: The Washington Post,
April 22, 2002, p. A17.

that in the presidential election of 2000, "television tended to cover campaign themes more than any other medium—68% compared to 56% on the Internet and 53% in newspapers."[13]

New Media Technologies

During President Ronald Reagan's vacations at his ranch in Santa Barbara, California, CBS News assigned two technicians to sit in a truck parked on a hilltop three miles away for the sole purpose of monitoring a TV screen. The screen was wired to a camera with a lens three feet long and weighing over four hundred pounds, custom-made for photographing the President when he appeared outdoors. "I'm going to fake a heart attack and tumble off this horse to see how quickly they get down the mountain with the news," Reagan joked.[14]

High-tech cameras are just one of many innovations that have greatly changed the nature of television reporting. The box feature on the next page shows just how far news gathering has evolved since the 1962 taping of "A Tour of the White House with Mrs. John F. Kennedy." The show required nine tons of lights, cameras, and cables put into place by fifty-four technicians. In contrast, the 1990 NBC special, "A Day in the Life of the White House," was produced by a handful of technicians. It was filmed on a Monday, edited on a Tuesday, and broadcast that Wednesday. Later in the chapter you will learn in the new millennium feature just how high-tech journalism has become in the twenty-first century.

Satellites   An especially significant technological advance is the satellite. As a result of satellite technology, television has become an instantaneous means of worldwide communication, which may explain why the Pentagon purchased the exclusive rights to Space Imaging corporation, to control access. The cost of satellite relay links between the East and West Coasts of the United States has dropped significantly, and the cost of transmission links to formerly remote areas in the Far East and Middle East has been reduced by half. One effect has been an expansion in coverage of the president's activities, both in Washington and abroad. In the early 1980s the number of local news stations with Washington bureaus grew from fifteen to more than fifty.

In the 1970s, fewer than half of all television news stories were shown on the day they occurred. Today, as a result of satellite technology, it is rare for any news story other than special features to be more than a few hours, if not minutes, old. The use of videophones during the early stages of the war on terrorism brought live visual images back from distant Afghanistan. Satellites have also affected the political process. Senators and members of the administration, as well as candidates for office, are making increasing use of direct satellite links to bypass network news and appear on local television newscasts.

Cable TV   Cable television was developed in the 1950s to bring television programming to remote areas that could not be reached by normal VHF and UHF broadcast signals. By transmitting television signals through coaxial cable to individual receivers, cable television avoided the environmental and atmospheric disturbances that often plagued regular broadcast signals. Since the 1980s, cable TV has become almost universal throughout the United States; although in recent years it has faced a serious challenge from satellite dish systems. Both systems are more popular than regular broadcasting because they provide superior signal definition and a wider variety of programming choices than any single broadcast market could provide. Channels like C-SPAN, Cable News Network, and CNN Headline News, as well as specialty channels for sports, feature films, and cultural programming, compete vigorously with the established broadcast networks for viewer's attention.

Narrowcasting   Technological advances such as satellites, cable TV, low-power television broadcast stations, VCRs, and remote-control all make possible lower

FYI

Peggy Noonan, former speech writer and image maker for Ronald Reagan and George W. Bush (she wrote Bush's famous "thousand points of light" speech), observed about television's power over Americans, "Our sophistication means nothing; for all our knowledge of TV, it still fools us. We are like people who go to a magic show knowing it's all strings and mirrors and still being thrilled when the lady gets sawed in half."

Tools of the Trade: How TV News Gathering Evolved

1927: Philo Farnsworth patents his dissector tube, an important component in the development of all electronic television.

1939: NBC broadcasts the opening of the New York World's Fair.

1948: NBC launched a 10-minute weekday news program, "The Camel Newsreel Theater." John Cameron Swayze reads news reports while film images, largely from newsreel companies, fill the screen.

1951: A coaxial cable link connecting the East and West coasts is completed, allowing live coast-to-coast broadcasts.

1956: The Ampex Corporation introduces the videotape recorder, making it possible to record in studio interviews and delay the broadcast to the West Coast.

1958: Reversal film, which when processed yields a positive print rather than a negative, is introduced, speeding the process of editing for broadcast. By 1960 a shift to color reversal newsfilm has begun.

1960s: The Vietnam War becomes the "television war," with film relayed quickly by aircraft to the nearest television cable terminus to be fed to the network.

1962: Telstar I, a communications satellite, is launched, allowing live transmission of events from all corners of the world.

1968: Sony introduces 3/4-inch videocassettes to the consumer market. The arrival of the digital time bas connector in 1972 allows broadcast-quality taping, and film disappears from news programs.

1970s: Mobile television news units become common, using lightweight microwave electronics installed in small vans equipped with telescoping masts.

1971: Communications satellites carrying spot beam antennas are launched, allowing the satellites to focus on a small portion of the Earth for reception and transmission.

1980s: A new generation of satellites, called Ku-band, require less power for transmissions, permitting small (and less expensive) earth stations like mobile vehicles to send and receive video.

1990s: Digitalization and compression of satellite TV signals yields better quality and greater efficiency in transmission.

1991: The Persian Gulf War is covered live, with CNN broadcasting from Baghdad as air strikes begin.

Source: New York Times, January 31, 2002, p. E5. Reprinted by permission of *The New York Times.*

costs and increased usage. Collectively, these advances have resulted in what media expert Austin Ranney terms *narrowcasting.* Network television is based on a broadcasting system in which television signals are transmitted over the air, aimed at huge, heterogeneous audiences, and transmitted to wireless receivers in viewers' homes. Narrowcasting, in contrast, is a mass communications system "in which television signals are transmitted either by air or by direct wires to people's homes and are aimed at smaller, more narrowly defined, and more homogenous audiences."[15]

Narrowcasting involves more than a move toward greater programming efficiency; it has developed largely as a way to boost profits in an increasingly competitive media market. It is based on the idea that a more carefully targeted viewing audience is also a more homogeneous buying audience. Among the most successful experiments in narrowcasting are CNN (twenty-four-hour programming devoted exclusively to news and information), ESPN (twenty-four-hour sports programming), Nickelodeon (programming for children), and MTV (twenty-four-hour music and entertainment).

◄ The Internet brings the world, and democratic ideals, to even the most closed societies. Here an Azad University student in an Internet café in Tehran, Iran, uses the Internet to research a term paper.

World Wide Web   The World Wide Web and the Internet are playing an increasingly important role in obtaining and disseminating political information. Virtually all news organizations now have their own home page on the Web, and in the 2000 presidential nomination election, candidates found it a relatively inexpensive way to reach voters. Every Republican and Democratic challenger in the 2000 primaries constructed a home page on the Web where their platforms, programs, and information could easily be accessed. The Democratic and Republican National Committees did the same. Today, as you can tell by navigating through the *Approaching Democracy* home page (http://www.prenhall.com/berman), virtually every government agency, lobbying group, interest group, newspaper, and television station have Web pages with easily accessed information. The Web promises to be the great equalizer in American politics, what one political analyst described as "keypad democracy."[16]

Functions of the Media

Social scientists are in general agreement that the mass media perform three basic functions: (1) surveillance of world events, (2) interpretation of events, and (3) socialization of individuals into cultural settings. "The manner in which these . . . functions are performed," writes political scientist Doris Graber, "affects the political fate of individuals, groups, and social organizations, as well as the course of domestic and international politics."[17]

Surveillance

In their surveillance role, the media function, as Marshall McLuhan observed, as "sense extensions" for people who do not participate directly in events.[18] From the media we learn about world conditions, cultural events, sports, weather, and much else. In many respects, the mass media have helped transform the world into a global community. Citizens of the now-united Germany watched the dismantling of the Berlin Wall at the same time as citizens of the United States did. Millions of viewers watched the changing of the millennium and the debate over the fate of Elian Gonzalez. When President George W. Bush, inadvertently referred to the Japanese devaluation rather than deflation, the yen immediately fell and did not correct itself until the White House retraction.

Every afternoon, television news anchors and their staffs sift through the myriad stories, tapes, and bits of information that have been funneled to them during the day to identify the most important information and events. What they select will be relayed to the public in evening news broadcasts. Thus, the news anchors actually define what is newsworthy.

THE ROAD TO DEMOCRACY

The Internet Scoop That Started It All

THAT WAS THEN . . .

It started late Saturday night, when Web-newsie Matt Drudge filed this breathless report on his site. "At the last minute, at 6 p.m. on Saturday evening, *Newsweek* magazine killed a story that was destined to shake official Washington to its foundation: A White House intern carried on a sexual affair with the President of the United States!" Drudge explains that "reporter Michael Isikoff developed the story of his career, only to have it spiked by top *Newsweek* suits hours before publication."

The scandal moves to television Sunday morning. *Weekly Standard* Editor William Kristol strategically inserts it in a discussion of the Paula Jones case during the round-table section of ABC's *This Week with Sam and Cokie*. It is approximately 12:45 P.M. EST, about a half-day after the Drudge eruption. Other "incidents" of Clinton philandering may surface, Kristol says, and "the media is going to be an issue here." He continues, "The story in Washington this morning is that *Newsweek* magazine was going to go with a big story based on tape-recorded conversations, which a woman who was a summer intern at the White House, an intern of Leon Panetta's—"

Monday brings more postings on various Websites: The *Drudge Report* updates the story—and the story behind the story. Drudge names Monica Lewinsky as Clinton's alleged paramour. *Slate* mentions the Kristol-Stephanopoulos-Donaldson exchange in "Pundit Central" and the alleged spiking of the *Newsweek* story in "In Other Magazines." The Webzine *The Underground* makes it the day's feature story. CNBC's *Rivera Live* airs a few choice rumors about the scandal. By Tuesday, Matt Drudge speaks his piece on CBS Radio's *Mary Matalin Show* and keeps filing on the Web. Tuesday night, Drudge writes that federal investigators possess taped phone conversations that substantiate the rumors of a presidential affair. And from the print media? Not a peep until Wednesday morning.

THIS IS NOW . . .

Matt Drudge earned his reputation by posting unconfirmed reports of political skullduggery and sex in the Clinton White House. Whether you think that Matt Drudge is Walter Winchell reincarnated or just the class gossipmonger of American politics, DrudgeReport.com has long been a site to be reckoned with. After the attacks on the World Trade Center, Drudge's site has become an ad domain to be reckoned with.

For the week ending Sept. 16, 2001, the Drudge Report was the no. 20 ad domain, according to Nielson/NetRatings, with 10,757,000 impressions, reaching 0.76 percent of the internet audience. This marks the first time that the popular site has ranked as a top ad domain.

▲ Internet political reporter Matt Drudge has helped to change the face of reporting with his online columns.

The sudden surge in impressions appears to relate to the attacks on the World Trade Center and the Pentagon. In the week ending Sept. 9, according to Nielson/NetRatings' data, the site attracted 535,000 unique visitors.

After the attacks, the number of weekly unique visitors to DrudgeReport.com jumped almost 38 percent, to 734,000 unique visitors in the week ending Sept. 16.

According to DrudgeReport.com, the site has received 90 million visits. But high traffic volume is nothing new for the stripped-down site. Following the presidential elections, so many people clogged the site that it was all but inaccessible.

Source: Seth Stevenson, "How the Story Everyone Is Talking About Stayed Out of the Papers," http://www.drudgereport.com, and Marty Beard, "Matt Drudge's rise as a hot ad domain," *Media Life*, http://www.medialifemagazine.com/pages/templates/scripts.prfr.asp.

APPROACHING DEMOCRACY AROUND THE GLOBE

The Proliferation of the Internet

Approximately 498 million people currently enjoy access to the Internet from their home computers, while millions more use the information superhighway at coffee shops and other commercial kiosks around the world. Even more astounding, the rate of growth in the number of people using the Internet at home is doubling every business quarter. These findings were based on the Nielsen/NetRatings Global Internet Trends service, a company compiling quarterly Internet statistics, taken from surveys between October and December of 2001.

A similar pattern of widespread and growing Internet use has extended abroad as well. In the Middle East, Africa, and Europe use of the Web on personal computers has mushroomed beyond all expectation. In Asia, South Korea and Singapore led the vanguard of at-home use, closing the gap on Hong Kong, the most dominant user.

Certain types of households use the Internet more than others. In Europe, Internet access at home is dominated by households headed by men with University degrees. The same pattern exists for households in the United States and Asia Pacific. Both in Europe and in Latin America, households with the most Internet users are headed by someone 35 or younger. Brazil, a nation with one of the youngest and most impoverished populations in Latin America, boasts the largest at-home Internet use of any nation in the southern hemisphere—three in four Brazilians with home computers use them to access the Internet. Mexico has recently experienced an 8% growth in people using their own computers to get online. Today, more than half of home personal computers are used to gain access.

Although many countries are seeing a surge in at-home use of the Internet, many are not. Some nations that list a vibrant growth also admit that particular segments of their population, such as American Indians living on isolated and rural reservations in the U.S., are having difficulty gaining access.

Stemming from poverty and an embryonic infrastructure, India has left millions of its rural agricultural population (most villages lack electricity) behind. India is the only country in Asia Pacific that lists only single-digit home access rates. Only one in fourteen households with telephones have Internet access. The rest of Asia Pacific fared better: 80% of homes use their personal computers to link to the Internet.

Source: Business Wire, "Nielsen/Net Ratings Reports a Record Half Billion People Worldwide now Have Home Internet Access," http://www.newsfactor.com/perl/story/17684.html.

The ability of the media to decide what constitutes news is a controversial aspect of their surveillance role. The media not only bring certain matters to public attention but also doom certain others to obscurity. During election campaigns, for example, the press is the "great mentioner," repeating the names of certain individuals who are being mentioned as possible candidates, or applying labels such as "dark horse" or "long shot." "At any given time in this country," writes journalist David Broder, "there are several hundred persons who are potential candidates for nomination.... Who is it that winnows this field down to manageable size? The press—and particularly that small segment of the press called the national political reporters."[19]

Question for Reflection: Can you name three current national political reporters? Three current network television and/or cable news anchors? How much do you actually know about these individuals who are shaping what is considered news and noteworthy in America?

"There are few checks on the media's surveillance role," writes Doris Graber. "The power of the media to set the civic agenda is a matter of concern because it is not controlled by a system of formal checks and balances as is power at various levels of government. It is not subject to periodic review through the electoral process. If media emphases or claims are incorrect, remedies are few."[20] Surveillance can occur at the private as well as public level. Despite the appeals from many in the administration and slain *Wall Street Journal* reporter Daniel Pearl's family, CBS decided to show the non-graphic portions of the amateur video showing Pearl's murder; determining that the U.S. public had a right to understand the depth of the propaganda war against the United States. The complete graphic soon turned up on the Internet.

Interpretation

The media do much more than provide public and private surveillance of events. They also interpret those events by giving them meaning and context, and in the process often shape opinions. Psychologist Hadley Cantril illustrates this point with the following example:

> Three umpires describe their job of calling balls and strikes in a baseball game. First umpire: "Some's balls and some's strikes and I calls 'em as they is." Second umpire: "Some's balls and some's strikes and I calls 'em as I sees 'em." Third umpire: "Some's balls and some's strikes but they ain't nothin' 'till I calls 'em."[21]

According to Cantril, very few journalists are like the first umpire, believing that the "balls and strikes" they count represent what is happening in the real world. Some journalists may admit to the second method of umpiring, using their judgment to "call them as they see them." The third umpire's style is the most controversial when applied to mass media coverage of significant events. For if, like the third umpire, journalists in print and television actually make the decisions regarding which actors or events are in or out of the "strike zone" or even determine their own "strike zone" or context for news, the potential power of the media becomes immense, and assertions of media "objectivity" sound rather hollow.

Actually, the process of gathering, evaluating, editing, producing, and presenting news involves each of the three umpiring styles. Some reporters may pursue a case against a prominent public figure or institution in the belief that their article will finally expose the "reality" of corruption, scandal, or wrongdoing. And every journalist—from reporters on the street to editors behind desks—exercises some judgment over which events are most "newsworthy;" an event is neither a curve ball in the dirt nor a fastball on the outside corner until some journalistic "umpire" makes the decision to cover it.

Political scientist Shanto Iyengar has developed a theory of media "framing effects" that is particularly relevant to television news coverage. In a series of carefully controlled experiments, Iyengar and his colleagues found that the way television portrays events and actors has a significant influence on the opinions of those who watch the coverage. For example, coverage of terrorism that emphasizes the violence and brutality of a terrorist act without attempting to explain the motivations behind it is likely to influence viewers to consider all such actions brutal and violent, regardless of the motivations or historical explanations. This is an important point. Since the constraints of time tend to dictate relatively brief, often superficial coverage of important news, viewers are likely to form equally superficial opinions.[22]

Investigative Journalism   Journalism may have changed since the days of the muckrakers, as the technology and political culture of America have changed, but the spirit of the muckraker can still be seen in the practice of **investigative journalism.** Investigative journalism differs from standard press coverage in the depth of coverage sought, the time spent researching the subject, and the shocking findings that often result from such reporting. Like their muckraking predecessors, today's investigative journalists turn their reportorial skills to the uncovering of corruption, scandal, conspiracy, and abuses of power in government and business.

The most familiar historical example of such reporting occurred during the Watergate scandal of the 1970s and developed out of extensive interviewing and analysis by two reporters for the *Washington Post*, Carl Bernstein and Bob Woodward. The editor of the *Post*, Ben Bradlee, risked his professional reputation and the reputation of his paper by running a series of investigative articles on the Watergate break-in and its connection to the White House. Although the *Post* articles, which began raising questions in the months before the 1972 presidential election, did not affect its outcome, they eventually uncovered a scandal that led to the resignation of President Richard Nixon.

investigative journalism The uncovering of corruption, scandal, conspiracy, and abuses of power in government and business; differs from standard press coverage in the depth of the coverage sought, the time spent researching the subject, and the shocking findings that often result from such reporting.

◀ Greta Van Susteren joined Fox News Channel in February 2002 and is the host of *On the Record with Greta Van Susteren*. Prior to joining FNC, Van Susteren hosted CNN's *The Point,* a primetime news and analysis program as well as the daytime legal affairs show, *Burden of Proof.* She joined CNN in 1991 as a legal analyst and commentated on several high profile cases for the network, including the O.J. Simpson civil and criminal trials.

Like the print media, television also developed a tradition of investigative journalism, drawing on the early work of Edward R. Murrow, whose most famous piece may have been his 1952 exposé of the vicious practices of Senator Joseph McCarthy. Today, such programs as *60 Minutes* continue this tradition. Sometimes televised "watchdog" journalism creates internal controversy, as was the case in a 1998 CNN broadcast "Valley of Death" on its *Newsstand* program. The story alleged that in 1970 U.S. Special Forces in Operation Tailwind dropped lethal sarin gas to suppress enemy fire while friendly forces were evacuated. CNN quickly retracted the story and fired several of the show's producers, but the producers were later vindicated in March 2002 when the Ninth Circuit Court issued an 18-page opinion regarding the Tailwind report. The court found no evidence of inaccurate reporting or coerced testimony.[23]

Socialization

The media play an important role in **socialization,** the process by which people learn to conform to their society's norms and values. As we noted in Chapter 8, most of the information that children acquire about their world comes from the mass media, either directly or indirectly through the media's influence on parents, teachers, or friends. The mass media also provide information that enables young people to develop their own opinions. MTV provides a forum, "Choose or Lose" that enables young people to learn about politics, issues, and candidates. It also served as a forum for Secretary of State Colin Powell to urge condom use—only to meet criticism from conservatives who argued that this was inconsistent with the President's position of promoting abstinence.

Studies of the effects of exposure to mass media have found that higher reliance on television as the primary source of information seems to correlate with a greater fear of crime and random violence, even when controlling for the socioeconomic status, education, and living conditions of the individual. Although such findings are tentative and subject to interpretation, they indicate that the medium on which most Americans rely for most of their information about the rest of the world—television—may contribute to a growing sense of unease. Yet more Americans feel that television news, as compared to newspapers, is the most reliable and honest source of news.

Much of the impact of the mass media seems to involve reinforcing prevailing norms and values rather than creating new ones. Until the dissolution of the former Soviet Union in 1990, most commentary on socialism, communism, Eastern Europe, and the USSR simply reinforced the Cold War perspective in support of free-market capitalism and against communism; public opinion surveys indicate that this message was clearly received. Now that the Soviet Union has been broken up,

socialization The process by which people learn to conform to their society's norms and values.

most coverage of Eastern Europe as Chapter 16 will show, tends to emphasize the transition and approaches to democracy. Opinion polls indicate that Americans are no longer as concerned about the potential "menace" of communism, and public opinion data shows a growing acceptance of Russia.

The power of the media as a socializing agent is reflected in public concern about media violence, particularly in children's television programming. While analysts remain sharply divided about the actual impact of violent programming, efforts have been made to regulate the frequency and intensity of violent and sexually explicit media content. For example, in the wake of the assassinations of Robert Kennedy and Martin Luther King, Jr., television programmers canceled a number of popular but violent shows or changed the programs to reflect less explicit violence.

In recent years the television networks have begun to voluntarily rate their shows for violent or adult content. Televised screenings of feature films containing explicit violence or sexual content have adopted the motion picture precedent of rating these programs and including viewer discretion warnings. Cable stations that air films "uncut" provide the original film rating and generally restrict the airing of such programming to the late evening, when children are more likely to be asleep. Although such attempts to regulate the socializing influence of mass media are controversial, they demonstrate widespread agreement that freedom of expression must sometimes be limited to avert social harm.

Limits on Media Freedom

The First Amendment to the Constitution states that "Congress shall make no law . . . abridging the freedom . . . of the press." Ideally, the media would investigate, report, provide information, and analyze political events without being subject to government-imposed restrictions. Such restrictions are commonplace in many other nations, where the media are subject to various degrees of restraint,

---

APPROACHING DIVERSITY

Young People up to Speed on Terrorism News

The post–9/11 era has seen a sharp rise in the public's appetite for serious news. Even a majority of young people, who traditionally lag well behind their elders in news attentiveness and knowledge, have stayed on top of terrorism-related developments. That has raised hoped that young people will now become more avid consumers of all news and, as a result, better informed and more engaged citizens. Twenty-somethings are remarkably well-briefed on terrorism and even the geopolitics of central Asia, even as they continue to have a poor grasp of politics in this country.

What the Generations Know

In a November survey by the Pew Research Center, 59% of the 25-and-under group correctly identified Turkey (from a list that also included Pakistan and Russia) as a nation that does not possess nuclear weapons. Older Americans were no better informed on this point. And young people's awareness of facts relating to anthrax and Muslim support for the war was on par with their elders.

When it comes to elementary political facts, however, many young Americans are still in the dark. Only about half (51%) could identify Dick Cheney as the vice president of the United States. That is not only less than any other age group, it is well below the 64% of those 25 and under who correctly identified Al Gore as vice president in a 1994 survey.

While most young people say their overall news interest has increased because of the attacks, there is a considerable generation gap in attentiveness to non-terrorism news. For example, fewer than three in ten young people reported paying close attentions to economic news, compared with better than four-in-ten of the rest of the public.

Source: Andrew Kohut for America Online. The Pew Research Center, http://www.people-press.org/commentary/display.php3?AnalysisID=36.

prohibition, or censorship. Americans take pride in the tradition of a free press, yet that freedom is not absolute. Not only are there laws against libel, slander, and obscenity, but the media are regulated by a government agency, the **Federal Communications Commission (FCC),** and are subject to certain limitations imposed by the judiciary. The nature of media ownership also plays a role in limiting media freedom.[24]

Regulating the Media

Regulation of the media began after World War I, in the heyday of radio. During that period large consortiums like the Radio Corporation of America (RCA) established networks to broadcast news, information, and entertainment, and millions of amateur "radio hams" were buying or building simple broadcast receivers and sending their own gossip, sermons, monologues, and conversations over the increasingly congested airwaves. In 1927 the federal government stepped in to clean up the chaotic radio waves. Congress created the five-member Federal Radio Commission (FRC) to allocate frequencies and regulate broadcasting procedures. Essentially, the objective of the FRC was to organize radio broadcasting and constrain the growing radio broadcast industry to prevent monopolization and other unfair practices.

In 1934 Congress passed the Federal Communications Act, in which the jurisdiction of the FRC was expanded to include telephone and telegraph communications, the panel was enlarged to seven members (eventually reduced again to five in 1982), and the agency was renamed the Federal Communications Commission (FCC). As broadcast and cable television (CATV) developed, they too came under the scrutiny and jurisdiction of the FCC. The most recent communications innovations—multipoint distribution service (MDS), direct broadcast satellites (DBS), and satellite master antenna television (SMATV)—have also come under the umbrella of FCC regulation.

The electronic media are regulated by four sets of guidelines:

1. Rules limiting the number of stations owned or controlled by a single organization
2. Examinations of the goals and performances of stations as part of periodic licensing
3. Rules mandating public service and local interest programs
4. Rules guaranteeing fair treatment to individuals and protection of their rights

Regulation of the electronic media has been consistently upheld by the Supreme Court under the scarcity doctrine. While there is no limit on the number of newspapers that can be published in a given area, two radio or television stations cannot broadcast signals at the same time and at the same frequency without jamming each other. Thus it is clearly in the public interest that government allocate frequencies to broadcasters. Broadcasting is viewed as a public resource, much like a national park, and the government establishes regulations designed to promote "the public convenience, interest, or necessity."

The scarcity doctrine, with its implications for the public interest, is the basis for the FCC's regulation of the political content of radio and television broadcasts. This regulation takes the form of three rules of the airwaves: the equal opportunities rule, the fairness doctrine, and the right to rebuttal.

The Equal Time Rule Although a station is not required to give or sell airtime to a candidate seeking a specific office, whenever it provides time to one candidate—whether for a price or for free—it must give equal time to all candidates running for the same office. This **equal time rule** holds whether there are two or two hundred candidates for office; each is entitled to equal time. Section 315 (a) of the Federal Communications Act stipulates:

Federal Communications Commission (FCC) A government commission formed to allocate radio and TV frequencies and regulate broadcasting procedures.

equal time rule A requirement that radio and TV stations allow equal time to all candidates for office.

If any licensee shall permit any person who is a legally qualified candidate for any public office to use a broadcasting station, he shall afford equal opportunities to all other such candidates for that office in the use of such broadcasting station.

The equal time rule has become important in recent presidential campaigns. In the 1992 presidential elections when Ross Perot bought large blocks of time for his "infomercials" on various campaign issues, the networks involved were required to make similar blocks of time available to George Bush and Bill Clinton. However, the rule does not require that the candidates actually take advantage of the available time, only that they have the opportunity to purchase it on an equal basis with all other candidates.

The Fairness Doctrine The **fairness doctrine,** now abandoned, required radio and television stations to provide a reasonable percentage of time for programs dealing with issues of public interest. Stations were also required to provide time for those who wished to express opposition to any highly controversial public issue aired or discussed on the station. Defining what is controversial had traditionally been left to the administrative courts, but the FCC has ruled that "two viewpoints" satisfies the licensee's obligation. The fairness doctrine was upheld by the Supreme Court in 1969 in *Red Lion Broadcasting v. FCC.* A federal court of appeals later ruled that the doctrine was not law and could be repealed without congressional approval. Congress then passed a bill that would have made the fairness doctrine permanent. But President Ronald Reagan vetoed the bill on grounds that federal policing of editorial judgment of journalists was an outrage. Following the veto, the FCC negated the doctrine.[25]

The Right of Rebuttal When the honesty, integrity, or morality of persons or groups is attacked on a station, they have the **right of rebuttal**—the right to refute the allegations, free of charge, within a reasonable time. The FCC operates under the assumption that a maligned person deserves a chance to reply, and the public has a right to hear that response. The rule does not apply to attacks on foreign groups or leaders, to personal attacks made by legally qualified candidates or their representatives, or to live, on-the-spot broadcasts.

Prior Restraint versus the Right to Know

In 1971 former government employee Daniel Ellsberg gave the *New York Times* copies of classified documents on the Vietnam War. The documents had been prepared in 1968 during the presidency of Lyndon Johnson, and they revealed the concerns of senior Defense Department officials during the Kennedy and Johnson years. The government sought to suppress the publication of the documents by obtaining a judicial restraining order, an action known as **prior restraint.** President Richard Nixon maintained that publication of the papers would threaten the lives of servicemen and servicewomen, intelligence officers, and military plans that were still in operation in Vietnam.

The case eventually reached the Supreme Court, which decided in favor of the *Times.* In his concurring opinion on the case, Justice Hugo Black offered a strong argument for absolute freedom of the press:

Paramount among the responsibilities of a free press is the duty to prevent any part of the Government from deceiving the people and sending them off to distant lands to die of foreign fever and foreign shot and shell. . . . *The New York Times* and the *Washington Post* and other newspapers should be commended for serving the purpose that the Founding Fathers saw so clearly. In revealing the workings of government that led to the Vietnam War, the newspapers nobly did precisely that which the Founders hoped and trusted they would do.[26]

In another case, when CNN broadcast recorded phone conversations involving Panamanian general Manuel Noriega as he awaited trial in Miami in 1990, the

fairness doctrine A policy, now abandoned, that radio and TV stations provide time to all sides in programs of public interest.

right of rebuttal The right to refute the allegations presented on a radio or TV station, free of charge, within a reasonable time.

prior restraint An action in which the government seeks to ban the publication of controversial material by the press before it is published; censorship.

Supreme Court refused to block a lower court's injunction banning all future broadcasts that CNN planned to air. The controversy raised important constitutional questions. At issue were Noriega's right to a fair trial as well as freedom of the press. What made the issue more intriguing was that the Court decided to suppress publication despite the fact that the U.S. government was responsible for the taping of the phone conversations in the first place.[27]

Other cases have been concerned with the media's right to cover a trial and whether that coverage would threaten the fairness of the trial. Should *Court TV,* for example, be permitted to broadcast the trial of Zacarias Moussaoui, who is believed to be the 20th hijacker on September 11 and is the only person charged in the attacks. In January 2002 a federal judge rejected cable television's request. In his ruling, Judge Leonie M. Brinkema cited procedural and security reasons for denying the request to overturn a ban on television broadcasts of federal criminal trials.

The case of *Miami Herald Publishing Co. v. Tornillo* (1974) brought up the issue of whether statutory guidelines implemented by Florida state law require newspapers to publish specific replies from political candidates attacked in their columns rather than merely publishing retractions. The Court ruled against the "right to reply" law, stating that it "turns afoul the elementary First Amendment proposition that government may not force a newspaper to print copy which, in the journalistic discretion, it chooses to leave on the newspaper floor."[28] That is, even when accused of publicly defaming a political figure, newspapers could not be required by law to print the responses of the defamed figure, since this was to "force a newspaper to print copy" in violation of the constitutional guarantee of a free press. As Chief Justice Warren E. Burger noted, "A responsible press is an undoubtedly desirable goal, but press responsibility is not mandated by the Constitution, and like many other virtues, it cannot be legislated."

Even with a relatively broad guarantee of freedom, there are laws restricting just how the press may cover news. Journalists are allowed wide latitude in levying charges against whomever they choose and may even print facts or accusations that subsequently prove untrue, as long as they do not *knowingly* publish untruths or print intentionally damaging statements known as **libel.** Anyone attempting to sue a newspaper for libel must also prove that the publication in question actually caused damage. As you will see in Chapter 13, libel is very difficult to prove, especially for public figures whose reputation may be affected by any number of things besides a single journalistic "hit piece" and who have an opportunity to make a reply. In general, as long as journalists do not set out to attack a public figure with malice, they are not subject to prevailing laws against libel.

Ideological Bias and Media Control

Many observers believe that the mass media display bias in the way they select and present news. While the majority of reporters in both print and electronic media are fairly liberal, their bosses—the magazine and newspaper publishers and network executives—tend to be more conservative, sometimes decidedly so. Most of the statistical evidence supporting conservative charges of a liberally biased "media elite" does not clearly differentiate between the reporters, the editors, and the publishers and owners of media outlets; sometimes the only analysis is of the reporters, a peculiarly well educated, well-paid, and liberal cohort of the American public. In the often-cited studies of Robert Lichter, Linda Lichter, and Stanley Rothman, for example, the "media elite" includes reporters, editors, and executives, but only as an aggregate population with no distinctions regarding the differences that might exist within this elite. Simply establishing the liberal leanings of reporters does not prove liberal press bias.[29]

In 2002 a new book was published by former CBS journalist Bernard Goldberg that engendered heated debate. In *Bias,* Goldberg argues that real media bias is the result of how those in the media see the world and how their bias directly effects

libel Published material that damages a person's reputation or good name in an untruthful and malicious way. As such it is not protected by the First Amendment.

— have to have facts

▲ Here's a presidential photo opportunity: President Bush leaves the White House carrying one of his favorite books, *Bias,* by former CBS reporter Bernard Goldberg, which claims that a liberal bias permeates the news media.

how we all see the world. Goldberg maintains that there is an elitist culture at the networks that is out of touch with conservative America. According to research surveys, 55 percent of journalists consider themselves liberal, compared with about 23 percent of the population as a whole. And on a number of issues, such as government regulation, abortion, and school prayer, the media's liberal attitudes are pervasive. Do these attitudes affect news coverage?[30]

In a *Times Mirror* survey of more than 250 members of the press, a substantial majority (55 percent) of American journalists who followed the 1992 presidential campaign believed that former President George Bush (41) was harmed by press coverage. "Only 11 percent felt that Bill Clinton's campaign was harmed by press coverage. Moreover, one out of three journalists (36 percent) thought that the media helped Clinton win the presidency, while a mere 3 percent believed that the press coverage helped the Bush effort." During the waning days of the campaign, President Bush frequently waved a red bumper sticker that stated, "Annoy the Media: Reelect Bush." The evidence confirms that Bush did indeed get more negative evening news coverage on CBS, ABC, and NBC than did Clinton and Perot.

This pattern again appeared in the 1996 Clinton-Dole presidential race. But the press appears to be getting better grades from the public; 53 percent thought that press coverage of the 1996 presidential election campaign was unbiased. Of those who saw bias, 14 percent felt the press favored Republicans and 22 percent felt it favored Democrats. Republicans were more apt to see a Democratic bias (40 percent) than Democrats were to see a Republican bias (20 percent). The press received similar grades in their coverage of the 2000 election.[31]

Although these findings are interesting, they do not make a conclusive case for significant liberal or conservative media bias in news coverage. A Pew Center national survey conducted in November 2001 found that the public image of the news had improved for the first time in sixteen years in response to the way the media covered the terrorist attacks. According to Pew Director Andrew Kohut, "Americans held more favorable opinions of the press' professionalism, patriotism, and morality than before September 11."[32]

Media Diversity

First of all, we must recall that the word *media* is plural. There are differences among the various communications media that make lumping them all together inaccurate. For example, print media tend to offer considerably more breadth of

▶ *Meet the Press,* America's longest-running television series, premiered on NBC-TV 6 on November 1947. The program was the first to bring Washington politics into American living rooms. As host of *Meet the Press,* Tim Russert is one of the most influential journalists working in Washington today. As NBC's senior vice president and Washington bureau chief, he has helped shape the way today's news is reported and analyzed. *Washingtonian* magazine named Russert the most influential journalist in Washington in 2001.

opinion than television. While newspapers and magazines can boast a number of popular conservative and liberal publications, television tends to offer a much more homogeneous, mainstream view. There is, however, some diversity even within the relatively narrow ideological parameters of television, particularly on the cable stations. But for the most part, television aspires to represent a mainstream, status quo perspective.

What many critics fail to mention in their attacks on "liberal" media is the almost total absence of an outlet for far left opinion, especially in television. While socialist and even communist magazines, newspapers, and newsletters have come and gone, leftist viewpoints have been almost invisible on television. Throughout the history of network television, no program featuring a socialist or social democratic point of view has ever appeared as a regular part of television programming. The absence of far left programming becomes more striking when we realize that the success of the Religious Right in capturing much of the Republican social agenda during the 1980s and 1990s owes much to the power of television. Popular televangelists like Jerry Falwell, Jimmy Swaggart, and onetime Republican presidential candidate Pat Robertson garnered most of their political following from regularly scheduled religious broadcasting. It was these leaders who Republican presidential candidate John McCain called "agents of intolerance" and "evil," a charge that cost him support among the voters of the far right.

Media Ownership and Control

Another reason to avoid making too much of the evidence of media "bias" concerns the economics of mass communication—specifically, the ownership and control of mass media outlets. Many recent analyses suggest that the overwhelming bias of the mass media is neither liberal nor conservative but corporate. William Greider maintains that the dissemination of information is so dominated by large media conglomerates and lobbyists for special interests who can afford to spend huge amounts of money that there can be no real dialogue because those without money, e.g. the far left, have little chance of bringing their viewpoints into the public debate.

Media scholar Ben Bagdikian has written extensively on the development of what he calls a "private ministry of information" created by the formation of a "media monopoly." Bagdikian's studies reveal that most of America's daily newspapers, magazines, television broadcasting, books, and motion pictures are controlled by only twenty-three corporations. As control of media slips into fewer and fewer hands, Bagdikian argues, the content of those media becomes increasingly similar because the overall interests of corporate executives tend to coincide, especially since many of them sit on the boards of directors of the same companies. The result is a disturbingly homogenous version of "reality," tempered by the priorities of large corporations that own and advertise through major media outlets. Consequently, the media are reluctant to attack their own corporate masters. An example is the refusal of NBC's *Today* show to include in its story on national boycotts of large corporations one of the largest—General Electric—which happens to own NBC. The same was true when ABC news programs refused in 1999 to do negative stories on Disney Corporation, its parent company.[33]

Since World War II, the profits of the news media business have steadily increased. This increase has been accompanied by a decrease in competition. With the exception of CNN, Fox, and a few cable programs, the three major television networks enjoy a monopoly over news and commercial sponsorship. The same process is at work in the newspaper industry, where large groups such as Gannett, Thomson, and Knight-Ridder control over 80 percent of the daily circulation of all newspapers.

More recently, an increase in cross-ownership of media—newspapers, television networks, book publishing, and Internet service providers all owned by conglomerates—has occurred. For example, Time merged with Warner Brothers to form

QUOTE ... UNQUOTE

"A popular government, without popular information, or the means of acquiring it, is but a prologue to a farce or a tragedy . . . a people who mean to be their own governors must arm themselves with the power which knowledge gives."

James Madison

Time Warner. The conglomerate then acquired Turner Broadcasting (CNN, Headline News, and TNT cable networks). And then Time Warner, in turn, was acquired by America Online. In the same vein, Disney purchased Capital Cities, which owns ABC, which in turn owns a host of cable stations like ESPN. By 1989 Capital Cities/ABC owned the ABC television network, twenty-nine affiliated radio and television stations, as well as ten daily newspapers, seventy-seven weeklies, and eighty specialized periodicals. NBC and CBS are owned by major conglomerates anchored by General Electric and Westinghouse, respectively.

These mergers have been highly beneficial to the autonomy of the media. By putting itself on solid financial footing, the mass media do not have to fear dependency on others, most notably politicians. In addition, this independence has increased news-gathering capabilities. However, some contend that the high concentration of media in the hands of a few can limit the expression of alternative views, further dilute news coverage, and limit criticism of the status quo. In February 2002, the Court of Appeals for the District of Columbia nullified the FCC's cross-ownership rule, which prevents one company from owning a cable system and local broadcast station in the same market. A consequence may be the opening of a door to a new wave of mergers among cable conglomerates and broadcast companies. The ruling was a huge victory for media giants like AOL, Time Warner, Inc., Viacom and News Corporation, which have long maintained that the regulation prevented expansion. "This is earth shattering," said Gene Kimmelman, co-director of the Washington office of the Consumers Union. "The end result could be the most massive consolidation in media this nation has ever seen."[34]

Question for Reflection: Much of the media's work is protected by the First Amendment. As our democracy evolves, what is the likelihood of a system of formal checks and balances, beyond the Federal Communications Commission guidelines being established?

Media-Government Symbiosis

A final problem with establishing a basis for ideological bias involves the symbiotic, or interdependent, relationship between the press and government. Just as the media have close ties with the largest American—and some international—corporations, so are they closely tied to the very government they are so often accused of attacking or treating unfairly. Reporters in all media rely overwhelmingly on "official sources," usually well-placed public officials, when reporting government events. Journalist Philip Weiss has observed that, when such "official" sources are consulted, a common practice among reporters is to allow these sources to exercise considerable approval over the way their statements are used in stories. Certainly the practice of "quote approval" is not restricted to government officials alone, and it may be an attempt to ensure journalistic "objectivity" by allowing interviewees to verify the intentions as well as the language behind what they express in interviews. But practices like quote approval can draw reporters into an uncomfortably intimate relationship with the very individuals about whom they are supposed to be unbiased. Only rarely are strong opponents of a government's foreign and domestic policy ever granted significant coverage in the mass media.[35]

▲ How often have you heard a reporter say, "According to an anonymous administration source. . . ." Former White House Press Secretary Mike McCurry decided to parody that dodge by showing up at a briefing wearing a bag over his head: "A briefing today from an anonymous source. . . . This is what they call . . . a senior White House official who is so helpful to so many of you all the time. I just thought I'd bring him out here."

The Media and Elections

No discussion of the media and politics would be complete without an examination of the uses of mass communication in elections. It is important here to distinguish between two types of media use in elections: coverage of the campaign by the media, and exploitation of media by candidates in the form of political advertising and "infomercials."

Press Coverage

The amount of media coverage can influence the outcome of an election campaign. By focusing on particular candidates or issues, the media often ignore others. Indeed, the media have been accused of focusing on the "horse race" nature of politics. Most of the coverage in any given campaign is devoted to the race itself rather than to the policies and issues around which the race revolves. As primary campaigns unfold, the press often gets caught up in reporting candidates' standing in the race. Coverage tends to be limited to the front-runners, thereby delivering the message that only the front-runners are worthy of public attention.

Polling

As we discussed in Chapter 8, over the last fifteen years media use of opinion polls has expanded dramatically. Not only are newspapers and television networks using more polls from the larger survey organizations like Gallup, Harris, and Roper; increasingly, major media outlets are conducting their own surveys. Large circulation newspapers and magazines like the *New York Times, USA Today,* and *Newsweek,* as well as CNN and the major broadcast television networks, are constantly conducting public opinion surveys on a variety of national issues. Much subsequent news coverage is based on these in-house polls. How significant is the impact of such coverage?

There is no solid evidence to suggest that media polling significantly affects public opinion; that is, such polling does not appear to change opinions. However, published accounts of consistently high or low public responses or sudden shifts of opinion can affect the political process. If candidates do not do well in published polls, they have much more trouble raising the contributions necessary to run expensive campaigns. And elected legislators, ever watchful for trends within their constituencies, obviously pay close attention to published opinion data concerning their states or districts. If we recall that polling techniques can sometimes distort public opinion simply by the way questions are worded, we are faced with the possibility that campaign contributors and legislators may sometimes be taking their cues from data that do not accurately reflect public preferences.

There has also been growing controversy regarding published results of early exit polls during the national elections that are aired before the polls close. Many of Jimmy Carter's supporters complained that network broadcasting of early exit polls, which projected an easy victory for Ronald Reagan, actually discouraged Carter's supporters on the West Coast from voting. The 2000 election exit polls created one of the great embarrassments when NBC, CBS, and CNN announced that Al Gore had won Florida. ABC and FOX quickly followed suit. All of this was based on the Voter News Service (VNS) statistical analysis was corrected for 2002.

Yet, the 2002 mid-term elections brought embarrassment and questions for Voter News Service. Just hours before the polls were scheduled to close, VNS abandoned its state and national exit poll results of voter attitudes. Projections were based on actual returns and not voter attitudes from exit polls. Citing server and system overload, faulty operator data input, and inadequately trained precinct workers, VNS pulled the plug. Networks and viewers did not know how the economy or the possibility of war impacted voter decisions. This was a major setback for a system that had been rebuilt and redesigned after the 2000 election fiasco, and there is no guarantee that the system will be ready for the 2004 presidential election.

Talk Shows

The proliferation of call-in radio and television talk shows presents an interesting bridge between press coverage of campaigns and media utilization by the candidates. Today there are more than ten thousand radio stations and eleven hundred commercial television stations; 99 percent of all households have a radio; 95 percent of all cars have a radio; and 57 percent of all adult Americans have a radio at work.

During the 1992 election, talk shows on radio and television emerged as a new platform in political campaigns and as the primary mode of discourse between candidates. Independent candidate H. Ross Perot decided to bypass journalists and appeal directly to the people on *Larry King Live*. By the end of the 1996 campaign, candidates had appeared on MTV, MSNBC, the three network morning shows, CNN, and radio talk shows.

Radio talk shows are believed to have significantly influenced the results of the 1994 congressional elections that ushered in a Republican majority. With their call-in format and no-holds-barred commentary, they provided an outlet where Americans dissatisfied with the Clinton administration and a Congress controlled by Democrats could vent their frustration.

The most successful of the talk show hosts, Rush Limbaugh, is broadcast over 800 radio stations. Calling the press "willing accomplices to the liberal power base in Washington," Limbaugh and other hosts (70 percent of whom call themselves conservative) led the movement to transform Congress into a Republican stronghold. Listeners turned out to vote in droves. Polls showed that more than half the voters surveyed at polling places said they listened to talk radio, and frequent listeners voted Republican by a 3 to 1 ratio. Other surveys found that while dedicated listeners make up only about 10 percent of the population, they have the highest level of voter registration.

What explains the effectiveness of talk radio? It appears that a major factor is public discontent. According to Andrew Kohut, director of the Times Mirror Center for the People and the Press, listeners, "tune into a community of similar attitudes and discontent, and they reinforce one another's views about how bad things are in Washington." Steve Wagner of Luntz Research, a Republican polling organization, adds that talk radio, "flourishes best on the fundamental sense that things are not going well."[36]

There is more to it than that, however. Some analysts believe talk radio may be performing a function that was formerly the domain of political parties, unions, and civic groups, giving people a feeling of connection with the political process. With a simple phone call they have an opportunity to express their views to a wide audience. Talk radio is, in short, a forum for political discussion. Often, however, the discussion is one-sided, and opposing views are not presented.

Television and Presidential Elections

The acronym ADI, meaning "area of dominant influence," is part of the everyday lexicon of the media strategists who have replaced party members as campaign organizers. The United States is divided into approximately sixty ADIs, which are further subdivided into DMAs, "local designated marketing areas." Every presidential campaign is geared to capturing this TV market. Candidates travel from one ADI to another, where "the old-fashioned political advance man now provides not only the proper crowds, but also the proper pictorial sites to silhouette his candidate's personality or proposal." Days before the candidate arrives, advance staff are checking acoustics, traffic patterns, photo opportunities, even the position of the sun at various times of the day.[37]

The use of television by presidential candidates is geared toward a major goal: getting the candidate's message on the evening news. This is accomplished through a variety of techniques, of which the most effective is the **sound bite.** A sound bite is a very brief statement, usually a snippet from a speech that conveys the essence of a longer statement and can be inserted into a news story. Lines such as "You're no Jack Kennedy," uttered by Lloyd Bentsen during the 1988 vice-presidential debate with Dan Quayle, and "Are you better off now than you were four years ago?" asked by Ronald Reagan in his 1980 debate against Jimmy Carter, have become part of political lore because of their effectiveness in targeting a specific issue or sentiment.

sound bite A very brief statement, usually a snippet from a campaign speech, that conveys the essence of a longer statement and can be inserted into a news story.

Today candidates come to debates prepared with one-liners they hope will be turned into sound bites and reported in the next day's news.[38]

Over the years sound bites have become progressively shorter. In 1968 a presidential candidate averaged 43 seconds of uninterrupted speech on the evening news. The average sound bite during the 1984 presidential campaign was only 14.79 seconds. By 1988 the average was down to 9 seconds, and by 1992 it was 8.4 seconds. A voter rarely hears a potential president utter a complete paragraph on the evening news.

Question for Reflection: Why do you think the length of a sound bite has so drastically decreased over the decades? What, if any, impact do you think this reduction has on our democracy?

How much useful information about a policy or issue can a candidate relay to the viewer in a nine-second sound bite? Not much, according to NBC News anchor Tom Brokaw, who has described sound bites as a cancer. Alternative news broadcasts such as *The News Hour with Jim Lehrer* on PBS often devote up to thirty minutes of coverage to a single issue, but this show is watched by a very small number of viewers. Some recently added cable news shows also attempt in-depth discussion and debate. In certain areas of the country, public television stations are making available the *BBC World News* which covers world events in greater depth and incorporates much longer sound bites, often excerpting comments made by U.S. government officials that did not even air on U.S. network television.

The 1996 election was marked by a few noteworthy innovations. Perhaps the most interesting is what we call "civic journalism," premised on the belief that journalists tend to focus too much on what they, not the people, think is important. The resulting news stories tend to address the agendas of elites, not the common person in the street. In an effort to redress this problem, several news organizations now devote time to local focus groups and issues. CBS news actually created a segment, "In Touch with America: Issues That Matter to You."

The 2000 presidential campaign was notable for the movement of the campaign into popular entertainment culture. Seeking to mobilize "undecided" voters to their side, both George Bush and Al Gore took a page from Bill Clinton's appearance on Arsenio Hall's now defunct late night show to play his saxophone and made multiple appearances on television shows hosted by Jay Leno, David Letterman, Rosie O'Donnell, Oprah Winfrey, and Regis Philbin. Political satire on shows such as MTV's "Indecision 2000" with Jon Stewart (as it turns out, a very apt title for the result) and Saturday Night Live had such a definite impact on the voters that Gore's advisers actually had him watch Darrell Hammond's adept impersonation of him in the presidential debate to help improve his performance. While both candidates resisted the offer to appear on the World Wrestling Foundation, these other appearances and the one on SNL's Election Special made clear that for better or worse the presidential candidates have now become just entertainers plugging their product on various television shows.

Political Advertising

The use of sound bites on television news contributes to the increasing focus on the candidates themselves at the expense of major issues facing the nation. This tendency is carried over into political advertising, which may refer to issues but is geared primarily to depicting the positive qualities of the candidate and the negative—even sinister—characteristics of opposing candidates.

In political advertising, everything hinges on image, and the image-maker's playground is the TV commercial, or "spot." Among the most memorable, and infamous, images of recent campaigns have been the work of image-makers. In 1964, for example, an anti-Goldwater spot was produced in which a little girl counted daisy petals. When she finished counting, the frame froze, a nuclear device was detonated, and a giant mushroom cloud dominated the TV screen, with a voice-over: "These are the stakes, to make a world in which all God's children can live, or to go into the darkness. Either we must love each other or we must die." The ad was aired only once, but that was more than enough. The impression had been established that Goldwater was a danger to the future.[39]

Such gripping, even terrifying, imagery is risky. Usually, therefore, media consultants try to establish some balance between their negative and positive political spots. Thus, not all political spots are as intensely negative as the one just described. The 1960 presidential campaign featured a number of spots showing John Kennedy sailing his yacht, riding horses, and frolicking with his family to demonstrate his "common" appeal, despite his uncommon wealth and social position. President Jimmy Carter made use of similar spots in 1976 and 1980; they showed him helping his daughter Amy with her homework and toiling away in shirtsleeves behind his desk in the Oval Office. Even the normally stiff, formal Richard Nixon tried to infuse his image with more warmth by allowing a film crew to capture him casually strolling along a California beach. The effect became unintentionally hilarious when reporters noticed that Nixon was wearing dress shoes.

Some of the most compelling positive advertising appeared in 1984, when incumbent Ronald Reagan ran under the theme "Morning in America." Hiring the same advertising agency that had produced a successful series of Coca-Cola commercials, Reagan's image management team crafted a series of spots showing smiling small-town men and women going about their daily business, secure in the knowledge that America was "back." That America had had to "return" from some worse place constituted a hint of negative advertising within an otherwise positive spot. These elegantly filmed, carefully designed spots are generally conceded to have played a major part in reinforcing Reagan's already formidable public support. The expected result of positive ads is that undecided voters will watch the warm, homey images of these potential national leaders and embrace them not as abstract political ideas but as people. George W. Bush tried to use this strategy in the 2000 nomination race when, upon seeing the success of reformer John McCain, he began touting a new theme called "Reform with Results."

As often as not, however, media consultants employ more combative imagery. Negative advertising usually involves a harsh attack on a political opponent, implying that the opponent is dishonest, corrupt, ignorant, or worse. This kind of political mudslinging is as old as American politics itself. Research shows that voters are more willing to believe negative information about public officials than positive information. Negative ads are also more memorable than positive messages.

Perhaps the most damaging negative ad in recent elections was aired in 1988 by the Bush campaign. It portrayed Willie Horton, a convicted rapist who had committed murder while on parole, and implied that Democratic candidate Michael Dukakis was so soft on crime and criminals that the public safety was endangered. Later, however, Bush himself fell victim to negative advertising by Bill Clinton in 1992.

Recent studies of the effect of negative advertising in campaigns suggests that negative advertising decreases voter turnout. As individuals become more cynical about politicians and the electoral and governing processes, they are less likely to want to vote. So, while negative advertising may be a useful technique in a campaign context, in the aggregate it tends to further increase feelings of distrust and lower individual levels of efficacy. As a result, in the 2000 presidential nomination campaign, candidates spent as much time promising not to use negative ads and on of the consequences appears to be a great increase in "position" voting.

In the United States, information about politics is routinely transmitted to the public through the electronic and print media as well as through faxes and electronic mail. Americans can read local, regional, national, and international newspapers; and twenty-four-hour news stations and coverage of local, state, and national public officials on television provide a firsthand look at the political process. But in a democratic polity the media must do more than bring political information to a broad audience. They must report events accurately and truthfully, free from control or censorship by government agencies. Freedom of the press and other media is essential in a free society.

No other nation in the world, even among the industrialized democracies, enjoys the degree of media freedom found in the United States. Yet, as we have seen in this chapter, there are a variety of limits on the independence of the media. They range from government-imposed restrictions, both foreign and domestic, to more subtle forms of censorship resulting from the symbiosis between reporters and "official sources" within the government. Thus, while media freedom in the United States represents a closer approach to democracy than has been achieved in any other nation, it is far from absolute.

DEMOCRACY IN THE NEW MILLENNIUM

The Impact of New Technology on Journalism

It looks like a cross between a large backpack and a portable space-rocket. But it's really a highly sophisticated news-reporting prototype, the *Mobile Journalist Workstation,* the product of the hard work of graduate students in computer engineering and journalism at Columbia University. In recent years, major advances in computer technology have revolutionized the idea of news reporting from abroad. Now reporters in the field, using expensive and corporate owned MJW systems, will be able one day to send messages back instantaneously to viewers at home, rather than wait hours or days to discover and report the news.

The Mobile Journalist Workstation (or MJW) is designed to help reporters find a story. It weighs twenty-five pounds and consists of a series of high-speed computers that link with the vital Global Positioning System (GPS) and its satellites in outer space. Attached with Velcro to the back of a reporter or cameraman, the device also includes a set of goggles that display vital information regarding local geographic position to enable the reporter to find the location of a news event and report back to the central news agency. Blips on the screen resemble Arnold Swartzeneger's character in *The Terminator* (1984). The MJW is expected to take another decade, however, before it reaches widespread production.

Another Star-Trek-like device is the videophone, which most Americans became very familiar following September 11 and the bombing of civilians in Afghanistan. Reporters used the new device to beam images back rapidly from the lobbies of hotels during the war. Invented in the early 1960s, the videophone was originally thought to one day revolutionize personal communications and has been widely used by the military and convert security agencies. The videophone still beats the time and price it would take for dropping an expensive satellite truck and engineering team into a war-torn region.

Gadgets like the videophone and the MJW reveal that the relationship of news reporting and advances in computer science is still incomplete—television news technology has advanced in mobility and coverage, but the technology that underlay the transmission of messages over long distances has lagged much farther behind. Today's journalism schools are interdisciplinary marriages with computer science departments. At Columbia University's Graduate School of Journalism—http://www.jrn.columbia.edu/—faculty and students work with engineering and computer science professors to develop a wearable computer for reporters. The Institute for Cyber-Information at Kent State University is an interdisciplinary research center whose mission is to promote the application and integration of digital content, design, and technologies through partnerships and outreach programs with business and educational communities—http://www.ici.kent.edu/.

▲ The Mobile Journalist Workstation tracks a reporter by satellite and feeds information that can be read inside the goggles.

Source: Susan Reed, "Equipment Check; Backpack, Goggles . . . ," *Washington Post,* January 31, 2002, B5; Susan Reed, "Reporting Live, From Almost Anywhere," *New York Times,* January 31, 2002, E1.

SUMMARY

1. The mass media consist of the various means, such as newspapers, radio, and television, through which information is transferred from its source to large numbers of people.

2. Early political leaders saw newspapers as the key to educating the public about political affairs and gaining support for their parties' positions. Mass-circulation newspapers first appeared in the 1830s. At the end of the nineteenth century, the desire for dramatic stories led to muckraking, which attempted to expose the power and corruption of the rich, and yellow journalism, which sought to entertain the masses with little regard for the truth.

3. Of all the mass media, magazines offer the widest variety of subject matter and political opinion. The most successful news magazine is *Time;* there are also numerous magazines of political opinion.

4. Radio was very popular between the two World Wars, largely because events could be described as they were happening. Politicians and public officials soon learned the value of speaking directly to the American people in radio broadcasts.

5. Television is more persuasive and effective than any other form of mass communication. It is an almost universal source of entertainment and the primary source of news for most Americans. New technologies such as satellites have expanded television coverage to permit instantaneous reporting of events throughout the world. Cable television has made possible a much wider range of programming choices, including entire channels aimed at specially targeted audiences.

6. One function of the mass media is surveillance of events throughout the world. This means that the media decide what events are newsworthy. The media also interpret events by giving them meaning and context, and thereby shape opinions. The third major function of the media is socialization, in which the members of a society learn to conform to society's norms and values. In general, the media serve to reinforce existing values rather than create new ones.

7. The electronic media are regulated by the Federal Communications Commission, which establishes regulations designed to protect the public interest. The FCC's rules of the air include the equal opportunities rule (for political candidates), the fairness doctrine (now abandoned), and the right of rebuttal.

8. On occasion the government has attempted to prevent the publication of information on the grounds that doing so would pose a threat to national security. This is done through a judicial restraining order, an action known as prior restraint. The media are also restricted by laws against libel and slander.

9. It is often said that the media have a liberal bias. However, there are numerous conservative publications, and many radio and television commentators, as well as publishers and network executives, are distinctly conservative. Corporate control of the media tends to produce middle-of-the-road coverage tempered by the concerns of advertisers. Another factor is the symbiosis between reporters and "official sources" within the government.

10. Media coverage of campaigns can influence the outcome of elections. The media are often accused of focusing on the "horse race" aspect of campaigns, implying that only the front-runners are worthy of coverage. The increasing use of data from opinion polls can also affect the political process.

11. In recent campaigns radio talk shows have taken on increasing importance. This was especially true in 1994, when conservative talk show hosts led the movement to replace many Democrats in Congress with Republicans.

12. Television takes center stage in presidential elections. Candidates travel from one ADI (area of dominant influence) to another, giving speeches in settings designed to make them look good on the evening news. The news broadcasts usually contain only snippets of candidates' speeches, known as sound bites.

13. Political advertising takes the form of commercials designed by image makers. The right image can have a tremendous impact on the voting public. Media consultants try to achieve a balance between positive and negative images, but because negative advertising appears to be more effective, there is a growing trend toward the use of such advertising. A recent variant on the commercial is the infomercial, which combines commercial advertising with an informational discussion.

KEY TERMS

spin	socialization	right of rebuttal
mass media	Federal Communications	prior restraint
muckraking	Commission (FCC)	libel
yellow journalism	equal time rule	sound bite
investigative journalism	fairness doctrine	

SUGGESTED READINGS

ARNETT, PETER. *Live from the Battlefield: From Vietnam to Baghdad.* New York: Simon & Schuster, 1994. The memoir of one correspondent's thirty-five years of news reporting from the war zones of the world, including his controversial television reports from Baghdad during the Gulf War.

BAGDIKIAN, BEN H. *The Media Monopoly.* 4th ed. Boston: Beacon Press, 1994. A fascinating analysis of the continuing concentration of ownership of mass media outlets into fewer hands.

GOLDBERG, BERNARD. *Bias: A CBS Insider Exposes How the Media Distort the News.* Washington, D.C.: Regency Publishing, 2001. Former Emmy-award winning broadcast journalist reveals a corporate news structure that responds to liberal opinions.

HALBERSTAM, DAVID. *The Powers That Be.* New York: Dell, 1979. A classic account of the rise of major media figures in America, written by one of America's foremost political journalists.

IYENGAR, SHANTO. *Is Anyone Responsible? How Television Frames Political Issues.* Chicago: University of Chicago Press, 1991. A scholarly analysis of the power of television to "frame" political issues and influence the way viewers respond to and think about those issues.

ANN COULTER. *Slander: Liberal Lies About the American Right.* New York: Crown 2002. Conservative commentator Ann Coulter critiques the so-called "liberal bias" of news media run by "cultural elite."

13 CIVIL LIBERTIES

CHAPTER OUTLINE

Approaching Democracy Case Study:
  The Constitution and the War on Terrorism

Introduction: Civil Liberties and Democracy

Defining and Examining Civil Liberties
  and Civil Rights

The Dawn of Civil Liberties and Civil Rights
  in America

A History of the Application of Civil Liberties
  to the States

Freedom of Religion

Freedom of Speech

Freedom of the Press

The Rights of Defendants

The Expanding Nature of Implied Rights

APPROACHING DEMOCRACY CASE STUDY

The Constitution and the War on Terrorism

"You can't protect the Constitution and respect it without also protecting lives." So spoke Attorney General John Ashcroft in defending the Bush administration's program of rooting out and prosecuting suspected terrorists on American soil. The result, says *Newsweek* magazine is either "a broad array of tactics that supporters are calling necessary tools in the war on terrorism . . . [or what] critics are attacking as the sharpest curtailment of civil liberties in decades." And the centerpiece of this program is the "Uniting and Strengthening America by Providing

Appropriate Tools Required to Intercept and Obstruct Terrorism Act," better known by its acronym, the "U.S.A. Patriot Act" which was signed into law by President Bush after a speedy Congressional passage on October 26, 2001.

Fueled by information that the F.B.I. was on the trail of some of the terrorists who launched the September 11 attack but was unable to stop them because of constitutional limitations on their search and seizure and arrest powers, the Attorney General asked for broad powers to conduct investigations: "one stop shopping" for a search warrant that covers all jurisdictions rather than separate warrants for each one, wiretaps for all telephones used by suspects, not just specific phones (thus dealing with the problem of tracking throw away cell phones), computer searches for Internet activity and seizure of suspects' voice mail, "sneak and peek" or "black bag" searches in which the suspect is never told that a search of his home or office has been conducted if it would negatively affect future investigations, detaining suspects indefinitely, and monitoring the communications between a suspect and his attorney. An outcry was raised that this law would create a modern version of the old British "writ of assistance" by which the authorities could proceed on a fishing expedition for any evidence of criminal activity. The Bush administration argued compellingly that only speed and certainty of such investigations could prevent future attacks on American soil, a claim that was strengthened when questioning of nearly 5,000 visiting aliens in the United States produced new leads and an expected immediate second attack by the terrorists did not materialize.

After minimal Congressional discussion, the act was passed by the House of Representatives by an overwhelming 357–66, while members complained that they had not yet even read the final bill. As it turns out, the bill which was passed had been negotiated behind closed doors by House Judiciary Committee Chairman F. James Sensenbrenner Jr. (R.-WI), House Speaker J. Dennis Hastert, (R.-IL), and members of the Bush administration. The Senate was equally hasty in its consideration of the measure. The Senate bypassed the Judiciary Committee, sending a measure hammered out by a group of top Committee members from both parties, the Administration, and the Senate leadership to the floor, and debated a scant four hours before passing the measure by a staggering 98–1 vote.

The result was a measure that gave authorities almost everything that the Attorney General had requested except for the unlimited detention of suspects before filing charges. However, if a suspect is determined to represent a threat to national security he or she can be detained indefinitely. In one of the most controversial provisions, the "sneak and peek" searches, done even on computer files without notice to the suspect for a "reasonable" time, were approved for use if authorities could argue that they had "reasonable cause to believe" that by giving notice to the suspect being searched it would have an "adverse" result to future investigations. In addition, rather than having to get a search warrant from a judge to conduct electronic surveillance, authorities can secure warrants from a Foreign Intelligence Surveillance Court using a lower probable cause standard to justify the search. "This legislation is not perfect," said Rep. Sensenbrenner, "However these are difficult times that require steadfast leadership and an expeditious response. The legislation is desperately needed."

Interestingly, while no case was immediately brought to test the new law in Court, even Laura Murphy, the director of the ACLU acknowledged that a direct challenge would be tough to win: "The courts may give more of a wink and nod about this. Courts historically have given greater deference to Congress when we've been involved in war." Thus, scholars and lawyers will look to a "war on drugs" case, involving a police sweep search of two suspects on a bus, called *United States v. Drayton,* to see just how far the Supreme Court might go in allowing such searches. Here police confronted two suspects on a bus heading from Tallahassee, Florida, to Detroit, Michigan, and after searching their bags for drugs, patted down the baggy clothing of the two men to reveal drugs in their possession. The Court was left to determine whether this kind of a search was justified under the prevailing "reasonable suspicion" standard for Fourth Amendment encounters. Their ruling here, allowing such a search without police having to inform suspects they were free to refuse the search, providing that under the "totality of circumstances" in the case that a reasonable person would understand that he or she is free to

▲ While Senator Patrick Leahy (D.-VT) recorded the moment for history, President George Bush signed the "U.S.A. Patriot Act" into law on October 26, 2001, thus launching the domestic legal war on terrorism.

refuse the search, sends a signal that the Court might be inclined in counter-terrorist searches to allow such profiling of suspects in public places for search so long as it can be justified under the prevailing "reasonable suspicion" standard for Fourth Amendment encounters. Justice Anthony Kennedy ruled for the majority that he believed that the "coerciveness" of the police encounter would have been acceptable had it occurred on the street. Solicitor General Ted Olson, who lost his wife Barbara in the attack on the Pentagon and is now directing the Bush administration's legal campaign before the Supreme Court against terrorism, pointed out that, "In the current environment, [these searches] may also become an important part of preventing other forms of criminal activity that involve travel on the nation's system of public transportation."[1]

By August 2002, though, the federal courts were not so willing to back the Bush administration. The secret court that oversees the Foreign Intelligence Surveillance Act, or FISA, rebuked the Bush administration for supplying erroneous information in more than 75 applications for search warrants and wiretaps over a two year period.

Question for Reflection: How much has the constitutional standard for Fourth Amendment searches been lowered by the "war on drugs" and what will happen to the search and seizure protections if all of those rulings are transferred over to the "war on terrorism"? How much should the level of Fourth Amendment search and seizure protection be lowered during wartime or a time of crisis?

INTRODUCTION: CIVIL LIBERTIES AND DEMOCRACY

The U.S.A. Patriot Act illustrates the challenge of defining and interpreting civil liberties, especially in times of crisis. The quality of a democracy can be measured by the degree to which it protects the rights of all its citizens, including those with unpopular views. Frequently, this task is left to the Supreme Court of the United States, which may find itself safeguarding the rights of individuals charged with heinous crimes or with engaging in socially unpopular acts. In a democracy, the fundamental rights of such individuals are given the same protection as those of any other citizen.

The fundamental rights of U.S. citizens are set forth in the Bill of Rights—the first ten amendments to the Constitution—and we often speak of the "protection" provided by that document. However, individual rights are always in jeopardy if they are not zealously safeguarded by all the institutions of society. When the Alabama Supreme Court Chief Justice places a 5,280 pound granite monument containing the Ten Commandments in the rotunda of the Alabama Supreme Court, freedom of religion is at issue. When Congress bans "indecent material" being transmitted over the Internet, freedom of speech is at issue. When the Supreme Court says that a student can grade the paper of another student, the question of the right to privacy is at issue. And, when a police officer stops you in your car and asks to search the trunk, the Fourth Amendment search and seizure provision is at issue. All of these situations and hundreds more are governed by the Bill of Rights.

In this chapter we explore the historical development of civil liberties. We begin with the framers' vision of the Bill of Rights, which was much less protective of individual freedoms than you might realize. We then explore the gradual expansion of civil liberties to the states over the course of our nation's history. We also analyze how civil liberties have been defined and how they have expanded and contracted over the last sixty-five years. These topics provide a dramatic demonstration of how the United States has approached democracy in the area of individual rights.

FYI

A poll by *USA Today* in November 2002 revealed that only 15% of the American people could identify the name of the Chief Justice of the United States (William Rehnquist).

Defining and Examining Civil Liberties and Civil Rights

Although the terms *civil liberties* and *civil rights* are often used interchangeably, they are not synonymous. **Civil liberties** are the individual freedoms and rights that are guaranteed to every citizen by the Bill of Rights and the due process clause of the Fourteenth Amendment. They include the most fundamental rights of Americans, such as freedom of speech and religion. **Civil rights** are concerned with protection of citizens against discrimination because of characteristics such as gender, race, ethnicity, or disability; they are derived largely from the equal protection clause of the Fourteenth Amendment.

One way to distinguish between civil liberties and civil rights is to view them in terms of governmental action. Civil liberties are best understood as *freedom from* any government interference with, or violation of, individual rights. This is a "negative" freedom in the sense that people are understood to have a right to certain liberties, such as freedom of speech, which can be exercised without government interference. For this reason, the First Amendment begins with the words, "Congress shall make no law. . . ."

In contrast, civil rights may be understood as *freedom to* exercise certain rights that are guaranteed to all U.S. citizens under the Constitution and cannot be removed by the government. This is a "positive" freedom in that the government is expected to provide the conditions under which certain rights can be exercised. Examples include the right to vote, the right to equal job or housing opportunities, and the right to equal education. We look more closely at civil rights in Chapter 14; in this chapter, we focus on civil liberties.

One reason the terms *civil liberties* and *civil rights* have become almost interchangeable in popular speech is that many issues involve aspects of both positive and negative freedom.[2] For example, consider the abortion issue, in which a woman seeks to choose the termination of a pregnancy, a civil liberty, while others seek to preserve the life of the potential being, a civil right.

Cases involving civil liberties nearly always come down to a conflict between the individual, seeking to exercise a certain right in a democracy, and the state, seeking to control the exercise of that right so as to preserve the rights of others. The judiciary is charged with drawing the lines between acceptable individual actions and permissible governmental controls.

But how are those lines drawn? You will recall from Chapter 6 that "activist" jurists tend to uphold the rights of individuals over those of the state, while "self-restraint" jurists tend to defer to the state. The great majority of jurists fall in neither camp and are called "balancers" because they look for the point at which the rights of the individual are overridden by the rights of society. If the Court is dominated by a "self-restraint" group of jurists, control by national and state governments will be upheld. If the Court is dominated by an "activist" group of jurists, citizens' rights will likely be expanded and new rights will be created.

The Dawn of Civil Liberties and Civil Rights in America

Many think that America's history of civil liberties and civil rights protection began in 1791 with the ratification of the Bill of Rights to the Constitution, but in fact the process did not begin in earnest until 1938 and really accelerated in the 1960s. Prior to that time, the Bill of Rights was not seen by the Supreme Court as a tool for protecting individual liberty, and before 1897 none of the Bill of Rights applied to the states. The Court's interest in civil liberties and civil rights began with these

FYI

According to the decision in *New Jersey v. T.L.O.* the standard for searches by school personnel in high schools is not probable cause but reasonable suspicion, which gives school authorities wider leeway when searching students' lockers or personal property.

civil liberties The individual freedoms and rights that are guaranteed to every citizen in the Bill of Rights and the due process clause of the Fourteenth Amendment, including freedom of speech and religion.

civil rights The constitutionally guaranteed rights that may not be arbitrarily removed by the government. Among these rights are the right to vote and equal protection under the law.

words in the footnote of an obscure 1938 economics case called *United States v. Carolene,* which dealt with Congress's regulation of "filled milk," the amount of additives added to milk to make the product more profitable to sell during the Depression. After explaining that the Court would continue to defer to the legislative body in matters of economic regulation, in a three paragraph footnote, the Court sent a billboard to those attorneys and litigants seeking justice under the Constitution: "There here may be narrower scope for operation of the presumption of constitutionality when legislation appears on its face to be within a specific prohibition of the Constitution, such as those of the first ten amendments, which are deemed equally specific when held to be embraced within the Fourteenth.... It is unnecessary to consider now whether legislation which restricts those political processes which can ordinarily be expected to bring about repeal of undesirable legislation, is to be subjected to more exacting judicial scrutiny under the general prohibitions of the Fourteenth Amendment than are most other types of legislation.... Nor need we enquire whether similar considerations enter into the review of statutes directed at particular religious, or racial minorities, whether prejudice against discrete and insular minorities may be a special condition, which tends seriously to curtail the operation of those political processes ordinarily to be relied upon to protect minorities, and which may call for a correspondingly more searching judicial inquiry."

This may read like incomprehensible gibberish to you, but it actually tells you which kinds of cases the Court might be willing to accept on appeal and consider seriously ruling in favor of the individual in litigation against the government and other actors. The first sentence says that any dispute that touches on the Bill of Rights or the Fourteenth Amendment may get special protection from the Supreme Court. The second sentence promises that any case that touches on the political process will receive special protection. Finally, the third sentence promises that any case that touches on "discrete and insular minorities" may receive special protection. In short, the Court is promising the launching of a **"double standard"** in which civil liberties will be judicially protected, but in economic cases the Court will defer to the legislature. The reason is that without Court protection, those who are politically disenfranchised or in the minority will be unable to protect themselves through the voting process or the legislature.[3]

Since the United States's approach to democracy in the area of civil liberties is relatively recent, we will focus on how these rights were created and expanded by the Warren Court (1953–69), partially cut back by the Burger Court (1969–86), and finally placed under full attack by the Rehnquist Court (1986–present). First, however, we will explore the history of the development of civil liberties and their application to the states and to the national government.

A History of the Application of Civil Liberties to the States

The history of civil liberties is one of gradual expansion of the protection of personal rights guaranteed by the Bill of Rights. This evolution occurred through a series of Supreme Court decisions that applied portions of the first ten amendments to the states, thereby protecting citizens from state action in relation to specific individual rights. This evolutionary process, summarized in Table 13.1 on pages 452–453, illustrates that it did not begin until 1897 and did not really take hold until the 1960s.

In the early years of the nation's history, the Bill of Rights provided far less protection for individual rights than is the case today. For example, the guarantee of freedom of speech did not prevent the Federalist party from passing the Alien and Sedition Acts in 1798, which jailed opponents of John Adams's administration for vigorously questioning the patriotism of Federalists in their criticism.[4] And the right to counsel guaranteed by the Sixth Amendment did not prevent the passage of the Federal Crimes Act of 1790, which instructed courts to provide defendants with counsel for capital offenses only.

double standard The varying level of intensity by which the Supreme Court considers cases by which it protects civil liberties claims while also deferring to the legislature in cases dealing with economic claims.

But as narrow as these protections were individually, in the 1833 case of *Barron v. Baltimore,* the Supreme Court severely limited their collective impact.[5] Silt unearthed by excavation and construction undertaken on behalf of the city of Baltimore was washed by rains and swollen rivers into Baltimore harbor, rendering a wharf owned by John Barron unusable. Barron claimed that he was entitled to money damages under the Fifth Amendment's "eminent domain" clause, which guarantees that the taking of private property by government for public use will result in "just compensation" from the state.

Even the normally nationalist-oriented Chief Justice John Marshall refused to extend the protections of the Bill of Rights to the states in denying Barron's claim. The Bill of Rights, he ruled, "contains no expression indicating an intention to apply them to the state governments [so] this Court cannot so apply them." The First Amendment, by stating that "Congress shall make no law . . . ," indicates that the Bill of Rights applies *only* to the national government. Unable to use the Fifth Amendment to sustain his claim, Barron had no case. The entire Bill of Rights would not be applied to the states for another century. During that time civil liberties varied from state to state, depending on the protections afforded by that state's constitution and existing laws.

The Fourteenth Amendment

With the passage of the Fourteenth Amendment in 1868, the issue of state responsibility relative to civil liberties was raised once again. The Fourteenth Amendment was one of the so-called *Civil War Amendments,* which were designed to free the slaves and protect their rights as citizens. It reads: "No State shall make or enforce any law which shall abridge the privileges or immunities of citizens of the United States; nor shall any State deprive any person of life, liberty, or property, without due process of law; nor deny to any person . . . the equal protection of the laws."

Since the Fourteenth Amendment began with the words "No State shall make or enforce any law . . . ," some believed that it was intended to reverse the Barron ruling and extend the Bill of Rights to the states. Initially, the Supreme Court was asked to rule on whether the "privileges or immunities" clause of the amendment would accomplish this aim. However, the Court ruled that this language did not protect state rights of citizenship, such as property rights, but only national rights of citizenship, such as petitioning Congress for a redress of grievances and being protected from piracy on the high seas.[6]

In later cases the Court was asked whether some or all of the Bill of Rights could be defined as "due process" of law and thus be extended to the states under the language of the Fourteenth Amendment. This approach, in which the Bill of Rights would be absorbed into the due process clause by the simple act of redefinition, was called the **incorporation** of the Bill of Rights.[7] The argument was that under the Fourteenth Amendment the states must protect due process, and since some or all of the Bill of Rights could be defined as due process, the states must also protect those portions of the Bill of Rights.

However, in the late 1800s and early 1900s the Court was dominated by conservative jurists who were more concerned with protecting property rights than with extending personal civil rights by making this definitional leap. Did California's practice of using a list of evidence called a bill of information to indict people rather than the grand jury proceeding promised in the Fifth Amendment violate due process of law? No, said the Court, ruling that the "new" procedure can be just as fair as the "old" grand jury guarantee.[8] Did New Jersey's practice of allowing a judge to comment on a defendant's unwillingness to take the stand in his own defense, which a jury might interpret as an indication of guilt, violate the Fifth Amendment's guarantee that no person shall be "compelled . . . to be a witness against himself"? No, ruled the Court, because this was not a "fundamental" right that must be applied to the states.[9]

The Court's position became known as **no incorporation,** since it was unwilling to define the Bill of Rights as part of the Fourteenth Amendment and thus to apply

incorporation The process whereby the protections of the Bill of Rights have been found by the Supreme Court to apply to the states.

no incorporation An approach in which the states would be bound only by the dictates of due process contained in the Fourteenth Amendment.

Table 13.1 ■ The Incorporation of the Bill of Rights

CASE	ISSUE	INCORPORATED
Chicago, Burlington and Quincy Railway Co. v. Chicago (1897)	Taking of private property by the state for public use without just compensation	Fifth Amendment guarantee of eminent domain
Gitlow v. New York (1925)	Arrest for speech threatening the state government	First Amendment guarantee of free speech
Near v. Minnesota (1931)	Prior restraint (censorship) of press	First Amendment guarantee of free press
Powell v. Alabama (1932)	Right to counsel in capital crimes. This was the famous *Scottsboro* case, in which seven young black males were accused and convicted without the aid of counsel of raping two white females	Sixth Amendment guarantee of right to counsel in capital cases where a "fair hearing" was lacking
Hamilton v. Regents of the University of California (1934)	Challenged public institution's mandatory military drills on basis of religious objections	First Amendment guarantee of freedom of religion
De Jonge v. Oregon (1937)	Peaceful assembly of Communist party members in Oregon	First Amendment guarantees of free assembly and of right to petition the government for a redress of grievances
Palko v. Connecticut (1937)	Twice being tried for same offense. In this case, Justice Cardozo devised his famous "honor roll of superior rights"	None, but it was Cardozo's insistence that superior rights should be incorporated that begins "selective incorporation"
Cantwell v. Connecticut (1940)	Whether religious groups (Jehovah's Witnesses) should have to be licensed to promote their religion	First Amendment guarantee of free exercise of religion
Everson v. Board of Education of Ewing Township (1947)	State aid to bus children to parochial schools.	First Amendment requirement that church and state be separate
In re Oliver (1948)	Whether a judge can act simultaneously as a grand jury and a trial judge to find a defendant guilty without a proper trial	Sixth Amendment guarantee to a public trial
Louisiana ex. rel. Francis Resweber (1947)	Whether a convicted man could be executed again after an electric chair failure	Cruel and unusual punishment
Wolf v. Colorado (1949)	Whether patient names from an appointment book of suspected abortionist gained by illegal search of doctor's office can be used in trial	The "core" of the Fourth Amendment, defined as "arbitrary invasions of privacy by the police"

its amendments to the states. The states would be bound only by the dictates of due process contained in the Fourteenth Amendment. The only exception came in an 1897 case involving a railroad company's objection to the right of eminent domain under the Fifth Amendment against a state taking its property without just compensation, which because it protected property rights was extended to the states.[10] Opposing the majority was Justice John Harlan, who in arguing that the protections in the Bill of Rights were so fundamental that all of them should be applied to the states, and thus created the position known as **total incorporation.**

The Clear and Present Danger Test

The battle over the application of the Bill of Rights to the states was resumed during World War I, when the government was anxious to restrict certain individual liberties. Concern with wartime treason, spying, and obstruction of the military draft led in 1919 to *Schenck v. United States*, the first important case involving freedom of speech. Charles T. Schenck had been convicted of circulating pamphlets against

total incorporation An approach arguing that the protections in the Bill of Rights were so fundamental that all of them should be applied to the states by absorbing them into the due process clause of the Fourteenth Amendment.

CASE	ISSUE	INCORPORATED
NAACP v. Alabama (1958)	Whether groups must register with the state and file membership names and addresses	First Amendment guarantee of freedom of association
Mapp v. Ohio (1961)	Use of the fruits of an illegal search and seizure without a proper search warrant in trial	Fourth Amendment prohibition on unreasonable search or seizure, and its exclusionary rule
Robinson v. California (1962)	A California statute providing a mandatory 90-day jail sentence for conviction of addiction to narcotics without any evidence of drug use	Eighth Amendment guarantee against the infliction of cruel or unusual punishment
Gideon v. Wainwright (1963)	Legal counsel availability when someone is on trial for a misdemeanor, non-capital offense	Sixth Amendment guarantee of counsel was expanded to include all felony-level criminal cases
Malloy v. Hogan and *Murphy v. Waterfront Commission of New York* (1964)	Whether investigation into gambling offenses after serving a jail sentence for the crime resulted in self-incrimination	Fifth Amendment prohibition against self-incrimination
Pointer v. Texas (1965)	Whether the accused has the right to confront witnesses against him instead of a transcript of their earlier testimony during a trial	Sixth Amendment guarantee that the accused shall be confronted by the witnesses against him
Griswold v. Connecticut (1965)	Legality of use and counseling on the use of birth control by married couples	First, Third, Fourth, and Ninth Amendments (and their penumbras) right of privacy
Parker v. Gladden (1966)	Whether bailiff statements rendered the jury unable to produce an impartial verdict	Sixth Amendment guarantee that the accused shall be judged by an impartial jury
Klopfer v. North Carolina (1967)	Whether a state can place a live case on inactive status only to take the case up again when it has more time and resources	Sixth Amendment guarantee of a speedy trial
Washington v. Texas (1967)	Whether a defendant can compel witnesses in his favor to appear in trial	Sixth Amendment right to compulsory process for obtaining witnesses
Duncan v. Louisiana (1968)	Whether state must offer trial by jury in noncapital cases	Sixth Amendment guarantee of a trial by jury in all criminal cases above the petty level
Benton v. Maryland (1969)	Whether a state must provide a guarantee against two trials for the same crime	Fifth Amendment guarantee against double jeopardy

the draft. In upholding the conviction, Justice Oliver Wendell Holmes argued that the state could restrict speech when "the words used are of such a nature as to create a clear and present danger that they will bring about the substantive evils that Congress has a right to prevent." In short, in some cases, such as falsely shouting "Fire!" in a crowded theater, the circumstances and nature of speech, or its effect, may justify restriction of this liberty. In ignoring the fact that there was no evidence showing that Schenck's "speech" had affected the draft, Holmes was saying that a wartime crisis was sufficient cause for restrictions on freedom of speech.[11]

Question for Reflection: How does the 1919 Supreme Court ruling on restriction of freedom of speak when "the words used are such a nation to create a *clear and present danger . . .* " compare with the 2001 U.S.A. Patriot Act which allows for covert searches without notice to the suspect if the authorities can argue that they have *"reasonable cause to believe"* that giving notice would have an adverse result on future investigations?

▶ Jacob Abrams (far right) with fellow anarchists (from left to right) Samuel Lipman, Hyman Lachowsky, and Mollie Steamer, are shown in 1921 shortly before being deported to Russia at their own expense, having served two years in jail. A fifth colleague, Jacob Schwartz, died in prison.

Two subsequent cases that also came to the Supreme Court in 1919 dealing with federal restrictions of freedom of speech revealed the problems of applying the **clear and present danger test** to other circumstances. When Jacob Frohwerk was convicted for writing scholarly articles on the constitutionality and merits of the military draft for a German-language newspaper in Missouri, the Court upheld the conviction in *Frohwerk v. United States*.[12] And when socialist Eugene Debs spoke out against the draft after signing an "Anti-war Proclamation and Program" in St. Louis, the conviction was upheld by the Court. The Court ruled in *Debs v. United States,* that Debs was impeding the war effort.[13] Thus, the Court had convicted one man for writing for a tiny minority and another for the thoughts he might have had while speaking, neither of whom had any demonstrable effect on the draft.

Seeing the censorship effect of his test, Holmes changed his views. In the fall of 1919, when an anarchist named Jacob Abrams appealed his conviction for circulating pamphlets imploring American workers to go on strike in sympathy with Russian workers hurt by the revolution there, seven members of the Court upheld the conviction in *Abrams v. United States* because Abrams's actions posed a *clear and present danger* to the war effort. However, Holmes, the inventor of the test, together with Louis D. Brandeis, dissented. They argued that Abrams was nothing more than a "poor and puny anonymity" whose "silly leaflet" represented no clear and present danger to the state.[14] Thus America's approach to freedom of speech had begun, but it still had a long way to go.

The Beginnings of Incorporation

Unlike the federal government, which passed laws against certain actions resulting from speech but did not attempt to control speech directly, some states, including New York, chose to outlaw the words themselves. In 1925 a radical named Benjamin Gitlow was convicted under New York's Criminal Anarchy Act of advocating the overthrow of the government. In *Gitlow v. New York,* the Supreme Court ruled for the first time that the First Amendment guarantee of freedom of speech could be applied to the states; however, it upheld Gitlow's conviction, deferring to the state of New York's belief that certain speech had a "bad tendency."[15]

Why would the Court be willing to apply the free speech guarantee to the states but not use it to protect Gitlow himself? Because it had learned that the right of free speech could be used to protect businesses—for example, when a business refuses to give reasons for firing an employee. The Court was therefore setting a precedent

QUOTE ... UNQUOTE

"The most stringent protection of free speech would not protect a man in falsely shouting fire in a theatre and causing a panic."

Justice Oliver Wendell Holmes, *Schenck v. United States* (1919)

clear and present danger test A free speech test allowing states to regulate only speech that has an immediate connection to an action states are permitted to regulate.

that could be used to protect the status quo without actually condoning speech aimed against these very same interests.

In the early 1930s the Court applied three other parts of the Bill of Rights to the states. In 1931, when the Minnesota legislature passed a law censoring the *Saturday Press,* a muckraking tabloid printed by Jay Near, the Court in a landmark case called *Near v. Minnesota* incorporated the guarantee of freedom of the press into the Fourteenth Amendment, thus applying it to the states, and overturned the Minnesota law.[16]

A year later the Court was called upon to rule in the case of the "Scottsboro Boys," in which a group of black youths had been unjustly accused of raping two white women on a train and had been convicted in a trial in which, instead of assigning a defense attorney, the judge asked "the entire bar of the county" to defend them. (In other words, they had no defense.) In its decision the Court incorporated and applied to the states the notion of a "fair hearing" implied in the Sixth Amendment, thus guaranteeing the right to counsel, but only for capital crimes like this one.[17]

Finally, in 1934, when the University of California required that courses in military training be taken by everyone on its campus, including religious pacifists, the Court incorporated the freedom of religion provision and applied it to the states while still leaving the program intact.[18]

The Court made clear in all of these cases that extending rights to the states did not necessarily mean increased rights for individuals. States were still free to punish the press after, rather than before, publication, to deny the right to counsel in non-capital criminal cases, and to require even pacifist students to take courses in military training. Thus, the question remained whether a more general rule applying the Bill of Rights in a meaningful way to the states could be established.

Selective Incorporation of the Bill of Rights

It was not until 1937, the year of F.D.R.'s failed Court-packing plan and one year before the Carolene Products footnote, in the landmark case of *Palko v. Connecticut,* that the first step was taken toward establishing a rule for determining whether to incorporate a right into the Fourteenth Amendment due process clause and apply

By Steve Kelley, Copley News Service, © *The San Diego Union-Tribune.*

it against the states.[19] Frank Jacob Palko had been convicted of the second degree murder of two police officers, and he objected to the state's plan to retry him because of procedural errors in the earlier trial for first degree murder, which carried the death penalty. Palko claimed that a retrial would deny him the Fifth Amendment's protection against **double jeopardy,** that is, the guarantee that a person may not be tried twice for the same crime. However, the Supreme Court had not yet applied this right to the states. The Court ruled that only rights that were "implicit in the concept of ordered liberty" would be applied to the states. According to Justice Benjamin Cardozo, those rights were fundamental freedoms such as freedom of speech, the right to fair trial, and freedom of thought; the double jeopardy protection was not one. Palko lost his appeal, and, with no double jeopardy right to worry about, the state retried him, convicted him, and put him to death. It was surely little comfort to him that his name was now associated with a new incorporation standard, **selective incorporation,** in which some portions of the Bill of Rights, but not all, were now part of the Fourteenth Amendment's due process clause and thus guaranteed against invasion by the states.

Gradually over the next forty-five years all but a handful of the provisions contained in the Bill of Rights were applied to the states by way of the Fourteenth Amendment. This judicial redefinition of civil liberties, particularly during the 1960s, was the greatest expansion of the power of the national government in the federal structure since the decisions in the 1930s that extended the interstate commerce power to the states.

Several amendments or portions thereof—including the Second, Third, and Seventh, the grand jury provision of the Fifth, and the excessive bails and fines provision of the Eighth—have not been, and probably will not be, incorporated. Since other rights that are not contained in the Bill of Rights, such as the right to privacy, have also been applied to the states, the best characterization of the approach now used by the Court might be "selective incorporation plus."

Once a provision of the Bill of Rights was incorporated, the question was raised whether these provisions meant the same at the state level as at the federal level. For example, once the right to trial by jury in the Sixth Amendment was applied to the states, did states have to observe the same twelve-person, unanimous-verdict rules as at the federal level? In this case, the Court decided that they did not.[20] Additional questions such as exactly what a provision meant and how much protection it extended to the individual need to be resolved. In the case of freedom of religion, for example, are religious practices protected if they violate other laws, such as the ban on polygamy? In the case of freedom of speech, is only actual speech protected, or is symbolic speech, such as flag burning, protected as well?

Freedom of Religion

Few issues were closer to the framers' hearts than those involving religion. Many of the nation's earliest European settlers were religious zealots seeking independence from the state-run Anglican Church of England. Accordingly, they either established state religions of their own or supported various religions without giving preference to any of them. It was not uncommon for state laws to be passed disenfranchising some religious groups, such as Catholics, Jews, agnostics, or atheists. Since the potential for fragmentation of the new nation into different religious communities fighting for governmental control was too dangerous to be ignored, the guarantee of freedom of religion was placed early in the Bill of Rights.

For the framers, religion was a matter of personal choice and conscience, not an area for governmental control. However, by restricting government's "establishment" of religion while simultaneously guaranteeing the "free exercise" of religion, the framers created contradictory goals.[21] For example, if the government provides tax-exempt status for religious organizations, as it does for other charitable institutions, thus promoting "free exercise of religion," does this constitute an "establishment of religion"? On the other hand, if government fails to grant such tax

double jeopardy Being tried twice for the same crime; banned by the Fifth Amendment.

selective incorporation An incorporation standard in which some portions of the Bill of Rights, but not all, were made part of the Fourteenth Amendment's due process clause and thus guaranteed against invasion by the states.

relief, would this result in the closing of some churches, thus restricting the free exercise of religion for some people?[22] Because of questions like these, the Supreme Court has chosen to rely more on the establishment clause rather than on the free exercise clause.

Establishment of Religion

In deciding whether particular governmental practices would have the effect of "establishing" a religion, the Court has searched for the proper balance between two opposing views of the relationship between government and religion. These are known as the *high wall of separation* position and the *government accommodation* position.

The high wall of separation position originated with the author of this constitutional provision, James Madison, who was reacting to the fact that half the colonies had adopted laws that provided support for religious institutions and practices.[23] Fearing that such laws could lead to religious persecution, he called for strict separation between church and state. However, there were too many connections between church and state to bar them all. In the government accommodation view, the government would be allowed to assist religion, but only if the aid was indirect, available to all other groups, and religiously neutral.

The government accommodation position was first articulated in 1947 in the case of *Everson v. Board of Education of Ewing Township*. A local school board, spurred by the desire to aid Catholic parochial schools, had provided funds to enable children to travel to parochial school on city buses. The Court ruled that the state's policy did not violate the establishment clause because it was the children, not the church, who received the benefit. According to Justice Hugo Black, the transportation assistance was similar to other basic services, such as police and fire protection. Black was unpersuaded by the arguments of the dissenters that such assistance made it possible for children to attend the church schools, thereby indirectly aiding religion.[24]

The high wall of separation doctrine was best described in 1962 in the case of *Engel v. Vitale*, in which the Court ruled that a brief nondenominational prayer led by a teacher in a public school was unconstitutional. For the Court, the mere chance that a student might feel compelled to worship a God that he or she did not believe in was precisely the kind of establishment of religion that the framers had sought to avoid.[25]

Partly because of the public outcry after the *Engel* decision, the Court began to search for a middle ground between separation and accommodation. It took a step in this direction one year later in the case of *Abington School District v. Schempp*. In ruling on this case, which involved the reading of selections from the Bible in Pennsylvania public schools, the Court adopted a *strict governmental neutrality* rule, under which a state was barred from doing anything that either advanced or inhibited religion. Since school-directed Bible reading clearly advanced religion, the practice was ruled unconstitutional.[26]

During the 1960s the Court continued to search for the proper test for judging cases involving state aid to religious schools. If bus money could be provided to parochial school students, what about books? Since the books were loaned, the Court found this practice constitutional. Could the same be said for state aid to parochial school teachers teaching nonreligious subjects? This question was raised by the 1971 case of *Lemon v. Kurtzman*. In deciding that case, the Court created a new test, called the **Lemon test,** for determining the permissible level of state aid for church agencies. For such aid to be considered constitutional, the state had to prove that (1) the law had a secular purpose; (2) the primary purpose and effect of the law were neither to advance nor to inhibit religion; and (3) the law did not foster an "excessive governmental entanglement with religion." Since the aid in this case was for teachers of nonreligious subjects, the first two conditions were met. However, the only way the state could judge whether the funded teachers were aiding religion would be to monitor their classes; the law therefore violated the "excessive entanglement" provision of the test.[27]

Lemon test A test from the Supreme Court case *Lemon v. Kurtzman* in 1971 for determining the permissible level of state aid for church agencies by measuring whether the purpose of the state aid is nonreligious in nature, whether it neither advances or inhibits religion, and whether it results in the excessive entanglement of the church and state.

THE ROAD TO DEMOCRACY
Questioning the Death Penalty

The 2002 Supreme Court term may provide hope for those on death row. And this news comes in the wake of many other changes, such as Larry Ollins, Omar Saunders, and Calvin Ollins emerging from death row in Joliet, Illinois after 15 years on death row for the rape and murder of a 23-year-old medical student, Lori Roscetti near a Chicago Housing Project only to be given gilt-edged placques reading: "The first day of the rest of your life." Their story was like that of Ricky McGuinn, who was staring at what he feared would be his last meal of a double cheeseburger, French fries and a Dr. Pepper, just 18 minutes from being put to death by lethal injection in Huntsville, Texas for the rape and murder of his 12-year-old stepdaughter when he was pardoned by then-Governor George W. Bush because DNA testing still needed to be done to ensure his guilt. These men, and scores of others had been cleared by DNA evidence showing that they could not have committed the crimes for which they were about to be killed.

THAT WAS THEN . . .

But these men are not alone. Since the Court upheld the Death Penalty in 1976 so long as it is not administered in an "arbitrary and capricious manner," more than 760 prisoners have been put to death and over 3,700 people currently sit on death row, a disproportionate number of them minorities, but both federal and state studies now show that the standards for determining who will live and who will die vary widely around the nation. In July 2000, President Bill Clinton postponed the first federal execution in nearly 40 years of convicted multiple drug-related murderer Juan Raul Garza when a federal study determined that more than three-quarters of the defendants in federal capital cases were minorities. In the 2001 term the United States Supreme Court considered the issue of whether the retarded can be put to death in the case of Johnny Paul Penry. Penry, a man with an IQ of 60, was convicted of raping, stomping, and fatally stabbing a woman named Pam Moseley Carpenter in 1979. But is the execution of a mentally-deficient person "cruel and unusual punishment" because the jury was never asked to consider this factor in issuing its sentence?

Discretion as to the imposition of the death sentence is evident everywhere. Nearly half of the federal cases in which the death penalty was an option came from just five districts, two of those in New York. The administration of the federal death penalty is like a "rigged lottery," said one defense attorney, with the outcome determined by "the color of your skin and where you purchased your ticket." For the Supreme Court, which ruled in the 1970s that the death penalty would have to be imposed fairly and not in a biased manner to be constitutional under the Eighth Amendment's "cruel and unusual punishment" guarantee, this had to be a disturbing direction.

THIS IS NOW . . .

Things were no better in individual states. In March 2000, Governor George Ryan of Illinois placed a moratorium on the use of the death penalty in his state when 13 men were cleared by new evidence and released from death row. One case was particularly galling. Anthony Porter went through all of his appeals on death row and was just 48 hours away from execution when the state court granted him a stay because a psychologist's test determined that Porter had an I.Q. of about 50, raising doubts about his mental competency. At this point the undergraduate students of David Protess, a journalism professor at Northwestern University, found evidence that both cleared Porter of the murder and led to the conviction of another man. Problems with the imposition of the death penalty are nationwide, as shown by a 2002 study showing that states which issue the highest numbers of death penalty sentences have had overall reversal rates of over two out of every three cases.

Fully 98 people were cleared of their death penalty offenses for rape and murder on the basis of DNA evidence after going on death row. While only two states—Illinois and New York—grant inmates the right to have their DNA

▲ Northwestern journalism professor David Protess shares a laugh with Anthony Porter, a former death row inmate who was freed as a result of investigations by Professor Protess's class. That class has helped to clear more than a dozen prisoners thus far.

During the past two decades this three-pronged so called *Lemon* test, has been applied in all cases involving the establishment of religion. However, its application has varied over the years depending on the composition of the Court. During the

tested, now over 90 percent of the American people want to have that right guaranteed to suspects. Even now, ten years after coal miner Roger Keith Coleman was put to death in Virginia for the rape and murder of his sister-in-law that he said he did not commit, supporters are trying to secure DNA testing of his corpse seeking to prove his innocence.

In June of 2000, the most extensive study of the death penalty in the United States found that nearly two out of every three death penalty convictions were overturned on appeal because of incompetent lawyers or overzealous police investigators. Indeed, in the case of the Ollins cousins and Saunders, it is feared that their convictions resulted from untruthful testimony by a forensic scientist and the coercion of confessions by investigators who were operating from a profiler's theory. The study from 1973 to 1995, examining nearly 5,800 death penalty convictions, also uncovered that 75 percent of those whose death penalties were set aside were later given a lesser sentence on retrial. Only 18 percent of those cases that were overturned resulted in another death penalty sentence.

The effect of all of this new evidence about the unfairness of the death penalty is influencing public opinion. Gallup polls have showed that public support for the punishment has slipped to 66 percent, the lowest point since 1978. With only a handful of nations still using the death penalty (including China, Turkey, and Iraq), the European Union firmly opposed to it, and the mounting evidence of the penalty's unfairness, the question of the future of this form of punishment in the United States will be a source of continued debate.

But change may be under way. Thanks in large part to the efforts of Justice John Paul Stevens the Supreme Court in mid-2002 issued two major rulings on the death penalty indicating that this sentence may be under review. The Court ruled by a 7 to 2 vote in *Ring v. Arizona* that juries and judges must decide whether or not a convicted murderer should be given the death penalty. And, the Court also ruled by a 6 to 3 vote in *Atkins v. Virginia* that executing a "mentally retarded" defendant would constitute "cruel and unusual punishment" in violation of the Eighth Amendment.

In their view, the recent passage by 18 of the 38 states with death penalty laws of provisions banning the execution of mentally-challenged defendents indicated a growing national consensus against this practice.

Sources: Jodi Wilgoren, "Three Cleared by DNA Tests Enjoy Liberty After 15 Years," *New York Times,* December 6, 2001, p. A20; Henry Weinstein, "Death Penalty Study Suggests Errors," *Los Angeles Times,* February 11, 2002; David G. Savage, "'92 Execution Haunts Death Penalty Foes," *Los Angeles Times,* July 22, 2001; Jonathan Alter, "The Death Penalty on Trial," *Newsweek,* June 12, 2000, pp. 24–35; Raymond Bonner and Marc Lacey, "U.S. Plans Delay in First Execution in Four Decades," *New York Times,* July 7, 2000, p. 1; and Fox Butterfield, "Death Sentences Being Overturned in 2 of 3 Appeals," *New York Times,* June 12, 2000, p. 1.

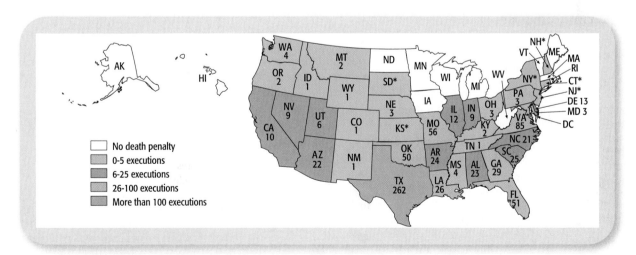

Death Row Executions Since 1976

*States that have the death penalty but have had no executions.

Source: Death Penalty Information Center, from *The New York Times,* June 12, 2000, p. A23. Copyright © 2000 by the New York Times Co. Reprinted by permission. Updated with data from Death Penalty Information Center, http://www.deathpenaltyinfo.org/executionmap.html, March 15, 2002.

early years of the Burger Court, the justices were sharply divided on the question of state aid to religious schools. States could supply standardized tests to parochial schools[28] and provide grants to all colleges, even church-related ones.[29] But in 1973

▲ Alabama Supreme Court Chief Justice Roy Moore showed what he thought of the First Amendment's call for the separation of church and state when he moved this Ten Commandments granite monument into the lobby of the state's Supreme Court building. Federal District Court Judge Myron Thompson ordered its removal.

the Court ruled in the *Committee of Education v. Nyquist* case that the state of New York could not offer tuition reimbursement of between $60 and $100 to impoverished students because there was no effort "to guarantee the separation between secular and religious educational functions and to ensure that State financial aid supports only the former," thus potentially causing religious strife.[30] Later, it ruled that the government could also not reimburse students for taking the New York State Regents exams,[31] or provide auxiliary services, such as counseling and speech therapy, to parochial school students.[32]

In the early 1980s changes in the makeup of the Court produced a shift toward a more accommodationist position. The parents of private, public, and parochial school students in Minnesota were permitted in *Mueller v. Allen* to take an income tax deduction for the costs of tuition, textbooks, and transportation;[33] a chaplain could open the daily proceedings of the Nebraska legislature;[34] and a crèche could be placed in a public park in Pawtucket, Rhode Island, as part of a larger Christmas display. It was here that Justice Sandra Day O'Connor offered her suggestion for replacing the *Lemon* test, saying that the Christmas display was permissible for her because it offered "no endorsement" of a particular religion or religion in general.[35] On the other hand, certain practices were disallowed: the state of Kentucky was barred from posting the Ten Commandments in school classrooms;[36] the state of Alabama was barred from requiring a moment of silent meditation in public schools if the teacher suggested that students use the time to pray or even suggested the wording of a prayer;[37] public school teachers could not be sent to parochial schools to teach secular subjects;[38] and the state of Louisiana could not require the teaching of creationism as a way of providing a perspective different from Darwinian evolution.[39] Religious groups around the country mounted the "Hang Ten" movement, seeking to post the Ten Commandments on the walls of public schools and public buildings. In 2002, for the second time in a year, a deeply divided court refused to hear an appeal of Indiana Governor Frank O'Bannon, who had been prevented by a lower court from placing a 7-foot stone monument containing the Ten Commandments on the statehouse lawn, a situation reminiscent of a similar effort by Justice Roy Moore in the Alabama Supreme Court building rotunda. These cases have led to the removal of memorials around the country.[40] An order by the federal court in November 2002 to remove the Alabama monument made it unclear whether this practice could continue.

The Rehnquist Court has stood ready to modify or reverse many of these decisions. The crèche that had been acceptable in Pawtucket five years earlier was now unacceptable on the grand staircase of the Allegheny County Courthouse in Pittsburgh. On the other hand, the placing of a menorah next to a Christmas tree and a sign saluting liberty just outside the City-County Building in the same city was acceptable.[41] A nondenominational prayer at a Rhode Island graduation was ruled unconstitutional in an opinion by Justice Anthony Kennedy because, in his alternative to the *Lemon* test, it might have a "psychological coercion" effect on nonbelievers who were present, and might even induce some students not to attend their graduation for religious reasons.[42]

In 2000 the Court decided a case from the Santa Fe Independent School District near Galveston, Texas, in which a student-led prayer before a football game had been banned by a federal district court judge. A six-member majority ruled that it made no difference that this was a student-led prayer at a football game. Because students feel social pressure to attend such events and might feel coerced by school-sponsored prayer to express a belief in religion that they did not hold, the Court ruled that prayer should be private and not led by schools.[43]

The continued viability of the *Lemon* test, and whether the Court will turn to a test along the lines of those proposed by Justices O'Connor, Kennedy, or some third approach, may well depend on the views of the new justices appointed by President Bush. While five members of the current Court have expressed some reservations about the test, seeing it as too separationist in its impact, it remains to be seen whether they can agree on a more accommodationist test. Until then, in the 2001 term the current Court tested the full limits of the *Lemon* test to schools when it heard an appeal from Cleveland, Ohio raising the question of whether school vouchers were constitutional. This voucher program was passed by the Ohio legislature, offering $2,250 in state aid to impoverished students, 99% of whom would use the money to attend religious schools. With more than twenty-five state legislatures considering bills that would offer public money to parents wishing to send their children to religious schools, this was a landmark case in the making. The U.S. Supreme Court seemed in the oral arguments to be evenly balanced on the issue of church-state separation, with four justices voting for separation and four for more government accommodation, and Sandra Day O'Connor in the middle. The question was whether they would follow the *Nyquist* precedent and strike the plan down because it violated the *Lemon* test, follow the *Mueller* case upholding the Minnesota tax credit for parochial schools because of the lack of "excessive entanglement" between the state and religion, or develop some new test to determine the constitutionality of state aid to religion-based schools. Would they agree with the state of Ohio that this plan presented "an educational lifeline" to "the poorest of the poor," or a scheme to funnel millions in state money to foster religion in parochial schools. In a narrow 5–4 ruling, Chief Justice Rehnquist upheld the Cleveland program, arguing that since it gave parents the option of sending their children to public charter or magnet schools as well as nonreligious private schools, it did not coerce them into subjecting children to religious instruction. Justice David Souter, in an unusual denunciation of the court's decision delivered orally from the bench, called it a "major devaluation" of the court's church-state rulings and "not only mistaken, but tragic."[44] This ruling will likely give energy to the effort by the Bush administration to fund "faith-based initiatives," such as soup kitchens and day care centers run by religious organizations that might now be seeking government funding.

This decision will certainly not end the fight over government spending for religious schools, just shift the legal battle to the state level. Some 37 states have so-called "Blaine Amendments," named for the anti-Catholic Maine Republican Congressman of the 1850s James G. Blaine, who tried to secure passage of an amendment to the United States Constitution banning any government funding for parochial schools. When that failed, states used it as a model for their own anti-religious school funding amendments to their constitution, sometimes barring both direct and indirect financial aid. Both sides in the voucher battle vowed to use litigation over these state provisions to continue the fight as to whether government funding of religious schools will be allowed.

Question for Reflection: Should state and federal funding be made available for religious schools that admittedly teach religion without any restrictions as to its use?

Free Exercise of Religion

Issues involving the free exercise of religion are particularly vexing because they most often involve disputes of liberty versus liberty, or the right of one person to practice religion in the face of another who seeks to avoid religion. One look at some of the practices of government—the "In God We Trust" motto on its currency, the chaplain's invocation that opens sessions of Congress, and even the admonition "God save this honorable Court" that opens each session of the Supreme Court—tells us that religion is pervasive in American politics. But do these practices place limits on the free exercise of religion? And, even if they do, is it possible politically to change them? These questions over the symbolic use of religious symbols in state-funded locations were made very clear in June 2002 when a 3-judge panel of the Ninth Circuit Court ruled that the "under God" provision of the pledge of allegiance made its use in public schools unconstitutional because it coerced non-religious students to express a religious belief that they did not hold. The nationwide

FYI

In 1997 Muslim groups tried to convince the Supreme Court to have the engraving of Muhammad looking down on the courtroom removed as being offensive to their religion. The Court refused. However, a Court's brochure now reads: "This figure is a well-intentioned attempt by the sculptor to honor Muhammad, and it bears no resemblance to Muhammad. Muslims generally have a strong aversion to sculptured or pictured representations of their Prophet."

storm of controversy that resulted from this decision caused the entire Court of Appeals to announce that it would reconsider its decision. If the case should ever reach the Supreme Court it will almost certainly be reversed.[45]

Free exercise cases usually involve a law that applies to everyone but is perceived as imposing a hardship on a particular religious group. For example, can laws against mail fraud be used to prosecute religious groups that make dubious claims in letters to potential donors? In such cases the Court will not inquire into the nature of the religion, but it will examine whether the actions that result from that belief contravene the law. This so-called **secular regulation rule** holds that there is no constitutional right to exemption on free exercise grounds from laws dealing with nonreligious matters. This rule was applied in 1878 in a case involving the practice of polygamy (taking multiple wives) by Mormons in the Utah Territory. The Court ruled that religious beliefs did not provide immunity from the law, in this case the law enforcing monogamy.[46]

Subsequently, it became clear that the secular regulation rule did impose undue hardship on religious groups in some instances. For example, the so-called "blue laws," under which all businesses were required to close on Sunday, put Muslim or Jewish business owners who observed the Sabbath on Friday or Saturday at a competitive disadvantage because their businesses had to be closed on Sunday as well. Accordingly, the Court invented a new test—the **least restrictive means test**—in which the state was asked to find another way, perhaps through exemptions, to enforce its regulations while still protecting all other religions.[47]

This "live and let live" position on issues of free exercise prevailed until 1990, when the Rehnquist Court decided a case in which two Native Americans working as unemployment counselors in Oregon were held to have violated the state's antidrug laws by smoking peyote, a hallucinogenic drug, as part of a religious observance. The Court felt that it was more important to defer to the state's efforts to control drug use than to protect the free exercise of religion in this instance.[48] Although the Court refused to use this precedent to allow the state of Florida to rely on its public health and animal anticruelty laws to specifically ban religious sacrifices of animals,[49] this decision was then used by government authorities to justify even greater incursions into religious behavior: autopsies were ordered contrary to religious beliefs, and an FBI agent who refused a work assignment for religious reasons was fired.[50]

The Oregon peyote use ruling was reversed by Congress in the Religious Freedom Restoration Act (RFRA), and in 1997 the Supreme Court overturned this law in the case of *City of Boerne v. Flores*. In this case, the congregation of the St. Peter Catholic Church in Boerne, Texas, wanted to expand its beautiful historic stone structure to accommodate its growing membership, but was blocked by the city's Historic Landmark Commission. This decision was challenged under RFRA, and the Court overturned the law, thus returning the standard to the *secular regulation rule*, saying that it was not within Congress's power to legislatively void judicial decisions, because

> "When the Court has interpreted the Constitution, it has acted within the province of the Judicial Branch, which embraces the duty to say what the law is. When the political branches of the Government act against the background of a judicial interpretation of the Constitution already issued, it must be understood that . . . the Court will treat its precedents with the respect due them under settled principles . . . and contrary expectations must be disappointed. RFRA was designed to control cases and controversies, such as the one before us; but as the provisions of the federal statute here invoked are beyond congressional authority, it is this Court's precedent, not RFRA, which must control."[51]

secular regulation rule Rule that holds that there is no constitutional right to exemption on free exercise grounds from laws dealing with nonreligious matters.

least restrictive means test A free exercise of religion test in which the state was asked to find another way, perhaps through exemptions, to enforce its regulations while still protecting all other religions.

Eventually, the city and the church later came to an agreement that allowed the church to expand the structure.

In sum, while the principle of freedom of religion appears straightforward on the surface, in practice it raises a variety of complex issues that have been resolved in various ways over the course of our history. It appears not to be possible to erect a high wall of separation between church and state, but the degree of accommodation of government practices involving religious organizations may vary, depending on the composition of the Court and the specific test applied in each instance. The same is true in the area of free exercise, where the composition of the Court determines the degree of freedom afforded to religious groups against state regulations. In the last several years, the Court signaled its willingness to protect the free speech and free exercise rights of religious organizations. In 2001 the Court ruled that public schools that allowed nonreligious groups to meet for activities in their buildings after school hours must also open their building to religious groups for their meetings, in this case an after-school Bible Club for young children.[52]

This direction was continued by the Court's 8 to 1 ruling in 2002 that Jehovah's Witnesses should not be subject to the town solicitation regulations of Stratton, Ohio, requiring door-to-door advocates to secure a permit and reveal the names of missionaries before going door-to-door to proselytize.[53]

Freedom of Speech

One of the hallmarks of a democratic state is the guarantee of freedom of speech. But just where does the state draw the line between a person's right to speak and other rights, such as the speech rights of others? Over the years the Supreme Court has taken two different approaches in attempting to solve this dilemma. One approach was suggested by Alexander Meiklejohn, a legal theorist who argued that although public, or political, speech on matters of public interest must be absolutely protected to preserve a democratic society, private speech, or speech intended for one's own purposes, can be restricted to protect the interests of other members of society.[54] On the other hand, Justice Oliver Wendell Holmes argued that democracy requires a "free marketplace of ideas" in which *any* view may be expressed, allowing the audience to decide what to believe. For Holmes, limits on freedom of speech were justified only when the consequences of speech endangered the state.[55]

 but can be restricted

Caught between these absolutist and balancing approaches, the Court has ruled in ways that protect certain kinds of speech but not others. All speech is afforded First Amendment protection unless it is offensive or obscene or poses a threat to

◄ The United States Senate, meeting in a special session held in New York City in 2002, offered its dissenting opinion to 9th Circuit Court of Appeals Court Judge Alfred T. Goodwin's decision to ban the recitation of the Pledge of Allegiance in public schools because it contains the words "one Nation under God."

national security. Since such utterances either convey no worthwhile ideas or do more harm to society than good, they are not deemed worthy of protection. Despite these guidelines, however, the degree of protection afforded to particular forms of speech has varied considerably.

Political Speech

Where does the government draw the line between promoting full political discussion and protecting the government's right to exist? The Court faced this challenge in the early 1950s, when the tensions of the Cold War led to fears that Communist party members in the United States were actively seeking to overthrow the government. No longer were these "poor and puny anonymities," the government argued in prosecuting twelve Communist party leaders, but members of a worldwide organization calling for full-scale revolution.

In *Dennis v. United States* the Court reviewed the convictions of Communist party leaders under the Smith Act, which made it a crime to teach or advocate overthrow of the government or to organize and conspire with those who do so. Did these actions pose a "clear and present danger" to the nation? In view of the tiny and disorganized nature of the American Communist party, the Court was unable to conclude that its actions created such a danger. However, the Court was anxious to uphold the convictions, and therefore it invented a new *sliding-scale test* in which the state needed to prove less about the probable results of speech if the potential threat involved was significant enough. In this case, since the Communists' goal was to overthrow the government, all that was now needed to convict them was the presence of their names on a list of the party membership and some evidence that they were involved in the organization's activities, not that they were actively plotting the government's overthrow.[56]

Not until 1957 did the Court become willing to protect the speech of Communists as long as they were not actively plotting to overthrow the government.[57] By 1967 the Court had made it virtually impossible to deny First Amendment rights to someone for just being a Communist.[58] At the time of Earl Warren's retirement in 1969, the Court had moved a considerable distance toward absolutism in protecting political speech. For example, when the leader of the Ku Klux Klan in Ohio was convicted for advocating unlawful methods of terrorism because he had appeared with a gun at a cross-burning rally that was filmed on television, the Court invented a new test. It would uphold convictions only for speech that incited "imminent lawless action" and was "likely to produce such action." On this basis, the conviction was reversed.[59]

In the 1999 term, the Supreme Court opened the door for further campaign finance reform by ruling in a Missouri case that limits on individual contributions are constitutional. The limits of $1,075 for contributions to statewide candidates, similar to laws in two-thirds of the states, were ruled not to be a limit on free speech.[60] The following term, the Court indicated once more its concern about the effect of money on political campaigns when it ruled against the request of the Colorado State Republican Party's request to be exempted from the federal limits on the amount of money that political parties can spend to assist their candidates' campaigns.[61] These decisions on campaign finance reform took on added importance in 2002 given the passage of the Bipartisan Campaign Finance Act banning soft money and "issue ads" shortly before elections and Kentucky Senator Mitch McConnell's comment that, "There is litigation ahead, meaning that the law would soon be tested in court." When the Court placed this law on a fast track for appeal it seemed likely that its constitutionality would be tested in the 2002–2003 term.

Public Speech

States have passed many laws to protect those who might be offended or threatened by certain kinds of speech. Disturbing the peace, disorderly conduct, inciting to riot, terroristic threats, and fighting-word statutes are designed to preserve public order and safety. The main problem with such statutes is that sometimes they are crafted or enforced specifically to exclude certain ideas or groups.

Laws involving public speech place the Supreme Court in the position of weighing the right of the speaker to say what he or she wishes against the right of the state to maintain law and order. Over the years the Court has developed three standards in this area. First, it asked whether a particular form of speech comes under the protective umbrella of the First Amendment. Thus, while controlled protests in public places such as the state library and state capitol are protected, calling a police officer "a goddamned racketeer" and "a damned fascist" is not; such expressions are considered **fighting words.**[62] The Court looked next at the nature of the statute itself. Is the law overbroad, including some protected forms of speech among the proscribed ones? Or is it underinclusive, failing to regulate some speech that should also be barred? For instance, a "disturbing the peace" law was used to arrest an anti-Semitic priest for making an inflammatory speech. The conviction was overturned because the law was used to punish speech that merely "invited dispute" or created "a condition of unrest;" it did not actually cause a riot.[63] The same standard is used today in determining the degree of protection that may be given to **hate speech**—speech and symbolic actions, such as cross-burning, that are laced with negative views toward certain groups of people. In two cases the Court ruled that government cannot selectively ban such speech based on its content, but it can increase punishment for those who physically assault minorities.[64]

Finally, assuming that a particular form of speech is protected and the statute is precisely and narrowly drawn, the Court will examine the facts of the case to see if the state's interests override those of the speaker. Can the state demonstrate that the dangers posed by the speech were significant enough to override the free speech interests involved (meaning that the regulation would be upheld)? Or did the police make arrests because of their objection to the speech itself rather than the resulting action (meaning that the arrest would be overturned)? Thus, picketing on the state-owned jailhouse grounds, which risked causing a riot inside the jail, would constitute trespassing, and the arrests of the picketers would be upheld.[65] But arresting a civil rights leader the day after he had made a protest speech in front of a courthouse, claiming that he might have caused a riot, would not be allowed.[66]

Symbolic Speech

Not all speech involves words. Some actions, such as burning the American flag, take the place of speech and are commonly called **symbolic speech.** In a 1971 case, *Cohen v. California,* the Court expanded its protection to these types of protests. Paul Cohen had appeared in a courthouse wearing a leather jacket bearing the words "F——K THE DRAFT. STOP THE WAR." The Court might have argued that these were *fighting words*—controllable actions or obscenity forced upon a captive audience—but instead it ruled that because the offensive speech was meant to convey a larger symbolic meaning, the behavior was protected under the First Amendment. It was this protective view of symbolic speech that led the Court in 1989 to uphold Gregory Lee Johnson's right to burn the American flag, even though many people found the action objectionable.[67]

Some symbolic speech, however, crosses the line into objectionable conduct, which can be regulated under the Constitution. In a series of cases dealing with so-called hate speech, including actions and protests that tend to defame or are intended to intimidate ethnic or religious groups, such as the burning of crosses or the painting of swastikas, the Court ruled that while these symbols were objectionable, state laws had to be carefully drawn to proscribe them. Since a St. Paul, Minnesota, city ordinance that banned any symbol that was likely to arouse "anger, alarm, or resentment in others on the basis of race, color, creed, religion or gender" was both underinclusive, banning too few kinds of speech, and overinclusive,

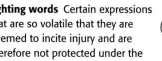

fighting words Certain expressions that are so volatile that they are deemed to incite injury and are therefore not protected under the First Amendment.

hate speech Speech or symbolic actions intended to inflict emotional distress, defame, or intimidate people.

symbolic speech Some actions, such as burning the American flag, that take the place of speech because they communicate a message.

banning too many kinds, a unanimous Court overturned it.[68] However, a unanimous Court upheld state laws that enhanced penalties for such hate speech behavior.[69]

In the 1990s this issue of symbolic protests, and whether they become regulatable conduct or are protected free speech, led the Court to examine the behavior of anti-abortion protesters. In an effort to protect women seeking abortion counseling and procedures at abortion clinics from antiabortion protesters who were demonstrating and sometimes trying to block passage into the facility, the Rehnquist Court in 1995 upheld a thirty-six-foot "no approach buffer zone" around a Florida clinic into which no antiabortion protester could tread.[70] Two years later, the Court revisited this issue when a lower court had created a fifteen-foot "fixed buffer zone" around a New York clinic's doorways and parking lot entrances in which no protesting would be allowed, permitted two antiabortion "sidewalk counselors" to enter the zone at any time unless the target of their conversation asked them to "cease and desist," and also created a fifteen-foot "floating buffer zone" around anyone entering or leaving the facility—a sort of "no-protest bubble." The Supreme Court struck down the floating no-protest bubble as a violation of the free speech of the protesters, but upheld the fifteen-foot "fixed no protest" zone around the clinic.[71]

In the 1999 term, the Court took another step in protecting abortion rights by upholding an unusual Colorado "bubble" law that established a one-hundred-foot "no approach" zone around a "health care facility" and prevented people from approaching others within eight feet to protest or pass out literature. For the Court, individuals had a "right to be left alone."[72]

? Question for Reflection: Should people be permitted to protest anywhere they want, on any topic that they choose, given the First Amendment's mandate that "Congress shall make no law . . . abridging Freedom of Speech?"

Freedom of the Press

Decisions in cases involving freedom of the press must establish a balance between the public's right to know and (1) the government's right to secrecy, (2) an individual's right to personal reputation and/or privacy, (3) a defendant's right to a fair trial, or (4) an individual's personal and moral sensibilities. To illustrate this point, ask yourself whether the public's "right to know" about a controversial criminal trial like that of Sean "P. Diddy" Combs or Robert Blake overrides both the defendant's right to receive a fair trial and society's right to maintain law and order. Some see the press as a critical "fourth branch," keeping a watchful eye on the government. But what if the revelation of certain government activities could be damaging to national security?

Prior Restraint

Often the balance between these two sets of rights depends on the kinds of laws used to restrict the press. **Prior restraint** (censorship) laws prevent the press from revealing information *before* publication of that information by the government. Prior restraint cases generally involve issues of national security, but they may also involve "gag orders" intended to preserve the right to a fair trial. In contrast, **subsequent punishment** laws punish writers and editors *after* the publication of certain information. Such laws are used to ban libel and obscenity because they are harmful to reputations or public sensibilities. The framers were more concerned with prior restraint than with subsequent punishment, believing that a trial by a jury of peers could deal with the latter, but in reality both can be equally harmful. A significant enough punishment threatened after publication can lead the press to censor itself prior to publication.

Probably the most significant case involving prior restraint was the 1971 *Pentagon Papers* case. A Defense Department researcher named Daniel Ellsberg, who had

prior restraint An action in which the government seeks to ban the publication of controversial material by the press before it is published; censorship.

subsequent punishment Laws that would punish someone for an action after it has taken place. For example, laws such as those banning libel and obscenity because they are harmful to reputations or public sensibilities punish writers, editors, and publishers after an item appears in print.

worked on a study called "A History of the United States Decision-Making Process on Vietnam Policy" (the Pentagon Papers), had leaked almost all of the forty-seven-volume report to the *New York Times*, which in turn eventually passed excerpts on to the *Washington Post*. When the newspapers planned to publish excerpts from the study, the government took the extraordinary step of seeking a court injunction to prevent their publication, claiming that it would be damaging to national security. Because of its controversial nature, the case went through the federal courts and reached the Supreme Court in the extraordinarily brief time of fifteen days. The Court ruled against prior restraint. In a concurring opinion, Justice Potter Stewart argued that prior censorship can be justified only when publication "will surely result in direct, immediate, and irreparable damage to our Nation or its people." Since the Pentagon Papers were strictly historical documents, Stewart failed to see the potential for such harm.[73]

However, a closer analysis of the four concurring and three dissenting opinions reveals that the decision was not as great a victory for the press as it seemed. Five of the justices implied that if the government had tried to punish the press after publication, using laws barring the release of secret documents, the convictions would have been upheld. Accordingly, later administrations passed and enforced a series of administrative regulations and laws to prevent the divulging of secret information.

Another area in which the press is subject to restraints is its coverage of criminal proceedings. Judges sometimes issue gag orders barring the media from publishing information about an ongoing criminal case. In 1976 the Court ruled that a gag order issued by a Nebraska court in the pretrial hearing of a multiple-murder case was a prior restraint of the press and hence violated the First Amendment.[74] Because the Court extended its ruling in 1980 to open criminal trials to the press and public "absent an overriding interest to the contrary," gag orders are far less common today.[75]

Libel

In a democracy, the free flow of ideas must sometimes be prevented or limited when it is untruthful, malicious, or damaging to a person's reputation or good name. Speech that has these effects is termed **slander;** if it appears in written form, it is termed **libel.** The Supreme Court has ruled that slander and libel are not protected by the First Amendment. But how does one determine whether a published statement is libelous? Some published statements may be intended to defame a person's reputation, but in some instances defamation is a result of negligence, or failure to take reasonable care in verifying information before publication. Do the latter instances also constitute libel?

The Court addressed this question in 1964, when the *New York Times* printed an advertisement that was critical of the racial views of unnamed public officials in Alabama. An elected commissioner in Montgomery, Alabama, L. B. Sullivan, filed suit in an Alabama court, claiming that the ad libeled him personally; he won the case under an Alabama law requiring newspapers to establish the truth of material before publishing it. The *New York Times* appealed the case to the Supreme Court. Seeking to balance the newspaper's right to publish against Sullivan's right to maintain his reputation, the Court took careful notice of Sullivan's status as a public official. Unlike private individuals, public officials have opportunities to respond to published statements through such means as press conferences. On the other hand, if the press were prevented from publishing statements that are critical of political figures, it would be unable to fulfill its role as a watchdog of government. So the Court ruled that convictions in cases involving libel against public officials, expanded in later cases to public figures, could be upheld only if the defamatory article had been printed with "knowledge that it was false or reckless disregard whether it was false or not." In short, the untrue and defamatory piece would have to be printed without any effort to check the facts.[76] Making no effort to check facts, supermarket tabloids are able to print outrageous articles about movie stars and public figures, generally without fear of retribution.

slander Speech that is untruthful, malicious, or damaging to a person's reputation or good name and thus not protected by the free speech clause of the First Amendment.

libel Published material that damages a person's reputation or good name in an untruthful and malicious way. As such it is not protected by the First Amendment.

Seeking to restrict the press, the Burger and Rehnquist Courts launched a two-pronged attack against the Sullivan standard. The class of people defined as "public figures" was narrowed,[77] and the press was instructed to turn over materials indicating its "state of mind" when publishing an article that was claimed to be libelous.[78] These changes had the effect of increasing the burden on the press to prove that it had not been negligent or malicious in publishing a statement that was challenged as being libelous.

One trend to watch in the future is the willingness of companies to resort to libel-like suits to attempt to silence their critics. The Food Lion grocery chain sued ABC's *Primetime Live* for a report on the chain's sales of spoiled food. Rather than sue for libel, the firm sued for fraud, breach of loyalty, and trespass because the reporters were undercover. While the grocery firm won $5.5 million in damages, most of it was reversed on appeal, leaving Food Lion with a $2 award. The Court ruled that such an end run of the First Amendment could not be used.[79] Yet another type of case will likely arise from the Internet, where statements in various Websites might cause damage to named people or businesses. Court decisions will need to explore what kind of speech exists in this format and whether it is protected.

Obscenity

Although the publication of obscene material is not protected by the First Amendment guarantee of freedom of the press, it is difficult to establish a definition of obscenity, and thus to judge whether a particular publication is obscene. In a 1957 case, *Roth v. United States,* the Supreme Court stated that material could be judged to be obscene if "the average person, applying contemporary community standards, [determines that] the dominant theme of the material, taken as a whole, appeals to the prurient interest."[80] Thus, a book like *Lady Chatterley's Lover* or *Peyton Place* could not be declared obscene because of a few scattered passages that might be offensive to a few highly susceptible people. In 1966 the Court added to the *Roth* standard the requirement that a work could be banned only if it was "utterly without redeeming social value."[81]

During the 1960s the Warren Court developed a *variable obscenity test* in which the definition of obscenity changed according to the circumstances of the material's use or sale. Material was judged to be obscene if it was thrust upon a "captive audience"—for example, a pornographic outdoor drive-in movie that was visible from the street—or sold to unsuspecting customers such as children. In addition, material that was geared specifically toward customers with alternative sexual lifestyles could be banned.[82]

Because of the confusion and uncertainty resulting from this variable standard, the Burger Court tried to create a clearer standard in the 1973 case of *Miller v. California*. Henceforth, the definition of material as obscene would depend on "whether the average person applying contemporary community standards would find the work taken as a whole, appeals to the prurient interest; whether the work depicts or describes, in *a patently offensive way*, sexual conduct specifically defined by the applicable state law; and whether the work taken as a whole *lacks serious literary, artistic, political, or scientific value*."[83] In contrast to the *Roth* standard, the *Miller* standard considered local tastes. But this distinction did not solve the problem of defining obscenity. Each locality now had its own standard and applied it in varying ways to nationally distributed work. For example, the movie *Carnal Knowledge*, which did not depict sexual activity, but contained a great deal of dialogue on the subject, was judged to be obscene in Georgia but not elsewhere.[84]

The Rehnquist Court has made little progress toward establishing a clear definition of obscenity. The only clarity has come in the area of child pornography, for which the Court has so little tolerance that it has permitted convictions for even the possession of obscene videos of clothed children.[85] The question of how to determine whether a particular book or other published material is obscene, and thus to prevent or punish the publication of such material, remains unanswered.

One thing that the Court has answered for the moment, however, concerns attempts to regulate alleged pornography on the Internet; such regulations will not be allowed. In 1996 Congress passed the Communications Decency Act (CDA) seeking to protect those under the age of eighteen from "obscene or indecent" messages or "patently offensive" communications "knowingly" sent over the Internet. Although the Court in the case testing this act was very committed to "protecting children from harmful materials," it found the definition of speech restricted by the Communications Decency Act to be too vague and the law to be so vague that parents could be prosecuted for the nature of their own children's use of the family computer. Thus Justice John Paul Stevens wrote for the majority that the First Amendment protects the Web's "vast democratic fora . . . where any person with a phone line can become a town crier." Thus, he explained, "in the absence of evidence to the contrary, we presume that governmental regulation of the content of speech is more likely to interfere with the free exchange of ideas than to encourage it."[86]

But Congress was not finished with its efforts to regulate the Internet in order to shield children from pornography and. Neither was the Court with its determination to make this form of restricting free speech difficult. In 1996 Congress passed the Child Pornography Prevention Act, which made it a crime to create or distribute virtual images of child pornography, that is simulated computer images rather than real children engaging in sexual acts, on the Internet. In the 2001–2002 term, the Supreme Court struck down this law, ruling that the law was so broad that it could be used to block the simulated teen-aged sexual acts found in movies such as "Titanic" and "Traffic."[87]

Whether this posture by the Supreme Court will continue remains to be seen because of its decision in a new case. In 1998, Congress passed the Child Online Protection Act, which required all commercial Websites, not just those marketing pornography, to use some service to protect children under 17 from material deemed "harmful to minors." After the enforcement of this law was blocked by a federal appeals court in Philadelphia, the Supreme Court ruled in its 2001 term that the lower court had not correctly applied the "contemporary community standards" provision of the obscenity test because this was a World Wide Web. So, the lower court was instructed to re-examine the substantive provisions of the law, a ruling that will likely be revisited by the High Court.[88] Then, Congress went beyond the regulation of an individual's use of the Web to pass the Children's Internet Protection Act of 2000, which requires all schools and libraries to place filters on their computers in order to protect child users from pornographic Websites, or face the loss of millions of dollars in federal funding. After a three-judge federal court panel ruled that this law was unconstitutional because the filter process could ban constitutionally protected sites, the Supreme Court agreed to review it in the 2002–2003 term.[89] The interesting part of this battle, given the difficulty of defining pornography on the Web in a manner that is acceptable to the federal courts under the First Amendment, will come if Congress moves to expand its Internet regulatory efforts to deal with sites believed to be harming national security.

The Rights of Defendants

To the framers, fearful of the kinds of abuses that had prevailed under British rule, protection of the rights of defendants was vital. The Bill of Rights therefore contains several safeguards against government oppression, including the right to be left alone in one's home (Fourth Amendment), the right to remain silent (Fifth Amendment), and the right to be represented by counsel (Sixth Amendment). Remarkably, despite many changes in the technology of police work, these guarantees remain as vital today as they were two hundred years ago. Whether searches involve ransacking one's belongings under a writ of assistance or using technology to monitor one's computer or one's conversations, the balance is still between the rights of

APPROACHING DEMOCRACY AROUND THE GLOBE

Justice, China Style

A new drive in China to crack down on crime is putting police under real pressure to solve crimes quickly by securing confessions rather than searching for tangible evidence. The result is a loss of civil liberties for suspects who are being accused of crimes they did not commit. In six provinces from 1997 to 1999, a state report found that 221 confessions had been extorted from suspects with 21 of those cases resulting in the death of the suspects. Suspects have virtually no rights, not being allowed access to an attorney, or contact with the outside world, during police questioning. Questioning can go on indefinitely, around-the-clock. Suspects can be retried as many times as the state chooses to do so. If the suspect is "convicted" execution often occurs by gunfire at point-blank range without family members learning about the sentence until after the fact.

Because of this aggressive prosecution process, it is left to defense attorneys to protect the suspects. But now in China, it is hard to find attorneys who are willing to defend suspects. The reason can be understood in the case of Liu Jian, an idealistic attorney from Nanjing who was sent to a trial 200 miles away by his law firm to represent a local official accused of taking bribes.

Liu worked around the clock in Binhai to round up his witnesses, interview them, examine documents, and, when the police would allow, consult with his client. But when court convened, almost none of his thirty-seven witnesses showed up for trial and at the end of the trial it was the lawyer, Liu, who was in police custody, charged with "illegally obtaining evidence."

For five months Liu was held in detention and subjected to beatings and daylong interrogations without food or rest. Shortly, thereafter he was arrested and held in solitary confinement; he was beaten in an attempt to gain a confession. "Because of the mental pressure I was under, I was forced to admit to their charges," he said. So he confessed and received a sentence of time served. His criminal record now bars him from practicing law. It was the end of his desire to be an attorney. "I've tried not to have any contact with the criminal law since," he said, adding, "I've really lost confidence in the system."

For years China has tried to overhaul its legal system, training thousands of new lawyers and trying to expand their role in the justice process by passing new laws. For the first time, defendants are given the right to consult with counsel, and lawyers are able to conduct pretrial investigations. But the results have been mixed in the rural areas, where the judges and police do not want to follow the rules. As a result, it is not uncommon for the new lawyers to end up in jail defending themselves.

As a result, attorneys face many challenges in conducting their duties in trials. Despite the fact that the law gives attorneys the right to meet with their clients within forty-eight hours, very often the police refuse to let them do so. Lawyers are not given the legally guaranteed access to court materials such as confessions and witness lists. Witnesses are often intimidated by the police and prosecutors, with the result that they refuse to show up at trial. During the trial the use of confessions by torture is very common. Sometimes those confessions are obtained by the police in a two-week period before the defendants can see their lawyers, and other times they occur during the trial itself. Transcripts of police interrogations often show breaks in the questioning where "education takes place." Then, when the session resumes, a confession is offered.

"Because of these problems, it's sometimes hard to find a lawyer for criminal cases," says Professor Li. "Many lawyers are scared they could become implicated in the case and lose their livelihood." As a result, many turn to the more lucrative and professionally safer practice of business law.

This is the third crackdown on crime in China since the 1976 Cultural Revolution. When Deng Xiaoping announced the "strike hard" campaign in 1983, estimates were offered that as many as 10,000 people died in a single year. When the second "strike hard" campaign was announced in 1996, thousands more were killed. With broad support for these campaigns among the Chinese population, the approach to democracy in the criminal justice area does not seem near.

Sources: Based on Craig S. Smith, "Chinese Fight Crime With Torture and Executions," *New York Times,* September 9, 2001, p. 1; Elisabeth Rosenthal, "In China's Legal Evolution, the Lawyers Are Handcuffed," *New York Times,* January 6, 2000, p. 1.

---

the individual and the rights of society. However, as in many other areas involving civil liberties, this balance depends on the composition of the Supreme Court at any given time. No issue better illustrates this fact than the shifting nature of Fourth Amendment protection over the past three decades.

The Fourth Amendment

The Fourth Amendment tries to balance two rights: the individual's reasonable expectation of privacy and society's right to control crime and protect the public.

Over the years the Supreme Court has devised different rules for establishing this balance. During the 1960s the Warren Court "revolution" greatly expanded the protection provided by the expectation of privacy, but in subsequent decades the Burger and Rehnquist Courts shifted the balance back toward the state (that is, the police). These shifts have had significant effects on both the nation's approach to, and recession from, democracy as expressed by the constrained and then increased power of the state to investigate and imprison people.

Many issues related to Fourth Amendment protections stem from the amendment's lack of an explicitly written remedy. What can a judge do if the police go too far in conducting a search? Can the evidence uncovered by such an illegal search be used in a trial? In other words, can the police break the law to uphold the law? As Justice Benjamin Cardozo put it, should "the criminal . . . go free because the constable had blundered"?[90] Debates over this issue center on the creation of an **exclusionary rule,** whereby evidence gathered by illegal means cannot be used in later trials. Under another doctrine, the *fruit of the poisonous tree,* no other evidence gathered as a result of other searches or investigations based on an initially illegal search can be used either.

The exclusionary rule was created in 1914 in the case of *Weeks v. United States,*[91] which prevented federal courts from using illegally gathered evidence in a trial. This rule, it was argued, not only protected the privacy rights of the individual defendant but also deterred the authorities from conducting illegal searches in future cases. However, the rule gave rise to problems that were both legal and symbolic. In some cases it prevented the use of hard, observable evidence, thus possibly allowing guilty individuals to go free.[92]

Since the Fourth Amendment did not yet apply to the states, the exclusionary rule could be used only in federal cases. In ruling on the admissibility of illegally seized evidence in state cases, the Supreme Court used the Fourteenth Amendment's due process clause. It held that only the results of searches that "shocked the conscience" of the justices could be barred from use in trials. The problem here was that different justices were "shocked" by different things. Justice Felix Frankfurter, the inventor of this test, was "shocked" by a case in which police officers broke into the office of a doctor suspected of performing abortions to find his patient book, which would then be used in making up a list of witnesses, and by a case in which a man's stomach was pumped to retrieve two morphine capsules,[93] but not by a case involving the taking of blood from an unconscious man to determine whether he was drunk.[94] Many of Frankfurter's fellow justices disagreed with his views. Not until after Frankfurter's retirement in 1962 did the Court begin to consider extending the exclusionary rule guarantee of the Fourth Amendment to defendants in state courts.

The Due Process Revolution It was in the case of Dollree Mapp in 1961 that the Warren Court made its landmark ruling on the nature of the Fourth Amendment and its application to the states. The case began when the Cleveland police received a tip from a "reliable authority" that a "suspected bomber of a house porch and bookmaker" was in Mapp's home. When Mapp refused to let the police in, three officers broke into the house, waving a blank piece of paper in the air and claiming that it was a search warrant. After Mapp stuffed the "warrant" inside her blouse, the officers tried to retrieve it and handcuffed Mapp for resisting their search. The search through the house produced no bomber or bookmaker, but the officers arrested and the court convicted Mapp for possessing obscene materials.[95]

While this episode might have "shocked the conscience" of the justices in an earlier day, in this case the Court made the *Weeks* exclusionary rule part of the Fourth Amendment and then incorporated it into the Fourteenth Amendment to apply it to the states. By this means the exclusionary rule was made uniform among the states and between the state and federal levels of government. Mapp's conviction was reversed and her case was sent back to the state court for a retrial, but with the pornographic materials now excluded from the new trial, the state had no choice but to drop the charges.

Mapp v. Ohio
- illegal search

LITTLE-KNOWN FACT

The "reliable informant" in the Mapp case was Don King, later to become a boxing promoter and manager for heavyweight champion Mike Tyson. The "bombing suspect" King was calling about was former boxing champion Archie Moore.

exclusionary rule Rule whereby evidence that was gathered by illegal means, and any other evidence gathered as a result, cannot be used in later trials.

Limiting the Exclusionary Rule   During the Burger Court years the justices were unhappy that under the exclusionary rule even the most minor police violations resulted in the loss of all the evidence. The Court began to argue that the exclusionary rule should be restricted or eliminated, saying that it had little or no deterrent effect on police.[96] It began to question whether any possible deterrent effect of the rule outweighed the harm to society that might result from allowing guilty individuals to go free because of the exclusion from trial of improperly gathered evidence.

After limiting the use of the exclusionary rule in various criminal justice proceedings, such as the grand jury[97] and habeas corpus proceedings in which convicted defendants were seeking a new trial,[98] the Court greatly reduced its application in the 1984 case of *United States v. Leon.* Federal authorities had received a warrant to search some houses and cars for drugs on the basis of an unreliable informer's outdated tips. For the Warren Court this would have voided the search and excluded the use of its evidence. But the Burger Court ruled that since the police believed they had a valid search warrant, the resulting evidence could be used in a trial.[99] This reasoning became known as the *good faith exception* to the Fourth Amendment. "Good faith" was not defined, but the watering-down effect on the exclusionary rule was clear. Evidence that once could have been excluded was now allowed to be used if the Court was persuaded through "reasonably objective" criteria that the police believed the search to be valid.

The Rehnquist Court appears to be willing to extend the good faith exception to cases in which no search warrant was issued. In *Illinois v. Rodriguez,* for example, officers relied on the word of a woman who said that she had a right to enter her exboyfriend's apartment. Searching the apartment with her consent, they found illegal drugs. Despite the fact that the woman actually had no right to admit the police, the Court ruled that since the police had relied on her word in good faith, the search was permissible.[100]

Warrantless Searches   Another way in which the Court can affect Fourth Amendment rights is by broadening or contracting the nature of searches in which judges have not issued warrants, or warrantless searches. The Fourth Amendment defines a proper search as one in which a proper search warrant has been issued after the police have demonstrated to a neutral judge that there is **probable cause,** or enough evidence to convince a reasonable person that a search should be undertaken because a crime has been or is about to be committed, and evidence of such a crime is likely to be found at a particular location. Only then will the judge issue a warrant stating specifically what can be searched for and where the police can search. But in some cases there isn't time to obtain a warrant. To cover these cases, the amendment adds that the people are protected against unreasonable searches. The question then becomes, what is a "reasonable search"?

Suppose a police officer stops a car, suspecting that it is carrying illegal weapons. Obviously, there is no time to get a warrant. If the officer can later demonstrate that the search was "reasonable," it will be allowed under a *movable automobile exception* to the Fourth Amendment.[101] The rationale in such a case is that the officer's safety might be in jeopardy and valuable evidence might be lost if the search is delayed until after the issue of a warrant, thus allowing the car and evidence to escape. On the other hand, what if a police officer enters a private house to speak with the occupant about a problem in the neighborhood and sees a Sidewinder missile hanging above the mantel? As long as the officer can give a valid reason for being there, justifiably believes what he sees to be incriminating, and can legally proceed to that evidence, what is in "plain view" can be seized as evidence even without a warrant.

In all Fourth Amendment cases, then, the central issue is whether a suspect's "expectation of privacy" is outweighed by the state's need to control crime by preserving evidence and ensuring the safety of police officers. As the Court said in *Katz v. United States,* a case ruling electronic surveillance of public phone booths to be unconstitutional: "The Fourth Amendment protects people, not places. What a person knowingly exposes to the public, even in his own home or office, is not a subject

▲ Not all unwarranted searches and seizures are illegal or suspect. In many states it is implied that drivers have to take a breathalyzer test to check possible impairment from alcohol.

probable cause A reasonable belief that a crime has been, is being, or is about to be committed. In cases of searches there must also be a belief that evidence of that crime may be located in a particular place. Police must establish this to a judge to secure a search warrant or retroactively justify a search that has already taken place.

of Fourth Amendment protection. . . . But what he seeks to preserve as private, even in an area accessible to the public, may be constitutionally protected."[102] However, many other exceptions to the Fourth Amendment have been created, including searches incident to a lawful arrest (on the person and within the person's reach), consent searches (if the suspect permits the search, the Fourth Amendment protection is waived), searches of fleeing suspects who might destroy evidence, and various kinds of administrative searches (for example, in airports and at national borders).[103] The 2001 U.S.A. Patriot Act gave significant latitude to civil authorities in their investigations of alleged terrorism, enabling them to search multiple locations using "one stop shopping" warrants and wiretaps for all phones used by suspects (including public phones).

The pattern of expanding and contracting Fourth Amendment rights can be seen in the evolution of the *stop-and-frisk exception*. A stop-and-frisk case is one in which the police detain a person and conduct a *pat-down search* of that person's outer clothing without a warrant or an arrest, basing their action on observed, potentially criminal conduct. The Warren Court first defined the constitutional limits of such searches in 1968 in *Terry v. Ohio*, in which an experienced Ohio police officer had observed two men apparently planning to burglarize a store. The officer approached the men, asked them some questions, and then patted down their clothing; the search revealed revolvers and bullets concealed under their jackets, and the officer thereupon arrested the men. The Court ruled that even though the officer did not have probable cause to arrest the suspects for the robbery until after he had conducted a full search, the initial frisk was legal because he could justify stopping the suspects in the first place.[104]

During the Burger and Rehnquist Court years the individual's protections under the Fourth Amendment have been watered down. First, the Court has developed a notion of *reasonable suspicion* or reasonableness of a search, balancing the expectation of privacy interests of the defendant against the investigation interests of the state. In the 1985 case, *New Jersey v. T.L.O*, the Supreme Court lowered the standard for searching in public schools in a case involving the search of the purse carried by a female student, who was suspected of smoking because she was stopped after leaving a women's rest room which had smoke billowing out of its vents into the hallway. At the same time as he saw the cigarettes, the school administrator saw a package of rolling papers that led him to search further for drugs. When the subsequent search of her purse revealed other drug paraphernalia, and a large amount of money, and the search of a zipped-shut pocket in the side of the purse uncovered lists of student names with dollar amounts next to them, leading to the suspension of the student for drug sales, the Court held this to be a justifiable search because the vice-principal had "reasonable suspicion." In response to the Court's holding that there were two searches here, one justified by smoke and the other by the rolling papers, Justice William Brennan argued that there was a third search, of the zipped pocket, where the student had a greater "expectation of privacy."[105]

In 1991 the Rehnquist Court decided two cases involving stop-and-frisk searches. In the first, the Court ruled that police need only make a "show of authority" by ordering a person to halt; if the person runs away, the police have the right to "seize" the person and "search" his or her possessions.[106] In the second case, the Court allowed the practice of "working the buses," in which police officers board a bus carrying a person suspected of possessing drugs and announce that they are going to search the belongings of everyone aboard. According to Justice Sandra Day O'Connor, as long as each of the passengers feels free to decline the officers' request for a search "or otherwise terminate the encounter," such a search is legal.[107]

By 1995, the Court, speaking through Antonin Scalia, expanded the *T.L.O.* case to uphold the random drug-testing of all student athletes in Vernonia, Oregon's public schools because the "war on drugs" was a problem, and the school administration had determined that this was the only way to root out the drug culture that they believed existed in the athletic community. In dissent, Justice Sandra Day O'Connor argued that the appellant, Jamie Acton, had absolutely no history of

The Rehnquist Court: Jurists or Activists?

The Supreme Court under William Rehnquist is very different from the one under Earl Warren in the 1950s and 1960s. Gone is the Court that was willing to take the lead in the fight against the racists in the South in a search for equality for all. In its stead, the Court is now a group of professional judges seeking to reflect the norms of society. Gone is the self-consciously loud political voice calling on other institutions and the people to follow. Now the justices use restrained language and do not use eloquent language to provoke political and public support. This Court neither looks beyond the words of the Constitution nor seeks to influence the morals and mores of the nation. Gone now is the notion that the Court should act in concert with the president and Congress to end the suffering of the poor and the disenfranchised. Today, the Court uses boundaries for its power that are less protective of individual rights. The Rehnquist Court is known for a narrow interpretation of the Constitution and the federal statutes, and produces narrow legal documents rather than issuing calls to action.

"The current majority decides only the case before it, focusing on the legal contours of the problem, rather than addressing larger dilemmas or treading where the rest of the nation has not yet gone," writes Joan Biskupic of the *Washington Post*. With each new case the justices will carefully parse the words of each law to ask what Congress truly intended in passing it. The one true agenda of a majority of the Court—to curb the reach of the federal government and restore authority to the state governments—is driven by their concern that governmental structures, and not individual lives, need to be readjusted. No one is sure about the overall impact of this movement since the Court has only modestly affected Congress's overall statutory power.

The transformation of the Court is a product of our times, as well as the composition of the institution. Paramount among those reasons is the chief justice—William Rehnquist—who was appointed by Richard Nixon in 1971 as a devout conservative and rose from "the Lone Ranger," a justice speaking only for himself, to become the Chief leading the Court in 1986. While Rehnquist is a conservative, he has no active agenda and does not try to persuade his colleagues to vote with him as William Brennan and Earl Warren did in the 1960s. In 1989, Rehnquist came within an inch of writing an opinion that would, in effect, have overturned the *Roe v. Wade* abortion decision. But days before the judgment was announced, Sandra Day O'Connor switched her vote and deprived him of his majority. Unlike his predecessor, Warren Burger, who used to punish justices for such transgressions, Rehnquist did not vent any wrath on O'Connor. Rather, it was the volatile Antonin Scalia who attacked her personally in his opinion, saying that her reasoning was "not [to] be taken seriously."

While Scalia seems capable of becoming a moral activist on the Court, the rest of the justices follow a pragmatic course. Justice Ruth Bader Ginsburg describes her approach as being "rooted in the place of the judiciary in our democratic society . . . apart from the political fray." For his part, Anthony Kennedy told a group of high school students, "Do I make policy? Was I appointed for life to go around answering these great questions and suggesting answers to Congress? That's not our function. . . . And we also think it's very dangerous for people who are not elected, who have lifetime positions to begin taking public . . . stances on issues that political branches of government must wrestle with." These matters must be left to the elected legislature, the Rehnquist Court now says, a position very different from that of the Warren Court.

While the justices on this Court seem to be uncomfortable with the way that each of their opinions is dissected, and they would like to avoid doing what William Brennan and his colleagues did in trying to move the people, they can never remove themselves from the center of the action. That is the result of their constitutional task—to decide the ultimate law of the land.

Source: Based on Joan Biskupic, "They Want to Be Known as Jurists, Not Activists." *Washington Post*, January 9, 2000, p. B3.

---

drugs personally, meaning that the school lacked the "individualized suspicion" to require this test.[108] Schools across the nation began expanding their drug-testing programs beyond athletes to students in extracurricular activities, and even those students who were seeking parking privileges on school grounds. The breadth of the Court's holding was tested in 2002 in a challenge involving the program of a small town near Oklahoma City which randomly drug tested all students in any competitive extra-curricular activity (including debate, choir, school plays, and the Future Homemakers of America). Said Lindsey Earls, now a student at Dartmouth but tested in high school because she was in the marching band, "I know the Supreme Court, in the *Vernonia* case, talked about how athletes have a risk of physical harm. But we're not going to hurt ourselves in choir."[109] Here the Court ruled by a narrow 5-4 margin in that such drug testing was constitutional because it was the only way that the school officials believed that drugs could be controlled in their school district.[110] This ruling takes on even more importance given the program of drug testing all public school students in some places around the country. The Court's allowance of sweeping searches like this in public schools citing a "war on drugs" resembles the similarly sweeping searches, using other techniques, approved by the 2001 U.S.A. Patriot Act and conducted in our "war on terrorism."

Seeking to expand the police's searching powers, the Court also relied on the wording of the concurring opinion by Justice John Harlan in the *Katz* case to develop another exception to the *expectation of privacy standard*. In trying to explain why a person could justifiably expect privacy in a glass-enclosed, public phone booth, Harlan argued: "There is a twofold requirement, first that a person have exhibited an actual (subjective) expectation of privacy and, second, that the expectation be one that society is prepared to recognize as 'reasonable.'"[111] Harlan was only trying to say that the phone booth was "a temporarily private place whose momentary occupants' expectations of freedom from intrusion are recognized as reasonable." In recent years, conservative jurists have been seizing on that "societal expectation of privacy" language to argue that society would not accept the claims of other privacy rights to be reasonable.

For a crime-control oriented justice, it becomes very hard to construct a search scenario that cannot in some way be justified using these "societal expectation of privacy" or "reasonable suspicion" standards. This was made clear in 2000 when the Court ruled that running at the mere sight of a police officer in a high-crime area will justify police in stopping and searching the suspect because the act of running constituted "reasonable suspicion."[112] It appeared that this trend took a brief detour in 2001 when the Court ruled that police use of a thermal-imaging device to determine by the concentrated heat evident in one room that marijuana was being grown in a house was an "unreasonable search and seizure." For them, the Constitution's Framers would have required that a warrant be issued for such technological search advances. However, Justice Antonin Scalia also added that his decision depended on the availability of this technology to the general public, leading one to wonder whether the inevitable sale of these devices by Radio Shack, and increasing availability to the nation's firefighters, will result in a change in the Court's decision.[113] In 2002, the Court used these concepts of "reasonable suspicion" and "societal expectation of privacy" to rule on the practice of police sweeps for drugs and weapons on buses, with one officer kneeling at the front of the bus while two others worked their way forward questioning and searching passengers without first informing them that they had the right to refuse permission to be searched. The Court ruled that this practice was constitutional because under the "totality of circumstances" rule such a search would be permissible if the police wished to make a similar kind of search of a suspect off the bus.[114] All of these decisions led a special federal appeals court to rule in November 2002 that the Justice Department can apply for counter intelligence wiretaps under the U.S.A. Patriot Act.

The Fifth and Sixth Amendments

The safeguards contained in the Fifth and Sixth Amendments were designed to prevent some of the worst practices of early English criminal law, such as secret interrogation and torture. In addition to guaranteeing the right not to be compelled to be a witness against oneself in a criminal trial, the Fifth Amendment provides the right to a grand jury, protection against double jeopardy (being tried twice for the same offense), and a guarantee against state government's taking of one's property for public use without due process of law and just compensation. To the guarantee of a right to counsel in criminal cases, the Sixth Amendment adds the rights to a speedy and public trial by an impartial jury, to be informed of the nature of the charges against oneself, to be confronted with the witnesses against oneself, and to compel the appearance of witnesses in one's defense. Such safeguards are vital to a

▲ Clarence Earl Gideon, a self-described "drifter" in Florida, became the subject in 1963 of a landmark Supreme Court case that required states to provide attorneys for poor people. Gideon became one of the very few people to get his case heard by the Supreme Court on the basis of his own handwritten appeal.

Orwell's Justice: The War on Drugs and Terrorism

The Supreme Court has been paving the road for constitutionally approving the war on terrorism for years with its decisions in the war on drugs. And they have been using precedents from the Warren Court in the 1960's to accomplish this goal. Knowing how difficult it is for the police to search for tiny granules, herbs and dust-like substances, beginning in the 1980s the Court loosened the definition of "unreasonable" in "search and seizure standard" of the Fourth Amendment to allow for more investigative leeway. A policeman no longer needs "probable cause" to conduct a search without a warrant, now all that is needed is either "reasonable suspicion," meaning would a reasonable person agree with the suspicion leading to the search, (a standard used in the *Terry v. Ohio* case in 1968) or a "societal expectation of privacy," meaning would the general population agree that a person has no basis for privacy in a situation (a standard in the *U.S. v. Katz* case in 1967).

For the police these two standards have been interpreted to allow searches of any container in an automobile if the container is big enough to house the item being sought (a small sealed pill box would work for drugs), sealed opaque garbage bags on the property street corner can be searched (they are no longer the owner's property and could be opened up by roaming animals), planes and helicopters can fly over a property to search in fenced-in backyards for growing marijuana plants, and suspects can be searched if they simply run away from the police (meaning that they must have something to hide). In the helicopter case, Justice Brennan complained that this loosened Fourth Amendment would establish "George Orwell's dread vision of life in the 1980's" when he wrote: "In the far distance a helicopter skimmed down between the roofs, hovered for an instant like a bluebottle, and darted away again with a curving flight. It was the Police Patrol, snooping into people's windows." While the Court would not allow the use of thermal imaging cameras to spot marijuana hothouses in rooms within houses because this technology is not available yet to the general public, one wonders how the Court might deal with the use of remote-controlled aircraft as was used searching for the Washington sniper.

The key to these decisions is revealed in the school search cases, which in 1995 were extended to allowing drug tests of competing athletes in public high schools. For Justice Antonin Scalia it was enough to know that drugs are a problem in society, that the school administration saw drugs as a problem in their school, believed that the athletes were involved in the drug culture and should be role models, and thought that this was the only way to solve the problem. In 2002, when the Court extended permissible public school drug testing to all students involved in competitive extracurricular activities, it seemed inevitable that eventually a case would reach the High Court testing whether such a program for all students was permissible. The 2001 U.S.A. Patriot Act has laid the groundwork for an even greater range of allowable searches and seizures. Cases questioning these broader interpretations of the Fourth Amendment are sure to come to the Supreme Court in the near future.

FYI

Ernesto Miranda was retried and convicted on the basis of his girlfriend's testimony. However, after his parole, he was killed at age 34 in a barroom stabbing by an illegal alien who objected to his effort to raise the price of his autographed "Miranda cards" from one dollar to two dollars.

democratic society and constitute a basic difference between democracies and totalitarian governments.

Like all the other civil liberties discussed in this chapter, the rights of accused persons have been subject to interpretation by the Supreme Court. Before the Fifth and Sixth Amendments were applied to the states, the Court used the due process clause of the Fourteenth Amendment in deciding cases involving police interrogations.[115] In such cases the justices examined the totality of circumstances of an interrogation to determine the "voluntariness" of a confession. If the "totality of circumstances" (the conditions under which the defendant had been questioned) indicated that a confession was not voluntary, it would not be allowed in a trial. If on the other hand, the suspect had done something like flagging down a police car or walking into a station house and starting to confess before a question could be asked, or even after statements had been made by the police, the confession would be considered voluntary. "Voluntariness" was an elusive concept, defying clear measurement, however. In one case a defendant was judged to have been compelled to confess because he had been refused the right to call his wife before talking to the police.[116]

After the protections of the Fifth and Sixth Amendments were extended to the states, the Court began to explore whether a person could be compelled to

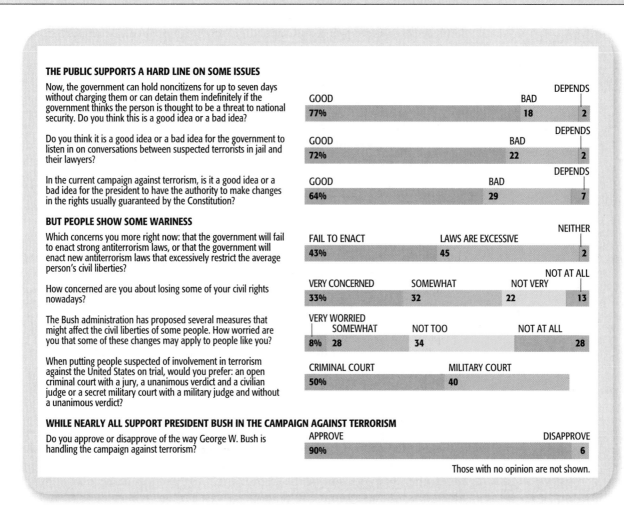

THE PUBLIC SUPPORTS A HARD LINE ON SOME ISSUES

Now, the government can hold noncitizens for up to seven days without charging them or can detain them indefinitely if the government thinks the person is thought to be a threat to national security. Do you think this is a good idea or a bad idea?

GOOD	BAD	DEPENDS
77%	18	2

Do you think it is a good idea or a bad idea for the government to listen in on conversations between suspected terrorists in jail and their lawyers?

GOOD	BAD	DEPENDS
72%	22	2

In the current campaign against terrorism, is it a good idea or a bad idea for the president to have the authority to make changes in the rights usually guaranteed by the Constitution?

GOOD	BAD	DEPENDS
64%	29	7

BUT PEOPLE SHOW SOME WARINESS

Which concerns you more right now: that the government will fail to enact strong antiterrorism laws, or that the government will enact new antiterrorism laws that excessively restrict the average person's civil liberties?

FAIL TO ENACT	LAWS ARE EXCESSIVE	NEITHER
43%	45	2

How concerned are you about losing some of your civil rights nowadays?

VERY CONCERNED	SOMEWHAT	NOT VERY	NOT AT ALL
33%	32	22	13

The Bush administration has proposed several measures that might affect the civil liberties of some people. How worried are you that some of these changes may apply to people like you?

VERY WORRIED	SOMEWHAT	NOT TOO	NOT AT ALL
8%	28	34	28

When putting people suspected of involvement in terrorism against the United States on trial, would you prefer: an open criminal court with a jury, a unanimous verdict and a civilian judge or a secret military court with a military judge and without a unanimous verdict?

CRIMINAL COURT	MILITARY COURT
50%	40

WHILE NEARLY ALL SUPPORT PRESIDENT BUSH IN THE CAMPAIGN AGAINST TERRORISM

Do you approve or disapprove of the way George W. Bush is handling the campaign against terrorism?

APPROVE	DISAPPROVE
90%	6

Those with no opinion are not shown.

Mixed Views on Civil Liberties

Source: New York Times, December 12, 2001. p. B9. Reprinted by permission of *The New York Times.*

confess simply by being confronted by the police. This question was the central issue in a 1964 case, *Escobedo v. Illinois,* in which a man had been arrested for the murder of his brother-in-law and questioned by police without being allowed to see his attorney, who was then in the police station. The Supreme Court ruled that police questioning of suspects for the purpose of gaining a confession was just as important as the trial itself. Once the police had gone beyond the general investigation phase of their interrogation by seeking to secure a confession, they had shifted "from the investigatory to the accusatory" phase, and under the Sixth and Fourteenth Amendments the suspect had the right to have counsel present.[117]

But should defendants be warned of their "right to silence," and just how far may the police go in their questioning? The answers came two years later in the case of *Miranda v. Arizona.* If you watch movies or television you have surely seen police officers recite the so-called **Miranda warning** to a suspect before questioning:

> You have the right to remain silent. Anything you say can and will be used against you. You have the right to an attorney. If you cannot afford an attorney, one will be provided for you. Do you understand these rights and are you willing to speak with us?

Miranda warning A warning that must be recited by police officers to a suspect before questioning: "You have the right to remain silent; anything you say can and will be used against you. You have the right to an attorney. If you cannot afford an attorney, one will be provided for you. Do you understand these rights and are you willing to speak with us?" Established in *Miranda v. Arizona,* 1966.

The requirement that suspects be informed of their rights stems from the *Miranda* case, in which a slightly psychotic produce worker given to flights of fantasy had confessed to a kidnapping and rape after only two hours of questioning in which the police lied in saying that the victim had identified him. The Court ruled that all police questioning was "inherently compulsory" and that confessions were therefore "inherently untrustworthy." Before questioning a suspect who had been taken into custody or "deprived of his freedom in any significant way," the police had to offer the warning just described. Otherwise, statements made by the accused could not be used in a trial or to gather related evidence.[118]

This ruling was highly controversial. It looked as if the Court was legislating new rules that would make convicting known felons impossible. In reality, the Court was just applying to the states the practices that the Federal Bureau of Investigation had long used in interrogating suspects. Still, the outcry against the "criminal-coddling Warren Court" did serious damage to the Court's prestige and led some critics to demand that the decision be reversed.

Rather than overturning *Miranda* directly, the Burger and Rehnquist Courts chipped away at its underpinnings to such an extent that very little of it remains in force. The Burger Court increased the number of situations in which confessions could be used in a trial even if the suspect had not been read the Miranda warning, such as to impeach the credibility of a witness.[119] Hints of the Court's future direction seemed to be apparent in a 1974 case called *Michigan v. Tucker* which involved a suspect who was convicted partly on the basis of an alibi witness he had named to the police in a statement that was offered without being given full observance of the *Miranda* guarantees. In the majority opinion upholding the use of the evidence, William Rehnquist argued that *Miranda* was not required by the Fifth Amendment right against self-incrimination, but merely a "prophylactic standard," or a protective device, that could be replaced by other means to safeguard the voluntariness of a suspect's statements to the police. Rehnquist seemed to be saying that if he had the votes *Miranda* could be overturned. In later cases, police were also given more leeway to encourage a suspect to confess, such as by making statements in his presence rather than questioning the suspect directly;[120] asking a suspect only where his or her weapon was located for the purposes of securing "public safety;"[121] and questioning a suspect twice, reading him or her the warning after a "voluntary" confession had been secured.[122]

For William Rehnquist, after his ascension to the Chief Justiceship, overturning the *Miranda* precedent seemed to become his personal odyssey. The Rehnquist Court seemed to be on the road toward overturning *Miranda* in the 1991 case of *Arizona v. Fulminante,* in which a prisoner confessed to the murder of his stepdaughter to a prison inmate who offered to protect him from harm but was in fact working as an informer with the FBI. The Court ruled that such confessions, even this arguably involuntary one because the defendant did not realize that he was speaking to an agent of the police, could be used in trials.[123]

In 2000, the Court and Chief Justice Rehnquist were presented with the opportunity to reconsider *Miranda* directly in the case of Charles Thomas Dickerson. Dickerson was interrogated by an FBI agent in January 1997 about a bank robbery in Alexandria, Virginia. After a few hours of questioning, Dickerson admitted that he knew about the robbery. While the officer said that the *Miranda* warnings had been given before the incriminating statement was made, Dickerson said that the warnings came after he had made his statement—meaning that the confession should be invalidated.

This case tested the constitutionality of Section 3501 of Title 18 of the United States Code, called the Omnibus Crime Control and Safe Streets Act, which was passed just two years after *Miranda* and stated that confessions could be admitted into federal trials if they were given "voluntarily," based on an examination of the "totality of circumstances" of the questioning. While this contradicted Chief Justice Earl Warren's argument that any questioning by police was "inherently compulsory," it was widely anticipated that Chief Justice Rehnquist, and the conservative majority, would take this opportunity to overturn *Miranda*.

To the surprise of many, the Court upheld the *Miranda* case by a 7 to 2 vote, with even its most vocal critic, Chief Justice Rehnquist, voting with the majority and writing the opinion. In overturning Section 3501, Justice Rehnquist argued as the Court did in the *City of Boerne Free Exercise of Religion* case that, "*Miranda*, being a constitutional decision of this Court, may not be in effect overruled by an act of Congress." Rehnquist further explained that the *Miranda* warnings should continue because they "have become part of our national culture" and have "become embedded in routine police practice." Since the warnings caused no measurable difficulties for prosecutors, there was no reason to overturn the case.[124] Just why the Chief Justice wrote the majority opinion in this way is not clear, but while *Miranda* still exists as a legal precedent, studies have found that police continually search for ways to avoid having suspects "lawyer up" in their questioning.[125]

In sum, while most of the basic rights of accused persons are protected in the Fourth, Fifth, and Sixth Amendments, the full nature and precise limits of those rights are subject to judicial interpretation. This tension between the rights of the accused and the safety of the public makes the civil liberties of defendants a source of continuing debate.

The Expanding Nature of Implied Rights

Are there rights beyond those set forth in the language of the Bill of Rights that should be safeguarded against governmental intrusion? If so, what are they, and what are their limits? These are difficult questions that involve moral and ethical positions as well as legal and constitutional judgments.

Privacy

The right of privacy is not explicitly mentioned in the Constitution. Is this right implied in the Fourth Amendment's protection against "unreasonable searches and seizures"? Or did the framers intend it to be one of the "rights retained by the people" in the Ninth Amendment? Or was it so obvious and important that it did not need to be mentioned at all? And, assuming that such a right exists, what exactly does it encompass?

These issues were explored in a landmark 1965 case, *Griswold v. Connecticut,* in which Estelle T. Griswold, the director of a New Haven birth control clinic opened by the Connecticut Planned Parenthood League, was charged with violating a state statute that prohibited the use, and medical counseling about the use, of birth control.[126] This law had been passed in response to the concerns of its author, the entrepreneur P. T. Barnum, who wished to control the spread of adultery and unsavory diseases.[127] Private citizens, however, argued that the state had no business regulating personal conduct in the bedroom, especially the marital bedroom.

The Supreme Court ruled that the behavior of married people in their bedrooms is protected by the right of privacy. According to Justice William O. Douglas, such a right, while not explicitly stated, can be seen in the "penumbras, formed by emanations," or shadows of shadows, of the First, Third, Fourth, Fifth, and Ninth Amendments; these, he said, create several "zones of privacy." To dissenting justices and students of law, this statement was somewhat confusing, in that the right of privacy could be glimpsed in several amendments but was not stated in any of them. Many felt that Douglas was inserting his own value preferences into the Constitution. Three months after the decision, Griswold and Dr. Lee Buxton reopened their New Haven birth control clinic. The Griswold decision has stood as the basis for the expansion of privacy rights, to the dismay of judicial conservatives and self-restraint advocates such as Robert Bork, who do not support rights that are not explicitly written into the Constitution and its amendments.[128]

QUOTE … UNQUOTE

"We do not sit as a super-legislature to determine the wisdom, need, and propriety of laws that touch economic problems, business affairs, or social conditions."

Justice William O. Douglas, *Griswold v. Connecticut* (1965)

Once privacy became an accepted part of constitutional interpretation, many additional rights could be created. It was not long before the right of privacy was extended to unmarried persons.[129] This constitutional privacy right became a central element in debates over rights related to abortion, homosexuality, AIDS, drug testing, and euthanasia. And, when states began the process of threatening this right to privacy by trying to remove legal and constitutional protection for those pursuing alternative lifestyles—in this case by passing a state constitutional amendment in Colorado forbidding localities from enacting ordinances outlawing discrimination against gays and lesbians—the Supreme Court made clear in *Romer v. Evans* in 1996 that such action was not constitutional. As Justice Anthony Kennedy said in arguing

APPROACHING DIVERSITY

Courting Justice: Gay Rights and the Supreme Court

Securing the protections for gays and lesbians promised by the *Carolene Products* footnote in 1938 has not been an easy road. Since 1957 gays have been before the Supreme Court seeking justice, but early on it was without success. Following an initial victory in 1958 ruling that *One* magazine, a gay magazine, was not pornographic and could thus be shipped through the U.S. mails, for nearly 30 years of the Court avoided rulings on this topic until 1987, when the best opportunity for gays and lesbians to have the Court extend to them the same privacy rights that had been extended in previous cases to married and single heterosexual individuals and couples came in the case of *Bowers v. Hardwick*.

▲ James Dale, who was expelled as an assistant scoutmaster of a New Jersey Boy Scout troop ten years ago because he was gay, saw his discrimination case go all the way to the Supreme Court. The Court ruled in favor of the Boy Scouts, arguing that under the First Amendment Freedom of Association the organization could set the requirements for membership.

On July 5, 1982, twenty-eight-year-old Michael Hardwick, a bartender at a gay nightclub in Atlanta known as The Cove, was cited by officer Keith Torrick for having an open container of liquor. "I'm counting on you to show up [in court]. If you don't, I'll take it that you're laughing in my face. And I will come find you. And I will lock you up," promised Torrick. Several hours after Hardwick failed to appear in court, Torrick went to Hardwick's house to serve the arrest warrant. As soon as Hardwick learned what had happened, he raced down to the court clerk's office, paid the $50 fine, and forgot about the incident.

Three weeks later, however, Officer Torrick came to the door once more with the arrest warrant. A houseguest told Torrick to 'look around' for the owner. So Torrick marched down the hall, found the back bedroom door slightly ajar, looked in, and saw Hardwick having sex with his male lover. Torrick then arrested Hardwick for violating Georgia Code Section 16-6-2, which outlaws sodomy.

For gay organizations this became the perfect opportunity to challenge Georgia's antisodomy law, and similar laws in twenty-three other states, and show that such laws violate constitutional guarantees of privacy. The Supreme Court had established the privacy rights of married couples and unmarried heterosexual couples; the hope was that such precedents would be extended to homosexual couples.

But Fulton County district attorney Lewis Slaton was not willing to give the ACLU this opportunity. He dropped the charges after the initial hearing on the case. Hardwick and the ACLU were not ready to give up, though, and filed a civil suit asking for a declaratory judgment, or a legal pronouncement that Georgia's law was an unconstitutional violation of the privacy rights safeguarded by the U.S. Constitution. What had begun as an encounter between a cop and a bartender was now a nationally prominent court case.

After Hardwick won in both the district court and the U.S. court of appeals, Georgia appealed to the Supreme Court. The case, *Bowers v. Hardwick*, was accepted by the Court for review. As with many cases in the deeply divided Burger Court, the result hinged on the vote of centrist Justice Lewis Powell. The initial vote was 5 to 4 to overturn the antisodomy law, with liberal justice Harry Blackmun assigned to write the opinion.

that this was a violation of the equal protection clause of the Fourteenth Amendment: "We must conclude that Amendment 2 [to the Colorado constitution] classifies homosexuals not to further a proper legislative end but to make them unequal to everyone else. This Colorado cannot do."[130]

Protection for gays was changed dramatically in 2000 at both the state and federal levels. Voters in California passed Proposition 22 which denied the protections for married couples to same-sex partners who had been married in other states. As we saw in Chapter 3, though, Vermont passed a law allowing same-sex couples to receive legal protections by creating "civil unions." That same year the U.S. Supreme Court ruled in a New Jersey case that the Boy Scouts could keep gays from being

The Blackmun majority viewed this as a privacy case, arguing that the nature of an individual's private, consensual sexual activity should be left to the individual, not to the government. The minority, led by Byron White, viewed this not as a case dealing with privacy but as one dealing with homosexual sodomy, which they argued was already banned as a criminal activity in twenty-four states. Powell had provided the fifth vote for overturning the law, saying he was troubled by the prospect of a twenty-year jail sentence for violation of this Georgia law. Several days later, though, Powell changed his vote. The reason, scholars have now learned, is that Powell, who thought he had never met a gay person even though one book has reported that several of his law clerks had been gay, gave the case for analysis to Michael Mosman, a conservative Mormon who was married with three children, rather than Carter Cabell Chinnis, Jr. a more moderate conservative law clerk who was also gay.* Powell reasoned from the fact that Hardwick's criminal case had been dropped and he was merely suing to test the antisodomy law. As a result, the votes swung to the conservatives, and White, now speaking for the majority, upheld Georgia's law, arguing that the Constitution does not confer a fundamental right of privacy to homosexuals engaging in sodomy. The four-justice dissent, led by Blackmun, responded that if the constitutional right to privacy means anything, it means that Georgia cannot prosecute its citizens for private consensual sexual activity.

The ruling on privacy rights puzzled many, with the *New York Times* titling its account: "60 Years of Expansion Interrupted by Ruling." The gay community reacted to the decision with great distress. But several months later, Jeff Levi, executive director of the National Gay and Lesbian Task Force, noted that his organization was receiving an outpouring of public support and funds and said, "Five to ten years down the line, we may thank Byron White for writing that opinion."** A few years later, Justice Powell admitted to an audience that he now regretted his decision in this case: "I think I probably made a mistake in that one. When I had the opportunity to reread the opinions. . . . I thought the dissents had the better of the arguments."†

Initially, these words seemed to be prophetic. When the Court later reviewed "Amendment 2" of the Colorado Constitution, which prohibited all governmental protection at either the state or the local level for gays and lesbians, it overturned this provision because "the amendment imposes a special disability upon those persons alone," an action which is "unprecedented in our jurisprudence."†† Having now ruled in both directions, the road to democracy for gays continued in the 1999 Supreme Court term, when it accepted the New Jersey case of *Boy Scouts of America v. Dale*. The New Jersey Supreme Court had ruled here that the Boy Scouts could not exclude a gay troop leader because it would violate the state laws that prohibit discrimination, making it the first state high court to so rule. The State Court had ruled that the Boy Scouts were a public enterprise, open to all boys, and as such could not discriminate based on sexual orientation. The Boy Scouts responded that their code of conduct requires "morally straight" behavior, so the inclusion of gays violates their First Amendment right to establish the message of their organization and freely associate as they wish. The Court ruled that the Boy Scouts program could exclude people based on sexual orientation because forcing it to do otherwise against the tenets of the organization would violate the group's freedom of association. For Chief Justice Rehnquist, it was "the freedom not to associate."††

The next landmark case will be decided in 2003 as *Lawrence v. Texas* gives the justices the chance to consider reversing *Bowers* when it hears Texas' ban on same-sex sodomy. In recent years many states, including Georgia, have already repealed or found unconstitutional their laws banning this practice.

*This box relies on the excellent volume; Joyce Murdoch and Deb Price, *Court Justice: Gay Men and Lesbians v. the Supreme Court*, (New York: Basic Books, 2001); Art Harris "The Unintended Battle of Michael Hardwick," *Washington Post*, August 21, 1986, p. 1, 4.

**Lisa Leif, "Gay Cause Is Gaining Attention, Leaders Say," *Washington Post*, August 26, 1986, p. 21.

†Quoted in John C. Jeffries, Jr., *Justice Lewis E. Powell, Jr: A Biography*, (New York: Charles Scribner's Sons, 1994), p. 530.

††*Boy Scouts of America v. Dale*, 530 US 640 (2000).

scout leaders. For the Court, opposition to homosexuality is part of the group's "expressive message." So the organization's Freedom of Association overrode the gay scout leader's right to privacy.[131]

Abortion

If the constitutional right of privacy allows people to choose to prevent conception, does it also allow them to terminate a pregnancy after conception? Before 1973 states were free to set restrictions on a woman's right to obtain an abortion, and many banned abortion entirely. As a result of differences in state laws, vast numbers of women went across state lines or out of the country to obtain abortions, and many others placed themselves in the hands of dangerous "back-alley" abortionists to terminate unwanted pregnancies.

In the 1973 case of *Roe v. Wade* the Supreme Court reviewed a Texas law that limited a woman's right to obtain an abortion. The Court ruled that the right of privacy gave a woman the right to obtain an abortion. But as with all rights, limitations could be placed on the exercise of this right. Those limitations were dictated by the interests of others—in this case, the right of the state to protect the health of the mother and the rights of the unborn fetus.[132]

The rights of the unborn fetus were the focal point in the *Roe* case. Some religious groups argue that the fetus is a living human being; for them, therefore, abortion constitutes murder. Other groups use the findings of medical science to argue that life begins when a fetus can be sustained by medical technology outside the mother's womb; this argument leads to a different set of limitations on the abortion procedure. Opposed to both of these arguments are those who claim that because the right of privacy gives a woman the unfettered right to control her own body, a woman has a right to choose to have an abortion.

In his majority opinion Justice Harry Blackmun attempted to strike a balance among these competing arguments by segmenting the term of the pregnancy into three trimesters. In the first three months, the woman has an absolute right to obtain an abortion, and the state has no legitimate interest in controlling a routine medical procedure. In the second trimester, the interests of the state become more important as the abortion procedure becomes more risky; thus, states may regulate abortions to ensure the woman's safety, but not to the extent of eliminating them. In the final three months, when the fetus has become viable and has interests that must be safeguarded, abortions can be banned completely.

▶ The matter of abortion arouses intense feelings in both pro-life and pro-choice advocates, such as these women engaged in a violent argument at a pro-life demonstration.

Roe left open a number of questions. As medical technology advances and fetuses can survive outside the womb earlier, can abortions be banned at an earlier stage of pregnancy? On the other hand, will the line move in the other direction as medical technology also makes abortions safer at later stages of pregnancy? And what will happen as new reproductive technologies make it possible for a fetus to develop outside of the womb?

Since the *Roe* decision some states, such as Louisiana, Utah, Ohio, and Pennsylvania, have limited and regulated abortions in various ways, including requiring notification of the parents of minors seeking abortions, establishing rules for determining which physicians and facilities are qualified to perform abortions, requiring notification of prospective fathers, and requiring a woman to follow a series of steps to inform herself about the nature of abortions before undergoing the procedure.

At the federal level, the debate has centered on whether government medical assistance to the poor should cover the cost of abortions. Opponents of abortion argue that public funds should not be used to pay for a procedure that some taxpayers find objectionable. Since 1976 Congress has passed various measures limiting federal assistance for abortions except in cases of rape or incest and when the health of the mother is in jeopardy. Some states have followed suit. In 1980 the Supreme Court upheld these restrictions, essentially denying poor women their constitutional right to obtain an abortion.[133]

Initially, the Burger Court was inclined to strike down restrictions such as the requirement that a woman's husband, or her parents if she is a minor, be informed if she seeks an abortion.[134] In 1983, the Court further reaffirmed the *Roe* decision in a case involving a number of regulations passed by the city of Akron, Ohio. The Court ruled that laws regulating abortion must be designed to protect the health of the mother. Justice Sandra Day O'Connor dissented, arguing that the Court should be concerned only with whether the law represents an "undue burden," or a severe obstacle, on the right to obtain an abortion.[135]

The Rehnquist Court has considered several cases involving abortion, beginning with the 1989 case of *Webster v. Reproductive Health Services*. The state of Missouri had passed one of the most restrictive of all state abortion laws: physicians performing abortions more than five months into the pregnancy were required to determine whether the fetus was viable; public employees or facilities could not be used to perform abortions; and public funds could not be spent to counsel women to seek abortions. The appointments of Justices Antonin Scalia and Anthony Kennedy had created an activist-conservative Court that seemed to have the votes to overturn the *Roe* decision; however, Justice O'Connor was still unwilling to do so. Thus, the Court upheld all the components of the Missouri law but allowed *Roe* to remain in force.[136]

In 1992 the abortion issue again came before the Court, this time in a case dealing with a restrictive Pennsylvania statute. In a surprising action three jurists—O'Connor, Kennedy, and Souter—broke from their conservative colleagues and wrote a centrist opinion upholding *Roe* because of its long-standing value as a precedent.[137] Shortly thereafter, two judges who seemed to support abortion rights—Ruth Bader Ginsburg and Stephen Breyer—were appointed to the Court. For the moment, the right to obtain an abortion, though restricted in some instances, seemed safe. This was further demonstrated in 1998, when the Supreme Court refused to rule on a federal court decision voiding a ban in Ohio on late-term abortions. Thus, the federal courts blocked state versions of legislation that was twice passed by Congress and twice vetoed by President Clinton.[138] Pro-abortion advocates won a major victory in June 2000 when the Court declared a Nebraska law, similar to ones in thirty other states, banning partial-birth (late-term) abortions to be unconstitutional as well. Still, the narrow 5–4 vote and the problems with the wording of this law make it uncertain whether the court would strike down future laws of this type.[139]

Given the president's view on this issue—George W. Bush is pro-life—and the likelihood of one or more new appointments to the Court in the near future, the Court's rulings could change dramatically in the future.

▲ This representative of the Hemlock Society, which advocates legal choice of suicide, leads a demonstration on behalf of Dr. Jack Kevorkian. For these demonstrators, the choice to end a life is just another form of personal privacy.

The Right to Die

As advances in medical technology allow people to live longer, questions arise about the quality of life experienced by those who are kept alive by artificial means. Should relatives and loved ones be allowed to turn off the life-support systems of critically ill patients? On another front, the efforts of a Detroit doctor, Jack Kevorkian, to assist the suicides of terminally ill patients raised the question of whether people have a right to conduct their own mercy killing.

During its 1989 term the Supreme Court heard arguments in the case of a Missouri woman, Nancy Cruzan, who had been in a coma for several years and was being kept alive by life-support equipment; because there was no hope that she would recover, her parents sought to have the life support removed. The Court ruled that because the state of Missouri requires clear and convincing evidence that a person maintained on life support would not wish to be kept alive by such means, the life-support system could not be disconnected in the absence of such evidence. However, Chief Justice Rehnquist noted that "the principle that a competent person has a constitutionally protected liberty interest in refusing unwanted medical treatment may be inferred from our prior decisions."[140]

Are physician-assisted suicides equivalent to murder, or do they simply represent the ultimate individual right stemming from the right of privacy? The Court refused in two cases in 1997 to find in the Constitution a "fundamental liberty" of the right to die. Thus states were permitted to decide for themselves whether to allow physician-assisted suicides. Laws in Washington and New York forbidding this practice were allowed to stand.[141] However, a majority of the Court seemed to indicate in these cases that they might in the future be willing to hear an appeal from a terminally ill patient who is suffering greatly and is seeking the right to end his or her life. Perhaps at that time the Court will rule in favor of this practice.

As the composition of the Court has changed, so have the decisions of the justices and, hence, the nature of the protections and limitations on individual rights. In the area of civil liberties, the United States has traveled a considerable distance in approaching democracy, but with each new controversy we can see that it has a way yet to travel. Only the continued interest of the citizenry in their constitutional

---

DEMOCRACY IN THE NEW MILLENNIUM

Preserving DNA Privacy?

Imagine that you are an insurance agency faced with the prospect of having to pay off on future claims for carpal tunnel syndrome. Wouldn't you like to figure out who might be prone to this disease and then find a way to deny them coverage in the first place? That prospect has arisen because of the development of two seemingly unrelated technological advances—the evolution of computer data bases and the scientific race to map the human DNA—and a change in the Bush administration's medical privacy guidelines. On March 21, 2002, the Bush administration proposed an alteration in a Clinton administration federal safeguard that required written permission from patients before their medical information was disclosed to doctors, hospitals, pharmacies and insurance companies. The new regulations would only require that users of your medical information notify you that they have done so.

How does this help the insurance company? By using information gathered as a result of the race between the Human Genome Project and the Celera company to map the human DNA, insurance companies could learn which genes lead to a tendency to develop certain diseases. Then they can match that up to patients who are seeking insurance coverage. So, after learning what genetic trait causes carpal tunnel syndrome, the insurance company can investigate your medical information, based on prior blood tests and examinations, determine that you have a tendency to develop that disease, and then deny you coverage on that basis.

For more information see: www.lbl.gov, www.cuinfo.cornell.edu/CPL/privacy.htm, and www.ornl.gov.

Note: With thanks to Lafayette student Adam Glickman for providing the idea for this feature.

rights, by their votes for the president and senators who choose and confirm the judges and their continued interest in the Court's rulings, helps to ensure that the evolution toward democracy over the last two centuries (but mainly the last 65 years) will continue.

SUMMARY

1. Although the terms civil liberties and civil rights are often used interchangeably, they are not synonymous. Civil liberties are the individual freedoms and rights that are guaranteed to every citizen by the Bill of Rights and the due process clause of the Fourteenth Amendment. Civil rights are concerned with protection of citizens against discrimination because of characteristics such as gender, race, ethnicity, or disability and are derived largely from the equal protection clause of the Fourteenth Amendment.

2. The history of civil liberties is one of gradual expansion of the degree of protection provided by the Bill of Rights. This evolution occurred initially through a series of Supreme Court decisions that applied portions of the first ten amendments to the states, thereby protecting citizens against state action in relation to specific individual rights. Those decisions centered on the question of incorporation of the Bill of Rights into the Fourteenth Amendment. Later cases then expanded the protection of these guarantees by judicial interpretation.

3. The Court's process of applying the Bill of Rights to the states by incorporating some, but not all of them, into the Fourteenth Amendment due process clause was a slow one. Between 1884 and 1925 the Court refused to apply most of them, saying that they were not "fundamental principles lying at the base of our civil and political institutions." In 1937 the Court began the process of "selective incorporation" by ruling that some of these rights were "implicit in the concept of ordered liberty." The real incorporation revolution, though, did not occur until the 1960s. Now, all but five parts of the Bill of Rights have been incorporated.

4. Issues involving freedom of religion are of two main types: those involving establishment, or governmental preference for one religion over others, and those involving free exercise or individual religious practices. In deciding whether certain governmental actions would have the effect of establishing a religion, the Supreme Court has searched for the proper balance between complete separation of church and state, known as the high wall of separation doctrine, and government accommodation, in which the government would be allowed to assist religious organizations indirectly and in a neutral manner. In deciding free exercise cases, the Court's protection of religious freedom against state regulation has varied depending on which justices have been on the Court when various cases were considered.

5. In cases involving freedom of speech, the Court has ruled in ways that protect certain kinds of speech but not others. Political speech is protected if it is not likely to incite imminent lawless action. Public speech is protected unless it consists of fighting words or can be shown to create a dangerous situation. Symbolic speech such as flag burning is also protected.

6. Issues involving freedom of the press hinge on the balance between the public's right to know and other rights, such as the government's right to secrecy or an individual's right to personal reputation. The Supreme Court has tended to rule against the state in cases of prior restraint, or censorship before publication, but not in cases of punishment after publication. In ruling on charges of libel, or the publication of statements that are untruthful and damaging to a person's reputation, the Court requires evidence of actual malice or reckless disregard for the truth. Cases involving obscenity have been most problematic because of the extreme difficulty of defining obscenity.

7. Many early debates over the Fourth Amendment's ban on unreasonable searches centered on the creation of an exclusionary rule whereby evidence gathered by illegal means cannot be used in later trials. Later, by defining "unreasonable searches" the Supreme Court has alternately expanded and limited the application of the Fourth Amendment; while generally protecting suspects against unreasonable searches, it has permitted a variety of exceptions that give the police some leeway in the methods used to obtain evidence.

8. The Fifth and Sixth Amendments contain several provisions designed to protect the rights of defendants. Of these, the most controversial have to do with the right to silence governing confessions resulting from police questioning. Since 1966 police officers have been required to read the so-called Miranda warning to suspects before questioning them; if they do not, statements made by the accused cannot be used in a trial. In recent years, however, the Court has increased the number of exceptions to this rule, and the absence of the Miranda warning will no longer result in the automatic overturning of a conviction.

9. The right of privacy is not explicitly mentioned in the Constitution, but the Supreme Court has ruled that such a right is implied by the wording of several provisions in the Bill of Rights. This right has been extended to cover a woman's right to obtain an abortion in the first three months of pregnancy. The Court has, however, allowed states to place certain restrictions on abortion. The right of privacy has also been extended to cover the right to die in cases involving patients kept alive by life-support equipment, provided that there is evidence that the patient would not have wished to be kept alive by such means.

KEY TERMS

civil liberties	selective incorporation	subsequent punishment
civil rights	*Lemon* test	slander
double standard	secular regulation rule	libel
incorporation	least restrictive means test	exclusionary rule
no incorporation	fighting words	probable cause
total incorporation	hate speech	Miranda warning
clear and present danger test	symbolic speech	
double jeopardy	prior restraint	

POLISIM ACTIVITY

Civil Liberties

In this simulation you are the Mayor of the City. You will have to make decisions and policies for a number of situations dealing with civil liberties. The City has been in an uproar over political events lately. When political conflict occurs, you are expected to keep public order and at the same time respect the civil liberties of the people involved. The toughest part about being the Mayor of the City is that the City newspaper has little to write about other than your latest actions, especially the mistakes. Good luck trying to control conflict while guarding everyone's rights.

SUGGESTED READINGS

ABRAHAM, HENRY J., and BARBARA A. PERRY. *Freedom and the Court: Civil Rights and Liberties in the United States.* 7th ed. New York: Oxford University Press, 1998. A comprehensive and highly readable survey of the Supreme Court's development of civil rights and liberties in the United States since the 1930s.

ALDERMAN, ELLEN, and CAROLINE KENNEDY. *In Our Defense: The Bill of Rights in Action.* New York: Avon Books, 1991. A timely journalistic account of the background and outcome of several cases covered by the first ten amendments.

CRAY, ED. *Chief Justice: A Biography of Earl Warren.* New York: Simon & Schuster, 1997. An eminently readable and informed biography of one of the greatest chief justices of all time and the man who presided over the Court that is responsible for many of our civil liberties and rights today.

FRIENDLY, FRED W., and MARTHA J. H. ELLIOTT. *The Constitution, That Delicate Balance: Landmark Cases That Shaped the Constitution.* New York: Random House, 1984. A fascinating account of sixteen major cases in civil liberties. Designed as a companion volume to the excellent videotape PBS series by the same name.

GARROW, DAVID, JR. *Liberty and Sexuality: The Right to Privacy and the Making of Roe v. Wade.* New York: Macmillan, 1994. A superb historical study of the Supreme Court's development of the right to privacy from *Griswold v. Connecticut* through *Roe v. Wade.*

JEFFRIES, JOHN C., JR. *Justice Lewis F. Powell: A Biography.* New York: Scribner's, 1994. A wonderful biography of the justice who served as the "swing member" on the contentious Burger Court and was responsible for so many crucial decisions and nondecisions.

LAZARUS, EDWARD. *Closed Chambers.* New York: Times Books, 1998. A fascinating account of life on the Supreme Court in the 1988–89 term by a Blackmun law clerk, revealing the role of the clerks in the production of opinions that year.

LEWIS, ANTHONY. *Gideon's Trumpet.* New York: Vintage Press, 1966. Still the best one-volume account of a single Supreme Court case, in this instance the *Gideon v. Wainwright* case, which extended the right to counsel protections of the Sixth Amendment to state criminal defendants.

———. *Make No Law: The Sullivan Case and the First Amendment.* New York: Random House, 1991. An account of the development of the *New York Times v. Sullivan* case, in which the Supreme Court established the standards for libel by the press in cases involving public figures.

MURDOCH, JOYCE and DEB PRICE. *Courting Justice: Gay Men and Lesbians v. the Supreme Court.* New York: Basic Books, 2001. A highly readable history of the Supreme Court's effort to avoid and then mishandle the issue of gay rights in cases throughout the decades.

MURPHY, BRUCE ALLEN. *Wild Bill: The Legend and Life of William O. Douglas.* New York: Random House, 2003. A biography of the most controversial Justice, and advocate of civil liberties, ever to have served on the Supreme Court.

NEWMAN, ROGER. *Hugo Black: A Biography.* New York: Pantheon Books, 1994. A fine biography of the justice who fought for so many years to implement his vision of an absolute and literal reading of the Bill of Rights.

O'BRIEN, DAVID M. *Constitutional Law and Politics.* Vol. 2, *Civil Rights and Civil Liberties.* New York: Norton, 1997. An excellent casebook containing cuttings of Supreme Court cases mixed with historical information and comprehensive charts showing the development of case law.

PRITCHETT, C. HERMAN. *Constitutional Civil Liberties.* Englewood Cliffs, N.J.: Prentice Hall, 1984. A complete survey of all of the case law in civil liberties broken down by amendment and subcategories within each amendment.

REHNQUIST, WILLIAM H. *All the Laws But One: Civil Liberties in Wartime.* New York: Alfred A. Knopf, 1998. A very readable history of the Supreme Court's unwillingness to protect civil liberties and civil rights during times of crisis, because "In time of war the laws are silent."

ROSEN, JEFFREY. *The Unwanted Gaze: The Destruction of Privacy in America.* New York: Random House, 2000. An interesting and disturbing examination of our loss of privacy, and control over the use of our personal information, on the computer and in cyberspace.

SAVAGE, DAVID G. *Turning Right: The Making of the Rehnquist Supreme Court.* New York: Wiley, 1992. A well-researched journalistic, behind-the-scenes account by the *Wall Street Journal's* court reporter on the effort by the Rehnquist Court to shape legal doctrine in the civil rights and liberties area.

SIMON, JAMES F. *The Center Holds: The Power Struggles Inside the Rehnquist Court.* New York: Simon & Schuster, 1995. An interesting account of the decision-making process of the current Supreme Court during the service of Chief Justice William Rehnquist.

THOMAS, ANDREW PEYTON. *Clarence Thomas: A Biography.* San Francisco: Encounter Books, 2001. An expansive full-length biography of the most elusive and enigmatic Justice now on the Supreme Court.

WEINREB, LLOYD L. *Leading Constitutional Cases on Criminal Justice.* Westbury, N.Y.: Foundation Press, 2001. A superb casebook on criminal justice cases illustrating the development of legal doctrine in each of the amendments.

14

CIVIL RIGHTS AND POLITICAL EQUALITY

CHAPTER OUTLINE

Approaching Democracy Case Study: Divided We Stand: Whither Affirmative Action?

Introduction: Civil Rights and Democracy

Establishing Constitutional Equality

Creating Legal Segregation

Establishing Legal Equality

The Civil Rights Movement

Affirmative Action

Women's Rights

Civil Rights and Other Minorities

Emerging Minority Groups Seek Prominence

Civil Rights and the War on Terrorism

Civil Rights and Approaching Democracy

APPROACHING DEMOCRACY CASE STUDY

Divided We Stand: Whither Affirmative Action?

All Barbara Grutter and Jennifer Gratz wanted was to attend the University of Michigan, but their desires may go down in history as the strongest legal cases testing affirmative action in America. Grutter, a white professional woman with children, had applied to the University Michigan law school, and Jennifer Gratz, a white co-ed, had applied to the undergraduate program at the University of Michigan. When they were denied admission and similarly credentialed minorities were accepted, Grutter and Gratz filed lawsuits alleging race discrimination.

Their lawsuits might well give the Supreme Court a chance to rule for the first time since 1978 on whether affirmative action programs should continue in educational institutions across the nation.

For years affirmative action programs have been restricted in this area. "The status of student body diversity as a compelling interest justifying a racial preference in university admissions is an open question," wrote Judge Stanley Marcus, an 11th Circuit Court of Appeals judge in a case striking down the University of Georgia's use of race as a slight advantage (about one-half of a point in the ratings) for applicants in its college admissions decisions. And, he added, that the issue "is one that, because of its great importance, warrants consideration by the Supreme Court." Indeed, federal judges cannot agree on the constitutionality of affirmative action either among or even within appellate circuits.

Thus, while the University of Georgia chose to change its admission process rather than to appeal the decision, the time may well come for the Supreme Court to weigh in on the issue of affirmative action in cases coming from the University of Michigan, a school with no history of discrimination. In fact its affirmative action admissions program is one of the strongest in the nation. Indeed, a study from 1995 to 2000 showed that a minority student had a 234.5 times greater chance of being admitted to the University of Michigan law school than a majority student, and minority students were given an extra 20 points out of 150 required in the admissions process. The federal district courts disagreed on how to rule in these cases. One federal district court judge ruled in Grutter's suit that the law school's affirmative action program violated the constitution because "a racially diverse student population . . . is not a compelling state interest," and "even if it were, the law school has not narrowly tailored its use of race to achieve that interest." Meanwhile, another federal district court judge ruled in Gratz's case that the undergraduate affirmative action program was constitutional because it provided diversity in the class that benefited the educational process. Both cases were then sent to the Sixth Circuit Court of Appeals.

The precedents nationally had been to greatly limit or end affirmative action programs. In 1999, voters in Washington passed the state Civil Rights Act that ended affirmative action in that state for both African Americans and women. The Federal Appeals Court in the Fifth Circuit voted in 2001 in the case of Cheryl Hopwood to end affirmative action in the Texas law school by saying that race could not be used as a factor in admissions. Following that, the Texas attorney general, Dan Morales, ruled that race would no longer be used as a basis for admissions to undergraduate schools or for scholarship programs in that state. Shortly thereafter, voters in California passed Proposition 209, which ended affirmative action in state hiring, education

programs, and government contracts based on race, sex, or ethnic origins. Seeking "to restore true color-blind fairness," the Regents of California's state university system eliminated affirmative action programs in graduate and, later, in undergraduate admissions decisions. Politicians moved quickly to adjust to the new legal climate. Then Governor George W. Bush of Texas and Governor Gray Davis of California, both announced affirmative action programs would end in state schools in favor of guaranteed admission for varying percentages of top students from the state regardless of race. In November 1999, Florida Governor Jeb Bush inaugurated by executive order his "One Florida" program. This program would guarantee admission to state colleges and universities to the top 20 percent of graduating seniors in the state, increase financial aid and test preparation assistance for poor students, and end the "racial set-aside" programs for minorities seeking government contracts. "The time has come to eliminate these legally suspect practices, that never fully achieved their purpose to begin with," said Governor Jeb Bush. By doing this, the governor had derailed the statewide vote on affirmative action.

Bush's action caused a storm of controversy in Florida. African American leaders protested, two African American legislators staged a sit-in in the lieutenant governor's office in the Capitol, and in March 2000, thousands of protesters marched at the Capitol to protest the plan while Bush was giving his State of the State address. But the governor was undaunted. "By September," said Jeb Bush, "what you will see is an increased number of students attending our university systems and an increased number of African Americans and Hispanics attending the university system. That's the synthesis of what this rule is about." Indeed, by the early fall of 2001

▲ Jennifer Gratz's suit against the University of Michigan, challenging its affirmative action undergraduate admissions program, could have historic consequences.

489

the "One Florida" program appeared to be sustaining the minority admissions rate in the Florida State School system, with the ten universities and New College in the state enrolling 5% more minorities. But at the same time, when the University of Florida decided to stop awarding any race-based scholarships, it was revealed that the school was running nearly 5% behind its normal rate of admission of minority students.

The University of Michigan cases continue to move forward in the judicial process toward the Supreme Court. The federal Sixth Circuit Court of Appeals ruled in May 2002 by a 5 to 4 vote that the University of Michigan affirmative action program for its law school was constitutional, because it allowed for needed diversity in educational programs. With that both Grutter and Gratz filed for an en banc hearing by the Circuit, or one considered by all of the judges. By accepting these two cases for review in December 2002, the Supreme Court will decide for the first time since 1978 the direction of affirmative action in higher education.[1]

? Question for Reflection: Established in 1965, affirmative action programs attempted to provide a "boost" to minority applicants relative to white applicants with roughly the same qualifications. How will the elimination of this "boost" with emphasis now placed on academic achievement and the introduction of education assistance for minorities, affect America's search for racial equality?

INTRODUCTION: CIVIL RIGHTS AND DEMOCRACY

The fight over civil rights and affirmative action did not begin with Jennifer Gratz and Barbara Grutter. When Rosa Parks refused to move from her seat on a bus in Montgomery, Alabama, in 1955, she set off a boycott that eventually led to a federal court ruling, affirmed by the Supreme Court, that the city of Montgomery could not maintain its policy of segregated transportation. Despite the resolve and bravery of those involved in the boycott, however, the legal process took almost thirteen months before culminating in the decision that African Americans would be allowed to sit at the front of a bus. Nor did the story end there; in fact, it was only beginning.

Over forty years after the Supreme Court told the nation's public schools to desegregate "with all deliberate speed" in the landmark case of *Brown v. Board of Education of Topeka, Kansas* [347 U.S. 483 (1954)], we see that the goal still seems to be out of reach. Today we are debating whether we should try to equalize rights, even at the expense of someone else's job or college admission. With such an acrimonious debate over affirmative action programs, is there any hope of approaching a democratic system of "equal rights for all" and "full participation by all" in the government?

In this chapter we trace the history of civil rights in the United States, a history that did not really begin until the second half of the nineteenth century, when a nation recovering from a devastating Civil War sought to establish equality of rights under the Constitution. But the real change did not come until nearly a century later. The period from 1896 to 1954 was spent debating the notion of legal equality; then from 1954 to 1968 the debate turned to the question of achieving actual equality through governmental policies. In the nearly thirty years that followed, the debate centered on whether actual equality should be achieved, and if so, how. But for the last several years, the discussion over a "color blind" policy has raised questions as to whether those policies will be reversed or even abandoned.

Before discussing the history of civil rights, however, we need to clarify exactly what we mean by civil rights, equality, and discrimination.

Defining Civil Rights

Most people agree that to truly approach democracy it is necessary to eliminate **discrimination,** that is, unequal treatment based on race, ethnicity, gender, and other distinctions. The primary means for achieving equal treatment is ensuring full protection of **civil rights,** the constitutionally guaranteed and protected rights that may not be arbitrarily removed by the government. These rights are often referred to as personal, natural, or inalienable rights; they are believed to be granted by God or nature to all human beings. It was these rights that Thomas Jefferson had in mind when he wrote in the Declaration of Independence, "We hold these truths to be self-evident, that all men are created equal, that they are endowed by their Creator with certain unalienable Rights, that among these are Life, Liberty and the pursuit of Happiness." These rights become statutory ones when they are established by legislation.

Several groups within the U.S. population have suffered from discrimination at various periods in the nation's history, and many still do today. Although in much of this chapter we focus on the civil rights of African Americans and women, we also discuss the efforts of other groups, such as Hispanics and Native Americans, to obtain equal treatment. Not all of these groups are minorities. Women, for example, are not a numerical minority, but they have experienced discrimination throughout the nation's history and continue to encounter unequal treatment in the workplace and elsewhere.

Civil rights are closely linked with the ideal of equality. There are two basic forms of equality: equality before the law (legal equality) and actual equality. Equality before the law, also called **de jure equality,** requires that there be no legally mandated obstacles to equal treatment, such as laws that prevent people from voting, living where they want to, or taking advantage of all the rights guaranteed to individuals by the laws of the federal, state, and local governments. Actual equality, also called **de facto equality,** looks at results: Do people live where they want to? Do they work under similar conditions? In a diverse and complex society like that of the United States, it is often difficult to achieve de jure equality; it is even more difficult to create the conditions that will lead to de facto equality. In the course of the nation's history there have been many turns along the road to equality, and while de jure equality has been achieved in some respects, de facto equality remains a distant objective.

discrimination Unequal treatment based on race, ethnicity, gender, and other distinctions.

civil rights The constitutionally guaranteed rights that may not be arbitrarily removed by the government. Among these rights are the right to vote and equal protection under the law.

de jure equality Equality before the law. It requires that there be no legally mandated obstacles to equal treatment, such as laws that prevent people from voting, living where they want to, or taking advantage of all the rights guaranteed to individuals by the laws of the federal, state, and local governments.

de facto equality Equality of results, which measure whether real-world obstacles to equal treatment exist. Some examples are: Do people actually live where they want to? Do they work under similar conditions? etc.

◄ Compare the two drinking fountains established under the Supreme Court's 1896 doctrine of "separate but equal" facilities in the segregated South, and ask yourself about the fairness of that policy.

Establishing Constitutional Equality

Although the Constitution was written to "secure the Blessings of Liberty to ourselves and our Posterity," those blessings did not extend to African American slaves. This was not surprising; all references to slavery had been stricken from the Declaration of Independence, written eleven years before. Why did the Constitution's framers ignore the plight of the slaves? And why did they choose to count "other persons"—that is, slaves—as only three-fifths of a person, with no rights at all? As we saw in Chapter 2, to create a constitution that would be ratified by a majority of the states, the framers were forced to compromise. To preserve the economic position of the southern states, they allowed slavery to continue. But in doing so, they also ensured that future battles would be fought over slavery.

Even for free African Americans, legal status varied in different regions of the country. By 1804 many northern states had either banned slavery or passed laws under which the children of slaves would be free. However, the right to vote, generally granted on the basis of property qualifications, was placed beyond the reach of most African Americans as well as nonproperty owning white males. In the South, measures were enacted that made the release of slaves extremely difficult.[2] At the federal level, Congress passed the Fugitive Slave Act (1793), which allowed runaway slaves to be captured (even in parts of the nation where slavery was outlawed) and returned to slave owners. Even Article VI, Section 2, of the Constitution mandated the return of fugitive slaves. African Americans were excluded by law from a procedure that enabled immigrants to become citizens (1790), from service in militias (1792), and from the right to carry the mail (1810).

In 1820, when the proposed introduction of Missouri as a slave state threatened to upset the equal division of slave and free states, the *Missouri Compromise* was passed. Missouri was admitted as a slave state along with the free state of Maine, and slavery was prohibited in the remainder of the Louisiana Purchase territory north of Missouri's southern border.

While some African Americans submitted to their condition, many others did not. The most famous slave revolt occurred in August 1831, when Nat Turner led a rebellion of about seventy slaves in Southampton County, Virginia. In twelve hours of turmoil, Turner's men killed dozens of whites. Eventually the insurgents were defeated by hundreds of soldiers and militiamen, and Turner was executed, along with scores of other slaves.

The *Compromise of 1850*, which admitted California as a free state, eliminated the slave trade in the District of Columbia, but continued to permit slavery there, while the territories of New Mexico and Utah were given no federal restrictions on slavery. As part of the compromise Congress passed a stronger Fugitive Slave Act and provided for hundreds of additional federal officials to enforce it. The political prospects for equality seemed more remote than ever.

The *Dred Scott* Case

In 1857 the Supreme Court decided a case with far-reaching implications for the civil rights of African Americans. A slave named Dred Scott had been taken by his master from Missouri into the free state of Illinois and the free territory of Wisconsin. When his master died and Scott was returned to Missouri, he claimed that because he had lived in areas where slavery was illegal, he was now a free man.

The case of *Dred Scott v. Sandford* reached the Court at a time when the justices were seeking to define the legality of slavery, particularly in the territories, as a means of solving the political dispute between the North and the South. In a highly controversial decision, the Court ruled that Scott could not sue in federal court because no African American, free or enslaved, could ever become a citizen of the United States. According to Chief Justice Roger Taney, even if Scott were free, he could not sue because African Americans were "not included, and were not

QUOTE ... UNQUOTE

"Our Constitution is color-blind, and neither knows nor tolerates classes among citizens. In respect of civil rights, all citizens are equal before the law. The humblest is the peer of the most powerful. The law regards man as man, and takes no account of his surroundings or of his color when his civil rights as guaranteed by the supreme law of the land are involved."

Justice John Harlan, 1896

Apologizing for the Past: Considering Slavery Reparations

While Yale University celebrated its 300th anniversary, and Brown and Harvard Universities continue their proud tradition of academic excellence, a debate still rages as to how these schools began. Three scholars, all doctoral candidates at Yale at the time, argue that Yale's first scholarships, endowed professorships and library endowment were derived from slave-trading money, leading to the names of two-thirds of its residential colleges, and subjects of the "Worthies" honored by the stained glass windows on Harkness Tower in the center of campus, reflecting the names of slave-owner donors. Two slave traders, Nicholas and John Brown, helped found Brown University, and portions of the money used to endow Harvard Law School came from the selling of slaves in the cane fields of Antigua. These three Ivy League schools of the North, all with proud recent histories of working to improve race relations, became part of one of the hottest debates in the race relations field: should America apologize for its slavery past by paying reparations to the victims of this practice?

Apologizing for past actions is not new for the American government. The surviving Scottsboro Boys, a group of young African American males who were put on trial for their lives in Alabama on allegations of raping two white girls on a train, were sentenced to life in prison but eventually pardoned when evidence of their innocence was uncovered. In 1988, embarrassed by the legacy of the Japanese-American Internment policy in World War II, by which 110,000 citizens were removed from their land and lives on the Pacific Coast and imprisoned in the southwest United States on the pretext of keeping the nation secure, Congress passed the Civil Liberties Act in 1988 offering $20,000 in reparations and a letter of apology to all of those still alive who were imprisoned. In 1999, the United States government agreed to pay what could amount to $2 billion in a landmark legal settlement to African-American farmers because of the discriminatory practices in issuing USDA federal farm loans by the Department of Agriculture. In Europe, similar $1.25 billion reparations judgements have been made by three Swiss banks to victims of the Holocaust and families of those forced into slave labor. Yet some argue that America has not fully acknowledged its history of slavery, a practice so pervasive in the nation's founding that it was legal in all 13 colonies during Revolutionary times.

The questions now are whether the nation should or how the nation should acknowledge and apologize for a practice that kept people in bondage. The issue began in

earnest in 1969 when Civil Rights activist James Forman marched into the Riverside Church in New York City and read his "Black Manifesto" demanding the payment of $500,000 in reparations for slavery from the largely white congregation (an action which initially gained him a police summons but eventually got some support from members of the church who established a $300,000 fund to benefit the urban poor.)

Seeking justice, a series of class-action lawsuits were filed in 2002 on behalf of the 35 million descendents of slaves against two insurance companies: Fleet Boston Financial Corporation and Aetna, Inc, who are accused of writing insurance policies on slaves. Another suit is being planned by Harvard Law Professor Charles J. Ogletree, co-coordinator of the Reparations Coordinating Committee, and defense attorney Johnny Cochran, against the United States Government and private companies who they claim gained "unjust enrichment" from the practice of slavery. Supporters of government reparations argue that only by acknowledging the mistakes of our past can American democracy move ahead in its effort to include all people, and only in this way can African Americans be compensated for the difficult economic situation that can be traced to slavery. Opponents of reparations argue that one should not impose today's morality on past events, that the statute of limitations has run on these events, and that there are few direct descendants to slavery now who were harmed by these practices.

Whether the drive for reparations will succeed is much in doubt. In 1995 a $100 million lawsuit seeking reparations was dismissed in a California federal district court on the basis of the sovereign immunity of government actors and the passage of time since those events. Yet each year since 1988 Rep. John Conyers, (D.-MI) has unsuccessfully introduced legislation calling for a federal commission to study the feasibility of slave reparations. The question now is whether the federal courts will do what Congress has not.

Sources: Kate Zernike, "Slave Traders in Yale's Past Fuel Debate on Restitution," *New York Times,* August 13, 2001, section B1; Tatsha Robertson, "For Slavery: Old Idea Goes Mainstream," *Boston Globe,* April 4, 2002; Matthew Kauffman and Kenneth R. Gosselin, *"Slavery Reparations Effort Just Beginning: Win or Lose, Experts Say the Discussion is Worth Having,"* The Hartford Courant, April 2, 2002; David Brion Davis, "The Enduring Legacy of the South's Civil War Victory," *New York Times,* August 26, 2001, Section 4, p. 1.

intended to be included, under the word 'citizens' in the Constitution" and therefore had no rights under that document. Finally, the chief justice ruled that the Missouri Compromise was unconstitutional because Congress could not deprive people of their property rights, in this case their slaves, under the due process clause of the Fifth Amendment.[3]

The Civil War and Reconstruction

The *Dred Scott* case closed the door to judicial remedies for African Americans seeking legal protection. Political remedies were still open, however. By freeing the slaves in the areas still in rebellion, President Abraham Lincoln's Emancipation Proclamation of 1863 renewed the possibility of "equality for all." But for Lincoln's executive order to be implemented, the Union had to win the Civil War and Congress had to support freedom for slaves with legal authority. Thus, in the period following the Civil War, Congress played a pivotal role in efforts to establish equality for African Americans.

In one series of actions Congress drafted three constitutional amendments, known as the Civil War Amendments. The Thirteenth Amendment, which abolished slavery, was ratified in 1865. It reads as follows:

> Section 1. Neither slavery nor involuntary servitude, except as a punishment for crime whereof the party shall have been duly convicted, shall exist within the United States, or in any place subject to their jurisdiction.
>
> Section 2. Congress shall have power to enforce this article by appropriate legislation.

Congress had already passed legislation allowing African Americans to testify against whites in federal courts (1864), granting equal pay and benefits to all soldiers (1864), and establishing the Freedmen's Bureau (1865), an agency of the War Department that was authorized to assist the newly freed slaves in making the transition to freedom.

But southern states were already passing laws, known as the **black codes,** that restricted the civil rights of blacks and enforced oppressive labor practices designed to keep them working on plantations. Led by the so-called Radical Republicans, Congress undertook to counteract these measures. Over President Andrew Johnson's vetoes, the Radical Republicans gave the Freedman's Bureau additional powers to settle labor disputes and nullify oppressive labor contracts. It also passed the Civil Rights Act of 1866, which made African Americans U.S. citizens and empowered the federal government to protect their civil rights.

Since many members of Congress feared that the new law might not stand up in court, they then drafted the Fourteenth Amendment to the Constitution, making African Americans citizens and giving them rights of that citizenship. Section 1 of the amendment states:

> All persons born or naturalized in the United States, and subject to the jurisdiction thereof, are citizens of the United States and of the State wherein they reside. No State shall make or enforce any law which shall abridge the privileges or immunities of citizens of the United States; nor shall any State deprive any person of life, liberty, or property, without due process of law; nor deny to any person within its jurisdiction the equal protection of the laws.

Section 5 of the amendment gave Congress the "power to enforce, by appropriate legislation, the provisions of this article." The new citizens were thus supposed to have the same rights as others, as well as be treated with fairness and equality under law.

Congress acted quickly. It required southern states to ratify this amendment, and later the Fifteenth Amendment, before they could rejoin the Union. The Fifteenth Amendment, granting African Americans **suffrage,** or the right to vote, reads:

> The right of citizens of the United States to vote shall not be denied or abridged by the United States or any State on account of race, color, or previous condition of servitude.

black codes Laws restricting the civil rights of blacks.

suffrage The right to vote.

Again, Congress was given the power to "enforce this article by appropriate legislation." To break the power of the Ku Klux Klan and other terrorists who attacked, beat, and sometimes killed African Americans who tried to vote or otherwise claim their rights, Congress also passed the Ku Klux Klan Acts of 1870 and 1871, making it a federal offense for two or more persons to conspire to deprive citizens of their equal protection and voting rights.

But the legislative branch of government could only create the tools for establishing legal equality. It remained to be seen whether the executive branch would enforce them and how the judicial branch would interpret them.

Creating Legal Segregation

In the post–Civil War period the Supreme Court showed little interest in the rights of African Americans. In *United States v. Cruikshank* (1876), for example, the Court considered the constitutionality of the Ku Klux Klan Act of 1870. William Cruikshank was part of a white mob that had murdered sixty African Americans in front of a courthouse. Since murder was not a federal offense and the state authorities had no intention of prosecuting anyone for the crime, the members of the mob were indicted on federal charges of interfering with the murdered men's right to assemble. However, the Court ruled that under the Fourteenth Amendment only **state action,** or action by the state government under the color of law to deprive rights, was subject to decisions by the federal court.[4] In other words, the federal government could not prosecute private individuals. This ruling left the states free to ignore lynchings, assaults, and mob actions against African Americans within their borders.

Separate But Equal?

In the *Civil Rights Cases* (1883), the Supreme Court applied its new *state-action doctrine* to overturn the Civil Rights Act of 1875, which prohibited racial segregation in transportation, inns, theaters, and other places of public accommodation and amusement.[5] The southern states thereupon passed a series of **Jim Crow laws,** which separated the races in public places. This legal separation was challenged in the 1896 case of *Plessy v. Ferguson*.[6]

Homer Adolph Plessy, who was one-eighth African American, had sought to ride in a railroad car designated as "whites only," rather than in the car at the end of the train designated for "coloreds only," as required by law, and had been arrested. The Supreme Court upheld the arrest, stating that the Fourteenth Amendment regulated only political equality and not social equality.

The logical consequences of the Plessy ruling were revealed in *Cumming v. County Board of Education* (1899), in which the Court approved "separate but equal" public schools in Georgia. Though the facilities were not really "equal," by claiming that public schools were a subject for state rather than federal jurisdiction, the Court could let segregation stand.[7] It was not long before legally enforced segregation pervaded every other area of social life.

The Disenfranchisement of African American Voters

Seeking to disenfranchise African American voters, southern politicians invented loopholes in the voting laws, thus circumventing the Fifteenth Amendment. Since many freed slaves owned no land, *property qualifications* kept some of them off the voting rolls; *literacy tests* did the same for those who could not read. When these loopholes were found to exclude many poor whites, an *understanding clause* was used: people were permitted to vote only if they could properly interpret a portion of the state constitution. (Of course, there were different sections of the constitution and different standards for "proper interpretation" depending on the race of the test taker.)

state action Action that is taken by state officials or sanctioned by state law.

Jim Crow laws Laws passed by southern states that separated the races in public places such as railroads, streetcars, schools, and cemeteries.

Another loophole was the *grandfather clause,* which exempted from property qualifications or literacy tests anyone whose relatives could have voted in 1867, thus excluding the freed slaves. Some southern states also implemented a **poll tax,** that is, a fee for voting, which would exclude poor African Americans. Finally, since the Democratic party was, in effect, the only party in the South, states utilized *whites-only primaries* to select the Democratic candidate, making the votes of African Americans in the general election irrelevant.[8] Thus, while African Americans were citizens of the United States, they were denied a voice in its government.

Establishing Legal Equality

African Americans reacted to end discrimination and oppression in a variety of ways. In 1895 Booker T. Washington, a former slave who had founded Tuskegee Institute, argued that racism would eventually end if African Americans would accept their situation, work hard, and improve their education. On the other hand, W.E.B. DuBois, the first African American to earn a Ph.D. from Harvard, argued that all forms of racial segregation and discrimination should be aggressively attacked and eradicated.

In 1909, DuBois, with other African Americans and concerned white people, formed the National Association for the Advancement of Colored People (NAACP) to litigate on behalf of racial equality. In a series of cases decided between 1905 and 1914, the NAACP convinced the Court to use the Thirteenth Amendment to strike down **peonage,** in which employers advanced wages and then required workers to remain on their jobs, in effect enslaving them, until the debt was satisfied.[9]

Encouraged by these successes, the NAACP challenged Oklahoma's law effectively exempting whites from the literacy test required for voting. In *Guinn v. United States* (1915), the Supreme Court struck it down using the Fifteenth Amendment.[10] Then, in 1927, the Court found that Texas's white-primary law violated the equal protection clause of the Fourteenth Amendment.[11] Still, the southern states continued to disenfranchise blacks by reenacting the offending laws or inventing new loopholes. Clearly, a more general approach to protecting the civil rights of African Americans was needed.

The White House and Desegregation

During World War II the obvious inequity of expecting African Americans to fight for a country that did not afford them full protection of their civil rights gave rise to new efforts to achieve equality. This time the White House took the lead. President Franklin D. Roosevelt issued an executive order prohibiting discrimination in defense businesses and creating a temporary wartime agency, the Fair Employment Practices Committee (FEPC), to investigate allegations of, and provide compensation for, such discrimination. In 1946, spurred by a spate of racial lynchings, President Harry Truman established a panel of citizens to examine the problem and recommend solutions.[12] He also issued an executive order making the FEPC a permanent executive branch agency.

poll tax A voting fee, now unconstitutional, that was used to prevent African Americans from voting in the South.

peonage A system in which employers advance wages and then require workers to remain on their jobs, in effect enslaving them, until the debt is satisfied.

desegregation The elimination of laws and practices mandating separation of the races.

But Truman's most significant action in relation to **desegregation** came in 1948, when he issued an executive order prohibiting segregation in the military and in federal employment. Truman also asked Congress to ban discrimination by private employers and labor unions, outlaw poll taxes, pass a federal anti-lynching law, create a permanent civil rights commission, and compel fair elections. However, these efforts were doomed by the opposition of conservative southerners who had split from the Democratic party under the leadership of South Carolina's Strom Thurmond to form the Dixiecrats. The struggle for equality now turned to the public school system.

Question for Reflection: What impact did the creation of the Dixiecrats have on the strength of the Democratic Party and its attempts to achieve racial equality for African Americans?

Seeking Equality in the Schools

NAACP attorneys had long been planning a comprehensive legal attack on segregation in the public schools. Initially, their strategy was to work within the separate but equal standard, using a series of test cases to show that certain educational facilities were not, in fact, equal. In 1938 the NAACP challenged a Missouri statute that met the state's separate but equal requirement by offering tuition refunds to African Americans who attended an out-of-state law school. The Supreme Court overturned the law, stating that students who were required to go to out-of-state schools would be burdened by inconveniences and costs not imposed on students who attended law schools in their home state.[13]

In 1950, under the leadership of Thurgood Marshall, the NAACP challenged the University of Texas law school's separate but equal plan, in which African American students were taught in the basement of an Austin office building rather than at the highly regarded state university. The justices agreed that the two "separate" schools were not "equivalent" in any respect, and for the first time the Court went beyond such physical differences to point out the constitutional importance of the intangible psychological differences represented by the differing academic environments, such as the differences in the prestige of the faculty, the students, the library, and the law review.[14] On the same day, the Court ruled that Oklahoma could not satisfy its separate but equal requirement for graduate schools by forcing an African American student to sit in the doorway during class, study in a special section of the library, and eat at a table in the cafeteria labeled "For Colored Only."[15]

> ### QUOTE ... UNQUOTE
>
> "Without [Thurgood Marshall] the whole civil rights movement and the legal enfranchisement of blacks might not have happened when it did. . . . That was the man's monument."
>
> **Author Richard Kluger, 1993**

◄ Lawyers George E. C. Hayes, Thurgood Marshall, and James M. Nabrit of the NAACP Legal Defense Fund congratulate each other outside the Supreme Court Building on May 17, 1954, after the announcement that they had won the case of *Brown v. Board of Education.*

Now that the Court had ruled that psychologically "separate" facilities could not be considered equal in graduate education, Marshall and the NAACP were ready to take direct aim at overturning the separate but equal doctrine as applied to public schools. Suits were initiated to challenge the segregated school districts of four states (Kansas, Delaware, South Carolina, and Virginia) and the District of Columbia. The NAACP's strategy was to attack the *Plessy* decision by focusing on the intangible psychological effects of separate but equal public school facilities.

Because so many of the precedents supported *Plessy,* the most effective way to convince the Court to change its position was to present evidence from social science research on the effects of segregation. An example was a series of studies by psychologist Kenneth Clark, who discovered that when African American schoolchildren were shown white and black dolls and asked which one they would prefer to be, they invariably chose the white doll. On the basis of such findings, Marshall argued that segregation had a devastating effect on African American children's self-esteem, and that therefore the education received in separate educational facilities could never be equal.

In 1952 the Supreme Court decided to combine the four state cases and rule on them under *Brown v. Board of Education of Topeka, Kansas.* Rather than handing down a decision, however, it called for reargument of the case. At about this time Chief Justice Fred Vinson, unsympathetic to the attack on segregation, died suddenly, leading Justice Felix Frankfurter, who realized the impact of this change for the *Brown* case, to confess, "This is the first indication I have ever had that there is a God." The new chief justice, former California governor Earl Warren, was far more willing to use his political skills to persuade all of the justices, even Kentuckian Stanley Reed, to rule against segregation.

On May 17, 1954, Warren announced the Court's unanimous decision that the separate but equal standard was henceforth unconstitutional. Warren argued that the importance of education in contemporary society was greater than it had been at the time of the *Plessy* ruling. Because segregated schools put African American children at a disadvantage, he stated, they violated the equal protection clause of the Fourteenth Amendment.[16] On the same day, relying on the Fifth Amendment's due process clause to deal with schools under federal government supervision, the Court also struck down segregation in Washington, D.C.'s, public schools.[17]

A year later the Court issued a second statement on *Brown v. Board of Education* (commonly referred to as *Brown II*) dealing with implementation of the decision.[18] All of the cases were ordered back to the lower federal courts, which in turn would supervise plans for desegregation, or the elimination of laws and practices mandating segregation "with all deliberate speed." Missing from the Court's statement was a direct order to compel **integration,** efforts to balance the social composition of the schools.

State and Federal Responses

State governments responded to the *Brown* decision in a variety of ways. In Washington, D.C., Kansas, and Delaware legalized segregation was largely eliminated. In the Deep South, however, violence was directed against African American activists who tried to implement this ruling. In some places mobs gathered to block African Americans from attending previously segregated public schools and universities. State legislatures also took steps to fight the *Brown* decision. Some forbade state officials to enforce the decision, while others closed the public schools in some districts and paid the private school tuitions of Caucasian children.[19] If any uniform progress was to be made toward desegregation in the South, it would be up to the federal government.

Initially, with the exception of fifty-eight courageous federal district court judges in the South, the federal government was no more willing to take desegregation action than the states had been.[20] Southern politicians took President Dwight Eisenhower's ambivalence as a signal to continue their discriminatory practices without

▲ Nine-year-old Linda Brown and her family in Topeka, Kansas, in 1954, who became the subject of the landmark Supreme Court case *Brown v. Board of Education.* The case began when Linda's father, a clergyman, took her to the all-white school, where she was denied admission.

integration Government efforts to balance the racial composition in schools and public places.

White House interference. Only reluctantly did the president decide to send federal troops to Little Rock, Arkansas, to help nine African American students desegregate the region's Central High School in the face of strong opposition, which included the deployment of state National Guard units to prevent the students from entering the school.

President Eisenhower signed into law the Civil Rights Act of 1957, which created a Civil Rights Commission to recommend legislation and gave the Justice Department the power to initiate lawsuits on behalf of African Americans who were denied the right to vote. Then, in the Civil Rights Act of 1960, the attorney general was authorized to call in federal officials to investigate voter registration in areas where discrimination may be occurring. While the Eisenhower administration did not use its new power vigorously, it did demonstrate that the federal government could be effective, if it wished, in protecting civil rights. In the meantime, however, the struggle for equality was carried on by the people most affected—African Americans themselves.

The Civil Rights Movement

The modern civil rights protests began with Rosa Park's refusal to give up her seat on a bus, which led to the bus boycott in Montgomery, Alabama, in 1955–56. Shortly afterward, African American activists founded the Southern Christian Leadership Conference (SCLC), which was headed by a charismatic leader, the Reverend Martin Luther King, Jr. Like Mahatma Gandhi of India, King preached **civil disobedience,** that is, breaking the law in a nonviolent fashion and being willing to suffer the consequences, even to the point of going to jail, to publicly demonstrate that a law is unjust. For example in the Montgomery bus case, protesters might **boycott,** or refuse to patronize, a business that practices segregation. Another kind of demonstration is the **protest march,** in which people walk down a main street carrying signs, singing freedom songs, and chanting slogans. During the early years of the civil rights protests, counter protesters frequently lined the streets to jeer at the

civil disobedience Breaking the law in a nonviolent fashion and being willing to suffer the consequences, even to the point of going to jail, in order to publicly demonstrate that the law is unjust.

boycott Refusal to patronize any organization that practices policies that are perceived to be unfair for political, economic, or ideological reasons.

protest march March in which people walk down a main street carrying signs, singing songs, and chanting slogans.

◀ Fifteen-year-old Elizabeth Eckford calmly ignores the taunts of the jeering crowd as she becomes one of the "Little Rock 9" in 1957 who integrated Central High School. "I tried to see a friendly face somewhere in the mob—someone who maybe would help me. I looked into the face of an old woman and it seemed a kind face, but when I looked at her again, she spat at me."

marchers, and law enforcement officials, blaming the protesters for the disturbances, would break up the protest, using everything from clubs to firehoses.

The concept of civil disobedience was not confined to the SCLC. Inspired by the Montgomery boycott, in 1958 Oklahoma City's NAACP Youth Council decided to protest the segregation of lunch counters by sitting down on the stools and refusing to leave when they were not served. This protest technique became known as a **sit-in,** and it proved to be very effective. In 1960 four African American students used this technique, entering a Woolworth store in Greensboro, North Carolina, and sitting down at the segregated lunch counter. When they were refused service, they simply sat there and studied until the store closed. During the following days others, both African American and white, joined the protest, and soon more than a thousand people were sitting-in at segregated eating establishments in Greensboro. The Greensboro protest gained national attention, and college students throughout the South began engaging in sit-ins. Many of the protesters were arrested, convicted, and jailed, thereby drawing further attention to the movement. The tide of public opinion turned, and eating establishments throughout the South began to desegregate.

Beginning in 1961, civil rights activists, called **freedom riders,** began traveling throughout the South on buses to test compliance with the Supreme Court's mandate to integrate bus terminals accommodating interstate travelers. In Anniston, Birmingham, and Montgomery, Alabama, the freedom riders were attacked by mobs while local police made themselves scarce.

During the same period the federal government worked with civil rights leaders to register African American voters in the hope of creating a legal revolution from within the system. With the aid of the Justice Department, the privately funded Voter Education Project began a campaign to enforce the voting rights provisions of the Civil Rights Act of 1957. As a result of these efforts, African American voter registration in the South rose from 26 to 40 percent between 1962 and 1964.[21]

Meanwhile, the civil rights movement was encountering increasingly violent resistance. When extremists began harassing and even killing civil rights activists, the White House was forced to act. In the spring of 1963, Martin Luther King Jr. decided to protest segregation in Birmingham with a series of demonstrations and marches designed to trigger a response by the segregationist police commissioner, Theophilus Eugene "Bull" Connor. The protest began with marches and sit-ins at segregated businesses, to which Connor responded by arresting protesters, including King himself, and obtaining a court injunction to prevent further demonstrations. Finally, after Connor attacked nonviolent protesters with vicious police dogs and firehoses, President John F. Kennedy sent Justice Department officials to Birmingham to work out a compromise, and business leaders agreed to desegregate their establishments. However, the night after the compromise was announced, bombs went off at the hotel where King was staying. Riots broke out, and peace was not restored until President Kennedy sent federal troops to a nearby fort and threatened to dispatch them to Birmingham if the violence continued.

▲ A young Reverend Martin Luther King, Jr., is arrested in Montgomery, Alabama in 1958 for "loitering" near the courthouse where one of his civil rights allies was being tried. King later charged that once out of sight of the cameras he was beaten and choked by the arresting officers.

sit-in A protest technique in which protesters refuse to leave an area.

freedom riders Civil rights activists who traveled throughout the South on buses to test compliance with the Supreme Court's mandate that transportation facilities accommodating interstate passengers be integrated.

The Civil Rights Acts

The civil rights movement made great progress toward equality in the early 1960s, but there was still a long way to go. To succeed, it needed more effective legal tools. In 1963 President Lyndon Johnson urged Congress in the name of the assassinated President Kennedy to "enact a civil rights law so that we can move forward to eliminate from this nation every trace of discrimination and oppression that is based upon race or color." And Congress responded. The Twenty-fourth Amendment, which prohibited the use of poll taxes in federal elections, was passed by Congress in 1962 (ratified 1964). Then, after a fifty-seven-day filibuster led by southern senators that was finally broken by the arm-twisting of President Johnson, Congress passed the Civil Rights Act of 1964.

The 1964 act was extremely comprehensive and greatly increased the federal government's ability to fight discrimination. Because the government could withhold funds from segregated schools and the attorney general was empowered to initiate school desegregation suits, African Americans would no longer have to rely on the slow, case-by-case approach to end school segregation. Moreover, by creating the Equal Employment Opportunity Commission (EEOC) and placing authority in the hands of the Commissioner of Education, the act put the power of the federal bureaucracy behind efforts to end discrimination.

The Voting Rights Act of 1965 was another step toward racial equality. Areas where less than 50 percent of the population had been registered to vote or had voted in the 1964 presidential election were automatically found to be in violation of the law. In those areas the use of literacy tests and similar devices was prohibited, and no new voting qualifications could be imposed without the approval of the attorney general. The law also mandated that federal examiners be sent to those areas to assist in the registration of voters and to observe elections.

In addition to calling for this legislation, President Johnson, a former Texas Senator, issued executive orders that brought the federal bureaucracy into the fight for civil rights. Among other things, Johnson instructed the Civil Service Commission to guarantee equal opportunity in federal employment, directed the secretary of labor to administer nondiscrimination policies in the awarding of government contracts, and ordered the attorney general to implement the section of the Civil Rights Act of 1964 that withdrew federal funds from any racially discriminatory programs.

By 1965 the federal government was clearly at the forefront of the struggle to end discrimination and guarantee the civil rights of all Americans. However, it remained to be seen whether the provisions of the new laws were constitutional.

The Supreme Court and Civil Rights

Less than six months after Congress passed the Civil Rights Act of 1964, two cases challenging its constitutionality reached the Supreme Court. In *Heart of Atlanta Motel v. United States,* the proprietor of a motel claimed that as a private businessman and not a "state actor," he was not subject to Congress's power to enforce the Fourteenth Amendment. The Court ruled that since the motel was accessible to interstate travelers, and thus was engaging in interstate commerce, Congress could regulate it under the interstate commerce clause of Article I.[22] In *Katzenbach v. McClung,* the justices noted that although Ollie's Barbecue (in Birmingham, Alabama) had few interstate customers, it obtained supplies through interstate commerce; therefore it, too, was subject to congressional regulation.[23] After these decisions, private businesses began voluntarily ending their discriminatory practices rather than risk losing costly lawsuits.

In 1966, in the case of *Harper v. Virginia Board of Elections,* the Court held that all poll taxes, even those imposed by states, violated the equal protection clause of the Fourteenth Amendment.[24] By the end of the 1960s the number of African American voters in the Deep South had almost doubled.[25] This new voting bloc eventually defeated segregationist candidates, changed the views of politicians who had formerly favored segregation, and elected many African Americans to office at all levels of government. But while African Americans were gaining de jure equality, they were still far from de facto equality.

De Jure versus De Facto Discrimination

The "War on Poverty" declared by President Johnson in 1964 was in part an attempt to address the problem of racial inequality. But African American communities continued to be plagued by poverty, and it became evident to people throughout the nation that discrimination and its effects were not limited to the South. When civil rights groups began to concentrate on the discrimination that existed in the North,

THE ROAD TO DEMOCRACY

Jackson, Mississippi: Freedom Rides the Span of 40 Years

Forty years after 350 Freedom Riders, beaten and firebombed on the buses in which they rode, were jailed in Jackson, Mississippi, Governor Ronnie Musgrove welcomed back 80 of the original group on Veteran's Day 2001, many of whom had not been in Mississippi since their release from prison, and declared it "Freedom Riders' Day." "We salute the heroic efforts in 1961 of the freedom riders and their role as an inspiration to others to follow on the long, often perilous road to end segregation," said Governor Musgrove. The year earlier, thousands of protestors had gathered in Selma, Alabama to celebrate the 35th anniversary of the bloody attack on protestors in that city by Alabama state troopers. So much has changed, everyone agreed, since that day in 1961 when the brutal racism of the South flared up for all to see. But so many challenges in the search for equality still remain.

THAT WAS THEN . . .

Before the protestors, who were riding the integrated buses through the South to test a Supreme Court decision that banned segregated interstate public transportation facilities, arrived in Jackson, police in other locations had unleashed a fierce attack with clubs, firehoses, bullwhips, cattle prods, and tear gas.

When the buses arrived in Jackson, the police sought to avoid making such a public demonstration of oppression; instead, they did so in private. The protestors were arrested as soon as they entered the Greyhound bus station, eventually transferred to a maximum-security prison, and forced

▲ Firefighters turn their firehoses full blast on African American civil rights demonstrators in the 1960s. At times the water came with such force, even on children demonstrating, that it literally tore the bark off fully grown trees.

to sleep either on concrete floors or on the metal bed frames. Their 40-day jail stay was made even more difficult when guards turned up the air-conditioning seeking to freeze the prisoners. The protestors passed the time by singing "We Shall Overcome" and playing chess and checkers using small pieces of cornbread and biscuits as game pieces. "If you weren't scared, you were crazy," recalls

their arguments changed considerably. In the South, segregation had been de jure, or sanctioned by law. In the North, however, segregation was more likely to be de facto; that is, it had developed out of social, economic, and other nongovernmental factors.

As efforts to fight discrimination continued, a major tragedy, the assassination of Martin Luther King, Jr., was turned into a dramatic achievement. One week after King's death on April 4, 1968, President Johnson signed into law the Civil Rights Act of 1968, which banned housing discrimination of all types. A few weeks later the Supreme Court upheld the government's power to regulate private housing by relying on the Civil Rights Act of 1866, which guaranteed all citizens the rights "to inherit, purchase, lease, sell, hold, and convey real and personal property." Justice Potter Stewart linked this law to the Thirteenth Amendment's guarantee to eliminate "badges and incidents of slavery," saying that discrimination in housing "herds men into ghettos and makes the ability to buy property turn on the color of their skin."[26] As a result, a home owner who wished to sell a house was required to sell it to any financially qualified buyer. But the question of what could be done about the racially divided neighborhoods that already existed, and about the segregated schools that resulted from those divisions, remained.

In 1969 the Supreme Court, tired of the continuing delay in school desegregation fifteen years after the *Brown* decision, ruled in *Alexander v. Holmes County Board of Education* that every school district must "terminate dual school systems at once

[handwritten note in left margin:] MLK's non-violent movement for civil rights

ex-freedom rider, Mary Davidoff, now a professor at St. Thomas University in St. Paul, Minnesota.

When Attorney General Robert Kennedy tried to secure the protestors' release, the Reverend Martin Luther King, Jr. persuaded him not to do so believing that if the jails became filled with Civil Rights activists the southern states would give up the fight.

But the fight continued. Four years later, and following scores of pitched battles between protestors and police throughout the South, bus-riding protestors in Selma, Alabama were attacked and blocked from crossing Edmund Pettus Bridge. "I thought I was going to die," recalled John Lewis, who had been badly beaten when he tried to cross the bridge named for a Confederate general. Now, Mr. Lewis is a Democratic congressman from Georgia who returned to Selma with a delegation of colleagues. "I'm thinking about all the tear gas and the horses," said Frank Spivey, 53, who was toward the back of the march in 1965. "The wind was blowing and the tear gas burned our eyes. All you could do was run." The violent clash in Selma, broadcast nationally on television, caught the attention of millions of Americans and set off a chain of events that altered the region's social and political landscape. Two weeks later, the Rev. Martin Luther King, Jr., led a march from Selma to the state capital, Montgomery, prompting Congress later that year to pass the Voting Rights Act.

THIS IS NOW . . .

"It was a moment of blessed human solidarity," said Professor Davidoff at the commemorative celebration in Jackson 40 years later, "It's a fight that we gave each other." To which, another ex-freedom rider, Reverend John R.

▲ Dr. Robert Singleton and Reverend John R. Washington reminisce about their landmark protests 40 years earlier in Jackson, Mississippi, on behalf of desegregating the city's Greyhound bus stations.

Washington, added: "It was something I had to do because my very personhood, my very salvation, was tied up not only with African-Americans being oppressed, but also with white people."

Sources: Steve Ritea, "Again They Ride," *New Orleans Times-Picayune,* November 10, 2001; "Mississippi Welcomes Freedom Riders," *New York Times,* November 10, 2001; "Looking Back at a Day in Selma, 35 Years On," *New York Times,* March 6, 2000.

and . . . operate now and hereafter only unitary schools."[27] In other words, they must desegregate immediately. School districts in the South complied within eight years, becoming the most integrated schools in the nation.[28] But in northern cities, where de facto segregation still existed, there was little progress.

How far would a school district have to go to end segregation? Did the Court's command require that school districts undertake to integrate schools? Did it mean that schools would have to bus children of different races to schools outside their neighborhoods to achieve racial balance? In 1971 the Court considered these questions in the case of *Swann v. Charlotte-Mecklenburg Board of Education.* It held that busing, numerical quotas for racial balancing, and other techniques were constitutionally acceptable means of remedying past discrimination.[29] Two years later, in *Keyes v. School District #1, Denver, Colorado,* the Court ruled that even if there had previously been no law mandating segregation in the schools, school districts could be found to have discriminated if they had adopted other policies that led to segregation.[30]

In the early 1970s the political and legal climate changed, and the civil rights movement suffered a setback. After ruling unanimously in every racial case since *Brown,* the Supreme Court became increasingly divided. Encouraged by this division, people who felt that their neighborhood schools were threatened by busing and other integration programs made their views known, and political opposition to desegregation grew. In 1972 and 1974, congressional efforts to restrict the use of busing to remedy segregation were narrowly defeated. In 1976, however, opponents of busing managed to remove the power of the Department of Health, Education and Welfare (HEW) to cut off federal funds for school districts that refused to use busing as a remedy.

Amid the turmoil surrounding busing, the Supreme Court heard the case of *Milliken v. Bradley* (1974), which asked whether the courts could go beyond the city limits of Detroit—in other words, outside an individual school district—in requiring busing programs to remedy segregation. In Detroit as in many other cities, whites had left the inner city to live in the suburbs, and only a plan that bused suburban children to inner-city schools or inner-city children to suburban schools would achieve racial balance. However, arguing that the local operation of schools is a "deeply rooted" tradition, the Court ruled that since there had been no official acts of discrimination by the suburban school districts (though there had by the city schools and the state), the Detroit desegregation plan did not need to include the suburban school districts.[31]

? Question for Reflection: Many parents in poor, low academic success rated urban school districts enroll their children in the more academically successful religious schools in their neighborhoods. Might this be seen as an attempt at *de facto equality* and should the government support this placement financially?

During the 1980s busing remained so controversial that the Justice Department turned instead to other measures, such as the creation of "magnet schools," or schools with special curricula designed to attract interested students from all parts of a city. But the struggle for de facto equality was not limited to public schools. Discrimination in other areas of social life, such as employment and higher education, was coming under increased public scrutiny. Much of that scrutiny focused on efforts to make up for past discrimination through an approach known as **affirmative action.**

affirmative action Programs that attempt to improve the chances of minority applicants for jobs, housing, employment, or graduate admissions by giving them a "boost" relative to white applicants with roughly the same qualifications.

▶ Some of the most violent and protracted fights against integration took place in northern cities such as Boston, Detroit, and Denver. In this powerful image, a white protester against busing white students in South Boston into Roxbury to integrate the school system turns his flag on a poor African American man who was just on his way to work.

Affirmative Action

We now turn to one of the most controversial aspects of the search for equality: programs that seek to increase equality but create temporary inequalities in the process. Such programs are collectively known as affirmative action, or programs that make exceptions to the standard operating procedures for the benefit of a previously discriminated against minority.[32] They attempt to improve the chances of minority applicants for jobs, housing, employment, government contracts, or school admissions by giving minority applicants a "boost" relative to white applicants with roughly the same qualifications. This action is needed, it is argued, because past discrimination has made it impossible for members of minority groups to achieve equality without such a boost. The problem, of course, is that such efforts appear to discriminate against white applicants. Affirmative action thus raises difficult questions about the nation's commitment to equality and the extent to which the civil rights of all citizens can be protected.

QUOTE ... UNQUOTE

"If the Senate can find in Title VII ... any language which provides that an employer will have to hire on the basis of percentage or quota related to color ... I will start eating the pages [of the Congressional Record] one after another, because it is not there."

Senator Hubert H. Humphrey, in the debate over the 1964 Civil Rights Act

Seeking Full Equality: Opportunity or Result?

At the beginning of the chapter we distinguished between legal equality and actual equality. Much of the discussion so far has described the history of efforts to remove obstacles to legal equality. We have seen that removing legal obstacles does not automatically result in actual equality; often, doing so gives rise to a new set of questions. In particular, does "actual equality" mean **equality of opportunity** or equality of result?

Underlying the goal of equality of opportunity is the idea that "people should have equal rights and opportunities to develop their talents."[33] This implies that all people should begin at the same starting point in a race. But what if life's circumstances make that impossible, placing members of different groups at different starting points, some much farther behind others? For example, a person born into a poor minority family in which no one has ever graduated from high school is likely to be much less prepared for admission to college than a person born into a highly educated family. Because of such differences, many people feel that the nation should aim instead for **equality of result.** All forms of inequality, including economic disparities, should be completely eradicated. This may mean giving some people an advantage at the start so that everyone will complete the race at the same point.

These two forms of equality—opportunity and result—are often in conflict. In a democracy, does providing rights or resources for one group take away rights from others? And if it does, would the action be undemocratic, or would it further approach democracy by improving the well-being of all? For example, the court can order the Piscataway, New Jersey, school system to integrate its high school business department, but can it force the creation of integrated public housing and schools in an effort to seek actual equality? Even if it does take this action, the justices cannot personally change the attitudes of those who think that protecting the civil rights of others will diminish their own rights.

Affirmative action was a logical extension of the desegregation effort. Its proponents argued that in allowing minority candidates to compete on a more level playing field by first tilting the field in their favor, affirmative action would eventually produce equality. In some programs, called **quota programs,** the concept was taken a step further to guarantee a certain percentage of admissions, new hires, or promotions to members of minority groups. Opponents of affirmative action, however, labeled this "reverse discrimination" and argued that the provision of benefits solely on the basis of membership in a minority group would deny those benefits to other, more deserving candidates who had not themselves discriminated against minorities. In other words, equality of result for minorities took away equality of opportunity for majority applicants.

equality of opportunity The idea that "people should have equal rights and opportunities to develop their talents," that all people should begin at the same starting point in a race.

equality of result The idea that all forms of inequality, including economic disparities, should be completely eradicated; this may mean giving some people an advantage at the start so that everyone will complete the race at the same point.

quota programs Programs that guarantee a certain percentage of admissions, new hires, or promotions to members of minority groups.

Affirmative action programs began with an executive order issued by President Johnson in 1965 requiring that federal contractors in the construction industry and later in the business community give a slight edge to minority applicants who were not quite equal to nonminority applicants. Between 1968 and 1971 the newly created Office of Federal Contract Compliance Programs (OFCCP) issued guidelines for federal contractors establishing certain "goals and timetables" if the percentages of African Americans and women they employed were lower than the percentages of those groups in similar positions in the local work force. Although the OFCCP's requirements originally dealt only with federal contractors, in 1972 Congress passed the Equal Employment Opportunity Act, which gave the Equal Employment Opportunity Commission the power to take private employers to court if they did not eliminate discrimination in their hiring practices.

Those who supported affirmative action hailed these actions; they believed that discrimination that had nothing to do with job performance could be eliminated by these means. Those who opposed affirmative action believed that these "guidelines" and "goals" amounted to quotas that would exclude more qualified white applicants. They argued that the Constitution was, and should be, "color-blind." Even the ultraliberal William O. Douglas expressed the opinion that the Fourteenth Amendment should be used "in a racially neutral way."[34]

The issue of affirmative action and quota programs reached the Supreme Court in 1978 in the case of *Regents of the University of California v. Bakke.* At issue was a voluntary policy of the University of California at Davis medical school, in which sixteen of the school's one hundred openings were set aside for minorities, who were given an advantage in admissions. Allan Bakke, a white male, claimed that the policy had deprived him of admission, even though he was more qualified than some of the minority candidates who had been admitted. Four of the justices wanted to rule that the University of California's policy violated the Civil Rights Act of 1964 because the use of quotas discriminated on the basis of "race, color, religion, sex, or national origin." Four other justices wanted to uphold the university's policy of affirmative action as an appropriate remedy for the nationwide scarcity of African American doctors. The deciding vote was cast by Justice Lewis Powell, who agreed in part with both groups. Powell argued that the university's admissions policy violated both the Civil Rights Act and the Fourteenth Amendment's equal protection clause, because its quota program provided specific benefits for students solely on the basis of race. However, Powell also argued that since schools had "a substantial interest" in promoting a diverse student body, admission policies that took race, ethnicity, and social and economic factors into account, while not employing strict quotas, could be constitutional.[35]

Confusion reigned after the *Bakke* decision. The Court tried a year later to refine its mandate in a case involving the use of affirmative action in employment. In *United Steelworkers v. Weber,* it considered an affirmative action program at the Kaiser Aluminum Chemical Corporation, which had previously discriminated against African Americans. The program was designed to increase the number of African Americans employed in skilled jobs by means of a training program that guaranteed that half of the openings at its plant in Gramercy, Louisiana, would be filled by African Americans until the proportion of minority workers matched their proportion in the local labor force. The Court ruled that the Kaiser plan did not violate the Civil Rights Act, since the purpose of the act was to remedy the effects of past discrimination.[36] In 1980 the Court reinforced this judgment in upholding a program in which 10 percent of the grants in the 1977 Public Works Employment Act were set aside for minority-owned businesses.[37]

Almost forty years since its inception, affirmative action remains controversial today. Even some who might benefit from the policy oppose it, believing that it stigmatizes individuals who wish to compete on their own merits. According to one critic, affirmative action programs "entail the assumption that people of color cannot at present compete on the same playing field with people who are white."[38] Nevertheless, proponents of affirmative action continued to argue that because of the effects of past discrimination, true equality will not be achieved until those effects are overcome by transition programs giving minorities a temporary advantage. Thus, in the area of affirmative action, the approach to democracy is hampered by lack of agreement not only over which goal is most democratic but also over which means represent the best approach.

Affirmative Action in the Reagan-Bush Era

Shortly after coming to office in 1981, President Ronald Reagan appointed officials who challenged many of the nation's civil rights policies. In reexamining affirmative action, his administration took the position that the various civil rights acts prohibited all racial and sexual discrimination, including discrimination against white males. It further argued that only employers found to have discriminated should be required to remedy their discriminatory practices and that they should be required to hire or promote only individuals who could prove that they had been discriminated against.

A key issue was raised by programs in which recently hired minority employees were protected from "last-hired/first-fired" union layoff rules. White workers with more seniority who now faced layoffs argued that abrogation of those rules was a violation of their civil rights. In 1984 the administration persuaded the Supreme Court to overturn a ruling by a federal district court requiring a fire department to suspend seniority rules when laying off employees.[39]

In 1986 the Court overturned a program in which public school teachers with more seniority in a district with no history of discrimination were laid off in favor of minority teachers.[40] However, it rejected the Reagan administration's position that race should never be a criterion for layoffs, ruling that such a plan may be justified in situations where it could be shown that there had been an *intent* to discriminate.[41]

Shortly thereafter, in another case, the Court accepted the use of a 29 percent hiring quota, which reflected the percentage of minorities in the local work force in that case, because it was being used to remedy blatant past discrimination by the local sheet metal union.[42] And in a 1987 case involving state troopers in Alabama, where not a single African American had reached the rank of corporal, the Court ruled that quotas could be used in promotion decisions when there had been blatant discrimination in the past.[43]

In general, the Court was saying that affirmative action could be used in states and localities only in cases where there was demonstrable evidence of specific discrimination and the program was "narrowly tailored" to meet that offense. A similar pattern prevailed during the George Herbert Walker Bush administration, as can be seen in the Rehnquist Court's rulings on six cases:

1. In *Martin v. Wilks* the Court held that even affirmative action programs that had been acceptable to employees and minority workers could later be challenged by nonminority workers.[44]

2. In *City of Richmond v. Croson* the Court held that a state contract with a set-aside affirmative action plan could be designed only to remedy specific instances of past discrimination.[45]

3. In *Patterson v. McLean Credit Union* the Court held that once a private employment contract was made, employers could not be held liable for issues such as racial harassment and discrimination, because such issues were subsequent to the "making" of that contract.[46]

4. In *Lorance v. AT&T Technologies* the Court reduced the amount of time available to plaintiffs wishing to bring employment discrimination suits.[47]

5. In *Independent Federation of Flight Attendants v. Zipes* the Court limited the right of recovery of attorneys' fees in employment discrimination cases.[48]

6. In *Wards Cove Packing Co. v. Antonio* the Court held that employees claiming employment discrimination had the burden of proving that employment qualifications were not necessary for the jobs they sought.[49]

Seeing the resegregating pattern of these judicial decisions, civil rights leaders turned for help to Congress, which was dominated by a combination of liberal Democrats and southerners who depended on the African American vote for reelection. In February 1990 a bill was introduced that sought to overturn the Court's decisions in the six cases just described. Both houses of Congress passed the law, but President Bush vetoed it, claiming that it would support "quotas." However, after extensive negotiations, a few minor changes in wording, and passage of the new bill, the President agreed to sign it into law as the Civil Rights Act of 1991.

The Future of Civil Rights

The direction of the government's policy toward civil rights during the Clinton administration was difficult to determine. While Clinton's initial rhetoric indicated a sensitivity toward further integrating American society, when the congressional Republicans' hostility toward affirmative action programs became clear, the President placed all of these programs "under review," leading several women's groups to march in Washington shouting "No retreat! No retreat!" The president later pledged full support for such programs, perhaps with an eye toward the 1996 election.

At the same time, in early 1995 the federal courts were sending mixed messages on racial equality. Faced with thirty-eight historically black publicly financed colleges in nineteen states that historically had segregated higher education systems, the federal court in Mississippi began to consider a case that has been termed the *Brown v. Board of Education* of higher education. Was the state's system of five historically white and three historically black universities constitutional? District court judge Neal B. Biggers, Jr., ruled the state's practice of historically different admission standards for the different schools to be unacceptable and ordered the state to spend more money to upgrade the black colleges. With similar legal challenges under way in states such as Alabama, Louisiana, and Tennessee, however, it was unclear how widespread the effect of this ruling would be.[50] At the same time, the Supreme Court let stand a lower federal court ruling that overturned the University of Maryland's program of blacks-only scholarships despite the school's admission that this program was designed to remedy its past discrimination. (One of those who had been discriminated against was Thurgood Marshall.) Once again, just what effect this ruling would have on similar programs in nearly half of the nation's other colleges is unclear.

Then, in a key 1995 decision involving a small business administration program in Colorado giving a Hispanic-owned company an affirmative action advantage in bidding for a highway contract, the Supreme Court for the first time refused to uphold the federal program. Instead, the Court ruled that, like state and local affirmative action programs, it would now use the *strict scrutiny test*, meaning that federal programs must serve a compelling governmental interest and must be designed to remedy specific instances of past discrimination, rather than just overall societal discrimination. This test will make it much more difficult to uphold federal affirmative action programs.[51]

In 1997 it was the unwillingness of the Court to review key actions and lower court decisions that led to the diminution of the affirmative action programs. As the case study makes clear, the Fifth Circuit Court of Appeals ruled in the case of Cheryl Hopwood that such race-based preference programs in admissions were unconstitutional. Shortly thereafter, voters in the state of California passed Proposition 209 by an overwhelming majority.[52] When the Supreme Court refused to accept either of these appeals, thus leaving the lower court and government actions in force, it appeared that affirmative action was in jeopardy of being eliminated.[53]

The battle over state-sponsored preference programs continued in the 1998 elections when voters in Washington state overwhelmingly approved a referendum that the government should be "prohibited from discriminating or granting preferential treatment based on race, sex, color, ethnicity, or national origin" in education, public employment, or contracting. This success may encourage similar efforts to terminate affirmative action in other states, but the question remains whether voters would want to eliminate such programs. These rulings, other refusals to make rulings by the Court, voter initiatives, and actions by governors such as Jeb Bush in Florida make clear that America's approach to democracy in the area of civil rights will continue to be debated year after year.

As outlined in the case study, this debate continued after the election of George W. Bush to the presidency. With literally thousands of racial preference laws hanging in the balance at the local, state, and national levels, the Supreme Court is narrowly balanced 5–4 for curbing such programs, with Sandra Day O'Connor holding the swing vote. The *Gratz* and *Grutter* cases will test the affirmative action program for admissions at the University of Michigan when the Supreme Court rules on them in its 2002–2003 term, and in doing so provides guidance for such programs in all educational institutions.

Women's Rights

In the early 1800s women in the United States were not permitted to vote, serve on juries, find profitable employment, attend institutions of higher education, or own land in their own name. Moreover, the English common law notion of *coverture*, which held that upon marriage a woman lost her separate legal identity, had been adopted in the United States. As a consequence, married women could not sue in their own name, divorce an alcoholic or abusive spouse, own property independently, or enter into contracts.

When Elizabeth Cady Stanton and Lucretia Mott were not seated as duly elected delegates at an international antislavery meeting in London in 1840, they decided to take action. They organized a movement to attain full legal rights for women. At a convention held in Seneca Falls, New York, in 1848, the movement borrowed the language of the Declaration of Independence in issuing a Declaration of Sentiments concerning the "natural rights" of women:

> We hold these truths to be self-evident: that all men and women are created equal; that they are endowed by their Creator with certain inalienable rights; that among these are life, liberty, and the pursuit of happiness.[54]

The convention passed twelve resolutions calling for political and social rights for women.

? Question for Reflection: What, if any, impact would it have on our approach to democracy if women were represented in leadership positions in government and business at the levels equivalent to their percentage of the total U.S. population?

In response to lobbying by women activists, the New York State legislature passed the Married Women's Property Act of 1848. The law gave women control even after marriage over property they received through gifts and inheritance. Encouraged by this success, Stanton, Susan B. Anthony, and other feminist leaders began to lobby for further reforms in New York and other states. Their efforts bore fruit in 1860, when New York passed a civil rights law that gave women control over their wages and inheritances, guaranteed them an inheritance of at least one-third of their husband's estate, granted them joint custody of their children, and allowed them to make contracts and sue in their own name.[55]

Two Steps Forward, One Step Back

The early successes of the women's rights movement were followed by some setbacks. In 1862 the New York State legislature rescinded and modified the earlier women's rights laws. Realizing that it was necessary to maintain constant pressure

▲ Susan B. Anthony and Elizabeth Cady Stanton, shown in 1870, were early leaders of the fight for women's rights and women's suffrage. As a result of their efforts, women got the vote in 1920 with ratification of the Nineteenth Amendment.

on legislators, Anthony and Stanton tried to further link their cause with that of African Americans; they formed the National Woman's Loyal League to advocate a constitutional amendment to prohibit slavery. Soon thereafter they joined with supportive men to form an abolitionist alliance called the American Equal Rights Association.

The new group put aside its feminist goals to promote the Fourteenth Amendment. This move proved to be a tactical error, as the amendment introduced the word "male" into the Constitution for the first time. When language giving women the vote was not included in the Fifteenth Amendment, Stanton and Anthony decided to form another organization designed to push solely for women's suffrage. In 1869 they formed the National Woman Suffrage Association and began a campaign for a constitutional amendment giving women the right to vote. Meanwhile, Lucy Stone, another longtime activist, formed the American Woman Suffrage Association, which sought to achieve suffrage on a state-by-state basis.

Just how far women had yet to go to achieve equality was made clear in 1873, when the first women's rights case reached the Supreme Court. In sustaining a law that barred women from the practice of law, Justice Joseph Bradley stated:

> Man is, or should be, woman's protector and defender. The natural and proper timidity and delicacy which belongs to the female sex evidently unfits it for many of the occupations of civil life. . . . [The] paramount destiny and mission of women are to fulfill the noble and benign offices of wife and mother. This is the law of the Creator.[56]

That "law" became the law of the land as well.

The Struggle for Suffrage

The question of whether the Fourteenth and Fifteenth Amendments were inclusive enough to permit women to vote still remained. In a test case that reached the Supreme Court in 1875, *Minor v. Happersett,* Virginia Minor's husband (since women could still not sue in their own names) argued that the new "privileges and immunities" clause protected his wife's right to vote. However, the Court disagreed, arguing that this privilege was reserved only for men by the Constitution and the state laws.[57]

Despite such setbacks at the federal level, gradual progress was being made at the state level. In 1869 and 1870 the Wyoming and Utah Territories granted full suffrage to women. Nebraska (1867) and Colorado (1876) gave women the right to vote in school elections. In 1890 Alice Stone Blackwell brought together the two rival suffrage organizations to form the National American Woman Suffrage Association, and lobbying for women's suffrage became more organized. By 1910, though, only four states (Colorado, Idaho, Utah, and Wyoming) had provided for full women's suffrage.

The new president of the National American Woman Suffrage Association, Carrie Chapman Catt, advocated the use of a coordinated grass-roots strategy, that is, decentralized action by ordinary citizens, to seek suffrage. This strategy paid off, and by 1918 more than fifteen states, including New York and California, had given women the vote.

This progress was too slow for some. For five years Alice Paul had been running the Congressional Union (later to become the National Woman's Party) to fight for a constitutional amendment permitting women's suffrage. Arguing that the party in power should be held accountable for the continued disenfranchisement of women, the Congressional Union began picketing the White House and putting pressure on Congress to pass an amendment by touring the country with a replica of the Liberty Bell wrapped in chains. But it was World War I that put the suffrage movement over the top. Women argued that their wartime service to the nation should be rewarded with the right of suffrage, and Congress agreed, passing the amendment in June 1919. The Nineteenth Amendment was ratified by the states in 1920, fifty-two years after ratification of the Fourteenth Amendment granting African American males the right to vote and eighty years after Elizabeth Cady Stanton and Lucretia Mott began their quest for full legal rights.

The Road to Equality

Women successfully used their new electoral clout to secure congressional passage of the Married Women's Independent Citizenship Act of 1922, which granted women citizenship independent from their husbands. However, having achieved its main goal of suffrage, the lobbying coalition fell apart, and actual equality for women would have to wait for decades.

Sex discrimination, also called **sexism,** could be seen in many areas of American society, but especially in education and employment. In 1961 the uproar that resulted when President Kennedy appointed only two women to governmental positions spurred him to issue an executive order creating the President's Commission on the Status of Women, chaired by Eleanor Roosevelt. At the suggestion of the commission, Congress passed the Equal Pay Act of 1963, which mandated equal pay for equal work—that is, salaries for men and women performing the same job had to be the same. Although this was a victory for women, the law's effectiveness was limited because employers were still free to create different job classifications with varying rates of pay.

It was the Civil Rights Act of 1964, originally intended to bring about equality for African Americans, that represented the greatest advance for women's rights, poetic justice perhaps, since the movement for full legal rights for women did much to further the causes of African Americans in the 1800s. Ironically, the change came at the behest of a southern congressman, who proposed adding sex to the bill's language in the hope of killing the bill, only to see the measure passed with the language intact. The act barred discrimination against any person on the basis of "race, color, religion, sex, or national origin."

Overburdened by an immense caseload, however, the EEOC was slow to enforce the provisions of the 1964 act. In 1966, outraged by the EEOC's inaction, several women organized the National Organization for Women (NOW). Borrowing techniques from the civil rights movement, NOW organized demonstrations and even picketed the *New York Times* because of its policy of printing a separate section advertising jobs for women. NOW also pressured the EEOC to hold hearings on regulations concerning sex discrimination. In the 1972 Federal Education Amendments, Congress amended the 1964 Civil Rights Act with Title VI, threatening a denial of federal funds to public and private programs that discriminated against women, and Title IX, which called for equal athletic opportunities for women in schools. As the box on Title IX shows, this law has resulted in great changes in college sports.

Leaders of the women's movement still hoped for a constitutional standard establishing equality for women. In 1967 NOW proposed the Equal Rights Amendment (ERA). Women's rights advocates entered the 1970s with the hope that the amendment would be passed and quickly ratified. However, despite congressional approval of the amendment in 1972 and the support of Presidents Nixon and Carter, the ERA fell three states short of the thirty-eight required for ratification. As a result, people are often surprised to learn that women are not specifically mentioned in, and thus not specifically protected by, the Constitution.

Seeking Equality Through the Courts

The quest for equal rights now turned to the courts. The focus of this effort was the Fourteenth Amendment, which states that "No state shall . . . deny to any person within its jurisdiction the equal protection of the laws." It seemed reasonable that a woman could be defined as a person and thus be included in the equal protection

sexism Prejudice against the female gender.

APPROACHING DIVERSITY

Leveling the Playing Fields

When the University of Connecticut women's basketball team beat the University of Oklahoma to win the NCAA championship in 2002, after a perfect 39–0 season, and some people not so kiddingly commented that this team would be a formidable opponent in the men's tournament, it was the culmination of thirty years of change. Alumni recalled the day in the 1970s when women competed at Storrs, Connecticut without scholarship, for the fun of the game, not in spacious Gampel Pavilion but in a field house where buckets were used to catch leaks in the roof, and the men's basketball team got all of the benefits of being an athlete in a major college while the women's team got none. Now with both professional women's basketball and soccer organizations in existence, it is time to reflect on the 30-year history of the federal law that helped create this condition.

The difference only began in 1972, as Title IX of the Federal Education Amendments promised that "No person in the United States shall, on the basis of sex, be excluded from participation in, be denied the benefits of, or be subjected to discrimination under any education program or activity receiving federal financial assistance." As a result, every federally funded college and university had to provide opportunities for men and women in their varsity sports roughly equal to the proportion of each gender in the school, unless they could prove some overriding reason for not doing so. In addition, the school had to give out scholarships to male and female varsity athletes in substantially the same proportion as those participating in the sports.

But change takes time. Despite the promise afforded by this law, in the 1991–92 academic year Donna Lopiano, the women's athletic director at the University of Texas,

▲ Continuing the positive legacy of Title IX of the 1972 Federal Education Amendments, the University of Connecticut's undefeated women's basketball team celebrate their 2002 national championship victory over the University of Oklahoma.

noticed that the school's football team had more athletes than did the entire women's athletic program. And Texas was hardly the only school to be in this situation. Seeking a remedy, Lopiano left her position to direct a national group promoting women in sports. As a result of a class action lawsuit against the school, which was successfully settled out of court in July 1993, the University of Texas was on the verge of meeting its goal of devoting 44 percent of its varsity athletic rosters to women's sports four years later.

Across the nation, schools are adding women's sports, such as softball, soccer, lacrosse, and field hockey, to meet the goal of equality. Sometimes when funding is tight, men's college athletic programs that generate little or no income are cut or trimmed, such as gymnastics, wrestling, swimming, or track. In some schools where the large size of a football program makes it difficult to achieve equality, the

clause. The key to this strategy would be the Supreme Court's interpretation of *equal protection,* or treating people in different categories equally unless the state can demonstrate some constitutional reason for doing otherwise.

For many years sex discrimination cases had been decided by the **test of reasonableness,** or whether a reasonable person would agree that law had a *rational basis,* thus making it constitutional. The burden was placed on the woman to prove that a law that discriminated by gender was arbitrary, capricious, and totally unjustifiable. Under this test, it was nearly impossible for women to win discrimination cases, because an acceptable rationale for the law could always be found or invented by the state. Thus, when the state of Michigan in the 1940s barred women from obtaining a bartender's license unless they were "the wife or daughter of the male owner," the Supreme Court accepted the state's rationale that it wanted to protect the sensibilities of women.[58] And when the state of Florida in the late 1950s declined to put women on jury lists unless they specifically asked to be included, the Court upheld the law because a "woman is still regarded as the center of home and family life" and had "special responsibilities" in this capacity.[59]

test of reasonableness Test in court cases of what reasonable people would agree to be constitutional because the law has a rational basis for its existence.

schools are creating unisex rifle teams in an effort to achieve the goals of the legislation.

But despite problems, the results of this drive for women's equality have been dramatic. Female athletes not only have the same chance to compete as men, but many are now able to get their education on scholarship. Since the 1970s when Title IX was introduced, there are nearly three million girls playing competitive sports in high school, in 1972 there were fewer than 300,000. In the last decade, the number of women's college athletic teams has risen from 2,159 to 2,613, and the total number of female athletes has risen from 35,557 to 47,124.

The positive results are most clearly evident in women's basketball. Once women's basketball was a barely noticed sport, with only a handful of college teams dominated by tiny Immaculata College, a Jesuit college in suburban Philadelphia, whose coach was the legendary Cathy Rush, wife of a National Basketball Association referee. Today Ms. Rush's former players are highly successful coaches for college teams around the country in a national women's NCAA league whose yearly playoffs rival the men's. The game is played on national television to sold-out audiences from Texas to Iowa and California to New York. Not only is there an interest in a women's United States Olympic basketball program but also in the recently created professional WNBA league, which quickly drafted members of UConn's championship team.

And this progress is not being eroded. In 1996 a federal rule clarifying the 1972 Title IX law dictated that equality in team sports would be judged by numbers of actual athletes rather than spots allotted to a team, or money allocated to men's and women's sports. The following year, the Supreme Court, by refusing to take an appeal, affirmed a decision that Brown University had to equalize its sports funding based on gender. In 2000, with 80 percent of the people supporting Title IX, schools everywhere were being compelled to equalize funding for sports based on gender. And in Georgia, Governor Roy Barnes signed a gender equity law ensuring that Title IX would result in equalizing funding for gender in state high schools. One indication of the progress under Title IX to equalize college sports by gender, even at the cost of some men's programs being eliminated, was the new trend by men's wrestlers and their coaches to begin suing in federal court alleging that the law was being violated by the elimination of men's programs to equalize sports program.

While it appeared that the future for gender equity funding for sports looks brighter, when the Bush administration announced in late June 2002, that a fifteen-member committee would be reviewing Title IX of the Federal Education Amendments, seeking recommendations on ways that the law could be changed to ensure "fairness for all college athletes," the nation's women's groups immediately objected. Would the advances for women over the last three decades now be rolled back, or in some way slowed down? Says Secretary of Education Rod Paige, who is directing the study: "Some would like to settle this in the courts. But we believe the better approach is to discuss all the questions openly, in a forum where all voices and viewpoints can be heard." The decision here, though, will determine whether female athletes will still have the opportunity to settle things on the field.

Sources: Erik Brady, "Bush Picks Panel to Review Title IX," *USA Today,* June 28, 2002, p. C. 1; Darryl Campagna McGrath, "Pioneer Players of the '70s Set Stage for Women's Basketball Today, *Buffalo News,* April 7, 2002; Amy Shipley, "Playing Field Levels at Texas," *Washington Post,* July 6, 1997, p. 1; David Nakamura, "Equity Leaves Its Mark on Male Athletes," *Washington Post,* July 7, 1997, p. 1; and Derrick Gould, "LSU Women Win Court Ruling," *New York Times,* June 2, 2000, p. 1.

Women's rights advocates decided to seek a change in the legal standard by which the Court decided cases involving sex discrimination, one that shifted the burden of proof to the state, thus making it more possible for women to win their suits. Ruth Bader Ginsburg, a lawyer for the American Civil Liberties Union (ACLU), designed a campaign modeled on that led by Thurgood Marshall twenty years earlier for the NAACP to end racial segregation in the public schools. The idea was to move the Court incrementally, on a case-by-case basis, toward abandoning the reasonableness test and replacing it with a new test more favorable to the women's cause.

The first case, decided by the court in 1971, involved an Idaho law requiring that in naming the executor of a will a male must be chosen over equally qualified females. Under this law a divorced mother named Sally Reed had been prevented from supervising the will of her deceased son. It seemed likely that the law would be upheld under the reasonableness test. The state's "rational basis" for the law was that men know more than women about business, and it was unnecessary for the courts to hold additional hearings to prove this fact.[60]

Ginsburg decided to use the *Reed v. Reed* case to persuade the Supreme Court to use a different test, known as the **strict scrutiny test,** in dealing with cases of sex discrimination. Under this test, laws that discriminate on the basis of a characteristic that is "immutable [or unchangeable] by birth," such as race or nationality, are considered "suspect." In cases involving such laws, the burden of proof shifts from the plaintiff to the state, which must demonstrate a "compelling state interest" to justify the discriminatory law. That is, the state must show that there was no other means of accomplishing a goal than to treat these classes of people unequally.

Because sex, like race and national origin, is "immutable by birth," Ginsburg hoped that the Court would add it to the list of suspect categories. She was only partially successful. The Court still used the reasonableness test to decide the case, but for the first time it could not find an acceptable justification for the state's discriminatory policy. The law thus violated the equal protection clause of the Fourteenth Amendment. The *Reed v. Reed* case is considered by some to be the equivalent for women's rights of the *Brown v. Board of Education* case for African Americans.

In 1973 the Court considered the case of Sharron Frontiero, a married air force lieutenant, who objected to a federal law that automatically provided benefits to dependents of married men in the armed forces while the husbands of women in the military received benefits only if they could prove that they were dependent on their wives. Four of the justices were now ready to expand the strict scrutiny test to include women. However, just as he would do later for homosexual rights, the "swing justice," Lewis Powell, was not yet ready to do so, because the Equal Rights Amendment was then being considered for ratification. Thus, the less protective reasonableness test continued to be the standard, which became even more important when the ERA failed to be ratified.[61]

In an unusual turn of events, the next case in the series involved a man, Mel Kahn, who claimed to have been discriminated against on the basis of his sex by a Florida law that provided $500 more in property tax exemption for widows than for widowers. Although the ACLU lost the case, it had made an important step forward. Rather than pressing for the strict scrutiny test or accepting the reasonableness test, Ginsburg asked the Court to create an intermediate **heightened scrutiny test,** which would be used for laws that created benevolent forms of discrimination. Such a standard would force the state to prove more than just the "reasonableness" of the law, though not its "compelling" nature, to justify it. Thus, a law would now be upheld if the rights of the plaintiff were deemed on balance to be more important than the state's interests as represented in the law.[62]

The present legal status of women was finally achieved in a 1976 case called *Craig v. Boren* that on the surface did not look like material for a landmark constitutional decision. An underaged fraternity boy and the Honk 'n' Holler convenience store had teamed up to challenge an Oklahoma statute under which eighteen-year-old girls could buy weak 3.2 beer (3.2 percent alcohol, as opposed to the 3.5–6 percent), but boys could not do the same until they were twenty-one. The state justified the law on the basis of differential driving records for the two groups. According to Ginsburg, this was a "nonweighty interest pressed by thirsty boys," but it nonetheless led to a legal victory. In striking down the law as an unconstitutional violation of the equal protection clause, the Supreme Court applied the heightened scrutiny test. Under this test, laws that classify people according to their sex must now "serve important governmental objectives and must be substantially related to the achievement of those objectives."[63]

In 1996 more progress was made for women's rights when the Supreme Court ruled that the Virginia Military Institute (VMI), a state-run, all-male military college, had to admit women or lose state funding. VMI had argued that its 157-year tradition of single-sex education—highlighted by its "rat line" whereby new cadets get crew cuts and face the taunts and face-to-face inquisitions of upperclassmen—justified the single-sex approach. But Justice Ginsburg ruled, "We find no persuasive evidence in this record that VMI's male-only admission policy 'is in furtherance

▲ Members of the senior class at the previously all-male Virginia Military Institute, standing in their "rat line," greet new cadet Megan Smith, properly attired with her military-style crew cut, as she becomes one of thirty women in the school's first coeducational class under court order.

strict scrutiny test Test of laws which discriminate on the basis of a characteristic that is "immutable [or unchangeable] by birth," such as race or nationality; in such cases, the burden shifts from the plaintiff to the state forcing the government to show the compelling reasons for the law. That is, the state must show that no other possible way existed to accomplish this regulation.

heightened scrutiny test A middle-level standard that would force the state to prove more than just the reasonableness of a law, though not its compelling nature, in order to justify it. For women's rights cases this means proving the important governmental objectives of the law's goals and linking it to the wording of the law.

APPROACHING DEMOCRACY AROUND THE GLOBE

Women of the House: Britain vs. Afghanistan

When considering the position of women in the legislative assemblies around the world it is a case of "where you stand, depends on where you sit." No better evidence of the political effect wrought by the American military operation in Afghanistan after September 11, 2001, is the fact that women began running for the legislative body there, but in higher numbers than in the British House of Commons.

In 1997, when women in Afghanistan were wearing full-length burka veils, and were not permitted to work or be educated, a record 101 women were elected to the British House of Commons in the landslide led by Tony Blair and the Labor Party. Very quickly these women were dubbed "Blair's Babes."

Perhaps this label was sign of the uphill battle these newly elected women faced in the British House. They soon discovered the working conditions were so bad that they could more easily buy bottles of whiskey in the Parliament building than fax a document. "In terms of the physical working conditions, I can honestly say they were the worst working conditions I have ever had in a long working life," said M.P. Jenny Jones. The Parliament building was not modernized, the hours went until near midnight, and while the building had a chess room and ribbons for one's sword on a personal coat hook, the new female members did not have offices, phones, desks, or a daycare center. When one new mother asked to breast feed her baby during long Parliament debates, some of the more senior male members "all but fell off their leather benches in horror." So few women chose to run for re-election in Britain in June 2001 that for the first time in two decades the number of women in Parliament declined. As former Member of Parliament Tess Kingham put it, she wanted "a productive working life, not a cultural experience in a gentlemen's club."

Meanwhile, since the American military routed the Taliban and the al-Qaeda, ex-king Mohammad Zaher Shah announced that he would return to Afghanistan after nearly three decades in exile in Italy and call into session the new assembly or loya jirga. More than 160 seats of the 1,500

▲ British Prime Minister Tony Blair is surrounded by some of the 101 women who were elected to the House of Commons along with him, thus becoming what the British Press labeled "Blair's Babes."

person assembly were guaranteed for women, women now clothed in brightly colored attire without veils, with daughters now admitted to local schools. "Our endeavor has been aimed at ensuring the rights of the Afghan people to freely choose their own destiny and political future," said Ismael Qasimyar, head of the independent commission in charge of planning the new nationwide assembly.

Some in Great Britain were just as hopeful about women in the Parliament. "I actually think we have brought the shaft of light into the House of Commons," said former M.P. Jenny Jones, who chose to retire from politics in 2001. But the changes needed for British women to succeed in government are less overt than allowing women to discard their floor length burkas.

Sources: Sarah Lyall, "With a Parting Swipe, Women of the House Exit," *New York Times,* May 18, 2001, p. A4; Pamela Constable, "Afghans Enjoy a Gala No Longer Banned," *Washington Post,* March 22, 2002, and Pamela Constable, "Panel Unveils Rules for Afghan Assembly," *Washington Post,* April 1, 2001.

of a state policy of diversity.'" "Rather," she added, "neither the goal of producing citizen-soldiers nor VMI's implementing methodology is inherently unsuitable to women."[64] While VMI and the Citadel, a formerly all-male military academy in South Carolina, both admitted women to their incoming classes, the tradition of the "rat line" has continued.[65] The progress of women in the service academies became even more evident in 2002 when George W. Bush spoke to the graduating class at West Point, which included a female valedictorian. The nation's only three all-male colleges—Hampden-Sydney in Virginia, Wabash in Indiana, and Morehouse in Georgia—are private ones.

Much progress has been made toward equal rights for women in the United States, but it is clear that there is much progress yet to be made. Many of the gains have been evident in the political world. In the past five presidential administrations, 20 cabinet heads have been women. The Bush administration benefits from the advice of more women in influential positions in the top levels of the executive branch than any prior president. National Security Advisor Condoleeza Rice, "the most powerful woman to work on a White House staff," helps to shape foreign policy, Karen Hughes was one of the most influential presidential counselors before leaving the staff to return to Texas, though she still helps to shape some policy, and Environmental Protection Agency head, Christie Todd Whitman, is spearheading the Bush administration's changes in environmental policy. With over 50 congressional seats, 19,000 elective posts nationwide, 22.6 percent of the state legislative posts (up from only 4.5 percent in 1971), and 2,500 state and federal judicial posts (not to mention numerous college presidencies and state governorships) all being filled by women, progress seems evident when measured against the days when Sandra Day O'Connor and Ruth Bader Ginsburg were only offered positions as legal secretaries after their distinguished law school careers.

This progress became even more clear in 1998 when the Supreme Court clarified its rules on sexual harassment. Confusion had reigned in the federal courts for years after the Supreme Court ruled in 1986 that sexual harassment was a form of sex discrimination covered by Title VII of the 1964 Civil Rights Act. In time, lower federal courts came to require that, an alleged victim prove the loss of a job or an anticipated promotion, a difficult task, in order to win restitution.

In June 1998, the Court handed down two 7 to 2 decisions, one involving a lifeguard in Boca Raton, Florida, and the other a marketing representative for Burlington Industries in Chicago. The Court ruled that employers were deemed to be responsible for the sexual misconduct of supervisors, even if they had no knowledge of it. Moreover, the victims of the abuse should not have to prove that they were denied a promotion or were fired because they rejected a boss's advances; rather, the pervasiveness or continued severity of any threats or abuse were enough for a lawsuit. In some cases, though, companies could defend themselves by proving that they took reasonable steps to prevent harassment in the workplace. As Justice David Souter wrote: "It is by now well recognized that . . . sexual harassment by supervisors (and, for that matter, co-employees) is a persistent problem in the workplace."

In the same term the Court also ruled that sexual harassment claims can be filed even in same-sex situations. And finally, students in public school who claimed sexual harassment by teachers were ruled not to be able to sue the school district unless school officials had direct knowledge of the harassment and were deliberately indifferent to it.[66]

As we saw in Chapter 3, in 2000 the Court ruled it unconstitutional for a college student who had been raped in her Virginia college dorm room by two football players to sue the alleged perpetrators under the 1994 Violence Against Women Act in federal court. The states were left to provide criminal and civil remedies for such attacks.[67] In 2000, though, Congress reauthorized VAWA and expanded it to include date rape, but those victims were still not able to sue their attackers in federal court.

Civil Rights and Other Minorities

Hispanic Americans

Immigrants to the United States from Mexico, Cuba, Puerto Rico, and other Spanish-speaking countries throughout South America and the Caribbean islands have experienced forms of discrimination similar to those faced by African Americans, though to different degrees. Mexican Americans have been robbed of their land, attacked by the Ku Klux Klan and rioting mobs, excluded from labor unions, and discriminated against in employment, housing, and education. Puerto Ricans,

QUOTE ... UNQUOTE

"Under our constitutional system courts stand against any winds that blow as havens of refuge for those who might otherwise suffer because they are helpless, weak, outnumbered, or because they are nonconforming victims of prejudice and public excitement."

Supreme Court Justice Hugo Black, *Chambers v. Florida,* 1940

Cubans and Columbians, have also suffered from discrimination and de facto housing segregation.

In 1929 Mexican Americans founded the League of United Latin American Citizens (LULAC), seeking to gain more equal treatment in American society. Then in the 1950s they formed organizations that stressed electoral politics and attempted to reclaim lost lands in New Mexico. Perhaps the most famous aspect of the movement was the formation of a union of migrant Mexican American farm workers under the leadership of Cesar Chavez. Through strikes, boycotts, pickets, and political action, the United Farm Workers drew national attention to the conditions endured by migrant farmworkers.

In the late 1960s the Mexican American Legal Defense and Education Fund (MALDEF) was created. Through litigation and lobbying, MALDEF campaigned for integration, equal school financing, and full protection of voting rights and against discrimination in employment. The success of MALDEF led to the creation of the Puerto Rican Legal Defense Fund. Other Hispanic American groups, such as the National Council of La Raza, have also fought for increased voter registration and electoral participation.

Along with African Americans, Hispanic Americans benefited from the Supreme Court's rulings on segregation, the Civil Rights Act of 1964, and the Voting Rights Act of 1965. In *Katzenbach v. Morgan*, for example, the Court upheld a portion of the Voting Rights Act of 1965 that outlawed the use of an English literacy test in New York.[68] Through the actions of MALDEF and other groups, the Voting Rights Act was extended to protect Hispanic Americans and "other language" minorities.

The effort to achieve greater education equality for Hispanic and other minority children living in poor communities suffered a setback in 1973 in the case of *San Antonio Independent School District v. Rodriguez*.[69] The Court was unwilling to overturn the use of property taxes to finance state school systems, despite the resulting inequality in educational resources between wealthy and poor communities in the state of Texas. Nevertheless, several other state supreme courts subsequently used their own state constitutions as a basis for requiring equal financing of education. Then, in 1982, the Court ordered that all children must be provided with schooling regardless of whether their parents were legal immigrants.[70]

Hispanic Americans continue to struggle against discrimination and poverty. Now numbering over 35 million people, up a remarkable 58% over the 22 million present in this country in 1990, and with half having been born outside this country, it is predicted that by the mid-twenty-first century Hispanic Americans will make up nearly one-third of the U.S. population.[71] Hispanic Americans are now the largest minority in the United States, outnumbering African Americans by less than a million people. So achievement of legal and actual equality for this group deserves high priority. Evidence of this demand has been seen in the effort by the Bush administration to have conservative Hispanic American Miguel Estrada confirmed by the Senate for the U.S. Court of Appeals for the District of Columbia. Presidential Counselor, Alberto Gonzalez, and Emilio Garza of the Fifth Circuit are also being mentioned for possible appointment to the Supreme Court.

Native Americans

The history of discrimination and segregation against Native Americans is well known but virtually ignored throughout America's history. Native American tribes have been removed from their land, treaties have been broken, and Native Americans have been denied the basic right of citizenship. In 1884 the Supreme Court ruled that Native Americans were not citizens of the United States and therefore were neither protected by the Fourteenth Amendment nor granted the right to vote.[72] In the early 1900s Native Americans strove to attain both citizenship and tribal autonomy, while during the 1920s they struggled against attempts to establish reservations that could be exploited by miners. Finally, in 1924 Congress passed the Indian Citizenship Act, which gave Native Americans the right to vote.

QUOTE ... UNQUOTE

The "Constitution is not a panacea for every blot upon the public welfare, nor should this Court, ordained as a judicial body, be thought of as a general haven for reform movements."

Supreme Court Justice John Marshall Harlan, *Reynolds v. Sims,* 1964

► Descendants of Chief Spotted Elk and his people commemorate the one-hundredth anniversary of the Battle of Wounded Knee, South Dakota, where on December 29, 1890, some three hundred women, children, and elderly people were massacred by the U.S. Army Seventh Regiment, Custer's old regiment, who were seeking revenge for the Battle of the Little Bighorn.

Native Americans have resisted various attempts to assimilate them into the mainstream culture of American society over the years. In the 1940s, the National Congress of American Indians was formed to fight for education and legal aid. During the 1960s, Native Americans engaged in acts of civil disobedience such as delaying dam construction, occupying government offices, and holding sit-ins and other demonstrations to fight against discrimination. The American Indian Movement (AIM) occupied buildings and staged demonstrations, and in 1973 AIM played a major part in the well-publicized occupation of Wounded Knee on the Pine Ridge Reservation in South Dakota. Unfortunately, however, the Native American cause has yet to generate the support found for other minority groups.[73]

Native Americans face a challenge that most other minorities do not: they are divided into two movements with different aspirations. The ethnic movement shares the aspirations of other ethnic minorities to achieve equality in American society. In contrast, the separatist tribal movement seeks separate citizenship and a system of government based on the tribe, the Indian culture decimated by the United States' growth. Whereas the ethnic movement wishes to participate in American democracy, the goal of the tribal movement is to create its own concept of democracy, removed from a democratic government that in the past too often failed to live up to its treaties (for more, see the *"Echoes from Ghost Ridge"* box).

During the 1960s Native Americans made some progress with regard to tribal sovereignty and treaty rights, as well as changing public perceptions of "Indians." In recent years tribes in Rhode Island, Connecticut, and elsewhere have even used the exemption of their reservation lands from state laws to create highly profitable gambling enterprises, thus helping to raise money for their communities and create political clout. This success, however, is relatively isolated and discrimination has not been eliminated. Equality is still an elusive goal as the Native American population remains among the poorest and least represented in government in the nation.

Emerging Minority Groups Seek Prominence

Americans with Disabilities

Unlike other minority groups, Americans with disabilities, which by some definitions now number 43 million people, have been extremely successful in persuading Congress to pass legislation barring discrimination against them. However, since

Echoes from Ghost Ridge: *Cobell v. Norton*

"I swear I am not going to let them break my spirit, I'm not going to let them break my son's spirit. I'm not going to let them break my grandchildren's spirit. We have to be strong." So spoke five-foot-four-inch Native American activist Elouise Cobell, who explained why she was suing the federal government on behalf of her Blackfeet Nation, seeking reparations of up to $137 billion for her people and possibly a jail sentence for Secretary of the Interior Gale Norton.

The idea for the lawsuit began with the stories Cobell, who was awarded a MacArthur Foundation "genius award" even though she had never graduated from college, heard of her ancestors' plight in the history of the United States. Once the Blackfeet Nation ruled the northern plains hunting massive herds of buffalo, but like the other native Indian tribes, the Blackfeet were forced to sign treaties with the United States government that promised reservation lands, rations and equipment in return for peace. While the Native Americans kept their part of the bargain, the government's promises were left unfulfilled. Five hundred Blackfeet died of starvation on Ghost Ridge in the winter of 1883–84 when the United States government did not honor its promise of delivering winter food rations and instead sold them on the open market for profit.

As part of the peace treaty signed with the United States government, individual members of the Blackfeet Nation, including Cobell's parents, were given reservation lands with the understanding that all mining, oil, timber and grazing rights would be leased out, and the money realized would be held in trust for them by the Bureau of Indian Affairs. This money was supposed to be distributed to the Blackfeet landholders, but only intermittently did they see any government checks. The problem was that the United States government never clearly identified the property lines, so the Blackfeet people, unsure as to where their land holdings were, remained ignorant of the billions of dollars being made from their land's use.

Ms. Cobell filed a class-action lawsuit representing 500,000 Native American litigants against the federal government and then–Secretary of the Interior Bruce Babbitt in 1996. When two Cabinet members refused to produce the trust documents as ordered by the Court, they were held in contempt of Court by U.S. District Court Judge

▲ Native American activist Eloise Cobell stands in front of one of the oil wells on land owned according to treaty by her Blackfeet Nation, but whose mineral rights profits have been going elsewhere, leading to her $137-billion law suit against the United States government.

Royce Lambert, who said that he had "never seen more egregious conduct" by the federal government, who itself had "engaged [in a] shocking pattern of deception of the court." The government was ordered to pay fines of $600,000. The judge also ruled that the government had not fulfilled its obligations under the trust agreement, but it was yet to be determined how much should be paid to members of the tribe, with some estimates ranging from $40 to $137 billion.

When the government, after employing a variety of delaying tactics, revealed that many of the documents involved have been lost or destroyed, Secretary of the Interior Gale Norton and Bureau of Indian Affairs Director Neal McCaleb were scheduled to be put on trial for contempt of court. For Cobell, who frequently reminds herself of the historical importance of her mission by walking near the mass grave on Ghost Ridge, all that she wants of the United States government is to "do the right thing."

Sources: "Eloise Cobell" "UPCLOSE," ABCNEWS, 2002 ABCNEWS Internet Ventures, found at www.abcnews.com, last checked July 13, 2002, and Richard Williams, "Settling the Trust Issue," *Denver Post*, December 5, 2001.

1999, the Supreme Court has, in a number of rulings, been making it more and more difficult for these people to obtain federal government protection.

In 1948, likely stirred by the memory of the wheelchair-bound late president, Franklin D. Roosevelt, Congress passed a law prohibiting discrimination against the physically handicapped in the civil service. In 1968 it passed the Architectural Barriers Act, which required that all buildings constructed with federal money or leased by the federal government be made accessible to the handicapped. Congress acted again in 1973, when it mandated that federal contractors and programs that received federal funds adopt policies of nondiscrimination and affirmative action for the disabled. When Congress passed the Civil Rights Restoration Act of 1988, it barred any institution that discriminated on the basis of race, sex, age, or handicap from receiving federal funds.

Despite the passage of these and other statutes that protect the rights of the disabled, Americans with disabilities continue to be deprived of many basic civil rights. For example, they still face discrimination by private employers and establishments. Some progress was made in 1990, when Congress passed the Americans with Disabilities Act (ADA). Under the provisions of this act, firms with more than twenty-five employees are barred from discriminating against disabled individuals in hiring or promotion. In addition, companies are required to make "reasonable accommodations" for disabled employees, such as providing readers for blind workers or wider doors for those in wheelchairs. Interestingly, these laws that bar unlawful discrimination against people with disabilities are being interpreted by the Court to say that government and industry must make exceptions in favor of those groups. The law thus becomes the largest and most expensive affirmative action program in the nation. Recent studies have shown, however, that this law rarely helps the disabled seeking jobs. Instead, in over one-third of the complaints, it is being used to deal with such relatively minor problems as back pain, psychological stress, and substance abuse.[74]

As we discussed in Chapter 3, the Supreme Court in 1999 ruled in five separate cases that the ADA would have a much narrower reach than many expected. Noting that Congress intended to reach 43 million people with the law, the Court ruled that this law did not apply to people with correctable impairments, such as high blood pressure or bad eyesight, which would have expanded the reach of the law to 160 million people. As a result, attorneys seeking disabilities protection will now turn to the states, such as California, for greater protection.[75] In the 2001–2002 term, the Court continued the states' rights direction of its rulings by deciding against disabled litigants who were seeking federal judicial protection in four separate cases. Among these decisions, the Court ruled that states are constitutionally immune from lawsuits for damages under the ADA. The Court ruled that Congress had not sufficiently demonstrated in the legislative record for the law that states discriminated against handicapped persons, and that Congress had no power to require states to implement such a law.[76]

While states were not governed by the United States Constitution in its dealings with handicapped persons, the Court also ruled that the Professional Golf Association (P.G.A.) could not prevent golfer Casey Martin, who has a debilitating leg injury, from riding a golf cart during tournaments, all of which normally require their participants to walk the course. For the Court, this was a "reasonable accommodation" for players which did not fundamentally alter the game's competitiveness.[77]

Why has the struggle for equality been relatively easy for the disabled when compared with other minority groups? One reason is that laws requiring access to facilities are viewed as providing equality of opportunity, a goal on which most Americans agree. Another reason is that the experiences of the disabled are very close to all of us, including politicians such as Franklin D. Roosevelt and Robert Dole, who themselves have disabilities or who have relatives with disabilities. The ADA demonstrates how far the United States can travel along the road to democracy when it is unified about the direction it wants to take.

Another set of questions deals with just how inclusive society should be in approaching democracy. Inevitably, other minority groups that face discrimination will demand greater equality. Two such groups are the elderly and homosexuals. With an ever-increasing percentage of Americans in the oldest age groups, there will be growing demands for protection of the civil rights of the elderly. While the Age Discrimination in Employment Act (ADEA) covers many of the elderly, new issues will undoubtedly arise and will be pressed on the government by the 30-million-member American Association of Retired Persons (AARP). In 2000, this group lost ground from a narrow 5 to 4 Supreme Court ruling that Congress lacked the power to make state governments liable to federal lawsuits brought under the Age Discrimination in Employment Act to remedy discrimination against older workers.[78]

The challenge for the gay and lesbian community, as seen by the controversy in 2002 when talk show host Rosie O'Donnell announced that she was gay, is unlike that faced by any other minority group in American society. A high percentage of the estimated 25 million to 30 million homosexual Americans live their lives in secret, undetected and unsuspected by a "straight" society that is prone to homophobia. While some states and localities attempt to protect the civil rights of homosexuals, the federal government and many states now do not. The impact of Proposition 22 in California and the reversal in Hawaii of its same-sex marriage law, while Vermont now allows legal protection for same-sex unions, illustrate how these rights vacillate. For them, the fight for equal protection will be an uphill one. However, one wonders whether there will one day be a judicial decision with the same impact on legal equality as *Brown* for this community.

Civil Rights and the War on Terrorism

Facing discrimination will demand greater equality. But the immediate question for the nation is whether we can preserve the civil rights of any individual under investigation during a time of crisis. While Chapter 13 considered how to preserve the legal and trial safeguards for people who are arrested in the "war on terrorism," what of those under investigation simply because of their ethnic background.

Perhaps the greatest test of America's approach to democracy with respect to civil rights since September 11, 2001, is the issue of ethnic profiling in conducting antiterrorism investigations, airport searches, immigration interviews and secret detentions of Muslim men who came from nations where the al-Qaeda network is considered to be active. Within days after the attacks on the World Trade Center and the Pentagon, over 1,200 Muslim men were arrested on minor immigration violations, such as overstaying their visas, and jailed without legal representation or their names being released. The passage of the U.S.A. Patriot Act later allowed for this kind of detention of others. Two months after the attack nearly 5,000 Arab men, between the ages of 18 and 33 who entered the United States after January 1, 2000 on non-immigrant visas, were requested to "voluntarily" present themselves for interviews by Justice Department and Immigration and Naturalization Service representatives. "We are merely seeking to solicit their assistance to obtain any information they may have regarding possible terrorists or potential terrorist acts," explained Attorney General John Ashcroft. Nearly 2,500 of the men could not be found, and these interviews resulted in fewer than two dozen arrests while revealing minimal information. Still, the Justice Department was encouraged by the level of cooperation of those interviewed and the nature of the information it gathered. So, early in 2002, over the objections of civil rights groups who feared that these interviews carried with it the dual risks of racial profiling and potential deportation, the government requested that another 3,000 visitors who entered this country more recently, present themselves for interviews. Years of dealing with charges of "racial profiling" in New Jersey, California, and other locations around the country as the police have used their discretion in stopping and questioning African Americans, now took a twist as authorities in airports and mass transportation centers began targeting Arab-Americans, persons of Arabian descent, and Arab visitors, for questioning, searching, and even detention. While authorities have tried to use random search techniques, thousands of complaints were lodged nationwide concerning racial profiling. Profiled individuals were being forced to leave planes, one of them a Secret Service agent for President Bush, because of fears by the pilots, flight attendants, or even passengers about traveling with them.[79]

These actions eventually led to challenges in federal court. Realizing that by mid-February 2002 over 300 men were still being detained in federal prisons without legal representation, many of them in northern New Jersey, a New Jersey state judge

DEMOCRACY IN THE NEW MILLENNIUM

Engineering a New Diversity

How do you promote diversity in your student body when the federal courts have limited or even ended your ability to use race as a factor in making admissions decisions with the intention of crafting a diverse class? The answer may well be to engineer a diverse class by constructing a new socioeconomic "diversity index" to be used in making admissions decisions. The effort to computerize heterogeneity in classes began in San Francisco, California after school officials were forced by a 1999 federal court settlement not to use race in the assignment of students to schools but still to maintain desegregated schools in the city. In order to fill the 112 public schools, school officials devised a complex ranking system of a variety of socioeconomic factors including: whether the student lives in public housing, is proficient in English, participates in the free lunch program, has a mother who finished high school, and/or previously attended a poorly performing school. On this basis, students are classified according to socioeconomic status and assigned to schools on that basis. "It's a noble attempt to maintain diversity," says one parent, "But the success of this is going to depend a lot on other aspects of the school system." Still, if race is ruled out as a possible factor for college admissions, it is not hard to imagine the addition of SAT scores and other factors, including neighborhood background descriptions and the quality of high schools attended, to compose a similar "diversity index," perhaps even including factors such as gender, for college admissions that might also "engineer diversity." The Council on Legal Education Opportunity (CLEO) attempted to construct just such a socioeconomic index for law school admissions, which resulted in successful improvement in minority admissions. When the federal government decided to cut its funding, CLEO was privatized. For more, see http://aad.english.ucsb.edu, http://www. feminist.org/ other/ccri/cahome.html, and http://www.amatecon.com/ etext/aar/aar.html.

set a deadline for the release of their names. The Immigration and Naturalization service ordered the state and local governments not to release the names, saying that the move could endanger both national security and the welfare of those being detained. By the middle of April a civil rights group sued the federal government on the detainees' behalf, alleging that hundreds of Muslim men were being held in prison on minor immigration violations, being subjected to harsh treatment, and not being given hearings to determine their legal status. When the case reached District Court Judge Gladys Kessler in the District of Columbia Circuit in August 2002, she ordered the names of these prisoners to be released, ruling that "The requirement that arrest books be open to the public is to prevent any 'secret arrests,' a concept odious to a democratic society."[80] In short, this practice receded from, rather than approached, democracy. Despite this ruling, the United States government continued to refuse to release the names of prisoners. By October 2002 it began to release a few of the prisoners, who were deemed to have little intelligence value, from the Guantanamo Bay holding facility. Meanwhile, many anticipated that the Supreme Court would begin hearing cases that would test the constitutionality of the government's war on terrorism. Still, one controversial practice by the government was the decision to seal the records of hundreds of deportation hearings if they were deemed to be of "special interest" after the September 11 attacks. The Bush administration's policy of holding secret deportation hearings was ruled by the the Sixth Circuit Court of Appeals to be unconstitutional. The court ruled that the public and press's right to access to deportation hearings can only be overcome if the government's are of the highest order. "Open proceedings, with a vigorous and scrutinizing press, serve to ensure the durability of our democracy," ruled the Sixth Circuit judges, who relied on the First Amendment's right of access to government proceedings.[81]

As other lawsuits work their way through the Courts the question is whether the government can show that the benefits to the security of the nation of such law enforcement supercedes the civil rights of the people under investigation. Lessons will be drawn from the civil rights fights of African Americans and women, the Japanese internment policy in the 1940s, and the "red scare" period in the 1950s, as the federal courts and the American people decide the nature of civil rights in times of crisis. In the end, the question will be asked whether the actions taken to preserve security will preserve the democratic goals of the nation or lead instead to a nation which no longer approaches the very democratic vision that it claims to be seeking.

Civil Rights and Approaching Democracy

After two hundred years of civil rights battles, how much farther do we need to go to achieve full equality for all Americans? Clearly, the Gratz, Grutter, and other affirmative action cases illustrate that the struggle is not over. Another set of questions deals with just how inclusive society should be in approaching democracy.

We have seen that at various times the protection of civil rights has fallen to the Supreme Court, at other times the Congress, and at still other times to the president. Throughout the struggle, the force behind the effort to achieve equal rights had been the "people power" of the civil rights movement, the women's movement, and others. Yet there is much left to be done. America will continue to approach democracy by guaranteeing legal and actual rights, but the road will not be a straight or smooth one.

SUMMARY

1. Discrimination is unequal treatment based on race, ethnicity, gender, and other distinctions. The primary means for achieving equal treatment is ensuring full protection of civil rights, the constitutionally guaranteed rights that may not be arbitrarily removed by the government.

2. Equality before the law, or de jure equality, requires that there be no legally mandated obstacles to equal treatment. Actual equality, or de facto equality, refers to results—the actual conditions of people's lives.

3. Although black slaves were freed during the Civil War, their civil rights did not gain legal protection. By the end of the nineteenth century the races were strictly segregated by Jim Crow laws, and in *Plessy v. Ferguson* the Supreme Court ruled that separate but equal facilities did not violate the Fourteenth Amendment. Although African Americans had been granted the right to vote, state voting laws contained many loopholes that effectively disfranchised blacks. In the early decades of the twentieth century the NAACP won several lawsuits that advanced the cause of racial equality.

4. During and after World War II the White House issued executive orders prohibiting discrimination in the defense business and the military. The battle for desegregation of the public schools was led by the NAACP and culminated in the historic *Brown v. Board of Education of Topeka Kansas* ruling that struck down the separate but equal doctrine.

5. Beginning with the Montgomery bus boycott in 1955, the civil rights movement employed techniques such as boycotts, protest marches, and sit-ins to publicly demonstrate the injustice of unequal treatment based on race. During the 1960s Congress passed several laws designed to eliminate discrimination, including the Civil Rights Act of 1964 (which focused on discrimination in public accommodations, voter registration, and employers), the Voting Rights Act of 1965, and the Civil Rights Act of 1968, which focused on discrimination in housing. Several cases decided by the Supreme Court during this period dealt with the specific means used to desegregate schools.

6. Affirmative action programs attempt to improve the chances of minority applicants for jobs, housing, employment, and graduate admissions by giving them a slight advantage over white applicants with similar qualifications. Such programs seek to increase equality but can create temporary inequalities in the process, and therefore are controversial. Underlying the controversy is a disagreement over the meaning of actual equality; some feel that the goal should be equality of opportunity, while others believe that the nation should strive for equality of result.

7. The Reagan administration challenged many of the nation's civil rights policies, claiming that the various Civil Rights Acts prohibited all racial and sexual discrimination, including discrimination against white males. In a series of cases the Supreme Court set specific limits on the use of affirmative action.

8. The movement for women's rights began with the Declaration of Sentiments drawn up at a convention held in Seneca Falls, New York, in 1848. Progress toward equality was slow and uneven throughout the next several decades; women gained control over their property but were unable to vote. It was not until 1920 that the Nineteenth Amendment to the Constitution granted women the right of suffrage.

9. In response to complaints of sex discrimination in education and employment, Congress passed the Equal Pay Act of 1963, which required equal pay for equal work. The Civil Rights Act of 1964 also barred discrimination on the basis of sex. However, efforts to pass the Equal Rights Amendment to the Constitution, which would have given full protection to the civil rights of women, were unsuccessful.

10. In the 1970s efforts to gain equal protection for women's rights turned to the courts and focused on the standard used to determine whether a state law is constitutional. In a series of cases the Supreme Court gradually shifted from a reasonableness test, which upheld a law if the state could provide an acceptable rationale for the law, to a heightened scrutiny test, in which laws that classify people according to their sex must serve important governmental objectives and be substantially related to the achievement of those objectives.

11. Hispanic Americans have made considerable progress toward equal treatment, particularly in the area of voting rights, but they continue to struggle against discrimination and poverty. Native Americans have also organized to demand the basic rights of citizenship and to fight against discrimination. In contrast to these and other minority groups, Americans with disabilities have been extremely successful in persuading Congress to pass legislation barring discrimination against them.

12. The ongoing investigation in the war on terrorism has raised the question of racial profiling of people of middle-Eastern descent. While the government has tried to use random searches to avoid complaints, it will be left to future litigation to determine whether the proper balance is being made between civil rights and national security. In an early indication of the federal court's holdings, the Bush administration's practice of holding secret deportation hearings was ruled unconstitutional.

KEY TERMS

discrimination	peonage	affirmative action
civil rights	desegregation	equality of opportunity
de jure equality	integration	equality of result
de facto equality	civil disobedience	quota programs
black codes	boycott	sexism
suffrage	protest march	test of reasonableness
state action	sit-in	strict scrutiny test
Jim Crow laws	freedom riders	heightened scrutiny test
poll tax		

POLISIM ACTIVITY

Travel the Civil Rights Timeline

Using this timeline of significant events in the civil rights struggle, you will access a wealth of information and multimedia to further explain the struggle. In addition the timeline will highlight all major events (good & bad), speeches, conflicts that are part of the civil rights story including Constitution disputes of slavery, abolition, women's suffrage, John Crow laws, and major sociological changes, to name a few.

SUGGESTED READINGS

ABRAHAM, HENRY J., and BARBARA A. PERRY. *Freedom and the Court: Civil Rights and Liberties in the United States*. 7th ed. New York: Oxford University Press, 1998. An analysis of the development of American civil rights and liberties by the Supreme Court and the lower federal courts.

BOK, DEREK and WILLIAM BOWEN, *The Shape of the River: Long-term consequences of Considering Race in College and University Admissions*. Princeton, N.J.: Princeton University Press, 1998. A powerful critique of the affirmative action program in American education.

BRANCH, TAYLOR. *Parting the Waters: America in the King Years, 1954–63*. New York: Simon & Schuster, 1988. A Pulitzer Prize winner, this is the first of three projected volumes on Martin Luther King Jr. and the civil rights movement in the United States.

BRANCH, TAYLOR. *Pillar of Fire: America in the King Years, 1963–65*. New York: Simon & Schuster, 1998. The second of three planned volumes on the life and times of Martin Luther King, Jr., covering events in the civil rights movement from the March on Washington to the demonstrations in Selma, Alabama.

BROWN, DEE ALEXANDER. *Bury My Heart at Wounded Knee: An Indian History of the American West*. New York: Holt, Rinehart & Winston, 1971. A highly readable history of the sad treatment of Native Americans by the United States government and its people.

CARTER, STEVEN L. *Reflections of an Affirmative Action Baby*. New York: Basic Books, 1991. A learned critique of the affirmative action programs by an African American law professor from Yale who benefited from them.

GARROW, DAVID J. *Bearing the Cross: Martin Luther King, Jr., and the Southern Christian Leadership Conference*. New York: Morrow, 1986. A landmark biography of King that won a Pulitzer Prize.

HALBERSTAM, DAVID. *The Children*. New York: Random House, 1998. Offers a dramatic account of the young civil rights freedom riders who desegregated the buses and restaurants in 1961 and tracks what happened to them in later life.

KEYSSAR, ALEXANDER. *The Right to Vote: The Contested History of Democracy in the United States*. New York: Basic Books, 2000. A pathbreaking study of the meandering expansion of voting rights throughout this nation's history.

KLUGER, RICHARD. *Simple Justice*. New York: Knopf, 1976. The compelling story of the cases that made up the landmark *Brown v. Board of Education* case. Included is the remarkable story of the legendary NAACP attorney Thurgood Marshall.

MANSBRIDGE, JANE J. *Why We Lost the ERA*. Chicago: University of Chicago Press, 1986. An examination of the reasons for the failure of the Equal Rights Amendment.

McGLEN, NANCY E., and KAREN O'CONNOR. *Women's Rights: The Struggle for Equality in the Nineteenth and Twentieth Centuries*. New York: Praeger, 1983. A useful history and analysis of the development of legal rights for women in America.

NIEMAN, DONALD G. *Promises to Keep: African-Americans and the Constitutional Order, 1776 to the Present*. New York: Oxford University Press, 1991. An informative history of the development of legal rights for African Americans.

O'BRIEN, DAVID M. *Constitutional Law and Politics*. Vol. 2, *Civil Rights and Civil Liberties*. New York: Norton, 1991. A comprehensive casebook of the development of civil rights by the Supreme Court.

PELTASON, JACK W. *Fifty-eight Lonely Men*. New York: Harcourt Brace Jovanovich, 1961. A study of the courageous southern federal district court judges charged with implementing the *Brown v. Board of Education* school desegregation decision.

STAVANS, ILAN. *The Hispanic Condition: Reflections on Culture and Identity in America*. New York: Harper-Collins, 1995. An up-to-date examination of the situation in America for the nation's fastest-growing minority group.

VERBA, SIDNEY, and GARY R. ORREN. *Equality in America: The View from the Top*. Cambridge, Mass.: Harvard University Press, 1985. An analysis of how close the United States has come to achieving true racial equality.

WILLIAMS, JUAN. *Eyes on the Prize: America's Civil Rights Years, 1954–1965*. New York: Penguin, 1987. The companion book to the PBS series on the history of the civil rights movement in the United States.

WOODWARD, C. VANN. *The Strange Career of Jim Crow*. New York: Oxford University Press, 1957. An important history of the development of the segregated legal society in the United States by one of this nation's premier historians.

15 DOMESTIC AND ECONOMIC POLICY

CHAPTER OUTLINE

Approaching Democracy Case Study: Tax Cuts and Approaching Democracy: "The First Major Achievement of a New Era"

Introduction: Public and Economic Policy and Democracy

The Policy-Making Process

Getting onto the Public Agenda

Regulatory Policy

Social Welfare Policy

Economic Policy

The Goals of Economic Policy

The Politics of the Federal Budget

Taxing

Spending

The Politics of International Economic Policy

APPROACHING DEMOCRACY CASE STUDY

Tax Cuts and Approaching Democracy: "The First Major Achievement of a New Era"

In a major moment of political success, President Bush signed into law the third largest tax cut since World War II, a $1.35-trillion-dollar tax cut on June 7, 2001. The signing took place in a public ceremony in the East Room and was steeped in the type of tradition reserved for important moments of national legislative history. As the Marine Corps band played "Hail to the Chief," President Bush signed the tax cut (see Figure 15.1 on page 528), using a different pen to sign each letter of his name.[1]

In signing the bill, President Bush fulfilled a campaign promise that many observers believed he could not achieve—"the first major achievement of a new era," as President Bush optimistically described the tax cut. "Today, for the first time since the landmark tax relief championed 20 years ago by President Ronald Reagan, and 40 years ago by President John F. Kennedy, an American President has the wonderful honor of letting the American people know significant tax relief is on the way," President Bush said.[2]

In addition to $300 for adults filing single tax returns and $600 for joint returns, the tax cut calls for gradual reductions in the tax rate. The credit provided to tax filers with children will increase, as will a new ten percent tax bracket at the bottom of the income scale. Tax filers will also be able to increase the amount of money contributed to retirement plans, 401(k)s, and accounts used to save for education expenses.

President Bush largely deserves credit for passage of the tax cut. No doubt recalling the lessons of his father who lost his second bid for office by breaking the "big" promise of "read my lips: no new taxes," the younger Bush intended to implement what he said—a major tax break for the American people. The new law was also a victory for conservatives in general because, "cutting taxes is the public policy precondition to expanding freedom, limiting government growth and promoting prosperity."[3] The Bush tax cut was a victory for each of these principles of conservatism.

President John F. Kennedy in the early 1960s engineered an enormous tax cut; so did President Ronald Reagan in the early 1980s. Like both previous tax cuts, the Bush plan drew heavily on bipartisan support. Conservative Democrats such as Senator John B. Breaux (LA) and Zell Miller (GA) steered the tax cut through an acrimonious Congress for Bush. One of the most ardent supporters of the cut was Senator Max Baucus (D-MT). As Chairman of the Finance Committee, Baucus occupied the important seat necessary for Bush to win approval of his tax plan. According to Baucus, working with the president on the controversial tax plan was politically necessary to ensure Democratic party competitiveness in the important 2002 congressional elections: "It's a good tax cut. It's a healthy tax cut. It's a big tax cut. And it's a fair tax cut."[4]

Not all Democrats agreed, Senate Democratic Leader Thomas Daschle warned that, "the policy implications . . . will be felt for decades to come. What this means is that the Social Security and Medicare trust funds are no longer viable. What this means is that we won't have the resources to make the commitment to education, prescription drug cost and the other priorities of the American people. But most sadly what this means is that we could be back into the days of debt in the not too distant future, all because many could not find the prudence and the balance to limit their appetite for tax cuts."[5]

Congress attached a caveat to the tax bill—the tax cut expires on December 31, 2010. This was in keeping with rules passed by Congress to limit spending bills that reach over a decade into the future. In June 2002 the House began debate on a Bush proposal to make permanent the "death-tax" as Republicans called it. "Failure to make the tax cuts permanent would increase the taxes on 104 million Americans," said Bush spokeswomen Claire Buchan.[6] An opponent of extending the tax cut, Representative Henry Waxman (D-California), asked his staff to assemble a chart depicting how members of the Bush cabinet would benefit if the estate tax were permanently eliminated. Waxman's staff did the same calculations for former Enron executives and for executives from other companies.[7] These are exhibited in Table 15.1 "The State of the Estate Tax" on page 529.

The bill that would have made the tax cuts permanent fell six votes short in the Senate, leading Carl Rove, the President's senior advisor to declare, "Don't look at it as a defeat. This is a war and we need to make an ongoing commitment to winning the effort to repeal the death tax."[8] This so-called "war" is likely to define much of the battleground following the 2002 midterm election and could very well define much of the 2004 presidential contest as well. Whatever the political outcome, most Americans will pay less taxes during the Bush administration than they did during the Clinton administration.

Question for Reflection: What is the relationship between taxes and public policy? What conditions need to be in place for adequate social programs as well as reasonable taxing policies to co-exist?

▲ "Tax relief is a great achievement for the American people. Tax relief is the first achievement produced by the new tone in Washington, and it was produced in record tme," said President Bush at a White House ceremony for signing the historic $1.35-trillion tax cut bill in June 2001.

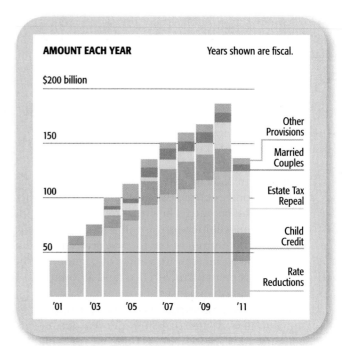

Figure 15.1
The Tax Cut Becomes Law
Note: Does not include an accounting change that shifts some corporate tax payments from one fiscal year to another.

INTRODUCTION: PUBLIC AND ECONOMIC POLICY AND THE DEMOCRATIC PROCESS

Public policies are the decisions, actions, and commitments of government. They are the means by which government attempts to solve problems and make life easier and safer for its citizens. Regulation of the national economy is one of the most crucial roles for modern government. This responsibility is important not only for the multiple benefits it yields to specific corporations and entrepreneurs, but also because a stable, growing economy provides an environment for a stable, orderly, and healthy democratic society.

By looking more closely at public policies, we can better understand both how government operates and how well it does so. In this chapter we begin by outlining the policy-making process. We then consider the politics of policy making and explore recent trends in American public policy, asking whether these policies are leading in an increasingly democratic direction. Finally, we will look at the world of taxing and spending policy to see how politics and economics are intertwined.

Types of Policies

Public policies enacted by the national government have four aims:

1. To regulate key industries and aspects of American life, such as the tobacco industry, savings and loan industry, or the meat-packing industry, in the interests of public safety.

2. To protect Americans from actual or potential enemies at home and abroad by providing a powerful national defense.

3. To encourage the accomplishment of important social goals by providing such programs as Head Start for preschool children and Pell grants for college students.

4. To assist a wide range of American citizens, such as farmers (through grain subsidies), low-income families (through Temporary Assistance for Needy Families), and state and local governments (through highway construction funds).

public policies The decisions, actions, and commitments of government.

Table 15.1 ■ The State of the Estate Tax

BUSH ADMINISTRATION OFFICIAL	ASSETS	ESTIMATED ESTATE TAX SAVINGS
President Bush	$11.1 million–$21.6 million	$4.6 million–$9.9 million
Vice President Cheney	$19.3 million–$81.8 million	$8.7 million–$40 million
Defense Secretary Donald H. Rumsfeld	$61 million–$242.5 million	$29.6 million–$120 million
Treasury Secretary Paul H. O'Neill	$62.8 million–$103.3 million	$30.5 million–$50.7 million
OMB Director Mitchell E. Daniels Jr.	$18.1 million–$75.3 million	$8.1 million–$36.7 million
Secretary of State Colin L. Powell	$19.5 million–$68.9 million	$8.8 million–$33.5 million
Commerce Secretary Donald L. Evans	$11.4 million–$45.1 million	$4.8 million–$21.6 million
EPA Administrator Christine Todd Whitman	$6.4 million–$20.3 million	$2.3 million–$9.2 million
U.S. Trade Representative Robert B. Zoellick	$3.3 million–$13 million	$555,000–$5.6 million
Labor Secretary Elaine L. Chao	$2.3 million–$5.4 million	$123,000–$1.8 million
HUD Secretary Mel R. Martinez	$1.6 million–$4 million	$0–$870,000 million
VA Secretary Anthony J. Principi	$1.6 million–$3.6 million	$0–$690,000
HHS Secretary Tommy G. Thompson	$1.3 million–$3.3 million	$0–$555,000
Attorney General John D. Ashcroft	$1.1 million–$3.3 million	$0–$555,000
Education Secretary Roderick R. Paige	$1.1 million–$2.9 million	$0–$377,000
Agriculture Secretary Ann M. Veneman	$680,000–$2 million	$0
Interior Secretary Gail A. Norton	$207,000–$681,000	$0
Energy Secretary Spencer Abraham	$224,000–$664,000	$0
Transportation Secretary Norman Y. Mineta	$220,000–$655,000	$0
COMPANY EXECUTIVES		
Gary Winnick (Global Crossing)	$734 million	$366 million
L. Dennis Kozlowski (Tyco Intl.)	$300 million	$149 million
Kenneth L. Lay (Enron)	$119 million	$59 million
Charles Watson (Dynegy)	$112 million	$55 million
Bernard J. Ebbers (WorldCom)	$78 million	$38 million
Michael Saylor (MicroStrategy)	$54 million	$26 million
Richard McGinn (Lucent)	$25 million	$12 million

Sources: The Washington Post, June 6, 2002, p. A29. Copyright © 2002 *The Washington Post.* Reprinted by permission. See also: www.house.gov/reform

Public policy can be divided into two major categories: regulatory policy and social welfare policy. **Regulatory policy** involves the use of police powers by the federal government to supervise the conduct of individuals, businesses, and other governmental agencies. It is essentially a set of *negative incentives* put into place by government to prevent certain kinds of behavior. For this reason, regulatory policy often focuses on social "villains"—industrial polluters, crooked savings and loan executives, unscrupulous railroad barons and meat packers and tobacco companies.[9] An interesting example of regulators moving into a new area involves the Federal Trade Commission's efforts toward requiring cigar and chewing tobacco manufacturers to report how much they spend on advertising and promotions as well as mandating that all cigars and chewing tobacco packages carry a health warning from the U.S. Surgeon General. These moves are the first step in narrowing the regulatory gap between cigars, chewing tobacco, and cigarettes.

In contrast to regulatory policy, **social welfare policy** uses *positive incentives*—cash assistance, stipends, entitlements, grants—to promote or encourage basic social

regulatory policy Policy that involves the use of police powers by the federal government to supervise the conduct of individuals, businesses, and other governmental agencies.

social welfare policy Policy that uses positive incentives (cash assistance, stipends, entitlements, grants, etc.) to promote or encourage basic social and economic fairness.

THE ROAD TO DEMOCRACY

Where Have You Gone, Joe Camel?

THAT WAS THEN . . .

"We are here to announce what we believe is the most historic public health achievement in history," said Michael Moore, attorney general for Mississippi, in June 1997, when announcing that a global settlement had been reached with the tobacco industry. "This is really the beginning of the end for the way the tobacco industry has treated the American public and probably the people of the world," observed Moore. The terms of the deal between the tobacco industry and the states were truly historic. The tobacco companies agreed to pay $363 billion for the next twenty-five years, as well as dramatically overhaul their marketing practices aimed at youth. In return, the industry would receive protection against future lawsuits bearing on tobacco-related diseases.

Just four years earlier, tobacco executives had vehemently denied the existence of any research that might suggest that their product was hazardous to anyone's health or even addicting. At congressional hearings in 1993, for example, James W. Johnston, then chief executive officer of R. J. Reynolds, laughed that the word "addiction" could be associated with cigarettes, going so far as to say that smoking was a pleasurable habit, like eating sweets or drinking.

The tobacco industry's credibility was also weakened by the release of internal documents from the 1970s showing how tobacco companies had targeted children as potential users for their products. These previously secret documents were part of a California lawsuit alleging that the Joe Camel advertising campaign was an unlawful and unfair business practice because it targeted minors and led them to purchase cigarettes illegally. The Joe Camel cartoon icon is recognized almost as readily by schoolchildren as is Mickey Mouse. The documents showed that in states where the Joe Camel campaign was introduced, cigarette purchases by minors increased dramatically. One internal R. J. Reynolds memo focused on young smokers as representing "tomorrow's cigarette business." T-shirts and other promotional items with brand-name logos were sold and given away on beaches. The secret documents also revealed that even when the tobacco companies had given public assurances that they would market cigarettes with lower nicotine, tobacco researchers were secretly involved in projects that would increase its potency.

In July 2000, a Miami-Dade County jury awarded the largest damage award in U.S. history—$145 billion—in punitive damages to 500,000 Florida smokers. The Florida decision opened the floodgates and eventually five out of seven plaintiffs would be awarded damages. While the tobacco industry had previously been successful in defeating lawsuits brought by individual smokers, it began to suffer significant setbacks.

THIS IS NOW . . .

On June 11, 2002, a jury in Miami, Florida ordered three cigarette makers to pay $37.5 million in damages to a lawyer who lost his tongue to cancer. John Lukas will not be able to spend his money; however, doctors have given him only seven months to live. Also in June 2002, a California judge ruled that R. J. Reynolds had violated its 1997 agreement to overhaul their marketing practices aimed at adolescents by continuing an advertising campaign that still promoted youth smoking. The company was fined $20 million. On June 20, 2002, a Miami jury awarded $5.5 million in damages to Lynn French, a flight attendant who does not smoke but as a result of spending years in smoke-filled planes suffers from chronic sinus problems. The judgment was the first defeat in a secondhand case for the nation's largest tobacco companies, paving the way for future secondhand smoke cases. In October 2002 a Los Angeles jury awarded a 64-year-old woman $28 billion after she developed lung cancer from cigarettes sold by Philip Morris. The $28 billion in punitive damages was calculated by multiplying $1 million times the 28,000 persons in the United States who die each year from lung cancer linked to smoking.

Sources: "Florida Smoker Awarded $37.5 million," *AP, Washington Post,* June 12, 2002, p. A2. Greg Winter, "Tobacco Company Reneged on Youth Ads, Judge Rules," *New York Times* June 7, 2002. Quoted in Robert Weissman, "The Great Tobacco Bailout," *Multinational Monitor* 18, nos. 7–8 (July/August 1997): *Washington Post* editorial; quoted in Steven F. Goldstone, "Don't Let the Tobacco Deal Go Up in Smoke," *Wall Street Journal,* February 20, 1998, p. 1. See Saundra Torry and John Schwartz, "Contrite Tobacco Executives Admit Health Risks before Congress," *Washington Post,* January 30, 1998, p. A14. See also "Tobacco Execs Urge Lawsuit Immunity," *USA Today,* January 29, 1998, p. 1. See "Court Papers Reveal Teen Smoking Targets," *USA Today,* January 15, 1998, p. 1; "Hundreds of Tobacco Industry Documents Released," *USA Today,* January 15, 1998, p. 8. "Cigarette Makers Manipulated Nicotine," *USA Today,* January 29, 1998, p. 1; Barry Meier, "Cigarette Maker Manipulated Nicotine, Its Record Suggests," *New York Times,* February 23, 1998, p. A1. "Clinton Pushes Anti-Tobacco Measures," *USA Today,* February 13, 1998, p. 1. See also Sandra Sobieraj, "Cigarette Tax May Cut Teen Smoking," *Washington Post,* February 13, 1998, p. 1. "Feds Vow to Push Anti-Tobacco Legislation," *USA Today,* April 12, 1998, p. 1. Greg Winter. "Jury Awards $5.5 million In a Secondhand Smoke Case," *New York Times,* June 20, 2002, p. A16.

---

fairness. Long-standing American social welfare objectives include aiding disadvantaged groups, such as people living below the poverty line, older Americans, people of color, women, military veterans, and educationally, emotionally, or physically challenged Americans.

APPROACHING DIVERSITY

No Child Left Behind Act of 2001: Reauthorization of the Elementary and Secondary Education Act

The reauthorization of the Elementary and Secondary Education Act of 1965 became a landmark education reform for President George W. Bush's first term in office. Signed into law on January 8, 2002, *No Child Left Behind* was the result of a bipartisan plan between Republican President Bush and Democratic Sen. Edward M. Kennedy of Massachusetts, and Rep. George Miller of California.

As a vow to make education of every child his number one domestic priority, President Bush promised that bipartisan education reform would be the cornerstone of his Administration. Conservatives in Congress favored the decentralization, local flexibility and parental choice aspects of the plan and compromised on federally dictated testing and spending. The president cooperated with Sen. Kennedy and Rep. Miller by agreeing to keep primary responsibility for education within the federal government.

The *No Child Left Behind Act* restructures elementary and secondary education programs to redefine "the federal role in K–12 education and will help to close the achievement gap between disadvantaged and minority students and their peers." A main aspect of the educational reform is to increase children's reading and math performance, allowing for provisions where parents of children from disadvantaged backgrounds will have the option to "participate in public school choice programs" or obtain services such as

tutoring. Federal efforts to close the achievement gap allows state and local schools greater flexibility and choice in the use of federal dollars in return for greater accountability of results through annual testing and state-mandated standards of children's performance.

To "leave no child behind" is to provide a quality education to each and every child by: "increased accountability for results" by State standards and annual testing; providing more choices for parents and students by increasing choices available to students and parents attending low-performance schools; increased flexibility for States, school districts, and schools to use federal funds to reflect each States' own local needs; and an overall focus on what works calling for States and school districts to use funds to implement programs based on scientific research. Based on four basic principles, the *No Child Left Behind Act* aims for "stronger accountability for results, increased flexibility and local control, expanded options for parents, and an emphasis on teaching methods" that work.

President Bush's Education Bill "gives students a chance, parents a choice, and schools a charge to be the best in the world." Implementation of the *No Child Left Behind Act* of 2001, provides the opportunity for American educational equality in the twenty-first century.

Sources: www.whitehouse.gov, April 8, 2002; http://www.nochildleftbehind.gov/start/index.html.

The Policy-Making Process

Policy scholars have developed several process models that try to capture the flavor and substance of policy making. One such model views the policy-making process as a *life cycle*. This model is especially useful in analyzing how an issue can be moved into the spotlight of the national agenda. These concepts of a public policy agenda and a policy life cycle are part of a relatively new approach to studying public policy that centers on the *process* by which the agenda of public policy is established. It seeks to discover how certain conditions, events, or situations come to be viewed as political problems requiring a policy response from government.[10]

Stated differently, how do public policies arise? How are they "born"? How long do they live? Why do some have long "lives," while others "die" quick deaths? Why do some ideas never become policies at all, while others travel quickly through the early stages of the policy life cycle, only to be stopped later in the process? The policy life cycle consists of eleven steps or stages, which can be illustrated by utilizing the evolution of federal funding for AIDS research.[11]

The Life Cycle of Policy Making

1. *Redefinition of a public or private "condition" as a public "problem."* In the case of the AIDS crisis, it took six years for the condition—a disease affecting certain subgroups of the population who did not support the Reagan Administration—to be defined as a problem to be addressed by public policy. Consequently, the administration chooses to ignore the problem.

▶ "We've got to get the public schools right," President Bush said during this visit to an elementary school in Michigan. On January 8, 2002, President Bush signed into law the *No Child Left Behind Act* of 2001. The act is the most sweeping reform of the Elementary and Secondary Education Act (ESEA) since ESEA was enacted in 1965. It redefines the federal role in K–12 education and will help close the achievement gap between disadvantaged and minority students and their peers. It is based on four basic principles: stronger accountability for results, increased flexibility and local control, expanded options for parents, and an emphasis on teaching methods that have been proven to work.

2. *Placement of the problem on the national policy agenda.* In the case of AIDS, this did not happen until the death of President Ronald Reagan's close friend, Rock Hudson.

3. *Emergence of the problem as a "public issue" requiring government action.* Only when Surgeon General C. Everett Koop announced that the problem was widespread did AIDS become a public issue. Prior to this, budget cutters in the Reagan administration were not inclined to allocate funds to fight a disease they thought was afflicting only drug users, Haitian immigrants, and the gay community.

4. *Formulation of a public policy response, usually followed by a pledge of action.* President Reagan announced that he would appoint a commission to study the epidemic.

5. *One or more reformulations of the proposed policy.* Every year the question of how much funding would be provided for AIDS research led to a reformulation of the policy.

6. *Placement of the proposed policy on the formal agenda of government.* Despite the unwillingness of the Reagan administration to push for major funding for AIDS research, the public, the press, and Congress would not let the issue die.

7. *Enactment of part or all of the proposed policy.* In 1986 Surgeon General C. Everett Koop released a report that made AIDS the key item on the administration's legislative agenda.

8. *Implementation of the policy.* Funding for AIDS research continued to grow. The government was now committed to fighting the disease—some six years following the first article on the mysterious disease.

9. *Impacts caused by implementation of the policy.* Activist groups ranging from coalitions of celebrities to congressional members emerged to help raise funds.

10. *Evaluation of the impact of the policy.* During the 1992 presidential nominating convention, AIDS funding was one of the many issues used by challenger Bill Clinton to attack the Bush administration's policies.

11. *Termination or continued implementation and evaluation of the policy.* Although the government continues to fund AIDS research at high levels, the disease is still the primary cause of death for men between the ages of twenty-five and forty-five in cities throughout the United States. Successfully attacking the HIV/AIDS epidemic requires a full-scale approach, which includes funding for prevention, research, housing, and care. We have come a long way, but have a long road ahead, especially as AIDS has spread worldwide in epidemic proportions in Africa and other countries. In June 2002, President Bush announced an

initiative that would help fund the fight against AIDS by spending $500 million in three years for prevention measures, with an emphasis on preventing transmission of AIDS from mother to child.

Getting onto the Public Agenda

Why do certain issues and not others become subjects for governmental action? That is, how do they get onto the agenda of the political world? Before they can enter the policy-making process, potential subjects of public policy must undergo a radical redefinition in the eyes of **policy elites**—members of Congress, the president, Supreme Court justices, cabinet officers, heads of key agencies and departments, leading editorial writers, and influential columnists and commentators. Such a redefinition changes the way the topic is viewed and places it on the **public agenda,** the set of topics that are a source of concern for policy elites, the general public, or both.

The public agenda can be viewed as the informal agenda of government. It should not be confused with the **formal agenda,** that is, the policies that are actually scheduled for debate and potential adoption by Congress, the president, the Supreme Court, or executive departments and agencies. For example, the harmful effects of nicotine have also been on the public agenda for quite some time, but not until the recent legal challenges and released documents did it reach the current threshold.

From Problems to Issues   How do social concerns become translated or redefined into matters that are important enough to be placed on the public agenda? The distinction between *problems* and *conditions* is critical for understanding public policy making. Citizens and policy makers are willing to live with various *social conditions*—pollution, high crime rates, low voter turnout, high rates of unemployment, or poverty rates—as long as those conditions do not come to be perceived as immediate threats to safety or financial security. When a condition is redefined as a problem, however, the government is expected to do something about it.

For a *condition* to be redefined as a *problem,* it must eventually come to be framed as an *issue.* There are two key ways in which social conditions become redefined as problems requiring governmental policy responses. First, a dramatic event may serve as a **triggering mechanism.** A triggering mechanism is a critical development that converts a routine problem into a widely shared, negative public response. It can transform a *condition* into a *problem* in the minds of the American public and political leadership alike. The tragic killings at Columbine High School triggered a national debate on gun control. The destruction of the World Trade Center buildings triggered a national debate on airline safety and student visas for foreign students.[12]

A potential policy can also reach the public agenda through the activities of **policy entrepreneurs,** individuals or groups that are instrumental in "selling" a program or policy to a policy-making body. American political history offers many examples of policy entrepreneurs who succeeded in placing a potential policy issue on the public agenda. In the 1950s and 1960s Martin Luther King, Jr., the Congress on Racial Equality, the Southern Christian Leadership Conference, the Student Non-Violent Coordinating Committee, and the National Association for the Advancement of Colored People used nonviolent tactics that successfully placed the issue of civil rights on both the public agenda and the formal agenda of the national government.

In the case of the civil rights movement, the policy entrepreneurs used a variety of tactics. Lawsuits challenged the "separate but equal" doctrine in public education. Confrontational demonstrations such as the civil rights marches in Montgomery, Birmingham, Selma, and Washington, D.C., and rallies and speeches such

policy elites Members of Congress, the president, Supreme Court justices, cabinet officers, heads of key agencies and departments, leading editorial writers, and influential columnists and commentators.

public agenda The set of topics that are a source of concern for policy elites, the general public, or both.

formal agenda The policies that are actually scheduled for debate and potential adoption by Congress, the president, the Supreme Court, or executive departments and agencies.

triggering mechanism A critical development that converts a routine problem into a widely shared, negative public response.

policy entrepreneurs Leaders who invest in and who create the conditions for a potential group to become an actual interest group. Ralph Nader stands as a classic example of a policy entrepreneur.

▶ Friends of the Earth put up this globe on the Washington mall for the thirtieth anniversary of Earth Day in April 2000. The event has gone from a limited public agenda to one of worldwide recognition.

as the famous "I Have a Dream" speech, given on the steps of the Lincoln Memorial by Martin Luther King, Jr., made the civil rights movement more visible to the American public. The assassinations of President John F. Kennedy, Martin Luther King, Jr., and Robert Kennedy served as triggering mechanisms for the passage of additional civil rights acts covering other areas of life. Thus, the efforts of a dedicated core of organizers and advocates stimulated actions and events that underscored existing problems in American society; the policy entrepreneurs then worked to promote specific solutions to those problems in the form of proposed policies.[13]

Getting onto the Formal Agenda

A policy reaches the formal agenda when it is actually scheduled for debate and potential adoption by policy-making bodies such as Congress. In the process, it is generally formulated and reformulated several times. In a formal sense, Congress actually enacts or passes legislation, but policy is "enacted"—constructed, debated, and put into effect—by all of the branches of the federal government.

Courts also formulate and reformulate public policy. Abortion is a case in point. In 1973 the Supreme Court adopted a policy position in the case of *Roe v. Wade,* arguing that women have an absolute right to choose an abortion in the first trimester of a pregnancy. More recently, in cases such as *Webster v. Reproductive Health Services* (1989), the Court modified the earlier *Roe* policy in favor of a more restrictive policy on abortion. It is possible that the Bush Supreme Court may overturn *Roe,* in which case abortion will surely be back on the public agenda.[14]

Policies are often formulated and reformulated in the committees and subcommittees of Congress, as well as during the process of debate and amendment on the floor of the House and Senate. For example, in 1998 the Senate decided not to rush into a vote on whether to ban human cloning. The issue of cloning raised questions ranging from the specter of genetic engineering of a master race to the cloning of specific tissue types or organs that could help in treating and possibly curing such diseases as Alzheimer's, heart disease, leukemia, and diabetes. As a policy, cloning involves ethical, moral, medical, and, of course, political concerns, which, at the moment, few members of Congress fully understand. By 2002 anticloning bills were stalled in the Senate, lacking the necessary sixty votes for passage; Republicans were expected to support a compromise two-year moratorium on cloning of human embryos.[15]

Policy formulation also occurs in the government agencies that implement laws enacted by Congress. Those agencies often issue regulations explaining how the agency will enforce and interpret the new law. These regulations are issued in tentative form and subsequently modified as part of a regular hearing and appeal process. In the case of the environment, for example, the Environmental Protection Agency will develop new microbiological testing criteria for coastal waters and then discuss them in public forums or provide analysis on the causes and effects of global warming.

Implementing a Policy

Once a policy has been enacted, it must be implemented. **Implementation** is the actual execution of a policy. Some policies are relatively easy to implement. For example, when Congress enacted a national highway speed limit of fifty-five miles per hour to conserve gasoline, the government quickly achieved full implementation of the policy by denying federal funds for highway construction to any state that did not enforce the new speed limit.

Other policies, however, are more difficult to implement. An example is court-mandated school desegregation, which was first ordered in 1954 by the Supreme Court in *Brown v. Board of Education of Topeka.* The next year the Court ordered that desegregation should proceed "with all deliberate speed," in part to soften the blow for the conservative and historically segregationist southern states, which were powerfully represented in Congress. However, it soon became apparent that the ambiguous phrase "all deliberate speed" meant one thing to the justices of the Supreme Court and another to state and local officials who were reluctant to implement the policy.[16]

Why are some federal policies easier to implement than others? The difficulty of implementing federal policies is a result of the "three Cs of implementation": *complexity, cooperation,* and *coordination.* Desegregating public schools is a far more complex process than changing the highway speed limit. Efforts to achieve full desegregation of public schools have had to confront the racial and ethnic hostilities in the American public, "white flight" to suburban communities surrounding urban areas, and declining funds for public schools.

Another obstacle to implementation of the *Brown* decision was that the actual plans for desegregating the schools required the cooperation of local and state officials. The involvement of more individuals and groups with the power to stop or delay a policy, such as officials of school districts and elected school boards, means more obstacles to full implementation of the policy. Some school districts, including those in Los Angeles and Boston, were actually turned over to "federal masters" appointed by federal courts to supervise desegregation in their areas.[17]

As the difficulty of desegregating public schools increased, so did problems of coordination. In the cases of Los Angeles and Boston, coordination among the federal courts, the court-appointed "masters," the elected school boards, as well as the parents and students, presented one of the greatest implementation challenges ever faced by the federal government.

As the examples of highway speed limits and school desegregation illustrate, implementation of public policies is far from automatic. The probability of full implementation of any public policy is inversely related to the complexity, cooperation, and coordination required by the proposed policy. Complex policies requiring extensive cooperation and a great deal of coordination have much less chance of achieving full implementation than simpler policies.

implementation The act of providing the organization and expertise required to put into action any policy that has become law; also refers to the actual execution of a policy.

Evaluating a Policy

All policies have an impact of some kind, though not all achieve the impact intended by those who proposed and enacted them. It is difficult to generalize about which policies have greater impact and why, but scholars have been able to identify some characteristics that contribute to the effectiveness of public policies: (1) a clearly written law or policy statement; (2) strong presidential support for the policy; and (3) local cooperation in the implementation of the policy. Policies that combine all three of these basic ingredients have the greatest chance of achieving their full impact. Most federal policies require a period of monitoring and analysis following implementation known as **policy evaluation.** Policy evaluation at the federal level is a mixture of scientific and political considerations. A good example is provided by the June 2002, EPA decision to relax clean air enforcement rules governing coal-fired power plants and refineries that would preclude government lawsuits when costly antipollution equipment to control smog, acid rain and soot was not installed. The industry had been complaining that aggressive enforcement under the Clinton administration had hindered or discouraged investment in power-generating plants. Environmentalists see the new EPA decision as a roll back of the 1970 Clean Air Act. Senator James Jeffords, (I-VT), then–Chairman of the Senate Environment and Public Works Committee said that the EPA decision was "a victory for outdated polluting power plants and a devastating defeat for public health and our environment."[18]

Terminating a Policy

Following evaluation, policies are either terminated or continued. If they are continued, they enter what social scientists call the *feedback loop*. Information about the consequences of a policy can be "fed back" into the cycle to help in the formulation of new policies. Policies may be terminated when they lose the political support of the general public, the president, the Supreme Court, or members of Congress. Termination of a policy is the end of the policy life cycle. But policies must be strongly supported by policy entrepreneurs in the government and by interest groups outside the government to be enacted in the first place, and these individuals and groups presumably benefit from the policy. As a result, public policies, once enacted, are rarely terminated.[19]

In the rare cases in which policies are terminated, it is usually because one of three scenarios takes place. First, the policy or program may come to be viewed as out of date and no longer important in light of new developments. An example is the nuclear-targeting policy of "mutual assured destruction" (MAD). The targeting of civilian areas such as Moscow as part of a strategy to protect the United States against the threat of a nuclear strike by the Soviet Union was rendered obsolete after the breakup of the Soviet Union in 1991.

Second, the policy or program may fail to perform effectively, or an alternative policy may be viewed as performing better than the original policy. An example is the Aid to Families with Dependent Children (AFDC) program, a sixty-year-old entitlement to federal cash assistance for mothers and children at the poverty level that was redesigned by the 1996 Welfare Reform Law. Today, block grants to states, designated as Temporary Assistance for Needy Families (TANF), provide assistance, but with a five-year lifetime limit on benefits (see Figure 15.2).

Continuing a Policy

Some policies have been in effect for a long time. They are implemented, evaluated, and continuously refined or modified by key actors in the national policy-making process—the president, Congress, or the courts. Policies that survive the early stages of the policy life cycle and are actually implemented are still subject to periodic review and possible modification over time. For example, the basic mission

policy evaluation The required period of monitoring and analysis of federal policies following their implementation.

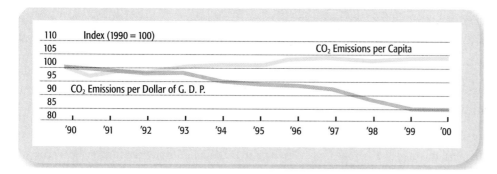

Figure 15.2
Carbon Emissions and the Economy
Source: Energy Information Administration.

of the National Aeronautics and Space Administration (NASA) has changed over time, from catching up with the Soviets (during the 1950s), to space exploration (1960–90), to analysis of the earth's weather and environmental patterns from space.

Several factors make public policy making a highly political process. They include the fragmentation created by a federal system of government; temporary political alliances (*logrolling*), policies that benefit particular states or districts (*pork barrel legislation*); *iron triangles,* or informal relationships among legislative committees, executive agencies, and interest groups; and *issue networks,* in which large numbers of participants take an active interest in a particular policy.

Regulatory Policy

Regulatory policies are designed to regulate conduct and protect the health and welfare of all Americans. As political scientist Kenneth Meier has noted, "Regulation is any attempt by the government to control the behavior of citizens, corporations, or sub-governments."[20]

The national government engages in six different kinds of regulatory activity. It may regulate (1) the price that can be charged for a good or service; (2) franchising or licenses granted to individuals or businesses; (3) performance of safety standards; or (4) resources such as water or electricity from federal dams and hydroelectric projects available to citizens or businesses. It may also (5) provide or withhold operating subsidies; or (6) use regulatory commissions such as the Federal Trade Commission (FTC) or the Securities and Exchange Commission (SEC) to regulate vital industries and promote fair competition among individuals and businesses.

▲ Government tests such as this one, a side impact test on a Ford Taurus, are part of the effort to regulate public safety.

Regulatory activity by the federal government has increased gradually during the past century after being almost nonexistent during the first hundred years of the nation's history. The first significant regulation occurred in response to the political pressures of the Granger and muckraker movements in the late 1800s and early 1900s. Another surge of regulatory activity occurred in the 1930s as a result of the problems created by the Great Depression. The highest levels of regulation were reached in the 1960s and 1970s in response to the consumer, civil rights, and environmental movements.

Beginning in the mid-1970s, regulatory activity by the federal government declined and a movement toward *deregulation* emerged. The government sold ("privatized") government-owned railroads to private investors and acted to deregulate the trucking, banking, and airline industries. Beginning in the late 1980s, however, there was a swing back toward increased regulation, a pattern that continues to this day (see Table 15.2).

Question for Reflection: Historically regulatory activity was most often spurred by social need. What impact do you think the deregulation activity of the 1970–80s had on America's approaching democracy?

Table 15.2 ■ A Regulatory Timeline

1970–74
President Richard M. Nixon signs an order creating the EPA and legislation establishing the Occupational Safety and Health Administration, the Consumer Product Safety Commission, and the National Highway Traffic Safety Administration.

January 1976
President Gerald R. Ford promises in his State of the Union address to cut red tape and address "the petty tyranny of massive government regulation."

1977–80
President Jimmy Carter deregulates the airline, trucking, and railroad industries. He also issues an executive order calling for regulatory agencies to be more sensitive to the concerns of those being regulated. Carter signs the Paperwork Reduction Act (P1 96-511), which directs the Office of Management and Budget (OMB) to eliminate unnecessary federal paperwork requirements. In addition, the bill creates the Office of Information and Regulatory Affairs with OMB. Carter also signs the Regulatory Flexibility Act (PL 96-354), which requires federal agencies to consider cost-benefit analysis when writing rules.

February 17, 1981
President Ronald Reagan issues an executive order barring agencies from issuing a major rule unless OMB decides its benefits outweighs its costs. It also requires OMB approval before a rule can be published.

January 1985
President Reagan issues an executive order requiring OMB to approve agencies' annual regulatory agenda.

1986
Reacting to complaints that the Office of Information and Regulatory Affairs overruled too many agency decisions and allowed industry groups excessive influence over rulemaking, Congress includes in the final omnibus continuing resolution (PL 99-591) requiring its administration to be confirmed by the Senate. The law also restricts the agency's oversight functions to the "sole purpose" of reviewing information collection requests contained in proposed regulations.

January 1992
President George Bush imposes a moratorium on new regulations and instructs agencies to change existing rules or programs that create regulatory burdens.

September 1993
President Bill Clinton issues an executive order allowing agencies to issue regulations only when benefits "justify" costs. All major rules must be submitted for OMB review, but only those with an annual economic effect of $100 million or more require its approval.

1996
Congress passes the Small Business Regulatory Enforcement Fairness Act (P1 104-121), which requires agencies to help small businesses comply with rules and allows for waivers of civil fines. The law includes language establishing the Congressional Review Act, which requires agencies to submit new rules to Congress and the General Accounting Office and gives lawmakers an expedited way to reject them.

January 20, 2001
On his first day in office, President George W. Bush orders a 60-day hold on the effective dates of all published Clinton regulations not yet in effect so the new administration can review them.

March 7, 2001
Congress passes a resolution (S J Res 6) repealing ergonomics rules issued by the Clinton administration; Bush later signs it into law (PL 107-5).

Source: CQ Weekly, May 5, 2001 p. 994. Reprinted by permission of Congressional Quarterly Press, through the Copyright Clearance Center.

Regulating the Environment

Environmental policy provides a good illustration of regulatory policy making. Americans became vitally interested in environmental issues in the 1960s and 1970s, and the federal government responded by enacting several key pieces of environmental legislation. The triggering mechanism for environmental policy making at the federal level was the publication of *Silent Spring* by Rachel Carson in 1962. In this pathbreaking book Carson argued that the widely used pesticide DDT was poisoning fields, streams, fish, and wildlife, and ultimately the American consumer. The book spurred a scientific search to develop less hazardous pesticides, as well as a search by federal policy makers for environmentally sensitive policies and programs.[21]

In a landmark piece of legislation, the National Environmental Policy Act of 1969, Congress required that government agencies issue an environmental impact statement listing the effects that proposed agency regulations would have on the environment. In 1970 Congress created the Environmental Protection Agency (EPA) to administer environmental programs and issue environmental regulations. It also enacted the Clean Air Act of 1970, which directed the EPA to monitor industrial air pollution and enforce compliance with existing pollution laws. The Department of Transportation was assigned the responsibility for monitoring and reducing pollution associated with automobile emissions.

In 1972, Congress passed the Water Pollution Control Act, which was aimed at reducing pollution in the nation's rivers and lakes. Congress soon added ocean dumping of wastes to the policy agenda with the Marine Protection Research Act, which was followed in 1976 by legislation regulating the dumping of hazardous waste. The 1976 Resource Conservation and Recovery Act not only regulated the disposal of hazardous waste but also sought to reduce the volume of waste by encouraging recycling, on-site disposal, incineration, and disposal of hazardous waste in safe landfills. The enormous expense associated with cleaning up hazardous-waste sites led to the enactment in 1980 of the Superfund Law, which created a fund to pay for toxic-site cleanups and authorized the EPA to order polluters to clean up sites where necessary. Congress later enacted the Safe Water and Toxic Enforcement Act of 1986, regulating discharges into surface water and groundwater; the Toxic Substances Control Act of 1987, requiring the removal of carcinogenic material such as asbestos from buildings; and the Clean Air Act Amendments of 1990, which resolved a long-running conflict between coal-producing and auto-manufacturing states, such as West Virginia and Michigan, and states such as Maine and California, whose residents and local economies were more favorably inclined toward environmental protection.

The Clean Air Act of 1990 set strict limitations on pollution from utilities and automobile emissions, mandated the use of less polluting fuels, and authorized inspections of potential polluters ranging from automobiles to wood-burning stoves. In addition, the 1990 act authorized the EPA to set standards for allowable pollutants by industries and to limit emissions of sulfur dioxide, the primary cause of acid rain. Still, many American cities do not yet meet the air quality standards established in the original Clean Air Act of 1970. Much will depend on the willingness of the EPA to enforce the regulations aggressively.

A second set of concerns has to do with the fact that pollution and the need for environmental regulation spill over state and national borders into the arena of international politics. The first international conference on the environment was held in 1992 in Rio de Janeiro, Brazil. The United States was the only major nation that would not sign the Rio Accords, which committed nations to strict environmental goals and required them to allocate a fixed percentage of their national budgets to take action on environmental concerns. The United States did not sign because pro-business interests did not like international entanglements that would cut into their profits, and conservative politicians had a general suspicion of multinational agreements like this one.

In late 1997 representatives of more than 150 nations gathered in Japan to discuss how best to counter the threat of global warming. The meeting produced the *Kyoto Protocol*—a commitment by developed nations to bring their emissions down to specific levels by specific dates (see Table 15.3). The parties agreed to reduce greenhouse gas emissions; the specific limits vary from country to country, but the framework and targets were based largely on U.S. proposals.[22]

In June 2002, the fifteen-member European Union ratified the Kyoto Protocol, raising the likelihood that the pact will become law even though the United States, the world's largest polluter, opposes it. The Bush administration specifically opposes the mandatory cuts in emissions that would result in the loss of billions of dollars and five million lost jobs (see Figure 15.3 on page 540).[23]

A third challenge facing environmental regulation is the increasing complexity of regulatory policy. *Offset policies* are a case in point. They allow a potential polluter

Table 15.3 ■ Targets and Timetables of the Kyoto Protocol

	Target	Summary
United States	Reduce emissions to 1990 levels between 2008 and 2012; unspecified reductions below 1990 levels after that. Applies to all six greenhouse gases: carbon dioxide, methane, nitrous oxide, hydrofluorocarbons, perfluorocarbons, and sulfur hexachloride.	Imposes a cap on average emissions for the period 2008 through 2012. A system of tradable permits between companies and credits for reductions before then. Supports a similar worldwide trading system. Insists that developing countries make some "meaningful" commitment on emissions levels.
European Union	At least 7.5 percent below 1990 levels by 2005; 15 percent below by 2010.	Cleaning up the former East Germany's industrial base and Britain's conversion from coal to natural gas has given the European Union a running start.
Developing nations and China	Reduction to 1990 levels by 2000; 7.5 percent below 1990 by 2005; 15 percent below 1990 by 2010; 35 percent below by 2020. Applies to carbon dioxide, methane, and nitrous oxide.	Rejects specific and legally binding targets and global trading system for developing nations at this time. Calls for a fund to compensate poorer countries harmed by climate change or for any economic losses caused by emissions cuts in richer nations (for example, oil-exporting countries).
Japan	5 percent below 1990 by 2008–2012.	Proposal allows some countries to adopt lower targets, depending on economic and social factors like high-energy efficiency (which would apply to Japan) or population growth (which could apply to the United States).
Alliance of Small Island States	20 percent below 1990 by 2005.	Generally overlooked on the global stage, these island nations in the Pacific and Indian Oceans and the Caribbean face the gravest threat from any rise in sea levels.

Source: New York Times, December 1, 1997, p. 3. Copyright © 1997 The New York Times Co. Reprinted by permission of *The New York Times.*

to build a facility that otherwise would not be allowable by "offsetting" the increased pollution with lower pollution elsewhere. For example, the 1990 Clean Air Act created *pollution credits.* Industries and companies that fail to meet their emission standards can "buy" extra pollution "credits" from companies whose emissions are below the allowable level. While the overall level of pollution in a particular area must remain below the established limit, there can be significant differences among industries and businesses in the amounts of polluting substances they emit. How should such a "market" in pollution credits be regulated, and will it require further monitoring and regulation as it develops?

In June 2002 the Bush administration sent a document, "U.S. Climate Action Report 2002," to the United Nations that detailed the effects global warming would inflict on the environment. The government report blamed human actions for global warming, primarily burning of fossil fuels that send heat-trapping greenhouse gases into the atmosphere. Still, the administration proposed no response other than voluntary action by industry and also reaffirmed it's opposition to the Kyoto Protocol. "The Bush administration now admits that global warming will change America's most unique wild places and wildlife forever," said Mark Van Putten, the president of the National Wildlife Federation, a private environmental group. How can it acknowledge global warming is a disaster in the making and then refuse to help solve the problem, especially when solutions are so clear." In an act of political containment, President Bush then dismissed the report as having been "put out by the bureaucracy," in this case the Environmental Protection Agency, EPA, an agency of the federal government headed by a Bush appointee.[24]

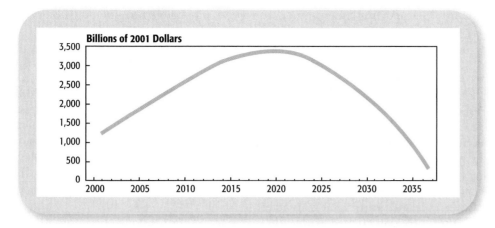

Billions of 2001 Dollars

Figure 15.3
Balance at the End of the Year
All revenues from the Social Security payroll tax and part from taxing some Social Security benefits are credited to the trust funds for the Old-Age and Survivors Insurance and Disability Insurance programs. Social Security benefits are paid from those funds. The trust funds serve mainly as accounting mechanisms to track revenues and spending for Social Security.
Sources: Social Security Administration, *The 2001 Annual Report of the Board of Trustees of the Federal Old-Age and Survivors Insurance and Disability Inusrance Trust Funds* (March 19, 2001), Table VI.E8 (intermediate assumptions).

Social Welfare Policy

The second major category of public policy, social welfare policy, is intended to alleviate the numerous problems associated with poverty in contemporary American society. Although poverty has existed in the United States since the early colonial days, it first reached the public agenda in the early 1900s as a result of works by muckraking journalists (see Chapter 12). Two books, Lincoln Steffens's *Shame of the Cities* and Robert Hunter's *Poverty,* both published in 1904, were influential in elevating poverty to the status of a political issue. In his study of tenement dwellers in Boston and New York, Hunter shocked turn-of-the-century readers by estimating that between 12 and 25 percent of all Americans lived in poverty.[25]

Before we consider the sources of poverty and the government's attempts to improve **poverty levels,** it is necessary to understand the history of social welfare policy in the twentieth century, beginning with the Social Security Act of 1935.

The Social Security Act

The Social Security Act was the centerpiece of President Franklin D. Roosevelt's New Deal legislative program. Even today, Social Security—the largest single non-defense item in the federal budget—is at the heart of social welfare policy in the United States. The Social Security Act established a safety net to catch those falling into poverty. It did so through a system of **entitlements**—government-sponsored benefits and cash payments—for which individuals might qualify by virtue of being poor, elderly, disabled, or a child living in poverty. The act created four major programs: Social Security retirement benefits, unemployment compensation, a public assistance or welfare program, and a series of aid programs for blind, disabled, or otherwise ineligible senior citizens.

The key provision of the act was Old Age Survivors Disability Insurance (OASDI), which provided a *contributory* program of retirement and unemployment benefits. The payments were available to workers who retired at age sixty-two or later, or to their dependents in the event of death. The money to fund the program came from a *payroll tax* shared equally by employers and employees. In subsequent years the act was modified to include self-employed persons, some employees of state and local governments, agricultural workers, and other workers not protected under the original act. Each state administers a separate unemployment insurance system. Workers who lose their jobs are eligible for twenty-six weeks of payments, although Congress has, on occasion, extended the eligibility period in times of high unemployment. Congress has made several efforts to apply **means testing** to Social Security entitlements—that is, to link benefits to income and provide payments only to the "truly disadvantaged"—but such efforts have failed owing to successful lobbying by senior citizen groups. Social Security benefits therefore remain

poverty level The federally determined level of income below which the government considers the person eligible to receive assistance.

entitlements Government-sponsored benefits and cash payments to those who meet eligibility requirements.

means testing The changing of the eligibility for entitlement benefits from everyone receiving benefits to only those with earnings and savings below a predetermined level in an attempt to save money.

▲ Saving Social Security is perhaps the most important issue on the minds of all citizens and politicians.

non-means-tested entitlements; they are paid to *any* eligible recipient, regardless of his or her financial status.

Social Security was established as a pay-as-you-go system, but recent projections of the ratio of working people to retirees indicate that the trust fund will not be able to meet its obligations in the future, when the majority of baby boomers will be entitled to collect full benefits. (see Figure 15.3). "By 2038, the 'trust fund' will run out of 'money' completely," writes David John, senior policy analyst for social security at the The Heritage Foundation. Moreover, a CNN/Gallup/USA poll conducted from May 28–29, 2002, found that 80% of the American public were "extremely" or "very" concerned about the future of social security.[26] In this chapter's Democracy in the New Millennium feature you can obtain information about your own social security benefits and make on-line calculations about your own future—it's never too early to know what is at stake!

A third program created by the 1935 act was a public assistance program, Aid to Families with Dependent Children (AFDC). Commonly referred to as "welfare," this program proved to be far less popular and more controversial than OASDI. AFDC was a *noncontributory* entitlement program that provided cash assistance to families below the official poverty line; this program has been terminated by federal legislation as part of the Clinton administration's welfare reforms of 1996.

The fourth program created by the Social Security Act of 1935 was actually a series of programs, now known as Supplemental Security Income (SSI), that provide aid to needy senior citizens who had not contributed to Social Security payroll taxes, as well as to blind or disabled citizens. Unlike the other programs just described, SSI is funded entirely by the federal government.

The War on Poverty

Along with other New Deal legislation, the Social Security Act was spurred by the massive economic dislocation caused by the Great Depression. In other words, the Depression acted as a triggering mechanism to translate the economic *condition* of poverty into a political *issue* to be addressed by policy makers in the national government. Three decades later poverty again reached the formal agenda of national government, influenced by the civil rights movement—in particular, by Martin Luther King, Jr.'s, call for civil rights and jobs for black Americans and also by Michael Harrington's description of the "invisible poor" in *The Other America*. President John F. Kennedy called for the creation of a "New Frontier" in which poverty would be attacked and overcome. Kennedy was assassinated before his program could be enacted, but his successor, Lyndon Johnson, launched a "War on Poverty" with two major pieces of legislation: the Economic Opportunity Act (1964) and the Medicare Act (1965).

▲ President Lyndon Baines Johnson, shown here with former President Harry S. Truman who first proposed the measure, signs the legislation that created Medicare, part of his War on Poverty.

The Economic Opportunity Act created the Job Corps to train the long-term unemployed; the Neighborhood Youth Corps to train neighborhood and inner-city unemployed youth for jobs; literacy programs to help adults learn to read and prepare for the job market; Head Start preschool programs to help poor children gain the skills necessary to do well in school; and work-study programs for low-income college students. Unlike Social Security, these community action programs (CAPs) were designed to be run with the "maximum feasible participation" of people in poor neighborhoods.

"Maximum feasible participation" proved to be highly controversial. Many members of Congress believed the federal government had too little control over vast sums of CAP money; mayors and other local officials believed they should control funds targeted for their cities; local community activists running CAP programs complained of insufficient funding and interference by local and federal officials. In the words of one key participant, Senator Daniel Patrick Moynihan of New York, maximum feasible participation quickly evolved into "maximum feasible misunderstanding."[27] Congress responded by passing the Hyde Amendment, which required

Your Hamburger: 41,000 Regulations

Protesting "overregulation" is a popular pastime of Americans. The 41,000 regulations that accompany a hamburger may seem an obvious example of the absurdity of too much regulation. But the issue is more complicated than it seems at first glance. If the government does not regulate pesticide use on crops, there is a significant risk of serious illness to consumers who eat the crops. If the government does not inspect to make sure livestock are free of tuberculosis, the incidence of TB bacteria in meat will be higher.

When examined closely, most of the regulations have a plausible rationale. But regulation is not free. In 1990 the cost of regulating hamburger was about 8 to 11 cents per pound. Today that cost has increased significantly. Is there too high a cost? It depends on the probability of contracting a serious disease and the value you as a consumer place on having some confidence in the quality of the products you buy.

Source: U.S. News & World Report, February 11, 1980, p. 64. Copyright 1980, U.S. News and World Report, Inc.

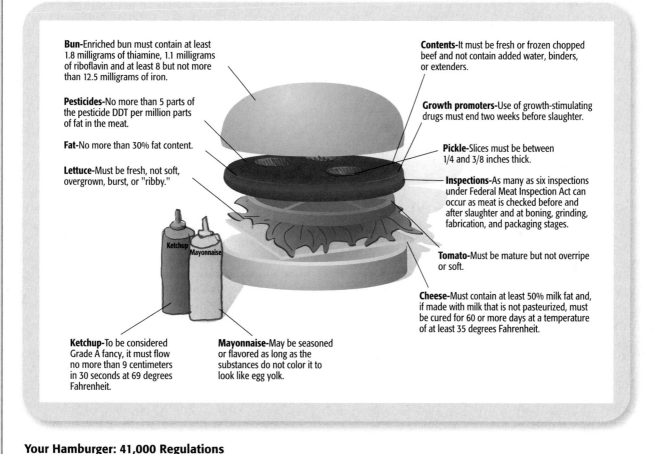

Bun-Enriched bun must contain at least 1.8 milligrams of thiamine, 1.1 milligrams of riboflavin and at least 8 but not more than 12.5 milligrams of iron.

Pesticides-No more than 5 parts of the pesticide DDT per million parts of fat in the meat.

Fat-No more than 30% fat content.

Lettuce-Must be fresh, not soft, overgrown, burst, or "ribby."

Ketchup-To be considered Grade A fancy, it must flow no more than 9 centimeters in 30 seconds at 69 degrees Fahrenheit.

Mayonnaise-May be seasoned or flavored as long as the substances do not color it to look like egg yolk.

Contents-It must be fresh or frozen chopped beef and not contain added water, binders, or extenders.

Growth promoters-Use of growth-stimulating drugs must end two weeks before slaughter.

Pickle-Slices must be between 1/4 and 3/8 inches thick.

Inspections-As many as six inspections under Federal Meat Inspection Act can occur as meat is checked before and after slaughter and at boning, grinding, fabrication, and packaging stages.

Tomato-Must be mature but not overripe or soft.

Cheese-Must contain at least 50% milk fat and, if made with milk that is not pasteurized, must be cured for 60 or more days at a temperature of at least 35 degrees Fahrenheit.

Your Hamburger: 41,000 Regulations
Source: U.S. News & World Report, February 11, 1980, p. 64. Copyright 1980. U.S. News and World Report, Inc.

that more control be given to local officials in deciding how CAP money would be spent.

The other major thrust of the "War on Poverty" was the Medicare Act, enacted in 1965, which added health insurance to the Social Security program. Medicare provides basic health care and hospitalization coverage for people over sixty-five years old. A related program, Medicaid, provides health care coverage for needy individuals under age sixty-five. The federal government pays a percentage of Medicaid costs, with state and local governments sharing the balance. Medicaid covers people who were not covered by Medicare, especially the blind, the disabled, and children living in poverty. In his 1998 State of the Union Address, President Clinton proposed opening Medicare to people fifty-five to sixty-four years old. A fierce political battle followed over whether this proposal to widen Medicare will pay for itself or will eventually need subsidies.[28]

In 1988, in a major revision of social welfare policy, Congress enacted the Family Support Act. The act's chief legislative architect, Senator Daniel Patrick Moynihan of New York, described it as "a new social contract" between the poor—who agree to work in exchange for benefits—and society—which agrees to support the poor at a livable wage.

The Family Support Act attempted to address the trend toward the feminization of poverty, which resulted from the increase in the number of working women, higher divorce rates, higher rates of illegitimate births, and a dramatic increase in the number of single-parent households. The act promoted **workfare**—programs to assist welfare recipients in making the transition into the work force. It provided for federal assistance in obtaining child support payments from absent fathers. It also created the Jobs program, which was designed to eventually replace AFDC with a program in which recipients (except mothers with children under three years old) must work in exchange for cash assistance. Recipients must be willing to engage in job training and job search activities as a condition for receiving benefits.

The Family Support Act was but the first step in welfare reform, which culminated on August 22, 1996, when President Clinton signed perhaps the most controversial legislation of his presidency—welfare reform legislation that signaled the end of cash assistance to dependent children by the federal government. "This is not the end of welfare reform, this is the beginning," said President Clinton when signing the legislation that "ended welfare as we know it." The new welfare reform law—the Personal Responsibility and Work Opportunity Reconciliation Act of 1996—ushered in a national commitment to the concept "from welfare to work." The new program did much more than redesign AFDC; it made broad changes in federal programs and policies. Under the terms of the legislation, each state must submit a state plan to the Department of Health and Human Services for certification in order to receive TANF block grant funds. The law restricted recipients to five years on federal benefits in their lifetime and required states to enroll 30 percent of their recipients in work programs in 1998, a rate that grows to 50 percent by 2002.[29]

In May 2002, the Department of Health and Human Services reported that while the federal rolls were still shrinking, the decline during 2001 was the smallest since 1994. Since President Clinton signed the welfare bill in 1996, the number of people on welfare has dropped from 12.2 million to 5.2 million, a 57 percent reduction (see Figure 15.4). Tommy G. Thompson, the Secretary of Health and

workfare The requirement that recipients of welfare programs like AFDC work on public works if they are unable to gain employment elsewhere.

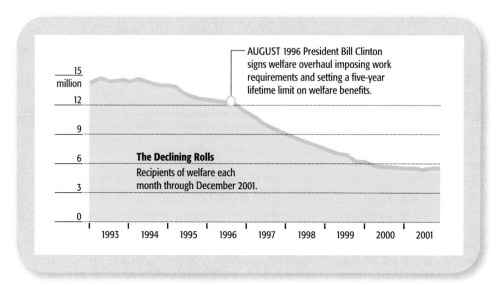

Figure 15.4
Source: Department of Health and Human Services, Administration for Children and Families (recipients).

Human Services, said, "Despite the soft economy and the tragic events of September 11, the national welfare caseload did not increase. Our reformed welfare system rose to the challenge. It continued to help recipients move toward work, and it continued to provide aid when needed."[30]

Still, the federal poverty level—the dollar amount of annual earnings below which a family is considered poor—has not been significantly reduced (see Table 15.4). This figure is established by the Census Bureau and used to generate official government estimates of the number of Americans living in poverty. There are actually two slightly different versions of the federal poverty measure: *poverty thresholds* and *poverty guidelines.* The thresholds are used for statistical purposes in preparing estimates of the numbers of Americans in poverty each year; the guidelines are used for administrative purposes in determining financial eligibility for certain federal programs.[31]

Social welfare policy making, like regulatory policy making, has a long political history and faces tremendous challenges. There is no easy formula for providing equal resources for all, a fair chance for all to succeed, and the opportunity for all to flourish financially and personally. How well national policy makers respond to these challenges—and how democratic the policies are—will remain crucial questions as American government continues its task of approaching democracy.

Question for Reflection: Social welfare policy has an impact on both the taxpaying public as well as the country's poor. A downturn in the economy, a natural disaster, or a massive terrorist attack on your nation can alter your position within society. In this give and take relationship, what are some of the key elements to consider when preparing democratic social welfare policies?

Economic Policy

"It's the economy, stupid." That was the personal reminder that focused former President Clinton's successful presidential campaign in 1992. A strong economy brought him reelection in 1996.[32] By 2000, the president's job approval ratings

---

Table 15.4 ■ What Is Poverty?

2002 Federal Poverty Guidelines for the 48 Contiguous States and the District of Columbia

Number in Family	Gross Yearly Income	Gross Monthly Income*	Approximate Hourly Income**
1	$8,860	$738	$4.26
2	$11,940	$995	$5.74
3	$15,020	$1,252	$7.22
4	$18,100	$1,508	$8.70
5	$21,180	$1,765	$10.18
6	$24,260	$2,022	$11.65
7	$27,340	$2,278	$13.14
8	$30,420	$2,535	$14.63
Over 8 add for each child	+$3,080	+257	+$1.48

Source: Federal Register Vol. 67, No. 31, February 14, 2002, pp. 6931–6933. Monthly and hourly data calculated by OCPP. Reprinted by permission of the Oregon Center for Public Policy.

*Rounded to the nearest dollar.

**Assumes a full-time job for a full year (2080 hours)

remained high because voters liked Clinton's management of the economy. Low unemployment rates, low interest rates, and no inflation or recession proved to be boons for the American public. In return, the public gave the president the benefit of the doubt on matters of character because, "it was the economy, stupid."

One of the most crucial roles for modern government is the regulation of the national economy. This responsibility is important not only for the multiple benefits it yields to specific corporations and entrepreneurs, but also because a stable, growing economy—one in which levels of employment are high, prices are reasonable, and families are afforded a modest degree of economic security—provides the environment for a stable, orderly, and healthy democratic society (see Figure 15.5).

When we look at the world of taxing and spending policy, we see very clearly that politics and economics are fundamentally intertwined. In studying American politics, then, we need to understand how politics and economics are woven together to present opportunities and obstacles in the United States' continuing approach to democracy. Both Republicans and Democrats believe in a strong, healthy economy. Where they differ is on how best to achieve this goal. Within each party differences exist regarding broad goals and specific policies, differences that have important consequences for government's ability to make coherent budgetary policy and for the lives of every American citizen.

The federal government influences the economy in many ways, both directly and indirectly. Government policies that affect the economy are categorized as fiscal policy, monetary policy, regulatory policy, and international economic policy.

Fiscal policy has the clearest impact through decisions that are reflected in the budget. Government budgetary choices concerning when and how much to tax, spend, subsidize, and borrow affect the economic lives of all citizens.

Monetary policy is the range of actions taken by the Federal Reserve Board to influence the level of the gross domestic product (GDP) or the rate of inflation. In an open economy, monetary policy will affect the level of imports, such as Japanese cars in the United States.

Regulatory policy is also pervasive. Government regulates aspects of the workplace to achieve health, safety, and environmental goals.

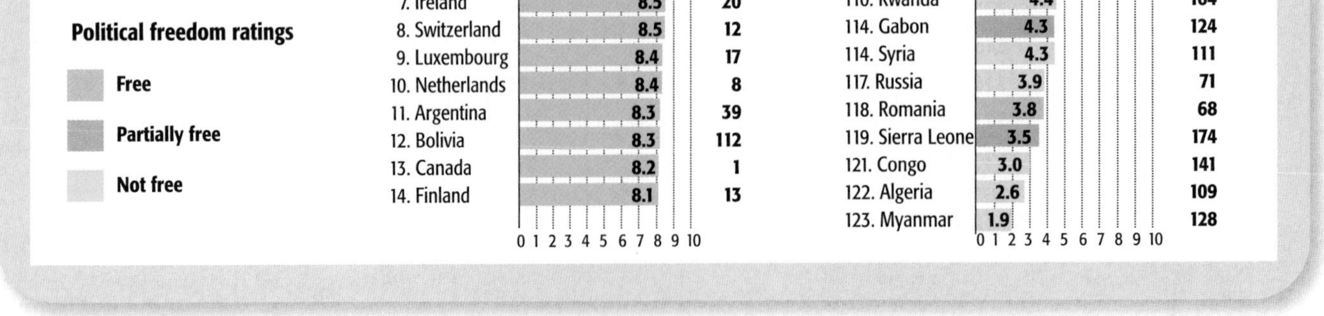

Economic freedom index

The index of economic freedom is based on 21 criteria, including freedom of personal choice, protection of private property and freedom of exchange.

Political freedom ratings

- Free
- Partially free
- Not free

The top-ranked countries:	Index number	Quality of life rank
1. Hong Kong	9.4	24
2. Singapore	9.3	22
3. New Zealand	8.9	18
4. Britain	8.8	10
5. United States	8.7	3
6. Australia	8.5	7
7. Ireland	8.5	20
8. Switzerland	8.5	12
9. Luxembourg	8.4	17
10. Netherlands	8.4	8
11. Argentina	8.3	39
12. Bolivia	8.3	112
13. Canada	8.2	1
14. Finland	8.1	13

Other selected countries:	Index number	Quality of life rank
20. Japan	7.9	4
62. Mexico	6.5	50
72. Indonesia	6.2	105
81. China	5.8	98
92. India	5.3	132
Some of the lowest-ranked countries:		
110. Rwanda	4.4	164
114. Gabon	4.3	124
114. Syria	4.3	111
117. Russia	3.9	71
118. Romania	3.8	68
119. Sierra Leone	3.5	174
121. Congo	3.0	141
122. Algeria	2.6	109
123. Myanmar	1.9	128

Figure 15.5 Freedom and Prosperity

[1]Political freedom rankings are based on Freedom House's Freedom in the World survey, which provides an annual evaluation of political rights and civil liberties.

[2]Quality of life ranking is based on the Human Development Index, which ranks nations based on criteria that include health, life expectancy, education and economic data.

Sources: Cato Institute, Freedom House, U.N. Development Program.

International economic policy influences economic relations with other countries through exchange rates, trade negotiations, and international economic institutions like the World Bank, the International Monetary Fund (IMF), and the World Trade Organization (WTO) and its predecessor, the General Agreement on Tariffs and Trade (GATT).

The Goals of Economic Policy

The primary goal of **economic policy** is to produce a vibrant, healthy, and growing economy.[33] The federal government's role in making economic policy has increased since World War II. Conditioned by the experience of 25 percent unemployment rates during the Great Depression of the 1930s and the very high *inflation rates* (rate of increase in prices) and commodity shortages of the war years of the 1940s, Congress adopted the Employment Act of 1946, which formalized the federal government's responsibility to guide the economy to achieve three primary economic goals: *stable prices* (low or zero inflation), *full employment* (an unemployment rate of 4 percent or less), and *economic growth* (substantial and sustained growth in the economy as measured by increases in the gross domestic product). The conditions necessary to achieve these three goals, as the postwar record shows, were often lacking, and the U.S. economy experienced periods of high unemployment, high inflation, and slow or even negative economic growth.

Developing an economic policy that can achieve these goals is difficult and complex, because actions that affect one goal also affect the others, often in undesirable ways. Policies that raise interest rates to push inflation down, for example, may discourage spending, which can raise unemployment rates and may also reduce investment spending and the adoption of new technology, which can, in turn, affect the rate of economic growth. Economic trade-offs must thus be considered in addition to political trade-offs.

To make matters worse, it appears that to achieve the goals of stable prices, full employment, and economic growth, we also need to attain a secondary set of economic goals, such as low and stable interest rates, stable exchange rates, and reduced federal budget **deficits** (annual shortfalls between what government takes in and spends) and balance-of-trade deficits. Progress toward these secondary economic goals seems necessary to achieve the rising living standards that are embodied in the nation's principal economic goals.[34]

The Politics of the Federal Budget

There is perhaps no better place to observe how economic policy and political factors intertwine than the case of the federal budget. We have already discussed some of the ways government uses its power to tax and spend to influence the economy. Yet government also taxes and spends to provide services for its citizens. How policy makers attempt to provide these services—and, more important, who pays for them and who receives them—gets to the very heart of the politics of the federal budget. Figure 15.6 shows the history of the federal budget from 1789 to the present.

The President Proposes, Congress Disposes

Stated simply, the national budget is a document that proclaims how much the government will try to collect in taxes and how those revenues will be spent on various federal programs. Yet, despite this seemingly simple definition, the preparation of the budget and its subsequent passage are both complex and profoundly political activities. The budget sets policy priorities by establishing the amount of money each program is slated to receive. Some programs are created, some receive more support than others, and still others are reduced or eliminated. The budget thus provides a policy blueprint for the nation.[35]

QUOTE ... UNQUOTE

"The good news is that a busload of supply-side economists plunged over a cliff. The bad news is that three seats were unoccupied at the time."

Morris Udall

QUOTE ... UNQUOTE

"There are two things that can disrupt the American economy. One is a war. The other is a meeting of the Federal Reserve Board."

Will Rogers

QUOTE ... UNQUOTE

"The final budget was a compromise in the sense that being bitten in half by a shark is a compromise with being swallowed whole."

P. J. O'Rourke

economic policy Policy aimed at producing a vibrant, healthy, and growing economy.

deficit The annual shortfall between the monies that government takes in and spends.

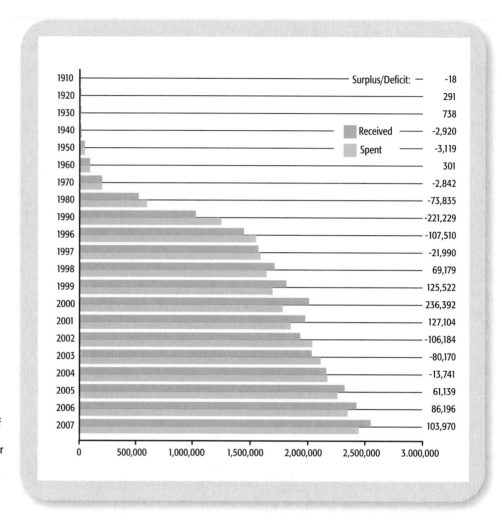

Figure 15.6
Budget Balance
The federal government in its first 112 years, 1789 through 1900, collected $15.622 billion, spent $16.543 billion and ran a deficit of $921 million. Receipts, expenditures and surpluses or deficits over the past century, with estimates for 2002 through 2007, in millions of dollars.

Source: Associated Press.

The law requires that by the first Monday in February, the president must submit to Congress his proposed federal budget for the next fiscal year. It is only after the Congress passes and the president signs the required spending bills that the government has a budget. Figure 15.7 shows a breakdown of President Bush's 2003 federal budget. The President has threatened to veto any spending that he thinks will undermine the war on terrorism. "We must not repeat the mistakes of the 60's when increased spending required by war was not balanced by slower spending in the rest of government," warned the President.

How the Budget Is Prepared

Budgetary politics involves many actors, the most important being the president and Congress. While in a strict constitutional sense Congress has sole power to authorize spending of any federal monies, the modern-day practice is for Congress to follow the lead of the president. The Budget and Accounting Act of 1921 conferred this responsibility upon the president, greatly enhancing the president's power in domestic affairs. First, the law requires government agencies to send their budget requests to the president for consideration. The president ultimately decides whether to include these requests in the budget plan. Second, the act created an executive budget office, the Bureau of the Budget (BOB), which became the **Office of Management and Budget (OMB)** under President Richard Nixon. The director of the OMB has cabinet-level status and is one of the president's top advisers and policy strategists.[36]

Office of Management and Budget (OMB) The unit in the Executive Office of the President that has primary responsibility for preparing and administering the president's annual budget. It is through the budget process that a president and the OMB can shape policy, since the process determines which departments and agencies grow, get cut, or remain the same as the year before.

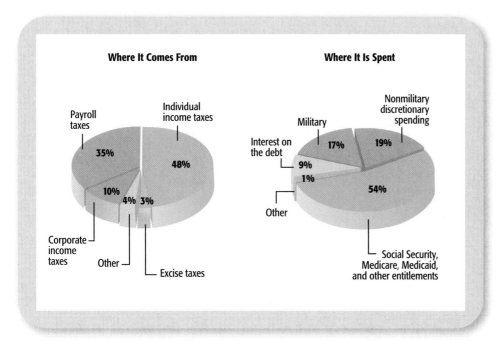

Figure 15.7
Breaking Down the Budget
President Bush's budget proposal for the 2003 fiscal year calls for total spending of $2.13 trillion and projects three years of deficits beginning in the 2002 fiscal year.
Source: Office of Management and Budget.

After first providing each agency with instructions and guidelines reflecting presidential budgetary priorities, the OMB analyzes the budgetary requests made by the agencies. This process takes place during the spring and fall of the year, after which the OMB director goes to the president with a budget—a set of estimates for both revenues and expenditures. But this procedure is not simply a matter of adding up numbers. Agency heads submit budgetary figures that represent their goals, their ideologies, and even their own personal ambitions. This is an extremely political undertaking, with plenty of political maneuvering and overt lobbying geared toward protecting and enhancing each agency's share of the budgetary pie. Finally, in January, after adjustments by the president, the budget of the U.S. government is submitted to Congress. With the help of the OMB, the president is able to submit to Congress a budget plan that outlines the national priorities, the president's vision for the policy agenda of the country. It is in this context that we see the workings of the old budgetary adage: "The president proposes and Congress disposes," for it is Congress that must approve the budget, turning the president's vision into tangible law. Congress uses its oversight authority to assess the performance of government agencies but also to check the president's power (see Figure 15.8).[37]

However, by 1973 it had become increasingly difficult for Congress to formulate a comprehensive, substantive alternative to the president's plan. Congress was often left with little control over the budget, making only incremental and marginal adjustments to what is clearly the president's plan for the nation. As we saw in Chapter 4, Congress is a highly decentralized and fragmented institution, one that allows its individual members to pursue their own personal policy and reelection goals. Although the institutional setup of Congress works to the advantage of individual members, it is a detriment to Congress's ability to produce a collective vision of national priorities to balance that of the president.

Partly in response to recurring budget battles with President Richard Nixon and partly to reassert its constitutional mandate to use the budget as an expression of its own policy vision, Congress passed the Budget and Impoundment Control Act of 1974. **Impoundment** refers to either the president's refusal to spend appropriated funds or his deferral of such expenditures. The first executive impoundment occurred in 1803, when Thomas Jefferson refused to spend $50,000 appropriated by Congress for gunboats on the Mississippi. President Nixon argued that he would

impoundment The president's refusal to spend funds appropriated by Congress.

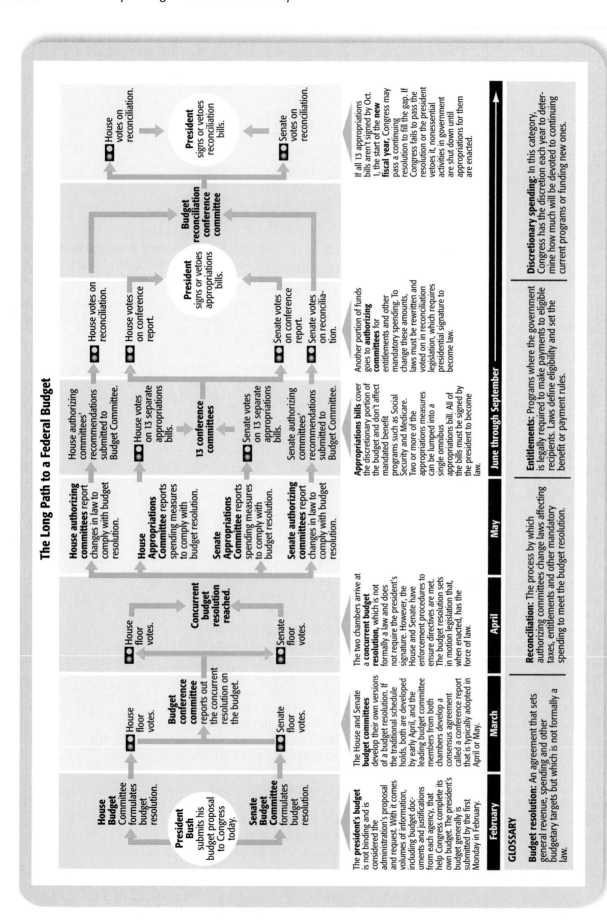

Figure 15.8
The Long Path to a Federal Budget

Sources: House Budget Committee, Office of Management and Budget, Congressional Research Service.

not be faithful to his oath to take care that the laws are faithfully executed if spending money appropriated by Congress would create an inflationary spiral. From 1969 to 1973, Nixon impounded approximately 20 percent of controllable funds appropriated by Congress.

In essence, the Impoundment Control Act sought to provide Congress a procedure, independent of the president, to gain more control and give it the ability to make comprehensive appropriations and spending decisions. The act modified the budget process by allowing Congress to establish overall levels for taxing and spending, including breakdowns for national defense, foreign aid, health, infrastructure, and agriculture. Congress established Budget Committees in the House and Senate to carry out these tasks and to hold hearings on the president's proposed budget. Congress set up the Congressional Budget Office (CBO), a staff of budgetary experts to provide both houses with their own source of budgetary data, enhancing their independence from the executive branch OMB. The House and Senate Budget Committees examine the president's budget. The committees send a budget to each chamber in the form of resolutions, and a conference committee then hashes out a single congressional budget that can reward or punish different agencies. Figure 15.9 shows two views of President George W. Bush's budget.

The reform worked well for several years, increasing the congressional role in budget formation. For the most part, recent budgets have reflected multiyear commitments to agencies and programs. At the same time, budgets have been more sensitive to macroeconomic changes.

By the mid-1980s a new problem was emerging, one that eventually led to further reform of the budgetary process. The combined tax cuts and increased military spending of the Reagan administration dramatically increased the existing budget deficit. In the same period, the percentage of the budget committed to *entitlement programs* (benefits to which people are entitled because they fall into a particular category, such as Medicaid or Medicare) also grew, taking much of the budgetary flexibility away from both the White House and Congress.

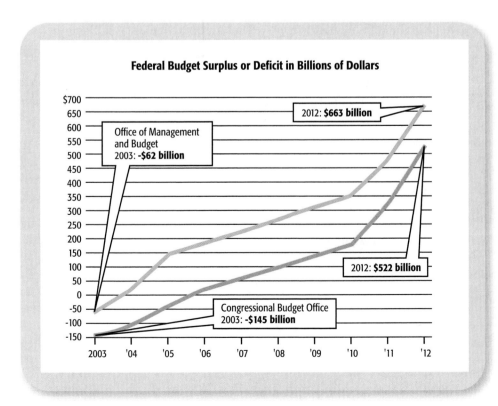

Figure 15.9
Two Views of the Budget
OMB numbers do not include White House policy proposals not yet enacted.

Taxing

While all citizens want their fair share of the budgetary pie—whether for better highways or more police protection—almost nobody wants to foot the bill for these services. Therein lies the strain in the politics of taxing and spending, a strain that is profoundly political. The president's ideas about where government revenues should be spent and who should shoulder the burden of paying led to serious battles. Policy makers decide who will benefit from government programs and who will pay for them, and neither these benefits nor the burden of paying for them are distributed evenly across society. The 2001 tax cut with its standard rebates was the Bush administration's attempt at giving back money to the highest percentage of the tax paying U.S. population.

Governments have never been able to meet public needs by relying on voluntary contributions alone. Most of us want—and in fact, expect—government to provide us with certain things. From highly targeted benefits like subsidies for farmers, to broad intangible things like national security, we look to our government as a provider. Most American's fail to realize that the "government's money" is predominantly the accumulated tax dollars collected annually. So when the government reaches into our pockets to pay for these services, we balk, we complain, and some of us even risk stiff penalties by trying to evade paying our "fair share." Such is the relationship between a government and its people where taxes are concerned.

This unwillingness to fork over hard-earned dollars is understandable. The idea of a free, democratic society is challenged when governments demand and take private property, including portions of the profits of corporations and the modest wages of workers. It was only early in this century that the federal government began to use its power to collect taxes from private corporations (1909) and from individuals (1913). Before these new tax levies, money to run the government came primarily from **tariffs,** taxes on goods imported into the country.

The power to tax has not always been easy to swallow for many U.S. citizens, leading to periodic "tax revolts." In 1978 the citizens of California staged one such revolt when they passed Proposition 13, a measure designed to permanently cap local property taxes. Antitax sentiment has appeared since then as well. Tax cuts were a central feature of the Reagan administration and led subsequently to former George Bush's now infamous pledge of "Read my lips. No new taxes." And the case study made clear that George W. Bush understood better than anyone the lesson of embracing and signing the historic tax cut.[38]

Sources of Tax Dollars

At least a partial answer to these questions comes from examining the sources and outlays of federal revenues—the government relies to a significant degree on the personal income tax. This puts the federal government in a position to benefit from the increases in personal income that accompany a healthy economy. The better the economy, the more revenues generated by the income tax. Interestingly, reliance on the income tax can also act as a buffer during economic downturns, in that the national pool of taxpayers means that economic slumps affecting some parts of the country are at least partially offset by greater prosperity in other parts. This heavy reliance on individual taxpayers rather than large corporations can impose severe, some argue unfair, tax burdens, particularly for middle-class citizens.[39]

(?) Question for Reflection: In the ideal, a government funded by the people is the ultimate in approaching democracy. Since the government relies to a significant degree on the personal income tax for federal revenues what impact does this have on how the country is run?

When we evaluate the importance of income taxes, it is important to recognize that not all taxes are created equal. Different types of taxes affect different groups

FYI

"Taxes are what we pay for civilized society," declared Oliver Wendell Holmes, Jr., in a famous phrase now chiseled on the Washington headquarters of the Internal Revenue Service (IRS).

tariffs The imposition of import taxes on foreign goods in an attempt to protect a nation's industry and/or labor.

of people. One way to judge income taxes, therefore, is according to whom they affect and how much. **Progressive taxes,** which tax those who make more money at a higher rate, are often considered the fairest, as they place a larger burden on those people with the greatest ability to pay. In general, the greater the number of tax brackets—steps in which the percentage rate of tax increases—the more progressive the tax. **Regressive taxes,** on the other hand, tax all people by the same amount, thereby taking a higher fraction of the income of lower-income taxpayers. These rates are generally seen as less fair. The **capital gains tax** (tax on unearned income from rents, stocks, and interest) is an example of a progressive tax, since most of the revenue it gathers comes from a tiny portion of the wealthiest Americans. Taxes on consumer goods such as gasoline, cigarettes, and alcoholic beverages are generally regressive, since most of the consumption of these goods—hence most of the taxes paid—comes from the relatively larger group of middle-and lower-class Americans.

Tax Reform

Periodic attempts to reform the tax structure are typically related to the issue of fairness. After prolonged political battles over who would benefit and who would pay, Congress passed the Tax Reform Act of 1986. The purpose of the reform was to simplify an unwieldy tax structure and promote greater fairness. The first goal was advanced by reducing the number of tax rates from fifteen categories to three, including a zero rate for low-income individuals. The remaining brackets dropped the highest rate from 50 to 28 percent and the lowest rate to 15 percent. Thus, on the face of things, tax rates were actually lowered for higher-income individuals, suggesting that the tax structure actually became more regressive.

Yet the tax reform of 1986 included another important aspect, one that helped increase revenues and retain a degree of progressivity. In addition to changing tax rates, the reform also eliminated many tax deductions, or what are technically called **tax expenditures.** Tax expenditures are amounts taxpayers have spent for items that they are allowed to subtract from their income when filing their tax returns. The effect of these deductions (some call them loopholes) is to reduce the amount of income that is actually subject to taxes, resulting in losses of government revenue. Some of the most common tax expenditures are interest paid on home mortgages or business equipment and business-related entertainment. Critics of tax expenditures argue that they are a drain on the federal treasury and specifically benefit the relatively wealthy. After all, only those who can afford to buy a home can benefit from the mortgage interest reduction.

In the end, the 1986 reforms changed many of these deductions, eliminating deductions for state sales taxes, interest paid on credit card and other personal debt, and interest on mortgages on third or fourth homes, while reducing deductions for medical expenses and business entertainment, among others. The result was a simplified, more progressive tax code, in which many taxpayers paid lower taxes and a greater burden was placed on upper-middle-income individuals. Critics argue, however, that the reform did not go far enough and that as some deductions were eliminated, new deductions sprang up to take their place, effectively reducing the impact of any attempts to increase the degree of progressivity or fairness of the reforms.

Unfortunately for George H. W. Bush, these tax reforms had another effect. They did not bring in enough revenue to cover federal spending. The result was further increases in the annual budget deficit. Thus, in 1990, former President Bush was forced to renege on his "Read my lips. No new taxes" promise and enact a modest tax increase on wealthier Americans. Republicans who had supported Bush, in 1988 were enraged by this tax increase, and it is likely that Bush paid a price for reneging on his pledge, as many Republicans voted for Ross Perot in 1992.

One major goal of ex-president Clinton's tax strategy was for the tax structure to be more equitable, to make good on his campaign promise to make wealthier

"I've been thinking about the flat tax and how it would inflict hardship on the poor, and I can live with that."

© 1996 The New Yorker Collection. J. B. Handelsman from cartoonbank.com. All Rights Reserved.

progressive taxes System of taxation in which those who make more money are taxed at a higher rate; an example is the income tax.

regressive taxes System of taxation in which taxes take a higher fraction of the income of lower-income taxpayers; examples are taxes on gasoline, cigarettes, and alcohol.

capital gains tax Tax on unearned income from rents, stocks, and interest.

tax expenditures Tax deductions that reduce the amount of income that is subject to taxes like home mortgages, business equipment, or business-related entertainment.

people "pay their fair share." Clinton introduced a greater degree of progressivity in income taxes by changing the tax structure: individuals making over $115,000 saw their tax rates rise from 31 to 36 percent; those making over $250,000 became subject to a 10 percent surcharge, making their tax-effective rate 39.6 percent. Clinton's plan resulted in actual income tax increases for fewer than 2 percent of all taxpayers, with the greatest hit being taken by the wealthiest, and tax cuts going to the poorest Americans.

The next largest source of federal revenue comes from Social Security taxes paid by employers and their employees. While not raising the effective tax rate for these taxes, Clinton's plan did tax a larger percentage of Social Security benefits from relatively wealthy recipients. Finally, Clinton's plan placed greater emphasis on a traditionally small part of federal revenue raised from excise taxes. **Excise taxes** are charges on the sale or manufacture of certain products, such as cigarettes, alcohol, and gasoline. Despite the concern of members of Congress from oil-producing states, Clinton won passage of an increased excise tax on gasoline.

Spending

Just as deciding who pays taxes and how much is a profoundly political question, so is deciding where to spend those revenues. While most of us balk at picking up the bill, we are also quite ready to hold out our hands for our fair share (or more) from the federal treasury. Be it low-cost student loans, government-subsidized health care, or cleaning up the environment, everyone wants his or her program to receive funding, and the more funding the better.

The way federal tax revenues are spent is often taken as a sign of a government's priorities. Ronald Reagan sought to boost the prestige and visibility of the U.S. military, and he achieved this goal by dramatically increasing spending for national defense, with much of the money coming from cuts in social programs and a resulting increase in the deficit. Of course, priorities change from year to year and administration to administration. George W. Bush's 2003 budget, for example, proposed a set of priorities dramatically different from Bill Clinton's final budget.

Discretionary spending accounts for 33 percent of all federal spending; this is what Congress and the president must decide to spend for the next year through thirteen annual appropriations bills. Examples of discretionary money are funding for the Federal Bureau of Investigation and the Coast Guard, housing and education, space exploration and highway construction, defense and foreign aid. The law currently imposes a cap through the year 2002 on total annual discretionary spending, but Congress and the president may change the spending levels under the cap from year to year.

Mandatory spending accounts for approximately 70 percent of all spending and is authorized by permanent laws, not the appropriations bills. It includes entitlements such as Social Security, Medicare, food stamps, and veterans' benefits, through which individuals receive benefits because they are eligible based on age, income, or other criteria. Mandatory spending also includes the interest on the **national debt**—the cumulative unpaid total of all annual budget deficits. The law requires that legislation that raises mandatory spending or lowers revenues from levels in existing laws be offset by spending cuts or revenue increases. This requirement is known as "pay as you go" because it is designed to prevent new legislation from increasing the deficit.

The Politics of International Economic Policy

As the global economy becomes increasingly integrated, nations are becoming increasingly interdependent. To a greater extent than ever before, the United States must take account of global forces in making economic policy, as the 2002 crisis in Argentina demonstrated.

excise taxes Charges on the sale or manufacture of products such as cigarettes, alcohol, and gasoline.

discretionary spending The spending Congress actually controls; entitlements such as Social Security, Medicare, and Medicaid; 33 percent of all spending.

mandatory spending Spending that must be allocated by law rather than by appropriations for entitlements like Social Security, Medicare, and Medicaid; 67 percent of the budget.

national debt The cumulative total of all budget deficits.

APPROACHING DEMOCRACY AROUND THE GLOBE

A Global Education Plan For All

Is it possible to provide a primary school education to 125 million children in the world's poorest countries? A group of global financial leaders have endorsed a World Bank plan aimed at ensuring that by 2015 all children in poor countries will have access to at least a primary school education. "Education for All" believes that education is the ultimate liberator of the human potential. It can free people from the handcuffs of poverty, giving them the power to greatly improve their lives and take a productive place in society. It can also free communities and countries, allowing them to leap forward into periods of wealth and social cohesion that otherwise would not be possible. A majority of these children are girls and it is believed that education will generate related benefits such as improved childcare and nutrition knowledge.

Only 32 countries were seen as being at risk of not achieving education on the basis of enrollment rates. But, that number rises to 88 if the criteria are adjusted to "five years of class completion." It is believed that fifty-nine of the 88 countries at risk can reach universal primary completion by 2015 if they bring the efficiency and quality of their education systems into line with benchmarks observed in higher-performing systems. The World Bank plan is based on the idea that the developing countries develop their own blueprints, rather than the donors, and that 10 countries would be selected for fast tracking based on their proposals. "We believe the World Bank and other donors should be prepared to significantly increase funding for basic education in those countries with strong policy and financial commitments to this sector," said Treasury secretary Paul O'Neill. Yet, the United States has still not committed any resources to the program—despite the Bush administration's emphasis on education evidenced by passage of the *No Child Left Behind Act.*

In June 2002, the Group of Seven G-7 industrial nations met in Canada to consider a proposal to spend as much as $10 billion a year on the plan. The World Bank proposal offers "the potential to be a watershed event if the G-7 countries step to the plate financially and coordinate their efforts," said Gene Sperling, director of the Forum on Universal Education at the Brooking Institution. This new plan for achieving global education calls on governments to show their commitment by transforming their education systems.

The meeting delegates also concluded that achieving success in universal primary education depends on integrating education into a broader poverty eradication program as well as ensuring educational access to all with special attention to girls and disadvantaged children.

Source: Paul Blustein, "Global Educations Plan Gains Backing," *Washington Post,* April 22, 2002, p. A15; "A New Focus on Education for All," *Official Document,* G8 Summit Meeting–Kananaskis, Canada, June 2002. http://www.g7.utoronto.ca/g7/summit/2002kananaskis/education.html.

In January of 2002, after three years of stagnation, Argentina was forced into debt default and currency devaluation. The destabilizing effects of which spread to its neighbors by mid-year. However, in August 2002, with no agreement on whether it would support and the IMF would provide further loans, the Bush administration agreed to extend trade benefits to Argentina allowing exporters from the country easier access to the U.S. market.

Many issues are involved in international economic policy. They deal with international trade, international monetary problems (including exchange-rate policy), international finance and debt problems, and the actions of international economic institutions such as the World Bank, the International Monetary Fund (IMF), and the World Trade Organization (WTO). Some economic issues are global in scope; others are multilateral, involving groups of nations; still others are bilateral, between two nations. In the area of trade, for example, U.S. policy influences global trade policy through the General Agreement on Tariffs and Trade (GATT) and the WTO, and regional trade policy through the North American Free Trade Agreement (NAFTA). The United States also engages in bilateral trade negotiations with many nations, most notably Japan.

International economic policies, like their domestic counterparts, are influenced both by political concerns and by broad philosophical and theoretical concerns. When policy makers determine their support for international policies, they must consider both how their constituents will be affected and whether the policy is broadly beneficial, given their understanding of the way the international economy works. How these two sets of forces play against each other can be seen in the politics of international trade in the 1990s.

The GATT Uruguay Round

In 1994 Congress considered the GATT agreement that resulted from the Uruguay Round of multilateral trade negotiations. (GATT has since been superseded by the **World Trade Organization (WTO)** as a forum for negotiating global trade agreements.) The Uruguay Round of GATT negotiations started under President Reagan in 1986, continued under former President Bush and concluded under President Clinton. The United States had sought in GATT to exchange further opening of its own markets to international goods and services for greater access to foreign markets, greater security for U.S. technology abroad, and more open access for U.S. exports. The GATT agreements gave the United States some but not all that it sought in this regard.

In considering the GATT agreement, Congress weighed the laissez-faire argument that free trade is a global "invisible hand" that will benefit all nations against the argument that open markets are not in the national interest because of their impact on certain groups, especially low-wage manufacturing workers. Members of Congress understood that some individuals and businesses in their districts might be harmed by foreign competition, but that other individuals and firms would gain from increased exports. In the end, after some dramatic skirmishing, the theory of free trade triumphed, and the GATT treaty was ratified—but not without criticism of the policy-making authority invested in the new World Trade Organization. Many feared that the WTO might overrule and thus weaken U.S. trade laws and undermine hard-won environmental protections.

The NAFTA Treaty

The politics of international trade were somewhat different in 1993, when Congress was asked to ratify the **North American Free Trade Agreement (NAFTA).** NAFTA was begun under President Reagan as a trade agreement between the United States and Canada. Negotiations continued under former President Bush and were concluded under President Clinton, with Mexico being added to the free-trade zone. NAFTA goes beyond GATT in its ardor for regional free trade. When fully implemented in several years, NAFTA will make trade among the United States, Canada, and Mexico as free and easy as that among Ohio, Indiana, and Illinois.

The NAFTA vote was far more dramatic than the later GATT tally. Republican members of Congress voted as a block in favor of NAFTA largely because of its laissez-faire origins. For many of these representatives, NAFTA meant less government interference in international trade, which they favored. Many Democrats, however, opposed NAFTA, despite President Clinton's strong support of the measure. In many cases, opposition was based on a calculation of local effects. NAFTA would create only a few jobs in each district, they figured, but it could produce great economic and political hard times in those sectors where the effect of competition with Canada or Mexico would be the greatest. Ironically, given all the controversy it raised, NAFTA was approved by a large margin.

The Need for International Policy Coordination

The politics of international economic policy illustrates that these types of decisions are based on some mix of economic theories and on local as well as national political concerns. As the U.S. economy becomes less distinctly national and more firmly connected to the global web of commercial enterprises, it is increasingly difficult for the United States to make economic policy. The United States must take the policies of other nations into account when setting its own, and attempt, when possible, to coordinate its policies with the European Union, Japan, and other nations.

To see why policy coordination is more important now among nations, consider for a moment this simple analogy. Think of the economy as a bathtub. In previous years, each nation had its own small bathtub, which was connected to others in only

World Trade Organization (WTO) International economic organization that monitors trade and ensures "fair" practices such as no tariffs.

North American Free Trade Agreement (NAFTA) An agreement between the United States, Mexico, and Canada that allows for free trade without tariffs and restrictions between these nations.

◀ Secretary of State Colin Powell urged coalition partners in the fight against terrorism to expand their campaign to nations that proliferate weapons of mass destruction. "We all have to stay focused on this campaign against terrorism and make sure it is rooted out wherever it exists," Powell said at the World Economic Forum's Annual Meeting 2002. "We have to look at those nations that proliferate weapons of mass destruction—states that might lend or provide all kinds of weapons to terrorist organizations. We can't just stop at a single terrorist organization, we have to go through the whole system," Powell added.

a few ways. It was possible in this situation for governments to use monetary and fiscal policy like water faucets, to regulate the flow of water in their own bathtub economy without much regard to what other nations did. Domestic economic policy reigned supreme.

These days, however, the economies are increasingly global in scope. Markets span national borders through trade, finance, and telecommunications. People buy goods from around the world, invest money around the world, and participate in global culture. *Globalization* means that all the nations are, to a certain extent, now part of one big bathtub economy. A large nation like the United States can have some effect on the flow of economic activity, but much less than before. It is difficult to get the water in its end of the bathtub to a higher level without raising the level for everyone else.

In these days of "global bathtubs," individual nations have much less ability to alter their own economic fates through monetary and fiscal policies. The most effective way to change the economy is to coordinate their economic policies with those of other nations. The need for coordinated action among national governments, however, conflicts with the ideal of an independent democratic process within nations. The effective economic policies of, say, the nation of France depend increasingly on the corresponding economic policies of Germany, Great Britain, and the United States.

The tension between domestic democratic processes and global economic forces was illustrated in 1995, when Mexico experienced sudden and unanticipated foreign debt problems, which caused the peso's value to fall from about thirty to fifteen cents over the course of a few days. Recognizing the interdependence of the U.S. and Mexican economies, especially after adoption of NAFTA, the Clinton administration quickly organized a plan to help finance some of Mexico's debt. His plan had to be withdrawn, however, when congressional leaders made it clear that they would not support this program because of negative voter sentiments. The administration of George W. Bush has placed great importance on improved relations with Mexico, specifically in immigration and labor issues.

The fact of international economic interdependence has not destroyed the concept of domestic democracy, but it has changed it. On critical matters of economic policy, the fundamental nature of the relationship among voters and elected officials, together with the policies they enact and the impact of those policies, has changed in subtle and important ways.

Economic policy making is a vital role of government. The decisions made by elected and un-elected officials can influence the economic well-being of the nation as a whole, as well as every single individual, whether rich or poor, Republican or Democrat. Moreover, these decisions are often rooted in those officials' conception of the proper role of government in the lives of citizens—who should be taxed

DEMOCRACY IN THE NEW MILLENNIUM

Making On-Line Calculations for a Secure Retirement

If you are the traditional college student, age 18–22, this may not seem important to you today, be we can guarantee you that it is not only going to be important, but that your parents are as concerned as we are about this issue. A secure, comfortable retirement is every worker's dream. Your Social Security benefits are the foundation on which you can build a secure retirement. Most financial advisors say you'll need about 70 percent of your pre-retirement earnings to comfortably maintain your pre-retirement standard of living. Under current law, if you have average earnings, your Social Security retirement benefits will replace only about 40 percent, so you'll need to supplement your benefits with a pension, savings, or investments.

In addition, Social Security will need changes if it is to continue to meet the demands of the times ahead. More than 79 million "baby boomers" will start retiring in about 2010 and, in about 30 years, there will be nearly twice as many older Americans as there are today and less young people. Social Security now takes in more in taxes than it pays out in benefits. The excess funds are credited to Social Security's trust funds, which are expected to grow to over $4 trillion before we need to use them to pay benefits to the baby boomer generation. In 2017, we will begin to pay out more in benefits than we collect in taxes. By 2041, the trust funds will be exhausted and the payroll taxes collected will be enough to pay only about 73 percent of benefits owed.

The Social Security Administration has developed a Social Security retirement planner that provides detailed information about your Social Security retirement benefits under current law and points out things you may want to consider as you prepare for the future. You can use the calculators to test out different retirement ages or different future earnings amounts. There is also information about how members of your family may qualify for benefits with you. At http://www.ssa.gov/retirement you will be directed to resources that will allow you to:

- Calculate your retirement benefits using different retirement scenarios.
- Find out how certain types of earnings and pensions can affect your retirement benefits.
- See if your spouse and children will be eligible for Social Security benefits on your record.
- Discover your options if you are close to retirement age.

Also go to http://www.ssa.gov/planners/calculators.htm; http://www.ssa.gov/planners/.

---

and how these revenues should be spent—and thus policies are likely to change as individuals representing different philosophies and political constituencies assume the reins of government. Managing the economy takes you to the very heart of the relationship between a government and its people. Voters know this, and they make their feelings known come election time.

The politics of economic policy have changed in recent years due to the rising importance of international economic policy. As economic matters have become increasingly global, the very nature of democracy has changed with respect to international economic policies. These forces make the political analysis of international economics more and more complex, even as they become more and more important in our daily lives.

Politicians know very well that they will be rewarded for good economic times and punished for economic downturns, although the 2002 midterm elections illustrated that voters' national security concerns took priority over a slumping market and a growing budget deficit. Politics and economics are thus fundamentally intertwined, and it is this linkage, with all of its multiple uncertainties, that provides the economic signposts on the road that America follows in its continuing approach to realizing its democratic potential.

SUMMARY

1. Public policies are the decisions, actions, and commitments of government. They have four key aims: to regulate key industries and aspects of American life, to protect citizens from foreign powers and other potential enemies, to encourage the accomplishment of important social goals, and to assist citizens and state and local governments.

2. The policy life cycle consists of eleven stages: (a) redefinition of a condition as a public problem, (b) placement of the problem on the public agenda, (c) emergence of the problem as an issue requiring government action, (d) formulation of a public policy response, (e) reformulation of the proposed policy, (f) placement of the policy on the formal agenda of government, (g) enactment of the policy, (h) implementation of the policy, (i) impacts caused by implementation of the policy, (j) evaluation of the impacts, and (k) termination or continued implementation and evaluation of the policy.

3. To reach the public agenda, a potential subject of public policy must undergo a radical redefinition in the eyes of policy elites; that is, it must be labeled as a problem to be solved by the government. A potential policy reaches the issue stage when it is framed in terms of a yes-or-no policy option. A dramatic event may serve as a triggering mechanism that causes a condition to be redefined as a problem, or an issue can reach the public agenda through the activities of policy entrepreneurs who "sell" it to a policy-making body. A policy reaches the formal agenda when it is actually scheduled for debate and potential adoption by a policy-making body.

4. Implementation is the execution of a policy. Some policies are difficult to implement because of their complexity, the cooperation required, and the need for coordination. Most federal policies require a period of monitoring and analysis known as policy evaluation. Following evaluation, policies are either terminated or continued. Once a policy has been enacted, however, it is often difficult to terminate.

5. Regulatory policy involves the use of police powers by the federal government to supervise the conduct of individuals, businesses, and other governmental agencies. The national government may regulate prices, franchising or licenses, performance or safety standards, and resources available to citizens or businesses. It may also provide or withhold operating subsidies or use regulatory commissions to regulate vital industries and promote fair competition.

6. Regulatory activity by the federal government began in the late 1800s and increased during the Great Depression. The highest levels of regulation were reached in the 1960s and 1970s and were followed by a movement toward deregulation. Beginning in the late 1980s there was a swing back toward increased regulation.

7. Social welfare policy uses positive incentives to promote or encourage basic social fairness. Much social welfare policy is intended to alleviate the problems associated with poverty. The federal poverty level—the dollar amount of annual earnings below which a family is considered poor—is used to generate official government estimates of the number of Americans living in poverty.

8. The first major piece of social welfare legislation was the Social Security Act of 1935, which created four major sets of entitlements: Old Age Survivors Disability Insurance, unemployment insurance, Aid to Families with Dependent Children, and Supplemental Security Income. Additional social welfare legislation was enacted during the 1960s as part of the "War on Poverty."

9. During the 1970s and 1980s entitlements increased, only to be scaled back during the Reagan administration. The Family Support Act of 1988 introduced work requirements for recipients of welfare benefits. The Personal Responsibility and Work Opportunity Reconciliation Act of 1996 ended the welfare system as we knew it and set the stage for ongoing reforms on a state-by-state basis.

10. Government policies that affect the economy can be organized into four groups: fiscal policy (decisions to tax and spend), monetary policy (the Fed's influence over the rate of inflation), regulatory policy (policies designed to achieve health, safety, and environmental goals), and international economic policies (policies dealing with exchange rates, trade negotiations, and international economic institutions).

11. The three main goals of economic policy are stable prices, full employment, and economic growth. Achieving these goals involves achieving certain secondary goals as well, such as low and stable interest rates, stable exchange rates, and reduced federal budget deficits and balance-of-trade deficits. Because of the complex interactions among these goals, economic policy makers often trade off one goal against another.

12. The federal budget is prepared by the Office of Management and Budget, which analyzes the budgetary requests made by every government agency. The president submits the budget to Congress in February of each year. The Budget Committees in the two

houses consider the president's proposals and establish overall levels for taxation and for various areas of government spending.

13. The federal personal income and capital gains taxes are progressive; that is, those who make more money are taxed at a higher rate. Taxes on consumer goods such as gasoline and cigarettes are regressive because they take a higher fraction of the income of lower-income taxpayers. Periodic attempts to reform the tax structure typically give rise to major political battles over who will benefit and who will pay more.

14. Discretionary spending covers appropriations for government operations. The largest proportion of federal spending consists of mandatory spending or direct payments to individuals through entitlement programs such as Social Security.

15. When policy makers consider international economic policies, they must consider both how their constituents will be affected and whether the policy is beneficial to the country as a whole. Thus, in considering the GATT agreement Congress weighed the potential benefits of free trade for all nations against the potential impact on certain groups, especially low-wage manufacturing workers. In considering the North American Free Trade Agreement, it weighed the benefits of reduced government interference in international trade against the possibility that large numbers of jobs would be moved to Mexico.

16. Increasingly, the United States must take the policies of other nations into account when making economic policy and must try to coordinate its policies with those of the European Union, Japan, and other nations.

KEY TERMS

public policies	entitlements	capital gains tax
regulatory policy	means testing	tax expenditures
social welfare policy	workfare	excise taxes
policy elites	economic policy	discretionary spending
public agenda	deficit	mandatory spending
formal agenda	Office of Management and	national debt
triggering mechanism	Budget (OMB)	World Trade Organization
policy entrepreneurs	impoundment	(WTO)
implementation	tariffs	North American Free Trade
policy evaluation	progressive taxes	Agreement (NAFTA)
poverty level	regressive taxes	

POLISIM ACTIVITY

Balancing the Nation's Checkbook: What Can You Get for $4 Trillion
The federal government's budget process begins nearly two years in advance, when the various departments and agencies estimate their needs and propose their budgets to the president. Agency officials take into account not only their needs but also the overall presidential program and the probable reactions of Congress. In this simulation you are the director of the Office of Management and Budget and need to make recommendations for budget cuts to make up for the president's tax.

SUGGESTED READINGS

FRIEDMAN, MILTON, and WALTER HELLER. *Monetary versus Fiscal Policy*. New York: Norton, 1969. Classic presentation of the pros and cons of monetary and fiscal policy given by a noninterventionist (Friedman) and an advocate of federal government intervention in the economy (Heller).

GREIDER, WILLIAM. *Secrets of the Temple: How the Federal Reserve Runs the Country*. New York: Simon & Schuster, 1987. A fascinating account of how the Federal Reserve Board actually conducts its business.

HARRINGTON, MICHAEL. *The Other America.* New York: Macmillan, 1994. The most widely read essay about poverty in the United States.

JENCKS, CHRISTOPHER. *Rethinking Social Policy: Race, Poverty, and the Underclass.* Cambridge, Mass.: Harvard University Press, 1992. A series of essays by a leading sociologist on social welfare policy and poverty.

MURRAY, CHARLES. *Losing Ground: American Social Policy, 1950–1980.* New York: Basic Books, 1984. A popular and controversial book that addresses the idea that social welfare programs for the poor have made things worse, not better.

ODELL, JOHN S. *Negotiating the World Economy.* Ithaca, N.Y.: Cornell University Press, 2000. An original analysis of strategies used by negotiators to get maximum payoffs.

SAVAGE, JAMES. *Balanced Budgets and American Politics.* Ithaca, N.Y.: Cornell University Press, 1988. A scholarly account of the history of ways the political environment affects budgeting in the United States.

SLEMROD, JOEL, and JON BAKIGA. *Taxing Ourselves.* 2d ed. Cambridge, Mass.: MIT Press, 2000. An excellent citizen's guide to the debate on taxation and reform.

16   FOREIGN POLICY

CHAPTER OUTLINE

Approaching Democracy Case Study:
   Operation Enduring Freedom: Building an
   International Coalition to Defeat Terrorism
Introduction: Foreign Policy and Democracy
An Overview of American Foreign Policy
The Constitution and Foreign Policy
The Foreign Policy Bureaucracy
Democratic Checks on Foreign Policy

APPROACHING DEMOCRACY CASE STUDY

Operation Enduring Freedom: Building an International Coalition to Defeat Terrorism

I n the wake of the September 11 attacks on the World Trade Center and the Pentagon, President Bush undertook the leadership challenge of building an international coalition aimed at defeating international terrorism as well as its network of financial support. The Pentagon named its military campaign "Operation Enduring Freedom," replacing an earlier name that was considered offensive to Muslims ("Operation Infinite Justice," because in the Islamic faith such finality is provided only by Allah.).[1]

In the weeks following the attack, Great Britain and other sympathetic countries quickly supported U.S. resolve to bomb Taliban positions in Afghanistan, the stronghold of the al-Qaeda network. The new coalition of nations formed an International Security Assistance Force, or ISAF, led by Great Britain with the mission of bringing security to Kabul, the capital of Afghanistan. Much of the Arab world remained wary of supporting a controversial and possibly long-term war against fellow Muslims. General Sharif of Pakistan, for example, faced momentous difficulties in retaining the loyalty of his people while helping the United States defeat Islamic terrorism in adjacent Afghanistan.

The international coalition showed signs of weakening during early 2002 when the military strikes with mounting civilian deaths continued far longer than many allied nations expected. International enthusiasm for the American-led military effort further waned, as the new Afghani government took power and began taking its first steps in approaching democracy. Secretary of Defense Donald Rumsfeld criticized the lack of help provided by other nations, particularly the dearth of monetary assistance and allied troops in the field. Afghanistan emerged from five years of totalitarian Taliban rule a much-divided nation where warlords and tribal law held sway over international justice. The need to train a national army to provide security for the new Afghanistan tested the resolve of the international coalition. As nations began to balk over American expectations of a continuation of international cooperation, Rumsfeld stated, "We are not the only country on the face of the Earth who can do things, and there are other countries who are perfectly capable of doing things as well. And it's an awful lot easier to stand back and point a finger and say why isn't something bigger, better or longer or richer or more of this, than it is to say, 'OK, I'll line up and help'."[2]

When Turkey took over the international peacekeeping force in Kabul in 2002, more money was needed from other countries to police the divided nation. Many countries feared taking part in a long-term occupation of Afghanistan. Even the Turkish government was highly divided about taking over the momentous peacekeeping task. The $28 million necessary to train and equip an Afghan national army of 200,000 fighters daunted nations like Japan and Argentina who were embroiled in severe economic slowdowns. The United States agreed to pay $20 million dollars to offset Turkey's role in taking over the ISAF.

As the world's remaining superpower, the U.S. was facing a high price tag to defeat international terrorism. But that cost is a necessary one because so many of the cold war doctrines of containment and deterrence are today irrelevant. "If we wait for threats to fully materialize, we will have waited too long," said President Bush, speaking at the commencement of the 204th graduating class of West Point, the nation's oldest military academy. "We must take the battle to the enemy, disrupt his plans and confront the worst threats before they emerge. The only path to safety is action. And this nation will act."[3]

The ability to act against ruthless and resourceful enemies is the new challenge facing American leadership in the formulation of a foreign policy. "In defending the peace, we face a threat without precedent," President Bush told the West Point graduating class. The President explained that America needed partners to preserve the peace; his words speak directly to our theme of approaching democracy:

> In the last few decades we've seen nations from Chile to South Korea build modern economies and freer societies, lifting millions of people out of despair and want. And there's no mystery to this achievement. The 20th century ended with a single surviving model of human progress based on non-negotiable demands of human dignity, the rule of law, limits on the power of the state, respect for women and private property, and free speech, and equal justice and religious tolerance. America cannot impose this vision. Yet, we can support and reward governments that make the right choices for their own people. In our development aid, in our diplomatic efforts, in our international broadcasting and in our educational assistance, the United States will promote moderation and tolerance and human rights. And we will defend the peace that makes all progress possible.[4]

Question for Reflection: How does the ISAF (International Security Assistance Force) compare with the United Nations Peacekeeping forces? Why do both forces need to exist?

▲ General Tommy Franks, commander in chief of U.S. Central Command, runs the day-to-day operations of the U.S. military campaign in Afghanistan.

INTRODUCTION: FOREIGN POLICY AND DEMOCRACY

Foreign policy refers to actions taken by the U.S. government on behalf of its national interests abroad to ensure the security and well-being of Americans and the strength and competitiveness of the U.S. economy. A secure citizenry requires protection of recognized national boundaries, a strong economy, and a stable, orderly society, but the case study provides ample evidence that foreign policy is linked with domestic security as well as shifting coalitions of interests.[5]

Since the end of World War II, U.S. foreign policy has been a cautious balancing act between American democratic ideals and U.S. military and economic interests. Much of the history is rooted in the concept of what is called American exceptionalism. "We shall be as a City upon a Hill," proclaimed Puritan leader John Winthrop more than three centuries ago. Indeed, it is this core value that comes closest to our theme of approaching democracy.[6] "On every continent democracy is securing for more and more people the basic freedoms we Americans have come to take for granted," observed President Bill Clinton in his 1998 address to the Joint Chiefs of Staff and Pentagon staff about the situation in Iraq. President Bush reiterated this theme following the September 11 terrorist attacks when he observed that the enemies of the United States hate us for the freedoms that we possess.[7]

The end of the Cold War and the breakup of the Eastern bloc may have nearly eliminated the threat of a global nuclear war, but it perhaps also stimulated increasing hostility, violence, and warfare. The collapse of the Soviet Union set the stage for a violent showdown between Russian president Boris Yeltsin and his own parliament. The breakup of the former Yugoslavia triggered a genocidal war between various ethnic factions. The massive 1991 U.S. deployment in the Persian Gulf War with Iraq would have been almost unthinkable a decade earlier, when the Soviet Union was still a potential force to be reckoned with. Without the policy priority of anticommunism, the United States has had to weigh carefully both its own interests and its commitments to democracy and human rights before developing a foreign policy response.

Moreover, following the collapse of the Soviet Union, the United States shifted its military focus to combat other international threats to American safety. Considered to be 'rogue' for challenging the hegemony of American foreign policy, these nations command a minor amount of weapons capable of inflicting "massive destruction" like the nuclear weapons possessed by the United States. Following the September 11 attacks of the Pentagon and World Trade Center, the idea of 'rogue' nations striking the United States came to be seen as an imminent possibility. In his State of the Union Address after the attacks, President Bush named an "axis of evil" that included North Korea, Iraq, and Iran.[8]

In his June 1, 2002, West Point Commencement address, the President observed that, "in defending the peace we face a threat with no precedent. Enemies in the past needed great armies and great industrial capabilities to endanger the American people and our nation. The attacks of September the 11 required a few hundred thousand dollars in the hands of a few dozen evil and deluded men. All of the chaos and suffering they caused came at much less than the cost of a single tank . . . The gravest danger to freedom lies at the perilous crossroads of radicalism and technology. When the spread of chemical and biological and nuclear weapons, along with ballistic missile technology, occurs weak states and small groups could attain a catastrophic power to strike great nations. Our enemies have declared this very intention and have been caught seeking these terrible weapons. They want the capability to blackmail us or to harm our friends. And we will oppose them with all our power."[9]

foreign policy Policy adopted and actions taken by the U.S. government on behalf of U.S. national interests abroad. The president is the country's chief foreign policy maker.

In this chapter we look at American foreign policy, its history, how it is made, and by whom. Perhaps the best way to start is by identifying the core goals of American foreign relations:

1. *Survival and independence:* A country's foreign relations are guided first and foremost by national security—the protection of those interests deemed necessary for the country's safety. Independence and survival are the irreducible, fundamental security objectives of the United States.

2. *Territorial integrity and acquisition of new territory:* The preservation of territorial integrity is the mirror image of survival and always a national security priority.

3. *Military security:* Military security for any nation depends on a variety of factors that includes weaponry, capabilities and intentions of other nations, advantages and disadvantages of geography, resources, and demographic trends.

4. *Economic security:* Two persistent themes of American foreign policy have been to keep the door open for trade wherever profit beckoned and be ready to employ costly economic measures to achieve goals. Economic advantage has long stood as an objective of U.S. foreign policy.

5. *Democratic values and ideals:* The promotion of democratic values and ideals worldwide has defined the national purpose of the United States's role in world affairs.[10]

An Overview of American Foreign Policy

We can distinguish between two eras in U.S. foreign policy. The first, from the founding of the republic until approximately World War I, might be described as a period of isolationism from Europe, but with vigorous expansion in the Western Hemisphere. The second is characterized by an increasing globalization of American interests and commitments including: two world wars, a Cold War, and a post-Cold War period of redefinition and refocusing of American national interests in foreign policy.

Isolation and Regionalism

Once free of the domination of Great Britain, the United States was not eager to reestablish binding ties with European empires; however, the newly independent country was not about to commit economic suicide by cutting off lucrative ties with the great trading centers of Europe. A pattern of **isolationism** was gradually established in which the United States fostered economic relations with Europe without committing itself to strategic alliances that might draw the country into a European war. Initially, such a policy was easily pursued, since the United States had virtually no standing army and few military resources upon which European countries could call. The United States also enjoyed a favorable geographic isolation, situated as it was between two vast oceans in a time of slow and dangerous sea travel.

The **Monroe Doctrine,** enunciated by President James Monroe in his December 2, 1823, State of the Union Address, reinforced the country's isolationism by proclaiming the North and South American continents to be in the United States' *sphere of influence* and therefore out of bounds for European aspirations. In return, the United States agreed not to become involved in European affairs. The Monroe Doctrine also contributed to another crucial ideal of U.S. foreign policy: vigorous territorial expansion within its own continental land-mass that belied any absolute isolation of America. Under the banner of *Manifest Destiny,* U.S. foreign policy makers in the first half of the nineteenth century invoked divine guidance to take control of what is now the continental United States. Then, at the end of the century, the United States looked south, to Central America, the Caribbean, and South America, turning from internal expansion to an enhanced role for America overseas.

isolationism A pattern in which the United States fosters economic relations abroad without committing to strategic alliances that might draw the country into a war.

Monroe Doctrine A doctrine enunciated by President James Monroe in 1823 that proclaimed North and South America to be in the United States' sphere of influence, hence out of bounds for European aspirations. It reinforced isolationism by promising not to interfere in the internal concerns of European states.

By this time U.S. governmental and private agencies controlled vast oil fields in Mexico and plantations in the Dominican Republic and Cuba. American businesses and diplomats were also looking toward the reluctantly opening door to China. Yet U.S. foreign policy was still regional, with a clear priority given to the resources and potential of the Western Hemisphere. In 1898, the United States went to war against Spain, and in the process seized the Philippines and Puerto Rico. In the same year, it annexed the Hawaiian Islands. In the first years of the twentieth century, under the leadership of President Theodore Roosevelt the United States emerged as policeman of the Western Hemisphere. Roosevelt not only launched the Panama Canal project, but also mediated the Russo-Japanese War and accelerated the development of the United States Navy.

World War I

With the start of World War I in Europe in 1914 and the collapse of the Russian monarchy three years later, the United States began to position itself as a player of global rather than regional stature. Despite strong isolationist and pacifist movements at home and the country's policy of neutrality, the United States clearly favored Britain and the Allied Powers over Germany and the Central Powers. But as long as trans-Atlantic shipping lanes remained unviolated, the United States was reluctant to commit more than indirect support. Then, in 1915, a German submarine sank the ocean liner *Lusitania,* and the death toll included American citizens. Many historians argue that the *Lusitania* was not really a "neutral" vessel, since evidence suggests that a large cache of munitions was in her hold. For U.S. policy makers, though, this act of aggression demonstrated the horrors of Germany's policy of unrestricted submarine warfare and the impossibility of containing the war within Europe. When Germany resumed unrestricted submarine warfare in 1917, the United States declared war, and the country's departure from its historic isolationism was rationalized as a commitment to "make the world safe for democracy" while fighting a "war to end all wars." U.S. forces, while undoubtedly turning the tide against Germany, suffered over 120,000 casualties. Despite the rhetoric heralding the United States entry into the war, neither antidemocratic nor warlike forces were vanquished in World War I.

With the end of hostilities in 1918, Americans were eager to put the horrors of war behind them. President Woodrow Wilson campaigned vigorously for an international organization of states to "outlaw" the sort of aggression that had triggered the war. While his efforts ultimately led to the founding of the League of Nations, Wilson was unable to get the U.S. Senate, which had to approve the peace treaty, to join the League. The prevailing mood favored a return to isolationism.

But the conditions leading to World War I and its consequences drew the United States into inevitable conflict with another European country: the newly founded Soviet Union. In the midst of wartime chaos, a small but determined Bolshevik party, led by Vladimir Ulyanov, better known as Lenin, had seized control of Russia. What would become the Union of Soviet Socialist Republics (USSR) was founded in 1917, the first large-scale attempt to form a modern socialist state and, since it was designed as an alternative to liberal capitalism, an ideological adversary of the United States. With little public knowledge, Wilson dispatched approximately ten thousand Americans to aid other Allied troops in the disruption of the revolutionary regime. This invasion set the stage for a growing hostility between the United States and the USSR that would not be fully apparent until after another world war.

Question for Reflection: How do you think the United States's role in international affairs would be different today if the Senate had approved the joining of the League of Nations?

World War II

Tensions between the United States and USSR were briefly tabled with the outbreak of World War II. Hitler invaded Poland in 1939, violating a nonaggression pact between Germany and the Soviet Union, but President Franklin D. Roosevelt refused to commit American military might to help stop the German advance. As in World War I, the United States was reluctant to encumber itself with strategic alliances, pursuing instead a policy of economic aid to the Allies. Only after Germany's Pacific ally, Japan, bombed the U.S. naval base at Pearl Harbor, Hawaii, on December 7, 1941, did the United States formally enter the war and send troops to Europe and the Pacific. This "Day of Infamy" galvanized Americans in an outrage that overcame the nation's traditionally isolationist orientation.

The wartime fates of the United States and the Soviet Union were strikingly different. For the United States, not yet recovered from the Great Depression, the expanded industrial production and employment demanded by wartime industrial mobilization actually helped to jump-start an economic boom. Beyond the initial destruction at Pearl Harbor, the country suffered no attacks on its home territory. In stark contrast, the Soviet Union was devastated. The Soviet Red Army stopped the eastward advance of Germany, but at tremendous cost; 20 million military personnel and civilians died, either from combat or through disease or starvation. As with most of battle-scarred Europe, the Soviet Union had the look of a defeated nation.

Given the striking differences between the United States and the Soviet Union at the end of World War II, it is surprising that the Soviet Union would emerge as the chief U.S. rival. So awesome would the dominance of the two countries become that they inspired a new concept—**superpower.** The term was intended to convey the disproportionate power—economic and military—that distinguished the United States and the Soviet Union from all other countries in the postwar era. And so pervasive was the superpower rivalry that relations between the United States and the USSR affected virtually every country in the world.

> **QUOTE ... UNQUOTE**
>
> "The 1920s taught us a clear lesson. Aggressive conduct, if allowed to go unchecked and unchallenged, ultimately leads to war."
>
> John F. Kennedy
> on the Cuban missile crisis

superpower The disproportionate power—economic and military—that distinguished the United States and the Soviet Union from all other countries in the postwar era.

◀ The December 7, 1941, Japanese bombing of Pearl Harbor galvanized the United States in outrage and subsequent willingness to enter World War II. Here, a motor launch rescues a survivor from the torpedo-damaged and surken U.S.S. *West Virginia.*

Globalism and the Cold War

Nothing in the international arena would be as it had been before the Second World War. The United States emerged as the only major power with a completely intact infrastructure, booming industrial production, and a monopoly on the most revolutionary weaponry ever created—the atomic bomb. Two atomic bombs had been dropped on Japan at the end of World War II, not only to shock the Japanese into complete surrender but, some believe, to send a message to the Soviet Union that the United States not only possessed such military might but was prepared to use it.[11]

U.S. foreign policy after 1946 was guided by the doctrine of **containment,** a concept delineated by George Kennan, then a State Department Soviet expert. Kennan observed that the USSR's expansionist foreign policy "moves along the prescribed path, like a persistent toy automobile wound up and headed in a given direction, stopping only when it meets some unanswerable force." According to Kennan, that "unanswerable force" must be the United States, and Soviet aggression must be "contained by the adroit and vigilant application of counterforce at a series of constantly shifting geographical and political points." Somewhat prophetically, Kennan argued that if the United States could contain the Soviet Union without weakening itself politically or economically, the result would be "either the break-up or the gradual mellowing of Soviet power."[12]

But the ultimate "breakup" and "mellowing" of the Soviet Union were still decades away. Both the United States and the Soviet Union had joined the new international organization, the United Nations (UN), upon its creation in 1945, but the two countries remained adversaries. Soviet forces controlled all of Eastern Europe, installing virtual puppet regimes behind an "iron curtain" of military might and political resolve. The United States applied the counterforce of billions of dollars in economic aid to Western Europe under the Marshall Plan of postwar reconstruction as well as through numerous strategic treaties and agreements.

In a historic address to Congress on March 12, 1947, President Harry Truman invoked the doctrine of containment in a pledge to halt the spread of communism through economic and military aid to Greece and Turkey. This intention to assist free, democratic nations beat back the threat of totalitarianism became known as the *Truman Doctrine.* At home, the National Security Act of 1947 created the Central Intelligence Agency (CIA) and the National Security Council (NSC), signaling the readiness of the United States to move beyond regionalism to **globalism.** Now the American "sphere of influence" included virtually every corner of the globe where U.S. interests might be affected.

In 1949, the United States secured the commitment of eleven European nations to form the **North Atlantic Treaty Organization (NATO).** The NATO charter also signaled the end of American isolationism and regionalism. Charter signatories agreed that an armed attack against one or more of them in Europe or North America would be interpreted as an attack against all. In the event of such an attack, the treaty bound all members of NATO to assist the attacked country, employing "forthwith, individually and in concert with the other Parties, such action as it deems necessary, including the use of armed forces," but as we saw in the recent call by the United States to defeat international terrorism, some NATO members resisted placing their troops in the field.[13]

Also in 1949, the U.S. monopoly of nuclear weapons ended when the Soviets detonated their first atomic bomb. In the same year, the American-backed regime in China collapsed and a communist state was created under the direction of Mao Zedong. In April 1950, members of the NSC drafted what was to become the "blueprint" for waging the **Cold War** during the next twenty years: National Security Council Paper 68 (NSC 68). NSC 68 outlined a sweeping mobilization of American economic and human resources in the effort to contain Soviet communism. It was the first major document to acknowledge the bipolar struggle between the American and Soviet superpowers.[14]

LITTLE-KNOWN FACT

The term cold war was first used by Herbert Bayard Swope (1882–1958) in speeches he wrote for Bernard Baruch (1870–1965). After Baruch told the Senate War Investigating Committee on October 24, 1948, "Let us not be deceived—today we are in the midst of a cold war," the press picked up the phrase, and it became part of everyday speech.

---

containment A term coined in 1946 by George Kennan, who believed that Soviet aggression must be "contained by the adroit and vigilant application of counterforce by the United States."

globalism View in which the U.S. sphere of influence has expanded beyond the western hemisphere to include virtually every corner of the globe where U.S. interests might be affected.

North Atlantic Treaty Organization (NATO) Charter signed by the United States, Canada, Turkey, and eleven European nations in 1949 agreeing that an armed attack against one or more of them would be interpreted as an attack against all.

Cold War The bipolar struggle between the United States and the Soviet Union that began in the 1950s and ended in the 1990s.

Bipolarity refers to the fundamental division of economic and military power between the poles of Western capitalism and Eastern communism. NSC 68 recommended against negotiation with the Kremlin and advocated the development of a more powerful nuclear arsenal, rapid expansion of conventional military resources, and the full mobilization of American society within a "government-created consensus" against the evils of communism. The document also called for a dramatic American commitment to international strategic and economic alliances against the Eastern bloc, indicating yet another push away from isolation and regionalism toward globalism. In 1955 the Soviet Union and its East European allies (called satellites) formed the **Warsaw Pact,** a military alliance to counter NATO.

In June 1950, just months after the drafting of NSC 68, war in Korea became a major test of the containment policy. Ironically, the challenge here was posed not by the Soviet Union but by the new communist regime in China. Ultimately, the Korean conflict proved a political and military stalemate. The decade closed with the declaration of a socialist revolution only ninety miles off the coast of Florida in Cuba and the ascension of Fidel Castro.

The Nuclear World   The nuclear age began with the U.S. bombing of Hiroshima and Nagasaki in August 1945. In September 1949, the exploding of a Soviet-made atomic device triggered a superpower arms race with frightening global implications. Over the next forty years, both the United States and the Soviet Union poured billions of dollars into the development of ever more powerful nuclear weapons, just as they devoted increasing intellectual resources to the development of foreign policies tailored to the new "nuclear world" that they had created.

The most dangerous nuclear confrontation of the Cold War occurred in 1962. Soviet Premier Nikita Khrushchev had begun construction of missile bases in Cuba, an act seen by U.S. leaders as a direct provocation, despite the fact that the United States had installed similar missile bases in Turkey aimed at the Soviet Union. After several tense days of secret debates within the U.S. national security establishment, President John Kennedy took the unprecedented step of going before the American people and announcing a naval blockade of Cuba aimed at keeping Soviet supply ships out. In a televised speech Kennedy demanded the immediate dismantling and removal of the bases. Ultimately, Khrushchev backed down and the bases were dismantled. Plans for a "hot line," providing a communications link between the two leaders, were continued, and a Limited Test Ban Treaty was negotiated in 1963. But the threat of a nuclear exchange continued.[15]

Mounting an Economic Offensive   Cold War policy makers did not restrict their activity to military planning. In line with the Truman doctrine, U.S. **foreign aid** continued to increase as a hedge against Soviet advances into less developed countries of the Third World. One such U.S. effort during the Kennedy administration was the **Peace Corps.** Volunteers sent to all parts of the globe were involved in everything from improving literacy and building roads and schools to starting immunization and other health programs. The Peace Corps remains the country's foremost experiment in fusing the aims of foreign policy with the resources of government and the initiative and expertise of private individuals.[16]

A second program initiated at this time, focusing on Latin America, was the *Alliance for Progress.* The policy really began in the last year of the Eisenhower administration with the formation of the Inter-American Development Bank, but it was popularized in 1961 under President Kennedy. In exchange for a commitment of $20 billion over ten years, the United States asked participating Latin American countries to liberalize their tax, land distribution, and social policies, which major players such as Argentina, Brazil, and Mexico were reluctant to do. In the end, the Alliance never lived up to its potential, either as a social and economic boon to Latin America or as a hedge against the blossoming of socialist and communist regimes in the region. By 1966, the Alliance had all but vanished. The U.S.

bipolarity The fundamental division of economic and military power between the poles of Western capitalism and Eastern communism.

Warsaw Pact Treaty signed by the Soviet Union and the Eastern bloc in Europe agreeing to mutual defense, in reaction to NATO.

foreign aid Small portion of the federal budget that goes to nonmilitary aid abroad, initially to mitigate against Soviet expansion.

Peace Corps Organization formed by President Kennedy to help with development in the Third World by having American volunteers live and work in needy communities.

Understanding the ABM Treaty

The History

- The Antiballistic Missile Treaty was signed by President Nixon and Leonid I. Brezhnev, the leader of the Soviet Union, on May 26, 1972 in Moscow. It was ratified by the United States Senate on Aug. 3, 1972, and entered into force on Oct. 3 of the same year. It is a relatively short treaty, consisting of 16 articles that fit, single-spaced, onto five sheets of paper.

Provisions for Withdrawal

- Article XV provided that either party, with six months notice, could withdraw from the treaty "if it decides that extraordinary events related to the subject matter of this Treaty have jeopardized its supreme interests."

What It Prohibits

- Article I prohibits the two nations from putting in place systems capable of defending their entire territories from intercontinental ballistic missile attacks.
- Article V prohibits the development, testing or deployment of sea-, air-, space- or mobile land-based antiballistic missile systems.

What It Allows

- Article III, as later amended, allows each country to build a single, fixed, land-based missile defense site, either to protect the nation's capital or to defend one of its intercontinental ballistic missile sites. The Soviet Union chose to build an antimissile system around Moscow, while the United States built a missile defense site in North Dakota, later shut down by then-Secretary of Defense Donald H. Rumsfeld in 1976.
- The treaty does not prohibit the two nations from developing defenses against shorter range, or theater, missiles that might be launched against a country's forward based troops.
- It also does not prohibit flight testing of stationary, land-based antiballistic missile systems and their components—the kind of testing the Pentagon has been conducting for the past several years.

Source: The New York Times, December 12, 2001, p. A14.

commitment to foreign aid for the developing world continued, but not at the level envisioned by the Kennedy administration.[17]

During the Bush administration a true crisis developed when on April 12, 2002, the administration's comments appeared to welcome the overthrow of Venezuela's elected President, Hugo Chavez, and to deny that there had been a military coup. These statements threatened to undermine over two decades of U.S. encouragement of democratic government in Latin America. Both Mexico and Argentina refused to recognize the new government. Confidence in the United States commitment to constitutional order was threatened. "There is anxiety in Brazil and the rest of Latin America because the U.S. no longer seems so committed to democratic principles," observed former Brazilian Foreign Minister Luiz Felipe Lampreia. Chavez was soon restored to power, but the United States lost much credibility in the region.[18]

Vietnam At the height of the Cold War, the United States entered what would prove to be its most damaging military intervention. In the southeastern Asian country of Vietnam, nationalist forces from the north, led by Ho Chi Minh, had defeated French colonial forces at Dienbienphu in 1954. In Geneva, where international talks on Korea were proceeding, Vietnam was partitioned into a communist north and a capitalist south, with the promise of elections in two years that could unify the country. The elections never materialized, as the struggle between the two Vietnams intensified. Determined to halt the spread of communism, the United States supported the corrupt but capitalist regime in the south.

Beginning early in the Kennedy administration, first hundreds and then thousands of U.S. military "advisers" were sent to South Vietnam. There was little public information about or discussion of U.S. policy in Southeast Asia, and policy makers were left to pursue their own course, which proved to be a mounting commitment of military personnel and equipment.

Within a few weeks of each other in November 1963, both South Vietnamese Prime Minister Ngo Dinh Diem and President Kennedy were assassinated. Lyndon Johnson assumed the presidency with public declarations of no desire to "widen" the war in Vietnam. Yet he convinced Congress to support a massive military buildup in Southeast Asia. On August 2, 1964, the U.S. destroyer *Maddox* was returning from an electronic espionage mission when North Vietnamese torpedo boats fired on it. The attack was repulsed. Rather than withdrawing U.S. ships from this danger zone, Johnson ordered another destroyer, the *C. Turner Joy,* to join the *Maddox* in the Gulf of Tonkin. On August 4, both the *Maddox* and the *C. Turner Joy* reportedly came under attack by torpedo boats. Considerable doubt exists about this second attack, as weather conditions were so bad and tensions aboard ship so high that Johnson later quipped, "For all I know, our Navy was shooting at whales out there." But circumstantial evidence was all Johnson needed for ordering reprisals against North Vietnam. The **Gulf of Tonkin Resolution,** passed by Congress in August 1964, provided President Johnson with broad legal authority to combat North Vietnamese aggression.

In July 1965, Lyndon Johnson chose to Americanize the war by increasing U.S. combat strength in Vietnam from 75,000 to 125,000, with additional U.S. forces to be sent when requested by field commander General William Westmoreland. "Now," Johnson wrote in his memoirs, "we were committed to major combat in Vietnam. We had determined not to let that country fall under Communist rule as long as we could prevent it."[19]

By the early 1970s the American military was mired in the Asian jungles, at a cost of billions of dollars and tens of thousands of lives. The U.S. national interest in the region was no longer clear, and the antiwar movement grew until the United States was hopelessly split on the issue. Finally, a treaty with the North Vietnamese government allowed the United States to withdraw in 1973. Ultimately, the war in Vietnam not only ravaged a nation and a people but cost more than fifty-eight thousand American lives and helped destroy the credibility of much of the U.S. foreign policy apparatus.[20]

Detente   In the wake of the withdrawal from Southeast Asia, the American people became profoundly anti-international and antimilitary. "No more Vietnams" became the rallying cry for those opposed to military intervention in Africa and Central America. Richard Nixon, ironically as anticommunist a president as ever existed, initiated a policy of **detente,** an attempt to relax the tensions between the United States and the USSR. Each side began to discuss ways to reduce the nuclear threat. A series of strategic arms limitations talks culminated in the signing of the first **Strategic Arms Limitation Treaty (SALT)** in 1972 to reduce the worldwide threat of nuclear war. But the conflict between the two superpowers heated up with the Soviet invasion of Afghanistan in December 1979, the failure by both countries to ratify the SALT II agreements, and the continuation of the arms race, now more sophisticated and involving weapons deployment in Europe.[21]

Some argue that the end of detente came with President Ronald Reagan's announcement in 1983 of plans to devise a new satellite-based laser defense system, the Strategic Defense Initiative (SDI), popularly known as "Star Wars." SDI was a program that the Soviets could not match financially or technologically, but many critics insisted that it was a "pie-in-the-sky" scheme that even the Americans could not pull off. Beyond the technological challenges of SDI, both the United States and the Soviet Union had seriously undermined their own economies through decades of military buildup. By the end of the 1980s the USSR had bankrupted itself, and the United States was over a trillion dollars in debt.[22]

In May 2002, President Bush and President Vladimir V. Putin signed an historic arms reduction treaty that commits both countries to reducing their arsenals from

Gulf of Tonkin Resolution Resolution passed by Congress that granted President Johnson authority to pursue the war in Vietnam, supposedly based on a naval attack by North Vietnamese ships.

detente An attempt to relax the tensions between the United States and the Soviet Union through limited cooperation.

Strategic Arms Limitation Treaty (SALT) Treaty signed by the United States (under President Nixon) and the Soviet Union to limit various classes of nuclear weapons.

▶ The World War II Normandy American Cemetery and Memorial is situated on a cliff overlooking Omaha Beach and the English Channel in Colleville-sur Mer, France. It contains the graves of 9,386 American military dead, most of whom gave their lives during the landings and ensuing operations of World War II. On the walls of the semicircular garden on the east side of the memorial are inscribed the names of 1,557 American missing who gave their lives in the service of their country, but whose remains were not located or identified. President Bush visited the cemetery on Memorial Day 2002 and delivered a somber yet moving speech.

about 6,000 warheads each to no more than 2,200 by 2012. According to Article 1 of the treaty:

"Each party shall reduce and limit strategic nuclear warheads, as stated by the President of the United States of America on November 13, 2001, and as stated by the President of the Russian Federation on November 13, 2001, and December 31, 2001, respectively, so that by December 31, 2012, the aggregate number of such warheads does not exceed 1,700–2,200 for each party. Each party shall determine for itself the composition and structure of its strategic offensive arms, based on the established aggregate limit for the number of such warheads . . . we are achieving a new strategic relationship. The era in which the United States and Russia saw each other as an enemy or strategic threat has ended . . . We recognize that the security, prosperity and future hopes of our peoples rest on a benign security environment, the advancement of political and economic freedoms and international cooperation."[23] Table 16.1 shows the history of arms reduction pacts between the United States and Moscow.

Table 16.1 ■ Limiting Nuclear Weapons						
	SALT I	**SALT II**	**START I**	**START II**	**START III**	**New Treaty**
Warhead limit	No limit	No limit	6,000	3,000–3,500	2,000–2,500	1,700–2,200
Missile limit	U.S.: **1,710** USSR: **2,347**	2,250	1,600	No limit	No limit	No limit
Status	Expired	Never entered into force	In force	Never entered into force	Never negotiated	Signed, awaits ratification
Date signed	May 26, 1972	June 18, 1979	July 31, 1991	Jan. 3, 1993	Not applicable	May 24, 2002
Entered into force	Oct. 3, 1972	Not applicable	Dec. 5, 1994	Not applicable	Not applicable	Not applicable
Reduction deadline	Not applicable	Dec. 31, 1981	Dec. 5, 2001	Dec. 31, 2007	Dec. 31, 2007	Dec. 31, 2012
Expiration	Oct. 3, 1977	Dec. 31, 1985	Dec. 5, 2009	Dec. 5, 2009	Not applicable	Dec. 31, 2012

Source: The Washington Post, July 7, 2002 p A8. Copyright © 2002 *The Washington Post.* Reprinted by permission.

The Post–Cold War Era

The year 1989 saw a remarkable change in world politics. Eastern European communist regimes that had been in power at the start of the year were gone by its end. Then, between August and December 1991, the Soviet Union—the focal point of U.S. foreign policy during the Cold War—ceased to exist. With its demise, the Soviet threat to the United States disappeared, the Cold War came to an end, and the basic premise that drove U.S. foreign policy for almost fifty years—containment—ceased to be relevant.[24]

The threat of cataclysmic nuclear war largely ceased to be a pressing issue, although there was a continuing threat of proliferation of nuclear, biological, and chemical weapons as countries like India and Pakistan developed their own atomic bombs (see Figure 16.1 for countries with high risks of instability). The "predators of the twenty-first century" is how former President Clinton described rogue states that seek to build "arsenals of nuclear, chemical, and biological weapons and the missiles to deliver them."[25]

In his 2002 State of the Union Address, President Bush named an "axis of evil" that included North Korea, Iraq, and Iran. In this address, President Bush listed seven 'rogue' nations as intended targets of nuclear weapons when insurmountable hostilities develop between them and the United States. This was followed by publication of a comprehensive rationale for shifting American military strategy to a pre-emptive action against hostile states and terrorist groups. This new Bush doctrine states that "while the United States will constantly strive to enlist the support of the international community, we will not hesitate to act alone, if necessary, to exercise our right of self-defense by acting pre-emptively against such terrorists."[26]

The New World Order   The end of the Cold War brought with it a dizzying array of complicated foreign policy issues. Policy makers no longer have clear guideposts to determine the relative merits of issues and no clear formula for how to address them. Before the Cold War was over, the United States, through the United Nations and with the help of a broad international coalition of nations, embarked on a large-scale war against Iraq. On August 2, 1990, Iraqi forces invaded Kuwait. The invasion followed a summer of escalating tension between Iraq and Kuwait on economic disputes about oil production and pricing. Following the invasion, President George H. W. Bush sought and obtained international backing for United Nations Security Resolution 660, under which Iraq faced economic sanctions and a naval blockade. A military response, Desert Shield, was initiated on August 7, involving a limited deployment of air and ground forces. Iraq was given until January 15, 1991, to withdraw its forces from Kuwait. On January 17, 1991, Operation Desert Storm began, and by February 26, 1991, the coalition led by the United States restored sovereignty to Kuwait. Iraq withdrew its remaining troops on February 27. The United States led the charge to make sure Iraq went no further, and President George H. W. Bush heralded the beginning of a "New World Order."[27]

The outlines of this New World Order never came clearly into focus, and the concept means different things to different people. At a minimum, President George H. W. Bush seemed to have in mind the end of the bipolar order and the start of a new order involving the United Nations but actually led by the United States, the world's dominant military power. Just what the relationship between the United States and the UN should be—and even whether there should be a relationship at all—continues to be debated, particularly in light of controversial military operations in Somalia, Bosnia, Haiti, and Iraq.[28]

NATO   Just about the only thing for certain is that NATO, the North Atlantic Treaty Organization, will be getting bigger—what the Bush administration describes as "a robust enlargement." The fifth enlargement of the NATO Alliance was

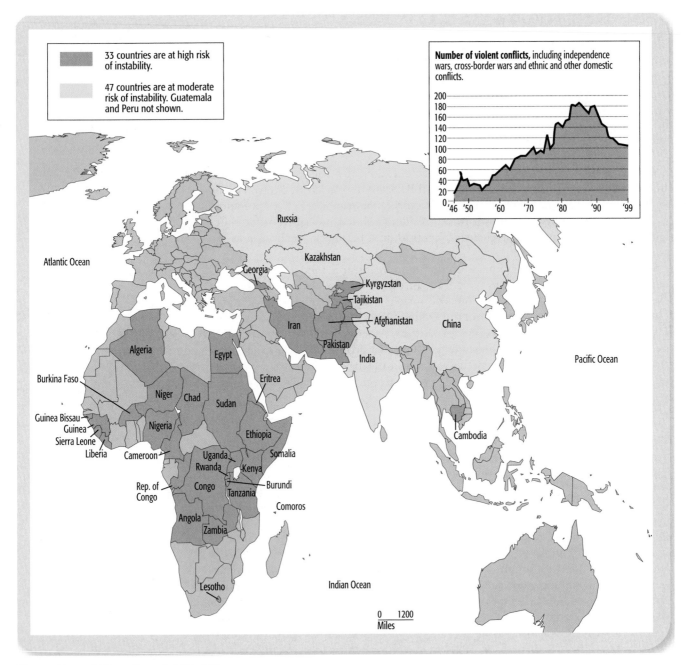

Figure 16.1   A More Peaceful World?

Source: CICDM University of Maryland. *The Washington Post,* January 17, 2001, p. A13.

formally announced at the Prague Summit in November 2002. The newest additions to the NATO Alliance are expected to join by 2004 and include Bulgaria, Estonia, Latvia, Lithuania, Romania, Slovakia, and Slovenia. NATO Ministers have also approved a new body, the Russia-NATO Council, in which old enemies sit together in areas such as counter-terrorism, ballistic missile defense, peacekeeping, arms proliferation, and emergency planning. "We believe we can lay the foundation for new cooperation between NATO and Moscow while fully protecting the alliance's ability to act independently," observed Secretary of State Colin Powell. "We must now together build the new world order, and this will be a long process, a difficult process."[29]

APPROACHING DEMOCRACY AROUND THE GLOBE

An Alliance with a Future: Vaclav Havel's Vision

"A long time ago, when I was part of the opposition to Communist dictatorship, I thought that if the Iron Curtain ever fell, communism collapsed and the Warsaw Pact was dissolved, NATO would also lose its raison d'etre as a principal tool of the policy of "containment." But once the Iron Curtain did indeed begin to fall, and I entered practical politics, I soon realized how naive I had been and how important was NATO's continued existence.

In fact, I came to feel that NATO had just arrived at its great historic test: Whether it would have the courage to embrace new European democracies and thus prove its genuine commitment to protecting the values it was called upon to defend at its founding. The alternative would be to show that it lacked that courage and was still rigidly entrenched in its Cold War ways—unwilling to be involved in creating a new world order.

But it seems that many of those who were, in the late 1980s and early 1990s, the most fervent advocates of NATO's continued existence now wonder whether it has outlived its purpose. Conversely, many who doubted that the Alliance would be meaningful in the future are now among its greatest defenders.

I am among those who sincerely believe the Alliance does have an irreplaceable role, now and likely in the future. And the deeper NATO goes in reflecting on its role, the more significant that role will be. Indeed, there are signs that we are coming to an era in which NATO must ponder its future thoroughly and then act quickly to translate its vision into a number of specific and audacious steps.

First and foremost, NATO will probably have to redefine itself and once again describe its position in today's world. NATO is known to have a cultural, historical, "value-based"—in more lofty terms, "civilizational"—identity alongside its geographic and strategic identity. Its membership is composed of democratic countries located in the Euro-Atlantic area, in what is referred to as "the West." Let me illustrate: No one would think of inviting New Zealand to join NATO, as close as its values and culture are to the NATO world, simply because New Zealand belongs to a different geographic space.

Conversely, it would make no sense to consider Russia for membership in NATO, even though its location and civilization are not far distant from the West. That is because, for various historical and geographic reasons, Russia is a world in itself. It is as large as all NATO members put together—a huge Eurasian empire with which we must enjoy the best possible partnership. And it is such a clearly independent part of today's world that its only relationship with NATO can and will be that of a separate entity.

If the future world order is really to defend peace and secure the survival of humankind, it will have to be based on equal and close cooperation among several regions. Such cooperation is possible only if these individual entities succeed in defining themselves—which requires, among other things, an understanding of where they begin and end. Many conflicts have been caused by insecure self-identification that leads to a blurred concept of one's "outer limits" and to diverging views of "spheres of interest."

In order to redefine itself, NATO will have to do two things: First, the Alliance must arrive at a new and unequivocal definition of its approach to other parts of the planet, infuse such an approach with the spirit of absolute equality, and begin to deepen it by institutional as well as practical cooperation. NATO is attempting to change the quality of its relations with Russia, which is certainly worthwhile; but, in doing so, it must not raise even a shadow of suspicion that the more affluent northern hemisphere is somehow ganging up on the other parts of the world and thus widening the gap that divides it from the southern part of the globe. It is for this reason—but certainly not only for this reason—that NATO must build its relations with China, India, Africa and other parts of the world.

Second, NATO must, in its own interest, open its doors to new European democracies, while at the same time setting a limit on its possible future enlargement. Otherwise, no future enlargement will make sense. (All the Balkan countries and all the "neutral European democracies" are undoubtedly considered possible candidates for future membership.) Saying that drawing such a borderline will create a new Iron Curtain means being mired in a Cold-War world, in which the only conceivable border is the one that separates us from our enemies and, therefore, has to be barb-wired.

In addition, NATO will have to significantly accelerate its internal transformation. Sept. 11 has, one hopes, made everyone understand that the single powerful and clearly situated strategic enemy of the past, "the Evil Empire," has long since been replaced by what is perhaps an even more dangerous enemy: a dispersed evil that is sophisticated yet hard to grasp, whose empire, focal point or axis I would dare not identify (though some regimes certainly serve evil more than others)."

? **Question for Reflection:** The Cold War ended fifty years of the U.S. foreign policy of containment and the changes resulting are placing the international community on the road to a new world order. What changes to NATO might enhance progress on approaching democracy internationally?

▶ The leaders who placed their signatures on the accord between the North Atlantic Treaty Organization and Russia in May 2002 celebrate the historic occasion. In the bottom row, second from the left, is President Vaclav Havel of the Czech Republic, a reminder of how our world approaches democracy.

A Policy of "Enlargement" A response to the new global economic environment has been to stress the policy of enlargement to replace the policy of *containment*. The idea behind enlargement is simply that the United States should support enlarging the sphere of market-oriented democracies on the assumption that additional open, democratic, and free-market societies will further the interests of the United States. They are good for peace (based on the belief that democracies do not easily go to war with one another) and good for business (based on the belief that more market economies will expand the global market and global economic well-being).[30]

By the 1990s, Asia had been the world's economic miracle for at least three decades. South Korea, Singapore, Hong Kong, Taiwan, Malaysia, Indonesia, and the Philippines achieved remarkable rates of economic success and growth. But by the middle of the decade these former "economic miracles" were struggling with collapsing currencies and plunging stock markets. The International Monetary Fund had to issue emergency loans to Thailand, Indonesia, and South Korea. How did it happen? The most straightforward explanation for the crisis was debt. Businesses had borrowed huge sums of money during the time of economic expansion. Most of the money was borrowed in U.S. dollars because our interest rates were much lower than their own currencies. The exchange rates were pegged against the dollar. All this was fine until 1995, when the dollar started to rise against most of the world's economies. Since Asian currencies were pegged to the dollar, their currencies rose with the dollar, and Asia's exports became more expensive and less competitive on world markets.[31]

▲ U2 rock star Bono and President George W. Bush met at the White House to discuss Bono's chief causes, the AIDS epidemic and financial assistance to poor countries.

Foreign Aid and Economic Sanctions These two traditional tools of foreign policy have also come under scrutiny and debate in the post–Cold War world. Since the end of World War II, foreign aid had been used to help support U.S. allies and interests abroad. Making up a tiny portion of the total federal budget, foreign aid programs—such as aid to Russia, Israel, Egypt, Africa, and Latin America—have come under fire during this period of tight budgets and are likely to be curtailed. Those who favor such programs argue that eliminating them would have severe negative consequences for U.S. interests around the world. In May 2002, the traveling odd-couple—rock star Bono of U2 and Treasury Secretary Paul O'Neill arrived in sub-Saharan Africa on a fact-finding mission that would determine how

The Slow Odyssey of China

China's drift towards democracy has primarily manifested itself at the local level of community politics. The National People's Congress, China's supreme legislative body, draws support and leadership from thousands of national congresses that link Chinese urban and rural dwellers. At the local level, Chinese men and women are increasingly vying for office without backing from the national government. Moreover, the local congresses are becoming increasingly responsive to Chinese popular sentiment. In 1992 sweeping changes initiated by the national government increased the power of local congresses, making them more activist than ever before. According to a member of the Guangdong People's Congress, "Ten years ago, whatever the local government submitted to us we would approve. Even if we saw great need for a certain type of legislation, all we did was wait." But now local congresses review laws, write laws, hold hearings, and review budgets. These are major changes for a political system that since World War II has given local governments little choice but to rubber-stamp all actions taken by the totalitarian regime.

In Guangdong Province, the People's Congress has become a showcase for the expanding power of Chinese democracy. Members of the congress were successful in 2002 in compelling the national government to lower the price of water and clean up rampant corruption in the local environmental office. Several powerful politicians were removed from office for their role in failing to close factories violating pollution control acts.

Other more active attempts to infuse democracy into provincial politics have been more controversial. In the city of Shenyang, local members of the legislature denied approval of a government study on the judiciary. In Heilongjiang Province, members of the People's Congress demanded that all government agencies reveal internal records to prove that corruption was spreading within the People's Republic of China. Some local legislators have even asked for reforms in China's legal system, long regarded as one of the world's most oppressive. China's "re-education for labor" program, the sentencing of political dissidents to three years of hard labor without a trial, has come under fire from democratic-minded Chinese who want to interject human rights into the Chinese political tradition.

As grassroots activism of Chinese people continue to push the Chinese government to embrace democratic traditions, the nation's supreme leaders face a difficult balancing act. The road to greater freedom is fraught with peril for the government as well as the Chinese people. As the recent crackdown on the Falung-Gong religious sect makes clear, full-blown religious and ideological freedom is often met with stiff government resistance. Still, China's leaders face a difficult bind: they must extend democratic traditions at the local level to meet the expectations of the populace, but not too much to inspire hope and another rebellion against government autocracy.

In November 2002, Hu Jintao became leader of the Communist Party of China. Mr. Hu was innovative enough to install broadband Internet access at the Communist Party School and encouraged debates about democracy and separation of powers. Only time will tell whether he continues the approach to democracy.

Source: Elisabeth, Rosenthal, "Far from Beijing, a Semblance of Democracy," *The New York Times*, March 8, 2002, A3; Joseph Kahn, "Mystery Man at the Helm," *The New York Times*, November 15, 2002, p. A1.

$50 billion in aid would be spent. Bono believes that aid saves lives and raises living standards, O'Neill is a doubter, believing it created dependency.[32]

Economic sanctions have also been the subject of debate. A case in point involves Cuba and normalizing of relations by lifting the trade embargo. Here is how former President Jimmy Carter, who visited Cuba and favors unrestricted trade, explained the political dilemma: "A newspaper cartoon published while I was in Cuba showed me alone in a small lifeboat in the Caribbean, surrounded by sharks. The caption was, 'I shouldn't have asked President Bush for a ride home.'"[33]

In Carter's view, "one approach is to continue the four-decade effort to isolate and punish Cuba with restricted visits and an economic embargo. The other is for Americans to have maximum contact with Cubans, let them see clearly the advantages of a truly democratic society, and encourage them to bring about orderly changes in their society."[34]

In an economically interdependent world, the use of economic sanctions is often seen as a useful tool of foreign policy. But while sanctions logically seem appropriate to force policy change inside a targeted state, they are difficult to use. Sanctions may have helped force South Africa to eliminate its system of apartheid (strict racial

economic sanctions The use of embargoes and boycotts rather than military force to compel compliance.

▶ Fidel Castro and Jimmy Carter prepare to toss out the first pitch in a baseball game in Havana. The former U.S. President became the first U.S. president — in or out of office — to visit the communist country since the 1959 revolution that put Fidel Castro in power. Carter said he was visiting "as friends of the people of Cuba and hope to know Cubans from different walks of life."

segregation) and move in a more democratic direction, but sanctions against Iraq, Haiti, Bosnia, Serbia, and Cuba, for example, have not achieved their intended effect while clearly hurting ordinary citizens by depriving them of goods or the opportunity to trade and earn a profit. The sanctions imposed on Iraq after its defeat in the Persian Gulf War clearly hurt his people, but Saddam Hussein continued to build more lavish palaces and invest in costly weapons. Unless policy makers in a target state are moved by the suffering of their people to alter their course, or unless they are overthrown, sanctions can fail to have the desired result. The United States and its allies struggle with questions about the propriety and effectiveness of economic sanctions in Iraq. Yet *coercive diplomacy*, the effort to compel policy change in a target state by means of economic sanctions and trade embargoes, will probably continue, especially against rogue states like Iran and North Korea.[35]

The Use of Force and the Limits of Diplomacy   Paradoxically, the end of the Cold War has had the effect of making the use of force by the United States more rather than less likely. Cases in point include American military involvement in Panama, Bosnia, Somalia, Haiti, Iraq, Afghanistan, and possibly Iraq again.[36] Even while some talk of the new diplomacy based upon economics, the old diplomacy based upon the use of force is alive and well. To avoid war, Iraq must produce a full and accurate list of nuclear, chemical, and biological weapons and ballistic missile developments. Saddam Hussein must serve as the agent of his own disarmament.

President Bush's style of diplomacy has been characterized as "ranch-house style"—making the human or personal connection. "Good diplomacy really depends on good personal relations," the president observed. "As you know, I rely on personal diplomacy a lot. I think it's easy when people find areas of mutual respect to work together."[37] The President was at his best on September 12, 2002, when he addressed the United Nations and challenged the Security Council to meet the threat to international security and peace posed by Iraq's efforts to develop weapons of mass destruction. In November, the Security Council voted 15–0 to endorse Resolution 1441, setting the stage for the return of U.N. Weapons inspectors to Baghdad on November 18, 2002. "Noncompliance is no longer an option," said John Negroponte, the United States Ambassador to the United Nations. Saddam had been given a diplomatic option which he would ignore at his own risk. "His cooperation must be prompt and unconditional or he will face the severest consequences," warned President Bush. U.N. Secretary General Kofi Annan added, "If Iraq's defiance continues . . . the Security Council must face its responsibility."[38]

The Security Council vote on Resolution 1441 was a remarkable achievement in diplomacy for the Bush administration. Yet, not all diplomatic initiatives have met with similar success. The Israeli-Palestinian conflict makes clear, there are limits to what a president can accomplish in foreign policy. In 1973, President Nixon intervened successfully in helping to settle the Yom Kippur War between Israel and Egypt. In 1982, President Reagan intervened to halt the Israeli destruction of Beirut during its short-lived invasion of Lebanon. A decade later, James A. Baker, as Secretary of State under President George H.W. Bush, flew repeatedly to Madrid to streamline the Middle East peace conference. In 1993 the Oslo Accords, an agreement between Israel and Palestinians, was sanctified by the U.S. in a signing ceremony led by President Clinton at the White House.

The Israeli–Palestinian conflict of 2002 presented a challenge for the foreign-policy team of the Bush administration. Vice President Dick Cheney told the press "there isn't anybody but us." Conditions became more urgent when terrorist attacks by Palestinians increased and little reform existed in the Palestinian authority. Israel's unwillingness to withdraw forces from the West Bank fueled the combustible situation. President Bush instructed his Secretary of State Colin Powell to make less of a commitment to future negotiations.[39]

The Constitution and Foreign Policy

As you learned in Chapter 2, the Constitution designates certain formal powers that are especially significant for foreign policy to the president and Congress. The president was given four types of broad authority in foreign policy:

1. As the commander in chief, the president has the power to commit troops to foreign lands.
2. The president has the power to negotiate treaties with other countries.
3. The president appoints United States ambassadors and the heads of all of the executive departments that make foreign policy.
4. The president decides whether to receive ambassadors—a decision that determines which nations the United States will formally recognize.

Congress also has significant foreign policy powers, including the power to declare war, appropriate money, and make laws. Congress also has the power to raise and support the armed forces. Thus, it has the power to decide whether to back presidential initiatives abroad. Through the advise and consent powers, the Senate has the power to ratify treaties and confirm presidential appointments.[40]

This division of powers reveals how the framers envisioned the roles of these two branches of government in the foreign policy arena. Remembering the problems of dealing with other countries under the Articles of Confederation, the framers gave the president power to conduct negotiations and use troops. Fearing the potential for tyranny, the framers gave Congress significant power to check and balance presidential decisions.

The President versus Congress

If the executive is the driving force behind U.S. foreign policy, Congress acts as the brakes on the president's initiatives. Through its constitutional powers to control the nation's purse strings, to ratify treaties and approve certain officials, and to make war, Congress can counterbalance the considerable power of the president. This allows Congress to have a very real impact on the direction of U.S. foreign policy. Much of this influence, however, depends upon the ever-changing willingness and ability of members of Congress to overcome partisanship and work together. Thus, Congress's influence in foreign policy has fluctuated greatly since World War II.

The very nature of Congress limits its ability to influence foreign policy. Congress is a domestically oriented institution whose members are primarily interested in issues that directly influence their constituents. This orientation dampens their interest in foreign policy and tends to warp policy to favor the narrow interests of individual districts. Furthermore, its size, procedures, and dispersed leadership make it difficult for Congress to act with the speed often necessary for foreign policy decisions. The slow, deliberative procedures that characterize Congress mean that, on issues of urgency, it cannot compete with a president who is able to respond quickly and decisively to international events.

Finally, the president, as the head of the executive branch, enjoys access to the expertise of the executive bureaucracy, which coordinates and implements policy. Traditionally, Congress has felt inferior in this respect and has tended to defer to the executive on substantive foreign policy matters. However, Congress has increased its access to foreign policy information since the Vietnam War. The professional staff serving congressional committees has more than doubled since the early 1970s, now totaling about ten thousand. In addition to undertaking research, these staffers provide an important link between Congress and the foreign policy bureaucracy. As such ties between Congress and the bureaucracy have strengthened, the view that foreign policy is the exclusive domain of the president has diminished. Although Congress is not and cannot be an expert on foreign policy, it has strengthened its oversight of presidential actions by passing specific legislation.

Beyond Congress's constitutionally granted powers, Congress can have an impact on foreign policy through **legislative oversight.** It can hold hearings, pass laws, and dictate the appropriation of money in an attempt to influence or rein in a president's foreign policy initiatives.

The War Powers Resolution

The War Powers Resolution   Congress passed the **War Powers Resolution** of 1973 in an attempt to restore the balance of power with the executive branch and prevent military involvement without congressional approval. After passage of the legislation, a president could no longer commit troops for longer than sixty days without specific congressional authorization. An optional thirty-day extension was included for issues involving troop safety. These provisions limited President Clinton's options in regard to human rights violations in Haiti.[41]

In one respect the War Powers Resolution sought to reverse the trend toward presidential domination of foreign affairs and fulfill the intent of the framers by ensuring "the collective judgment of the Congress and the President." But the act was also a response to the general expansion of presidential powers at the expense of legislative authority, an attempt to reassert congressional oversight over presidential actions and enhance the power of the legislature.

The "success" of the War Powers Resolution is difficult to gauge. Presidents have generally ignored its reporting requirement, seeing it as an unconstitutional infringement on the powers of the president as commander in chief. President Bush worked hard to gain a joint resolution authorizing the use of U.S. armed forces against Iraq.

The Power of Money: Appropriations

The Power of Money: Appropriations   Congress's control over federal spending gives it a powerful tool in foreign policy. Restrictions on foreign aid, military spending, and intelligence funding can severely restrict the executive branch's foreign policy efforts. Congress uses each of these levers to varying degrees, depending on the electorate's mood and Congress's relationship with the president at the time. Military spending appropriations also give Congress an important role in determining the direction of U.S. foreign policy. On the whole, however, Congress has deviated little from the defense funding requests of the executive branch.

Congress's ability to control foreign aid appropriations is one example of its power in foreign affairs. Foreign aid in the form of cash, food, or other economic resources is one of the more benevolent policy options. The United State's annual commitment

legislative oversight The power that Congress has to oversee the operation of various federal agencies.

War Powers Resolution A highly controversial measure passed over President Nixon's veto that stipulated that presidential commitments of U.S. military forces cannot extend beyond sixty days without specific congressional authorization.

to foreign aid is generally less than one-half of one percent of the federal budget (see Figure 16.2), but it represents a large infusion of economic resources to the rest of the world.

The popularity of foreign aid programs has declined in the United States since the mid-1970s. Not surprisingly, they are a popular target today for budget cuts, in large part because such funding is typically of no concern to a legislator's constituency and thus provides a "painless" cut in the budget.

The Foreign Policy Bureaucracy

Assisting the president in foreign policy development and implementation are some thirty-eight separate government departments and agencies. We will look at four core national security areas and the organizations within each:

1. *Foreign affairs:* This is primarily the domain of the Department of State, with other related agencies playing supporting roles. These other agencies include the Agency for International Development, the Arms Control and Disarmament Agency, and the United States Information Agency (which includes Radio Free Europe, Voice of America, and Radio Liberty).
2. *Defense:* National security issues related to defense are dominated by the Department of Defense. In matters relating to nuclear energy, the Department of Energy is also involved.
3. *Intelligence:* While dominated by the Central Intelligence Agency (CIA), the intelligence community also includes the State Department's Bureau of Intelligence and Research, the Defense Department's Defense Intelligence Agency, the National Reconnaissance Office, the intelligence components of the individual military services, the Federal Bureau of Investigation (FBI), and the National Security Agency, a highly secret intelligence-gathering organization.
4. *Economic agencies:* Fierce global economic competition has increased the importance and influence of the departments and agencies responsible for developing and implementing U.S. trade policies, negotiating tariffs with other governments, and representing the United States in various trade forums. Involved are the Department of the Treasury, the Departments of Commerce and of Agriculture, and the Office of the United States Trade Representative.

The Department of State

The Department of State is the oldest and preeminent department of the foreign policy bureaucracy. It is responsible for managing foreign affairs on a daily basis, including pursuing diplomatic relations with other countries and international organizations, protecting American citizens and their interests abroad, and gathering and analyzing information bearing on U.S. foreign policy. The department's embassies, foreign service officers, and representatives to international organizations make it the only department in the executive bureaucracy with a global view. Despite its important role, however, the Department of State, with twenty-five thousand employees, is fairly small.[42]

Critics of the State Department have charged that its global perspective encourages it to focus more on what is happening abroad than at home, leading it to place the interests of other countries ahead of those of the United States. Secretary Colin Powell has certainly done much to represent United States interests vis-a-vis several shifting international coalitions.

The Department of Defense

The secretary of defense is the principal military adviser to the president and is responsible for the formulation of general defense policy and all matters of direct concern to the Department of Defense. Under the direction of the president, the secretary exercises authority, direction, and control over all American military activity.

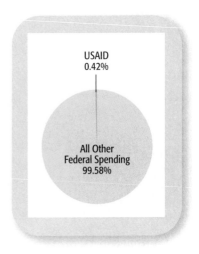

Figure 16.2 Foreign Aid as a Percentage of Federal Outlays
Source: U.S. Agency for International Development, http://www.usaid.gov/press/releases/2000/budget2001.html.

▲ Much has been written about tensions between the moderate and pragmatic Secretary of State Colin Powell and the more ideologically conservative members of the Bush administration such as Secretary of Defense Donald Rumsfeld and Vice President Dick Cheney. This animated discussion on Afghan reconstruction, with National Security advisor Condoleeza Rice looking on, leaves the impression that Powell is intent on making his point.

The Defense Department is composed of four service branches (army, navy, air force, and marines) that often compete with each other for influence, authority, and resources. Each branch of the service is headed by a chief of staff. Heading all four branches is the chair of the Joint Chiefs of Staff, who acts as the voice of the military (as opposed to civilian) side of the Pentagon. The chair of the Joint Chiefs is one of the president's principal military advisers.

Each of the four service branches also reports to a civilian secretary. Civilian agencies within the Defense Department handle functions such as logistics and communications. This combination of military and civilian personnel often results in overlapping duties and some confusion over the roles each is supposed to play in the operation of the department.

In many of the areas where the State Department is weak, the Defense Department is exceptionally strong, making it a powerful force in foreign policy making. With nearly a million individuals employed by defense-related industries, the Defense Department has many people with a vested interest in its financial well-being. A cut in defense spending can mean the loss of a job for a welder in Lubbock, Texas, while a new air force base can turn a ghost town into a boom town. Thus, the Defense Department is an integral part of American social, political, and economic life. It has an impact in both the domestic and international spheres, which the State Department, with its exclusively global orientation, lacks. The Defense Department is much larger than the State Department, with around three million military and civilian employees.[43]

The Defense Department's strongest influence in foreign policy has historically been the result of the close ties between the Pentagon and the corporations that dominate the U.S. weapons industry. Even as early as 1961, President Dwight Eisenhower, in his Farewell Address, warned of the growing power and influence resulting from the "conjunction of an immense military establishment and a large arms industry." Eisenhower called this phenomenon the **military-industrial complex.** Its development meant that, "the potential for the disastrous rise of misplaced power exists and will persist."[44]

With their seemingly insatiable appetite for more and better firepower, Pentagon officials are the defense industry's best—and sometimes only—customers. In turn, large corporations argue that their weapons production plants produce thousands of jobs and stimulate the economy at both the local and the national levels. Members of Congress are drawn into this relationship, either to protect local jobs by ensuring defense contracts or to appear sufficiently supportive of the military to satisfy their constituents back home. Together, the Pentagon, defense contractors, and key legislators form a strong lobby in support of sustained defense spending for the U.S. military and for export to other nations. However, since the collapse of the Soviet Union, the power of the military-industrial complex has begun to wane.

? **Question for Reflection:** The military-industrial complex was an outgrowth of WWII and the Cold War; its existence helped pull the U.S. from the depths of the Depression, yet in 1961 President Eisenhower warned of its influence over policy. If the use of force as a diplomatic strategy were seriously curtailed, what impact would this have?

The National Security Council

The National Security Council (NSC) was created in 1947 to provide the president with advice on all domestic, foreign, and military policies relating to national security. Members of the NSC include the president (as chair), the president's national security adviser, who acts as the special assistant for national security, the vice president, and the secretaries of state and defense, with the director of the CIA and the chair of the Joint Chiefs of Staff sitting in as advisers. Various other cabinet and agency heads, such as the secretary of the treasury, the attorney general, and the U.S. ambassador to the United Nations, participate as needed.

military-industrial complex What President Eisenhower in 1961 called the growing power and influence resulting from the "conjunction of an immense military establishment and a large arms industry."

Through the NSC the president coordinates the different government agencies dealing with foreign or defense policy. The NSC became especially active under President Kennedy and his special assistant for national security, McGeorge Bundy. Under Bundy the staff became the president's key personal foreign policy "team." What emerged was an informally structured organization for the formulation and implementation of foreign policy that has persisted to this day. Such an organization works both for and against the executive branch, however, affording a base for quick and secretive executive-level responses to national security problems but allowing a sometimes dangerous policy-making latitude to unelected and relatively unaccountable decision makers. For example, it was in the NSC that the controversial Iran-Contra "arms-for-hostages" operation was conceived and run by Lieutenant Oliver North.[45]

By decreasing the president's reliance on the bureaucracy for information and advice, the NSC adviser and staff can become a "screen" between the president and the rest of government, reducing the president's direct influence and personal leadership. This intervention has led to serious rivalries among the national security adviser, the secretaries of state and defense, the director of the CIA, and their staffs. The relative influence and access of each organization often depend upon the personal relationship between each department head and the president.

The role of the national security adviser has changed over the years, based on the personality of the appointee to the post. Presidents have shaped the position to fit their personal management styles. On the whole, however, the national security adviser remains an extremely influential, although often anonymous, policy maker.

The CIA and Intelligence Gathering

The Central Intelligence Agency (CIA) is the dominant force in the intelligence community. It was established after World War II to be the president's nonpartisan resource for coordinated intelligence analysis. However, its mission quickly expanded to include covert operations such as espionage, psychological warfare, paramilitary maneuvers, and political and economic intervention.

The CIA's most important function, however, is information gathering although it failure to process intelligence information relating to the attacks on September 11 has raised serious charges of incompetence. It is responsible for collecting information about the state of leadership in other countries, the political situation and stability, military capabilities, strengths and weaknesses, and possible intentions in the political, economic, and military spheres. All of this information is analyzed and reported to policy makers so they can make better decisions on foreign policy issues.

In addition to its international role, the CIA has expanded its activities on the domestic front, leading to concerns about the potential for abuse. Concerns about illegal activities against American citizens and dubious operations in foreign countries have led to the CIA being overseen by Congress. However, this has proven less than effective. Under the Reagan administration, for example, the CIA supported Nicaraguan insurgents and their mining of Nicaragua's harbors—activities that went unreported to Congress, despite legal requirements to keep Congress "fully and currently informed" of all intelligence activities. Congress could do little more than scold the CIA director for his disobedience. Faced with an inability to control the CIA, a member of the House Intelligence Committee at the time lamented, "We are like mushrooms. They keep us in the dark and feed us a lot of manure."[46]

The Agencies Behind Economic Policy Making

In the 1960s the overwhelming economic superiority of the United States began to dwindle, caused in part by the economic dislocations triggered by financing the Vietnam War. But, more important, this period also witnessed the first stirrings of real economic strength from the European and Asian economies that had been ravaged by World War II and rebuilt with considerable assistance from the United States. As the economies of Europe and Japan expanded, the corresponding American share of world markets decreased. In addition, with the end of the Cold War and the absence of the ready reference point of containment, priorities of U.S. foreign policy changed. Such global economic shifts and political changes led to similar shifts in the balance of influence among the government organizations involved in foreign policy. The power and influence of several departments not traditionally associated with foreign policy decision-making have increased. Instead of a foreign policy establishment dominated by the NSC, the State Department, and the Pentagon, U.S. policy making now features such actors as the Department of Commerce and the Office of the Trade Representative in roles of unprecedented prominence. Economic power is the overriding issue for these agencies.

These departments and agencies play highly specialized roles in making foreign policy. The Department of Labor, for example, represented the United States in international negotiations on the General Agreement on Tariffs and Trade (GATT, now the World Trade Organization), the Organization for Economic Cooperation and Development (OECD), and the International Labor Organization (ILO). The Department of Agriculture has its own Foreign Agricultural Service, which is responsible for formulating, administering, and coordinating the department's programs overseas. The Department of Energy is responsible for conducting nuclear weapons research as well as development, production, and surveillance operations.

The Departments of Treasury and Commerce, in particular, are central figures in the making of economic policy in the global arena. The Treasury Department is primarily concerned with the development of financial policy. It focuses on trade regulations, exchange rates, and the balance of payments. Unlike the State Department, which judges nations largely on the basis of their political systems, or Defense, which looks at military strength, the Treasury Department is concerned with a foreign nation's economic system and how it affects the U.S. economy. For example, is a nation's exchange rate fair? Is its tariff structure conductive to U.S. exports? How do American exports to a particular nation compare with American imports from it?

While the Treasury Department develops U.S. financial policy, the Commerce Department is responsible for expanding and protecting U.S. commerce abroad, which it does through the Foreign Commercial Service. Similar to the State Department's Foreign Service, the Foreign Commercial Service works through U.S. embassies and consulates, advising foreign businesses on their U.S.-related business activities. The Commerce Department also maintains nearly fifty offices in the United States to encourage U.S. firms to export their products.

Much of the actual foreign policy making takes place within the nooks and crannies of the State Department, the Pentagon, and other agencies and departments, as career bureaucrats exercise their delegated and undelegated discretionary decision making power to develop policy. Because these bureaucrats have the expertise to analyze the immense volume of foreign policy information, a president needs the support of the bureaucracy to be successful in foreign policy.

The bureaucracy also assists with policy implementation. This task is a far-flung process in terms of geography and the vast array of departments and agencies that must cooperate on a given issue. Officials in the field, for example, especially the State Department's Foreign Service officers, tend to believe that those in Washington, D.C., far removed from the problems of their post, do not understand the realities of their situation.

At all but the lowest levels of the foreign policy bureaucracy are individuals who owe their jobs to the political process, political appointees who form a large and powerful contingent within the foreign policy bureaucracy: deputy secretaries, undersecretaries, assistant secretaries, and directors of the various departments and agencies. As a group, political appointees are ambitious people who want to have a hand in shaping U.S. foreign policy. Thus, they have to play the bureaucratic game in a way that will keep them involved in the action for as long as possible; they perform a delicate dance to maintain and expand their sphere of influence. The end of the Cold War has brought about the need to reexamine the institutions of U.S. foreign policy and national security policy making. Under examination are the structure of the State Department and the future of the Arms Control and Disarmament Agency, the U.S. Information Agency, and the U.S. Agency for International Development. Special commissions have been put in place to examine the roles and missions of both the Defense Department and the intelligence community.

Democratic Checks on Foreign Policy

In no other realm of government activity is the exercise of democratic control less apparent than in the making of foreign policy. Both the complex nature of global affairs and the crisis atmosphere that sometimes prevails can lead the national security establishment to ignore public opinion. Similarly, the increasing use of executive agreements and covert operations means that decisions often unfold out of public view and without any opportunity for public debate except after the fact.

Although the president is the primary initiator of foreign policy, there are important checks on the president's power to make foreign policy. We have already looked at how Congress can check presidential foreign policy making using its oversight power to force open the decision-making process. The press and public opinion can also act as a check on foreign policy outcomes.

The Press

The press plays a very important role in the surveillance, investigation, criticism, and advocacy of the government's foreign policy activities. The media provide American citizens with most of their knowledge of the rest of the world. While the media are ostensibly neutral and objective, they typically mirror the opinions of the foreign policy establishment. However, the media sometimes offer competing perspectives on international affairs. On occasion, individual reporters have questioned or strongly opposed government policies, stimulating public opposition. Press criticism of the Johnson administration's direction of the Vietnam War, while not widespread, served to chip away at the "monopoly of information" enjoyed by the White House, challenging the government version of reality and stimulating public criticism of U.S. involvement in Southeast Asia.[47]

More commonly, though, the press serves as a conduit for the opinions of various actors involved in the policy process. The leak, a calculated release of controversial information, is used by individuals at all levels of the bureaucracy for a variety of purposes. The right words at the right time can stir up Congress, the public, and foreign governments and put an end to a controversial foreign policy initiative. Key players in the foreign policy process often release information to friendly reporters to test the waters of public response to policy options under consideration.

With very few exceptions, the American press is reluctant to strongly oppose the actions of the U.S. government, particularly where the deployment of American troops is involved. Throughout most of the Vietnam War, the press, like most of the general public, supported the U.S. presence in Southeast Asia, breaking with the official version of U.S. policy in Vietnam only when the inconsistencies and contradictions of that policy had become glaringly apparent. This supportive role was even more apparent during more recent actions, including the U.S. invasions of Grenada, Panama, and Iraq. In each case, most media analysts relied on government sources, accepted government explanations, and focused predominantly on tactical and technical, rather than ethical or moral, analysis.

For example, mainstream press coverage of the Panama invasion and Noriega's capture tended to emphasize the size and power of the forces deployed, the peculiarities of Noriega's personal life, and the apparent effectiveness of the operation.

Absent from most reports was the history of U.S. ties to the Panamanian dictator, the specific link between Noriega and George H. W. Bush, or the fact that many of the casualties suffered by U.S. forces were the result of "friendly fire" from other U.S. military personnel. Since neither the White House nor the Pentagon wished to stress such negative details, the press reliance on government sources denied U.S. citizens access to the kind of information they needed to formulate a more balanced perspective on a complex policy. In such cases, the "watchdog" can become a "lapdog."

Nonetheless, the media can be credited with providing Americans with a wealth of information, thereby helping them to become better informed citizens. And the constitutional guarantees of a free press and free speech afford American citizens a small but sometimes persistent and influential voice in the otherwise elite-dominated foreign policy process.[48]

The Public

Often overlooked in analyses of foreign policy decision-making is the role played by the public and public opinion. In some cases, the voice of public opinion can penetrate the carefully encrypted speech and muffled secrecy of foreign policy making to have an impact. Popular discontent with Vietnam is an example of the government abiding by public opinion to reverse a long-standing policy. The validity of this claim is open to argument, but the fact remains that typically the foreign policy-making process is among the least democratic in the American system. Historically, U.S. citizens have had little significant influence on the foreign policy created by their government.[49]

Table 16.2 shows how Americans and Europeans differ on foreign policy issues. There exists a vast opinion gulf between the American public and people elsewhere.

The public tends to rally around the president in times of national crisis, such as war or international confrontation, reducing the likelihood of any sizable public

Table 16.2 ■ Transatlantic Assessment of U.S. Policies	Fra %	Ger %	Ita %	GB %	US %
Approve of Bush's international policy					
Today	32	35	44	40	69
August, 2001	16	23	29	17	45
Bush makes decisions mainly on US interests					
Today	85	69	71	80	—
August, 2001	85	73	74	79	—
Approve of . . .					
Foreign aid increase	90	86	95	90	53
War in Afghanistan	64	61	59	73	83
Mideast peace effort	67	76	88	75	77
Disapprove of . . .					
Axis of evil rhetoric	62	74	60	55	34
Steel import tariff	81	74	58	65	27
Mideast policies	63	63	51	39	26

Source: http://people-press.org/reports/display.php3?ReportID=153. Reprinted by permission of the Pew Research Center for the People and the Press.

Released April 20, 2002.

DEMOCRACY IN THE NEW MILLENNIUM

The U.S.–Afghanistan War and New Military Technology

Nations embroiled in war by necessity develop new military technology to protect national interests at home and around the globe. Like the secret Manhattan project born in World War II that accelerated the development of the nuclear bomb, major weapons are often developed completely by the executive branch and without feedback from the American people in Congress. Justified by wartime needs, many new war technologies, such as the tank and radar, often become the centerpiece of the U.S. military in future conflicts.

Following the September 11, 2001, bombing of the World Trade Center and Pentagon by al-Qaeda operatives, the U.S. federal government accelerated weapon-development programs to meet the pressing needs of a new and difficult physical threat from abroad. Federal officials in the Pentagon working on research and engineering immediately came together to decide which of the 150 new weapons currently in development required massive government funding. Working in secret at major military installations throughout the nation, scientists, biologists, and nuclear specialists then created new tools of defense and attack. Billions of dollars in federal funding, through an increase in the military budget by President Bush, went to national defense and to make weapons of massive destruction in 2002.

Military units of Taliban fighters in Afghanistan were the first to receive the full force of the latest military technology produced by the United States in the wake of the September 11 attacks. In March of 2002 a group of fighters hiding in a deep cave complex in the mountains of northern Afghanistan were hit during Operation Anaconda by a new "thermobaric" bomb dropped by an American F-15. Designed to send shock waves deep into caves to kill humans without blowing up non-human material, the bomb failed to destroy the target due to a faulty guidance system. Although the bomb required further testing to perfect its killing power, its main purpose was to enable American intelligence officials to enter the cave complexes to retrieve valuable information.

Other advancements in new weapon technology were directly linked to the U.S. War in Afghanistan. With help from the Central Intelligence Agency, the U.S. military developed unmanned drone planes known as the *Predator* and *Global Hawk* to gather intelligence and drop bombs on people and hardware. Used for the first time in Afghanistan, the new planes enabled the U.S. to more closely safeguard both ground personnel and pilots who normally risked their lives to attack the enemy. Other military advancements in the field of laser technology in bomb guidance systems and communication helped to more accurately link military observers on the ground with pilots to hit targets from great distances.

Like the thermobaric bomb, however, problems arose in the immediate use of the new technology. One of the Global Hawk unmanned planes crashed in the deserts of Afghanistan, at the hefty cost of $30 million dollars to the American people. Several friendly-fire incidents and glitches in improved technology of laser-guided "smart" bombs led to the deaths of three American soldiers and wounded two dozen others. Nevertheless, Pentagon officials believe the duration of the U.S. War in Afghanistan has proved invaluable in helping to perfect new technologies of warfare. A valuable resource on the Revolution in Military Affairs (RMA) is http://www.comw.org/rma. Also visit the Center for Strategic and Budgetary Assessments— CSBA online at http://www.csbaonline.org/.

Source: Vernon Loeb, "Afghan War Is a Lab for U.S. Innovation," *The New York Times*, March 26, p. A16.

---

opposition. The greatest likelihood of any widespread, sustained public outcry against foreign policies occurs during prolonged and stalemated military actions when Americans watch their young men and women fight and die but see no tangible gains. Public support will be strongest when the conflict in question is relatively brief, decisive, and victorious, and when information is carefully controlled by the military rather than left to the freewheeling inquiry of individual reporters. Table 16.2 shows how Americans and Europeans differ widely on foreign policy issues.

The United States faces an impressive array of foreign policy challenges. Policy makers and the public must cope with forces of change in politics, economics, technology, and demographics. The United States must assess not only its interests in world affairs but also its proper role. In this quickly changing world, questions about foreign policy abound. How will the United States lead in the post–Cold War era? What is the role of NATO, and how and at what pace should it expand? What is the proper relationship between the United States and the United Nations? What should be the future role of peacekeeping operations and foreign aid programs?

How will the United States balance economic and political interests when they collide? How will it balance economic and political interests against humanitarian and environmental concerns?

As we have seen throughout this text, the United States must respond to such questions in the context of its ongoing experiment in self-government. Indeed, there are really two related challenges for U.S. foreign policy today. First, the United States must try to determine its course in a complicated and changing international environment, one that involves an appropriate balance of commitments and resources. Second, it must do so within the democratic limits established in the Constitution. Ultimately, then, the paramount challenge is how to balance the interests of security and the requirements of democracy.

Understanding the link between foreign policy and democracy requires that we first recognize the dramatically altered world environment in the wake of the Cold War and the new terrorist threat that faces all democratic nations, as well as those taking first steps in approaching democracy. Afghanistan is a case in point. In mid-April 2002, delegations from 16 villages in northern Afghanistan met in the village of Mardyan to select candidates to join the national assembly that will choose the country's next government. This is Afghanistan's first attempt to select a leader by democratic means.[50]

Today, there is a new well-defined threat to anchor U.S. foreign policy—international terrorism from rogue states. The challenge is to establish a new psychological basis for engaging the nation in the world, and develop principles to guide the use of diplomatic, economic, and military tools abroad. We face a set of novel, diffused, and unfamiliar foreign policy problems, such as small peripheral states armed with weapons of mass destruction threatening regional and global security, and unconventional challenges posed by narco-terrorists, religious fundamentalist movements, the export of sensitive military and satellite technology to China and international terrorist networks.

SUMMARY

1. Foreign policy refers to actions the government takes abroad to ensure the security and well-being of Americans and the strength and competitiveness of the U.S. economy. Foreign policy making is often complex because of the need to balance democratic ideals against military and economic interests.

2. Before World War I, U.S. foreign policy was characterized by isolationism, in which the United States fostered trade with Europe without committing to strategic alliances. Despite its policy of neutrality, the United States clearly favored Britain and the Allies at the beginning of World War I and entered the war after Germany resumed unrestricted submarine warfare. Following the war, however, isolationism again prevailed.

3. The United States was initially reluctant to enter World War II but did so after Japan's surprise bombing of Pearl Harbor. After the war its primary foreign policy goal was the *containment* of communism, which placed it in direct opposition to the Soviet Union in what came to be known as the Cold War.

4. After 1949 both the United States and the Soviet Union poured vast amounts of money into the development and deployment of nuclear weapons. During the same period U.S. foreign aid commitments were increased in an effort to prevent Soviet advances in less developed countries.

5. During the 1960s the effort to contain communism gradually drew the United States into a full-scale war in Vietnam, a war that was a disaster for both military and foreign policy. After the war the United States entered into a *detente* with the Soviet Union and began discussing ways to reduce the nuclear threat.

6. In 1991 the Soviet Union ceased to exist, thereby ending the Cold War and clearing the way for what President Bush (41) hoped would be a New World Order.

7. The strategies of foreign policy are also changing. The use of foreign aid has come under fire, as has the use of economic sanctions as a means of forcing a target nation to change its policies. The temptation to find military solutions to political problems remains strong.

8. The Constitution gives the president the authority to commit troops to foreign lands, negotiate treaties, appoint ambassadors, and decide whether to receive ambassadors, an action designating formal resignation. Congress has the power to declare war, appropriate money, and make laws, thereby deciding whether to back presidential initiatives abroad. The Senate also has the power to ratify treaties and confirm presidential appointments.

9. The president determines the general direction of foreign policy and the effectiveness of its implementation by the bureaucracy. The president's influence has been increased by additional powers granted by Congress during emergencies. In addition, presidents have often entered into executive agreements with foreign governments instead of treaties, thereby avoiding the need for ratification by the Senate.

10. Congress tends to be oriented toward domestic policy and cannot respond quickly and decisively to international events. It has attempted to strengthen its oversight of foreign policy through legislation. Congress can also restrict the executive branch's foreign policy efforts by limiting appropriations for foreign aid, military spending, and intelligence gathering.

11. Although the Department of State has primary responsibility for the development and implementation of foreign policy, the Department of Defense also plays an important role because it commands a large share of the federal budget and has considerable political clout. For information and policy planning, however, the president depends on the National Security Council, consisting of the president, the national security adviser, the vice president, and the secretaries of state and defense.

12. The Central Intelligence Agency, along with several other agencies, is responsible for gathering and analyzing intelligence about the activities of foreign governments. It also engages in covert operations such as espionage, psychological warfare, and paramilitary operations. Concern about possible abuses of power by the CIA has led to attempts to restructure the agency and bring it under greater congressional and executive control.

13. Most of the detailed analysis and development of foreign policy is done by career bureaucrats in the State Department. At the higher levels are political appointees such as deputy secretaries and undersecretaries.

14. The press plays an important role in surveillance, investigation, criticism, and advocacy of foreign policy activities, although it is usually reluctant to oppose the actions of the U.S. government overseas. Public opinion does not seem to have had a major influence on foreign policy.

KEY TERMS

foreign policy	Cold War	Strategic Arms Limitation
isolationism	bipolarity	Treat (SALT)
Monroe Doctrine	Warsaw Pact	economic sanctions
superpower	foreign aid	legislative oversight
containment	Peace Corps	War Powers Resolution
globalism	Gulf of Tonkin Resolution	military-industrial complex
North Atlantic Treaty	detente	
Organization (NATO)		

POLISIM ACTIVITY

The Impact of Foreign Aid

The primary foreign policy goal of the United States remains, as it has been, to maintain our security and freedom. You are the Chief of Staff to the Secretary of State of the United States of America. In this simulation, you are presenting and arguing for the budget allocations for the next fiscal year for military aid, development aid, and human welfare.

SUGGESTED READINGS

GERTZ, BILL, *Breakdown: How America's Intelligence Failures Led to September 11th*. Regency Publishing, 2002. *New York Times* author shows how America's intelligence community completed broke down in the years prior to the attacks on the World Trade Center and Pentagon. He calls it the greatest intelligence failure since Pearl Harbor.

LEVITE, ARIEL E., BRUCE W. JENTLESON, and LARRY BERMAN, eds. *Foreign Military Intervention: The Dynamics of Protracted Conflict*. New York: Columbia University Press, 1992. Six case studies that examine the similarities and differences among nation-states that use military might to intervene in civil wars and otherwise reshape the domestic political order of weakened states.

LITWAK, ROBERT S. *Rogue States and U.S. Foreign Policy*. Washington, D.C.: Woodrow Wilson Center Press and The Johns Hopkins University Press, 2000. A seminal contribution to the discussion of so-called rogue states. President Clinton and other U.S. policy makers have warned that "rogue states" pose a major threat to international peace in the post–Cold War era. But what exactly is a "rogue state" and does the concept provide a useful approach to foreign policy?

NYE, JOSEPH S., JR. *The Paradox of American Power: Why the World's Only Superpower Can't Go It Alone*. New York: Oxford University Press, 2002. An analysis of American foreign policy that pits America's preeminent position against the need to recognize and account for the interdependent global system.

REITER, DAN and ALLAN C. STAM. *Democracies at War*. Princeton: Princeton University Press, March 2002. A study of why 80% of the time democracies win the wars they fight.

WALTER, BARBARA F. *Committing to Peace: The Successful Settlements of Civil Wars*. Princeton: Princeton University Press, February 2002. An in-depth look at the competing theories about why some civil wars have successfully implemented peace settlements and others have not.

APPENDICES

1 PRESIDENTS AND CONGRESSES,
1789–2002   592

2 SUPREME COURT
JUSTICES   594

3 DECLARATION
OF INDEPENDENCE   596

4 THE FEDERALIST,
NO. 10   598

5 THE FEDERALIST,
NO. 51   601

6 INTRODUCING THE CONCEPT
OF APPROACHING DEMOCRACY   603

APPENDIX 1

Presidents and Congresses, 1789–2001

TERM	PRESIDENT AND VICE PRESIDENT	PARTY OF PRESIDENT	CONGRESS	MAJORITY PARTY HOUSE	MAJORITY PARTY SENATE
1789–97	**George Washington**	None	1st	N/A	N/A
	John Adams		2d	N/A	N/A
			3d	N/A	N/A
			4th	N/A	N/A
1797–1801	**John Adams**	Fed	5th	N/A	N/A
	Thomas Jefferson		6th	Fed	Fed
1801–09	**Thomas Jefferson**	Dem Rep	7th	Dem Rep	Dem Rep
	Aaron Burr (1801–5)		8th	Dem Rep	Dem Rep
	George Clinton (1805–9)		9th	Dem Rep	Dem Rep
			10th	Dem Rep	Dem Rep
1809–17	**James Madison**	Dem Rep	11th	Dem Rep	Dem Rep
	George Clinton (1809–12)[1]		12th	Dem Rep	Dem Rep
	Elbridge Gerry (1813–14)[1]		13th	Dem Rep	Dem Rep
			14th	Dem Rep	Dem Rep
1817–25	**James Monroe**	Dem Rep	15th	Dem Rep	Dem Rep
	Daniel D. Tompkins		16th	Dem Rep	Dem Rep
			17th	Dem Rep	Dem Rep
			18th	Dem Rep	Dem Rep
1825–29	**John Quincy Adams**	Nat'l Rep	19th	Nat'l Rep	Nat'l Rep
	John C. Calhoun		20th	Dem	Dem
1829–37	**Andrew Jackson**	Dem	21st	Dem	Dem
	John C. Calhoun (1829–32)[2]		22d	Dem	Dem
	Martin Van Buren (1833–37)		23d	Dem	Dem
			24th	Dem	Dem
1837–41	**Martin Van Buren**	Dem	25th	Dem	Dem
	Richard M. Johnson		26th	Dem	Dem
1841	**William H. Harrison**[1]	Whig			
	John Tyler (1841)				
1841–45	**John Tyler**	Whig	27th	Whig	Whig
	(VP vacant)		28th	Dem	Whig
1845–49	**James K. Polk**	Dem	29th	Dem	Dem
	George M. Dallas		30th	Whig	Dem
1849–50	**Zachary Taylor**[1]	Whig	31st	Dem	Dem
	Millard Fillmore				
1850–53	**Millard Fillmore**	Whig	32d	Dem	Dem
	(VP vacant)				
1853–57	**Franklin Pierce**	Dem	33d	Dem	Dem
	William R. D. King (1853)[1]		34th	Rep	Dem
1857–61	**James Buchanan**	Dem	35th	Dem	Dem
	John C. Breckinridge		36th	Rep	Dem
1861–65	**Abraham Lincoln**[1]	Rep	37th	Rep	Rep
	Hannibal Hamlin (1861–65)		38th	Rep	Rep
	Andrew Johnson (1865)		38th	Rep	Rep
1865–69	**Andrew Johnson**	Rep	39th	Union	Union
	(VP vacant)		40th	Rep	Rep
1869–77	**Ulysses S. Grant**	Rep	41st	Rep	Rep
	Schuyler Colfax (1869–73)		42d	Rep	Rep
	Henry Wilson (1873–75)[1]		43d	Rep	Rep
			44th	Dem	Rep
1877–81	**Rutherford B. Hayes**	Rep	45th	Dem	Rep
	William A. Wheeler		46th	Dem	Dem
1881	**James A. Garfield**[1]	Rep	47th	Rep	Rep
	Chester A. Arthur				
1881–85	**Chester A. Arthur**	Rep	48th	Dem	Rep
	(VP vacant)				
1885–89	**Grover Cleveland**	Dem	49th	Dem	Rep
	Thomas A. Hendricks (1885)[1]		50th	Dem	Rep
1889–93	**Benjamin Harrison**	Rep	51st	Rep	Rep
	Levi P. Morton		52d	Dem	Rep

TERM	PRESIDENT AND VICE PRESIDENT	PARTY OF PRESIDENT	CONGRESS	MAJORITY PARTY HOUSE	SENATE
1893–97	**Grover Cleveland**	Dem	53d	Dem	Dem
	Adlai E. Stevenson		54th	Rep	Rep
1897–1901	**William McKinley**[1]	Rep	55th	Rep	Rep
	Garret A. Hobart (1897–99)[1]		56th	Rep	Rep
	Theodore Roosevelt (1901)				
1901–09	**Theodore Roosevelt**	Rep	57th	Rep	Rep
	(VP vacant, 1901–05)		58th	Rep	Rep
	Charles W. Fairbanks (1905–09)		59th	Rep	Rep
			60th	Rep	Rep
1909–13	**William Howard Taft**	Rep	61st	Rep	Rep
	James S. Sherman (1909–12)[1]		62d	Dem	Rep
1913–21	**Woodrow Wilson**	Dem	63d	Dem	Dem
	Thomas R. Marshall		64th	Dem	Dem
			65th	Dem	Dem
			66th	Rep	Rep
1921–23	**Warren G. Harding**[1]	Rep	67th	Rep	Rep
	Calvin Coolidge				
1923–29	**Calvin Coolidge**	Rep	68th	Rep	Rep
	(VP vacant, 1923–25)		69th	Rep	Rep
	Charles G. Dawes (1925–29)		70th	Rep	Rep
1929–33	**Herbert Hoover**	Rep	71st	Rep	Rep
	Charles Curtis		72d	Dem	Rep
1933–45	**Franklin D. Roosevelt**[1]	Dem	73d	Dem	Dem
	John N. Garner (1933–41)		74th	Dem	Dem
	Henry A. Wallace (1941–45)		75th	Dem	Dem
	Harry S. Truman (1945)		76th	Dem	Dem
			77th	Dem	Dem
			78th	Dem	Dem
1945–53	**Harry S. Truman**	Dem	79th	Dem	Dem
	(VP vacant, 1945–49)		80th	Rep	Rep
	Alben W. Barkley (1949–53)		81st	Dem	Dem
			82d	Dem	Dem
1953–61	**Dwight D. Eisenhower**	Rep	83d	Rep	Rep
	Richard M. Nixon		84th	Dem	Dem
			85th	Dem	Dem
			86th	Dem	Dem
1961–63	**John F. Kennedy**[1]	Dem	87th	Dem	Dem
	Lyndon B. Johnson (1961–63)				
1963–69	**Lyndon B. Johnson**	Dem	88th	Dem	Dem
	(VP vacant, 1963–65)		89th	Dem	Dem
	Hubert H. Humphrey (1965–69)		90th	Dem	Dem
1969–74	**Richard M. Nixon**[3]	Rep	91st	Dem	Dem
	Spiro T. Agnew (1969–73)[2]		92d	Dem	Dem
	Gerald R. Ford (1973–74)[4]				
1974–77	**Gerald R. Ford**	Rep	93d	Dem	Dem
	Nelson A. Rockefeller[4]		94th	Dem	Dem
1977–81	**Jimmy Carter**	Dem	95th	Dem	Dem
	Walter Mondale		96th	Dem	Dem
1981–89	**Ronald Reagan**	Rep	97th	Dem	Rep
	George Bush		98th	Dem	Rep
			99th	Dem	Rep
			100th	Dem	Dem
1989–93	**George Bush**	Rep	101st	Dem	Dem
	J. Danforth Quayle		102d	Dem	Dem
1993–2001	**William J. Clinton**	Dem	103d	Dem	Dem
	Albert Gore, Jr.		104th	Rep	Rep
			105th	Rep	Rep
			106th	Rep	Rep
2001	**George W. Bush**	Rep	107th		
	Richard Cheney				

[1] Died in office.
[2] Resigned from the vice presidency.
[3] Resigned from the presidency.
[4] Appointed vice president.

APPENDIX 2

Supreme Court Justices

Name[1]	Years on Court	Appointing President
JOHN JAY	1789–1795	Washington
James Wilson	1789–1798	Washington
John Rutledge	1790–1791	Washington
William Cushing	1790–1810	Washington
John Blair	1790–1796	Washington
James Iredell	1790–1799	Washington
Thomas Jefferson	1792–1793	Washington
William Paterson	1793–1806	Washington
JOHN RUTLEDGE[2]	1795	Washington
Samuel Chase	1796–1811	Washington
OLIVER ELLSWORTH	1796–1800	Washington
Bushrod Washington	1799–1829	J. Adams
Alfred Moore	1800–1804	J. Adams
JOHN MARSHALL	1801–1835	J. Adams
William Johnson	1804–1834	Jefferson
Brockholst Livingston	1807–1823	Jefferson
Thomas Todd	1807–1826	Jefferson
Gabriel Duvall	1811–1835	Madison
Joseph Story	1812–1845	Madison
Smith Thompson	1823–1843	Monroe
Robert Trimble	1826–1828	J. Q. Adams
John McLean	1830–1861	Jackson
Henry Baldwin	1830–1844	Jackson
James M. Wayne	1835–1867	Jackson
ROGER B. TANEY	1836–1864	Jackson
Philip P. Barbour	1836–1841	Jackson
John Cartron	1837–1865	Van Buren
John McKinley	1838–1852	Van Buren
Peter V. Daniel	1842–1860	Van Buren
Samuel Nelson	1845–1872	Tyler
Levi Woodbury	1845–1851	Polk
Robert C. Grier	1846–1870	Polk
Benjamin R. Curtis	1851–1857	Fillmore
John A. Campbell	1853–1861	Pierce
Nathan Clifford	1858–1881	Buchanan
Noah H. Swayne	1862–1881	Lincoln
Samuel F. Miller	1862–1890	Lincoln
David Davis	1862–1877	Lincoln
Stephen J. Field	1863–1897	Lincoln
SALMON P. CHASE	1864–1873	Lincoln
William Strong	1870–1880	Grant
Joseph P. Bradley	1870–1892	Grant
Ward Hunt	1873–1882	Grant
MORRISON R. WAITE	1874–1888	Grant
John M. Harlan	1877–1911	Haves
William B. Woods	1881–1887	Haves
Stanley Matthews	1881–1889	Garfield
Horace Gray	1882–1902	Arthur
Samuel Blatchford	1882–1893	Arthur
Lucious Q. C. Lamar	1888–1893	Cleveland
MELVILLE W. FULLER	1888–1910	Cleveland
David J. Brewer	1890–1910	B. Harrison
Henry B. Brown	1891–1906	B. Harrison
George Shiras, Jr.	1892–1903	B. Harrison
Howel E. Jackson	1893–1895	B. Harrison

Name[1]	Years on Court	Appointing President
Edward D. White	1894–1910	Cleveland
Rufus W. Peckman	1896–1909	Cleveland
Joseph McKenna	1898–1925	McKinley
Oliver W. Holmes	1902–1932	T. Roosevelt
William R. Day	1903–1922	T. Roosevelt
William H. Moody	1906–1910	T. Roosevelt
Horace H. Lurton	1910–1914	Taft
Charles E. Hughes	1910–1916	Taft
EDWARD D. WHITE	1910–1921	Taft
Willis Van Devanter	1911–1937	Taft
Joseph R. Lamar	1911–1916	Taft
Mahlon Pitney	1912–1922	Taft
James C. McReynolds	1914–1941	Wilson
Louis D. Brandeis	1916–1939	Wilson
John H. Clarke	1916–1922	Wilson
WILLIAM H. TAFT	1921–1930	Harding
George Sutherland	1922–1938	Harding
Pierce Butler	1923–1939	Harding
Edward T. Sanford	1923–1930	Harding
Harlan F. Stone	1925–1941	Coolidge
CHARLES E. HUGHES	1930–1941	Hoover
Owen J. Roberts	1930–1945	Hoover
Benjamin N. Cardozo	1932–1938	Hoover
Hugo L. Black	1937–1971	F. Roosevelt
Stanley F. Reed	1938–1957	F. Roosevelt
Felix Frankfurter	1939–1962	F. Roosevelt
William O. Douglas	1939–1975	F. Roosevelt
Frank Murphy	1940–1949	F. Roosevelt
HARLAN F. STONE	1941–1946	F. Roosevelt
James F. Brynes	1941–1942	F. Roosevelt
Robert H. Jackson	1941–1954	F. Roosevelt
Wiley B. Rutledge	1943–1949	F. Roosevelt
Harold H. Burton	1945–1958	Truman
FREDERICK M. VINSON	1946–1953	Truman
Tom C. Clark	1949–1967	Truman
Sherman Minton	1949–1956	Truman
EARL WARREN	1953–1969	Eisenhower
John Marshall Harlan	1955–1971	Eisenhower
William J. Brennan, Jr.	1956–1990	Eisenhower
Charles E. Whittaker	1957–1962	Eisenhower
Potter Stewart	1958–1981	Eisenhower
Byron R. White	1962–1993	Kennedy
Arthur J. Goldberg	1962–1965	Kennedy
Abe Fortas	1965–1970	L. Johnson
Thurgood Marshall	1967–1991	L. Johnson
WARREN E. BURGER	1969–1986	Nixon
Harry A. Blackmun	1970–1994	Nixon
Lewis F. Powell, Jr.	1971–1987	Nixon
William H. Rehnquist	1971–1986	Nixon
John Paul Stevens	1975–	Ford
Sandra Day O'Connor	1981–	Reagan
WILLIAM H. REHNQUIST	1986–	Reagan
Antonin Scalia	1986–	Reagan
Anthony Kennedy	1988–	Reagan
David Souter	1990–	Bush
Clarence Thomas	1991–	Bush
Ruth Bader Ginsburg	1993–	Clinton
Stephen Brever	1994–	Clinton

[1]Capital letters designate Chief Justices
[2]Never confirmed by the Senate as Chief Justice

APPENDIX 3

THE DECLARATION OF INDEPENDENCE

IN CONGRESS, JULY 4, 1776
(The unanimous Declaration of the Thirteen United States of America)

Preamble

When, in the course of human events, it becomes necessary for one people to dissolve the political bands which have connected them with another, and to assume, among the powers of the earth, the separate and equal station to which the laws of nature and of nature's God entitle them, a decent respect to the opinions of mankind requires that they should declare the causes which impel them to the separation.

We hold these truths to be self-evident; that all men are created equal, that they are endowed by their Creator with certain unalienable rights, that among these are life, liberty, and the pursuit of happiness.

That, to secure these rights, governments are instituted among men, deriving their just powers from the consent of the governed.

That whenever any form of government becomes destructive of these ends, it is the right of the people to alter or to abolish it, and to institute new government, laying its foundation on such principles, and organizing its powers in such form, as to them shall seem most likely to effect their safety and happiness. Prudence, indeed will dictate that governments long established should not be changed for light and transient causes; and accordingly all experience hath shown that mankind are more disposed to suffer while evils are sufferable, than to right themselves by abolishing the forms to which they are accustomed. But when a long train of abuses and usurpations, pursuing invariably the same object, evinces a design to reduce them under absolute despotism, it is their right, it is their duty, to throw off such government, and to provide new guards for their future security.

Such has been the patient sufferance of these colonies; and such is now the necessity which constrains them to alter their former systems of government. The history of the present king of Great Britain is a history of repeated injuries and usurpations, all having in direct object the establishment of an absolute tyranny over these states. To prove this, let facts be submitted to a candid world.

He has refused his assent to laws, the most wholesome and necessary for the public good.

He has forbidden his governors to pass laws of immediate and pressing importance unless suspended in their operation till his assent should be obtained; and when so suspended, he has utterly neglected to attend to them.

He has refused to pass other laws for the accommodation of large districts of people, unless those people would relinquish the right of representation in the legislature, a right inestimable to them, and formidable to tyrants only.

He has called together legislative bodies at places unusual, uncomfortable, and distant for the depository of their public records, for the sole purpose of fatiguing them into compliance with his measures.

He has dissolved representative houses repeatedly, for opposing, with manly firmness, his invasions on the rights of people.

He has refused, for a long time after such dissolutions, to cause others to be elected; whereby the legislative powers incapable of annihilation, have returned to the people at large for their exercise; the state remaining, in the meantime, exposed to all the dangers of invasion from without and convulsions within.

He has endeavored to prevent the population of these states; for that purpose obstructing the laws of naturalization of foreigners, refusing to pass others to encourage their migration hither, and raising the conditions of new appropriations of lands.

He has obstructed the administration of justice, by refusing his assent to laws for establishing judiciary powers.

He has made judges dependent on his will alone for the tenure of their offices, and the amount and payment of their salaries.

He has erected a multitude of new offices, and sent hither swarms of officers to harass our people and eat out their substance.

He has kept among us, in times of peace, standing armies, without the consent of our legislature.

He has affected to render the military independent of, and superior to, the civil power.

He has combined with others to subject us to jurisdiction foreign to our constitution and unacknowledged by our laws, giving his assent to their acts of pretended legislation:

For quartering large bodies of armed troops among us;

For protecting them, by a mock trial, from punishment for any murders which they should commit on the inhabitants of these states;

For cutting off our trade with all parts of the world;

For imposing taxes on us without our consent;

For depriving us, in many cases, of the benefits of trial by jury;

For transporting us beyond seas, to be tried for pretended offenses;

For abolishing the free system of English laws in a neighboring province, establishing therein an arbitrary government, and enlarging its boundaries, so as to render it at once an example and fit instrument for introducing the same absolute rule into these colonies;

For taking away our charters, abolishing our most valuable laws, and altering, fundamentally, the forms of our governments;

For suspending our own legislatures, and declaring themselves invented with power to legislate for us in all cases whatsoever.

He has abdicated government here, by declaring us out of his protection and waging war against us.

He has plundered our seas, ravaged our coasts, burned our towns, and destroyed the lives of our people.

He is at this time transporting large armies of foreign mercenaries to complete the works of death, desolation, and tyranny already begun with circumstances of cruelty and perfidy scarcely paralleled in the most barbarous ages and totally unworthy of the head of a civilized nation.

He has constrained our fellow-citizens, taken captive on the high seas, to bear arms against their country, to become the executioners of their friends and brethren, or to fall themselves by their hands.

He has excited domestic insurrections among us, and has endeavored to bring on the inhabitants of our frontiers the merciless Indian savages, whose known rule of warfare is an undistinguished destruction of all ages, sexes, and conditions.

In every stage of these oppressions we have petitioned for redress in the most humble terms; our repeated petitions have been answered only by repeated injury. A prince whose character is thus marked by every act which may define a tyrant is unfit to be the ruler of a free people.

Nor have we been wanting in attention to our British brethren. We have warned them, from time to time, of attempts by their legislature to extend an unwarrantable jurisdiction over us. We have reminded them of the circumstances of our emigration and settlement here. We have appealed to their native justice and magnanimity; and we have conjured them, by the ties of our common kindred, to disavow these usurpations, which would inevitably interrupt our connections and correspondence. They, too, have been deaf to the voice of justice and of consanguinity. We must, therefore, acquiesce in the necessity which denounces our separation, and hold them, as we hold the rest of mankind, enemies in war, in peace, friends.

We, therefore, the representatives of the United States of America, in General Congress assembled, appealing to the Supreme Judge of the world for the rectitude of our intentions, do, in the name and by authority of the good people of these colonies, solemnly publish and declare, that these united colonies are, and of right ought to be, free and independent states; that they are absolved from all allegiance to the British crown, and that all political connection between them and the state of Great Britain is, and ought to be, totally dissolved; and that, as free and independent states, they have full power to levy war, conclude peace, contract alliances, establish commerce, and do all other acts and things which independent states may of a right do. And, for the support of this declaration, with a firm reliance on the protection of Divine Providence, we mutually pledge to each other our lives, our fortunes, and our sacred honor.

APPENDIX 4

THE FEDERALIST, NO. 10, JAMES MADISON

To the People of the State of New York: Among the numerous advantages promised by a well-constructed union, none deserves to be more accurately developed than its tendency to break and control the violence of faction. The friend of popular governments, never finds himself so much alarmed for their character and fate, as when he contemplates their propensity of this dangerous vice. He will not fail, therefore, to set a due value on any plan which, without violating the principles to which he is attached, provides a proper cure for it. The instability, injustice, and confusion introduced into the public councils, have, in truth, been the mortal diseases under which popular governments have everywhere perished; as they continue to be the favorite and fruitful topics from which the adversaries to liberty derive their most specious declamations. The valuable improvements made by the American constitutions on the popular models, both ancient and modern, cannot certainly be too much admired; but it would be an unwarrantable partiality, to contend that they have as effectually obviated the danger on this side, as was wished and expected. Complaints are everywhere heard from our most considerate and virtuous citizens, equally the friends of public and private faith, and of public and personal liberty, that our governments are too unstable; that the public good is disregarded in the conflicts of rival parties; and that measures are too often decided, not according to the rules of justice, and the rights of the minor party, but by the superior force of an interested and overbearing majority. However anxiously we may wish that these complaints had no foundation, the evidence of known facts will not permit us to deny that they are in some degree true. It will be found, indeed, on a candid review of our situation, that some of the distresses under which we labor have been erroneously charged on the operations of our governments; but it will be found, at the same time, that other causes will not alone account for many of our heaviest misfortunes; and, particularly, for that prevailing and increasing distrust of public engagements, and alarm for private rights, which are echoed from one end of the continent to the other. These must be chiefly, if not wholly, effects of the unsteadiness and injustice, with which a factious spirit has tainted our public administrations.

By a faction, I understand a number of citizens, whether amounting to a majority of the whole, who are united and actuated by some common impulse of passion, or of interest, adverse to the rights of other citizens, or to the permanent and aggregate interests of the community.

There are two methods of curing the mischiefs of faction: the one, by removing its causes; the other, by controlling its effects.

There are again two methods of removing the causes of faction: the one, by destroying the liberty which is essential to its existence; the other, by giving to every citizen the same opinions, the same passions, and the same interests.

It could never be more truly said, than of the first remedy, that it was worse than the disease. Liberty is to faction what air is to fire, an aliment without which it instantly expires. But it could not be a less folly to abolish liberty, which is essential to political life, because it nourishes faction, than it would be to wish the annihilation of air, which is essential to animal life, because it imparts to fire its destructive agency.

The second expedient is as impracticable, as the first would be unwise. As long as the reason of man continues fallible, and he is at liberty to exercise it, different opinions will be formed. As long as the connection subsists between his reason and his self-love, his opinions and his passions will have a reciprocal influence on each other; and the former will be objects to which the latter will attach themselves. The diversity in the faculties of men, from which the rights of property originate, is not less an insuperable obstacle to an uniformity of interests. The protection of these faculties is the first object of government. From the protection of different and unequal faculties of acquiring property, the possession of different degrees and kinds of property immediately results; and from the influence of these on the sentiments and views of the respective proprietors, ensues a division of the society into different interests and parties.

The latent causes of faction are thus sown in the nature of man; and we see them everywhere brought into different degrees of activity, according to the different circumstances of civil society. A zeal for different opinions concerning religion, concerning government, and many other points, as well of speculation as of practice; an attachment to different leaders ambitiously contending for preeminence and power; or to persons of other descriptions whose fortunes have been interesting to the human passions, have, in turn, divided mankind into parties, inflamed them with mutual animosity, and rendered them much more disposed to vex and oppress each other, than to cooperate for their common good. So strong is this propensity of mankind, to fall into mutual animosities, that where no substantial occasion presents itself, the most frivolous and fanciful distinctions have been sufficient to kindle their unfriendly passions and excite their most violent conflicts. But the most common and durable source of factions, has been the various and unequal distribution of property. Those who hold, and those who are without property, have ever formed distinct interests in society. Those who are creditors, and those who are debtors, fall under a like discrimination. A landed interest, a manufacturing interest, a mercantile interest, a moneyed interest, with many lesser interests, grow up of necessity in civilized nations, and divide them into different classes, actuated by different sentiments and views. The regulation of these various and interfering interests forms the principal task of modern legislation, and involves the spirit of the party and faction in the necessary and ordinary operations of the government.

No man is allowed to be a judge in his own cause; because his interest will certainly bias his judgment, and, not improbably, corrupt his integrity. With equal, nay, with greater reason, a body of men are unfit to be both judges and parties at the same time; yet what are many of the most important acts of legislation, but so many judicial determinations, not indeed concerning the right of single persons, but concerning the rights of large bodies of citizens? And what are the different classes of legislators, but advocates and parties to the causes which they determine? Is a law proposed concerning private debts? It is a question to which the creditors are parties on one side, and the debtors on the other. Justice ought to hold the balance between them. Yet the parties are, and must be, themselves the judges; and the most numerous party, or, in other words, the most powerful faction, must be expected to prevail. Shall domestic manufacturers be encouraged, and in what degree, by restrictions on foreign manufacturers? Are questions which would be differently decided by the landed and the manufacturing classes; and probably by neither with a sole regard to justice and the public good. The apportionment of taxes, on the various descriptions of property, is an act which seems to require the most exact impartiality; yet there is, perhaps, no legislative act, in which greater opportunity and temptation are given to a predominant party to trample on the rules of justice. Every shilling, with which they overburden the inferior number, is a shilling saved to their own pockets.

It is in vain to say, that enlightened statesmen will be able to adjust these clashing interests, and render them all subservient to the public good. Enlightened statesmen will not always be at the helm, nor, in many cases, can such an adjustment be made at all, without taking into view indirect and remote considerations, which will rarely prevail over the immediate interest which one party may find in disregarding the rights of another, or the good of the whole.

The inference to which we are brought is, that the causes of faction cannot be removed; and that relief is only to be sought in the means of controlling its *effects*.

If a faction consists of less than a majority, relief is supplied by the republican principle, which enables the majority to defeat its sinister views, by regular vote. It may clog the administration, it may convulse the society; but it will be unable to execute and mask its violence under the forms of the Constitution. When a majority is included in a faction, the form of popular government, on the other hand, enables it to sacrifice to its ruling passion or interest, both the public good and the rights of other citizens. To secure the public good, and private rights, against the danger of such a faction, and at the same time to preserve the spirit and the form of popular government, is then the great object to which our inquiries are directed. Let me add, that it is the great desideratum, by which alone this form of government can be rescued from the opprobrium under which it has so long laboured, and be recommended to the esteem and adoption of mankind.

By what means is this object attainable? Evidently by one of two only. Either the existence of the same passion or interest in a majority, at the same time, must be prevented; or the majority, having such coexistent passion or interest, must be rendered, by their number and local situation, unable to concert and carry into effect schemes of oppression. If the impulse and the opportunity be suffered to coincide, we well know that neither moral nor religious motives can be relied on as an adequate control. They are not found to be such on the injustice and violence of individuals, and lose their efficacy in proportion to the number combined together; that is, in proportion as their efficacy becomes needful.

From this view of the subject, it may be concluded, that a pure democracy, by which I mean a society consisting of a small number of citizens, who assemble and administer the government in person, can admit of no cure for the mischiefs of faction. A common passion or interest will, in almost every case, be felt by a majority of the whole; a communication and concert, results from the form of government itself; and there is nothing to check the inducements to sacrifice the weaker party, or an obnoxious individual. Hence, it is, that such democracies have ever been spectacles of turbulence and contention; have ever been found incompatible with personal security, or the rights of property; and have in general been as short in their lives, as they have been violent in their deaths.

Theoretic politicians, who have patronized this species of government, have erroneously supposed, that by reducing mankind to a perfect equality in their political rights, they would, at the same time be perfectly equalized and assimilated in their possessions, their opinions, and their passions.

A republic, by which I mean a government in which the scheme of representation takes place, opens a different prospect, and promises the cure for which we are seeking. Let us examine the points in which it varies from pure democracy, and we shall comprehend both the nature of the cure and the efficacy which it must derive from the union.

The two great points of difference, between a democracy and a republic, are, first, the delegation of the government, in the latter, to a small number of citizens, elected by the rest; secondly, the greater number of citizens, and greater sphere of country, over which the latter may be extended.

The effect of the first difference is, on the one hand, to refine and enlarge the public views, by passing them through the medium of a chosen body of citizens, whose wisdom may best discern the true interest of their country, and whose patriotism and love of justice, will be least likely to sacrifice it to temporary or partial considerations. Under such a regulation, it may well happen, that the public voice, pronounced by the representatives of the people, will be more consonant to the public good, than if pronounced by the people themselves, convened for the purpose. On the other hand the effect may be inverted. Men of factious tempers, of local prejudices, or of sinister designs, may by intrigue, by corruption, or by other means, first obtain the suffrages, and then betray the interest of the people. The question resulting is, whether small or extensive republics are most favourable to the election of proper guardians of the public weal; and it is clearly decided in favour of the latter by two obvious considerations.

In the first place, it is to be remarked that, however small the republic may be, the representatives must be raised to a certain number, in order to guard against the cabals of a few; and that however large it may be, they must be limited to a certain number, in order to guard against the confusion of a multitude. Hence, the number of representatives in the two cases not being in proportion to that of the constituents, and being proportionally greatest in the small republic, it follows, that if the proportion of fit characters be not less in the large than in the small republic, the former will present a greater option, and consequently a greater probability of a fit choice.

In the next place, as each representative will be chosen by a greater number of citizens in the large than in the small republic, it will be more difficult for unworthy candidates to practice with success the vicious arts, by which elections are too often carried; and the suffrages of the people being more free, will be more likely to centre in men who possess the most attractive merit, and the most diffusive and established characters.

It must be confessed, that in this, as in most other cases, there is a mean, on both sides of which inconveniences will be found to lie. By enlarging too much the number of electors, you render the representatives too little acquainted with all their local circumstances and lesser interests; as by reducing it too much, you render him unduly attached to these, and too little fit to comprehend and pursue great and national objects. The federal constitution forms a happy combination in this respect; the great and aggregate interests being referred to the national, the local and particular to the state legislatures.

The other point of difference is, the greater number of citizens, and extent of territory, which may be brought within the compass of republican, than of democratic government;

and it is this circumstance principally which renders factious combinations less to be dreaded in the former, than in the latter. The smaller the society, the fewer probably will be the distinct parties and interests composing it; the fewer the distinct parties and interests, the more frequently will a majority be found of the same party; and the smaller the number of individuals composing a majority, and the smaller the compass within which they are placed, the more easily will they concert and execute their plans of oppression. Extend the sphere, and you take in a greater variety of parties and interests; you make it less probable that a majority of the whole will have a common motive to invade the rights of other citizens; or if such a common motive exists, it will be more difficult for all who feel it to discover their own strength, and to act in unison with each other. Besides other impediments, it may be remarked, that where there is a consciousness of unjust or dishonourable purposes, communication is always checked by distrust, in proportion to the number whose concurrence is necessary.

Hence, it clearly appears, that the same advantage, which a republic has over a democracy, in controlling the effects of faction, is enjoyed by a large over a small republic—is enjoyed by the union over the states composing it. Does this advantage consist in the substitution of representatives, whose enlightened views and virtuous sentiments render them superior to local prejudices, and to schemes of injustice? It will not be denied that the representation of the union will be most likely to possess these requisite endowments. Does it consist in the greater security afforded by a greater variety of parties, against the event of any one party being able to outnumber and oppress the rest? In an equal degree does the increased variety of parties, comprised within the union, increase the security? Does it, in fine, consist in the greater obstacles opposed to the concert and accomplishment of the secret wishes of an unjust and interested majority? Here, again, the extent of the union gives it the most palpable advantage.

The influence of factious leaders may kindle a flame within their particular states, but will be unable to spread a general conflagration through the other states; a religious sect may degenerate into a political faction in a part of the confederacy; but the variety of sects dispersed over the entire face of it, must secure the national councils against any danger from that source: a rage for paper money, for an abolition of debts, for an equal division of property, or for any other improper or wicked project, will be less apt to pervade the whole body of the union than a particular member of it; in the same proportion as such a malady is more likely to taint a particular county or district, than an entire state.

In the extent and proper structure of the union, therefore, we behold a republican remedy for the diseases most incident to republican government. And according to the degree of pleasure and pride we feel in being republicans, ought to be our zeal in cherishing the spirit, and supporting the character of federalists.

APPENDIX 5

THE FEDERALIST, NO. 51, JAMES MADISON

To what expedient, then, shall we finally resort, for maintaining in practice the necessary partition of power among the several departments as laid down in the Constitution? The only answer that can be given is that as all these exterior provisions are found to be inadequate the defect must be supplied, by so contriving the interior structure of the government as that its several constituent parts may, by their mutual relations, be the means of keeping each other in their proper places. Without presuming to undertake a full development of this important idea I will hazard a few general observations which may perhaps place it in a clearer light, and enable us to form a more correct judgment of the principles and structure of the government planned by the convention.

In order to lay a due foundation for that separate and distinct exercise of the different powers of government, which to a certain extent is admitted on all hands to be essential to the preservation of liberty, it is evident that each department should have a will of its own; and consequently should be so constituted that the members of each should have as little agency as possible in the appointment of the members of the others. Were this principle rigorously adhered to, it would require that all the appointments for the supreme executive, legislative, and judiciary magistracies should be drawn from the same fountain of authority, the people, through channels having no communication whatever with one another. Perhaps such a plan of constructing the several departments would be less difficult in practice than it may in contemplation appear. Some difficulties, however, and some additional expense would attend the execution of it. Some deviations, therefore, from the principle must be admitted. In the constitution of the judiciary department in particular, it might be inexpedient to insist rigorously on the principle: first, because peculiar qualifications being essential in the members, the primary consideration ought to be to select that mode of choice which best secures these qualifications; second, because the permanent tenure by which the appointments are held in that department must soon destroy all sense of dependence on the authority conferring them.

It is equally evident that the members of each department should be as little dependent as possible on those of the others for the emoluments annexed to their offices. Were the executive magistrate, or the judges, not independent of the legislature in this particular, their independence in every other would be merely nominal.

But the great security against a gradual concentration of the several powers in the same department consists in giving to those who administer each department the necessary constitutional means and personal motives to resist encroachments of the others. The provision for defense must in this, as in all other cases, be made commensurate to the danger of attack. Ambition must be made to counteract ambition. The interest of the man must be connected with the constitutional rights of the place. It may be a reflection on human nature that such devices should be necessary to control the abuses of government. But what is government itself but the greatest of all reflections on human nature? If men were angels, no government would be necessary. If angels were to govern men, neither external nor internal controls on government would be necessary. In framing a government which is to be administered by men over men, the great difficulty lies in this: you must first enable the government to control the governed; and in the next place oblige it to control itself. A dependence on the people is, no doubt, the primary control on the government; but experience has taught mankind the necessity of auxiliary precautions.

This policy of supplying, by opposite and rival interests, the defect of better motives, might be traced through the whole system of human affairs, private as well as public. We see it particularly displayed in all the subordinate distributions of power, where the constant aim is to divide and arrange the several offices in such a manner as that each may be a check on the other—that the private interest of every individual may be a sentinel over the public rights. These inventions of prudence cannot be less requisite in the distribution of the supreme powers of the State.

But it is not possible to give to each department an equal power of self-defense. In republican government, the legislative authority necessarily predominates. The remedy for this inconveniency is to divide the legislature into different branches; and to render them, by modes of election and different principles of action, as little connected with each other as the nature of their common functions and their common dependence on the society will admit. It may even be necessary to guard against dangerous encroachments by still further precautions. As the weight of the legislative authority requires that it should be thus divided, the weakness of the executive may require, on the other hand, that it should be fortified. An absolute negative on the legislature appears, at first view, to be the natural defense with which the executive magistrate should be armed. But perhaps it would be neither altogether safe nor alone sufficient. On ordinary occasions it might not be exerted with the requisite firmness, and on extraordinary occasions it might be perfidiously abused. May not this defect of an absolute negative be supplied by some qualified connection between this weaker department and the weaker branch of the stronger department, by which the latter may be led to support the constitutional rights of the former, without being too much detached from the rights of its own department?

If the principles on which these observations are founded be just, as I persuade myself they are, and they be applied as a criterion to the several State constitutions, and to the federal Constitution, it will be found that if the latter does not perfectly correspond with them, the former are infinitely less able to bear such a test.

There are, moreover, two considerations particularly applicable to the federal system of America, which place that system in a very interesting point of view.

First. In a single republic, all the power surrendered by the people is submitted to the administration of a single government; and the usurpations are guarded against by a division of the government into distinct and separate departments. In the compound republic of America, the power surrendered by the people is first divided between two distinct governments, and then the portion allotted to each subdivided among distinct and separate departments. Hence a double security arises to the rights of the people. The different governments will control each other, at the same time that each will be controlled by itself.

Second. It is of great importance in a republic not only to guard the society against the oppression of its rulers, but to guard one part of the society against the injustice of the other part. Different interests necessarily exist in different classes of citizens. If a majority be united by a common interest, the rights of the minority will be insecure. There are but two methods of providing against this evil: the one by creating a will in the community independent of the majority—that is, of the society itself; the other, by comprehending in the society so many separate descriptions of citizens as will render an unjust combination of a majority of the whole very improbable, if not impracticable. The first method prevails in all governments possessing an hereditary or self-appointed authority. This, at best, is but a precarious security; because a power independent of the society may as well espouse the unjust views of the major as the rightful interests of the minor party, and may possibly be turned against both parties. The second method will be exemplified in the federal republic of the United States. Whilst all authority in it will be derived from and dependent on the society, the society itself will be broken into so many parts, interests and classes of citizens, that the rights of individuals, or of the minority, will be in little danger from interested combinations of the majority. In a free government the security for civil rights must be the same as that for religious rights. It consists in the one case in the multiplicity of interests, and in the other in the multiplicity of sects. The degree of security in both cases will depend on the number of interests and sects; and this may be presumed to depend on the extent of country and number of people comprehended under the same government. This view of the subject must particularly recommend a proper federal system to all the sincere and considerate friends of republican government, since it shows that in exact proportion as the territory of the Union may be formed into more circumscribed Confederacies, or States, oppressive combinations of a majority will be facilitated; the best security, under the republican forms, for the rights of every class of citizen, will be diminished; and consequently the stability and independence of some member of the government, the only other security, must be proportionally increased. Justice is the end of government. It is the end of civil society. It ever has been and ever will be pursued until it be obtained, or until liberty be lost in the pursuit. In a society under the forms of which the stronger faction can readily unite and oppress the weaker, anarchy may as truly be said to reign as in a state of nature, where the weaker individual is not secured against the violence of the stronger; and as, in the latter state, even the stronger individuals are prompted, by the uncertainty of their condition, to submit to a government which may protect the weak as well as themselves; so, in the former state, will the more powerful factions or parties be gradually induced, by a like motive, to wish for a government which will protect all parties, the weaker as well as the more powerful. It can be little doubted that if the State of Rhode Island was separated from the Confederacy and left to itself, the insecurity of rights under the popular form of government within such narrow limits would be displayed by such reiterated oppressions of factious majorities that some power altogether independent of the people would soon be called for by the voice of the very factions whose misrule had proved the necessity to it. In the extended republic of the United States, and among the great variety of interests, parties, and sects which it embraces, a coalition of a majority of the whole society could seldom take place on any other principles than those of justice and the general good; whilst there being thus less danger to a minor from the will of a major party, there must be less pretext, also, to provide for the security of the former, by introducing into the government a will not dependent on the latter, or, in other words, a will independent of the society itself. It is no less certain that it is important, notwithstanding the contrary opinions which have been entertained that the larger the society, provided it lie within a practicable sphere, the more duly capable it will be of self-government. And happily for the *republican cause,* the practicable sphere may be carried to a very great extent by a judicious modification and mixture of the *federal principle.*

APPENDIX 6

INTRODUCING THE CONCEPT OF APPROACHING DEMOCRACY

Excerpts of a Speech by Vaclav Havel, President of the Czech Republic to a Joint Session of the U.S. Congress, Washington, D.C., February 21, 1990

Dear Mr. Speaker, dear Mr. President, dear senators and members of the House, ladies and gentlemen:

I've only been president for two months, and I haven't attended any schools for presidents. My only school was life itself. Therefore, I don't want to burden you any longer with my political thoughts, but instead I will move on to an area that is more familiar to me, to what I would call the philosophical aspect of those changes that still concern everyone, although they are taking place in our corner of the world.

As long as people are people, democracy in the full sense of the word will always be no more than an ideal; one may approach it as one would a horizon, in ways that may be better or worse, but it can never be fully attained. *In this sense you are also merely approaching democracy*. You have thousands of problems of all kinds, as other countries do. But you have one great advantage: You have been approaching democracy uninterruptedly for more than 200 years, and your journey toward that horizon has never been disrupted by a totalitarian system. Czechs and Slovaks, despite their humanistic traditions that go back to the first millennium, have approached democracy for a mere twenty years, between the two world wars, and now for three and a half months since the 17th of November of last year.

The advantage that you have over us is obvious at once.

The Communist type of totalitarian system has left both our nations, Czechs and Slovaks as it has all the nations of the Soviet Union, and the other countries the Soviet Union subjugated in its time a legacy of countless dead, an infinite spectrum of human suffering, profound economic decline, and above all enormous human humiliation. It has brought us horrors that fortunately you have not known.

At the same time, however unintentionally, of course it has given us something positive: a special capacity to look, from time to time, somewhat further than someone who has not undergone this bitter experience. A person who cannot move and live a normal life because he is pinned under a boulder has more time to think about his hopes than someone who is not trapped in this way.

What I am trying to say is this: We must all learn many things from you, from how to educate our offspring, how to elect our representatives, all the way to how to organize our economic life so that it will lead to prosperity and not poverty. But it doesn't have to be merely assistance from the well educated, the powerful, and the wealthy to someone who has nothing to offer in return.

We too can offer something to you: our experience and the knowledge that has come from it.

This is a subject for books, many of which have already been written and many of which have yet to be written. I shall therefore limit myself to a single idea.

The specific experience I'm talking about has given me one great certainty: Consciousness precedes Being, and not the other way around, as Marxists claim.

For this reason, the salvation of this human world lies nowhere else than in the human heart, in the human power to reflect, in human humbleness and in human responsibility.

Without a global revolution in the sphere of human consciousness, nothing will change for the better in the sphere of our Being as humans, and the catastrophe toward which this world is headed, whether it be ecological, social, demographic or a general breakdown of civilization, will be unavoidable. If we are no longer threatened by world war or by the danger that the absurd mountains of accumulated nuclear weapons might blow up the world, this does not mean that we have definitively won. We are in fact far from definite victory.

We are still a long way from that "family of man;" in fact, we seem to be receding from the ideal rather than drawing closer to it. Interests of all kinds: personal, selfish, state, national, group and, if you like, company interests still considerably outweigh genuinely common and global interests. We are still under the sway of the destructive and thoroughly vain belief that man is the pinnacle of creation, and not just a part of it, and that therefore everything is permitted. There are still many who say they are concerned not for themselves but for the cause, while they are demonstrably out for themselves and not for the cause at all. We are still destroying the planet that was entrusted to us, and its environment. We still close our eyes to the growing social, ethnic and cultural conflicts in the world. From time to time we say that the anonymous megamachinery we have created for ourselves no longer serves us but rather has enslaved us, yet we still fail to do anything about it.

In other words, we still don't know how to put morality ahead of politics, science and economics. We are still incapable of understanding that the only genuine backbone of all our actions if they are to be moral is responsibility. Responsibility to something higher than my family, my country, my firm, my success. Responsibility to the order of Being, where all our actions are indelibly recorded and where, and only where, they will be properly judged.

The interpreter or mediator between us and this higher authority is what is traditionally referred to as human conscience.

If I subordinate my political behaviour to this imperative, I can't go far wrong. If on the contrary I were not guided by this voice, not even ten presidential schools with 2,000 of the best political scientists in the world could help me.

This is why I ultimately decided after resisting for a long time to accept the burden of political responsibility.

I'm not the first nor will I be the last intellectual to do this. On the contrary, my feeling is that there will be more and more of them all the time. If the hope of the world lies in human consciousness, then it is obvious that intellectuals cannot go on forever avoiding their share of responsibility for the world and hiding their distastes for politics under an alleged need to be independent.

It is easy to have independence in your programme and then leave others to carry out that programme. If everyone thought that way, soon no one would be independent.

I think that Americans should understand this way of thinking. Wasn't it the best minds of your country, people you could call intellectuals, who wrote your famous Declaration of Independence, your Bill of Rights, and your Constitution, and who above all took upon themselves the practical responsibility for putting them into practice? The worker from Branik in Prague, whom your president referred to in his State of the Union message this year, is far from being the only person in Czechoslovakia, let alone in the world, to be inspired by those great documents. They inspire us all. They inspire us despite the fact that they are over 200 years old. They inspire us to be citizens.

When Thomas Jefferson wrote that "Governments are instituted among Men, deriving their just powers from the Consent of the Governed," it was a simple and important act of the human spirit.

What gave meaning to that act, however, was the fact that the author backed it up with his life. It was not just his words, it was his deeds as well.

I will end where I began. History has accelerated. I believe that once again, it will be the human spirit that will notice this acceleration, give it a name, and transform those words into deeds.

GLOSSARY

actual groups Interest groups that have already been formed; they have headquarters, an organizational structure, paid employees, membership lists, and the like.

administration Performance of routine tasks associated with a specific policy goal.

administrative discretion The latitude that an agency, or even a single bureaucrat, has in interpreting and applying a law.

affirmative action Programs that attempt to improve the chances of minority applicants for jobs, housing, employment, or education by giving them a "boost" relative to white applicants with roughly the same qualifications.

amicus curiae briefs Legal briefs that enable groups or individuals, including the national government, who are not parties to the litigation but have an interest in it, to attempt to influence the outcome of the case; literally, "friend of the court" briefs.

Antifederalists Strong states' rights advocates that organized in opposition to the ratification of the U.S. Constitution prior to its adoption.

appellate court The court that reviews an appeal of the proceedings of the trial court, often with a multijudge panel and without a jury; it considers only matters of law.

appellate jurisdiction The authority of a court to hear a case on appeal after it has been argued in and decided by a lower federal or state court.

appointment power The president's power to name some three thousand agency officials, of whom about seven hundred are in policy-making positions, such as cabinet and subcabinet officials and bureau chiefs.

appropriations bill A separate bill that must be passed by Congress to fund measures that require spending.

Articles of Confederation The first constitutional framework of the new United States of America. Approved in 1777 by the Second Continental Congress, it was later replaced by the current Constitution.

authoritarian regime An oppressive system of government in which citizens are deprived of their basic freedom to speak, write, associate, and participate in political life without fear of punishment.

bicameral legislature A legislative system consisting of two houses or chambers.

Bill of Rights The first ten amendments to the Constitution, added in 1781.

bipolarity The fundamental division of economic and military power between the poles of Western capitalism and Eastern communism.

black codes Laws restricting the civil rights of blacks.

block grant A federal grant that provides money to states for general program funding with few or even no strings attached.

Boston Massacre A 1770 incident in which British soldiers fired a volley of shots into a crowd of hecklers who had been throwing snowballs at the redcoats; five colonists were killed.

Boston Tea Party A 1773 act of civil disobedience in which colonists dressed as Native Americans dumped 342 chests of tea into Boston Harbor to protest increased taxes.

boycott Refusal to patronize any organization that practices policies that are perceived to be unfair for political, economic, or ideological reasons.

briefs Written arguments to the court outlining not only the facts and legal and constitutional issues in a court case, but also answering all of the anticipated arguments of the opposing side.

bureaucracy A large and complex organizational system in which tasks, roles, and responsibilities are structured to achieve a goal.

bureaucrats People who work in a bureaucracy, not only the obscure, faceless clerks normally disparaged by critics of government but also "street-level bureaucrats" such as police officers, social workers, and schoolteachers.

cabinet Group of presidential advisers including secretaries of the major departments of the bureaucracy and any other officials the president designates.

cabinet departments Major administrative units whose heads are presidential advisers appointed by the president and confirmed by the Senate. They are responsible for conducting a broad range of government operations.

capital gains tax Tax on unearned income from rents, stocks, and interest.

casework Favors done as a service for constituents by those they have elected to Congress.

categorical grant The most common type of federal grant, given for specific purposes, usually with strict rules attached.

caucus Meeting of party adherents who gather to discuss, to deliberate, and finally to give their support to a candidate for president. They then select delegates who will represent their choices at higher-level party meetings; eventually, their votes get reflected at the national convention itself. Also means a conference of party members in Congress.

checks and balances Systems that ensure that for every power in government there is an equal and opposite power placed in a separate branch to restrain that force.

chief of staff The president's top aide.

civil cases Noncriminal cases in which courts resolve disputes among individuals and parties to the case over finances, property, or personal well-being.

civil disobedience Breaking the law in a nonviolent fashion and being willing to suffer the consequences, even to the point of going to jail, in order to publicly demonstrate that the law is unjust.

civil liberties The individual freedoms and rights that are guaranteed to every citizen in the Bill of Rights and the due process clause of the Fourteenth Amendment, including freedom of speech and religion.

civil rights The constitutionally guaranteed rights that may not be arbitrarily removed by the government. Among these rights are the right to vote and equal protection under the law.

civil service A system of hiring and promoting employees based on professional merit, not party loyalty.

class action suit A single civil case in which the plaintiff represents the whole class of individuals similarly situated, and the court's results apply to this entire class.

clear and present danger test A free speech test allowing states to regulate only speech that has an immediate connection to an action the states are permitted to regulate.

closed primary A system of conducting primary elections in which only citizens registered as members of a particular political party may participate in that party's primary.

cloture A procedure through which a vote of 60 senators can limit debate and stop a filibuster.

coattails effect "Riding the president's coattails into office" occurs in an election when voters also elect representatives or senators of a successful presidential candidate's party.

Cold War The bipolar power struggle between the United States and the Soviet Union that began in the 1950s and ended in the 1990s.

collective action The political action of individuals who unite to influence policy.

Committees of Correspondence Formed in Boston in 1772, the first institutionalized mechanism for communication within and between the colonies and foreign countries.

Common Sense Thomas Paine's pamphlet of January 1776, which helped crystallize the idea of revolution for the colonists.

compact A type of agreement that legally binds two or more parties to enforceable rules.

concurrent powers Powers that are shared by both national and state levels of government.

concurring opinion A written opinion of a justice who agrees with the majority decision of the Court but differs on the reasoning.

conditions of aid National requirement that must be observed.

confederation A league of sovereign states that delegates powers on selected issues to a central government.

conference committees Committees that reconcile differences between the versions of a bill passed by the House and the Senate.

congressional agenda A list of bills to be considered by Congress.

Congressional Budget Office (CBO) A government office created by Congress in 1974 to analyze budgetary figures and make recommendations to Congress and the president.

constitutional courts Courts mentioned in Article III of the Constitution whose judges are life-tenured.

constructionist A view of presidential power espoused by William Howard Taft, who believed that the president could exercise no power unless it could be traced to or implied from an express grant in either the Constitution or an act of Congress.

containment A term coined in 1946 by George Kennan, who believed that Soviet aggression must be "contained by the adroit and vigilant application of counterforce by the United States."

contingency election An election held in the House if no candidate receives the required majority in the electoral college.

continuing resolution A bill passed by Congress and signed by the president which enables the federal government to keep operating under the previous year's appropriations.

cooperative federalism A cooperative system in which solutions for various state and local problems are directed and sometimes funded by both the national and state govern-

ments. The administration of programs is characterized by shared power and shared responsibility.

council of revision A combined body of judges and members of the executive branch having a limited veto over national legislation and an absolute veto over state legislation.

creative federalism An initiative that expanded the concept of the partnership between the national government and the states under President Lyndon Johnson in the 1960s.

criminal cases Cases in which decisions are made regarding whether or not to punish individuals accused of violating the state or federal criminal code.

culture theory A theory that individual preferences "emerge from social interaction in defending or opposing different ways of life."

de facto equality Equality of results, which measures whether real-world obstacles to equal treatment exist. Some examples are: Do people actually live where they want to? Do they work under similar conditions?

de jure equality Equality before the law. It requires that there be no legally mandated obstacles to equal treatment, such as laws that prevent people from voting, living where they want to, or taking advantage of all the rights guaranteed to individuals by the laws of the federal, state, and local governments.

dealignment The moving away from partisanship.

Declaration of Independence A formal proclamation declaring independence, approved and signed on July 4, 1776.

deficit The annual shortfall between the monies that government takes in and spends.

delegated powers Powers that are expressly granted or enumerated in the Constitution and limited in nature.

delegates Congress members who feel bound to follow the wishes of a majority of their constituents; they make frequent efforts to learn the opinions of voters in their state or district.

democracy A system of government in which the people rule, either directly or through elected representatives.

desegregation The elimination of laws and practices mandating separation of the races.

detente An attempt to relax the tensions between the United States and the Soviet Union through limited cooperation.

deviating election Election in which the minority party captures the White House because of short-term intervening forces, and thus a deviation from the expectation that power will remain in the hands of the dominant party.

devolution Reducing the size and authority of the federal government by returning programs to the states.

devolution revolution A trend initiated in the Reagan administration and accelerated by Newt Gingrich as Speaker to send programs and power back to the states with less involvement by the national government.

direct democracy A type of government in which people govern themselves, vote on policies and laws, and live by majority rule.

discretionary spending The spending Congress actually controls; entitlements such as Social Security, Medicare, and Medicaid; 33 percent of all spending.

discrimination Unequal treatment based on race, ethnicity, gender, and other distinctions.

dissenting opinion A written opinion of a justice who disagrees with the holding of the Court.

docket The Supreme Court's agenda of cases to consider.

double jeopardy Being tried twice for the same crime; banned by the Fifth Amendment.

double standard The varying level of intensity by which the Supreme Court considers cases by which it protects civil liberties claims while also deferring to the legislation in cases with economic claims.

dual federalism A system in which each level of power remains supreme in its own jurisdiction, thus keeping the states separate and distinct from the national government.

economic policy Policy aimed at producing a vibrant, healthy, and growing economy.

economic sanctions The use of embargoes and boycotts rather than military force to compel compliance.

elections The institutions that give people the opportunity to participate in public life.

electoral college The group of 538 electors who meet separately in each of their states and the District of Columbia on the first Monday following the second Wednesday in December after a national presidential election. Their majority decision officially elects the president and vice president of the United States.

electoral college system Votes in the national presidential elections are actually indirect votes for a slate of presidential electors pledged to each party's candidate. Each state gets one elector for each of its representatives and senators. The winning slate of electors casts their votes in their state's capital after the public election. In the United States, election of the president and vice president is dependent upon receiving a majority (270) of the votes cast in the electoral college.

en banc Proceedings in which all of the appeals judges in a particular circuit serve as a tribunal.

enrolled act (or **resolution**) The final version of a bill, approved by both chambers of Congress.

entitlements Government-sponsored benefits and cash payments to those who meet eligibility requirements.

equal time rule A requirement that radio and TV stations allow equal time to all candidates for office.

equality A state in which all participants have equal access to the decision-making process, equal opportunity to influence the decisions made, and equal responsibility for those decisions.

equality of opportunity The idea that "people should have equal rights and opportunities to develop their talents," that all people should begin at the same starting point in a race.

equality of result The idea that all forms of inequality, including economic disparities, should be completely eradicated; this may mean giving some people an advantage at the start so that everyone will complete the race at the same point.

excise taxes Charges on the sale or manufacture of products such as cigarettes, alcohol, and gasoline.

exclusionary rule Rule whereby evidence that was gathered by illegal means, and any other evidence gathered as a result, cannot be used in later trials.

executive agreement A government-to-government agreement with essentially the same legal force as a treaty. However, it may be concluded entirely without the knowledge and/or approval of the Senate.

executive branch The branch of the government that executes laws.

Executive Office of the President (EOP) Created in 1939, this office contains all of the staff units that serve to support the president in his administrative duties.

executive privilege The implied or inherent power of the president to withhold information on the ground that to release such information would affect either national security or the president's ability to discharge his official duties.

exit polls Polls that question voters as they leave the voting booth to predict the outcome of an election.

express powers Powers delegated specifically to the national government by the Constitution.

factions According to James Madison in *The Federalist*, no. 10: "A number of citizens, whether amounting to a majority or a minority of the whole, who are united and actuated by some common impulse or passion or . . . interests."

fairness doctrine A policy, now abandoned, that radio and TV stations provide time to all sides in programs of public interest.

faithless elector Member of the electoral college who casts his or her vote for someone other than the state's popular vote winner.

Federal Communications Commission (FCC) A government commission formed to allocate radio and TV frequencies and regulate broadcasting procedures.

federal mandate A direct order from Congress to the states to fulfill.

federal matching funds System under which presidential candidates who raise a certain amount of money in the required way are able to apply for and are given a matching sum of money from the federal government.

Federal Reserve System Created in 1913, it is the nation's principal overseer of monetary policy.

federalism The relationship between the centralized national government and the individual state governments.

Federalists Those in favor of the Constitution, many of whom were nationalists at the Convention.

fighting words Certain expressions that are so volatile that they are deemed to incite injury and are therefore not protected under the First Amendment.

filibuster A technique that allows a senator to speak against a bill, or talk about nothing at all, just to "hold the floor" and prevent the Senate from moving forward with a vote. He or she may yield to other like-minded senators, so that the marathon debate can continue for hours or even days.

First Continental Congress The meeting of fifty-six elected members (from provincial congresses or irregular conventions) that took place in Philadelphia's Carpenter's Hall in 1774. It resulted in a resolution to oppose acts of the British Parliament and a plan of association for the colonies.

foreign aid Small portion of the federal budget that goes to nonmilitary aid abroad, initially to mitigate against Soviet expansion.

foreign policy Policy adopted and actions taken by the U.S. government on behalf of U.S. national interests abroad. The president is this country's chief foreign policy maker.

formal agenda The policies that are actually scheduled for debate and potential adoption by Congress, the president, the Supreme Court, or executive departments and agencies.

formal rules In a bureaucracy, clearly defined procedures governing the execution of all tasks within the jurisdiction of a given agency.

formula grant A grant based on a prescribed legislative formula to determine how money will be distributed to eligible governmental units (states or big cities).

formula/project grant A grant in which competitive grants are awarded but also restricted by use of a formula.

franking privilege The free mailing of newsletters and political brochures to constituents by members of Congress.

free press Media characterized by the open reporting of information without censorship by the government.

free riders Members who do not invest money or time in an interest group but still share in the collective benefits of group action.

freedom A value that suggests that no individual should be within the power or under the control of another.

freedom riders Civil rights activists who traveled throughout the South on buses to test compliance with the Supreme Court's mandate to integrate bus terminals and public facilities accommodating interstate travelers.

frontloading The process by which most party primaries and caucuses are held early in the nomination schedule so that the majority of the delegate support is locked up early.

gender gap A difference in the political opinions of men and women.

general revenue sharing (GRS) A system of the New Federalism program in which money was given to the states with no restrictions on how it could be spent.

generational effect Socialization patterns in which a generation of adults who grew up during a certain decade or period appears to have its own outlook, differentiating itself from the previous age.

gerrymander Any attempt during state redistricting of congressional voting boundaries to create a safe seat for one party.

Gibbons v. Ogden The 1824 decision by Chief Justice John Marshall that gave Congress the power, under the "interstate and commerce" clause, to regulate anything that "affects" interstate commerce.

globalism View in which the U.S. sphere of influence has expanded beyond the western hemisphere to include virtually every corner of the globe where U.S. interests might be affected.

going public Actions taken by presidents to promote themselves and their policies to the American people.

good-character test A requirement that voting applicants wishing to vote get two or more registered voters to vouch for their integrity.

government corporation A semi-independent government agency that administers a business enterprise and takes the form of a business corporation.

grant-in-aid Money paid to states and localities to induce them to implement policies in accordance with federally mandated guidelines.

grass-roots activity The rallying of group members, as well as the public, behind a lobby's cause.

Great Compromise (also called the **Connecticut Compromise**) A plan presented at the Constitutional Convention that upheld the large-state position for the House, its membership based on proportional representation, balanced by the small-state posture of equal representation in the Senate, where each state would have two votes.

gridlock A condition in which major government initiatives are impossible because a closely balanced partisan division in the government structure, accompanied by an unwillingness to work together toward compromise, produces a stalemate.

group maintenance Activities by an interest group designed to affect policy. Includes enrolling new members and providing benefits for them.

Gulf of Tonkin Resolution Resolution passed by Congress that granted President Johnson authority to pursue the war in Vietnam, supposedly based on a naval attack by North Vietnamese ships.

Hatch Act Approved by Congress in 1939 and named for its author, Senator Carl Hatch of New Mexico, a list of political dos and don'ts for federal employees; designed to prevent federal civil servants from using their power or position to engage in political activities to influence elections, thereby creating a nonpartisan, nonpolitical, professionalized bureaucracy.

hate speech Speech or symbolic actions intended to inflict emotional distress, defame, or intimidate people.

hearings Formal proceedings in which a range of people testify on a bill's pros and cons.

heightened scrutiny test A middle-level standard that would force the state to prove more than just the *reasonableness* of a law, though not its *compelling* nature, in order to justify it. For women's rights cases this means proving the important governmental objectives of the law's goals and linking it to the wording of the law.

hierarchy A clear chain of communication and command running from an executive director at the top down through all levels of workers.

hold A request by a senator not to bring a measure up for consideration by the full Senate.

House majority leader The person elected by the majority party caucus who serves as the party's chief strategist and floor spokesperson.

impeachment The process by which government actors can be removed from office for "treason, bribery, or other high crimes and misdemeanors." The House of Representatives first votes on the charges and then the trial takes place in the Senate.

implementation The act of providing the organization and expertise required to put into action any policy that has become law; also refers to the actual execution of a policy.

implied powers Powers not specifically stated in the Constitution but can be inferred from the express powers.

impoundment The president's refusal to spend funds appropriated by Congress.

incorporation The process whereby the protections of the Bill of Rights have been found by the Supreme Court to apply to the states.

incumbents Individuals who currently hold public office.

independent agencies Agencies established to regulate a sector of the nation's economy in the public interest.

independent expenditures Loophole in the campaign finance law involving no limits to funds that are dispersed independently by a group or person in the name of a cause and not coordinated by a candidate.

indirect democracy A type of government in which voters designate a relatively small number of people to represent their interests; those people, or representatives, then meet in a legislative body and make decisions on behalf of the entire citizenry.

inherent powers Powers that do not appear in the Constitution but are assumed because of the nature of government. Also refers to a theory that the Constitution grants authority to the executive, through the injunction in Article II, Section 3, that the president "take care that the Laws be faithfully executed."

initiative A proposal submitted by the public and voted upon during elections.

integration Government efforts to balance the racial composition in schools and public places.

intensity In public opinion, a measure of the depth of feeling associated with a given opinion.

interest groups Formal organizations of people who share a common outlook or social circumstance and who band together in the hope of influencing government policy.

Intolerable Acts A series of punitive measures passed by the British Parliament in the spring of 1774 as a response to the Boston Tea Party.

investigative journalism The uncovering of corruption, scandal, conspiracy, and abuses of power in government and business; differs from standard press coverage in the depth of the coverage sought, the time spent researching the subject, and the shocking findings that often result from such reporting.

iron triangles The informal three-way relationships that develop among key legislative committees, the bureaucracy, and interest groups with a vested interest in the policies created by those committees and agencies.

isolationism A pattern in which the United States fosters economic relations abroad without committing to strategic alliances that might draw the country into a war.

issue advertising Advertisements in a political campaign funded by an interest group advocating a position on an issue but technically not supporting a specific candidate.

issue advocacy The process of campaigning to persuade the public to take a position on an issue.

issue networks Networks composed of political actors in a particular policy area, usually including bureaucrats, congressional staffers, interest groups, think-tank researchers or academic experts, and media participants, all of whom interact regularly on an issue.

issue stage A stage reached by a potential policy when it is framed in terms of a yes-or-no policy option.

Jim Crow laws Laws passed by southern states that separated the races in public places such as railroads, streetcars, schools, and cemeteries.

joint committees Groups of members from both chambers who study broad areas that are of interest to Congress as a whole.

judicial activism An approach in which justices create new policy and decide issues, to the point, some critics charge, of writing their own personal values into law.

judicial restraint An approach in which justices see themselves as appointed rather than elected officials, who should defer to the legislature and uphold a law or political action if at all possible.

judicial review The power of the Supreme Court established in *Marbury v. Madison* to overturn acts of the president, Congress, and the states if those acts violate the Constitution. This power makes the Supreme Court the final interpreter of the Constitution.

judiciary The branch of the government that interprets laws.

"King Caucus" The process of selecting candidates for president in the early nineteenth century in which the members of each party's delegation in Congress did the nominating.

latency In public opinion, feelings that are unspoken, suggesting the potential for an attitude or behavior, but only when the right circumstances occur.

least restrictive means test A free exercise of religion test in which the state was asked to find another way, perhaps through exemptions, to enforce its regulations while still protecting all other religions.

legislative branch The branch of the government that makes laws.

legislative courts Courts designed to provide technical expertise on specific subjects based on Article I of the Constitution.

legislative oversight The power that Congress has to oversee the operation of various federal agencies.

legislative veto A legislative action that allows the president or executive agencies to implement a law subject to the later approval or disapproval of one or both houses of Congress.

***Lemon* test** A test from the Supreme Court case *Lemon v. Kurtzman* in 1971 for determining the permissible level of state aid for church agencies by measuring whether the purpose of the state aid is nonreligious in nature, whether it neither advances or inhibits religion, and whether it results in the excessive entanglement of the church and state.

libel Published material that damages a person's reputation or good name in an untruthful and malicious way. As such, it is not protected by the First Amendment.

limited government A type of government in which the powers of the government are clearly defined and bounded, so that governmental authority cannot intrude in the lives of private citizens.

line item veto The power given to the president to veto a specific provision of a bill involving taxing and spending. Previously the president had to veto an entire bill. Declared unconstitutional by the Supreme Court in 1998.

literacy test A requirement that voting applicants had to demonstrate an understanding of national and state constitutions. Primarily used to prevent blacks from voting in the South.

lobbying The formal, organized attempt to influence legislation, usually through direct contact with legislators or their staff.

lobbyists People paid to pressure members of Congress to further the aims of some interest group.

local party organization The initial point of entry for those seeking involvement in politics as volunteers, organizers, or candidates.

logrolling A temporary political alliance between two policy actors who agree to support each other's policy goals.

machine politics An organizational style of local politics in which party bosses traded jobs, money, and favors for votes and campaign support.

maintaining election Election in which the majority party of the day wins both Congress and the White House, maintaining its control of government.

majority-minority district A congressional district that has been drawn to include so many members of a minority group that the chance of a minority candidate to be elected is greatly improved.

majority opinion A decision of the Supreme Court that represents the agreed-upon compromise judgment of all the justices in the majority.

majority rule A decision-making process in which, when more than half of the voters agree on an issue, the entire group accepts the decision, even those in the minority who voted against it.

mandatory spending Spending that must be allocated by law rather than by appropriations for entitlements like Social Security, Medicare, and Medicaid; 67 percent of the budget.

Marbury v. Madison The 1803 case in which Chief Justice John Marshall established the power of judicial review.

margin of error The measure of possible error in a survey, which means that the number for the *entire population* of voters will fall within a range of plus or minus several points of the number obtained from the small but representative sample of voters.

markup session A session held by a subcommittee to revise a bill.

mass media The various media—newspapers, magazines, radio, television, and the Internet—through which information is transferred from its sources to large numbers of people.

McCulloch v. Maryland The 1819 decision by Chief Justice John Marshall that expanded the interpretation of the "necessary and proper" clause to give Congress broad powers to pass legislation and reaffirmed the national government's power over the states under the supremacy clause.

McGovern-Fraser Commission Democratic party commission that after the 1968 national convention opened up meetings and votes to a large variety of party activists, made primaries rather than caucuses the common means of choosing convention delegates, weakened the power of party leaders, and set up rules to ensure that a wide range of party members could participate fully in all party operations.

means testing The changing of eligibility for entitlement benefits from everyone receiving benefits to only those with earnings and savings below a predetermined level, in an attempt to save money.

midterm elections Elections in which Americans elect members of Congress but not presidents; 2002, 2006, and 2010 are midterm election years.

military-industrial complex What President Eisenhower in 1961 called the growing power and influence resulting from the "conjunction of an immense military establishment and a large arms industry."

minor parties (or **third parties**) Parties in the American system other than the Democrats or Republicans.

minority leader The leader of the minority party in Congress.

minority rights Rights given to those in the minority; based on the idea that tyranny of the majority is a danger to human rights.

Miranda warning A warning that must be recited by police officers to a suspect before questioning: "You have the right to remain silent; anything you say can and will be used against you. You have the right to an attorney. If you cannot afford an attorney, one will be provided for you. Do you understand these rights and are you willing to speak with us?" Established in *Miranda v. Arizona*, 1966.

Monroe Doctrine A doctrine enunciated by President James Monroe in 1823 that proclaimed North and South America to be in the United States sphere of influence, hence out of bounds for European aspirations. It reinforced growing isolationism by promising not to interfere in the internal concerns of European states.

muckraking A word used to describe a style of investigative reporting that uncovered many scandals and abuses.

multiparty system A political system in which five to ten or more parties regularly compete in elections, win seats, and have some chance of gaining power. Promoted by systems with proportional representation and is characteristic of most democratic nations.

national debt The cumulative total of all budget deficits.

national party convention The national meeting of the party every four years to choose the ticket for the presidential election and write the platform for the party.

national party organization Party organization at the national level whose primary tasks include fund raising, distribution of information, and recruitment.

necessary and proper clause A clause in Article I, Section 8, Clause 18, of the Constitution stating that Congress can "make all Laws which shall be necessary and proper for carrying into Execution the foregoing Powers."

New Deal coalition Brought together by Franklin Roosevelt in 1932, a broad electorate made up of the urban working class, most members of the newer ethnic groups, the bulk of American Catholics and Jews, the poor, the South, and liberal intellectuals.

"New Democrat" A conservative Democrat who supports states' rights and a less activist national Government.

New Federalism A program under President Nixon that decentralized power as a response to New Deal centralization.

New Jersey Plan A plan presented to the Constitutional Convention of 1787 designed to create a unicameral legislature with equal representation for all states. Its goal was to protect the interests of the smaller, less populous states.

no incorporation An approach in which the states would be bound only by the dictates of due process contained in the Fourteenth Amendment.

nomination A candidate's "sponsorship" by a political party.

North American Free Trade Agreement (NAFTA) An agreement between the United States, Canada, and Mexico that allows free trade without tariffs and restrictions between those nations.

North Atlantic Treaty Organization (NATO) Charter signed by the United States, Canada, Turkey, and eleven European nations in 1949 agreeing that an armed attack against one or more of them in Europe or North America would be interpreted as an attack against all.

nullification A nineteenth-century theory that upholds that states faced with unacceptable national legislation can declare such laws null and void and refuse to observe them.

Office of Management and Budget (OMB) The unit in the Executive Office of the President whose main responsibilities are to prepare and administer the president's annual budget. It is through the budget process that a president and the OMB can shape policy, since the process determines which departments and agencies grow, get cut, or remain the same as the year before.

omnibus legislation A large bill that combines a number of smaller pieces of legislation.

open primary A system of conducting primary elections in which citizens vote in whichever party's primary they choose.

opinion A written version of the decision of a court.

order A condition in which the structures of a given society and the relationships thereby defined among individuals and classes comprising it are maintained and preserved by the rule of law and police power of the state.

original jurisdiction The authority of a court to be the first to hear a case.

override The two-thirds vote of both houses of Congress required to pass a law over the veto of the president.

oversight Congressional function that involves monitoring the effectiveness of laws by examining the workings of the executive branch.

participation Mass political involvement through voting, campaign work, political protests, civil disobedience, among many others.

party caucus A conference of party members in Congress.

party identification A psychological orientation, or long-term propensity to think positively of and vote regularly for, a particular political party.

party platform The statement of principles and policies; the goals that a party pledges to carry out if voters give it control of the government.

Peace Corps Organization formed by President Kennedy to help with development in the Third World by having American volunteers live and work in needy communities.

peonage A system in which employers advance wages and then require workers to remain on their jobs, in effect enslaving them, until the debt is satisfied.

plea bargains Agreements in which the state presses for either a reduced set of charges or a reduced sentence in return for a guilty plea.

pluralism A system that occurs when those in the minority band together into groups based on particular interests and seek to influence policy by allying with other groups.

plurality opinion Less than a majority vote on an opinion of the Court; does not have the binding legal force of a majority opinion.

pocket veto Presidential refusal to sign or veto a bill that Congress passes in the last ten days of its session; by not being signed, it automatically dies when Congress adjourns.

police powers The powers to regulate the health, morals, public safety, and welfare, which are reserved to the states.

policy elites Members of Congress, the president, Supreme Court justices, cabinet officers, heads of key agencies and departments, leading editorial writers, and influential columnists and commentators.

policy entrepreneurs Leaders who invest in, and who create the conditions for, a potential group to become an actual interest group. Ralph Nader stands as a classic example of a policy entrepreneur.

policy evaluation The required period of monitoring and analysis of federal policies following their implementation.

policy networks Networks characterized by a wide-ranging discussion of options as issues are resolved, conveying a more inclusive and less conspiratorial image of the policy process than *iron triangles* do.

political action committees (PACs) Committees formed as the fund-raising and financial distribution arm of specific interest groups.

political culture A political perspective based on core values, political ideology, culture, and lifestyle.

political ideology A coherent way of viewing politics and government; ideological perspectives include beliefs about the military, the role of government, the proper relation between government and the economy, the value of social welfare programs, and the relative importance for society of liberty and order.

political parties Organizations that exist to allow like-minded members of the population to group together and magnify their individual voices into a focus promoting individual candidates and government action.

political socialization The process by which we learn about the world of politics and develop our political beliefs.

political violence Violent action motivated primarily by political aims and intended to have a political impact.

poll tax A fee that had to be paid before one could vote; was used to prevent African Americans from voting; now unconstitutional.

pork-barrel legislation Policies and programs designed to create special benefits for a member's district, such as bridges, highways, dams, and military installations, all of which translate into jobs and money for the local economy and improve reelection chances for the incumbent.

potential groups Interest groups that could come into being under the right circumstances; as yet, they have no substantive form and may never have one, but they cannot be discounted by political participants.

poverty level The federally determined income below which a family of four is considered poor.

precedents Previously decided court cases on an issue similar to the one being considered.

President of the Senate The vice president of the United States.

president pro tempore The majority party member with the longest continuous service in the Senate; serves as the chief presiding officer in the absence of the vice president.

primary election A pre-election that allows all members of a party, not just its leadership, to select the party's candidate for the general election in the fall.

primary system The system of nominating candidates in which voters in the state make the choice by casting ballots.

prior restraint An action in which the government seeks to ban the publication of controversial material by the press before it is published; censorship.

privatization The turning over of public responsibilities to privately owned and operated enterprises for regulation and for providing goods and services.

probable cause A reasonable belief that a crime has been, is being, or is about to be committed. In cases of searches, there must also be a belief that evidence of that crime may be located in a particular place. Police must establish this to a judge to secure a search warrant or retroactively justify a search that has already taken place.

progressive taxes System of taxation in which those who make more money are taxed at a higher rate. An example is the income tax.

project grant A grant not based on a formula, but distributed for specific purposes after a fairly competitive application and approval process.

proportional representation A system of representation popular in Europe whereby the number of seats in the legislature is based on the proportion of the vote received in the election.

proposal The first stage of the constitutional amendment process, in which a change is proposed.

protest Expression of dissatisfaction; may take the form of demonstrations, letters to newspapers or public officials, or simple "opting out" of the system by failing to vote or participate in any other way.

protest march March in which people walk down a main street carrying signs, singing freedom songs, and chanting slogans.

public agenda The set of topics that are a source of concern for policy elites, the general public, or both.

public interest groups Groups that focus not on the immediate economic livelihood of their members, but on achieving a broad set of goals that represent their members' vision of the collective good. Examples include the National Taxpayers Union, the League of Women Voters, and Common Cause.

public opinion The collective expression of attitudes about the prominent issues and actors of the day.

public policies The decisions, actions, and commitments of government.

quota programs Programs that guarantee a certain percentage of admissions, new hires, or promotions to members of minority groups.

random sample A strategy required for a valid poll whereby every member of the population has an equal chance of appearing in the sample.

ratify An act of approval of proposed constitutional amendments by the states; the second step of the amendment process.

realigning election Election characterized by massive shifts in partisan identification, as in 1932 with the New Deal coalition.

realignment A shift in fundamental party identification and loyalty caused by significant historical events or national crises.

reapportionment A process of redrawing voting district lines from time to time and adjusting the number of representatives allotted each state.

recruitment The process through which parties look for effective, popular candidates to help them win votes and offices.

red tape The excessive number of rules and regulations that government employees must follow.

redistricting The redrawing of boundary lines of voting districts in accordance with census data or sometimes by order of the courts.

referendum A proposal submitted by a state legislature to the public for a popular vote, often focusing on whether a state should spend money in a certain way.

regressive taxes System of taxation in which taxes take a higher fraction of the income of lower income taxpayers; examples are taxes on gasoline, cigarettes, and alcohol.

regulation The making of rules by an administrative body that must clarify and interpret legislation, its enforcement, and the adjudication of disputes about it.

regulatory policy Policy that involves the use of police powers by the federal government to supervise the conduct of individuals, businesses, and other governmental agencies.

representative democracy A system of government in which the voters select representatives to make decisions for them.

representative sample A sample that includes all the significant characteristics of the total population.

republic A system of government that allows indirect representation of the popular will.

reserved powers Powers not assigned by the Constitution to the national government but left to the states or to the people, according to the Tenth Amendment.

retrospective voting A particularly powerful form of issue voting in which voters look back over the last term or two to judge how well an incumbent or the "in party" has performed in office.

Revolution of 1800 The first election in the world in which one party (the Federalist party of John Adams) willingly gave up power because of a lost election to another party (the Republican party of Thomas Jefferson) without bloodshed.

rider An amendment to a bill in the Senate that is totally unrelated to the subject of the bill but is attached to a popular measure in the hopes that it too will pass.

right of rebuttal The right to refute the allegations presented on a radio or TV station, free of charge, within a reasonable time.

right to privacy The right to have the government stay out of the personal lives of its citizens.

rule of four A means of determining which cases will be heard by the Supreme Court; at least four justices must vote to hear a case and grant the petition for a writ of certiorari for the case to be put on the Court's docket.

rules The decisions made by the House Rules Committee and voted on by the full House to determine the flow of legislation—when a bill will be discussed, for how long, and whether amendments can be offered.

salience In public opinion, the extent to which people see an issue as having a clear impact on their own lives.

sampling bias A bias in a survey whereby a particular set of people in the population at large is more or less likely to appear in the final sample than other sets of people.

schemas Intellectual frameworks for evaluating the world.

Second Continental Congress A meeting convened on May 10, 1775, with all thirteen colonies represented. The purpose of the Congress was to decide whether or not to sever bonds with England and declare independence.

secular regulation rule Rule that holds that there is no constitutional right to exemption on free exercise grounds from laws dealing with nonreligious matters.

select committees (or **special committees**) Temporary congressional committees that conduct investigations or study specific problems or crises.

selective incorporation An incorporation standard in which some portions of the Bill of Rights, but not all, were made part of the Fourteenth Amendment's due process clause, and thus guaranteed against invasion by the states.

Senate majority leader A senator selected by the majority party whose functions are similar to those of the speaker of the House.

senatorial courtesy A procedure in which a president submits the names of judicial nominees to senators from the same political party who are also from the nominee's home state for their approval prior to formal nomination.

seniority An informal, unwritten rule of Congress that more senior members (those who have served longer than others) are appointed to committees and as chairpersons of committees. This "rule" is being diluted in the House as other systems are developed for committee appointments.

separation of powers State in which the powers of the government are divided among the three branches: executive, legislative, and judicial.

sexism Prejudice against the female gender.

single-member districts Districts in which a seat goes to the candidate with the most votes. In this system, small parties, say one that wins 10 percent in every district across the nation, do not get a single seat in the legislature.

sit-in A protest technique in which protesters refuse to leave an area.

slander Speech that is untruthful, malicious, or damaging to a person's reputation or good name and thus not protected by the free speech clause of the First Amendment.

social contract theorists A group of European philosophers who reasoned that the most effective way to create the best government was to understand human nature in a state prior to government.

social welfare policy Policy that uses positive incentives (cash assistance, stipends, entitlements, grants, etc.) to promote or encourage basic social and economic fairness.

socialization The process by which people learn to conform to their society's norms and values.

soft money Campaign contributions directed to advancing the interests of a political party or an issue in general, rather than a specific candidate.

solicitor general The third-ranking official in the Justice Department, appointed by the president and charged with representing the U.S. government before the Supreme Court.

sound bite A very brief statement, usually a snippet from a speech, that conveys the essence of a longer statement and can be inserted into a news story.

sovereignty The independence and self-government of a political entity.

Speaker of the House The only presiding officer of the House mentioned in the Constitution. The leader of the majority party in Congress and third in line for the presidency.

special revenue sharing A system of the New Federalism program in which groups of categorical grants-in-aid in related policy areas, such as crime control or health care, are consolidated into a single block grant.

specialization A principle that in a bureaucracy, specific tasks should be delegated to individuals whose training and experience give them the expertise to execute them. Also refers to a norm used to push legislation through Congress in which members who lack expertise in a particular policy area defer to policy specialists with more knowledge.

spin The interpretation placed on the news by those presenting it.

split-ticket ballots Ballots on which people vote for candidates from more than one party.

spoils system A system in which government jobs and contracts are awarded on the basis of party loyalty rather than social or economic status or relevant experience.

stability A condition that is resistant to sudden change or overthrow.

Stamp Act A British act of 1765 that required that revenue stamps be placed on all printed matter and legal documents, making it felt in every aspect of commercial life in the colonies.

standing committees Permanent congressional committees that determine whether proposed legislation should be sent to the entire chamber for consideration.

stare decisis A doctrine meaning "let the decision stand," or that judges deciding a case should adhere if at all possible to previously decided cases that are similar to the one under consideration.

state action Action that is taken by state officials or sanctioned by state law.

state party organizations Party organizations at the state level; they organize elections and provide the electoral college votes needed to win the presidency; they also supervise the various functions vital to state parties, such as fund raising, identifying potential candidates, providing election services, offering advice on reapportionment matters, and developing campaign strategies.

states' rights Those rights that have neither been granted to the national government nor forbidden to the states by the U.S. Constitution.

statutory construction The power of the Supreme Court to interpret or reinterpret a federal or state law.

stewardship An approach to presidential power that was articulated by Theodore Roosevelt and based on the presidencies of Lincoln and Jackson, who believed that the president had a moral duty to serve popular interests and did not need specific constitutional or legal authorization to take action.

straight-party ticket Ballots on which people vote for only one party.

Strategic Arms Limitation Treaty (SALT) Treaty signed by the United States (under President Nixon) and the Soviet Union to limit various classes of nuclear weapons.

straw poll A nonscientific method of measuring public opinion.

strict scrutiny test Test of laws that discriminate on the basis of a characteristic that is "immutable (or unchangeable) by birth," such as race or nationality; in such cases, the burden shifts from the plaintiff to the state, forcing the government to show the compelling reasons for the law.

subcommittees The subgroups of congressional committees charged with initially dealing with legislation before the entire committee considers it.

subsequent punishment Laws that would punish someone for an action after it has taken place. For example, laws such as those banning libel and obscenity because they are harmful to reputations or public sensibilities punish writers, editors, and publishers after an item appears in print.

suffrage The right to vote.

Sugar Act A British act of 1764 that levied a three-penny-per-gallon tax on molasses and other goods imported into the colonies.

superdelegates Delegates to the Democratic National Convention who are not bound to vote for any particular candidate; usually prominent members of the party or elected officials.

supermajority A majority vote required for constitutional amendments; consists of more than a simple majority of 50 percent plus one.

superpower The disproportionate power—economic and military—that distinguished the United States and the Soviet Union from all other countries in the postwar era.

supremacy clause A clause in Article IV of the Constitution holding that in any conflict between federal laws and treaties and state laws, the will of the national government always prevails.

symbolic speech Some actions, such as burning the American flag, that take the place of speech because they communicate a message.

tariffs The imposition of import taxes on foreign goods in an attempt to protect a nation's industry and/or labor.

task force An informal procedure used by Congress to get groups of legislators together to draft legislation and negotiate strategy for passing a bill.

tax expenditures Tax deductions that reduce the amount of income that is subject to taxes like home mortgages, business equipment, or business-related entertainment.

term limits A legislated limit on the amount of time a political figure can serve in office.

test of reasonableness Test in court cases of what reasonable people would agree to be constitutional because the law has a rational basis for its existence.

three-fifths compromise A compromise that stated that the apportionment of representatives by state should be determined "by adding to the whole number of free persons . . . three-fifths of all other persons" (Article I, Section 2); meaning that it would take five slaves to equal three free people when counting the population for representation and taxation purposes.

total incorporation An approach arguing that the protections in the Bill of Rights were so fundamental that all of them should be applied to the states by absorbing them into the due process clause of the Fourteenth Amendment.

town meeting A form of governance dating back to the 1700s in which town business is transacted by the consent of a majority of eligible citizens, all of whom have an equal opportunity to express their views and cast their votes at an annual meeting.

Townshend Revenue Acts A series of taxes imposed by the British Parliament in 1767 on glass, lead, tea, and paper imported into the colonies.

tracking polls Polls used by the media to track the support levels for candidates over time.

treaties Formal international agreements between sovereign states.

triad of powers Three constitutional provisions—the interstate commerce clause, the general welfare clause, and the Tenth Amendment—that help to continually shift the balance of power between the national and state governments.

trial court The point of original entry in the legal system, with a single judge and at times a jury deciding matters of both fact and law in a case.

triggering mechanism A critical development that converts a routine problem into a widely shared, negative public response.

trustees Congress members who feel authorized to use their best judgment in considering legislation.

Two Congresses A term denoting the differing views the public has toward Congress as a whole and their representative individual, noting that the opinions are more positive for the individual representative than for the body as a whole.

unanimous consent agreement The process by which the normal rules of Congress are waived unless a single member disagrees.

unicameral legislature A legislative system consisting of one chamber.

U.S. courts of appeals The middle appeals level of judicial review beyond the district courts; in 1999, consisted of 167 judges in 13 courts, 12 of which are geographically based.

U.S. district courts The trial courts serving as the original point of entry for almost all federal cases.

universal suffrage The requirement that everyone must have the right to vote.

veto Presidential power to forbid or prevent an action of Congress.

vice president The second-highest elected official in the United States.

Virginia Plan A plan presented to the Constitutional Convention; favored by the delegates from the bigger states.

voter turnout The percentage of eligible voters who actually show up and vote on election day.

War Powers Resolution A highly controversial measure passed over President Nixon's veto that stipulated that presidential commitments of U.S. military forces cannot extend beyond sixty days without specific congressional authorization.

Warsaw Pact Treaty signed by the Soviet Union and the Eastern bloc in Europe agreeing to mutual defense, in reaction to NATO.

welfare state A social system whereby the government assumes primary responsibility for the welfare of citizens.

whip Congress members charged with counting prospective votes on various issues and making certain that members have the information they need for floor action.

winner-take-all system A system in which the winner of the primary or electoral college vote gets all of the state's convention or electoral college delegates.

workfare The requirement that recipients of welfare programs like AFDC work on public works if they are unable to gain employment elsewhere.

World Trade Organization (WTO) International economic organization that monitors trade and ensures "fair" practices, such as no tariffs.

writ of certiorari A Latin term meaning "to be made more certain"; this is a writ that enables the Court to accept cases for review only if there are "special and important reasons therefore."

yellow journalism Brash, colorful, well-illustrated, often lurid and sensationalized organs of half-truth, innuendo, and sometimes outright lies, usually associated with the big-city daily newspapers of Joseph Pulitzer and William Randolph Hearst.

NOTES

CHAPTER 1

1. The case study is based on Rene Sanchez, "Honoring Chavez and Hispanic Clout," *Washington Post,* April 24, 2000, p. A3; http://ufw.org.

2. Eric Schmitt, "Census Shows Bid Gain for Mexican-American," *New York Times,* May 10, 2001, p. A22; Eric Schmitt, "Hispanic Voter Is Vivid in Parties' Crystal Ball," *New York Times,* April 5, 2001, p. A14; D'Vera Cohn, "Shifting Portrait of U.S. Hispanics," *The Washington Post,* May 10, 2001, p. A1, 20.

3. Kenneth Prewitt, "Demography, Diversity, and Democracy," *The Brookings Review,* Winter 2002, Vol. 20, No. 1, p. 6–9. In same issue see Jonathan Rauch, "Diversity in a New America," p. 4–5.

4. Congressional Record-House, February 21, 1990, p. H392–95.

5. See "Freedom in the World 2001–2002, Selected Data from Freedom House's Annual Global Survey of Political Rights and Civil Liberties." www.freedomhouse.org/research/survey2002.htm; Douglas Jehl, "Democracy's Uneasy Steps in Islam's World," *New York Times,* November 23, 2001, p. A1, 10; Barbara Crossette, "As Democracies Spread, Islam World Hesitates," *New York Times,* December 23, 2001, p. A15.

6. Alexis de Tocqueville, *Democracy in America* (first published 1835–40). Available in many editions. See also "The 2500 Anniversary of Democracy: Lessons of Athenian Democracy," *PS* (September 1993): p. 475–93.

7. See Thomas E. Cronin, *Direct Democracy: The Politics of Initiative, Referendum, and Recall* (Cambridge, Mass.: Harvard University Press, 1989).

8. From a letter from John Adams to John Taylor of Caroline, 1814, cited in Richard Hofstadter, *The American Political Tradition and the Men Who Made It* (New York: Vintage Books, 1948), p. 13.

9. Sheldon Wolin, "Democracy: Electoral and Athenian," *PS* (September 1993): p. 475–7.

10. Quoted in J. Roland Pennock, *Democratic Political Theory* (Princeton, N.J.: Princeton University Press, 1979), p. 20.

11. Isaiah Berlin, *Two Concepts of Liberty* (Oxford: Clarendon Press, 1958).

12. Sidney Verba and Gary R. Orren, *Equality in America: The View from the Top* (Cambridge, Mass.: Harvard University Press, 1985), p. 5; Robert Dahl, *Democracy and Its Critics* (New Haven, Conn.: Yale University Press, 1989). Friedrich A. Hayek, *The Constitution of Liberty* (Chicago: University of Chicago Press, 1960), pp. 103–17; Carole Pateman, *Participation and Democratic Theory* (Cambridge, Mass.: Cambridge University Press, 1970).

13. E. E. Schattschneider, *Two Hundred Million Americans in Search of a Government* (Hillsdale, Ill.: Dryden Press, 1969), p. 27.

14. Quoted in J. D. Richardson, ed., *Messages and Papers of the Presidents, 1789–1902,* 20 vols. (Washington, D.C., 1917), 1:309–12; Joshua Cohen and Joel Rogers, *On Democracy* (Harmondsworth, Middlesex: Penguin, 1983), pp. 48–73.

15. See Adam Michnik, "After the Revolution," *New Republic,* July 2, 1990, p. 28.

CHAPTER 2

1. William Rehnquist, *All the Laws But One: Civil Liberties in Wartime,* (New York: Alfred A. Knopf, 1998), passim; "Ashcroft's Counterterrorism Requests," *CQ Weekly,* September 29, 2001, p. 2264; Michael Kramer, "Ashcroft Takes Aim, Shoots Self in Foot," *New York Daily News;* William Safire, "Military Tribunals Modified," *New York Times,* March 21, 2001, p. A 37; Carl Schoettler, "A Time Liberties Weren't Priority," *The Baltimore Sun.*

2. See Gordon S. Wood, "The Origins of the Constitution," *This Constitution* 15 (Summer 1987): 4; Gordon S. Wood, "The Intellectual Origins of the American Constitution," *National Forum* 4 (Fall 1984): 5–8.

3. See George Brown Tindall, *America: A Narrative History* (New York: Norton, 1988), pp. 58–62; Alfred H. Kelly and Winfred A. Harbison, *The American Constitution: Its Origin and Development* (New York: Norton, 1976), pp. 7–16.

4. Quoted in Tindall, *America,* p. 168; Ronald W. Clark, *Benjamin Franklin: A Biography* (New York: Random House, 1983), pp. 107–8.

5. Quoted in Kelly and Harbison, *American Constitution,* p. 69; Tindall, *America,* pp. 194–95. See also Philip B. Kurland and Ralph Lerner, *The Founders Constitution* (Chicago: University of Chicago Press, 1987).

6. Brinkley, *Unfinished Nation,* p. 108.

7. James MacGregor Burns, *The Vineyard of Liberty* (New York: Vintage Books, 1983), p. 83.

8. Quoted in Tindall, *America,* pp. 206–7.

9. Ibid., pp. 207–8.

10. Brinkley, *Unfinished Nation,* p. 133.

11. For more on the motivations of the framers, see Richard B. Bernstein, with Kym S. Rice, *Are We to Be a Nation? The Making of the Constitution* (Cambridge, Mass.: Harvard University Press, 1987), passim.

12. Quoted in Bowen, *Miracle at Philadelphia,* p. 12.

13. The number of slaves at the time is taken from the notes of Convention delegate Charles Cotesworth Pinckney, July 10, 1787, found in *Supplement to Max Farrand's "The Records of the Federal Convention of 1787,"* ed. James H. Hutson (New Haven, Conn.: Yale University Press, 1987), p. 160.

14. Christopher Collier and James Lincoln Collier, *Decision in Philadelphia: The Constitutional Convention of 1787* (New York: Random House, 1986), p. 16.

15. Ibid., p. 94.

16. For more on this possible motivation, see John E. O'Connor, *William Paterson, Lawyer and Statesman, 1745–1806* (New Brunswick, N.J.: Rutgers University Press, 1979).

17. Quoted in *Supplement to Farrand's "Records,"* ed. Hutson, p. 305.

18. Robert A. Goldwin, "Why Blacks, Women and Jews Are Not Mentioned in the Constitution," *Commentary,* May 1987, p. 29.

19. Bowen, *Miracle at Philadelphia,* pp. 55–56; see also Collier and Collier, *Decision in Philadelphia,* chaps. 18 and 19.

20. Quoted in Bowen, *Miracle at Philadelphia,* p. 263.

21. George Washington, September 17, 1787, in *Supplement to Farrand's "Records,"* ed. Hutson, p. 276.

22. Collier and Collier, *Decision in Philadelphia,* pp. 255–56.

23. Alexander Hamilton, James Madison, and John Jay, *The Federalist Papers* (New York: New American Library, 1961), no. 51, p. 322.

24. David Ivanovich, "Senators Seek Enron–White House Communications," *Houston Chronicle,* March 22, 2002.

25. *Youngstown Sheet and Tube v. Sawyer,* 343 U.S. 579, p. 635 (1952).

26. Richard E. Neustadt, *Presidential Power: The Politics of Leadership from FDR to Carter* (New York: Wiley, 1980), p. 26.

27. Hamilton, Madison, and Jay, *Federalist Papers,* no. 10, p. 78.

28. Quoted in Charles L. Mee, Jr., *The Genius of the People* (New York: Harper & Row, 1987), p. 300.

29. Ibid., 299.

30. Quoted in Bowen, *Miracle at Philadelphia,* p. 310.

31. Herbert Mitgang, "Handwritten Draft of a Bill of Rights Found," *New York Times,* July 29, 1987, p. 1.

32. *Dillon v. Gloss,* 256 U.S. 368 (1921). The Court refused to rule in 1939 in a case involving time limits contained in a child labor amendment, saying that it was a "political question," or a matter for the political bodies to decide. *Coleman v. Miller,* 307 U.S. 433 (1939). Since 1939 the Supreme Court has refused to rule on such time limits.

33. The convention process was used because legislators in "dry" states were expected to be pressured by voters to vote against ratification. For more on the Eighteenth and Twenty-first Amendments and the entire amendment process, see Richard B. Bernstein, with Jerome Agel, *Amending America: If We Love the Constitution So Much, Why Do We Keep Trying to Change It?* (New York: Random House, Times Books, 1993), pp. 170–77, passim.

34. *Immigration and Naturalization Service v. Chadha,* 462 U.S. 919, p. 978 (1982).

35. Garry Wills, *Lincoln at Gettysburg: The Words that Remade America,* (New York: Simon and Schuster, 1992), p. 120.

CHAPTER 3

1. Eric Pooley, "Mayor of the World," *Time,* December 31, 2001, pp. 40–56; Dan Barry, "A Man More than a Mayor," *New York Times,* December 31, 2001, p. 1.

2. Alexander Hamilton, James Madison, and John Jay, *The Federalist Papers* (New York: New American Library, 1961), no. 10, p. 83. *The Federalist,* no. 10, is reprinted in the Appendix.

3. Richard A. Knox, "Health Reform Fizzling in States," *Boston Globe,* July 17, 1994, pp. 1, 16.

4. Melanie Markley and Karen Masterson, "Education Act Modeled after Texas Reforms," *The Houston Chronicle,* December 19, 2001.

5. *New State Ice Co. v. Liebmann,* 285 U.S. 262 (1932), p. 311.

6. *Heart of Atlanta Motel v. United States,* 379 U.S. 241 (1964); *Katzenbach v. McClung,* 379 U.S. 294 (1964).

7. In June 1987 the Supreme Court upheld the law, with Chief Justice William H. Rehnquist ruling that Congress has the power to act "indirectly under its spending power to encourage uniformity in the States' drinking ages. *South Dakota v. Dole,* 483 U.S. 203 (1987).

8. *United States v. E. C. Knight,* 156 U.S. 1 (1895); *Hammer v. Dagenhart,* 247 U.S. 251 (1918); *Carter v. Carter Coal,* 298 U.S. 238 (1936).

9. *United States v. Darby Lumber Co.,* 312 U.S. 100 (1941).

10. *Printz v. United States* and *Mack v. United States,* 117 S.Ct. 2635 (1997); "Symposium: American Federalism Today," in *Rockefeller Institute Bulletin* (1996): 1–23.

11. See *Pennsylvania v. Nelson,* 350 U.S. 497 (1956).

12. Tom Gorman, "Nev. Governor Faces Long Odds to Block Yucca Nuclear Dump," *Los Angeles Times,* April 19, 2002; Wayne Parry, "Detainees' Names to Remain Secret," *The Philadelphia Inquirer,* April 19, 2002, p. A15.

13. Brad Knickerbocker, "Assisted Suicide Movement Gets a Boost," *Christian Science Monitor,* April 19, 2002.

14. *McCulloch v. Maryland,* 4 Wheaton 316 (1819).

15. *Gibbons v. Ogden,* 9 Wheaton 1 (1824), p. 195.

16. *United States v. E. C. Knight Co.,* 156 U.S. 1 (1895).

17. *Hammer v. Dagenhart,* 247 U.S. 251 (1919), p. 274.

18. *Schechter Poultry Corp. v. United States,* 295 U.S. 495 (1935); *Carter v. Carter Coal Co.,* 298 U.S. 238 (1936); *United States v. Butler,* 297 U.S. 1 (1936)

19. *National Labor Relations Board v. Jones and Laughlin Steel Corp.,* 301 U.S. 1 (1937); and see *N.L.R.B. v. Fruehauf Trailer Co.,* 801 U.S. 1 (1937) and *N.L.R.B. v. Friedman-Harry Marks Clothing Co.,* 301 U.S. 58 (1937).

20. *United States v. Darby Lumber Co.,* 312 U.S. 100 (1941), p. 124.

21. For the Constitutional theory here, see *Marshall E. Dimock, Modern Politics and Administration: A study of the Creative State* (New York: American Book, 1937), pp. 54–55.

22. *National League of Cities v. Usery,* 426 U.S. 833 (1976); *Garcia v. San Antonio Metropolitan Transit Authority,* 469 U.S. 528 (1985); *South Carolina v. Baker,* 485 U.S. 505 (1988).

23. *Powell v. Alabama,* 287 U.S. 45 (1932).

24. *Brown v. Board of Education of Topeka,* 347 U.S. 483 (1954).

25. *Reynolds v. Sims,* 377 U.S. 533 (1964).

26. Tamar Lewin, "States Slow to Take U.S. Aid to Teach Sexual Abstinence," *New York Times,* May 8, 1997, p. 1.

27. See *United States v. Butler,* 297 U.S. 1 (1936); *Steward Machine Co. v. Davis,* 301 U.S. 548 (1937); *Wickard v. Filburn,* 317 U.S. 111 (1941).

28. Advisory Commission on Intergovernmental Relations (ACIR), *Characteristics of Federal Grant-in-Aid Programs to State and Local Governments: Grants Funded FY 1995* (Washington, D.C.: ACIR, 1996), pp. 1–2.

29. Ibid., p. 2.

30. Lawrence Mishel, "Changes in Federal Aid to State and Local Governments, as Proposed in the Bush Administration FY2002 Budget,"

Economic Policy Institute Briefing Paper, May 2001; and ———, "$20 Billion Anti-Terror Package Is on Bush's Desk," *St. Louis Post Dispatch,* December 21, 2001.

31. See http://www.cfda.gov/public/browse_by_typast.asp, last consulted May 3, 2002; see also *Advisory Commission on Intergovernmental Relations (ACIR), Characteristics of Federal Grant-in-Aid Programs to State and Local Governments: Grants Funded FY 1995* (Washington, D.C.: ACIR, 1996), p. 2.

32. Ibid., pp. 22–42.

33. Calculations from http://www.cfda.gov/public/browse by typast.asp and Ibid., p. 14.

34. Ibid.

35. "Federal Spending on the Elderly and Children," May 3, 2002; see http://www.cbo.gov.

36. John Kincaid, "De Facto Devolution and Urban Defunding: The Priority of Persons Over Places," *Journal of Urban Affairs,* Volume 21, Number 2, (1999) pp. 135–167, at p. 163.

37. ABC Nightly News, "American Agenda," October 27, 1993.

38. Senator Dick Kempthorne, "Getting Control over Unfunded Mandates," in "Symposium: American Federalism Today," p. 39.

39. Richard P. Nathan, "The 'Devolution Revolution': An Overview," in ibid., p. 12.

40. ACIR, "Reconsidering Old Mandates," in ibid., pp. 43–44.

41. David B. Walker, *Toward a Functioning Federalism* (Cambridge, Mass.: Winthrop, 1981), pp. 68, 79.

42. John E. Schwarz, *America's Hidden Success: A Reassessment of Public Policy from Kennedy to Reagan* (New York: Norton, 1988), pp. 17–71.

43. Jeffrey Pressman and Aaron Wildavsky, *Implementation* (Berkeley: University of California Press, 1973).

44. See Schwarz, *America's Hidden Success;* Allen Matusow, *The Unraveling of America: A History of Liberalism in the 1960s* (New York: Harper & Row, 1984).

45. Nathan, "'Devolution Revolution,'" pp. 8–9.

46. Ronald Reagan, Inaugural Address, January 20, 1981, in *A Documentary History of the United States,* ed. Richard D. Heffner (New York: Mentor Books, 1991), pp. 398–401.

47. Ronald Reagan, speech to Congress, February 18, 1981, reprinted in *Congressional Quarterly,* February 21, 1981, pp. 15ff, p. 16.

48. Marshall Kaplan and Sue O'Brien, *The Governors and the New Federalism* (Boulder, Colo.: Westview Press, 1991), p. 2.

49. Michael de Courcy Hinds, "80's Leave States and Cities in Need," *New York Times,* December 30, 1990, pp. 1, 16.

50. ACIR, Federal Grant-in-Aid Programs, p. 14.

51. Walker, *Toward a Functioning Federalism,* p. 114.

52. Peter Edelman, "The Worst Thing Bill Clinton Has Done," *Atlantic Monthly,* March 1997, p. 43; Richard P. Nathan, "'Devolution Revolution',," p. 12.

53. Alison Mitchell, "Wellstone Death Brings New Focus to Senate Battles," *New York Times,* October 27, 1997, p. 1; Ron Eckstein, "Federalism Bills Unify Usual Foes," *Legal Times,* October 18, 1999.

54. *New York v. United States,* 112 S. Ct. 2408, 2435 (1992). This entire discussion of the Court's recent stance on federalism benefited from Tinsley Yarbrough, "The Rehnquist Court and the 'Double Standard'," paper presented at the

annual meeting of the Southern Political Science Association, Norfolk, Va., November 6–8, 1997.

55. *United States v. Lopez,* 131 L. Ed. 2d 626 (1995).

56. *U.S. Term Limits v. Thornton,* 115 S. Ct. 1842 (1995).

57. *Seminole Tribe v. Florida,* 134 L. Ed. 2d 252 (1996).

58. *Printz v. United States,* 117 S. Ct. 2635 (1997), p. 2638.

59. *Reno v. Condon,* 528 US 141 (2000)

60. Herman Schwartz, "Supreme Court: Assault on Federalism Swipes at Women," *Los Angeles Times,* May 21, 2000. Joan Biskupic, "Ban on Guns Near Schools Is Rejected," *Washington Post,* April 27, 1995, p. 1; Linda Greenhouse, "Justices Step in as Federalism's Referee," *New York Times,* April 28, 1995, p. 1; Nina Burleigh, "A Gun Ban Is Shot Down," *Newsweek,* May 8, 1995, p. 85; George Will, "Rethinking 1937," *Newsweek,* May 15, 1995, p. 70.

61. Both quoted in Adam Clymer, "Switching Sides on States' Rights," *New York Times,* June 1, 1997, pp. E1, E6.

CHAPTER 4

1. Based on Diane Dwyre and Victoria A. Farrar-Myers. *Legislative Labyrinth: Congress and Campaign Finance Reform* (Washington, D.C: Congressional Quarterly, 2001); Alison Mitchell, "Sponsors Thwart Moves to Scuttle Soft-Money Bill," *New York Times,* February 14, 2002, p. 1: Alison Mitchell, "Campaign Finance Bill Wins Final Approval in Congress and Bush Says He'll Sign It," *New York Times,* March 21, 2002, p. 1.

2. See Morris P. Fiorina, *Congress: Keystone of the Washington Establishment* (New Haven, Conn.: Yale University Press, 1977).

3. On comparisons between the House and the Senate, see Ross K. Baker, *House and Senate,* 2d ed. (New York: Norton, 1995).

4. See *How Congress Works* (Washington, D.C.: Congressional Quarterly Press, 1994).

5. See *The Federalist,* nos. 17, 39, and 45, in Alexander Hamilton, James Madison, and John Jay, *The Federalist Papers* (New York: New American Library, 1961).

6. *Reno v. American Civil Liberties Union,* 117 S.Ct. 2329 (1997).

7. *Clinton v. New York,* 66 U. S. L. W. 4543 (1998).

8. *Dickerson v. United States,* 530 U.S. 428 (2000).

9. See Glenn R. Simpson, "Of the Rich, by the Rich, for the Rich: Will the Millionaires Turn Congress into a Plutocracy?" *Washington Post,* April 17, 1994, p. C4. and compare with, Allan Freedman, "Lawyers Take a Back Seat in the 105th Congress," *Congressional Quarterly Weekly Report,* January 4, 1997, p. 29.

10. See Hannah Fenichel Pitkin, *The Concept of Representation* (Berkeley: University of California Press, 1967).

11. Donna Cassata, "Freshman Class Boasts Résumés to Back Up 'Outsider' Image," *Congressional Quarterly,* November 12, 1994, pp. 9–12.

12. Gary C. Jacobson, *The Politics of Congressional Elections* (New York: HarperCollins, 1992), p.

13. Elaine R. Jones, "In Peril: Black Lawmakers," *New York Times,* September 11, 1994, p. E19; Ronald Smothers, "Fair Play or Racial Gerrymandering? Justices Study a 'Serpentine' District," *New York Times,* April 16, 1993, p. B12.

14. *Shaw v. Reno,* 509 U.S. 630 (1993), p. 637.

15. *Miller v. Johnson,* 132 L.Ed. 2d 762 (1995).

16. *Abrams v. Johnson,* 117 S.Ct. (1997).

17. "Race and Redistricting," *Washington Post,* June 23, 1997, p. A18; Roger H. Davidson and Walter J. Oleszek, *Congress and Its Members,* 8th ed. (Washington, D.C.: Congressional Quarterly Press, 2002), p. 55.

18. *Hunt v. Cromartie,* 143 L.Ed. 2d 791 (1999).

19. David E. Rosenbaum, "Fight Over Political Map Centers on Race," *New York Times,* Feb. 21, 2002. p. A18.

20. Charles Clapp, *The Congressman: His Job as He Sees It* (Washington, D.C.: Brookings Institution, 1963); Roger H. Davidson, *The Role of the Congressman* (Indianapolis, Ind.: Bobbs-Merrill, 1969).

21. John F. Kennedy, *Profiles in Courage* (New York: Harper & Row, 1956).

22. Davidson and Oleszek, *Congress and Its Members,* pp. 62; Cassata, "Freshman Class," p. 3237.

23. See David Mayhew, *Congress: The Electoral Connection* (New Haven, Conn.: Yale University Press, 1974).

24. For more on casework and Congress, see John R. Johannes, *To Serve the People: Congress and Constituency Review* (Lincoln: University of Nebraska Press, 1984); Morris P. Fiorina, *Congress: Keystone of the Washington Establishment,* 2d ed. (New Haven, Conn.: Yale University Press, 1989).

25. Davidson and Oleszek, *Congress and Its Members,* pp. 128–29.

26. Davidson and Oleszek, *Congress and Its Members,* p. 76.

27. David B. Magleby and Candice J. Nelson, *The Money Chase* (Washington, D.C.: Brookings Institution, 1990), p. 71.

28. *U.S. Term Limits v. Thornton,* 115 S. Ct. 1842 (1995).

29. *Arkansas Term Limits v. Donovan,* 138 L. Ed. 2d 874 (1997).

30. B. Drummond Ayres, Jr., "Term Limit Laws Are Transforming More Legislatures," *New York Times,* April 28, 1997, p. 1.

31. See "California Voters Soundly Reject Attempt to Kill Term Limits," *No Uncertain Terms,* April 4, 2002, vol. 10, no. 4, http://www.termlimits.org/Press/No_Uncertain_Terms/2002/0204nut.pdf.

32. Harris Poll #6, 1/30/02, accessed at www.//harrisinteractive.com/harris_poll/. See chart in *National Journal,* January 17, 1998, p. 111. Richard Morin, "Six Out of Ten Disapprove of Way Hill Does Its Job," *Washington Post,* July 3, 1994, pp. 1, 5.

33. *National Journal,* October 31, 1998, p. 2559.

34. See Davidson and Oleszek, *Congress and Its Members,* p. 407; Glenn R. Parker and Roger H. Davidson, "Why Do Americans Love Their Congressmen So Much More Than Their Congress?" *Legislative Studies Quarterly* 4 (February 1979): 53–61.

35. For the Democratic party, the names of these bodies are different: it is the Steering and Policy Committee that is chosen by the caucus.

36. Barbara Sinclair, *Majority Leadership in the U.S. House* (Baltimore: Johns Hopkins University Press, 1983).

37. Ward Sinclair, "High Theater Starring Tip and Cast of 434," *Washington Post,* August 20, 1982, p. 1.

38. For more on minority leaders, see Charles O. Jones, *Minority Party in Congress* (Boston: Little, Brown, 1970).

39. See Barbara Sinclair, *The Transformation of the U.S. Senate* (Baltimore: Johns Hopkins University Press, 1989).

40. Rowland Evans and Robert Novak, *Lyndon B. Johnson: The Exercise of Power* (New York: New American Library, 1966); Merle Miller, *Lyndon: An Oral Biography* (New York: Ballantine Books, 1980), chap. 2.

41. Harry McPherson, oral history, Lyndon Johnson Library, Austin, Tex., pp. 78–88; see also Robert A. Caro, *Master of the Senate,* (New York: Alfred A. Knopf, 2002).

42. *Washington Post,* June 12, 1985, p. 5.

43. Woodrow Wilson, *Congressional Government* (New York: Meridian, 1967), p. 28.

44. Davidson and Oleszek, *Congress and Its Members,* p. 349.

45. Lawrence D. Longley and Walter J. Oleszek, *Bicameral Politics: Conference Committees in Congress* (New Haven, Conn.: Yale University Press, 1995).

46. Richard F. Fenno, Jr., *Congressmen in Committees* (Boston: Little, Brown, 1973), p. 280.

47. The classic source on committees and the roles of members of Congress is ibid. See also Steven Smith and Christopher Deering, *Committees in Congress,* 2d ed. (Washington, D.C.: Congressional Quarterly Press, 1990).

48. Allan Freedman, "Returning Power to Chairmen," *Congressional Quarterly Weekly Report,* November 23, 1996, p. 3300.

49. Quoted in James T. Murphy, "Political Parties and the Porkbarrel: Party Conflict and Cooperation in House Public Works Committee Decision Making," in *Studies in Congress,* ed. Glen Parker (Washington, D.C.: Congressional Quarterly Press, 1985), pp. 237–38.

50. Davidson and Oleszek, *Congress and Its Members,* pp. 206.

51. See Leroy N. Rieselbach, *Legislative Reform: The Policy Impact* (Lexington, Mass.: Lexington Books, 1978).

52. Jill Abramson, "Tobacco Industry Steps Up Flow of Campaign Money," *New York Times,* March 8, 1998, p. 1.

53. Thomas E. Mann and Norman J. Ornstein, eds., *Renewing Congress: A Second Report* (Washington, D.C.: American Enterprise Institute and the Brookings Institution, 1993).

54. Walter J. Oleszek, *Congressional Procedures and the Policy Process* (Washington, D.C.: Congressional Quarterly Press, 1989).

55. Stanley Bach and Steven Smith, *Managing Uncertainty in the House of Representatives: Adaptation and Innovation in Special Rules* (Washington, D.C.: Brookings Institution, 1988).

56. D. B. Hardeman and Donald C. Bacon, *Rayburn: A Biography* (Lanham, Md.: Madison Books, 1987).

57. Quoted in David E. Rosenbaum, "Tax Bill Faces Fight, but First the Rules," *New York Times,* April 2, 1995, p. 20.

58. See Steven S. Smith, *Call to Order: Floor Politics in the House and Senate* (Washington, D.C.: Brookings Institution, 1989).

59. Helen Dewar, "As Senate Crunch Nears, Holdups Threaten," *Washington Post,* November 15, 1999, p. 21.

60. Quoted in Alison Mitchell, "Rule No. 1: My Way or No Way," *New York Times,* November 2, 1997, p. WK6.

61. Quoted in Sarah A. Binder and Steven S. Smith, "The Politics and Principles of the Senate

Filibuster," *Extensions* (Fall 1997); see also Sarah A. Binder and Steven S. Smith, *Politics or Principles? Filibustering in the U.S. Senate* (Washington, D.C.: Brookings Institution, 1997), p. 69.

62. See Fred R. Harris, *Deadlock on Decision: The U.S. Senate and the Rise of National Politics* (New York: Oxford University Press, 1993).

63. Donald Matthews, *U.S. Senators and Their World* (Chapel Hill: University of North Carolina Press, 1960), p. 54; see also Ross K. Baker, *House and Senate* 2d ed. (New York: W. W. Norton, 1995), chap. 2.

64. John E. Yang, "Notion of House Civility Gets a Push Backward," *Washington Post,* April 10, 1997, p. A23.

65. Frank Ahrens, "Putting 'Polite' into Politics," *Washington Post,* March 6, 1997, p. B1.

66. Burdett Loomis, "Civility and Deliberation: A Linked Pair?," Burdett Loomis, ed. *Esteemed Colleagues: Civility and Deliberation in the U.S. Senate,* Washington, D.C.: Brookings Institution Press, 2000), p. 1.

67. For more on the importance of seniority, apprenticeship, and political loyalty in Congress, see John R. Hibbing, *Congressional Careers: Contours of Life in the U.S. House of Representatives* (Chapel Hill: University of North Carolina Press, 1991), pp. 113–28; Donald Matthews, *U.S. Senators and Their World* (Chapel Hill: University of North Carolina Press, 1960), chap. 5.

68. John Ferejohn, "Logrolling in an Institutional Context: A Case of Food Stamp Legislation," in *Congress and Policy Change,* ed. Gerald C. Wright, Jr., Leroy Rieselbach, and Lawrence C. Dodd (New York: Agathon Press, 1986).

69. Davidson and Oleszek, *Congress and Its Members,* p. 271.

70. Anick Jesdanun, "Specter Gets 'Oinker' Award from Critical Citizens' Group," *Centre Daily Times,* March 11, 1998, p. 3A.

71. Quoted in Elsa C. Arnett, "Citizens, Interest Groups Fear New Round of Spending," *Centre Daily Times,* March 11, 1998, p. 3A.

72. Quoted in Donald G. Tacheron and Morris K. Udall, *The Job of the Congressman,* 2d ed. (Indianapolis, Ind.: Bobbs-Merrill, 1970), p. 18.

73. Douglas Arnold, *The Logic of Congressional Action* (New Haven, Conn.: Yale University Press, 1990), pp. 64–84; V. O. Key, Jr., *Public Opinion and American Democracy* (New York: Knopf, 1961), pp. 265–85.

74. William R. Shaffer, *Party and Ideology in the United States Congress* (Lanham, Md.: University Press of America, 1980); Norman Ornstein, Thomas E. Mann, and Michael Malbin, *Vital Statistics on Congress: 1993–94* (Washington, D.C.: Congressional Quarterly Press, 1994), p. 200.

75. Statistics taken from "President Support and Opposition: Senate," *Congressional Quarterly,* for the years 1992, p. 3897; 1991, p. 3785; 1990, p. 4209; 1989, p. 3566; 1988, p. 3348; 1987, p. 3213; 1986, p. 2688; 1985, pp. 741–46; 1984, pp. 2802–08; 1983, p. 2781; and 1982, p. 2796.

76. David Rohde, *Parties and Leaders in the Post-Reform House* (Chicago: University of Chicago Press, 1991); Robert L. Peabody, *Leadership in Congress* (Boston: Little, Brown, 1976).

77. Stephen Wayne and George Edwards III, *Presidential Influence in Congress* (San Francisco: Freeman, 1980); Stephen Wayne, *The Legislative Presidency* (New York: Harper & Row, 1978).

78. R. W. Apple, "In Pennsylvania, Feeling the Consequences of One Vote," *New York Times,* September 27, 1994, p. A22.

79. See Jeffrey Birnbaum, *The Lobbyists* (New York: Times Books, 1992); Jeffrey Birnbaum and Alan S. Murray, Showdown at Gucci Gulch (New York: Vintage Press, 1987).

80. See Harrison W. Fox, Jr., and Susan Webb Hammond, *Congressional Staffs: The Invisible Force in American Lawmaking* (New York: Free Press, 1977).

81. Richard Fenno, *Home Style: House Members in Their Districts* (New York: HarperCollins, 1987).

82. Donald R. Matthews and James A. Stimson, *Yeas and Nays* (New York: Wiley, 1975); David M. Kovenock, "Influence in the U.S. House of Representatives: A Statistical Study of Communications," *American Politics Quarterly* 1 (October 1973): 456ff.

83. John W. Kingdon, *Congressional Voting Decisions*, 3d ed. (Ann Arbor: University of Michigan Press, 1989); Aage R. Clausen, *How Congressmen Decide* (New York: St. Martin's Press, 1973).

84. Roughly ten thousand bills are introduced in each two-year session of Congress, and about six hundred laws are passed from that group. See Barry, "Bills Introduced and Laws Enacted," p. 2.

85. John W. Kingdon, *Agendas, Alternatives, and Public Policies* (Boston: Little, Brown, 1984).

86. See Paul Light, *Forging Legislation* (New York: Norton, 1992).

87. Longley and Oleszek, *Bicameral Politics*, passim.

88. Davidson and Oleszek, *Congress and Its Members*, p. 247.

89. Helen Dewar, "Campaign Finance Bill Dies in Senate," *Washington Post*, February 27, 1998, p. 1.

90. For more on the implications of the changes in the operations of the House rules by Newt Gingrich and the Republican Congress for the theory of legislating in Congress, see John H. Aldrich and David W. Rohde, "The Transition to Republican Rule in the House: Implications for Theories of Congressional Politics," *Political Science Quarterly* 112, no. 4 (1997–98): 541–67.

91. Davidson and Oleszek, *Congress and Its Members*, p. 226.

92. Ibid., p. 363.

93. Sinclair, *Transformation of the U.S. Senate*, passim.

94. Joel D. Aberbach, *Keeping a Watchful Eye: The Politics of Congressional Oversight* (Washington, D.C.: Brookings Institution, 1990); James Q. Wilson, *Bureaucracy: What Government Agencies Do and Why They Do It* (New York: Basic Books, 1991).

95. *Immigration and Naturalization Service v. Chadha*, 462 U.S. 919 (1983).

96. Aaron Wildavsky, *The New Politics of the Budgetary Process* (Glenview, Ill.: Scott, Foresman/Little, Brown, 1988); Allen Schick, *The Capacity to Budget* (Washington, D.C.: Urban Institute, 1990).

97. Ross Baker, quoted in Robin Toner, "Capitol Dynamic to Do the Framers Proud," *New York Times*, February 26, 1995, p. 1.

98. Jill Barshay, "A Year of Power Struggles and Common Purpose," *CQ Weekly*, December 22, 2001, p. 3018.

99. Charles Cook, "Election Day Unlikely to Transform Congress." Jennifer Duffy, "Senate Teeters on a Knife's Edge," and Amy Walter, "House Races Still Young," *The Cook Election Preview: A Supplement to the National Journal*, Spring 2002, pp. 3–14.)

CHAPTER 5

1. Ron Fournier, "From 'Accidental President' to Commander in Chief," *The Allentown Morning Call*, January 22, 2002; Dana Milbank, "In War, It's Power to the President," *The Washington Post*, November 20, 2001; Ramesh Ponnuru, "Rising Freshman," *National Review*, January 28, 2002. See Elisabeth Bumiller, "At First Year's End, Bush Cites Both Victories and Challenges," *New York Times*, December 30, 2001, B3. See also on-line *News Hour*, Shields and Books, "A President Expanded in Scope." http://www.pbs.org/newshour; "Assessment of Bush's First Year and Future," Brookings Institution National Issues Forum, January 30, 2002, http://www.brooking.edu/comm/transcripts/20020130nif.htm.

2. "There Is No Doubt in My Mind. Not One Doubt." Interviews with President Bush on December 20, 2001. *Washington Post*, A14; Helen Thomas, "President Bush Is a Wartime CEO," http://www.thebostonchannel.com/helenthomas/1133563/detail.html.

3. See David E. Rosenbaum, "When Government Doesn't Tell," *New York Times*, February 3, 2002, Section 4, p.1; Elisabeth Bumiller with David Sanger, "Taking Command in Crisis, Bush Wields New Power," *New York Times*, January 1, 2002, p. A1.

4. See Sidney M. Milkis and Michael Nelson, *The American Presidency: Origins and Development, 1776–1990* (Washington, D.C.: CQ Press, 1990); Thomas E. Cronin, ed., *Inventing the Presidency* (Albany: State University of New York Press, 1988), p. 20.

5. See Robert J. Spitzer, *The Presidential Veto: Touchstone of the American Presidency* (Albany: State University of New York Press, 1988), p. 20.

6. See Christopher Marquis, "Bush Hires Hard Liners to Handle Cuba Policy," *New York Times*, February 3, 2002, p. 5; "In Recess Appointment Bush Names Transport Security Chief," *New York Times*, January 8, 2002, p. A 16; "Bush Bypasses Senate on 2 More Nominees," *New York Times*, January 12, 2002, p. A10.

7. See Louis Fisher, *Constitutional Conflicts Between Congress and the President* (Lawrence: University Press of Kansas, 1991); Susan Benkleman, "Parsing the Veto Threat," *CQ Weekly*, June 23, 2001, p. 1480.

8. Gerald R. Ford, "Ford: I Had 'Fast-Track,' Clinton Deserves It, Too," *USA Today*, October 22, 1997, 15A; see "Clinton, Congress and Trade," *Legislate News Service*, November 10, 1997, p. 1.

9. See Lael Brainard and Hal Shapiro, "Fast-Track Trade Promotion Authority," Policy Brief #91, December 2001. Published on Brookings Website, November 30, 2001, http://www.brook.edu.

10. Deb Reichman, "Presidents Assert Executive Privilege," *WashingtonPost.com*, January 29, 2002; see Ellen Nakashima, "Bush Invokes Executive Privilege on Hill," *Washington Post*, December 14, 2001, p. A43.

11. See "Symposium on Executive Privilege and the Clinton Presidency," *William & Mary Bill of Rights Journal*, April 2000, vol. 8, issue 3, pp. 583–629.

12. See Mike Allen, "GAO to Sue Cheney within 2 or 3 weeks," *Washington Post*, January 31, 2002, A4. Dana Milbank, "Cheney Refuses Records Release," *Washington Post*, January 28, 2002, A 01.

13. Ibid.

14. See "Law and the War on Terrorism." *Harvard Journal of Law and Public Policy*, 25th Anniversary issue, Spring 2002, vol. 25, no. 2. See John Mueller, *Wars, Presidents and Public Opinion*, (New York: Wiley, 1970); Mueller, *Policy, Opinion and the Gulf War*, (Chicago: University of Chicago Press, 1994), p. 645; *United States v. Nixon*, 418 U.S. 683 (1974). See *The Washington Post* Series, "America's Chaotic Road to War," January 27, 2002–February 3, 2002.

15. Quoted in Richard Neustadt, "Presidency and Legislation: Planning the President's Program," *American Political Science Review* 49 (December 1955): 980–1021; Neustadt, "Presidency and Legislation: The Growth of Central Clearance," *American Political Science Review* 48 (September 1954): 641–71.

16. Clinton Rossiter, *The American Presidency*, rev. ed. (Baltimore: Johns Hopkins University Press, 1987), p. 52.

17. See James Carville. *We're Right, They're Wrong* (New York: Random House), 1996.

18. Quoted in George Wolfskill, *Happy Days Are Here Again!* (Hinsdale, Ill.: Dryden, 1974), p. 189. See also James MacGregor Burns, *Roosevelt: The Lion and the Fox* (New York: Harcourt Brace Jovanovich, 1956); Burns, *Roosevelt: The Soldier of Freedom, 1940–1945* (New York: Harcourt Brace Jovanovich, 1970); Frank Freidel, *Franklin D. Roosevelt*, 4 vols. (Boston: Little, Brown, 1952–53); Arthur Schlesinger, Jr., *The Age of Roosevelt*, 3 vols. (Boston: Houghton Mifflin, 1957–60).

19. Theodore Roosevelt, "The Stewardship Doctrine," in *Classics of the American Presidency*, ed. Harry Bailey (Oak Park, Ill.: Moore, 1980), pp. 35–36. See also *The Autobiography of Theodore Roosevelt* (New York: Scribner's, 1913), pp. 197–200.

20. John Morton Blum, *The Republican Roosevelt* (New York: Atheneum, 1962), pp. 129–30.

21. See Larry Berman, *The New American Presidency* (Little, Brown, 1986), pp. 54–56. See William Howard Taft, *Our Chief Magistrate and His Powers*, (New York: Columbia University Press, 1916), pp. 138–45.

22. See Stephen Skowronek, *The Politics Presidents Make: Leadership from John Adams to George Bush*, (Cambridge, Mass.: Harvard University Press, 1993).

23. One of President Bush's favorite books is by historian Edmund Morris, *Theodore Rex* New York: Random House, 2002.

24. See *INS v. Chadha*, 103 S. Ct. 2764 (1983); Harold Relyea, "Executive Power and the Chadha Case," *Presidential Studies Quarterly* 13 (Fall 1983): 651–53; Louis Fisher, "A Political Context for Legislative Vetoes," *Political Science Quarterly* 93 (Summer 1978): 241–54. See also Harvey C. Mansfield, Jr., *Taming the Prince: The Ambivalence of Modern Executive Power*, (Baltimore: Johns Hopkins University Press, 1993). Congressional Budget Office memorandum, "The Line Item Veto After One Year," http://www.CBO.gov. See Robert J. Spitzer, "The Constitutionality of the Presidential Line Item Veto," *Political Science Quarterly* 112, no. 2, 1997: 261; Judith A. Best, "The Item Veto: Would the Founders Approve?" *Presidential Studies Quarterly* (Spring 1984): 188.

25. *United States v. Curtiss-Wright*, 299 U.S. 304 (1936).

26. For detailed accounts of Johnson's views from White House tapes, see Michael Beschloss, *Reaching for Glory*, (New York: Simon & Schuster 2000).

27. See Arthur M. Schlesinger, Jr., *The Imperial Presidency* (Boston: Houghton Mifflin, 1973).

28. *Youngstown Sheet and Tube Co. v. Sawyer*, 343 U.S. 579 (1952). See Maeva Marcus, *Truman and the Steel Seizure Case* (New York: Columbia University Press, 1977); Alan Weston, *The Anatomy of a Constitutional Law Case* (New York: Macmillan, 1958).

29. See U.S. Congress, Senate, *Congressional Record*, 93rd Cong., 1st sess., 1973, p. 119. See also U.S. Congress, Subcommittee on International Security and Scientific Affairs, *The War Powers*

Resolution: Relevant Documents, Correspondence, Reports, 93rd Cong., 3rd sess., June 1981; Hardy, "Tug of War," 306–40.

30. See Louis Fisher and David Gray Adler, "The War Powers Resolution: Time to Say Goodbye," *Political Science Quarterly* 113, no. 1, 1998: 1–20. See David P. Auerswald and Peter F. Cowhey, "Ballotbox Diplomacy: The War Powers Resolution and the Use of Force," *International Studies Quarterly* 41, 1987:505–28; Larry Berman and Bruce W. Jentleson, "Bush and the Post-Cold War World: New Challenges for American Leadership," in *The Bush Presidency: First Appraisals,* ed. Colin Campbell and Bert A. Rockman (Chatham, N.J.: Chatham House, 1991), pp. 93–94.

31. W. Taylor Reveley III, "Presidential War Making: Constitutional Prerogative or Usurpation?" *Virginia Law Review* 55, (November 1969): 1243–1305; and Reveley, *"Resolved: That the Powers of the Presidency Should Be Curtailed," A Collection of Excerpts and Bibliography Relating to the Intercollegiate Debate Topic, 1974–75* (Washington, D.C.: U.S. Government Printing Office, 1974), pp. 91–133; U.S. Congress, Senate, Committee on Foreign Relations, *Powers of the President to Send Armed Forces Outside the United States,* 82d Cong., 1st sess., 1951. See Elisabeth Palmer, "Executive Powers in Crises Are Shaped by Precedent, Personality, Public Opinion," *CQ Weekly,* (September 15, 2001), pp. 2122–3.

32. See http://www.washingtonpost.com/wp-dyn/articles/A38075-2002Oct29.html; http://www.washingtonpost.com/ac2/wp-2002Sep19; http://www.whitehouse.gov/infocus/iraq/index.html; http://www.washingtonpost.com/ac2/wp-dyn/A33534-2002Oct16.

33. Samuel Kernell, *Going Public: New Strategies of Presidential Leadership* (Washington, D.C.: CQ Press, 1993); rev. ed. 1997. Jeffrey K. Tulis, *The Rhetorical Presidency* (Princeton, N.J.: Princeton University Press, 1977), pp. 61–87.

34. John Hart, *The Presidential Branch* (Chatham, N.J.: Chatham House, 1995), pp. 37–38; Peri Arnold, *Making the Managerial Presidency* (Princeton, N.J.: Princeton University Press, 1986).

35. Jack Valenti, "Life's Never the Same After the White House Power Trip," *Washington Post National Weekly Edition,* (March 19, 1984), p. 21.

36. Thomas Cronin, "Everybody Believes in Democracy Until He Gets to the White House: An Examination of White House-Departmental Relations," *Law and Contemporary Problems* 35, (Summer 1970): 573–625.

37. Fred I. Greenstein, *The Hidden-Hand Presidency: Eisenhower as Leader* (New York: Basic Books, 1982), p. 55.

38. Larry Berman, *The Office of Management and Budget and the Presidency, 1921–1977* (Princeton, N.J.: Princeton University Press), 1977.

39. Quoted in Alexander Groth, *Lincoln: Authoritarian Savior* (Lanham, Md.: University Press of America, 1996), pp. 130–131.

40. See Jeffrey E. Cohen, *The Politics of the U.S. Cabinet,* Pittsburgh: (University of Pittsburgh Press, 1988). See Bradley H. Patterson, Jr., *The Ring of Power* (New York: Basic Books, 1988). See Kathryn Dunn Tenpas and Stephen Hess, "Bush's 'A Team': Just like Clinton's, but More So," *Washington Post,* (January 27, 2002), B5., See also "The Bush White House: First Appraisals," http://www.brook.edu.

41. See Lizett Alverez and Eric Schmitt, "Cheney Ever More Powerful as Crucial Link to Congress," *The New York Times,* (May 13, 2001), A1; Alvin Felzenberg, "The Vice Presidency Grows Up," *Policy Review,* (January 31, 2002).

http://www/heritage.org; Susan Page, "Cheney Takes 'Backseat' in a Strong Way," *USA Today,* November 16, 2001, 13A.

CHAPTER 6

1. *Bush v. Gore.* 531 U.S. 98 (2000); Tony Mauro, "*Bush v. Gore* is Bound to Have an Impact on the Justices' Futures." *New Jersey Law Journal,* December 18, 2000; David Abel, "*Bush v. Gore* Case Compels Scholars to Alter Courses at U.S. Law Schools," *Boston Globe,* February 3, 2001; Michael Kirkland, "A Court in Search of a Theme." *San Diego Union-Tribune,* January 6, 2002; William Kristol, "Crowning the Imperial Presidency," *New York Times,* November 28, 2000. p. A29: David Kaplan, "The Secret Vote that Made Bush President," *Newsweek,* September 17, 2001, p. 34; and Stuart Taylor, Jr., "How History Will View the Court," *Newsweek,* September 17, 2001, p. 35

2. Alexander Hamilton, James Madison, and John Jay. *The Federalist Papers* (New York: New York American Library, 1961), no. 78. p. 465.

3. *Marbury v. Madison,* 5 U.S. 137 (1803). The U.S. court of appeals was not established by congressional act until 1891. Before this time, the appellate courts were staffed by a panel of two district court judges and one circuit-riding Supreme Court justice.

4. Edward S. Corwin, review of Benjamin F. Wright's *Growth of American Constitutional Law,* Harvard Law Review 56 (1942):487.

5. Henry J. Abraham, *The Judicial Process,* 6th ed (New York: Oxford University Press. 1993), p. 272. See also David O'Brien. *Constitutional Law and Politics,* vol 1, *Struggles for Power and Governmental Accountability,* (New York: Norton, 1991), p. 38.

6. ———. "Defining 'Disabled': The High Court Rejects a Loose Interpretation." *Pittsburgh Post Gazette,* January 15, 2002.

7. For more here, see William H. Rehnquist, *Grand Inquests: The Historic Impeachments of Justice Samuel Chase and President Andrew Johnson* (New York: Morrow, 1992).

8. Quoted in Nina Totenberg, "Judicial Vacancies: Politics," National Public Radio broadcast transcript, September 26, 1997, p. 1.

9. See John Aloysius Farrell, "Republicans Take Aim at the Federal Judiciary," *Boston Globe.* September 24, 1997: p. 1; David Kairys, "Clinton's Judicial Retreat," *New York Times,* September 7, 1997, p. C1.

10. Frank G. Scafidi, "F.B.I. to Congress: Don't Make a Federal Case Out of It," *Los Angeles Times,* September 9, 2001.

11. See Milton Heumann, *Plea Bargaining: The Experiences of Prosecutors, Judges and Defense Attorneys* (Chicago: University of Chicago Press. 1977); John H. Langbein, "Torture and Plea Bargaining, *Public Interest* vol. XXI (Winter 1980): 24–26.

12. Myron Levin, "Jury Hands Tobacco Firms a Key Victory," *Los Angeles Times,* November 15, 2001.

13. Jennifer Lin, "First Class-Action Lawsuit Filed Against Terrorists," *Pittsburgh Post-Gazette* February 20, 2002.

14. Carrie Johnson, "Testing the Limits," *Legal Times,* October 4, 1999, p. 1; Neil Lewis, "A Court Becomes a Model of Conservative Pursuits," *New York Times,* May 24, 1999, p. 1.

15. Abraham, *Judicial Process,* p. 163.

16. J. Woodford Howard, Jr., *Courts of Appeals in the Federal Judicial System* (Princeton, N.J.: Princeton University Press. 1981), p. 58.

17. William Glaberson, "Caseload Forcing Two-Level System for U.S. Appeals," *New York Times,* March 14, 1999, p. 1.

18. See Laurence H. Tribe, *God Save This Honorable Court* (New York: Random House, 1985), pp. 50–77; William H. Rehnquist, *The Supreme Court: How It Was, How It Is* (New York: Morrow, 1987), pp. 235–53. And see John B. Gates and Jeffrey E. Cohen, "Presidents, Supreme Court Justices and Racial Equality Cases: 1954–1984," *Political Behavior* 10, no. 1 (1994): 22–36.

19. Henry J. Abraham, *Justices and Presidents: A Political History of Appointments to the Supreme Court* (New York: Oxford University Press, 1992), p. 266.

20. Abraham, *Justices and Presidents,* p. 238.

21. See Barbara Perry, *A "Representative" Supreme Court? The Impact of Race, Religion, and Gender on Appointments* (New York: Greenwood Press, 1991).

22. Until the Bush administration there used to be an "exceptionally well qualified" rating as well.

23. For more on the role of the ABA in the appointment process, see Joel Grossman, *Lawyers and Judges: The ABA and the Politics of Judicial Selection* (New York: Wiley, 1965).

24. Quoted in Henry J. Abraham, *Justices and Presidents: A Political History of Appointments to the Supreme Court,* 3d ed. (New York: Oxford University Press, 1992). pp. 16–17.

25. For more on the Bork battle, see Ethan Bronner, *Battle for Justice: How the Bork Nomination Shook America* (New York: Norton. 1989).

26. For more on the Thomas confirmation battle, see Timothy M. Phelps and Helen Winternitz, *Capitol Games* (New York: Hyperion Books, 1991); Jane Mayer and Jill Abramson, *Strange Justice: The Selling of Clarence Thomas,* Boston: Houghton Mifflin, 1994); John C. Danforth, *Resurrection: The Confirmation of Clarence Thomas* (New York: Viking Press. 1994).

27. For more on the Fortas nomination, see Bruce Allen Murphy, *Fortas: The Rise and Ruin of a Supreme Court Justice* (New York: Morrow, 1988): for more on the confirmation process generally, see John Massaro. *Supremely Political: The Role of Ideology and Presidential Management in Unsuccessful Supreme Court Nominations* (Albany: State University of New York Press. 1990).

28. Henry J. Reske, "The Safe Debate," *ABA Journal,* vol. 48 (July 1994): 20.

29. Sheldon Goldman, "Bush's Judicial Legacy: The Final Imprint, *Judicature* 76, no. 6 (April/May 1993): 295.

30. For more on the appointment process for district court judges, see Neil McFeeley. *Appointment of Judges: The Johnson Presidency* (Austin: University of Texas Press, 1987); Harold Chase, *Federal Judges: The Appointing Process* (Minneapolis: University of Minnesota Press, 1972).

31. This information comes from Sheldon Goldman and Matthew D. Saronson, "Clinton's Nontraditional Judges: Creating a More Representative Bench," *Judicature* 78, no. 2 (September/October 1994): 73. See also Goldman. "Bush's Judicial Legacy": Goldman, "The Bush Imprint on the Judiciary: Carrying on a Tradition," *Judicature* 74, no. 6 (April/May 1991): 294–306.

32. Sheldon Goldman, "Reagan's Second Term Judicial Appointments: The Battle at Midway," *Judicature* 70, no. 4 (April/May 1987): 328–31.

33. Sheldon Goldman and Elliot Slotnik, "Clinton's First-Term Judiciary: Many Bridges to Cross," *Judicature* 80, no. 6 (May/June 1997): 270

34. Goldman and Saronson, "Clinton's Nontraditional Judges," p. 69.

35. Sheldon Goldman and Elliot Slotnick, "Picking Judges under Fire," *Judicature,* 86, no. 6 (May/June 1999): 265–78.

36. David O'Brien, *Storm Center: The Supreme Court in American Politics*, 4th ed. (New York: Norton 1996), pp. 165–66.

37. See Doris Marie Provine, *Case Selection in the United States Supreme Court* (Chicago: University of Chicago Press, 1980). This study also found that the Court gave special consideration to questions of federalism and organized labor issues. See also Joseph Tanenhaus, Marvin Schick, Matthew Muraskin, and Daniel Rosen, "The Supreme Court's Certiorari Jurisdiction: Cue Theory," in *Judicial Decision Making*, ed. Glendon Schubert (New York: Free Press. 1963), pp. 111–32.

38. Rehnquist, *Supreme Court*, p. 265. See also H. W. Perry, Jr., *Deciding to Decide: Agenda Setting in the United States Supreme Court* (Cambridge, Mass.: Harvard University Press, 1991); Gregory A. Caldeira and John R. Wright, "The Discuss List: Agenda Setting in the Supreme Court," *Law and Society Review* 24 (1990): 809–13.

39. Tony Mauro, "Justices Give Pivotal Role to Novice Lawyers," *USA Today*, March 13–15. 1998, pp. 1–2.

40. *Escobedo v. Illinois*, 378 U.S. 478 (1964).

41. *Miranda v. Arizona*, 384 U.S. 436 (1966). Besides the lead case, *Miranda*, the other appeals accepted were *Vignera v. New York*, *Westover v. United States*, and *California v. Stewart*. For the rest of the cases the Court had also decided there would be no "retroactivity;" that is, the broad protections would not be extended back to previously decided cases. See *Linkletter v. Walker*. 381 U.S. 618 (1965).

42. Liva Baker. *Miranda, Crime, Law, and Politics* (New York: Antheneum Press. 1983), p. 88.

43. Linda Greenhouse, "Court Had Rehnquist Initials Intricately Carved on Docket," *New York Times*, July 2, 2002, pp. 1, 16.

44. Cass R. Sunstein, "Supreme Caution," *Washington Post*, July 6, 1997, pp. C1, C5; and Linda Greenhouse. "Benchmarks of Justice." *New York Times*, July 1, 1997, pp. A1, A18.

45. David M. O'Brien, "The Rehnquist Court's Shrinking Plenary Docket," *Judicature* 81. no. 2 (September–October, 1997). pp. 58–65.

46. Tony Mauro, "Justices Give Pivotal Role to Novice Lawyers," *USA Today*, March 13–15, 1998, pp. 1–2.

47. Lincoln Caplan, "Uneasy Days in Court," *Newsweek*, October 10, 1994, pp. 62–64: Linda Greenhouse. "Which Counts, Congress's Intent or Its Words," *New York Times*, October 6, 1994, p. A18.

48. Joan Biskupic, "10th Justice States His Case," *Washington Post*, March 2, 1998, p. A15.

49. *Brown v. Board of Education*, 347 U.S. 483 (1954).

50. Richard Kluger, *Simple Justice* (New York: Knopf, 1975).

51. Joan Biskupic, "Nothing Subtle About Scalia, The Combative Conservative," *Washington Post*, February 18, 1997, p. A4.

52. Joan Biskupic, "Women Are Still Not Well Represented Among Lawyers Facing Supreme Test," *Washington Post*, May 27, 1997, p. A3; and Joan Biskupic, "Justices Growing Impatient with Imprecision," *Washington Post*, May 5, 1997, p. A7.

53. See letters from Robert Bradley, Chief Justice Rehnquist and Henry J. Abraham in American Political Science Association. "Law, Courts and Judicial Process Section Newsletters," 6, no. 4 (Summer 1989): 2–3, and 7, no. 1 (Fall 1989): 3. See also Abraham, *Judicial Process*. p. 196.

54. Linda Greenhouse, "Ruling Fixed Opinions," *New York Times*, February 22, 1988, p. A16.

55. Joan Biskupic, "Justices in Conference: A Tradition Wanes," *Washington Post*, February 2, 2000.

56. Phillip Cooper and Howard Ball, *The United States Supreme Court: From the Inside Out* (Upper Saddle River, N.J.: Prentice Hall, 1996), p. 218.

57. *Smith v. Allwright*, 321 U.S. 649 (1944).

58. Alpheus Thomas Mason, *Harlan Fiske Stone: Pillar of the Law* (New York: Viking Press, 1956), pp. 614–17.

59. *Roe v. Wade*, 410 U.S. 113 (1973).

60. *Planned Parenthood of Southeastern Pennsylvania v. Casey*, 112 S.Ct. 931 (1992).

61. David J. Garrow, "Justice Souter Emerges," *New York Times Magazine*, September 25, 1994. pp. 36–42.

62. See Joan Biskupic, "Ex-Supreme Court Clerk's Book Breaks the Silence," *Washington Post*, March 4, 1998, p. A8; see also Ed Lazarus, *Closed Chambers* (New York: Times Books, 1998).

63. Quoted in Nat Hentoff, "The Constitutionalist," *New Yorker*, March 12, 1990, p. 60.

64. Quoted in Walter Murphy, *Elements of Judicial Strategy* (Chicago: University of Chicago Press, 1964), pp. 51–52.

65. Harold Spaeth, *Studies in U.S. Supreme Court Behavior* (New York: Garland Press, 1990); Saul Brenner and Harold Spaeth, "Ideological Positions as a Variable in the Authoring of Dissenting Opinion," *American Politics Quarterly* 16 (July 1988): 17–28.

66. See *Webster v. Reproductive Health Services*, 492 U.S. 490 (1989), pp. 533–35. For the behind-the-scenes account of the battle, see David Savage, *Turning Right: The Making of the Rehnquist Supreme Court* (New York: Wiley, 1992), pp. 209–14, 255–72, 288–98, esp. pp. 292–93.

67. *Lamb's Chapel v. Center Moriches Union Free School District*, 124 L. Ed. 2d. 352 (1993), p. 365.

68. *New York Times Co. v. United States*, 403 U.S. 713 (1971).

69. Sandra L. Wood and Gary M. Gansle, "Seeking a Strategy, William J. Brennan's Dissent Assignments," *Judicature* 81. no. 2 (September–October 1997), pp. 73–75.

70. Bernard Schwartz, *The Ascent of Pragmatism* (Reading, Mass.: Addison-Wesley, 1990); Bob Woodward and Scott Armstrong, *The Brethren: Inside the Supreme Court* (New York: Avon Books, 1979).

71. *Stanley v. Georgia*, 394 U.S. 557 (1969).

72. *Payne v. Tennessee*, 59 Law Week, 4823 (1991).

73. Abraham, *Judicial Process*, p. 325.

74. See Herbert Wechsler, *Principles, Politics, and Fundamental Law* (Cambridge, Mass.: Harvard University Press, 1961). See also Alexander M. Bickel, *The Least Dangerous Branch* (Indianapolis, Ind.: Bobbs-Merrill, 1962); Raoul Berger, *Government by Judiciary: The Transformation of the Fourteenth Amendment* (Cambridge, Mass.: Harvard University Press, 1977); Jesse H. Choper, *Judicial Review and the National Political Process* (Chicago: University of Chicago Press, 1980); John Hart Ely, *Democracy and Distrust: A Theory of Judicial Review* (Cambridge, Mass.: Harvard University Press, 1980).

75. Jeffrey Segal and Albert Cover, "Ideological Values and the Votes of U.S. Supreme Court Justices," *American Political Science Review* 83 (1989): 557–65.

76. *West Virginia Board of Education v. Barnette*, 319 U.S. 624 (1943), pp. 646–47.

77. *United States v. O'Brien*,. 391 U.S. 367 (1968).

78. *Griswold v. Connecticut*, 381 U.S. 479 (1965).

79. *Sierra Club v. Morton*, 405 U.S. 727 (1972), pp. 742–43.

80. For a fine example of this argument detailing the problems of the Court as a "superlegislature," see Robert Bork, *The Tempting of America: The Political Seduction of the Law* (New York: Macmillan, 1990).

81. Hugo Black, *A Constitutional Faith* (New York: Knopf, 1968). p. 21; For more on Black's judicial philosophy, see Roger K. Newman, *Hugo Black: A Biography* (New York: Pantheon Books, 1994), p. 512.

82. Quoted in *New York Times Magazine*, October 5, 1986, p. 74.

83. David J. Danelski, "The Influence of the Chief Justice in the Decisional Process of the Supreme Court," in *Courts, Judges and Politics*, ed. Walter Murphy and Charles Herman Pritchett (New York: Random House, 1986), p. 568.

84. Quoted in *Newsweek*, October 12, 1992, p. 78.

85. Eisenhower was backing the decision by the Supreme Court to desegregate Central High School in Little Rock, Arkansas—*Cooper v. Aaron*, 358 U.S. 1 (1958).

86. The decision banning school prayer is *Engel v. Vitale*, 370 U.S. 421 (1962).

87. *Worcester v. Georgia*, 31 U.S. 515 (1832). See Albert Beveridge, *Life of John Marshall*, vol. 4 (Boston: Houghton Mifflin, 1919), p. 551. Presidential opposition is not unusual.

88. *Employment Division, Department of Human Resources of Oregon v. Smith*, 110 S.Ct. 1595 (1990).

89. David E. Anderson, "Signing of Religious Freedom Act Culminates Three-Year Push," *Washington Post*, November 20, 1993, p. C6.

90. *City of Boerne v. Flores*, 138 L. Ed. 2d 624 (1997), p. 633.

91. *Ibid.*

92. Thomas Marshall, *Public Opinion and the Supreme Court* (Boston: Unwin Hyman, 1989).

93. *Gideon v. Wainwright*, 372 U.S. 335 (1963).

94. Woodrow Wilson, *Constitutional Government in the United States* (New York: Columbia University Press, 1907), p. 142.

CHAPTER 7

1. "Parade," *Sacramento Bee*, January 27, 2002, pp. 4–6; "The Office of Homeland Security," www.whitehouse.gov/homeland; "Does Ridge Have the Clout To Carry It Off?" *Congressional Quarterly Weekly*, November 3, 2001, pp. 2586–87; Eric Pianin and Bradley Graham, "Ridge: Goal Isn't to Create Bureaucracy," *Washington Post*, October 4, 2001, p. A24.

2. See Alison Mitchell, "Disputes Erupt on Ridge's Needs for his Job," *New York Times*, November 4, 2001; Jedd Pillets and Adam Lisberg, "Terrorism Czar; Mandate Unclear," http://www.bergen.com/campaign/homeland200110021.htm; "Governor Ridge Speaks at Homeland Security and Defense Conference," http://www.whitehouse.gov/news/releases/2001/11/20011128-6.html; see also Mark Benjamin, "Ridge: Government Might Need Reorganizing," *United Press International*, February 7, 2002; Bill Miller, "$37.7 Billion for Homeland Defense Is a Start, Bush Says," *Washington Post*, January 25, 2002, p. A15; Bill Miller, "Ridge Lacks Power to Do His Job, Says Panetta at Hearing, Cabinet Rank, Budget Clout Urged," *Washington Post*, April 18, 2002, p. A 19; Joel Brinkley and Philip Shenon, "Ridge Meeting Opposition from Agencies," *New York Times*, February 7, 2002, p. A12; Elizabeth Becker, "Ridge Briefs Home Panel,

but Discord Is not Resolved," *New York Times,*
April 1, 2002, p. A17; Bill Miller, "Ridge Will
Meet Informally with 2 House Committees,"
Washington Post, April 4, 2002, p. A15.

3. President George W. Bush, transcript of a
speech reprinted as "The Plan: We Have Concluded that Our Government Must Be Reorganized," *New York Times,* June 6, 2002, p. A18.

4. The Department of Homeland Security, President George W. Bush, June 2002. http://www.
whitehouse.gov/homeland/.

5. Barry Bozeman, *Bureaucracy and Red Tape*
(Upper Saddle River, N.J.: Prentice Hall, 2000),
p. 1.

6. Anthony Downs, *Inside Bureaucracy* (Boston: Little, Brown, 1967), pp. 24–25.

7. See Max Weber, *Essays in Sociology,* trans. and ed.
H. H. Garth and C. Wright Mills (New York: Oxford University Press, 1958), p. 232.

8. John Marini, *The Politics of Budget Control: Congress, the Presidency, and the Growth of the Administrative State* (New York: Crane Russak, 1992),
p. 191.

9. David Frum, *Dead Right* (New York: Basic Books,
1994), pp. 42–43; "Kingsize Tribute," *The Sacramento Bee,* July 18, 1997, p. A16.

10. William L. Riordon, *Plunkitt of Tammany Hall*
(New York: Dutton, 1963), chapter 9.

11. Kenneth J. Meier, *Politics and the Bureaucracy: Policymaking in the Fourth Branch of Government,* 4th
ed. (Pacific Grove, Calif.: Brooks/Cole, 1993);
Hugh Heclo, *A Government of Strangers* (Washington, D.C.: Brookings Institution, 1974).

12. "Changes in Federal Civilian Employment: An
Update," June 1999, TRAC Data Services,
http://trac.syr.edu/aboutOrder/index.html.

13. See Ellen Nakashima, "The Shifting Federal
Workforce," *Washington Post,* September 21,
2001, p. A2.

14. See Wilson, *Bureaucracy,* chapter 7. See also Guy
Benveniste, *Bureaucracy* (San Francisco: Boyd
and Frasier, 1977).

15. Larry Hill, ed., *The State of Public Bureaucracy*
(New York: M. E. Sharpe, 1992).

16. Marrion Burros, "U.S. to Subject Organic Foods
Long Ignored to Federal Rules," *New York Times,*
December 15, 1997, p. A1.

17. See the OMB Website for "Rating Government's
Performance," www.whitehouse.gov/omb.

18. Ibid.; see also, Eric Schmitt, "Is This Any Way to
Run a Nation?" *NewsWeek in Review,* April 14,
2002, p. A4.

19. See "Postal Service Plans Layoffs and 3 Cent Rise
in Postage," *New York Times,* January 9, 2002,
p. A14.

20. Robert D. Hershey, Jr., "IRS Opens Its Doors Sat-
urdays for Problem Solving," *New York Times,* No-
vember 16, 1997, p. A20; see also Jacob M.
Schlesinger, "Help Wanted: Hated Bureaucracy
Seeks Real People to Raise Image," *Wall Street
Journal,* February 27, 1998, p. 1.

21. Emily Eakin, "Presidential Papers as Smoking
Guns," *New York Times,* April 13, 2002, p. A 17.

22. Quoted in Richard Heustadt, *Presidential Power*
(New York: Mentor, 1960), p.22.

23. See David Stockman, *The Triumph of Politics: The
Inside Story of the Reagan Revolution* (New York:
Avon, 1987).

24. See Glenn Kessler, "OMB Chief Signals New
Spending Goals," *Washington Post,* October 17,
2001, p. A3.

25. See Richard Nathan, *The Plot that Failed* (New
York: John Wiley & Sons Ltd., March 1975).

26. See Philip Shenon, "Agent Who Betrayed F.B.I.
Cites Its Laxity," *New York Times,* April 5, 2002,
p. A 7; Dan Eggen and Walter Pincus, "Russia
Complained About Spy Offer," *Washington Post,*
April 6, 2002, p. A2.

27. See John Lumpkin, "CIA Gets Big Boost in Bush
Budget," www.washingtonpost.com, February 4,
2002; see also, Walter Pincus and Vernon Loeb,
"CIA Resurfaces in the Oval Office," *Washington
Post,* July 29, 2001, p. A5.

28. "Who Can Be Trusted?" *Gallup Poll Monthly,* September 1992, p. 7; Larry B. Hill, "Refusing to
Take Bureaucracy Seriously" (paper presented
at the annual meeting of the Midwest Political
Science Association, Chicago, 1993).

29. See Arthur Schlesinger, Jr., "Government Isn't
the Root of All Evil," *Wall Street Journal,* January
30, 1998, p. A14; Anthony Downs, *Inside Bureaucracy* (Prospect Heights, Ill.: Waveland Press,
1994), pp. 100–101; Herbert Kaufman, *Red Tape:
Its Uses and Abuses* (Washington, D.C.: Brookings
Institution, 1997).

30. David Bullier and Joan Claybrook, "Regulations
That Work," *Washington Monthly,* April 1986,
pp. 47–54.

31. Bill Miller, "More Help Sought for Those Who
Blow Whistle," *Washington Post,* February 28,
2002, p. A21; see also "F.B.I. to Pay Whistle
Blower $1.1 Million in a Settlement," *New York
Times,* February 27, 1998, p. 15; Greg Schneider,
"No Whistle Blowing Protection for Airport Bag-
gage Screeners," *Washington Post,* February 8,
2002, p. A29.

32. See Thomas Joseph Powers, "A Man with Con-
nections—Thomas Joseph Ridge," *New York
Times.* November 26, 2002, A17; also "Bush Signs
Bill Creating Department for Security," *New York
Times.* November 26, 2002, A17.

CHAPTER 8

1. Quoted in Michael Wheeler, *Lies, Damn Lies,
and Statistics: The Manipulation of Public Opinion
in America* (New York: Dell, 1976), p. 82. See also
Albert Hadley Cantril with Mildred Strunk,
Public Opinion, 1935–1946 (Princeton, N.J.:
Princeton University Press, 1951), pp. 151–55.
See George Gallup, "Professor Gallup Describes
a New Way of Measuring Public Opinion,"
Independent Journal, November 15, 1935. See also
Gallup, "The Quintamensional Plan of Question
Design," *Public Opinion Quarterly* 11, no. 3 (Fall
1947): 385–93; Gallup, "Polls and the Political
Process: Past, Present and Future," *Public Opin-
ion Quarterly* 29, no. 4 (Winter 1965–66):
544–49.

2. See "Post Poll: 72% of Israelis for War," The In-
ternet *Jerusalem Post,* http://www.jpost.com/
Editions2002/04/05/News/News.46383.html.
See also Richard Morin and Claudia Deane,
"Public Voices Doubts on Mideast Role,"
Washington Post, April 23, 2002, p. A11.

3. See Walter Lippmann, *The Phantom Public* (New
York: Macmillan, 1927), pp 13–14.

4. Alexander Hamilton, James Madison, and John
Jay, *The Federalist Papers* (New York: New American Library, 1961), no. 10, p. 119. *The Federalist,*
no. 10, appears in the appendices.

5. William Flanagan and Nancy H. Zingale, *Political Behavior of the American Electorate* (Washington, D.C.: *Congressional Quarterly Press,* 1998), p.
179; Herbert Asher, *Polling and the Public: What
Every Citizen Should Know,* 4th ed. (Washington,
D.C.: *Congressional Quarterly Press,*) 1988.

6. Quoted in Gary Langer, "Responsible Polling in
the Wake of 9/11," *Public Perspective,*
March/April 2002, pp. 14–16.

7. See the discussion in Robert S. Erikson and
Kent L. Tedin, *American Public Opinion: Its Origins, Content, and Impact,* 5th ed. (Boston: Allyn
and Bacon, 1995), pp. 128–30.

8. "E-Government Poll," *Washington Post,* February
27, 2002. p. A21.

9. See Fred Greenstein, *Children and Politics* (New
Haven, Conn.: Yale University Press, 1965),
p. 119.

10. Urie Bronfenbrenner, *Two Worlds of Childhood:
U.S. and USSR.* (New York: Simon and Schuster,
1970).

11. Robert D. Putnam, "Bowling Alone: America's
Declining Social Capital," *Journal of Democracy* 6
(1995): 65–78.

12. See http://people-press.org for finding a guide
to these polls. We have made extensive use of resources from The Pew Research Center for the
People and the Press.

13. Todd Gitlin, *The Whole World Is Watching: Mass
Media in the Making and Unmaking of the New Left*
(Berkeley: University of California Press, 1980),
p. 201. See also Gitlin, *Watching Television: A Pantheon Guide to Popular Culture* (New York: Pantheon Books, 1986).

14. http://www.zogby.com/index.cfm.

15. Benjamin I. Page and Robert Y. Shapiro, *The Rational Public* (Chicago: University of Chicago
Press, 1992), p. 201; see also William Flanagan,
Political Behavior of the American Electorate (Washington, D.C.: Congressional Quarterly Press,
1988), p. 174

16. William H. Flanagan, *Political Behavior of the
American Electorate,* (Washington, D.C.: Congressional Quarterly Press, 1998) p. 174.

17. See http://www.gendergap.com.

18. James Gibson, "The Political Consequences of
Intolerance: Cultural Conformity and Political
Freedom," *American Political Science Review* 86
(June 1992): 338–56.

19. Ibid., p. 341.

20. Elizabeth Noelle-Neumann, *The Spiral of Silence*
(Chicago: University of Chicago Press, 1984).

21. See William H. Flanagan and Nancy H. Zingale,
Political Behavior of the American Electorate, 8th ed.
(Washington, D.C.: *Congressional Quarterly Press,*
1994), p. 132.

22. Norman R. Luttbeg and Michael M. Gant,
American Electoral Behavior, 1952–1992, 2d ed.
(Itasca, Ill.: Peacock, 1995), esp. pp. 91–164; see
also Aaron Wildavsky, "Choosing Preferences by
Constructing Institutions: A Cultural Theory of
Preference Formation," *American Political Science
Review* 81 (March 1987): 3–23.

23. Walter Lippmann, *The Phantom Public.* (New
York: Macmillan, 1927), pp. 13–14.

24. Joseph Schumpeter, *Capitalism, Socialism and
Democracy* (New York: Harper & Bros., 1950), p.
262 Luttbeg and Gant, *American Electoral Behavior,* esp. chaps. 3–4, p. 67. See also Philip E. Converse, "Information Flow and the Stability of
Partisan Attitudes," *Public Opinion Quarterly* 26,
no. 4 (Winter 1962): 578–99.

25. See Michael Kagay, "In Judging Polls, What
Counts Is When and How Who Is Asked What,"
New York Times, September 12, 1988, p. A12; see
also Kagay, "As Candidates Hunt the Big Issue,
Polls Can Give Them Clues," *New York Times,* Oc-
tober 20, 1991, p. E3.

26. Benjamin Page and Robert Shapiro, *The Rational Public: Fifty Years of Trends in Americans' Policy
Preference* (Chicago: University of Chicago Press,
1992); see also Paul Brace and Barbara Hinck-
ley, *Follow the Leader: Opinion Polls and Modern*

Presidents (New York: Basic Books, 1992), pp. 97–115.

27. See Angus Campbell, Philip Converse, Warren Miller, and Donald Stokes, *The American Voter* (New York: Wiley, 1960).

28. "Bush Outperforms GOP," *Washington Post.* February 17, 2002. p A5.

29. Benjamin Page, *Choices and Echoes in Elections: Rational Man and Electoral Democracy* (Chicago: University of Chicago Press, 1978), chap. 8; see also Sidney Verba and Norman H. Nie, *Participation in America: Political Democracy and Social Equality* (New York: Harper & Row, 1972), pp. 25–26.

CHAPTER 9

1. Douglas Waller, "How Jeffords Got Away," *Time,* June 4, 2001, pp. 36–40; Mike Christensen, "Anguished Transformation from Maverick to Outcast," *CQ Weekly,* May 26, 2001, pp. 1242–46; Jim Jeffords, *My Declaration of Independence,* (New York: Simon and Schuster, 2001).

2. See E. E. Schattschneider, *The Semisovereign People* (New York: Holt, 1960); V. O. Key, Jr., Politics, Parties, and Pressure Groups (New York: Crowell, 1964).

3. Quoted in *National Party Conventions, 1831–1988* (Washington, D.C.: Congressional Quarterly Press, 1991), p. 2. See also Michael Nelson, ed., *Guide to the Presidency* (Washington, D.C.: Congressional Quarterly Press, 1989), pp. 268–69.

4. Quoted in Noble E. Cunningham, *The Making of the American Party System, 1789 to 1809* (Englewood Cliffs, N.J.: Prentice Hall, 1965); see also Cunningham, *The Jeffersonian Republicans* (Chapel Hill: University of North Carolina Press, 1957).

5. See Warren E. Miller, "Party Identification, Realignment, and Party Voting: Back to the Basics," *American Political Science Review* 85 (1991): 557.

6. See Ralph Ketcham, *Presidents Above Party* (Chapel Hill: University of North Carolina Press, 1984).

7. See Frank Freidel, *Franklin D. Roosevelt: The Triumph* (Boston: Little, Brown, 1956), pp. 248–49.

8. James David Barber, *The Pulse of Politics* (New York: Norton, 1980), pp. 238–63.

9. See William Leuchtenburg, *In the Shadow of FDR* (Ithaca, N.Y.: Cornell University Press, 1983).

10. Cite John Kohut, "GOP Fighting the Tide," Charles Cook, *The Cook Election Preview, National Journal,* April 27, 2002, p. 15.

11. The Harris Poll No. 8, February 13, 2002, at http://www.harrisinteractive.com, and "Battleground 2002 (XXI), The Tarrance Group, Inc., Study #8794, http://www.azwins.org/Battleground%202002.pdf.

12. Charles Babington, "Divided Outcome Extends to State Legislatures Too," *Washington Post,* November 9, 2000, supplemented by author's calculations of the party balance in the Washington State and Oregon legislatures from the Websites of those states' legislatures.

13. Jonathan Alter, "Independents' Day," *Newsweek,* August 28, 1995, pp. 34–37; E. J. Dionne, Jr., "Perot and Those Pandering Pols," *Washington Post National Weekly Edition,* August 21–27, 1995, p. 29.

14. See Austin Ranney, *The Doctrine of Responsible Party Government: Its Origins and Present State* (Urbana: University of Illinois Press, 1962); Samuel J. Eldersvald, *Political Parties in American Society* (New York: Basic Books, 1982).

15. See L. Sandy Maisel, *Parties and Elections in America* (New York: McGraw Hill, 1992).

16. See John Aldrich, *Before the Convention: Strategies and Choices in Presidential Nomination Campaigns* (Chicago: University of Chicago Press, 1980).

17. See American Political Science Association, Committee on Political Parties, "Toward a More Responsible Two-Party System," *American Political Science Review* 64 (1950).

18. Edmond Constantini and Linda Ol Valenty, "The Motives-Ideology Connection Among Political Party Activists," and Peter B. Clark and James Q. Wilson, "Incentive Systems: A Theory of Organization," *Administrative Science Quarterly* 6 (1961): 129–66.

19. See William L. Riordan, *Plunkitt of Tammany Hall* (New York: Knopf, 1963); Harold Gosnell, *Machine Politics* (Chicago: University of Chicago Press, 1939).

20. See Xandra Kayden and Eddie Mahe, Jr., *The Party Goes On: The Persistence of the Two-Party System in the United States* (New York: Basic Books, 1985).

21. See Howard Reiter, *Parties and Elections in Corporate America* (New York: Longman, 1973).

22. Sandra Sobieraj, "President Pushes 2002 Fund-Raising Tally for Himself, Cheney Over $100 Million Mark," *Allentown Morning Call,* June 22, 2002, p. A 23.

23. See Byron E. Shafer, *Quiet Revolution: The Struggle for the Democratic Party and the Shaping of Post-Reform Politics* (New York: Russell Sage Foundation, 1983).

24. Paul West, "An Early Start for Democrats," *The Baltimore Sun,* February 4, 2002; Richard L. Berke, "Nominees May Be Chosen Quickly in Rare Competitive Primary Season," *New York Times,* January 2, 2000, p. 22.

25. See Theodore H. White, *The Making of the President, 1968* (New York: Atheneum, 1969).

26. See David E. Price, *Bringing Back the Parties* (Washington, D.C.: Congressional Quarterly Press, 1983).

27. Thomas B. Edsall, "GOP Gains Advantage on Key Issues, Poll Says," *Washington Post,* January 27, 2002, p. A4; Juliet Eilperin, "After McCain-Feingold, A Bigger Role for PACs," *Washington Post,* June 1, 2002, p. 1, 7.

28. See Samuel Patterson, "The Etiology of Party Competition," *American Political Science Review* 78 (1984): 691.

29. The tendency of single-member district systems to be found in conjunction with two parties, while multimember districts correlate with a system of many parties, is often known as Duverger's Law. It is named for a well-known French political scientist, Maurice Duverger, who first enunciated this theory in his book *Political Parties* (London: Methuen, 1954).

30. See Everett Carl Ladd, *American Political Parties: Social Change and Political Response* (New York: Norton, 1970); James L. Sundquist, *Dynamics of the Party System* (Washington, D.C.: Brookings Institution, 1973).

31. See Warren E. Miller, "Party Identification," in *Political Parties and Elections in the United States: An Encyclopedia,* ed. L. Sandy Maisel (New York: Garland, 1991).

32. See Frank Smallwood, *The Other Candidates: Third Parties in Presidential Elections* (Hanover, N.H.: University Press of New England, 1983); Steven J. Rosenstone, Roy L. Behr, and Edward H. Lazarus, *Third Parties in America: Citizen Response to Major Party Failure* (Princeton, N.J.: Princeton University Press, 1984).

33. See Byron Shafer, ed., *Beyond Realignment? Interpreting American Electorial Eras* (Madison: University of Wisconsin Press, 1991).

34. Roger H. Davidson and Walter J. Oleszek, *Congress and Its Members,* 8th ed. (Washington, D.C.: Congressional Quarterly Press, 2002), p. 276; William R. Shaffer, *Party and Ideology in the United States Congress* (Lanham, Md.: University Press of America, 1980); Norman Ornstein, Thomas E. Mann, and Michael Malbin, *Vital Statistics on Congress, 1993–94* (Washington, D.C.: Congressional Quarterly Press, 1994), p. 200.

35. David Broder, *The Party's Over* (New York: Harper & Row, 1971).

36. "Battleground 2002 (XXI)," Study #8794, The Tarrance Group, Inc., found at www.azwins.org/Battleground%202002.pdf, and Thomas B. Edsall, "GOP Gains Advantage on Key Issues, Polls Say," *Washington Post,* January 27, 2002, p. A4.

CHAPTER 10

1. See Peter Baker, "Motor Voter Apparently Didn't Drive Up Turnout," *Washington Post,* November 6, 1996, p. B7. Also see B. Drummond Ayres, Jr., "Law to Ease Voter Registration Has Added 5 Million to the Polls," *New York Times,* September 3, 1995, p. A1; "'Motor Voter' Bill Enacted after 5 Years," *CQ Almanac* 49 (1993): 199–201. See Executive Summary of the Federal Election Commission's Report to the Congress on "The Impact of the National Voter Registration Act of 1993 on Federal Elections, 1999–2000." http://www.fee.gov./pages/nvrareport2000/nvrareport2000.htm.

2. Raymond Wolfinger and Jonathan Hoffman, "Requesting and Voting with Motor Voter," *PS* (March 2001): pp. 85–92.

3. See U.S. Census Bureau, United States Department of Commerce. http://www.census.gov cited in CALTECH/MIT Voting Technology Report "What Is; What Could Be," July 2001 Fast Facts.

4. "National Commission on Federal Election Reform," *Summary of Principal Recommendations,* The Century Foundation. http://www.tcf.org/Press Releases/ElectionReform.html 1/30/02.

5. Sidney Verba and Norman H. Nie, *Participation in America: Political Democracy and Social Equality* (New York: Harper & Row, 1972); see Karen M. Arlington and William L. Taylor, eds., *Voting Rights in America: Continuing the Quest for Full Participation* (Lanham, Md.: University Press of America, 1992); See Francis Fox Piven and Richard A. Cloward, *Why Americans Don't Vote* (New York: Pantheon, 1988); Raymond E. Wolfinger and Steven J. Rosenstone, *Who Votes* (New Haven, Conn.: Yale University Press, 1980).

6. Larry Berman and Bruce Murphy, *Approaching Democracy,* 3rd ed. (Upper Saddle River, NJ: Prentice Hall, p. 368).

7. See Dan Keating and John Mintz, "Florida Black Ballots Affected Most in 2000," *Washington Post,* November 13, 2001, p. A3; Ford Fessenden, "Ballots Cast by Blacks and Older Voters Were Tossed in Far Greater Numbers," *New York Times,* November 12, 2001, p. A47.

8. See Caltech-MIT/Voting Technology Project, http://www.vote.caltech.edu/.

9. Steven J. Rosenstone and Raymond E. Wolfinger, "The Effect of Registration Laws on Voter Turnout," *American Political Science Review* 72 (March 1998): 25–30.

10. See Richard G. Niemi and Herbert F. Weisberg, eds., *Controversies in Voting Behavior,* 3d ed.

(Washington, D.C.: Congressional Quarterly Press, 1993); Richard Morin, "The Dog Ate My Forms, and, Well, I Couldn't Find a Pen," *Washington Post National Weekly Edition,* November 5–11, 1990, p. 38. See George Will, "In Defense of Nonvoting," *Newsweek,* October 10, 1983, p. 96.

11. Michael Kagay, "The Mystery of Nonvoters and Whether They Matter," *New York Times,* August 27, 2000, Section 4, p. 1. See Michael M. Grant and William Lyons, "Democratic Theory, Nonvoting, and Public Policy: The 1972–1988 Presidential Elections," *American Politics Quarterly* 21 (April 1993): 185–204; Priscilla L. Southwell, "Alienation and Nonvoting in the United States: A Refined Operationalization," *Western Political Quarterly* 38 (December 1985): 663–75.

12. Richard Berke, "Nonvoters Are No More Alienated Than Voters, Survey Shows," *New York Times,* May 30, 1996. For the complete survey and analysis, visit the League of Women Voters home page at http://www.lwv.org. Angus Campbell, Philip E. Converse, Warren E. Miller, and Donald Stokes, et al., *The American Voter* (New York: Wiley, 1960).

13. See National Initiative News, The Democracy Foundation, http://p2dd.org/ nationalinitiative/newsletter/.

14. See IRI. Initiative and Referendum Institute, http://www.iandrinstitute.org/home.asp. This website and www.ballot.org were created to provide in-depth nonpartisan and nonpolitical information about the initiative and referendum process at the local, state, and national level as well as to provide a glimpse of what is happening with initiative and referendum around the world.

15. See Stanley Kelley, Jr., *Interpreting Elections* (Princeton, N.J.: Princeton University Press, 1983). See also, Morris P. Fiorina, *Retrospective Voting in American National Elections* (New Haven. Conn.: Yale University Press, 1979). See Nelson Polsby and Aaron Wildavsky, *Presidential Elections,* 9th ed. (New York: Free Press, 1995).

16. See M. Margaret Conway, *Political Participation in the United States* (Washington, D.C.: Congressional Quarterly Press, 1991), p. 8, Table 1–2.

17. Martin Diamond, *The Electoral College and the American Idea of Democracy* (Washington, D.C.: American Enterprise Institute, 1977).

18. See Michael Glennon, *When No Majority Rules: The Electoral College and Presidential Succession,* (Washington DC: CQ Press, 2000, 2002); Verba and Nie, *Participation in America,* pp. 25–40.

19. See www.fee.gov/, "Campaign Finance," a report and study by the League of Women Voters at http://www.lwv.org. Also see Common Cause website, www.commoncause.org.

20. *Buckley v. Valeo,* 424 U.S. 1 (1976); *Federal Election Commission v. National Conservative Political Action Committee,* et al., 450 U.S. 480 (1985); see also Larry Sabato, *The Party's Just Begun* (Glenview, Ill.: Scott, Foresman/Little, Brown, 1988), p. 125.

21. See "Charting the Health of American Democracy," a report by the League of Women Voters, June 1997 http://www.lwv.org.

22. See Campaign Finance Reform, www.fee.gov/.

23. David E. Rosenbaum. "Foes of New Campaign Law Bring Two Suits Against it," *The New York Times,* March 28, 2002, p. A21.

CHAPTER 11

1. The case study is based on Liz Marlantes, "Democrats Tone Down Gun-Control Stance,"

Christian Science Monitor, May 10, 2002; ——, "Million Moms: Group Must Focus on Election Day," *Minneapolis Star Tribune,* May 12, 2002; Gina Holland, "Supreme Court Allows Judges to Toughen Sentences When Guns Used in Crimes, *Boston Globe,* June 24, 2002; Thomas B. Edsall, "NRA Puts Faith in Turnout," *Washington Post,* May 22, 2000, p. A3; Susan Levine, "Many Moms' Voices Are Heard on Mall," *Washington Post,* May 15, 2000, p. 1; and Helen Dewar, "Democrats' Pressure Spurs Lott to Allow Votes on Gun Control," *Washington Post,* May 17, 2000, p. A6.

2. See Jeffrey M. Berry, *The Interest Group Society,* 3d ed. (New York: Longman Press, 1997); Allan J. Cigler and Burdett A. Loomis, eds., *Interest Group Politics,* 4th ed. (Washington, D.C.: Congressional Quarterly Press, 1995).

3. Alexis de Tocqueville, *Democracy in America* (New York: Knopf, 1991), p. 485.

4. James Madison, *The Federalist,* no. 10, is reprinted in the Appendix.

5. See Arthur F. Bentley, *The Process of Government* (Chicago: University of Chicago Press, 1906); David Truman, *The Governmental Process* (New York: Knopf, 1951); E. E. Schattschneider, *The Semi-Sovereign People* (New York: Holt, 1960).

6. Tocqueville, *Democracy in America,* p. 487.

7. See Burdett A. Loomis and Allan J. Cigler, "The Changing Nature of Interest Group Politics," in *Interest Group Politics,* ed. Loomis and Cigler, pp. 1–31; Jack Walker, *Mobilizing Interest Groups in America* (Ann Arbor: University of Michigan Press, 1991).

8. See Mancur Olson, Jr., *The Logic of Collective Action* (Cambridge, Mass.: Harvard University Press, 1965), pp. 5–52; Dennis Chong, *Collective Action and the Civil Rights Movement* (Chicago: University of Chicago Press, 1991).

9. See David Vogel, *Fluctuating Fortunes: The Political Power of Business in America* (New York: Basic Books, 1989); William Greider, *Who Will Tell the People? The Betrayal of American Democracy* (New York: Simon & Schuster, 1992).

10. See Jeffrey H. Birnbaum and Alan S. Murray, *Showdown at Gucci Gulch* (New York: Vintage Books, 1988); Kay Lehman Schlozman and John T. Tierney, *Organized Interests and American Democracy* (New York: Harper & Row, 1986).

11. See the argument in John Kenneth Galbraith, *American Capitalism: The Concept of Countervailing Power* (Boston: Houghton Mifflin, 1952).

12. See Lawrence S. Rothenberg, *Linking Citizens to Government: Interest Group Politics at Common Cause* (New York: Cambridge University Press, 1992); Andrew S. McFarland, *Common Cause: Lobbying in the Public Interest* (Chatham, N.J.: Chatham House, 1984).

13. *Garcia v. San Antonio Metropolitan Transit Authority,* 469 U.S. 528 (1985).

14. See Karen O'Connor, *Women's Organizations' Use of the Courts* (Lexington, Mass.: Lexington Books, 1980); Mark P. Petracca, ed., *The Politics of Interests* (Boulder, Colo.: Westview Press, 1992).

15. Olson, *Logic of Collective Action.* See also Robert H. Salisbury, "An Exchange Theory of Interest Groups," *Midwest Journal of Political Science* 13 (1969): 1–32.

16. For an extended discussion of the reasons why people decide to get involved in full-time political activity, including work within interest groups, see James L. Payne et al., *The Motivation of Politicians* (Chicago: Nelson-Hall, 1984).

17. See Jeffrey M. Berry, *Lobbying for the People* (Princeton, N.J.: Princeton University Press, 1977).

18. See Ronald J. Hrebenar and Clive S. Thomas, "The Japanese Lobby in Washington: How Different Is It?" in *Interest Group Politics,* ed. Cigler and Loomis, pp. 349–68; Pat Choate, *Agents of Influence: How Japan's Lobbyists in the United States Manipulate America's Political and Economic System* (New York: Knopf, 1990).

19. See Laura Woliver, *From Outrage to Action* (Urbana: University of Illinois Press, 1993).

20. James L. Guth, et al., "Onward Christian Soldiers: Religious Activist Groups in American Politics," in *Interest Group Politics,* ed. Cigler and Loomis, pp. 42–75.

21. See Frank J. Sorauf, "Adaptation and Innovation in Political Action Committees," in *Interest Group Politics,* ed. Cigler and Loomis, pp. 175–92; Dan Clawson, Alan Neustadt, and Denise Scott, *Money Talks: Corporate PACs and Political Influence* (New York: Basic Books, 1992).

22. *United States v. Harris,* 347 U.S. 612 (1954).

23. Jonathan D. Salant, "Highlights of the Lobby Bill," *Congressional Quarterly Weekly Report,* December 2, 1995, p. 3632.

24. Jonathan Rauch, *Demosclerosis: The Silent Killer of American Government* (New York: Random House, 1994).

25. Arthur Bentley, *The Process of Government, A Study of Social Pressures* (Chicago: University of Chicago Press, 1908).

26. David B. Truman, *The Governmental Process* (New York: Knopf, 1951).

27. Theodore Lowi, *The End of Liberalism* (New York: Norton, 1979). See also Robert Dahl, *Preface to Democratic Theory* (Chicago: University of Chicago Press, 1956).

28. Hugh Heclo, "Issue Networks and the Executive Establishment," in *The New American Political System,* ed. Anthony King (Washington, D.C.: American Enterprise Institute, 1978), pp. 55–82.

29. John P. Heinz, Edward O. Lauman, Robert L. Nelson, and Robert H. Salisbury, *The Hollow Core* (Cambridge, Mass.: Harvard University Press, 1993).

30. *Colorado Republican Federal Campaign Committee v. Federal Election Commission,* 135 L.Ed. 2d 795 (1996), p. 803.

31. Quoted in Richard L. Berke, "Interest Groups Prepare to Spend on Campaign Spin," *New York Times,* January 11, 1998, p. 1.

32. Adam Clymer, "The Supreme Court: Campaign Money," *New York Times,* June 26, 2001; discussing *Federal Election Commission v. Colorado Republican Federal Campaign Committee* 533 U.S. 431 (2001).

33. Federal Election Commission reports issued on October 30, 2002, for the fund-raising between January 1, 2001 and September 30, 2002, as reported by the Center for Responsive Politics, found at http://www.opensecrets.org/ overview/.

34. ——"Editorials by Any Other Name," *The Christian Science Monitor,* October 30, 2002.

CHAPTER 12

1. See Marvin Kalb, "How to Cover a War," *New York Times,* October 17, 2001, p. A31.

2. Howard Hurtz, "War Coverage Takes a Negative Turn," *Washington Post,* February 7, 2002, p. A14; Michael R. Gordon, "Military Putting Heavier Limits on Reporter Access," *New York Times,* October 21, 2001, p. B3.

3. See Roberto J. Gonzalez, "Ignorance Is Not Bliss," SF Gate, http://www.sfgate.com/

cgi-bin/article.cgi?f-/c/a/2002/01/02/
ED232248.DTL, January 2, 2002, pp. 1–3.

4. See Jane Perlez, "Southeast Asia's Press Is Under Pressure," *New York Times*, April 4, 2002, p. A10; Mark Lacey, "Eritrea Puts a Tight Lid on its Press," *New York Times*, May 5, 2002, p. A4.

5. Quoted in Harold W. Chase and Allen H. Lerman, *Kennedy and the Press* (New York: Crowell, 1965), p. 26.

6. Robert M. Entman, *Democracy Without Citizens: Media and the Decay of American Politics* (New York: Oxford University Press, 1989), p. 8; Shanto Iyengar, *Is Anyone Responsible? How Television Frames Political Issues* (Chicago: University of Chicago Press, 1991); W. Russell Newman, *The Paradox of Mass Politics* (Cambridge, Mass.: Harvard University Press, 1986).

7. Thomas Jefferson, quoted in Samuel Kernell, *Going Public* (Washington, D.C.: Congressional Quarterly Press, 1993), p. 94; George Washington, quoted in Jeffrey K. Tulis, *The Rhetorical Presidency* (Princeton, N.J.: Princeton University Press, 1987), p. 131.

8. Ronald Berkman and Laura W. Kitch, *Politics in the Media* (New York: McGraw-Hill, 1986); Deane E. Alger, *The Media and Politics* (Englewood Cliffs, N.J.: Prentice Hall, 1989). See W. Russell Neuman, Marion R. Just, and Ann N. Crigler, *Common Knowledge: News and the Construction of Political Meaning* (Chicago: University of Chicago Press, 1992); Stephen Ansolabehere, Roy Behr, and Shanto Iyengar, *The Media Game: American Politics in the Television Age* (New York: Macmillan, 1993).

9. David Halberstam, *The Powers That Be* (New York: Dell, 1979), p. 72.

10. Richard E. Neustadt, *Presidential Power and the Modern Presidents: The Politics of Leadership from Roosevelt to Reagan* (New York: Free Press, 1990), p. 260. See also Todd Gitlin, ed., *Watching Television* (New York: Pantheon, 1986).

11. Frank Rich, "The Weight of an Anchor," http://web.dailycamera.com/opinion/editorials/2beancho.html.

12. PBS Anchor Lehrer says network news is expendable; Rips Koppel. http://drudgereport.com/flash9.htm, May 19, 2002.

13. Project for Excellence in Journalism, "Differences in Medium," http://www.journalism.org.

14. See Todd Gitlin, ed., *Watching Television* (New York: Pantheon, 1986). See Thomas E. Patterson, *Out of Order* (New York: Knopf, 1993); Patterson, *The Mass Media Election: How Americans Choose Their President* (New York: Praeger, 1980); *1-800-President: The Report of the Twentieth-Century Fund Task Force on Television and the Campaign of 1992* (New York: Twentieth-Century Fund Press, 1993). Sig Mickelson, *The Electric Mirror* (New York: Dodd, Mead, 1972), p. 154. See also Larry Speakes, *Speaking Out: The Reagan Presidency from Inside the White House* (New York: Scribner's, 1988), p. 111.

15. Austin Ranney, *Channels of Power: The Impact of Television on American Politics* (New York: Basic Books, 1983), p. 144.

16. See Lawrence Grossman, *The Electronic Republic* (New York: Viking, 1995), p. 60.

17. Doris Graber, *Mass Media and American Politics* (Washington, D.C.: Congressional Quarterly Press, 1989), p. 12.

18. Marshall McLuhan, *Understanding Media: The Extensions of Man* (New York: McGraw-Hill, 1965).

19. David Broder, *Behind the Front Page: A Candid Look at How News Is Made* (New York: Simon & Schuster, 1987), p. 114. See also Jay Rosen and Paul Taylor, *The New News v. the Old News: The Press and Politics in the 1990s* (New York: Twentieth-Century Fund, 1992).

20. Graber, *Mass Media and American Politics*, p. 20.

21. Cited in Thomas Dye, Harmon Zeigler, and S. Robert Lichter, *American Politics in the Media Age* (Pacific Grove, Calif.: Brooks/Cole, 1992), p. 5.

22. Iyengar, *Is Anyone Responsible?* See also Douglas Kellner, *Television and the Crisis of Democracy* (Boulder, Colo.: Westview Press, 1990). See also, Eric Barnouw, *Tube of Plenty: The Evolution of American Television* (New York: Oxford University Press, 1982), p. 415.

23. See Jeff Cohen and Norman Solomon, "CNN's 'Tailwind' and Selective Media Retractions," http://www.fair.org/extra/9808/tailwind.html.

24. Ben Bagdikian, *The Media Monopoly*, 4th ed. (Boston: Beacon Press, 1994).

25. *Red Lion Broadcasting v. FCC*, 395 U.S. 367 (1969).

26. *New York Times Co. v. United States*, 403 U.S. 714, p. 717 (1971).

27. Mark Cook and Jeff Cohen, "The Media Go to War: How Television Sold the Panama Invasion," *FAIR 3*, no. 2 (January/February 1991): pp. 22–25.

28. *Miami Herald Publishing Co. v. Tornillo*, 418 U.S. 241 (1974).

29. Robert Lichter, Stanley Rothman, and Linda Litcher, *The Media Elite* (Bethesda, Md.: Alder and Alder, 1986).

30. Bernard Goldberg, *Bias* (Regency Publishers, 2001).

31. See Jeff Cohen, "Maybe the Public- Not the Press- Has a Leftist Bias," http://www.fair.org/articles/liberal-media.html.

32. Andrew Kohut, "Listen Up, Bias Mongers! The Audience Doesn't Agree." Columbia Journalism Review On-line, http://www.cjr.org/year/02/2/kohut.asp.

33. Bagdikian, *Media Monopoly*. See also, William Greider, *Who Will Tell the People? The Betrayal of American Democracy* (New York: Simon & Schuster, 1992).

34. See Christopher Stern, "Limits on Media Ownership Voided," *Washington Post*, February 20, 2002, pp. E1, E3. See also, "Protecting Media Diversity." *New York Times*, February 23, 2002, p. A 30.

35. Howard Kurtz, "The Media Anoint Clinton: But How Do They Know That He's the Front-Runner?" *Washington Post Weekly*, January 20–26, 1992, p. 13; Sidney Blumenthal, "The Anointed," *New Republic*, February 3, 1992, pp. 24–27. See also, "Campaign 2000 Highly Rated," The Pew Research Center for the People and the Press, November 16, 2000, http://www.people-press.org/reports/display.php3?ReportID=23. Richard Sobel, ed., *Public Opinion in U.S. Foreign Policy*. (Latham, Md.: Rowan and Littlefield, 1993). Richard Morin, "Maybe the Messenger Should Re-Think the Message: Is the Media Polluting Our Politics?" *Washington Post Weekly*, November 29–December 5, 1993, p. 37.

36. See Timothy Egan, "Triumph Leaves Talk Radio Pondering Its Next Targets," *New York Times*, January 1, 1995, p. 22. Quoted in Robin Toner, "Election Jitters in Limbaughland," *New York Times*, November 3, 1994, p. A29.

37. Theodore White, *America in Search of Itself* (New York: Harper & Row, 1982), pp. 165–66. See also Roland Perry, *Hidden Power: The Programming of the President* (New York: Beaufort, 1984).

38. Daniel Hallin, "Sound Bite News: Television Coverage of Elections, 1968–1988," Media Studies Project Occasional Paper (Washington, D.C.: Woodrow Wilson International Center for Scholars, 1990); Mickey Kaus, "Sound-Bitten," *New Republic*, October 26, 1992, pp. 16–18; Kiku Adatto, "The Incredible Shrinking Sound Bite," *New Republic*, May 28, 1990, pp. 20–21.

39. Edwin Diamond and Stephen Bates, *The Spot: The Rise of Political Advertising on Television* (Cambridge, Mass.: MIT Press, 1992).

CHAPTER 13

1. The case study is based on Elizabeth A. Palmer, "Terrorism Bill's Sparse Paper Trail May Cause Legal Vulnerabilities," *Congressional Quarterly Weekly*, October 27, 2001, pp. 2533–35; and Anne Gearan, "Supreme Court to Hear Clarifying Police Power During Bus Searches," *The Legal Intelligencer*, January 7, 2002; Evan Thomas and Michael Isikoff, "Justice Kept in the Dark," *Newsweek*, December 10, 2001, pp. 37–43; ——— "Terrorism Bill's Sparse Paper Trail May Cause Legal Vulnerabilities," *CQ Weekly*, October 27, 2001, pp. 2533–64; and Dan Eggen and Susan Schmidt, "Secretive Court Balks at Anti-Terrorism Plan," *Allentown Morning Call*, August 23, 2002, p. 1.

2. For more on this argument, see Henry J. Abraham and Barbara A. Perry, *Freedom and the Court: Civil Rights and Liberties in the United States*, 7th ed. (New York: Oxford University Press, 1998), pp. 3–9.

3. *United States v. Carolene Products Co.*, 304 U.S. 144; 58 S. Ct. 778; 1938, Louis Lusky, *By What Right* (Charlottesville, Va.: The Michie Company, 1974)

4. See Leonard W. Levy, *Freedom of Speech and Press in Early American History: Legacy of Suppression* (New York: Harper & Row, 1963).

5. *Barron v. Baltimore*, 32 U.S. 243 (1833).

6. *Slaughterhouse Cases*, 83 U.S. 36 (1873).

7. For more on this process, see *Palko v. Connecticut*, 302 U.S. 319 (1937); *Adamson v. California*, 332 U.S. 46 (1947).

8. *Hurtado v. California*, 110 U.S. 516 (1884).

9. *Twining v. New Jersey*, 211 U.S. 78 (1908).

10. *Chicago, Burlington and Quincy Railway Co. v. Chicago*, 166 U.S. 226 (1897).

11. *Schenck v. United States*, 249 U.S. 47 (1919).

12. *Frohwerk v. United States*, 249 U.S. 204 (1919).

13. *Debs v. United States*, 249 U.S. 211 (1919).

14. *Abrams v. United States*, 250 U.S. 616 (1919).

15. *Gitlow v. New York*, 268 U.S. 652 (1925).

16. *Near v. Minnesota*, 283 U.S. 697 (1931).

17. *Powell v. Alabama*, 287 U.S. 45 (1932).

18. *Hamilton v. Regents of the University of California*, 293 U.S. 245 (1934).

19. *Palko v. Connecticut*, 302 U.S. 319 (1937).

20. See *Williams v. Florida*, 399 U.S. 78 (1970); *Apodaca v. Oregon*, 406 U.S. 404 (1972); *Johnson v. Louisiana*, 406 U.S. 356 (1972).

21. For more, see Anson Phelps Stokes and Leo Pfeffer, *Church and State in the United States* (New York: Harper & Row, 1964).

22. *Walz v. Tax Commission*, 397 U.S. 664 (1970).

23. Abraham and Perry, *Freedom and the Court*, pp. 220–320.

24. *Everson v. Board of Education of Ewing Township*, 330 U.S. 1 (1947).

25. *Engel v. Vitale*, 370 U.S. 24 (1962).

26. *Abington School District v. Schempp*, 374 U.S. 203 (1963).

27. *Lemon v. Kurtzman*, 403 U.S. 602 (1971).

28. *Wolman v. Walter*, 433 U.S. 229 (1977).

29. *Roemer v. Board of Public Works of Maryland*, 426 U.S. 736 (1976).

30. *Committee for Public Education v. Nyquist*, 413 U.S. 756 (1973).

31. *Levitt v. Committee for Public Education and Religious Liberty*, 413 U.S. 472 (1973).

32. *Meek v. Pittenger*, 421 U.S. 349 (1975).

33. *Mueller v. Allen*, 463 U.S. 388 (1983).

34. *Marsh v. Chambers*, 463 U.S. 783 (1983).

35. *Lynch v. Donnelly*, 465 U.S. 668 (1984).

36. *Stone v. Graham*, 449 U.S. 39 (1980).

37. *Wallace v. Jaffree*, 472 U.S. 38 (1985).

38. *Grand Rapids School District v. Ball*, 473 U.S. 373 (1985).

39. *Edwards v. Aguillard*, 482 U.S. 578 (1987).

40. Patty Reinert, "Commandment Case Rejected," *Houston Chronicle*, February 26, 2002.

41. *County of Allegheny v. Greater Pittsburgh ACLU*, 497 U.S. 573 (1989).

42. *Lee v. Weisman*, 112 S.Ct. 2649 (1992).

43. *Santa Fe Independent School District v. Jane Doe*, 530 US 290 (2000).

44. *Zelman v. Simmons-Harris*, 153 L.Ed.2d 604 (2002), David Savage, "School Vouchers Win Backing of High Court," *Los Angeles Times*, June 28, 2002, p. 1.

45. David Von Drehle, "Judge Blocks Decision During Appeals," *The Washington Post*, June 28, 2002.

46. *Reynolds v. United States*, 98 U.S. 145 (1879).

47. See *Braunfeld v. Brown*, 366 U.S. 599 (1961); *McGowan v. Maryland*, 366 U.S. 420 (1961); *Sherbert v. Verner*, 374 U.S. 398 (1963).

48. *Oregon Department of Human Resources v. Smith*, 294 U.S. 872 (1990).

49. *Church of Lukumi Babalu Aya v. Hialeah*, 508 U.S. 520 (1993).

50. Bob Cohn and David A. Kaplan, "A Chicken on Every Altar?" *Newsweek*, November 9, 1992, p. 79.

51. *City of Boerne v. Flores*, 117 S.Ct. 2157 (1997). Ibid., p. 2162.

52. *Good News Club v. Milford Central School*, 533 US 98 (2001).

53. *Watchtower Bible and Tract Society of New York v. Village of Stratton, Ohio*, 153 L.Ed.2d 205 (2002); see Tony Mauro, "In God's Hands," *Legal Times*, February 25, 2002, p. 1.

54. See Alexander Meiklejohn, *Free Speech and Its Relation to Self-Government* (New York: Harper, 1948).

55. *Abrams v. United States*, 250 U.S. 187 (1919).

56. *Dennis v. United States*, 339 U.S. 494 (1951).

57. *Yates v. United States*, 354 U.S. 298 (1957).

58. See *Scales v. United States*, 367 U.S. 203 (1961); *United States v. Robel*, 389 U.S. 258 (1967).

59. *Brandenburg v. Ohio*, 385 U.S. 444 (1969).

60. *Nixon v. Shrink Missouri Gov't PAC*, 528 US 377 (2000). Discussed in Warren Richey, "Court Affirms Campaign Finance Laws," *Christian Science Monitor*, January 25, 2000, p. 1. See also, *Buckley v. Valeo*, 424 U.S. 1 (1976).

61. *Federal Election Commission v. Colorado Republican Federal Campaign Committee*, 533 US 431 (2001).

62. See *Edwards v. South Carolina*, 372 U.S. 229 (1963); *Brown v. Louisiana*, 383 U.S. 131 (1966); *Chaplinsky v. New Hampshire*, 315 U.S. 568 (1942).

63. *Terminiello v. Chicago*, 337 U.S. 1 (1949).

64. *RAV v. City of St. Paul*, 505 U.S. 377 (1992); *Wisconsin v. Mitchell*, 508 U.S. 476 (1993).

65. *Adderly v. Florida*, 385 U.S. 39 (1967).

66. *Cox v. Louisiana*, 379 U.S. 569 (1965).

67. *Cohen v. California*, 403 U.S. 15 (1971) and *Texas v. Johnson* 491 U.S. 397 (1989).

68. *RAV v. City of St. Paul, Minnesota*, 505 U.S. 377 (1992).

69. *Wisconsin v. Mitchell*, 508 U.S. 476 (1993).

70. *Madsen v. Women's Health Center*, 115 S.Ct. 2338 (1995).

71. *Schenck v. Pro-Choice Network of Western New York*, 117 S.Ct. 855 (1997).

72. Bill McAllister, "Two Victories for Abortion Rights," *Denver Post*, June 29, 2000, p. 1.

73. *New York Times Co. v. United States*, 403 U.S. 713 (1971).

74. *Nebraska Press Assn. v. Stuart*, 427 U.S. 539 (1976).

75. *Richmond Newspapers Inc. v. Virginia*, 448 U.S. 555 (1980).

76. See *New York Times v. Sullivan*, 376 U.S. 254 (1964); *Curtis Publishing Co. v. Butts*, 388 U.S. 130 (1967).

77. *Gertz v. Robert Welch Inc.*, 418 U.S. 323 (1974); *Rosenbloom v. Metromedia*, 403 U.S. 29 (1971).

78. *Herbert v. Lando*, 441 U.S. 153 (1979).

79. "First Amendment Decision: The Press Wins," *New York Times*, October 23, 1999, p. 1.

80. *Roth v. United States*, 354 U.S. 476 (1957).

81. *Memoirs v. Massachusetts*, 383 U.S. 413 (1966).

82. *Ginzburg v. United States*, 383 U.S. 463 (1966); *Ginsberg v. New York*, 390 U.S. 629 (1968); *Mishkin v. New York*, 383 U.S. 502 (1966); *Redrup v. New York*, 386 U.S. 767 (1967).

83. *Miller v. California*, 413 U.S. 15 (1973).

84. *Jenkins v. Georgia*, 418 U.S. 153 (1974).

85. *Knox v. United States*, 114 S.Ct. 375 (1993).

86. *Reno v. American Civil Liberties Union*, 117 S.Ct. 2329 (1997); see also Greg Miller, "Law to Control Online Porn Creates Strange Bedfellows," *Los Angeles Times*, February 15, 1999, p. 1; and Greg Miller, "Court Rejects Child Online Protection Act," *Los Angeles Times*, June 23, 2000, p. 1.

87. *Ashcroft v. Free Speech Coalition*, 152 L.Ed. 2d 403 (2002).

88. *Ashcroft v. American Civil Liberties Union* 535 U.S. 564 (2002).

89. Lyle Denniston, "Justices to Weigh Library Web Access," November 13, 2002. Robert O'Harrow, Jr. "U.S. Court Overturns Internet Smut Law Ruling in Library Case is 3rd Loss for Congress," *Boston Globe*, June 1, 2002. And see, Michael S. Romano, "Putting Up a Filter for the Kids," *New York Times*, April 4, 2002.

90. *People of New York v. Defore*, 242 N.Y. 13, pp. 19–25 (1927).

91. *Weeks v. United States*, 232 U.S. 383 (1914).

92. For more, see David Fellman, *The Defendant's Rights Today* (Madison: University of Wisconsin Press, 1976), pp. 292–97.

93. *Wolf v. Colorado*, 338 U.S. 25 (1949); *Rochin v. California*, 342 U.S. 165 (1952).

94. *Breithaupt v. Abram*, 352 U.S. 432 (1957).

95. *Mapp v. Ohio*, 367 U.S. 643 (1961).

96. Dissent by Warren Burger, *Bivens v. Six Unknown Named Agents of Federal Bureau of Narcotics*, 403 U.S. 388 (1971).

97. *United States v. Calandra*, 414 U.S. 338 (1974).

98. *Stone v. Powell*, 428 U.S. 465 (1976).

99. *United States v. Leon*, 468 U.S. 902 (1984).

100. *Illinois v. Rodriguez*, 110 S.Ct. 2793 (1990).

101. See *Carroll v. United States*, 267 U.S. 132 (1925); *United States v. Chadwick*, 433 U.S. 1 (1977); *Cady v. Dombroski*, 413 U.S. 433 (1973).

102. *Katz v. United States*, 389 U.S. 347 (1967), p. 351.

103. See *Chimel v. California*, 395 U.S. 752 (1969); *Coolidge v. New Hampshire*, 403 U.S. 443 (1971); *Schneckloth v. Bustamonte*, 412 U.S. 218 (1973); *United States v. Cortez*, 449 U.S. 411 (1981).

104. *Terry v. Ohio*, 391 U.S. 1 (1968).

105. *New Jersey v. T.L.O.* 469 US 325 (1995).

106. *California v. Hodari D.*, 111 S.Ct. 1547 (1991).

107. *Florida v. Bostick*, 111 S.Ct. 2382 (1991).

108. *Vernonia School District 47J v. Acton*, 515 US 646 (1995).

109. Tamar Lewin, "Schools Across U.S. Await Ruling on Drug Tests," *New York Times*, March 20, 2002.

110. *Board of Education v. Earls*, 153 L.Ed. 2d 735 (2002).

111. *Katz v. United States*, 389 U.S. 347 (1967), p. 361.

112. *Illinois v. Wardlow*, 528 US 119 (2000).

113. *Kyllo v. United States*, 533 US 27 (2001).

114. *United States v. Drayton* 153 L.Ed. 2d 242 (2002).

115. *Brown v. Mississippi*, 297 U.S. 278 (1936).

116. *Haynes v. Washington*, 373 U.S. 503 (1963).

117. *Escobedo v. Illinois*, 378 U.S. 478 (1964).

118. *Miranda v. Arizona*, 384 U.S. 436 (1966).

119. *Harris v. New York*, 401 U.S. 222 (1971).

120. *Rhode Island v. Innis*, 446 U.S. 291 (1980); see also *Michigan v. Tucker*, 417 U.S. 433 (1974).

121. *New York v. Quarles*, 467 U.S. 669 (1984).

122. *Oregon v. Elstad*, 470 U.S. 298 (1985).

123. *Arizona v. Fulminante*, 111 S.Ct. 1246 (1991).

124. *United States v. Dickerson*, 530 US 428 (2000).

125. Jan Hoffman, "Police Tactics Chipping Away at Suspects' Rights," *New York Times*, March 29, 1998, p. 1; and Jan Hoffman, "As Miranda Rights Erode, Police Get Confessions from Innocent People," *New York Times*, March 30, 1998, p. 32.

126. *Griswold v. Connecticut*, 381 U.S. 479 (1965).

127. See David J. Garrow, *Liberty and Sexuality: The Right to Privacy and the Making of* Roe v. Wade (New York: Macmillan, 1994), pp. 16–195.

128. See Robert Bork, *The Tempting of America* (New York: Free Press, 1989); Ethan Bronner, *Battle for Justice: How the Bork Nomination Shook America* (New York: Norton, 1989).

129. *Eisentadt v. Baird*, 405 U.S. 438 (1972); *Doe v. Bolton*, 410 U.S. 179 (1973).

130. *Romer v. Evans*, 116 S.Ct. 1620 (1996), p. 1629.

131. *Boy Scouts of America v. Dale* 530 US 640 (2000), see also Linda Greenhouse, "Supreme Court Backs Boy Scouts," *New York Times*, June 29, 2000, p. 1.

132. *Roe v. Wade*, 410 U.S. 113 (1973).

133. *Harris v. McRae*, 448 U.S. 297 (1980).

134. *Planned Parenthood of Central Missouri v. Danforth*, 428 U.S. 52 (1976).

135. *Akron v. Akron Center for Reproductive Health,* 462 U.S. 416 (1983).

136. *Webster v. Reproductive Health Services,* 492 U.S. 490 (1989).

137. *Planned Parenthood of Southeastern Pennsylvania v. Casey,* 112 S.Ct. 2791 (1992).

138. Linda Greenhouse, "U.S. Court Voids Ohio Ban on Late-Term Abortion," *New York Times,* November 19, 1997.

139. *Stenberg v. Carhart,* 530 US 914 (2000).

140. *Cruzan by Cruzan v. Director, Missouri Department of Health,* 110 S.Ct. 2841 (1990).

141. *Washington v. Glucksberg,* 117 S.Ct. 2258 (1997), and *Vacco v. Quill,* 117 S.Ct. 2293 (1997).

CHAPTER 14

1. The case study is based on David J. Garrow, "How Much Weight Can Race Carry?", *New York Times,* May 19, 2002, p. 4 wk; Mark Clayton, "Michigan Affirmative Action Case Will Reverberate Widely," *Christian Science Monitor,* October 23, 2001; Ben Feller, "One Florida Sustains Universities' Diversity," *Tampa Tribune,* September 6, 2001; Barry Klein, "UF Ends Race-Based Scholarship Program," *St. Petersburg Times,* August 31, 2001; Travis Gosselin, "Divided We Stand: Affirmative Action: Why It Should Remain," *St. Louis Post Dispatch,* April 11, 2001; David J. Garrow, "The Path to Diversity? Different Differences," *New York Times,* September 2, 2001, p. 4; Peter Kilborn, "Jeb Bush Roils Florida on Affirmative Action," *New York Times,* February 4, 2000.

2. Donald G. Nieman, *Promises to Keep: African Americans and the Constitutional Order, 1776 to the Present* (New York: Oxford University Press, 1991), pp. 3–5.

3. *Dred Scott v. Sandford,* 19 Howard 393 (1857).

4. *United States v. Cruikshank,* 92 U.S. 214 (1876).

5. *Civil Rights Cases,* 109 U.S. 3 (1883).

6. *Plessy v. Ferguson,* 163 U.S. 537 (1896).

7. *Cumming v. County Board of Education,* 175 U.S. 528 (1899).

8. C. Vann Woodward, *Origins of the New South: 1877–1913,* 2d ed. (Baton Rouge: Louisiana University Press, 1987), pp. 331–38, 372–75.

9. *Bailey v. Alabama,* 219 U.S. 219 (1911).

10. *Guinn v. United States,* 238 U.S. 347 (1915). See also Nieman, *Promises to Keep,* pp. 123–27.

11. *Nixon v. Herndon,* 273 U.S. 536 (1927).

12. Richard Kluger, *Simple Justice* (New York: Knopf, 1976), p. 250.

13. *Missouri ex rel. Gaines v. Canada,* 305 U.S. 337 (1938).

14. *Sweatt v. Painter,* 339 U.S. 629 (1950).

15. *McLaurin v. Oklahoma State of Regents,* 339 U.S. 637 (1950).

16. *Brown v. Board of Education of Topeka, Kansas,* 347 U.S. 483 (1954).

17. *Bolling v. Sharpe,* 347 U.S. 497 (1954).

18. *Brown v. Board of Education of Topeka, Kansas,* 349 U.S. 294 (1955).

19. Alfred H. Kelly and Winfred A. Harbison, *The American Constitution: Origins and Development,* 4th ed. (New York: Norton, 1970), p. 940.

20. Jack W. Peltason, *Fifty-Eight Lonely Men* (New York: Harcourt Brace Jovanovich, 1961).

21. Nieman, *Promises to Keep,* pp. 166–76.

22. *Heart of Atlanta Motel v. United States,* 379 U.S. 241 (1964).

23. *Katzenbach v. McClung,* 379 U.S. 294 (1964).

24. *Harper v. Virginia Board of Elections,* 383 U.S. 663 (1966).

25. Nieman, *Promises to Keep,* p. 180.

26. *Jones v. Alfred H. Mayer,* 329 U.S. 409 (1968).

27. *Alexander v. Holmes County Board of Education,* 396 U.S. 19 (1969).

28. Nieman, *Promises to Keep,* p. 179.

29. *Swann v. Charlotte-Mecklenburg Board of Education,* 402 U.S. 1 (1971).

30. *Keyes v. School District #1, Denver, Colorado,* 413 U.S. 189 (1973).

31. *Milliken v. Bradley,* 418 U.S. 717 (1974).

32. Leslie Goldstein, "Affirmative Action Toward the 21st Century," address to the graduate seminar "The Constitution and Bill of Rights in the New Millennium," August 1, 1997, Freedom's Foundation, Valley Forge, Pa.

33. Sidney Verba and Gary R. Orren, *Equality in America: The View from the Top* (Cambridge, Mass.: Harvard University Press, 1985), p. 5.

34. *DeFunis v. Odegaard,* 416 U.S. 312 (1974).

35. *Regents of the University of California v. Bakke,* 438 U.S. 265 (1978).

36. *United Steelworkers v. Weber,* 443 U.S. 193 (1979).

37. *Fullilove v. Klutznick,* 448 U.S. 448 (1980).

38. Steven L. Carter, *Reflections of an Affirmative Action Baby* (New York: Basic Books, 1991), p. 69.

39. *Firefighters Local Union No. 1784 v. Stotts,* 467 U.S. 561 (1984).

40. *Wygant v. Jackson Board of Education,* 476 U.S. 267 (1986).

41. *Local Number 93, International Association of Firefighters v. City of Cleveland,* 478 U.S. 501 (1986).

42. *Local 28 of the Sheet Metal Workers' International Association v. EEOC,* 478 U.S. 421 (1986).

43. *U.S. v. Paradise,* 480 U.S. 149 (1987).

44. *Martin v. Wilks,* 109 S.Ct. 2180 (1989).

45. *City of Richmond v. Croson,* 488 U.S. 469 (1989).

46. *Patterson v. McLean Credit Union,* 109 S.Ct. 2363 (1989).

47. *Lorance v. AT&T Technologies,* 490 U.S. 900 (1989).

48. *Independent Federation of Flight Attendants v. Zipes,* 491 U.S. 754 (1989).

49. *Wards Cove Packing Co. v. Antonio,* 109 S.Ct. 2115 (1989).

50. Ronald Smothers, "Mississippi Mellows on Issue of Bias in State Universities," *New York Times,* March 13, 1995, p. A14.

51. *Adarand Constructors v. Pena,* 115 S. Ct. 2097 (1995).

52. Rene Sanchez and Sue Anne Pressley, "Universities Admit Fewer Minorities," *Washington Post,* May 19, 1997, p. A1.

53. Ibid.

54. Quoted in Nancy E. McGlen and Karen O'Connor, *Women's Rights: The Struggle for Equality in the Nineteenth and Twentieth Centuries* (New York: Praeger, 1983), pp. 389–91.

55. Ibid., pp. 272–74.

56. *Bradwell v. State of Illinois,* 83 U.S. 130 (1873).

57. *Minor v. Happersett,* 88 U.S. 162 (1875).

58. *Goesaert v. Cleary,* 335 U.S. 464 (1948).

59. *Hoyt v. Florida,* 368 U.S. 57 (1961).

60. *Reed v. Reed,* 404 U.S. 71 (1971).

61. *Frontiero v. Richardson,* 411 U.S. 677 (1973).

62. *Kahn v. Shevin,* 416 U.S. 351 (1974).

63. *Craig v. Boren,* 429 U.S. 190 (1976).

64. *United States v. Virginia,* 116 S.Ct. 2264 (1966).

65. Donald P. Baker and Tod Robberson, "Admit Women, Keep 'Rat Line,' VMI Alumni Say," *Washington Post,* July 2, 1996, p. B1; Michael Janofsky, "Citadel, Bowing to Court, Says It Will Admit Women," *New York Times,* June 29, 1996, p. 6; Donald P. Baker, "By One Vote, VMI Decides to Go Coed," *Washington Post,* September 22, 1996, p. 1.

66. *Farragher v. Boca Raton,* 66 U.S.L.W. 4643 (1998); *Burlington Industries v. Ellerth,* 66 U.S.L.W. 4643 (1998); and Joan Biskupic, "Court Draws Line on Harassment," *Washington Post,* June 27, 1998, pp. 1, 11. See also *Meritor Savings Bank v. Vinson,* 477, U.S. 57 (1986); *Harris v. Forklift Systems,* 510, U.S. 510 (1993); *Oncale v. Sundowner Offshore Services,* 66 U.S.L.W. 4172 (1998); and *Gebser v. Lago Vista Independent School District,* 66 U.S.L.W. 4501 (1998).

67. *U.S. v. Morrison,* explained in Stuart Taylor, Jr., "The Tipping Point," *National Journal,* June 10, 2000, pp. 1810–19.

68. *Katzenbach v. Morgan,* 384 U.S. 641 (1966).

69. *San Antonio Independent School District v. Rodriguez,* 411 U.S. 1 (1973).

70. *Plyler v. Doe,* 457 U.S. 202 (1982).

71. U.S. Census figures found at *www.census.gov* last consulted July 13, 2002.

72. *Elk v. Wilkins,* 112 U.S. 94 (1884).

73. Dee Brown, *Bury My Heart at Wounded Knee: An Indian History of the American West* (New York: Holt, Rinehart & Winston, 1971).

74. Jay Mathews, "Landmark Law Failing to Achieve Workplace Goals," *Washington Post,* April 16, 1995, p. 1.

75. Marcia Coyle, "ADA: Clarified or Ruined?" *National Law Journal,* July 5, 1999, pp. 1, 10.

76. *Board of Trustees of the University of Alabama v. Garrett* 531 US 356 (2001).

77. *P.G.A. Tour, Inc. v. Martin* 121 S. Ct. 1879 (2001).

78. *Kimel v. Florida Board of Regents, 528 US 62 (2000).*

79. Michael A. Fletcher, "Diversity's Future?". *Washington Post,* March 18, 2002, p. 1.

80. *Center for National Security Studies v. United States Department of Justice,* 2002 U.S. Dist. LEXIS 14168, Civ. 01-2500 (D.D.C. August 2, 2002; Kessler, J.).

81. *Detroit Free Press v. John Ashcroft,* 303 F. 3d 681 (2002).

CHAPTER 15

1. David E. Sanger, "President's Signature Turns Broad Tax Cut, and a Campaign Promise, Into Law," *New York Times,* June 8, 2001, p. A18.

2. See http://www.whitehouse.gov/news/usbudget/blueprint/bud02.html.

3. Stephen Moore, "Bush Tax Cut: A Good First Step." *Human Events Online.* http://www.humaneventsonline.com/articles/06-11-01/moore.html.

4. See Gary Klott, "Congress Approves $1.35 Trillion Tax-Cut Plan," Tax Planet.com. http://www.taxplanet.com/taxnews/final52601/final52601.html.

5. David E. Sanger, "President's Signature Turns Broad Tax Cut, and a Campaign Promise, Into

Law," *New York Times,* June 8, 2001, p. A18. See also http://www.whitehouse.gov/news/usbudget/blueprint/bud02.html.

6. See Jackie Koszczuk, "GOP-Led House Votes to Make Bush Tax Cuts Permanent," *Washington Post,* June 7, 2002, p. A5; Carl Hulse, "Senate Leader, In Surprise Move, Opens Debate on Estate Tax Repeal," *New York Times,* June 12, 2002, p. A16; Helen Dewar and Juliet Eilperin, "Senate Votes Down Permanent Repeal of the Inheritance Tax," *Washington Post,* June 13, 2002, p. A5.

7. See http://www.house.gov/reform/min/pdfs/pdf_inves/pdf_admin_estate_tax_fact_sheet.pdf.

8. See Mike Allen, "Rove Urges 'War' for Permanent Repeal of Estate Tax," *Washington Post,* June 14, 2002, p. A5.

9. Larry Gerston, *Making Public Policy: From Conflict to Resolution* (Boston: Little, Brown, 1983), p. 6; see Bruce Ingersoll, "U.S. Regulators to Raise a Stink about Cigars," *Wall Street Journal,* February 9, 1998, p. B1.

10. Leading process models of policy making include Randall Ripley and Grace Franklin, *Congress, the Bureaucracy, and Public Policy,* 5th ed. (Pacific Grove, Calif.: Brooks-Cole, 1991); Ripley and Franklin, *Policy Implementation in the United States,* 2d ed. (Homewood, Ill. Dorsey Press, 1986); James E. Anderson, *Public Policymaking* (Boston: Houghton Mifflin, 1990); leading policy typologies include Theodore Lowi, "Four Systems of Policy, Politics, and Choice," *Public Administration Review* 32, July/August 1972:298–310; Paul Peterson, *City Limits* (Chicago: University of Chicago Press, 1981); John W. Kingdon, *Agendas, Alternatives, and Public Policies* (Boston: Little, Brown, 1984); Leading scholars in the agenda-setting approach to understanding public policy include Roger Cobb and Charles Elder, *Participation in American Politics: The Dynamics of Agenda-Building,* 2d ed. (Baltimore: Johns Hopkins University Press, 1983); Bryan Jones, *Governing Urban America: A Policy Focus* (Boston: Little, Brown, 1982); Barbara Nelson, *Making an Issue of Child Abuse* (Chicago: University of Chicago Press, 1984); and Robert Waste, *The Ecology of City Policymaking* (New York: Oxford University Press, 1989).

11. Christopher Bosso, *Pesticides and Politics: The Life Cycle of a Public Issue* (Pittsburgh: University of Pittsburgh Press, 1987) The examples are based on the excellent account in Randy Shilts, *And the Band Played On: Politics, People, and the Epidemic* (New York: St. Martin's Press, 1987); p. 20. See also John Kinsella, *Covering the Plague: AIDS and the American Press* (New Brunswick, N.J.: Rutgers University Press, 1989); "Clinton to Seek More Money for AIDS Drugs," *New York Times,* December 30, 1997, p. A16; "Funding for AIDS Programs in Final Stretch," http://www.thebody.com/aac/sep1897.html.

12. For a discussion of policy entrepreneurs, see Eugene Lewis, *Public Entrepreneurship: Toward a Theory of Bureaucratic Political Powers* (Bloomington: Indiana University Press, 1980). See also the discussion of policy entrepreneurs and "policy windows" in John Kingdon, *Policies, Politics, and Agendas,* 2d ed. (Chatham, N.J.: Chatham House, 1992). For an interesting account of policy entrepreneurs—some successful and some not—in the Great Depression, see Alan Brinkley, *Voices of Protest: Huey Long, Father Coughlin, and the Great Depression* (New York: Knopf, 1982).

13. See Henry J. Abraham, *Freedom and the Court* (New York: Oxford University Press, 1988); Richard Klugar, *Simple Justice* (New York: Knopf, 1976); Gerald Rosenberg, *The Hollow Hope: Can Courts Bring About Social Change?* (Chicago: University of Chicago Press, 1992).

14. *Roe v. Wade,* 413 U.S. 113 (1973); *Webster v. Reproductive Health Services,* 424 U.S. 490 (1989).

15. Lizette Alvarez, "Senate, 54–41, Rejects Republican Bill to Ban Cloning," *New York Times,* February 12, 1998, p. A18; see also William Powers, "A Slant on Cloning," *National Journal,* January 10, 1998, p. 58; "FDA Is Prepared to Block Unapproved Cloning Efforts," *New York Times,* January 20, 1998, p. A13; "Cloning Foes Consider Moratorium," *Washington Post.* June 12, 2002, p. A7; Helen Dewer, "Anti-Cloning Bills in Senate, Vote Unlikely Soon," *Washington Post,* June 14, 2002, p. A4; Rick Weiss, "Debate over Cloning Puts the Political in Science," *Washington Post,* June 10, 2002, p. A9.

16. *Brown v. Board of Education of Topeka,* 347 U.S. 483 (1954); *Brown v. Board of Education of Topeka,* 349 U.S. 294 (1955).

17. Jonathan Kozol, *Savage Inequalities: Children in America's Schools* (New York: Crown, 1991); see also Alex Kotlowitz, *There Are No Children Here* (New York: Doubleday, 1991); Tracy Kidder, *Among Schoolchildren* (New York: Avon, 1989).

18. Eric Planin, "EPA Proposes to Ease Rules on Clean Air," *Washington Post,* June 14, 2002, p. A1, A8.

19. For a case in point that agencies, programs, and policies are extremely difficult to terminate, see Fred Bergerson, *The Army Gets an Air Force: The Tactics of Bureaucratic Insurgency* (Baltimore: Johns Hopkins Press, 1976). The discussion of the demise of public policies draws heavily on the similar discussion of the reasons for the demise of public agencies in Anthony Downs, *Inside Bureaucracy* (Boston: Little, Brown, 1959).

20. Kenneth J. Meier, *Regulation: Politics, Bureaucracy, and Economics* (New York: St. Martin's Press, 1985), p. 1; see also Michael D. Reagan, *The Politics of Policy* (Boston: Little, Brown, 1987). This discussion of the types of regulatory activity used by the federal government draws heavily upon the discussion of regulatory activity in Meier, *Regulation,* pp. 1–2.

21. Rachel Carson, *Silent Spring* (Boston: Houghton Mifflin, 1962); see also Kent E. Portney, *Controversial Issues in Environmental Policy* (Newbury Park, Calif.: Sage, 1992). The best single account of environmental policy making in this period is the agenda-setting study by Bosso, "Pesticides and Politics." See also Thomas Dunlap, *DDT: Scientists, Citizens, and Public Policy* (Princeton, N.J.: Princeton University Press, 1981); Charles O. Jones, *Clean Air: The Policies and Politics of Pollution Control* (Pittsburgh: University of Pittsburgh Press, 1975).

22. William Stevens, "In Kyoto, the Subject Is Climate; the Forecast Is for Storms," *New York Times,* December 1, 1997, p. D1; see also "The Kyoto Protocol on Climate Change." http://www.epa.gov/globalwarming.

23. Colum Lynch, "EU Ratifies Global Warming Treaty," *Washington Post,* June 1, 2002, p. A15.

24. "White House Warns on Climate Change," *New York Times Online,* June 3, 2002. http://www.nytimes.com/aponline/n.../AP-Climate-change.html?pagewanted=print&position=to, 6/4/02; see also, George Archobald, "White House Defends U-Turn on Global Warming," *Washington Times,* June 4, 2002. http://www.washingtontimes.com/national/20020604-15929206.htm. Quoted in Marc Lacey, "Clinton Targets Polluted Runoff to Clean Up Water," *Sacramento Bee,* February 20, 1998, p. A10.

25. Lincoln Steffens, *The Shame of the Cities* (New York: McClure, 1904); Robert Hunter, *Poverty* (New York: Macmillan, 1904); see also William Julius Wilson, *The Truly Disadvantaged* (Chicago: University of Chicago Press, 1987). For

documentation that public opinion is strongly in favor of supporting programs in aid of the needy, see Theodore R. Marmor, Jerry L. Mashaw, and Philip L. Harvey, *America's Misunderstood Welfare State* (New York: Basic Books, 1990).

26. David, John. "Social Security: The Crisis Is Real," *The Heritage Foundation Online.* 4/26/02, http://www.heritage.org/press/commentary/ed042602.cfm.; The CNN/Gallup USA Poll can be found at http://www.socialsecurity.org/.

27. Daniel Patrick Moynihan, *Maximum Feasible Misunderstanding: Community Action and the War on Poverty* (New York: Free Press, 1969).

28. Two dated but still excellent accounts of the policy-making battles surrounding the enactment of Medicare are Robert Alford, *Health Care Politics* (Chicago: University of Chicago Press, 1975); Theodore Marmor, *The Politics of Medicare* (Chicago: Aldine, 1973).

29. See Mary Jo Bane, "Welfare as We Know It," *American Prospect,* no. 30 January/February 1997: 47–53, http://www.epn.org/prospect/30/30bane.html; "Welfare Reform" http://www.libertynet.org/~edeivic/welfref.html.

30. Robert Pear, "Federal Welfare Rolls Shrink, But Drop Is Smallest Since '94," *New York Times,* May 21, 2002, p. A12.

31. See Pamela Winston, *Welfare Policy in the States* (Georgetown University Press, 2002).

32. Christopher Georges, "Clinton's Budget Recalls His '92 Agenda," *Wall Street Journal,* February 3, 1998, p. A3.

33. Aaron Wildavsky, *The New Politics of the Budgetary Process* (New York: HarperCollins, 1991).

34. Adam Smith, *An Inquiry into the Wealth of Nations* 1776; reprint (New York: Bobbs Merrill, 1961); John Maynard Keynes, *The General Theory of Employment, Interest, and Money* (Cambridge: Cambridge University Press, 1936); Milton Friedman and Walter Heller, *Monetary versus Fiscal Policy* (New York: Norton, 1969).

35. James L. Gosling, *Budgetary Politics in American Governments* (New York: Longman, 1992), pp. 73–74; Howard E. Shuman, *Politics and the Budget: The Struggle between the President and the Congress* (Englewood Cliffs, N.J.: Prentice Hall, 1988), p. 220.

36. Larry Berman, *The Office of Management and Budget and the Presidency, 1921–1979* (Princeton, N.J.: Princeton University Press, 1979).

37. James Pfiffner, ed., *The President and Economic Policy* (Philadelphia: Institute for Human Issues, 1986).

38. Denise E. Markovich and Ronald E. Pynn, *American Political Economy: Using Economics with Politics* (Monterey, CA: Brooks Cole, 1988), p. 214; John T. Woolley, *Monetary Politics: The Federal Reserve and the Politics of Monetary Policy* (London: Cambridge University Press, 1984); Kevin Phillips, *The Politics of Rich and Poor: Wealth and the American Electorate in the Reagan Aftermath* (New York: Random House, 1990); Donald F. Kettl, *Deficit Politics* (New York: Macmillan, 1992); Robert Heilbronce and Peter Bernstein, *The Debt and Deficit* (New York: Norton, 1989).

39. Benjamin Friedman, *Day of Reckoning: The Consequences of American Economic Policy under Reagan and After* (New York: Random House, 1988); David S. Stockman, *The Triumph of Politics: Why the Reagan Revolution Failed* (New York: Harper, 1986); Kevin Phillips, *Boiling Point: Democrats, Republicans, and the Decline of Middle Class Prosperity* (New York: Random House, 1993); Herbert Stein, *Presidential Economics: The Making of Economic Policy from Roosevelt to Reagan and Beyond,* 2d ed. (Washington, D.C.: American Enterprise Institute, 1988).

CHAPTER 16

1. Reuters News, "Saudis Praise Bush, Urge Speedy Action on Middle East, *New York Times*, April 28, 2002. Also see "Pentagon Now Calls It 'Enduring Freedom'," www.washingtonpost.com, p. A7.

2. UPI, "Do-Little 'Allies' Anger U.S." www. NewsMax.com Wires, March 29, 2002.

3. See Mike Allen and Karen DeYoung, "Bush: U.S. Will Strike First at Enemies," *Washington Post*, June 2, 2002, p. A1, A8.

4. The complete text of the President's West Point Commencement speech can be found at www. whitehouse.gov, June 1, 2002; see also "Text of Bush's Speech at West Point," *New York Times*, June 1, 2002; www.nytimes.com, June 1, 2002.

5. See Hans Morgenthau, *Politics Among Nations: The Struggle for Power and Peace*. New York: Knopf, 1973; Robert C. Johansen, *The National Interest and the Human Interest: An Analysis of U.S. Foreign Policy* (Princeton, N.J.: Princeton University Press, 1980).

6. See Bruce W. Jentleson and Thomas G. Paterson, *Encyclopedia of U.S. Foreign Relations* (New York: Oxford University Press, 1997), vol. 1, preface for these core values.

7. "In Clinton's Words: Containing the Predators of the 21st Century," *New York Times*, February 18, 1998, p. A12.

8. See Walter Pincus, "'Rogue' Nations Policy Builds on Clinton's Lead," *Washington Post*, March 12, 2002, p. A4. See also Thomas G. Paterson and J. Garry Clifford, *America Ascendant: U.S. Foreign Relations since 1939* (Lexington, Mass.: D.C. Heath, 1995).

9. The complete text of the President's West Point Commencement speech can be found at www. whitehouse.gov, June 1, 2002; see also "Text of Bush's Speech at West Point," *New York Times*, June 1, 2002; www.nytimes.com, June 1, 2002.

10. See Ernest K. King, *The Making of the Monroe Doctrine* (Cambridge, Mass.: Harvard University Press, 1975); David F. Ronfeldt, "Rethinking the Monroe Doctrine," *Orbis* 28 (Winter 1985): 38–41; Bruce W. Jentleson and Thomas G. Paterson, Encyclopedia of U.S. Foreign Relations (New York: Oxford University Press, 1997) vol. 1, preface.

11. See Barton J. Bernstein, "Roosevelt, Truman, and the Atomic Bomb, 1941–1945," *Political Science Quarterly* 40 (Spring 1975): 61.

12. George F. Kennan, "The Sources of Soviet Conduct," *Foreign Affairs* 25 (July 1947): 566–82.

13. NATO Charter, quoted in Walter LaFeber, *America, Russia, and the Cold War, 1945–1990*, 6th ed. (New York: McGraw-Hill, 1991), p. 82.

14. See The National Security Archive at www.gwu.edu/~nsarchiv/ and the Cold War International History Project at http://wwics.si.edu/.

15. See Ernest R. May and Philip D. Zelikow, eds., *The Kennedy Tapes: Inside the White House* (Boston: Harvard University Press, 1997). Graham Allison, *Essence of Decision: Explaining the Cuban Missile Crisis* (Boston: Little, Brown, 1971); Robert Kennedy, *Thirteen Days* (New York: Signet Books, 1969), pp. 38–39; James G. Blight, Joseph S. Nye, Jr., and David A. Welch, "The Cuban Missile Crisis Revisited," *Foreign Affairs* 66 (Fall 1987): 170–88.

16. See Gerald T. Rice, *The Bold Experiment: JFK's Peace Corps* (Bloomington: University of Indiana Press, 1985).

17. Students should read President Kennedy's address at the White House reception for Latin American diplomats and members of Congress, March 13, 1961. "Preliminary Formulations of the Alliance for Progress," www.fordham.edu/halsall/mod/1961kennedy-afp1.html.

18. See Arturo Valenzuela, "Bush's Betrayal of Democracy," *Washington Post*, April 16, 2002, p. A19; Jennifer McCoy, "Chavez's Second Chance," *New York Times*, Op-Ed, April 18, 2002; Peter Hakim, "Democracy and U.S. Credibility," *New York Times*, News of the Week, April 21, 2002. p. 4.

19. See Larry Berman, *Planning a Tragedy: The Americanization of the War in Vietnam* (New York: Norton, 1982); Larry Berman, *Lyndon Johnson's War: The Road to Stalemate in Vietnam* (New York: Norton, 1989).

20. See Larry Berman, "No Peace, No Honor: Nixon, Kissinger and Betrayal in Vietnam," *The Free Press*, 2001. Also see, Arnold Issacs, *Without Honor: Defeat in Vietnam and Cambodia* (Baltimore: Johns Hopkins University Press, 1984); Townsend Hoopes, *The Limits of Intervention* (New York: Norton, 1987).

21. Raymond L. Garthoff, *Détente and Confrontation: American–Soviet Relations from Nixon to Reagan* (Washington, D.C.: Brookings Institution, 1985); Beth A. Fischer, "Toeing the Hardline? The Reagan Administration and the Ending of the Cold War," *Political Science Quarterly* 112, no. 3 (1997): 477–96.

22. McGeorge Bundy, George F. Kennan, Robert S. McNamara, and Gerard Smith, "The President's Choice: Star Wars or Arms Control," *Foreign Affairs* Winter 1984–85.

23. See "A Treaty to 'Reduce and Limit' Warheads and a Declaration of a New Relationship," *New York Times*, May 25, 2002, p. A7.

24. See Larry Berman and Bruce W. Jentleson, "Bush and the Post–Cold War World: New Challenges for American Leadership," in *The Bush Presidency: First Appraisals*, ed. Colin Campbell and Bert Rockman (Chatham, N.J.: Chatham House, 1991), pp. 93–94.

25. See Robert Litwak, *Rogue States and U.S. Foreign Policy: Containment After the Cold War* (Woodrow Wilson Center Press, 2000).

26. "'Rogue' Nations Policy Builds on Clinton's Lead, *Washington Post*, March 12, 2002, p. A4; David E. Sanger, "Bush to Outline Doctrine of Striking Foes First," *New York Times*, September 20, 2002, p. A2.

27. Bruce W. Jentleson, *With Friends Like These* (New York: Norton, 1994).

28. Larry Berman and Emily O. Goldman, "Clinton's Foreign Policy at Midterm," in *The Clinton Presidency: First Appraisals*, eds. Colin Campbell and Bert A. Rockman (Chatham, N.J.: Chatham House, 1996), p. 324.

29. See David Sanger, "NATO Formally Welcomes Russia as a Partner," *New York Times*, May 29, 2002, p. A1, A7; Tom Roam, "NATO Embraces Russia as Partner," *Chicago Tribune*, May 28, 2002, www.chicagotribune.com. Steven Erhanger, "For NATO, Little Is Sure Now But Growth," May 19, 2002, p. A8; Vernon Loeb, "U.S. Looks Eastward in New NATO," *Washington Post*, May 28, 2002, p. A10; see also *NATO Update*, http://www.nato.int/docu/update/2002/11-november/e11z1c.htm.

30. National Security Advisor Anthony Lake, "From Containment to Enlargement," speech at Johns Hopkins University, September 21, 1993, http://www.whitehouse.gov/.

31. David E. Sanger, "U.S. Treasury Chief Offers Plan to Avoid Crises Like Asia's," *New York Times*, April 15, 1998, p. A13.

32. Paul Blustein, "Treasury Bonds with Bono," *Washington Post*, Style, p. C1.

33. Jimmy Carter, "Opening to Cuba," *Washington Post*, May 14, 2002, p. A35.

34. Kevin Sullivan, "Carter Begins Historic Trip," *Washington Post*, May 13, 2002, p. A7.

35. David J. Richardson, "The Political Economy of Strategic Trade Policy," *International Organization* 44 (Winter 1990): 101–35.

36. Alexander L. George, *Forceful Persuasion* (Washington, D.C.: U.S. Institute of Peace Press, 1991).

37. Karen DeYoung, "Presidential Diplomacy, Ranch-Home Style," *Washington Post*, May 23, 2002, p. A22.

38. See Julia Preston, "Security Council Votes, 15–0, for Tough Iraq Resolution; Bush Calls It a 'Final Test'," *New York Times*, November 9, 2002, p. A1.

39. Peter Slevin and Glenn Frankel, "If U.S. Wants to Engage, Analysts See Many Options," *Washington Post*, March 31, 2002, p. A10; see also Bob Woodward, *Bush at War*, (New York: Simon and Schuster, 2002).

40. See James M. Lindsay, *Congress and the Politics of U.S. Foreign Policy* (Baltimore: Johns Hopkins University Press, 1994).

41. Michael J. Glennon, "The War Powers Resolution Ten Years Later: More Politics Than Law," *American Journal of International Law* 78 (July 1984): 52–79.

42. Barry Rubin, *Secrets of State: The State Department and the Struggle over U.S. Foreign Policy* (New York: Oxford University Press, 1985).

43. James Fallows, *National Defense* (New York: Random House, 1981).

44. See Donald Bletz, *The Role of the Military Professional in U.S. Foreign Policy* (New York: Praeger, 1972); Asa A. Clark IV, Peter W. Chiarelli, Jeffery S. McKitrick, and James W. Reed, *The Defense Reform Debate* (Baltimore: Johns Hopkins University Press, 1984); James Clotfelter, *The Military in American Politics* (New York: Harper & Row, 1973); Adam Yarmolinsky, *The Military Establishment* (New York: Harper & Row, 1971). Quoted in Robert J. Art, "Restructuring the Military-Industrial Complex: Arms Control in Institutional Perspective," *Public Policy* 22 (Fall 1974).

45. See Theodore Draper, *A Very Thin Line: The Iran-Contra Affairs* (New York: Simon & Schuster, 1991).

46. See Rhodri Jeffreys-Jones, *The CIA and American Democracy* (New Haven, Conn.: Yale University Press, 1989); Loch K. Johnson, *America's Secret Power: The CIA in a Democratic Society* (New York: Oxford University Press, 1989); John Prados, *President's Secret Wars: CIA and Pentagon Covert Operations Since World War II* (New York: Morrow, 1986). Quoted in Kegley and Wittkopf, eds., *Perspectives on American Foreign Policy*, p. 383.

47. Daniel C. Hallin, *The Uncensored War: The Media and Vietnam* (New York: Oxford University Press, 1986).

48. Philip M. Taylor, *War and the Media* (New York: Manchester University Press, 1992).

49. John Mueller, *Policy and Opinion in the Gulf War* (Chicago: University of Chicago Press, 1994); Miroslov Nincic, "Domestic Costs, the U.S. Public, and the Isolationist Calculus," *International Studies Quarterly* 41 (1997): 593–610.

50. Susan Glasser, "Afghans Take a First Step toward Democracy," *Washington Post*, April 16, 2002, p. 12; Pamela Constable, "Voting Ends for Afghan Assembly," *Washington Post*, June 9, 2002, p. A22.

PHOTO CREDITS

INDEX

A

Abacha, Sani, 119
ABC, 438, 468
Abdullah, Prince of Saudi Arabia, 286
Abington School District v. Schempp, 457
abortion, 482–83
    limitations on, 483
    party platforms, 326
    policy making, 534–35
    protecting right of, 466
    protests against, freedom of speech
        and, 466
Abraham, Spencer, 154
Abrams, Jacob, 454
Abrams v. United States, 454
absentee voting, 354
absolutist activists, 232
activist judges, 232–33, 449
Acton, Lord, 164
actual groups, 385
Adams, Abigail, 39
Adams, John, 13, 19, 21, 37, 38,
    203–4, 450
    death of, 66
    electoral college and, 369
    on political parties, 313–14
Adams, John Quincy, 37, 314
Adams, Samuel, 35, 37
Adams, Sherman, 191
ad hoc coalitions, 392
ADI (area of dominant influence), 440
administration, by bureaucracy, 257
Administration for Children and
    Families, 271
administrative discretion, 256–57
administrative oversight, 267
Administrative Procedure Act of 1936,
    263, 265
advertising
    issue, 411, 464
    political, 438, 441–43
"advice and consent," of Congress, 267
Advisory Commission on
    Intergovernmental Relations
    (ACIR), 100
affirmative action, 505–8
    constitutionality of, 488–90
    defined, 504
    equality and, 505
    future of, 508–9
    history of, 506
    strict scrutiny test, 508
Afghanistan, 8–9, 10, 416–18
    U.S. campaign against, 562–63
    women in legislative assembly, 515
AFL-CIO, 391, 393, 407
Africa
    democracy in, 352
African Americans, 3–4, 5. *See also* civil
    rights; civil rights movement
    affirmative action and, 489–90
    citizenship of, 494
    civil rights movement, 389, 390

civil rights of, 490–509
in Congress, 122
Congressional districts and, 124–26
discrimination against, 22–23
disenfranchisement of, 351, 495–96
legal settlement to farmers, 493
opinion formation by, 291, 293
rights of slaves, 315
trust in government by, 299
voter registration, 499, 500, 501
voting rights, 19, 349–50, 492, 494–96
age
    voting behavior and, 359
    voting rights, 349, 351
age discrimination, 520–21
Age Discrimination in Employment Act
    of 1967, 19, 520
agricultural interest groups, 394–95
Agriculture Department, 258, 259,
    270, 584
Agriculture Labor Relations Act, 3
AIDS policy making, 531–33
Aid to Families with Dependent
    Children (AFDC), 103, 536, 541–42
Air Force 1, 175
Akaka, Daniel K., 122
Albany Plan, 32, 37
Albright, Madeleine, 172, 581
*Alexander v. Holmes County Board of
    Education,* 502–3
Alien and Sedition Acts, 18, 450
Al-Jazeera television, 417
"all deliberate speed," 535
Allen, Woody, 406
Alliance for Marriage, 82
Alliance for Progress, 569
amendments, to Constitution, 54. *See
    also* specific amendments
    amendment process, 68–69
    Bill of Rights, 64, 66–67
    procedures for, 61
    ratification of, 67, 68–69
American Association of Retired Persons
    (AARP), 400, 520
American Association of University
    Professors (AAUP), 400
American Bar Association, 213
American Civil Liberties Union (ACLU),
    239, 397, 400, 447, 480, 513
American Conservative Union
    (ACU), 397
American Independent party, 337, 339
American Indian Movement (AIM), 518
American Revolution, 32–36. *See also*
    Colonial America
Americans for Democratic Action
    (ADA), 340, 397
Americans with Disabilities Act (ADA) of
    1990, 19, 205, 520
American Woman Suffrage
    Association, 510
America Online, 438
amicus curiae briefs, 223, 404

anarchy, 42
Anderson, John, 337
Andre, John, 239
Anthony, Susan B., 509–10
Antiballistic Missile (ABM) Treaty, 570
Antifederalists
    defined, 61
    Federalists *vs.,* 62–64
    ratification of the Constitution
        and, 65–66
    writings of, 62
antinationalists, 46
apathy, 299
appeals courts, 209–11
appellate courts, 208–9
appellate jurisdiction, 203, 220
appointment power, of president,
    169, 266
apprenticeship, in Congress, 142
Approaching Democracy Web site, 427
appropriations
    bills, 149
    foreign policy and, 580–81
Architectural Barriers Act, 519
area of dominant influence (ADI), 440
Argentina, 555, 570
Arizona v. Fulminante, 478
Arnold, Benedict, 239
Arthur Andersen, 394–95
Articles, of the Constitution, 57–61
    Article I, 57–58
    Article II, 58–60
    Article III, 60
    Article IV, 57, 60–61
    Article V, 57, 61
    Article VI, 57, 61
    Article VII, 57, 61
Articles of Confederation, 32, 41–43, 52
Ashcroft, John, 27–28, 88–89, 164, 220,
    269, 395, 521
Asian Americans, 122
assignment of opinions, 227–28
association, freedom of. *See* freedom of
    association
Association for Postal Commerce, 264
Athenian democracy, 14, 28
Atkins v. Virginia, 459
atomic bomb, 568, 569
attainder, bills of, 89
Attucks, Crispus, 34
authoritarian regime, 9, 10
automobile industry, regulation
    of, 271–73
Aviation and Transportation Security Act
    (ATSA), 248
"axis of evil," 564, 573

B

Babbitt, Bruce, 216, 519
bad tendency, 454–55
Bagdikian, Ben, 437
Baker, Ross, 153

Bakke, Allan, 506
Balanced Budget Amendment, 150–51
balance of powers, 58–59
Baldwin, Abraham, 49
banks, national, 89–90
Barber, James David, 316
Barnes, Roy, 99, 513
Barron, John, 451
Barron v. Baltimore, 451
Barry, Marion, 390
Baruch, Bernard, 568
Bass, Lance, 263
Baucus, Max, 527
BBC World News, 441
Bentley, Arthur, 409
Benton v. Maryland, 453
Bentsen, Lloyd, 440
Berlin, Isaiah, 15–16
Bernstein, Carl, 430
Berry, John W., 73
bias, of the media, 435–38
Bias (Goldberg), 435–36
bicameral legislature, 29, 117
Biden, Joseph, 154, 220
Biggers, Neal B., Jr., 508
Bill of Rights, 64, 295
    adoption of, 66–67
    defined, 67
    expansion of rights guaranteed
        by, 450–56
    framers' view of, 448
    incorporation of, 95, 451–53
    no incorporation of, 451–52
    rights set forth in, 448
    selective incorporation of, 455–56
    states and, 67, 94–95
    total incorporation of, 452
bills. *See* lawmaking
bipolarity, 569
birth control, 479
Bismarck, Otto von, 137
Black, Hugo, 229, 234, 434, 457, 516
black codes, 494
Black Farmers and Agriculturist
    Association, 393, 395
Blackfeet Nation, 519
"Black Manifesto," 493
Blackmun, Harry, 216, 217, 224, 230,
    233, 234, 235, 397, 480–81, 482
Black Panthers, 390
Blackwell, Alice Stone, 510
Blaine, James G., 461
Blaine amendments, 461
blanket primaries, 328
Blek, Mary Leigh, 383
Bliley, Thomas J., Jr., 137
block grants, 97, 102, 104
blue laws, 462
Bob Jones University, 291
"boll weevils," 131
Bond, Christopher "Kit," 220
Bonior, David, 145
Bonner, Jack, 412
Bono, 576–77
Bono, Mary, 128
Bono, Sonny, 128
Bork, Robert, 146, 213, 215, 219, 223,

224, 231, 233, 234, 479
Boston Committee of
    Correspondence, 35
Boston Massacre, 34, 35
Boston Tea Party, 35–36
Bowdoin, James, 40
Bowen, Catherine Drinker, 72
Bowers v. Hardwick, 480
boycotts, 3, 499
Boy Scouts of America v. Dale, 480–82
Bradley, Bill, 324, 330, 331, 336, 372
Bradley, Joseph P., 201
Brady, James, 383
Brady Campaign to Prevent Gun
    Violence, 383, 384
Brady handgun control law, 107
Brandeis, Louis D., 83, 213, 220,
    229, 454
Brazil, 429
Bread for the World, 399
Breaux, John B., 527
Brennan, William, 212, 228, 229, 233,
    234, 235, 473, 474
Breyer, Stephen G., 201, 226, 233, 234,
    235, 411, 483
    appointment of, 169, 212, 213,
        216, 217
bribery, 402
briefs, filing, 224
Brinkema, Leonie M., 435
British East India Company, 35
Broder, David, 320, 341
Brokaw, Tom, 333, 441
Bronfenbrenner, Urie, 288
Brown, Edmund (Jerry), 3, 386
Brown, Linda, 202
Brownlow Commission, 190
Brown University, 493
*Brown v. Board of Education of Topeka,
    Kansas*, 96, 224, 236, 237, 240, 490,
    495, 498, 535
    Brown II, 498
Bryan, William Jennings, 315, 316
Brzonkala, Christy, 108–9
"bubble" law, 466
Buchanan, James, 167
Buchanan, Patrick, 336, 408
Buckley v. Valeo, 374
budget. *See* federal budget
Budget and Accounting Act of 1921, 548
Budget and Impoundment Control Act
    of 1974, 185
"bully pulpit," 188
Bumpers, Dale, 263
Bundy, McGeorge, 583
Bundy, Ted, 224
Bunker Hill, Battle of, 37
bureaucracy, 244–75, 246–47
    accountability of, 265
    administration by, 257
    cabinet departments, 259
    characteristics of, 247–49,
        255–56, 275
    civilian, 255–56
    civil service, 252–55
    congressional control over, 267–68
    constraints on, 262–65

criticism of, 270–72
    defined, 248
    democracy and, 246–47, 274–75
    foreign policy, 581–85
    formal rules in, 248–49
    functions of, 256–58
    goals and, 264
    government corporations, 261–62
    growth of, 249–52
    hiring and advancement in, 253, 254
    implementation by, 256–57
    independent agencies, 259–60
    independent regulatory
        commissions, 260–61
    managers, 264
    morale of, 258
    national security, 244–46, 268–69
    performance review of, 259–60, 274
    presidential control over, 265–67
    problems inherent in, 249
    public attitudes toward, 247–48,
        270–72
    reform of, 252, 264, 272–74
    regulation by, 257–58
    size of, 250, 252, 256, 268
    specialization in, 248
    structure of, 259–62
    waste by, 270
    Web sites, 274
bureaucrats, 248
Bureau of Alcohol, Tobacco, and
    Firearms (ATF), 268
Bureau of Consular Affairs, 271
Bureau of Indian Affairs, 271, 273
Bureau of the Budget (BOB), 193
Burger, Warren, 216, 224, 227, 229–30,
    435, 450, 459, 471, 483
Burke, Edmund, 34, 126
Burns, James MacGregor, 36
Burr, Aaron, 39, 314, 369
Burton, Dan, 174
Burton, Philip, 145
Burton, Sala, 145
bus boycotts, 499
Bush, George H. W., 163, 172, 185, 318
    affirmative action and, 507–8
    campaign spending, 374
    coattails effect and, 367
    economy and, 177
    federal aid and, 104–5
    international economic policy, 556
    judicial appointments, 206, 217, 218,
        219, 221
    media coverage of, 436
    Persian Gulf War and, 176
    regulatory policy, 538
    solicitor general under, 223
    Supreme Court appointments, 212,
        213, 215, 216, 235
    tax policy, 552, 553
    as vice president, 195
    voter evaluation of, 362
Bush, George W., 8, 21, 22, 26–28, 56,
    72, 176, 181, 185, 291, 515
    abortion and, 483
    affirmative action and, 489
    appointees, 516

appointments, 169, 172, 194, 206, 212, 219
bureaucracy and, 259, 266, 267
campaign finance reform and, 374, 377
civil rights and, 98, 509
Congress and, 116, 122
death penalty and, 458
education program, 82–83, 168, 531, 532
2000 election and, 200–202, 336, 351, 355, 370
emergency powers, 163–65, 175, 177, 187
Enron and, 394, 395
environmental policy, 540
executive orders issued, 178
executive privilege use, 58–59, 174
faith-based initiatives, 461
federal aid and, 96, 106
federal budget, 548, 549, 551
federalism and, 96, 106, 110
FirstGov.org, 196
first year as president, 162–65
foreign policy, 564, 570–73, 576, 578, 579
fundraising by, 325, 333
Hispanic voters and, 334
international economic policy, 557
legislation and, 176
media and, 427, 441
Military Tribunals, 211
national security and, 269
political advertising, 442
political ideology, 298–99
regulatory policy, 538
Republican party and, 321
social welfare policy, 541
spending policy, 554
staff, 191, 192
support for, 188–89, 295
supremacy clause and, 88–89
tax policy, 526–27, 552
vetoes, 149, 169
war on terrorism and, 239, 244–46, 248, 416–17, 562–63
war powers, 71, 194
Bush, Jeb, 489, 509
Bush v. Gore, 200–202, 214, 221, 223, 231
business
    interest groups, 393–95, 407
Business Roundtable, 393
bus segregation, 22–23
Butler, Pierce, 220
Byrd, Robert, 59, 133, 143
Byrnes, James F., 212

C

cabinet, 193–94, 194, 259
Cabinet Secretariat, 194
cable television
    development of, 425
    history of, 425
    news viewership, 419, 424
    regulation of, 433
Cabranes, Jose, 517

Caltech/MIT Voting Technology Report, 351–52, 354
Cambridge Agreement, 29
Campaign Finance Law of 1974, 114, 141
campaign finance reform, 114–16
    contribution limits, 464
    foreign contributions, 376
    freedom of speech and, 464
    history of, 373–74
    independent expenditures, 376–77
    issue advocacy, 376
    legislation, 151, 376–78
    soft money and, 374, 376, 378
Campaign Finance Reform Act of 2002, 114–16, 142, 153–55, 156, 325, 333, 408, 411, 464
campaign specialists, 363
Campbell, Ben Nighthorse, 122, 144
Canada, 92
Cannon, Joseph, 131
Cantril, Hadley, 430
Cantwell, Maria, 154
Cantwell v. Connecticut, 452
Capital Cities, 438
capital crimes, right to counsel and, 455
capital gains taxes, 553
Card, Andrew, 191, 192
Cardozo, Benjamin, 220, 471
career civil servants, 253
Caribbean, 565–66
Carnahan, Mel, 154
Carolene Products, 455
"carrot-and-stick" programs, 85
"carrot" approach, Supreme Court, 228
Carson, Rachel, 538
Carswell, G. Harrold, 215
Carter, Jimmy, 169, 185, 348, 351, 440
    bureaucracy and, 266
    coattails effect and, 367
    creative federalism, 102–3
    economy and, 179
    electoral college and, 372
    foreign policy, 577, 578
    gender differences in support for, 294
    judicial appointments, 217, 218
    media polls and, 439
    political advertising by, 442
    regulatory policy, 538
    voter evaluation of, 362
    women's rights and, 511
Carville, James, 177
casework, for Congressional constituents, 127
Castle, Michael N., 136, 154
Castro, Fidel, 578
categorical grants, 96–97
Catholics, 291–93
Catt, Carrie Chapman, 510
caucuses, 327
CBS News, 425, 438
censorship, 419
census, redistricting, 124
Central Agreement on Tariffs and Trade (GATT), 584
Central America, 565–66

Central Intelligence Agency (CIA), 260, 268, 269, 568, 583, 587
Certification Day, 370
"cert pool," 224–25
Chafee, Lincoln, 311
Challenger space shuttle, 262–63
Chancellor, John, 330
Chao, Elaine L., 259
Chase, Samuel, 206
Chavez, Cesar, 2–3, 5, 9, 16, 119, 517
Chavez, Hugo, 570
Checci, Al, 373
checks and balances, 54–56
    Constitution and, 54–57
    defined, 46
    media and, 429
    Montesquieu's views on, 30
    presidential power and, 185
Cheney, Dick, 59, 155, 174, 239, 394–95, 432, 579
    role of, 195, 196
Chen Shui-bian, 119
Chian Kai-shek, 322
Chicago, Burlington and Quincy Railway Co. v. Chicago, 452
Chicago Seven, 330, 332–33
chief justice, 229–30
chief of staff, White House, 191
chief of state, president as, 175
Child Internet Pornography Act (CIPA), 73
child labor, 93
Child Online Protection Act, 469
child pornography, 468–69
Child Pornography Prevention Act, 469
children, federal spending on, 97
Children's Internet Protection Act of 2000, 469
China
    civil liberties in, 470
    democracy and, 8, 9, 577
Chretien, Jean, 92
Christian Coalition, 412
Christian Left, 399
Chrysler Corporation, 393–94
church and state, separation of, 457
Church Arson Prevention Act of 1996, 209
Churchill, Winston S., 8, 349
circuit courts, 210–11
Citadel, 515
citizen participation, 388
Citizens Against Government Waste, 143
City of Boerne v. Flores, 462, 479
City of Richmond v. Croson, 507
civic journalism, 441
civil cases, 209
civil disobedience, 365–66, 389, 499–500
civilian civil service employees, 255–56
Civilian Conservation Corps (CCC), 251
civil liberties, 446–85
    around the world, 470
    civil rights *vs.,* 449
    clear and present danger test, 452–54
    crises and, 27
    defined, 449

democracy and, 448, 484–85
Fourteenth Amendment, 451–52
freedom of religion, 456–63
freedom of speech, 463–69
history of, 449–51
implied rights, 479–84
incorporation of Bill of Rights,
    454–56
rights of defendants, 469–79
war on terrorism and, 446–48
Civil Liberties Act of 1988, 493
civil rights, 488–523
affirmative action, 488–90, 505–9
of African Americans, 490–509
civil liberties *vs.*, 449
Civil War and reconstruction, 494–95
constitutional equality, 492–95
defined, 449, 491
de jure *vs.* de facto discrimination,
    501–4
democracy and, 490, 523
desegregation, 496–99
equality and, 491, 505–8
freedom riders, 502–3
future of, 508–9
of Hispanics, 516–17
history of, 449–50, 490
interest groups, 398–99
legal equality, 496–99
legal segregation, 495–96
legislation, 499–501
of Native Americans, 517–18, 519
of people with disabilities, 518–20
slavery reparations and, 493
Supreme Court and, 501
war on terrorism and, 521–23
of women, 509–16
Civil Rights Act of 1866, 494, 502
Civil Rights Act of 1957, 139, 499
Civil Rights Act of 1960, 499
Civil Rights Act of 1964, 19, 500–501,
    506, 511
    interstate commerce clause and, 85
    Title VII, sexual harassment, 516
Civil Rights Act of 1968, 502
Civil Rights Act of 1991, 508
Civil Rights Act of 1999 (Washington
    State), 489
Civil Rights Cases, 495
Civil Rights Commission, 499
civil rights movement, 2–3, 389, 390,
    499–504, 499–509
    Parks and, 22–23
    Supreme Court and, 407
Civil Rights Restoration Act of 1988, 520
civil service, 252–55
    defined, 253
    machine politics and, 324
    political campaign activities and,
        254–55
Civil Service Commission, 253
Civil Service Reform Act, 253, 272
civil union laws, 81, 82–83
Civil War
    civil liberties and, 27, 56
    civil rights and, 494
    military commission trials, 239

Civil War Amendments, 451, 494
Clark, Kenneth, 224, 234, 498
Clark, Lois A., 273
Clark, Tom, 217
class action suits, 209
Clay, Henry, 314, 315
Clean Air Act of 1970, 539
    Amendments of 1990, 539, 540
clear and present danger test,
    452–54, 464
Cleveland, Grover, 315, 316, 370
Clinton, Bill, 56, 95, 145, 154, 187, 290,
    307, 334, 339, 412
    appointments by, 172
    bureaucracy and, 265
    campaign finance reform and,
        114–15, 325, 374
    civil rights and, 508
    death penalty and, 458
    Democratic party and, 177
    economic policy, 545
    executive privilege use, 58, 174
    fast-track authority and, 173
    foreign policy, 564, 573
    impeachment, 135–36, 153, 166, 311,
        339–40
    international economic policy, 556
    judicial appointments, 206, 217, 219,
        220, 221
    Lewinsky scandal, 115, 153, 174,
        185, 428
    media coverage of, 436
    minorities and, 291
    moral leadership and, 177
    political ideology of, 298
    realignment and, 373
    regulatory policy, 538
    social welfare policy, 544
    spending policy, 554
    support for, 294
    Supreme Court and, 212, 217, 235,
        236–37
    tax policy, 553–54
    veto use, 149, 169, 171
    voter evaluation of, 362
Clinton, Hillary Rodham, 56, 122,
    355, 383
Clinton v. Jones, 185
cloning, 534–35
Closed Chambers (Lazarus), 228
closed primary elections, 328
cloture, 140–41
Clymer, George, 38
CNN, 424, 426, 431, 434–35
Coast Guard, 247
coattails effect, 367
Cobell v. Norton, 519
Cochran, Johnny, 493
Coercive Acts, 36
coercive diplomacy, 578
Cohen, Paul, 465
Cohen v. California, 465
Colby, Charles, 274
Cold War, 568–72, 584
collective action, 389–90
colleges and universities
    affirmative action in, 488–90

promoting diversity in, 522
Collins, Susan, 311
Colonial America. *See also* American
    Revolution
    Boston Massacre, 34, 35
    Boston Tea Party, 35–36
    British taxation, 32–36
    causes of rebellion, 32–36
    Committees of Correspondence, 35
    early governments, 29–30
    First Continental Congress, 36–37
    Second Continental Congress, 37
    self-government of, 32
    social contract theory and, 30–31, 38
    Townshend Revenue Acts, 34
    voting rights, 29–30
commander in chief, president as, 175
Commanger, Henry Steele, 62
Commerce Department, 259, 270, 584
Committee of Education v. Nyquist, 460, 461
committee of the whole, 148
Committee on Administrative
    Management, 190
Committees of Correspondence, 35
Commodity Futures Trading
    Commission, 394
Common Sense, 38
Communications Decency Act (CDA) of
    1996, 120, 389, 469
Communist party, 464
community action programs, 542
Community Services Organization, 3
compact, 29
compassionate conservatism, 298–99
compensatory damages, 209
Compromise of 1850, 492
Comstock, George, 339
Concord Coalition, 397
concurrent powers, 87–88
concurrent resolutions, 186
concurring opinions, 229
conditions of aid, 95
Confederate flag, display of, 98–99
confederations, 32
confederation system of government, 80
conference committees, 133
confessions
    police questions and, 477, 478
    by torture, 470
    voluntariness of, 476, 478–79
Congress, 114–57. *See also* House of
    Representatives; legislative branch;
    Senate
    administrative oversight by, 267
    "advice and consent" role, 267
    Budget Committees, 551
    budget-control powers, 152
    bureaucracy controlled by, 267–68
    Constitution and, 117–18
    declaration of war by, 187
    delegation of power to president,
        182, 184
    democracy and, 116–30
    emergencies and, 176
    First, 121
    foreign policy role, 579–81
    impeachment powers, 153

interest groups and, 340–41, 406
judicial review and, 120
lawmaking, 114–16, 139–43, 146–52
leadership, 130–33
legislative oversight, 580
limitations on, 117–18, 120
lobbyists and, 403
majority leaders, 131, 132
minority leaders, 131
oversight functions, 152–53
powers of, 117–20, 267
president and, 120, 186
public confidence in, 129–30, 238
reapportionment, 122–24
Republican Revolution, 127, 153–56
rules and norms of, 138–43
size of, 122
Speaker of the House, 130–31
staff, 146
strength of, 156
structure of, 117–18
Supreme Court and, 205–6, 236–37
term limits, 128–29
Two Congresses view of, 129–30
whips, 131
Congressional Accountability Act, 137
congressional agenda, 147
Congressional Budget and
  Impoundment Control
  Act of 1974, 152
Congressional Budget Office (CBO),
  152, 256, 551
Congressional committees, 133–38
  chairs, 135
  conference, 134
  consideration of bills by, 147–49
  joint, 134
  power of, 136
  purposes of, 135
  select (special), 134
  seniority and, 142–43
  standing committees, 133
  subcommittees, 133, 137–38, 534
Congressional districts, 122–26
  gerrymandering, 124, 125
  majority-minority districts, 124–26
  reapportionment, 122–24
  single-member, 335
Congressional elections, 366–67
  costs of, 128
  interest groups and, 411
  2002 results, 155–56, 341–42,
    342, 411
Congressional Hispanic Caucus, 4, 5
Congressional members, 121–40
  apprenticeship, 142
  casework, 127–28
  characteristics of, 121–23
  Constitution and, 117–18
  ethnic and minority group, 122
  finances of, 128
  franking privilege, 127
  incumbents, 127–28
  name recognition of, 127–28
  reciprocity of, 143
  roles of, 126–27
  seniority of, 142

specialization of, 143
title use, 142
turnover rate, 129
voting decisions of, 144–46
Web sites of, 156
women, 122
Congressional Record, 147
Congressional Union, 510
Connecticut Compromise, 49–50,
  117–18
Connor, Theophilus Eugene "Bull," 500
consensus
  interest groups and, 410
  majority rule and, 17
"consensus model" of Congressional
  voting behavior, 146
conservative interest groups, 388, 397
conservative magazines, 423
conservatives
  defined, 297
  gender and, 294
  in the media, 435, 437
  political party ideology and, 340
  religion and, 291–93
  Supreme Court justices, 231–35
  trends, 298
  views of, 297–98
constituents. *See also* voters
  Congressional voting behavior
    and, 144
  views of Congress, 129–30
Constitutional Convention, 43–57
  future conventions, 68
  Great Compromise, 48–50
  key events, 44
  large/small-state debate, 48–49
  mission of, 44
  New Jersey Plan, 47–48
  participants, 44–46
  presidency, 51–53
  results of, 53–57
  slavery issue, 43, 50–51
  Virginia Plan, 46–47
constitutional courts, 209–10
Constitution of the United States
  amendment process, 68–69
  amendments to, 54, 237
  articles, 57–61
  Bill of Rights, 64
  Congress and, 117–18
  core values embodied in, 295–96
  crises and, 27
  distribution of power and, 54–57
  drafting, 14
  equality and, 71
  evolution of, 71–72
  federalism in, 84–86
  foreign policy and, 579–81
  judicial interpretation, 69–71, 203–4
  original intent theory, 231
  preamble, 53
  presidential elections and, 314
  ratification, 61, 65–66, 420
  republican form of government
    and, 53–54
  slavery and, 71
  strict construction, 231

supremacy clause, 48
Supreme Court and, 203, 204, 231
text of, 78–93
updating, 67–71
voting rights and, 71
women and, 71
writing by hand, 71
constitutions, state, 40–41
constructionist approach to
  presidency, 181
Consumer Product Safety Commission
  (CPSC), 251, 258
containment, 568, 576
Continental Congress, 41–43
contingency elections, 371
continuing resolutions, 151
Contract with America, 60, 100, 135,
  141, 150, 152, 298, 341
Cook, Charles, 155–56
Cooley, Thomas N., 261
Coolidge, Calvin, 393
cooperative federalism, 94, 100
copyright protection, 73
core values, 295–97
corporate interest groups, 384, 393. *See
  also* interest groups
Corwin, Edward S., 204
Corzine, Jon, 128, 334
Coughlin, Charles, Father, 423
Council of Economic Advisors, 193
council of revision, 47
Council on Legal Education
  Opportunity (CLEO), 522
court system. *See also* federal court
  system; judiciary
  case types, 209
  court types, 208
  establishment of, 203
  federal courts, 206, 208
  organization of, 208
  state and local courts, 206, 208
Court TV, 435
coverture, 509
Craig v. Boren, 514
creative federalism, 100–101
Crewe, Ivor, 361
Criminal Anarchy Act (New York), 454
criminal cases, 209. *See also* defendants'
  rights
  defendants' rights, 469–79
  gag orders, 467
Cronin, Thomas, 179, 191
cross-ownership, of the media, 437–38
Cruzan, Nancy, 484
Cuba, 569, 577
cue structure, 146
culture theory, 299
*Cumming v. County Board of
  Education,* 495
Czechoslovakia, 5, 8

D

Dale, James, 480
Daley, Richard, 332–33
Danforth, John, 216
Daniels, Mitchell E., Jr., 259, 267

Daschle, Tom, 79, 116, 140, 155, 163, 311, 335, 527
    Congressional committees and, 136
    leadership role, 132, 154
Daughters of Liberty, 35–36
Davis, Gray, 3, 489
Dawes, William, 37
Day, William R., 91
dealignment, 373
death and dying
    death penalty, 458–59
    right to die, 484
"death-tax," 527, 528
Debs, Eugene, 27, 339, 454
Debs v. United States, 454
debtors' prison, 40
Declaration of American Rights, 37
Declaration of Independence, 38–40, 66, 71–72
Declaration of Sentiments, 509
Declaratory Act, 34
de facto discrimination, 501–4
de facto equality, 491
defendants' rights, 469–79
    due process and, 471
    exclusionary rule and, 471–72
    Fifth Amendment and, 469, 475–79
    Fourth Amendment and, 469–75
    right to counsel, for capital crimes, 455
    right to silence, 476–78
    Sixth Amendment and, 450, 469, 475–79
    warrantless searches, 472–77
Defense Appropriation Act, 412
Defense Department, 258, 259, 270, 581–82
Defense Intelligence Agency (DIA), 268
Defense of Marriage Act, 61, 82, 88
defense policy, 528
deficits, 547
De Jong v. Oregon, 452
de jure discrimination, 501–4
de jure equality, 491
DeLay, Thomas, 115, 131, 135, 142, 145, 206
delegated powers, 57, 86
delegates
    committed, 326
    Congress members as, 126–27
    to national party conventions, 325–27
    superdelegates, 331
    uncommitted, 326
Dellinger, Walter, 223
Del Polito, Gene, 264
democracy
    in Africa, 352
    around the world, 9, 119, 348, 352, 398, 577
    Athenian, 14, 28
    bureaucracy and, 246–47, 274–75
    civil liberties and, 448–49, 484–85
    civil rights and, 523
    Congress and, 116–30
    cultural commitment to, 22–23
    defined, 9, 10, 23
    development of, 8–9, 29–32

    direct, 12–13
    dynamic nature of, 17
    economic policy and, 557–58
    elements of, 19–23
    as evolutionary process, 5–23
    fear of, 28
    foreign policy and, 565, 587–88
    freedom and, 10
    Greek concept of, 28
    indirect, 12, 13
    informed citizenry and, 418–19
    interest groups and, 384–88, 409–10, 411–12
    judiciary and, 202, 204, 207
    media and, 418–19, 442–43
    political participation and, 348–51
    political parties and, 312
    president and, 164–66, 195, 197
    public opinion and, 280, 304–7
    public policy and, 528
    representative, 13
    Roman concept of, 28
    roots of, 14–15
    spread of, 119
    Supreme Court and, 202, 238–40
Democracy in America (Tocqueville), 9, 281
democratic ideals, 15–19
    equality, 15–16
    freedom, 15–16
    majority rule, 17–18
    minority rights, 17–18
    order, 16–17
    participation, 18–19
    stability, 16–17
Democratic National Convention (Chicago, 1968), 329–30, 332–33
Democratic party
    candidate Web sites, 427
    decline in cohesiveness of, 333–34
    defined, 317
    economic policy, 546
    2000 election and, 368
    fundraising by, 325, 332–33, 378
    Hispanics and, 342
    history of, 313–19
    identification with, 302, 318, 355
    ideology of, 340–41
    interest groups and, 320–21
    Jeffords and, 311
    majority control by, 311–12, 318
    media coverage of, 436
    minorities and, 291
    party platform, 326
    structure of, 325
    Supreme Court appointments and, 212
    symbol of, 315
    Web site, 342
Democratic Progressive party, Taiwan, 322
Democratic-Republican party, 18, 63, 313, 317
Dennis v. United States, 464
Den Xiaoping, 470
Department of Energy (DOE), 251, 259, 267

deregulation, 537
desegregation, 496. *See also* racial desegregation
Desert Shield, 573
detente, 571–72
Devanter, Willis Van, 220
deviating elections, 372–73
devolution, 57, 86
devolution revolution, 97
Dickerson, Charles Thomas, 478
Dickerson case, 227, 230, 233, 236, 237
Dickinson, John, 45
digital divide, 377
Digital Millennium Copyright Act (DMCA), 73
Dillinger, John, 268
Diouf, Abdou, 119
diplomacy. *See also* foreign policy
    coercive, 578
    limits of, 578–79
    presidential role in, 176
direct broadcast satellites (DBS), 433
direct democracy, 12–13, 348
    defined, 12, 23
    initiatives and referenda, 359–60
direct-mail, 405–6
disabilities, people with, 518–20
disaster assistance programs, 96
discretionary grants, 97
discretionary spending, 554
discrimination, 491. *See also* racial discrimination
Disney, 438
dissenting opinions, 229
distinguishing cases, 230
District of Columbia, 351
diversity
    census classifications, 6–7
    in members of Congress, 121–22
    in policies, 81–83
    promoting, 522
    teaching, 297
DNA testing
    evidence, 458–59
    insurance companies and, 484
docket, 219
Dodd, Christopher, 311, 325
Dole, Robert, 105, 132, 290, 335, 520
    Congressional committees and, 142–43
    electoral college and, 370
domestic policy
    democracy and, 527
    economic, 545–57
    formal agenda and, 534–35
    policy continuation, 536–37
    policy evaluation, 536
    policy implementation, 535
    policy-making process, 530–37
    policy termination, 536
    political agenda and, 533–34
    public policies, 528–30
    regulatory, 529–30, 537–40
    social welfare, 530, 541–45
double jeopardy, 456, 475
double standard, 450

Douglas, William O., 15, 212, 216, 227, 229, 232, 233, 234, 479, 496, 506
    appointment of, 213
Dred Scott v. Sandford, 201, 315, 492–93
drinking age, 85
Drivers Privacy Protection act, 107
drone planes, 587
Drudge, Matt, 428
Drudge Report, 422, 428
Drug Enforcement and Administration (DEA), 268
drug searches, 473–75, 476
drug-testing programs, 473–75
dual federalism, 91, 93, 94
Duberstein, Kenneth M., 318
DuBois, W. E. B., 496
due process clause, Fifth Amendment, 475, 493, 498
due process clause, Fourteenth Amendment, 471, 476
Dukakis, Michael J., 374, 442
Dulaney, Daniel, 34
Duncan v. Louisiana, 453

E
economic equality, 2–3, 96, 296
economic growth, 547
economic interest groups, 393–95
Economic Opportunity Act of 1964, 542
economic policy, 545–47
    agencies involved in, 583–85
    democracy and, 527, 557–58
    federal budget, 547–52
    fiscal policy, 546
    goals of, 547
    international, 547, 554–57
    monetary policy, 546
    presidential role in, 177, 179
    regulatory policy, 546
    spending, 554
    taxation, 526–27, 552–54
economic sanctions, 577
education
    affirmative action in, 488–90
    equality in, 497–98
    federal funding of, 101
    for Hispanics and other language minorities, 517
    No Child Left Behind Act, 82–83, 106, 176, 531, 532
    party platforms, 326
    political socialization and, 287
    promoting diversity, 522
    school busing, 504
    school desegregation, 498–99, 502–4, 535
    school segregation, 490
    separate but equal doctrine and, 495, 497–98
    sex discrimination in, 514–15
    voting behavior and, 290, 359
educational testing, 82–83
Education Department, 259, 266
Education for All, 555
Education Reform Act, 116, 155
Edwards, John, 335

Eighteenth Amendment, 68, 69, 70
Eighth Amendment, 67
Einstein, Albert, 552
Eisenhower, Dwight D., 98, 332
    cabinet, 194
    civil rights and, 498–99
    cooperative federalism and, 100
    executive privilege use, 173
    foreign policy, 582
    legislation and, 176
    political appeal of, 361
    Republican party and, 316
    staff, 191
    Supreme Court and, 212, 236
elastic clause, 85. *See also* necessary and proper clause
elderly
    civil rights of, 520
    federal spending on, 97
    voting habits, 285
election campaigns. *See also* campaign finance reform
    civil servants and, 254–55
    electoral college and, 371–72
    federal matching funds for, 375
    funding issues, 373–78
Election.com, 377
elections. *See also* primary elections
    Congressional, 128, 155–56, 341–42, 366–67, 411
    contingency, 371
    defined, 20
    deviating, 372–73
    maintaining, 372
    nomination process, 325–235
    political party organization of, 319–20
    presidential, 367–73
    primary system, 316
    public opinion polls, 278–79
    realigning, 373
    timing of election day, 359
electoral college, 51–53, 166, 335–36, 368–72
    campaign strategies and, 371–72
    defined, 368
    electors, 369
    faithless electors, 369–70
    framers' intent, 368–69
    operation of, 369–71
    process, 370
    reform of, 372
electronic voting system, House of Representatives, 149
Elementary and Secondary Education Act (ESEA), 101, 531, 532
Eleventh Amendment, 70
Ellsberg, Daniel, 434, 466–67
Emancipation Proclamation, 184, 494
emergencies
    presidential powers and, 164, 181, 182
    presidential role in, 175–76
Emergency Price Control Act, 185
emerging democracy, 10
Emerson, Jo Ann, 169
EMILY's List, 405

eminent domain clause, Fifth Amendment, 451, 452
employment
    affirmative action in, 506–7
    full, 547
Employment Act of 1946, 193
en banc proceedings, 211
Energy Department. *See* Department of Energy (DOE)
Engel, Steven, 202
Engel v. Vitale, 457
enlargement policy, 576
enrolled act (resolution), 149
Enron Corporation, 56, 59, 116, 152, 174, 393
    lobbying activities of, 394–95
entitlement programs, 541, 551
Environmental Defense Fund (EDF), 399
environmental interest groups, 392
environmental policy, 538–40
Environmental Protection Agency (EPA), 251, 257, 258, 260, 535, 539, 540
Equal Employment Opportunity Act of 1972, 506
Equal Employment Opportunity Commission (EEOC), 258, 501, 506
equality
    affirmative action and, 505
    civil rights and, 491, 492–99, 505–8
    constitutional, 492–95
    Constitution and, 71
    de facto, 491
    defined, 12
    de jure, 491
    as democratic ideal, 15–16
    economic, 2–3, 96, 296
    in education, 497–98
    Gettysburg Address and, 72
    legal, 496–99
    national standards for, 96
    of opportunity, 15–16, 296, 505
    political, 296
    of result, 16, 505
    in town meeting, 12
Equal Pay Act f 1963, 511
equal protection clause, Fourteenth Amendment, 201, 496, 498, 501, 514
Equal Rights Amendment, 61, 511, 514
equal rights amendment (ERA), 68
equal time rule, 433–34
Era of Good Feelings, 314
Eritrea, 418
Escobedo v. Illinois, 222, 477
ESPN, 426, 438
establishment of religion, 456–61
    government accommodation position, 457, 460
    high wall of separation position, 457
estate tax, 527, 528
Ethics in Government Act of 1978, 408
ethnic groups. *See also* minorities
    opinion formation and, 290–91
    redistricting and, 124
ethnicity. *See also* specific ethnicities

census classifications, 6
ethnic profiling, 521–23
evangelists, 437
Evans, Donald L., 394
Everson v. Board of Education of Ewing Township, 452, 457
evidence
    DNA, 458–59
    exclusionary rule and, 471–72
    illegally gathered, 471
    warrantless searches and, 472–73
excessive entanglement provision, 457
excise taxes, 554
exclusionary rule, 471, 472
executive branch
    cabinet, 193–94
    checks and balances and, 54–56
    Constitutional powers, 58–60
    defined, 46
    Executive Office of the President, 191–93
    foreign policy role, 580
    powers of, 71
    staff, 190
    vice president, 195, 196
    wartime powers, 58–59
    Web sites, 196
    White House office, 190–91
Executive Office of the President (EOP), 191
executive orders, 177
    Executive Order 13803, 105
    issued by G. W. Bush, 178
executive privilege
    balance of powers and, 58–59
    defined, 173
    political scandal and, 185
    use of, 173–74
exit polls, 284, 439
Ex Parte Quirin, 239
expectation of privacy standard, 475
ex post facto laws, 89

F

factions
    defined, 63
    Madison's concerns about, 63–64, 386–87, 392, 408
    political parties as, 313, 387
Fair Employment Practices Committee (FEPC), 496
fair hearing, under Sixth Amendment, 455
Fair Labor Standards Act, 397
fairness doctrine, 434
fair trial, rights to, 435
faith-based initiatives, 461
faithless electors, electoral college, 369–70
Falwell, Jerry, 437
family, political socialization and, 286–87
Family Support Act, 544
Farley, James, 278–79, 279
fast-track authority, 173
federal aid
    block grants, 97

Bush, George H. W. and, 104–5
Bush, George W. and, 106
"carrot-and-stick" approach to, 85
Carter and, 102–3
categorical grants, 96–97
Clinton and, 105–6
conditions of aid for, 95
creative federalism and, 100–101, 102–3
Eisenhower and, 100
formula grants, 96–97
formula/project grants, 96–97
grants-in-aid, 95
Johnson and, 100–101
Nixon and, 102
policy making through, 98–99
project grants, 96–97
Reagan and, 103–4
Roosevelt and, 100
September 11, 2001 terrorist attacks and, 79–80
trends in, 96
Truman and, 100
Federal Aviation Administration, 273
federal budget, 547–51
    balancing, 548
    Congressional control over, 152
    deficits, 547, 551
    impoundment, 549, 551
    national debt, 554
    president and, 547–48
Federal Bureau of Investigation (FBI), 211, 268–69, 272, 447
Federal Campaign Finance Act of 1971, 408
Federal Campaign Finance Act of 1974, 408
Federal Communications Act of 1934, 433
Federal Communications Commission (FCC), 251, 257, 261
    cross-ownership rule, 438
    defined, 433
    establishment of, 433
federal court system, 208. *See also* judiciary
    appeals courts, 209–11
    appointments, 206, 217–19
    circuit courts, 210–11
    constitutional courts, 209–10
    courts of appeals, 209–11
    en banc proceedings, 211
    establishment of, 203
    interest groups and, 407
    jurisdiction of, 203
    organization of, 206, 208, 209–11
    staffing, 217–19
    U.S. district courts, 209–10
Federal Crimes Act of 1790, 450
Federal Deposit Insurance Corporation (FDIC), 251
Federal Election Campaign Act (FECA) of 1971, 373–74, 407, 409, 410–11
Federal Election Commission (FEC), 338, 347, 373, 407
Federal Emergency Management Agency (FEMA), 96, 257

Federal Energy Administration (FEA), 251
Federal Energy Office (FEO), 251
Federal Financial Management Improvement Act of 1996, 261
Federal Financial Managers Integrity Act of 1982, 261
federal government. *See also* bureaucracy
    desegregation of, 496
    top fifty achievements of, 19, 20
federal grants, 96–99
Federal Highway Administration, 258
federalism
    advantages of, 81–84
    Canada and, 92
    Constitution and, 84–89
    cooperative, 100
    creative, 100–101
    defined, 56, 80–81
    development of, 89–100
    disadvantages of, 84
    dual, 91
    experimentation and, 83–84
    future of, 106–8
    Hamilton's and Jefferson's views on, 89–90
    national power under, 89–91
    ongoing debate over, 108–10
    policy diversity and, 81–83
    in post-New Deal era, 94–95
    power distribution and, 83
    presidents and, 100–106
    purpose of, 81
    state-centered view of, 91
    Supreme Court and, 106–8
Federalism Accountability Act, 105–6
Federalism Act, 105
Federalist Papers, The, 61–62
    newspaper publication of, 420
    no. 10, 62, 63, 81, 281, 386
    no. 27, 107
    no. 51, 54, 62, 88
    no. 55, 28
    no. 73, 168
    no. 78, 203
Federalist party, 63
Federalists, 313
    Antifederalists *vs.,* 62–64
    defined, 31, 61
    ratification of the Constitution and, 65–66
    writings of, 61–62
federal mandates, 99–100
federal matching funds, 375
Federal National Mortgage Association (FNMA, or "Fannie Mae"), 251
federal questions, 220–21
Federal Radio Commission (FRC), 433
Federal Registration of Lobbying Act of 1946, 408
Federal Reserve Board (FED), 56, 261
federal spending. *See* spending
Federal Trade Commission (FTC), 261
feedback loop, 536
Feingold, Russell, 115, 153–55
feminism, 39. *See also* women's rights
Fenno, John, 420

Fifteenth Amendment, 19, 54, 70, 349
  African American voting rights
    and, 496
  circumvention of, 495–96
  women's rights and, 510
Fifth Amendment, 67, 205
  defendants rights, 469, 475–79
  double jeopardy and, 456
  due process clause, 475, 493, 498
  eminent domain clause, 451, 452
  extending to states, 476–77
fighting words, 465
filibusters, 139–41
First Amendment, 15, 67. *See also*
    freedom of speech; freedom of the
    press
  campaign contributions and, 374
  Communications Decency Act
    and, 120
  crises and, 27–28
  digital copyright protection and, 73
  freedom of speech, 385, 411,
    454–55, 463
  freedom of the press, 434–35
  interest groups and, 385
  Internet and, 73, 469
First Continental Congress, 36–37
FirstGov.org, 196, 274
fiscal policy, 546
flag burning, 465
Fleischer, Ari, 164, 187
flimsies, 222
Food and Drug Administration
    (FDA), 257
Food Lion grocery chain, 468
Forbes, Steve, 373, 375
Ford, Gerald R., 185, 318, 348, 351
  electoral college and, 372
  fast-track authority and, 173
  federal aid programs, 102
  Nixon pardon, 175
  regulatory policy, 538
  Supreme Court appointments, 235
  voter evaluation of, 362
  war powers, 186
foreign aid, 569, 576–77, 580–81
Foreign Intelligence Surveillance Act
    (FISA), 448
Foreign Intelligence Surveillance
    Court, 447
foreign policy, 562–88
  Cold War, 568–69
  Congressional role in, 579–81
  Constitution and, 579
  defined, 564
  democracy and, 564–65, 565, 587–88
  detente, 571–72
  economic policy and, 569–70,
    576–78, 583–85
  "enlargement" policy, 576
  European assessment of U.S.
    policies, 586
  federal agencies involved in, 581–85
  globalism, 568
  goals of, 565
  isolationism, 565
  media and, 585–86

NATO, 574, 575
  New World Order, 573
  nuclear age, 569, 571–72
  post–Cold War era, 573
  presidential role in, 184–87, 579–80
  president's right to conduct, 173
  public opinion and, 586–87
  regionalism, 565–66
  use of force, 578–79
  Vietnam War, 570–71
  War Powers Resolution, 580
  World War I, 566
  World War II, 567
Forest Service, 271
formal agenda, 533, 534–35
formal rules, in bureaucracy, 248–49
Forman, James, 493
Forman, Michele, 311
formula grants, 96–97
formula/project grants, 96–97
Fortas, Abe, 215, 234
four-cell method, for classifying justices,
    232–33
Fourteenth Amendment, 70
  affirmative action and, 506
  civil liberties and, 450
  due process clause, 471, 476
  equal protection clause, 201, 496,
    498, 501, 514
  incorporation of Bill of Rights and,
    455–56
  purpose of, 494
  racial segregation and, 495
  women's rights and, 510, 511–12, 514
Fourth Amendment, 67
  defendants rights, 469, 470–75
  exceptions to, 472–73
  good faith exception to, 472
  incorporation of, 471
  "reasonable suspicion" standard,
    447–48
  search and seizure and, 448
  warrantless searches, 472–75
Fox, Michael J., 402
Fox, Vincente, 92, 180, 578
framing effects, of media, 430
Frankfurther, Felix, 206, 214, 216, 227,
    228, 232, 234, 471, 498
franking privilege, 127
Franklin, Benjamin, 32, 37, 38, 40, 52–53
  Constitution and, 53
  ratification of Constitution and, 65
Franklin Printing Company, 398
Franks, Robert D., 334
Franks, Tommy, 417
Fraser, Don, 333
Frear, Allen, 132
Freedmen's Bureau, 494
freedom
  classification of countries by, 9, 63
  as core value, 295
  defined, 15
  in democracies, 10
  evolution of, 63
  "from" *vs.* "to," 449
  government and, 36
  institutionalization of, 19

  in Islamic and non-Islamic
    countries, 11
  limits on, 15–16
  negative, 15
  positive, 15
  prosperity and, 546
  twentieth-century spread of, 63
Freedom House, 11
Freedom of Access to Clinic Entrances
    Act of 1994, 209
freedom of association
  First Amendment, 385
  freedom not to associate, 480–82
  interest groups and, 385
Freedom of Information Act of 1966,
    263–64, 265
freedom of religion, 456–63
  establishment of religion, 456–61
  free exercise of religion, 456–57,
    461–63
  incorporation of, 455
freedom of speech, 463–66
  application to states, 454–55
  bad tendency and, 454–55
  interest groups and, 385, 411
  libel, 467–68
  obscenity, 468–69
  political speech, 463, 464
  private speech, 463, 465–66
  public speech, 463, 464–65
  symbolic speech, 463, 465–66
  wartime restriction on, 453
freedom of the press, 21, 466–69
  interest groups and, 385
  prior restraint (censorship)
    laws, 466–67
  subsequent punishment laws, 466
  Supreme Court and, 434–35
freedom riders, 500, 502–3
"Freedom to Farm" Act, 143
"free marketplace of ideas," 463
free press
  around the world, 420
  defined, 21
  democracy and, 419
free rider, 400–401
Free Soil party, 315
French and Indian War, 32
Frohwerk, Jacob, 454
Frohwerk v. United States, 454
Frost, Martin, 136
fruit of the poisonous tree doctrine, 471
Fugitive Slave Act, 492
full employment, 547
"full faith and credit clause," 82–83

G

Gage, Thomas, 36, 37
gag orders, 467
Galbraith, John Kenneth, 393, 397
Gallman, James, 98
Galloway, George, 37
Gallup, George, 282
Gallup Organization, 307
Gambia, 11
"Gang of Five," 155

Garcia v. San Antonio Metropolitan Transit Authority, 94, 396–97
Garfield, James, 253
Garza, Emilio, 517
gays and lesbians
 civil rights of, 520
 civil union laws, 81, 82–83
 discrimination against, 480–82
 same-sex marriage, 60–61, 81, 82–83, 89, 480–81, 521
 sexual harassment among, 516
 Supreme Court and, 480–81
Gazette of the United States, 420
gender. *See also* women
 opinion formation and, 294–95
 voting behavior and, 355
gender-motivated violence, 108
General Accounting Office (GAO), 56
General Agreement on Tariffs and Trade (GATT), 555
 Uruguay Round, 556
General Electric, 438
general revenue sharing (GRS), 102
General Services Administration, 260
general welfare clause, 84, 85
generational effect, 287
generation gap, 287
Generation X, 288
Genovese, Michael, 179
Genuine Information (Martin), 62
George III, king of England, 33, 36, 37, 39
Gephardt, Dick, 145, 155, 340
Germany, 566
Gerry, Elbridge, 45, 124
gerrymandering, 124–25
Gettysburg Address, 71–72
Gibbons, Sam, 142
Gibbons, Thomas, 90–91
Gibbons v. Ogden, 90–91
Gideon, Clarence Earl, 475
Gideon v. Wainwright, 238, 453
Gingrich, Newt, 97, 105, 334
 Congressional committees and, 135, 136, 137
 Contract with America, 150, 152
 leadership role, 153–54
 as Speaker of the House, 131
Ginsburg, Ruth Bader, 72, 215, 225–26, 226, 233, 234, 235, 474, 483, 513–15, 516
 appointment of, 169, 212, 213, 214, 217
Gitlin, Todd, 108
Gitlow, Benjamin, 454
Gitlow v. New York, 452, 454
Giuliani, Rudolph, 78–79
"global bathtubs," 557
globalism, 568
globalization, 557
Global Positioning System (GPS), 443
global warming, 540
going public, 188
Goldberg, Arthur, 216, 234
Goldberg, Bernard, 435–36
Goldman, Sheldon, 219
Goldwater, Barry, 441–42

Gonzales, Alberto, 72, 212, 517
Gonzalez, Elian, 427
good character test, for voting, 350
Goode, Virgil, 319
good faith exception to Fourth Amendment, 472
Goodwin, Alfred T., 463
Gore, Al, 22, 52, 56, 270, 432
 campaign fundraising by, 374
 2000 election and, 331, 336, 351, 355
 gender differences in support for, 295
 media polls and, 439
 media use by, 441
 as vice president, 195
Gorton, Slade, 154
government accommodation position, 457, 460
Government Accountability Project, 273
Government Accounting Office (GAO), 174
government corporations, 261–62
government interest groups, 396–97
Government in the Sunshine Act of 1976, 264, 265
government-media relationships, 438
government overthrow, 464
government regulation. *See* regulation
Graber, Doris, 427
Gramm, Philip, 394
Grams, Rod, 154
grandfather clause, voting rights and, 496
Grant, Ulysses S., 402
grants-in-aid, 95–99. *See also* federal aid
 defined, 95
grantsmanship, 101
grass-roots activity, 404–6
Gratz case, 488–90, 509
Grayson, William, 44
Great Britain
 American Revolution and, 36–40
 taxation of American colonies by, 32–36
 women in House of Commons, 515
Great Compromise, 49–50
Great Depression, 251, 316, 542
Great Society program, 100–101, 251
Greece, 14, 28, 348
Green, Theodore F., 132
Green party, 336, 338–39, 396
Gregg, Judd, 311
Greider, William, 437
Grenville, George, 33, 36
gridlock, 410
Griswold, Estelle, 202
Griswold v. Connecticut, 232, 453, 479
gross national product, 102
group maintenance, 400
Grutter case, 488–90, 509
Guinn v. United States, 496
Guiteau, Charles, 253
Gulf of Tonkin Resolution, 571
gun control
 interest groups and, 382–84
 Supreme Court and, 106–7

Gun-Free School Zones law, 106–7
gun-rights advocates, 382–84, 402

H

habeas corpus, writ of. *See* writ of *habeas corpus*
Habibie, B. J., 119
Hagel, Chuck, 59
Halberstam, David, 422
Haldeman, H. R., 191
Hamilton, Alexander, 39, 42–43, 45, 65
 Federalist Papers, 61, 107, 168, 203, 420
 on political parties, 313
 views on federalism, 89–90
Hamilton v. Regents of the University of California, 452
Hammer v. Dagenhart, 91
Hammond, Darrell, 441
Hancock, John, 38, 66
Hang Ten movement, 460
Hansen, James V., 412
Hanssen, Robert P., 269
Harding, Warren, 167
Hardwick case, 230
Harlan, John Marshall, 206, 234, 452, 475, 492, 517
Harper v. Virginia Board of Elections, 501
Harrington, Michael, 542
Harrison, Benjamin, 38
Harris v. United States, 384
Hart, Gary, 333
Hart-Teeter telephone surveys, 284
Harvard University, 391, 493
Hastert, J. Dennis, 130, 131, 135, 152, 154, 155, 335, 447
Hatch, Carl, 254
Hatch, Orrin, 206, 213, 219, 220
Hatch Act, 253–55
hate speech, 465
Hatfield, Mark, 144
Havel, Vaclav, 5, 8, 9, 15, 71, 575, 576
Hayden, Tom, 330, 333, 390
Hayes, George E. C., 497
Hayes, Rutherford B., 201
Haynsworth, Clement, 215
Hays, Lawrence Brooks, 127
Head Start program, 101, 256–57, 542
Health, Education and Welfare, U.S. Department of, 504
Health and Human Services Department, 257, 259, 544
health care, 326
hearings, subcommittee, 147
Hearst, William Randolph, 421
Heart of Atlanta Motel v. United States, 501
Helms, Jesse, 139, 143, 155
Hemlock Society, 484
Henry, Patrick, 36, 66
hierarchy, in bureaucracy, 246, 248
high wall of separation position, 457
Hill, Anita, 215
Hill, Arthur, 258
Hine, Lewis, 421
Hispanics
 affirmative action and, 489
 civil rights of, 2–3, 491, 516–17

in Congress, 122
Congressional districts and, 124
Democratic party and, 342
interest groups and, 406
opinion formation by, 291
Republican party and, 334
Hobbes, Thomas, 30–31, 32
Ho Chi Minh, 570
Hoffman, Abbie, 333
Hoffman, Jonathan, 347
holds, 139–40
Holmes, Oliver Wendell, 27, 212, 229, 231–32, 453, 454, 463, 552
homeland defense programs, 110
Homeland Security, Department of, 194, 195, 256, 266, 268
    establishment of, 244–45
    functions of, 247
    funding of, 246
    organizational structure of, 247
    personnel management, 255
homosexuals. *See* gays and lesbians
Honda, Mike, 156
Hoover, Herbert, 278, 316
    economy and, 177
    executive power and, 182
Hoover, J. Edgar, 265, 268
hopper, 147
horizontal powers, 54–56
Horton, Willie, 442
House majority leader, 131
House of Representatives. *See also*
    Congress; Congressional
    committees; Congressional
    members
    Budget Committee, 551
    compared to Senate, 121
    Constitutional Convention and, 49
    Constitution and, 53, 117–18
    decentralization of power in, 137
    election costs, 373
    elections settled in, 314
    gender-related voting behavior
        and, 355
    House majority leader, 131
    House Rules committee, 138–39
    lawmaking process, 147–49
    leadership, 130–31
    minority leader, 131
    representativeness of, 13, 64
    Rules Committee, 131
    size of, 122
    Speaker of the House, 130–31
Housing and Urban Development,
    Department of, 257
Hoyer, Steny H., 145
Hruska, Roman, 215
Huang, John, 376
Hughes, Charles Evans, 93, 220, 229
Hughes, Karen, 516
Humphrey, Hubert, 132, 330, 339, 397, 505–8
    Democratic National Convention,
        1968, and, 332–33
    Democratic party and, 316
Hunter, Robert, 541
Hussein, Saddam, 21, 578

Hyde, Henry J., 137, 153
Hyde Amendment, 542–43

I

Ibrahim, Jeremy Gonzales, 334
ideological bias, of the media, 435–38
ideological interest groups, 397
Illinois v. Rodriquez, 472
immigrants, political parties and, 315–16
Immigration and Naturalization Service
    (INS), 268
    performance of, 273
    September 11 terrorist attacks
        and, 250
    war on terrorism and, 521–22
"imminent lawless action," 464
impeachment
    of Clinton, 135–36, 153, 166, 311, 339–40
    Congressional power of, 153
    defined, 153
    of Nixon, 153
    of president, 166
    of Supreme Court judges, 205
Imperial Presidency, The (Schlesinger), 185
implementation
    by bureaucracy, 256–57
    of public policies, 535
    three C's of, 535
implied powers, 86
impoundment, 60, 549, 551
Impoundment Control Act, 551
income
    opinion formation and, 290
    voting behavior and, 359
incorporation, of Bill of Rights, 95, 451–53, 455–56
incumbents, 127
independent agencies, 259–60
Independent Counsel Act of 1978, 185
independent expenditures, 376–77
*Independent Federation of Flight Attendants
    v. Zipes,* 507
independent regulatory agencies,
    260–61
independents, 301, 311–12, 360
    election process and, 319
    minor parties, 337
India, 348, 429
Indian Citizenship Act, 517
indirect democracy, 12, 13, 23
Indonesia, 119
inflation, 547
information
    about terrorism, 419, 583
    access to information, 365, 437–38
    from interest groups, 390–92
    from Internet, 365
    from lobbyists, 403
    from media, 365, 418–19
    political knowledge, 365
    public interest in, 288–89
informed citizenry, 418–19
inherent powers, 86
initiatives, 359–60
inner cabinet, 193

Inouye, Daniel K., 122
In re Oliver, 452
inside strategy, 152
insurance companies, DNA testing
    and, 484
INS v. Chadha, 184, 186
integration, 498
intellectual property protection, 73
intelligence, 583, 587
intensity, of opinion, 303
Inter-American Development Bank, 569
"*Inter arma silent leges*", 27
interest group liberalism, 409
interest group rating scheme, 340–41
interest groups, 382–412
    actual, 385
    ad hoc coalitions, 392
    campaign contributions by, 374
    characteristics of, 399–402
    civil rights, 398–99
    collective action through, 389–90
    Congress and, 406–7
    Congressional voting decisions and,
        145–46, 340–41
    conservative, 388, 397
    court system and, 407
    defined, 21, 384, 385–86
    democracy and, 384–88, 409–10,
        411–12
    Democratic party fundraising and,
        332–33
    economic, 393–95
    effectiveness of, 401–2
    2002 election and, 411
    environmental, 392
    functions of, 38–392
    future of, 410–11
    government, 397
    grass-roots activity, 404–6
    growth of, 386, 409–10, 412
    gun control and, 382–84
    history of, 385, 386–87
    ideological, 397
    impacts of, 391–92, 409–10
    information provided through,
        390–92
    liberal, 388, 397
    lobbying by, 402–4
    membership in, 399–401
    organized labor, 392
    political action committees, 407–8
    political parties and, 320–21
    potential, 385
    program implementation and, 257
    public attitudes toward, 384–85
    public interest, 395–96
    recent trends, 387–88
    regulation of, 408–9
    religious, 392, 397
    single-interest, 399
    strategies of, 402–7
    student groups, 392
    types of, 392–99
intergovernmental transfers, 95
Interior Department, 259, 273
Internal Revenue Service (IRS), 249,
    257, 265, 273, 552

international economic policy, 547, 554–57
International Labor Organization (ILO), 584
International Monetary Fund (IMF), 119, 555, 576
International Republican Institute (IRI), 398
International Security Assistance Force (ISAF), 563
Internet. *See also* Web sites
copyright protection and, 73
First Amendment and, 73, 469
grass-roots organizing through, 412
growth of, 429
libel and, 468
"netizens" organizations, 389
as news source, 427
online voter registration, 358
online voting, 377
political coverage on, 427, 428
regulation of, 433
as source of political information, 365
worldwide access to, 429
interpretation role, of media, 430
interstate commerce clause, 84–85
civil rights laws and, 501
gun control and, 106–7
intrastate commerce and, 90–91
regulation of, 84–85
interstate highway system, 98
interviewer bias, in public opinion polls, 284
Intolerable Acts, 36, 37
intolerance, 296–97
intrastate commerce, 90–91
investigative journalism, 430–31
investigative oversight, by Congress, 152
Iran, 119, 564, 573
Iraq, 21, 564, 573, 578
iron triangles, 268, 410, 537
isolationism, 565
Israel, 579
issue advertising, 115, 116, 411, 464
issue advocacy, 376
issue networks, 268, 537
issue-oriented voting behavior, 361–62
Istook, Ernest J., Jr., 59
Iyengar, Shanto, 430

J

Jackson, Andrew, 167, 272, 317
civil service and, 252–53
election of, 370
executive power and, 181
executive privilege use, 174
patronage system and, 272
political party system and, 315
staff, 190
Supreme Court and, 236
Jacksonian Democrats, 315
Japanese-American Internment policy, 493
Jay, John, 37, 41, 203
Federalist Papers, 61, 420

Jefferson, Thomas, 14, 18, 21, 36, 38, 39–40, 41, 50, 138, 206
Antifederalists and, 63
Constitution and, 67–68
death of, 66
electoral college and, 369
executive power and, 60, 181
federalism and, 89–90
impoundment by, 549
on natural rights, 491
newspapers and, 420, 421
on political information, 365
on political parties, 313–14
political parties and, 317
on presidency, 185
Jeffersonian Republicans, 313
Jeffersonians, 316
Jefferson-Jenkins, Carolyn, 377
Jeffords, Jim, 106, 116, 155, 163, 206, 213, 221, 310–12, 319, 321, 335, 343, 536
Jehovah's Witnesses, 463
Jenner-Butler Bill, 206
Jews, 291–93
Jim Crow laws, 495
Job Corps, 542
Joe Camel, 530
John, David, 542
Johnson, Andrew, 153, 187, 494
Johnson, Lyndon B., 132, 206, 330
bureaucracy and, 251
civil rights and, 500–501
Congress and, 116, 142
creative federalism and, 100–101
Democratic party and, 316
electoral college and, 372
federal aid, 97
federalism and, 97, 100–101, 109
foreign policy, 571
media and, 585
poverty program, 542
staff, 191
war powers, 185–86
"Johnson rule," 142
"Johnson Treatment," 132
"Join 3," 223
Joint Chiefs of Staff, 582
joint committees, 134
Jones, Gordon S., 136
Jones, Paula Corbin, 185
J.P. Morgan Chase, 395
judicial conference, 227
judicial restraint, 231–32
judicial review
of Congressional legislation, 120
Constitution and, 55–56, 69–71
defined, 21, 70, 204
democracy and, 204
judiciary, 200–240. *See also* court system; federal court system; Supreme Court
case types, 209
checks and balances and, 54–56
Constitutional powers, 60
court appointments, 211–19
courts types, 208–9
defined, 46

democracy and, 202, 207
development of judicial power, 203–5
federal courts, 209–11
independence of, 205–6, 207–8, 238–40
judicial activism, 232
organization of, 206
origins of judicial power, 203–4
Supreme Court decisions, 230–38
Supreme Court operations, 219–30
wartime and, 239
Judiciary Act of 1789, 203, 204
jurisdiction, 203
appellate, 203
original, 203
Justice Department, 257, 259, 521–22

K

Kagay, Michael, 359
Kaiser Aluminum Chemical Corporation, 506
Kamhawi, Lahib, 119
Katz, Sam, 307
Katzenbach, Nicholas, 81
Katzenbach v. McClung, 501
Katzenbach v. Morgan, 517
Katz v. United States, 472, 475
Kazakhstan, 398
Keating Owen Act, 91
Kennan, George, 568
Kennedy, Anthony M., 126, 201, 214, 216, 226, 227–28, 231, 233, 234, 235, 237, 460, 474, 480–81, 482, 483
Kennedy, Edward M. (Ted), 121, 216, 335, 531
Kennedy, John F., 127, 165, 176, 360, 534, 567, 571
bureaucracy and, 267
civil rights and, 500
coattails effect and, 367
foreign policy, 569
media and, 419
political advertising by, 442
poverty program, 542
Supreme Court and, 216, 236
tax policy, 527
women's rights and, 511
Kennedy, Robert F., 330, 332, 432, 503, 534
Kernel, Samuel, 188
Kerrey, Bob, 132
Kessler, Gladys, 522
Kettl, Don, 108
Kevorkian, Jack, 484
Keyes v. School District #1, Denver, Colorado, 504
"keypad democracy," 427
Khameni, Ayatollah Ali, 119
Khatami, Mohammad, 119
Khrushchev, Nikita, 569
Kimmelman, Gene, 438
Kincaid, John, 97
King, Don, 471
King, Martin Luther, Jr., 2, 22–23, 268, 366, 401, 432, 499, 502, 503, 534, 542

King, Rodney, 366
King Caucus, 315
Kingdon, John, 146
Klain, Ronald, 225
Klopfer v. North Carolina, 453
Kluger, Richard, 497
Knox, Henry, 173
Kohl, Herb, 139–40
Kohut, Andrea, 436
Kohut, Andrew, 440
Korea, 569, 570
Korematsu v. United States, 201
Kozinski, Alex, 224
Kramer, David, 334
Kristol, William, 201
Kuberua, 11
Ku Klux Klan, 494–95
Ku Klux Klan Acts of 1870/1871, 495
Kunstler, William, 333
Kuwait, 573
Kyoto Protocol, 539, 540

L

Labor Department, 259, 584
Lachowsky, Hyman, 454
Lambert, Royce, 519
Lamm, Richard, 338
Landon, Alf, 279
language minorities, 517
latency, of opinion, 303–4
Latin America, 429, 569
Latinos. *See* Hispanics
law clerks, Supreme Court, 224–25
lawmaking
    amendments to bills, 139
    cloture, 140–41
    Congress and, 147–49
    debate, 147–48
    filibusters, 139–41
    holds, 139–40
    House Rules Committee
        and, 138–39
    influences on, 144–46, 147
    line item veto, 139
    lobbyists, 147
    logrolling and, 143
    markup session, 147
    obstacles, 149–52
    political nature of, 114–16, 142
    pork-barrel legislation, 143
    president and, 149, 176
    process, 146–52
    riders to bills, 139
    subcommittees, 147
Lay, Kenneth L., 394, 395
Lazarus, Edward, 224, 228
Lazio, Rick, 355
League of Nations, 172, 377, 566
League of United Latin American
    Citizens (LULAC), 517
League of Women Voters, 359
Leahy, Patrick, 134, 154, 206, 219, 221
leaks, 585
least restrictive means test, 462
Lee, Richard Henry, 38
Legal Services program, 101

legislative branch. *See also* Congress;
    House of Representatives; Senate
    checks and balances and, 54–56
    Constitutional powers, 57–58
    defined, 46
    executive privilege and, 58–59
    powers of, 71
    war declaration and, 71
legislative courts, 211
legislative oversight, 152, 580
Legislative Reorganization
    Act of 1946, 152
legislative veto, 152, 184
legislature
    bicameral, 29, 117
    state, 42
    unicameral, 47
Lehrer, Jim, 424
Lemon test, 228, 457–61
Lemon v. Kurtzman, 228, 457
Lenin, 566
Lesotho, 352
Letters of Brutus (Yates), 62
Leviathan (Hobbes), 30
Levin, Carl, 98
Lewinsky, Monica, 56, 58, 115, 153, 174,
    185, 428
Lewis, John, 503
Lewis, Lawrence, 190
Libby, Lewis, 195
libel, 435, 467–68
liberal interest groups, 388, 397
liberal magazines, 423
liberals
    defined, 297
    gender and, 294
    in the media, 435, 437
    political party ideology and, 340
    religion and, 291–93
    Supreme Court justices, 231–35
    trends, 298
    views of, 297–98
liberty. *See* freedom
Liberty party, 315
Lichter, Linda, 435
Lichter, Robert, 435
Light, Paul C., 273
Lightner, Candy, 386
Limbaugh, Russ, 440
limited democracy, 10
limited government, 31
Limited Test Ban Treaty, 569
Lincoln, Abraham, 27, 55, 70, 167,
    315, 494
    assassins of, 239
    emergency powers, 164, 181
    Gettysburg Address, 71–72
    moral leadership by, 177
    Republican party and, 315, 317
    war powers, 184
Lincoln, Benjamin, 40
"Lindbergh" law, 87
Lindsey, Bruce, 58
Lindsey, Lawrence B., 59
line item veto, 60, 120, 144
Lipman, Samuel, 454
Lippmann, Walter, 299, 301

literacy tests, for voting, 350, 495, 501, 517
Literary Digest political polls, 278–79, 282,
    283, 284
Little Rock, Arkansas, school
    desegregation, 498–99
Livingston, Bob, 131
lobby-agents, 402
lobbying, 147, 402–4
    defined, 402
    registration of lobbyists, 408
    regulation of, 408–9
    tactics, 403–4
Lobbying Disclosure Act, 409
local elections, voter turnout, 372
local governments
    policy variations, 81
    Supreme Court effects on, 237
local party organization, 321, 323
Locke, John, 31–32, 38
Lodge, Henry Cabot, 139
logrolling, 143, 537
Loomis, Burdett, 142
Lorance v. AT& Technologies, 507
Lott, Trent, 140, 151, 153–55, 206, 335
    campaign finance reform and, 115
    Congressional Committees and, 136
    Jeffords and, 310, 311
    lawmaking and, 152
    pork-barrel legislation and, 143
    Senate leadership and, 132
Louisiana ex. rel. Francisco Resweber, 452
Louisiana Purchase, 181
lower-court system, 208
Lowi, Theodore, 409
loyalists, 35
Luce, Henry, 422
Lusitania, 566
Luttig, Michael, 224
lynchings, 495, 496

M

MacArthur, Douglas, General, 21–22
machine politics, 316, 323–24
Madison, James, 14, 28, 39, 41,
    42–43, 167
    on access to information, 437–38
    checks and balances and, 56
    concerns about factions, 63–64,
        386–87, 392, 408
    Constitutional Convention and,
        45–46, 48
    Federalist Papers, 54, 61–64, 81, 88,
        281, 386, 420
    on House of Representatives, 117
    ratification of Constitution and, 66
    on separation of church and
        state, 457
    War of 1812 and, 184
magazines, 422–23, 436–37
Magna Carta, 28
Maher, Bill, 436
maintaining elections, 372
majoritarianism, 17
majority leader, 131
majority-minority districts, 124–26
majority opinions, 229–29

majority rule
defined, 12
minority rights and, 12, 16–17
in town meeting, 12
Mali, 352, 353
Malloy v. Hogan, 453
mandatory spending, 554
Manifest Destiny, 565
Mann, Thomas, 59, 155
Mao Zedong, 322
Mapp, Dollree, 202, 471
Mapp v. Ohio, 453
Marbury, William, 203–4
Marbury v. Madison, 21, 70, 203–4, 237
Marcus, Stanley, 489
Marcy, William, 253
margin of error, 282
Margolies-Mezvinsky, Marjorie, 145
Marine Protection Research Act, 539
markup session, subcommittee, 147
marriage, same-sex, 60–61, 81, 82–83, 89
Married Women's Independent
Citizenship Act of 1922, 511
Married Women's Property
Act of 1848, 509
Marshall, John, 70, 204, 229, 230, 497
on application of Bill of Rights to
states, 451
constitutionality of national bank
and, 90
Marshall, Thurgood, 234, 235, 495,
497–98, 508, 513
appointment of, 213
martial law, during Civil War, 27
Martin, Casey, 520
Martin, Luther, 46, 49, 62
Martin v. Wilks, 507
Martz, Judy, 355
Mason, George, 39, 45, 66
Massachusetts Bay Company, 29
mass media, 419. *See also* media
Matalin, Mary, 195
Matthew, Donald, 142
Mauritania, 11
Mauro, Tony, 224
"maximum feasible participation," 542
Mayaguez, 186
Mayflower Compact, 28, 32
McAuliffe, Christa, 262–63
McAuliffe, Terry, 325, 340, 342
McCain, John, 153–55, 324, 335,
437, 442
campaign finance reform and, 115,
116, 374
Confederate flag and, 98
McCaleb, Neal, 519
McCarthy, Eugene, 330, 332–33
McCarthy, Joseph, 431
McConnell, Mitch, 115, 116, 374, 464
McCormack, John, Jr., 144
McCulloch v. Maryland, 90
McCurry, Mike, 438
McGovern, George, 329, 330, 331
McGovern-Fraser Commission,
330–31, 333
McKinley, William, 173, 315, 316
McKinney, Cynthia, 125, 126

McLuhan, Marshall, 427
McReynolds, James C., 220
means testing, 541
media, 416–53. *See also* television
cable television, 419, 424, 425, 433
censorship, 419
checks and balances and, 429
conservatives in, 435, 437
corporate control of, 437–38
cross-ownership of, 437–38
democracy and, 418–19, 442–43
diversity of, 436
election coverage by, 368, 438–42
emergence of, 419–27
equal time rule, 433–34
fairness doctrine and, 434
foreign policy and, 585–86
framing effects of, 430
functions of, 427–32
government relations with, 438
government restrictions on, 416–18
ideological bias and, 435–38
independence of, 419
information provided by, 365, 418–19
Internet, 427
interpretation role of, 430
investigative role of, 430–31
leaks, 585
liberals in, 435, 437
limits on freedom of, 432–35
magazines, 422–23, 436–37
manipulation of facts by, 431
narrowcasting, 425–26
newspapers, 419, 420–22, 430, 436–37
"official sources" for, 438
polling by, 439
prior restraint and, 434–35
radio, 423, 433, 439–40
right of rebuttal, 434
satellite technology and, 425
scarcity doctrine, 433
socialization role of, 431–32
surveillance function of, 427, 429
technology and, 425–27, 443
television, 423–25, 440–41
war on terrorism and, 416–18
Medicaid, 96, 101, 103, 104
Medicare, 101
Medicare Act of 1965, 542, 543–44
Meehan, Marty, 115
"megabills," 151
Meier, Kenneth, 537
Meiklejohn, Alexander, 463
mentally challenged defendants, death
penalty and, 458
merit-based hiring and
advancement, 253
Merit Systems Protection Board,
253, 254
Merryman, John, 27
Mexican American Legal Defense and
Education Fund (MALDEF), 517
Mexican Americans, 3, 516
Mexico, 570
federalism and, 92
Internet access in, 429
president, 180

*Miami Herald Publishing Company v.
Tornillo*, 435
Michigan, University of, 488–90
Michigan Qualified Voter File
(QVF), 358
Michigan v. Tucker, 478
Michnik, Adam, 19
Middle East
democracy in, 119
peace efforts, 579
midterm elections, 366–67
migrant laborers, 3
military
civilian control of, 21–22
courts, 211
desegregation of, 496
tribunals, 211, 239
military-industrial complex, 582
Mill, John Stuart, 9, 281
Miller, George, 531
Miller, Zell, 527
Miller v. California, 468
Milliken v. Bradley, 504
Million Mom March, 383–84, 409, 412
Miner, Ruth, 355
minorities. *See also* African Americans;
Hispanics
cloture and filibusters and, 141
Congressional members, 122
distribution by county, 11
judicial appointments of, 218
opinions of, 281–82, 290–91
Supreme Court appointments,
213, 214
voting rights, 349–50
minority leader, 131
minority-owned businesses, 506
minority rights, 12, 16–17, 18
minor parties, 304, 337–39, 339
Minor v. Happersett, 510
Minton, Sherman, 217
Miranda, Ernesto, 202, 476
Miranda v. Arizona, 201, 222, 227, 230,
233, 236, 477–79
Miranda warning, 477
Missouri Compromise, 492, 493
Mitchell, George, 132
Mobile Journalist Workstation
(MJW), 443
Model Cities program, 101
moderates
political party ideology and, 340
Supreme Court justices, 231–35
monarchy, 10
monarchy/limited democracy, 10
Mondale, Walter, 195
monetary policy, 546
money bills, 49
monopoly, in the media, 437–38
Monroe, James, 314, 565
Monroe Doctrine, 565
Montesquieu, Charles de, 30
Moore, Archie, 471
Moore, Roy, 460
Moorhead, Carlos J., 137
moral leadership, as presidential
role, 177

Morella, Constance A., 406
Morris, Gouverneur, 45
Morris, Robert, 38, 39, 45
Mothers Against Drunk Driving, 85, 386
Motor-Voter Law (National Voter Registration Act (NVRA) of 1993), 346–47, 353, 355
Mott, Lucretia, 509
Moussaoui, Zacarias, 435
movable automobile exception, to Fourth Amendment, 472
Moynihan, Daniel Patrick, 220, 542, 544
MTV, 426, 431
Mueller case, 461
Mugabe, Robert, 364
multiparty system, 335–39. *See also* political parties
    cultural factors affecting, 336
    institutional factors affecting, 335–36
    minor parties, 337–39
    party identification and, 336–37
multipoint distribution service (MDS), 433
Munoz, Cecilia, 250
Murphy, Frank, 217
Murphy, Laura W., 239, 447
Murphy v. Waterfront Commission of New York, 453
Murrah, Alfred P., Federal Building, 205, 270
Murrow, Edward R., 423, 431
Musgrove, Ronnie, 502
Muslims
    culture, 460
    ethnic profiling of, 521–22
    war on terrorism and, 562–63
mutual assured destruction (MAD), 536

N

NAACP v. Alabama, 453
Nabrit, James M., 497
Nader, Ralph, 336, 338, 386, 396
name recognition, 128, 361
narrowcasting, 425–26
Nast, Thomas H., 253, 315
Nation, 423
National Aeronautics and Space Administration (NASA), 260, 262–63, 271, 537
National American Women Suffrage Association, 510
National Association for the Advancement of Colored People (NAACP), 98–99, 398, 496, 497–98, 500
National Association of Manufacturers (NAM), 393, 408
national bank, 89–90
national chair, political parties, 324
National Commission on Federal Election Reform, 348, 351
National Conference of State Legislatures, 360
National Congress of American Indians, 518

National Council of La Raza, 517
national debt, 554
National Democratic Institute (NDI), 398
National Economic Council, 193
National Emergencies Act, 187
National Enquirer, 422
National Environmental Policy Act of 1969, 264, 538–39
National Federation of independent Business, 412
National Gay and Lesbian Task Force, 481
National Gazette, 421
National Guard, 247
national health care, 105
Nationalist Party, Taiwan, 322
nationalists, 45–46
National Labor Relations Board (NLRB), 251, 261
National Labor Relations Board (NLRB) v. Jones and Laughlin Steel, 93
National League of Cities v. Usery, 94
National Organization for Women (NOW), 398–99, 404–5, 511
national party conventions, 315, 324–27
national party organization, 324–25. *See also* political parties
National Review, 423
National Rifle Association (NRA), 383, 389, 399, 404, 412
National Right to Life Committee, 115
National Science Foundation, 259, 261
National Security Act of 1947, 269, 568
national security advisor, 583
National Security Agency (NSA), 268
national security bureaucracy, 244–46, 268–69. *See also* Homeland Security, Department of
National Security Council (NSC), 192, 568, 582–83
National Security Council Paper 68 (NSC 68), 568–69
national standards, interest groups and, 383
National Taxpayers Union, 401
National Transportation Safety Board (NTSB), 261
national unity, September 11 attacks and, 288, 300
National Voter Registration Act (NVRA) of 1993 (Motor-Voter Law), 346–47, 353, 355
National Weather Service, 259, 271
National Wildlife Federation, 540
National Woman's Loyalty League, 510
National Woman's Party, 510
National Woman Suffrage Association, 510
Native Americans, 3
    civil rights of, 491, 517–18, 519
    in Congress, 122
    ethnic movement, 518
    religious freedom of, 462
    separatist tribal movement, 518
natural rights, 491
NBC, 438

Near, Jay, 455
Near v. Minnesota, 452, 455
necessary and proper clause, 58, 85, 118
negative incentives, regulatory policy as, 529
"negative pork," 143
Neighborhood Youth Corps, 542
Nelson, Thomas, 38
"netizens" organizations, 389
Neustadt, Richard, 424
New Deal, 93–94
    bureaucracy and, 251
    coalition, 316
    dual federalism and, 93
    political party realignment and, 301
    Supreme Court and, 216–17
New Democrat, 105
New Federalism, 102
New Hampshire primary, 328–29
New Jersey Plan, 47–48
New Jersey v. T.L.O., 473
new media, 425–27
New Republic, 423
News Corporation, 438
news coverage
    cable television, 419, 424
    government restrictions on, 416–18
    Internet, 427
    public television, 441
    television, 419, 424, 426, 441
    war on terrorism, 416–17, 418
    youth interest in, 432
newspapers, 420–22
    diversity of, 436–37
    history of, 420–21
    investigative journalism by, 430
    muckraking, 421
    number and circulation of, 421
    readership of, 419
    yellow journalism, 421–22
Newsweek, 428, 439
New World Order, 573
New York City, terrorist attacks and, 78–80
New York Independent Journal, 420
New York Sun, 421
New York Times, 434, 439, 467, 511
New York Times Co. v. United States, 229
New York v. United States, 106
Ngo Dinh Diem, 571
Nicaragua, 583
Nichols, Terry, 205
Nickelodeon, 426
Nickles, Don, 132
Nie, Norman, 348–49
Nigeria, 119, 353
Nineteenth Amendment, 19, 54, 70, 350, 510–11
Ninth Amendment, 67, 120
Nixon, Richard, 56, 164, 287, 318, 333
    campaign finance reform and, 374
    coattails effect and, 367
    electoral college and, 372
    executive privilege use, 58, 60, 174
    federal aid programs, 102
    federal budget, 548, 549
    foreign policy, 571, 579

impeachment and, 153
impoundment by, 549, 551
investigation of, 152
minor parties and, 339
pardoning of, 175
political advertising, 442
regulatory policy, 538
Supreme Court appointments, 216
war powers, 186
Watergate and, 430
women's rights and, 511
"no approach buffer zone," 466
nobility titles, 89
No Child Left Behind Act, 82–83, 106, 176, 531
no incorporation, of Bill of Rights, 451–52
nomination
caucuses, 327
defined, 325
primary elections, 327–29
process, 325–235
reform of, 329–35
nonpartisan elections, 360–61
nonvoting, 355, 357–58
Noonan, Peggy, 425
Noriega, Manuel, 434–35, 585–86
norms
of bureaucratic culture, 262–63
media socialization and, 431
North, Oliver, 583
North American Free Trade Agreement (NAFTA), 555, 556
North Atlantic Treaty Organization (NATO), 568, 574–75, 576
North Korea, 564, 573
Norton, Gale, 273, 519
nuclear weapons, 570
arms control, 570–72, 572
atomic bomb, 568, 569
Cold War and, 568, 569
policy making, 536
nullification, 91

O

O'Bannon, Frank, 460
Obasanjo, Olusegun, 119
Obey, David R., 142
O'Brien, David, 223, 232
obscenity, 468–69
Observations on the New Constitution. . . by a Colombian Patriot (Warren), 62
Occupational Safety and Health Administration (OSHA), 251
O'Connor, Sandra Day, 72, 106, 216, 226, 228, 231, 233, 234, 235, 460, 461, 473, 474, 482, 483, 509, 516
appointment of, 213, 214, 217
O'Donnell, Rosie, 383, 521
Office of Emergency Preparedness, 251
Office of Faith-Based and Community Initiatives, 191
Office of Federal Contract Compliance Programs (OFCCP), 506
Office of Homeland Security. *See* Homeland Security, Department of

Office of Management and Budget (OMB), 193, 548–49, 551
oversight of bureaucracy by, 259–60, 261, 266–67
Office of Personnel Management, 253
Office of Strategic Influence, 419
Office of Strategic Initiatives, 191
Office of Trade Representatives, 584
"official sources," 438
offset policies, 539–540
Ogden, Aaron, 90–91
Ogletree, Charles J., 493
Old Age Survivors Disability Insurance (OASDI), 541, 542
Olive Branch Petition, 37
Oliver, Jack, 334
Olson, Barbara, 448
Olson, Mancur, Jr., 400
Olson, Theodore, 223, 448
Omnibus Budget Reconciliation Act, 103
Omnibus Crime Control and Safe Streets Act, 236, 478
Omnibus Highway Spending Bill, 143
omnibus legislation, 151
O'Neill, Paul H., 394, 555, 576–77
O'Neill, Thomas ("Tip"), 131, 143, 403
"one-person, one-vote" standard, 96
"one stop shopping" search warrants, 447
On Liberty (Mill), 281
Open Housing Act of 1968, 19
open primary elections, 328
Operation Desert Storm, 573. *See also* Persian Gulf War
Operation Rescue, 407
Operation Tailwind, 431
opinions
announcing, 228–29
assignment of, 227–28
concurring, 229
defined, 227
dissenting, 229
drafting process, 228
intensity of, 303
latency of, 303–4
majority, 228–29
plurality, 229
salience of, 304
social variables affecting formation of, 289–93
opportunity, equality of, 15–16, 505, 526
oral argument, Supreme Court, 225–26
order, 16–17
O'Reilly, Bill, 424
Organization for Economic Cooperation and Development (OECD), 584
organized labor interest groups, 392, 393–94
original intent theory, 231
original jurisdiction, 203, 221
Ornstein, Norman J., 311
O'Rourke, R. J., 547
Orwell, George, 418
Oslo Accords, 579
outside strategy, 152
oversight, by Congress, 152–53
administrative, 267
investigative, 152

legislative, 152, 580
overturning Supreme Court decisions, 230

P

"packages," 151
PACs. *See* political action committees (PACs)
Page, Ben, 300
Paige, Rod, 513
Paine, Thomas, 38
Pakistan, 563
Palestinians, 579
Palko v. Connecticut, 452, 455
Panama, 585–86
Panama Canal, 181
pardons, presidential, 175
Parker v. Gladden, 453
Parks, Rosa, 22–23, 490, 499
participation, 18–19. *See also* political participation
citizen participation programs, 388
defined, 348
system for, 20–21
partisanship. *See* political party identification
party caucuses, 131
party-line voting, 360, 362
party platform, 324
Party's Over, The (Broder), 341
Pataki, George E., 78–80, 177
pat-down searches, 473
Paterson, William, 46
patronage system, 253, 272
Patterson v. McLean Credit Union, 507
Paul, Alice, 510
Peace Corps, 260, 569
Pearl, Daniel, 429
Pearl Harbor, 567
peers, political socialization and, 288
Pelosi, Nancy, 131, 145
Pendleton Act of 1883, 253
penny press, 421
Pentagon Papers, 466–67
peonage, 496
People for the American Way, 397
Perot, H. Ross, 303–4, 336, 337–38, 339, 386, 553
media time purchases, 434
use of talk shows by, 440
Persian Gulf War, 417, 564, 578
Personal Responsibility and Work Opportunity Reconciliation Act, 544
persuasion
controlling bureaucracy with, 267
by lobbyists, 403
Peru, 11
petit courts, 208
Pew Research Center, 307, 368, 432, 436
Phillips, Carter, 224
Pickering, Charles W., 220, 221
Pinckney, Charles, 52, 369
Pitt, William, 34
Planned Parenthood of Southeastern Pennsylvania v. Casey, 227, 482

Plato, 281, 282
plea bargains, 209
pledge of allegiance, 461, 463
Plessy v. Ferguson, 22, 201, 495, 498
pluralism, 18
plurality opinions, 229
pocket vetoes, 149, 168, 170
Pointer v. Texas, 453
"poison pill" amendments, 115
police, civilian control of, 21–22
police powers, 57, 86
policy elites, 533
policy entrepreneurs, 386, 533
policy evaluation, 536
policy making
    "carrot-and-stick" approach to, 85
    life cycle of, 531–33
    process of, 531–33
    public agenda and, 533–37
    through federal aid, 98–99
policy networks, 410
policy termination, 536
political action committees (PACs),
    332–33, 396
    Congressional voting decisions and,
      145–46
    defined, 332, 388
    growth of, 407–8
political activists, 321, 323
political advertising, 438
    negative, 441–42
    in presidential campaigns, 441–43
political awareness, 299–300
political campaigns
    campaign specialists, 363
    spending limits, 410–11
    volunteer workers, 363–64
    voting behavior and, 363
political candidates
    appeal of, 361
    equal time rule and, 433–34
    exploitation of media by, 438–42
    media coverage of, 438–42
    political advertising by, 438, 441–43
    recruitment of, 320
    use of talk shows by, 439–40
    Web sites of, 365, 427
political caucuses, 315
political culture, 295–99
    core values, 295–96, 295–97
    political ideology, 297–99, 340–41
political equality, as core value, 296
political ideology, 297–99. *See also*
    political parties
    Congressional voting decisions
      and, 144
    political parties and, 340–41
political information. *See* information
political issues, voting behavior and,
    361–62
political knowledge, sources of, 365
Politically Incorrect with Bill Maher, 436
political opinions. *See* public opinion
political participation, 299–300. *See also*
    direct democracy; interest groups;
    representative democracy; voters;
    voting behavior; voting rights

activists, 349
campaign activities, 363–65
congressional elections, 366–67
continuum of, 348–49
democracy and, 348–51
electoral college and, 368–72
funding and, 373–79
growth of, 388
inactive, 349
Motor-Voter Law and, 346–47
presidential elections, 366–67,
    372–73
protest, 365–66
value of, 378–79
voting behavior, 349–63
political parties, 310–43. *See also*
    multiparty system
antagonism between, 115
balance of, 310–12
campaign committees, 132
Congressional voting decisions
    and, 144
dealignment, 373
defined, 20, 312
democracy and, 312, 342–43
2002 election and, 341–42
election process and, 319–20
as factions, 313, 387
functions of, 312, 319–21, 339
future of, 341–42
government institutions and, 339–40
history of, 313–19
ideologies of, 340–41
independents and, 301
interest groups and, 320–21
local party organization, 321, 323
loyalty to, 142, 153–55
machine politics, 316, 323–24
major parties, 317
minor parties, 337–39
multiparty system, 335–39
national chair, 324
national conventions, 315, 324–25
organization of, 321–25
party-line voting, 360, 362
party platforms, 324
presidential elections and, 325–35
presidential leadership of, 177
public opinion of, 341–43
realignment, 301, 313, 318–19, 373
recruitment by, 320
state party organization, 323
Supreme Court appointments
    and, 212
third, 304
two-party system, 335–37
voters and, 320, 321
political party identification, 286, 301–2,
    336–37, 341–42, 355
    defined, 360
    with Democratic party, 302, 318, 355
    multiparty system and, 336–37
    with Republican party, 302, 318, 355
    as schema, 301–2
    voters and, 301–2, 336–37, 360–61
political power, dispersal of, 83, 84
political protest, 365–66

political satire, 441
political scandals
    Lewinsky scandal, 115, 153, 174,
      185, 428
    media and, 430
    presidential power and, 185
    Watergate scandal, 56, 430
    Whitewater investigation, 56
political socialization, 285–89
    defined, 285
    education and, 287
    family and, 286–87
    peers and, 288
    television and, 288–89
political speech, 463, 464
political violence, 366
politicos, Congress members as, 127
Polk, James, 167
polling. *See* public opinion polls
poll taxes, 350, 496, 500
polygamy, 462
population, U.S.
    by age, gender, race/ethnicity, and
      region, 4
    distribution of minorities by
      county, 11
    representative government and, 48
population, world
    by freedom status, 9
pork-barrel legislation, 143, 537
pornography, 468–69
Porter, Anthony, 458
portest
    against World Trade Organization
      (WTO), 391, 392
positive incentives, social welfare policy
    as, 531
Posner, Richard, 201, 224
Postal Service, U.S., 264, 271, 273
potential groups, 385–86
poverty, women and, 544
poverty guidelines, 545
poverty levels, 541, 545
poverty programs
    Great Society, 101
    war on poverty, 542–45
poverty thresholds, 545
Powell, Colin, 72, 431, 557, 574, 582
Powell, Lewis, 216, 220, 234, 480,
    506, 514
Powell v. Alabama, 452
power of the purse, of Congress, 267
precedent, Supreme Court decisions
    and, 230
president, 162–97
    bills considered by, 149
    bureaucracy and, 265–67
    Congress and, 120, 144–45
    Constitutional Convention and,
      51–53
    Constitutional powers, 166, 167–75
    democracy and, 164–66, 195, 197
    eligibility, 167
    emergencies and, 162–64
    federal budget and, 547–48
    federal court appointments, 217–19
    federalism and, 100–106

foreign policy role, 579–80
functional roles, 175–80
impeachment, 166
job approval ratings, 189
line of succession, 195
oratory of, 188
persuasive powers of, 267
powers of, 180–89
public support for, 187–89, 238
ranked by historians, 183
selection of, 166
staff assistance, 190–94
statistics, 167
Supreme Court and, 205, 211–17, 236
term of office, 166
Presidential Campaign Fund, 375
presidential decrees, 177
presidential elections, 367–73
costs of, 373–78
decided in the House of
Representatives, 314
2000 election, 52, 200–202, 351–52,
354, 368, 371, 425
electoral college and, 51–53, 368–72
financing, 373–78
gender and, 295
interpreting, 372–73
media coverage, 425
political advertising in, 441–43
popular vote for, 314
television and, 440–41
voter turnout, 372
presidential power, 167–75
activist presidents and, 181–82
appointment power, 169, 266
commander in chief, 175
Congress and, 182, 184
Constitution and, 167, 180–81
constructionist approach to, 181
in emergencies, 163–64
executive agreements, 173
executive privilege, 173–74
fast-track authority, 173
foreign policy, 173
growth in, 164–65, 180–82, 185
pardons, 175
public opinion and, 188
stewardship approach to, 181
as threat to democracy, 164
treaty power, 169–73
veto power, 168–69
war powers, 71, 184–87
presidential roles, 175–79
chief diplomat, 176
chief executive, 177
chief legislator, 176–77
chief of state, 175
commander in chief, 175
crisis leader, 175–76
economic leader, 177, 179
moral leader, 177
multiple roles of, 179
party leader, 177
president of the senate, 132
president pro tempore, 132
President's Commission of the Status of
Women, 511

press, freedom of. *See* freedom of the
press
Prewitt, Kenneth, 5
Price, Tom, 412
primary elections, 316, 327–29
blanket, 328
closed, 328
defined, 327
frontloading, 328
history of, 328
machine politics and, 324
open, 328
proportional representation, 328
voting behavior and, 361
whites-only, 496
winner-take-all system, 327–28,
371–72
prior restraint, 434–35, 466–67
privacy
expectation of, 475, 476
Fourth Amendment and, 470–71
implied rights, 479–82
right to, 21, 448
Supreme Court and, 107
Privacy Act of 1974, 264
private speech, 463, 465–66
privatization, 272–73
privileged legislation, 138
probable cause, 472
pro bono cases, 226
Progressive era, 250
magazines, 423
newspapers, 421
Progressive party, 337
progressive taxes, 553
Prohibition, 69, 397
Project for Excellence in Journalism,
424–25
project grants, 96–97
property qualifications, for voting, 495
property rights, 451
property taxes, 552
proportional representation
defined, 46–47
primary elections, 328
proposal of amendment, 68
Proposition 13 (California), 552
Proposition 209 (California), 489, 508
proprietary colonies, 29
Protess, David, 458
protest
abortion, 466
political, 365–66
protest marches, 499
by students, 390–91, 392
against taxation, 552
against Vietnam War, 330, 366, 390
violence and, 366
public agenda
defined, 533
issues, 533–34
policy making and, 533–37
Public Citizen, 396
public communication, by
president, 188
public figures, libel against, 467
public interest groups, 395–96

Public Interest Research Groups
(PIRGs), 396
public officials, libel against, 467
public opinion, 278–307
of bureaucracy, 270
defined, 281–82
democracy and, 280, 304–7
factors affecting political
socialization, 285–89
foreign policy and, 586–87
formation of, 301–2
measuring, 282–84
media polling and, 439
political awareness and involvement,
299–300
political culture, 295–99
of political parties, 341–43
of president, 187–89
public policy and, 304–7
as social control, 297
social factors influencing, 289–95
stability and change in, 302–4
Supreme Court and, 237–38
public opinion polls
accuracy of, 278–79
close-ended questions, 284
exit polls, 284
importance of, 284
interviewer bias in, 284
by the media, 439
open-minded questions, 284
question wording, 284
random sampling, 283
reliability of, 284
representative samples for, 282
sample size for, 282–83
sampling bias in, 279, 283
straw polls, 282
telephone polls, 283, 284
tracking polls, 284
voting behavior and, 307
public policy
continuing, 536–37
defense policy, 528
defined, 528
diversity of, 81–83
economic policy, 545–57
evaluation of, 536
experimentation in, 83–84
foreign policy, 173, 184–87
formal agenda, 534–35
goals of, 528
implementation, 536
public agenda, 533–37
public opinion and, 304–6
regulatory, 528
social welfare, 528
termination, 536
types of, 528
public speech, 463, 464–65
public television news, 441
Publicus, 61
Public Works Employment
Act of 1977, 506
Puerto Rican Legal Defense Fund, 517
Pulitzer, Joseph, 421
punitive damages, 209

Putin, Vladimir, 571–72, 575
Putnam, Robert, 288

Q

Quayle, Dan, 440
Quinn, Kevin, 79
quota programs, 505, 506–8

R

race. *See also* African Americans;
    Hispanics; minorities
  census classifications, 6
  Congressional districts and, 124–26
  opinion formation and, 290–91
racial desegregation
  Confederate flag and, 98
  implementation of, 535
  presidential actions affecting, 496
  in schools, 502–4
racial discrimination
  affirmative action as, 488–90
  in crises, 26–27
  defined, 491
  de jure *vs.* de facto, 501–4
  in education, 490
  in housing, 502
  reparations for, 493
  in transportation, 490
racial integration, 498
racial profiling, 521
racial segregation
  effects of, 498
  legal, 495–96
  separate but equal doctrine and, 22,
      495, 497–98
  state-action doctrine and, 495
Radical Republicans, 494
radio
  effectiveness of, 423
  regulation of, 433
  talk shows, 423, 439–40
Radio Corporation of America
    (RCA), 433
"rally effect," 176
Randolph, Edmund, 39, 46, 52, 66
random digit dialing (RDD), 283
random sampling, 283
Rankin, Jeannette, 122
Rather, Dan, 333
ratification
  of amendments, 67, 68–69
  of Constitution, 61, 65–66
Rational Public, The (Page and
    Shapiro), 300
Rayburn, Sam, 131, 142
Reagan, Ronald, 21, 131, 167, 318, 440
  affirmative action and, 507
  appointments by, 172
  bureaucracy and, 252, 266
  coattails effect and, 367
  election of, 370
  fairness doctrine and, 434
  federal aid programs, 103–4
  federalism and, 103–4, 109–10
  foreign policy, 571, 579
  investigation of, 152

  judicial appointments, 206, 217, 218
  media and, 425, 439
  national security and, 269
  political advertising by, 442
  political ideology of, 298
  public communication by, 188
  realignment and, 373
  regulatory policy, 538
  solicitor general under, 223
  spending policy, 554
  support for, 294, 361
  Supreme Court appointments, 169,
      214, 215, 216
  tax policy, 527, 552
  veto use, 169
Reagan, Ronald, Building and
    International Trade Center, 252
realigning elections, 373
realignment, 301, 313, 318–19, 373
reapportionment, 122–24, 123
Reapportionment Act of 1929, 122
reasonable suspicion standard, 447–48,
    473, 475
rebuttal, right of, 434
recess appointments, 169
reciprocity, in Congress, 143
Reconstruction, 494–95
recruitment, by political parties, 320
redistricting, 124–26
Red Lion Broadcasting v. FCC, 434
red tape, 270
Reed, Stanley, 227, 498
Reed, Thomas, 131
Reed v. Reed, 513–14
Reeves, Christopher, 402
referenda, 9, 359–60
Reform party, 336, 338–39
*Regents of the University of California v.
    Bakke*, 506
regional differences, opinions and,
    293–94
regionalism, in foreign policy, 565–66
regressive taxes, 553
regulation
  bureaucracy and, 257–58
  of food industry, 543
  independent agencies, 260–61
  of media, 433–34
  value of, 271–72
regulatory policy, 528, 537–40
  defined, 529
  deregulation, 537
  economic policy, 546
  environmental, 538–40
  types of, 537
Rehnquist, William, 27, 86, 201, 209,
    214, 215, 216, 217, 222, 226, 227,
    229, 230, 233, 234, 235, 450, 460,
    466, 471, 474, 478, 479, 483, 484
  appointment of, 474
  Supreme Court under, 106–9
Reich, Otto J., 169
Reid, Harry, 132, 311
religion. *See also* freedom of religion
  establishment of, 456–61
  free exercise of, 456–57, 461–63
  opinion formation and, 291–93

  Supreme Court appointments
      and, 213
Religious Freedom Restoration Act
    (RFRA), 236–37, 397, 462
religious interest groups, 392, 397
Religious Right, 437
religious schools, aid to, 459–61
Reno, Janet, 56
representation
  Declaration of Independence and,
      39–40
  political parties and, 320
  virtual, 33–34
representative democracy
  Constitution and, 53–54, 72
  defined, 13
  political participation and, 348
  voting and, 346
representative samples, 282
republic
  Constitution and, 53–54
  defined, 13, 28
  Roman, 28
Republican National Guard (Iraq), 21
Republican party, 63
  campaign spending limits and,
      410–11
  candidate Web sites, 427
  defined, 317
  economic policy, 546
  2000 election and, 368
  fundraising by, 325, 333, 378
  Hispanic voters and, 334
  history of, 315–19
  identification with, 302, 318, 355
  ideology of, 340–41
  interest groups and, 320–21
  Jeffords and, 311–12
  majority control by, 318
  media coverage of, 436
  party platform, 326
  structure of, 325
  Supreme Court appointments
      and, 212
  symbol of, 315
  trend toward, 318–19
Republican Revolution, 127, 153–56
Republicans (Jeffersonian
    Republicans), 313
reserved powers, 57, 86
resolution, 149
Resource Conservation and Recovery
    Act, 539
result-oriented judges, 232
retrospective voting, 362
revenue sharing, 102
Revere, Paul, 35, 37
reverse discrimination, 505
Revolution of 1800, 314
Reynolds v. Sims, 96, 126, 517
Rice, Condaleeza, 58–59, 72, 516, 582
riders, to bills, 139
Ridge, Tom, 58–59, 194, 244–46, 247,
    256, 266
right of rebuttal, 434
right to die, 484
right to privacy, 21, 448

"right to reply" law, 435
Riley, Joseph P., 98
Ringe, Tom, 110
Ring v. Arizona, 459
Rio Accords, 539
Roberts, Owen, 93, 220
Robertson, Pat, 437
Robinson v. California, 453
Rockefeller, Jay, 121
Rockefeller, Nelson, 195
Roe, Jane, 202
Roe v. Wade, 201, 214, 227, 237, 240, 474, 482–83, 534
Rogan, James, 135–36
Rogers, Will, 321, 547
Rogers, William, 262
Rogers Commission, 262–63
"rogue" nations, 564, 573, 588
Roman republic, 28
Romer, Roy, 325
Romer v. Evans, 480–81
Roosevelt, Eleanor, 397
Roosevelt, Franklin D., 27, 71, 332, 359, 411, 519, 520, 541, 567
    bureaucracy and, 250–51, 266
    campaign finance reform and, 374
    civil rights and, 496
    cooperative federalism and, 100
    court-packing plan, 86, 93, 206
    Democratic party and, 316
    election polls, 278–79
    emergency powers, 164
    executive power and, 181, 185
    federalism and, 100, 109
    fireside chats, 423
    judicial appointments, 218
    New Deal, 93
    public communication by, 188
    staff, 190
    Supreme Court and, 201, 212, 213
    Tenth Amendment and, 86
    war powers, 184–85
Roosevelt, Theodore, 167, 173, 304, 565
    bureaucracy and, 251
    executive power and, 181, 182
    presidential power and, 185
    Progressive party, 337
    public communication by, 188
Roper, Elmo, 282
Rossiter, Clinton, 177
Roth, William, 154
Rothman, Stanley, 435
Roth v. United States, 468
Rove, Karl, 221, 527
royal grants, 29
Rubin, Jerry, 330, 333
Rubin, Peter J., 214
rule of four, 222
rules, bureaucratic regulation, 257–58
rules, Congressional, 138–43
    closed, 138
    committees and, 148
    defined, 138
    informal, 142–43
    norms, 142–43
    open, 138
    restrictive, 138

Speaker of the House and, 138–39
Rumsfeld, Donald, 239, 563, 570, 582
run-off elections, 372
Rush, Benjamin, 66
Russia, 63, 566
Russia-NATO Council, 574
Russian Space Agency, 263
Rust, Roland, 274
Rutledge, John, 45, 224
Rutledge, Wiley, 213, 217
Ryan, George, 458

S

safe seats, 124
Safe Water and Toxic Enforcement Act of 1986, 539
salience, of opinion, 304
same-sex marriage, 521
    bans, 60–61
    civil union laws, 81, 82–83
    Constitution and, 89
same-sex sexual harassment, 516
samples
    margin of error, 282–83
    random sampling, 283
    representative, 282
    size of, 282–83
    telephone bias, 283
sampling bias, 279, 283
Samuelson, Robert, 63
San Antonio Independent School District v. Rodriguez, 517
Sanders, Bernard, 319
satellite master antenna television (SMATV), 433
satellites, media coverage and, 425
Saturday Night Live, 441
Saturday Press, 455
Scalia, Antonin, 107, 216, 226, 227, 228, 229, 233, 235, 473, 474, 475, 476, 483
    appointment of, 217
Scalia, Eugene, 169
scarcity doctrine, 433
scarlet letter provision, 128
Schattman, Michael, 221
    221
Schattschneider, E. E., 17
schemas
    defined, 301
    party identification as, 301–2
Schenck, Charles T., 452–53
Schenck v. United States, 452–53, 454
Schieffer, Bob, 333
Schiff, Adam, 334
Schlesinger, Arthur M., Jr., 185
school busing, 504
school desegregation, 498–99, 502–4, 535
school drug searches, 473–75, 476
school prayer, 460
school segregation, 490, 495, 497–98
school vouchers, 461
Schuck, Perter, 6
Schumer, Charles, 382–83
Schumpeter, Joseph, 299

Schwartz, Jacob, 454
Schwarzkopf, H. Norman, 417
Scott, Dred, 315
Scottsboro Boys, 455, 493
Scottsboro case, 96
search and seizure
    counter-terrorist, 446–48
    Fourth Amendment and, 448
    illegal, 471
    "one stop shopping," 447
    probable cause for, 472
    "reasonable suspicion" standard, 447–48
    "sneak and peek," 447
    warrantless searches, 472–75
Second Amendment, 67, 382–83
Second Amendment Sisters, 383, 409
Second Continental Congress, 37, 41
"Second Declaration of Independence," 72
secrecy, government and, 417
secret ballot, 324
secular regulation rule, 462–63
Securities and Exchange Commission (SEC), 56, 251, 395
segregation. *See* racial discrimination; racial segregation
Seguin, Yves, 92
selective incorporation, of Bill of Rights, 456
select (special) committees, 133
self-realization, 63
self-restrained justices, 232–33, 449
Seminole Indians, 107
Senate. *See also* Congress; Congressional committees; Congressional members
    Budget Committee, 551
    Constitutional Convention and, 49
    Constitution and, 53, 118
    election costs, 373
    elections, 118
    House of Representatives and, 121
    lawmaking process, 147–49
    leadership, 132–33
    people represented by, 64
    representative democracy and, 13
    selection of senators, 118
    Supreme Court and, 214–15
    treaties and, 170, 172
Senate majority leader, 131, 147
Senate National Security Working Group, 152
senatorial courtesy, 217
Seneca Falls women's rights convention, 350
Senegal, 119
Senior Executive Services (SES), 272
seniority, in Congress, 142
Sensenbrenner, F. James, Jr., 250, 447
separate but equal doctrine, 22, 491
    in education, 497–98
    establishment of, 495
separation of powers
    Constitution and, 54
    defined, 47
    horizontal powers, 54–56

vertical powers, 56–57, 84
September 11, 2001 terrorist attacks,
    26–28. *See also* terrorism; terrorism,
    war on
    anti-terrorism funding, 96
    bureaucratic response to, 244–46
    Bush and, 163–64, 175
    class action suits, 209
    Congressional unity and, 155
    federal aid and, 79–80, 106, 110
    foreign policy and, 564
    intelligence information and, 583
    national unity and, 288, 300
    New York City and, 78–80
    presidential powers and, 184
Sessions, Jefferson Beauregard, 206
Seventeenth Amendment, 19, 54, 68, 70
Seventh Amendment, 67
Seven Years' War, 32
sex discrimination, 509–16
    strict scrutiny test, 514
    Supreme Court cases, 511–16
    test of reasonableness, 512
sexism, 511
sexual harassment, 516
sexually explicit material, television self-
    rating of, 432
shadow government, 59
Shaheen, Jeanne, 355
Shallus, Jacob, 71
Shapiro, Robert, 300
Shaw v. Reno, 124
Shays, Christopher, 115
Shays, Daniel, 40–41
Shays's Rebellion, 40–41, 42, 57
Shelby, Richard, 144, 319
Sherman, Roger, 45, 46, 49, 66
Shinawarta, Thaksin, 418
Shriver, Mark K., 406
Shuster, Bud, 143
Shuttleworth, Mark, 263
Sierra Club, 399, 400, 401
Sierre Leone, 352
Silberman, Laurence, 224
Silver, Sheldon, 79
Simon, Arthur, 399
single-interest interest groups, 399
single-member districts, 335
sit-ins, 500
Sixteenth Amendment, 70
Sixth Amendment, 67, 96, 450
    defendants' rights, 469, 475–79
    extending to states, 476–77
    fair hearing under, 455
Sklyarov, Dmitri, 73
slander, 467
slavery
    Confederate flag display and, 98–99
    Constitutional Convention and, 43,
        49–50
    Constitution and, 71
    Declaration of Independence and,
        39–40
    interstate commerce and, 91
    proposed reparations for, 493
    Republican party and, 315
slaves

rights of, 315, 492
    voting and, 349
sliding-scale test, 464
Slotnick, Elliot, 219
Small Business Administration (SBA),
    260
Smith Act, 464
Smith v. Allwright, 227
"smoke-filled rooms," 315, 316
"sneak and peek" searches, 447
Snowe, Olympia, 311
soccer moms/dads, 294
social class
    opinion formation and, 290
    voting behavior and, 359
social contract theorists, 30–31, 38
socialization role, of media, 431–32
social policy, 528
Social Security, 541–42
    calculating benefits, 558
    Medicare, 543–44
    party platforms, 326
    taxes, 554
Social Security Act of 1935, 83–84, 251,
    541–42
Social Security Administration, 265, 271
social welfare policy, 528, 529, 541–45
    defined, 531
    party platforms, 326
    Social Security, 541–42
    war on poverty, 542–45
soft money, 114–16, 151, 325, 333, 464
    campaign finance reform and, 374,
        376, 378
    defined, 376, 407
    issue advertising and, 411
    political action committees and, 407
solicitor general, 223
Solidarity movement, 19
Solomon, Erich, 220
Somalia, 417
sound bites, 419, 440–41
Souter, David, 106–7, 109, 226, 227–28,
    234, 235, 461, 482, 483, 516
    appointment of, 212, 216
South America, 565–66
South Carolina v. Baker, 94
Southeast Asia, 570–71
Southeast Asia resolution, 186
Southern Christian Leadership Council
    (SCLC), 499
Southern Utah Wilderness Alliance
    (SUWA), 412
sovereigns, 31
sovereignty, 30
Soviet Union
    collapse of, 564
    detente with, 571–72
    dissolution of, 573
    World War I and, 566
    World War II and, 567
Space Imaging Corp., 417, 425
space program, 262–63
Speaker of the House
    defined, 130
    lawmaking and, 147
    role of, 130–31

Rules Committee and, 138–39
    term limits for, 128
special interest groups
    campaign reform and, 115
    Constitutional amendment process
        and, 69
specialization
    in bureaucracy, 248
    in Congress, 143
special revenue sharing, 102
Specter, Arlen, 215, 311
speech, freedom of. *See* freedom of
    speech
speed limits, 81, 95, 535
spending, 554
    foreign aid, 580–81
    pork-barrel legislation and, 143, 537
sphere of influence, 565
spin, 419
spiral of intolerance, 297
spiral of silence, 297
spiral of tolerance, 297
split-ticket ballots, 360
spoils system, 253
St. Clair, Arthur, 173–74
stability, 16–17
Stamp Act, 33–34
standing committees, in House and
    Senate, 133
Stanley v. Georgia, 230
Stanton, Elizabeth Cady, 509–10
Starr, Kenneth, 56, 58, 153
"Star Wars," 571
state-action doctrine, 495
state aid, to religious schools, 459–60
state and local courts
    organization of, 206, 208
    Supreme Court effects on, 237
State Department, 249, 259, 581
    foreign policy and, 584–85
State of the Union Address, 190, 289
state party organization, 323
state powers
    constitutional guarantees of, 87
    constitutional limits on, 87
    division of powers and, 86–89
    general welfare clause and, 84, 85
    interstate commerce clause and,
        84–85
    nullification, 91
    preemption of, 88–89
    prohibited, 88–89
    Rehnquist Court and, 106–9
    taxation of federal entities, 90
    Tenth Amendment and, 85–86
states
    application of Bill of Rights to, 67,
        451–53
    Articles of Confederation and, 41–43
    constitutions, 40–41
    devolution revolution and, 97
    federal aid trends in, 103
    interstate relations, 60–61
    large- and small-state interests,
        48–49, 117
    legislative term limits, 129
    legislatures, 42

New Federalism and, 102
policy variations, 81
political party organization, 321, 323
racial desegregation and, 498–99
ratification of Constitution by, 65–66
Tenth Amendment and, 85–86
states' rights
Antifederalists and, 61–63, 66
Confederate flag and, 98–99
defined, 80
federalism and, 80
Supreme Court and, 106–9
Steamer, Mollie, 454
Steffens, Lincoln, 421, 541
Stevens, John Paul, 60, 128, 200, 221, 224, 226, 233, 234, 235, 459, 469
Stevens, Ted, 59
stewardship approach to presidency, 181
Stewart, Jon, 441
Stewart, Potter, 234, 467, 502
"stick" approach, Supreme Court, 228
Stone, Harlan Fiske, 220, 227, 229
stop-and-frisk searches, 473
Story, Joseph, 212
straight-party ticket, 360
Strategic Arms Limitation Treaty (SALT), 571
SALT II, 571
Strategic Defense Initiative (SDI) ("Star Wars"), 571
straw polls, 282
Street, John, 307
strict construction, 231
strict government neutrality rule, 457
strict scrutiny test, 508, 514
Struck, Doug, 417
Student Nonviolent Coordinating Committee (SNCC), 390
student protest, 390–91, 392
Students for a Democratic Society (SDS), 390
Subcommittee Bill of Rights, 137
subcommittees, Congressional, 133, 137–38
hearings, 147
policy making and, 534
subsequent punishment, 466
Suffolk Resolves, 37
suffrage. See also voting rights
for African Americans, 494
defined, 494
for women, 510–11
Sugar Act, 33–34
Suharto, 119
Sullivan, L. B., 467
Sullivan standard, 467–68
superdelegates, 331
Superfund Law, 539
supermajority, 68
superpowers, 567
Super Tuesday, 329
Supplemental Security Income (SSI), 542
supremacy clause, 57
of the Constitution, 48
defined, 86
federal use of, 88–89

Supreme Court. See also specific cases
affirmative action and, 506–7
appeals received by, 219–21
appellate jurisdiction, 220
Bill of Rights and, 94–95
briefs, 224
case selection, 221–23
civil liberties and, 448, 449
civil rights and, 501
Congressional influence on, 205–6, 236–37
Constitutional basis of authority, 203, 231
constitutionality of laws and, 204, 205
Constitutional updating and, 68–69
costs of taking cases to, 226
criticism of, 201
death penalty and, 458–59
democracy and, 202, 238–40
distinguishing cases, 230
docket, 219
dual federalism and, 94
2000 election and, 200–202
establishment of, 203
executive privilege and, 174
fairness doctrine and, 434
federalism and, 106–8
federal questions and, 220–21
freedom of the press and, 434–35
gay rights and, 480–81
Hispanic member proposed, 334
implementation of decisions by, 235–36
independence of, 205–6
interest groups and, 407
judicial activism, 232
judicial conference, 227
judicial restraint, 231–32
judicial review, 21, 120
law clerks, 224–25
legislative veto and, 152
media's right to cover a trial and, 434–35
New Deal and, 216–17
opinions, 227–29
oral argument, 225–26
overturning decisions, 230
photograph, 220
political parties and, 212
precedent and, 230
presidential influence on, 169, 205, 236
presidential powers and, 58–59, 184, 185
public approval of, 201, 238
public opinion and, 237–38
racial segregation and, 495, 502–4
redistricting and, 126
refusal to review a case, 205
on regulation of the media, 433
representative democracy and, 13
representativeness of, 212–13
Roosevelt's court-packing plan for, 86, 93
"self-inflicted wounds" to, 201–2
staff, 221–22
state and local effects, 237–38

states' rights and, 106–9
statutory construction power, 205
Tenth Amendment and, 86
term limits and, 128
women's rights and, 510–16
Supreme Court appointments
American Bar Association and, 213
effect of presidential selections, 216–17
political parties and, 212
presidential selections, 169, 215–16
process, 211–16
representativeness of, 212–13
"safe" candidates, 215–16
Senate confirmation of, 205, 215–16
Senate opposition to, 215
women and minorities, 213, 214
Supreme Court justices
absolutist activists, 232
activist, 232–33, 449
character and interaction, 233
chief justice, 229–30
conservatives, 231–35
four-cell method for classifying, 232–33
jurisprudential posture of, 231–32
liberals, 231–35
moderates, 231–35
political ideology of, 231
result-oriented, 232
self-restrained, 232–33, 449
"swing justices," 201
voting blocs, 233–35
Surratt, Mary, 239
surveillance function of media, 427, 429
Sutherland, George, 184, 220
Swaggart, Jimmy, 437
Swann, James, 202
Swann v. Charlotte-Mecklenburg Board of Education, 504
"swap and turnback program," 103
"swing justices," 201
Swope, Herbert Bayard, 568
symbolic speech, 463, 465–66
Synar, Mike, 144

T

Taft, William Howard, 167, 181, 337
executive power and, 181–82
as Supreme Court judge, 216
Taft-Hartley Act, 374
Taiwan, 119, 322
Taliban, 8
talk shows
political candidates and, 439–40
Taney, Roger Brooke, 27
Tarbell, Ida, 421
tariffs, 552
task forces
lawmaking and, 151–52
taxation, 552–44
of American Colonies, 32–36
in Canada, 92
capital gains, 553
estate tax ("death-tax"), 527, 528
excise taxes, 554

of federal entities, by states, 90
party platforms, 326
progressive taxes, 553
protests against, 552
public policy, 526–28
regressive taxes, 553
sources of tax dollars, 552–43
tariffs, 552
tax reform, 543–54
"taxation without representation," 33–34
tax expenditures, 553
Tax Reform Act of 1986, 553
Tea Act, 35
Teamsters, 393
technology
   media and, 425–27, 443
   voting and, 358
telephone polls, 283, 284
television, 423–25
   cable, 419, 424, 425, 433
   diversity and, 437
   election coverage by, 368
   investigative journalism by, 431
   political satire, 441
   political socialization and, 288
   power of, 425
   presidential elections and, 440–41
   regulation of, 433
   self-rating systems, 432
   talk shows, 439–40
television news
   cable viewership, 419, 424
   credibility of, 424
   history of, 426
   political coverage, 424
   public television, 441
   viewership, 419
temperance groups, 69
Temporary Assistance for Needy
   Families (TANF), 536, 544
Ten Commandments, 460
Tenet, George, 269
Tennessee Valley Authority (TVA), 251,
   261–62
Tenth Amendment, 67, 84, 85–86, 91,
   106, 120
   New Deal and, 94
term limits, 128–29, 320
terrorism
   foreign policy and, 588
   media coverage of, 430, 436
terrorism, war on. See also Homeland
   Security, Department of
   anti-terrorist laws, 247
   Bush and, 239, 244–46, 248, 416–17,
      562–63
   civil rights and, 446–48, 521–23
   federal funds for, 110
   homeland defense programs, 110,
      194, 195, 244–45, 256, 266, 268
   media and, 416–18
   military tribunals, 239
   news coverage and, 418
   plan to distribute false information
      on, 419
   program funding, 96
   technology and, 587

Terry v. Ohio, 473, 476
test of reasonableness, 512
Thailand, 418
theocracy, 10
thermobaric bombs, 587
Third Amendment, 67
third parties. See minor parties
Thirteenth Amendment, 19, 70
   housing discrimination and, 502
   purpose of, 494
Thomas, Clarence, 107, 226, 233, 235
   appointment of, 212, 213, 215, 216,
      217, 220, 223, 311
Thompson, Tommy G., 544–45
three-fifths compromise, 50–51
Thurmond, Strom, 132, 134, 139, 143,
   155, 496
Tilden, Andrew, 370
Tillman Act of 1907, 374
Time magazine, 422
Times Mirror, 436
Time-Warner, Inc., 437–38
Title IX, 511, 512–13
Title VI, 511
Tito, Dennis, 263
tobacco industry, 393, 529, 530
Tocqueville, Alexis de, 9, 281, 295,
   296, 385
tolerance, as core value, 296–97
Tonkin Gulf Resolution, 186
Torricelli, Robert, 132
total incorporation, of Bill of Rights, 452
Towey, Jim, 191
town meetings, 12, 13
Townshend Revenue Acts, 34
Toxic Substances Control
   Act of 1987, 539
tracking polls, 284
trade agreements, 173
trade associations, 393
Trade Promotion Authority (TPA), 173
Traficant, James A., Jr., 156
transfer payments, 252
transitional government, 10
Transportation Department, 259
Transportation Security Administration
   (TSA), 248
Treasury Department, 249, 257
   foreign policy and, 584
   Presidential Campaign Fund, 375
treaties
   arms control, 569, 570, 571–72
   defined, 169–70
   presidential power to negotiate,
      169–73
   Senate and, 170, 172
   World War I, 172
triad of powers, 84–86
   defined, 84
   general welfare clause, 84, 85
   interstate commerce clause, 84–85
   Tenth Amendment, 84, 85–86
trial courts, 208
trials
   media's right to cover, 434–35
   right to a fair trial, 435
   Sixth Amendment rights, 475

Tribe, Laurence, 72, 83
triggering mechanisms, 533
Trinidad and Tobago, 11
"troika," 193
Truman, David, 409
Truman, Harry, 21–22, 194, 542, 568
   bureaucracy and, 265
   campaign finance reform and, 374
   civil rights and, 496
   cooperative federalism and, 100
   economy and, 177, 179
Truman Doctrine, 568
trustees, Congress members as, 126–27
Turkey, 563
Turner, Nat, 492
Turner Broadcasting, 438
Twelfth Amendment, 70, 314, 369
Twentieth Amendment, 70
Twenty-fifth Amendment, 70
Twenty-first Amendment, 68, 69, 70
Twenty-fourth Amendment, 19, 54,
   70, 500
Twenty-second Amendment, 70, 166
Twenty-sixth Amendment, 19, 54, 70,
   351, 390
Twenty-third Amendment, 19, 54, 70, 351
Two Congresses, 129–30
Two Treatises on Government (Locke),
   31–32
Tyler, John, 167
Tyson, Mike, 471

U
Udall, Morris, 547
unanimous consent agreements, 139
understanding clause, for voting, 495
Unfunded Mandates Reform Act of
   1995, 100
unicameral legislature, 47
unitary system of government, 80
United Farm Workers (UFW), 3, 16, 517
United Nations, 172
United Nations (UN), 568, 573
United States v. Carolene, 450, 480
United States v. Cruikshank, 495
United States v. Curtiss-Wright, 184
United States v. Darby Lumber Co., 94
United States v. Drayton, 447
United States v. E. C. Knight, 91
United States v. Leon, 472
United States v. Lopez, 106
United States v. Nixon, 185
United Steelworkers v. Weber, 506
United Students Against
   Sweatshops, 391
United We Stand America, 338, 386
universal suffrage, 18
Uruguay Round, General Agreement on
   Tariffs and Trade (GATT), 556
U.S.A. Patriot Act, 27, 59, 116, 117, 155,
   209, 473, 475, 476, 521–22
   civil liberties and, 447, 448
U.S. Agency for International
   Development (USAID), 398
U.S. Census Bureau, 6–7, 347
U.S. Chamber of Commerce, 393

U.S. Court of Appeals, 210
  for the Federal Circuit, 210
  for the Ninth Circuit, 210, 222
U.S. district courts, 209–10
U.S. Postal Service, 249
USA Today, 439

V

Valenti, Jack, 191
values
  core, 295–96
  media socialization and, 431
variable obscenity test, 468
Venezuela, 119, 570
Ventura, Jesse, 319
Verba, Sidney, 348–49
vertical powers, 56–57, 84
Veterans Affairs Department, 259
vetoes
  Congressional override of, 149
  Constitutional basis of, 166
  defined, 168
  legislative, 152, 184
  pocket, 149, 168
  presidential, 149, 168–69, 170, 171
  subcommittees and, 138
Viacom, 438
vice president, 195, 196
  election of, 314, 369
videophones, 443
Vietnam War, 185–86, 570–71, 583–84
  media and, 419, 434, 585
  protest against, 330, 366, 390
  public opinion and, 586
Vinson, Fred, 229, 498
violence
  as political protest, 366
  television self-rating of, 432
Violence Against Women Act (VAWA),
    108–9, 516
Virginia Military Institute (VMI), 514–15
Virginia Plan, 46–47, 48
virtual representation, 33–34
voluntariness of confessions, 476
volunteer workers, in political
    campaigns, 363–64
Voter News Service (VNS), 295, 439
voter registration
  of African Americans, 499, 500, 501
  difficulties of, 355, 357
  2000 election and, 354
  encouraging, 346–47, 358
  Motor-Voter Law, 346–47, 353, 355
voters
  Hispanic, 334
  political awareness and involvement
      of, 299–300
  political opinion formation by, 301–2
  political parties and, 320, 321
  political party identification and,
      301–2, 336–37
  public policy formation and, 304–6
  stability and change in views of,
      302–4
  voting behavior, 307
voter turnout, 352–57

defined, 352
  explanations of, 353–57
  international, 353, 355, 356
  in midterm elections, 366–67
  Motor-Voter Law and, 347
  presidential elections and, 372
voting behavior, 351–63
  attitudes of nonvoters, 359
  campaigns and, 363
  candidate appeal and, 361
  coattails effect, 367
  decision-making, 360–63
  education and, 290
  gender and, 355, 368
  income and, 290
  issue-oriented, 361–62
  machine politics and, 323–24
  nonvoters, 355, 357–58
  online voting, 377
  party identification and, 360–61
  policies and issues and, 361–62
  polls and, 307
  retrospective, 362
  split-ticket ballots, 360
  straight-party ticket, 360
voting blocs, in Supreme Court, 233–35
voting rights, 18–19, 20
  of African Americans, 492, 494–96,
      495–96
  in Colonial America, 29–30
  Constitutional Convention and,
      44–45
  Constitution and, 71
  good character test, 350
  history of, 349–51
  of Native Americans, 517
  poll taxes, 350
  property requirements, 349
  restrictions on, 349–50
  of women, 349
Voting Rights Act of 1965, 5, 19, 126,
    350, 390, 501, 503, 517

W

Wagner Act, 251
Wahid, Abdurraham, 119
Wallace, George, 81, 247, 337, 339
  Confederate flag and, 98
war
  military tribunals, 239
  power to declare, 71, 186–87
  restrictions of freedom of speech
      during, 453
  war cabinet, 194
  war powers, of president, 58–59,
      184–87
War Department, 249
Wards Cove Packing Co. v. Antonio, 507
War of 1812, 184
"War of the Worlds" radio broadcast, 423
War Powers Act of 1973, 185, 186, 580
warrantless searches, 472–75
Warren, Earl, 227, 229, 234, 450, 464,
    474, 498
  appointment of, 212
Warren, Mercy Otis, 62

Warsaw Pact, 569
wartime media coverage, 416–18
Washington, Booker T., 496
Washington, George, 21, 37, 38, 41, 42,
    49, 51, 53, 167, 420
  bureaucracy and, 249
  Constitution and, 67–68
  electoral college and, 368, 369
  executive privilege use, 173–74
  moral leadership by, 177
  on political parties, 313–14
  ratification of Constitution and, 66
  staff, 190
  treaty power and, 170
Washington Post, 417, 430, 467
Washington v. Texas, 453
Watergate scandal, 56, 430
Water Pollution Control Act of 1972, 539
Watkins, Sherron, 394
Watts, J. C., 156
Waxman, Henry A., 138, 527
Waxman, Seth, 108
weapons
  atomic bomb, 568, 569
  technology and, 587
weapons agreements
  Antiballistic Missile (ABM) Treaty,
      570
  arms reduction treaty, 571–72
  Strategic Arms Limitation Treaty
      (SALT), 571
  Strategic Arms Limitation Treaty II
      (SALT II), 571
Weather Underground, 390
Weber, Max, 248, 249
Weberg, Brian, 360
Web sites. *See also* Internet
  Approaching Democracy, 427
  of bureaucratic offices, 274
  of Congressional members, 156
  of Democratic party, 342
  of Democratic party candidates, 427
  of executive branch, 196
  of political candidates, 365
  of Republican party candidates, 427
  of White House, 196
Webster, Daniel, 315
Webster, William, 269
Webster v. Reproductive Health Services, 483,
    534
Weeks v. United States, 471
Weiss, Philip, 438
Welfare Reform Law of 1996, 151, 536
welfare state, 250–52
  defined, 251
  machine politics and, 324
Welles, Orson, 423
Wertheimer, Fred, 409
Westinghouse, 438
Westmoreland, William, 571
Whig party, 63, 315, 317
whips, 131
Whistleblower Protection Act of 1989,
    272
whistle-blowers, 272, 273
White, Byron, 71, 217, 230, 234
White, Edward, 216

White, Ronnie, 220
"white ethnic" voters, 291
White House
    chief of staff, 191
    office, 190–91
    Web site, 196
Whitehurst, Frederick, 272
whites-only primaries, 496
Whitewater investigation, 56
Whitman, Karen Todd, 516
Whittaker, Charles Evans, 234
Wilkie, Wendell, 332
Willis, Garry, 72
Wilson, James, 52, 71
Wilson, Woodrow, 27, 56, 70, 133, 136,
    238, 316, 566
    executive power and, 181, 182
    Treaty of Versailles, 172
    on vice president, 195
winner-take-all system, 327–28, 371–72
Winthrop, John, 29, 564
Wirth, Timothy, 410–11
WISH, 405
Wolfinger, Raymond, 347
Wolf v. Colorado, 452
women
    cabinet positions, 273
    civil rights of, 491
    in Congress, 122
    Constitution and, 71

    in legislative assemblies, 515
    opinion formation by, 294–95
    poverty and, 544
    presidential candidates, 167
    on Supreme Court, 213, 214
    violence against, 108–9
    voting behavior of, 355, 368
    voting rights, 349
women's rights, 509–16
    suffrage, 350, 510–11
    Supreme Court and, 510–16
women's sports, 511, 512–13
Woodhull, Victoria, 167
Woodward, Bob, 430
workfare, 544
World Bank, 555
World Trade Center, 79, 175. *See also*
    September 11, 2001 terrorist attacks
    terrorist attacks on, 79
World Trade Organization (WTO), 555,
    556, 584
    defined, 556
    protest against, 391, 392
World War I, 172, 566
    civil liberties and, 27, 56
World War II, 567–68, 572
    bureaucracy and, 251
    civil liberties and, 27
    military tribunals, 239
World Wide Web. *See also* Internet;

Web sites
    as news source, 427
    political coverage on, 427, 428
Wounded Knee, Battle of, 518
Wright, James, 131
writ of assistance, 447
writ of certiorar, 221, 222
writ of *habeas corpus*, 27, 56, 70, 239
writs of assistance, 36

Y

Yale University, 493
Yates, Robert, 62
yellow journalism, 421–22
*Youngstown Sheet and Tube Company v.
    Sawyer,* 186
youth
    interest in news by, 432
    political knowledge of, 432
    youth culture, 288
Yugoslavia, former, 564

Z

Zaire, 352
Ziglar, James W., 250
Zimbabwe, 11, 364
Zogby, John, 293